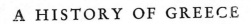

A HISTORY OF GREECE

A
HISTORY OF GREECE

TO THE

DEATH OF ALEXANDER THE GREAT

▶▶▶

BY

J. B. BURY, D.Litt., LL.D., F.B.A.

REGIUS PROFESSOR OF MODERN HISTORY, AND FELLOW OF KING'S COLLEGE,
IN THE UNIVLRSITY OF CAMBRIDGE

▶▶▶

THE MODERN LIBRARY
NEW YORK

Distributed in Canada
by Random House of Canada Limited, Toronto

THE MODERN LIBRARY
is published by RANDOM HOUSE, INC.

Manufactured in the United States of America by H. Wolff

JOHN BAGNELL BURY

(1861-1927)

A NOTE ON THE AUTHOR OF "A HISTORY OF GREECE"

As a student at Foyle College, in Derry, Ireland, J. B. Bury's first interest in antiquity was awakened by Freeman's *History of Federal Government in Greece and Italy*. After winning a fellowship at Trinity College, Dublin, he wrote, when he was but twenty-seven, *A History of the Later Roman Empire from Arcadia to Irene*. This work was acclaimed by scholars and became widely popular. His love of Pindar's poetry led him to edit the *Nemean* and *Isthmian Odes*. In 1893, he was made Professor of History at Trinity College and wrote *A History of the Roman Empire from Its Foundation to the Death of Marcus Aurelius*. Seven years later he issued his major work, *A History of Greece*, and was appointed Regius Professor at Cambridge. In addition to his monumental classical research and translations, he found time to write a *Life of Saint Patrick*. In 1908, he lectured at Harvard University, and thereafter continued to add to his stature as a teacher and scholar. His last work, published in 1923, carried forward his Roman historical chronicle to the death of Justinian. Ill health forced him to abandon his labors and go to Rome, where he died on June 1, 1927.

PREFACE TO THE 1913 EDITION

THE excavations of Sir Arthur Evans at Cnossus began in the year in which the first edition of this History of Greece appeared (1900). His amazing discoveries there, followed and supplemented by the work of other explorers on many other prehistoric sites in Crete, have transformed our knowledge of the Aegean civilisation of the second millennium, and placed in a new focus the problems of early Greece. In consequence of these discoveries, and of other researchs (among which I may mention especially Professor Ridgeway's *Early Age of Greece* and Mr. Leaf's *Troy*), it has been necessary to rewrite the greater part of Chapter I. An account of Cretan civilisation is included; the view that the pre-Achaean inhabitants of Greece were not Greeks, which it seems to me no longer possible to maintain, is abandoned; and the Trojan War is recognised to be an historical event.

Outside Chapter I, a few minor changes have been made. I need only mention that the accounts of the battles of Salamis and Plataea have been partly rewritten

J. B. B.

PREFACE TO FIRST EDITION

In determining the form and character of this book, I have been prompted by two convictions. One is that while, in writing a history based on the original authorities and from one's own personal point of view, it is natural and certainly easier to allow it to range into several volumes, its compression into a single volume often produces a more useful book. In the case of a new history of Greece, it seemed worth while to undertake the more laborious task. The other opinion which I venture to hold is this. So far as history is concerned, those books which are capable of enlisting the interest of mature readers seem to me to be best also for informing younger students. Therefore, while my aim is to help education, this book has in view a wider circle than those merely who are going through a course of school or university discipline.

It was a necessary consequence of the limitations of space which I imposed upon myself, that literature and art, philosophy and religion, should be touched upon only when they directly illustrate, or come into some specially intimate connexion with, the political history. It will be found that I have sometimes interpreted this rule liberally; but it is a rule which could be the more readily adopted as so many excellent works dealing with art, literature, and philosophy are now easily accessible. The interspersion, in a short political history, of a few unconnected chapters dealing, as they must deal, inadequately with art and literature seems useless and inartistic.

The existence of valuable handbooks, within the reach of all, on constitutional antiquities has enabled me, in tracing the development of the Athenian state or touching on the institutions of other cities, to omit minor details. The reader must also seek elsewhere for the sagas of Hellas, for a geographical description of the country, for the topography of Athens. On the topography of Athens, and on the geography of Greece, he will find excellent works to his hand.

There are two cautions which I must convey to the reader, and it will be most convenient to state them here. The first concerns the prehistoric age, which is the subject of the first chapter of this work. The evidence gathered by the researches

ix

of archaeologists on the coasts and islands of the Aegean during the last twenty years, as to the civilisation of prehistoric Greece, brought historians face to face with a set of new problems, for which no solutions that can be regarded as certain have yet been discovered. The ablest investigators differ widely in their views. Fresh evidence may at any hour upset tentative conclusions and force us to seek new interpretations of the data. The excavations which are now to be undertaken in Crete, at last restored to its own Greek world, may lead to unexpected results that may transform the whole question. Thus prehistoric Greece cannot be treated satisfactorily except by the method of discussion, and in a work like this, since discussion lies outside its scope, a writer can only describe the main features of the culture which excavation has revealed, and state with implied reserve the chief general conclusions, which he considers probable, as to the correlation of the archaeological evidence with the literary traditions of the Greeks. He must leave much vague and indefinite. The difficulty of the problems is increased by the circumstance that the literary evidence concerning the doings and goings of the early Greek folks is largely embedded in myth and harder to extract from its bed than buried walls or tombs from their coverings of earth. The importance of the pre-Greek inhabitants of Greece, the mixed ethnical character of the historical Greeks, the comparatively early date of the "Ionian" migration, the continuity of Aegean civilisation, the relation of the so-called "Mycenaen" culture to the culture described by Homer— these are the main points which I have been content to emphasise.[1]

The second caution applies to all histories of Greece that have been written since the days of Ephorus. The early portion of Greek history, which corresponds to the seventh and sixth centuries B.C., is inevitably distorted and placed in a false perspective through the strange limitations of our knowledge. For at that time (as well as in the centuries immediately preceding, which are almost quite withdrawn from our vision) the cities of the western coast of Asia Minor formed the most important and enlightened part of the Hellenic world, and of those cities in the days of their greatness we have only some disconnected glimpses. Our knowledge of them hardly begins till Persia advances to the Aegean and they sink to a lower place in Greece. Thus the pages in which the Greeks of Asia should have the supreme

---

[1] It has been a disappointment to me that Professor Ridgeway's promised work on the "Mycenaean" age has not yet appeared.

place are monopolised by the development of elder Greece; and the false impression is produced that the history of Hellas in the seventh and sixth centuries consisted merely or mainly of the histories of Sparta and Athens and their immediate neighbours. Darkness also envelops the growth of the young Greek communities of Italy and Sicily during the same period. The wrong, unfortunately, cannot be righted by a recognition of it. Athens and Sparta and their fellows abide in possession. *Les absents ont toujours tort.*

In the Notes and References at the end of the volume I have indicated obligations to modern research on special points. Here I must acknowledge my more general obligations to the histories of Grote, Freeman (*History of Sicily*), Busolt, Beloch, E. Meyer (*Geschichte des Altertums*), and Droysen. Though other histories of high reputation, both English and foreign, have been respectfully consulted, it is to those mentioned that I am chiefly indebted. But I owe perhaps a deeper debt to the writings of one who, though he has never written a formal history of Greece, has made countless invaluable contributions to its study—Professor U. von Wilamowitz-Möllendorff. With some of his conclusions I do not agree, but I would express here deep sympathy with his methods and admiration for the stimulating virtue of his writings.

Several friends have been good enough to help me. The book has had the advantage of the criticisms of a master of the subject, Mr. Mahaffy, who most kindly read through the proof-sheets. The first chapter is enriched by a small map of the "Mycenaen" sites of Crete, marked for me by Mr. J. L. Myres. Mr. Cecil Smith assisted me in the matter of illustrations taken from antiquities in the British Museum; and Professor Percy Gardner superintended the preparation of some photographs from busts in the Oxford Galleries.

All the plans and many of the maps (including Bactria and North-Western India) were roughly sketched by myself and then properly drawn by the skilful chartographers Messrs. Walker and Boutall. In the case of a plan or map that is not current, I have stated in the List of Illustrations to what work I am indebted. Nearly all the reproductions of coins are from coins in the British Museum.

My obligations to Messrs. R. and R. Clark will be understood by those who have had the good fortune to have had works printed at their press.

J. B. BURY.

CONTENTS

INTRODUCTORY

CHAPTER I

THE BEGINNINGS OF GREECE AND THE HEROIC AGE

CHAPTER II

THE EXPANSION OF GREECE

CHAPTER III

GROWTH OF SPARTA

xiii

CHAPTER IV

THE UNION OF ATTICA AND THE FOUNDATION OF
THE ATHENIAN DEMOCRACY

CHAPTER V

GROWTH OF ATHENS

CHAPTER VI

THE ADVANCE OF PERSIA TO THE AEGEAN

CHAPTER VII

THE PERILS OF GREECE. THE PERSIAN AND PUNIC
INVASIONS

CHAPTER VIII

THE FOUNDATION OF THE ATHENIAN EMPIRE

CHAPTER IX

THE ATHENIAN EMPIRE UNDER THE GUIDANCE OF PERICLES

CHAPTER X

THE WAR OF ATHENS WITH THE PELOPONNESIANS
(431-421 B.C.)

CHAPTER XI

THE DECLINE AND DOWNFALL OF THE ATHENIAN EMPIRE

CHAPTER XII

THE SPARTAN SUPREMACY AND THE PERSIAN WAR

CHAPTER XIII

THE REVIVAL OF ATHENS AND HER SECOND LEAGUE

CHAPTER XIV

THE HEGEMONY OF THEBES

CHAPTER XV

THE SYRACUSAN EMPIRE AND THE STRUGGLE WITH CARTHAGE

CHAPTER XVI

RISE OF MACEDONIA

ILLUSTRATIONS

xix

MAPS

A HISTORY OF GREECE

INTRODUCTORY

GREECE AND THE AEGEAN

THE rivers and valleys, the mountains, bays, and islands of Greece will become familiar, as our story unfolds itself, and we need not enter here into any minute description. But it is useful at the very outset to grasp some general features which went to make the history of the Greeks what it was, and what otherwise it could not have been. The character of their history is so intimately connected with the character of their dwelling-places that we cannot conceive it apart from their land and seas.

Of Spain, Italy and Illyricum, the three massy promontories of which southern Europe consists, Illyricum in the east would have closely resembled Spain in the west, if it had stopped short at the north of Thessaly and if its offshoot Greece had been sunk beneath the waters. It would then have been no more than a huge block of solid land, at one corner almost touching the shores of Asia, as Spain almost touches the shores of Africa. But Greece, its southern continuation, has totally different natural features, which distinguish it alike from Spain the solid square and Italy the solid wedge, and make the eastern basin of the Mediterranean strikingly unlike the western. Greece gives the impression of a group of nesses and islands. Yet in truth it might have been as solid and unbroken a block of continent, on its own smaller scale, as the massive promontory from which it juts. Greece may be described as a mountainous headland broken across the middle into two parts by a huge rift, and with its whole eastern side split into fragments. We can trace the ribs of the framework, which a convulsion of nature bent and shivered, for the service, as it turned out, of the human race. The mountains which form Thessaly's eastern barrier, Olympus, Ossa, and Pelion; the mountains of the long island of Euboea; and the string of islands which seem to hang to Euboea as a sort of tail, should have formed a perpetual mountainous chain—the rocky eastern coast of a solid promontory. Again, the ridges of Pindus which divide Thessaly from Epirus find their prolongation in the heights of Tymphrestus and Corax, and then, in an oblique south-eastward line, deflected from its natural direc-

The Illyrian (or Balkan) peninsula.

Character of Greece:

the Gulf of Corinth;

the mountain ribs;

tion, the chain is continued in Parnassus, Helicon, and Cithaeron, in the hills of Attica, and in the islands which would be part of Attica, if Attica had not dipped beneath the waters. In the same way the mountains of the Peloponnesus are a continuation of the mountains of Epirus. Thus restoring the framework in our imagination and raising the dry-land from the sea, we reconstruct, as the Greece that might have been, a lozenge of land, ribbed with chains of hills stretching south-eastward far out into the Aegean. If nature had given the Greeks a land like this, their history would have been entirely changed; and by imagining it we are helped to understand how much they owed to the accidents of nature. In a land of capes and deep bays and islands it was determined that waterways should be the ways of their expansion. They were driven as it were into the arms of the sea.

The most striking feature of continental Greece is the deep gulf which has cleft it asunder into two parts. The southern half ought to have been an island—as its Greek name, "the island of Pelops," suggests—but it holds on to the continent by a narrow bridge of land at the eastern extremity of the great cleft. Now this physical feature had the utmost significance for the history of Greece; and its significance may be viewed in three ways, if we consider the existence of the dividing gulf, the existence of the isthmus, and the fact that the isthmus was at the eastern and not at the western end. 1. The double effect of the gulf itself is clear at once. It let the sea in upon a number of folks who would otherwise have been inland mountaineers, and increased enormously the length of the seaboard of Greece. Further, the gulf constituted southern Greece a world by itself; so that it could be regarded as a separate land from northern Greece—an island practically, with its own insular interests. 2. But if the island of Pelops had been in very truth an island, if there had been no isthmus, there would have been from the earliest ages direct and constant intercourse between the coasts which are washed by the Aegean and those which are washed by the Ionian Sea. The eastern and western lands of Greece would have been brought nearer to one another, when the ships of trader or warrior, instead of tediously circumnavigating the Peloponnesus, could sail from the eastern to the western sea through the middle of Greece. The disappearance of the isthmus would have revolutionised the roads of traffic and changed the centres of commerce; and the wars of Grecian history would have been fought out on other lines. How important the isthmus was may perhaps be best illustrated by a modern instance on a far mightier scale. Remove the bridge which joins the southern to the northern conti-

[margin notes:]

maginary reconstruction.

[IMPORTANT GEOGRAPHICAL FEATURES. I. The Great Inlet (Gulf of Corinth).

nent of America, and contemplate the changes which ensue in the routes of trade and in the conditions of naval warfare in the great oceans of the globe. 3. Again, if the bridge which attached the Peloponnesus to the mainland had been at the western end of the gulf, the lands along either shore of the inlet would have been accessible easily, and sooner, to the commerce of the Aegean and the orient; the civilisation of north-western Greece might have been more rapid and intense; and the history of Boeotia and Attica, unhooked from the Peloponnesus, would have run a different course.

The character of the Aegean basin was another determining condition of the history of the Greeks. Strewn with countless islands it seems meant to promote the intercourse of folk with folk. The Cyclades, which, as we have seen, belong properly to the framework of the Greek continent, pass imperceptibly into the isles which the Asiatic coast throws out, and there is formed a sort of island bridge, inviting ships to pass from Greece to Asia. The western coast of Lesser Asia belongs, in truth, more naturally to Europe than to its own continent; it soon became part of the Greek world; and the Aegean might be considered then as the true centre of Greece. II. The Aegean.

The west side of Greece too was well furnished with good harbours, and though not as rich in bays and islands as the east, was a favourable scene for the development of trade and civilisation. It was no long voyage from Corcyra to the heel of Italy, and the inhabitants of western Greece had a whole world open to their enterprise. But that world was barbarous in early times and had no civilising gifts to offer; whereas the peoples of the eastern seaboard looked towards Asia and were drawn into contact with the immemorial civilisations of the Orient. The backward condition of western as contrasted with eastern Greece in early ages did not depend on the conformation of the coast, but on the fact that it faced away from Asia; and in later days we find the Ionian Sea a busy scene of commerce and lined with prosperous communities which are fully abreast of Greek civilisation. The west

The northern coast of Africa, confronting and challenging the three peninsulas of the Mediterranean, has played a remarkable part in the history of southern Europe. From the earliest times it has been historically associated with Europe, and the story of geology illustrates the fitness of this connexion. Western Europe and northern Africa were once in days long past united together by bridges of continuous land; and this ancient continent, which we might call Europo-Libya, was perhaps inhabited by peoples of a III. Position of Greece in regard to Africa. Land-bridges in the Mediterranean in the pliocene homogeneous race, who were severed from one another when the ocean was let in and the Mediterranean assumed its present shape. Sicily, a remnant of the old land-bridge, has always been for Italy a step to, or a step from, Africa; while Spain needs no island to bridge her strait.

Greece is a land of mountains and small valleys; it has few plains of even moderate size and no considerable rivers. It is therefore well adapted to be a country of separate communities, each protected against its neighbours by hilly barriers; and the history of the Greeks, a story of small independent states, could not have been wrought out in a land of dissimilar formation. The political history of all countries is in some measure under the influence of geography; but in Greece geography made itself pre-eminently felt, and fought along with other forces against the accomplishment of national unity. The islands formed states by themselves, but, as seas, while like mountains they sever, may also, unlike mountains, unite, it was less difficult to form a sea than a land empire. In the same way, the hills prevented the development of a brisk land traffic, while, as we have seen, the broken character of the coast and the multitude of islands facilitated intercourse by water.

There is no barrier to break the winds which sweep over the Euxine from the Asiatic continent towards the Greek shores and render Thrace a chilly land. Hence the Greek climate has a certain severity and bracing quality, which promoted the vigour and energy of the people. Again, Greece is by no means a rich and fruitful country. It has few well-watered plains of large size; the cultivated valleys do not yield the due crop to be expected from the area; the soil is good for barley but not rich enough for wheat to grow freely. Thus the tillers of the earth had hard work. And the nature of the land had consequences which tended to promote maritime enterprise. On one hand, richer lands beyond the seas attracted the adventurous, especially when the growth of the population began to press on the means of support. On the other hand, it ultimately became necessary to supplement home-grown corn by wheat imported from abroad. But if Demeter denied her highest favours, the vine and the olive grew abundantly in most parts of the country, and their cultivation was one of the chief features of ancient Greece.

CHAPTER I

THE BEGINNINGS OF GREECE AND THE HEROIC AGE

SECT. I. THE ORIGIN OF THE GREEKS

OUR European civilisation had its origin in Greece, and we must date its beginnings to more than three thousand years ago. We know that in the thirteenth century B.C. the Greek tongue was spoken throughout the Greek peninsula, from the mountain walls which protect the plains of Thessaly in the north to the southern bays of Argos, Laconia, and Messenia. But when we try to reach further back and to discover whence the Greek-speaking folks came and how long they had possessed their country, we find little that is certain.

Our earliest written record, the *Iliad* of Homer, refers to the peoples and civilisation of Greece in the thirteenth century, and shows us the Achaeans as being at that time the most prominent and powerful among the Greeks. But it was only recently that they had attained to this power and prominence; and before them other Greek peoples may have attained to similar though hardly to equal greatness. Thus the Pelasgians were an ancient people who, according to tradition, were once dominant in many parts of Greece, but it has been disputed whether they were of Greek origin, and it was believed by some that they spoke a tongue which was not Greek. The inhabitants of the hilly uplands of Arcadia, who spoke a purely Greek language, had been there since time immemorial; they boasted that they had lived among their mountains before the birth of the moon.

Greece was in-habited by Greeks long be-fore the Achaean conquests.

But although we conclude that it had become Greek long before the Achaean age (13th and 12th centuries), the Greek peninsula was not always Greek. The original coming of the Greeks was utterly forgotten by their descendants, and we are unable to fix its date. The old home of the invaders is supposed to have lain in the northwest regions of the Balkan peninsula. They must have come southward in such numbers as to extinguish ultimately the native speeches which they found in their new country. The men whom the Greeks conquered learned the new tongue and forgot their own. But they had given to many a hill and rock the name which was to abide with

Coming o, the Greeks.

The pre-Greek popula-tion.

5

it for ever. Corinth and Tiryns, Parnassus and Olympus, Arne and Larisa, are names which the Greeks seem to have received from the ancient inhabitants. And some of these names which are also found in the western parts of Asia Minor suggest that the primeval inhabitants belonged to a race which was diffused on both sides of the Aegean.

We shall not perhaps be far astray if we conjecture that the Greeks descended into Greece in the course of the third millennium. Their conquest may have been a gradual infiltration of people after people rather than the single migration of a vast host and may have extended over many years. And it is not improbable that by 2000 B.C. Zeus, the great Indo-European lord of Heaven, was invoked and worshipped throughout the length and breadth of the land.

The Greeks of history who had completely forgotten this far-distant past were not exclusively the descendants of these Greek invaders. For it is not to be supposed that the conquered people was abolished or obliterated. The idea that the older inhabitants were entirely crushed out and a clear field left for the newcomers is due to exactly the same kind of false inference from language to race, which makes out Greeks and Romans, Celts and Germans, Slavs and Illyrians, Phrygians and Armenians, Persians and ancient Indians, to be the posterity of common Aryan ancestors, because they all spoke kindred tongues. The Greek language is vigorous and masterful, as its subsequent history has shown.[1] It made a complete conquest of the languages of the older inhabitants; in whatever land the Greeks settled, it became exclusively the language of the land. But the extermination of the older tongues does not mean the extermination of the older races. The men among whom the Greeks settled, or whom they conquered, learned the new tongue and forgot their own. There was fusion of the old and the new;[2] and the Indo-European gods of the invaders had to make terms with the deities of the natives.

Sect. 2. Aegean Civilisation. Crete.

If Greece, as we may fairly believe, was Greek since days to which we cannot reach back, there flourished close to its shores a

---

[1] 1. Its vigour is proved by its survival with comparatively little change. There is less difference between the Greek of to-day and the Greek of the days of Xenophon, than between the English of to-day and the English of Gower's age. 2. Its masterfulness is illustrated by the victory it gained over its Slavonic sister in the Middle Ages. The Slavs who settled in the Peloponnesus lost their own tongue and adopted Greek. It failed, however, to master Albanian.

[2] It may be conjectured that the mixture of the Greeks with the native peoples had a decisive effect in differentiating the Greek dialects. Subsequent invasion of Illyrians and others carried the process further.

great non-Greek civilisation which had a decisive influence on its fortunes and of which we know far more than of the contemporary Greeks. It is only recently that we have become aware of this "Aegean" civilisation, as it is called, which had grown steadily in Crete and in Melos and other islands of the Aegean, from remote

FIG. 1.—Two sides of a white steatite Seal, with writing (Crete).

beginnings in the stone age, until towards the end of the third millennium Crete entered upon a period of power and brilliancy which rivals in interest the more famous civilisations of Egypt and Babylon. The monuments which reveal the great age of Crete have been dug out of the earth; and although Greek tradition remembered that Crete was once a strong sea power, no one suspected that this island had been the home of a life and art highly developed and various, and the centre of a culture which spread far over the Mediterranean Sea. **Crete.**

In the course of the third millennium Crete had passed from the age of stone into the age of metal. The remains of a homogeneous culture have been found all over the island, but the leading settlements, the seats of the most powerful rulers, were Cnossus and Phaestus. Nearly at the middle of the north coast, the hill of Cnossus is situated a few miles from the sea, close to the banks of a stream (Cairatos). About 2000 B.C. a great palace was erected on this hill; and at Phaestus, in the south of the island, a palatial residence arose much about the same time. These palaces endured for several centuries; and in this period the development of Cretan art was marked by the perfection of polychrome (many-coloured) pottery. We have some beautiful examples of what Cretan artists could do, such as a fresco picture of a little boy, who is painted in blue, picking white crocuses and placing them in a vase. **Cnossus and Phaestus; the first palaces c. 2000 B.C.**

One of the most interesting facts about the civilisation of the Cretans is that they could write. We find first a method of picture writing, in which each pictorial symbol, such as an ox head, or a **Systems of writing. (1) Hiero-glyphic**

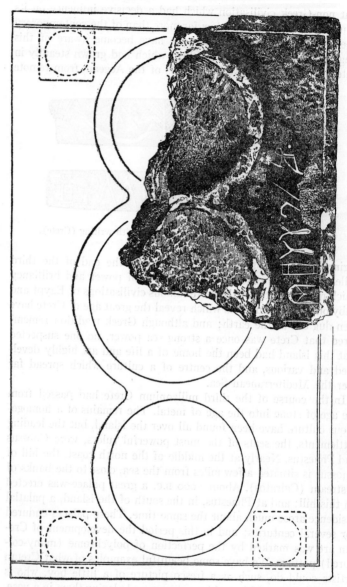

Fig. 2.—Table of Offerings, with inscription, found in the Dictaean Cave (Crete).

gate, or an eye, represented a word;[3] but at a later period there was likewise used a system of "linear" signs, of which each probably stood for a syllable. A table of drink offerings, inscribed with signs of this kind, was found in the cave of Mount Dicte, already a holy place and afterwards to be associated with the birth of Zeus.

We have no clue to the language of these documents. It seems unlikely that it was Indo-European; it seems most likely that it was cognate with the tongues of the Lycians and other ancient peoples of western Asia Minor. In eastern Crete a strange language was still spoken in late times when the rest of the island had become Greek; we have some slight records of it which can be read but cannot be interpreted;[4] and it would be natural to suppose that this was the same language which prevailed in the pre-Hellenic period.

It was about 1700 B.C that the end of this brilliant period of Cretan history was marked by the partial destruction of the palaces of Cnossus and Phaestus. It seems probable that this was the consequence of a revolution within the island, and not of foreign invasion. At the same time the intercourse between Egypt and Crete, which had been close, seems to have been interrupted for a hundred years or more. But a new dynasty was soon to take possession of the Cnossian hill, to develop further the native civilisation and inaugurate a still more brilliant period in the island's history.

Aegean civilisation attained its highest bloom in Crete, but it had developed independently in the islands of the Archipelago, especially in Melos, where its continuous growth can be traced in the important settlement of Phylakopi. Melos produces obsidian, which in the stone age and later was in great request for the manufacture of knives and spear-points, and her export of this product, which was taken for instance to Egypt, may explain her early prosperity. Remains have been found which show that the eastern coast of Greece was not unaffected by this insular civilisation.

We have still to glance at a great stronghold which towards the end of the third millennium stood on the hill of Troy, commanding the entrance of the Hellespont. It was not the first city that had been reared on that illustrious hill, which rises to the height

Marginal notes:

(before 2000 B.C.) (2) Early linear (before 1600 B.C.)

Language

End of first palace of Cnossus. c. 1700 B.C.

"Cycladic" civilisation.

Melos.

Troy (the hill now called Hissarlik, "fortress"). The oldest city

---

[3] A most remarkable document of pictorial writing found in Crete is a small terra-cotta disc from Phaestus, entirely covered on both sides with picture-characters running in a continuous spiral line. It seems to have been intended for use as a die; and it has been conjectured that the text is a religious hymn. But there is reason for thinking that it is not of Cretan origin, but was imported, perhaps from Lycia.

[4] See below, p. 130.

of about 160 feet, not far from the banks of the Scamander. The earliest settlement, fortified by a rude wall of unwrought stone, can still be traced; and some of its primitive earthware and stone implements have been found. An axe-head of white nephrite seems to show that in those remote days there was a line of traffic, however slow and uncertain, between the Mediterranean and the Far East; for this white jade must have come from Central Asia. On

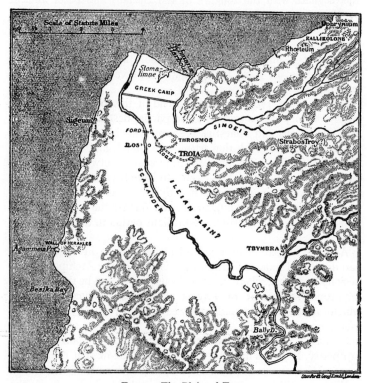

FIG. 3.—The Plain of Troy.

The
SECOND
CITY.

the ruins of this primeval city arose a great fortress, girt with a wall of sun-baked brick, built on strong stone foundations. There were three gates, and the angles of the walls were protected by towers. The inhabitants of this city lived in the stone and copper age; bronze was still a rarity. Their pottery was chiefly hand-made. But a treasure of golden ornaments, wrought by skilful craftsmen, shows that the place was wealthy. The most important feature to be noted is the outline of the palace in this ancient city.

Here at the very outset of Aegean civilisation we find the general plan of the main part of the house exactly the same as that which is described, more than a thousand years later, in the poems of Homer. From an outer gate we pass through a courtyard, in which an altar stood, into a square preliminary chamber; and from it we enter the great hall, in the centre of which was the hearth.[5]

An enemy's hand destroyed the castle by fire, and no tradition of its existence has survived. When we come down seven or eight centuries, to the famous city of which it was the precursor, we shall learn the probable secret of the prosperity of its kings.

De-stroyed, c. 2000 B.C.

It may be asked how, without the guidance of literary records, we can fix the successive stages of Aegean civilisation in an ordered series and assign approximate dates to its period. When we have started with the capital division of time between the age of stone and the age of bronze, the potter's art is the chief clue for establishing a relative chronology within each of those ages. The clay vessels, from the most simple and primitive moulded by hand to the most artistic and elaborate wrought by wheel, can be arranged in a definite series; and thus the things which are found in the same stratum as a particular class of sherds can be assigned to a definite place in this succession. Such things, found in association with particular stages in the development of pottery, may then become themselves additional criteria for dating remains. The history of Cretan civilisation from the end of the stone age has by this means been arranged in three chief ages, called Early, Middle, and Late "Minoan," and each of these has been subdivided into three periods.[6]

CHRON-OLOGY: Relative·

It is to the intercourse of Crete with Egypt that we are indebted for the means of determining roughly the absolute dates of its history, or, in other words, of correlating its chronology with the gen-

Absolute.

---

[5] In an adjacent building we find not only the preliminary chamber (πρόδο-μος), but the vestibule outside it, as described by Homer.

[6] The following table, assigning rough dates to the Middle and Late Minoan periods, with some Egyptian synchronisms, may be useful:

MM 1. B.C. 2100-1900 (Dynasty XI. 2160-2000).
MM 2. " 1900-1700 (Dynasty XII. 2000-   ).
MM 3. " 1700-1600.
LM 1. " 1600-1500 (Dynasty XVIII. 1580-   ).
LM 2. " 1500-1400 (Thothmes III. 1500-   ;
                    Amenhotep II. 1450-   ;
                    Amenhotep III. 1414-   ).
                    Fall of Cnossus c. 1400.
LM 3. " 1400-1100 (Amenhotep IV.=Ikhnaton, between 1375 and 1360.
                    (Dynasty XIX. 1321-   :
                    Ramses II. 1292-   ;
                    Mernptah 1225-1215;
                    Ramses III. 1198-1167).

eral chronology of the world. Thus a polychrome Cretan vessel found in the tomb of King Senusert III. (Sesostris) at Egyptian Abydos enables us to conclude that the Second period of the Middle Minoan age was approaching its close about B.C. 1880. Again, the statuette of an Egyptian in diorite stone, inscribed with his name in Egyptian characters, was found in a court of the Cnossian palace, and its style makes it probable that it was wrought under the XIIth or XIIIth Dynasty, perhaps in the second half of the nineteenth century B.C.[7]

The later palace of Cnossus. It was probably about 1600 B.C that kings, perhaps of a new dynasty but not of a new race, began to rule on the hill of Cnossus. The palace had been rebuilt on a grander scale, and adapted to more sumptuous needs, though there was no change in the general architectural style; and about 1500 B.C. it seems to have been extensively remodelled. It covered an area of about five acres. It was not fortified by an exterior wall; its lords seem to have trusted to their ships for defence against foreign invaders. To the east and to the west of a great central court were extensive labyrinths of rooms and passages, and the remains of staircases show that in some parts the building rose to the height of three or four storeys. The principal halls were lit at one end by open shafts or "light-wells," walled in on three sides, and on the fourth open to the hall from which they were separated by two or three columns. There were bathrooms, and there was an excellent system of drainage by pipes, superior perhaps to any of the contrivances that have been since in use till quite recent times. If the palace had merely served as the habitation of the royal household it need not have been so large; but it was much more. It was the seat of a government which controlled not merely the neighbouring regions or even the island, but a maritime empire. The administration of this empire was conducted on careful business lines as is shown by the financial documents found in the archives. We may fairly surmise that there existed a well-developed system of administrative machinery which needed considerable room for its offices. The rich tributes which the kings derived from their dependencies were stored in the palace, and various industries were carried on within its walls for the private needs of the monarch and also probably for purposes of commerce. The discovery of an olive press and great jars for

[7] The dates of the XIth, XIIth, and following dynasties have been much disputed, but the view has recently gained ground that the XIIth (to which Sesostris belongs) began about 2000 B.C., and the XIth may be placed about 2160-2000 B.C.

oil-storage suggests that not only did the palace supply itself with the oil required for its cooking and its lamp-fuel, but that the king himself may have traded in oil, which seems at this time to have been one of the principal Cretan exports. Then there was accommodation for the sculptors and painters who were employed in the royal service; there is evidence that the paints were manufactured on the spot, and a sculptor's workshop has been discovered.

One of the most notable rooms in this spacious palace was the Chamber of the Throne, entered through an anteroom from the central court. The throne is a stone seat adorned with a painted design, and on either side are benches along the wall. Here the king may have sat in council with his ministers. Adjoining this apartment was a room open to the air, containing a tank, and its walls showed a picture of Egyptian character, a landscape with river, sedge, and palms. Most of the principal chambers and corridors were decorated with fresco paintings, representing solemn processions, gay groups of men and women, scenes of town-life, less often of war. The fashions of the time are vividly portrayed in a series of miniature frescoes, showing us women, idling in courts or on balconies, with their hair elaborately dressed, wearing costumes which look as if they had been modelled on quite modern fashions, puffed sleeves, flounced skirts, bodices tightly drawn in round the waist. One of the most striking pictures which have survived is that of a tall, handsome cupbearer, evidently belonging to the same race as the Cretans (Keftiu) who are represented in a painting of Egyptian Thebes as bringing offerings to King Thothmes III. in the fifteenth century.

Near the northern entrance to their palace the later lords of Cnossus constructed a theatre, capable of holding about 400 spectators. This was not a new thing; a theatre of an earlier period has been discovered in the palace of Phaestus. The orchestral area in these early theatres was not circular as in those of later times, but rectangular; and the performances were probably religious dances in honour of the great Cretan goddess, and perhaps boxing matches. The space was not large enough for bull fights, which seem to have been a favourite amusement of the Cretans if we may judge from scenes depicted on wall-paintings and gems, which present acrobats grappling with bulls. Women took part in this dangerous sport. In one painting we see a girl in the air caught on the horns of a bull. The kings had also quieter recreations. A magnificent inlaid gaming board of very beautiful design was found in the palace, made of pieces of ivory overlaid with gold foil, and

Throne Room.

Painting.

Fashions.

(Thothmes B.C. 1500-1450.)

Theatres.

Bull fights.

crystals coloured alternately blue and white by means of blue-paste (*kyanos*) and silver foil on which they were set.[8]

The little palace at Cnossus. Beneath the great palace, close to the river bank and about 130 yards east of the northern entrance gate, was a smaller palace which, it has been conjectured, may have been used by the king as a summer retreat. On its smaller scale it seems to have been as sumptuous as the greater dwelling. Here was found, fallen from a room on an upper storey, a superb painted jar, showing the highest point to which the art of the Cnossian potters could attain in the sixteenth century. The decoration, displaying sprays of papyrus and rosettes, is effected by the combination of colour and relief. Here, too, there was a throne-room—a remarkable pillared hall, more than 12 yards long, resembling in its arrangement the Roman basilica or law-court.

The palace of Phaestus. The rebuilding of the palace of Phaestus fell perhaps in the sixteenth century. Like that of Cnossus it was unfortified, and it was built on a very similar plan, and in the same fashion of architecture. Here, too, there was a large court in the centre, surrounded by pillared reception halls and store-rooms, and a smaller court in the west of the building. The residence of Phaestus was distinguished by an imposing entrance, with a flight of twelve steps forty-five feet broad; and though it was much smaller in extent than the rival palace of Cnossus, and its walls were not adorned with such rich and various paintings, its external appearance seems to have been more imposing, for it was built upon the slope of a hill, and rose, roof above roof, on different levels. About two miles off, at a place now called Hagia Triada, a well-built house has been found which seems to have served as a pleasure-residence for the potentates of the neighbouring palace.[9]

Cretan towns. Not far from the palace of Cnossus there must have been a populous town. Whole Cretan towns have been excavated in eastern Crete, and much has been found to illustrate the town life of the common people and the artisans; for instance, the house of a carpenter, with all his tools, his chisels, saws, awls,

---

[8] Another Aegean gaming table, made of ivory, was found at old Salamis (Enkomi) in Cyprus; and some crystal plaques in one of the graves on the acropolis of Mycenae are surmised to be the remains of a similar board. What appear to be ivory pieces for playing the unknown game have also been found in the Cnossian palace.

[9] It is remarkable that while valuable art treasures of the sixteenth century have been found at Hagia Triada, few objects of interest have been unearthed at Phaestus itself.

and nails.[10] But of the appearance of a flourishing town, such as Cnossus must have been, we can better gain an idea from the façades of private houses which are represented on mosaic plaques of porcelain discovered in the palace. The houses were of several storeys; some had two doors, others one; the windows above might have four or six panes; and there seem to be un-windowed openings in the upper storeys, which might serve the purposes of balconies. These Cretan houses show considerable likeness to contemporary houses in Egypt.

Religion.

There seems to be no evidence that there were public temples in Crete at this period. There were sanctuaries in the palaces, and perhaps the Cretans generally performed their religious duties in domestic shrines. The chief divinity whom they worshipped was a nature-goddess, the goddess whom the Greeks called Rhea, and this indeed may have been her Cretan name. Scenes of worship were frequently depicted in art; the goddess is represented sometimes guarded by lions, sometimes associated with doves who were symbolic of the descent of a deity; she was served by priestesses. She was closely connected with a male divinity, whether her consort or her son, who seems to have been sub-ordinate to her. In later times the Greeks conceived this god as Zeus, son of Rhea and nurtured in the Idaean cave. Both the goddess and the god were associated with the double-axe, a fetish in which the deity was supposed to dwell. We find the same worship of the double-axe in western Asia Minor among the Carians.

Mother-Goddess.

This symbol was so frequently represented on the walls of the Cnossian palace that it might almost be called the palace of the double-axe; and, as the Carian name for the double-axe was *labrys*, it has been suggested that the palace was known as the *labyrinthos*. This would explain the origin of the curious Greek legend that Minos, king of Cnossus, kept in a labyrinth the monstrous Minotaur who devoured the tribute of youths and virgins brought from overseas. The intricate plan of the palace might well suggest a maze.

Laby-rinth.

We have seen that the art of writing was long familiar to the Cretans. In this later period a new and more advanced system of linear signs was in use. The kings kept accurate records and accounts. Hundreds of written documents have been found in the Cnossian palace, consisting of small rectangular tablets of clay,

Later linear writing.

---

[10] At Gournia (ancient name unknown), which seems to have been burned down about 1500 B.C. Palaikastro, where the plan of a town has also been laid bare, was the ancient Heleia.

which were preserved in wooden boxes secured by seals. As we have no clue to the language they cannot be read; but the numerical symbols can be identified. The arithmetical system was decimal, and there were signs for fractions. It has been inferred from the frequent occurrence of numerals, and from the insertion of figures representing objects, that many of the documents are accounts relating to the stores. The Cretans possessed a system of weights, and here they seem to have been indebted, through whatever intermediate channel, to the kingdom of Babylonia, for their standard was derived from what is known as the light Babylonian talent. And they had a metal currency. Pieces of gold and silver, and bronze ingots have been found, which can only have been used for the purpose of exchange.

The power and splendour of the kings of Cnossus were at their height in the fifteenth century. These kings were undoubtedly the richest and most powerful in Crete, and it is not improbable that they now exercised overlordship over the rulers of Phaestus and over the other towns of the island, in many of which striking remains of Aegean civilisation have been unearthed. Their fleets controlled the Aegean sea; they dominated the islands; and their civilisation spread, as we shall see, to the mainland of Greece. But Cretan influence radiated to more distant shores, by trade and even by colonisation. The commercial intercourse with Egypt, which had existed from primitive times, became probably more regular and frequent; oil and pottery were exported to the lands of the Nile; "the kings of the country of the Keftiu and the isles of the great sea" brought offerings to the great monarchs of the XVIIIth Dynasty. And the influence of Egypt can be traced in the Cretan culture of the time. The Philistines who settled in southern Palestine are now supposed to have been colonists from Crete;[11] and remains found in Sicily and Spain testify that the island of Minos sent products and offshoots of its civilisation far to the west.

The later Greeks associated the Cretan supremacy in the Aegean with the name of the great sea-lord Minos. There is, however, a difficulty about Minos. In Homer he appears as an Achaean ruler in Crete, two generations before the Trojan War (that is, in the thirteenth century). It was thought by some Greeks in later times that there were two kings of this name, of whom the earlier reigned towards the end of the fifteenth century. But

Weights.

Money.

Extent of Cretan power and influence.

Keftiu, Egyptian name for Cretans.

Minos.

[11] Minoa was an ancient name of Gaza. The same name, in Amorgos, Siphnos, and Paros, is a record of Cretan rule over the Aegean islands.

there is no early evidence for the existence of the supposed Minos I.[12]

SECT. 3. MYCENAEAN CIVILISATION (1600-1100 B.C.)

The rise of a civilisation on Greek soil, very similar to Cretan, and undoubtedly under Cretan influence, began probably in the sixteenth century and lasted till the end of the twelfth. Its records are monuments of stone which have remained for more than three thousand years above the face of the earth, or have been brought to light by the spade; and the objects of daily use and luxury which were placed in the houses of the dead and have been unearthed, chiefly in our days, by the curiosity of Europeans seeking the origins of their own civilisation. And for the later stage of this period we have the Homeric poems.

The records of Mycenaean civilisation.

The most numerous and significant records have been found in the east of the Peloponnesus, in the plain of Argos,—at Mycenae, which keeps guard in the mountains at the northern end of the plain, and at Tiryns, its lowlier fellow close to the sea. The richest and strongest city on the coasts of the Aegean seems for a long time to have been Mycenae; and the whole civilisation to which its greatness belongs has been called *Mycenaean*.[13] Remains of the royal palaces, built early in the 14th century to replace earlier residences, have been found both at Mycenae and Tiryns.

Tiryns was the older of the two fortresses, and had played its part in the earlier epoch before the Aegean peoples had yet emerged from the stone age. It stands on a long low rock about a mile and a half from the sea, and the land around it was once a marsh. From north to south the hill rises in height, and was shaped by man's hand into three platforms, of which the southern and highest was occupied by the palace of the king. But the whole acropolis was strongly walled round by a structure of massive stones laid in regular layers but rudely dressed, the crevices being filled with a mortar of clay. This fashion of building has been called Cyclopean from the legend that masons called Cy-

The fortress of Tiryns.

"Cyclopean" masonry. The gate

[12] So far as the Catalogue in *Iliad* ii. may be regarded as preserving a record of the relative resources of the Greek states *c.* 1200 B.C., it does not suggest that Crete at this time had an exceptionally strong fleet. Crete sent 80 ships, less than Pylos which sent 90, not to speak of Argolis (180, besides 50 lent to the Arcadians) and Thessaly (220).

[13] This designation, which had come into use before the discoveries in Crete, is convenient to distinguish the civilisation of the Greek mainland (from the 16th to the 11th century) from the *Minoan* civilisation of the island.

clopes were invited from Lycia to build the walls of Tiryns. The main gate of entrance, on the east side, was approached by a passage between the outer wall of the fortress and the wall of the palace; and the right, unshielded side of an enemy advancing to the gate was exposed to the defenders on the castle wall. On the west side there was a postern, from which a long flight of stone steps led up to the back part of the palace. But one curious feature in the castle of Tiryns sets it apart from all the other ancient fortresses of Greece. On the south side the wall deepens for the purpose of containing store-chambers, the doors of which open out upon covered galleries, also built inside the wall, and furnished with windows looking outward.

The stronghold of Mycenae, about twelve miles inland, at the north-eastern end of the Argive plain, was built on a hill which rises to 900 feet above the sea-level in a mountain glen. The shape of the citadel is a triangle, and the greater part of the wall is built in the same "Cyclopean" style as the wall of Tiryns. Another fashion of architecture, however, also occurs. The gates and some of the towers are built of even layers of stones carefully hewn into rectangular shape.[14] No store-rooms or galleries like those of Tiryns have been found at Mycenae; but on the north-east side a vaulted stone passage in the wall led by a downward subterranean path to the foot of the hill, where a cistern was supplied from a perennial spring outside the walls. Thus the garrison was furnished with water in case of a siege. Mycenae had two gates. The chief was on the west, ensconced in a corner of the wall which at this point running in south-eastward then turned outward due west, and thus enclosed and commanded the approach to the gate. The lintel of the doorway is formed by one huge square block of stone, and the weight of the wall resting on it is lightened by the device of leaving a triangular space. This opening is filled by a sculptured stone relief representing two lionesses standing opposite each other on either side of a pillar, on whose pedestal their fore-paws rest.[15] They are, as it were, watchers who ward the castle, and from them the gate is known as the Lion gate.

The ruins on the hill of Tiryns enable us to trace the plan of the palace of its kings. One chief principle of the construc-

The wall-chambers.

Mycenae.

The wall.

Ashlar masonry.

The cistern.

The Lion gate (beginning of 14th century).

Palace of Tiryns (early in 14th cent.)

---

[14] There is also in the western wall polygonal masonry in which the blocks do not form horizontal rows, but are polygons of various sizes, so sharply cut and accurately set as to leave no crevices. But this work is of a far later date.

[15] The same heraldic scheme is found on gems, and in some cases a male figure takes the place of the pillar. This points to pillar—or, as it is called "baetyl"—worship.

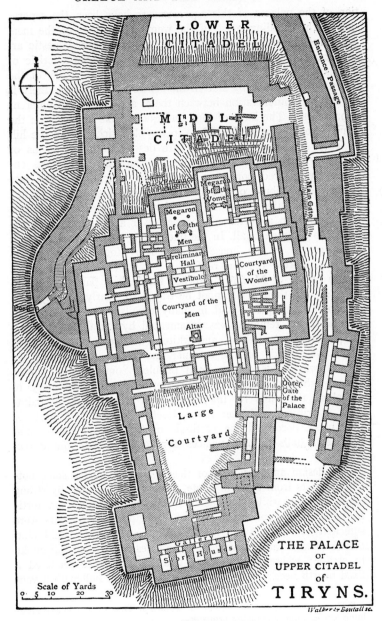

LOWER CITADEL

MIDDLE CITADEL

Megaron of the Women

Megaron of the Men

Preliminary Hall

Vestibule

Courtyard of the Men

Altar

Courtyard of the Women

Inner Gate

Outer Gate of the Palace

Large Courtyard

Postern

Entrance Passage

Main Gate

Gallery
Store Houses

THE PALACE
or
UPPER CITADEL
of
TIRYNS.

Scale of Yards
0   5   10   20   30

Walker & Boutall sc.

FIG 4·

tion of the palaces of this age seems to have been the separa-
'ion of the dwelling-house of the women from that of the men,
—a principle which continued to prevail in Greek domestic architecture in historical times. But the striking characterisic of
Tiryns is that, while the halls of the king and the halls of the
queen are built side by side in the centre of the palace, there is
no direct communication between them, and they have different
approaches.[16] The halls of king and queen alike are built on the
same general plan as the palace in the old brick city on the hill
of Troy and the palaces which are described in the poems of

Courtyard
(αὐλή).
Portico
(αἴθουσα).
Prelimi-
nary hall
(πρόδομος)
(λάϊνος
οὐδός.)
Hall
(μέγαρον)

Homer. An altar stood in the men's courtyard which was enclosed by pillared porticoes; the portico which faced the gate
being the vestibule of the house. Double-leafed doors opened
from the vestibule into a preliminary hall, from which one
passed through a curtained doorway over a great stone thresh-
hold into the men's hall. In the midst of it was the round hearth
—the centre of the house—encircled by four wooden pillars
which supported the flat roof.[17]

Palace of
Mycenae
(c. 1400
B.C.).

The palace of Mycenae crowned the highest part of the hill,
and its plan, though it cannot be traced so clearly or fully, was
in general conception, and in many details, alike. The hearth,
of which part remains, was ornamented by spiral and triangular patterns in red, blue, and white. The floors of the covered
rooms were made of fine cement; and in the open courts the
cement was hardened by small pebbles. Sometimes the floors

Decora-
tion.

were brightened with coloured patterns. It was customary to
embellish the walls by inlet sculptured friezes and by paintings. A brilliant alabaster frieze, inset with *cyanus* or paste of
blue glass, decorated the vestibule of the hall at Tiryns, and
the men's halls in both palaces were adorned with mural pictures.

Differ-
ences
between
Cretan
and My-
cenaean
palaces.

The design and structure of these palaces differ in some notable respects from those of Crete. They were protected by strong
exterior walls, while Cnossus and Phaestus had no such fortifications. In the milder climate of Crete portable braziers were
sufficient for heating the rooms, and the architects could plan
their houses without having to make holes in the roof for smoke
to escape; whereas the severer weather of Greece rendered a
fixed hearth necessary in the centre of the chief hall with a vent

---

[16] The identification of the hall of the women at Tiryns is not indeed absolutely certain, but it is highly probable.
[17] Or rather a portion raised above the flᴖt ⸗ᴖᴄᶠ for the purpose of letting
the smoke of the fire escape.

above for the smoke. This hall, with its pillared portico, became the most important part of the palace, and it was lit from above. The "light-wells," characteristic of Cnossus and Phaestus, were not used in the castles of the mainland.

Besides their castle and palace, and burying-places of the kings of Mycenae are their most striking memorials. The men with whom we are now dealing bestowed their dead in tombs; there is no trace of the practice of burning corpses. At one time the lords of the citadel and their families were buried on the castle hill. Close to the western wall, south of the Lion gate, the royal burial circle has been discovered, within which six tombs cut vertically into the rock had remained untouched by the hand of man since the last corpses were placed in them. Weapons were buried with the men, some of whose faces were covered with old masks. The heads of the women were decked with gold diadems; rich ornaments and things of household use were placed beside them. There was a stêlê or sepulchral stone over each tomb, and some of these slabs were sculptured.

But a day came when this simple kind of grave was no longer royal enough for the rich princes of Mycenae, and they sought more imposing resting-places; or else, as some believe, they were overthrown by lords of another race who brought with them a new fashion of sepulchre. Nine sepulchral domes, hewn in the opposite hillside, have been found not far from the Acropolis. The largest of them is generally known as the "Treasury of Atreus," a name which arose from a false idea as to its purpose. These tombs, which are found, as we shall see, in other places in Greece, consist of three parts—the passage of approach, the portal, and the dome. A stone causeway leads up to the portal which admits into a round vaulted chamber built into the hollowed slope of a hill; and in some tombs (but this is exceptional) there is also a square side-chamber. The portal of the Treasury of Atreus had a striking façade, being clad with slabs of coloured marble and framed by dark grey alabaster pillars with zigzag and spiral patterns and carved capitals. The two massive lintel-stones were relieved by the same device which was adopted in the architecture of the Lion gate, and the triangle was filled by red porphyry. The vaulted room of beehive shape is formed by rings of well-joined and well-chiselled stones, which grow narrower as they rise, and a roof-stone. The walls were adorned with bronze rosettes arranged in some pattern. A door, similar to that of the portal and framed with pillars, admits to the side-chamber, which is hewn into the rock; its walls were decorated with sculptured alabaster

The sepulchres.

The shaft-tombs of the citadel (16th cent.).

The round vaulted tombs (15th and 14th centuries).

Tomb known as Treasury of Atreus. *Dromos, stomion,* and *tholos*

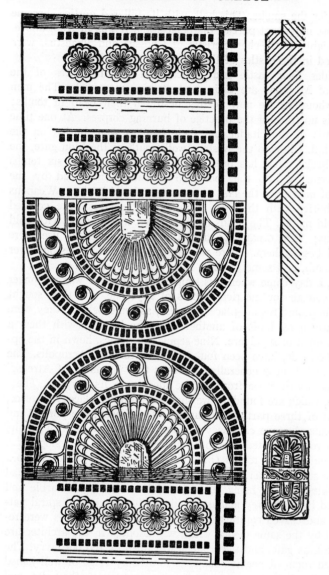

Fig. 5.—Frieze, alabaster and cyanus, of Palace of Tiryns.

plates. The doorway of another tomb [18] was framed by two alabaster columns, fluted like the columns of a Doric temple.

But besides the stately burying-places of the kings, the humbler tombs of the people have been discovered. The town of Mycenae below the citadel consisted of a group of villages, each of
which preserved its separate identity; each had its own burying-ground. Thus Mycenae, and probably other towns of the age,
represented an intermediate stage between the village and the
city—a number of little communities gathered together in one
place, and dominated by a fortress. The tombs in these village
burying-grounds resemble in plan the royal vaults. They are
square chambers cut into the rock; they are approached by a
passage which leads up to a doorway. The difference is that they
are not round and have gabled roofs. Some of the things found in
these sepulchres indicate that most of them are of later date than
the royal tombs of the citadel and contemporary with the vaulted
tombs below.

Tombs of the people.

We have seen how in the royal graves on the castle hill treasures of gold, long hidden from the light of day, revealed the
wealth of the Mycenaean kingdom. Treasures would perhaps have
been found also in some of the great vaulted tombs if they had
not been rifled by plunderers in subsequent ages. But for us the
works of the potter, and the implements of war and peace fashioned by the bronze-smith, are of more value than the golden ornaments for studying this early civilisation; and things of daily
use have been found in the lowlier rock-tombs as well as in the royal sepulchres of hill or plain. From the implements which the
people used, and also from the representations which artists
wrought, we can win a rough picture of their dress, armour, and
ornaments, and form an idea of their capacity in art.

Their civilisation belonged to the age of bronze and copper.
Even in its later period iron was still so rare and costly that it was
used only for ornaments—rings, for instance, and possibly for
money. And in its earlier period, the stone age had not been quite
forgotten; obsidian was still employed for the heads of arrows.
But, in general, bronze was used in Greece for all implements
throughout this age. The arms with which the men of Mycenae attacked their foes were sword, spear, and bow. Their defensive armour consisted of huge helmets, probably made of leather; shields
of ox-hide reaching from the neck almost to the feet—complete
towers of defence, but so clumsy that it was the chief part of a military education to manage them. The princes went forth to war in

Bronze age.

---

[18] That which is popularly known as the Tomb of Clytemnestra.

two-horsed war chariots, which consisted of a board to stand on and a breastwork of wicker.[19] The fragment of a silver vessel (found in one of the rock-tombs of Mycenae) shows us a scene of battle in front of the walls of a mountain city, from whose battlements women, watching the fight, are waving their hands. Round

Fig. 6.—Column from the portal of the "Treasury of Atreus" (Mycenae).

Fig. 8.—Gold Intaglio, with combat of warriors, showing shape of shield.

Fig. 7.—Prehistoric Swords (Mycenae).

shields came into use later. Among the pottery discovered at Mycenae there is a large jar, on one side of which we see a woman looking after six warriors with round shields marching forth to battle armed from head to foot, and on the other, less clearly, men

[19] The horse had probably come into common use in the Aegean countries by the middle of the second millennium. An impression of a seal, found at Cnossus, and probably of the sixteenth century, represents the embarkation of a horse on a boat.

engaged in battle—black-brown figures on a yellow ground.[20] On gems and seal-stones we also find representations of armed men. One of the most striking pictures of the warriors of this age is a group of five spearmen with round shields on a painted gravestone.

Men wore long hair, not, however, flowing freely, but tied or plaited in tresses. Razors have been found in the tombs, but in contrast with the Cretans who always shaved, they often let the beard grow. It is not certain that they ever went naked with mere loin aprons, like the Cretans. In later times they wore a close-fit-

Dress.

FIG. 9.—Siege-scene on a silver vessel; shield above in left corner (Mycenae).

ting tunic and a cloak fastened by a clasp-pin. High-born dames wore tight bodices and wide gown-skirts. Frontlets or bands round the brow were a distinction of their attire, and they wore their hair high coiled in rings, letting the ends fall behind. The ornaments which have been found in the royal tombs show that the queens of Mycenae appeared in glittering gold array.

The "Mycenaean" pottery has given a clue for fixing the earlier and later epochs of the civilisation which produced it, and enables

Relative chronology

[20] The shields on this vase are round at the top, but cut short below so as to form a crescent and leave the thigh uncovered.

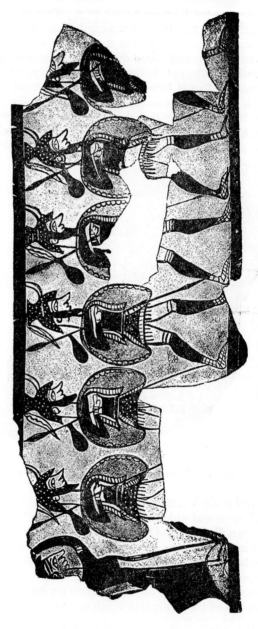

Fig. 10.—Warrior Vase (Mycenae).

; to say that, for instance, the vaulted sepulchres of the plain were subsequent to the shaft sepulchres on the castle hill of Mycenae.

The painted vessels of the second millennium fall into two general classes, unglazed and glazed. The unglazed, ornamented chiefly with lines and spirals, were older, and, when the glazed style attained its perfection, went almost entirely out of use. In the varnished jars, the development of the handicraft from the cruder work of the earlier potters can be traced through the best period into an age of decadence, when the Mycenaean comes into com-

of this period. Pottery: Unglazed ware:

Glazed ware.

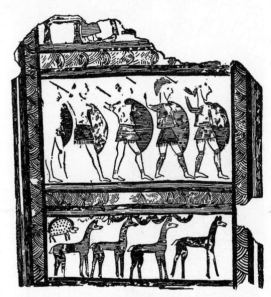

FIG. 11.—Painted Tombstone with Warriors (Mycenae, lower town).

petition with other and newer styles. The colour of these vessels, in the best age, is warm, varying from yellow to dark brown, and sometimes burnt into a rich deep red. A new impulse of decoration has come upon the potters. The ornaments are no longer lines and spirals, but vegetables and animals, especially of the sea kingdom, fishes, polypods, seaweeds. On the other hand, sphinxes, griffins, lotus flowers, and other oriental and Egyptian subjects, though common elsewhere in Mycenaean ornament, are hardly ever copied by the workers in clay. The curious "false-necked" jars which have no opening above the neck, but a spout at the side, are one of the

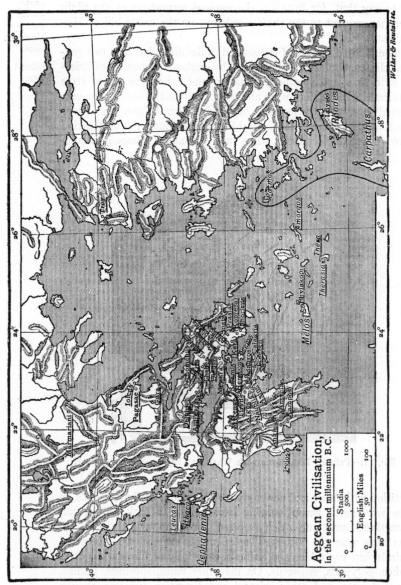

Aegean Civilisation,
in the second millennium B.C.

Stadia
0   500   1000

English Miles
0   50   100

Fig. 12.

Walker & Boutall sc.

most characteristic products of the potteries, which we call Mycenaean.

Other marks for fixing the relative dates of "Mycenaean" troves
are stone tools and iron. If, for example, we find in one tomb obsidian spear-heads and no trace of iron, and in another no stone
implements but iron rings, it is a safe inference that the first is
older than the second. The occurrence of iron is a mark of comparative lateness.

Stone im-
plements;
iron.

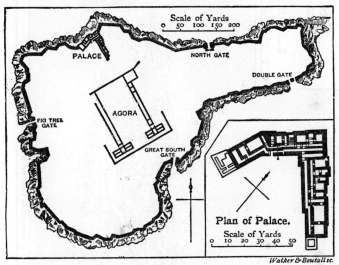

FIG. 13.—Plan of Gla.

It is by such marks as these that we are able to say that the
kings of the shaft graves reigned before the kings who were buried
in the vaulted tombs, and that remains which have been found in
the island of Thera belong to the beginning of the "Mycenaean
age."

The remains at Mycenae and Tiryns are, taken in their entirety,
the most impressive of the memorials of the civilisation of the
Greek mainland in the bronze age. Close to Sparta, on high ground
on the east bank of the Eurotas, there was an unwalled stronghold
which perished in a conflagration, and in later times was associated
with the name of king Menelaus. And not far to the south, at Amyclae, which was in early ages perhaps the most important place in
the Laconian vale, there has been discovered a lordly tomb, which,
unlike the Treasury of Atreus, was never invaded by robbers. In
this vault, among other costly treasures, were found the most prec-

Mene-
laion.

Amyclae.

Tomb at
Vaphio.

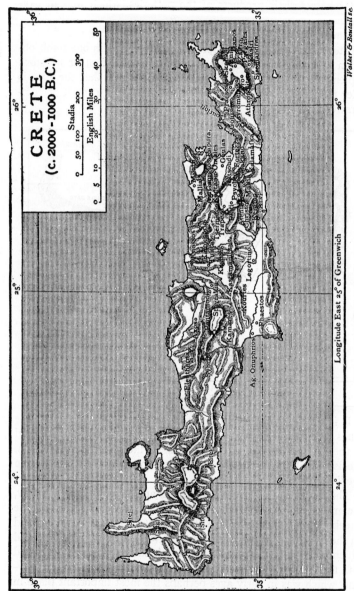

FIG. 14.

ious of all the works of Cretan art that have yet been drawn forth from the earth; two golden cups on which a metal-worker of matchless skill has wrought vivid scenes of the snaring and capturing of wild bulls.

'The bull-cups.

In Attica there are many relics. On the Athenian Acropolis there are a few stones supposed to belong to a palace of great antiquity, but we can look with more certainty on some of the ancient foundations of the fortress wall. This wall was called Pelargic or Pelasgic by the Athenians; and it seems likely that the word preserves the name of the ancient inhabitants of the place, the Pelasgoi.[21] But the Pelasgians of Athens were not the only people of the Athenian plain. Towards the northern end of this plain, a vaulted tomb seems to record ancient princes of Acharnae. The lords of Thoricus had tombs of the same fashion; and at Eleusis there is similar evidence. In many other places in Attica graves of this period have been found; at Prasiae a number of remarkable rock-tombs resembling those in the lower town of Mycenae.

Attica;

Athens;

Acharrae (Menici); Thoricus; Eleusis; Prasiae (Porto Rafti).

In Boeotia there are some striking memorials. Remains of a palace, with some traces of wall paintings, have been found on Cadmeia, the citadel of historic Thebes. On the western shores of the great Copaic marsh a people dwelled, whose wealth was proverbial; and their city Orchomenus shared with Mycenae the attribute of "golden" in the Homeric poems. Paintings on the walls of their palace represented scenes from the sports of the bull-ring, and pillar shrines, which must have been executed by artists of the same school as those who wrought at Cnossus. One of their kings built a great sepulchral vault under the hill of the citadel, and later generations took it for a treasury. It approached, though it did not quite attain to, the size of the Treasure-house of Atreus itself; and it had a second chamber covered by a stone ceiling which was adorned with a curious design in low relief, an arrangement of meandering spirals and fan-shaped leaves bordered by rosettes, producing the effect of a carpet. The same design which decked the burying-place of Orchomenus in stone was used by the painters of some lord of Tiryns to adorn the walls of his palace; and one is tempted to see both in the ceiling and in the sepulchre the work of craftsmen from Crete. But in any case, the common design of ceiling and painting is borrowed from Egypt,[22] for we find almost the

Cadmeia.

Orchomenus, ruled by the Minyae.

Egyptian influence.

---

[21] The most simple explanation of the name Pelargikon is that it was formed by popular etymology (with a suggestion of πελαργός, "stork,") from Pelasgikon.

[22] The same design has been observed also on the dress of a goddess on the walls of the temple of Thothmes III. over against Wadi Halfa, and on the ceiling of a rock-tomb in Nubia.

same design on the ceilings of tombs at Egyptian Thebes. The lords of Orchomenus were probably the mightiest lords in Boeotia, but they had neighbours—were they rivals or friends?—in another fastness of the Copaic marsh. While Orchomenus was situated by the western shores, this primeval stronghold was built on

The castle in Lake Copais (known as Gla).

a rock rising out of the waters. The ruins of the mighty fortress-walls which girded the edge of the rock are still there, and the foundations of the palace of these island princes; but the name of the place is unknown.[23] To the lords of this nameless castle and to the princes of Orchomenus, the curious habits of their spacious lake were a matter of perpetual concern. The lake or morass which fertilised their land has no river to bear its water to the sea, and its only outlets are underground clefts piercing Mount Ptôon, which rises on its northern banks, a barrier between the lake and

Drainage of Lake Copais.

the sea. To help the water to reach these passages, men made canals through the lake, and guarded them by fortresses.

Fig. 15.—Inlaid Dagger-blade, with Nile scene (Mycenae).

Western Greece.

Remains have also been found, especially at Pylus and in Leucas and Cephallenia, which show that the coasts and islands of the Ionian sea, which in Homeric poetry are associated with Nestor and Odysseus, were not outside the "Mycenaean" circle.

Ialysus in Rhodes.

At the extreme south-east of the Aegean there was a "Mycenaean" community at the beginning of the fourteenth century—at Ialysus in Rhodes. An old burying-place has been dug out, and revealed horizontal rock-graves with the arrangement of avenue, doorway, and four-sided chamber, resembling those of Mycenae. The vases found here belong to the best kind of Mycenaean glazed ware; and the absence of earlier pottery suggests that this stage of civilisation had not been reached by a gradual development in the place, but that settlers had brought their civilisation with them.

Thessaly.

In Thessaly the rude life of the stone age, survived long after Cretan civilisation had transformed southern Greece. The land

---

[23] It has been conjectured to be Arne.

remained comparatively barbarous, and even when in the late "Aegean" period the civilisation of the south began to penetrate, it never throve. Thessaly can show no wealthy cities or mighty walls; a few small beehive tombs are the chief record of the heroic age.

Tombs at Dimini, near Pagasae, Marmariani, etc.

From this brief survey of the character and range of the "Mycenaean" civilisation, it will be seen that it was an outgrowth of Cretan civilisation, marked by peculiarities of its own. The period within which it flourished and declined fell between the sixteenth and the eleventh centuries. The end came with the beginning of the iron age, and in Greece iron did not come into general use for weapons and ordinary purposes before the eleventh century. Here too, as in Crete, Egypt supplies evidence bearing on the chronology. Early in the sixteenth century Mycenaean vases were represented on a wall-painting at Egyptian Thebes. At Gurob, a city which was built in the fifteenth century and destroyed two or three hundred years later, a number of "false-necked" jars imported from the Aegean have been found; and they belong not to the earlier but to the later period of Mycenaean pottery. And Egyptian evidence is found not only on Egyptian soil, but on both sides of the Aegean. Three pieces of porcelain, one inscribed with the name, the two others with the "cartouche," of Amenhotep III. of Egypt, and a scarab with the name of his wife, Taia, have been found in the chamber-tombs of Mycenae. It is a curious coincidence that a scarab of the same Amenhotep was discovered in the burying-place of Ialysus in Rhodes. The single occurrence of such a scarab in one place might be an unsafe basis for an argument; but the coincidence seems to point to some special epoch of active intercourse with Egypt in this king's reign. It would follow that early in the fourteenth century at latest the period of the chamber-tombs and the vaulted tombs began. But the earlier sepulchres also supply testimony to Egyptian influence. On an inlaid dagger-blade, found in one of the rock-tombs on the Mycenaean citadel, we see represented a scene from Egyptian life—ichneumons catching ducks in a river which can only be the Nile. The workmanship is Aegean, not Egyptian; but the Aegean artist knew Egypt.

16th to 13th centuries, later periods of Mycenaean pottery.

Egyptian evidence in the Aegean. Scarabs and porcelain with name of Amenhotep III. (1414-1383 B.C.) discovered at Mycenae and Ialysus: five objects in all.

The simplest way of explaining the rise of this civilisation is to suppose that the Cretans, when their power expanded after 1600 B.C., descended on various parts of Eastern Greece, and establishing themselves especially in Argolis and Boeotia planted their own culture among the Greeks. There is some evidence for Cretan settlements and Cretan lordships. For instance, the name of the island Minoa opposite to Megara seems to record a settlement from the island of Minos.[24] In the legend of Cadmus and Europa, the founders of Thebes, Europa is mother of Minos, daughter of Phoenix; and the tradition that Cadmus was the inventor of writing may commemorate the introduction of a Cretan script. Though the story represents Europa as a Phoenician, she was, in the original version, a Cretan princess. As daughter of Phoenix, she was transferred to Phoenicia, because the Greeks had forgotten that, long before they were acquainted with the traders of Tyre and Sidon, they had been wont to designate the brown-skinned Cretans as *Phoenikes,* "red men." But these arguments are valid only if we assume that the name of Minos was already connected with Crete in the 16th or 15th century.

Probably some of the principalities which were founded under the aegis of Crete grew strong enough to fling off the authority of the Minoan sovrans and refuse to pay tribute. But in all that concerns the relations of Cnossus to Mycenae and her fellows, the history of the fifteenth century is hidden from us. Then about 1400 B.C. Cnossus fell and the glory of Crete departed. The splendid palace was destroyed by fire, and the other great settlements in the island seem to have been overwhelmed in the same catastrophe.[25] This common destruction seems to show that the disaster was the work of invaders, and of invaders who had come simply to destroy and to sail away when the work of ruin was complete.

Destruction of Cnossus c. 1400 B.C.

Uncertain who destroyed it.

But who the destroyers were we cannot say for certain. Some think that they were the Achaeans, who, as we shall see, rose to great power in Greece, in the thirteenth century, and also made settlements and bore rule in Crete. But although it is possible that Achaeans may have been concerned in the destruction of Cnossus, and although they were the predominant people in Crete a century and a half later, there is no proof that they had come southward so early. There was no break-up of the old Cretan civilisation; it lived on under less wealthy rulers and declined. The palaces of Cnossus and Hagia Triada were reoccupied and partly rebuilt. It is not impossible that the ruin of the Cretan power was wrought by the lords of the Argolid plain, who had become rivals of the Cnossian kings. At all events, after the fall of Cnossus pre-Achaean Argolis became the most powerful seat of Aegean civilisation.

We can make out little as to the mutual relations of the small

---

[24] There was another Minoa on the east coast of Laconia.

[25] The latest dated relic of the great age of Crete is a scarab of Queen Taia, found at Hagia Triada

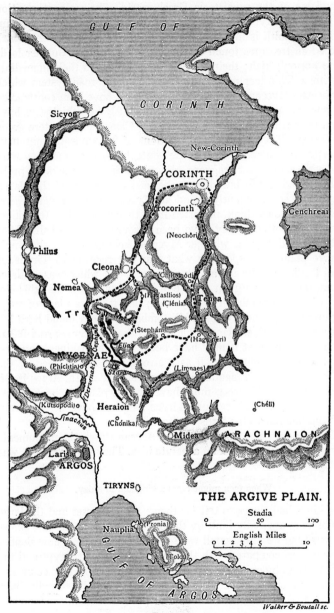

THE ARGIVE PLAIN.

Stadia

Walker & Boutall sc.

FIG. 16.

kingdoms of the prehistoric Greek world. The eminent position

of "golden" Mycenae herself seems to be established. Her comparative wealth is indicated by the treasures of her tombs which exceed all treasures found elsewhere in the Aegean. But her lords were not only rich; their power stretched beyond their immediate territory. This fact may be inferred from the road system which connected Mycenae with Corinth, and must have been constructed

The high-
roads
from
Mycenae
to the
Isthmus.

by one of her kings. Three narrow but stoutly built highways have been traced, the two western joining at Cleonae, the eastern going by Tenea. They rest on substructions of "Cyclopean" masonry; streams are bridged and rocks are hewn through; and as they were not wide enough for waggons, the wares of Mycenae were probably carried to the Isthmus on the backs of mules. If the glazed clay-ware, so abundantly found at Mycenae, was wrought there, and not, as some think, imported from the islands, then the industry of her potteries may have been a source of her wealth. It is not easy to determine whether Mycenae held sway over the whole Argive plain and especially what was her relation to Tiryns. A

road leading southward as far as a small hill which was, in later times, famous for a great temple of Hera, may show that this site was under the dominion of Mycenae; and it was a place of some importance, for three vaulted hill-tombs have been found hard by.

Tiryns was an older place of habitation than Mycenae; and it has been suggested that it may have been Tirynthian kings who first selected the Mycenaean hill as a strong post at the head of the plain and a bulwark against invaders from the north. Argos itself,

under the hill of Larisa, must have been a place of importance, and in the thirteenth century Tiryns seems to have belonged not to Mycenae but to the lords of Argos.[26]

Of the power and resources of the Aegean states, the monuments hardly enable us to form an absolute idea. They were small; it was an age

> When men might cross a kingdom in a day.

The kings had slaves to toil for them; the fortresses and the large tombs were assuredly built by the hands of thralls. One fact shows in a striking way how small were these kingdoms, and how slender their means, compared with the powerful realms of Egypt and the Orient. If Babylonian or Egyptian monarchs, with their command of slave-labour, had ruled in Greece, they would assuredly have cut a canal across the Isthmus and promoted facilities for com-

---

[26] If we may trust the Catalogue in *Iliad* ii., Tydeus was king of Argos and Tiryns, Atreus of Mycenae.

merce by joining the eastern with the western sea. That was an undertaking which neither the small primitive states, nor the small Greek states which came after, ever had the means of carrying out.

SECT. 4. THE ACHAEANS AND THE TROJAN WAR

It is uncertain at what time the Achaeans[27] began to become prominent in the Greek peninsula. While the traditions of the Greeks all point to their being an old Greek people who lived originally in Thessaly and the plain of the Spercheus, it has been held in recent years by some that they were not Greeks, but belonged to a people of Indo-European speech who came down from the regions of the Danube and made conquests in north Greece, perhaps in the fifteenth century B.C.; that they were soon assimilated in speech and manners to their Greek subjects; that they did not work destruction, but carried on the traditions of the civilisation which they found in Thessaly poor and backward, in the Peloponnesus wealthy and luxurious; that in the later remains of "Mycenaean" civilisation their presence or influence can be recognised by some new features which they brought with them from the north—such as the use of long swords, round shields, and brooches (*fibulae*). This bold assumption of an invasion of foreigners, of which the Greeks had not the faintest memory, does not seem required to explain the rise of the Achaeans to power and rule in various parts of Greece; nor are there any facts which necessarily point to an immigration of strangers from the north at this period. It is safer to assume that the Achaeans were Greeks, and that movements within Greece itself raised them to kingship in the south.

It is certain that by the thirteenth century Achaeans had both risen to power in Argos and made settlements in Crete. The dynasty from which the Homeric kings, Agamemnon and Menelaus, sprang was founded, according to Greek tradition, early in the thirteenth century, by Pelops, a Phrygian.[28] His son was Atreus, father of Agamemnon and Menelaus, who represent the Achaean stock,[29] and the meaning of the Phrygian relationship is not clear.

The
Achaeans

---

[27] There is no reason to suppose that the Achaeans generally were fair-haired because Homer calls Menelaus ξανθός (which means probably brown). Among the later Greeks there were two marked types distinguished by light and dark hair. The fair complexion was rarer and more prized. This is illustrated by the fact that women and fops used sometimes to dye their hair yellow or red—the κόμης ξανθίσματα mentioned in the *Danaë* of Euripides.

[28] Pelops married Hippodamia daughter of Oenomaus; Menelaus, Helen daughter of Tyndareus.

[29] That the Cretan Achaeans came from Thessaly is suggested by tradition. Idomeneus was the chief potentate in Crete at the beginning of the twelfth

However it came about, Achaeans had risen to power in many lands, and were the most prominent Greek rulers in the thirteenth and twelfth centuries; and the kings who held sway in Argolis were the most powerful. It is significant that the minstrels of the twelfth century used both "Achaeans" and "Argives" to designate all the Greeks. They used also, in the same sense, the obscure name *Danaoi,* which legend associated especially with the Argolid, and which perhaps belonged to the original Greek inhabitants of that district.[30]

The Achaeans of north Greece, of the land which was later to be Thessaly, seem to have been the great sea-adventurers of the heroic age. With this country were connected the memories of early Greek exploration of the Euxine, in the legend of the ship Argo. We do not know to which Achaeans we are to refer the earliest notice which preserves the Achaean name in a historical document. An Egyptian writing tells us that they came in company with other peoples [31] "from the lands of the sea" and invaded Egypt in the year 1223 B.C., when Mernptah was king. But the great achievement which made the Achaeans illustrious was one in which southern and northern Greece combined—the expedition against Troy.

The Achaean name is specially associated with the land of Phthia in southern Thessaly [32] and the country to the south, including the plain of the river Spercheus, as far as Mount Oeta. The Spercheus region has a particular interest as the original land of *Hellas.* Here dwelled the Hellênes, a small folk, who would one day give their name to all the Greeks. They were probably the old Greek population who had been subdued by the Achaean invaders.

If we may judge from the ancient names of places, which the Greeks preserved, it would seem that languages closely akin were at one time spoken on both sides of the Aegean and in the isles; the coastmen and highlanders of western Asia Minor called their

Western
Asia
Minor,
from the
Troad to
Lycia, is
outside
the
Aegean
civilisa-
tion.

century; and his father's name was Deucalion. Now the name Deucalion was a home in north Greece (Thessaly): it belonged to the mythical father of the mythical Hellên. We may suppose that the Achaeans won their power in Crete much about the same time as they won it in Argolis, and much in the same way, by intermarriage.

[30] The legend associated Danaus, the name-sire of the Danaoi, with Egypt, and it has been supposed that this people should be identified with the Danauna, who appear in Egyptian documents as early as 1400 and as late as *c.* 1200 as mercenaries and raiders.

[31] Namely: Luku = Lycians, Shardana, Shakalsha, Tursha. It has been proposed to connect these three peoples with names which we afterwards find in the western Mediterranean—Sardinians, Sikels, Tyrrhenians.

[32] The realm of Achilles (*Iliad,* ii. 681) included the Pelasgian Argos (in Thessaly), Phthia, and Hellas.

capes and hills and streams by names which resemble in root and formation names which we find on the coast and in the highlands of Greece, and in islands of the intermediate sea. But the strange thing is that the diffusion of the civilisation which we have been examining stopped short at the margin of the Asiatic shore. It extended to Rhodes, and to the small islands north and south of Rhodes, but it did not, until the days of its decline, touch the opposite continent. The peoples who held the seaboard of Asia Minor between the Troad in the north and Lycia in the south were the Maeonians, the Carians, and the Leleges. It is a fact of importance that these lands lay outside the Mycenaean world, notwithstanding the affinities of race which bound the inhabitants of those countries to the folks of the Aegean islands and Greece. South of Troy, which stood quite by itself, there are no palaces or fortresses of the Mycenaean age along the east Aegean coast, nor in the large islands of Lesbos, Chios, and Samos. The relics even of commerce with the western Aegean, though one would expect such commerce to have been brisk and constant, are few and rare. There was, therefore, an obstinate resistance on the part of the inhabitants of these regions to the reception of the Aegean civilisation of the bronze age.

The most probable explanation of this fact is that a great inland power exercised control over Asia Minor down to the coast and excluded foreign settlements. This power was the empire of the Hittites. The ruins of their capital have been found at Boghaz-Keui in north-western Cappadocia. Their kingdom seems to have lasted from about 2000 to 800 B.C., and about the time of the fall of Cnossus they extended their power southward by conquering north Syria, where they established a second capital at Carchemish. They had close political relations with Babylonia, as is shown by the clay tablets in two languages, Hittite and Babylonian, which have been excavated at Boghaz-Keui. Their lordship extended in some form to the Troad and the western coast of Asia Minor. The conjecture may be hazarded that they were the people who destroyed the great brick fortress of Troy. Many of the influences which passed to and fro between the Aegean world and Mesopotamia may have been transmitted through the Hittites. Their southward expansion meant wars with the Egyptians who also aspired to dominate Syria. In a battle which was fought at Cadesh in 1287 B.C. between the two rival powers, we find among others the Dardanians of the Troad fighting for their Hittite lords. But about this very time the Hittite power was declining, and north-western Asia Minor as far as the valley of the Sangarius was

The Hittite Empire.

(Pteria.)

Phrygian invasion (13th cent.).

wrested from their rule by swarms of new invaders from Europe. These were the Phrygians to whose race the Dardanians belonged, and who were so closely akin to the Thracians that we may speak of the Phrygo-Thracian division of the Indo-European family.

After the destruction of early Troy, centuries had passed during which no attempt was made to restore its vanished splendour. Three different settlements indeed succeeded one another on its site, but they were insignificant, villages rather than castles. We may account for this long interval by the jealous policy of the Hittite kings. These were followed by a stone fortress, of which we

The Fifth City.

know nothing. It also disappeared, and then not long afterwards, apparently towards the end of the sixteenth century B.C., arose the great stronghold which Priam would one day rule—the Troy of legend and history.

Troy: the SIXTH CITY.

The new Troy, through whose glory the name of the spot was to become a household word for ever throughout all European lands, was built on the levelled ruins of the older towns. The circuit of the new city was far wider, and within a great wall of well-

The wall.

wrought stone the citadel rose terrace upon terrace to a highest point. On that commanding summit, as at Mycenae, we must pre-

The houses.

sume that the king's palace stood. The houses of which the foundations have been disclosed within the walls have the same simple plan that we saw in the older brick city and in the palaces of Mycenae and Tiryns. The wall was pierced by three or four gates, the chief gate being on the south-east side, guarded by a flanking

Trojan masonry.

tower. The builders were more skilful than the masons of the ruder walls of the fortresses of Argolis which belong to an earlier age.

Trojan subjects.

To the Trojan realm were reckoned not only the men of the Trojan plain, but the Dardanians in the upper valley of the Scamander, among the hills of Ida—the country of the Homeric Aeneas —and, to the east, the inhabitants of the plains of the Granicus and the Aesepus. And south of Mount Ida were a number of strongholds inhabited by "Pelasgian tribes," who represented the original inhabitants of the country whom the Trojans had subdued.[33]

Source of Trojan power and wealth.

The lords of Troy did not owe their power and wealth to the fertility of the soil or to any natural products of the region in which they had fixed their abode. The little plain, watered by the Scamander, has no advantages in itself to attract settlers; and its

---

[33] The most important of these cities were Larisa on the west coast, Pedasos (the later Assos), Lyrnessos (the late Antandros), and Thebe. Among the Pelasgian tribes some were Leleges, others Cilices.

coasts offer no good harbourage for ships. To account for the fortune of Troy it has been suggested that it was due to the way in which its rulers took advantage of the difficulties of navigation which beset mariners trading between the Aegean and the Euxine. The prevailing summer winds, from north, north-east, and north-west, used to detain sailing ships for days or weeks at the mouth of the Hellespont. The sailors wanted anchorage, and they wanted fresh water which was to be got from the Scamander and also on the west coast at Besika Bay. These things the masters of the Scamander plain had it in their power to grant or withhold. Hence Troy was in a position to control the trade which passed through the Hellespont. And here a number of converging lines of traffic met. From Thrace and Paeonia came wine, swords, white horses, and perhaps gold. From Paphlagonia and the southern coasts of the Euxine came timber, silver, vermilion, wild asses. Southward there was the commerce of the Maeonians and Carians and Lycians. The Maeonians, who were noted as slave-dealers, dwelled in the land which was afterwards to be Lydia, on the banks of the Hermus and in the plain of Sardis. The Carians possessed Miletus, where there were skilful workers in ivory, and the districts of the Maeander. The Lycians may have held much of the carrying trade from Egypt and Syria to the northern coasts of the Aegean.

Lines of trade:

north;

east;

south.

The policy of Troy was to levy a toll upon all the traffic which converged on the Hellespontine shores. It has been conjectured that there was held a great yearly market in the Trojan plain, to which traders from all quarters came by sea or land with their merchandise, an arrangement which was exceedingly profitable to the Trojan king who received the market dues. But there is no evidence for such a yearly international gathering at Troy.[34]

But while, in the absence of any positive evidence, we cannot accept this particular theory, it is clear that a strong power, entrenched at the entrance of the Dardanelles, could interfere with the free access of other powers to the Propontis and the Euxine. That Troy had been found to be an obstacle to Greek enterprise in those seas may well be reflected in the legend of the sack of Troy by Heracles, which was connected with the story of the Argonauts. Heracles embarked at Iolcus with the other heroes in the Argo, and leaving the ship during the voyage destroyed Troy, of which Laomedon, Priam's father, was king.

(Argonautic expedition.)

Troy was the strongest power on the west coast of Asia Minor, and it was to the interest of Troy in the north, and of Lycia in the

[34] It is to be observed that in the Trojan War the various peoples whose merchandise came to the Hellespont appear to have been the allies of Troy.

The
Trojan
War:
(tradi-
tional
date of
fall of
Troy 1183
B.C.;
approxi-
mately
correct).

south, to oppose attempts of the Achaeans to expand eastward.
That they desired to make settlements on the Asiatic coasts and
adjacent islands is shown by the fact that such settlements began
soon after the fall of Troy.

It was probably at the beginning of the twelfth century that the
Achaeans made ready a great expedition to exterminate the power
which was the chief obstacle to eastward expansion.[35] It is uncertain how far the Greek states of the time can be described as a
federation or an empire, but most of them recognised the supremacy of Mycenae, and there seems no reason to doubt that the
Achaean king of Mycenae, whose name was Agamemnon, son of
Atreus, succeeded in enlisting the co-operation of the chief kings
and princes of northern as well as southern Greece; it looks, indeed, as if the Achaean lords of Phthia and Thessaly—the country
from which the Argo sailed—had a particular interest in the enterprise. All sailed to the plain of Troy. The peoples of the west coast
of Asia, including the Lycians, all rallied to the help of Priam. It
was a war between both sides of the Aegean Sea. According to the
tradition of the poets the siege lasted nine years; and, however it
came about, Priam's city was destroyed. Its fall was the necessary
prelude to the opening of the Propontis and the Euxine sea to
Greek enterprise, and Greek colonisation on the eastern coasts and
islands of the Aegean would soon begin. The hill of Troy would be
again inhabited, but it would be of small importance, little more
than a place of famous memories.

SECT. 5. THE HOMERIC POEMS

The later period of the heroic age, its manners of life, its material environment, its social organisation, its political geography,
are reflected in the Homeric poems. Although the poets who composed the *Iliad* and the *Odyssey* probably did not live before the
ninth century,[36] they derived their matter from older lays which
must have belonged to the generations immediately succeeding the
Trojan War. After the age of bronze had passed away, and the
conditions of life and the political shape of the Greek world had
been utterly changed, it would have been impossible for any
one, however imaginative,—unless he were a scientific antiquar-
ian with abundance of records at his command,—to create a

---

[35] It is quite possible that the motive which the poets assigned for the Trojan War—to recover Helen, the wife of Menelaus, king of Sparta, carried off
by Paris, son of Priam,—had some historical basis; but if such an incident occurred it served only as a pretext for the war.

[36] See below, p. 61.

consistent picture of a vanished civilisation. And the picture which Homer presents is a consistent picture, closely corresponding, in its main features and in remarkable details, to the evidence which has been recently recovered from the earth and described in the foregoing pages. The Homeric palace is built on

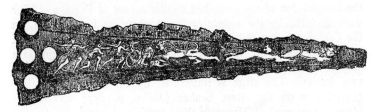

FIG. 17.—Inlaid Dagger-blade, with lion-hunt (Mycenae).

the same general plan as the palaces that have been found at Mycenae and Tiryns, at Troy and in Boetia. The equipment of the Homeric heroes and the man-screening Homeric shield receive their best illustration from Mycenaean gems and jars. The blue inlaid frieze in the vestibule of the hall of Tiryns proves that the poet's frieze of cyanus in the hall of Alcinous was not a fancy; and he describes as the cup of Nestor a gold cup with doves perched on the handles, such as one which was found in a royal tomb at Mycenae. The subjects wrought on the shield which the master-smith made for Achilles may be illustrated by works of art found at Mycenae and in Crete. The shield, wrought in bronze, tin, silver, and gold, is round and has a ringed space in the centre, encompassed by three concentric girdles. In the middle is the earth, the sea, and the heaven, with "the unwearied sun and the moon at her full, and all the stars wherewith heaven is crowned." The subject of the first circle is Peace and War. Here are scenes in a city at peace—banquets, brides borne through the streets by torchlight to their new homes, the elders dealing out justice; there is another city besieged, and scenes of battle. The second circle shows scenes from country-life at various seasons of the year: ploughing in spring, the ploughman drinking a draught of wine as he reaches the end of the black furrow; a king watching reapers reaping in his meadows, and the preparations for a harvest festival; a bright vintage scene, "young men and maids bearing the sweet fruit in wicker baskets," and dancing, while a boy plays a lyre [37] and sings the song

The shield of Achilles (in Iliad xviii.) made by Hephaestus.

[37] The Cretans had seven-stringed lyres. Thus in a funeral scene on a sarcophagus found at Hagia Triada a man is playing this instrument.

of Linus; herdsmen with their dogs pursuing two lions which had carried off an ox from the banks of a sounding river; a pasture and shepherds' huts in a mountain glen. The whole was girded by the third, outmost circle, through which "the great might of the river Oceanus" flowed—rounding off, as it were, the life of mortals by its girdling stream. The whole conception is due to the imagination of the poet, but similar scenes of Peace and War were depicted by the artists of the Aegean; as for instance, on the Cretan plaques (which probably adorned the cover of a chest of cypress-wood) on which we saw a city represented, and on a vase of steatite decorated by a picture of what is probably a harvest festival. The siege is illustrated by the scene of the leaguered city on the silver beaker (above, p. 25); and dagger blades discovered at Mycenae show brilliant examples of the art of inlaying on metal.

See above, p. 14.
Vase found at Hagia Triada.

The art of writing, too, is mentioned in the *Iliad*, in the story of Bellerophon, who carries from Argos to Lycia "deadly symbols in a folded tablet." The fact, which was doubted till a few years ago, that writing was practised in the heroic age, shows that the poet was guilty of no anachronism.

σήματα λυγρά.

There is indeed one striking difference in custom. The Mycenaean tombs reveal few traces of the habit of burning the dead, which the Homeric Greeks invariably practised; while, beyond what is implied in a single mention of embalming, the poems completely ignore the practice of burial. In later times both customs existed in Greece side by side. The explanation of this discrepancy is still uncertain.

Burial and cremation.

Heroic minstrelsy was probably an old institution in Greece, and in the twelfth century lays commemorating the Trojan War were sung throughout Greece. The glorification of Achilles and other features of the *Iliad* point to northern Greece, where was the kingdom of Achilles in Phthia, as the home of one of these early minstrels. In southern Greece too, in the royal palaces of Mycenae and Argos, Sparta and Pylos, lays of Troy, which would long afterwards inspire the epic poetry of Homer, must have been often sung.

Minstrelsy.

Odyssey.

Sect. 6. Political and Social Organisation of the Early Greeks

Old Aryan institutions.

The Homeric poems give us our earliest glimpse of the working of those political institutions which were the common heritage of most of the children, whether children by adoption or by birth, of the Aryan stock,—of Greek, Roman, and German alike. They show us the King at the head. But he does not govern wholly of his own will; he is guided by a Council of the chief men of the community whom he consults; and the decisions of the Council and King deliberating together are brought before the Assembly of the whole people. Out of these three elements— King, Council, and Assembly—the constitutions of Europe have grown; here are the germs of all the various forms of monarchy, aristocracy, and democracy.

But in the most ancient times this political organisation was weak and loose. The true power in primitive society was the family. When we first meet the Greeks they live together in family communities. Their villages are habitations of a *genos*, that is, of a clan, or family in a wide sense; all the members being descended from a common ancestor and bound together by the tie of blood. Originally the chief of the family had the power of life and death over all who belonged to the family; and it was only as the authority of the state grew and asserted itself against the comparative independence of the family, that this power gradually passed away. But the village communities are not, as they were in the Asian foreworld, isolated and independent; they are part of a larger community which is called the *phylē* or tribe. The tribe is the whole people of the kingdom, in the kingdom's simplest form; and the territory which the tribe inhabited was called its deme. When a king became powerful and won sway over the demes of neighbouring kings, a community consisting of more than one tribe would arise; and, while each tribe had to merge its separate political institutions in the common institutions of the whole state, it would retain its separate identity within the larger union.

It was usual for several families to group themselves together into a society called a *phratra* or brotherhood, which had certain common religious usages. The organisation of clan and tribe, with the intermediate unit of the phratry, was a framework derived from Aryan forefathers, shared at least by other Aryan races. For we find the same institutions among the Romans and among the Germans. The clan is the foundation of Roman society; the Julian *gens,* for instance, has exactly the same social significance as the *genos* of the Alcmaeonids of Attica. The *phyle* is the Roman tribe; and the phratry corresponds to the Roman *curia,* and to our own English *hundred.* The importance of the brotherhood is illustrated by Homer's description of an outcast. as one who has no "brothers" and no hearth.

Family organisation.

γένος, gens.

φυλή, tribus.

δῆμος.

φράτρα. Clan, phratry, and tribe were Aryan institutions.

Family property in land.

The importance of the family is most vividly shown in the manner in which the Greeks possessed the lands which they conquered. The soil did not become the private property of individual freemen, nor yet the public property of the whole community. The king of the tribe or tribes marked out the whole territory into parcels, according to the number of families in the community; and the families cast lots for the estates. Each family then possessed its own estate; the head of the family administered it, but had no power of alienating it. The land belonged to the whole kin, but not to any particular member. The right of property in land seems to have been based, not on the right of conquest, but on a religious sentiment. Each family buried their dead within their own domain; and it was held that the dead possessed for ever and ever the soil where they lay, and that the land round about a sepulchre belonged rightfully to their living kinsfolk, one of whose highest duties was to protect and tend the tombs of their fathers.

The Basileus or king.

The king was at once the chief priest, the chief judge, and the supreme war-lord of the tribe. He exercised a general control over religious ceremonies, except in cases where there were special priesthoods; he pronounced judgment and dealt out justice to those who came to his judgment-seat to have their wrongs righted, and he led forth the host to war. He belonged to a family which claimed descent from the gods themselves. His relation to his people was conceived as that of a protecting deity; "he was revered as a god in the deme." The kingship passed from sire to son, but it is probable that personal fitness was recognised as a condition of the kingly office, and the people might refuse to accept a degenerate son who was unequal to the tasks that his father had fulfilled. The sceptred king had various privileges—the seat of honour at feasts, a large and choice share of booty taken in war and of food offered at sacrifices. A special close of land was marked out and set apart for him as a royal domain, distinct from that which his family owned.

σκηπτ-οῦχος βασιλεύς.

The bulê or council.

The royal functions were vague enough, and a king had no power to enforce his will if it did not meet the approval of the heads of the people. He must always look for the consent and seek the opinion of the deliberative Council of the Elders. Strictly, perhaps, the members of the Council ought to have been the heads of all the clans, and they would thus have represented the whole tribe, or all the tribes if there were more than one. But we must take it for granted, as an ultimate fact, which we have not the means of explaining, that certain families had come to hold a privileged position above the others—had, in fact, been marked out as noble, and claimed descent from Zeus; and the Council was composed of this nobility. In the puissant authority of this Council of Elders lay the germ of future aristocracy.

Class of nobles.

More important than either King or Council for the future growth of Greece was the Gathering of the people, out of which democracy was to spring. All the freemen of the tribe—all the freemen of the nation, when more tribes had been united—met together, not at stated times, but whenever the king summoned them, to hear and acclaim what he and his councillors proposed. To hear and acclaim, but not to debate or propose themselves. As yet the Gathering of the folk for purposes of policy had not been differentiated from the Gathering for the purpose of war. The host which the king led forth against the foe was the same as the folk which assented, by silence or applause, to the declarations of his will in the Agŏra. The Assembly was not yet distinguished as an institution from the army; and if Agamemnon summons his host to declare his resolutions in the plain of Troy, such a gathering is the Agora in no figurative sense, it is no mere military assembly formed on the model of a political assembly; it is in the fullest sense the Assembly of the people—the fellow institution of the Roman *comitia,* our own *gemot,* derived all three from the same old Aryan gatherings.

Agora, or Gathering of the folk.

The army is the assembly.

The king was surrounded by a body of Companions, or retainers, who were attached to him by personal ties of service, and seem often to have abode in his palace. The Companions are the same institution as the thanes of our English kings. And if kingship had held its ground in Greece, the Companions might possibly, as in England, have developed into a new order of nobility, founded, not on birth, but on the king's own choice for his service.

The king's Companions.

Though the monarchy of this primitive form, as we find it reflected in the Homeric lays, generally passed away, it survived in a few outlying regions which lagged behind the rest of the Hellenic world in political development. Thus the Macedonian Greeks in the lower valley of the Axius retained a constitution of the old Homeric type till the latest times—the royal power continually growing. At the close of the tale of Greek conquest and expansion, which began on the Cayster and ended on the Hyphasis, we shall come back by a strange revolution to the Homeric state. When all the divers forms of the rule of the few and the rule of the many, which grew out of the primitive monarchy, have had their day, we shall see the Macedonian warrior, who is

Survival of old form of monarchy in Macedonia.

Alexander the Great.

to complete the work that was begun by the Achaean conquerors of Troy, attended by his Companions like Agamemnon or Achilles, and ruling his people like an Achaean king of men.

The constitutional fabric of the Greek states was thus simple and loose in the days of Homer. Perhaps few large communities had come into Greece, but larger communities were constantly formed in the course of the conquest. In the later part of the royal period a new movement is setting in which is to decide the future of Greek history. The city begins to emerge and take form and shape out of the loose aggregate of villages. The inhabitants of a plain or valley are induced to leave their scattered villages and make their dwellings side by side in one place, which would generally be under the shadow of the king's fortress. At first the motive would be to gain the protection afforded by joint habitation in unsettled times; just as we find in an earlier age villages grouped under the citadel of Mycenae. Sometimes the group of villages would be girt by a wall; sometimes the protection of the castle above would be deemed enough. The change from village to city life was general, but not universal; many communities continued to live in villages, and did not form cities till long afterwards. The movement was promoted by the kings; and it is probable that strong kings often brought it about by compulsion. But in promoting it they were unwittingly undermining the monarchical constitution, and paving the way for their own abolition. A city-state naturally tends to be a republic.

In the heroic age, then, the state had not fully emerged from the society. No laws were enacted and maintained by the state. Those ordinances and usages which guided the individual man in his conduct, and which are necessary for the preservation of any society, were maintained by the sanction of religion. There were certain crimes which the gods punished. But it was for the family, not for the whole community, to deal with the shedder of blood. The justice which the king administered was really arbitration. A stranger had no right of protection, and might be slain in a foreign community, unless he was bound by the bond of guest friendship with a member of that community, and then he came under the protection of Zeus the Hospitable. Wealth in these ages consisted of herds and flocks; for, though the Greeks were tillers of the soil and had settled in a country which was already agricultural, the land was not rich enough to bestow wealth. The value of a suit of armour, for instance, or a slave was expressed in oxen. Piracy was a common trade, as was inevitable in a period when there was no organized maritime power

[margin notes]

Beginning of the CITY: 10th to 9th cent. B.C.

Some peoples (e.g. the Eleans) continue to live in villages.

The state not yet differentiated. (θέμιστες.)

Manslaughter avenged by kinsfolk. Attitude to strangers. (Zeus Xenios.) Wealth.

Piracy.

strorg enough to put it down. So many practised this means of livelihood that it bore no reproach; and when seamen landed on a strange strand, the natural question to ask them was: "Outlanders, whence come ye? are ye robbers that rove the seas?"

SECT. 7. THE DORIAN CONQUEST

The heroic age of Greece may be said to have come to an end within two generations after the Trojan War. A dark period of about two centuries followed, which were marked by the disappearance of the old civilisation, by the expansion of the Greek race over the Aegean, and by wide political changes in the mother country. The transition to the new period corresponds to the transition from the bronze to the iron age. The old Aegean fashions of pottery are replaced by a style distinguished by geometrical decorations; and hence in the history of art the "Geometric age" is often used as a convenient designation.

Iron age.

The pressure of Illyrian peoples across the northern frontiers of Greece seems to have been the principal cause of the changes. The Dorians who appear upon the scene and play the leading part in transforming Greece were probably of Illyrian stock. Unlike the earlier northern invaders, the Achaeans, they destroyed instead of adopting the civilisation which they found. The Dorians did not come with horses, they fought on foot; and their weapons were iron.

Illyrian invasions.

The southward pressure of the Illyrians was fatal to Aetolia. In the Homeric poems we have a reflected glimpse of the prosperity of the Aetolian coast-land. We see that "Pleuron by the sea and rocky Calydon" and the other strong cities of that region were abreast of the civilisation of the heroic age; and the Aetolian myth of Meleager and the hunting of the Calydonian boar became a part of the heritage of the national legend of Greece. Maritime Aetolia was then a land of wine; its pride in its vineyards is displayed in the name of its mythic kings. But in the later ages of Greek history all this is changed. We find Aetolia regarded as a half barbarous country, the abode of men who speak indeed a Greek tongue, but have lagged ages and ages behind the rest of Greece in science and civilisation. And we find the neighbouring countries in the same case. Epirus, or the greater part of it, had been hellenized when the worship of Zeus was introduced at Dodona, to become famous and venerable throughout the Greek world. Suddenly it lapses into comparative barbarism, and the sanctuary of Dodona remains a lonely outpost

I. Destruction of Aetolian civilisation.

(Oenomaus, Oeneus.)

The explanation of this falling away is the irruption and conquest of Illyrian invaders. It was not through laziness or degeneracy, or through geographical disadvantages, that the Greeks of Epirus and Aetolia fell out of the race; it was because they were overwhelmed by a rude and barbarous people, who swamped their civilisation instead of assimilating it. The Aetolians and Epirots of later history are mainly of Illyrian stock.

The Eleans.

This invasion naturally drove some of the Greek inhabitants to seek new homes elsewhere. It was easy to cross the gulf, and Aetolian emigrants made their way to the river Peneus, where they settled and took to themselves the name of Eleans or "Dalesmen." They won dominion over the Epeans, the first Greek settlers, and gradually extended their power to the Alpheus. Their land was a tract of downs with a harbourless coast, and they never became a maritime power. The people in this western plain of the peninsula were distinguished by their veneration of the hero Pelops. His worship had taken deep root at Pisa on the banks of the river Alpheus. It was a spot which in a later age, when the Greeks had spread over-seas into distant lands, was to become one of the holiest seats of Greek religion, where the greatest of the Aryan, the supremest of the Hellenic, gods was to draw to his sacred precinct men from all quarters of the Greek world to do him honour with sacrifices and games. But even when Pisa had come to be illustrious as Olympia, even when the temple and altar of the Olympian Zeus had eclipsed all other associations of the place, Pelops still received his offering.

Origin of the name Peloponnesus.

But though Pelops himself was remembered only as a legendary figure, except in one or two places like Olympia where his old worship survived, his name is living still in one of the most familiar geographical names of Greece.[38] It is in the regions near the mouth of the Corinthian Gulf, where the existence of the bridge at Corinth may be easily unremembered, that men would be most tempted to call the great peninsula an island. And so, when Pelops was still widely worshipped, the name "island of Pelops" may have originated on that side—not, probably, in the peninsula itself, but on the opposite shores, in Aetolia for example; and then it made its way into universal use and clung henceforward to southern Greece.

II. The Thessalian

The pressure of the Illyrians in Epirus may be associated with two movements of great consequence, the Thessalian and the

---

[38] Some suppose that Pelops is the eponymous ancestor of a people called the Pelopes, and that Peloponnesus meant the island of the Pelopes. This seems unlikely. The inference from Cecrops in Attica is on a different footing.

Boeotian migration. A backward Greek folk named Petthăloi, but called by men of other dialects Thessaloi, crossed the hills and settled in the western corner of the land which is bounded by Pelion and Pindus. They gained the upper hand and spread their sway over the whole plain. They drove the Achaeans southwards into the mountains of Phthia, and henceforward these Achaeans play no part of any note in the history of Greece. The Thessalian name soon spread over the whole country, which is called Thessaly to the present day. Crannon, Pagasae, Larisa, and Pherae, became the seats of lords who reared horses and governed the surrounding districts. The conquered people were reduced to serfdom and were known as the Labourers; they cultivated the soil, at their own risk, paying a fixed amount to their lords; and they had certain privileges; they could not be sold abroad or arbitrarily put to death. But they gained one victory over their conquerors; the Achaean language prevailed. The Thessalians gave up their own idiom and learned, not indeed without modifying, the speech of their subjects, so that the dialect of historic Thessaly bears a close resemblance to the tongue which we find spoken by the Achaean settlers in Asia Minor. When they had established themselves in the lands of the Peneus, the Thessalians pressed northward against the Perrhaebi, eastward against the Magnetes, and southward against the Achaeans of Phthia, and reduced them all to tributary subjection. We know almost nothing of the history of the Thessalian kingdoms; in later times we find the whole country divided into four great divisions: Thessaliotis, in the south-west, the quarter which may have been the first settlement and home of the Thessalian invaders; Phthiotis of the Achaeans in the south; Pelasgiotis, a name which records the survival of the Pelasgians, one of the older peoples [39]; and Histiaeotis, the land of the Histiaeans, who have no separate identity in history. All the lordships of the land were combined in a very loose political organisation, which lay dormant in times of peace; but through which, to meet any emergency of war, they could elect a common captain, with the title of *tāgos*.

But all the folk did not remain to fall under the thraldom imposed by the new lords. A portion of the Achaeans migrated southward to the Peloponnesus and founded settlements along the

[39] The origin and significance of the name *Pelasgian* have not yet been cleared up. In Greece we find it in connexion with Epirus (Dodona), Thessaly, Attica, and the Peloponnesus. There are two main views. (1) The Pelasgians were a pre-Greek people. (2) They were pre-Achaean Greeks. Against (2) is the fact that the Leleges and other subjects of the Trojans are described as Pelasgians (see above, p. 40).

southern
Achaeans
in the
Pelopon-
nesus.
Histiaea
and
Eretria in
Euboea,
founded
by His-
tiaeans
and
others.
III. The
Boeotian
conquest.

strip of coast which forms the southern side of the Corinthian Gulf, and was henceforth called Achaea. Thus there were two Achaean lands, the old Achaea in the north, now shrunk into the mountains of Phthia, and the new Achaea in the south. There was also apparently a movement to Euboea, in consequence of the Thessalian invasion: according to tradition, Histiaea in the north of the island and Eretria in the centre owed their origin to settlers from Thessaly, and there is independent evidence that there was truth in this tradition.

The lands of Helicon and Cithaeron experienced a similar shock to that which unsettled and changed the lands of Olympus and Othrys; but the results were not the same. The old home of the Boeotians was in Mount Boeon in Epirus; the mountain gave them their name. Their dialect was probably closely akin to the original dialect of the Thessalians, being marked by certain characters which enable us to distinguish roughly a "north-western" group of dialects from those spoken by the earliest invaders of Greece. Coming from the west, or north, the Boeotians first occupied places in the west of the land which they were to make their own.[40] From Chaeronea and Coronea they won Thebes, the city of the Cadmeans. Thence they sought to spread their power over the whole land. They spread their name over it, for it was called Boeotia, but they did not succeed in winning full domination as rapidly as the Thessalians succeeded in Thessaly. The rich lords of Orchomenus preserved their independence for hundreds of years, and it was not till the sixth century that anything like a Boeotian unity was established. The policy of the Boeotian conquerors, who were perhaps comparatively few in number, was unlike that of the Thessalians; the conquered communities were not reduced to serfdom. On the other hand they did not, like the Thessalians, adopt or adapt the speech of the older inhabitants; but the idioms of the conquerors and conquered coalesced and formed a new Boeotian dialect.

Impulse
given by
the
Boetian
conquest
to mi-
gration.

The Boeotian conquest, there can be little doubt, caused some of the older peoples to wander forth to other lands; and it may explain the participation of the Cadmeans and the men of Lebadea and others in some of the Ionian settlements in Asia Minor. Moreover, the coming of the Boeotians probably unsettled some

[40] The Greeks, when they came to meditate on their history, neatly connected the Boeotian with the Thessalian conquest as effect with cause. They thought, and attempted to prove, that the Boeotians lived in Thessaly and moved southward under the pressure of the Thessalians. There is certainly something to be said for the view that the Boeotians, before they reached Boeotia, sojourned for a while in Thessaly.

of the neighbouring peoples and drove them to change their abodes.[41]

West of Boeotia, in the land of the Phocians amid the regions of Mount Parnassus, there were dislocations of a less simple kind. Hither came the Dorians. For a while, it would seem, a large space of mountainous country between Mount Oeta and the Corinthian Gulf, including a great part of Phocis, became Dorian land. The greater part of them soon went forth to seek fairer abodes in distant places. But a few remained behind in the small basin-like district between Mount Oeta and Mount Parnassus, where they preserved the illustrious Dorian name throughout the course of Grecian history in which they never played a part. It would seem that the Dorians also took possession of Delphi, the "rocky threshold" of Apollo, and planted some families there who devoted themselves to the service of the god. After the departure of the Dorian wanderers the Phocians could breathe again; but Doris was lost to them, and Delphi, which, as we shall see, they often essayed to recover. And the Phocians had to reckon with other neighbours. In later times we find the Locrians split up into three divisions, and the Phocians wedged in between. One division, the Ozolian Locrians, are on the Corinthian Gulf, to the west of Phocis; the other two divisions are on the Euboean sea, to the north-east of Phocis. The Ozolians were one of the most backward peoples of Greece. The Locrians of the north play a part in the *Iliad*, under the leadership of their hero Ajax, who ruled over Thronion as well as over Opus; and Locris was probably a continuous strip along the coast of the Euboean straits. The Phocians wanted an outlet to the sea and severed it into two parts.

The departure of the Dorians from the regions of Parnassus was probably gradual, and it was accomplished by sea. They built ships—perhaps the name of Naupactus, "the place of the ship-building," is a record of their ventures; and they sailed round the Peloponnesus to the south-eastern parts of Greece. One band of adventurers brought a new element to Crete, the island of many races; others settled in Thera and in Melos. Others sailed away eastward, beyond the limits of the Aegean, and found a home on the southern coast of Asia Minor, where, surrounded by barbarians and forgotten by the Greek world, they lived a life apart, taking no share in the history of Hellas.

Margin notes:

IV. The DORIANS.

Doris.

The Dorian priesthood of Delphi. Phocis.

Locris,—
(1) Ozolian,
(2) Opuntian,
(3) Epicnemidian.

Dorian settlements in Crete and islands. Pamphylia.

---

[41] The Abantes are said to have moved from Phocis to north Euboea, the Dryopes from the regions of Mount Oeta to south Euboea, whence they colonised Asine and Hermione on the Argolic coast.

{Pam-
phyloi.)
But they preserved their Hellenic speech, and their name, the Pamphylians, recorded their Dorian origin, being the name of one of the three tribes by which the Dorians were everywhere recognised.

The next conquests of the Dorians were in the Peloponnesus. They had found it impossible to attack on the north and west; they now essayed it on the south and east. There were three distinct conquests—the conquest of Laconia, the conquest of Argolis, the conquest of Corinth. The Dorians took possession of the rich vale of the Eurotas, and, keeping their own Dorian stock pure from the mixture of alien blood, reduced all the inhabitants to the condition of subjects. It seems probable that the Dorian invaders who subdued Laconia were more numerous than the Dorian invaders elsewhere. The eminent quality which distinguished the Dorians from other branches of the Greek race was that which we call "character"; and it was in Laconia that this quality most fully displayed and developed itself, for here the Dorian seems to have remained more purely Dorian.

Dorian
conquest
of
Laconia.

In Argolis the course of things ran otherwise. The invaders, who landed under a king named Temenos, had doubtless a hard fight; but their conquest took the shape not of subjection but of amalgamation. The Argive state was indeed organised on the Dorian system, with the three Dorian tribes—the Hylleis, Pamphyli, and Dymanes; but otherwise few traces of the conquest remained. It is to the time of this conquest that the overthrow of Mycenae is probably to be referred. Certain it is that both Mycenae and Tiryns were destroyed suddenly and set on fire. Henceforward Argos under her lofty citadel was to be undisputed queen of the Argive plain. Greater, indeed, was the feat which the Dorians wrought in their southern conquest, the feat of making lowly Sparta, without citadel or wall, the queen of the Laconian vale.

Conquest
of Argos.

Destruction of
fortresses
of My-
cenae and
Tiryns.

Dorian ships were also rowed up the Saronic Gulf. It was the adventure of a prince whom the legend calls Errant, the son of Rider. He landed in the Isthmus and seized the high hill of Acrocorinth, the key of the peninsula. This was the making of Corinth. Here, as in Argolis, there was no subjection, no distinction between the conquerors and the conquered. The geographical position of Corinth between her seas determined for her people a career of commerce, and her history shows that the Dorians had the qualities of bold and skilful traders.

Conquest
of
Corinth.
'Αλήτης
son of
'Ιππότης.

From Argos the Dorians made two important settlements in the north, on the river Asopus—Sicyôn on its lower, and Phliûs

Sicyon
and
Phlius

on its upper banks. And beyond Mount Geraneia another Dorian city arose, we know not how, on the commanding hill which looks down upon the western shore of Salamis. Its name was Nisa. But the hill had been crowned by a royal palace in the heroic age, and so the place came to be called Megara "the Palace," and in historical times no other name was known, though the old name[42] lurked in the name of the harbour Nisaea. In later days, Dorian Megara was associated politically with the Peloponnesus rather than with northern Greece; in pre-Dorian days it had been reckoned as part of Boeotia, separated though it was from that

Nisa = Megara.

Nisa's harbour.

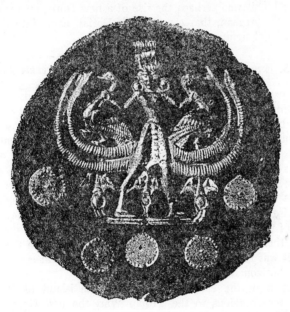

FIG. 18.—Gold Pendant, ninth century (found in Aegina).

country by the western portion of the massive range of Cithaeron.

The island, whose conical mountain in the midst of the Saronic waters is visible to all the coasts around, was also destined to become a Dorian land. Aegina was conquered by Dorian settlers from Epidaurus, but the conquest was perhaps not effected for two hundred years or more after the subjugation of Argolis. In Aegina too there was, doubtless, a fusion of the old inhabitants and the new settlers; and we may be sure that it had been be-

Aegina dorized, c. 800 B.C.(?)

[42] Preserved in the catalogue in the *Illiad*, Bk. ii. l. 508.

fore, as it was after, the change an island of bold and adventurous sailors.

In Crete and Laconia we meet, as we shall see, some peculiar institutions, which seem to have been characteristically Dorian, but are not found in Argos or Corinth. Yet all the Dorian settlements remembered their common Dorian origin; and the conquerors of Laconia, at least, looked with emotions of filial piety towards the little obscure Doris in the highlands of Parnassus as their mother-country. The evidence of the three Dorian tribes might help to maintain the consciousness of a Dorian section of Greece; but it was perhaps the rise of a new Doris, on the other side of the Aegean, that elevated the Dorian name into permanent national significance.

Sect. 8. Expansion of the Greeks to the Eastern Aegean

The expansion of the Greeks over the Aegean islands and the plantation of Greek settlements along the western coast of Asia Minor began when the heroic age was drawing to a close, and continued for about a century and a half. This movement was promoted and in some of its stages directly caused by the consequences of the Dorian invasion and the migrations in north Greece; but it may have begun, without any external pressure, perhaps on account of over-population, and partly in a spirit of enterprise which was tempted by the fertile river valleys and plains of the Asiatic coast, where there was now no great power to oppose them. The Hittite empire had fallen back from the west, which it was never to reach again; it does not appear even on the distant horizon in the Homeric poems.

Apart from the early settlements in the island of Rhodes, which were previous to the Trojan War, the first Greeks who sailed across the Aegean to find new homes were the Achaeans and their fellows from the hills and plains of Thessaly and the plain of the Spercheus. Their expeditions probably started from the land-locked bay of Pagasae, and tradition long afterwards associated the first sea-ventures of the Greeks with the port of Iavolkos.[43]

(Gulf of Volo.)

(Iólkos.)

The Aeōlians.

Along with the Achaeans there sailed as comrades and allies the Aeōlians. Some indeed believe that "Aeolian" was simply another name for "Achaean";[44] but it seems safer to regard the

---

[43] From which the legendary *Argo* sailed, manned by Thessalian heroes, on the quest of the golden fleece.

[44] Αἰόλος (Αἰολεύς) being a "short name" for Ἀχ-αιός.

Aeŏlians as distinct from, though closely related to, the Achaeans. It is impossible to determine whether those who crossed the
Aegean were settlers in Thessaly, and not rather some of the Aeolians who lived beyond the mountains by another seaboard, on
the northern shore of the Corinthian Gulf. We know that in early
times these Aeolians were engaged in constant warfare with the
Aetolians, who ultimately won the upper hand and gave their
name to the whole country. And perhaps the pressure of these
foes induced some of them to throw in their lot with the Achaeans who were sailing in search of new homes beyond the sea.

It was to the northern part of Asia Minor, the island of Lesbos *Achaeo-*
and the opposite shores, that the Achaean and Aeolian adventur- *Aeolian*
ers steered their ships. Here they planted the first Hellenic settle- *colonisa-*
ments on Asiatic soil—the beginning of a movement which, before *tions.*
a thousand years had passed away, was to carry Greek conquerors to the Indian Ocean. The coast-lands of western Asia Minor *Physical*
are, like Greece itself, suitable for the habitations of a sea-faring *character*
people. A series of river-valleys are divided by mountain chains *of coast of*
which run out into promontories so as to form deep bays; and *Asia*
the promontories are continued in islands. The valleys of the *Minor.*
Hermus and the Caicus are bounded on the north by a chain of
hills which run out into Lesbos; the valley of the Hermus is parted from that of the Cayster by mountains which are prolonged in
Chios; and the valley of the Cayster is separated from the valley
of the Maeander by a chain which terminates in Samos. South of
the Maeander valley there are bays and islands, but the mountains of the mainland are broken by no rivers. The Greek occupation of the lower waters of the Hermus and Caicus is known to
us only by its results. The invaders won the coast-lands from the
Mysian natives and seized a number of strong places which they
could defend—Pitane, Myrina, Cyme, Aegae, Old Smyrna.
They pressed up the rivers, and on the Hermus they founded
Magnesia under Mount Sipylus. All this, needless to say, was not
done at once. It must have been a work of many years, and of
successive expeditions from the mother-country.

The Achaean wave of emigration was succeeded by another
wave, flowing mainly from the coasts of Attica and Argolis, and
new settlements were planted south of the elder Achaean settlements. The two-pronged peninsula between the Hermus and
Cayster rivers, with the off-lying isle of Chios, the valleys of the
Cayster and Maeander, with Samos and the peninsula south of
Mount Latmos, were studded with communities which came to
form a group distinct from the older group in the north. Each

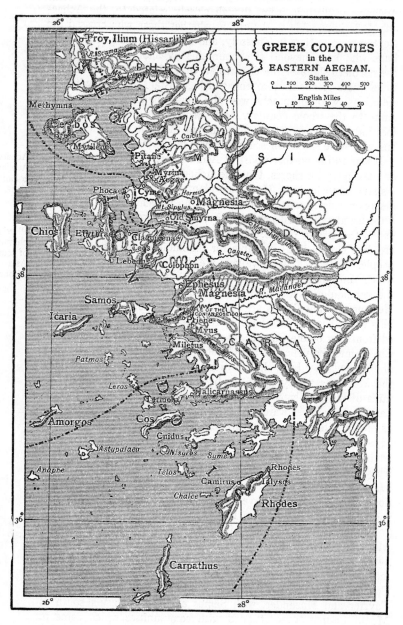

GREEK COLONIES
in the
EASTERN AEGEAN.

Stadia
0   100   200   300   400   500

English Miles
0   10   20   30   40   50

FIG. 19.

group of settlements came to be called by a collective name. As
the Achaeans were the most illustrious of the settlers in the
north, one might expect to find the northern group known as
Achaean. But it is not thus that names are given in primitive
times. A number of cities or settlements, which have no political
union and are merely associated together by belonging to the
same race and speaking the same tongue, do not generally choose
themselves a common name. It rather happens that when they
get a common name it is given to them by strangers, who, looking from the outside, regard them as a group and do not think of
the differences of which they are themselves more vividly conscious. And it constantly happens that the name of one member of
the group is, by some accident, picked out and applied to the
whole. Thus it befell that the Aeolian and not the Achaean name
was selected to designate the northern division of the Greek
settlements in Asia; just as our own country came to be called
not Saxony but England. The southern and larger group of colonies received the name of Iāvŏnes—or Iōnes, as they called
themselves, when they lost the letter *v*. The Iavones "with flowing tunics," who are mentioned in the *Iliad* in association with
the Boeotians, refers to the Athenians; but the name itself, perhaps, is not Greek and was first given to the Greek colonists on
Asiatic soil.

But it would probably be a mistake to regard these two groups
as well-defined from the first. To begin with, it is possible that
they overlapped chronologically. The latest of the Aeolian settlements may have been founded subsequently to the earliest of the
Ionian. In the second place, the original homes of the settlers
overlapped. Though the Aeolian colonists mainly came from the
lands north of Mount Oeta—apart from those who came from
Aetolia—they included some settlers from the coasts of Boeotia
and Euboea. Thus Cyme in Aeolis derived its name from Euboean Cyme. And, on the other hand, though the Ionian colonies
were chiefly derived from the coasts of Attica and Argolis—apart
from some contingents from Crete and other places in the south
—there were also some settlers from the north. Thirdly, the two
groups ran into each other geographically. Phocaea, for example,
which is geographically in Aeolis, standing on the promontory
north of the Hermus river, was included in Ionia. Its name shows
that some of the men who colonised it were Phocians. And some
of the places in north Ionia—Teos, for instance—had received
Achaean settlements first, and were then re-settled by Ionians.

The
AEOLIAN
group.

The
IONIAN
group.

Distinc-
tion of the
two
groups
and their
over-
lappings.

In Chios, which was afterwards fully in Ionia, a language of Aeolic complexion was once spoken.

Of the foundation of the famous colonies of Ionia, of the order in which they were founded, and of the relations of the settlers with the Lydian natives, we know as little as of the settlements of the Achaeans. Clazomenae and Teos arose on the north and south sides of the neck of the peninsula which runs out to meet Chios; and Chios, on the east coast of her island, faces Erythrae on the mainland—Erythrae, "the crimson," so called from its purple fisheries, the resort of Tyrian traders. Lebedus and Colophon lie on the coast as it retires eastward from Teos to reach the mouth of the Cayster; and there was founded Ephesus, the city of Artemis. By the streams of the Cayster was a plain called "the Asian meadow," which destiny in some odd way selected to bestow a name upon one of the continents of the earth. South of Ephesus and on the northern slope of Mount Mycale was the religious gathering-place of the Ionians, the temple of the Heliconian Poseidon, which, when once the Ionians became conscious of themselves as a sort of nation and learned to glory in their common name, served to foster a sense of unity among all their cities from Phocaea in the north to Miletus in the south. Samos faces Mount Mycale, and the worship of Hera, which was the religious feature of Samos, is thought to point to men of Argos as participators in its original foundation. South of Mycale the cities of Myus and Priene were planted on the Maeander. Then the coast retires to skirt Mount Latmos and breaks forward again to form the promontory, at the northern point of which was Miletus with its once splendid harbour. There was one great inland city, Magnesia on the Maeander, which must not be confused with the inland Aeolian city, Magnesia on the Hermus. Though counted to Ionia, it was not of Ionian origin, for it was founded by the Magnētes of Thessaly. And settlers from Euboea and Boeotia took part in the colonisation of Ionia, as well as the Ionians of Argolis and Attica.[45] The old inhabitants—Leleges,

[45] The following list will illustrate the Ionian colonisation. Phocaea—Phocians; Clazomenae—Cleonae and Phlius; Samos—Argolis; Chios—Euboea; Erythrae—Boeotia and Euboea; Teos (first, Achaeans from Thessaly)—Attica and Boeotia; Lebedos—Boeotia; Colophon—Pylus (in Messenia); Ephesus—Argolis, and various; Priene—Cadmeans and Arcadians; Myus—Attica; Miletus—Attica. These twelve cities were called the Ionian dodecapolis. The best test of Ionian race was the celebration of the feast of *Apaturia;* and the fact that this feast was not held at Ephesus and Colophon shows that the Ionian element in these cities was very small. The Ionian dialect embraces the idioms which were spoken in Euboea, the Cyclad islands, and the Ionian colonies. Euboean speech was much influenced by neighbouring dialects (especially the Boeotian); but the language of the Cyclades is close

Matonians, Carians—probably offered no prolonged resistance to the invaders, and in some places, as the Carians for example at Miletus, they mixed with the Greek strangers.

The colonists carried with them into the new Greece beyond the seas traditions of the old civilisation which in the mother country was being overwhelmed by the Dorian invaders; and those traditions helped to produce the luxurious Ionian civilisation which meets us some centuries later when we come into the clearer light of recorded history. And they carried with them their minstrelsy, their lays of Troy, celebrating the deeds of Achilles and Agamemnon and Odysseus. The heroic lays of Greece entered upon a new period in Ionia, where a poet of supreme genius arose, and the first and greatest epic poem of the world was created. It was probably in the ninth century that Homer composed the *Iliad*. His famous name has the humble meaning of "hostage," and we may fancy, if we care, that the poet was carried off in his youth as a hostage in some local strife. Possibly he lived in rugged Chios, and he gives us a local touch when he describes the sun as rising over the sea. From him the Homerid family of the bards of Chios were sprung. He took as his main argument the wrath of Achilles leading up to the death of Hector, and wrought into his epic many other episodes derived from the old lays on the theme of Troy. Tradition made Homer the author of both the great epics, the *Odyssey* as well as the *Iliad*. Whether this is so or not, no great length of time need separate the composition of the two poems.

Many critics think that the *Iliad* we have is not the original *Iliad* of Homer, but that his poem was a much shorter work and was remoulded and expanded by succeeding poets in a way that was not entirely to its advantage. Similar views are held about the *Odyssey*. This is the "Homeric question," and no agreement has yet been reached. In any case, even if the whole *Iliad* was not his work—and this has not been proved—Homer was the father of epic poetry, in the sense in which we distinguish an epic poem with a large argument from a short heroic lay. His work was thoroughly artificial—conscious art, as the greatest poetry always is; and it is possible that he committed the *Iliad* to writing.[46] As he and his successors sang in Ionia, at the courts of

Homer (c. 850 B.C.)

The Iliad written

enough to that of Ionia, one of the chief differences being that Ionia lost the *spiritus asper*. Herodotus says that there were four distinct sub-dialects in Ionia itself. He probably refers to the speech of the common people. So far as the evidence of inscriptions goes, the local differences in the written language were insignificant.

[46] See below, p. 70.

Ionian princes, he dealt freely with the dialect of the old Achaean poems. The *Iliad* was arrayed in Ionic dress, and ultimately became so identified with Ionia that the Achaean origin of the older poetry was forgotten. The transformation was not, indeed, perfect, for sometimes the Ionian forms did not suit the metre, and Aeolian forms were used. But the change was accomplished with wonderful skill. It is probable that the Ionian poet also did much to adapt the epic material which he used to the taste and moral ideas of a more refined age. The *Iliad* is notably free from the features of crude savagery which generally mark the early literature of primitive peoples; only a few slight traces remain to show that there were in the background ugly and barbarous things over which a veil has been drawn. In other respects, the Ionian poets have faithfully preserved the atmosphere of the past ages of which they sung. They preserved its manners, its environment, its geography. Only an occasional anachronism slips in, which in the otherwise consistent picture can easily be detected. Unwittingly, for instance, the poet of the *Odyssey* allows it to escape that he lived in the iron age, for such a proverb as "the mere gleam of iron lures a man to strife" could not have arisen until iron weapons had been long in use. But he is at pains to preserve the weapons and gear and customs of the bronze age.

Homer preserved the memory of the Trojan War as a great national enterprise. The *Iliad* was regarded as something of far greater significance than an Ionian poem; it was accepted as a national epic, and was, from the first, a powerful influence in promoting among the Greeks community of feeling and tendencies towards national unity. The *Odyssey*, affiliated as it was to the Trojan legend, became a national epic too; although the scene of one-third of the story is laid in fairyland, and it has not as a whole any national significance. And the interest awakened in Greece by the idea of the Trojan war was displayed by the composition of a series of epic poems, dealing with those events of the siege which happened both before and after the events described in the *Iliad,* and with the subsequent history of some of the Greek heroes. These poems were ascribed to various obscure authors; [47] some of them passed under the name of Homer. Along with the *Iliad* and *Odyssey,* they formed a chronological series which came to be known as the Epic Cycle.

The Ionic settlements did not complete the Greek colonisation of Asia Minor. The Dorian conquest of the eastern Peloponnesus was followed by a Dorian expansion beyond the seas and a colo-

[47] As to the last, see below, p. 110.

nisation of the Asiatic coast, to the south of Ionia. The Carians had spread over this region down to the border of Lycia and had pressed the older inhabitants into the promontory which faces the island of Calymna. Here the Leleges participated in the latest stages of the Aegean civilisation, as we know by the pottery and other things which have been discovered at Termera in chamber-tombs. These round tombs, not hewn out of the earth, like the vaulted sepulchres of Mycenae, but built above ground, are found in many parts of the peninsula and remain as the most striking memorial of the Leleges.

The Leleges confined to the Myndian promontory.

Chamber tombs at Termera (Assarlik); "late Mycenaean."

The bold promontories below Miletus, the islands of Cos and Rhodes were occupied by colonists from Argolis, Laconia, Corinth, and Crete. On the mainland Halicarnassus was the most important Dorian settlement, but it was formed in concert with the Carian natives, and was half Carian. This new Doris eclipsed in fame, and shed a new lustre on the old Doris under Mount Oeta; all the settlements were independent, but they kept alive their communion of interest and sentiment by the common worship of the Triopian Apollo. The Carians were a vigorous people. They impressed themselves upon their land, and soon men began to forget that it had not been always Caria. They took to the sea, and formed a maritime power of some strength, so that in later ages a tradition was abroad that there was once upon a time a Carian sea-supremacy, though no one could mention anything that it had achieved. The Carians also claimed to have made contributions to the art of war by introducing shield-handles, and the crested helmet, and the emblazoning of shields—claims which we cannot test.

Caria.

The Greek fringe of western Asia Minor was complete. It was impossible for Doris to creep round the corner and join hands with Pamphylia; for the Lycians presented an insuperable barrier. The Lycians were not a folk of Aryan speech, as a widely-spread error supposed them to have been; their language is related to the Carian. Their proper name was Trm̃mili; but the name Lycian seems to have been given them by others as well as by the Greeks who recognised in the chief Tremilian deity their own Apollo Lykios.[48] But, though Lycia was not colonised, the Aegean was now entirely within the Greek sphere, excepting only its northern margin, where Greek enterprise in the future was to find a difficult field. It is important to observe that the process

Lycia.

---

[48] This fact need not exclude the view (now generally accepted) that the Luku, who appear as invaders of Egypt in the reigns of Ramses II. and Mernptah, were Lycians.

by which Asiatic Greece was created differs in character from the
Dorian invasion of the Peloponnesus. The settlements of Ionia
and Doris are examples of colonisation. Bands of settlers went
forth from their homes to find new habitations for themselves,
but they left a home-country behind them. The Dorian movements, on the other hand, partake of the character of a folk-
wandering. The essential fact is that a whole people dispersed to
seek new fields and pastures. For the paltry remnant which remained in the sequestered nook beyond Parnassus could not be
called the parent-people except by courtesy; the people, as a
whole, had gone elsewhere.

Before the completion of the Greek occupation of the western
coast of Asia Minor, another migration left the shores of the

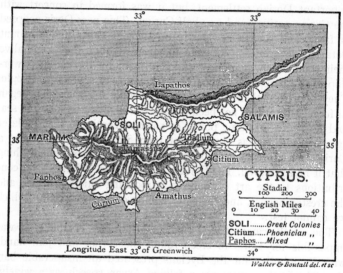

FIG. 20.

Peloponnesus to seek a more distant home. Cyprus, an island
whose geographical position marks it out to be contested between
three continents, was now to receive European settlers. Throughout the bronze age it played an important part in supplying the
Aegean countries with copper, and it exported timber, but it did
not begin to share in the advanced civilisation of the Aegean till
the very last days of Cnossian supremacy. Then it received colonists from the Aegean and developed an art which shows the
characteristics of Cretan and Mycenaean art, with its own local
peculiarities. At Salamis, in the east of the island, sepulchres

Cyprus:
Aegean
civilisa-
tion in.
(Enkomi.)

have been found which show how Aegean culture flourished in Cyprus in the fourteenth century. The Cypriotes presently learned the craft of manufacturing iron, which was beginning to come into use. Their position, near Asia Minor, Syria, and Egypt gave them favourable opportunities for commerce which brought them wealth. The island was destined, however, to play a part in the world's debate as a wrestling-ground between the European and the Asiatic; and the first Europeans who went forth for the struggle were Peloponnesian Greeks whom, we may suspect, the events of the Dorian invasion incited to wander. Much about the same time the Phoenicians also began to plant settlements in the island, mainly in the centre—Amathus, Cition, Idalion, Tamassus, Lapathus—and some places seem to have been colonised jointly by Phoenicians and Greeks, just as on the coast of Asia Minor Greeks and Carians mingled. A new Cypriot culture arose out of the intermingling of the two races and the old inhabitants. The worship of the Great Mother Goddess, attended by doves, was native to Cyprus as to Crete; and the Greeks identified her with Aphrodite, who became universally known as the Cyprian goddess.

The Greek colonisation, 11th cent. Phoenician colonies.

Graeco-Phoenician civilisation. Aphrodite Cypris.

The settlers in Cyprus spoke the Arcadian dialect, but this does not prove that their old homes were in Arcadia. Before the Dorians came and developed new dialects, the Arcadian speech with but slight variations seems to have prevailed in the coast-lands as well as in the centre of the peninsula; and some of the Cypriot Greeks went forth from Laconia and Argolis.[49] Some sailed from Salamis in the Attic bay and gave their name to Salamis in Cyprus. The colonists found already established a mode of linear writing, which exhibits close resemblances to the Cretan systems and had probably been imported with the rest of Aegean civilisation. This syllabic system was ill-adapted to express the Greek language; but the colonists adapted it to their use. And, although nothing is clumsier than a Greek writing in the Cypriot character, yet the Greeks of Cyprus clung to it when the rest of their race had learned the use of a finer instrument.

Cypriot dialect.

Salamis.

Cypriot syllabary.

If we look back now upon the early history of the Greeks, we see that though we can establish a probable chronology, there is only a single date which can lay claim to precision, and this concerns an event of minor importance—an Achaean raid on Egypt.

Chronology.

[49] Paphos seems to have been an Arcadian, Lapathus a Loconian, and Curion an Argolic foundation. But doubtless each settlement was mixed. Tradition connected the Cypriot Soli with Attica.

For all the leading changes and movements we must be content with approximate limits:—

Greek-speaking peoples occupy Greece . .	3rd millennium.
Crete leading power in Aegean	*c.* 2200-1400 B.C.
Advanced Aegean civilisation in Greece .	from *c.* 1600 B.C.
Fall of Cnossus	*c.* 1400 B.C.
Achaeans found principalities in Peloponnesus	1300-1250 B.C.
Achaeans join in raid on Egypt . . .	*c.* 1223 B.C.
Trojan war	early in 12th century.

Thessalian conquest

Boeotian conquest

Beginnings of Achaean migration

    to Asia Minor

} towards end of 12th century.

Ionian colonisation in Asia Minor begins

Dorian conquests in Peloponnesus and Crete

Dorian colonisation in Asia Minor begins

Greek colonisation of Cyprus

} 11th century.

Sect. 9. Fall of Greek Monarchies and Rise of the Republics

What the kings did for Greece.

Under their kings the Greeks had conquered the coasts and islands of the Aegean, and had created the city-state. These were the two great contributions of monarchy to Grecian history. In forwarding the change from rural life in scattered thorps to life in cities, the kings were doubtless considering themselves as well as

Effects of city-life.

their people. They thought that the change would consolidate their own power by bringing the whole folk directly under their own eyes. But it also brought the king more directly under the eye of his folk. The frailties, incapacities, and misconduct of a weak lord were more noticed in the small compass of a city; he was more generally criticised and judged. City-life too was less appropriate to the patriarchal character of the Homeric "shepherd of the people." Moreover, in a city those who were ill-pleased with the king's rule were more tempted to murmur together, and able

Decline of monarchy: causes.

more easily to conspire. Considerations like these may help us to imagine how it came about that throughout the greater part of Greece in the eighth century the monarchies were declining and disappearing, and republics were taking their place. It is a transformation of which the actual process is hidden from us, and we can only guess at probable causes; but we may be sure that the deepest cause of all was the change to city-life. The revolution was general; the infection caught and spread; but the change in different states must have had different occasions, just as it took different shapes. In some cases gross misrule may have led to the violent deposition of a king; in other cases, if the succession to the sceptre devolved upon an infant or a paltry man, the nobles may have taken it upon themselves to abolish the monarchy. In many places perhaps the change was slower. The kings who had already sought to strengthen their authority by the foundation of cities must have sought also to increase or define those vague powers which belonged to an Aryan ruler—sought, perhaps, to act of their own freewill without due regard to the Council's advice. When such attempts at magnifying the royal power went too far, the elders of the Council might rise and gainsay the king, and force him to enter into a contract with his people that he would govern constitutionally. Of the existence of such contracts we have evidence. The old monarchy lasted into late times in remote Molossia, and there the king was obliged to take a solemn oath to rule his people according to law. In other cases the rights of the king might be strictly limited, in consequence of his seeking to usurp undue authority; and the imposition of limitations might go on until the office of king, although maintained in name, became in fact a mere magistracy in a state wherein the real power had passed elsewhere. Of the survival of monarchy in a limited form we have an example at Sparta; of its survival as a mere magistracy we have an example at Athens. And it should be observed that the functions of the monarch were already restricted by limits which could easily be contracted further. Though he was the supreme giver of dooms, there might be other heads of clans or tribes in the state who could give dooms and judgment as well as he. Though he was the chief priest, there were other families than his to which certain priesthoods were confined. He was therefore not the sole fountain of justice or religion.

There is a vivid scene in Homer which seems to have been painted when kings were seeking to draw tighter the reins of the royal power. The poet, who is in sympathy with the kings, draws a comic and odious caricature of the "bold" carle with the gift of fluent speech, who criticises the conduct and policy of the kings. Such an episode could hardly have suggested itself in the old days before city-life had begun; Thersites is assuredly a product of the town. Odysseus, who rates and beats him, announces, in another part of the same scene, a maxim which has become as famous as Thersites himself: "The sovereignty of many is not good; let there

Episode of Thersites (in Iliad ii.).

be one sovereign, one king." That is a maxim which would win applause for the minstrel in the banquet-halls of monarchs who were trying to carry through a policy of centralisation at the expense of the chiefs of the tribes.

Rise of the republics.

Where the monarchy was abolished, the government passed into the hands of those who had done away with it, the noble families of the state. The distinction of the nobles from the rest of the people is, as we have seen, an ultimate fact with which we have to

Rule of the nobles.

start. When the nobles assume the government and become the rulers, an aristocratic republic arises. Sometimes the power is won, not by the whole body of the noble clans, but by the clan to which the king belonged. This was the case at Corinth, where the royal family of the Bacchiads became the rulers. In most cases the aristocracy and the whole nobility coincided; but in others, as at Corinth, the aristocracy was only a part of the nobility, and the constitution was an oligarchy of the narrowest form.

At this stage of society the men of the noble class were the nerve and sinew of the state. Birth was then the best general test of excellence that could be found, and the rule of the nobles was a true aristocracy, the government of the most excellent. They practised the craft of ruling; they were trained in it, they handed it down from father to son; and though no great men arose—great men are dangerous in an aristocracy—the government was conducted with knowledge and skill. Close aristocracies, like the Corinthian, were apt to become oppressive; and, when the day approached for aristocracies in their turn to give way to new constitutions, there were signs of grievous degeneration. But on the whole the Greek republics flourished in the aristocratic stage, and were guided with eminent ability.

Two achievements of aristocracies: 1. Colonisation (see below, Chap. II. sects. 1-3.)

The rise of the republics is about to take us into a new epoch of history; but it is important to note the continuity of the work which was to be done by the aristocracies with that which was accomplished by the kings. The two great achievements of the aristocratic age are the planting of Greek cities in lands far beyond the limits of the Aegean sea, and the elaboration of political machinery. The first of these is simply the continuation of the expansion of the Greeks around the Aegean itself. But the new movement of expansion is distinguished, as we shall see, by certain peculiarities in its outward forms,—features which were chiefly due to the fact that city-life had been introduced before the colonisation began. The beginning of colonisation belonged to the age of transition from monarchy to republic; it was systematically promoted by the aristocracies, and it took a systematic shape. The creation of political machinery carried on the work of consolidation which the kings had begun when they gathered together into cities the loose elements of their states. When royalty was abolished or put, as we say, "into commission," the ruling families of the republic had to substitute magistracies tenable for limited periods, and had to determine how the magistrates were to be appointed, how their functions were to be circumscribed, how the provinces of authority were to be assigned. New machinery had to be created to replace that one of the three parts of the constitution which had disappeared. It may be added that under the aristocracies the idea of law began to take a clearer shape in men's minds, and the traditions which guided usage began to assume the form of laws. In the lays of Homer we hear only of the single dooms given by the kings or judges in particular cases. At the close of the aristocratic period comes the age of the lawgivers, and the aristocracies had prepared the material which the lawgivers improved, qualified, and embodied in codes.

2. Political organisation.

Growth of law.

SECT. 10. PHOENICIAN INTERCOURSE WITH GREECE

The Greeks were destined to become a great seafaring people. But sea-trade was a business which it took them many ages to learn, after they had reached the coasts of the Aegean; it was long before they could step into the place of the old sea-kings of Crete. For several centuries after the Trojan War the trade of the Aegean with the east was partly carried on by strangers. The men who took advantage of this opening were the traders of the city-states of Sidon and Tyre on the Syrian coast, men of that Semitic stock to which Jew, Arab, and Assyrian alike belonged. These coast-landers, born merchants like the Jews, seem to have migrated to the shores of the Mediterranean from an older home on the shores of the Red Sea. The Greeks knew these bronzed Semitic traders by the same name, Phoenikes or "red men," which they had before applied to the Cretans. This led to some confusion in their traditions. We have seen how the Cretan Cadmus and Europa were transferred to Phoenicia in the legend.

Period of Phoenician trade with Greece.

We have no warrant for speaking of a Phoenician sea-lordship in the Aegean. The evidence of the Homeric poems shows clearly that between the commercial enterprise of the heroic age and the commercial enterprise of the later Greeks there was an interval of perhaps two hundred years or thereabouts, during which no Greek state possessed a sea-power strong enough to exclude foreign merchants from Greek seas, and trade was consequently shared by

No Phoe-
nician set-
tlements
in Greece;
only some
trading
stations.

Greek and Tyrian merchants. It was not only Phoenician carriers who came to Greece; the Greeks also sailed to Syria and Cyprus; [50] and the Carians developed a considerable sea-power. We shall see in the next chapter how the men of Tyre and Sidon made a new Phoenicia in the western Mediterranean; but on the shores of the Aegean they seem to have made no serious attempts, or at least to have succeeded in no attempts, to plant permanent settlements, except at Camirus in Rhodes, and possibly in the island of Cythera. It may be that they had stations at the purple fisheries of Cos and Nisyros and Erythrae and elsewhere; it has been supposed that they were the first to tap the gold-mines of Siphnos and Thasos and even the silver-mines of Attica. It has been held that there were Phoenician settlements on the Isthmus of Corinth, under the Acropolis of Athens, and even at inland Thebes. There is no assurance or probability that such settlements were ever made. The Phoenicians, doubtless, had marts here and there on coast or island; but there is no reason to think that Canaanites ever made homes for themselves on Greek soil or introduced Semitic blood into the population of Greece. It was not here that the struggle was to be fought out between Baal and Zeus. Their ships were ever winding in and out of the Aegean isles from south to north, bearing fair naperies from Syria, fine-wrought bowls and cups from the workshops of Sidonian and Cypriot silversmiths, and all manner of luxuries and ornaments; and this constant commercial intercourse lasting for two centuries is amply sufficient to account for all the influence that Phoenicia exerted upon Greece. In the worship of Aphrodite and other Greek goddesses we see the influence of the cult of Syrian Astarte. It is a mistake to suppose that the Phoenician god Melkart was taken into Greek mythology as Melicertes, but he was identified in many places with the Greek god Heracles. The briskest trade was perhaps driven with the thriving cities of Ionia, and the Phoenicians adopted the Ionian name, and diffused it in Syria, as the general designation of all the Greeks.

Iavan (=
Iavones),
oriental
name for
Greeks.
The Greek
alphabet
(derived
from the
Phoeni-
cian) in-
vented
10th to
11th cent

These things were of slight concern compared with one inestimable service which the Phoenicians rendered to Hellas and thereby to Europe. They gave the Greeks the most useful instrument of civilisation, alphabetic writing. It was perhaps at the beginning of the ninth century, hardly later, that the Phoenician alphabet was

---

[50] The predominance of Sidon seems to have ceased about the tenth century; the date is uncertain. Then there was a short period in which the Philistines who overthrew Sidon were dominant; and then the period of Tyre's power began.

moulded to the needs of the Greek language. In this adaptation the Greeks showed their genius. The alphabet of the Phoenicians and their Semitic brethren is an alphabet of consonants; the Greeks added the vowels. They took some of the consonantal symbols for which their own language had no corresponding sounds, and used these superfluous signs to represent the vowels. Several alphabets, differing in certain details, were diffused in various parts of the Hellenic world, but they all agree in the main points, and we may suppose that the original idea was worked out in Ionia. In Ionia, at all events, writing was introduced at an early period, and was perhaps used by poets of the ninth century. Perhaps the earliest example of a Greek writing that we possess is on an Attic jar of the seventh century; it says the jar shall be the prize of the dancer who dances more gaily than all others.[51] But the lack of early inscriptions is what we should expect. The new art was used for ordinary and literary purposes long before it was employed for official records. It was the great gift which the Semites gave to Europe.

Sect. 11. Greek Reconstruction of Early Greek History

We must now see what the Greeks thought of their own early history. Their construction of it, though founded on legendary tradition and framed without much historical sense, has considerable importance, since their ideas about the past affected their views of the present. Their belief in their legendary past was thoroughly practical; mythic events were often the basis of diplomatic transactions; claims to territory might be founded on the supposed conquests or dominions of ancient heroes of divine birth.[52]

At first, before the growth of historical curiosity, the chief motive for investigating the past was the desire of noble families to derive their origin from a god. For this purpose they sought to connect their pedigrees with heroic ancestors, especially with Heracles or with the warriors who had fought at Troy. The Trojan war was, with some reason, regarded as a national enterprise; and Heracles—who seems originally to have been specially associated with Argolis—was looked on as a national hero. The consequence

*Gene-
alogies.*

[51] ὃς νῦν ὀρχηστῶν πάντων ἀταλώτατα παίζει
το[ῦ]το δεκά[ν] μιν (?)
[52] Grote has illustrated this from our own history. The belief in the descent of the kings of England from Brute the Trojan was still robust in the seventeenth century. It figured in a state document drawn up in A. D. 1301 to uphold the rights of the English crown in the dispute with Scotland.

was that the Greeks framed their history on genealogies and determined their chronology by generations, reckoning three generations to a hundred years. The later Homeric poets must have contributed a great deal to the fixing of the mutual relations of legendary events; but it was the poets of the school of Hesiod in the eighth century who did most to reduce to a historical system the legends of the heroic age. Their poems are lost, but they were worked up into still more complete and elaborate schemes by the prose logographers or "storywriters" of the sixth and fifth centuries, of whom perhaps the most influential were Hecataeus of Miletus and Acusilaus of Argos. The original works of the logographers have also perished, but their teaching has come down to us fully enough in the works of later compilers and commentators.

In the first place, it had to be determined how the various branches of the Greek race were related. As soon as the Greeks came to be called by the common name of Hellenes,[53] they derived their whole stock from an eponymous ancestor, Hellēn, who lived in Thessaly.[54] They had then to account for its distribution into a number of different branches. In Greece proper they might have searched long, among the various folks speaking various idioms, for some principle of classification which should determine the nearer and further degrees of kinship between the divisions of the race, and establish two or three original branches to which every community could trace itself back. But when they looked over to the eastern Greece on the farther side of the Aegean, they saw, as it were, a reflection of themselves, their own children divided into three homogeneous groups—Aeolians, Ionians, and Dorians. This gave a simple classification; three families sprung from Aeolus, Ion, and Dorus, who must evidently have been the sons of Hellen. But there was one difficulty. Homer's Achaeans had still to be accounted for; they could not be affiliated to Aeolians, or Ionians, or Dorians, none of whom play a part in the *Iliad*. Accordingly it was arranged that Hellen had three sons, Aeolus, Dorus, and Xuthus; and Ion and Achaeus were the sons of Xuthus.[55] It was easy enough then, by the help of tradition and language, to fit the

---

[53] See below, p. 98.

[54] Hellen and his sons were placed in Thessaly because the Hellenes of Homer lived in Thessalian regions. Hellen was variously represented as the son of Zeus and the son of Deucalion (who was the son of Prometheus and Pandora).

[55] The motive for making Ion and Achaeus brothers may have been the belief that in consequence of the Dorian invasion Achaeans and Ionians had together left the Peloponnesus and colonised Asia Minor.

ethnography of Greece under these labels; and the manifold dialects were forced under three [56] artificial divisions.

The two great events on which everything turned and to which all other events were related were the Trojan war and the Dorian conquest of the Peloponnesus. A most curious version of the Dorian conquest was invented in Argos and won its way into general belief; it is a striking illustration of the motives and methods of the Greeks in reconstructing their past. The Temenids, the royal family of Argos, derived themselves from Aegimius, to whom the foundation of the Dorian institutions was ascribed. But as the fame and glory of Heracles waxed great, the Temenids desired to connect themselves with him. The problem was solved with wonderful skill. The eponymous ancestors of the three Dorian tribes, Hyllus, Pamphylus, and Dyman, were naturally regarded as the sons of Aegimius. According to the new story Hyllus was really the son of Heracles. It was said that Heracles fought against the Lapiths for Aegimius who was Dorian king in Thessaly, and that he received a third of the kingdom as a reward for his valiant service. On his death his children were protected by Aegimius, who adopted Hyllus, and confirmed him in the possession of his father's third. The sons of Hyllus failed in their attempts to recover the possessions of Heracles in the Peloponnesus; the achievement was reserved for his great-grandchildren, Temenus, Cresphontes, and Aristodemus. With a Dorian host they crossed from Naupactus, under the guidance of a one-eyed Aetolian man named Oxylus, and conquered all the Peloponnesus exept Arcadia. They gave Elis to Oxylus for his pains. Those of the Achaean inhabitants of the peninsula, who did not migrate beyond the sea, retreated to the northern coast-land—the historical Achaea. The other three parts of the Peloponnesus fell by lot to the three brothers, Messenia to Cresphontes, Laconia to Aristodemus, and Argos to Temenus. An explanation was added how there were two royal houses at Sparta. Aristodemus died prematurely, and Laconia was divided between his twin sons Eurysthenes and Procles.[57]

Thus the Dorian invasion was justified as a recovery of usurped rights; and the royal houses of Argos and Sparta renounced their Dorian origin and connected themselves by blood with Heracles, who was associated with the pre-Dorian lords of Argolis.

Every place in Greece had its own local legends, which grew up

The Dorian conquest conceived as the Return of the Heraclidae.

---

[56] Not four, for the Achaeans had been partly dorized and partly ionized.

[57] See below, p. 114. Agis and Eurypon, the ancestors of the royal families, the Agids and Eurypontids, were made sons of Eurysthenes and Procles.

quite independently. Sometimes they were adapted and modified to suit the legendary scheme of the poets and "story-writers"; but often they lived on, unscrupulously accepted notwithstanding all incompatibilities. In several cases we find in the poems of Homer and Hesiod legends which are inconsistent with those which became currently accepted. Thus Cadmus was the founder of Thebes according to the current legend; but in the *Odyssey*, Thebes is built by Amphion and Zethus. The origin of Corinth was traced on one hand to Ephyre, daughter of Ocean; on the other to Sisyphus, the son of Aeolus. The received genealogy of pre-Dorian Argos had no connexion with Hellen and his sons. Argos derived its origin from Inachus—a personification of the stream of Inachus which flows by the town—who, like most rivers, was regarded as a son of Ocean; Argos was his great-grandson; Io, from whom the Danaoi were descended, was his daughter. Thus it emerges that the pre-Dorian Argives were not Hellenes, for they were not derived from Hellen. If the legend had been true to history they should have been traced from Ion, as there was probably a large Ionian element in Argolis.

The Aeolids.

But for most of the Greeks connexions with Hellen and his sons were manufactured. It was to Aeolus that most descents were traced. He had seven sons and five daughters, and it was not difficult to work out more or less plausible connexions. Aetolian legends fastened themselves on to his daughter Calyce. His son Sisyphus founded Corinth. The Thessalian heroes, Admetus and Jason, were

The Neleids.

derived from another son, Cretheus. Perhaps the most interesting instance is the genealogy which was established for the Codrid families of Miletus and other cities of Ionia. They traced up their lineage to Poseidon and at the same time derived themselves from Hellen. The story was that Salmoneus, son of Aeolus, had a daughter who bore to Poseidon twin sons, Pelias and Neleus. As Pelias won the Thessalian kingdom of Iolcus, Neleus went forth from the land and founded a kingdom for himself at Pylus in the southwest of the Peloponnesus. He was succeeded by Nestor, who in his old age bore a part in the Trojan war. Nestor's fourth successor Melanthus was ruler of Pylus when the Dorians came down into the

$Νειλεύς$
(Ionic),
$Νηλεύς$
(Aeolic).

Peloponnesus, and he retreated before their attack to Athens, where he became king and was the father of Codrus. Then Neleus, a son of Codrus, led the Ionian migration to Asia Minor. Thus a number of different traditions were wrought into a narrative, which, originating in Ionia, was accepted in Attica and influenced the ideas of the Athenians about a part of their own early history.

The Greeks were not content that their legends should be confined to the range of their own country and their own race; and, in curious contrast with that exclusive pride which drew a hard and fast line between Greek and barbarian, they brought their ancestors and their myths into connexion with foreign lands. Thus the myth of Io made the Danaoi of Argos cousins of the Egyptians. By her amour with Zeus, Io became the grandmother of Danaus and Aegyptus, the eponymous ancestors of the two peoples. Cadmus, the name-sire of the Cadmeians of Thebes, was represented as a Phoenician, who went forth from his own land in quest of his sister Europa and settled in Boeotia. The tale which gained widest belief made Pelops son of the Phrygian Tantalus, king of Sipylus, whence he migrated to the Peloponnesus and founded the royal line of Argos, from which Agamemnon was sprung. A Corinthian legend brought the early history of Corinth into connexion with Colchis, representing Aeetes, offspring of the Sun, as the first Corinthian king, and his daughter Medea as heiress to the land. The true home of the Greeks before they won dominion in Greece had passed clean out of their remembrance, and they looked to the east, not to the north, as the quarter from which some of their ancestors had migrated.

Egypt.

Phoenicia.

Phrygia.

Colchis.

Of the legends which won sincere credence among the Greeks, and assumed as we may say a national significance, none is more curious or more obscure in its origin than that of the Amazons. A folk of warrior women, strong and brave, living apart from men, were conceived to have dwelt in Asia in the heroic age, and proved themselves worthy foes of the Greek heroes. An obvious etymology of their name, "breastless," suggested the belief that they used to burn off the right breast that they might the better draw the bow. In the *Iliad* Priam tells how he fought against their army in Phrygia; and one of the perilous tasks which are set to Bellerophon is to march against the Amazons. In a later Homeric poem, the Amazon Penthesilea appears as a dreaded adversary of the Greeks at Troy. To win the girdle of the Amazon queen was one of the labours of Heracles. All these adventures happened in Asia Minor; and, though this female folk was located in various places, its original and proper home was ultimately placed on the river Thermodon near the Greek colony of Amisus. But the Amazons attacked Greece itself. It was told that Theseus carried off their queen Antiope, and so they came and invaded Attica. There was a terrible battle in the town of Athens, and the invaders were defeated after a long struggle. At the feast of Theseus the Athenians used to sacrifice to the Amazons; there was a building called the Amazoneion in the western quarter of the city; and the episode

Legend of the Amazons

In the Iliad (iii. 186 and vi. 152).
In the Aethiopis

Amazon invasion of Attica

was believed by such men as Isocrates and Plato to be as truly an historical fact as the Trojan war itself. The battles of Greeks with Amazons were a favourite subject of Grecian sculptors; and, like the Trojan war and the adventure of the golden fleece, the Amazon story fitted into the conception of an ancient and long strife between Greece and Asia.

The details of the famous legends—the labours of Heracles, the Trojan war, the voyage of the Argonauts, the tale of Cadmus, the life of Oedipus, the two sieges of Thebes by the Argive Adrastus, and all the other familiar stories—belong to mythology and lie beyond our present scope. But we have to realise that the later Greeks believed them and discussed them as sober history, and that many of them had a genuine historical basis, however slender. The story of the Trojan war has more historical matter in it than any other; but we have seen that the Argonautic legend and the tale of Cadmus contain dim memories of actual events. It is quite probable that the heroic age witnessed rivalry and war between Thebes and Argos.

Two powerful generating forces of these historic myths had been the custom of families and cities to trace their origin to a god, and the instinct of the Greeks to personify places, especially towns, rivers, and springs. Then, when men began both to become keenly conscious of a community of race and language, and to speculate upon the past, attempts were naturally made to bring the various myths of Greece into harmony; since they were true, they must be reconciled. Ultimately they were reduced into chronological systems, which were based upon genealogical reckonings by generations. Hecataeus of Miletus counted a generation as forty years; but it was more usual to reckon three generations to a hundred years. According to the scheme which finally won the widest acceptance, Troy was taken in 1184 B.C., and the Dorians invaded the Peloponnesus under the leadership of the Heraclids in 1104 B.C., and both these dates accord more closely than one might expect, considering the method by which they were obtained, with the general probabilities of the case.

LEADING DATES ACCORDING TO THE SYSTEM OF ERATOSTHENES
(c. 220 B.C.)

Cadmus	B.C.	1313
Pelops	”	1283
Heracles	”	1261-1209
Argonauts	”	1225

Seven against Thebes . . .	B.C.	1213
Fall of Troy	”	1184

Leading Dates according to the System of Eratosthenes
(c. 220 b.c.)—continued

Thessalian conquest ⎫ . . .		
Boeotian ” ⎬ . . .	B.C.	1124
Aeolic migration ⎭		
Return of Heraclidae . . .	”	1104
Death of Codrus	”	1044
Ionic migration	”	1044
Lycurgus at Sparta . . .	”	885

NORTHERN
GREECE.

Stadia
0 100 200 300 400 500 600

English Miles
0 10 20 30 40 50 60

FIG. 21.

CHAPTER II

THE EXPANSION OF GREECE

Secr. 1. Causes and Character of Greek Colonisation

The expansion of the Greeks beyond Greece proper and the coasts of the Aegean, the plantation of Greek colonies on the shores of Thrace and the Black Sea, in Italy and Sicily, even in Spain and Gaul, began it is uncertain when, and was completed in the sixth century. But it must not be regarded as a single or isolated phenomenon. It was the continuation of the earlier expansion over the Aegean islands and the coast of Asia Minor, the details of which were forgotten by the Greeks themselves, and are consequently unknown to us.

The cause of Greek colonisation is not to be found in mere trade interests. These indeed were in most cases a motive, and in some of the settlements on the Black Sea they were perhaps a leading motive. But the great difference between Greek and Phoenician colonisation is that, while the Phoenicians aimed solely at promoting their commerce, and only a few of their settlements, notably Carthage, became more than mere trading-stations or factories, Greek colonisation satisfied other needs than desire of commercial profit. It was the expression of the adventurous spirit which has been poetically reflected in the legends of the "Sailing of the Argo" and the "Home-coming of Odysseus"—the same spirit, not to be expressed in any commercial formula, which prompted English colonisation.

Difference of Greek and Phoenician colonisation.

Trade, of course, sometimes paved the way. Colonists followed in the paths of trade, and the merchants of Miletus, who adventured themselves in the dangerous waters of the Euxine, observed natural harbours and inviting sites for cities, and when they returned home organised parties of settlers. The adventurous, the discontented, and the needy were always to be found. But in the case of the early colonies at least, it was not over-population of the land, so much as the nature of the land-system, that drove men to emigrate. In various ways, under the family system, which was ill suited to independent and adventurous spirits, it would come

Causes of Greek colonisation: (1) trade: (2) the land-system;

about that individual members were excluded from a share in the common estate, and separated from their kin. Such lacklands were ripe for colonial enterprise. Again, the political circumstances of most Greek states in the eighth and seventh centuries favoured emigration. We have seen that at this time the aristocratic form of government generally prevailed. Sometimes a king was formally at the head, but he was really no more than the first of peers; a body of nobles were the true masters. Sometimes there was an aristocracy within an aristocracy; or a large clan, like the Bacchiads at Corinth, held the power. In all cases the distinction between the members of the ruling class and the mass of free citizens was widened and deepened. It was the tendency of the rulers to govern in their own interest and oppress the multitude, and they cared little to disguise their contempt for the mass of the people. At Mytilene things went so far that the Penthilids, who had secured the chief power, went about in the streets, armed with clubs, and knocked down citizens whom they disliked. Under these conditions there were strong inducements for men to leave their native city where they were of little account and had to endure the slights, if nothing worse, of their rulers, and to join in the foundation of a new *polis* where they might themselves rule. The same inducement drew nobles who did not belong to the inner oligarchical circle. In fact, political discontent was an immediate cause of Greek colonisation; and conversely it may be said that colonisation was a palladium of aristocracy. If this outlet had not existed, or if it had not suited the Hellenic temper, the aristocracies might not have lasted so long, and they wisely discerned that it was their own interest to encourage colonisation.

But while we recognise the operation of general causes we must not ignore special causes. We must, for instance, take into account the fact that Miletus and the south Ionian cities were unable to expand in Caria, as the north Ionian cities expanded in Lydia, because the Carians were too strong for them; and Lycia presented the same kind of barrier to Rhodes. Otherwise, perhaps neither Rhodes nor Miletus would have sent settlers to distant lands.

Wherever the Greek went, he retained his customs and language, and made a Greek "polis." It was as if a bit of Greece were set down on the remote shores of the Euxine or in the far west on the wild coasts of Gaul or Iberia. The colony was a private enterprise, but the bond of kinship with the "mother-city" was carefully fostered, and though political discontent might have been the cause which drove the founders forth, yet that solemn departure for a distant land, where a new city-state, protected by the same gods, was to spring up, always sealed a reconciliation. The emigrants took fire from the public hearth of their city to light the fire on that of their new home. Intercourse between colonies and the mother-country was specially kept up at the great religious festivals of the year, and various marks of filial respect were shown by the daughter to the mother. When, as frequently befell, the colony determined herself in turn to throw off a new shoot, it was the recognised custom that she should seek the *oecist* or leader of the colonists from the mother-city. Thus the Megarian colony, Byzantium, when it founded its own colony, Mesembria, must have sought an oecist from Megara. The political importance of colonisation was sanctified by religion, and it was a necessary formality, whenever a settlement was to be made, to ask the approbation of the Delphic god. The most ancient oracular god of Greece was Zeus of Dodona. The Selli, his priests and "interpreters," are mentioned in the *Iliad;* and in the *Odyssey* Dodona appears as a place to which a king of the west might go to ask the will of Zeus "from the lofty oak," wherein the god was conceived to dwell. But the oak-shrine in the highlands of Epirus was too remote to become the chief oracle of Greece, and the central position of Delphi enabled the astute priests of the Pythian Apollo[1] to exalt the authority of their god as a true prophet to the supreme place in the Greek world. There were other oracular deities who foretold the future; there was, not far off, Trophonius at Boeotian Lebadea; there was Amphiaraus in the land of the Graes, not yet Boeotian. But none of these ever became even a rival of the Delphian Apollo, who by the seventh century at least had won the position of adviser to Greece.[2]

Oracles

It is worthy of notice that colonisation tended to promote a feeling of unity among the Greek peoples, and it did so in two ways. By the wide diffusion of their race on the fringe of barbarous lands, it brought home to them more fully the contrast between Greek and barbarian, and, by consequence, the community of the Greeks. The Greek dwellers in Asia Minor, neighbours of not-Greek peoples, were naturally impressed with their own unity in a way which was strange to dwellers in Boeotia or Attica, who were surrounded on all sides by Greeks and were therefore alive chiefly to local differences. With the diffusion of their sons over various parts of the world, the European Greeks acquired a stronger sense of unity. In the second place, colonisation led to

Consciousness of Greek unity promoted by colonisation, through (1) intercourse with non Greeks:

(2) joint enterprises.

---

[1] The Delphic oracle is also mentioned in the *Odyssey,* for instance in viii. 80.
[2] The influence of the oracle is another question. See below, p. 152.

the association of Greeks of different cities. An oecist who decided to organise a party of colonists could not always find in his own city a sufficient number of men willing to take part in the enterprise. He therefore enlisted comrades from other cities; and thus many colonies were joint undertakings and contained a mixture of citizens of various nationality. This feature was not indeed confined to the later epoch of colonisation; it is one of the few facts about the earlier settlements on the Asiatic coast of which we can be certain.

SECT. 2. COLONIES ON THE COASTS OF THE EUXINE, PROPONTIS, AND NORTH AEGEAN

Legend of
the Argo.

The voyage of the Argonauts in quest of the golden fleece commemorates in a delightful legend the memorable day on which Greek sailors for the first time burst into the waters of the Euxine Sea. Accustomed to the island straits and short distances of the Aegean, they fancied that when they had passed the Bosphorus they were embarking on a boundless ocean, and they called it the "Main," *Pontos*. Even when they had circumnavigated its shores it might still seem boundless, for they knew not where the great rivers, the Ister, the Tanais, the Danapris, might lead. The little preliminary sea into which the Hellespont widens, to contract again into the narrow passage of the Bosphorus, was appropriately named the "vestibule of the Pontus"—*Propontis*. Full of creeks and recesses, it is happily described by Euripides as the "bayed water-key of the boundless Sea." The Pontus was a treacherous field for the barques of even experienced mariners, and it was supposed to have received for this reason its name "Euxine," or Hospitable, in accordance with a habit of the Greeks to seek to propitiate adverse powers by pleasant names.[3] It was when the compass of the Euxine was still unknown, and men were beginning shyly to explore its coasts, that the tale of the wanderings of Odysseus took form. He was imagined to have sailed from Troy into the Pontus, and, after having been driven about in its waters, to have at last reached Ithaca by an overland journey through Thrace and Epirus. In the *Odyssey,* as we have it now, compounded of many different legends and poems, this is disguised; the island of Circe has been removed to the far west, and the scene of the Descent to the Underworld translated to the Atlantic Ocean. But Circe, the daughter of the Sun, and sister of King Aeetes who possessed the golden fleece, belongs to the seas of Colchis; and the

The
Pontos
(Black
Sea).

Propontis.

Signifi-
cance of
the
Odyssey.

---

[3] But this explanation is by no means certain.

world of shades beyond the Cimmerians is to be sought near the
Cimmerian Bosphorus. The mention of Sicily in some of the later
parts of the poem, and the part played by Ithaca, which, with the
other islands of the Ionian Sea, lay on the road to the western
Mediterranean, reflect the beginning of the expansion of Greece in
that direction. But the original wanderings of Odysseus were connected, not with the west, but with the exploration of the Euxine. (Straits of Azov).

A mist of obscurity hangs about the beginnings of the first Greek
cities which arose on the Pontic shores. Here Miletus was the
pioneer. Merchants carrying the stuffs which were manufactured
from wool of Milesian sheep may have established trading-stations
along the southern coast. Flax from Colchis, steel and silver, slaves
were among the chief products which their wool bought. But the
work of colonisation beyond the gate of the Bosphorus can hardly Megarian colonies:
have fully begun until the gate itself was secured by the enterprise
of Megara, which sent out men, in the first part of the seventh
century, to found the towns of Chalcedon and Byzantium. Byzan- Byzan-tium [660 B.C.]
tium could command the trade of the Black Sea, but the great
commercial and political importance of her situation was not fully
appreciated until a thousand years had passed, when she became
the rival and successor of Rome and took, in honour of her second
founder, the name Constantinople. This is the first appearance of
the little state of Megara in Greek history; and none of her contemporaries took a step that was destined to lead to greater things
than the settlement on the Bosphorus. The story was that Chal- Chal-cedon;
cedon was founded first, before the Megarians perceived the striking advantages of the opposite shore, and the Delphic oracle, which
they consulted as a matter of course, chid them as "blind men."
Westward from Byzantium they also founded Selymbria, on the Selym-bria; Heraclea.
north coast of the Propontis; eastward they established "Heraclea
in Pontus," on the coast of Bithynia.

The enterprise of the Megarians stimulated Miletus, and she Milesian colonies:
determined to anticipate others in seizing the best sites on the
Pontic shore. At the most northerly point of the southern coast a
strait-necked cape forms two natural harbours, an attractive site
for settlers, and here the Milesians planted the city Sinope.[4] Sinope;
Farther east, half-way to that extreme eastern point of the sea
where the Phasis flows out at the foot of Mount Caucasus, arose
another Milesian colony, Trapezus. At the Bosphorus the Mile- Trebi-zond;

---

[4] This city claimed to date from the eighth century, to have been swept
away in the invasion of the Cimmerians, and to have risen again in the seventh; but it is highly improbable that any of the Pontic cities were older than
the towns of the Bosphorus and Propontis.

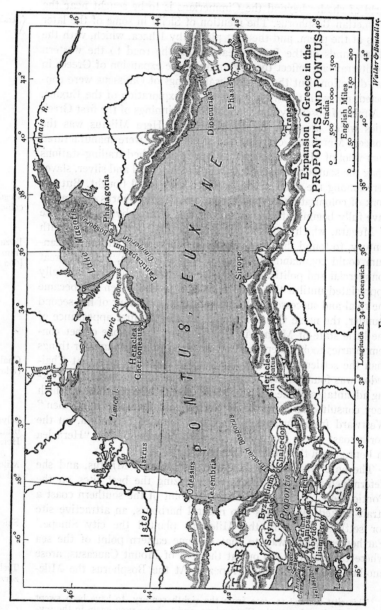

Walker & Boutall sc.

Expansion of Greece in the
PROPONTIS AND PONTUS

Stadia
0   500   1000   1500

English Miles
0   50   100   150   200

Longitude E. 34 of Greenwich

FIG. 22.

sians had been anticipated by Megara, but they partly made up for this by planting Abydos on the Hellespont opposite Sestos, and they also seized a jutting promontory on the south coast of the Propontis, where a narrow neck, as at Sinope, forms two harbours. The town was named Cyzicus, and the peninsula was afterwards transformed into an island; the tunny-fish on the coins of the city shows what was one of the chief articles of her trade. Lampsacus, at the northern end of the Hellespont, once a Phoenician factory, was colonised by another Ionian city, Phocaea, about the same time, and the winged sea-horse on Lampsacene coins speaks of naval enterprise which led afterwards to wealth and prosperity. The foundation of Parion was due to a joint undertaking of Miletus and Erythrae; and Clazomenae joined Miletus in planting Cardia at the neck of the Thracian Chersonese, in the important position of an advance fort against Thrace. On the southern side of the Hellespont the lands of the Scamander invited the Greeks of Lesbos, and a number of small Aeolian settlements arose.

Greek settlements also sprang up in the more remote parts of the Euxine. Dioscurias and Phasis were founded in the far east, in the fabled land of Colchis. On the Tauric Chersonesus or "peninsula" (now the Crimea), Panticapaeum was founded over against Phanagoria at the entrance to the Maeotic lake, and Tanais at the mouth of the like-named river. Heraclea, or Chersonesus, on the western side of the peninsula, was destined to preserve the municipal forms of an old Greek city for more than a thousand years. Olbia at the mouth of the Dnieper, Odessus, Istrus, Mesembria were only some of the Greek settlements which complete the circuit of the Black Sea.

This sea and the Propontis were the special domain of the sea-god Achilles, whose fame grew greater by his association as a hero with the legend of Troy. He was worshipped along the coasts as "lord of the Pontus"; and in Leuce, the "shining island" near the Danube's mouth, the lonely island where no man dwelled, he had a temple, and the birds of the sea were said to be its warders.

If Miletus and Megara took the most prominent part in extending the borders of the Greek world eastward of the Hellespont, the northwestern corner of the Aegean was the special domain of Euboea. The barren islands of Sciathus and Peparethus were the bridge from Euboea to the coast of Macedonia, which, between the rivers Axius and Strymon, runs out into a huge three-pronged promontory. Here Chalcis planted so many towns that the whole promontory was named Chalcidice. Some of the chief cities, however, were founded by other states, notably Corinthian Potidaea

Abydos;

Cyzicus.

Phocaean colony: Lampsacus.

Milesian and Erythraean colony: Parion. Cardia.

Other settlements on the Pontus: Dioscurias, Puasis, Panticapaeum Tanais, Heraclea Olbia, Odessus, Mesembria. Worship of Achilles in the Pontus. Ποντάρχης. Temple at Leuce.

Chalcidian colonisation.

Chalcidice.

Corinth-
ian
colony:
Potidaea.

on the most westerly of the three prongs, which was called Pallene. Sithonia was the central prong, and Acte, ending in Mount Athos, the eastern. Some of the colonies on Pallene were founded by Eretria, and those north of Acte by Andros, which was dependent on Eretria. Hence we may regard this group of cities as Euboean, though we cannot regard it as Chalcidian. On the west side of the Thermaic Bay, two Euboean colonies were planted, Pydna and Methone, on Macedonian soil.

Pydna
and
Methone.

Sect. 3. Colonies in the Western Mediterranean

The earliest mention of Sicilian and Italian regions in literature is to be found in some later passages of the *Odyssey*, which should perhaps be referred to the eighth century. There we meet with the Sicels, and with the island of Sicania; while Temesa, where Greek traders could buy Tuscan copper, has the distinction of being the first Italian place mentioned by name in a literary record. By the end of the seventh century Greek states stood thick on the east coast of Sicily and round the sweep of the Tarentine Gulf. These colonies naturally fall into three groups:

(1) The Euboean, which were both in Sicily and in Italy.

(2) The Achaean, which were altogether on Italian soil.

(3) The Dorian, which were with few exceptions, in Sicily.

The chronology is uncertain, and we cannot say whether the island or the mainland was first colonised.

Odysseus
in the
west.

The oldest stories of the adventures of Odysseus were laid, as we have seen, in the half-explored regions of the Black Sea. Nothing shows more impressively the life of this poetry, and the power it had won over the hearts of the Greek folks, than the fact that when the navigation of the Italian and Sicilian seas began, these adventures were transferred from the east to the west; and in the further growth of this cycle of poems a new mythical geography was adopted. At a time when the Greeks knew so little of Italy that the southern promontories could be designated as "sacred islands,"[5] the straits of Messana were identified with Scylla and Charybdis, Lipara became the island of Aeolus, the home of the Cyclopes was found in the fiery mount of Aetna. Then Scheria, the isle of the Phaeacians, was fancied to be Corcyra; an entrance to the under-world was placed at Cumae; and the rocks of the Sirens were sought near Sorrento. And not only did the first glimpses of western geography affect the transmutation of the *Odyssey* into its final shape, but the *Odyssey* reacted on the geography of the

[5] The expression is preserved in the Catalogue of the Hesiodic Theogony.

west. That the promontory of Circei in Latin territory bears the name of the sorceress of Colchis, is an evidence of the spell of Homeric song. Odysseus was not the only hero who was borne westward with Greek ships in the eighth century. Cretan Minos and Daedalus, for example, had links with Sicily. Above all, the earliest navigation of the western seas was ascribed to Heracles, who reached the limits of the land of the setting sun, and stood on the ledge of the world looking out upon the stream of Oceanus. From him the opposite cliffs which form the gate of the Mediterranean were called the Pillars of Heracles.

The earliest colony founded by Greek sailors in the western seas was said to have been Cyme on the coast of Campania. Tradition assigned to it an origin before 1000 B.C., a date which modern criticism has called in question. But even if we place its origin much later, the tradition that it was the earliest Greek city founded in the middle peninsula of the Mediterranean may possibly be true. It was at all events one of the oldest, and it had an unique position. Chalcis, Eretria, and Cyme, a town on the eastern coast of Euboea, which at that time had some eminence but afterwards sank into the obscurity of a village, joined together, and enlisted for their expedition some Graeans who dwelled on the opposite mainland in the neighbourhood of Tanagra. The colonisers settled first on the island of Pithecusae, and soon succeeded in establishing themselves on a rocky height which rises above the sea just where the Italian coast is about to turn sharply eastward to encircle the bay of Naples. The site was happily chosen. It was a strong post, and though there was no harbour, the strangers could haul up their ships on a stretch of sand below. Subsequently they occupied the harbour which was just inside the promontory, and established there the town of Dicaearchia which afterwards became Puteoli; farther east they founded Naples, "the new city."

The people in whose midst this outpost of Greek civilisation was planted were the Opicans, one of the chief branches of the Italic race. The colonists were eminently successful in their intercourse with the natives; and the solitary position of Cyme in these regions —for no Greek settlement could be made northward on account of the great Etruscan power, and there was no rival southward until the later plantation of Posidonia—made her influence both wide and noiseless. Her external history is uneventful; there are no striking wars or struggles to record; but the work she did holds an important and definite place in the history of European civilisation. To the Euboeans of Cyme we may say that we owe the alphabet which we use to-day, for it was from them that the Latins

EUBOEAN COLONIES: Cyme.

Its date.

Founders.

Site.

Dicaearchia. Neapolis

Importance of Cyme in European history.

Italian alphabet.

learned to write. The Etruscans also got their alphabet independently from the same masters, and, having modified it in certain ways to suit themselves, passed it on to the Oscans and Umbrians. Again, the Cymaeans introduced the neighbouring Italian peoples to a knowledge of the Greek gods and Greek religion. Heracles, Apollo, Castor, and Polydeuces became such familiar names in Italy that they came to be regarded as original Italian deities. The oracles of the Cymaean Sibyl, prophetess of Apollo, were believed to contain the destinies of Rome.

Introduction of Greek gods.

To Cyme, too, western Europe probably owes the name by which she calls Hellas and the Hellenes. The Greeks, when they first came into contact with Latins, had no common name; Hellenes, the name which afterwards united them, was as yet merely associated with a particular tribe. It was only natural that strangers should extend the name of the first Greeks with whom they came in contact to others whom they fell in with later, and so to all Greeks whatsoever. But the curious circumstance is that the settlers of Cyme were known, not by the name of Chalcis or Eretria or Cyme itself, but by that of Graia. *Graii* was the term which the Latins and their fellows applied to the colonists, and the name *Graeci* is a derivative of a usual type from Graii. It was doubtless some trivial accident which ruled that we to-day call Hellas "Greece," instead of knowing it by some name derived from Cyme, Eretria, or Chalcis. The west has got its "Greece" from an obscure district in Boeotia; Greece itself got its "Hellas" from a small territory in Thessaly. This was accidental. But it was no accident that western Europe calls Greece by a name connected with that city in which Greeks first came into touch with the people who were destined to civilise western Europe and rule it for centuries.

Origin of the name Greece—

from the Boeotian Graeans.

The next settlement of the Euboean Greeks was on Sicilian, not Italian, ground. The island of Sicily is geographically a continuation of Italy—just as the Peloponnesus is a continuation of the great eastern peninsula; but its historical importance depends much more on another geographical fact. It is the centre of the Mediterranean; it parts the eastern from the western waters. It has been thus marked out by nature as a meeting-place of nations; and the struggle between European and Asiatic peoples, which has been called the "Eternal Question," has been partly fought out on Sicilian soil. There has been in historical times no native Sicilian power. The greatness of the island was due to colonisation—not migration—from other lands. Lying as a connecting link between Europe and Africa, it attracted settlers from both sides; while its

Sicily; its position in history.

ciose proximity to Italy always rendered it an object of acquisition to those who successively ruled in that peninsula.

The earliest inhabitants of the island were the Sicans. They believed themselves to be autochthonous, and we have no record at
what time they entered the island or whence they came or to what
race they belonged. The nature of things makes it probable that
they entered from Italy. From them the island was called Sicania.
The next comers were the Sicels, of whom we can speak with more
certainty. As we find Sicels in the toe of Italy, we know that tradition correctly described them as settlers from the Italian peninsula,
and there is some slight evidence to show that they spoke the same
language as that group of Italic peoples, to which the Latins belonged. The likeness of the names Sicel and Sican has naturally led
to the view that these two folks were akin in race and language.
But likeness of names is deceptive; and it is a remarkable fact
that the Greeks, who were only too prone to build up theories on
resemblances of words, always carefully distinguished the Sican
from the Sicel as ethnically different. Still a connexion is possible,
if we suppose that the Sicels were Sicans who remaining behind in
Italy had in the course of centuries become Italicised by intercourse with the Latin and kindred peoples, and then, emigrating in
their turn to the island, met without recognition the brethren from
whom they had parted in the remote past. But all this is uncertain.
The Sicels, however, wrested from the Sicans the eastern half of
the island, which was thus cut up into two countries, Sicania in the
west, Sicelia in the east. In the *Odyssey* we read of Sicania; perhaps the Greeks of Cyme knew it by this name. At a very early
time Sicania was invaded by a mysterious people named Elymians,
variously said to have come from Italy and from the north of Asia
Minor. The probability is that they were of Iberian race. They
occupied a small territory in the north-west of the island.

These were the three peoples who inhabited this miniature continent, soon about to become the battlefield of Greek and Phoenician. The Sicels were the most numerous and most important. The
only Sican town of any significance in historical times was *Hyk-
kara* on the north-west promontory. *Minôa,* originally Sican on the
south coast, became Greek. *Camicus,* at some distance inland in
the same region, was in early days an important stronghold. The
Elymian settlements at *Segesta* and *Eryx* became of far greater importance than the Sican. The eastern half of the isle, the original
Sicelia, was thickly set with Sicel fortresses from *Cephaloedium*
(the modern Cefalù), at the centre of the northern coast, to
Motyca, an inland town in the southeastern corner. Among the

SICANS.

SICELS.

Were
Sicans
and Sicels
kinsfolk?
Answer
uncertain.

ELY-
MIANS.

Sican
places.

Elymian
towns.

Sicel
towns.

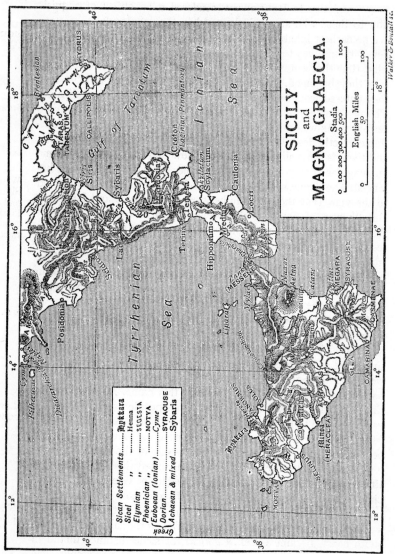

SICILY
and
MAGNA GRAECIA.

Stadia
0 100 200 300 400 500 · · · 1000

English Miles
0 · · · 50 · · · 100

Sican Settlements......Henna
Sicel   „   ......SEGESTA
Elymian   „   ......NOTYA
Phoenician „   ......Cyme
(Euboean (Ionian)
Dorian............SYRACUSE
Achaean & mixed ......Sybaris
Greek

most famous were *Agyrium, Centuripa, Morgantina,* and above all *Henna.*

PHOENI-CIANS:

At an early age merchants from Phoenicia planted factories on the coasts of the island. At first they did not make any settlements of a permanent kind,—any that could be called cities. For Sicily was to them only a house to call at, lying directly on their way to the land of the farthest west, when they went forth to win the golden treasures of Tarshish and planted their earliest colony, Gades, outside the straits which divide Europe from Africa. Their next colonies were on the coast of Africa over against Sicily, and this settlement had a decisive influence on the destinies of the island. The Phoenician trading-stations on the east coast of Sicily were probably outposts of old Phoenicia, but some at least of those in the west seem to have come from the new and nearer Phoenicia. The settlements of Hippo and Utica, older than Carthage, were probably the parents of the more abiding Phoenician settlements in Sicily.[6] In the east of the island the Phoenicians had no secure foothold. They were not able to dispossess the Sicel natives, or to make a home among them; they appeared purely in the guise of traders. Hence when the Greeks came and seriously set to work to plant true cities, the Phoenicians disappeared and left few traces to show that they had ever been there.

Colonies
in Spain
(Gades).
Africa.

(Hippo,
Utica.)

Stations
in Sicily.

Sicilian, like Italian history, really opens with the coming of the Greeks. They came under the guidance of Chalcis and the auspices of Apollo. It was naturally on the east coast which faces Greece that the first Greek settlement was made, and it is to be noticed that of the coasts of Sicily the east is that which most resembles in character the coast-line of Greece. The site which was chosen by the Chalcidians, and the Ionians of Naxos who accompanied them, was not a striking one. A little tongue of land, north of Mount Aetna, very different from the height of Cyme, was selected for the foundation of Naxos. Here, as in the case of Cyme, the Chalcidians who led the enterprise surrendered the honour of naming the new city to their less prominent fellow-founders. The first of all the Greek towns of Sicily, Naxos was not destined to live for much

GREEKS.

Naxos
[tradi-
tional
date,
735 B.C.].

---

[6] See below, p. 94. There is no clear evidence for the date of the Phoenician colonies in western Sicily. It might be argued that they were later than the Greek colonies, on the ground that the Phoenicians, if their colonisation had begun earlier than Greek colonisation, would have occupied the excellent sites which the Greeks seized. But this argument is not conclusive. For one thing, the Sicels had to be reckoned with. It was probably an easier task to gain a footing on Sican soil; and the Phoenicians may have tried and failed on Sicel soil where the Greeks succeeded. Or again, if Phoenician city-settlements grew out of mere factories, the Greeks may have abolished such factories, which might, if they had been left to themselves, have grown into cities.

more than three hundred years. It was to be destroyed not by the
fire of the dangerous mountain which dominated it, but by a
human foe. A sort of consecration was always attached to Naxos
as the first homestead of the Hellenes in the island which was to
become a brilliant part of Hellas. To Apollo Archēgĕtes an altar
was erected on the spot where the Greeks first landed,—driven, as
the legend told, by contrary winds, through Apollo's dispensation,
to the Sicilian shores. It was the habit of ambassadors from old
Greece as soon as they arrived in Sicily to offer sacrifice on this
altar. In the fertile plain south of Aetna the Chalcidians soon afterwards founded Catane, close to the sea and protected by a low
range of hills behind, but under the power of Aetna which was to
unmake the place again and again; and inland Leontini at the
south end of her plain between two hills, with an eastern and a
western acropolis. These sites, Leontini certainly if not Catane,
were wrested from the Sicels. The Chalcidians also won possession
of the north-east corner, and thus obtained command of the straits
between the island and the mainland. Here Cymaeans and Chalcidians planted Zancle on a low rim of land, which resembles a
reaping-hook and gave the place its name. The haven is formed by
the curving blade; and when Zancle came in afterdays to mint
money she engraved on her coins a sickle representing her harbour
and a dolphin floating within it. A hundred years later the city
was transformed by the immigration of a company of Messenians,
and ultimately the old local name was ousted in favour of Messana.
From Zancle the Euboeans established the fortress of Mylae on the
other side of the north-eastern promontory; and in the middle of
the seventh century they founded Himera, the only Greek city on
the northern coast, destined to live for scarce two centuries and a
half, and then to be swept away by the Phoenician. It was important for Zancle that the land over against her, the extreme
point of the Italian peninsula, should be in friendly hands, and
therefore the men of Zancle incited their mother-city to found
Rhegion; and in this foundation Messenians took part.

While this group of Chalcidian colonies was being formed in
north-eastern Sicily, Dorian Greeks began to obtain a footing in
south-eastern Sicily, which history decided should become the
Dorian quarter. The earliest of the Dorian cities was also the greatest. Syracuse, destined to be the head of Greek Sicily, was founded
by Corinthian emigrants under the leadership of Archias before
the end of the eighth century. Somewhere about the same time
Corinth also colonised Corcyra; the Ionian islands were half-way
stations to the west. Which colony was the elder, we know not;

tradition did not attempt to decide, for it placed both in the same year. But in both cases Corinth had to dispossess previous Greek settlers, and in both cases the previous settlers were Euboeans. Her colonists had to drive Eretrians from Corcyra and Chalcidians from Syracuse. date, 734 B.C.].

The great Haven of Syracuse, with its island and its hill, formed the most striking site on the east coast, and could not fail to invite the earliest colonists. Chalcidians occupied the island of Ortygia (Isle of quails) as it was called—they must have won it from the Sicel or possibly from the Phoenician—and held it long enough to associate it for ever with the name of a fountain in their old home, Arethusa. It is highly probable that the Chalcidian occupation was effected very soon after that of Naxos, and it is possible that the Corinthians did not supersede the Chalcidians till many years later. But when they once held Syracuse, they effectually prevented any Chalcidian expansion south of Leontini. The Island, Ortygia.

Fountain of Arethusa.

FIG. 24.—Coin of Zancle, early (obverse). Harbour of Zancle, with a dolphin [legend: ΔANK(λαίων)]. FIG. 25.—Coin of Himera, early (obverse). Cock. FIG. 26.—Coin of Syracuse, early (obverse). Head of Arethusa; dolphins [legend: ΣΥΡΑΦΟΣΙΟΝ].

At an early date Megarians also sailed into the west to find a new home. After various unsuccessful attempts to establish themselves, they finally built their city on the coast north of Syracuse, beside the hills of Hybla, and perhaps Sicel natives joined in founding the western *Megara*. It was the most northerly Dorian town on the east coast. But, like her mother, the Hyblaean Megara was destined to found a colony more famous than herself. In the middle of the seventh century the Megarians sent to their metropolis to invite co-operation in planting a settlement in the southwestern part of the island. This settlement, which was to be the farthest outpost of Greek Sicily, was Selinus, the town named of wild celery as its own coins boasted, situated on a low hill on the coast. Megara had been occupied with the goodwill of the Sicel; Selinus was probably held at the expense of the Sican. In the mean- Megara (Hyblaean) [trad. date, 728 B.C.].

Selinus [628 B.C.]

time the south-eastern corner was being studded with Dorian cities, though they did not rise by any means so rapidly as the Chalcidian in the north. The Sicels seem to have offered a stouter resistance here. At the beginning of the seventh century, Gela—the name is Sicel—was planted by Rhodian colonists with Cretans in their train. This city was set on a long narrow hill which stretched between the sea and an inland plain. At a later time Acrae and Casmenae were founded by Syracuse. They were over-shadowed by the greatness of the mother-city, and never attained as much independence as more distant Camarina which was planted from the same metropolis about half a century later.

The latest Dorian colony of Sicily was only less conspicuous than the first. The Geloans sought an oecist from their Rhodian metropolis and founded, half-way between their own city and Selinus, the lofty town of Acragas, which soon took the second place in Greek Sicily and became the rival of Syracuse. It was perched on a high hill near the sea-shore. The small poor haven was at some distance from the town; "flock-feeding Acragas" never became a maritime power. The symbols on its coins were the eagle and the crab.

In planting their colonies and founding their domination in Sicily, the Greeks had mainly to reckon with the Sicels. In their few foundations in the farther west they had to deal with the Sicans. These older inhabitants were forced to retire from the coasts, but they lived on in their fortresses on the inland hills. The island was too large and its character too continental to invite the newcomers to attempt to conquer the whole of it. With the Phoeni-cians the Greeks had no trouble. Their factories and temples had not taken root in the soil, and on the landing of a stranger who was resolved to take root they vanished. Traces of their worship some-times remained, here as in the Aegean. But they did not abandon the western corner of the island, where the Greeks did not attempt to settle. There they maintained three places which now assumed the character of cities. These were Panormus, Solus, and Motya—the Haven, the Rock, and the Island. Panormus or "All-haven" in a fertile plain is protected on the north by Mount Hercte, now the Pilgrim Mount, and on the east by Solus. Motya is on an island in a small bay on the west coast. The Elymian country lay be-tween Motya and Panormus. The chief town of the Elymians, Segesta (which in Greek mouths became Egesta), was essentially a city, while Eryx farther west, high above the sea but not actually on it, was their outpost of defence. On Eryx they wor-shipped some goddess of nature, soon to be identified with the

---

Side notes (left margin):

Rhodian Gela [trad. date, 688 B.C.].

Syracusan Acrae and Casmenae and Camarina [595 B.C.].

Geloan Acragas (Roman Agrigentum, now Girgenti) [581 B.C.].

The Sicans.

Three Phoeni-cian cities: Panor-mus,

Solûs, Motya.

The Elymians and their towns.

Greek Aphrodite. The Elymians were on good terms with the Phoenicians, and western Sicily became a Phoenician corner. While the inland country was left to Sicel and Sican, the coasts were to be the scene of struggles between Phoenician and Greek. And here the natural position of the combatants was reversed, for the Asiatic power was in the west and the European in the east. In the seventh century this struggle was still a long way off, Sicily was still large enough to hold both the Greek and the Canaanite in peace.

The name by which we know the central of the three great peninsulas of the Mediterranean did not extend as far north as the Po in the time of Julius Caesar, and originally it covered a very small area indeed. In the fifth century Thucydides applies the name Italy to the modern Calabria—the western of the two extremities into which the peninsula divides. This extremity was inhabited, when the Greeks first visited it, by Sicels and Oenotrians. But the heel was occupied by peoples of that Illyrian race which had played, as we dimly see, a decisive part in the earliest history of the Greeks. The Illyrian was now astride of the Adriatic; he had reached Italy before the Greek. The Calabrians, who gave their name to the heel, were of Illyrian stock; and along with these were the Messapians, some of whose brethren on the other side of the water seem to have thrown in their fortunes with the Greeks and penetrated into Locris and Boeotia and perhaps into the Peloponnesus. It was on the seaboard of the Sicels and Oenotrians that the Achaeans of the Peloponnesus, probably towards the close of the eighth century, found a field for colonisation. It has been already remarked that the Ionian islands are a sort of stepping-stone to the west, and just as we find Corinthians settling in Corcyra, so we find Achaeans settling in Zacynthus. The first colonies which they planted in Italy were perhaps Sybaris and Croton, famous for their wealth and their rivalry. Sybaris on the river Crathis, in an unhealthy but most fruitful plain, soon extended her dominion across the narrow peninsula and, founding the settlements of Laos and Scidros on the western coast, commanded two seas. Thus having in her hands an overland route to the western Mediterranean, she could forward to her ports on the Tyrrhenian sea the valuable merchandise of the Milesians, whom Chalcidian jealousy excluded from the straits between Italy and Sicily. Thus both agriculture and traffic formed the basis of the remarkable wealth of Sybaris, and the result was an elaboration of luxury which caused the Sybarite name to pass into a proverb. Posidonia, famous for its temples and its roses, was another colony on the western sea, founded from Sybaris. It is said to have been formed by Troe-

ACHAEAN COLONIES. Original meaning of the name Italy.

Messapioi or Metapioi.

Sybaris [trad. date, 721 B.C.].

Posidonia

zenians who were driven out from that city by the Achaeans.

Croton
[trad.
date,
703 B.C.].

A good way to the south of Sybaris you come to Croton, before the coast, in its southern trend, has yet reached the Lacinian promontory, on which a stately temple of Hera formed a central place of worship for the Greek settlers in Italy. Unlike the other Achaean colonies, Croton had a good harbour, the only good harbour on the west side of the gulf, but her prosperity, like that of her fellows, rested not on maritime traffic but on the cultivation of land and the rearing of cattle. The Delphic god seems to have taken a more than wonted interest in the foundation of this city, if we may judge from the Delphic tripod which appears on its earliest coins. Like Sybaris, Croton widened its territory and planted colonies of its own. On the Tyrrhenian sea, Terina and Temesa were to Croton what Laos and Scidros were to Sybaris.[7]

FIG. 27.—Early coin of Poseidonia (obverse). Poseidon with trident. FIG. 28.—Early coin of Caulonia. Obverse: Apollo with bough, small figure on his arm; stag [legend: ΚΑΤΛΟ]. Reverse: incuse, back of these figures.

Caulonia.
Locrian
colonies.
Epizephy-
rian
Locri.

Caulonia, perhaps also a Crotoniate settlement, was the most southerly Achaean colony and was the neighbour of the western Locri. This town was founded in the territory of the Sicels, it is not certain by which of the three Locrian states; perhaps it was a joint enterprise of all three. It was agricultural, like its Achaean neighbours, and like them it pushed over to the western sea and founded Medma and Hipponion on the other coast.

Medma.
Hip-
ponion.

The Achaeans and Locrians might quarrel among themselves, but they had more in common with each other than either had with the Dorians, and we may conveniently include Locri in the Achaean group. Thus the southern coast of Italy would have been almost a homogeneous circle if a Dorian colony had not been established in a small sheltered bay at the extreme north point of the gulf to which it gave the name it still bears, Taras or Taren-

Dorian
colonies.
Taras
[trad.
date,
707 B.C.].

[7] Another colony of Croton was Pandosia, and it conquered the Ionian town of Scylletion (Scylacium).

tum. Taras was remarkable as the only foreign settlement ever made by the greatest of all the Dorian peoples. The town—called, like Sybaris, after the name of a neighbouring stream—was founded by the *Partheniae*, a name which has not yet been explained. There are reasons for thinking that these first founders were pre-Dorian Greeks from the Peloponnesus. But Laconian settlers occupied the place at some unknown date and made of it a Dorian city. A legend then grew up which connected the Partheniae with Sparta, and a historical episode, taking various forms, was manufactured. It was said that in a war with the Messenians, when the Spartans were for many years absent from home, the women bore sons to Helots, and that this progeny, called Partheniae or "Maidens' Children," conspired against the state, and being driven out of the country were directed by the oracle to settle at Taras. The hero Phalanthus, who seems to have been originally a local sea-god, degraded to the rank of a hero at the coming of Poseidon, was worshipped by the Tarentines, and his ride overseas on a dolphin was represented on their coins, The framers of the story of the Partheniae made him the leader of the colonists from Laconia.

First founders, the Partheniae. Second founders, the Laconians. Legend linking the two sets of founders.

Phalanthus— Poseidon

The prosperity of the Tarentines depended partly on the cultivation of a fruitful territory, but mainly on their manufacturing industry. Their fabrics and dyed wools became renowned, and their pottery was widely diffused. Taras in fact must be regarded as an industrial rather than as an agricultural state. Her position brought her into contact with inhabitants of the Calabrian peninsula, and she had a foe in the Messapian town of Brentesion. She founded the colonies of Callipolis and Hydrus on the eastern coast where she had no Greek rivals. But on the other side, her possible advance was foreseen and hindered by the prudence of the Sybarites. They feared lest the Dorian city might creep round the coast and occupy the fertile lands which are watered by the Bradanus and the Siris. So they induced the Achaeans of old Greece to found a colony at Metapontion on the Bradanus, a place which had derived its name from Messapian settlers; and this the most northerly of the Achaean cities flourished as an agricultural community and cut off the westward expansion of Taras. But in the meantime another rival seized the very place from which the Achaeans had desired to exclude the Dorians. In the middle of the seventh century Colophonians planted a colony at Siris, and this Ionian state threatened to interrupt the Achaean line of cities and cut off Metapontion from her sisters. This solitary instance of an Ionian attempt to found a colony at this period in these regions is rendered

Brundusium.

Achaean Metapontion, Metapontum (="place of the Metapians," or Messapians). Siris.

interesting through the probability that the poet Archilochus took part in the expedition. But the attempt seems to have failed. There are reasons for thinking, though the evidence is not clear, that the place was seized by its Achaean neighbours and became an Achaean town. Siris, like Sybaris, Croton, and Locri, had her helpmate, though not a daughter, on the Tyrrhenian sea. By the persuasion of common interest she formed a close connexion with Pyxus; the two cities issued common coins; and perhaps organised a rival overland route.

Pyxus (Policastro).

Thus the western coast of the Tarentine gulf was beset with a line of Achaean cities, flanked at one extremity by Western Locri, on the other by Dorian Taras. The common feature, which distinguished them from the cities settled by the men of Chalcis and Corinth, was that their wealth depended on the mainland, not on the sea. Their rich men were landowners, not merchants; it was not traffic but rich soil that had originally lured them to the far west. The unwarlike Sicels and Oenotrians seem to have laid no obstacles in the way of their settlements and to have submitted to their rule. The Iapygians and Messapians of Calabria were of different temper, and it is significant that it was men from warlike Sparta who succeeded in establishing Taras.

ἡ μεγάλη Ἑλλάς (Magna Graecia).

These cities, with their dependencies beyond the hills, on the shores of the Tyrrhenian sea, came to be regarded as a group, and the country came to be called Great Hellas. We might rather have looked to find it called Great Achaia, by contrast to the old Achaean lands in Greece; but here, as in other cases, it is the name of a lesser folk which prevails. If the Hellenes, the old Greek inhabitants of the plain of the Spercheus, had been conquered by the Achaeans, the conquest was forgotten, and the two peoples had gone forth together to found new cities in the west; and here the Hellenic name rose to celebrity and honour. It was no small thing in itself that the belt of Greek settlements on the Tarentine gulf should come to be called Great Hellas. But it was a small thing compared with the extension of the name Hellenes to designate all peoples of Greek race. There was nothing to lead the Greeks of their own accord to fix on Hellenes as a common name; if they had sought such a name deliberately, their natural choice would have been Achaeans, which Homer had already used in a wide sense. The name must have been given to them from without. Just as the barbarian peoples in central Italy had taken hold of the name of the Graes, so the barbarians in the southern peninsulas took hold of the name of the Hellenes, and used it to denote all settlers and strangers of the same race. Such a common name, applied by bar-

Conjectured origin of the name Hellenes = Greeks.

barian lips to them all alike, brought home to Greek traders the significance of their common race; and they adopted the name themselves as the conjugate of *barbarians*. So the name Hellenes, obscure when it had gone forth to the west, travelled back to the east in a new sense, and won its way into universal use. The fictitious ancestor Hellên became the forefather of the whole Greek race; and the fictitious ancestors of the Dorians, Ionians, and Aeolians were all derived from him. The original Hellenes lost their separate identity as completely as the original Aeolians and Ionians had lost theirs; but their name was destined to live for ever in the speech of men, while those of their greater fellows had passed into a memory.

Sect. 4. Growth of Trade and Maritime Enterprise

The age of the aristocratic republics saw the face of the Greek world completely transformed. The colonial expansion of Greece eastward and westward was itself part of this transformation, but it also helped signally to bring about other changes. For, while the colonies were politically independent of their mother-states, they reacted in many ways on the mother-country.

Family system of property in land.

We have seen how the system of family property was favourable to colonial enterprise. But the colonists, who had suffered under that system, were not likely to introduce it in their new settlements, and thus the institution of personal landownership was probably first established and regulated in the colonies. Their example reacted on the mother-country, where other natural causes were also gradually undermining the family system. In the first place, as the power of the state grew greater the power of the family grew less; and when the head of the state, whether king or republican government, was felt as a formidable authority, the prestige of the head of the family, overshadowed by the power of the state, became insensibly weaker. In the second place, it was common to assign a portion of an estate to one member of the family, to manage and enjoy the undivided use of it; and although it did not become his and he had no power of disposing of it, yet the natural tendency would have been to allow it on his death to pass to his son on the same conditions. It is clear that such a practice tended to the ultimate establishment of personal proprietorship of the soil. Again, side by side with the undivided family estate, personal properties were actually acquired. At this period there was much wild unallotted land, "which wild beasts haunt," especially on the hill-slopes, and when a man of energy reclaimed a portion of this land for tillage, the new fields became his own, for they had belonged to no man. We can thus see generally how inevitable it was that the old system should disappear and the large family estates break up into private domains; but the change was not accomplished by legislation, and the gradual process by which it was brought about is withdrawn from our eyes. It was only when private landownership had become an established fact, that the law came in and recognised it by regulating sales of land and allowing men to bequeath it freely.

The life of farmers in Boeotia, 8th century, described in Hesiod's Works and Days.

The Boeotian poet Hesiod has given us a picture of rural life in Greece at this period. He was a husbandman himself near Ascra, where his father, who had come as a stranger from Cyme in Aeolis, had put under cultivation a strip of waste land on the slopes of Helicon. The farm was divided between his two sons, Perses and Hesiod, but in unequal shares; and Hesiod accuses Perses of winning the larger moiety by bribing the lords of the district. But Perses managed his farm badly and it did not prosper. Hesiod wrote his poem the *Works* to teach such unthrifty farmers as his brother true principles of agriculture and economy. His view of life is profoundly gloomy, and suggests a condition of grave social distress in Boeotia. This must have been mainly due to the oppression of the nobles, "gift-devouring" princes as he calls them. The poet looks back to the past with regret. The golden age, the silver, and the bronze, have all gone by, and the age of the heroes who fought at Troy; and mankind is now in the iron age, and "will never cease by day or night from weariness and woe." "Would that I did not live in this generation, would that I had died before, or were born hereafter!" The poem gives minute directions for the routine of the husbandman's work, the times and tides of sowing and reaping, and the other labours of the field, the fashion of the implements of tillage; and all this is accompanied by maxims of proverbial wisdom.

Historical significance of Hesiod's poem.

Apart from the value of his poem as a social picture, Hesiod has a great significance as the first spokesman of the common folk. In the history of Europe, his is the first voice raised from among the toiling classes and claiming the interest of mankind in their lot. It is a voice indeed of acquiescence, counselling fellow-toilers to make the best of an evil case; the stage of revolt has not yet been reached. But the grievances are aired, and the lords who wield the power are exhorted to deal just judgments, that the land may prosper. The new poet is, in form and style, under the influence of the Homeric poems, but he is acutely conscious that he is striking new notes and has new messages for men. He comes forward, unlike

Homer, in his own person; he contrasts himself with Homer when he claims that the Muses can teach truth as well as beautiful fiction. In another poem, the *Theogony*, we are told that the daughters of Zeus taught Hesiod as he fed sheep on the hill-sides of Helicon; they gave him for staff a branch of bay. The staff was now the minstrel's emblem; for the epic poems were no longer sung to the lyre, but were recited by the "rhapsode" standing with a staff in his hand. Then the Muses breathed into the shepherd of Ascra the wizard power of declaring the future and the past, and set him the task of singing the race of the blessed gods. In the *Theogony* he performs this task. He sings how the world was made, the gods and the earth, the rivers and the ocean, the stars and the heaven; how in infinite space which was at the beginning there arose Earth and Tartarus and Love the cosmic principle; and it is notable how he introduces amongst the eldest-born powers of the world such abstractions as love itself, memory, sleep. These speculations on the origin of the universe, and the attempt to work up the popular myths into a system, mark a new stage in the intellectual development of Greece. There were other works composed by various bards who merged their identities under Hesiod's name; and, as we have seen,[8] these Hesiodic poems had a decisive influence in moulding the ideas of the Greeks as to the early history of their race.

The Theogony.

Hesiod's cosmic system.

Hesiodic school.

Boeotia was always an unenterprising country of husbandmen, and Hesiod had no sympathy with trade or foreign venture, though his father had come from Aeolis. But the growth of trade was the most important fact of the time, and here too the colonies reacted on the mother-country. By enlarging the borders of the Greek world they invited and facilitated the extension of Greek trade and promoted the growth of industries. Hitherto the Greeks had been mainly an agricultural and pastoral people; many of them were now becoming industrial. They had to supply their western colonies with oil and wool, with metal and pottery, and they began to enter into serious competition with the Phoenician trader and to drive eastern goods from the market.

Greek trade moved chiefly along water-ways, and this is illustrated by the neglect of road-making in Greece. There were no paved roads, even in later times, except the Sacred Ways to frequented sanctuaries like that from Athens to Eleusis and Delphi, or that from the sea-coast to Olympia. Yet the Greeks were still timorous navigators, and it was deemed hazardous to sail even in the most familiar waters, except in the late summer. Hesiod expresses in vivid verses the general fear of the sea: "For fifty days after the

Roads in Greece.

Danger of navigation.

[8] Above, p. 72.

solstice, till the end of the harvest, is the tide for sailing; then you will not wreck your ship, nor will the sea wash down your crew, un-less Poseidon or Zeus wills their destruction. In that season winds are steady and Ocean kind; with mind at rest, launch your ship and stow your freight; but make all speed to return home, and await not the new wine and the rain of the vintage-tide, when the winter approaches, and the terrible South-wind stirs the waves, in fellow-ship with the heavy autumnal rain of Zeus, and makes the sea cruel." About this time, however, an important advance was made in seacraft by the discovery of the anchor.

Development of ship-building.

Seafaring states found it needful to build warships for protection against pirates. The usual type of the early Greek warship was the penteconter or "fifty-oar," a long, narrow galley with twenty-five benches, on each of which two oarsmen sat. The penteconter hardly came into use in Greece before the eighth century. The Homeric

The pen-teconter.

Greeks had only smaller vessels of twenty oars, but we can see in the Homeric poems the penteconter coming within their ken as a strange and wonderful thing. The ocean deity, Briareos, called by

Aegaeus.

the name of the Aegean, appears in the *Iliad;* and he is probably no other than the new racer of the seas, sped by a hundred hands. In the *Odyssey* the Phaeacians, who are the kings of seacraft, have ships of fifty oars. But before the end of the eighth century a new idea revolutionised shipbuilding in Phoenicia. Vessels were built

The bireme.

with two rows of benches, one above the other, so that the number of oarsmen and the speed were increased without adding to the length of the ship. The "bireme," however, never became common in Greece, for the Phoenicians had soon improved it into the "tri-reme," by the superposition of another bank of oars.[9] The trireme,

The trireme comes into more general use in Greece not long before 500 B.C. The beak (embolos).

propelled by 170 rowers, was ultimately to come into universal use as the regular Greek warship, though for a long time after its first introduction by the Corinthians the old penteconters were still gen-erally used; but the unknown shipwright who invented the bireme deserves the credit of the new idea. Whatever naval battles were fought in the seventh century were fought mainly, we may be sure, with penteconters. But penteconters and triremes alike were affect-ed by the new invention of the bronze ram on the prow, a weapon of attack which determined the future character of Greek naval warfare.

Tradition of an ancient

The Greeks believed that the first regular sea-fight between two Greek powers was fought before the middle of the seventh century

[9] The secret of building this kind of galley has been lost. Modern ship-wrights cannot reproduce a trireme. In later times the Greeks built ships of many banks—five, ten, even forty.

between Corinth and her daughter city Corcyra. If the tradition is true, we may be sure that the event was an incident in a struggle for the trade with Italy and Sicily and along the Adriatic coasts. The chief competitors, however, with Corinth in the west were the Euboean cities, Chalcis and Eretria. In the traffic in eastern seas the island city of Aegina, though she had no colonies of her own, took an active part, and became one of the richest mercantile states of Greece. Athens too had ships, but her industries were still on a comparatively small scale, and it was not till a much later period that her trade was sufficient to involve her in serious rivalry with her neighbours. But the most active of all in industry and commerce were the Greeks of Ionia.

naval battle between Corinth and Corcyra (664 B.C.).

Sect. 5. Influence of Lydia on Greece

The Greeks of the Asiatic coast were largely dependent, for good or evil, on the adjacent inland countries. The inland trade added to their prosperity, but at any moment if a strong barbarian power arose their independence might be gravely menaced. At the beginning of the seventh century active intercourse was maintained between the Greeks and the kingdoms of Phrygia and Maeonia. The Phrygian king Midas dedicated a throne to the god of Delphi; both the Phrygians and the Lydians adopted the Greek alphabet, while the Greeks adopted their modes of music and admitted Phrygian legends into Greek mythology.

Dedication of Midas (c. 700?).

A considerable Phrygian element had won its way into Lydia, and had gained the upper hand. In the Homeric poems we nowhere read of Lydians but only of *Maeonians,* and there can be no doubt that this name represents the Phrygian settlers or conquerors. A Maeonian dynasty ruled in Lydia at the beginning of the seventh century, and the king bears a Maeonian name, Candaules, "houndchoker." The Aryan conquerors—conquerors, that is, who spoke an Aryan tongue—had occupied the throne for centuries; and Greek tradition afterwards derived the origin of the family of Candaules from Heracles himself. But they had become degenerate, and Gyges, a native Lydian, of the clan of the Mermnadae, succeeded in slaying Candaules and seizing the crown. This revolution ushered in a new period for the Lydian, as it was now called, no longer Maeonian, kingdom. The dominion of the Maeonian sovereign had probably extended southward to the valley of the Maeander. Gyges extended his power northward to the shores of the Propontis, where he founded Dascylion, and conquered the Troad. But he also designed to make the Aegean his western boundary and bring the

The Maeonian dynasty (so-called Heraclidae) of Lydia.

Usurpation of Gyges 687-652 B.C.

His conquests.

Greek cities under his lordship. He pressed down the valley of the Hermus against Smyrna; down the valley of the Cayster against Colophon; down the valley of the Maeander against Miletus and Magnesia. Of these enterprises only the faintest hints have come down to us. It may be that Colophon was actually captured, and perhaps Magnesia; but the other cities beat back the enemy. The poet Mimnermus sings how a warrior, perhaps his own grandfather, wrought havoc in the ranks of the Lydian horsemen in the plain of the Hermus.

But the plans of Gyges against his Greek neighbours were suddenly interrupted by a blow, which descended, as it were from the other side of the world, upon Greeks and Lydians alike. The regions round about Lake Maeotis, on the northern coast of the Black Sea, were inhabited by the Cimmerians, who appear in the marvellous wanderings of Odysseus. They were now driven forth from their abodes, to which, however, their name clung and still clings, by a Scythian folk, the Scolotae, who came from the east. Homeless, the Cimmerians wandered to the opposite side of the Euxine; but whether they travelled by the eastern or the western route, by the Caucasus or by the Danube, is not known for certain. On one hand, they seem to have appeared first in eastern Asia Minor; on the other, they seem to have associated with themselves some Thracian peoples—the Trerians, Edonians, and Thynians. The truth may be that they came round by the eastern coast; and that afterwards, when they made their incursions into western Asia Minor, they invited allies from Thrace to help them. Having defeated the Milesians of Sinope, they chose this place to be their chief settlement. They ventured to attack the great Assyrian empire, and King Assarhaddon himself tells how "I smote the Cimmerian Teuspa with all his army." But they overthrew the realm of Phrygia under its last king Midas, and towards the middle of the seventh century they attacked Lydia. To meet this danger, Gyges sought help from Assyria. The warlike Assarhaddon had been succeeded at Nineveh by Assurbanipal, a peaceful and literary prince, whose refined luxury is caricatured in the Greek conception of Sardanapalus. The lord of Lydia acknowledged the overlordship of the lord of Assyria. He gained a victory over the Cimmerians, and sent their chiefs in chains to Nineveh. But he did not long brook to be the vassal of another sovereign. He threw off his allegiance to Assyria, and sent Ionian and Carian mercenary soldiers to Egypt, to help that country also to free itself from Assyrian dominion. At this moment, perhaps, Gyges was at the height of his power. His wealth was famous, and he too, like Phry-

Cimmerian invasions.

(Crimea.)

Cimmerians defeated by Assyrians, 679 B.C.

Power and wealth of Gyges.

gian Midas, sent gifts—among them, six golden mixing-bowls—to
the Delphian god. The poet Archilochus, who witnessed his career,
makes one of his characters declare that he "cares not for the
wealth of golden Gyges."

But the Cimmerians presently renewed their attack, and fortune
changed. Gyges was slain in battle; his capital Sardis was taken, **Death of Gyges.**
except the citadel; and it was some satisfaction to Assurbanipal to
record that Lydia was in the hands of the Cimmerians. It was not
long before they swooped down upon the Greek cities. Callinus, a **Cimmerian attack of Ionia.**
poet of Ephesus, heard the trample of their horses and roused his
fellow-citizens to battle; Ephesus defied their attack, but the

FIG. 29.—The Cimmerians: Frieze on a sarcophagus of Clazomenae (British
Museum).

temple of Artemis outside the walls was burned down. They and
their allies from Thrace destroyed Magnesia on the Maeander.
The barbarians made a deep impression. The swords which they
swept down upon their enemies were enormous; they were
equipped with large quivers, and wore the curved caps of the Scythians; fierce hounds ran with their horses. Such was their appearance as they were portrayed by a Greek artist of a later genera-
tion on a painted sarcophagus found at Clazomenae. But the dan- **Ardys, king of Lydia.**
ger passed away. Ardys succeeded Gyges on the Lydian throne,
and he finally not only drove out the Cimmerians from the land,
but perhaps succeeded in extending his power into Cappadocia, as
far as the Halys.

In the meantime Lydia had made an invention which revolu- **Lydian coinage**
tionised commerce. It is to Lydia that Europe owes the invention
of coinage. The Babylonians, Phoenicians, and Egyptians made
use of weighed gold and silver as a medium of exchange, a certain
ratio being fixed between the two metals. A piece of weighed metal
becomes a coin when it is stamped by the State and is thereby
warranted to have its professed weight and purity. This step was
first taken in Lydia, where the earliest money was coined somewhere about the beginning of the seventh century, probably by
Gyges. These Lydian coins were made of the native white gold, or

electron—a mixture of gold and silver in which the proportion of gold was greater. A bar of the white gold of Sardis was regarded as ten times the value of a silver bar, and three-fourths of the value of a gold bar, of the same weight.[10] Miletus and Samos soon adopted the new invention, which then spread to other Asiatic towns. Then Aegina and the two great cities of Euboea instituted monetary systems, and by degrees all the states of Greece gave up the primitive custom of estimating value in heads of cattle, and most of them had their own mints. As gold was very rare in Greece, not being found except in the islands of Siphnos and Thasos, the Greeks coined in silver. This invention, coming at the very moment when the Greeks were entering upon a period of great commercial activity, was of immense importance, not only in facilitating trade, but in rendering possible the accumulation of capital. Yet it took many generations to supersede completely the old methods of economy by the new system.

Fig. 30.—Coin of Halicarnassus, sixth century. Obverse: stag [legend: ΦΑΝΟΣ ΕΜΙ ΣΕΜΑ]. Reverse: incuse. Fig. 31.—Coin of Cyzicus, fifth century (obverse). Kneeling Heracles with bow and club; tunny-fish.

The Greeks had derived their systems of weight from Babylonia and Phoenicia. But, when Aegina and the Euboean cities fixed the standard of their silver coinage, they did not adopt the silver standard of either of those countries. The heavier statêr (as the standard silver coin was named) of Aegina weighed 192 grains, and slightly exceeded a florin in value; and this system was adopted throughout the Peloponnese and in northern Greece. The lighter statêr of Euboea weighed 130 grains, which was the Babylonian standard of gold. This system, at first confined to Euboea, Samos, and a few other places, was adopted in the seventh century by Corinth in a modified form, and afterwards by Athens.[11]

It was highly characteristic of the Greeks that their coinage was marked from the beginning by religious associations; and it has been supposed that the priests of their temples had an important

---

[10] The Lydians had two scales: one for domestic intercourse, based on a standard which they derived from Babylonia, and one for foreign commerce based on a standard derived from Phoenicia through the Greeks.

[11] See below, p. 175.

share in initiating the introduction of money. It was in the shrines of their gods that men were accustomed to store their treasures for safe-keeping; the gods themselves possessed costly dedications; and thus the science of weighing the precious metals was naturally studied by the priesthoods. Every coin which a Greek state issued bore upon it a reference to some deity. In early times this reference always took the shape of a symbol; in later times the head of the god was often represented. The Lydian coins of Sardis, the coins of Miletus and other Ionian cities, bore a lion; those of Eretria showed a cow with a sucking calf; Aegina displayed a tortoise, and Cyzicus a tunny-fish; and all these tokens were symbols of the goddess who, whether under the name of Aphrodite or Hera or Artemis, was identified by the Greeks with Astarte of Phoenicia.

SECT. 6. THE OPENING OF EGYPT

Thus the merchants of Miletus and her fellows grew rich. They were the intermediaries between Lydia and the Mediterranean; while the Lydians carried *their* wares to the interior parts of Asia Minor and the far east. Their argosies sailed to the far west, as well as to the coasts of the Euxine. But a new field for winning wealth was opened to them, much about the same time as the invention of coinage revealed a new prospect to the world of commerce. The jealously guarded gates of Egypt were unbarred to Greek trade.

The greatest exploit of the Assyrian monarch Assarhaddon was the conquest of Egypt. The land had been split up into an endless number of small kingdoms, and the kings continued to govern as vassals of Assyria. But the foreign domination did not last for much more than a quarter of a century. One of the kings, Psammetichus of Sais, in Lower Egypt, probably of Libyan stock, revolted against Assurbanipal, who, in the last year of his reign, was occupied in subduing an insurrection of the Elamites of Susiana. We have seen how mail-clad soldiers of Ionia and Caria were sent by the lord of Lydia to assist Psammetichus. With the help of these "bronze men who came up from the sea," he reduced the other kings and brought the whole of Egypt under his sway. This Libyan dynasty kept Sais as their capital, and their power was supported by foreign mercenaries, Greeks and Carians, Syrians and Phoenicians. Psammetichus built the fortress of Daphnae—for so Greek speech graciously altered into Greek shape the Egyptian name Defenneh—and entrusted it to

Assyrian conquest of Egypt. c. 672. Egypt recovers independence, c. 645.

Psammetich I.

Fort of Defenneh, 664 to c. 570 B.C.

his Greek soldiers. Relics of this foreign garrison have been dug up among the ruins of Daphnae. Psammetichus and his successors completely departed from the narrow Egyptian policy of the Pharaohs, and were the forerunners in some respects of the Greek dynasty of the Ptolemies, who three centuries hence were to rule the land. They opened Egypt to the trade of the world and allowed Greeks to settle permanently in the country. Necho, the son of Psammetichus, connected the Red Sea with the Nile by a canal, and began a work, which it was reserved for our own time to achieve, the cutting of a channel through the isthmus which parts the Red Sea from the Mediterranean. His war-fleets sailed both in the Cypriot and in the Arabian seas; and a party of Phoenician explorers sent out by him accomplished the circumnavigation of Africa—a feat which two thousand years later was regarded as a wild dream.

Foundation of Naucratis.

The Milesians founded a factory on the western or Canobic channel of the Nile, not very far from Sais; and around it a Greek city grew up, which received the name of Naucratis, "sea-queen." This colony became the haven of all Greek traders; for though at first they seem to have moved freely, restrictions were afterwards placed upon them and they were not permitted to enter Egypt except by the Canobic mouth. At Naucratis, the Milesians, the Samians, and the Aeginetans had each their own separate quarter and their own sanctuaries; all the other Greek settlers had one common enclosure called the Hellenion, girt by a thick brick wall and capable of holding 50,000 men. Here were their market-place and their temples. All the colonists of Naucratis were Greeks of the Asiatic coast, whether Ionians, Dorians, or Aeolians, excepting alone the Aeginetans.

640-30 B.C.

Greek soldiers at Abusimbel [Psammetich II. 594-89 B.C.].

Egypt, as we see, offered a field not only for traders but for adventurous soldiers, and thus helped to relieve the pressure of over-population in Ionia. At Abusimbel in Upper Egypt we have a relic of the Greek mercenaries, who accompanied King Psammetichus II., Necho's successor, in an expedition against Ethiopia. Some of them scratched their names on the colossal statues of the temple; and the very triviality of this relic, at such a distance of time, perhaps makes it the more interesting.

They write their names.

Sect. 7. Cyrene

Foundation of Cyrene, c. 630 B.C.

Not long after Egypt was thrown open to Greek trade, there arose to the west of Egypt a new Greek city. Civil dissension in the island of Thera between the older population, who called themselves by the obscure name of Minyae, and the later Dorian settlers led to an emigration of the Minyae—some Dorians among them; and the exiles, having increased their band by Cretan adventurers, sailed for the shores of Barca. They made their first settlement on the little island of Platea off the coast; their second on the opposite coast of the mainland; and when this too proved a failure, they founded their abiding settlement about eight miles from the sea near an abundant spring of water, on two white hills, which commanded the encompassing plain. The city was named Cyrene, and it was the only Greek colony on the coast of Africa which attained to eminence and wealth. The man who led the island folk to their new home became their king; his name seems to have been Aristoteles, but he took the strange name of Battus, which is said to mean "king" in the Libyan language, while its resemblance to the Greek word for "stammer" gave rise to the legend that Battus I. stammered in

FIG. 32.—Coin of Cyrene, early (obverse). Silphion; silphion seed; lion's head.
FIG. 33.—Electron coin of Lydia (beginning of seventh century). Obverse: striated surface. Reverse: oblong and two square sinkings.

his speech. His son was Arcesilas; and in the line of the Cyrenaean kings Battus and Arcesilas succeeded each other in alternation. Under Battus II. the new city was reinforced by a large incoming of new settlers whom he invited, chiefly from the Peloponnese and Crete; and this influx changed the character of the place, since the original "Minyan" element was outnumbered. The lands which the Greeks took from the Libyan inhabitants were made fruitful by the winter rains; Pindar describes them as plains over which dark clouds hover. There was excellent pasturage, and the men of Cyrene became famous for rearing horses and for skill as riders and charioteers. They were naturally the intermediaries between Greek merchants and the Libyan natives; but the chief source of the wealth of the Cyrenaean kings was the export of silphion, a plant which acquired a high repute for medicinal virtues. In those days it grew luxuriantly in the regions of Barca; now it is extinct. The sale of silphion was a monopoly of the king; and on a fine Cyrenaean cup we can see

Arcesilaus.

Arcesilas II. himself watching the herb being weighed and packed. It was in the reign of this king that Barca was founded, farther west. He quarrelled with his brothers, and they left Cyrene and founded a town for themselves.

Cyrene held her head high in the Greek world though she was somewhat apart from it. A Cyrenaean poet arose, and continued

FIG. 34.—The Arcesilas Vase.

The
Telegony
of Eugam-
mon,
c. 600 B.C.

the *Odyssey* and described the last adventures of Odysseus. His poem was accepted by Greece as winding up the Epic Cycle which was associated with the name of Homer. His work was distinguished by local pride and local colouring. He gave Odysseus a son Arcesilaus, and connected the royal line of Cyrene with the great wanderer. And he introduced a flavour of those Libyan influences which modified Cyrenaean civilisation, just as the remote cities of the Euxine received influences from Scythia.

Sect. 8. Popular Discontent in Greece

The advance of the Greeks in trade and industry produced many consequences of moment for their political and social development. The manufactures required labour, and a sufficient number of free labourers was not to be had. Slaves were therefore indispensable, and they were imported in large numbers from Asia Minor and Thrace and the coasts of the Euxine. The slave-trade became a profitable enterprise, and the men of Chios made it their chief pursuit. The existence of household slaves, generally war-captives, such as we meet in Homer, was an innocent institution which would never have had serious results; but the new organised slave-system which began in the seventh century was destined to prove one of the most fatal causes of disease and decay to the states of Greece.

At first the privileged classes of the aristocratic republics benefited by the increase of commerce; for the nobles were themselves the chief speculators. But the wealth which they acquired by trade undermined their political position. For, in the first place, their influence depended largely on their domains of land; and when industries arose to compete with agriculture, the importance of land necessarily declined. In the second place, wealth introduced a new political standard; and aristocracies resting on birth tended to transform themselves into aristocracies resting on wealth. The proverb "money makes the man" now came into vogue. As nobility by birth cannot be acquired, whereas wealth can, such a change is always a step in the direction of democracy.

On the other hand, the poorer freemen at first suffered. How heavily the transition from the old systems of exchange to the use of money bore upon them, we shall find illustrated when we come to the special history of Athens. But their distress and discontent drove them into striving for full political equality, and in many cases they strove with success. The second half of the seventh century is marked in many parts of Greece by struggles between the classes; and the wiser and better of the nobles began themselves to see the necessity of extending political privileges to their fellow-citizens. The centralisation in towns, owing to the growth of industries and the declining importance of agriculture, created a new town population and doubtless helped on the democratic movement.

In this agitated period lived a poet of great genius, Archilochus of Paros. It has been truly said that Archilochus is the first Greek

Increase of trade and industry.

Slavery.

Decrease of importance of agriculture. Wealth becomes a power in politics.

The voice of the people begins to be heard.

Archilochus.

"of flesh and blood" whom we can grasp through the mists of antiquity. Son of a noble by a slave mother he tried his luck among the adventurers who went forth to colonise Siris in Italy, but he returned having won an experience of sea-faring, which taught him to sing of the "bitter gifts of Poseidon" and the mariner's prayers for "sweet home." Then he took part in a Parian colonisation of Thasos, and was involved in party struggles which rent the island. It has been thought that he witnessed at Thasos an eclipse of the sun at noontide which he describes, the eclipse of the 6th of April 648 B.C., but it is very doubtful whether he is really referring to this eclipse. All the evils of all Hellas are here, he exclaims; and "Thasos is not a fair place nor a desirable, like the land round the stream of Siris." He announces that he is "the servant of the lord of battle and skilled in the delicious gift of the Muses." But when he fought in a war which the Thasians waged with the Thracians of the opposite coast, he ran for his life and dropped his shield; "never mind, he said, I will get me another as good." Poor, with a stain on his birth, tossed about the world, soured by adversity, Archilochus in his poetry gave full expression to his feelings, and used it to utter his passionate hatred against his enemies, such as the Parian Lycambes, for instance, who refused him his daughter Neobule. Had fortune favoured him, he would have been a noble of the nobles; ill-luck drove him to join the movement against aristocracy. His poems present a complete contrast to the epic style and even to Hesiod. He addressed himself to the people; used colloquial language; and perfected iambic and trochaic measures for literary purposes. His influence may be judged from the fact that his poems were recited by the rhapsodes along with Homer and Hesiod.

The ills of Greece, which were reflected in the poems of Archilochus, were to lead to the development of equality and freedom. But success in the struggle would in most cases depend on military efficiency; and a revolution in the art of warfare, which was brought about at the same period, was therefore of immense importance. This takes us to the history of Sparta.

Fig. 35.—Early coin of Gortyna (obverse). Europa on bull. Fig. 36.—Early coin of Phocaea, (obverse). Seal (phôkê).

CHAPTER III

GROWTH OF SPARTA. FALL OF THE ARISTOCRACIES

Sect. 1. Sparta and her Constitution

THE Dorian settlers from the north, who took possession of the valley of the Eurotas, established themselves in a number of village communities throughout the land, and bore the name of Lacedaemonians. In the course of time, a city-state grew up in their midst and won dominion over the rest. The town was formed by the union of five villages [1] which, after their union, still continued to preserve their identity, as separate units within the larger unity. The city was called Sparta, and took the dominant place in Laconia which had been formerly held by Amyclae. The other Lacedaemonian communities were called the *perioeci*, or "dwellers round about" the ruling city, and, though they were free and managed their local affairs, they had no political rights in the Spartan state.[2] The chief burdens which fell on them were military service and the farming of the royal domains.

The Spartans were always noted for their conservative spirit. Hence we find in their constitution, which was remarkable in many ways, survivals of an old order of things which existed in the days of Homeric poetry, but has passed away in most places when trustworthy history begins. The most striking of these survivals was royalty; Sparta was nominally ruled by kings.

This conservative spirit of the Spartans rendered them anxious to believe, and others willing to accept the view, that their constitution had existed from very ancient times in just the same shape and feature which it displayed in the days of recorded history. We are, however, forced to suspect that this was not the case. There can be

Origin of the Spartan state.

Subject communities; perioikoi.

Conservative spirit of Sparta.

Spartan belief in the antiquity of the constitution.

[1] Pitane, Messoa, Limnae, Konoûra, and Dyme.
[2] There is some evidence that in later times they were under the supervision of Spartan harmosts; but even this evidence chiefly concerns the island of Cythera, which, from a military point of view, required special arrangements.

little doubt that the Spartan state developed up to the end of the seventh century on the same general lines as other Greek states, though with some remarkable peculiarities. There can be little doubt that, like most other states, it passed through the stages of royalty and aristocracy; and that the final form of the constitution was the result of a struggle between the nobles and the people. The remarkable thing was that throughout these changes hereditary kingship survived.

The machine of the Spartan constitution, as we know it when it was fully developed, had four parts: the Kings, the Council, the Assembly, and the Ephors. The first three are the original institutions, which were common, as we saw, to the whole Greek race; the Ephors were a later institution, and were peculiar to Sparta.

I. The kings.

We saw that towards the end of the Homeric period the powers of the king were limited, and that this limited monarchy then died out, sometimes leaving a trace behind it, perhaps in the name of a magistracy—like the king-archon at Athens. In a few places it survived, and Sparta was one of them. But, if it survived here, its powers were limited in a twofold way. It was limited not only by the other institutions of the state, but by its own dual character. For there were two kings at Sparta, and had been since the memory of men. It seems possible that the origin of this double kingship lay in the coalition of two distinct communities, each of which had its own king. One tribe dwelt about Sparta, and its kings belonged to the clan of the Agidae. The other tribe, we may guess, was settled somewhere in southern Laconia, and its royal clan was that of the Eurypontidae. These two tribes must have united to form a large city-state at Sparta; and the terms of the union may have been that neither tribe should give up its king, but two kings, with coequal authority, should rule over the joint community. The kingship passed from father to son in the two royal houses of the Agids and Eurypontids; and if the Agid kings possessed a slight superiority in public estimation over their colleagues, this may have been due to the fact that the Eurypontids were the strangers who migrated to Sparta.[3] According to a pedigree which was made out for them in later days, when the myth of the Return of the Heraclidae had become current, both dynasties traced themselves back to Heracles.

Origin of the dual kingship.

(At Amy-clae?).

Limitation of the royal powers.

It seems probable that it was partly because there were two kings, the one a check upon the other, that kingship was not abolished in Sparta, or reduced to a mere magistracy. But the powers

[3] The relation of the five villages to these two communities must remain obscure; and also the question of the coalition of yet another tribe or clan(?) the Aegidae, who, however, did not retain their own king.

of the kings were largely curtailed; and we may suppose that the limitations were introduced by degrees during that epoch in which throughout Greece generally, monarchies were giving way to aristocratic republics. Of the religious, military, and judicial functions, which belonged to them and to all other Greek kings, they lost some and retained others.

They were privileged to hold certain priesthoods; [4] they offered solemn sacrifices for the city every month to Apollo; they prepared the necessary sacrifices before warlike expeditions and battles; they were priests, though not the sole priests, of the community.

Religious functions.

They were the supreme commanders of the army. They had the right of making war upon whatever country they chose, and penalties were laid on any Spartan who presumed to hinder them. In the field they had unlimited right of life and death; and they had a bodyguard of a hundred men. It is clear that these large powers were always limited by the double nature of the kingship. But at a later period it was defined by law that only one of the kings, to be chosen on each occasion by the people, should lead the army in time of war, and moreover they were made responsible to the community for their conduct in their campaigns.

Military functions.

c. 500 B.C

But while they enjoyed this supreme position as high-priests and leaders of the host, they could hardly be considered judges any longer. The right of dealing out dooms like the Homeric Agamemnon had passed away from them; only in three special cases had they still judicial or legal powers. They presided at the adoption of children; they decided who was to marry an heiress whose father had died without betrothing her; and they judged in all matters concerning public roads.

Judicial functions.

There were royal domains in the territory of the *perioeci* from which the kings derived their revenue. But they also had perquisites at public sacrifices; on such occasions they were (like Homeric kings) given the first seat at the banquet, were served first, and received a double portion of everything, and the hides of the slaughtered beasts. The pious sentiment with which royalty, as a hallowed institution, was regarded, is illustrated by the honours which were paid to the kings when they died. "Horsemen," says Herodotus, "carry round the tidings of the event through all Laconia, and in the city women go about beating a cauldron. And at this sign, two free persons of each house, a man and a woman, must put on mourning garb, and if any fail to do this great pains are imposed." The funeral was attended by a fixed number of the perioeci, and it was part of the stated ceremony that the dead king

Funeral honours.

[4] Of Zeus Lacedaemon and Zeus Uranios.

should be praised by the mourners as better than all who had gone before him. Public business was not resumed for ten days after the burial. The king was succeeded by his eldest son, but a son born before his father's accession to the kingship had to give way to the eldest of those who were born after the accession. If there were no children, the succession fell to the nearest male kinsman, who was likewise the regent in the case of a minority.

I. Gerusia, or Council of Elders (or Gerontia).

The *gerontes* or elders whom we find in Homer advising the king and also acting as judges have developed at Sparta into a body of fixed number, forming a definite part of the constitution, called the *gerusia*. This Council consisted of thirty members, including the two kings, who belonged to it by virtue of their kingship. The other twenty-eight must be over sixty years of age, so that the council was a body of elders in the strict sense of the word. They held their office for life and were chosen by acclamation in the general assembly of citizens, whose choice was supposed to fall on him whose moral merits were greatest; membership of the Council was described as a "prize for virtue." The Council prepared matters which were to come before the Assembly; it exercised, as an advising body, a great influence on political affairs; and it formed a court of justice for criminal cases.

But though the Councillors were elected by the people, they were not elected from the people. Nobility of birth retained at Sparta its political significance; and only men of the noble families could be chosen members of the Council. And thus the Council formed an oligarchical element in the Lacedaemonian constitution.

III. Apella, or Assembly of the People.

Every Spartan who had passed his thirtieth year was a member of the *Apella*, or Assembly of Citizens, which met every month between the bridge of Babyka and the stream of Knakion. In old days, no doubt, it was summoned by the kings, but in historical times we find that this right has passed to the ephors. The assembly did not debate, but having heard the proposals of kings or ephors, signified its will by acclamation. If it seemed doubtful to which opinion the majority of the voices inclined, recourse was had to a division. The people elected the members of the Gerusia, the ephors and other magistrates; determined questions of war and peace and foreign politics; and decided disputed successions to the kingly office. Thus, theoretically, the Spartan constitution was a democracy. No Spartan was excluded from the apella of the people; and the will of the people expressed at their apella was supreme. "To the people," runs an old statute, "shall belong the decision and the power." But the same statute granted to the executive authorities —"the elders and magistrates"—a power which restricted this apparent supremacy of the people. It allowed them "to be seceders, if the people make a crooked decree." It seems that the will of the people, declared by their acclamations, did not receive the force of law, unless it were then formally proclaimed before the assembly was formally dissolved. If the elders and magistrates did not approve of the decision of the majority of the assembly, they could annul the proceedings by refusing to proclaim it—"seceding" and dissolving the meeting, without waiting for the regular dissolution by king or ephor.

The five ephors were the most characteristic part of the political constitution of Sparta. The origin of the office is veiled in obscurity; it was supposed to have been instituted in the first half of the eighth century.[5] But we must distinguish between the first institution of the office and the beginning of its political importance. It is probable that, in the course of the eighth century, the kings finding it impossible to attend to all their duties were constrained to give up the civil jurisdiction, and that the ephors or "overseers" were appointed for this purpose.[6] The number of the ephors would seem to be connected with the number of the five demes or villages whose union formed the city; and perhaps each one of the ephors was assigned originally to one of the villages. But it cannot have been till the seventh century that the ephors won their great political power. They must have won that power in a conflict between the nobility who governed in conjunction with the kings, and the people who had no share in the government. In that struggle the kings represented the cause of the nobility, while the ephors were the representatives of the people.[7] A compromise, as the result of such a conflict, is implied in the oaths which were every month exchanged between the kings and the ephors. The king swore that he would observe the laws of the state in discharging his royal functions; the ephor that he would maintain the royal power undiminished, so long as the king was true to his oath. In this ceremony we have the record of an acute conflict between the government and people. The democratic character of the ephorate appears from the

Ephorate

[5] The Alexandrines seem to have had an ephor-list reaching as far back as 757 B. C. ; but we cannot build much on this. It is perhaps of more importance that the ephorate existed in the Laconian colony at Thera; but what most of all proves its antiquity is its close inter-connexion with the whole framework of the Spartan constitution.

[6] We have no knowledge of the local institutions in the towns of the *perioeci*, which would probably throw some light on details of the Spartan constitution. Polemon's work, *On the Cities in Lacedaemon,* has unfortunately not survived.

[7] The Eurypontid kings probably smoothed the way for the compromise. It has been suggested that such names as Archi*damos,* which occur among the Eurypontids but not among the Agids, allude to their popular attitude.

fact that any Spartan might be elected. The mode of election, which is described by Aristotle as "very childish," was practically equivalent to an election by lot. When the five ephors did not agree among themselves, the minority gave way.

The ephors entered upon their office at the beginning of the Laconian year, which fell on the first new moon after the autumnal equinox. As chosen guardians of the rights of the people, they were called upon to watch jealously the conduct of the kings. With this object two ephors always accompanied the king on warlike expeditions. They had the power of indicting the king and summoning him to appear before them. The judicial functions which the kings lost passed partly to the ephors, partly to the Council. The ephors were the supreme civil court; the Council, as we have seen, formed the supreme criminal court. But in the case of the Perioeci the ephors were criminal judges also. They were moreover responsible for the strict maintenance of the order and discipline of the Spartan state, and, when they entered upon office, they issued a proclamation to the citizens to "shave their upper lips and obey the laws."

Character of Spartan constitution.

This unique constitution cannot be placed under any general head, cannot be called kingdom, oligarchy, or democracy, without misleading. None of these names is applicable to it, but it participated in all three. A stranger who saw the kings going forth with power at the head of the host, or honoured above all at the public feasts in the city, would have described Sparta as a kingdom. If one of the kings themselves had been asked to define the constitution, it is probable that he would have regretfully called it a democracy. Yet the close Council. taken from a privileged class, exercising an important influence on public affairs, and deferring to an Assembly which could not debate, might be alleged to prove that Sparta was an oligarchy. The secret of this complex character of the Spartan constitution lies in the fact that, while Sparta developed on the same general path as other states and had to face the same political crises, she overcame each crisis with less violence and showed a more conservative spirit. When she ought to have passed from royalty to aristocracy, she diminished the power of the kings, but she preserved hereditary kingship as a part of the aristocratic government. When she ought to have advanced to democracy, she gave indeed enormous power to the representatives of the people, but she still preserved both her hereditary kings and the Council of her nobles.

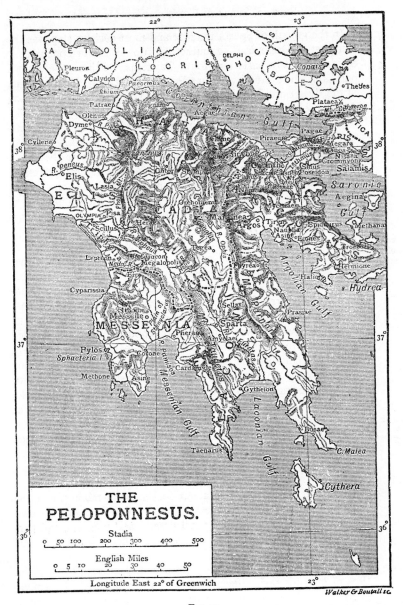

FIG. 37.

Sect. 2. Spartan Conquest of Messenia

Messenia.

In the growth of Sparta the first and most decisive step was the conquest of Messenia. The southern portion of the Peloponnesus is divided into two parts by Mount Taygetus. Of these, the eastern part is again severed by Mount Parnon into two regions: the vale of the river Eurotas, and the rugged strip of coast between Parnon and the sea. The western country is less mountainous, more fruitful, and blessed by a milder climate, nor is it divided in the same way by a mountain chain; the hills rise irregularly, and the river Pamisus waters the central plain of Stenyclarus where the Greek invaders are said to have fixed their abode. The natural fortress of the country was the lofty rock of Ithome which rises to the west of the river. It is probable that under its protection a town grew up at an early period, whose name Messene was afterwards transferred to the whole country.

Early conquest of Messenia.

The fruitful soil of Messenia, "good to plant and good to ear," as a Spartan poet sang, could not but excite the covetousness of her martial neighbours. It is impossible to determine the date of the First Messenian War with greater precision than the eighth century. Legends grew up freely as to its causes and its course. All that we know with certainty is that the Spartan king, under whose auspices it was waged, was named Theopompus; that it was decided by the capture of the great fortress of Ithome; and that the eastern part of the land became Laconian. A poet writing at the beginning of the seventh century would have naturally spoken of Messene or Pherae as being "in Lacedaemon." When the Second War broke out towards the end of the seventh century, it was either history or legend that the previous war had lasted twenty years. Legends grew up around it in which the chief figure was a Messenian hero named Aristodemus. The tale was that he offered his daughter as a sacrifice to save his country, in obedience to the demand of an oracle. Her lover made a despairing effort to save her life by spreading a report that the maiden was about to become a mother, and the calumny so incensed Aristodemus that he slew her with his own hand. Afterwards, terrified by evil dreams and portents, and persuaded that his country was doomed, he killed himself upon his daughter's tomb.

Legend of Aristodemus.

Condition of the Messenians.

As the object of the Spartans was to increase the number of the lots of land for their citizens, many of the conquered Messenians were reduced to the condition of Helots, and servitude was hard though their plight might have been harder. They paid to their lords only one-half of the produce of the lands which they tilled, whereas in Attica at the same period the free tillers of the soil had to pay five-sixths. The Spartan poet Tyrtaeus describes how the Messenians endured the insolence of their masters:—

> As asses worn by loads intolerable,
> So them did stress of cruel force compel,
> Of all the fruits the well-tilled land affords,
> The moiety to bear to their proud lords.

For some generations they submitted patiently, but at length, when victorious Sparta felt secure, a rebellion was organised in the northern district of Andania. The rebels were supported by their neighbours in Arcadia and Pisatis, and they are said to have found an able and ardent leader in Aristomenes, sprung from an old Messenian family. The revolt was at first successful. The Spartans fared ill, and their young men experienced the disgrace of defeat. The hopes of the serfs rose, and Sparta despaired of recovering the land. But a leader and a poet arose amongst them. The lame Tyrtaeus is recorded to have inspired his countrymen with such martial vigour that the tide of fortune turned, and Sparta began to retrieve her losses and recover her reputation. Some scraps of the poems of Tyrtaeus have been preserved, and they supply the only trustworthy material we have for the history of the Messenian wars; and he won such fame by the practical successes of his art that at a later time the Athenians sought to claim him as one of their sons and gave out that Sparta, by the counsel of an oracle, had sent for him. The warriors advanced to battle singing his "marches" to the sound of flutes, while his elegies, composed in the conventional epic dialect, are said to have been recited in the tents after the evening meal. But we learn from himself that his strategy was as effective as his poetry, and the Messenians were presently defeated in the Battle of the Great Foss. They then retired to the northern stronghold of Eira on the river Nedon, which plays the same part in the second war that Ithome played in the first, while Aristomenes takes the place of Aristodemus. As to Eira, indeed, we possess no record on the contemporary authority of Tyrtaeus, whose extant fragments notice none of the adventures, nor even the name, of the hero Aristomenes. Yet Eira may well have been the place where the last stand was made; for the Spartans had rased the fortifications of Ithome, which is not mentioned in connection with the second war. At Eira the defenders were near their Arcadian supporters and within reach of Pylos which seems not to have been yet Lacedaemonian. But Eira fell; legend says that it was beleaguered for eleven years. Aristomenes was the soul of the defence, and his wonderful

Their rebellion: "Second War" (c. end of 7th cent.)

Tyrtaeus

Capture of Eira.

escapes became the argument of a stirring tale. On one occasion he was thrown, with fifty fellow-countrymen, captured by the Spartans, into a deep pit. His comrades perished, and Aristomenes awaited certain death. But by following the track of a fox he found a passage in the rocky wall of his prison and appeared on the following day at Eira. When the Spartans surprised that fortress, he made his escape wounded to Arcadia. He died in Rhodes, but two hundred and fifty years later, on the field of Leuctra, he reappeared against the Spartans to avenge his defeat.

Those Messenians who were left in the land were mostly reduced again to the condition of Helots, but the maritime communities and even a few in the interior remained free, as perioeci, in the possession of their estates. Many escaped to Arcadia, while some of the inhabitants of the coast-towns may have taken ship and sailed to other places.

At this time Sparta, like most other Greek states, suffered from domestic discontent. There was a pressing land question, with which Tyrtaeus dealt in a poem named *Eunomia*, or *Law and Order*. This question was partly solved by the conquest of the whole land of Messenia, and doubtless the foundation of the colony of Taras in southern Italy was undertaken for the purpose of relieving an excessive population.

The Messenian war, as recorded by Tyrtaeus, shows us that the power of the privileged classes had already been undermined by a great change in the method of warfare. The fighting is done, and the victory won, by regiments of mailed foot-lancers, who march and fight together in close ranks. The secret had been discovered that such well-drilled spearsmen—hoplites as they were called—were superior to cavalry; and much about the same period in Ionia, we find the infantry of Smyrna holding their own against the Lydian horsemen of Gyges. The recognition of serried bodies of foot, as a useful weapon in battle, can be traced in the later parts of the *Iliad;* but it was in Sparta first that their value was fully appreciated. There they became the main part of the military establish-

ment. The city no longer depended chiefly on her nobles in time of war; she depended on her whole people. The progress of metalsmiths in their trade, which accompanied the general industrial advance of Greece, rendered possible this transformation in the art of war. Every well-to-do citizen could now provide himself with an outfit of armour and go forth to battle in panoply.[8] The transfor-

---

[8] The metal breast-plate had been introduced; metal greaves were worn, and thigh-pieces. The round shield borne on the arm had superseded the clumsy shoulder-swung shield of the heroic period.

mation was distinctly levelling and democratic; for it placed the noble and the ordinary citizen on an equality in the field. We shall not be wrong in connecting this military development with those aspirations of the people for a popular constitution, which resulted in the investment of the ephorate with its great political powers.

From Sparta, where it was brought to a perfection which in the days of Tyrtaeus it had not yet attained, the institution of the heavy foot-lancers spread throughout Greece, and its natural tendency everywhere was to promote the progress to democracy. It is significant that in Thessaly, where the system of hoplites was not introduced and cavalry was always the kernel of the army, democratic ideas never made way.

Sect. 3. Internal Development of Sparta and her Institutions

In the seventh century one could not have foretold what Sparta was destined to be. Her nobles lived luxuriously, like the nobles of other lands; the individual was free, as in other cities, to order his life as he willed. She showed some promise of other than military interests. Lyric poetry was transported from its home in Lesbos to find for a while a second home on the banks of the Eurotas. Songs to be sung at banquets, at weddings, at harvest feasts, and at festivals of the gods, by single singers or choirs of men or maidens, were older than memory could reach; but with the development of music and the improvement of musical instruments the composition of these songs became an art, and lyric poetry was created. The lyre of seven strings was an ancient invention, but it was attributed to Terpander of Lesbos, who was at all events an historical person, and both a poet and a musician. He visited Sparta, and is said to have instituted the musical contest at the Carnea, the great festival of Lacedaemon. His music was certainly welcomed there, and Sparta soon had a poet, who, though not her own, was at least her adopted, son. Alcman from Lydian Sardis made Sparta his home, and we have some fragments of songs which he composed for choirs of Laconian maidens. Sparta had her epic poet too in Cinaethon. But this promise of a school of music and poetry was not to be fulfilled.

When Sparta emerges in to the full light of history we find her under an iron discipline, which invades every part of a man's life and controls all his actions from his cradle to his death-bed. Everything is subordinated to the art of war, and the sole aim of the state is to create invincible warriors. The martial element was doubtless,

Character of Sparta in early times.

Terpander (c. 700 B.C.). (Feast of Carnean Apollo.)

Transformation of Sparta (7th-6th cent.)

from the very beginning, stronger in Sparta than in other states; and as a city ruling over a large discontented population of subjects and serfs, she must always be prepared to fight; but we shall probably never know how, and under what influences, the singular Spartan discipline which we have now to examine was introduced. Nor can we, in describing the Spartan society, distinguish always between older and later institutions.

The whole Spartan people formed a military caste; the life of a Spartan citizen was devoted to the service of the state. In order to carry out this ideal it was necessary that every citizen should be freed from the care of providing for himself and his family. The nobles owned family domains of their own; but the Spartan community also came into possession of common land, which was divided into a number of lots. Each Spartan obtained a lot, which passed from father to son, but could not be either sold or divided; thus a citizen could never be reduced to poverty.[9] The original inhabitants, whom the Lacedaemonians dispossessed and reduced to the state of serfs, cultivated the land for their lords. Every year the owner of a lot was entitled to receive seventy medimni of corn for himself, twelve for his wife, and a stated portion of wine and fruit. All that the land produced beyond this, the Helot was allowed to retain for his own use. Thus the Spartan need take no thought for his support; he could give all his time to the affairs of public life. Though the Helots were not driven by taskmasters, and had the right of acquiring private property, their condition seems to have been hard; at all events, they were always bitterly dissatisfied and ready to rebel, whenever an occasion presented itself. The system of Helotry was a source of danger from the earliest times, but especially after the conquest of Messenia; and the state of constant military preparation in which the Spartans lived may have been partly due to the consciousness of this peril perpetually at their doors. The *Krypteia* or secret police was instituted—it is uncertain at what date—to deal with this danger. Young Spartans were sent into the country and empowered to kill every Helot whom they had reason to regard with suspicion. Closely connected with this system was the remarkable custom that the ephors, in whose hands lay the general control over the Helots, should every year on entering office proclaim war against them. By this device, the youths could slay dangerous Helots without any scruple or fear of the guilt of manslaughter. But notwithstanding these precautions serious revolts broke out again and again. A

Marginal notes: Land: private and public. Lots. The Helots. (105 bushels?). Krypteia.

[9] In the fourth century, however, some Spartans had been impoverished, from what cause is unknown.

Spartan had no power to grant freedom to the Helot who worked on his lot, nor yet to sell him to another. Only the state could emancipate. As the Helots were called upon to serve as light-armed troops in time of war, they had then an opportunity of exhibiting bravery and loyalty in the service of the city, and those who conspicuously distinguished themselves might be rewarded by the city with the meed of freedom. Thus arose a class of freedmen called *neodamōdes,* or new demesmen. There was also another class of persons, neither serfs nor citizens, called *mothōnes,* who probably sprang from illegitimate unions of citizens with Helot women.

Neo-damōdes and Mothōnes (or Mothakes) Education (ἀγωγή).

Thus relieved from the necessity of gaining a livelihood, the Spartans devoted themselves to the good of the state, and the aim of the state was the cultivation of the art of war. Sparta was a large military school. Education, marriage, the details of daily life were all strictly regulated with a view to the maintenance of a perfectly efficient army. Every citizen was to be a soldier, and the discipline began from birth. When a child was born it was submitted to the inspection of the heads of the tribe, and if they judged it to be unhealthy or weak, it was exposed to die on the wild slopes of Mount Taygetos. At the age of seven years, the boy was consigned to the care of a state-officer, and the course of his education was entirely determined by the purpose of inuring him to bear hardships, training him to endure an exacting discipline, and instilling into his heart a sentiment of devotion to the state. The boys, up to the age of twenty, were marshalled in a huge school formed on the model of an army.[10] The captains and prefects who instructed and controlled them were young men who had passed their twentieth year, but had not yet reached the thirtieth, which admitted them to the rights of citizenship.[11] Warm friendships often sprang up between the young men and the boys whom they were training; and this was the one place in Spartan life where there was room for romance.

(Paido-nómos.)

Iranes.

At the age of twenty the Spartan entered upon military service and was permitted to marry. But he could not yet enjoy home-life; he had to live in "barracks" with his companions, and could only pay stolen and fugitive visits to his wife. In his thirtieth year, having completed his training, he became a "man," and obtained

---

[10] They were divided into "herds" (βόυαι), and each herd consisted of a certain number of "pens" or troops (ἴλαι). The youth who commanded the *bua* was a *buagor,* the captain of the *ila* an *ilarch.*

[11] The elder youth from eighteen to twenty was called a *melliran,* for he was soon, on completing his twentieth year, to enter into the ranks of the *iranes,* or young men over twenty and under thirty. The younger members of this class were called *first iranes (protiranes);* the eldest, who were about to become "men," were *sphaireis;* and there were probably intermediate classes.

the full rights of citizenship. The *Homoioi* or peers, as the Spartan citizens were called, dined together in tents in the Hyacinthian Street. These public messes were in old days called *andreia,* or "men's meals," and in later times *phiditia.* Each member of a common tent made a fixed monthly contribution, derived from the produce of his lot, consisting of barley, cheese, wine, and figs, and the members of the same mess-tent shared the same tent in the field in time of war. These public messes are a survivial, adapted to military purposes, of the old custom of public banquets, at which all the burghers gathered together at a table spread for the gods of the city. Of the organisation of the Spartan hoplites in early times we have no definite knowledge. Three hundred "horsemen," chosen from the Spartan youths, formed the king's bodyguard; but though, as their name shows, they were originally mounted, in later times they fought on foot. The light infantry was supplied by the Perioeci and Helots.

Spartan discipline extended itself to the women too, with the purpose of producing mothers who should be both physically strong and saturated with the Spartan spirit. The girls, in common with the boys, went through a gymnastic training; and it was not considered immodest for them to practise their exercises almost nude. They enjoyed a freedom which was in marked contrast with the seclusion of women in other Greek states. They had a high repute for chastity; but if the government directed them to breed children for the state, they had no scruples in obeying the command, though it should involve a violation of the sanctity of the marriage-tie. They were, proverbially, ready to sacrifice their maternal instincts to the welfare of their country. Such was the spirit of the place.

Thus Sparta was a camp in which the highest object of every man's life was to be ready at any moment to fight with the utmost efficiency for his city. The aim of every law, the end of the whole social order was to fashion good soldiers. Private luxury was strictly forbidden; Spartan simplicity became proverbial. The individual man, entirely lost in the state, had no life of his own; he had no problems of human existence to solve for himself. Sparta was not a place for thinkers or theorists; the whole duty of man and the highest ideal of life were contained for a Spartan in the laws of his city. Warfare being the object of all the Spartan laws and institutions, one might expect to find the city in a perpetual state of war. One might look to see her sons always ready to strive with their neighbours without any ulterior object, war being for them an end in itself. But it was not so; they did not wage war

hiditia.

Army.

Spartan women.

Motive of Spartan discipline.

more lightly than other men; we cannot rank them with barbarians who care only for fighting and hunting. We may attribute the original motive of their institutions, in some measure at least, to the situation of a small dominant class in the midst of ill-contented subjects and hostile serfs. They must always be prepared to meet a rebellion of Perioeci or a revolt of Helots, and a surprise would have been fatal. Forming a permanent camp in a country which was far from friendly, they were compelled to be always on their guard. But there was something more in the vitality and conservation of the Spartan constitution, than precaution against the danger of a possible insurrection. It appealed to the Greek sense of beauty. There was a certain completeness and simplicity about the constitution itself, a completeness and simplicity about the manner of life enforced by the laws, a completeness and simplicity too about the type of character developed by them, which Greeks of other cities never failed to contemplate with genuine, if distant, admiration. Shut away in "hollow many-clefted Lacedaemon," out of the world and not sharing in the progress of other Greek cities, Sparta seemed to remain at a standstill; and a stranger from Athens or Miletus in the fifth century visiting the straggling villages which formed her unwalled unpretentious city must have had a feeling of being transported into an age long past, when men were braver, better, and simpler, unspoiled by wealth, undisturbed by ideas. To a philosopher, like Plato, speculating in political science, the Spartan state seemed the nearest approach to the ideal. The ordinary Greek looked upon it as a structure of severe and simple beauty, a Dorian city stately as a Dorian temple, far nobler than his own abode but not so comfortable to dwell in. If this was the effect produced upon strangers, we can imagine what a perpetual joy to a Spartan peer was the contemplation of the Spartan constitution; how he felt a sense of superiority in being a citizen of that city, and a pride in living up to its ideal and fulfilling the obligations of his nobility. In his mouth "not beautiful" meant "contrary to the Spartan laws," which were believed to have been inspired by Apollo. This deep admiration for their constitution as an ideally beautiful creation, the conviction that it was incapable of improvement—being, in truth, wonderfully effective in realising its aims—is bound up with the conservative spirit of the Spartans, showing so conspicuously in their use of their old iron coins [12] down to the time of Alexander the Great.

It was inevitable that, as time went on, there should be many fallings away, and that some of the harder laws should, by tacit

Greek admiration of Sparta.

[12] The *obel* and the *pelanor*.

agreement, be ignored. The other Greeks were always happy to point to the weak spots in the Spartan armour. From an early period it seems to have been a permitted thing for a citizen to acquire land in addition to his original lot. As such lands were not, like the original lot, inalienable, but could be sold or divided, inequalities in wealth necessarily arose, and the "communism" which we observed in the life of the citizens was only superficial. But it was specially provided by law that no Spartan should possess wealth in the form of gold or silver. This law was at first eluded by the device of depositing money in foreign temples, and it ultimately became a dead letter; Spartans even gained throughout Greece an evil reputation for avarice. By the fourth century they had greatly degenerated, and those who wrote studies of the Lacedaemonian constitution contrasted Sparta as it should be and used to be with Sparta as it was.

Degeneration of Sparta.

There is no doubt that the Spartan system of discipline grew up by degrees; yet the argument from design might be plausibly used to prove that it was the original creation of a single lawgiver. We may observe how well articulated and how closely interdependent were its various parts. The whole discipline of the society necessitated the existence of Helots; and on the other hand the existence of Helots necessitated such a discipline. The ephorate was the keystone of the structure; and in the dual kingship one might see a cunning intention to secure the powers of the ephors by perpetual jealousy between the kings. In the whole fabric one might trace an artistic unity which might be thought to argue the work of a single mind. And until lately this was generally believed to be the case; many still maintain the belief. A certain Lycurgus was said to have framed the Spartan institutions and enacted the Spartan laws about the beginning of the ninth century.

Unity of the constitution.

Vulgar date of Lycurgus 885 B.C.

But the grounds for believing that a Spartan lawgiver named Lycurgus ever existed have been questioned. The earliest statements as to the origin of the constitution date from the fifth century, and their discrepancy shows that they were mere guesses, and that the true origins were buried completely in the obscurity of the past. Pindar attributed the Lacedaemonian institutions to Aegimius, the mythical ancestor of the Dorian tribes; the historian Hellanicus regarded them as the creation of the two first kings of Sparta, Procles and Eurysthenes. The more critical Thucydides, less ready to record conjectures, contents himself with saying that the Lacedaemonian constitution had existed for rather more than 400 years at the end of the Peloponnesian war. Herodotus states that the Spartans declared Lycurgus to have been the guardian of

Statements of Pindar, Hellanicus. Thucydides [c. 804],

and Herodotus.

one of their early kings, and to have introduced from Crete their
laws and institutions. But the divergent accounts of this historian's
contemporaries, who ignore Lycurgus altogether, suggest that it
was only one of many guesses and not a generally accepted tradition. It may be added that if the old Spartan poet Tyrtaeus had
mentioned Lycurgus as a lawgiver, his words would certainly have
been quoted by later writers; and therefore it is argued [13] that he
knew nothing of such a tradition.

Silence of Tyrtaeus.

Hence the theory has arisen that Lycurgus (*Lyco-vorgos*) was
not a man; he was only a god. He was an Arcadian deity or
"hero,"—perhaps some form of the Arcadian Zeus Lycaeus, god
of the wolf-mountain; and his name meant "wolf-repeller." He was
worshipped at Lacedaemon where he had a shrine, and it is conjectured that his cult was adopted by the Spartans from the older
inhabitants whom they displaced. He may have also been connected with Olympia, for his name was inscribed on a very ancient
quoit—the so-called quoit of Iphitus—which was preserved there,
and perhaps dated from the seventh century. The belief that this
deity was a Spartan lawgiver, promoted by the Deiphic oracle,[14]
gradually gained ground and in the fourth century generally prevailed. Aristotle believed it, and made use of the old quoit to fix
the date of the Lycurgean legislation to the first half of the eighth
century. But while everybody regarded Lycurgus as unquestionably an historical personage, candid investigation confessed that
nothing certain was known concerning him, and the views about
his chronology were many and various.

Lycurgus deified.

Quoit of Iphitus

SECT. 4. THE CRETAN CONSTITUTIONS

Ancient Greek students of constitutional history were struck by
some obvious and remarkable resemblances between the Spartan

[13] This depends on a twofold argument from silence, but seems a fair inference; the probability is considerable that if Lycurgus had been remembered as
the original lawgiver in the poet's time, the poet would have mentioned him;
and it is probable that if he had mentioned him, some of the numerous extant
writers who deal with the Laconian state and Lycurgus would have appealed
to his venerable authority.

[14] Apollo himself debated whether Lycurgus was god or man in an oracle
cited by Herodotus (i. 65), which was to this effect:

> Well-come, Lycurgus, come to my rich shrine,
> Whom Zeus loves well, and all celestials love;
> Shall I declare thee human or divine?
> Surely a god, if I know aught thereof.

The decision of the god agrees with the result of modern criticism. There were
indeed two other lines of doubtful authenticity, which referred to his supposed legislation. Herodotus did not know them, but they are recorded by
Diodorus.

and the Cretan states, and it was believed by many that the Spartan constitution was derived from Crete, though there are notable differences as well as notable likenesses. It will be convenient to glance here at the political condition of this island, to which we shall seldom have to recur, since, owing to its geographical situation and the lack of political union, it was isolated and withdrawn from the main course of Greek history.

In a passage in the *Odyssey* the inhabitants of Crete are divided into five classes: Achaeans, Eteo-Cretans, Cydonians, Dorians, and Pelasgians. Of these the Eteo-Cretans may represent the original people who dwelled in the island before the Greeks came, like the Eteo-Carpathians of Carpathus. They survived chiefly in the eastern part of the island, and they continued to speak their own tongue in historical times, writing it, however, not in their ancient linear script but in Greek characters. A specimen of it—but we have no key to the meaning—has been preserved in some inscriptions [15] found at Praesus, their most important city. The people of Cydonia were perhaps also a remnant of the old population. The Achaeans and Pelasgians point to Thessaly, and there are some links which seem to connect Cretan towns with Perrhaebia. We may consider it probable that early settlers from Thessaly found their way to Crete.

But the most important settlers belonged to the Dorian branch of the Greek race, easily recognised by the three tribes, Hylleis, Pamphyli, and Dymanes, which always accompanied its migrations. These three tribes can be traced in many Cretan cities, and we saw that this island was one of the first places to receive the Dorian wanderers. But at a later time there seems to have been a further infusion of the "Dorian" element. New settlers came from Argolis and Laconia and mingled with the older inhabitants, refounding many cities. Thus Gortyn in the south of the island, in the valley of the river Lethaeus, was re-settled; and her neighbour Phaestos, distinguished by a mention in Homer, was invaded by newcomers from Argolis. "Well-built Lyttus," in its central site, also of Homeric fame, and Polyrrhenion, "rich in sheep," in the north-western corner, a haunt of the divine huntress Dictynna, were both colonised from Laconia. Cnossus "the great city" of

Marginal notes:
Genuine Cretans.

(Od. iii. 293.)

---

[15] One of these reads:—

$$
\ldots \nu\kappa\alpha\lambda\mu\iota\tau\kappa\iota
$$
$$
os \mid \beta\alpha\rho\xi\epsilon \mid a \ldots o
$$
$$
\alpha\rho\kappa\iota\alpha\pi\sigma\epsilon\tau \mid \mu\epsilon\gamma.
$$
$$
\alpha\rho\kappa\rho\kappa o\kappa\lambda\epsilon s—\gamma\epsilon\pi
$$
$$
\iota\alpha \ \sigma\epsilon\pi\gamma\nu\alpha\nu\alpha\iota\tau
$$

Minos, Cnossus "the broad," was repeopled by Dorians, and though it never attained to its former splendour, it remained the leading city in Crete.

(Od. xix. 178; Il. xviii. 590.)

The island then, colonised first by a folk closely akin to those who conquered Lacedaemon and Argos, colonised again by those very conquerors, may be said to be doubly "Dorian"; and there is thus a double reason for resemblances between Laconian and Cretan institutions. In the Cretan cities themselves there were of course many local divergences, but the general resemblances are so close, wherever we can trace the facts, that for our purpose we may safely follow the example of the ancients in assuming a general type of Cretan polity.

The population of a Cretan state consisted of two classes, warriors and serfs. In a few cases where one city had subjugated another, the people of the subject city held somewhat the same position as the Laconian Perioeci and formed a third class, but these cases were exceptional. In general, one of the main differences between a Cretan state and Sparta was that the Cretan state had no perioeci. There were two kinds of serfs, *mnoitai* and *aphamiotai*. The *mnoites* belonged to the state, while the *aphamiotes*, also called *clarotes* or "lot-men," were attached to the lots of the citizens, and belonged to the owners of the lots. These bondsmen cultivated the land themselves and could possess private property, like the Spartan Helots, but though we do not know exactly what their obligations were, they seem to have been in some ways in a better condition than the bondsmen of Laconia. If the *pastas* or lord of a Cretan serf died childless, the serf had an interest in his property. He could contract a legal marriage, and his family was recognised by law. The two privileges from which he was always jealously excluded were the carrying of arms and the practice of athletic exercises in the gymnasia. Unlike the Helots, the Cretan serfs found their condition tolerable, and we never hear that they revolted. The geographical conditions of the Cretans enabled them to excuse their slaves from military service.

The serfs.

Of the monarchical period in Crete we know nothing. In the sixth century we find that monarchy has been abolished by the aristocracies, and that the executive governments are in the hands of boards of ten annual magistrates, entitled *kosmoi*. The *kosmoi* were chosen from certain important clans (*startoi*), and the military as well as the other functions of the king had passed into their hands. They were assisted by the advice of the Council of elders which was elected from those who had filled the office of *kosmos*. The resolves of the *kosmoi* and Council were laid before

(Gerusia.)

the *agorai* or general assemblies of citizens, who merely voted and had no right to propose or discuss.

Comparison of Crete and Sparta. There is a superficial resemblance between this constitution, which prevailed in most Cretan cities, and that of Sparta. The Cretan *agora* answers to the Spartan *apella,* the Cretan to the Spartan *gerusia,* and the *kosmoi* to the ephors. The most obvious difference is that in Crete there was no royalty. But there is another important difference. The democratic feature of the Spartan constitution is absent in Crete. While the ephors were chosen from all the citizens, in a Cretan state only certain noble families were eligible to the office of *kosmos;* and, as the *gerusia* was chosen from the *kosmoi,* it is clear that the whole power of the state resided in a privileged class consisting of those families or clans. Thus the Cretan state was a close aristocracy.

Cretan education. The true likeness between Sparta and Crete lies in the circumstance that the laws and institutions of both countries aimed at creating a class of warriors. Boys were taught to read and write, and to recite certain songs ordained by law; but the chief part of their training was bodily, with a view to making them good soldiers. At the age of seventeen they were admitted into "herds," *agelai,* answering to the Spartan *buai,* which were organised by sons of noble houses and supported at the expense of the state. The members of these associations went through a training in the public gymnasia or *dromoi,* and hence were called *dromeis.* Great days were held, on which sham fights took place between these "herds" to the sound of lyres and flutes. The *dromeus* was of age in the eyes of the law, and he was bound to marry, but his wife continued to live in the house of her father or kinsmen, until he passed out of the state of a *dromeus* and became a "man." The men dined at public messes called *andreia,* corresponding to the Spartan *phiditia,* but the boys were also permitted to join them.[16] These meals were not defrayed altogether, as at Sparta, by the contributions of the members, but were partly at least paid for by the state; and the state also made provision for the sustenance of the women. The public income, which defrayed these and other such burdens and maintained the worship of the gods, must have been derived from public land cultivated by the mnoites, and distinct from the land which was apportioned in lots among the citizens.

We see then that in the discipline and education of the citizens, in the common meals of the men, in general political objects, there is a close and significant likeness between Sparta and Crete. But

[16] The citizens were divided into *hetairiai,* and each *hetairia* had its own *andreion.*

otherwise there are great differences. (1) In Crete there were, as a rule, no Perioeci; (2) the Cretan serfs lived under more favourable conditions than the Helots, and were not a constant source of danger; (3) kingship did not survive in Crete, and consequently (4) the functions which in Sparta were divided between kings and ephors were in Crete united in the hands of the *kosmoi;* (5) the Cretan state was an aristocracy, while Sparta, so far as the city itself was concerned, was a limited democracy; a difference which clearly reveals itself in (6) the modes of electing *kosmoi* and ephors; (7) there is a more advanced form of communism in Crete, in so far as state stores contribute largely to the maintenance of the citizens. If one city had become dominant in Crete and reduced the others to subjection, the resemblance between Laconia and Crete would have been much greater. A class of Cretan perioeci would have forthwith been formed.

SECT. 5. THE SUPREMACY AND DECLINE OF ARGOS. THE OLYMPIAN GAMES

The rebellion of Messenia had been especially formidable to Sparta, because the rebels had been supported by two foreign powers, Arcadia and Pisa. Part of Arcadia seems to have been united at this time under the lordship of the king of the Arcadian Orchomenus. The king of Pisa on the Alpheus had recently risen to new power and honour with the help of Argos; and Argos itself had been playing a prominent part in the peninsula under the leadership of her king Pheidon. The reign of this king was the last epoch of Argos as an active power of the first rank. We know little about him, but his name became so famous that in later times the royal house of distant Macedonia, when it reached the height of its success in Alexander the Great, was anxious to connect its line of descent with Pheidon.[17] Under his auspices a system of measures was introduced into Argos and the Peloponnesus. These measures were called after his name *Pheidonian,* and were likewise adopted at Athens; they seem to have been closely connected with the Aeginetan system of weights. But the only clear action of Pheidon is his expedition to the west. He led an Argive army across Arcadia to the banks of the Alpheus, and presided there over the celebration of the Olympian festival, which is now for the first time heard of in the history of Greece.

Pheidon of Argos (middle of 7th century).

Pheidonian measures.

Pheidon at Olympia.

The *altis* or sacred grove of Olympia lay, under the wooded mount of Cronus, where the river Cladeus flows into the Alpheus,

The Altis at Olympia

[17] In the interest of genealogy, he was placed more than a century before the time in which he really reigned.

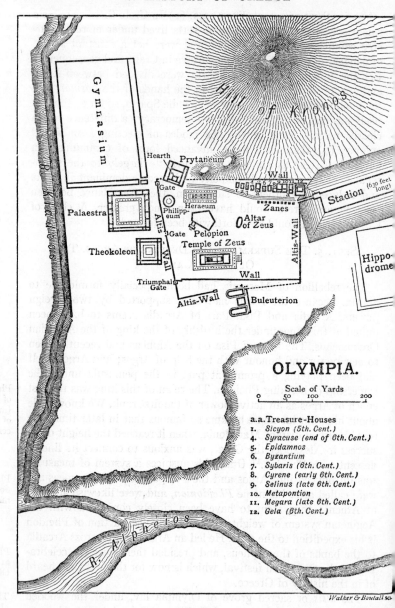

OLYMPIA.

Scale of Yards

0   50   100   200

a.a. Treasure-Houses

1. Sicyon (5th. Cent.)
4. Syracuse (end of 6th. Cent.)
5. Epidamnos
6. Byzantium
7. Sybaris (6th. Cent.)
8. Cyrene (early 6th. Cent.)
9. Selinus (late 6th. Cent.)
10. Metapontion
11. Megara (late 6th. Cent.)
12. Gela (6th. Cent.)

Walker & Boutall sc.

FIG. 38.

in the angle between the two streams. It was dedicated to the worship of Zeus; but the spot was probably sacred to Pelops, before Zeus claimed it for himself, and Pelops, degraded to the rank of a hero, kept his own sacred precinct within the larger enclosure. The sanctuary was in the territory of Pisa, and it is possible that the care of the worship and the conduct of the festivals belonged originally to the Pisan community. But the men of Elis, the northern neighbours of Pisa, set their hearts on having the control of the Olympian sanctuary, which, though it is not once mentioned, as Delphi and Dodona are mentioned, in the poems of Homer, must by the seventh century have won a high prestige in the Peloponnesus and drawn many visitors. As Elis was stronger than Pisa, the Eleans finally succeeded in usurping the conduct of the festival. Games were the chief feature of the festival, which was held every fourth year, at the time of the second full moon after midsummer's day. The games at first included foot-races, boxing, and wrestling; chariot-races and horse-races were added later. Such contests were an ancient institution in Greece. We know not how far back they go, or in what circumstances they were first introduced, but the funeral games of Patroclus, described in the *Iliad*, permit us to infer that they were a feature of Ionian life in the ninth century. We can see dimly into the political relations of Pheidon's age; but we can discern at least that Sparta lent her countenance to Elis in this usurpation, and that Argos, jealous of the growing power of Sparta, espoused the cause of Pisa. This was the purpose of king Pheidon's expedition to Olympia. He took the management of the games out of the hands of Elis and restored it to Pisa. And for many years Pisa maintained her rights. She maintained them so long as Sparta, absorbed in the Messenian strife, had no help to spare for Elis; and during that time she did what she could to help the foes of Sparta. But when the revolt was suppressed, it was inevitable that Elis should again, with Spartan help, win the control of the games, for Argos, declining under the successors of Pheidon, could give no aid to Pisa.

When king Pheidon held his state at Olympia, the most impressive shrine in the altis was the temple of Hera and Zeus; and this is the most ancient temple of which the foundations are still preserved on the soil of Hellas. It was built of sun-baked bricks, upon lower courses of stone, and the Doric columns were of wood. The days of stone temples were at hand; but it was not till two centuries later that the elder shrine was overshadowed by the great stone temple of Zeus. The temple of Hera is supposed by some to have been founded in the eleventh or tenth century; it is hardly

belongs to the Pisans.

Usurped by Eleans 572 B.C.

Pheidon restores Olympia to Pisa.

The temple of Hera and Zeus (Heraeum).

likely to be so old; but it was certainly very old, like the games of the place. The mythical institution of the games was ascribed to Pelops or to Heracles; and, when the Eleans usurped the presidency, the story gradually took shape that the celebration had been revived by the Spartan Lycurgus and the Elean Iphitus in the year 776 B.C., and this year was reckoned as the first Olympiad. From that year until the visit of Pheidon, the Eleans professed to have presided over the feast; and their account of the matter won its way into general belief.

It is possible that king Pheidon reorganised the games and inaugurated a new stage in the history of the festival. At all events, by the beginning of the sixth century the festival was no longer an event of merely Peloponnesian interest. It had become famous wherever the Greek tongue was spoken, and, when the feast-tide came around in each cycle of four years, there thronged to the banks of the Alpheus, from all quarters of the Greek world, athletes and horses to compete in the contest and spectators to behold them. During the celebration of the festival a sacred truce was observed, and the men of Elis claimed that in those days their territory was inviolable. The prize for victory in the games was a wreath of wild olive; but rich rewards always awaited the victor when he returned home in triumph and laid the Olympian crown in the chief temple of his city.

It may seem strange that the greatest and most glorious of all Panhellenic festivals should have been celebrated near the western shores of the Peloponnesus. One might have looked to find it nearer the Aegean. But situated where it was, the scene of the great games was all the nearer to the Greeks beyond the western sea; and none of the peoples of the mother-country vied more eagerly or more often in the contests of Olympia than the children who had found new homes far away on Sicilian and Italian soil. This nearness of Olympia to the western colonies comes into one's thoughts, when standing in the sacred altis one beholds the terrace on the northern side of the precinct, and the scanty remains of the row of twelve treasure-houses which once stood there. For of those twelve treasuries five at least were dedicated by Sicilian and Italian cities. Thus the Olympian festival helped the colonies of the west to keep in touch with the mother-country; it furnished a centre where Greeks of all parts met and exchanged their ideas and experiences; it was one of the institutions which expressed and quickened the consciousness of fellowship among the scattered folks of the Greek race; and it became a model, as we shall see, for other festivals of the same kind, which concurred in promoting a feeling of national unity.

The final success of Sparta in the long struggle with Messenia marks the period at which the balance of power among the Peloponnesian states began to shift. In the seventh century, Argos is the leading state. She has reduced Mycenae; she has annihilated Asine; she has made Tiryns an Argive fort; she has defeated Sparta at Hysiae. There can be little doubt that Pheidon's authority extended over all Argolis; moreover his influence was felt in Aegina, and the Laconian island of Cythera may have been an Argive possession, as well as the whole eastern coast of Laconia. But his reign is the last manifestation of the greatness of the southern Argos. Fifty years after the subjugation of Messenia, the Spartans become the strongest state in the Peloponnesus, and the Argives sink into the position of a second-rate power—always able to maintain their independence, always a thorn in the side of Sparta, always to be reckoned with as a foe and welcomed as a friend, but never leading, dominant, or originative.

(Battle of Hysiae; traditional date, 669-8 B.C.).

Decline of Argos and rise of Sparta.

Sect. 6. Democratic Movements. Lawgivers and Tyrants

It is clear that there is no security that equal justice will be meted out to all, so long as the laws by which the judge is supposed to act are not accessible to all. A written code of laws is a condition of just judgment, however just the laws themselves may be. It was therefore natural that one of the first demands the people in Greek cities pressed upon their aristocratic governments, and one of the first concessions those governments were forced to make, was a written law. It must be borne in mind that in old days deeds which injured only the individual and did not touch the gods or the state, were left to the injured person to deal with as he chose or could. The state did not interfere. Even in the case of bloodshedding, it devolved upon the kinsfolk of the slain man to wreak punishment upon the slayer. Then, as social order developed along with centralisation, the state took justice partly into its own hands; and the injured man, before he could punish the wrong-doer, was obliged to charge him before a judge, who decided the punishment. But it must be noted that no crime could come before a judge, unless the injured person came forward as accuser. The case of bloodshedding was exceptional, owing to the religious ideas connected with it. It was felt that the shedder of blood was not only impure himself, but had also defiled the gods of the community; so that,

Demand for written laws.

as a consequence of this theory, manslaughter of every form came under the class of crimes against the religion of the state.

Early law-givers (7th century).

The work of writing down the laws, and fixing customs in legal shape, was probably in most cases combined with the work of re-forming; and thus the great codifiers of the seventh century were also lawgivers. Among them the most famous were the misty figures of Zaleucus who made laws for the western Locrians, and Charondas the legislator of Catane; the clearer figure of the Athenia Dracon, of whom more will be said hereafter, and, most famous of all, Solon the Wise. But other cities in the elder Greece had their lawgivers too, men of knowledge and experience; the names of some are preserved but they are mere names. It is prob-able that the laws of Sparta herself, which she afterwards attributed to a god, were first shaped and written down at this period. The cities of Crete too were affected by the prevalent spirit of law-shaping, and some fragments are preserved of the early laws of Gortyn, which were the beginning of an epoch of legislative ac-tivity culminating in the Gortynian Code which has come down to us on tablets of stone.

Political struggles: demo-cratic move-ments.

In many cases the legislation was accompanied by political con-cessions to the people, and it was part of the lawgiver's task to modify the constitution. But for the most part this was only the beginning of a long political conflict; the people striving for free-dom and equality, the privileged classes struggling to retain their exclusive rights. The social distress, touched on in a previous chap-ter, was the sharp spur which drove the people on in this effort towards popular government. The struggle was in some cases to end in the establishment of a democracy; in many cases, the oligarchy succeeded in maintaining itself and keeping the people down; in most cases, perhaps, the result was a perpetual oscilla-tion between oligarchy and democracy—an endless series of rev-olutions, too often sullied by violence. But though democracy was not everywhere victorious—though even the states in which it was most firmly established were exposed to the danger of oligarchical conspiracies—yet everywhere the people aspired to it; and we may say that the chief feature of the domestic history of most Greek cities, from the end of the seventh century forward, is an en-deavour, here successful, yonder frustrated, to establish or main-tain popular government. In this sense then we have now reached a period in which the Greek world is striving and tending to pass from the aristocratic to the democratic commonwealth. The move-ment passed by some states, like Thessaly,—just as there had been some exceptions, like Argos, to the general fall of the monarchies;

while remote kingdoms like Macedonia and Molossia were not affected.

As usually, or at least frequently, happens in such circumstances, the popular movement received help from within the camp of the adversary. It was help indeed for which there was no reason to be grateful to those who gave it; for it was not given for love of the people. In many cities feuds existed between some of the power-holding families; and, when one family was in the ascendant, its rivals were tempted to make use of the popular discontent in order to subvert it. Thus discontented nobles came forward to be the leaders of the discontented masses. But when the government was overthrown, the revolution generally resulted in a temporary return to monarchy. The noble leader seized the supreme power and maintained it by armed might. The mass of the people were not yet ripe for taking the power into their own hands; and they were generally glad to entrust it to the man who had helped them to overthrow the hated government of the nobles. This new kind of monarchy was very different from the old; for the position of the monarch did not rest on hereditary right but on physical force.

Rise of new unconstitutional monarchies in some states.

Such illegitimate monarchs were called tyrants, to distinguish them from the hereditary kings, and this form of monarchy was called a tyrannis. The name "tyrant" was perhaps derived from Lydia, and first used by Greeks in designating the Lydian monarchs; Archilochus, in whose fragments we first meet "tyrannis," applied it to the sovereignty of Gyges. The word was in itself morally neutral and did not imply that the monarch was bad or cruel; there was nothing self-contradictory in a good tyrant, and many tyrants were beneficent. But the isolation of these rulers, who, being without the support of legitimacy, depended on armed force, so often urged them to be suspicious and cruel, that the tyrannis came into bad odour; arbitrary acts of oppression were associated with the name; and "tyrant" inclined to the evil sense in which modern languages have adopted it. For the Greek dislike of the tyrannis there was however a deeper cause than the fact that many tyrants were oppressors. It placed in the hands of an unconstitutional ruler arbitrary control, whether he exercised it or not, over the lives and fortunes of the citizens. It was thus repugnant to the Greek love of freedom, and it seemed to arrest their constitutional growth. As a matter of fact, this temporary arrest during the period when the first tyrannies prevailed may have been useful; for the tyrannis, though its direct political effect was retarding, forwarded the progress of the people in other directions.

The tyrannis

And even from a constitutional point of view it may have had its uses at this period. In some cases, it secured an interval of repose and growth, during which the people won experience and knowledge to fit them for self-government.

The period which saw the fall of the aristocracies is often called the age of the tyrants. The expression is unhappy, because it might easily mislead. The tyrannis first came into existence at this period; there was a large crop of tyrants much about the same time in different parts of Greece; they all performed the same function of overthrowing aristocracies, and in many cases they paved the way for democracies. But on the other hand, the tyrannis was not a form of government which appeared only at this transitional crisis, and then passed away. There is no age in the subsequent history of Greece which might not see, and did not actually see, the rise of tyrants here and there. Tyranny was always with the Greeks. It, as well as oligarchy, was a danger by which their democracies were threatened at all periods.

Ionia seems to have been the original home of the tyrannis, and this may have been partly due to the seductive example of the rich court of the Lydian "tyrants" at Sardis. But of the Ionian tyrannies we know little. We hear of factions and feuds in the cities, of aristocratic houses overthrown and despotisms established in various states. A tyrant of Ephesus marries the daughter of the Lydian monarch Alyattes. The most famous of these tyrants was Thrasybulus of Miletus, under whose rule that city held a more brilliant position than ever. Abroad, he took part in planting some of the colonies on the Black Sea, and successfully resisted the menaces of Lydia. At home, he developed the craft of tyranny to a fine art.

In Lesbian Mytilene we see the tyrannis and also a method by which it might be avoided. Mytilene had won great commercial prosperity; its ruling nobles, the Penthilids, were wealthy and luxurious and oppressed the people. Tyrants rose and fell in rapid succession; the echoes of hatred and jubilation still ring to us from relics of the lyric poems of Alcaeus. "Let us drink and reel, for Myrsilus is dead." The poet was a noble and a fighter; but in a war with the Athenians on the coast of the Hellespont he threw away his shield, like Archilochus, and it hung as a trophy at Sigeum. He plotted with Pittacus against the tyrant, but Pittacus was not a noble and his friendship with Alcaeus was not enduring. Pittacus however, who distinguished himself for bravery in the same war with Athens, was to be the saviour of the state. He gained the trust of the people and was elected ruler for a period of ten years in order to heal the sores of the city. Such a governor, possessing supreme power but for a limited time, was called an aesymnētes. Pittacus gained the reputation of a wise lawgiver and a firm, moderate ruler. He banished the nobles who opposed him, among others the two most famous of all Lesbians, the poets Alcaeus and Sappho. At the end of ten years he laid down his office, to be enrolled after his death in the number of the Seven Wise Men. The ship of state had reached the haven, to apply a metaphor of Alcaeus, and the exiles could safely be allowed to return.

holds office of aesymnetes [first years of 6th cent.?].

This was the brilliant period of the history of Lesbos, and a few surviving fragments of its two great poets, who struck new notes and devised new cadences of lyric song, give a glimpse of the free and luxurious life of the Aeolian island. The radiant genius of Sappho was inspired by her passionate attachments to young Lesbian maidens; the songs of Alcaeus, mirroring the commotions of party warfare, rang with the clatter of arms and the clinking of drinking-cups.

Sect. 7. The Tyrannies of Central Greece

About the middle of the seventh century, three tyrannies arose in central Greece in the neighbourhood of the Isthmus: at Corinth, at Sicyon, and at Megara. In each case the development was different, and is in each case instructive. In Sicyon the tyranny is brilliant and beneficent, in Corinth brilliant and oppressive, in Megara short-lived and followed by long intestine struggles.

The three Isthmian tyrannies

The ruling clan of the Bacchiads at Corinth was overthrown by Cypselus, who had put himself at the head of the people. A characteristic legend was formed at an early time about the birth of Cypselus, suggested by the connexion of his name with κυψέλα, a jar. His mother was a Bacchiad lady named Labda, who, being lame and consequently compelled to wed out of her own class, married a certain Eëtion, a man of the people. Having no children and consulting the Delphic oracle on the matter, Eetion received this reply:—

I. Corinth.

Cypselus: legend of his birth and name.

> High honour is thy due, Eetion,
> Yet no man doth thee honour, as were right.
> Labda thy wife will bear a huge millstone,
> Destined to fall on them who rule alone,
> And free thy Corinth from their rightless might.

The prophecy came to the ears of the Bacchiads and was confirmed to them by another oracle. So, as soon as Labda's child was born, they sent ten men to slay it. When the men came to the court of Eetion's dwelling they found that he was not at home, and they asked Labda for the infant. Suspecting nothing, she gave it to one of them to take in his arms, but, as he was about to dash it to the ground, the child smiled at him and he had not the heart to slay it. He passed it on to the second, but he too was moved with pity;

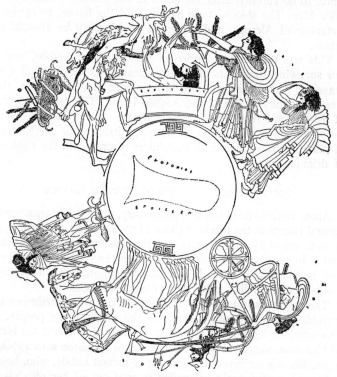

FIG. 39.—Eurystheus hiding from Heracles in a jar (red figured Vase, painted by Euphronius).

and so it was passed round from hand to hand, and none of the ten could find it in his heart to destroy it. Then giving the infant back to the mother, and going out into the courtyard, they reviled each other for their weakness, and resolved to go in again and do the deed together. But Labda listening at the door overheard what they said, and hid the child in a jar, where none of them thought of looking.[18] Thus the boy was saved, but the men falsely

[18] The hiding in the jar is illustrated by Euphronius' picture of Eurystheus hiding from Heracles in a jar.

reported to the Bacchiads that they had performed their errand.

The Bacchiads were banished and their property confiscated; dangerous persons were executed, and Cypselus took the reins of government into his own hands. Of the rule of Cypselus himself we know little; he is variously represented as harsh and mild. His son Periander succeeded, and of him more is recorded. The general features of the Cypselid tyrannis were a vigorous colonial and commercial policy, and the encouragement of art.

Colonial policy of the Cypselids. Corinth makes Corcyra subject.

One of the earliest triumphs of Cypselus was probably the reduction of Corcyra, which had formed a fleet of its own and had grown to be a rival of its mother in the Ionian seas. It has already been mentioned that the earliest battle of ships between two Greek states was supposed to have been fought between Corinth and Corcyra. The attempt of Corinth to form a colonial empire was an interesting experiment. The idea of Cypselus corresponded to our modern colonial system, in which the colonies are in a relation of dependence to the mother-country, and not to that of the Greeks, in which the colony was an independent sovereign state. Geographical conditions alone rendered it out of the question to apply the new principle to Syracuse, but the success at Corcyra was followed up by a development of Corinthian influence in the north-west of Greece. The Acarnanian peninsula of Leucas was occupied and made into an island by piercing a channel through the narrow isthmus. Anactorion was founded on the south side of the Ambracian gulf, and inland, on the north side, Ambracia. Apollonia was planted on the coast of Epirus; and farther north Corcyra, under the auspices of her mother-city, colonised Epidamnus. At a later period, and in another quarter of the Greek world, a son of Periander founded Potidaea in the Chalcidic peninsula.

Leucas. Anactorion. Ambracia. Apollonia. Epidamnus.

Cypselus and Periander did their utmost to promote the commercial activity of their city. In the middle of the seventh century the rival Euboean cities, Chalcis and Eretria, were the most important merchant states of Greece. But fifty years later they had somewhat declined; Corinth and Aegina were taking their place. Their decline was brought about by their rivalry, which led to an exhausting war for the Lelantine plain. It is said that this struggle assumed the larger proportions of a Greek mercantile war, involving on one side Corinth and Samos as allies of Chalcis, on the other Megara and Miletus as allies of Eretria. The dates are uncertain, but the fact seems to be that the strife was protracted and interrupted, and at some points in its course it may have led to consequences beyond Euboea. Archilochus sang how

Trade.

Decline of Eretria and Chalcis. War of the Lelantine Plain (end of 7th cent.)

Euboea's spear-famed lords
Shoot not with slings or bows, but smite with swords;

(c. 590?
at
earliest).

and Theognis of Megara at a much later date speaks of the end of the war as a recent event:—

> Cerinthus fallen; the Lelantine plain
> Waste, and the vineyards; all the Good have fled;
> The city in the power of evil men!
> O might the Cypselids even so be sped!

an utterance which shows that the end of the war was complicated by domestic factions. Eretria suffered most in the struggle; she lost her share in the Lelantine plain, and she presently lost also her continental territory, the plain of Oropus, which in the course of the sixth century passed under the power of Thebes. Moreover her sway over the islands of Andros, Tenos, and Ceos was undermined, and they came after a while under Athenian influence.

Oropus

The decline of Chalcis was perhaps promoted by a radical change in the foreign policy of Corinth. This city had formerly cultivated the alliance of Samos. She now deserted this alliance and formed a friendship with her old foe Miletus. The cause of this change was, at least in great measure, the natural sympathy of tyrannies. Thrasybulus the powerful tyrant of Miletus sympathised with Periander the powerful tyrant of Corinth. This change in policy is connected with the change in the balance of mercantile power. Corinth is more prosperous than ever; and Aegina is beginning to share with her the place which was hitherto held by the cities of Euboea.

Egyptian
name
of Peri-
ander's
nephew.

The foreign relations of Periander extended to Egypt, and there are two indications of his intercourse with the Egyptian monarchs Necho and Psammetichus II. His nephew and successor was called after the last-named king. Moreover we may guess that the canal works of Necho suggested to Periander undertakings of the same kind—the small canal which he actually cut at Leucas, and the great canal which he designed to cut through the isthmus of Corinth itself. But a Greek tyrant had not at his command the slave-labour of which an Egyptian king disposed, and the design fell through—an enterprise more than once attempted since, but not accomplished till our own day. Had Periander had the resources to carry out his idea, the subsequent history of Greek military and naval operations would have been largely changed.

Peri-
ander's
canals.

(Tyrants
patrons of
art and
litera-

While the most successful of the tyrants, like Periander, furthered material civilisation, they often manifested an interest in intellectual pursuits, and did something for the promotion of art.

A new form of poetry called the *dithyramb* was developed at Corinth during this period, the rude strains which were sung at vintage-feasts in honour of Dionysus being moulded into an artistic shape. The discovery was attributed to Arion, a mythical minstrel, who was said to have leaped into the sea under the compulsion of mariners who robbed him, and to have been carried to Corinth on the back of a dolphin, the fish of Dionysus.

ture.)
Dithy-
ramb.

In architecture, Corinthian skill had made an important contribution to the development of the temple. In the course of the seventh century men began to translate into stone the old shrine of brick and wood; and stone temples arose in all parts of the Greek world—the lighter "Ionic" form in Ionia, the heavier "Doric" in the elder Greece. By the invention of roof-tiles, Corinthian workmen rendered it practicable to give a considerable inclination to the roof; and thus in each gable of the temple a large triangular space was left, inviting the sculptor to fill it with a story in marble. The pediment, as we name it, was called by the Greeks the "eagle"; and thus it was said that Corinth had discovered the eagle.

Invention
of roof-
tiles.

ἀετός.

Seven great columns of limestone, which till the other day were almost the only sign that marked the site of ancient Corinth, are probably a relic of the reign of Periander. They belonged to the colonnade of a large Doric temple, with two separate chambers. It was a sanctuary of Apollo, and the second chamber was perhaps a treasury. The dedicatory offerings of the Cypselids at Delphi and Olympia were rich and remarkable. The treasure-house of the Corinthians at Delphi was ascribed to Cypselus. More famous, on account of the legend which was in later times attached to it, was a large chest of cedar-wood, which was dedicated, probably by Periander, in the shrine of Hera at Olympia. It was called the chest of Cypselus, and was said to have been the place in which Labda hid her child. This story overlooked the fact that a chest was an obvious place to search in, and fabricated the theory that the Corinthians called a chest a "jar." Three sides of the chest were ornamented with mythological scenes which ran round in five bands. It was still in existence eight centuries later, and a traveller who saw it then has left a minute description, which enables us to form a notion how Greek art in the days of Periander attempted the treatment of legend.

Old
temple of
Apollo.

Corinth-
ian
thêsauros
at Delphi

So-called
"Chest of
Cypselus'
(c. 600
B.C.).

Seen and
described
by
Pausanias
(2nd cent.
A.D.).

Judged by a modern standard, the government of Periander was strict, though in accordance with the practice in other cities and with the Greek views of the time. There were laws forbidding men to acquire large numbers of slaves or to live beyond their income;

Periander.

Laws
restricting

individual
liberty.

suppressing excessive luxury and idleness; hindering country people from fixing their abode in the city.

Tyranry
at Epi-
daurus.

In his home-life Periander was unlucky. He married Melissa, the daughter of Procles, who had made himself tyrant of Epidaurus. It was believed that he put her to death, and this led to an irreconcilable quarrel with his son Lycophron. The story is that Procles

Tale of
Lyco-
phron,
son of
Periander.

invited his two grandchildren, Lycophron and an elder brother, to his court. When they were departing he said to them, "Do ye know, boys, who killed your mother?" The elder was dull and did not understand; but the word sank into the heart of Lycophron, and henceforward he showed dislike and suspicion towards his father.

Periander
reduces
Epi-
daurus.

Periander, pressing him, discovered what Procles had said; and the affair ended, for the time, in a war with Epidaurus in which Procles was captured, and the banishment of Lycophron to Corcyra. As

Lyco-
phron at
Corcyra.

years went on and Periander was growing old, seeing that his elder son was dull of wit, he desired to hand over the government to Lycophron. But the son was implacable, and did not deign even to answer his father's messenger. Then Periander sent his daughter to intercede, but Lycophron replied that he would never come to Corinth while his father was there. Periander then decided to go himself to Corcyra and leave Corinth to his son, but the Corcyraeans were so terrified at the idea of having the tyrant among them that they slew Lycophron in order to foil the plan. For this act Periander chastised them heavily.

c. 586 B.C.

End of the
tyranny.

The great tyrant died and was succeeded by his nephew Psammetichus, who having ruled for a few years was slain. With him the tyranny of the Cypselids came to an end, and an aristocracy of merchants was firmly established. At the same time the Cypselid colonial system partly broke down, for Corcyra became independent and hostile, while the Ambraciots set up a democracy. But over her other colonies Corinth retained her influence, and was on friendly terms with all of them.

II.
MEGARA.

Thea-
genes,
c. 640 B.C.

The natural sympathy of tyrannies affected the relations of Corinth and Megara. Some time after the inauguration of the Cypselid tyranny, a similar constitutional change occurred at Megara, and a friendship sprang up between the two cities. The mercantile development of Megara, famous for her weavers, had enriched the nobles, who held the political power and oppressed the peasants with a grinding despotism. Then Theagenes arose as a deliverer and made himself tyrant. The example of Cypselus, and probably his direct influence and help, had something to do with the enterprise of Theagenes. A connexion between the tyrannies of Corinth and Megara seems implied in the rancorous reference which the Megarian poet Theognis makes to the Cypselids. Having obtained a bodyguard, Theagenes surprised and massacred the aristocrats. His term of tyranny was marked by one solid work, the construction of an aqueduct. He was overthrown and did not, like Cypselus, transmit his power to his descendants. Then followed a political struggle between the aristocracy, which had regained its power, and the people. But the time for an unmitigated aristocracy had gone by; the dêmos could not be ignored or brushed aside. Concessions were wrung from the government. The economical condition of the peasants was relieved by a measure which forced the capitalists to pay back the interest which they had extorted, while the political disabilities were relieved by extending citizenship to the country population and admitting the tillers of the soil to the Assembly. These conflicts and social changes are reflected in the poems of Theognis, who meditated and lamented them. He sang in the early part of the sixth century, pouring out his heart to Cyrnus, a young noble of the Polypaid family.[19] He had made an unsuccessful voyage, lost his land and fortune, and consequently his influence. He judges severely the short-sighted, greedy policy of his own caste, and sees that it is likely to lead to another tyranny. On the other hand, his sympathies are with an aristocratic form of government, and he discerns with dismay the growth of democratic tendencies, and the changed condition of the country folk, whom he regarded with true aristocratic contempt. The exclusiveness of the nobility was breaking down in the new circumstances, and mixed marriages were coming in. He cries:

[See above, p. 144.]

Theognis.

> Unchanged the walls, but, ah, how changed the folk!
> The base, who knew erstwhile nor law nor right,
> But dwelled like deer, with goatskin for a cloak,
> Are now ennobled; and, O sorry plight!
> The nobles are made base in all men's sight.

It was not long before the importance of Megara as a power in Greece dwindled. The war with Athens which resulted in the loss of the island of Salamis was decisive for her own decline and for the rise of her rival.[20]

Megara loses Salamis.

The rise of a tyranny in agricultural Sicyon seems to have occurred much about the same time as at mercantile Corinth. We know nothing of the circumstances. The name of the first founder, who was of low birth, is said to have been Orthagoras.[21] The first of

III. SICYON

Orthagoras (?)

---

[19] The Theognidea are a collection of poems of various ages—drinking songs, moral and political apophthegms. Those addressed to Cyrnus are from the genuine Theognis.

[20] See below, p. 182.

[21] Cleisthenes was the son of Aristonymus, the son of Myron, the son of Andreas, according to Herodotus, who does not mention Orthagoras.

Cleis-
thenes
c. 590.

Anti-
Argive
policy.

Story of
the new
phylae:
Hyatai,
Oneatai,
Choire-
atai, and
Archelaoi.

Story
of the
wooing of
Agarista.

the house of whom we have any historical record is Cleisthenes, who ruled in the first quarter of the sixth century. His hostility to Argos, which claimed lordship over Sicyon, the part he took in the Sacred War of Delphi, and the splendour of his court are the chief facts of which we know. He was engaged in an Argive war. He would not permit rhapsodists to recite the Homeric poems at Sicyon, because there was so much in them about Argos and Argives; and he did away with the worship of the Argive hero Adrastus, whose cult in Sicyon had been conspicuous. It is also stated that not wishing that the tribes of Sicyon and Argos should have the same names, he substituted for the Dorian tribes—Hylleis, Pamphyli, Dymanes—the insulting names Swine-ites, Assites, and Pigites, and called his own tribe Archelaoi, "Rulers"; and that this nomenclature endured for sixty years after his death, when the old Dorian names were restored and Archelaoi changed to Aigialeis. In this form the story seems highly unlikely, for such a change would have been a greater slight to the mass of the Sicyonians than to the Argives. But it is quite possible that the tyrant changed the name of his own tribe Aigialeis to Archelaoi, and we can understand how the story might have arisen out of a word spoken in jest: "I have changed my Goats (Αἰγι-αλεῖς) into Rulers of the folk; I have a mind to change those Argive *Hy*-lleis and the rest of them into Swine and Asses."

Cleisthenes married his daughter Agarista to an Athenian noble, Megacles, of the famous family of the Alcmaeonids. A legend is told of the wooing of Agarista which illustrates the tyrant's wealth and hospitality and the social ideas of the age. On the occasion of an Olympian festival at which he had himself won in the chariot-race, Cleisthenes made proclamation to the Greeks that all who aspired to the hand of his daughter should assemble at Sicyon, sixty days hence, and be entertained at his court for a year. At the end of the year he would decide who was most worthy of his daughter. Then there came to Sicyon all the Greeks who had a high opinion of themselves or of their families. From Sybaris and Siris in the far west, from Epidamnus and Aetolia, Arcadia and Elis, Argos and Athens, Euboea and Thessaly, the suitors for the hand of Agarista came. Cleisthenes tested their accomplishments for a year. He tried them in gymnastic exercises, but laid most stress on their social qualities. The two Athenians, Hippocleides and Megacles, pleased him best, but to Hippocleides of these two he most inclined. The day appointed for the choice of the husband came, and Cleisthenes sacrificed a hundred oxen and feasted all the suitors and all the folk of Sicyon. After the dinner, the wooers competed in music and general conversation. Hippocleides was the most brilliant, and, as his success seemed assured, he bade the flute-player strike up and began to dance. Cleisthenes was surprised and disconcerted at this behaviour, and his surprise became disgust when Hippocleides, who thought he was making a decisive impression, called for a table and danced Spartan and Athenian figures on it. The host controlled his feelings, but, when Hippocleides proceeded to dance on his head, he could no longer resist, and called out, "O son of Tisander, you have danced away your bride." But the Athenian only replied, "Hippocleides careth not," and danced on. Megacles was chosen for Agarista and rich presents were given to the disappointed suitors.

Sect. 8. The Sacred War. The Panhellenic Games

The most important achievement of Cleisthenes, and that which won him most fame in the Greek world, was his championship of the Delphic oracle.

The temple of Delphi, or Pytho, lay in the territory of the Phocian town of Crisa.[22] A Delphic Hymn tells how Apollo came "to Crisa, a hill facing to westward, under snowy Parnassus; a beetling cliff overhangs it, beneath is a hollow, rugged glen. Here," he said, "I will make me a fair temple, to be an oracle for men." The poet's picture is perfect. The sanctuary of "rocky Pytho" was terraced on a steep slope, hard under the bare sheer cliffs of Parnassus, looking down upon the deep glen of the Pleistus; an austere and majestic scene, supremely fitted for the utterance of the oracles of God. The city of Crisa lay on a vine-tressed hill to the west of the temple, and commanded its own plain which stretched southward to the sea. The men of Crisa claimed control over the Delphians and the oracle, and levied dues on the visitors who came to consult the deity. The Delphians desired to free themselves from the control of the Crisaeans, and they naturally looked for help to the great league of the north, in which the Thessalians, the ancient foes of the Phocians, were now the dominant member. The folks who belonged to this religious union were the "dwellers around" the shrine of Demeter at Anthela, close to the pass of Thermopylae; and hence they were called the *Amphictiones* of Anthela or Pylae. The league was probably old; it was formed, at all events, before the Thessalians had incorporated Achaean Phthiotis in Thessaly; for the people of Phthiotis were an independent member of the league,

Site of Delphi.

Site of Crisa.

The Amphictionic league.

[22] Crisa and Cirrha are different forms of the same name, and mean the same town. After the destruction of Crisa the name was applied to the port where the pilgrims used to land—mentioned simply as λιμήν in the Hymn to the Pythian Apollo, a work of the seventh century.

which included the Locrians, Phocians, Boeotians, and Athenians,
as well as the Dorians, Malians, Dolophians, Enianes, Thessalians,
Perrhaebians, and Magnetes. The members of the league were
bound not to destroy, or cut off running water from, any city
which belonged to it.

The Amphictions espoused warmly the cause of Apollo and his
Delphian servants, and declared a holy war against the men of
Crisa who had violated the sacred territory.[23] And Delphi found a
champion in the south as well as in the north. The tyrant of Sicyon
across the gulf went forth against the impious city. It was not
enough to conquer Crisa and force her to make terms or promises.
As she was situated in such a strong position, commanding the road
from the sea to the sanctuary, it was plain that the utter destruction of the city was the only conclusion of the war which could lead
to the assured independence of the oracle. The Amphictions and
Sicyonians took the city after a sore struggle, rased it to the
ground, and slew the indwellers. The Crisaean plain was dedicated
to the god; solemn and heavy curses were pronounced against whosoever should till it. The great gulf which sunders northern Greece
from the Peloponnesus, and whose old name "Crisaean" testified to
the greatness of the Phocian city, received, after this, its familiar
name "Corinthian" from the city of the Isthmus.

One of the consequences of this war was the establishment of a
close connexion between Delphi and the Amphictiony of Anthela.
The Delphic shrine became a second place of meeting, and the
league was often called the Delphic Amphictiony. The temple was
taken under the protection of the league; the administration of the
property of the god was placed in the hands of the Hieromnemones
or sacred councillors, who met twice a year in spring and autumn,
both at Anthela and at Delphi. Two Hieromnemones were sent as
its representatives by each member of the league. The oracle and
the priestly nobles of Delphi thus won a position of independence;

their great career of prosperity and power began. The Pythian
games were now reorganised on a more splendid scale, and the
ordering of them was one of the duties of the Amphictions. The festival became, like the Olympian, a four-yearly celebration, being
held in the middle of each Olympiad; gymnastic contests were introduced, whereas before there had been only a musical competition; and money-prizes were abolished for a wreath of bay. Cleisthenes won the laurel in the first chariot-race in the new hippo-
drome which was built in the plain below the ruins of Crisa. Hard

---

[23] It is said that Solon the Athenian took an active part in urging on the
war.

by was the stadion or racecourse in which the athletes ran and wrestled; and it was not till after many years had passed that the new stadion was built high up above Delphi itself, close under the cliffs. Cleisthenes was remembered as having taken a prominent part both in the Sacred War and in the institution of the games; and he commemorated the occasion of his victory by founding Pythian games at Sicyon, which afterwards, by a stroke of the irony of history, became associated with the hated hero Adrastus. Before the Sacred War it would seem that Sicyon had a treasure-house within the Delphic precinct; some traces of its round form, some traces possibly of its primitive sculptures, have been discovered; but not long after the war, the old building had to make way for a larger house in the shape of a Doric temple, and it is hard not to believe that it was Cleisthenes himself who erected this lordlier treasury for Sicyon.

Much about the same time two other Panhellenic festivals were instituted at Isthmus and at Nemea. It is uncertain whether the Isthmian games in honour of Poseidon were founded by Periander, or in commemoration of the abolition of tyranny at Corinth after the death of Psammetichus. The games in honour of Nemean Zeus were administered by the little town of Cleonae and seem to have been established by the influence of Argos. Both the Isthmian and the Nemean festivals were two-yearly. Thus from the beginning of the sixth century four Panhellenic festivals are celebrated, two in the Peloponnesus, one on the isthmus, one in the north; and throughout the course of Grecian history the prestige of these gatherings never wanes.

Isthmian games (586 or 582).

Nemean games (? 576).

These four Panhellenic festivals helped to maintain a feeling of fellowship among all the Greeks; and we may suspect that the promotion of this feeling was the deliberate policy of the rulers who raised these games to Panhellenic dignity. But it must not be overlooked that the festivals were themselves only a manifestation of a tendency towards unity, which had begun in the eighth century. We have already seen how this tendency was promoted by colonisation, and confirmed by the introduction of a common name for the Greek race. About the middle of the seventh century, we meet the name "Panhellenes" in a poem of Archilochus, and the phrase "Panhellenes and Achaeans" occurs in a passage, which may be still earlier, in the Homeric Catalogue of the Ships. The Panhellenic idea, the conception of a common Hellenic race with common interests, was encouraged by the poetical records of the heroic age. The Trojan war was remembered as a common enterprise, in which northern and southern Greece had joined; and the ancient poets

Growth of Hellenic unity: displayed by

(1) a common name;

(2) the conception of the Trojan war as Panhellenic·

had called the whole host "Achaeans" or "Argives" indifferently. The Homeric poems were a bond among all men of Greek speech, and the memory of Troy was an ingredient in a sentiment which, though we cannot call it national, was distinctly a sentiment of community. The feeling of community was also displayed in the recognition of the Pythian Apollo as the chief and supreme oracle of Greece. The growth of the prestige of the Delphic god might almost have been used as a touchstone for measuring the growth of the feeling of community. As a meeting-place for pilgrims and envoys from all quarters of the Greek world, Delphi served to keep distant cities in touch with one another, and to spread news; purposes which were effected in a less degree by the Panhellenic festivals. The tendencies to unity were also shown by the leagues, chiefly of a religious kind, which were formed among neighbouring states. The maritime league of Calauria is an instance;[24] the northern Amphictiony of Anthela is another; and we shall presently have a glimpse of the Ionic federation of Delos. Early in the sixth century we find the cities of Italy bound together by a sort of commercial league, which was indicated in the character of their coinage. We shall soon see Sparta uniting a large part of the Peloponnesus in a confederacy under her presidency.

(3) the Panhellenic position of Delphi (the "common hearth" of Greece);

(4) the Panhellenic games;

(5) partial minor unions, religious leagues.

These tendencies to unity never resulted in a political union of all Hellas. The Greek race never became a Greek nation; for the Panhellenic idea was weaker than the love of local independence. But an ideal unity was realised; it was realised in those beliefs and institutions which we have just been considering. They fostered in the hearts of the Greeks a lively feeling of fellowship and a deep pride in Hellas; though there was no political tie. And it is to be noted that the Delphic oracle made no efforts to promote political unity, though unintentionally it promoted unity of another kind. If it had made any such efforts, they would certainly have failed; for the oracle had little influence in initiation. Greek states did not ask Apollo to originate or direct their policy; they only sought his authority for what they had already determined.

Nature of Delphic influence.

We saw that the Boeotians were a member of the northern Amphictiony. The unity of Boeotia itself had taken the form of a federation, in which Thebes was the dominant power, being not only the federal capital, but—at all events in later times—being represented by two members on the board of Boeotarchs, as the federal magistrates were called, whereas each of the other cities returned only one Boeotarch. Its religious centre—for like all old Greek federations it was religious before it became political—was

The Boeotian confederacy.

[24] See below, p. 170. For the Ionic league of Delos, see p. 190.

the sanctuary of Poseidon at Onchestus. In the seventh century it did not yet include all Boeotia; Orchomenus still resisted. But at length Thebes forced Orchomenus to join, and in the course of the sixth century the Graian land of Oropus was annexed. The unity of Boeotia, thus completed, had its weak points; its maintenance depended upon the power of Thebes; some of the cities were reluctant members. Above all, Plataea chafed; she had kept herself pure from mixture with the Boeotian settlers, and her whole history—of which some remarkable episodes will pass before us—may be regarded as an isolated continuation of the ancient struggle between the elder Greek inhabitants of the land and the Boeotian conquerors.

Orchomenus joins Boeotian league (? c. 600 B.C.), [see below, p. 207]. Position of Plataea

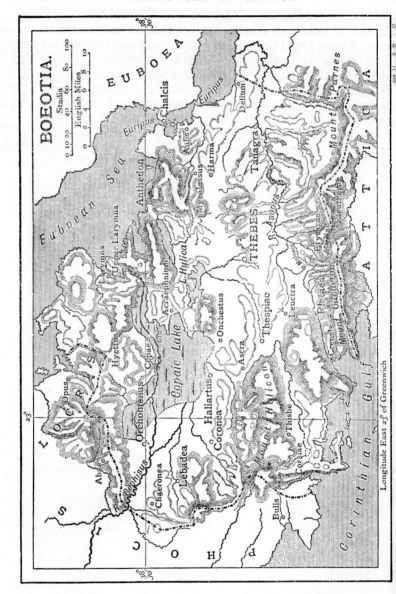

BOEOTIA.

CHAPTER IV

THE UNION OF ATTICA AND THE FOUNDATION OF THE ATHENIAN
DEMOCRACY

SECT. 1. THE UNION OF ATTICA

WHEN recorded history begins, the story of Athens is the story of Attica, the inhabitants of Attica are Athenians. But Attica, like its neighbour Boeotia and other countries of Greece, was once occupied by a number of independent states. Some of these little kingdoms are vaguely remembered in legends which tell of the giant Pallas who ruled at Pallene under the north-eastern slopes of Hymettus, of the dreaded Cephalus lord of the southern region of Thoricus, or of Porphyrion of mighty stature whose domain was at Athmonon under Mount Pentelicus. The hill of Munychia was, in the distant past, an island, and was crowned by a stronghold; the name *Piraeus* has been supposed to preserve the memory of days when the lords of Munychia looked across to the mainland and spoke of the "opposite shore." At a later stage we find neighbouring villages uniting themselves together by political or religious bonds. Thus in the north, beyond Pentelicus, Marathon and Oenoe and two other towns formed a *tetrapolis*. Again Piraeus, adjacent Phaleron, and two other places joined in the common worship of the god Heracles, and were called the Four-Villages. Of all the lordships between Mount Cithaeron and Cape Sunium the two most important were those of Eleusis and Athens, severed from one another by the hill-chain of Aegaleos.

Tetra-kômoi.

It was upon Athens, the stronghold in the midst of the Cephisian plain, five miles from the sea, that destiny devolved the task of working out the unity of Attica. This Cephisian plain, on the south side open to the Saronic gulf, is enclosed by hills, on the west by Aegaleos, on the north-west by Parnes, on the east by Hymettus, while the gap in the north-east, between Parnes and Hymettus, is filled by the gable-shaped mass of Pentelicus. The river Cephisus flows not far from Athens to westward, but the Acropolis was girt by two smaller streams, the Ilīsus and the Eridănus.[1] We have seen

The Acropolis

---

[1] This stream no longer exists, but its bed has been traced.

that it had been occupied as an abode of men in the third millennium, and that in the bronze age it was one of the strong places of Greece. There still remain pieces of the wall of grey-blue limestone with which the Pelasgian lords of the castle secured the edge of their precipitous hill.[2] The old wall was called the Pelargikon, but in later times this name was specially applied to the ground on the north-western slope. The Acropolis is joined to the Areopagus by a high saddle, which forms its natural approach, and on this side walls were so constructed that the main western entrance to the citadel lay through nine successive gates. At the north-western corner a covered staircase led down to the well of Clepsydra, which supplied the fortress with water; and on the north side there were two narrow "postern" descents into the plain, much steeper than that at Tiryns. We may take it that all these constructions were the work of the Pelasgians and were inherited by their Greek successors.

The first Greeks who won the Pelasgic acropolis were probably the Cecropes, and, though their name was forgotten as the name of an independent people, it survived in another form. For the later Athenians were always ready to describe themselves as the sons of Cecrops. This Cecrops was numbered among the imaginary prehistoric kings of Athens; he was nothing more than the fabulous ancestor of the Cecropes. But the time came when other Greek dwellers in Attica won the upper hand over the Cecropes, and brought with them the worship of Athena. It was a momentous day in the history of the land when the goddess, whose cult was already established in many other Attic places, took possession of the hill which was to be pre-eminently, and for all time, associated with her name. The Acropolis became Athēnai; the folks—whether Cecropes or Pelasgians—who dwelled in the villages around it, on the banks of the Ilīsus and Eridănus, became Athenians. The god whom the Cecropes worshipped on the hill, Poseidon Erechtheus, was forced to give way to the goddess. Legend told that Athena and Poseidon had disputed the possession of the Acropolis, and that each had set a token there, the goddess her sacred olive-tree, the god a salt-spring. The dethroned deity was not banished; there was a conciliation, characteristic of the Greek temper, between the old and the new. Erechtheus in the shape of a snake is permitted still to live on the hill of Athena, and the oldest temple that was built for the goddess, harboured also the god. In later times Athe-

Marginal notes:
Remains of Pelasgic wall on S. W. and S. E. of Acropolis.

Ennea-pylon.

The Cecròpes.

(Traditional date of Cecrops, 1581 B.C.)

Athens derives its name from Athena.

Legendary contest of Poseidon and Athena.

---

[2] Remains of prehistoric houses, and perhaps of the royal palace (see above, p. 20), have also been found on the north side of the Acropolis.

nian "history" transformed Erechtheus into a hero, and regarded him, like Cecrops, as one of the early kings.

There was another god who was closely associated in Attic legend with Athena, and Athens was distinguished by the high honour in which she held him. This was Hephaestus, the divine smith, the master and helper of handicraftsmen, the cunning giver of wealth. But we cannot say how far back his worship in Attica goes, or when his special feasts were instituted. It is probable that

FIG. 41.—Athena and Poseidon on a vase painted by Amasis.

his honour grew along with the prosperity of the craftsmen. An Athenian poet calls his countrymen "sons of Hephaestus," and, according to one myth, it was from his seed that all the earth-born inhabitants of Attica were sprung. At the feast of Apaturia, in the last days of autumn, when children were admitted into the Phratries by a solemn ceremony, the fathers used to light torches at the hearth and sing a hymn to the lord of fire.

The next great step in Attic history was the union of the land. We cannot be certain at what time this union took place; it recedes beyond the beginnings of recorded history; and we can only dimly discern how it was brought about. When the lords of the Acropolis had subdued their own Cephisian plain, from Mount Parnes to the

Athenians called Erech-theidae. Athenian worship of Hephaestus.

Feasts: Hephaestia and Chalkeia.

The Athenian conquest of Attica.

hill of Munychia, from the slopes of Hymettus to Aegaleos, they were tempted to extend their power eastward into the "Midlands" beyond Mount Hymettus, and subdue the southern "acté," or wedge of land which ends in the lofty cape of Sunium. The completion of this conquest was possibly the first great achievement of Athens, and the second was probably the subjugation of the northeastern plain of Marathon and the "tetrapolis." Thus the first stage in the union of Attica is the reduction of the small independent sovereignties throughout all the land, except the Eleusinian plain in the west, under the loose overlordship of Athens.

The Synoecism of Attica.

In the course of time the feeling of unity in Attica became so strong that all the smaller lordships, which formed parts of the large state, but still retained their separate political organisations, could be induced to surrender their home governments and merge themselves in a single community with a government centralised in the city of the Cephisian plain. The man of Thoricus or Aphidnae or Icaria now became a citizen of Athens and his political rights

(Feast of Synoikia.)

must be exercised there. The memory of this *synoecism* was preserved in historical times by an annual feast, and it was fitting that it should be so remembered, for it determined the whole history of

Historical importance of this constitutional change.

Athens. From this time forward she is no longer merely the supreme city of Attica. She is neither the head of a league of partly independent states, nor yet a despotic mistress of subject-communities. She is not what Thebes is to become in Boeotia, or what Sparta is in Laconia. If she had been, and she might well have been, either of these things, her history would have been gravely altered. She is the central city of an united state; and to the people of every village in Attica belong the same political rights as to the people of Athens herself. The man of Marathon or the man of Thoricus is no longer an Attic, he is an Athenian. It is generally supposed that the synoecism was the work of one of the kings. It was undoubtedly the work of one man; but it is possible that it belongs to the period immediately succeeding the abolition of the royal power.

Theseus.

In after-times the Athenians thought that the hero Theseus, whom they had enrolled in the list of their early kings,[3] was the author of the union of their country. But at the period when that union was brought about Theseus was not a national hero. He was a local god, worshipped in the Marathonian district and in the east

---

[3] Old Attic tradition (preserved by Herodotus) counted only four kings before Theseus, viz. Cecrops, Erechtheus, Pandion, and Aegeus. The four Cleisthenic tribes (see next chapter) which were named after Attic kings were named after these four. The augmentation of the list was due to Hellanicus.

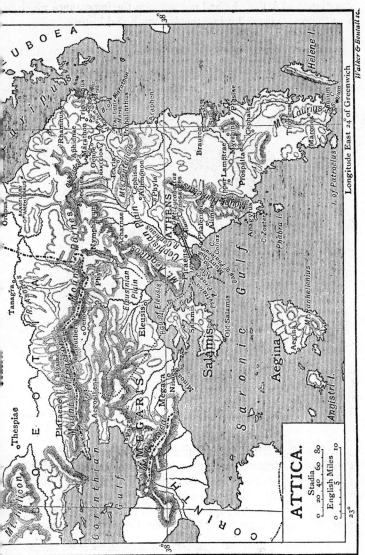

FIG. 42.

coastlands of Attica; he had not yet won the importance which he was to possess hereafter in Athenian myth and history.

SECT. 2. FOUNDATION OF THE ATHENIAN COMMONWEALTH

The early history of the Athenian constitution resembles that of most other Greek states, in the general fact that a royalty, sub-

FIG. 43.—Codrus, going forth to his last battle, bids a friend farewell (Bologna cylix).

jected to various restrictions, passes into an aristocracy. But the details of the transition are peculiar, and the beginning of the republic seems to have been exceptionally early. The traditional names of the Attic kings who came after the hero Theseus are certainly in some cases, and, it may be, in most cases, fictitious, the most famous of them being the Neleid Codrus,[4] who was said to

---

[4] Codrus was regarded by the Ionian cities as the leader of the Ionian colonisation; and therefore, as Athens claimed to be the mother city of the Ionian colonies, Codrus must needs be connected with Attica and made into an Athenian king. He was made the son of Melanthus, the eponymous hero of Melaenae. Now many Ionian families connected their origin with Messenia and the Neleids of Pylos; and it therefore became necessary for Athens, to the full establishment of her maternal relation to Ionia, to bring Neleids from Pylos to Attica. Consequently the hero Melanthus was explained to be a Neleid prince, a descendant of Nestor (see above, p. 74). It was said that the

have sacrificed himself to save his country on the occasion of an attack of invaders from the Peloponnesus. The Athenians said that they had abolished royalty, on the death of Codrus, because he was too good to have a successor—a curious reversal of the usual causes of such a revolution. But this story is a late invention.[5] The first limitation of the royal power effected by the aristocracy was the institution of a *polemarch* or military commander. The supreme command of the army, which had belonged to the king, was transferred to him and he was elected from and by the nobles. The next step seems to have been the overthrow of the royal house by the powerful family of the Medontids. The Medontids did not themselves assume the royal title, nor did they abolish it. They instituted the office of *archon* or regent, and this office usurped the most important functions of the king. Acastus, the Medontid, was the first regent. We know that he was an historical person; the archons of later days always swore that they would be true to their oath even as Acastus. He held the post for life, and his successors after him; and thus the Medontids resembled kings, though they did not bear the kingly name. But they fell short of royalty in another way too; for each regent was elected by the community; the community was only bound to elect a member of the Medontid family. The next step in weakening the power of this kingly magistrate was the change of the regency from a life office to an office of ten years. This reform is said to have been effected about the middle of the eighth century. It is uncertain at what time the Medontids were deprived of their prerogative and the regency was thrown open to all the nobles. With the next step we reach firmer ground. The regency became a yearly office, and from this time onward an official list of the archons seems to have been preserved.

But meanwhile there were still kings at Athens. The Medontids had robbed the kings of their royal power, but they had not done away with the kings; there was to be a king at Athens till the latest days of the Athenian democracy. It seems probable that, as some historical analogies might suggest, the Medontids allowed the shadow of royalty to remain in the possession of the old royal house, so that for some time there would have been life-kings existing by the side of the life-regents; it is not likely that from the very first

Marginal notes:

Fall of the kings.

Rule of the regents for life. (Traditional date of Medon, 1088 B.C.)

Ten-yearly regents (traditional date 753-7 B.C.).

Annual regents, 683-2 B.C.

Maintenance of the title Basileus.

Athenian king Thymoetes—the eponymous ancestor of the clan of the Thymoetadae—was compelled on account of his cowardice to resign the royal power to the brave stranger Melanthus.

[5] The popular story of Codrus visiting the camp of the Peloponnesians in peasant's dress, and seeking a quarrel in order that the enemy might slay him —an oracle having predicted that they would take Athens if they did not slay king Codrus—is also late. According to the older tradition Codrus fell in battle.

the kingship was degraded to be a yearly office, filled by election. This, however, was what it ultimately became.

The whole course of the constitutional development is uncertain; for it rests upon traditions, of which it is extremely hard to judge the value. But, whatever the details of the growth may have been, two important facts are to be grasped. One is that the fall of royalty, which does not imply the abolition of the royal name, happened in Athens at an earlier period than in Greece generally. The other is that the Medontids were not kings, but archons—the chiefs of an aristocracy. The great work of the Medontids was the foundation of the Athenian commonwealth; and perhaps one of their house is to be remembered for another achievement, not less great, which has been already described, the union of Attica.

Origin of the four Ionian tribes.

That union need not be older than the ninth century, and it is possible that the same republican movement which led to the downfall of the old royal house of the Acropolis, led to the synoecism of Attica. The political union of a country demands a system of organisation; and the statesmen who united Attica sought their method of organisation from one of those cities of Ionia, which Athens came to look upon as her own daughters. All the inhabitants were distributed into four tribes, which were borrowed from Miletus. The curious names of these tribes—Geleontes, Argadeis, Aigicoreis, and Hoplētes—seem to have been derived from the worship of special deities; for instance, Geleontes from Zeus Geleon. But the original meanings of the names had entirely passed away, and the tribes were affiliated to Apollo Patrōos, the paternal Apollo, from whom all Athenians claimed descent. The Brotherhoods seem to have been reorganised and arranged under the tribes—three to each tribe; so that there were twelve brotherhoods in the Attic state. At the head of each tribe was a "tribeking."

Twelve phratries. Phylobasileus.

The γένη.

We can see the clan organisation at Athens better than elsewhere. The families of each clan derived themselves from a common ancestor,[6] and most of the clan names are patronymics. The worship of this ancestor was the chief end of the society. All the clans alike worshipped Zeus Herkeios and Apollo Patrōos; many of them had a special connexion with other public cults. Each had a regular administration and officers, at the head of whom was an "archon." To these clans only members of the noble families belonged; but the other classes, the peasants and the craftsmen, formed similar organisations founded on the worship not of a com-

The orgeōnes

[6] And were therefore called *Homogalaktes*, "milk-fellows," descended from common *mothers*.

non ancestor, for they could point to none, but some deity whom they chose. The members of these were called *orgeōnes*. This innovation heralds the advance of the lower classes to political importance.

The brotherhoods, composed of families whose lands adjoined, united their members in the cult of Zeus Phratrios and Athena Phratria. In early times only clansmen belonged to the brotherhoods, but here again a change takes place in the seventh century, and orgeones are admitted. The organisation was then used for the purposes of census. Every child whose parents were citizens must be admitted into a brotherhood; and, if this rite is neglected, he is regarded as illegitimate. It should be observed that illegitimacy at Athens did not deprive a man of political rights, but he could not lay claim by right of birth to his father's inheritance.

At a much later time the constitutional historians of Athens made out that the clans were artificial subdivisions of the brotherhoods. They said that each tribe was divided into three brotherhoods, each brotherhood into thirty clans, and it was even added that each clan comprised thirty men. This artificial scheme is true, so far as the relation of the tribe to the brotherhood is concerned; but it is not true in regard to the clan, and is refuted by the circumstance that the tribes consisted of others than clansmen.

Sect. 3. The Aristocracy in the Seventh Century

Early in the seventh century, then, the Athenian republic was an aristocracy, and the executive was in the hands of three annually elected officers, the archon, the king, and the polemarch. The archon was the supreme judge in all civil suits. When he entered on office, he published a declaration that he would, throughout the term of his archonship, preserve the property of every citizen intact. At a later time this sphere of judicial power was limited and he judged mainly cases in which injured parents, orphans, heiresses were involved. He held the chief place among the magistrates, having his official residence in the Prytaneum where was the public hearth, and his name appeared at the head of official lists, whence he was called *epōnymus;* though the archonship was a later institution than that of polemarch, as is shown by the fact that no old religious ceremonies were performed by the archon, such as devolved upon the polemarch as well as upon the king. But the conduct of festivals instituted at later times was entrusted to him. Such was the Thargelia, the late-May feast of the first-fruits, the chief Athenian feast of Apollo, introduced from

Delos probably in the seventh century; such was the great Dionysia, which, as we shall see, were founded in the sixth. The polemarch had judicial duties, besides being commander-in-chief of the
army. He held a court in the Epilykeion on the banks of the Ilisus,
and judged there all cases in which non-citizens were involved.
Thus what the archon was for citizens, the polemarch was for the
class of foreign settlers who were called "metics." The king had his
residence in the royal Stoa in the Agora. His functions were confined to the management of the state-religion, and the conduct of
certain judicial cases connected with religion. He was president of
the Council, and thus had considerable power and responsibility in
the conduct of the judicial functions of that body.

The Bulê or Council was the political organisation through
which the nobles carried out, at Athens as elsewhere, the gradual
abolition of monarchy. This Council of Elders—a part as we saw
of the Aryan inheritance of the Greeks—came afterwards to be
called at Athens the Council of the Areopagus, to distinguish it
from other councils of later growth. This name was derived from
one of the Council's most important functions. According to early
custom, which we find reflected in Homer, murder and manslaughter were not regarded as crimes against the state, but concerned exclusively the family of the slain man, which might either
slay the slayer or accept a compensation. But gradually, as the
worship of the souls of the dead and the deities of the underworld
developed, the belief gained ground that he who shed blood was
impure and needed cleansing. Accordingly when a murderer satisfied the kinsfolk of the murdered by paying a fine, he had also to
submit to a process of purification, and satisfy the Chthonian gods
and the Erinyes or Furies, who were in the original conception, the
souls of the dead clamouring for vengeance. This notion of manslaughter as a religious offence necessarily led to the interference
of the state. For when the member of a community was impure,
the stain drew down the anger of the gods upon the whole community, if the unclean were not driven out. Hence it came about
that the state undertook the conduct of criminal justice. The
Council itself formed the court, and the proceedings were closely
associated with the worship of the Semnai. These Chthonian goddesses had a sanctuary, which served as a refuge for him whose
hand was stained with bloodshed, on the north-east side of the
Areopagus, outside the city wall. It is possible that the association
of this hill with the god Ares is merely due to a popular etymology,
for he had no shrine here; but the correct explanation of the name

Areiospagos is not known.[7] On this rugged spot, apart from but within sight of the dwellings of men, the Council held its sittings for cases of murder, violence with murderous intent, poisoning, and incendiarism. The accuser stood on the stone of Insolence, the accused on the stone of Recklessness, each a huge unhewn block. This function of the Council, which continued to belong to it after it had lost its other powers, procured it the name of Areopagus.

(ὕβρις.)
(ἀναίδεια.)

During the period of the aristocracy, the Council was the governing body of Athens. We may be certain that the magistrates were always members; but otherwise we do not know how it was composed, and therefore can form no clear idea how the constitution worked. The Council doubtless exercised direct control over the election of the chief magistrates; but we need have small doubt that the king, the archon, and the polemarch were either elected by the Ecclesia consisting of the whole body of citizens entitled to vote, or at all events were chosen by the Council out of a limited number nominated by the Assembly.

As an achievement of the aristocracy we may regard the annexation of Eleusis. The Eleusinian kingdom bound in by Athens on one side and Megara on the other—its little bay locked by Megarian Salamis—did not play any part in any portion of Greek history of which we have the faintest record. But of its independent existence we have a clear echo in a hymn which tells the Eleusinian story of Demeter. That goddess, wandering in quest of her lost daughter Persephone, came to Eleusis, where she was hospitably entertained by the king, and would have made his infant son immortal but for the queen's want of faith. This poem is thought to have been composed in the seventh century, and, if so, the days when Eleusis was independent had not yet passed out of men's memories then.

Conquest of Eleusis.

The coming of Demeter.

The middle of the seventh century is marked by a further constitutional change, which is the result of various social changes. The aristocracy of birth is forced to widen into an aristocracy of wealth. The general causes of this change are to be found in the new economical conditions which have been already pointed out as affecting the whole Greek world in the seventh century. But to understand their operation and political consequences at Athens, we must look more closely into the classes of the Attic population and the social structure.

[7] One suggestion is that the name is derived from Athena Areia, who had an altar on the hill, another that it means the hill of the *Arai* "curses," a name of the Semnai in Aeschylus.

Three
classes:
1. Eupa-
tridai,
2. Ge-
orgoi.
3. Demi-
urgoi.

Kerameis.

Freemen
without
civic
rights.

Hekte-
moroi or
Pelatai.

Pottery.

The
Dipylon
vases (9th
and 8th
centuries).

c. 650 (?).

Under the rule of the kings and the aristocracies, the free population fell into three classes: the *Eupatridae* or nobles; [8] the *Georgi*
or peasants who cultivated their own farms; and the *Demiurgi*
(public workers), those who lived by trade or commerce. The
Eupatrids originally lived in the country, and many Attic places
were called from their families, such as Paeonidae or Butadae.
After the synoecism, many of them came to live in the city. The
Demiurgi had their settlements in the neighbourhood of the city—
for example, there was the quarter of the "potters" north of the
Areopagus—and also villages in the country, such as *Pelekes* or
Daedalidae. But besides these classes of citizens, who had the right
of attending the Assembly, there was a mass of freemen who were
not citizens. Among these we can distinguish the agricultural
labourers, who, having no land of their own, cultivated the estates
of the nobles. In return for their labour they retained one-sixth of
the produce and were hence called "Sixth-parters" (Hektemoroi).
There were also the craftsmen who were employed and paid by the
Demiurgi, and doubtless small retail dealers and others.

Although Attica seems to have taken no part in the colonising
movements of the eighth and seventh centuries, the Athenians
shared in the trading activities of the period and were profoundly
affected by the economical revolution in the Greek world. The
cultivation of the olive was becoming a feature of Attica, and its
oil a profitable article of exportation. At the same time Attic potters were actively developing their industry on lines of their own,
and Attic pottery was in the course of another century to become
disseminated throughout the Mediterranean countries from Tuscany to Cyprus. Jars of this age have been found in tombs near
the Dipylon gate on the north-west side of Athens, and these Dipylon vases, as they are called, give us a glimpse of the Attic civilisation of the period. We not only see a new style of vase-painting,
with geometrical ornament and a symmetrical arrangement of the
space at the painter's disposal; but in the pictures of funeral processions we can observe with what pomp and cost the Attic nobles
buried their dead. In the graves where these vases were found,
offerings were laid beside the dead, pottery and sometimes gold
ornaments; and the sepulchral pit was surmounted not by a mound
but by a tall clay jar with an opening below, through which drink
offerings could be poured. But it must be noticed that soon after
this epoch, the influence of Ionia made itself felt in Attica, and the
custom was introduced of burning the dead; burial, however, was

[8] The generic name must be distinguished from the particular family of the
Eupatridae.

not discontinued; the two customs subsisted side by side. Ionia also influenced Athenian dress. The woollen peplos fastened with a pin was given up and the Ionian sleeved tunic or chiton, of linen, took its place.

It would be interesting if we might see in the rude representations of ships on some of the Dipylon vases an illustration of the beginnings of Attic seamanship. The sea traffic of Athens must have been rapidly growing in the first half of the seventh century. It is easy to see how the active participation of Athens in trade began to undermine the foundations of the aristocracy of birth, by

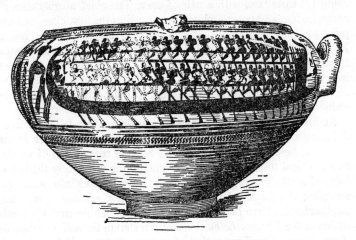

FIG. 44.—Dipylon Vase, with ship (British Museum).

introducing a new standard of social distinction. The nobles engaged in mercantile ventures with various success, some becoming richer, and others poorer; and the industrial folk increased in wealth and importance. The result would ultimately be that wealth would assert iself as well as birth, both socially and politically; and in the second half of the seventh century we find that, though the aristocracy has not been fully replaced by a *timocracy*, or constitution, in which political rights depend entirely on wealth, all the conditions are present for such a transformation. For we find the people divided into three classes according to their wealth. The principle of division was the annual yield of landed property, in corn, oil, or wine. The highest class was the *Pentacosiomedimni*. Before this name had any official meaning it was perhaps in popular use to designate those large proprietors whose income reached five hundred medimni of corn, at a time when oil and wine had not been much

Th ee classes: 1. Penta cosio medimni.

cultivated. When it acquired an official sense, it was defined to in
clude those whose land produced at least so many measures (me
dimni) of corn and so many measures (metrētae) of oil or wine a

2. Hippês.

together amounted to five hundred measures. The second clas
included those whose property produced more than three hundre
but less than five hundred such measures. These were calle
Knights, and so represented roughly those who could maintain .
horse and take their part in war as mounted soldiers. The minimun
income of the third class was two hundred measures, and thei

3. Zeu-
gitae.

name, *Teamsters,* shows that they were well-to-do peasants wh
could till their land with a pair of oxen. The chief magistracies o
archon, king, and polemarch were confined to the first class, but th
principle was admitted that a successful man, although not :
Eupatrid, was eligible for the highest offices if his income amounte
to 500 midemni. It was natural that the rating should be expresse
in terms of wealth derived from land; but it is not a necessary in
ference that the handicraftsmen were entirely excluded, or that ii
order to win political rights they were forced to purchase estates.

At first this concession of the Eupatrids to their fellow-citizen
did not practically amount to much. Most of the richest men in th
state still belonged to the old clans; but the recognition of wealtl
as a political test could not fail to undermine ultimately the privi
leges of birth. The organisation of the lower classes into bodies re
sembling the Clans of the nobles, and their admission into th

Six Thes-
mothetae
(? 650-630
B.C.).

Brotherhoods, have been mentioned. It is probable that the insti
tution of the *Thesmothetae* also marks a step in the self-assertion o
these classes. The Thesmothetae were a college of six judges, who
managed the whole judicial system of Athens. It was their duty to
examine, and call attention to defects in, the laws, and to keep a
record of judicial decisions; and they seem to have taken cogni
sance of all cases which belonged to the scope of the Council o
Areopagus, except trials for murder. In fact, it looks as if they were
practically a committee of that Council. They were elected an
nually, and it has been plausibly supposed that the number of si
was determined by the fact that they originated in a compromise
between the orders, three being Eupatrids, two Georgi, and one a
Demiurgos. They were soon associated with the three chief magis

"Nine
archons."

trates, the archon, basileus, and polemarch; and the nine came to
form a sort of college and were called the Nine Archons. Each of the
Nine when he entered on his office took an oath that he would act
in accordance with the laws, and vowed that if he committed any in
justice he would dedicate in gold a man's statue of life-size. It was a
penalty which no archon could have discharged.

Outside these classes were the smaller peasants who had land of their own, of which, however, the produce did not amount to two hundred measures of corn or oil, and the humbler handicraftsmen. These were called *Thêtes,* the name being perverted from its proper meaning of "labourers." The Thêtes were citizens, but had no political rights. Yet they were beginning to win a certain public importance. The conditions of a growing maritime trade led to the development of a navy. As the sea power grew, a new organisation was found necessary, and there can be little doubt that the duty of serving as marines in the penteconters mainly devolved upon the Thêtes. This gave them a new significance in the state, a significance which would strengthen their claim to political rights when the time for pressing that claim should come. We shall see hereafter how closely connected was the democracy of Athens with her sea power; and we can hardly be wrong in surmising the faint foreshadowings of that connexion at the very beginning of her naval history. Each of the four tribes was divided, for this purpose, into twelve districts called *Naucrariae;* each naucraria was probably bound to supply a ship. Thus the fleet consisted of forty-eight ships. The administration was directed by a body of naucrari, at the head of which were presidents; and the organisation might be found convenient for other than naval purposes. Thus the naucrari formed an important administrative council.

We see then that, in the middle of the seventh century, society in Attica is undergoing the change which is transforming the face of all the progressive parts of Hellas; wealth is competing with descent as a political test; and the aristocracy of birth seems to be passing into a timocracy. The power is in the hands of the three chief archons, who always belong to the class of wealthy nobles, and the Council of Areopagus, which is certainly composed of Eupatridae. But the classes outside the noble Clans, the smaller proprietors and the merchants, are beginning to assert themselves and make their weight felt; possibly the institution of the thesmothetae is due to their pressure. They also obtain admission into the Brotherhoods, which had been hitherto exclusive. Attic trade is rapidly growing. The commercial development promotes these democratic tendencies, and has also led to the creation of a fleet, which, since the poorest class of citizens are required to man it, renders that class important and prepares the way for its political recognition.

As yet, however, the naval establishment of Athens was but small compared with her neighbours Chalcis and Corinth, or her daughter cities of Ionia. And Aegina, which had come for a while

Thêtes.

Naucrariae. Council of naucrari: prytanies. (4 ?)

Recapitulation.

The worship of Poseidon at Calauria.

under the influence of Argos, outstripped her. It is interesting to find these two cities, Athens and Aegina, which were in later times to be bitter rivals for the supremacy in their gulf, in the seventh century taking part in an association for maintaining the worship of Poseidon in the little island of Calauria, over against Troezen. Other coast towns of the Saronic and Argolic bays—Epidaurus, Troezen, Hermione, Nauplia, Prasiae—belonged to this sacred union; and the Boeotian Orchomenus, by virtue of the authority which she still possessed over the sailors of Anthedon, was also a member. There was no political significance in the joint Calaurian worship of these maritime towns; their seamen propitiated Poseidon at Calauria, just as they sacrificed to Panhellenic Zeus on the far-seen Mountain of Aegina. And they were not grudging votaries. They built a house for the sea-god in his island; its foundations have been recently uncovered, and it is one of the earliest stone temples whose ruins have been found in Greece.

Temple at Calauria (? end of 7th cent.).

Money.

Attica, like the rest of the Greek world, was disturbed in her economic development by the invention of money. She had naturally been brought into close commercial relations with her neighbour Aegina, which at this time began to take a leading part in maritime enterprise. Accordingly we find Athens adopting the Aeginetan coinage, and using a system of weights and measures which was almost, if not quite, identical with the Aeginetan. The introduction of money, which was at first very scarce, and led to the accumulation of capital in the chests of successful speculators, was followed by a period of transition between the old system of the direct exchange of commodities and the new system of a metallic medium; and this transitional period was trying to all men of small means. But the inevitable economic crisis did not come at once, though all conditions of social distress were present, and a conflict between the rich and the poor was drawing steadily near. An event happened about thirty years before the end of the century which shows that the peasants were still loyal to the existing constitution.

Con-spiracy of Cylon, c. 632 B.C.

The example of tyranny was infectious, and, as it flourished at the very door of Athens—in Megara and Corinth,—it was unlikely that some attempt should not be made at Athens too. A certain Cylon, of noble family, married the daughter of Theagenes, tyrant of Megara; and, under Megarian influence and with Megarian help, he tried to make himself master of the city. Consulting the Delphic oracle, he was advised to seize the Acropolis on the greatest festival of Zeus. Cylon, an Olympic victor himself, had no doubt that the feast of Olympia was meant; but when his plot failed, it was explained that the oracle referred to the Athenian feast of the

Diasia in March, which was celebrated outside the city. Cylon enlisted in his enterprise a number of noble youths, and a band of Megarian soldiers were sent by Theagenes; he had no support among the people. He succeeded in seizing the Acropolis, but the sight of foreign soldiers effectually quenched any lurking sympathy that any of the Athenians might have felt for an effort to overthrow the government. The Council of the naucraries summoned the husbandmen from the country, and the summons was readily obeyed. Cylon was blockaded in the citadel, and, after a long siege when food and water began to fail, he escaped with his brother from the fortress. The rest were soon constrained to capitulate. They sought refuge in the temple of Athena Polias, and left it when the archons promised to spare their lives. But Megacles, of the Alcmaeonid family, was archon this year; and at his instigation the pledge was disregarded, and the conspirators were put to death. Some feud among the clans may have been at work here. The city was saved from a tyrant, but it had incurred a grave pollution. Such a violation of a solemn pledge to the suppliants who had trusted in the protection of the gods was an insult to the gods themselves; and the city was under a curse till the pollution should be removed. This view was urged by the secret friends of Cylon and those who hated the Alcmaeonids. And so it came to pass that while Cylon, his brother, and their descendants were condemned to disfranchisement and perpetual banishment, the Alcmaeonids and those who had acted with them were also tried on the charge of sacrilege and condemned to a perpetual exile, with confiscation of their property. And the bodies of those of the clan who had died between the deed of sacrilege and the passing of this sentence were exhumed and cast beyond the boundary of Attica. The banishment of the Alcmaeonids had consequences in the distant future, and we shall see how it comes into the practical politics of Athens two hundred years later. The tale is also told that the city required a further purification, and that a priest named Epimenides came from Crete and cleansed it. But it has been thought doubtful whether Epimenides is more than a mythical name like Orpheus, since another story brings him to Athens again, for similar purposes of atonement, more than a century afterwards; and then both tales are conciliated by ascribing to the seer a miraculous sleep of a hundred years.

Banishment of the Alcmaeonids.

Epimenides.

In the course of the next ten years, the state of the peasants seems to have changed considerably for the worse. The outbreak of a war with Megara, in consequence of the plot of Cylon, aggravated the distress of the rural population; for the Attic coasts suffered from the depredations of the enemy, and the Megarian market was closed to the oil-trade. Whether the peasants, who groaned under the existing system, found leaders and extorted concessions from the government, or whether the ruling classes themselves saw the danger, and tried to prevent it by a timely concession, it was at all events decided that a code of law should be drawn up and written down. Probably men had been clamouring long to obtain this security for life and property; and what the thesmothetae may have already done by recording judicial decisions in writing was not enough. Dracon was appointed an extraordinary legislator (Thesmothetes), and empowered to codify and rectify the existing law. We know only the provisions of that part of his criminal law which dealt with the shedding of blood; for these provisions were not altered by subsequent legislation. In later times it was thought that Dracon revealed to the Athenians how harsh their laws were, and his name became proverbial for a severe lawgiver. An Athenian orator won credit for his epigram that Dracon's laws were written not in ink but in blood. This idea arose from the fact that certain small offences, such as stealing cabbage, were punished by death. A broader view, however, of Dracon's code will modify this view. He drew careful distinctions between murder and various kinds of accidental or justifiable manslaughter. In Dracon's laws we meet a body of fifty-one judges, called the *Ephetae*. They were chosen from the Eupatrids, but it is not clear whether they formed a part of the Council of the Areopagus or were a wholly distinct body. Those cases of bloodshed which did not come before the court of the Areopagus were tried by the Ephetae, in case the shedder of blood was known. According to the nature of the deed the Ephetae held their court in different places: in the temple of the Delphinian Apollo, in the Palladion at Phaleron, or at Phreatto, a tongue of land on the Munychian peninsula. This last court was used in the case of those who were tried for manslaughter committed abroad, and as they might not set foot on the soil of their country, they had to answer the charge standing in a boat drawn up near the shore. When the shedder of blood was not known, the case came before the King in the Prytaneum.

It is unfortunate that we are not informed of Dracon's other legislation. We know that the laws relating to debtors were stringent; the creditor could claim the person of the insolvent debtor. In general, he was bound to provide for the interests of the rich powerholding class; but it was at all events an enormous gain for the poor that those interests should be defined in writing.

Dracon's Code, 621 B.C.

(Demādes.)

The Ephetae.

Sect. 4. The Legislation of Solon and the Foundation of Democracy

Dracon's code was something, but it did not touch the root of the evil. Every year the oppressiveness of the rich few and the impoverishment of the small farmer were increasing. Without capital, and obliged to borrow money, the small proprietors mortgaged their lands, which fell into the hands of capitalists, who lent money at ruinous interest. It must be remembered that money was still very scarce,[9] and that the peasants had now to purchase all their needs in coin. Even in Attica the small peasant could not cope with the larger proprietor. Thus the little farms of Attica were covered with stones, on which the mortgage bonds were written; the large estates grew apace; the black earth, as Solon said, was enslaved.

The condition of the free labourers was even more deplorable. The sixth part of the produce, which was their wage, no longer sufficed, under the new economical conditions, to support life, and they were forced into borrowing from their masters. The interest was high, the laws of debt were ruthless, and the person of the borrower was the pledge of repayment and forfeited to the lender in case of inability to pay. The result was that the class of free labourers was being gradually transformed into a class of slaves, whom their lords could sell when they chose.

The Hektemoroi,

reduced to slavery.

Thus while the wealthy few were becoming wealthier and greedier, the small proprietors were becoming landless, and the landless freemen were becoming slaves. And the evil was aggravated by unjust judgments, and the perversion of law in favour of the rich and powerful. The social disease seemed likely to culminate in a political revolution. The people were bitter against their remorseless oppressors, and only wanted a leader to rebel. To any student of contemporary politics, observing the development in other states, a tyranny would have seemed the most probable solution. A tyranny had already, once at least, and probably more than once, been averted; and now, as it happened, the masses obtained a mediator, not a demagogue, a reform, not a revolution. The tyranny, though it was ultimately to come, was postponed for more than thirty years. The mediator in the civil strife was Solon, the son of Execestides, a noble connected with the house of the Medontids. He was a merchant, and belonged to the wealthiest class in

Solon.

---

[9] The value of silver at this time may be judged from the fact that a sheep cost a drachma, a bushel of barley a drachma, an ox five drachmae. (A drachma = about a franc.)

the state. But he was very different from the Attic Eupatrids, rustic squires, of old fashions and narrow vision. We may guess that he had not been a home-keeping youth, but had visited the eastern coasts of the Aegean, whither mercantile concerns might have taken him. At all events, he had learned much from progressive Ionia. He had imbued himself with Ionic literature, and had mastered the art of writing verse in the Ionic idiom; so that he could himself take part in the intellectual movement of the day and become one of the sages of Greece. He was a poet, not because he was poetically inspired, like the Parian Archilochus of an earlier, or the Lesbian Sappho of his own, generation; but because at that time every man of letters was a poet; there was no prose literature. A hundred years later Solon would have used prose as the vehicle of his thoughts. His moderate temper made him generally popular; his knowledge gave him authority; and his countrymen called upon him, at last, to set their house in order. We are fortunate enough to possess portions of poems—political pamphlets—which he published for the purpose of guiding public opinion; and thus we have his view of the situation in his own words. He did not scruple to speak plainly. The social abuses and the sad state of the masses were clear to everybody, but Solon saw another side of the question; and he had no sympathy with the extreme revolutionary agitators who demanded a redistribution of lands. The more moderate of the nobles seem to have seen the danger and the urgent need of a new order of things; and thus it came to pass that Solon was solicited to undertake the work of reform. He definitely undertook the task and was elected archon,[10] with extraordinary legislative powers, for the purpose of healing the evils of the state, and conciliating the classes.

Instead of making the usual declaration of the chief magistrate, that he would protect the property of all men undiminished, he made proclamation that all mortgages and debts by which the debtor's person was pledged were annulled, and that all those who had become slaves for debt were free. By this proclamation in that summer, memorable for the rescue of hundreds of poor wretches into liberty and hope, the Athenians "shook off their burdens," and this first act of Solon's social reform was called the *Seisachtheia*. The great deliverance was celebrated by a public feast.

The character of the remedial measures of Solon is imperfectly known. After the cancelling of old debts he passed a law which for-

His Ionic culture.

Solon's archonship, 594-3 or 592-1 B.C.

Solon's inauguratory act: the Seisachtheia.

[10] The year of Solon's archonship is either 594-3 or 592-1 B.C.: There is evidence for both, perhaps the earlier is the more probable. In any case it seems certain that Solon's legislative activity extended over more than a single year, and likely that he was commissioned as an extraordinary lawgiver (nomothetês) to revise the constitution.

bade debtors to be enslaved. He fixed a limit for the measure of land which could be owned by a single person, so as to prevent the growth of dangerously large estates. And he forbade the exportation of Attic products, except oil. For it had been found that so much corn was carried to foreign markets, where the prices were higher, that an insufficient supply remained for the population of Attica. It is to be observed that at this time the Athenians had not yet begun to import Pontic corn.

All these measures hit the rich hard, and created discontent with the reformer; while, on the other hand, he was far from satisfying the desires and hopes of the masses. He would not confiscate and redistribute the estates of the wealthy, as many wished. And, though he rescued the tree labourer from bondage, he made no change in the Sixth-part system, so that the condition of these landless freemen was improved only in so far as they could not be enslaved, and in so far as the law limiting exportation affected prices. And Solon was too discreet to attempt to interfere seriously with the conditions of the money market by artificial restrictions. He fixed no maximum rate of interest, and his monetary reforms must be kept strictly apart from his social reforms. Hitherto the Athenians did not coin money of their own. They used the Aeginetan currency. Solon inaugurated a native coinage, but he adopted the Euboic, not the Aeginetan, standard. Thus 100 of the new Attic drachmae were equivalent in value to about 70 Aeginetan drachmae. The Attic coinage introduced by Solon is to be brought into connexion, not with the domestic reform, but with the foreign policy of Athens, to which new prospects were opening. The old coinage attached her to Aegina, with which her relations were strained, and to her foe Megara; the new system seemed to invite her into the distant fields beyond the sea, where Chalcis and Corinth had led the way in opening up a new world. A generation later, a new monetary reform introduced a distinct Attic standard, slightly higher than the Euboic.

What Solon did to heal the social sores of his country entitled him to the most fervent gratitude, but it was no more than might have been done by any able and honest statesman who possessed men's confidence. His title to fame as one of the great statesmen of Europe rests upon his reform of the constitution. He discovered a secret of democracy, and he used his discovery to build up the constitution on democratic foundations. The Athenian commonwealth did not actually become a democracy till many years later; but Solon not only laid the foundations, he shaped the framework. At first sight, indeed, the state as he reformed it might seem little

The hektemors.

Attic coinage begins; Euboic standard.

Attic standard introduced by Pisistratus.

Solon's reform of the Constitution.

more than an aristocracy of wealth—a timocracy—with certain democratic tendencies. He retained the old graduation of the people in classes according to property. But he added the Thêtes as a fourth class, and gave it certain political rights. On the three higher classes devolved the public burdens, and they served as cavalry or as hoplites. The Thetes were employed as light-armed troops or as marines. It is probable that Solon made little or no change in regard to the offices which were open to each class. Pentacosio-medimni were alone eligible to the archonship, and for them alone was reserved the financial office of Treasurer of Athena. Other offices [11] were open to the Hippês and the Zeugitae, but the distinction in privilege between them is unknown. The Thetes were not eligible to any of the offices of state, but they were admitted to take part in the meetings of the Ecclesia, and this gave them a voice in the election of the magistrates.

The opening of the Assembly to the lowest class was indeed an important step in the democratic direction; but it may have been only the end of a gradual process of widening, which had been going on under the aristocracy. The radical measure of Solon, which was the very corner-stone of the Athenian democracy, was his constitution of the courts of justice. He constituted a court out of all the citizens, including the Thetes; and as the panels of judges were enrolled by lot, the poorest burgher might have his turn. Any magistrate on laying down his office could be accused before the people in these courts; and thus the institution of popular courts invested the people with a supreme control over the administration. The people, sitting in sections as sworn judges, were called the *Heliaea*,—as distinguished from the Ecclesia, in which they gathered to pass laws or choose magistrates, but were required to take no oath. Having in its hands both the appointment of the magistrates and the control of their conduct, the people possessed theoretically the sovereignty of the state; and the meting out of more privileges to the less wealthy classes could be merely a matter of time. At first the archons were not deprived of their judicial powers, and the heliaea acted as a court of appeal; but by degrees the competence of the archons was reduced to the conduct of the proceedings preliminary to a trial, and the heliaea became both the first and the final court.

The constitution of the judicial courts out of the whole people was the secret of democracy which Solon discovered. It is his title

---

[11] The offices of the Pôlêtai (who farmed out public contracts, *e.g.* mines), the Eleven (heads of the executive of justice), the Kôlakretai (financial officers).

to fame in the history of the growth of popular government in Europe. Without ignoring the tendencies to a democratic development which existed before him, and without, on the other hand, disguising the privileges which he reserved to the upper classes, we can hardly hesitate to regard Solon as the founder of the Athenian democracy. It must indeed be confessed that there is much in the scope and intention of his constitution which it is difficult to appreciate, because we know so little of the older constitution which he reformed. Thus we have no definite record touching the composition of the Council of the Areopagus, touching its functions as a deliberative body and its relations to the Assembly, or touching the composition of the Assembly itself. We can, however, have little doubt that under the older commonwealth the Council of Elders exerted a preponderant influence over the Assembly, and that the business submitted to the Assembly, whether by the magistrates or in whatever way introduced, was previously discussed and settled by the Council. The founder of popular government could not leave this hinge of the aristocratic republic as it was. He must either totally change the character of the Council and transform it into a popular body, or he must deprive it of its deliberative functions in regard to the Assembly. Solon deprived the Council of Elders of these deliberative functions, so that it could no longer take any direct part in administration and legislation. But on the other hand he assigned to it a new and lofty rôle. He constituted it the protector of the constitution, and the guardian of the laws, giving it wide and undefined powers of control over the magistrates, and a censorial authority over the citizens. Its judicial and religious functions it retained. In order to bring it into harmony with the rest of his constitution, Solon seems to have altered the composition of the Council. Henceforward, at least, the nine archons at the end of their year of office became life-members of the Council of the Areopagus; and this was the manner in which the Council was recruited. Thus the Areopagites were virtually appointed by the people in the Assembly.

Solon's treatment of the Areopagus.

Having removed the Council of the Areopagus to this place of dignity, above and almost outside the constitution, Solon was obliged to create a new body to prepare the business for the Assembly. Such a body was indispensable, as the Greeks always recognised; and it is clear that in its absence enormous powers would have been placed in the hands of the magistrates, on whom the manipulation of the Assembly would have entirely devolved. The "probuleutic" Council which Solon instituted consisted of four hundred members; a hundred being taken from each of the four tribes, either chosen

The new Council of Four Hundred.

by the tribe itself or, more probably, picked by lot. All citizens of the three higher classes were eligible; the Thetes alone were excluded. In later days this Council—or rather a new Council which took its place—gained a large number of important powers, which made it to all intents an independent body in the state, but at first its functions seem to have been purely "probuleutic," and it has therefor rather the aspect of being merely a part of the organisation of the Assembly. It must always be remembered that it does not represent the Council of Elders of the Aryan foreworld; it does not correspond to the Gerusia of Sparta or the Senate of Rome. But it takes over certain functions which had before formed part of the duty of the Council of elders; it discusses beforehand the public matters which are to be submitted to the Assembly.

Lot.

The use of lot for the purpose of appointing public officers was a feature of Solon's reforms. According to men's ideas in those days, lot committed the decision to the gods, and was thus a serious method of precedure—not a sign of political levity, as we should regard it now. But a device which superstition suggested was approved by the reflexions of philosophical statesmen; and lot was recognised as a valuable political engine for security against undue influence and for the protection of minorities. It was doubtless as a security against the undue influence of clans and parties that Solon

Mixed method of election and lot.

used it. He applied it to the appointment of the chief magistrates themselves. But, religious though he was, he could not be blind to the danger of taking no human precautions against the falling of the lot upon an incompetent candidate. He therefore mixed the two devices of lot and election. Forty candidates were elected, ten from each tribe, by the voice of their tribesmen; and out of these the nine archons were picked by lot. It is probable that a similar mixed method was employed in the choice of the Four Hundred Councillors.

Danger in the tribes and clans.

Solon sought to keep the political balance steady by securing that each of the four tribes should have an equal share in the government. He could hardly have done otherwise, and yet here we touch on the weak point in the fabric of his constitution. The gravest danger ahead was in truth not the strife of poor and rich, of noble lord and man of the people, but the deep-rooted and bitter jealousies which existed between many of the clans. While the clan had the tribe behind it and the tribe possessed political weight, such feuds might at any moment cause a civil war or a revolution. But it was reserved for a future lawgiver to grapple with this problem. Solon assuredly saw it, but he had no solution ready to hand; and the evil was closely connected with another evil, the local parties which divided Attica. For these dangers Solon offered no remedy, and therefore his work, though abiding in the highest sense, did not supply a final or even a brief pacification of the warring elements in the state. He is said to have passed a law—so clumsy, so difficult to render effective, that it is hard to believe that such an enactment was ever made—that in the case of a party struggle every burgher must take a side under pain of losing his civic rights. Solon, if he was indeed the author of such a measure, sought to avert the possible issues of political strife by forcing the best citizens to intervene; it was a safeguard, a clumsy safeguard, against the danger of a tyranny.

It is interesting to observe that in some directions Solon extended and in others restricted the freedom of the individual. He restricted it by sumptuary laws and severe penalties for idleness; he extended it by an enactment allowing a man who had no heirs of his body to will his property as he liked, instead of its going to the next of kin.[12] One of Solon's first acts was to repeal all the legislation of Dracon, except the laws relating to manslaughter. His own laws were inscribed on wooden tables set in revolving frames called *axŏnes,* which were numbered, and the laws were quoted by the number of the axon. These tablets were kept in the Public hall. But copies were made on stone pillars, called in the old Attic tongue *kyrbeis,* and kept in the Portico of the King. Every citizen was required to take an oath that he would obey these laws; and it was ordered that the laws were to remain in force for a hundred years. **Preservation of Solonian laws.**

Solon had done his work boldly, but he had done it constitutionally. He had not made himself a tyrant, as he might easily have done, and as many expected him to do. On the contrary, one purpose of his reform was to forestall the necessity, and prevent the possibility, of a tyranny. He had not even become an aesymnetes—a legislator (like Pittacus) who for a number of years supersedes the constitution in order to reform it, and rules for that time with the absolute power of a tyrant. He had simply held the office of archon, invested, indeed, with extraordinary powers. To a superficial observer caution seemed the note of his reforms, and men were surprised, and many disgusted, by his cautiousness. His caution consisted in reserving the highest offices for men of property, and the truth probably is that in his time no others would have been fitted to perform the duties. But Solon has stated his **Solon's moderation.** **His caution.**

[12] This measure, we may probably assume, simply legalised an usage which had been introduced in practice long before.

own principle that the privileges of each class should be proportional to the public burdens which it can bear. This was the conservative feature of his legislation; and, seizing on it, democrats could make out a plausible case for regarding his constitution as simply a timocracy. When he laid down his office he was assailed by complaints, and he wrote elegies in which he explains his middle course and professes that he performed the things which he undertook without favour or fear. "I threw my stout shield," he says, "over both parties." He refused to entertain the idea of any modifications in his measures, and thinking that the reforms would work better in the absence of the reformer, he left Athens soon after his archonship and travelled for ten years, partly for mercantile ends, but perhaps chiefly from curiosity, to see strange places and strange men.

Character of Solon.

Though the remnants of his poems are fragmentary, though the recorded events of his life are meagre, and though the details of his legislation are dimly known and variously interpreted, the personality of Solon leaves a distinct impression on our minds. We know enough to see in him an embodiment of the ideal of intellectual and moral excellence of the early Greeks, and the greatest of their wise men. For him the first of the virtues was moderation, and his motto was "Avoid excess." He was in no vulgar sense a man of the world, for he was many-sided—poet and legislator, traveller and trader, noble and friend of the people. He had the insight to discern some of the yet undeveloped tendencies of the age, and could sympathise with other than the power-holding classes. He had meditated too deeply on the circumstances of humanity to find power a temptation; he never forgot that he was a traveller between life and death. It was a promising and characteristic act for a Greek state to commit the task of its reformation to such a man, and empower him to translate into definite legislative measures the views which he expressed in his poems.

The sequel.

Solon's social reforms inaugurated a permanent improvement. But his political measures, which he intended as a compromise, displeased many. Party strife broke out again bitterly soon after his archonship, and only to end, after thirty years, in the tyranny which it had been his dearest object to prevent. Of this strife we know little. It took the form of a struggle for the archonship, and two years are noted in which, in consequence of this struggle, no archons were elected, hence called years of *anarchy*. Then a certain archon, Damasias, attempted to convert his office into a permanent tyranny and actually held it for over two years. This attempt frightened the political parties into making a compromise of some

Years of anarchia, 589-8 (?) and 584-3 (?) B.C.

sort. It was agreed [13] that ten archons should be chosen, five Eupatrids, three Georgi, and two Demiurgi, all of course possessing the requisite minimum of wealth. It is unknown whether this arrangement was repeated after the year of its first trial, but it certainly did not lead to a permanent reconciliation.

Damasias, 583-581 B.C.

581-580 B.C.

The two great parties were those who were in the main satisfied with the new constitution of Solon, and those who disliked its democratic side and desired to return to the aristocratic government which he had subverted. The latter consisted chiefly of Eupatrids and were known as the men of the Plain. They were led by Lycurgus, and numbered among them the clan of the Philaidae—distinguished as the clan of Hippoclides, the wooer of Agarista, and destined to become more distinguished still as that of more than one Cimon and Miltiades. The opposite party of the Coast included not only the population of the coast, but the bulk of the middle classes, the peasants as well as the demiurgi, who were bettered by the changes of Solon. They were led by Megacles, son of Alcmaeon, the same Megacles who married Agarista. For one of Solon's measures was an act of amnesty which was couched in such terms that, while it did not benefit the descendants of Cylon, it permitted the return of the Alcmaeonidae. Their position severed them from the rest of the Eupatrids and associated them with the party which represented Solon's views.

Two parties:

the Plain (πεδιακοί);

the Coast (πάραλοι).

[13] We learn this from Aristotle's 'Αθηναίων Πολιτεία, and there is no longer any doubt about the reading. This unique arrangement superseded the Solonian constitution.

CHAPTER V

Sect. I. The Conquest of Salamis and Nisaea

In the midst of these domestic troubles and party struggles, there were a few statesmen who found time to attend to foreign affairs, and saw that the time had come for Athens to take a new step in her political career. Under her aristocracy, Athens had enjoyed a long period of development which may be called peaceful, if we compare the growth of some other states; and this prepared her to take her place in the general scene of Greek history. Though Attica was a poor country, scantily watered and with light soil, her prosperity in the oil trade might encourage her to look forward to becoming rich. But, if she was ever to become a political power, there was one thing to be achieved at all hazards. Every Athenian who stood on his strong hill and looked south-westward could see what this was. He descried, lying close to his own shore, an island which was not his own. And, if he walked across Mount Aegaleos, he saw how this foreign island blocked up the bay of what was now his own Eleusis. Almost equally distant from Athens and Megara, parted by a narrow water from both, Salamis in the hands of either must be a constant menace to the other. The possession of Salamis must decide the future history of both Megara and Athens. At this period Megara with her growing colonial connexions was a strong state and a formidable neighbour; and her expanding trade must have been viewed with alarm and jealousy by Athenian statesmen. A struggle with Megara, sooner or later, was inevitable, and the Cyclonian conspiracy, as we saw, furnished an occasion of war. Theagenes could not easily brook the slaughter of his men in violation of the promise which had been given to them, and he sent his ships to harry the Attic coast. The Athenians sought to occupy Salamis, but all their efforts to gain a permanent footing failed, and they abandoned the attempt in despair. Years passed away. At length Solon saw that the favourable hour had come. It was, perhaps, a quarter of a century after the year of his lawgiving; he had returned from his travels and was living at

Salamis.

Rivalry of Megara.

Megarian war (c. 629 B.C.).

Athens, one of the Council of the Areopagus. Megara was now weaker than in the days of Theagenes, and, whether she had given any new cause of offence to Athens or not, Solon and his friends decided that it was time to strike. The great legislator came forward now, not as before to assuage strife but to stir up to conquest. He composed a stirring poem which began: "I came myself as a herald from lovely Salamis, but with song on my lips instead of common speech." He blamed the peace policy of the "men who let slip Salamis," as dishonourable; and cried, "Arise and come to Salamis, to win that fair island and undo our shame." The poem of Solon was intended to have the effect which in later times, when "common speech" had been perfected to a fine art, would have been wrought by the eloquence of an orator in the Assembly. His appeal moved the hearts of his countrymen to a national effort, and an Athenian army went forth to lay the first stone of their country's greatness.

Solon's poem on Salamis.

An intimate friend of Solon took part in the enterprise,—Pisistratus, son of Hippocrates, whose home and estates were near Brauron. It has been thought that Pisistratus was the polemarch of the year, but it is more probable that he was only a general subordinate to the polemarch. He helped the expedition to a successful issue. Not only was the disputed island wrested from Megara, but he captured the port of Nisaea over against the island. We may conjecture that Nisaea was surprised first, and that its capture enabled the Athenians to occupy Salamis. Thus, though Pisistratus was associated with the conquest of Nisaea, not with the conquest of Salamis, it was to him, along with his friend Solon who inspired the enterprise, that the great achievement was really due. The seizure of her port was a great shock to the trade of Megara. It was indeed afterwards restored, when peace was made through the mediation of Sparta; but the hopes of Athenian policy, which its possession aroused, are reflected in the legend, created at this time, that Nisus the Megarian hero was a son of Pandion an early Athenian king. The two states agreed to submit their disputes to the arbitration of Sparta, and the award of the Spartans gave the island to Athens. In setting forth her case, Athens based her claims on a verse in Homer which she interpreted as proving that Salamis had formerly belonged to her (*Iliad* ii. 558). There is no reason to suppose that there was any truth in this prehistoric claim. But the fact of the appeal to Homer is interesting as showing the weight carried by Homer's authority. But Salamis now became permanently annexed to Attica. The island was afterwards divided in lots among Athenian citizens, who were called *cleruchs* or "lotholders." Salamis, unlike Eleusis, was not incorporated in Attica,

Pisistratus (polemarch), c. 570-65 B.C. Conquers Salamis and Nisaea.

(See above, p. 55.)

Cleruchs in Salamis.

though it was nearer Athens. There have been found fragments of a document inscribed on a stone-pillar, perhaps (but it is difficult to judge the dates of early Attic writings) eighty years or so later than the conquest,—a decree of the people which concerns the settle-

Athenian decree. ment of Salamis; one of the earliest scriptured stones of Athenian history, and the earliest example we possess of a decree of the Athenian people. The old inhabitants of the island were to pay the same taxes as the "Athenians" and to serve in the army, but they were to dwell on their farms in the island, and were not to let their lots to others under pain of a fine.

The conquest of Salamis was a decisive event for Athens. Her territory was now rounded off; she had complete command of the landlocked Eleusinian bay; it was she who now threatened Megara.

Sect. 2. Athens under Pisistratus

The conqueror of Nisaea was the hero of the day. By professing democratic doctrines and practising popular arts, he ingratiated himself with those extreme democrats who, being bitterly opposed to the nobles and not satisfied by the Solonian compromise, were outside both the Plain and the Coast. Pisistratus thus organised a new party which was called the Hill, as it largely consisted of the

The Hillsmen (Dia-krioi). poor hillsmen of the highlands of Attica; but it also included the hektemors, for whom Solon had done little, and many discontented men, who, formerly rich, had been impoverished by Solon's measure of cancelling old debts. With this party at his back, Pisis-

Pisi-stratus seizes the tyranny, 561-0 B.C. Archon-ship of Comeas. (κορυνη-φόροι.) tratus aimed at no less a thing than grasping the supreme power for himself. One day he appeared in the agora, wounded, he said, by a foul attack of his political foes—his foes because he was a friend of the people; and he showed wounds which he bore. In the Assembly, packed by the Hillsmen, a bodyguard of fifty clubsmen was voted to him on the proposal of Aristion. We have a monument, which we may associate with the author of this memorable act, in a sepulchral slab discovered near Brauron, on which is finely wrought

The stêlê of Aristion. in very low relief the portrait of "Aristion" standing armed by his tombstone; and it is hardly too bold to recognise in this con-temporary sculpture the friend of Pisistratus, when we remember that the home of the Pisistratid family was at Brauron. Having secured his bodyguard—the first step in the tyrant's progress—Pisistratus seized the acropolis, and made himself master of the state.

It was the fate of Solon to live long enough to see the establish-ment of the tyranny which he dreaded. We know not what part he had taken in the troubled world of politics since his return to Athens. The story was invented that he called upon the citizens to arm themselves against the tyrant, but called in vain; and that then, laying his arms outside the threshold of his house, he cried, "I have aided, so far as I could, my country and the constitution, and I appeal to others to do likewise." Nor has the story that he refused to live under a tyranny and sought refuge with his Cyprian friend the king of Soli, any good foundation. We know only that in his later years he enjoyed the pleasures of wine and love, and that he survived but a short time the seizure of the tyranny by Pisistratus, who at least treated the old man with respect.

Death of Solon (c. 560-59 B.C.).

The discord of parties had smoothed the way for the schemes of Pisistratus; but his success led in turn to the union of the two other parties, the Plain and the Coast, against him, and at the end of about five years they succeeded in driving him out. But new disunion followed, and Megacles the leader of the Coast seems to have quarrelled not only with the Plain but with his own party. At all events, he sought a reconciliation with Pisistratus and undertook to help him back to the tyranny on condition that the tyrant wedded his daughter. The legend is that the partisans of Pisistratus found in Paeania, an Attic village, a woman of loftier than common stature, whom they arrayed in the guise of the goddess Athena. Her name was Phye. Then heralds, on a certain day, entered Athens, crying that Pallas herself was leading back Pisistratus. Presently a car arrived bearing the tyrant and Phye; and the trick deceived all the common folk.

First exile of Pisistratus (556-5 B.C.).

Legend of Phye.

First restoration and second tyranny (550-49 B.C. ?).

But the coalition of Pisistratus with Megacles was not more abiding than that of Megacles with Lycurgus. By a former wife [1] Pisistratus had two sons—Hippias and Hipparchus; and as he desired to create a dynasty, he feared that, if he had offspring by a second wife, the interests of his older sons might be injured and family dissensions ensue. So, though he went through the form of marriage with the daughter of Megacles, as he had promised, he did not treat her as his wife. Megacles was enraged when the tyrant's neglect reached his ears; he made common cause with the enemies of Pisistratus and succeeded in driving him out for the second time, perhaps in the same year in which he had been restored.

The second exile lasted for about ten years, and Pisistratus

Second

---

[1] Her name is unknown. Pisistratus had also married Timonassa an Argive woman, whom, being a foreigner, Attic law did not recognise as a legal wife. The sons of Timonassa, Iophon and Hegesistratus, were therefore technically illegitimate, but socially, doubtless, no stain was attached to them. Hegesistratus seems to have been afterwards legitimised and made a citizen; perhaps it was on this occasion that he received his other name Thessalus.

exile (550-
49 B.C. ?).

spent it in forming new connexions in Macedonia. On the Thermaic gulf he organised the inhabitants of the neighbourhood of Rhaecelus into some sort of a city-state. He exploited the gold mines of Mount Pangaeus near the Strymon, and formed a force of mercenary soldiers, thus providing himself with money and men to recover his position at Athens. He was supported by Lygdamis, the tyrant of Naxos, and by the friendship of other Greek states, such as Thessaly, which he had cultivated in the days of his power. The aristocracy of Eretrian horsemen were well-disposed to him, and

Second
restora-
tion and
third
tyranny
(540-39–
528-7
B.C.)

their city was an admirable basis for an attack upon Athens. When he landed at Marathon, his adherents flocked to his standard. The citizens who were loyal to the constitutional government marched forth, and were defeated in battle at Pallene. Resistance was at an end, and once more Pisistratus had the power in his hands. This time he kept it.

The rule of Pisistratus may be described as a constitutional tyranny. He did not stop the wheels of the democracy, but he guided the machine entirely at his own will. The constitution of Solon seems to have been preserved in its essential features, though in some details the lapse of time may have brought modifications. Thus it is possible that even before the first success of Pisistratus the assessment according to measures of corn and oil had been converted into an assessment in money. And as money became more plentiful the earlier standards for the division of classes ceased to have the old significance. A man who at the beginning of the sixth century just reached the standard of the first class was passing rich; fifty years later he would be comparatively poor. But it was not to the interest of the tyrant to raise the census for political office. Various measures of policy were adopted by him to protect

(1) Influ-
ence on
the magis-
tracies.

his position, while he preserved the old forms of government. He managed to exert an influence on the appointment of the archons, so as to secure personal adherents, and one of his own family generally held some office. This involved the suspension or modification of the system of lot introduced by Solon. The tyrant kept up a

(2) Mer-
cenaries.

standing force of paid soldiers—among them, perhaps, Scythian archers, whom we see portrayed on Attic vases of the time. And he

(3) Host-
ages.

kept in his power, as hostages, the children of some noble families which he suspected. Most, indeed, of his more prominent opponents, including the Alcmaeonids, had left Attica, and the large estates which they abandoned were at his disposal.

These estates gave him the means of solving a problem which Solon had left unsolved, and of satisfying the expectations of a large number of his supporters. He divided the vacant lands into lots and gave them to the labourers who had worked on these and other estates. Thus the way was prepared for the total abolition of the hektemors. They became practically peasant proprietors, and they had to pay only the land-tax, amounting to one-tenth of the produce. Land was also given to many needy people who idled in the city, and loans of money to start them. The tax of a tenth, imposed on all estates, formed an important source of the tyrant's revenue, and it is generally supposed that he introduced it. But this is not probable. We may take it that this land-tax was an older institution which continued under Pisistratus, until either he or his sons were able, through an increase of revenue from other

Abolition
of the hek-
temoroi.

The
land-tax.

Fig. 45.—Troops at Athens (vase of age of Pisistratus).

sources, to reduce it to one-twentieth. It has been plausibly suggested that this increase of revenue came from the silver mines of Laurion, which now perhaps began to be more effectively worked. His possessions on the Strymon were another mainstay of the finance of Pisistratus. He exerted himself to improve agriculture, and under his influence the olive, which had long ago found a home in Attica, was planted all over the land.

Under Pisistratus Athens rested from the distractions of party strife, and the old parties gradually disappeared. The mass of discontented hektemors was absorbed in the class of peasant proprietors. Thus the people enjoyed a tranquil period of economical and political development. And as the free forms of the constitution were preserved, the masses, in the Assembly and in the Lawcourts, received a training in the routine at least of public affairs, which rendered them fit for the democracy which was to ensue when the tyranny was overthrown.

Abroad it was the consistent policy of Pisistratus to preserve

Foreign
policy.

peaceful relations with other states. Aegina indeed was openly the rival of Athens, and humbled Megara could hardly be aught save sullen. But Athens was on friendly terms with both the rival powers of the Peloponnesus, Sparta and Argos; and Thebes, and Thessaly, and the Eretrian knights had helped the tyrant in the days of his adversity. His influence extended to the banks of the Strymon and the coast of Macedonia, as we have already seen; and he had a subservient friend in Lygdamis of Naxos, whom he had installed as tyrant over the Naxian people.

Athens on the Propontis: the war for Sigeum.

It was doubtless with the object of injuring the Megarian trade in Pontic corn, and gaining some counterpoise to Megarian power in the region of the Propontis, that Athens made her first venture in distant seas. It was about forty years before Pisistratus became tyrant that Athens seized the Lesbian fortress of Sigeum on the shore of the Troad at the entrance to the Hellespont. The friendship of Miletus, mother of many Pontic colonies, favoured this enterprise, which however involved Athens in a conflict with Mytilene whose power and settlements extended along the shores of the straits. Mytilene, failing to recover the fortress, built another, the Achilleon, close by, which cut off the Athenians from the sea. It has been already told how the statesman Pittacus was engaged in this war and slew an Athenian commander in single combat, and how the poet Alcaeus threw away his shield. It would seem that while Athens was absorbed in her party conflicts at home, Sigeum slipped from her hands, and that the recapture of it was one of the achievements of Pisistratus. The tyrant showed the importance he attached to it by installing one of his sons as governor. The statesmen who first sent Athenian soldiers to the shores of the Hellespont had in truth opened up a new path for Athenian policy, and Pisistratus pursued that path. It was not long before a much greater acquisition than Sigeum was made in the same region; but this acquisition, though made with the good-will, and even under the auspices, of Pisistratus, was made by one who was his political rival and opponent. Miltiades, son of Cypselus, belonged to the noble family of the Philaids, and was one of the leaders of the Plain. It was after the usurpation of Pisistratus, that as he sat one day in the porch of his country-house at Laciadae on the road from Athens to Eleusis, he saw a company of men in Thracian dress, and armed with spears, passing along the road. He called out to them, invited them into his house, and proffered them hospitality. They were Dolonci, natives of the Thracian Chersonese, and they had come to Greece in search of a helper, who should have the strength and skill to defend them against their

(535-27 B.C.)

Acquisition of the Thracian Chersonese (559-6 ?). Miltiades.

northern neighbours, who were pressing them hard in war. They had gone to Delphi, and the oracle had bidden them invite the man who first offered them entertainment after they left the shrine. Miltiades, thus designated by the god, obeyed the call of the Thracians, not reluctant to leave his country fallen under a tyrant's rule.

The circumstances of the foundation of Athenian power in the Chersonese were thus wrought by the story-shaping instinct of the Greeks into a picturesque tale. The simple fact seems to have been that the Dolonci applied directly to Athens, inviting the settlement of an Athenian colony in their midst. Pisistratus was well pleased to promote Athenian influence on the Hellespontine shores; and the selection of Miltiades was not unwelcome to him, since it removed a dangerous subject. We may feel no doubt that it was as an oecist duly chosen by the Athenian people that Miltiades went forth, blessed by the Delphic oracle, to the land of his Thracian guests. But the oecist who went forth, as it was said, to escape tyranny, became absolute ruler in his new country. He ruled as a Thracian prince over the Dolonci; he ruled as a tyrant over his Athenian fellow-settlers. He protected the peninsula against invasions from the north by a wall which he built across the neck from Cardia to Pactye. We hear of his war with Lampsacus and his friendship with the king of Lydia.

It is not too much to say that Pisistratus took the first steps on the path which led Athens to empire. That path had indeed been pointed out to him by nameless predecessors; but his sword conquered Salamis; under his auspices Athens won a footing on both shores of the Hellespont. We cannot estimate too highly the statesmanship which sought a field for Athenian enterprise in the regions of the Propontis. The Ionian cities had forestalled Athens in venturing into the vast spaces of the eastern sea and winning the products of its shores. But though she entered into the contest late, she was destined to outstrip both her friend Miletus, and Megara her foe. Many years indeed were still to run before her ships dominated the Euxine; but it was much that she now set her posts as a watcher on either side of the narrow gate

Where the sea-ridge of Helle hangs heavier, and east upon west waters break.

Pisistratus strongly asserted the claim of Athens to be the mother and leader of the Ionian branch of the Greek race. The temple of Apollo in Delos, the island of his mythical birth, had been long a religious centre of the Ionians on both sides of the Aegean. There, as an ancient hymn sang, "the long-robed Ionians gather with their children and their wives," to honour Apollo with dance and

Importance of the settlements on the Hellespont.

The Delian festival.

song and games: "a stranger who came upon the Ionians in their throng, seeing the men and the fair-girdled women and the swift ships and all their wealth, whould say that they were beings free for ever from death and eld." Pisistratus "purified" the sacred spot by digging up all the tombs that were within sight of the sanctuary and removing the bones of the dead to another part of the island.

Purifica-
tion of
Delos.

Thus Athens took the famous Ionian festival under her special care. It was said, and has been believed by many both in ancient and in modern times, that Pisistratus or his enlightened son Hipparchus did a yet more important thing for the great Ionic epics, the *Iliad* and the *Odyssey*. The story is that a commission of literary men was appointed to collect and write down and revise the two poems of Homer, and it has thus been supposed that it was due to the initiative of the tyrants and the labours of the learned men whom they employed that the poems were for the first time written down. If this were so, it would be difficult to explain how the Athenians a generation before, in their dispute with Lesbos over the possession of Sigeum, could appeal to Homer as to the part they had played in the Trojan War, in the absence of a generally recognised text of the *Iliad*. As to the special verse in the Catalogue which they quoted to establish their claim to Salamis (see above, page 183) against Megara, it was alleged by Megarians in later times that it was spurious, having been fabricated and inserted by the Pisistratean commission in the interests of Athens. This accusation had a certain plausibility, because Onomacritus, who was the most prominent member of the commission, was not above suspicion in the matter of forgery. He was a teacher of the Orphic religion, and assisted Hippias, the tyrant's eldest son, in editing a collection of the oracles of soothsayers. But he was detected in introducing into the collection an oracle which he had invented, and was banished from Athens. The whole story, however, of the Homeric commission of Pisistratus, implying that our texts of the two poems only go as far back as the sixth century, is without good foundations and is highly improbable.

Alleged
Pisi-
stratean
edition of
Homer.

Pisistratus was indeed interested in Homer in another way. He made Homeric recitations a feature of the great Panathenaic festival, and he made a rule that the rhapsodes who competed should follow strictly the order of the poems in choosing the pieces they recited. The Panathenaic feast had been remodelled, if not founded, shortly before he seized the tyranny, and, on the pattern of the national gatherings at Olympia and Delphi, was held every fourth year. It was celebrated with athletic and musical contests,

The Pan-
athenaic
feast.
Temples
of Athena

but the centre and motive of the feast was the great procession which went up to the house of Athena on her hill, to offer her a robe woven by the hands of Athenian maidens. The "rich fane" of Athena, wherein she accorded Erechtheus a place, had the distinction of passing into the Homeric poems. It was situated near the northern cliff; and to the south of it a new house had been reared for the goddess of the city to inhabit, close to the ruins of the palace of the ancient kings. It had been built before the days of Pisistratus, but it was probably he who encompassed it with a Doric colonnade. From its length this temple was known as the House of the Hundred Feet, and many of the lowest stones of the walls, still lying in their places, show us its site and shape. The triangular gables displayed what Attic sculptors of the day could achieve. Hitherto the favourite material of these sculptors had been the soft marly limestone of the Piraeus, and by a curious stroke of luck some striking specimens of such work—Zeus encountering the three-headed Typhon, Heracles destroying the Hydra—have been partly preserved, the early efforts of an art which a hundred and fifty years would bring to perfection. But now —in the second half of the sixth century—Greek sculptors have begun to work in a nobler and harder material; and on one of the pediments of the renovated temple of Athena Polias the battle of the Gods and Giants was wrought in Parian marble. Athena herself in the centre of the composition, slaying Enceladus with her spear, may still be seen and admired.

But the tyrant planned a greater work than the new sanctuary on the hill. Down below, south-eastward from the citadel, on the banks of the Ilisus, he began the building of a great Doric temple for the Olympian Zeus. He began but never finished it, nor his sons after him. So immense was the scale of his plan that Athens, even when she reached the height of her dominion and fulfilled many of the aspirations of Pisistratus, never ventured to undertake the burden of completing it. A full completion was indeed to come, though in a shape far different from the old Athenian's plan; but not until Athens and Greece had been gathered under the wings of a power which had all Europe at its feet. The richly ornamented capitals of the few lofty pillars which still stand belong to the work of the Roman emperor, but we must remember that the generations of Athenians, with whom this history has to do, saw only plain Doric columns there, the monument of the wealth and ambition of the tyrant who had done more for their city than they cared to think.

Pisistratus was indeed scrupulous and zealous in all matters con-

(1) on the site of the later Erechtheum = house of Athena and Erechtheus, (2) the Hecatompedon = temple of Athena Polias. Peristasis and pediments added probably in Pisistratean age. Pedimental sculptures (? c. 600 B.C.). Use of marble in sculpture Gigantomachy in the Pisistratean pediment

Completed by the Emperor Hadrian.

cerned with religion, and his sons more than himself. But no act of his was more fruitful in results than what he did for the worship of Dionysus. In the marshes on the south side of the Areopagus the bacchic god had an ancient sanctuary, of which the foundations have been recently uncovered; but Pisistratus built him a new house at the foot of the Acropolis, and its ruins have not yet wholly disappeared. In connexion with this temple Pisistratus instituted a new festival, called the Great Dionysia of the City, and it completely overshadowed the older feast of the Winepress (Lenaea), which still continued to be held in the first days of spring at the temple of the Marshes. The chief feature of the Dionysiac feasts was the choir of satyrs, the god's attendants, who danced around the altar clothed in goat-skins, and sang their "goat song." But it became usual for the leader of the dancers, who was also the composer of the song, to separate himself from his fellows and hold speech with them, assuming the character of some person connected with the events which the song celebrated, and wearing an appropriate dress. Such performances, which at the rural feasts had been arranged by private enterprise, were made an official part of the Great Dionysia, and thus taken under state protection, in the form of a "tragic" contest, two or more choruses competing for a prize. It was the work of a generation to develop these simple representa-

tions into a true drama, by differentiating the satyric element. Legends not connected with Dionysus were chosen for representation, and the dancers appeared, not in the bacchic goat-dress, but in the costume suitable for their part in the story. This performance was divided into three acts; the dancers changed their costumes for each act; and only at the end did they come forward in their true goat-guise and perform a piece which preserved the original satyric character of "tragedy." Then their preponderant importance was by degrees diminished, and a second actor was introduced; and by a development of this kind, hidden from us in its details, the goat song of the days of Pisistratus grew into the tragedy of Aeschylus.

The popularity of the worship of Dionysus at Athens in the days of Pisistratus might be observed in the workshops of the potters. No subject was more favoured than Dionysiac scenes by the artists—Exekias and his fellows—who painted the black-figured jars of this period. There is another thing which the student of history may learn among the graceful vessels of the potters of Athens. On the jars of the Pisistratean age the deeds of Heracles are a favourite theme, while Theseus is little regarded. But before the golden age of vase-painting sets in, about the time of the fall of the Pisistratids, Theseus has begun to seize the popular imagination as the great Attic hero, and this is reflected in paintings on the cups of Euphronius and the other brilliant masters of the red-figured style. If we remember that Theseus was specially associated with the hill country of north Attica, which was the stronghold of the Pisistratean party, we may be tempted to infer that the glorification of Theseus was partly due to the policy of Pisistratus.

Theseus on red-figured cylixes, etc. (c. 510-470 B.C.).

But besides caring for the due honours of the gods, the tyrant busied himself with such humbler matters as the improvement of the water-supply of Athens. West and south-west of the Acropolis, in the rocky valley between the Areopagus and the Pnyx, his water-works have recently come to light. A cistern there received the waters which an aqueduct conveyed from the upper stream of the Ilisus. It is indeed on this side of Athens, south and west of the oldest Athens of all, that the chief stone memorials of the age of Pisistratus stood, apart from what he may have built on the Acropolis itself. But he not only built; he also demolished. He pulled down the old city-wall, and for more than half a century Athens was an unwalled town.

Aqueducts.

SECT. 3. GROWTH OF SPARTA, AND THE PELOPONNESIAN LEAGUE

While a tyrant was moulding the destinies of Athens, the growth of the Spartan power had changed the political aspect of the Peloponnesus. About the middle of the sixth century Sparta won successes against her northern neighbours Tegea and Argos; and in consequence of these successes she became the predominant power in the peninsula.

Eastern Arcadia is marked by a large plain, high above the sea-level; the villages in the north of this plain had coalesced into the town of Mantinea, those in the south had been united in Tegea. Sparta had gradually pressed up to the borders of the Tegean territory, and a long war was the result. This war is associated with an interesting legend based on the tradition that the Laconian hero Orestes was buried in Tegea. When the Spartans asked the Delphic oracle whether they might hope to achieve the conquest of Arcadia, they received a promise that the god would give them Tegea. Then, on account of this answer, they went forth against Tegea with fetters, but were defeated; and bound in the fetters which they had brought to bind the Tegeates were compelled to till the Tegean plain. Herodotus professed that in his day the very fetters hung in the temple of Athena Alea, the protectress of Tegea. War went on, and the Spartans, invariably defeated, at last con-

Tegeate war, c. 560-50 (?).

Legend of the conquest of Tegea and the bones of Orestes.

sulted the oracle again. The god bade them bring back the bones of
Orestes, but they could find no trace of the hero's burying-place,
and they asked the god once more. This time they received an oracle
couched in obscure enigmatic words:

> Among Arcadian hills a level space
>   Holds Tegea, where blow two blasts perforce
> And woe is laid on woe and face to face
>   Striker and counter-striker; there the corse
> Thou seekest lies, even Agamemnon's son;
> Convey him home and victory is won.

This did not help them much. But it befell that, during a truce
with the Tegeates, a certain Lichas, a Spartan man, was in Tegea
and entering a smith's shop saw the process of beating out iron. The
smith in conversation told him that wishing to dig a well in his
courtyard he had found a coffin seven cubits long and within it a
corpse of the same length, which he replaced. Lichas guessed at
once that he had won the solution of the oracular enigma, and
returning to Sparta communicated his discovery. The courtyard
was hired from the reluctant smith, the coffin was found, and the
bones brought home to Laconia. Then Tegea was conquered, and
here we return from fable to fact. The territory of the Arcadian
city was not treated like Messenia; it was not incorporated in the
territory of Lacedaemon. It became a dependent state, contributing a military contingent to the army of its conqueror; and it
bound itself to harbour no Messenians within its borders.

At this period the counsels of Sparta seem to have been guided
by Chilon, whose name became proverbial for wisdom. It was
much about the same time, perhaps shortly after the victory over
Tegea, that Sparta at length succeeded in rounding off the frontier
of Laconia on the north-eastern side by wresting the disputed territory of Thyreatis from Argos. The armies of the two states met in
the marchland, but the Spartan kings and the Argive chiefs agreed
to decide the dispute by a combat between three hundred chosen
champions on either side. The story is that all the six hundred
were slain except three, one Spartan and two Argives; and that
while the Argives hurried home to announce their victory, the
Spartan—Othryades was his name—remained on the field and
erected a trophy. In any case, the trial was futile, for both parties
claimed the victory and a battle was fought in which the Argives
were utterly defeated. Thyreatis was the last territorial acquisition
of Sparta. She changed her policy, and instead of aiming at gaining
new territory, she endeavoured to make the whole Peloponnesus a
sphere of Lacedaemonian influence. This change of policy was exhibited in her dealing with Tegea.

*Sparta
conquers
Thyreatis,
?. 550 B.C.*

The defeat of Argos placed Sparta at the head of the peninsula. All the Peloponnesian states, except Argos and Achaea, were enrolled in a loose confederacy, engaging themselves to supply military contingents in the common interest, Lacedaemon being the leader. The meetings of the confederacy were held at Sparta, and each member sent representatives. Corinth readily joined; for Corinth was naturally ranged against Argos, while her commercial rival, the island state of Aegina, was a friend of Argos. Periander had already inflicted a blow upon the Argives by seizing Epidaurus and thus cutting off their nearest communications with Aegina. The other Isthmian state, Megara, in which the rule of the nobles had been restored, was also enrolled. Everywhere Sparta exerted her influence to maintain oligarchy, everywhere she discountenanced democracy; so that her supremacy had important consequences for the constitutional development of the Peloponnesian states.

The Peloponnesian confederacy and Sparta's supremacy.

In northern Greece the power of the Thessalians was declining; and thus Sparta became the strongest state in Greece in the second half of the sixth century. She was on the most friendly terms with Athens throughout the reign of Pisistratus; but the tyrant was careful to maintain good relations with Argos also. With Argos herself indeed Athens had no cause for collision; but the rivalry which existed between Athens and Aegina naturally ranged Athens and Argos in opposite camps. It was, perhaps, not long before the accession of Pisistratus that the Athenians had landed forces in Aegina and had been repulsed with Argive help. The policy of Pisistratus avoided a conflict with his island neighbour and courted the friendship of Argos; but the deeper antagonism is shown by the embargo which Argos and Aegina placed upon the importation of Attic pottery. The excavations of the temple of the Argive Hera have illustrated this hostile measure; hardly any fragments of Attic pottery, dating from the period of Pisistratus or fifty years after his death, have been found in the precinct.

Athenian attack on Aegina (first half of 6th cent. ?).

SECT. 4. FALL OF THE PISISTRATIDS AND INTERVENTION OF SPARTA

When Pisistratus died, his eldest son Hippias took his place. Hipparchus helped him in the government, while Thessalus took little or no share in politics. The general policy of Pisistratus, both in home and foreign affairs, was continued. But the court of Athens seems to have acquired a more distinctive literary flavour. Hippias, who was a learned student of oracles, and Hipparchus were abreast

Death of Pisistratus (528-7 B.C.). His sons and their court.

of the most modern culture. The eminent poets of the day came to their court. Simonides of Ceos, famous for his choral odes; Anacreon of Teos, boon companion, singer of wine and love; Lasus of Hermione, who made his mark by novelties in the treatment of the dithyramb, and amused his leisure hours by composing "hissless hymns," in which the sound *s* did not occur—all these were invited or welcomed by Hipparchus. One of the most prominent figures in this society was Onomacritus, a religious teacher,[2] already mentioned in connexion with the alleged edition of Homer.

ὕμνος
ἄσιγμος.

The first serious blow aimed at the power of the tyrants was due to a personal grudge, not to any widespread dissatisfaction; but nevertheless it produced a series of effects which resulted in the fall of the tyranny. It would seem—but conflicting accounts of the affair were in circulation—that Hipparchus[3] gave offence to a comely young man named Harmodius and his lover Aristogiton. It is said that Hipparchus was in love with Harmodius, and, when his wooing was rejected, avenged himself by putting a slight on the youth's sister, refusing to allow her to "bear a basket" in the Panathenaic procession. Harmodius and Aristogiton then formed the plan of slaying the tyrants, and chose the day of that procession, because they could then, without raising suspicion, appear publicly with arms. Very few were initiated in the plot, as it was expected that when the first blow was struck, the citizens would declare themselves for freedom. But, as the hour approached, it was observed that one of the conspirators was engaged in speech with Hippias in the outer Ceramicus. His fellows leapt hastily to the conclusion that their plot was betrayed, and, giving up the idea of attacking Hippias, rushed to the market-place and slew Hipparchus near the Leokorion. Harmodius was cut down by the mercenaries, and Aristogiton, escaping for the moment, was afterwards captured, tortured, and put to death.

Conspir-
acy of
Harmo-
dius and
Aristo-
giton.

(514 B.C.)

Murder of
Hippar-
chus.

At the time no sympathy was manifested, little perhaps felt, for the conspirators. But their act led to a complete change in the government of Hippias. Not knowing what ramifications the plot might have or what dangers might still lurk about his feet, he became a hard and suspicious despot. He fortified Munychia, to have a post on the shore, from which he might at any hour flee overseas, and he began to turn his eyes towards Persia, where a new power had begun to cast its shadow over the Hellenic world. Then many Athenians came to hate him, and longed to shake off the reins

Harsh
rule of
Hippias.

[2] See below, p. 301.
[3] According to another story, Thessalus.

of tyranny; and they began to cherish the memory of Harmodius and Aristogiton as tyrant-slayers.

The overthrow of the tyranny was chiefly brought about by the Alcmaeonids, who desired to return to Athens, and could not win their desire so long as the Pisistratids were in power. They had taken care to cultivate an intimacy with the priesthood of Delphi, which they now turned to account. The old sanctuary of Apollo had been burned down by a mischance, and it was resolved to build a new temple at an enormous cost.[4] A Panhellenic subscription was organised, and by this means about a quarter of the needed money was raised; the rest was defrayed from the resources of Delphi. The Alcmaeonids undertook the contract for the work, and the story went that a frontage of Parian marble was added at their own expense, poros-stone having been specified in the agreement. The temple was not unworthy of the greatest shrine of Hellas. An Athenian poet has sung of the "glancing light of the two fair faces" of the pillared house of Loxias, and has vividly described sculptured metopes with heroes destroying monsters, and a pediment with the gods quelling the giants.[5] It must have been about the time when the new temple was approaching its completion, or soon after, that to the holy buildings of Delphi was added one of the richest of all. The islanders of Siphnos spent some of the wealth which they dug out of their gold-mines, in making themselves a treasury at the mid-centre of the earth, and its remains, recently recovered, show us the richness of its decoration. Perhaps this building marks the height of Siphnian prosperity. Before a hundred years had passed, their supply of precious metal was withdrawn; their miners had got below the sea-level, and the water filtering in cut them off from the sources of their wealth.

Large sums of money passed through the hands of the Alcmaeonids during the building of the temple, and their enemies said that this enabled them to hire mercenaries for their design on Attica. Their first attempt was a failure. They and other exiles seized Leipsydrion, a strong position on a spur of Mount Parnes looking down on Paeanidae and Acharnae; but they were too few to take the field by themselves, and the people had no desire to drive out the tyrant for the sake of setting up an oligarchy of nobles. They were soon forced to abandon their fortress and leave Attica. Convinced that

Temple of Delphi built by Alcmaeonids.

548-7 B.C.

Siphnian Treasury.

[4] 300 talents, perhaps £100,000, which, in those days when money was scarce and the fortunes of the richest were small, would correspond to six or seven times as much nowadays.

[5] Euripides, in the *Ion*, 185 *sqq*.

they could only accomplish their schemes by foreign help, they used their influence with the Delphic oracle to put pressure on Sparta. Accordingly, whenever the Spartans sent to consult the god, the response always was: "First free Athens."

It has already been said that the Pisistratids cultivated the friendship of Sparta, and after his brother's murder Hippias was more anxious than ever not to break with her. But the diplomacy of the Alcmaeonids, of whose clan Cleisthenes, son of Megacles, was at this time head, supported as it was by the influence of Delphi, finally prevailed, and the Spartans consented to force freedom upon Athens. Perhaps they thought the dealings of Hippias with Persia suspicious; he had married his daughter Archedice to a son of the tyrant of Lampsacus, who was known to have influence at the Persian court.

The
Spartans
invade
Attica.

Fall of the
Pisis-
tratids,
510 B.C.
(archon-
ship of
Harpac-
tides).

A first expedition of the Spartans under Anchimolius was utterly routed with the help of a body of Thessalian cavalry; but a second led by king Cleomenes defeated the Thessalians, and Hippias was blockaded in the Acropolis. When his children, whom he was sending secretly into safety abroad, fell into the hands of his enemies, he capitulated, and, on condition that they were given back, undertook to leave Attica within five days. He and all his house departed to Sigeum; and a pillar was set up on the Acropolis, recording the sentence which condemned the Pisistratids to perpetual disfranchisement (*atimia*).

Thus the tyrants had fallen, and with the aid of Sparta Athens was free. It was not surprising that when she came to value her liberty she loved to turn away from the circumstances in which it was actually won and linger over the romantic attempt of Harmodius and Aristogiton, which might be considered at least the prelude to the fall of Hippias. A drinking-song, breathing the spirit of liberty, celebrated the two friends who slew the tyrant; Harmodius and Aristogiton became household words. A skilful sculptor Antenor wrought a commemorative group of the two tyrant-slayers, and it was set up, not very many years later, above the market-place.

Athens in
the Pelo-
ponnesian
league.

The Athenian republic had to pay, indeed, something for its deliverance. It was obliged to enter into the Peloponnesian league, of which Sparta was the head; and thus Sparta acquired a certain right of interference in the affairs of Athens. This new obligation was destined to lead soon to another struggle.

Sect. 5. King Cleomenes and the Second Spartan Intervention

The birth
of Cleo-

It is necessary here to digress for a moment to tell of the strange manner of the birth of King Cleomenes, who liberated Athens. His father king Anaxandridas was wedded to his niece, but she had no children. The Ephors, heedful that the royal family of the Agids should not die out, urged him to put her away, and when he gainsaid, they insisted that he should take a second wife into his house. This he did, and Cleomenes was born. But soon afterwards his first wife, hitherto childless, bore a son, who was named Dorieus. When the old king died, it was ruled that Cleomenes as the eldest should succeed, and Dorieus, who had looked forward to the kingship, was forced to leave Sparta. He went forth to seek his fortune in lands beyond the sea; having attempted to plant a settlement in Libya, he led an expedition of adventure to the west; he took part in a war of Croton with Sybaris, and then fared to Sicily, with the design of founding a new city in the south-west country, yet he did not bring his purpose to pass, for he fell in a battle against the Carthaginians and their Elymian allies. It must also be told that after the birth of Dorieus his mother brought Anaxandridas two other sons, Leonidas and Cleombrotus, both of whom we shall meet hereafter.

After the expulsion of the tyrant, the Athenians had to deal with the political problems, whose solution, fifty years before, had been postponed by the tyranny. The main problem was to modify the constitution of Solon in such a way as to render it practicable. The old evils which had hindered the realisation of Solon's democracy reared their heads again as soon as Hippias had been driven out and the Spartans had departed. The strife of factions, led by noble and influential families, broke out; and the Coast and Plain seem to have risen again in the parties of the Alcmaeonid Cleisthenes [6] and

[6] Tree showing the relationships of eminent Alcmaeonids in the sixth and fifth centuries:

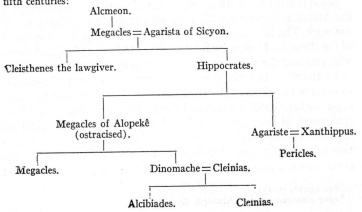

his rival Isagoras. As Cleisthenes had been the most active promoter of the revolution, Isagoras was naturally supported by the
secret adherents of the tyrant's house. The struggle at first turned
in favour of Isagoras, who was elected to the chief magistracy; but
it was only for a moment. Cleisthenes won the upper hand by enlisting on his side superior numbers. He rallied to his cause a host of
poor men who were outside the pale of citizenship, by promising to
make them citizens. Thus the victory of Cleisthenes—and the
victory of Cleisthenes was the victory of reform—was won by the
threat of physical force; and in the year of his rival's archonship he
introduced new democratic measures of law. Isagoras was so far
outnumbered that he had no recourse but appeal to Sparta. At his
instance the Lacedaemonians, who looked with disfavour on democracy, demanded that the Alcmaeonids, as a clan under a curse,[7]
should be expelled from Attica; and Cleisthenes, without attempting resistance, left the country. But this was not enough. King Cleomenes entered Attica for the second time; he expelled 700 families
pointed out by Isagoras, and attempted to dissolve the new consti-

tution and to set up an oligarchy. But the whole people rose in
arms; Cleomenes, who had only a small band of soldiers with him,
was blockaded with Isagoras in the Acropolis, and was forced to
capitulate on the third day "in spite of his Spartan spirit." [8] Cleisthenes could now return with all the other exiles and complete his
work. The event was a check for Lacedaemon. It was the first, but
it was not the last, time that Athenian oligarchs sought Spartan intervention and Spartan men-at-arms held the hill of Athena.

SECT. 6. REFORM OF CLEISTHENES

Solon created the institutions, and constructed the machinery, of
the Athenian democracy. We have seen why this machinery would
not work. The fatal obstacle to its success was the political strength
of the clans; and Solon, by retaining the old Ionic tribes, had therewith retained the clan organisation as a base of his constitution. In

order therefore to make democracy a reality, it was indispensable
to deprive the clans of political significance and substitute a new
organisation. Another grave evil during the past century had been
the growth of local parties; Attica had been split up into political
sections. The memorable achievement of Cleisthenes was the invention of a totally new organisation, a truly brilliant and, as the
event proved, practical scheme, which did away with the Ionic

---

[7] See above, p. 171.
[8] ὅμως Λακωνικὸν πνέων, Aristoph. Lys. 276.

tribes, abolished the political influence of the phratries and clans, and superseded the system of the Naucraries; thus removing the danger of the undue preponderance of social influence or local parties, and securing to the whole body of citizens a decisive and permanent part in the conduct of public affairs.

Abolition of old tribes.

Taking the map of Attica as he found it, consisting of between one and two hundred demes or small districts, Cleisthenes distinguished three regions: the region of the city, the region of the coast, and the inland. In each of these regions he divided the demes into ten groups called *trittyes,* so that there were thirty such trittyes in all, and each trittys was named after the chief deme which was included in it. Out of the thirty trittyes he then formed ten groups of three, in such a way that no group contained two trittyes from the same region. Each of these groups constituted a tribe, and the citizens of all the demes contained in its three trittyes were fellow-tribesmen. Thus Kydathenaion, a trittys of the city region, was combined with Paeania, a trittys of the inland, and Myrrhinus, a trittys of the coast, to form the tribe of Pandionis. The ten new tribes thus obtained were called after eponymous heroes chosen by the Delphic priestess.[9] The heroes had their priests and sanctuaries, and their statues stood in front of the senate-house in the Agora.

Three regions.

Thirty trittyes.

Ten tribes.

Distribution of demes among the tribes.

Both the tribes and the demes were corporations with officers, assemblies, and corporate property. The demarch or president of the deme kept the burgess list of the place, in which was solemnly entered the name of each citizen when he reached the age of seventeen. The organisation of the army depended on the tribes, each of which contributed a regiment of hoplites and a squadron of horse. The trittys had no independent constitution of this kind, no corporate existence, and consequently it appears little in official documents. But it was the scarce visible pivot on which the Cleisthenic system revolved, the link between the demes and the tribes. By its means a number of groups of people in various parts of Attica, without community of local interest, were brought together at Athens, and had to act in common. The old parties of Plain, Hill, and Coast were thus done away with; there was no longer a means of local political action. Thus an organisation created for a purely political purpose was substituted for an organisation which was originally social and had been adapted to political needs. The ten new tribes, based on artificial geography, took the place of the four old tribes, based on birth. The incorporate trittys, which had no independent existence, but merely represented the relation between

Demarchs. ($\lambda\eta\xi\iota\alpha\rho$-$\chi\iota\kappa\grave{o}\nu$ $\gamma\rho\alpha\mu\mu\alpha$-$\tau\epsilon\hat{\imath}o\nu$).

Importance of the trittys.

Effect of the new system;

contrast with the old.

[9] Names of the ten tribes: Erechthesis, Aegeis, Pandianis, Leontis, Acamantis, Oeneis, Cecropis, Hippothontis, Aeantis, Antiochis.

the tribe and the deme, took the place of the independent and active phratry. And the deme, a local unit, replaced the social unit of the clan. This scheme of Cleisthenes, with the artificial trittys and the artificially formed tribe, might seem almost too artificial to last. The secret of its permanence lay in the fact that the demes, the units on which it was built up, were natural divisions, which he did not attempt to reduce to a round number.

It must have taken some time to bring this reform into full working order. The first list of demesmen on the new system decided the deme of all their descendants. A man might change his home and reside in another deme, but he still remained a member of the deme to which he originally belonged. Henceforward in official documents men were distinguished by their demes instead of, as heretofore, by their fathers' names.[10] All Attica was included in this system except Eleutherae and Oropus on the frontier, which were treated as subject districts and belonged to no tribe.

Close connexion of this organisation with the Council. New council of Five Hundred and One. (460 B.C.)

The political purpose and significance of this reorganisation, which entitles its author to be called the second founder of the democracy, lay in its connexion with a reformed Council. As the existing Council of Four Hundred had been based on the four Ionic tribes, Cleisthenes devised a Council of Five Hundred based on his ten new tribes. Each tribe contributed fifty members, of which each deme returned a fixed number, according to its size. They were probably appointed by lot from a number of candidates chosen by each deme; but the preliminary election was afterwards abolished, and forty years later they were appointed entirely by lot. All those on whom the lot fell were proved, as to the integrity of their private and public life, by the outgoing Council, which had the right of rejecting the unfit. They took an oath when they entered upon office that they would "advise what is best for the city"; and they were responsible for their acts, when they laid it down.

(1) Administrative functions.

This Council, in which every part of Attica was represented, was the supreme administrative authority in the state. "In conjunction with the various magistrates it managed most of the public affairs." An effective control was exerted on the archons and other magistrates, who were obliged to present reports to the Council and receive the Council's orders. All the finances of the state were practically in its hands, and ten new finance officers called *apodektai* (one from each tribe) acted under its direction. It seems, moreover, from the very first to have been invested with judicial powers in matters concerning the public finance, and with the right of fining

[10] At a later period it became customary to give the father's name as well as the deme.

officials. Further, the Council acted as a ministry of public works, and even as a ministry of war. It may also be regarded as the ministry of foreign affairs, for it conducted negotiations with foreign states, and received their envoys. It had no powers of declaring war or concluding a treaty; these powers resided solely in the sovereign Assembly. But the Council was not only an administrative body, it was a deliberative assembly, and had the initiative in all lawmaking. No proposal could come before the Ecclesia unless it had already been proposed and considered in the Council. Every law passed in the Ecclesia was first sent down from the Council in the form of a *probuleuma*, and, on receiving a majority of votes in the Ecclesia, became a *psephisma*. Again, the Council had some general as well as some special judicial functions. It formed a court before which impeachments could be brought, as well as before the Assembly, and in these cases it could either pass sentence itself or hand them over to another court.

(2) Deliberative functions.

(3) Judicial functions. (εἰσαγγελίαι.)

It is obvious that the administrative duties could not conveniently be conducted by a body of five hundred constantly sitting. Accordingly the year of 360 days was divided into ten parts, and the councillors of each tribe took it in turn to act as a committee for carrying on public business during a tenth of the year.[11] In this capacity, as members of the acting committee of fifty, the councillors were called *Prytaneis* or presidents, the tribe to which they belonged was said to be the *presiding*, and the divisions of this artificial year were called *prytanies*. It was incumbent on the chairman, along with one trittys, of the committee, to live permanently during his prytany in the Tholos, a round building, where the presidents met and dined at the public expense. The Tholos or Skias was on the south side of the Agora, close to the Council-hall. The old prytaneion still remained in use as the office of the archon and the hearth of the city.

The Prytaneis and the civil year.

Epistates

Cleisthenes invented an ingenious arrangement for bringing his official year into general harmony with the civil year, so that the beginning of the one should not diverge too far from the beginning of the other. The civil year was supposed to begin as nearly as possible to the first new moon after the summer solstice; and the difference between the lunar twelvemonth and the solar revolution was provided for by a cycle of eight years, in the first, third, and sixth of which additional months were intercalated. The ordinary year

The Cleisthenic cycle, and the adjustment of the official and the civil years.

[11] At the same time some changes must have been made in the organisation of the Ecclesia, but we do not know what they were. As we find it working in later times, the Assembly met four times regularly in each prytany, and, when necessary, extraordinary meetings were held.

consisted of 354, the intercalated of 384 days. Cleisthenes, taking 360 as the number of days in his official year, was also obliged to intercalate, but not so often. He adopted a cycle of five years, and once in each cycle an intercalary month of 30 days was introduced. But this month was not always inserted in the same year of the cycle. It was here that Cleisthenes brought his quinquennial into line with the octennial system. The extraordinary official month was intercalated in the first year of the official cycle that coincided with an intercalary year of the civil cycle. The new institution of Cleisthenes began to work in 503-2 B.C.—the first year of an octennial cycle. The first Cleisthenic year began on the 1st of Hecatombaeon, the first month of the civil calendar; it would not begin on that day again till forty years hence.[12]

In opening the citizenship to a large number of people who had hitherto been excluded, Cleisthenes was only progressing along the path of Solon. He seems to have retained the Solonian restrictions on elegibility for the higher offices of state. It is just possible that he may have set the knights, in this respect, on a level with the Pentacosiomedimni; but the two lower classes were still excluded from the archonship; the third class remained ineligible for another half-century.[13] But this conservatism of Cleisthenes might be easily misjudged. We must remember that since the days of Solon time itself had been doing the work of a democratic reformer. The money value of five hundred medimni was a much lower rating at the end than it had been at the beginning of the sixth century. Trade had increased and people had grown richer.

[Till 458-7 B.C.]

Military reforms.

The new tribes of Cleisthenes led to a change in the military organisation. Each of the ten tribes was required to supply a regiment of hoplites and a squadron of horsemen; and the hoplites were commanded by ten generals [14] whom the people elected from each tribe. The office of general was destined hereafter to become the most important in the state; but at first he was merely the commander of the tribal regiment.

Ten generals.

The Council a popular representative body.

The Athenian Council instituted by Cleisthenes shows that Greek statesmen understood the principle of representative government. That Council is an excellent example of representation with a careful distribution of seats according to the size of the electorates;

---

[12] It is convenient to observe that the first year of a Cleisthenic quinquennium begins always in a year B.C. ending in 3 or 8 (503, 498, 493 B.C., etc.).

[13] In the appointment of archons the Solonian method had been discontinued (above, p. 186), and Cleisthenes does not seem to have reintroduced it.

[14] The office of stratêgos, as commander of a τάξις, was much older; but the institution of the ten statêgoi (501 B.C.) was a consequence of the reforms of Cleisthenes.

and it was practically the governing body of the state. But though Greek statesmen understood the principle, they always hesitated to entrust to a representative assembly sovereign powers of legislation. The reason mainly lay in the fact that, owing to the small size of the city-state, an Assembly which every citizen who chose could attend was a practicable institution; and the fundamental principle, that supreme legislative power is exercised by the people itself, could be literally applied. But while we remember that the Council could not legislate, although its co-operation was indispensable to the making of laws, we may say that its function will be misunderstood if it be either conceived as a sort of Second Chamber or compared to a body like the Roman Senate. It was a popular representative assembly, and from it were taken (though on a totally different principle) committees which performed in part the administrative functions of our "Government." It had a decisive influence on legislation; and here the influence of the Council on the Ecclesia must be rather compared to the influence of the Government on our House of Commons. But the ratification given by the Assembly to the proposals sent down by the Council was often as purely formal as the ratification by the Crown of bills passed in Parliament.

SECT. 7. FIRST VICTORIES OF THE DEMOCRACY

The Athenian republic had now become a democracy in the fullest sense, and the new government was hardly established before it was called upon to prove its capacity. King Cleomenes, who was the greatest man in Greece at the time, could not rest without attempting to avenge the humiliation which he had recently endured at the hands of the Athenian people. The man who had pulled down one tyrant now proposed to set up another. Isagoras, who had hitherto aimed at establishing an oligarchy, now, it would seem, came forward as an aspirant to the tyrannis. Cleomenes arranged with the Boeotians and the Chalcidians a joint attack upon Attica. While the Lacedaemonians and their allies invaded from the south, the Boeotians were to come down from Mount Cithaeron, and the men of Chalcis were to cross the Euripus; the land was to be assailed on three sides at the same moment.

The Peloponnesian host under the two kings, Cleomenes and Demaratus, passed the isthmus and occupied Eleusis; and the Athenians marched to the Eleusinian plain. But the peril on this side passed away without a blow. The Corinthians, on second thoughts, disapproved of the expedition, as unjust, and returned to Corinth. At this time Aegina was the most formidable commercial rival of Corinth, and it therefore suited Corinthian interests to

506 B.C.: the Peloponnesians invade Attica,

encourage the rising power of Aegina's enemy. This action of the Corinthians disconcerted the whole army, and the situation was aggravated by the discord between the Spartan leaders, Cleomenes **and retire.** and Demaratus. In the end the army broke up, and there was nothing left for Cleomenes but to return home. His attempt to thrust a tyranny had been as unsuccessful as his previous attempt to thrust an oligarchy upon Athens. For the second time the Athenian democracy had been saved from Spartan coercion. A hundred years hence, indeed, that coercion was to befall her; **(404 B.C.)** Cleomenes is the forerunner of Lysander, who will amply avenge him.

Plataea supported by Athens against Thebes. The Theban leaders of Boeotia had readily concurred in the Spartan plan, for they had a recent cause of offence against Athens. The town of Plataea, on the Boeotian slope of Mount Cithaeron, was determined to retain her independence and hold aloof from the Boeotian league, which was under the supremacy of Thebes. The Plataeans applied in the first instance to Sparta; but as Sparta was **510 9 B.C.** unwilling to interfere, they sought and obtained the help of Athens. This was the beginning of a long friendship between Athens and Plataea, based on mutual interest. Plataea depended on the support of Athens to maintain her independence in Boeotia; while it suited Athens to have a small friendly power on the other side of Cithaeron—a sort of watch-tower against Thebes. The Athenians went to the protection of Plataea, but the threatened conflict was averted by **Hysiae becomes Athenian.** the intervention of Corinth. The Corinthian arbitration ruled that Boeotian cities which did not wish to join the league must not be coerced. But, as they were departing, the Athenians were treacherously attacked by the Thebans, and, winning a victory, they fixed the river Asopus as the southern boundary of the territory of Thebes. The Athenians acquired, by this expedition, a post in Boeotia itself—the town of Hysiae, on the northern slope of Cithaeron.

Athenians defeat the Boeotians (506 B.C.). On the approach of the Peloponnesian army, the Boeotians had seized Hysiae, and crossing the pass of Cithaeron above it had taken Oenoe on the upper Attic slopes. When Cleomenes and the Peloponnesians retreated, the Athenian army marched northward to check the knights of Chalcis who were ravaging the northern demes of Attica. The Boeotian forces then withdrew into their own land and moved northwards too, in order to join the Chalcidians. But the Athenians, who must have been generalled by an able polemarch, succeeded in encountering their two foes singly. They intercepted the Boeotians near the straits and won a complete victory. Then they crossed the straits, for the Chalcidians had retired to their island, and fought another battle, no less decisive, with the horsemen of Chalcis. The defeat of the Chalcidians was so crushing that they were forced to cede to Athens a large part of that rich Lelantine plain whose possession in old days they had disputed so hotly with Eretria. But this was not all. A multitude of Chalcidians and Boeotians had been made prisoners; they were kept fettered in bitter bondage until their countrymen ransomed them at two minas a man. We cannot withhold our sympathy from the Athenian people if they dealt out hard measure to those whom the Spartan king had so unjustly stirred up against them. The "gloomy iron chains" in which "they quenched the insolence" of their foes were proudly preserved on the Acropolis, and with a tithe of the ransom they dedicated to Athena a bronze chariot.

A portico commemorative of this victory was set up within the sanctuary of Delphi. "The Athenians dedicated the portico, with the arms and figureheads which they took from their foes"—so runs the dedicatory inscription found in recent years on a step of the ruined building. It would appear from this that the Athenians captured and destroyed the ships of Chalcis. If the victory had been some twenty years later, Athens would have added them to her own fleet; but she had not yet come to discern that her true element was the sea.

The democracy had not only brilliantly defended itself, but had won a new territory. The richest part of the Chalcidian plain was divided into lots among two thousand Athenian citizens, who transported their homes to the fertile region beyond the straits—probably under the same conditions as the cleruchs of Salamis.

These outsettlers retained all their rights as citizens; they remained members of their demes and tribes. The Salaminians were so near Athens that it was easier for them than for most of the inhabitants of Attica to attend a meeting of the Ecclesia; and the plain of Chalcis was not farther than Sunium from Athens.

And not only beyond the sea was new territory acquired, but on the borders of Attica itself. This at least is the only occasion to which we can well assign the annexation of the march district of Oropus, the land of the people who gave to the Hellenic race its European name. It had come under the sway of Eretria, had adopted the Eretrian dialect which it was to retain throughout all future vicissitudes, and was the last part of Boeotia to be annexed by the Boeotian power of Thebes. This fertile little plain was destined to be a constant subject of discord between Boeotia and Athens, as it had before been a source of strife between Eretria and Boeotia; but it was now to remain subject to Athens for nearly a hundred years. Subject to Athens, not Athenian; the men of Oropus, like the men of Eleutherae, never became Athenian citizens.

and the Chalcidians.

(£8.)

Stoa at Delphi.

Cleruchies of Chalcis.

Acquisition of Oropus (which remains under Athens till 412 B.C.). The land of the Graes (see above, p. 153): under Eretria till some date subsequent to Lelantine war, then annexed to Boeotia.

CHAPTER VI

THE ADVANCE OF PERSIA TO THE AEGEAN

Sect. 1. The Rise of Persia and the Fall of the Lydian Kingdom

WHILE the Greeks were sailing their own seas, and working out in their city-states the institutions of law and freedom, untroubled by any catastrope beyond the shores of the Mediterranean, great despotic kingdoms were waxing and waning in the east. In the seventh century, the mighty empire of Assyria was verging to its end; the power destined to overthrow it had arisen. But the story of Assyria lies outside the story of Greece, since the Greeks, except in one outlying corner, came into no immediate contact with the lords of Nineveh. The Greek, as well as the Phoenician, communities of Cyprus were involved in the fortunes of the Syrian coastland. When in the last quarter of the eighth century Sargon, under whose sceptre Assyria reached the summit of her power, had conquered the lands of the sea-coast—the Phoenicians and the Philistines—seven kings who lived "at a distance of seven days in the middle of the western sea" trembled before him and offered their submission. They were the kings of Yatnan, as the Assyrians called Cyprus, and their act of fealty is recorded for us by Sargon himself on a pillar which he set up "in a valley of the land of Yatnan." Among the monarchs who submitted there were doubtless Greeks as well as Phoenicians, and a generation later we have the names of ten Cypriote kings who were subject to Assarhaddon and to Assurbanipal—Assarhaddon the great conqueror who voluntarily abdicated his throne, and Assurbanipal the peaceful sovereign, whom the Greeks remembered as Sardanapalus. Among the names of the vassals whom inscriptions of these two kings enumerate are those of Eteandros of Paphos and Pylagoras of Cition.[1] But if the story of Assyria touches only a remote fringe of the Hellenic world, it is otherwise with the story of those who destroyed the Assyrian empire. The Medes and Persians, folks of Aryan speech like the

[1] The other eight are the kings of Idalion, Salamis, Soli, Curion, Tamassus, a Cypriote Carthage (Kartihadaasti), Ledron (near Leucosia), and Nurii(?).

Greeks, were marked out by destiny to be the adversaries of the Greeks throughout the two chief centuries of Grecian history.

The land of Media lies east of Assyria. Its ancient history is shrouded in mist; but there are some reasons for guessing that in the second millennium it was part of a great Aryan kingdom which stretched far north-eastwards over the plains of Bactria, peopled by the Iranian branch, as it is called, of the Aryan stock. The Iranians worshipped the same gods of heaven and light as the other folks of their kindred; but their sun-worship developed into a very different shape from the religion of Zeus. They regarded the element of fire with deeper reverence than other sun-worshippers; they dreaded to pollute it by the touch of a dead body or the overflow of boiling water; their land was full of temples with altars of perpetual fire. But the religion of the fire-worshippers had been moulded into an almost philosophical form by their prophet Zoroaster, who, though his name is encompassed with legend and it is uncertain when he lived, was assuredly a real man and not a creation of myth. He diffused among the Iranians the doctrine that the world is the perpetual scene of a deadly strife between the powers of light and darkness, between Ormuzd, the Great Lord, and Ahriman, the principle of evil.

The
Medes.

It was towards the end of the eighth century that the Medes rebelled against the yoke of Assyria. They were led by Deioces, and after a struggle Media gained her independence, and the deliverer was elected king by the free vote of his people. He had not only freed but had united his countrymen, and he set the seal on the union of Media by building the great city of Ecbatana. His treasury and palace were in the centre of a fortress girdled by seven walls; and he is said to have lived in this stronghold, withdrawn from the sight of his people, who could approach him only by written petitions.

Deioces
(Da-
yaukku)
founds
kingdom
of Media,
c. 700 B.C.

The first successors of Deioces had enough to do in resisting the efforts of Assyria to recover her power over Media. But presently a king arose who was strong enough to extend his sway beyond the borders of his own land. Phraortes conquered the hilly land of Persia in the south; and thus a large Aryan realm was formed stretching from the Caspian to the Persian Gulf, east of Assyria and Babylonia. The next step was to conquer Assyria itself; and Cyaxares, the successor of Phraortes, prepared for the enterprise by a new organisation of the Median army. It was no hopeless task, for the Assyrian empire had been breaking up. Egypt had thrown off the yoke of the kings of Nineveh; and Nabopolassar had just arisen to do for Babylonia what Deioces had done for Media. Nabo-

Phraortes
(c. 650-25
B.C.) con-
quers
Persia.

New
kingdom
of Baby-
lonia.

Nabo-
polassar,
525-605.
Fall of
Assyrian
kingdom,
612.
Baby-
lonia
under
Nebucad-
nezar,
604-562
B.C.

polassar and Cyaxares joined hands; and the united forces of Media and Babylonia defeated the Assyrian army. The conquerors divided the empire. The south-western portion up to the borders of Egypt went to Babylonia; Assyria itself and the lands stretching westward into Asia Minor were annexed to Media.

The restored kingdom of Babylonia, under Nebucadnezar, the successor of its founder, rose into wonderful fame and brilliance. He drove the Egyptians out of Syria, smiting them in the great battle of Carchemish; he stormed Jerusalem and carried the Jews into captivity; he made Tyre on its rock tremble though he failed to take it; he invaded and overran Egypt. But more famous than his conquests abroad were his mighty works in his own land. He made Babylon the greatest city in the world; and the stray Greeks who visited it came back with amazing stories of the palaces and temples, and the "hanging gardens," a terraced park which was constructed by Nebucadnezar, though report ascribed it to the mythical queen Semiramis. But the gigantic walls which girt the city were the mightiest monument of Nebucadnezar; Greek travellers said that the circuit was more than fifty miles. It seems certain that few men have done more than this lord of Babylon to increase the sum of human misery, if we imagine the lives of countless thralls forced under the pitiless lash to spend their flesh and blood in unceasing and unsparing labour. Nebucadnezar went down to his grave, full of honours, after a long reign. He knew well on what side danger was to be feared for his kingdom. One of his works of fortification was a wall from the Tigris to the Euphrates, north of Babylon, to defend Babylonia against Media, her northern neighbour.

The exploits of the great Babylonian king affected Greece little.[2] The Greeks of Cyprus must have caught the echoes of the clash of arms at Carchemish; they must have been stirred by the tidings of the storming of Jerusalem and excited by the siege of Tyre. But the changes which had befallen the east were brought nearer to the ken of Greece by the advance of Media. Cyaxares drew under his power the eastern parts of Asia Minor as far as the banks of the Halys, and this river became the boundary between Media and Lydia. The conquest of Lydia was the next aim in the expansion of the Median power, and a pretext was found for declaring war. In the sixth year of the war a battle was fought, but in the midst of the combat the day was turned suddenly to night; and the darkening of the sun made such a deep impression on the minds of the combatants that they laid down their arms and a peace was concluded. But the solar obscuration of this May day has another association which has

War of
Lydia and
Media:
battle;
eclipse
of sun,
May 28,
585 B.C.,

[2] Greek mercenaries, indeed, took service under him.

a deeper interest for Europe than the warfare of Lydian and Mede. It was the first eclipse of which European science foretold when it should betide. Thales of Miletus, the father of Greek, and thereby of European, philosophy and science, had studied astronomy in Egypt; and he was able to warn the Ionians that before such a year had passed—his lore could not tell the day or the hour—the sun would be darkened. Thales was not only the first man of science; he was also the first philosopher: science and philosophy were not yet separated. If he looks over the ages to Copernicus, Newton, and Laplace, he looks likewise to Descartes, Berkeley, and Kant. He sought for a common substance, a single principle which should explain the variety of nature and reduce the world to unity and system; it is a small matter that he found this principle in water;[3] it is his eternal merit to have sought it.

predicted by Thales

Beginnings of Greek science and philosophy.

The Lydian king Alyattes wedded his daughter to Astyages, who succeeded to the throne of Media, and the kingdom of Lydia was saved for a generation, to enjoy the most brilliant period of its history. When Lydia recovered from the Cimmerian invasion, king Ardys renewed the efforts of Gyges to reduce the Greek cities of the coast. His chief success seems to have been the capture of Priene. His successors, Sadyattes and Alyattes, carried on a weary war against Miletus. They harried the Milesian territory every year, destroying the corn crops, and defeated the Milesians in two battles; but the strong walls of the coast-city defied them, as they had no fleet. At length Alyattes made peace with Miletus; possibly it was the outbreak of the war with Media that forced him to this step. At all events, he seems to have behaved liberally to his foes. He built two temples to Athena in the place of one which had been burned down when he was devastating the Milesian land. This act of reparation was quite in accordance with the reverence for the gods of Greece which the Lydian monarchs invariably displayed. The story is that, when Alyattes fell ill and consulted Apollo at Delphi, the oracle enjoined upon him to restore the temple. Ionian Miletus was saved, but the famous Achaean city of Smyrna was not only captured but destroyed, and in this volume its name will occur no more. Alyattes also conquered Bithynia, and drove the remnant of the Cimmerians out of Asia. He might think that Lydia would now take rank with one of the great monarchies of the south or the east, and he built himself an enormous sepulchre, an earth-mound on stone foundations, which in size at least might match the monuments of Egyptian or Babylonian kings.

Reign of Ardys in Lydia;

of Alyattes.

[3] Yet not so small. It was much to have fixed on fluid substance, and rejected the vulgar fallacy of ascribing to hardness a greater reality.

212   A HISTORY OF GREECE

Reign of
Croesus,
560-546
B.C.

It was reserved for Croesus, the son of Alyattes, to carry out fully the design of subjugating the cities of Eastern Greece. He attacked and subdued the cities, Ionian and Aeolian, one after another, all except Miletus, whose treaty with his father he respected, while Miletus on her part saved her freedom by withholding all help from her sister cities. The Dorian states of Caria were also forced to submit, and the empire of Croesus extended from the Halys to the Aegean. We saw before that Lydia exercised a distinct influence on the Greeks of Asia, but perhaps their influence upon her was even greater. The Greek language spread in Lydia, and we may suspect that it was heard in Sardis as much as the native idiom; the Greek gods were revered; the Greek oracles were appealed to. The kings were benefactors of Hellenic sanctuaries. In the new temple of Artemis, which arose at Ephesus during his reign, Croesus was the donor of the sculptured reliefs which encircled the Ionic pillars, and fragments of the three words, which recorded the gift "Dedicated by King Croesus," can still be read on the bases of the columns. Hence the Greeks never regarded the Lydians as utter barbarians; and they always cherished a curious indulgence and sympathy for Croesus, though he had enslaved and ruled as despot the cities of Asiatic Hellas. The court of Sardis was in truth more oriental than Hellenic, not only in wealth and luxury, but also in its customs, for instance, polygamy and the infliction of cruel punishments. Croesus carded alive a man who had opposed his succession to the throne. The Ionians had marvelled at the treasures of golden Gyges, but the untold wealth of Croesus became proverbial. It was furnished largely by the tributes of the Greek cities, as well as by the white gold of the Pactolus and the products of the mines of Pergamon. Croesus was the first to introduce, instead of the white gold money, a coinage of two metals, pure gold and silver, bearing to each other the fixed proportion of 3 to 40.

Croesus
and
Delphi.

There is no more striking proof of the political importance of the oracle of Delphi at this period than the golden offerings dedicated by Croesus, offerings richer than even the priestly avarice of the Delphians could have dared to hope for. Wealthy though the lord of Lydia was, genuine as was his faith in the inspiration of the oracle, he might hardly have sent such gifts if he had not wished to secure the political support of Apollo and believed that Apollo's support was worth securing. His object was to naturalise himself as a member of the Greek world; to appear, not as an outsider, but as an adopted son of Hellas, ruling over the Greeks whom he had subdued and those whom he still hoped to subdue. Nothing would be more helpful than the good word of the Delphic oracle to compass such a reputation. Moreover, if one of the Asiatic cities contemplated rebellion, a discouraging reply from the oracle, which would assuredly be consulted, might stand the despot in good stead.

Having extended his sway to the coast, Croesus conceived the idea of making Lydia a sea-power and conquering the islands. It was a perfectly feasible plan; and it was not till unforeseen events had frustrated it that the islanders could have found much comfort in the epigram that a Lydian king sailing against them with a fleet would be like themselves advancing against Lydia with a host of cavalry. The tale afterwards shaped itself that one of the wise men of Greece—it mattered little whether he was alive at the time or not .—used this witticism to dissuade Croesus from the enterprise. But Croesus was diverted from his western designs by something graver than an epigram. Events of great moment were happening in the east. His brother-in-law Astyages was hurled from the throne of Media by a hero, who was to become one of the world's mightiest conquerors. The usurper was Cyrus the Great, of the Persian family of the Achaemenids. The revolution signified indeed little more than a change of dynasty; the Persians and Medes were peoples of the same race and the same faith; the realm remained Iranian as before. But the Persians seem to have been the noblest part of the Iranian race; their bravery, temperance, and love of truth extorted the admiration of the Greeks.

Fall of Median Dynasty.

Cyrus.

The fall of Astyages was an opportunity for the ambitious Lydian to turn his arms to the east. The restoration of his brother-in-law was indeed a sufficient plea; and he might have good cause to fear that if he were not the first to strike, the Persian usurper would soon advance to the conquest of Lesser Asia. But Croesus certainly cherished hopes of extending the Lydian power into the interior parts of Asia, if not of succeeding himself to the Median throne. In undertaking such an enterprise he had to fear his Greek subjects, who might take advantage of his absence to throw off his yoke, and might even intrigue with the Persian. That the Greeks of Ionia had been long accustomed to regard Media as a resort against Lydia and to intrigue with the Median kings is shown by the word *medism*. For if such intriguing had first come into fashion after the rise of Persia and the fall of Lydia, the name chosen to designate it would naturally have been *persism*. The preparations of Croesus for an expedition to the east were welcome news to the lands of the Aegean. Desirous of probing the hidden event of the future, he consulted some of the oracles of Greece. There can be no question that the Delphic god gave him an answer which was meant to encourage him in his enterprise. It is said that the answer was that

Policy of Delphi.

if he crossed the Halys he would destroy a mighty empire—an answer which need not have been that which was actually given, but may have been circulated afterwards to justify the oracle when the expedition failed. But it is the policy of the oracle, not its methods of evasion, which has historical significance. The spirit of Delphi was favourable to Hellenic freedom, and it saw in the proposed expedition the probability of a long war with Persia and a chance for the eastern Greeks of retaining their independence. It did not foresee the complete conquest of Lydia and the subjection of the Greeks to a power which was utterly barbarian. The oracle took the occasion, however, to bring about a union between Croesus and the Lacedaemonians, by bidding him seek the aid of the most powerful state of Greece. An alliance was concluded, but led to nothing, and Lacedaemon sent no help.

Croesus, at the head of an army which included a force of Ionian Greeks, crossed the fateful Halys and invaded Cappadocia. He took the ancient city of Pteria, and in its neighbourhood fought an indecisive battle with the host of Medes and Persians which Cyrus had led against him. But the host of Cyrus seems to have been far superior in numbers, and Croesus retired before him into Lydia. Under the walls of the capital the invader won a decisive victory, and after a short siege Sardis was stormed and plundered. The life of Croesus was spared. Cyrus had given strict injunctions that he was on no account to be slain in the struggle of the capture; and the story went that a soldier, not recognising him, was about to cut him down, when the king's son, who had been dumb from birth, suddenly burst out into speech: "O man, slay not Croesus."

Capture
of Sardis,
546 B.C.

This was not the only tale which adorned the fall of the Lydian king. The capture of Sardis was an eventuality of which no one had seriously thought. So great had been the wealth and might of Croesus, so dizzy the height of his power, that none deemed his overthrow possible; and the sheer and sudden fall into nothingness made perhaps a deeper and more abiding impression on the imagination of Hellas than any other historical event. It was the most illustrious example that the Greeks had ever witnessed of their favourite doctrine that the gods visit with jealousy men who enjoy too great prosperity. And the personality of Croesus himself crept into their sympathies—the admirer of Hellenic art and wisdom, the adorer of Hellenic gods, the generous giver out of his abundant wealth. Never more than for the memory of Croesus did Greece put forth the power of that genius, which she possessed in such full measure, of weaving round an event of history tales which have a deep and touching import as lessons for the life of men.

Cyrus built a great pyre—so the story is told by Herodotus—and placed thereon Croesus bound in chains, with fourteen Lydian boys. And as Croesus was standing on the pile, in this extreme pass, there came into his mind a word which Solon had said to him, that no man could be called happy so long as he was alive. For the Athenian statesman had visited the court of Sardis in his travels—the art of the tale-weaver had no precise regard for the facts of time—and when he had seen the royal treasures and the greatness of the king-

Story of Croesus and Solon.

Fig. 46.—Croesus on the pyre (Attic vase).

dom Croesus asked him whom he deemed the happiest of men. Solon named some obscure Greeks who were dead; and when the king, unable to hide his wonder and vexation, exclaimed, "Is our royal fortune so poor, O Athenian stranger, that you set private men before me?" the wise Greek had discoursed on the uncertainty of life and the jealousy of the gods. Then Croesus, remembering this, groaned aloud and called thrice on the name of Solon. But Cyrus heard him call, and bade the interpreters ask him on whom he was calling. For a while Croesus would not speak, then he said: "One whom I would that all tyrants might meet and converse with." Pressed further he named Solon the Athenian, and repeated the wise man's words. The pyre was already alight, but when Cyrus heard the answer of his prisoner he reflected that he too was a man, and he commanded that the fire should be quenched and the victims set free. The flames were already blazing so strong and high that the men could not quench them. Then Croesus cried to Apollo for help, and the god sent clouds into the clear sky, and a tempestuous shower of rain extinguished the fire.

The story of the fate of Croesus, as told by Bacchylides.

Such is the tale as we read it in the history of Herodotus, who may have heard it at Athens. But we can almost see the story in the making. For, before the episode of Solon was woven in, the fate of Croesus had been wrought into a legend; this legend is related in a poem of Bacchylides. When the day of doom surprised the king, "he would not abide to endure the bitterness of bondage, but he raised a pyre before the palace court, and gat him up thereon with his wife and his weeping daughters. He bade the slippered thrall kindle the timber building; the maidens screamed, and stretched their arms to their mother. But as the might of the fire was springing through the wood, Zeus set a sable cloud above it and quenched the yellow flame. Then Apollo bore the old man with his daughters to the land of the Hyperboreans, to be his abiding place, for his piety's sake, because his gifts to Pytho were greater than all men's gifts." The moral of the tale clearly was, Bring gifts to Delphi; and we can hardly doubt that it originated under Delphic influence. But in the city of Solon it was transformed by a touch of genius into one of the great stories of the world.

Fate of Croesus.

As for Croesus it is certain that his life was spared, and it is possible that he spent his remaining days in Media, unconscious that a mythical association with the famous Athenian lawgiver would be his best assured claim on the memory of future ages.

SEC. 2. THE PERSIAN CONQUEST OF ASIATIC GREECE

The kingdom of Lydia had performed a certain function in the development of Greece. Besides the invention of coinage, which was its one great contribution to the civilisation of mankind; besides the influence which its luxury and "tyranny" exercised on Ionia; the mere existence of the Lydian realm, in its intermediate position between Greece and the east, was of considerable importance as a bulwark against the great oriental empires. It kept Greece from coming into direct contact with the empire of Assyria; it kept

Greece for sixty years from coming into direct contact with the empire of Media. When the barrier is swept away, a new period is opened in Grecian history. The Greeks now stand face to face with the power of a monarch whose dominion stretches far away beyond the Euphrates, beyond the Tigris, into lands which are totally unknown to them. The Asiatic Greeks are now to exchange subjection to a lord of Sardis for subjection to a potentate who holds his court in a city so distant that the length of the journey is told by months. This distance of the centre from the extremities of the empire was of the utmost significance. The king was obliged to leave his conquests in Asia Minor to the government of his satraps; and the Greeks were unable to exercise any influence upon him, as they might have done if he had ruled from Sardis or some nearer capital. This was all the more unfortunate, on account of another difference which distinguished the Persian from the Lydian kingdom. While the Lydians were outside the Aryan family, the Persians and Medes spoke a language of the same stock as that of the Greeks. It may be thought that if the Persians had come under Greek influence, Iranian history would have taken a different course. For the Persians were a people marked out to fall under the influence of others and not to hew an independent path for themselves. In their own highlands, like the Spartans in the Laconian vale, they might live unspotted from the world, a valiant, simple, and truthful race; but when they once went forth to conquer and to rule, it was their inevitable doom to be led captive by their captives and to adopt the manners and ideals of more intellectual and original peoples. If Cyrus had transported the centre of his empire to the west, the Greeks might have been the teachers of their Persian speech-fellows; but such an idea would have occurred to no Mede or Persian. Consequently the new Iranian kingdom fell under the relaxing influences of the corrupt Semitic civilisations of Babylonia and Assyria; and it had soon become a despotism so typically oriental that it is hard to remember that the ruling peoples spoke a tongue akin to the Greek. Hence the struggle of two hundred years, upon which we are now entering, between Greece and Persia, though strictly and literally it was a struggle between Aryan peoples,—peoples, that is, of Aryan speech,— assumes the larger character of strife between Europe and Asia, between east and west, between Aryan and non-Aryan; and takes its place as the first encounter in that still unclosed debate which has arrayed Europe successively against Babylonian, Phoenician, Saracen, and Turk.

At the beginning of the campaign against Lydia, Cyrus had

Disunion
of Ionia.

invited the Ionians who were in the army of Croesus to change sides. They had refused to "medize," not perhaps from loyalty to the rule of the Lydian, under which they chafed, but because they did not anticipate his utter overthrow and therefore feared his vengeance. This refusal annoyed Cyrus; and when, after the fall of Sardis, the Greek cities made overtures to the conqueror, he declined to make any conditions. Only with Miletus, which had not been subject to Lydia and had stood aloof from the contest, did he conclude a sort of treaty like that in which Croesus had recognised her independence. The others prepared to defend themselves. Cyrus himself had greater projects which recalled him to the far east; and he committed the lesser task of reducing the Asiatic Greeks to the lieutenants whom he left in Lydia. The want of unity among the Ionians was disastrous. They might meet in their Panionic assembly, but they seem to have been without the ability or the organisation to carry out any plan of common action. The most powerful of all the states, Miletus had gone her own path and stood quite apart. One of her citizens, Thales, the astronomer and philosopher, whom we have met before, is said to have ventured himself into the speculations of political, as well as of celestial, science. He saw the weakness of Ionia in its disunion, and the futility of the loose league of the Panionion; and he made the remarkable proposal that Ionia should form itself into an united nation, with one Hall of Council as well as one place of Assembly, each city surrendering her sovereignty and becoming merely a town or deme of the state; and he suggested Teos as the fitting place for the capital. The idea, whether it was put forward by Thales or not, was assuredly suggested by the political development of Attica, the mother country of the Ionians. It was an idea which the proposer can hardly have hoped to persuade the Ionians to adopt, but it had its value as a comment on the disunion of the Greeks in the one part of Greece where, above all others, there was needed a closer unity and a solid serried front, to resist the aggression of the great barbarian powers. Another proposal, which was made in one of the ineffectual meetings of the Panionion, receives the approval of the historian Herodotus. Bias, a statesman of Priene, advised all the Ionians to sail forth together to the west, to the great island of Sardinia, and there found an Ionian city-state, and live happy and free. This proposal illustrates the terror and despair of Ionia at the prospect of Persian rule.

Persian conquest of Greeks of Asia.

Disunited, the Asiatic Greeks were an easy prey. Harpagus, the general of Cyrus, reduced them one after another; tribute was imposed upon them and the burden of serving in the Persian armies, when such service was required; but no restrictions were placed upon the freedom of their commerce. To the inhabitants of two cities, exile seemed more endurable than this new slavery and they acted in the spirit of Bias. The people of Phocaea, or the most part of them, embarked in their penteconters and sailed to the island of Corsica, where their own settlement of Alalia received them. The Teians did likewise, but found a nearer home on the coast of Thrace, where they founded Abdera.

One common effort indeed the Aeolians and Ionians made for their defence. They made a common appeal to the most powerful state in the mother country. They sent an embassy to Lacedaemon, but the Spartans, whose horizon was bounded by the Peloponnesus, did as little for them as they had done for Croesus. Sparta had the curiosity, however, to send a ship to Ionia, to spy out the condition of the country and the power of Cyrus. The story is that one of her reconnoitrers went up to Sardis and standing before the Persian king forbade him to work harm to any Greek community, "since the Lacedaemonians will not permit it." The anecdote was doubtless invented by those who liked a jest at the expense of Sparta; but, if Cyrus might well ask "who are the Lacedaemonians?" his successors learned the answer to their cost.

Asiatic Greeks appeal to Sparta.

The conqueror of Lydia returned to the east to subdue the mightier power of Babylon. The conquest occupied some years; then the greatest city on earth was taken; and Cyrus took to himself the title of "king of Babel, Sumer, and Accad, and of the four quarters of the world," thus formally entering into the Babylonian inheritance. The dominion of Cyrus the Great extended in the east over Armenia and Hyrcania, Parthia and Bactria, and into the midst of Afghanistan; from the coasts of the Aegean to the banks of the Jaxartes. But his conquests lie outside our history. His last enterprise was the subjugation of the Massagetae, a Scythian folk near the Aral lake, and one story says that he was slain in battle against them, and that the savage queen placed his head in a basin of blood. All we know with certainty is that his body was buried in Persia, and two hundred years hence we shall visit his tomb at Pasargadae, in the company of a conqueror who was mightier even than he.

Fall of Babylon, 538.

Death of Cyrus.

SECT. 3. PERSIAN CONQUEST OF EGYPT. POLYCRATES OF SAMOS

The subjugation of Lydia and the Greek sea-board carried the borders of the Iranian empire, under its new dynasty, farther westward than the Assyrian conquest had ever reached. Two lords of

Sardis had indeed acknowledged the overlordship of the kings of Nineveh; but that relation had been of brief duration and slight significance, and Lydia can hardly be said to have ever formed a part of the Assyrian dominion. In subduing the Greeks of the coast, at all events, Cyrus broke entirely new ground; they had never paid submission in any shape to Assyria. But while he far outpassed the utmost limits of Assyria in some directions, he left unconquered the great kingdom of the south, which had once been part of the Assyrian empire. But his son Cambyses repaired the omission; it was inevitable that the new lords of Syria should seek to bring Egypt under their subjection. We saw how Egypt, like Media itself and Babylonia, threw off the Assyrian yoke and entered upon a new period of national prosperity under enlightened rulers. King Amasis who climbed the throne by a revolution maintained his power by a bodyguard of Ionian and Carian mercenaries, like a Greek tyrant. An Egyptian writing tells us how he loved the strong "wine of Kelebi of Egypt." He built great temples to the Egyptian gods like the Pharaohs of old; but in his patronage of Greece he may be compared to Croesus. He sent gifts to the Greek sanctuaries; he subscribed generously to the rebuilding of the temple at Delphi; he married a Greek princess of Cyrene; under him Naucratis rose to the rank of a city, though the only city where Greeks were allowed to trade. He had extended his sway over the island of Cyprus when the power of Babylonia was declining; but the Cypriots threw off his yoke when Cyrus entered into the Babylonian heritage, and made their submission to the Persian. Amasis trembled at the rise of the new power in the east, and he lived to witness with dismay the preparations of Cambyses; but he died a few months before the invasion, and the blow fell upon his son, Psammetichus. A fierce battle near Pelusium delivered Egypt into the hands of the Persians. The conqueror led his army up the Nile, and perhaps he extended the southern frontier of the Egyptian kingdom on the side of Nubia. The Egyptians said that he planned the conquest of all Ethiopia and was compelled to return through want of provisions, so that his enterprise came to nothing. But the Egyptians hated Cambyses, who openly scoffed at their religion; and it is possible that they may have represented as an inglorious failure what was really a successful effort to secure the southern frontier. The conquest of Egypt, which became a Persian satrapy, led to the submission of Greek Cyrene, even as the conquest of Lydia had led to the subjection of the Greeks of the neighbouring coasts.

Amasis and his son might have hoped, when the Persian danger threatened, that they could depend on the support of a powerful

Persian conquest of Egypt by Cambyses.

Amasis (Aahmes), 569 B.C.;

a phil-Hellene.

Naucratis.

Death of Amasis, 525 B.C.

(Psammetichus III.) Battle of Pelusium, 525 B.C. Ethiopian expedition of Cambyses.

Voluntary submission of Cyrene.

Polycrates, tyrant of Samos.

Greek friend, the lord of Samos. In that island, not long after the Persian conquest of Ionia, a certain Polycrates and his two brothers had established a joint tyranny over the state, with the help of Lygdamis of Naxos. But Polycrates removed his brothers by death and banishment and became sole tyrant. He organised a fleet of a hundred pentecomters and made Samos a strong power; as the Ionian mainland had fallen under Persian dominion, he had perhaps the strongest Greek sea-power in the Aegean. His luxurious court was brightened by the presence of the Bacchic poet Anacreon. He completed the building of the great temple of Hera, but the most famous of his works was the aqueduct which supplied this city with water from a spring beyond a hill. The engineering skill of the Megarian architect Eupalinus—who perhaps also constructed the waterworks of Pisistratus at Athens—carried the duct through the hill by a tunnel. In all that he put his hand to, Polycrates prospered; he defied the power of Persia; he extended his influence over some of the Ionian cities under Persian sway; he hoped perhaps to become the lord of all Ionia. It was natural that he and Amasis of Egypt should form a close alliance, based on the common interest of antagonism to Persia. But when the hour of peril came, when Cambyses moved upon Egypt, the Samian tyrant altered his policy. He felt that his navy was unequal to coping with the joint armaments of Phoenicia and Cyprus, and, instead of coming to the aid of his old friend's son, he sent forty ships to increase the fleet of the invader. These ships, however, never reached Egypt. The tyrant had manned them with those Samians whom he most suspected of hating himself and his tyranny; but his trick recoiled. At the island of Carpathus the crew took the resolve of sailing back to Samos and overthrowing the despot. Defeated in a battle they sought the aid of Sparta, and their appeal was strongly backed by the Corinthians, whose trade probably suffered from the pirate ships of Polycrates. The Lacedaemonians sent an armament to besiege Samos; it was their first expedition to the east, and it was a failure. Despairing of taking the city, and repulsed in a conflict, they returned home.

We cannot charge Polycrates with perfidy in espousing the cause of Persia against Egypt, since we are ignorant of his relations, not only with Psammetichus, but with Amasis in the last years of that monarch's reign. We might indeed gather from the story of the ring of Polycrates, that the alliance had ceased to exist, and that it was Amasis who had broken it off. Amasis hearing of his friend's marvellous prosperity, never varied by a reverse, wrote him a letter, expressing misgivings at a good fortune so great

526 B.C.

Spartan
attack on
Samos.

Story of
the ring of
Poly-
crates.

and enduring that it could not fail to draw down the envy of heaven, and counselling Polycrates to cast away whatever possession it would give him the most pain to lose: "Cast it away utterly, out of the world." Polycrates, taking the words to heart, manned a penteconter, and having rowed out to sea, cast into the waves the most precious thing he had, an emerald ring engraved by the gemcutter Theodorus. A few days later a fisherman came to his house and presented him with a huge fish; the ring was found inside it. Polycrates wrote to Amasis an account of what had happened, and Amasis, when he read the letter, discerned that it was impossible for any man to deliver another from that which was destined to befall him. Convinced therefore that Polycrates would come to no good end, and not wishing to have to grieve for a friend's misfortune, Amasis broke off the tie of guest-friendship which bound them. The forecast of the Egyptian was fulfilled. Soon after his repulse of the Lacedaemonian attack, Polycrates fell into a trap laid for him by the Persian satrap of Sardis, and was seized and crucified.

Death of Polycrates, c. 523 B.C.

SECT. 4. IONIA UNDER DARIUS

Death of Cambyses, 522 B.C.

King Cambyses was recalled from Egypt by a rebellion. He had put to death, on suspicions of disloyalty, his brother Smerdis, to whom he had entrusted the regency of some of the eastern provinces; and a usurper had arisen, pretending to be the dead Smerdis, to whom he bore a remarkable likeness. Cambyses went in haste to crush the false Smerdis. But, as he passed through Syria, he "found death by his own hand," as is related in a great writing on the rock of Behistun. The next heir to the Persian throne was a certain Hystaspes, who was satrap of Parthia and had a son named Darius. But Hystaspes made no attempt to secure his right, and the false Smerdis established himself so firmly that, as Darius wrote afterwards in that famous inscription of the rock, "No Persian nor Mede dared to oppose him." But Darius had different thoughts from his father; and conspiring with six nobles he killed the usurper and became king himself. In the first years of his reign his force and ability were proved in the task of quelling rebellions which broke out in almost all parts of the wide realm which Cyrus had put together. Elam, Babylonia, Media, Armenia revolted; a new false Smerdis arose; Babylon had to be twice besieged. Having established his power firmly and crushed all resistance, Darius recorded for future ages the hardly won successes of his first years, in an inscription on the lofty rock of Behistun on

Accession of Darius (Dârajavahuš), 521 B.C.

(Babylon taken, (1) Feb. 520 B.C., (2) 519 B.C.) Inscrip-

the upper course of the river Choaspes. The writing is in the Persian, the Susic, and the Babylonian languages.

By wedding Atossa, the daughter of Cyrus and widow of her brother Cambyses, Darius linked himself closely to the family of his predecessors. He proceeded to reorganise the administration of his dominion. He extended the system of satrapies or governments, and the whole realm was divided into twenty such satrapies. West of the Halys, the old kingdom of Lydia consisted of three provinces, but subject to two satraps: the Ionian and the Lydian under one governor who resided at Sardis; the Phrygian which included the Greek cities of the Propontis under a governor whose seat was at Dascylion. These satraps did not interfere in the local affairs of the Greek cities, which were ruled by despots; and the despots might do much as they pleased, so long as they paid tribute duly and furnished military contingents when required. The despots liked the Persian rule which secured their power, and this explains the noteworthy fact that the Greeks of Asia Minor made no attempt to shake off the Persian yoke during the troubles which ushered in the reign of Darius. It is possible too that their condition under the rule of Cambyses was better than under Darius; for Darius is said to have instituted a fixed yearly tribute instead of irregular contributions. Commerce, however, was furthered by this king's monetary reforms, and by his improvement of the road-system in Persia. He adopted the bimetallic coinage which Croesus had introduced in Lydia; the chief piece of Persian gold money was always known in Greece by the name *daric*. The Royal Road, by which the messengers between Susa and Sardis came and went, was divided into stages marked off by regular stations. Its length was over 1500 miles, and the way was counted a three months' journey for a man on foot. A Greek who had to visit Susa would land at Ephesus, and in three days reach Sardis. The road ran through the heart of Phrygia, by the tomb of Midas the golden king, past Pessinus and Ancyra and across the Halys to Pteria the ancient Cappadocian city which Croesus took, then across the Halys again, southward to Mazaka and Comana, to cross the Taurus and reach the Euphrates at Samosata. Beyond the Euphrates, it skirted the mountains which bound Mesopotamia on the north, passing Nisibis and reaching the Tigris at Nineveh, the ruined capital of Assyria. Beyond Arbela, it went south-eastward to the river Choaspes and Susa. A good and safe road, carefully maintained, brought central Asia nearer to the Aegean, and helped to open the east to western curiosity. The construction of the Royal Road must have had an incalculable effect in widening Greek ideas of geography. Its influence is shown by the importance which it assumed on the first Greek maps. Conceived as a straight line running east and west, it plays on one of the maps which were used by Herodotus practically the same part which is played in the modern Atlas by the Equator. The longitudes were determined by the conception that the Nile and the Danube, the two greatest rivers known within the range of the Greek world, were in the same meridian—the Danube being supposed to flow from north to south. This meridian line passed through Sinope. It was a principle of the early Greek geographers who arose about the end of the sixth century in Ionia that the features of the earth were symmetrically arranged. The attempt to apply mathematical principles to a small portion of the earth, very imperfectly observed, necessarily produced maps which to our fuller knowledge appear grotesque. But it would be hard to overestimate the intellectual activity of the Ionian investigators who made the new departure, Anaximander and Hecataeus, both citizens of Miletus. Anaximander constructed the first map, and Hecataeus wrote a Geography which served as a "text to Anaximander's map." Hecataeus was himself a traveller—he composed the earliest guide-book to the wonders of Egypt; and he could supplement his own observations by second-hand material gathered, in the great centre of trade where his home was, from travellers and strangers. This development of geography in Ionia was certainly forwarded by the Royal Road, and so far the Persian conquest of eastern Greece was an advantage to European civilisation.

Europe owes so much to the Ionian intellects which at this period were breaking new paths of progress that we may linger a moment longer over the movement of intellectual discovery before resuming the march of events. It was a movement of the most interesting kind, in which the instinct for speculation and the thirst for positive knowledge were closely united. For Anaximander, the first chartographer, map-making is only part of his wider work as a physical philosopher. Dissatisfied with the theory of Thales who found the first principle of the universe in water, he sought it in a more general conception which he designated, negatively, as the "Unlimited"—unlimited, that is, by qualities, and so capable of differentiation into all the kinds of definite matter which our senses perceive. Hecataeus is the founder of Greek history. He partly breaks with the old traditions, and criticises the Hesiodic school of theology. The heroes who appeared in legend as sons of the gods he regards as the bastard sons of women who, to shield their shame, ascribed the fatherhood to Zeus or Apollo. "The stories of the

Greeks," he says, "are, in my opinion, manifold and absurd." Thus reason was asserting itself against authority in the religious sphere; and Hecataeus was one of the pioneers. But more effective than he in pressing the claims of reason was another Ionian, his contemporary, Xenophanes of Colophon; and we shall have to consider the importance of his work in another connexion.

Xeno-
phanes
(see
below,
Chap.
VII,
sect. 14).

The remoteness of Susa from the Greek seas, and the homesickness of Greeks whom any chance transported to the far east, find an illustration in the curious story of the physician Democedes of Croton. This man's skill had earned high salaries, as public physician at Aegina and Athens, and higher still in the service of Polycrates of Samos. He was carried off as a prisoner to Susa, in consequence of a series of troubles which followed the death of that tyrant; and he was taken from his dungeon to try his craft for Darius, who had sprained a foot in the chase. His success gained him the king's favour, and there was nothing which he might not ask except the one thing which he desired, permission to return to Greece. One day he was summoned by Queen Atossa who was suffering from a tumour on the breast, and he made her swear that if he cured her she would do what he asked. Acting by his directions, she stirred up the king to cherish the project of conquering the Greeks, and suggested that he should send spies under the conduct of Democedes to travel through Greece and bring back a report. These counsels of the daughter of Cyrus carried weight with Darius, according to the story; and the plan of Democedes succeeded. He promised to return to Susa, and Darius gave him rich presents for his kinsfolk; the Persians who accompanied him were privately charged to see that he did not escape. When they came to Taras,—for the story assumes that Italiot Greece was included in the programme of the journey,—the lord of that city arrested the Persians as spies, and kept them in prison until Democedes had time to escape to his native town. When the Persians were released they followed him to Croton, but the Crotoniats refused to give him up; a Persian invasion of Italy was a contingency which they might reasonably risk. Such is the strange story, blended of fact and fiction, which men told of the first Greek physician who practised at the court of Susa. He was not the last; we shall meet hereafter a more famous leech, who did not yearn back to Greece and wrote the history of his adopted country.

The story
of Demo-
cedes.

(Ctesias.)

SECT. 5. THE EUROPEAN EXPEDITION OF DARIUS: CONQUEST OF THRACE

Cyrus had conquered the eastern coasts of the Mediterranean;

Cambyses had completed and secured that conquest on the south side by the subjection of Egypt; it remained for Darius to complete and secure his empire on the north side by the reduction of Thrace. The possession of the adjacent part of the European continent was of like importance to the lord of Asia Minor, as the possession of the adjacent part of the African continent to the lord of Syria. Having spent eight years in setting his house in order, Darius prepared for his European expedition. It seems probable that his original design was first to subdue the Thracian peoples as far as the Danube, so as to make that river the northern boundary of his empire, and secondly to extend his power westward over Macedonia. The Thracian race was warlike and the country is mountainous, so that the Persian enterprise was serious and demanded large forces and careful precautions. The skill of a Samian architect named Mandrocles was employed to throw a bridge of boats across the Bosphorus, north of Byzantium; and, when the Persian host had passed over, Darius ordered two pillars to be set up on the European side, inscribed with the names of the various peoples composing his army, in Greek and cuneiform characters. These pillars were seen by the historian Herodotus. And in the temple of Hera at Samos there was to be seen another monument of the crossing into Europe. Mandrocles spent a part of the reward which Darius gave him in setting up there a painting in which the bridge and the crossing over, with Darius seated in a prominent place, were portrayed. He inscribed on it four verses to this effect: "Having bridged the fishy Bosphorus, Mandrocles dedicated to Hera a memorial of his raft-bridge. A crown he set upon his own head, and glory upon the men of Samos; for the work he wrought pleased king Darius." A large fleet was also furnished by the Greek subjects of Persia, to sail along the Thracian coast of the Black Sea as far as the mouths of the Danube, and to support and co-operate with the army. The contingents of the various Greek cities were commanded by their despots, prominent among whom were Histiaeus of Miletus, Hippoclus of Lampsacus, and Miltiades of the Thracian Chersonesus.

No details of the warfare in Thrace are preserved. We are told that many tribes submitted, and the Getae signalised their love of freedom by refusing to surrender it without a struggle. It seems probable, however, that the Thracians made some preparations to meet the invader. North of the Danube, in the lands which are now called Walachia and Moldavia (between the Danube, the Carpathians, and the Pruth), lived tribes which were allied in many respects to the tribes south of the river. The Greeks included these

C. 5?? B.C.

tribes under the general name of Scythian, which they applied to the whole series of peoples who dwelled between the Carpathians and the Caucasus. While the most easterly of that series approximated in language to the Persian, the most westerly approximated to the Thracian. Nothing was more natural than that the people south of the Danube, threatened by an Asiatic invasion, should have taken steps to gain help from their neighbours on the north, to oppose the Persian advance. Such help would have been readily given, and Darius doubtless became aware before he reached the Danube that the hostility of the Scythian beyond the Danube— whose frozen waters invited them to cross in winter—might be a frequent trouble to Persian rule in Thrace. The Greek fleet sailed up the mouth of the river and a bridge of boats was thrown across. Darius and his army marched over into Scythia. But both the king's purpose and what he did, in this remote corner of the world, are hidden in a cloud of legend. That he may have wished to make a hostile demonstration and strike terror into the restless neighbours of Thrace is probable; but it is not the whole explanation. We may rather suppose that the chief object of the diversion beyond the Danube was to lay hands upon the gold mines of Dacia, which was then the land of the Agathyrsi, and to secure a route of communication between that land and the mouth of the Danube. For three facts seem to emerge from the mist. The first is that the Agathyrsi were active in opposing the march of the Persians; the second, that he erected forts on a river named the Oaros,—a name otherwise unknown, but evidently a tributary of the Danube; the third, that his communications with the fleet which awaited his return were for some time cut off, and the Greek commanders were tempted to sail away and leave him in the lurch. He afterwards showed his gratitude to them for the loyalty with which they supported him in this expedition. The fact is that it would have been entirely contrary to their own interests to inflict a blow on the power which maintained despotism in the Greek cities of Asia Minor. But their loyalty at this juncture was all the more precious to the Persian king when he found on returning through Thrace that Byzantium, Perinthus, and Chalcedon had revolted. These revolts forced him to avoid the Bosphorus. He marched to the Thracian Chersonese and crossed the Hellespont, but left behind him an army under Megabazus, which was ultimately to complete the conquest of Thrace, and immediately to reduce the Greek cities along the northern coast of the Propontis and the Aegean. Megabazus established Persian dominion actually as far as the Strymon, and nominally even farther west; for the Paeonians, between the

Why Darius crossed the Danube.

Persian sway in Europe.

Strymon and the Axius, were conquered, and Macedonia acknowledged allegiance to the Great King.

The Persian dominion over the eastern part of the Balkan peninsula lasted for about fifteen years, and it was increased by the acquisition of the islands of Lemnos and Imbros. The excursion of Darius beyond the Danube, so far as it was intended to make an impression on the Scythians, seems to have been effective. It is only when the Persian power is shaken by a Greek revolt and Thrace herself is able to throw off the yoke that we find Scythians overrunning Thrace and even driving Miltiades out of the Chersonese.

c. 496 B.C.

Legend of Scythian expedition.

The European expedition of Darius had thus been a distinct success, which might fearlessly be set beside the Egyptian expedition of Cambyses. But it has come down to us in a very different and totally fabulous shape. It is represented as not primarily an expedition against Thrace, but as an attempt to execute the mad project of incorporating the Scythians of the steppes of southern Russia in the Persian empire. In this story, which is told with all the art of Herodotus, Thrace appears merely as the way to Scythia; and the actual conquest of Thrace sinks into insignificance beside the ignominious failure of the Persian army to achieve the ultimate end of their wild enterprise, the conquest of Scythia. Darius, whose purpose is said to have been to take vengeance on the Scythians for their invasion of Media a hundred years before, dispatches the Greek fleet to the Ister simply for the purpose of throwing a bridge of boats across the river. His first idea was to break down the bridge when he had passed over and send the ships home; but by the advice of a prudent Greek he changed his plan. He took a cord, in which he tied sixty knots, and said to the Greek captains: "Untie one of these knots every day, and remain here and guard the bridge till they are all untied. If I have not returned at the end of that time, sail home." The Greek historian Herodotus then conducts Darius with his vast host through the steppes of Scythia "as it were through fairyland," without any regard to the rivers which had to be crossed, the leagues which had to be traversed, the want of supplies. He carries him to regions beyond the Don, and transports the river Oaros, on which Darius built his forts, from the neighbourhood of the Danube to the neighbourhood of the Maeotic sea; placing this imaginary march of the Persians in the midst of a poetical picture of the Scythian folks and the Scythian land. In returning to the Danube the Persians found themselves in sore straits, chased and harassed by the barbarians, and meanwhile the sixty days had passed. The Ionians waited at the river beyond the ordained time, and presently a band of Scythians arrived urging them to destroy the bridge, so that they might ensure the destruction of Darius and gain their own freedom. Miltiades the tyrant of the Chersonese strongly advocated the proposal of the Scythians, but the counter-arguments of Histiaeus of Miletus prevailed, for he pointed out that the power of the despots in the cities depended on the Persian domination. They pretended however to fall in with the Scythian proposal, and destroyed a part of the bridge on the northern side, so that the Scythians went their ways, satisfied that the retreat of Darius would be cut off. A little later, Darius arrived in the dark hours of the night, and was filled with terror when he could discover no bridge. An Egyptian with a loud voice shouted the name "Histiaeus!" across the water, and Histiaeus, who was himself keeping guard, heard the cry, brought up his boats, and renewed the missing portion of the bridge. Thus Darius, after an ignominious retreat, was saved by the good offices of Histiaeus; whereas, if the advice of Miltiades had been adopted, the subsequent Persian invasion of Greece might never have taken place.

Thus Greek imagination, inspired by Greek prejudice, has changed a reasonable and successful enterprise into an insane and disastrous expedition; and the transmutation was so skilfully wrought that the fiction was taken for history until the other day.

Sect. 6. The Ionic Revolt against Persia

The Persian conquest of Thrace and Macedonia was a step, though there is no reason for supposing it an intentional step, towards a Persian attempt to conquer Greece. The attempt on Greece was not made till more than twenty years later; and for the first twelve years after the return of Darius from Thrace, nothing occurred which seemed likely to bring on a great struggle between Asiatic autocracy and European freedom. Hippias, the banished tyrant of Athens, repaired to Sardis and tried to induce the satrap Artaphernes to aid him in recovering his power. Artaphernes went so far as to threaten the Athenians; envoys from Sardis said at Athens: "Take back Hippias, if you look for safety." But he did nothing to enforce his menace.

It was in consequence of events in which Hippias had no part that the expedition of the Persians against Athens was at last undertaken. The condition of politics in the island of Naxos led indirectly to an insurrection of the subject Greeks against the Persian power; and the part which Athens and other Greek cities played in connexion with this revolt was the proximate cause of the Persian expeditions against Greece.

In return for service rendered during the Thracian expedition Histiaeus of Miletus was rewarded by Darius with a boon of his own requesting. He asked for Myrcinus, a town with fertile land on the lower Strymon—near the place where the famous Amphipolis was to be built at a later date—where he desired to found a colony. He seems to have accompanied Megabazus in his western march, and he set to work to fortify the place at once. Myrcinus was in the neighbourhood of silver-mines, and there was abundance of wood suitable for shipbuilding. The Persian general thought it would be impolitic to allow a Greek colony to be planted in such a position, and communicated his views to the king who was still at
Sardis; and Darius sending for Histiaeus, on the plea that he was a friend whose company was indispensable, carried him off to Susa, with the full purpose of never allowing him to return to the Aegean. Thus the schemes of Histiaeus were cut short, and he spent twelve years in regrets at the court of Susa before he had an opportunity of resuming his connexion with the politics of the Aegean.

Miletus was governed by his son-in-law Aristagoras, a man whose ability fell short of his ambition, but famous in history as the originator of the revolt of the Ionian Greeks. To this man came a number of Naxian oligarchs, who had been expelled from their city by a democratic rising, begging for help to put down the people
and gain possession of the populous and wealthy island. Aristagoras discerned in the request a means for his own aggrandisement; but without Persian assistance the enterprise did not seem feasible. He therefore went up to Sardis, and unfolded to Artaphernes a project of reducing all the Cyclades and then perhaps Euboea itself, a project of which the occupation of Naxos was to be the first step. Artaphernes readily entered into the plan, the consent of Darius was obtained, and 200 ships under the command of Megabates were placed at the disposal of the Milesian. There is little doubt that the enterprise would have been entirely successful but for a quarrel between Aristagoras and Megabates. The Persian admiral spitefully warned the Naxians of the approaching danger; the islanders made such effectual preparations that they stood a siege of four months, and, as there was then no likelihood of reducing the city, the fleet returned to Ionia. This failure was fatal to the prospects of Aristagoras. He had wasted Persian money, forfeited the confidence of Artaphernes, and made a powerful enemy in Megabates. He resolved to retrieve his fortunes by inciting a revolt of the Asiatic Greeks against the Persian power.

The story was that his father-in-law Histiaeus, weary of his long exile beyond the Tigris, instigated Aristagoras to this step, by a secret message branded on the head of a faithful slave. This message is said to have reached Aristagoras just at the moment when he was meditating a rebellion and to have decided him. The motive of Histiaeus in desiring the revolt is supposed to have been the conviction that Darius would send him down to Ionia to restore order. But the story sounds improbable. Histiaeus, detained at Susa because he was already deemed dangerous to Persian interests in the Aegean, would rather have had reason to fear that a revolt promoted by his son-in-law would prove fatal to his credit with Darius. It was a surprising thing that Darius was afterwards induced to send down such a near relative of Aristagoras, and we may suspect that the story that Histiaeus instigated the rebellion was suggested by his subsequent conduct—possibly even invented by himself.

in the Ionic revolt?

There were the seeds of revolt in Ionia, which only needed kindling to burst into flame. It would be a superficial view to suppose that the rebellion was due to the ambition of Greek despots. On the contrary, its indispensable condition was the widespread hatred of a despotic constitution, which smouldered in the cities; and the despotic constitutions were part of the Persian system. An ambitious despot was indeed the means of calling this feeling into action; but in order to do so he had first to cease to be a despot.

The initial step in promoting the rebellion was to set up democracies in the Greek States and drive out the tyrants. Aristagoras himself resigned his position in Miletus, and in most cases the change seems to have been accomplished without the shedding of blood. Mytilene was an exception; there the tyrant had earned such deep hatred that he was stoned to death.

The next step was to obtain help from free Greece against the Persian power. Aristagoras undertook the mission. He went first to Sparta, but the Spartans refused to send help to free Ionia from Persian oppression, even as they had before refused to aid her against Persian invasion. In later days a delightful story was told of his visit. He went to king Cleomenes and showed him a map of the earth, graven on bronze, displaying the countries of the known world, the seas, and the rivers. Cleomenes had never seen a map before, and the plausible Ionian tried to convince him that Sparta ought to aspire to the conquest of the Persian empire. Cleomenes was impressed, but deferred his reply till the third day, and then asked Aristagoras the distance from Ionia to Susa. "Three months," said Aristagoras off his guard, and he would have described the road, but the king cut him short with the command, "Begone from Sparta, Milesian stranger, before the sun sets." Aristagoras made

Aristagoras at Sparta;

yet another attempt. Entering the house of Cleomenes as a suppliant, he sought to bribe him. Beginning with ten talents, he gradually raised his offers till he reached fifty. Then Gorgo, the king's daughter, a child of eight or nine years, cried out, "Father, the stranger will corrupt you"; and moved by her words Cleomenes left the room.

at Athens and Eretria. 498 B.C.

The Milesian stranger fared better at Athens and Eretria. Both these cities sent succour; Athens twenty ships—ships, says Herodotus, with the solemnity due to the historical significance of the moment, "which were the beginning of ills between Greeks and barbarians."

Advice of Hecataeus.

The prospects of success seemed unfavourable to those who were acquainted with the vast resources of the Persian empire. When Aristagoras consulted with the men of leading at Miletus, the geographer Hecataeus had tried to dissuade him. Seeing that Aristagoras and the others had made up their minds and disparaged his arguments, Hecataeus gave a second-best counsel: "If you do revolt, seize the treasure of the temple of Apollo at Didyma, and become masters of the sea; for if you do not, the enemy will." But the advice was not taken.

The Greeks at Sardis.

With his Athenian and Eretrian allies, Aristagoras marched up to Sardis and occupied the city, but they did not take the citadel. While they were there, a fire broke out and the town was burned to the ground. The Greeks left the smoking ruins and marched back to the coast; but near Ephesus they were met by a Persian force and defeated. The Athenians straightway returned home; and with this battle the part played by Athens in the Ionic revolt comes to an end. But the brief episode was to bring serious consequences upon her in the future. The burning of Sardis was important, not so much for the course of the revolt itself as for what the revolt was to lead to. It irrevocably compromised two states of European Greece in the eyes of Persia. The story is that Darius, being told that Athenians had helped to burn Sardis, asked, "The Athenians —who are they?" He then called for a bow and shooting an arrow into the air invoked heaven, that it might be given to him to punish the Athenians. Moreover he bade one of his slaves to say to him three times at dinner, "Sire, remember the Athenians." The story has no historical value, but it has artistic significance in the narrative of Herodotus. The historian (as has been well observed) marks, by the significant word and act, that he has entered on a new phase of his great subject, the strife between Greeks and barbarians.

Part played by Athenians in the revolt.

Anecdote of Darius and the Athenians.

The revolt extended southwards to Caria and to Cyprus, northwards to the Propontis. In Cyprus all the cities except Amathus threw off the Persian yoke, but a Phoenician fleet was sent and the island was recovered. The Hellespontine towns were also subdued. In Caria the insurgents, after suffering two serious defeats, succeeded in destroying a Persian army.

The revolt in the south.

But Aristagoras was a man of slight spirit, not meant by nature to be the leader of such a movement. Seeing that Persia prospered in dealing with the rebellion, he despaired of his cause and fled to Myrcinus in Thrace. It is said that he called a meeting of his adherents, to decide what they should do and whither they should flee. In that assembly it was proposed to sail to the distant shores of Sardinia; and here again Hecataeus is related to have offered advice, which Aristagoras and his friends rejected—the establishment of a fortress in the neighbouring island of Leros, from which, if fortune favoured, they might easily return to Miletus. Aristagoras soon met his fate at the siege of a Thracian town. His death did not affect the course of the rebellion, in which he had played a sorry part. He has hardly left the stage when his father-in-law appears; but the rôle of Histiaeus is even less important than that of Aristagoras. This adventurer persuaded, or professed that he had persuaded, Darius to send him down to the coast, by promising to suppress the insurrection before he changed his tunic, and to annex Sardinia to the dominion of the Great King. This promise of Histiaeus, though it may not be true to fact, is thoroughly characteristic of the Greek adventurers of that time, deceiving themselves and others with speculations on the remote island of Sardinia. When he came down to Sardis, Histiaeus found that he was deeply suspected by the satrap Artaphernes, and feeling himself unsafe he fled to Chios. There he embraced the cause of the rebels, asserting that *he* had instigated the revolt, and perhaps spreading the famous story of the message written on the slave's head. Having obtained some ships from Lesbos he adopted the congenial business of piracy, occupying Byzantium and seizing the ships that attempted to pass the straits, as long as the revolt lasted. In the end he was taken prisoner and crucified by Artaphernes.

Flight of Aristagoras.

Reappearance of Histiaeus.

his fate, 493 B.C.

The main and decisive event of the war was the siege of Miletus on which the Persians at length concentrated all their efforts. The town was blockaded by the squadron of 600 ships which had just reduced Cyprus. The Greek fleet was stationed off the island of Lade. It is said to have numbered 353 ships, but they were ill disciplined, and the contingents were not united under a single command, nor animated by a common spirit. In the battle which ensued, the Lesbians and Samians deserted; the men of Chios fought

494 B.C. Battle of Lade and capture of Miletus.

splendidly but they were too few. Miletus was then taken by storm; the men were slain and the women and children sent up to Susa. The temple of Apollo at Didyma, one of the chief oracular sanctuaries of the Greek world, was surrendered by the Branchidae, its hereditary priests, and was burnt down. Some of the statues which adorned the Sacred Way leading to the temple have partially survived. They are of great interest to the student of sculpture, but one of them is of interest also to the historian. It is a statue of Chares of Teichiussa, who was doubtless a tyrant set up in that city by Darius, and thus it is a monument of the Persian domination in Ionia.

We may suspect that the burning of Apollo's shrine was not approved of by Darius himself. The respect which the king of kings felt for the oracular god is attested in a letter of admonition which he addressed to a satrap of Ionia. The text of a Greek version of this letter is partly preserved on a stone, and records the remarkable testimony of the king that Apollo always "told the truth to the Persians."

The capture of Miletus was followed by the reduction of Caria, where the rebels had for a time prospered, and by the conquest of the islands. Presently the Phoenician navy appeared in the waters of the Hellespont; and the attempt of eastern Greece to regain her independence was completely crushed.

Though the Athenians had withdrawn from the movement in Ionia at an early stage, the tidings of the fall of Miletus produced at Athens a deep feeling of disappointment and sympathy, which found expression some time afterwards in the punishment of Phrynichus, a tragic poet, who made the catastrophe of Miletus the theme of a drama. The Athenians fined him for having recalled to their minds *their own* misfortunes. But in the meantime there had been won for them, from the Persian, what was destined to become afterwards a lasting possession. Miltiades, the tyrant of the Chersonese, took no part in the revolt, but he availed himself of it to strike for his own hand and to seize the isles of Lemnos and Imbros. When the revolt failed, feeling himself unsafe in the Chersonese, he fled to Athens. His son was captured by the Persians, but was kindly treated by Darius; and this proves that Miltiades in his earlier career had been on friendly terms with Persia. At Athens he professed that he had conquered Lemnos and Imbros for her; and, though these islands seem to have been reoccupied by the Persians for a time, they passed back under Athenian dominion.

Temple of the Branchidae.

Chares.

Letter of Darius to Gadates.

End of revolt.

Phrynichus fined 1000 drachmae for the Capture of Miletus.

Miltiades.

Lemnos and Imbros become Athenian.

Sect. 7. Second and Third European Expeditions of Darius. Battle of Marathon

Having suppressed the rebellion, Persia had three things to do. Greek Asia was to be reorganised; Persian Europe was to be reconquered; and those free Greek states which had made war on Persia and occupied Sardis were to be punished.

Artaphernes caused the territories of the Ionian cities to be measured and surveyed, and regulated the tributes accordingly. It was also ordained that the cities should no longer have the right of making war upon one another. But there was more to be done. The revolt had taught Persia that the system of tyrannies did not answer; and it was now resolved to make an experiment of the opposite policy. The despots were abolished and democratic governments were set up. The world may well have been surprised to see the great despotism of all favouring the institution of democracy; it was a concession to the spirit of the Greeks, which reflects credit on the wisdom of Darius.

The king's son-in-law, Mardonius, was sent to reassert Persian supremacy in Thrace and Macedonia; and through Macedonia he proposed to advance into Greece in order to punish the two cities which had helped the Ionian rebels. A fleet sailed along the coast and subdued the island of Thasos on its way. Thrace was reduced, and Macedonia, then under king Alexander, submitted—a submission which was to be avenged in distant days to come by a descendant and a namesake. But the Greek expedition could not be carried out, since a disaster had befallen the fleet which was partly wrecked in a storm off the perilous promontory of Athos. Mardonius returned; he had lost many ships, but he had fulfilled the more important parts of his task.

But Darius was sternly resolved that Athens and Eretria should not escape without chastisement. Their connexion with the burning of Sardis had deeply incensed him; it seemed an insult which the Great King's pride could not let pass unnoticed. Moreover Hippias, the banished tyrant, was at the court of Susa, urging an expedition against the city which had cast him out. It was decided that the new expedition should not be sent by way of Thrace and Macedonia, but should move straight across the Aegean sea. The cities of the Persian seaboard were commanded to equip warships and transports for cavalry; and heralds were sent to the chief cities of free Greece that were not at war with Persia, requiring the tokens of submission, earth and water. In most cases the tokens were given; and among others by Aegina, the enemy of Athens. The command of the army was entrusted to Datis and Artaphernes, a nephew of Darius; and they were accompanied by the aged tyrant Hippias, who hoped to rule once more over his native country. The armament—600 galleys strong, according to Herodotus—setting sail from Samos, made first for Naxos, the island where Aristagoras had failed. The inhabitants abandoned the city and fled up into the hills; and the Persians burned the town. The sacred island of Delos was scrupulously spared; but soon after the Persians had departed, it was shaken by an earthquake, and the unwonted event was noted as a sign of coming troubles. Having sailed from isle to isle, subduing the Cyclades, the fleet went up the channel between Euboea and Attica, and, reducing Carystus by the way, reached the territory of Eretria. It is strange to find that Athens and Eretria had made no common preparations to meet a common danger. Eretria was severed from Attica only by a narrow water, and yet there was no joint action. Athens indeed directed the colonists whom she had settled in the territory of her dependency Chalcis to assist their Eretrian neighbours, but she sent no other help. We hear of sharp engagements outside the walls of the Euboean city, but within seven days it was delivered over to the invaders by the treachery of some leading burghers. The flames which consumed the temples of Eretria were a small set off against the flames of Sardis. The inhabitants were enslaved. Of all the Greek towns which were involved in the strife between Europe and Asia, none was more ill-fated than Eretria.

The Persian generals had accomplished the lesser half of their task; it now remained to deal with the other city which had defied their king. Crossing over the strait they landed their army in the bay of Marathon. For the second time an exiled tyrant of Athens came down from Eretria to recover his power. The father had come, fifty years before, with but a few mercenaries; the son came now with the forces of Asia. Yet so far as winning support at Athens was concerned, the foreign host was the weakest argument of Hippias. The house of the Pisistratids had many bitter enemies, but none was more bitter than one who had also known what it was to rule as a tyrant, Miltiades, son of Cimon. We have seen how he returned from the Chersonese after the Ionic revolt. His enemies accused him of the crime of oppressive rule in the Chersonese, but he was acquitted by his fellow-citizens, to whom he had brought the gift of Lemnos and Imbros. His hatred of the Pisistratids was natural; they had put to death his father Cimon, celebrated as a victor in the Olympian chariot-race. It is not surprising that Miltiades. who was active as a party man, who was known to be a hot

Persians subdue Cyclades and Carystus,

burn Eretria.

land in Attica.

Miltiades.

foe of the tyrants, who had probably more first-hand knowledge of the Persians than any other man at Athens, was chosen as the strategos of his tribe. He was the soul of the resistance which his country now offered to the invader.

Athens had changed much since Hippias had been cast out, though a generation had not passed. Athenian character had been developed under free democratical institutions. It has been said that if the Athenians had not been radically different from their former selves Hippias would easily have recovered Athens. In other words, if the Persian invasion had happened twenty years sooner, the same stand would not have been made against it as Athens now made; the liberty of Greece would have succumbed. But it was no mere accident that the blow had not been aimed twenty years sooner. The Persian invasion was brought about by the same political causes which enabled Athens to withstand it. The Ionian Greeks would not have risen in revolt but for the growth of a strong sentiment against tyrannies,—the same cause which overthrew the Pisistratids and created Marathonian Athens. On the other hand, if the Ionic revolt had broken out before the expulsion of Hippias, Athens would have taken no part in it, and the Persian invasion of Greece might not have followed.

Energy of free Athens.

As the story is told by our historian, one would almost think that the enemy had already landed on Attic soil before the Athenians bethought themselves how they were to defend their city and their land. A fast runner was dispatched in hot haste to Lacedaemon to bear the news of the fall of Eretria and the jeopardy of Athens. The Lacedaemonians said that they would help Athens—they were bound to help a member of their league—but religious scruples forbade them to come at once; they must wait till the full moon had passed. But when the full moon had passed, it was too late.

Philippides sent to Sparta.

The whole army of the Athenians may have numbered about 9000. The commander-in-chief was Callimachus, the polemarch of the year; and the grave duty of organising the defence rested upon him and the ten generals of the tribal regiments, who formed a Council of War. Fortunately for Athens, Callimachus seems to have been willing to hearken to the counsels of Miltiades; and the joint authority of the polemarch and the most influential general outweighed the scruples of their less adventurous colleagues. The enemy had landed near Marathon and clearly intended to advance on unwalled Athens by land and sea. The question was whether the Athenian army should await their approach and give them battle within sight and reach of the Acropolis, or should more boldly go forth to find them. This was a question which it de-

Callimachus.

Decision to march to Marathon.

volved upon the Athenian people itself to decide. The hour when
the Assembly met to deliberate on this question was the most fateful moment in the whole episode. Miltiades proposed that the army
should march to Marathon and meet the Persians there. To have
proposed and carried this decree is probably the greatest title of
Miltiades to his immortal fame. But if the tyrants had not pulled
down the city walls, it would assuredly never have been carried.

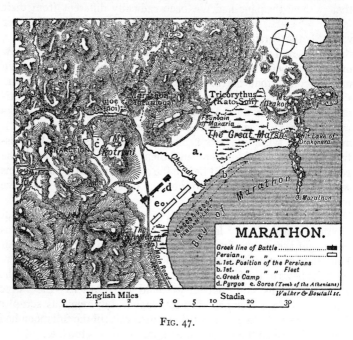

FIG. 47.

Field of
Mara-
thon.

The plain of Marathon, stretching along a sickle-shaped line of
coast, is girt on all other sides by the hills which drop down from
Pentelicus and Parnes. In the northern part, and on the extreme
south, the soil is marshy, and the plain is cleft into two halves by
the path of a torrent coming down from the hills through the northern valley, in which the village of Marathon is situated. Two roads
lead from Athens to Marathon. The main road, turning eastward,
passes between the mountains of Hymettus and Pentelicus; and,
traversing the deme of Pallene, skirting Mount Pentelicus, and then
turning due north when it reaches the coast, it enters the plain of
Marathon from the south. The other road, which is somewhat
shorter but more difficult, continues northward, past the deme of
Cephisia, and, running into the hills north of Pentelicus, finds two

issues in the Marathonian plain. It divides into two paths which encircle the hill of Kotroni: the northern path goes on to Marathon and descends into the plain from the north along the banks of the torrent; the other, passing by a sanctuary of Heracles, and descending the valley of Avlona, issues in the plain at its southwestern corner, close to the village which is now called Vraná.

Callimachus took the northern road by Cephisia, and encamped in the valley of Avlona, not far from the shrine of Heracles. The choice of this admirable position was more than half the victory. The Athenians were themselves unassailable, in the lower valley, except at a great disadvantage; and they commanded not only the mountain road by which they had come, but also the main road and the southern gate of the plain; for the Persians in attempting to reach that gate would be exposed to their flank attack. At this period Athens had accomplished strategists, and the brilliant campaign against Boeotia and Chalcis, sixteen years before, has prepared us for the ability which her commanders now displayed in the presence of a graver peril. The Persians had encamped on the north side of the torrent-bed, and their ships were riding at anchor beside them. It was to their interest to bring on a pitched battle in the plain as soon as possible. On the other hand, the Athenians had everything to gain by waiting in their impregnable position; if they waited long enough they might hope for help from Sparta. Help from another quarter had already come. When they reached the sanctuary of Heracles they were joined by a band of 1000 Plataeans, who, in gratitude for the protection of Athens against the Theban yoke, now came to help her in the hour of jeopardy.

Athenian position.

Persian position.

Some days passed, and then, as the Greeks remained immovable, the Persians would wait no longer. Having embarked a part of the army, including the whole body of their cavalry, they made ready to move upon Athens by land and sea. The land force must follow the main road by Pallen, and was therefore prepared for battle, in case the Greeks should attack them before they defiled from the plain. Another critical moment had come for the Athenians, but the polemarch and the generals had probably decided already what should be done when this contingency arose. That Miltiades, as before in the Assembly so now in the camp, urged the boldest course, we may well believe; but the supreme direction belonged to the polemarch, and he decided to attack the enemy as they marched southward.

Persians prepare to move.

Callimachus, whether he acted of his own wit or by the counsel of others, showed now a skill in tactics as consummate as the skill in strategy which we have already witnessed. Outnumbered by

Tactics of the Athenians.

the foe, if the Athenian line had formed itself in equal depth throughout, it would have swept the Persian centre into the sea, but then it would have been caught in a trap, between the sea and ships on one side and the Persian wings, which would have closed in, on the other. Accordingly Callimachus made his own centre long and shallow, so that it would cover the whole Persian centre, while his wings of the normal depth would be opposed to the wings of the enemy.

Battle of
Marathon
(Sept.).

The long Persian line crossed the bed of the torrent and advanced along the shore. A large portion was detached to mask the Greek position—a precaution which was dictated by elementary principles of strategy, in order either to prevent or to repel a flank attack. With these troops to cover them, the rest of the host might march securely past. The Greek army had perhaps already appeared in the recess of the hills at the mouth of the valley of Avlona. Callimachus himself led the right wing; the Plataean allies were posted on the extreme left. Among those who fought for their country on this day we must notice one who, though he held no post of command, was destined to hold a greater place in Athenian history than any of his fellow-warriors, Themistocles, the son of Neocles, who fought in the regiment of the Leontid tribe. Another of worldwide fame, Aeschylus the tragic poet, also bore shield and spear, and charged the Medes, on this memorable day. When the Greeks drew near to the line of the enemy, they were met by volleys of arrows from the eastern archers, and to escape this danger they advanced at a run into close quarters. The hoplites did not fail the generals; their valour secured the victory which masterly strategy and tactics had prepared. All fell out as had been foreseen. The Athenian centre was driven back towards the hills by the enemy's centre, where the best troops, including the Persians themselves, were stationed; but the Athenian wings completely routed the wings of their foe. Then, closing in—and leaving the vanquished to reach their ships if they could—they turned upon the victorious Persians, who were following the retreating Greek centre. Here again they were utterly victorious, breaking up the array of the enemy and pursuing them in confusion to the shore, where all who escaped the sword were picked up by the ships. Only a portion of the Persian army had been engaged; the main body doubtless embarked as soon as they saw the first signs of the disruption of the force on which they had relied to cover them from the enemy.

It was not a long battle. The Athenian loss was small, 192 slain; and the Persian loss was reckoned at about 6400, a number whose very moderation stamps it as probably near the truth. Datis and

Artaphernes had still an immense host, which might retrieve the
fortune of the campaign; Athens was not yet out of danger. The
Persian squadron sailed down the straits and rounded Cape
Sunium, while the victorious army, leaving one regiment on the field
of their triumph to guard the slain and the spoils, marched back to
defend Athens. They halted outside the city near the shrine of
Heracles in Cynosarges, on the banks of the Ilisus, and they beheld
the fleet of the enemy riding off Phaleron. But it did not put into
shore, and presently the whole squadron began to draw out to sea.
Datis had abondoned his enterprise. Perhaps he had sailed within
sight of Athens only on the chance of finding it undefended; and,
when he saw that the army was there, shrank from another conflict
with the hoplites. But a Spartan army, 2000 strong, cannot have
been far from Athens now; it had set out on the day after the full
moon, and it reached Athens soon after the battle. We may guess
that tidings of the approach of the Spartans, if not their actual
presence, had something to do with the sudden departure of the invaders, who, though they had received an unlooked-for check, had
not endured an overwhelming defeat.

*Persians
near
Phaleron:
the return
to Asia.*

*Arrival
of the
Spartans.*

The Spartans arrived too late for the battle. They visited the
field desiring to gaze upon the Persian corpses, and departed home
praising the exploit of the Athenians. The scene of the battle is still
marked by the mound which the Athenians raised over their own
dead; Callimachus was buried there, and Cynegirus (a brother of
the poet Aeschylus), who was said to have seized a Persian galley
and held it until his arm was severed by an axe. Legend grew up
quickly round the battle, and there was no historian to record at the
time what had actually happened; so that, when a generation had
passed, the facts were partly forgotten, and partly transfigured.
Three motives were at work in this transfiguration: the love of the
marvellous, the vanity of the Athenians, and the desire of his family
to exalt the services of Miltiades. Gods and heroes fought for
Athens, ghostly warriors moved among the ranks. The panic terror
of the Persians at the Greek charge was ascribed to Pan, and the
worship of this god was revived in a cave consecrated to him under
the north-west slope of the Acropolis. Out of this grew a story which
added a charming incident to the chain of Marathonian memories.
The fast runner Philippides, speeding through Arcadia on his way
to seek Spartan help, had been accosted by Pan himself, who had
asked why the Athenians neglected his worship, and promised them
favours in the future. But the supernatural can be easily allowed
for. It was more serious that the extraordinarily brilliant strategy
and tactics, to which the success was chiefly due, should have faded

*The
mound of
Mara-
thon.*

*The
Mara-
thonian
myth.*

*Worship
of Pan.*

out of the story, and that Marathon should have been regarded as entirely a soldiers' battle. It was soberly asserted and believed that those wonderful warriors had taken their enemy aback by advancing against them for a whole mile at a run. Miltiades, who was doubtless the heart and soul of the campaign, was raised by the Marathonian myth to be the commander-in-chief on the day of battle; and it was explained that the chief command each day devolved upon the generals in rotation. This was an arrangement which came into force a few years later, when the polemarch lost his importance; but it supplied the legend with a ready means of setting aside Callimachus in favour of Miltiades. We need not follow the myth further. The battle of Marathon was caught up into a cloud of glory, which obscured the truth of the events; and historical criticism has been able to rescue only the barest outline. Callimachus in particular received less than his due, overshadowed by the fame of Miltiades; and it is interesting to find that there was at least a stone in Athens—set up perhaps by his son—which recorded the services of "the polemarch of the Athenians" in the struggle with the Medes. A few precious words have been preserved.

The flashing of the shield.   One mysterious incident connected with the battle must be numbered among those historical puzzles which have never been cleared up. "When the Persians were already in their ships," a shield was flashed, as a signal to them, on the summit of Pentelicus. Who held up the shield, and what did the signal mean? The popular explanation, in later days, was that it invited the Persians to sail straight for Athens, and the enemies of the Alcmaeonids said that they were the treacherous authors of the signal. Herodotus doubted the explanation, but he was convinced that the flashing of the shield was a well-attested fact.

The Athenian treasury of Delphi.   In the holiest place of Greece, in the sanctuary of Delphi itself, have been found in recent years remains of the noblest monument of the victory of Marathon. Out of the Persian spoils, the Athenians built a little Doric treasure-house of marble from their own Pentelic quarries. It seems to have been a gem of architecture, worthy of the severe grace of the sculptured reliefs which ran round the inside of the building and have been safely preserved under its ruins. The sculptures represent the deeds of Theseus and of Heracles, and the battle of the gods and giants.

Picture of the battle in the Poikilē Stoa.   The descendants of the Marathonian warriors derived perhaps their most vivid idea of the combat from a picture of it which was painted about a quarter of a century later—one of the famous battle-pictures in the Portico of Frescoes in the market-place. In one scene the Athenians and Plataeans advanced against the trow-

sered barbarians; in a second the Persians in their flight pushed
each other into the marsh; and in the last, the Phoenician ships
were portrayed and the Greeks slaying the foemen who were striving to reach the ships. Callimachus, Miltiades, Datis and Artaphernes, Cynegirus seizing the prow of a ship, could all be recognised; and Theseus, who was believed to have given phantom aid
to the warriors, seemed to rise out of the earth. High above the rag-
ing strife, the artist—Micon was his name—showed the gods and
goddesses as they surveyed, from the tranquillity of Olympus, the
prowess of their Greeks smiting the profane destroyers of the holy
places of Eretria.

Fig. 48.—The Warning of Darius (scene on a vase, Naples). Darius, seated
among his nobles, is warned by one who stands in front of him against the
expedition to Greece.

The significance of the victory of Marathon, as a triumph for
Athens, for Greece, for Europe, cannot be gainsaid; but we must
take care not to misapprehend its meaning for Greece and for
Athens herself. That significance is unmistakable even if we mini-
mise the immediate peril which was averted. The Asiatic invader
had perhaps not yet come to annex; he had come only to chastise;
it was enough for him if the rest of the Greeks looked on with re-
spectful awe, while he meted out their doom to the two offending
cities. His work in Euboea had been purely a work of demolition;
he had not sought to annex territory or add a satrapy to the Persian
dominion. The Cyclad islands and Carystus had indeed been compelled to submit to the formal authority of the Great King; but it
is not proved that Darius thought of reducing the western coasts of
the Aegean to the subject condition of Ionia. Thus the danger which
menaced Athens may not have been subjection to an Asiatic despot.
Nor was she threatened by the doom of destruction and slavery
which befell Eretria. The Persian army had come to restore Hippias; and assuredly Darius did not purpose to restore his friend to
a city of smouldering temples. The Athenians would be condemned

*What the
victory of
Marathon
meant.*

to bow beneath the yoke of their own tyrant; they would not become, like their Eretrian fellows, the bondmen of a barbarian master. To be delivered over to an aged despot, thirsting for power and vengeance, embittered by twenty years of weary exile,—this was the punishment of the Athenians, and this was the fate which they escaped by their valour on the field of Marathon. If they had lost that battle and the rule of the Pisistratids had been restored, the work of twenty years ago would have had to be done again; but that it would have been done again there can be hardly a doubt. The defeat of the Athenians would have arrested, it would not have closed, their development. It might even be argued that it would have saved Greece the terrible trial of the later Persian invasion; if that invasion was undertaken solely to wipe out the ignominy of the repulse at Marathon. Probably, if Datis had been victorious, the subsequent attempt of Persia to conquer Greece would have assumed a different shape. But the attempt would assuredly have been made. The history of the world does not depend on proximate causes. The clash of Greece and Persia, the effort of Persia to expand at the cost of Greece, were inevitable. From the higher point of view it was not a question of vengeance; where Darius stopped, the successors of Darius would undoubtedly go on. The success of Marathon inspirited Greece to withstand the later and greater invasion; but the chief consequence was the effect which it wrought upon the spirit of Athens herself. The enormous prestige which she won by the single-handed victory over the host of the Great King gave her new self-confidence and ambition; history seemed to have set a splendid seal on her democracy; she felt that she could trust her constitution and that she might lift her head as high as any state in Hellas. The Athenians always looked back to Marathon as marking an epoch. It was as if on that day the gods had said to them, Go on and prosper.

The great battle immortalised Miltiades; but his latter end was not good. His services at Marathon could not fail to gain for him increased influence and respect at Athens. His fellow-citizens granted him, on his own proposal, a commission to attack the island of Paros. For the Parians had furnished a trireme to the armament of Datis, and had thereby made war upon Athens. Miltiades besieged the city of Paros for twenty-six days but without success, and then returned home wounded. The failure was imputed to criminal conduct of the general; his enemies, jealous of his exploits in the Marathonian campaign, accused him of deceiving the people; and he was fined fifty talents, a heavy fine. It is not known what his alleged wrongdoing was; but afterwards, when the legend of Mil-

Expedition to Paros.

Condemnation of Miltiades

tiades grew and the part which he played in the campaign of Marathon was unduly magnified, it was foolishly said that he persuaded the Athenians to entrust the fleet to him, promising to take them to a land of gold, and that he deceived them by assailing Paros to gratify a private revenge. At Paros itself, in the temple of Demeter, the tale was told that, when the siege seemed hopeless, he corrupted a priestess of the goddess, named Timo, and that, coming to meet her in a sanctuary to which only women were admitted, he was seized with panic and in his flight, leaping the fence of the precinct, hurt his leg. Certain it is that he returned wounded to Athens, however he came by the chance; appeared on a couch at his trial; and died soon after his condemnation.

His death

SECT. 8. STRUGGLE OF ATHENS AND AEGINA

At this time Aegina was the strongest naval power in the Aegean. Hostile feeling had long been the rule between her and Athens, and soon after the fall of the Pisistratids the island had been involved in the quarrel between Athens and Thebes. Legend said that the nymphs Aegina and Theba were sisters; but it was more than sisterly sympathy which drove Aegina to declare a state of standing war —a war without herald, as the Greeks called it—against her continental neighbour. Her ships ravaged Phaleron and the Attic coast. It was to be expected that Aegina would side with the Persian when he sailed against her foe, and would cordially desire the humiliation of Athens. The Athenians had some reason to fear that she would give the invader not only her goodwill but her active help. Accordingly, the Athenians sought the intervention of Sparta, complaining that Aegina was medizing and betraying Greece out of enmity to Athens. The complaint was listened to at Sparta, and king Cleomenes, proceeding to Aegina, seized ten hostages and deposited them with the Athenians. By this means the hands of Aegina were tied; she was hindered from lending help to the Persians or hampering the men of Athens in their preparations to meet the invaders.

Hostility of Aegina and Athens, 506 B.C.

($\pi\acute{o}\lambda\epsilon\mu os$ $\dot{a}\kappa\acute{\eta}\rho\nu\kappa\tau os$) 498 B.C.

Appeal of Athens to Sparta;

coercion of Aegina (before 491 B.C.).

This appeal of Athens to Sparta to interfere and exercise coercion in the common interests of Hellas, and the implied recognition of Sparta as the leading power, has been supposed to mark a climax in that feeling of deference towards her which had been growing up both within and without Greece. The episode has been described as "the first direct and positive historical manifestation of Hellas as an aggregate body with Sparta as its chief." This description is an exaggeration; for we must not lose sight of the fact—which is too often forgotten, and which Athens took pains to forget—that

Athens was, like Aegina, a member of the Peloponnesian league, and the appeal to the head of the league was therefore a matter of course.

Defeat of Argos.

494 B.C.

The prestige of Sparta had indeed been confirmed and increased by a decisive victory which she had won a few years before over her old rival Argos. The battle was fought at Sêpeia, near the hill of Tiryns. According to the story, the Argive generals acted with extraordinary folly and were easily overreached by Cleomenes. They listened for the commands which the herald proclaimed to the army of their enemies, and then issued those same commands to their own men. Learning this, Cleomenes gave secret orders that, when the herald gave the word for dinner, the soldiers should pay no heed but stand prepared for battle. The Argives dined in accordance with the command of the Spartan herald, and were immediately fallen upon and destroyed by their enemies. The disaster lamed the power of Argos for more than twenty years.

Feud of the Spartan kings.

The episode of the hostages of Aegina brought to a final issue the great scandal of Sparta, the bitter feud of her two kings, Cleomenes and Demaratus. King Demaratus entered into a private compact with the Aeginetans to thwart the intervention of king Cleomenes. Accordingly Cleomenes incited Leotychidas, the next heir of the Eurypontid line to which Demaratus belonged, to challenge the legitimacy of his rival's birth. A trial was held; a curious story touching the birth of Demaratus was manufactured and attested; and an oracle came from Delphi, declaring that Demaratus was not the son of his reputed father. Leotychidas consequently became king; Demaratus fled to the court of Darius—refuge of fallen potentates—where as the friend of medizing Aegina he found a good reception. Then Cleomenes and his new colleague went to Aegina and seized the hostages.

Fate of Cleomenes.

But the means which Cleomenes used to ruin Demaratus recoiled upon himself. It was discovered that he had tampered with the Pythian priestess at Delphi to bring about the dethronement of his enemy, and fearing the public indignation at this disclosure he fled first to Thessaly and then returned as far as Arcadia, where he conspired against his country. The Spartan government deemed it politic to invite him to return, and he accepted their offer of pardon. But his adventures had unhinged his mind; he became a violent madman, striking with his stick every one who approached, and his kinsfolk placed him in chains under the guard of a Helot. One day,

(? c. 489 B.C.]

having forced his keeper by means of threats to give him a sword, he wounded himself horribly and died.

Such was the curiously inglorious end of king Cleomenes, who, if he had not been a Spartan, might have been one of the greater figures in Grecian history. But his ambition was cabined and his abilities hampered by the Spartan system; whenever, if left to himself he might have pursued an effective policy, he was checked by the other king or the Ephorate. On important occasions during his life, Sparta was called upon to take action in foreign affairs; and on each occasion we find that the policy of Cleomenes falls short of the mark owing to the opposition of his royal colleague. Even as it is, he dominates in Spartan history for more than twenty years.

After his death, the Aeginetans sent envoys to Sparta, demanding the restoration of the hostages whom he and the other king Leotychidas had delivered over to Athens. Leotychidas had been the accomplice of Cleomenes in deposing Demaratus, and was consequently at this time under the shadow of public displeasure. The Spartans were ready, it is said, to hand him over to the Aeginetans as a prisoner, but the envoys preferred to ask that he should go with them to Athens and compass the restoration of the hostages. The Athenians flatly refused the demand. Aegina resorted to reprisals, and a war broke out. It began with the conspiracy of an Aeginetan citizen, named Nicodromus, who undertook with the help of Athens to overthrow the oligarchical government of his city. His plan failed because the Athenians came a day too late. The delay was due to the necessity of increasing their squadron of fifty triremes by a loan of twenty more from Corinth. These ships gained a victory and landed troops on the island to besiege the town. But the Aeginetans on their side obtained some troops from Argos, and overcame the Athenians. This defeat caused disorder in the fleet, which was then attacked and routed by the islanders. But the double repulse was not decisive, and warfare was protracted between the two cities by desultory plundering raids on their respective coasts. The necessity of protecting Attica from Aeginetan depredations, the ambition perhaps of ultimately reducing Aegina to subjection or insignificance, sensibly accelerated the conversion of Athens into a naval power.

War of Athens and Aegina.

487 B.C.

SECT. 9. GROWTH OF THE ATHENIAN DEMOCRACY

The Athenian constitution underwent several important modifications in the course of the twenty years which followed its reform by Cleisthenes; and there is reason for thinking that some of the changes which tradition ascribed to Cleisthenes were really not introduced by him. Under his scheme, the power of the archons remained very great; they were usually men deliberately elected for

Change in

their ability; and if the Council of Cleisthenes was a check upon them, they also were a check upon it. The natural development of things was to strengthen the Council and weaken the magistrates. And at length, some years after Marathon, this step was taken by means of a change in the mode of appointment. Henceforward they were appointed by lot. Five hundred men were elected by the demes—in the same way in which the Council itself was elected—and out of this body of five hundred the nine archons were taken by lot. The result of any system of lot in the appointment of offices is to secure average honesty and exclude more than average ability. Henceforward the chances against any prominent statesmen holding the office of chief archon are five hundred to one. It is obvious that the political importance of the chief magistracy now disappears. It is also obvious that a polemarch appointed by lot could no longer hold the post of commander-in-chief. That post must pass to those who were deliberately picked out as competent to hold it. The powers of the polemarch were therefore vested, not in a new officer, but in the body of the ten strategi who were hitherto elected each by his own tribe. Either now or not many years later a reform was introduced by which the whole people elected the Generals, but they endeavoured so far as possible to choose one from each tribe, and we know no instance in which the same tribe was represented by more than two. The evil of a divided authority was at first obviated by giving each strategos supreme command for a day—an experiment which to our modern notions seems almost childish. Routine business in time of peace might be transacted on such a system; but a daily change of command in time of war was naturally doomed to failure. There is no reason to suppose that it ever became the practice at the election of the Generals to assign to one of the ten a position of supreme authority over all his colleagues during their whole term of office. That would have been a reinstitution of the polemarch in another form. The danger of a divided command was avoided by a simpler expedient. Whenever the people voted a military or naval expedition, they decreed which of the Generals should conduct it, and assigned a position of leadership or presidency to one of those whom they chose. But this superior command was limited to the conduct of the particular expedition; and the General to whom it was assigned exercised it only over those of his colleagues who were specially associated with him.

We have no record touching the attitude of Cleisthenes to the venerable council of the Areopagus, nor do we hear anything about that body for a generation after the fall of the Pisistratids. But a new institution was originated during this period which weakened

method of appointing archons.

487-6 B.C.

Polemarch superseded by the Ten Generals.

Ostracism.

the position of the Areopagus by depriving it of its most important political function—that of guarding the constitution and protecting the state against the danger of a tyranny. The institution of ostracism is traditionally ascribed to Cleisthenes, but it was not made use of till two years after the battle of Marathon. The ordinance of the *Ostrakismos* was that in the sixth prytany of each civil year the question should be laid before the Assembly of the people whether they willed that an ostracism should be held or not. If they voted in the affirmative, then an extraordinary Assembly was summoned in the market-place in the eighth prytany. The citizens were grouped in tribes, and each citizen placed in an urn a piece of potsherd (*ostrakon*) inscribed with the name of the person whom he desired to be "ostracized." The voting was not valid unless 6000 votes at least were given, and whoever had most ostraka against him was condemned to leave Attica within ten days and not set foot in it again for ten years. He was allowed however to retain his property, and remained an Athenian citizen.

By this institution the duty of guarding against the dangerous ambitions of influential citizens was transferred from the paternal council of the Areopagus to the sovereign people itself.[4] If this clumsy and, it must be owned, oppressive institution was established by Cleisthenes, it would follow that for about fifteen years the Assembly declined every year to make use of it, though it is stated that the chief object of Cleisthenes was to banish a relation of the Pisistratids, Hipparchus the son of Charmus. And in fact this Hipparchus was ultimately banished, by the first ostracism that was ever practised; and in the following year Megacles, who though an Alcmaeonid had espoused the cause of the Pisistratid faction, suffered the same fate. In these acts, as well as in the constitutional reform affecting the archonship, we must see the work of the progressive democratic statesmen, of whom the three most prominent were Xanthippus, Aristides, and Themistocles. These leaders, however, had separate policies and separate parties, and the people were persuaded to ostracise Xanthippus, and, two years later, Aristides. It is clear that in these cases there was no fear or danger of a tyranny, but that ostracism was used as a convenient engine for removing the opposition of a statesman who hampered the adoption

Ostracism of Hipparchus, 487 B.C.; of Megacles, 486 B.C.;

of Xanthippus, 484 B.C.; of Aristides, 482 B.C.

[4] It is important to note that the law of ostracism did not leave it to the discretion of the Council of Five Hundred whether the question should be proposed to the Assembly or not, but ordained that it should be proposed as a matter of course at a fixed time every year. This was an additional safeguard to the people.—It has been suggested that ostracism was intended to replace Solon's law against neutrality (see above, p. 179), and was itself replaced by the Graphê Paranomôn (see below, p. 445).

of a popular measure. We cannot guess on what question Xanthippus stood in the way of Aristides or Themistocles, but it is possible that the ostracism of Aristides was connected with the bold naval policy which it was the great merit of Themistocles to have originated and carried through. An excellent anecdote is told of the ostracism of Aristides "the Just," as he was called. On the day of the voting an illiterate citizen chanced to be close to Aristides who was unknown to him by sight, and requested him to write down the name "Aristides" on the ostrakon. "Why," said Aristides, doing as he was asked, "do you wish to ostracise him?" "Because," said the fellow, "I am tired of hearing him called the Just."

SECT. 10. ATHENS TO BE A SEA-POWER

The work of Themistocles.

But the greatest statesman of this critical period in the history of Athens, greater than either of his two rivals, Xanthippus and Aristides, greater than the hero of Marathon himself, was Themistocles, the son of Neocles. It may be said that he contributed more than any other single man to the making of Athens into a great state. The pre-eminent importance of his statesmanship was due in the first place to his insight in discerning the potentialities of his city and in grasping her situation before any one else had grasped it; and then to his energy in initiating, and his adroitness and perseverance in following, a policy which raised his city, and could alone have raised her, to the position which she attained before his death. In the sixth century the Athenians were a considerable naval power, as Greek naval powers then went; but the fleet was regarded as subsidiary to the army. The idea of Themistocles was to sacrifice the army to the navy and make Athens a sea-state—the strongest sea-state in Greece. The carrying out of this policy in the face of scepticism and opposition was the great achievement of Themistocles. He began the work when he was archon and thus already a

493-2 B.C.

man of some prominence, two or three years before the battle of Marathon, by carrying a measure through the Assembly for the fortification of the peninsula of Piraeus. Hitherto the wide exposed strand of Phaleron was the harbour where the Athenians kept their triremes, hauled up on the beach, unprotected against the surprise of an enemy, but within sight of the Acropolis. At that time, after the quelling of the Ionic revolt, Persian warships were cruising about the Aegean, and the possibility of an attack on Phaleron seems to have opened the eyes of the Athenians to the need of re-forming their naval establishment. The hostility of Aegina was a nearer and more pressing motive. The Athenians had not to seek far for a suitable port. It seems strange that they had not before made use of "the Piraeus," the large harbour on the west side of the peninsula of Munychia, which could be supplemented by the two smaller harbours on the east side, Munychia and Zea. But the Piraeus was somewhat farther from the city, and was not within sight of the Acropolis like Phaleron. So long, therefore, as there was no fortified harbour, Phaleron was safer. The plan of Themistocles was to fortify the whole circuit of the peninsula by a wall, and prepare docks in the three harbours for the reception of the warships. The work was begun, but it was interrupted by the Persian invasion, and by the party struggles after Marathon. Then the war with Aegina broke out, and this, combined with the fear of another Persian invasion, helped Themistocles to carry to completion another part of his great scheme—the increase of the fleet. A rich bed of silver had been recently discovered at Maronea, in the old mining district of Laurion, and had suddenly brought into the public treasury a large sum, perhaps a hundred talents. It was proposed to distribute this among the citizens, but Themistocles persuaded the Assembly to apply it to the purpose of building new ships. Special contributions for the same object must have been made soon afterwards; more ships were built; and two years later we find Athens with nearly 200 triremes at her command—a navy which could be compared with those of Syracuse and Corcyra. The completion of the Piraeus wall was not attempted at this period, but was accomplished, as we shall see, after the final repulse of the Persians from the shores of Greece.

Harbours of Piraeus.

Increase of fleet.

(Camareza.)
483-2 B.C.
£27,000.
482 B.C.

CHAPTER VII

THE PERILS OF GREECE. THE PERSIAN AND PUNIC INVASIONS

THE
SECOND
PERSIAL/
WAR.

WE have now reached the threshold of the second and the greater Persian invasion—the second and the greater triumph of Hellas. The significance of this passage in their history was not lost upon the Greeks. Their defence of Europe against the barbarians of Asia, the discomfiture of a mighty oriental despot by a league of their free states, the defeat of a vast army and a large fleet by their far smaller forces,—these surprises made an enduring impression upon the Greek mind, and were shaped by Greek imagination into a wonderful dramatic story at a time when the critical instinct had not yet developed. No tale is more delightful than this tale as Herodotus tells it, when we take it simply as a tale; and none illustrates better the story-shaping genius of the Greeks. The historical criticism of it is another matter: we have to seek to extract what actually happened out of the bewildering succession of daring exaggerations, naïve anecdotes, fictitious motives, oracles, not to speak of miracles; in most of which the reflected light of later events is visibly altering the truth, while much is coloured by the prejudices and leanings of the Athenians, from whom Herodotus seems to have derived a great part of his record.

SECT. 1. THE PREPARATIONS AND MARCH OF XERXES

(490-80
B.C.)

The chief event in Persia during the ten years which elapsed between the first and second invasions of Greece was the death of king Darius. After the unexpected repulse of his forces at Marathon, he had determined to repeat the experiment and begun to make some preparations. Four years passed and then a revolt broke out in the province of Egypt which demanded immediate attention. But its suppression was delayed in consequence of the king's death, and was only accomplished under Xerxes, son of Atossa, who succeeded to the throne. The question then arose whether the design of an expedition against Greece, to avenge those who fell at Marathon and redeem the fame of Persian arms, should be carried out. It is related that Xerxes was himself undecided, but was over-persuad-

(486-5
B.C.)
Death of
Darius,
485 B.C.

Subjuga-
tion of
Egypt,
484-3 B.C.

ed by the impetuous counsels of his cousin Mardonius. On the other hand, his uncle Artabanus appears in the pages of Herodotus as the prudent and experienced adviser who weighs all the obstacles and foresees failure. Xerxes, swayed hither and thither between these opposing counsels, is finally determined to yield to the wishes of Mardonius by the peremptory command of a dream, which overcomes even the scruples of Artabanus. In this manner does Herodotus pretend to take us behind the curtain of the council chamber at Susa, representing—in the light of later events—the advice of Mardonius as youthful and foolish, although that advice merely amounted to the execution of the design which, according to Herodotus himself, the old and experienced Darius had initiated and prepared. Nevertheless the contrast of Mardonius and Artabanus, and the dreams divinely sent with evil purpose, are, though not historical, a most effective dramatic introduction to the episode of the invasion. Further pressure was brought to bear on the king by Greeks who visited his court—envoys from the Aleuad princes of Thessaly and members of the Pisistratid family who brought with them the seer Onomacritus to impress Xerxes by favourable oracles.

It was clear that the expedition must consist of a joint attack by sea and land. Preparations were begun by the difficult enterprise of digging a canal (about a mile and a half long) across the isthmus of Mount Athos. On the occasion of the expedition of Mardonius to Thrace and Macedonia, it will be remembered that a large part of the fleet had been wrecked in rounding that dangerous headland. But was it necessary for the fleet to venture on this occasion within the proximity of Cape Athos? Might it not sail straight across the Aegean to Greece? On these grounds Herodotus suggested that the cutting of Athos was undertaken for display rather than from necessity. This is an unsound criticism. It was a fundamental principle of Persian strategy in these expeditions that the army and navy should co-operate and never lose touch. The Thracian expedition of Darius, the Macedonian expedition of Mardonius, the Greek expedition of Xerxes illustrate this principle. The canal of Athos was intended to ensure that the ships should safely accompany the land forces along the coasts of Thrace.[1] It seems to be established that the work was completed and used, although later writers threw doubts on the "velification" of Athos. When it was finished, the workmen proceeded to lay a bridge over the Strymon for the pas-

Canal of Athos, 483 B.C.

---

[1] Once through Athos the fleet was sheltered from the dangerous north-east winds, and it was not necessary to cut through the flat-shored promontories of Sithonia and Pallene.

sage of the army, and preparations were made all along the line of route for the feeding of a vast host.

Xerxes came down from Susa to Sardis in the autumn. He met the oriental contingents of his army at Critalla in Cappadocia. At Celaenae it is recorded that Pythius, the richest man in the empire, entertained at his own cost the king and the whole army. His wealth amounted to four million gold darics, all but seven thousand, and Xerxes bestowed upon him seven thousand to make up the full sum. Xerxes spent the winter at Sardis. Pythius was so pleased with the king's graciousness that when the army was about to start for the Hellespont in the following spring he ventured to prefer the request that the eldest of his five sons who were serving in the army might be permitted to remain behind. Great was the king's wrath at what he regarded as the insolent demand of a "slave." The body of the eldest son was cut in two; one half was placed at each side of the gate of Sardis, through which the army was about to march forth. The anecdote illustrates the severity with which personal military service was enforced.

Crossing
of the
Helles-
pont,
April,
480 B.C.

It is impossible to suppose that the whole army wintered in Sardis with the king; it is probable that the place of mustering was at the Hellespont across which two bridges had been constructed, in the neighbourhood of Sestos and Abydos, by Phoenician and Egyptian engineers. But the strength of these bridges was not sufficient, and a tempest destroyed them. The wrath of Xerxes at this catastrophe was violent. He not only beheaded the engineers, but commanded that 300 lashes should be inflicted on the waters of the Hellespont. Those who carried out this strange order addressed the sea as they scourged it in these words: "O bitter water, our lord lays this punishment upon thee, for having done him wrong, who never did wrong to thee. King Xerxes will cross thee, whether thou wilt or not. Just is it that no man sacrifices to thee, for thou art a treacherous and briny river." These words are blamed by Herodotus as "un-Greek and impious." The reconstruction of the bridges was entrusted to new engineers. Two lines of ships were moored across the strait by anchors at prow and stern. The line nearer to the Propontis consisted of 360, the other of 314, triremes and penteconters mixed. Over each of these lines of ships six huge cables—two of flax, four of papyrus—were stretched; and in three places gaps were left between the ships and under the cables for small trading craft to pass between the Euxine and the Aegean. Planks were laid across the cables and kept in their places by a second layer of cables above. On this foundation a road was made with wood and earth, and at each side palisades were set, high enough to prevent the animals which

passed over from seeing the water. On a marble throne erected on
the shore Xerxes is said to have witnessed the passage of his army,
which began at the first moment of sunrise. The troops crossed
under the lash, and the crossing was accomplished in two days. But
when the size of the Persian host was magnified, in later years, to
the impossible figure of five millions, the story was that the crossing
of the Hellespont required seven days and seven nights—the favourite number of fiction—without a moment's pause.

The army was joined by the fleet at Doriscus in Thrace. Fleet
and army were henceforward to act together. In the plain of Doriscus Xerxes reviewed and numbered his forces. "What nation of
Asia," asks Herodotus, "did not Xerxes lead against Hellas?" He
enumerates forty-six peoples, with a picturesque description of their
array. The Persians themselves, who were under the command of
Otanes, wore coats of mail and trowsers; they had wicker shields,
large bows, and short spears. The Medes, Cissians, and Hyrcanians
were attired in the same way. Then there were Assyrians with brazen helmets, linen cuirasses, clubs, lances, and short swords; Bactrians with cane bows; trowsered Sacae with pointed hats, and
carrying axes; Indians clad in cotton, Caspians in goatskin; Saran-
gians wearing dyed garments and high boots; Ethiopians clad in
lion skins or leopard skins and armed with arrows whose stone
points transport us to a primitive age; Sagartians with dagger and
lasso; Thracians with foxskin caps; Colchians with cowskin shields.
The fleet was furnished by the Phoenicians, Egyptians, Cypriotes,
Cilicians, Pamphylians, Lycians, Carians, and subject Greeks. It is
said to have consisted of 1207 warships, with 3000 smaller vessels.
A curious story was told of the numbering of the army. Ten thousand men were packed together in a close space; a line was drawn
round them, and a wall built. All the infantry passed successively
into this enclosure. It was filled 170 times, so that the whole number
of fighting men was 1,700,000. The number of the cavalry was
80,000, and there were some additional troops not included. Adding
to these the crews of the ships—counting 200 to each larger and 80
to each smaller vessel—the total was obtained of 2,317,000 men.
This enormous number was further increased by fresh contingents
which joined during the march through Thrace and Macedonia.
Besides the fighting men were a vast number of servants, sutlers,
camp-followers, whom Herodotus considered to be quite as numerous as the soldiers. The whole host would consequently have
reached to upwards of 5,000,000, not including eunuchs and concubines.

It is needless to say that these numbers are wholly fabulous.

Descrip-
tion of
Persian
forces.

Fabulous
numbers.

The facts which Herodotus states as to the number of the fighting men are false, and the principle of his conjecture that the total number of the host was double that of the fighting men is also fallacious. The picked body of 10,000 troops, called the Immortals, had the privilege of travelling comfortably with their wives and baggage; but this was an exceptional privilege, and it cannot be supposed that the mass of the troops were accompanied by servants. There is reason for supposing that the land forces may have amounted to 300,000—hardly more. A larger force than that would have been unmanageable in a small mountainous country, and the difficulties of provisioning even this were formidable. The number of the fleet must also be considerably reduced—perhaps to 800 triremes.

From Doriscus, Xerxes proceeded to Therma with his fabulous host, in three divisions, drinking rivers dry in their march. At the crossing of the Strymon, near the place called the Nine Roads, he sacrificed nine native youths and virgins. At Therma he was rejoined by his fleet, which had been separated from him while it sailed round Sithonia and Pallene.

August,
480 B.C.

Tendencies of the Greek story

Most of the incidents which Herodotus recounts concerning this march of Xerxes are pleasing stories, designed to illustrate the historian's general view as to the great struggle of Greek and barbarian. The cruelty of Xerxes to Pythius, his barbarity and impiety in scourging the Hellespont, serve to characterise the barbarian and the despot. The enormity of the host which rolled over the straits to deluge Europe enhances the danger and the glory of Hellas. And to signify by a solemn portent the destined discomfiture of the Persian host, it is stated that as Xerxes was setting forth from Sardis the sun was darkened. This eclipse actually happened two years later; the tradition which Herodotus follows transposed its date to an impressive and significant occasion.

(Feb. 16,
478 B.C.).

SECT. 2. PREPARATIONS OF GREECE

In the meantime Greece was aware of the preparations of the Great King for her enslavement, and was making her counter-preparations. The digging at Athos had warned her betimes, and the coming down of the king to Sardis showed that the danger was imminent. Xerxes is said to have dispatched from Sardis heralds to all the Greek states, except Athens and Sparta, to demand earth and water. These two cities now joined hands to resist the invasion. They were naturally marked out as the leaders of Greece in Greece's greatest crisis; Sparta by virtue of that generally acknowledged headship which we have already seen, Athens by the prestige which she had won in resisting the Mede at Marathon. They jointly convened an Hellenic congress at the Isthmus to consult on the measures to be taken for common resistance to the threatened invasion. We have already observed certain indications of the growth of a Panhellenic feeling; but this is the first instance of anything that can be called a deliberate Panhellenic policy. It is an "attempt to combine all the scattered cities of the Greek world to withstand the power of Persia. It is a new fact in Grecian history, opening scenes and ideas unlike to anything which has gone before—enlarging prodigiously the functions and duties connected with that headship of Greece which had hitherto been in the hands of Sparta, but which is about to become too comprehensive for her to manage." [1] A large number of cities sent delegates to the congress, which was called the *Synedrion of Probuloi* or Congress of Representatives. It met at the Isthmus—a meeting-place marked out by its central position—under the presidency of Sparta. There the states which were represented, thirty-one in number, bound themselves together in a formal confederation by taking a solemn oath that they would "tithe those who uncompelled submitted" to the barbarian, for the benefit of the Delphic god. This was a way of vowing that they would utterly destroy such traitors. A great many states, the Thessalians, most of the Boeotian cities, besides the smaller peoples of northern Greece—Locrians, Malians, Achaeans, Dolophians, and others—took no part in this congress. Their inaction by no means meant that they had made up their minds to "medize." They were only waiting to see how things would turn out, and, considering their geographical position, their policy might be justified by the natural instinct of self-preservation. These northern states would be first invaded by the Persian, and it was hopeless for them to think of withstanding him alone. Unless they could absolutely rely on Sparta and her confederates to support them in defending the northern frontier of Thessaly, nothing would be left for them but to submit. And with this prospect, it would have been imprudent for them to compromise themselves by openly joining the confederacy. Events proved that if they had seriously relied on that confederacy throwing all its strength into the defence of northern Greece, they would have been cruelly deceived. And, as we shall see, they were ready to resist so long as there were hopes of support from the stronger states. In some cases there were parties or classes who were favourable to the Persian cause, for example, the oligarchs of Thebes and the Aleuadae of Thessaly.

[1] Grote.

One of the great hindrances to joint action was the existence of domestic disputes. There were feuds of old standing between Thessaly and Phocis, Argos and Lacedaemon, Athens and Aegina. The Congress attempted to reconcile such feuds, and Athens and Aegina laid aside their enmity to fight together for Grecian freedom. Another important question concerned the command of the confederate forces. The claim of Sparta to the leadership of the army was at once admitted. The question as to the fleet was not so clear. Sparta was not a naval power, and Athens, which would furnish more ships than any other state, had a fair claim. But the other cities were jealous of Athens; they declared that they would submit only to a Spartan leader. The Athenian representatives, when they saw the feeling of the allies, at once yielded the point.

Question of leadership.

The Congress made some other provisions. While spies were sent to observe the preparations of Xerxes in Asia Minor, envoys went forth to various Greek states to enlist new confederates—to win over Argos, which had sent no delegates to the Isthmus; and to obtain promises of assistance from Crete, Corcyra, and Syracuse. None of these embassies led to anything. Gelon, the great tyrant of Syracuse, was himself absorbed by the prospect of an attack of the Carthaginians, and, even if he had wished, could have sent no aid to the mother-country.

Appeal to Syracuse.

When the military preparations for the defence of Greece were made, and the generals appointed, the Congress of Representatives probably met again in spring, and then consigned the conduct of affairs to the military congresses of the commanders who used to meet together and decide on each movement under the presidency of the Spartan leaders. King Leonidas was leader of the confederate army, and Eurybiadas, a Spartan who did not belong to either of the royal families, was commander of the confederate fleet.

(480 B.C.).

The Greeks had abundance of time for their preparations—for strengthening their defences and building new ships. Athens probably threw herself with more energy into the work than any other city. One wise measure shows that she had risen to a full apprehension of the truth that a solemn hour in her history had arrived. She recalled those distinguished citizens whom the vote of ostracism had driven into banishment during the last ten years. Aristides and Xanthippus returned home; their feuds with Themistocles were buried in the presence of the great danger; and the city seems to have soon shown its confidence in their patriotism by choosing them as Generals. These leaders will each play his part in the coming struggle.

Athens recalls ostracized statesmen, spring, 480 B.C.

Sect. 3. Battles of Thermopylae and Artemisium

About the time when Xerxes reached the Hellespont, the Thessalians sent a message to the confederacy, suggesting that the pass of Tempe should be defended against the invading army. Accordingly 10,000 hoplites were sent. But when they arrived at the spot they found that there were other passes from Macedonia into Thessaly, by which the Persians would be more likely to come. There were the passes of Volustana and Petra which descended into the valley of the river Titaresius, and it was by one of these that Xerxes actually marched. Ten thousand hoplites were not enough to defend the three passes, and it seemed useless and dangerous to occupy this advanced post. Hence the defence of Tempe was abandoned, and the troops left Thessaly. This desertion necessarily drove all the northern Greeks—between Tempe and Thermopylae —to signify their submission to Xerxes by the offering of earth and water.

Northern passes left open.

The next feasible point of defence was Thermopylae, a narrow pass between the sea and mountain, separating Trachis from Locris. It was the gate to all eastern Greece south of Mount Oeta. At the eastern and at the western end the pass, in those days, was extremely narrow, and in the centre the Phocians had constructed a wall as a barrier against Thessalian incursions. Near the western end was Anthela, the meeting-place of the amphictionic council, while on the Locrian side one emerged from the defile near the village of Alpenoi. The retreat of the sea, and consequent enlargement of the Malian plain, have so altered the appearance of this memorable pass that it is hard to recognise its ancient description; the hot sulphur springs from which it derived its name and the sheer mountain are the two permanent features. It was possible for an active band of men, if they were debarred from proceeding by Thermopylae, to take a rough and steep way over the mountains and so reach the Locrian road at a point east of Alpenoi. It was therefore needful for a general who undertook the defence of Thermopylae to secure this path, lest a detachment should be sent round to surprise him in the rear.

Thermopylae, natural features.

The Greeks determined to defend Thermopylae, and Leonidas marched thither at the head of his army. He had about 7000 men, including 4000 from Peloponnesus, 1000 Phocians, 400 Thebans, 700 Thespians, and the Locrians in full force. It is possible that there may have been some other Boeotians who are not mentioned. Of the Peloponnesians more than half were Arcadians. Mycenae,

Greek troops at Thermopylae.

free at this moment from Argive control, sent 80 men. There were Corinthians and Phliasians; 1000 Laconians, and 300 Spartans. So far as the Peloponnesians were concerned, this was only a small portion of their forces, and we may suspect that but for Athens they would have abandoned northern Greece entirely and concentrated themselves at once on the defence of the Isthmus. But they were dependent on Athens because her fleet was so strong, and they were therefore obliged to consider her interests. To surrender Thermopylae and retire to the Isthmus meant the surrender of Attica.

Policy of Sparta.

But the hearts of the Spartans were really set on the ultimate defence of the Isthmus, and not on the protection of the northern states; their policy was narrow and Peloponnesian. They attempted to cover this selfish and short-sighted policy by the plea that they were hindered from marching forth in full force by the celebration of the Carnean festival, and that the Peloponnesians were delayed by the Olympic games; they alleged that the soldiers of Leonidas were only an advance guard, the rest would soon follow. Yet the feasts did not interfere with the movement of the confederate fleet.

Position of Greek fleet.

As the land arm and the sea arm of the Persian force always operated together, it was necessary that while the Greek hoplites held the pass under Mount Oeta, the Greek triremes should oppose the Persian fleet in the straits between Euboea and the mainland. The Persians would naturally attempt to sail between Euboea and Magnesia into the Malian gulf, and thence, accompanying the advance of the army, along the western shore of the long island, to the Euripus. The object of the Greeks was to prevent this, and support the garrison of Thermopylae by controlling the Malian gulf.

The Greek fleet, which numbered 324 triremes and 9 penteconters—the Athenians contributing 200—chose its station near Artemisium on the north coast of Euboea. Three ships were sent forward to reconnoitre in the Thermaic gulf, and two of them were destroyed by the Persians. This was the first collision in the war. The incident is said to have so depressed the Greeks that the whole squadron sailed back to the Euripus; but this is highly unlikely, for it was bound to remain at the mouth of the Malian gulf, so long as Leonidas held Thermopylae. It was however necessary that the Euripus should be guarded. For there was the possibility that the Persians might send round a detachment by the south of Euboea and so cut off their retreat. As fifty-three Athenian ships were absent during the first conflicts at Artemisium, it may be supposed that they were deputed to the service of keeping watch at the Euripus.

In the month of July the Persian army arrived at Thermopylae,

and the Persian navy at the Magnesian coast between Casthanaea
and Cape Sepias. Their ships were so many that they could not all
be moored at the shore, and had to range themselves in eight lines
parallel to the coast. While they were in this unsafe position a great
storm rose and destroyed, at the lowest computation, 400 ships.
Thus the gods intervened, to lessen the inequality between the Persian and the Greek forces. Encouraged by this disaster, the Greek
fleet returned to its station at Artemisium. In this account of Herodotus, the main fact is that the Persians suffered serious loss by a

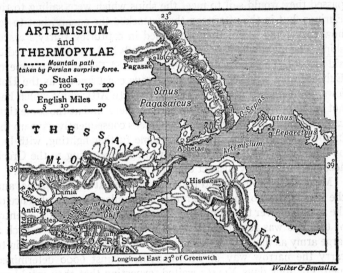

FIG. 49.

storm off the Magnesian coast. But the loss is exaggerated in proportion to the exaggeration of the original size of the fleet, and the
movements of the Greeks are probably misrepresented. The story
goes on that cowed by the numerical superiority of the Persians,
even after their losses, the Greek commanders wished to retreat
again and were restrained from doing so by Themistocles. The
Euboeans were naturally anxious that the fleet should remain where
it was, as a protection to themselves, and to secure this they gave
Themistocles thirty talents. Of this sum Themistocles distributed
eight in bribes to his colleagues and kept the rest. The facts of the
case throw doubt on this story, which was perhaps suggested by
what happened some weeks later at Salamis. For Eurybiadas and
the Peloponnesians were bound to stay at Artemisium so long as the
land army was at Thermopylae.

After the storm the Persians took up their station at Aphetae. They determined to cut off the Greek retreat, and secretly sent a squadron of 200 vessels to sail round Euboea. The news of this movement was brought to the Greek camp by Scyllias of Scione, the most remarkable diver of his time, who plunged into the sea at Aphetae and did not emerge above water till he reached Artemisium at a distance of ten miles. Herodotus, indeed, hesitates to accept this tale, and records his private belief that Scyllias arrived at Artemisium in a boat. The Greeks decided that when midnight had passed they would sail to meet the ships which were sailing to the Euripus, but in the afternoon they attacked the enemy, just to see how they fought, and they succeeded in capturing thirty Persian ships. The night was very stormy; the gods had again intervened to aid Greece. The 200 ships, having rounded the southern cape of Euboea, were wrecked off the dangerous coast known as the Hollows. Immediately afterwards the fifty-three Attic ships which had not yet appeared at Artemisium arrived there, and at the same time came the news of the disaster. The Greeks consequently gave up the intention of retreating. There was some further fighting, with loss on both sides; with no decisive advantage, according to the Greek account, but we may suspect that the Persians had the best of it.

Meanwhile Leonidas had taken up his post at Thermopylae, and the Phocians, who knew the ground, had undertaken the defence of the bye-road over the mountains. The old Phocian wall in the centre of the pass was repaired. It was a serious matter for even such a large army as that which was now encamped in the Malian plain to carry the narrow way of Thermopylae against 6000 determined men. For four days Xerxes waited, expecting that they would retreat, awed by the vision of his mighty host. On the fifth he attacked; and in the engagements which took place at the west end of the pass the Hellenic spearmen affirmed their distinct superiority to the Asiatic archers. On the following day the result was the same; the Immortals themselves made no impression on the defenders. Herodotus says that Xerxes "sprang thrice from his throne in agony for his army." It was then decided to send round the Immortals—hardly the whole 10,000—under their commander Hydarnes, by the mountain road to take the Greeks in the rear. A Malian Greek named Epialtes guided the band and so won the name of having betrayed Greece. At dawn they reached the highest point of the path, where the Phocians were posted. The Phocians fled to the heights, and the Persians went on paying no attention to them. Meanwhile deserters informed Leonidas of the Persian stratagem. He hastily called a council of war. The exact plan of action which was decided on is unknown. We only know that the Spartans, Thebans, and Thespians remained in the pass, while the rest of the Greeks retired southward. It was afterwards represented that they had deserted the defence of the position and returned home. But in that case, it was foolish, if splendid, of Leonidas to hold the pass between foes on both sides. The rational courses were either for the whole garrison to abandon the pass, or else, just as the Persians aimed at enclosing the Greeks, so to enclose the band of Hydarnes. We may suspect that this second plan was actually adopted. While part of the force, including Leonidas and the Spartans, remained in the pass, the rest (we may suppose) placed themselves at some distance east of the point where the mountain path descended to the road, so as to take Hydarnes in the rear. Of the 1400 who stood in the pass, some had to guard the eastern entrance against Hydarnes, others the western against the main army. Leonidas and his 300 undertook the western side. But they were no longer content with merely repelling assaults; they now rushed out upon the enemy. Their charge was effective, but Leonidas himself was slain, and a Homeric battle raged over his body. Two brothers of Xerxes fell. Many Persians were driven into the sea. But at length the defenders were forced back behind the wall. They drew together on a hillock where they made a last stand, to be surrounded and slain by overwhelming numbers. For the Immortals, having in the meantime routed the Greeks in their rear, had now forced their way into the pass. It was said that 4000 Greeks fell.

The valiant defence of Thermopylae made a deep impression upon Greece, and increased the fame of the Spartans for bravery. It was represented as a forlorn defence—Leonidas and his band devoting themselves to certain death, and clinging to their posts from that sense of military duty which was inculcated by the Spartan system from early youth. The brave Thespians would not desert the Spartans; while the Thebans are represented as detained by Leonidas against their will, because they were suspected of secret medism. The malicious tale adds that, having taken only a perfunctory part in the defence, the Thebans advanced to the enemy and asked for quarter, declaring that they were friends of the Great King and had come to Thermopylae against their will. Their lives were spared, but all, including the commander, were forced to suffer the shame of being branded as bad slaves. It is certain that this contrast between the Thespians and Thebans was invented in the light of the subsequent medism of Thebes. Nor is it clear that the defence of Themopylae, although eminently heroic, was, until the very end, desperate. If, as we suspected, an effort was made to

Behaviour of Thebans

meet the Immortals, then, if that effort had been more effectual, it might have been possible to hold the pass; and in that case a naval battle must have decided whether the Persians or the Greeks would be forced to retreat.

A column was afterwards erected at Sparta with the names of Leonidas and his 300. Among them was to be read the name of Diēnekes, reputed as the author of a famous *mot*, which displayed the lightheartedness of a Spartan soldier in the hour of peril. When it was observed to him that the Persian host was so enormous that their arrows hid the sun, he replied, "So much the better, we shall fight in the shade."

Retreat of Greek fleet.

The news of Thermopylae speedily reached the fleet at Artemisium. The Greeks forthwith weighed anchor and sailed through the Euripus to the shores of Attica.

Sect. 4. Battle of Salamis

480 B.C. (August).

Having thus succeeded in breaking through the inner gate of Hellas, and slain the king of the leading state, Xerxes continued his way and passed from Locris into Phocis and thence into Boeotia, meeting with no resistance. The Thebans and most of the other Boeotians now, unable to do otherwise, submitted to the Persians. The loss of Thermopylae forced them to this course, as the abandonment of Tempe had forced the Thessalians.

Delphic legend.

In later days a story was told at Delphi that a Persian band detached itself from the main host in Phocis, in order to proceed to Pytho and plunder the shrine of the god. "I think," says Herodotus, "that Xerxes knew its treasures better than his own." The Delphians fled up into the heights of Parnassus, leaving only sixty men and the prophet Acērătus in the temple. They did not remove the treasures, for the god said that he would protect his own. As soon as the barbarians approached, marvels began to happen. The prophet saw the sacred arms, which no man might touch, lying in front of the temple, carried out by some mysterious means. And when the Persians came to the shrine of Athena Pronaea, which stood not far from the Castalian fountain, lightning flashed; two crags rent from Parnassus fell with a loud crash, crushing many of them; and a war-whoop was heard from Athena's temple. The barbarians fled in terror, and told how two hoplites of superhuman size pursued them. These were Phylacus and Autonous, the native heroes of Delphi. Such was the legend told at Delphi of the Persian invasion.

The Athenians

When the Athenians returned from Artemisium they found that

the main body of the Peloponnesian army was gathered at the leave
Attica.
Isthmus and engaged in building a wall from sea to sea, instead of
advancing to the defence of Boeotia as had been previously arranged. Thus Boeotia and Attica were unprotected. Themistocles
and his Athenian colleagues decided to evacuate Athens. They made
a proclamation that all the citizens should embark in the triremes,
and that all who could should convey their families and belongings
to places of safety. This was done. The women and children were
transported to Troezen, Aegina, and Salamis. The council of
Areopagus helped at this crisis by distributing from the treasury of
Athena eight drachmae to each citizen who embarked. At the same
time the great natural strength of the Acropolis, though its walls
had been demolished after the expulsion of the tyrants, encouraged
the hope that it might be held against the Persians, and a small garrison was left to defend it. This bold and wise policy of embarkation
was dictated by the circumstances, but it was supposed to have been
based on an oracle, which foretold the utter destruction of Attica
with the sole exception of a "wooden wall." The wooden wall was
interpreted to mean the ships. And to suit this view it was represented that the garrison left on the Acropolis was merely a handful
of poor citizens who remained behind and barricaded themselves
there, because they adopted the more literal interpretation of a
wooden barricade. This explanation of the oracle was perhaps
suggested by subsequent events.

While the Athenians were thus showing that they were not bound
to their soil, the allied fleet had stationed itself in the bay of
Salamis, and it was reinforced by new contingents, so that it
reached the total strength of 378 triremes and seven penteconters.
The army at the Isthmus was now placed under the command of
Cleombrotus, brother of Leonidas and guardian of his son Pleistarchus, who was still a child.

Xerxes arrived at Athens about the same time that his fleet c. Sept.
17.
sailed into the roadstead of Phaleron. He found the town empty,
but for the small band which had entrenched itself on the Acro- Persians
capture
the
Acropolis.
polis. Persian troops occupied the lower height of the Areopagus,
which is severed from the Acropolis by a broad saddle, and succeeded in setting the wooden barricade on fire by means of burning arrows. The garrison rolled stones down on them, and such is
the natural strength of the Acropolis that the siege lasted two
weeks. Then the Persians managed to ascend on the precipitous
north side by the secret path which emerged close to the shrine of
Aglaurus. The Greeks were slain, the temples plundered and burnt.

After the fall of the Acropolis the Greek generals held a council Will the

Greek
fleet
fight at
Salamis
or the
Isthmus?

of war, and it was carried by the votes of the majority that they should retreat to the Isthmus and await there the attack of the Persian fleet. The advantage of this seemed to be that they would there be in close touch with the land forces and have the Peloponnesus as a retreat in case of defeat; whereas at Salamis they would be entirely cut off. This decision meant the abandonment of Aegina, Salamis, and Megara; and it was strenuously opposed by the Aeginetans, Athenians, and Megarians. Themistocles determined to thwart it. He went privately to Eurybiadas and convinced him that it would be much more advantageous to fight in the narrow waters of the Salaminian channel than in the open bay of the Isthmus, where the superior speed and number of the hostile ships would tell. A new council was summoned at which, it is said, hot words passed between the Athenian and the Corinthian general. When Themistocles opened the debate without waiting for the formal introduction of Eurybiadas, the Corinthian Adeimantus said, "O Themistocles, those who stand up too soon in the games are whipped." "Yes," was the reply, "but those who start late are not crowned." It is recorded that Themistocles, in order to carry his point, had to threaten that the Athenians, who were half the fleet, would cease to co-operate with their allies and seek new homes in some western land, if the retreat to the Isthmus were decided. Themistocles won his way; and when it was resolved to fight in Salaminian waters, the heroes of the island, Ajax and Telamon, were invoked, and a ship was sent to Aegina to fetch the other Aeacid heroes.

What
Dema-
ratus and
Dicaeus
saw in the
Thriasian
plain.

Of all the tales of signs and marvels which befell in these memorable days none perhaps was more attractive to the Athenians than the experience of two Greek exiles as they walked in the Thriasian plain. One was an Athenian named Dicaeus, and his companion was none other than Demaratus, the Spartan king, who had sought refuge at the Persian court. As they went, they saw a great dust afar off near Eleusis, such a dust as they thought might be raised by a host of thirty thousand men; and then they heard a voice suddenly from the midst of the dust, and it sounded like the cry of the mystic Iacchus which is cried at the Eleusinian festival. Demaratus asked his companion what it might be. "It is a token," said Dicaeus, "of some great disaster to the King's host. For since the plain is desolate of men, it is clear that the thing which uttereth the cry is divine,—and it is a thing coming from Eleusis to help the Athenians. If it turn to the Peloponnese, the peril menaces the army of the land, but if it wend toward the ships, then are the King's ships endangered." "Peace," said Demaratus, "for if these words of thine come to the King's ears, thou shalt lose thy head." Then the dust, wherein the voice was, turned to a cloud, and rising aloft moved towards the Greek fleet at Salamis: and so they knew that the fleet of Xerxes was doomed.

Meanwhile the Persians too had deliberated and determined to fight. According to a Halicarnassian story told by Herodotus, the Carian queen Artemisia alone gave sound advice—not to risk a sea fight but either to wait for the Greek fleet to disperse from want of provisions, or to advance by land into the Peloponnesus.

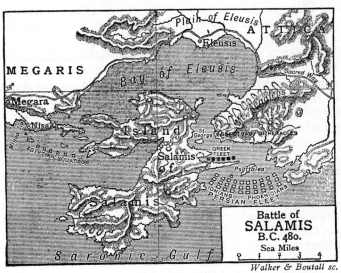

Walker & Boutall sc.

FIG. 50.

The southern entrance to the narrow sound between Salamis and Attica is blocked by the islet of Psyttalea and the long promontory which runs out from Salamis towards the mainland. The Greek fleet was anchored close to the town of Salamis, north of this promontory. It would be best for the Greeks if they could lure the Persian fleet to enter the Salaminian bay so that its flank would be exposed as it sailed through the narrow waters. It would be best for the Persians if they could force the Greeks out into the open sea. Xerxes foresaw the possibility that his enemies might attempt to escape at night, and to prevent this he moved his armament so as to enclose the ingresses of the two straits on either side of Psyttalea, and landed troops on that island, to rescue Persians and kill Greeks who should happen to swim to its shores in the expected battle.

These movements, carried out in the afternoon, alarmed the Greeks; the Peloponnesian commanders brought pressure to bear on Eurybiadas; another council was called, and Themistocles saw that the hard-won result of his previous exertions would now be overthrown. He therefore determined on a bold stroke. Leaving the council, he dispatched a slave named Sicinnus to the Persian camp bearing a message from himself, as a well-wisher to Xerxes, that the Greeks purposed to sail away in the night. If they were prevented from doing so, a Persian victory was certain, owing to the disunion which existed in the Hellenic camp. If the Persians attacked the Greeks where they were, the Athenians would turn against their allies. This message was believed, and Xerxes took his measures at nightfall to hinder the Greek fleet from escaping by the western straits between Salamis and the Megarid. He sent his 200 Egyptian ships to round the southern promontory of Salamis and place themselves so that they could bar the straits. And he decided to attack in the morning—a fatal decision, which only the prospect of the treachery of some of his foes could have induced him to take.

The Greek generals meanwhile were engaged in hot discussion. Suddenly Themistocles was called out from the council. It was his rival Aristides who had sailed across from Aegina and brought the news that the fleet was surrounded by the enemy. Themistocles made Aristides inform the generals of what had happened, and the tidings was presently confirmed by a Tenian ship which deserted from the Persians. There is no reason to question the sensational incident that Aristides brought the news; but we need not suppose that this was his first return from ostracism. It seems probable that he had been sent with the ship which fetched the Aeacids from Aegina and that he was one of the ten strategoi.

Themistocles had managed that a naval battle should be fought at Salamis, and under the conditions most favourable to the Greeks. The position and tactics of the two armaments have been the subject of much debate. According to the poet Aeschylus, who was an eyewitness of the battle, the Persian ships were drawn up in three lines outside the entrance into the sound. The extreme left wing was composed of the Ionian Greeks, while the right, towards the Piraeus, was the Phoenician squadron on which Xerxes chiefly relied. The Greek fleet was drawn up behind the promontory of Cynosura and facing northward; the Athenians on the left, near the town of Salamis; the Aeginetans probably near them; and the Lacedaemonians on the right. On the opposite mainland shore, un-

Artifice of Themistocles to bring on a battle.

Position of fleets on day before battle.

der Mount Aegaleos, a high throne was erected, from which Xerxes could survey the battle and watch the conduct of his men.

At break of day the Persians began to advance into the straits. The three lines converted their formation into three columns, and the Phoenicians led the way through the opening between Psyttalea and the mainland. The Ionians on the left would naturally move through the smaller channel between Psyttalea and Salamis. When the Phoenicians came into view, the Athenian squadron immediately advanced, assailed them in the flank, and cut them off from the rest of the fleet, driving them towards the Attic shore. The other Persian divisions crowded through the straits, and a furious mellay ensued, which lasted till nightfall. There was no room for the exercise of tactical skill in the crowded, narrow waters, where the fairway (between Cynosura and Attica) is little more than a mile in breadth. The valour of the Aeginetans was conspicuous. They seem to have completed the discomfiture of the Phoenicians, and to have dispersed the Ionians.

The battle, c. Sept. 20.

The Persians, under the eyes of their king, fought with great bravery, but they were badly generalled and the place of the combat was unfavourable to them. By sunset the great armament of Xerxes was partly destroyed, partly put out of action. Aristides, who with a force of Athenian hoplites was watching events on the shore of Salamis, crossed over to Psyttalea and killed the barbarians who had been posted there by Xerxes.

Causes of Persian defeat.

Among the anecdotes told about this battle the most famous is that which was current at Halicarnassus, of the signal bravery and no less signal good fortune of the Carian queen Artemisia. She saved herself by the stratagem of attacking and sinking another Carian vessel. Those who stood round Xerxes observed the incident, but supposed the destroyed trireme to be Greek. "Sire," they said, "seest thou how Artemisia has sunk an enemy's ship." And Xerxes exclaimed, "My men have become women, my women men."

Anecdote of Artemisia.

Sect. 5. Consequences of Salamis

The Greek victory of Salamis was a heavy, perhaps a decisive, blow to the naval arm of the Persian power. The wrath of Xerxes against the Phoenicians was boundless. On them he had relied, and to their infidelity he ascribed the loss of the battle; his threats so frightened the remnant of the Phoenician contingent that they deserted. But the prospects of the ultimate success of the invasion

Movements of the Persians after the defeat

were still favourable. The land army had met with no reverse, and was overwhelmingly superior in numbers. The only difficulty was to keep it supplied with provisions, and in this respect the loss of the command of the sea was a serious misfortune. The Greeks represented Xerxes as smitten with wild terror, fleeing back overland to the Hellespont and hardly drawing breath till he reached Susa. This dramatic glorification of the victory misrepresents the situation. Xerxes personally was in no jeopardy. The real danger lay not in Attica but in Ionia. The Persians had good reason to fear the effect which the news of the crushing defeat of their navy might have upon the Greeks of Asia, and if Xerxes dreaded anything, he dreaded the revolt which actually came to pass in the following year. It was all-important for him to secure his line of retreat, while he had no intention of relinquishing his enterprise of conquering Greece. These considerations explain what happened. The Persian fleet was immediately dispatched to the Hellespont to guard the bridge and the line of retreat. The land forces were placed under the command of Mardonius, who, as the season was now advanced, determined to postpone further operations till the spring and to winter in Thessaly. A force of 60,000 men was detached to accompany Xerxes to the Hellespont.

When he arrived there he found that the bridge had been destroyed by storms—the same storms which had wrecked his ships off Magnesia. The fleet took him across to Abydos, and he proceeded to Sardis which he made his headquarters. The convoy of 60,000 soldiers returned to the main army in Thessaly, and on their way they laid siege to two towns, which afterwards became famous, on the Pallene isthmus, Olynthus and Potidaea. Olynthus, then a Bottiaean town, was taken and handed over to the Chalcidians who had remained faithful to Persia. Potidaea successfully withstood a siege of three months.

Meanwhile the Greeks had failed to follow up their victory. Cleombrotus was about to advance from the Isthmus with the purpose of aiming a blow at the retreating columns of the Persian forces before they reached Boeotia. But as he was sacrificing, before setting out, two hours after noon on the second of October, the sun was totally eclipsed, and this ill-omen made him desist from his plan and march back to the Peloponnesus. Themistocles tried to induce the naval commanders to follow up their advantage by sailing after the Persian fleet to the Hellespont, that they might deal it another blow and break down the bridge. It might be expected that, if this were done, the Greeks of Ionia would revolt. But the Peloponnesians would not consent to sail to a distant part of the world, while the Isthmus was still threatened by the presence of the Persian army. The story goes that, having failed to get his advice adopted, Themistocles, with that characteristic adroitness which won the admiration of his contemporaries, determined to utilise his failure. The faithful Sicinnus was sent to Xerxes to assure the monarch of the goodwill of Themistocles, who had dissuaded the Greeks from pursuing the Persian fleet. Themistocles might expect that Xerxes, having been deceived before, would now disbelieve his announcement and therefore hasten back with all speed to reach the Hellespont, if possible, before the Greeks. But on a later day of his life, when he was an exile, he claimed Persian gratitude for this service. It was even represented that, with extraordinary longsightedness or treachery, he had in his view the contingency of being driven to seek Persian help or protection against his countrymen. But the tale need not be seriously criticised; it has all the appearances of an invention suggested by subsequent adventures of the subtle Athenian.

The island of Andros and the Euboean city Carystus had furnished contingents to the Persian fleet. Just as the Athenians, after the battle of Marathon, had sailed against Paros and demanded a war contribution, so now the Greeks acted against Andros and Carystus. They failed at Andros, just as Miltiades had failed at Paros; they devastated the territory of Carystus.

Great was the rejoicing in Greece over the brilliant victory which was so little hoped for. The generals met at Isthmus to distribute the booty, and adjudge rewards. The Aeginetans received the choice lot of the spoil on account of their pre-eminent bravery, and dedicated in the temple of Delphi, on Apollo's express demand, three golden stars set on a mast of bronze. For bravery the Athenians were adjudged the second place. Prizes were also proposed for individuals who had distinguished themselves for valour, or for wisdom. In adjudging the prizes for wisdom, each captain wrote down two names in order of merit and placed his tablet on the altar of Poseidon at Isthmus. The story is that each wrote his own name first and that of Themistocles second, and that consequently there was no prize, for a second could not be given, unless a first were also awarded. This ingenious anecdote reflects the reputation for cleverness which had been won by Themistocles.

The Corinthians who fell in the battle were buried in Salamis, and their sepulchral stêlê was inscribed with a simple distich telling the stranger that "Salamis the isle of Ajax holds us now, who once dwelled in the city of Corinth between her waters." The stone has been recently found. This is only one of many epitaphs composed

Andros and Carystus

Prizes of bravery to the warriors of Salamis.

The epitaphs.

by nameless authors in those days of joy and sorrow in various parts of Greece, all marked by the simplicity of a great age, whose reserve, as has been said truly, is the pride of strong men under the semblance of modesty. In later days, insensible to such reserve, it became the fashion to improve these epitaphs by the addition of boastful verses, which have imposed, till recently, upon posterity; and the epitaphs thus disfigured were all said to be the workmanship of the poet Simonides. The exposure of these two deceptions increases our admiration for Hellas at the time of the invasion. There were men everywhere capable of writing a simple appropriate inscription for a grave, and the tombstones of the fallen were not used for superfluous boasts.

But the triumph of Hellas had nobler memorials than the unassuming verses of the tombs. The barbarian invasion affected art and literature, and inspired the creation of some of the great works of the world. Men seemed to rise at once to the sense of the high historical importance of their experience. The great poets of the day wrought it into their song; the great plastic artists alluded to it in their sculptures. Phrynichus had now a theme which he could treat without any dread of another fine. Aeschylus, who had himself fought against the Mede, made the tragedy of Xerxes the argument of a drama, which still abides the one great historical play, dealing with a contemporary event, that exists in literature. But the Persian war produced, though not so soon, another and a greater work than the *Persians;* it inspired the "father of history" with the theme of his book—the contest of Europe with Asia. The idea was afloat in the air that the Trojan war was an earlier act in the same drama,—that the warriors of Salamis and Plataea were fighting in the same cause as the heroes who had striven with Hector on the plain of Troy. Men might see, if they cared, this suggestion in the scenes from the two Trojan wars, which were wrought by the master sculptors of Aegina to deck the pediments of the temple of Athena, whose Doric columns still stand to remind us that Aegina once upon a time was one of the great states of Greece. And in other temples, friezes and pediments spoke in the conventional language of sculptured legend—by the symbols of Lapiths and Centaurs, Gods and Titans—of the struggle of Greek and barbarian.

Marginal notes:
The Phoenissae of Phrynichus. The Persians of Aeschylus, acted 472 B.C. Herodotus.

Sculptures in the Aeginetan temple of Athena.

Sect. 6. Preparations for another Campaign

Marginal note: Prospects of Greece.

The words of the poet Aeschylus, that the defeat of the Persian sea-host was the defeat of the land-host too, were perfectly true for the hour. But only for the hour. The army, compelled after Salamis to retreat to the north, spent the winter in the plains of Thessaly, and was ready for action, though unsupported by a fleet, in the following spring. The liberty of Greece was in greater jeopardy than ever, and the chances were that the success of Salamis would be utterly undone. For in the first place the Greeks, especially the Lacedaemonians and Athenians, found it hard to act together. This had been shown clearly the year before, eminently on the eve of the Salaminian battle. The Peloponnesian interests of the Lacedaemonians rendered them unwilling to meet the enemy in northern Greece; while the northern Greeks, unless they were supported from the Peloponnesus, could not attempt a serious resistance, and were therefore driven to come to terms with the barbarians. And, in the second place, if these difficulties were overcome and a Panhellenic force were opposed to the Persians, the chances were adverse to the Greeks; not from the disparity of numbers, but from the deficiency of the Greeks in cavalry.

In spring Mardonius was joined by Artabazus and the troops who had conducted Xerxes to the Hellespont. The total number of the forces now at the disposal of Mardonius is unknown; it may perhaps have been 150,000. Meanwhile the Persian fleet, 400 strong, but without the Phoenician ships, was collected at Samos, with the purpose of guarding Ionia; and a Greek squadron of 110 ships gathered at Aegina under the command of the Spartan king Leotychidas, for the purpose of defending the coasts of Greece, but not intending to assume the offensive. With great difficulty some envoys from Chios induced Leotychidas to advance as far as Delos, but he could not be moved to sail farther east with a view to the liberation of Ionia, for "Samos seemed as far away as the Pillars of Heracles," and he dreaded the Persian waters teeming with unknown dangers. It seems probable that Athenian policy was working upon the Spartan admiral's inexperience in military affairs. The object of the Athenians was to secure their own land against a second Persian occupation. They therefore desired the protection of the fleet for their coasts; but there was a more important consideration still. If the fleet took the offensive and gained another naval victory, the Peloponnesus would be practically secured against a Persian attack, defended at once by a victorious navy and the fortifications of the Isthmus. The result would be that the Peloponnesians would refuse to take any further part in the defence of northern Greece and would leave Athens a prey to the army of Mardonius. It was therefore the policy of the Athenians to keep the fleet inactive until the war should have been decided by a

479 B.C

Inactivity of Greek fleet.

battle on land; and for this reason they equipped only a few of their ships.

Mardonius, well aware of this fatal division of interests between the Athenians and Peloponnesians, made a politic attempt to withdraw Athens from the Greek league. He sent an honourable ambassador, King Alexander of Macedon himself, with the most generous offers. He undertook to repair all the injuries suffered by Athens from the Persian occupation, to help her to gain new territory, and asked only for her alliance as an equal and independent power. In a desolated land, amid the ruins of their city and its temples, knowing well that their allies, indifferent to the fate of Attica, were busy in completing the walls of Isthmus, the Athenians might be sorely tempted to lend an ear to these seductive overtures. Had they done so, the fate of Peloponnesus would have been sealed,—as the Lacedaemonians knew. Accordingly envoys were sent from Sparta to counteract the negotiations of Alexander, and to offer Athens material help in the privations which she was suffering. Tempting as the proposals of Mardonius sounded, and good reason as they had to depend little on the co-operation of their allies, the Athenians were constrained by that instinct of freedom which made them a great people, to decline the Persian offer. "Tell Mardonius," they said to Alexander, "that the Athenians say: so long as the sun moves in his present course, we will never come to terms with Xerxes." This answer utters the spirit of Europe in the "eternal question" between the East and West—the spirit of the Senate when Hannibal was at the gates of Rome, the spirit of Roman and Goth when they met the riders of Attila on the Catalaunian Plain.

Thus the embassy of Alexander ought to have strengthened rather than weakened the Greek league. It ought to have made the Lacedaemonians more actively conscious of the importance of Athenian co-operation, and consequently readier to co-operate with Athens. It enabled Athens to exert stronger pressure on the Peloponnesians, with a view to the defence of northern Greece; and the Spartan envoys promised that an army should march into Boeotia. But still stronger pressure was needed to overcome the selfish policy of the Peloponnesians. Soon after the embassy of Alexander they had completed the walling of the Isthmus, and, feeling secure, they took no thought of fulfilling their promise. The Spartans alleged in excuse the festival of the Hyacinthia, just as the year before they had pleaded the Carnea. And in the meantime Mardonius had set his army in motion and advanced into Boeotia, with the purpose of reoccupying Attica. Once more the Athenians had been cruelly deceived by their allies; once more they had to leave their land and remove their families and property to the refuge of Salamis. Mardonius reached Athens without burning or harrying; he still hoped to detach the Athenians from the Greek cause; herein lay his best chance of success. If they would now accept his former offers he would retreat from their land, leaving it unravaged. But even at this extremity, under the bitter disappointment of the ill-faith of their allies, the Athenians rejected the insidious propositions which were laid by an envoy before the Council of the Five Hundred at Salamis. Immediately the three northern states which had not yielded to the Mede, Athens, Megara, and Plataea, sent ambassadors to Sparta, to insist upon an army marching at once to oppose Mardonius in Attica—a tardy redemption of their promises—with the threat that otherwise there would be nothing for it but to come to terms with the foe. Even now the narrow Peloponnesian policy of the Ephors almost betrayed Greece. For ten days, it is said, they postponed answering the ambassadors, and would have ultimately refused to do anything, but for the intervention of a man of Tegea, named Chileos, who impressively pointed out that the alliance of the Athenian naval power with the Persians would render the Isthmian fortifications on which the Ephors relied absolutely useless. One would have fancied that this was obvious even to an Ephor, without a prophet from Tegea to teach him. However it happened, the Lacedaemonian government suddenly changed its policy and dispatched a force of 5000 Spartans, each attended by some Helots, to northern Greece. Never since, never perhaps before, did so large a body of Spartan citizens take the field at once. They were followed by 5000 perioeci, each attended by one Helot. It was clear that Sparta had risen at last to an adequate sense of the jeopardy of the Peloponnesus. The command was entrusted to Pausanias, who was acting as regent for his child-cousin Pleistarchus, son of the hero of Thermopylae. At the Isthmus, the Lacedaemonian army was joined by the troops of the Peloponnesian allies, and by contingents from Euboea, Aegina, and western Greece; [2] in the Megarid they were reinforced by the Megarians, and at Eleusis by Aristides in command of 8000 Athenians and 600 Plataeans. It was entirely an army of foot soldiers, and the total number, including light armed troops, may have approached 100,000. The task of leading this host devolved upon Pausanias.

Sparta acts.

[2] (a) Peloponnesian: from Tegea, Orchomenus, Corinth, Sicyon, Phlius, Epidarus, Troezen, Hermione, Lepreon, Mycenae, and Tiryns. (b) Euboean: from Chalcis, Eretria, and Styra. (c) West Greek: from Ambracia, Leucas, Anactorion, Paleis in Cephallenia.

The strong fortress of Thebes, which he had abundantly supplied with provisions, was the base of Mardonius; and once the
Greek army was in the field, he could not run the risk of having
his communications with his base broken off and finding himself
shut up in Attica, a land exhausted by the devastation of the preceding autumn. Accordingly he withdrew into Boeotia, having completed the ruin of Athens, and having sent a detachment to make
a demonstration in the Megarid. He did not take the direct route
to Thebes, but marching northward to Decelea and by the north
side of Mount Parnes he reached Tanagra and the plain of the
Asopus. Marching up this stream, westward, he came to the spot
where it is crossed by the road from Athens to Thebes, at the point
where that road descends from the heights of Cithaeron. The river
Asopus was the boundary between the Theban and Plataean territories, and the destruction of Plataea was probably an object of the
Persians. But the main purpose of Mardonius in posting himself
on the Asopus was that he might fight with Thebes behind him.
The Persians had every cause to be sanguine. Not only had they
superior, though not overwhelmingly superior, forces, but they
had a general who was far abler than any commander on the side
of the Greeks. Mardonius was not anxious to bring on a battle. He
fully realised that his true strategy was to do as little as possible;
he knew that the longer the army of the Greeks remained in the
field, the more would its cohesion be relaxed through the jealousies
and dissensions of the various contingents. We need not take
too seriously the story which the Greeks were afterwards fain to believe, that at this moment there was a certain dispiritedness and
foreboding of disaster in the Persian camp. An anecdote told by
one of the guests at a Theban banquet was thought to illustrate this
gloomy mood. Attaginus, a Theban general, made a feast in honour
of Mardonius. A hundred guests were present, arranged on double
couches a Persian and a Boeotian on each. Thersander of Orchomenus was among the guests, and in after-days he told the historian
Herodotus that his Persian couch-fellow spoke these words to him:
"Since we have now shared the same table and wine, I wish to
leave thee a memorial of my opinion; that being forewarned thou
mayest look to thine own welfare. Seest thou these Persians feasting,—and the host which we left encamped by the river? In a little
while thou shalt see few of all these remaining." The Persian shed
tears as he spoke, and Thersander rejoined: "It behoves thee to tell
this to Mardonius"; but the Persian said: "Stranger, man cannot
avert what God hath ordained. No one would believe me. Many of
us Persians know it and follow the army under constraint. No

human affliction is worse than this: to know and to be helpless."

Mardonius had taken up his position and constructed a forti- Strategic
policy of
Mar-
donius.
fication on the north bank of the river Asopus, before the Greek
army had crossed Cithaeron. His plan was to act on the defensive.
He would wait for the Greeks to attack him, so that the issue might
be tried in a plain when he would be able to reap the full advantage
of his superiority in cavalry. It would, on the contrary, be to the
interest of the Greeks, when they descended from Cithaeron, if they
could by any means entice the enemy to give battle on the rough
and high ground south of the river where cavalry would be of little
use.

Sect. 7. Battle of Plataea

The field on which the fate of Greece was decided is bounded on August,
479 B.C.
the north by the river Asopus, on the south by Mount Cithaeron.
The town of Plataea stood in the south-west of this space, on the
most westerly of six ridges which connect the lower heights of the
mountain with the plain. Three roads descended here into Boeotia: The road:
of Cithae-
ron.
on the extreme east the road from Athens to Thebes; in the centre,
that from Athens to Plataea; on the west, that from Megara to
Plataea. The Greek army took the most easterly way, which after
a gradual ascent on the Attic side reaches the fortress of Eleutherae and the pass of the Oak's Heads, and then descends steeply
into the Boeotian land. They found when they reached the other
side that the road passed through the Persian camp, and they were First posi-
tion of the
Greeks.
forced to take up a position at the foot of the pass. Their right wing,
consisting of the Spartans and Tegeates, rested on the high bastion
of the mountain which rises above the town of Erythrae; their
centre on lower ground close to the town; and the left wing, where
the Athenians and Megarians were posted, was advanced right
down to the foot of the descent. Thus the position of the Greeks was
astride the road to Thebes. The only assailable point was the left
wing, and against it Mardonius sent cavalry under the command of
Masistius. Sore bestead by the darts and arrows of the enemy, and
with no cavalry to aid them, the Megarians required succour. Three
hundred Athenians (for the Athenians were also on the left wing)
went down to the scene of battle, and the fortune of the day was at
last changed when the general Masistius, a conspicuous figure in
the fight, fell from his wounded charger. He was slain with difficulty
by a spear which pierced his eye, for his armour was impenetrable;
and the Persian horsemen, after a furious and fruitless charge to
recover the body of their leader, abandoned the attack. The camp
of the Persians was filled with loud wailing and lamentation—echo-

ing, says Herodotus, all over Boeotia—for the death of Masistius.

But this success was far from dealing any solid advantage to the Greeks or serious injury to their foes. The Persians were well content to remain where they were; their great host still lay north of the Asopus. The Greeks, in order to obtain a better water supply, and knowing that there was no chance that the Persians would attack them in their present position, decided to occupy lower ground in the territory of Plataea. In order to do this they moved north-westward along the spurs of Cithaeron, past the towns of Erythrae and Hysiae. To understand the operations which ensued, it is to be observed that the region between Cithaeron and the Asopus falls into two parts separated by a depression in the ground. The southern part is marked by the six ridges already mentioned and the streams which divide them; while the northern tract is also hilly, being marked by three ridges between which rivulets flow into the Asopus. Westward the depression opens out into flat land, the only flat land here, which stretches northward from Plataea to the river and is traversed by the road to Thebes.

Second position of the Greeks. The Greek army ultimately arranged itself in order of battle between the Theban road and the Moloeis, a tributary stream of the Asopus. Their position was marked by the spring of Gargaphia, which afforded an abundant supply of fresh water, and the temple of the hero Androcrates. We are told that a dispute arose between the Tegeates and the Athenians for the occupation of the west wing, and that the Lacedaemonians decided in favour of the Athenians, who (as we have seen) were under the command of Aristides. The Tegeates were stationed next the Lacedaemonians on the right. Pausanias had now lost control of the eastern passes across Mount Cithaeron. The Persian general, as soon as the Greeks had left their first position, promptly occupied the roads, and cut off a provision train which was on its way to supply the Greek army. The Greek general hoped every day that the enemy would attack; but Mardonius, apart from cavalry skirmishing, remained persistently on the defensive.

It would seem that the Greeks remained about two days inactive in this weak position, harassed by the Persian cavalry, which crossed the river, hovered on the ridges, discharged darts into the camp, and finally succeeded in choking up the waters of the Gargaphia spring. The only course open to the Greeks was to fall back upon the mountain, and either take up a position on the ridges between Hysiae and Plataea, or seek to regain their former position The Greeks fall back. at the foot of the main pass. For they could not venture to cross the Asopus and brave the Persian cavalry. Pausanias held a council

of war, and it was determined that the army should fall back to a
position between Hysiae and Plataea, and that one division should
move up the mountain slope to recover command of the pass from
Plataea to Athens. The whole movement was to be carried out at

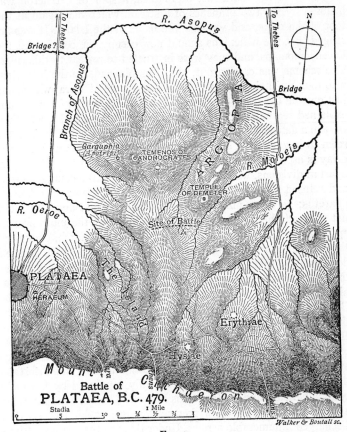

FIG. 51.

night. Perhaps Pausanias had received information that the Persian commander was growing impatient and was contemplating an
attack. In any case his plan of retreat proved fortunate, and though
it was not executed with precision, the Persians, even as at Salamis,
were induced to give battle in conditions chosen by their enemy
and unfavourable to themselves. We might understand why Mardonius decided to abandon the defensive strategy to which hitherto
he had adhered, if we knew something of the intrigues and divisions

in the Persian camp. There seems to have been disastrous rivalry between himself and his second in command, Artabazus, who in the ensuing battle did simply nothing, and probably desired that Mardonius should not win the glory of victory.

A little to the south-east of Plataea, a spur of Cithaeron was inclosed by the two branches of a stream which met again at the foot of the ridge, and went by the name of the Island. It was arranged that the Athenians should now occupy the centre next the Lacedaemonians, and they were instructed to retreat to this ridge. The scheme was carried out, at it was planned, by the left wing, who took up their post in front of the temple of Hera, which was just outside the walls of Plataea. But the Athenians, for some unexplained reason, failed to obey orders, and remained where they were in a dangerous and isolated position. The Lacedaemonians too seem to have wasted the precious hours of the short night. Their delay is ascribed to the obstinacy of the commander of one of the Spartan divisions, who had not been present at the council of war, and refused to obey the order to retreat. His name was Amompharětus; he was a man of blameless valour, and Pausanias could not persuade himself to leave him behind. But the morning was approaching, and at length Pausanias began his march, convinced that his stubborn captain would follow when he found himself deserted. And so it fell out. When they had moved about ten stades, the Spartans saw that Amompharetus was coming, and waited for him. But the day had dawned; the Persians had perceived that the Greek position was deserted, and Mardonius decided that now was the moment to attack when the forces of the enemy were divided. His cavalry came up and prevented the Lacedaemonians from proceeding. It was on the slopes under Hysiae, near the modern village of Kriekouki, that Pausanias was compelled to turn and withstand the Persian horsemen, who were speedily supported by the main body advancing under Mardonius himself. The Persians threw up a light barricade of their wicker shields, from behind which they discharged innumerable arrows. Under this fire the Greeks hesitated; for the victims were unfavourable. At length Pausanias, looking towards the temple of Hera, invoked the goddess; and after his prayer the prophets obtained good omens from the sacrifices. The Lacedaemonians no longer held back. Along with the Tegeates who were with them they carried the barricade and pressed the Persians backward towards the temple of Demeter which stood on a high acclivity above them. In this direction the battle raged hotly; but the discipline of the best spearmen of Greece approved itself brilliantly; and, when Mardonius fell, the battle was decided.

The Lacedaemonians and Tegeates had borne the brunt of the day. At the first attack, Pausanias had dispatched a hasty messenger to the Athenians. As they marched to the scene they were attacked by the Greeks of the left wing of the enemy's army, who effectually hindered them from marching farther. Meanwhile the tidings had reached the rest of the Greek army at Plataea, that a battle was being fought and that Pausanias was winning it. They hastened to the scene, but the action was practically decided before their arrival; some of them were cut off, on the way, by Theban cavalry. The defeated host fled back across the Asopus to their fortified camp; the Greeks pursued, and stormed it. The tent of Mardonius was plundered by the men of Tegea, who dedicated in the temple of Athena Alea in their city the brass manger of his horses; while his throne with silver feet and his scimitar were kept by the Athenians on the Acropolis, along with the breastplate of Masistius, as memorials of the fateful day. The body of Mardonius was respected by Pausanias, but it was mysteriously stolen, and none ever knew the hand that buried it. The slain Greek warriors, among whom was the brave Amompharetus, were buried before the gates of Plataea, and the honour of celebrating their memory by annual sacrifice was assigned to the Plataeans, who also agreed to commemorate the day of the deliverance of Hellas by a "Feast of Freedom" every four years. Pausanias called the host together, and in the name of the Spartans and all the confederacy guaranteed to Plataea political independence and the inviolability of her town and territory. The hour of triumph for Plataea was an hour of humiliation for Thebes. Ten days after the battle the army advanced against the chief Boeotian city and demanded the surrender of the leaders of the medizing party. On a refusal, Pausanias laid siege to the place, but presently the leaders were given up, by their own wish, for they calculated on escaping punishment by the influence of bribery. But Pausanias caused them to be executed, without trial, at Corinth. A Theban poet who sympathised with the national effort of Hellas might well feel "distressed in soul."

The battle had been won simply and solely by the discipline and prowess of the Spartan hoplites. The plans of the exceptionally able commander, who was matched indeed with a commander abler than himself, were frustrated once and again through the want of unity and cohesion in his army, through the want apparently of tactical skill—most of all perhaps through the half-heartedness of the Athenians. Never do the Athenians appear in such an ill light, as in the campaign of Cithaeron; and in no case

Spoils.

Festival of Eleutheria.

(Pindar.)

The legend of the battle;

have they exhibited so strikingly their faculty of refashioning history, in no case so successfully imposed their misrepresentations on the faith of posterity. They had no share in the victory; but they told the whole story afterwards so as to exalt themselves and to disparage the Spartans. They represented the night movements planned by Pausanias as a retreat before an expected attack of the enemy, and they invented an elaborate tale to explain how the attack came to be expected. Mardonius, they said, growing impatient of the delay, called a council of war, and it was decided to abandon defensive tactics and provoke a battle. Then Alexander of Macedon showed at this critical moment that his real sympathies were with Hellas and not with his barbarian allies. He rode down to the outposts of the Athenians, and, shouting, we must suppose, across the river, revealed the decision of the Persian council of war. Thus made aware of the Persian resolve to risk a battle, the Spartans proposed to the Athenians to change wings, in order that the victors of Marathon might fight with the Persians, whose ways of warfare they had already experienced, while the Spartans themselves could deal better with the Boeotians and other Greeks, with whose methods of fighting they were familiar. The proposal was agreed to, and as day dawned the change was being effected. But the enemy perceived it, and immediately began to make a corresponding change in their own array. Seeing their plan frustrated, the Greeks desisted from completing it; and both the adversaries resumed their original positions. Mardonius then sent a message to the Lacedaemonians, complaining that he had been deeply disappointed in them, for though they had the repute of never fleeing or deserting their post, they had now attempted to place the Athenians in the place of danger. He challenged them to stand forth as champions for the whole Greek host and fight against an equal number of Persians. To this proposal the Spartans made no reply. Then Mardonius began his cavalry operations which led to the retreat of the Greeks from their second position. The three striking incidents of this malicious tale, the night-visit of Alexander, the fruitless attempt of the Spartans to shirk the responsibility of their post on the right wing, the challenge of Mardonius, are all improbable in themselves; but nevertheless this story was circulated and believed, and has received a sort of consecration in the pages of Herodotus.

SECT. 8. BATTLE OF MYCALE AND CAPTURE OF SESTOS

The battle of Cithaeron shares with Salamis the dignity of being decisive battles in the world's history. Pindar links them together as the great triumphs of Sparta and Athens respectively, battles "wherein the Medes of the bent bows were sore afflicted." Notwithstanding the immense disadvantage of want of cavalry, the Lacedaemonians had turned at Plataea a retreat into a victory. The remarkable feature of the battle was that it was decided by a small part of either army. Sparta and Tegea were the actual victors; and on the Persian side, Artabazus, at the head of 40,000 men, had not entered into the action at all. On the death of Mardonius, that general immediately faced about and began without delay the long march back to the Hellespont. Never again was Persia to make a serious attempt against the liberty of European Greece; "a god," said a poet of the day—and the poet was a Theban—"turned away the stone of Tantalus imminent above our heads." For the following century and a half, the dealings between Greece and Persia will only affect the western fringe of Asia, and then the balance of power will have so completely shifted that Persia will succumb to a Greek conqueror, and Alexander of Macedon will achieve against the Asiatic monarchy what Xerxes failed to achieve against the free states of Europe.

One memorial of this victory of Europe over Asia has survived till to-day. The votive offering which the Greeks sent to Delphi was a tripod of gold set upon a pillar of three brazen serpents, with the names of the Greek peoples who offered it inscribed upon the base. The pillar still stands in Byzantium, whither it was transferred after that city had been renamed Constantinople by her second founder. The immense booty which was found in the Persian camp was divided, when portions had been set apart for the gods and for the general who had led the Greeks to victory.

its memorial. The tripod at Delphi.

The achievement of the Hellenic army under Mount Cithaeron, which rescued Greek Europe from the invader, was followed in a few days by an achievement of the Hellenic fleet which delivered the Asiatic Greeks from their master. The Greek fleet was still at Delos. We saw that it was the policy of the Athenians to remain inactive at sea until a battle had been fought on land. For a naval victory would probably have meant the retreat of the Spartans from northern Greece, on the calculation that the enemy would not attack Peloponnesus without the co-operation of the fleet. But the armament at Delos was drawn into action by a message from the Samians, seeking to join the Greek league, and begging help against the Persian. For the Persian fleet was at Samos, and hard by at Cape Mycale a large Persian army, including many Ionian troops, was encamped. The Samian request was granted; Leotychidas sailed to the island, and on his approach the Persian ships with-

Battle of Mycale (middle of August, 479 B.C.).

drew to the shelter of Cape Mycale and their army. The Greeks landed; attacked, carried, and burned the enemy's camp. Their victory was decided by the desertion of the Ionians, who won their freedom on this memorable day. Mycale followed so hard upon Plataea, that the belief easily arose that the two victories were won on the same afternoon. There is more to be said for the tradition that as the Athenians and their comrades assailed the entrenchments on the shore of Mycale the tidings of Plataea reached them and heartened them in their work.

The Athenians and Ionians, led by the admiral Xanthippus, followed up the great victory by vigorous action in the Hellespont, while the Peloponnesians with Leotychidas, content with what they had achieved, returned home. The difference between the Athenian and the Spartan character, between the cautious policy of Sparta and the imperial instinct of Athens, is here distinctly and, it is not too much to say, momentously expressed. The Lacedaemonians were unwilling to concern themselves further with the Greeks of the eastern and north-eastern Aegean; the Athenians were both capable of taking a Panhellenic point of view, and moved by the impulse to **Capture of Sestos, 478 B.C.** extend their own influence. The strong fortress of Sestos, which stands by the straits of Helle, was beleaguered and taken; and with this event Herodotus closes his history of the Persian wars. The independence of the Hellespontine regions was a natural consequence of the victory of Mycale, but its historical significance lies in the fact that it was accomplished under the auspices of Athens. The fall of Sestos is the beginning of that Athenian empire, to which Pisistratus and the elder Miltiades had pointed the way.

SECT. 9. GELON TYRANT OF SYRACUSE

While the eastern Greeks were securing their future development against the Persian foe, and were affirming their possession of the Aegean waters, the western Greeks had been called upon to defend themselves against that Asiatic power which had established itself in the western Mediterranean and was a constant threat to their **Struggle of Greek and Phoenician in western Mediterranean in sixth century.** existence. The Greeks had indeed, on their side, proved a formidable check and hindrance to the expansion of the dominion and trade of Carthage. The endeavours of this vigorous Phoenician state to secure the queenship of the western seas, from Africa to Gaul, from the coast of Spain to the shores of Italy, depended largely for their success on her close connexion and identity of interests with her sister-towns in Sicily; and secondly, on her alliance with the strong pirate power of Etruria. The friendly Phoenician ports of western Sicily—Motya, Panormus, and Solus—were an indispensable aid for the African city, both for the maintenance of her communications with Tuscany and for the prosecution of designs upon Sardinia and Corsica. In Corsican waters as well as in Sicily, the Phoenician clashed with the Greek. It was in the first quarter of the sixth century that Dorian adventurers from Cnidus and Rhodes sought to gain a foothold in the barbarian corner of Sicily, at the very gates of the Phoenicians. The name of their leader was Pentathlus. He attempted a plant a settlement on Cape Lilybaeum, hard by Motya,—a direct menace to the communications between Motya and Carthage. The Phoenicians gathered in arms, and they were supported by their Elymian neighbours; the Greeks were defeated and Pentathlus was slain. It was not the destiny of Lilybaeum to be the place of a Hellenic city; but long afterwards it was to become illustrious as the site of a Punic stronghold which would take the place of Motya, when Motya herself had been destroyed by a Greek avenger of Pentathlus. After their defeat the men of Pentathlus, casting about for another dwelling-place, betook themselves to the volcanic archipelago off the north coast of Sicily, and founded Lipara in the largest of the islands. This little state was organised on communistic principles. The soil was public property: a certain number of the citizens were set apart to till it for the common use; the rest were employed in keeping watch and ward on the coasts of their little home against the descents of Tuscan rovers. This system was indeed subsequently modified: the land was portioned out in lots, but was redistributed every twenty years.

The enterprise of Pentathlus, c. 580 B.C.

Foundation of Lipara.

Collectivism.

The attempt of Pentathlus, the occupation of the Liparaean group, the recent settlement of Acragas, pressed upon Carthage the need of stemming the Greek advance. Accordingly we find her sending an army to Sicily. The commander of this expedition, precursor of many a greater, was Malchus; and it is possible that he was opposed by Phalaris, who established a tyranny at Acragas. There was a long war, of which we know nothing except that the invader was successful and Greek territory was lost to the Phoenician. In the northern seas Carthage was also confronted by the Greeks. The Phocaeans of Massalia planted colonies and won influence on the coast of Spain. We are told that in the days of Cambyses "the Phocaeans gained repeated victories over the Carthaginians by sea." Moreover the new Phocaean settlement at Alalia in Corsica was a challenge to Carthage in what she regarded as her own domain. But Greek Alalia was short-lived. Carthage and her powerful Etruscan allies nearly annihilated the Phocaean fleet; and the crews which escaped were only able to rescue their families and goods. Alalia

Carthaginian expedition to Sicily under Malchus, c. 560-50 B.C.

The Phocaeans: of Massalia;

of Alalia.

Battle of Alalia, c. 535 B.C

was deserted; Corsica fell under the power of the Etruscans, and the coasts of Sardinia were gradually appropriated by Carthage. Thus the chance of establishing a chain of Greek settlements between Massalia and Sicily was frustrated.

It now remained for Carthage to establish and extend Phoenician power in Sicily. We have seen how Dorieus, son of a Spartan king, made an attempt to do somewhat the same thing which the Cnidian adventurer had essayed—to gain a footing in Sicily within the Phoenician circle. He too failed; but such incidents brought home to Carthage the need of dealing another and a mightier blow at the rival power in Sicily. She was occupied with the conquest of Sardinia and with a Libyan war, and the struggle was postponed; but the hour came at last, and the Carthaginians put forth all their power to annihilate colonial Greece at the very time when the Great King had poured forth the resources of Asia against the mother-country. It was, in the first instance, an accident that the two struggles happened at the same moment. The causes which led to the one were independent of the causes which led to the other. But the exact moment chosen by Carthage for her attack upon Sicily was probably determined by the attack of Xerxes upon Greece; and although the two struggles ran each its independent course, there is no reason to question the statement that the courts of Susa and Carthage exchanged messages, through the mediation of the Phoenicians, and were conscious of acting in concert against the same enemy.

In the second decade of the fifth century Greek Sicily was dominated by four tyrants. Anaxilas of Rhegium had made himself master of Zancle, which from this time forward is known as Messana, and he thus controlled both sides of the straits, which he secured against the passage of Etruscan pirates. Terillus, his father-in-law, was tyrant of Himera. Over against this family group in the north stood another family group in the south: Gelon of Syracuse and his father-in-law Theron of Acragas.

Gelon had been the general of Hippocrates, a tyrant of Gela, who had extended his sway, whether as lord or over-lord, over Naxos, Zancle, and other Greek cities, and had aimed at winning Syracuse. Hippocrates had defeated the Syracusans on the banks of the Helorus, and would have seized their city, if it had not been for the intervention of Corinth and Corcyra. But Syracuse was forced to cede her dependency, Camarina, to the victor. Hippocrates died in besieging Hybla; and the men of Gela had no mind to allow his sons to continue their father's tyranny. But Gelon, son of Deinomenes, a general who had often led the cavalry of Gela to victory, espoused

(See above, p. 199.)

Sicily menaced by Carthage.

Tyrants in Sicily.

Hippocrates, tyrant of Gela. [Battle of the Helorus, 492 B.C.]

Gelon, tyrant of

the cause of his master's heirs, and as soon as he had gained posses-
sion of the city brushed them aside and took the tyranny for him-
self. The new lord of Gela achieved what his predecessors had vain-
ly striven to accomplish. The *Gamori* or nobles of Syracuse had
been driven out by the commons, and they appealed to Gelon to re-
store them. The Syracusan people, unable to resist the forces which
Gelon brought against them, made terms with him, and he estab-
lished his power in Syracuse over oligarchs and democrats alike. It
seems probable that Gelon was either at once or at a later stage of
his rule appointed formally "General with full powers"; we find his
brother Hieron, who succeeded to his position, addressed by the
poet Bacchylides as "General" of the Syracusan horsemen.

Gela,
491 B.C.;

wins
Syracuse;

his posi-
tion there.

The tyrant of Gela now abandoned his own city and took up his
abode in Syracuse, making it the centre of a dominion which em-
braced the eastern part of the island. Gela had for a short space en-
joyed the rank of the first of Sicilian cities; she now surrendered it
to Syracuse, which was marked out by its natural site for strength
and domination. Gelon may be called the second founder of Syra-
cuse. He joined the Island of Ortygia with the fortified height of
Achradina which looked down upon it. In the course of the sixth
century a mole had been constructed connecting the Island with the
mainland, so that the city, though it was still called the Island, had
become strictly a peninsula. Gelon built a wall from the Achradina
fort down to the shore of the Great Harbour. Thus Achradina and
Ortygia were included within the same circuit of wall; Achradina
became part of the city, Ortygia remained the "acropolis." The
chief gate of Syracuse was now in the new wall of Gelon, close to
the Harbour; and near it a new agora was laid out, for the old
agora in the Island no longer sufficed. Hard by docks were built, for
Syracuse was to become a naval power. She was now by far the
greatest Greek city in the west.

He en-
larges
Syracuse;
his walls
and docks.

Gelon, belonging to a proud and noble family, sympathised and
most willingly consorted with men of his own class, and looked with
little favour on the people, whom he described in a famous phrase as
"a thankless neighbour." He held court at Syracuse like a king, sur-
rounded by men of noble birth. He tolerated the Syracusan com-
mons; he was not unpopular with them; but he showed elsewhere
what his genuine feelings were. One of his first needs was to find in-
habitants to fill the spaces of his enlarged town. For this purpose he
transplanted men on a large scale from other places of his domin-
ions. His own town Gela was sacrificed to the new capital; the half
of its citizens were removed to Syracuse. Harder was the fate of
luckless Camarina, which was now for the second time blotted out

his court
and class-
prejudice;

his treat-
ment of
other
cities;

from the number of Greek cities. Two generations had hardly passed since she had been swept away by the Syracusan republic; and now the Syracusan tyrant carried off all the inhabitants and made them burgesses of the ruling state. Megara, the next-door neighbour of Syracuse on the north, and Euboea higher up the coast, also contributed to swell the population of Gelon's capital. Megara became an outpost of Syracuse, while Euboea was so entirely blotted out that its very site is uncertain. But in both these cases the policy of Gelon strikingly displayed the prejudice of his class. He admitted the nobles of Megara and Euboea to Syracusan citizenship; he sold the mass of the commons in the slave market. In abolishing cities and transplanting populations Gelon set an example which we shall see followed by later tyrants. He also invited new settlers from elder Greece, and he gave the citizenship to 10,000 mercenary soldiers.

his family.

Gelon was supported in his princely power by his three brothers, Hieron, Polyzālus, and Thrasybulus. He entered into close friendship with Theron, his fellow-tyrant, who made Acragas in wealth a power second only to Syracuse itself. Thereon, like Gelon, was a noble, belonging to the family of the Emmenids, and his rule was said to have been mild and just Gelon married Damareta, the daughter of Theron; and Theron married a daughter of Polyzalus. The brilliant lords of Syracuse and Acragas, thus joined by close bonds, were presently associated in the glorious work of delivering Greek Sicily from the terrible danger which was about to come against her from over-seas.

SECT. 10. THE CARTHAGINIAN INVASION OF SICILY, AND THE BATTLE OF HIMERA

A quarrel between Theron of Acragas and Terillus tyrant of Himera led up to the catastrophe which might easily have proved fatal to the freedom of all the Sicilian Greeks. The ruler of Acragas crossed the island and drove Terillus out of Himera. The exiled tyrant had a friend in Anaxilas of Rhegium; but Rhegium was no match for the combined power of Acragas and Syracuse, and so Terillus sought the help of Carthage, the common enemy of all.

Terillus
invites in-
tervention
of Car-
thage.

Carthage was only waiting for the opportunity. She had been making preparations for a descent on Sicily, and the appeal of Terillus merely determined the moment and the point of her attack. Terillus urging the Phoenician against Himera plays the same part as Hippias urging the Persian against Athens, but in neither case is a tyrant's fall the cause of the invasion. The motive of the Carthaginian expedition against Sicily at this particular epoch is to be found in a far higher range of politics than the local affairs of Himera or the interests of a petty despot. There can hardly be a doubt that the Great King and the Carthaginian republic were acting in concert, and that it was deliberately planned to attack, independently but at the same moment, eastern and western Greece. While the galleys of the elder Phoenicia, under their Persian master, sailed to crush the elder Hellas, the galleys of the younger Phoenician city would cross over on her own account against the younger Hellas. In the Phoenicians of Tyre and Sidon, Xerxes had willing intermediaries to arrange with Carthage the plan of enslaving or annihilating Hellas.

Carthage and Persia.

Fig. 52.—Coin of Rhegion, fifth century (reverse). The Rhegine People seated [legend: ΡΕΓΙΝΟΣ]. Fig. 53.—Coin of Himera, fifth century (obverse). Himera, the nymph, sacrificing at altar; satyr bathing himself at a hot spring. Fig. 54.—Coin of Selinus, fifth century (obverse). River Silenus sacrificing at altar; cock, bull, leaf of selinon [legend: ΣΕΛΙΝΟΣ].

The western island mattered little to Xerxes; but it mattered greatly to him that the lord of Syracuse should be hindered from sending a powerful succour in men and ships to the mother-country. We have already seen how the mother-country sought the help of Gelon, and how the danger of Sicily forced him to refuse.

When the preparations were complete, Hamilcar, the shophet of Carthage, sailed with a large armament and landed at Panormus; for the call of Terillus determined that the recovery of Himera should be the first object. It is said that the army consisted of 300,000 men, conveyed by more than 200 galleys and 3000 transports; but we can lay no stress on these figures. From Panormus this great host moved along the coast to Himera, accompanied by the warships, and proceeded to besiege the city, which Theron was himself guarding with a large force. Hamilcar made two camps in front of the town. The sea camp lay on the low ground between the hill of Himera and the beach; the land camp stretched along the low hills on the western side of the town. A sally of the besieged resulted in loss, and Theron sent a message to Syracuse to hasten the coming of his son-in-law. With 50,000 foot-soldiers and 5000 horsemen

The Punic armament.

Gelon marched to the rescue without delay. He approached the town on the east side and formed a strong camp on the right bank of the river.

Battle of Himera, 480 B.C.

The decisive battle was brought about in a strange way, if we can trust the story. Hamilcar determined to enlist the gods of his foes

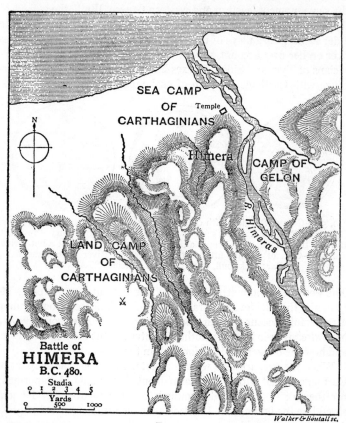

Fig. 55.

on his own side. He appointed a day for a great sacrifice to Poseidon near the shore of the sea. For this purpose it was needful to have Greeks present who understood how the sacrifice should be performed. Accordingly Hamilcar wrote to Selinus, which had become a dependency of Carthage, bidding that city send horsemen to the Punic camp by a fixed day. The letter fell into the hands of Gelon, and he conceived a daring stratagem. On the morning of the appointed day a band of Syracusan horsemen stood at the gate of the sea camp, professing to be the expected contingent from Selinus. The Carthaginians could not distinguish strangers of Syracuse from strangers of Selinus, and they were admitted without suspicion. They cut down Hamilcar by the altar of Poseidon, and they set fire to the ships. All this was visible from the high parts of the town above them, and men posted there signalled to Gelon the success of the plan. The Greek commander immediately led his troops round the south side of the city against the land camp of the enemy. There the battle was fought, a long and desperate struggle, in which the scale was finally turned in favour of the Greeks by a body of men which Theron sent round to take the barbarians in the rear. The victory was complete; the great expedition was utterly destroyed; the chief himself was slain.

Fig. 56.—Coin of Syracuse, fifth century. Obverse: head of Victory; dolphins [legend: ΣΤΡΑΚΟΣΙΟΝ]. Reverse: Quadriga crowned by Victory; below, a lion.

But of the death of that chieftain the Carthaginians had another and a far grander tale to tell. This tale does not explain how the battle was brought about. It simply gives us a splendid picture. The battle rages "from the morning till the late evening," and during that long day Hamilcar stands at the altar of Baal, in his camp by the sea. A great fire devours the burnt-offerings to the god; victim after victim, whole bodies of beasts and perhaps of men, are flung into the flames, and the omens are favourable to Carthage. But as he is pouring out a drink-offering, he looks forth, and behold his army is put to flight. The moment for a supreme sacrifice has come; he leaps into the fire and the flames consume him. The offering of his life did not retrieve the day; but hereafter Himera was destined to pay a heavy penalty for the death of Hamilcar.

The common significance of the battles of Salamis and Himera, or the repulse of Asia from Europe, was appreciated at the time and naïvely expressed in the fanciful tradition that the two battles were

Legend of Hamilcar's death.

fought on the same day. But Himera, unlike Salamis, was immediately followed by a treaty of peace. Carthage paid the lord of Syracuse 2000 talents as a war indemnity, but this was a small treasury compared with the booty taken in the camp. Out of a portion of that spoil a beautiful issue of large silver coins was minted and called "Damaretean," after Gelon's wife; and some pieces of this memorial of the great deliverance of Sicily are preserved.

The Damaretean decadrachms.

Sect. I. Syracuse and Acragas under Hieron and Theron

The enlargement of Acragas, 479-2 B.C.

Theron and Acragas had played an honourable part in the deliverance of Sicily, though it was a part which was second to that of Gelon and Syracuse. Thereon survived the victory by eight years, and during that time he was engaged in doing for Acragas what had been already done for Syracuse by his fellow-tyrant. The enlargement of the Syracusan and the Acragantine cities was effected by opposite processes. Syracuse had sprung up a hill; Acragas which was perched aloft on a height sprang down the slope. The enlarged city was encompassed by a wall, of which nature had already done half the building. The most striking feature of the new city was the southern wall, stretching between the rivers, and lined by a row of temples. Theron laid the foundations of the temples along the wall; but it was not till long after his death that they were completed, and the line of holy buildings shone forth in all its glory. In all this work, and in the watercourses which he also constructed, Theron had slave-labour in abundance—the barbarians who had been captured after the battle of Himera. Theron placed rescued Himera under the government of his son Thrasydaeus, who however, unlike Theron himself, proved an oppressor and was hated by the citizens.

Death of Gelon and succession of Hieron, 478 B.C.

Meanwhile Gelon died, and left the fruits of his enterprise and statesmanship to be enjoyed by his brother Hieron. While Hieron was to have the sovereign power, Gelon desired that Polyzalus, whom he ordered to marry his widow Damareta, should have the supreme command of the Syracusan army. The idea of this dual system was unwise; and it neccesarily led to fraternal discord. Polyzalus was popular at Syracuse, and his double connexion with Theron secured him the support of that tyrant. To Hieron he seemed a dangerous rival, and in the end he was compelled to seek refuge at Acragas. This led to an open breach between Hieron and Theron, but it did not come to actual war, and it is said that the lyric poet Simonides, who was a favourite at both courts, acted as peacemaker. War between the two chief cities of Sicily did not come till after Theron's death, and then it brought freedom to Acragas.

Hieron may be said to have completed the work of Himera by the defeat which he inflicted upon the Etruscans at Cyme. The Etruscans were the other rival power which, besides the Carthaginians, threatened the "Greater Greece" of the west. The possession of the northern outpost of Hellas on the Italian coast, the colony of Cyme, was one of the great objects of Etruscan politics; and, three or four years after the accession of Hieron, it was pressed hard by a Tuscan squadron. Hieron was a statesman of a sufficiently large view to answer the prayer of Cyme for help. The Syracusan fleet sailed to the spot and defeated the besiegers. From this time the Etruscan power rapidly declined and ceased to menace the development of western Greece. From the booty Hieron sent a bronze helmet to Olympia; and this precious memorial of one of the glorious exploits of Greece is now in the great London collection of antiquities. More precious still is the song in which Pindar of Thebes immortalised the victory.

It is perhaps from the hymns of Pindar that we win the most lively impression of the wealth and culture of the courts of Sicily in the fifth century. Pindar, like other illustrious poets of the day, Simonides and Bacchylides, and Aeschylus, visited Sicily, to bask in the smiles, and receive the gifts, of the tyrant. The lord of Syracuse—or king, as he aspired to be styled—sent his race-horses and chariots to contend in the great games at Olympia and Delphi, and he employed the most gifted lyric poets to celebrate these victories in lordly odes. Pindar and Bacchylides were sometimes set to celebrate the same victory in rival strains. These poets give us an impression of the luxury and magnificence of the royal courts and the generosity of the royal victors. Syracuse, on whose adornment her tyrants could spend the Punic spoils, and Acragas, "fairest of the cities of men," seemed wonderful to the visitors from elder Greece. Yet amid all their own magnificence and amid their absorbing political activity, the princes of this younger western world coveted above all things that their names should be glorious in the mother country. They still looked to the holy place of Delphi as the central sanctuary of the world, and they enriched it with costly dedications. The golden tripod, which Gelon and his brothers dedicated from Punic treasure, became, like the other golden things of Delphi, the loot of robbers; but we are reminded of that fraternal union by a precious bronze charioteer, which was dug up recently in the ruins of the Delphic sanctuary. It was dedicated by Polyzalus, perhaps in honour of a Pythian victory.

It were easy to be blinded by the outward show of these princely tyrants, which the genius of Pindar has invested with a certain dignity. But Pindar, himself born of a noble family, cherished the

Side notes:

Hieron defeats the Etruscans.

Battle of Cyme, 474 B.C.

Pindar's First Pythian.

Victories of Sicilian tyrants in Panhellenic games.

Ideals of Pindar.

ideas and prejudices of a bygone generation. He belonged to a class,
he wrote chiefly for a class, whose day was past: nobles whose sole
aim in life was to win victories at the public games. These men were
out of sympathy with the new ideas and the political tendencies of
their own age; they were belated survivals of an earlier society.
Pindar sympathised with them. He liked aristocracies best; he accepted monarchy even in the form of tyranny; but democracy he
regarded as the rule of a mob's passions. The despots of Sicily and
Cyrene supported the national games of Greece, and that was in
truth their great merit in the eyes of the poet. The chariot-race, the
athletic contests, seen in the midst of a gay crowd, then the choral
dance and song in honour of the victory, and the carouse, in the
hall perhaps of some noble Aeginetan burgher, these were "the delightful things in Hellas" which to Pindar were the breath of life.
He was religious to the heart's core; and all these things were invested with the atmosphere of religion. But allowing for this, we
feel that he takes the games too seriously, and that when Aeschylus
was wrestling with the deep problems of life and death, the day was
past for regarding an Olympian victory as the grandest thing in the
world. We must not be beguiled by Pindar's majestic art into ascribing to the tyrants any high moral purpose. It was enough that they
should aspire to an Olympian crown, and incur the necessary outlay, and seek immortality from the poet's craft; the poet could
hardly dare to demand a higher purpose.

Fair as the outside of a Syracusan state might seem to a favoured visitor who was entertained in the tyrant's palace, underneath
there was no lack of oppression and suspicion. The system of spies
which Hieron organised to watch the lives of private citizens, tells
its own tale. One of his most despotic acts was his dealing with the
city of Catane. He deported all the inhabitants to Leontini, peopled
the place with new citizens, and gave it the name of Aetna. His motive was partly vanity, partly selfish prudence. He aspired to be remembered and worshipped as the founder of a city; and he also intended Aetna to be a stronghold of refuge to himself or his dynasty,
in case a day of jeopardy should come. His son Deinomenes was installed as "King of Aetna." But the Dorian city of Aetna, so cruelly
founded, though it was celebrated in lofty phrases by Pindar and
had the still higher honour of supplying the motive of a play of
Aeschylus, had but a short duration; it was soon to become Catane
again.

At Acragas, the mild rule of Theron seems to have secured the
love and trust of his fellow-citizens; but at Himera he showed what
a tyrant might do, by slaughtering without any mercy those who

Founda-
tion of
Aetna.

ad showed their discontent at the rule of his son. Neither the Syracusan nor the Acragantine dynasty endured long. After Theron's death, Thrasydaeus misruled Acragas, as he had already misruled Himera. But for some unknown reason he had the folly to go to war with Hieron, who discomfited him in a hard-fought battle. This defeat led to his fall. Himera became independent, and Acragas adopted a free constitution. The deliverance of Syracuse came about five years later. When Hieron died, his brother Thrasybulus took the reins of government, and, being a less able and dexterous ruler than Hieron, he soon excited a revolution by his executions and confiscations. The citizens rose in a mass, and obtaining help from other Sicilian cities besieged the tyrant and his mercenaries in Syracuse. He was ultimately forced to surrender and retired into private life in a foreign land. Thus the tyranny at Syracuse came to an end, and the feast of *Eleutheria* was founded to preserve the memory of the dawn of freedom.

Death of Theron, 472-1 B.C. Thrasydaeus: his war with Hieron, and his fate. 471-0 B.C. Death of Hieron, 467 B.C

The rule of the despots seems to have wiped out the old feud between the nobles and the commons. But a new strife arose instead. The old citizens, nobles and commons alike, distrusted the new citizens, whom Gelon had gathered together from all quarters. A civil war broke out; for some time, the old citizens were excluded from both the Island and Achradina; but in the end all the strangers were driven out, and the democracy of Syracuse was securely established. One good thing the tyrants had done. They had obliterated the class distinctions which had existed before them; and thus the cities could now start afresh on the basis of political equality for all. The next half-century was a period of weal and prosperity for the republics of Sicily, especially for the greatest among them, Syracuse and Acragas, and for Selinus, freed from the Phoenician yoke. At Acragas the free people carried to completion the works which their beneficent tyrant had begun. The stately row of temples along the southern wall belongs to this period. "It was a grand conception to line the southern wall, the wall most open to the attacks of mortal enemies, with this wonderful series of holy places of the divine protectors of the city. It was a conception due, we may believe, in the first instance, to Theron, but which the democracy fully entered into and carried out." [3] But her sacred buildings brought less glory to Acragas than the name of the most illustrious of her sons. The poet and philosopher Empedocles was reared in what he describes as the "great town above the yellow river of Acragas." He was not only a profound philosopher, an inspired poet, a skilful physician, but he had lent his hand to the reform of the constitution of his

Republics in Sicily.

Empedocles.

[3] Freeman.

city. Unhappily his personality is lost in the dense covert of legends which quickly grew up around him. The true Empedocles who, banished from his home, died quietly in the Peloponnesus, becomes the seer and magician who hurled himself into the bowl of Aetna that he might become a god. A god indeed he proclaims himself to be, going about from city to city, crowned with Delphic wreaths, and worshipped by men and women.

Ducetius and the Sicels, 460-440 B.C.
His cities: (1) Menaenum (Mineo), (2) Palica, (3) Kalê Aktê.

For a time indeed the Siceliots were threatened with a remarkable danger, the revival of the native power of the Sicels. This revival was entirely due to the genius of one man, and the danger disappeared on his death. Ducetius organised a federation of the Sicel towns, and aspired to bring the Greek cities under Sicel rule. He displayed his talent in the foundation of new cities, which survived the failure of his schemes. His first settlement was on the hill-top of Menaenum, overlooking the sacred lake and temple of the Palici. As his power and ambitions grew, he descended from the hill and founded Palica close to the national sanctuary, to be the political capital of the nation. He captured Aetna, gained a victory over the Acragantines and Syracusans, but was subsequently defeated by Syracuse, and on this defeat his followers deserted him, and the fabric which he had reared collapsed. He boldly took refuge himself at the altar in the Syracusan market-place; his case was debated in the Assembly; and by an act of clemency, which we might hardly expect, he was spared and sent to Corinth. Five years later we find him again in Sicily, engaged in the congenial work of founding a third city, Kalê Aktê or Fairshore, on the northern coast, with the approbation of Syracuse. It is uncertain whether he dreamed of repeating his attempt at a national revival or had become convinced that the fortune of the Sicel lay in Hellenization. His foundations were more abiding than those of Hieron; one of them, Mineo, survives to-day. The career of Ducetius exhibited the decision of destiny that the Greek was to predominate in the island of the Sicels.

His failure, 450 B.C.

SECT. 12. RELIGIOUS MOVEMENTS IN THE SIXTH CENTURY

In the latter part of the sixth century, the expansion of the Persian power had suspended a stone of Tantalus over Hellas, and it seemed likely that Greek civilisation might be submerged in an oriental monarchy. We have seen how Greek generals, Greek spearmen, and Greek seamen averted this calamity. We have now to see how another danger was averted, a danger which, though it is not like the Persian invasion written large on the face of history, threatened Greece with a no less terrible disaster. This danger lay in the dissemination of a new religion, which, if it had gained the upper hand, as at one time it seemed likely to do, would have pressed with as dead and stifling a weight upon Greece as any oriental superstition. Spiritually the Greeks might have been annexed to the peoples of the orient.

The age of Solon witnessed not only a social and political movement among the masses in various parts of Greece, but also an intellectual and spiritual stirring. There was an intellectual dissatisfaction with the theogony of Hesiod as an explanation of the origin of the world; and the natural philosophy of Thales and his successors came into being in Ionia. But there was also a moral dissatisfaction with the tales of religious mythology, as they were handed down by the epic bards; and this feeling took the form of interpreting and modifying them, so as to make them conform to ethical ideals. The poet Stesichorus was a pioneer in this direction, and it was he who first imported into the legend of the house of Atreus—the murder of Agamemnon by his wife, and the murder of Clytaemnestra by her son—the terrible moral significance which Aeschylus and the Attic tragedians afterwards made so familiar. Further than this, men began to feel a craving for an existence after death, and intense curiosity about the world of shades, and a desire for personal contact with the supernatural. Both the scientific and the religious movements have the same object—to solve the mystery of existence; but the religious craving demanded a short road and immediate satisfaction. The craving led to the propagation of a new religion, which began to spread about the middle of the sixth century. We know not where it originally took shape, but Attica became its most active centre, and it was propagated to western Hellas beyond the sea. Based partly on the wild Thracian worship of Dionysus, this religion was called Orphic from Orpheus, poet and priest, who was supposed to have been born in Thrace and founded the bacchic rites; and it exercised a deep influence over not only the people at large, but even the thinkers of Greece. The Orphic teachers elaborated a theology of their own; a special doctrine of the future world; peculiar rites and peculiar rules of conduct. But they took up into their system, so far as possible, the old popular beliefs. The Orphic religion might almost be described as based on three institutions: the worship of Dionysus, the mysteries connected with the gods of the underworld, and the itinerant prophets; but Dionysus, the underworld, and the art of the seer and purifier, all acquired new significance in the light of the Orphic theology.

It was perhaps as early as the eighth century that the worship of Dionysus was introduced into northern Greece, and various legends

Beginning of rationalism.

Religious movement.

Elements in the Orphic religion.

Dionysiac worship.

record the opposition which was at first offered to the reception of the stranger. His orgies spread, especially in Boeotia and Attica The worshippers gathered at night on the mountains, by torchlight, with deer-skins on their shoulders and long ivy-wreathed wands in their hands, and danced wildly to the noise of cymbals and flutes. Men and women tore and devoured the limbs of the sacred victims. They desired to fall, and they often fell, especially the women, into a sort of frenzied ecstasy, in which their souls were thought to be in mystic communion with Dionysus. It was probably the influence of the Dionysiac worship that induced the Delphic god [4] to give his oracles through the mouth of a woman cast into a state of divine frenzy.

Itinerant seers.

Men could also deal with the supernatural world through the mediation of seers. Wise men and women, called *bakids* and *sibyls,* attached to no temple or sanctuary, travelled about and made their livelihood by prophesying, purifying, and healing. They practised these three arts through their intimacy with the invisible world of spirits; to which the causes of disease and uncleanness were ascribed. Epimenides was one of the most famous and powerful of these wizards; we saw how he was called upon to purify Athens.

Mysteries.

Mysteries, connected with the cult of the deities of the underworld, supplied another means of approaching the supernatural. The Homeric bards of Ionia may have lived in a society where life yielded so many pleasures that men could look forward with equanimity and resignation to that colourless existence in the grey kingdom of Persephone, which is described in the epics. But the conditions of life were very different in the mother-country in the seventh century. The strife for existence was hard, and the Boeotian poet must have echoed the groans of many a wretched wight when he cried

> The earth is full of ills, of ills the sea.

It was a time when men were ready to entertain new views of a future world, suggesting hopes that a tolerable existence, unattainable here, might await them there. These new hopes which begin to take shape in the course of the seventh century were naturally connected with the religion of the deities of the underworld. In Homer we find Persephone as queen in the realm of the ghosts, but we meet there no hint of a connexion between her worship and that of Demeter, the goddess of the fruits of the earth. But as the earth which yields

---

[4] Dionysus was worshipped from of old at Delphi, and was identified with Apollo. This identity comes out strikingly in the hymn to Dionysus Paean by a Locrian poet (338 B.C.), recently discovered at Delphi.

the sustenance of men's life also receives men into her bosom when they die, Demeter and Persephone came to be associated in many local cults throughout Greece, and there grew up the legend of the rape of Persephone, which was specially developed at Eleusis and was the subject of the Eleusinian Hymn to Demeter, composed in the seventh century. At Eleusis this *chthonian* cult acquired a peculiar character by the introduction of a new doctrine touching the state of souls in the life beyond the grave.

In the days of Eleusinian independence, the kings themselves were the priests of the two goddesses. When Eleusis became part of the Athenian state, the Eleusinian worship was made part of the Athenian state-religion; a temple of the two goddesses was built under the Acropolis and called the Eleusinion; and the Eleusinian Mysteries became one of the chief festivals of the Attic year, conducted by the king. The Mysteries, which were probably of a very simple nature in the seventh century, were subsequently transformed under Athenian influence. Two points in this transformation are especially to be noted. The old Eleusinian king Triptolemus is made more prominent, and is revered as the founder of agriculture, sent abroad by Demeter herself to sow seed and instruct folk in the art. But far more important is the association of the cult of Iacchus with the Eleusinian worship. Iacchus was a god of the underworld, who had a shrine in Athens. In the Mysteries he was borne to Eleusis and solemnly received there every year. He was originally distinct from the mystic Dionysus, with whom he was afterwards identified.

The Mysteries seem to have consisted of a representation in dumb show of the story of Persephone and Demeter. Mystic spells were uttered at certain moments in the spectacle, and certain sacred gear was exhibited. There was no explanation of any system of doctrine; the initiated were seers not hearers. When the scheme of the Mysteries was fully developed the order of the festival, which took place in September, was on this wise.[5] On the first day, the cry was heard in the streets of Athens—

> Seaward, O mystae, mystae, to the sea!

And the initiated went down to the shore and cleansed themselves in the sea water. Hence the day was called ἅλαδε μύσται. The next two days were occupied with offerings and ceremonies at Athens, and on the fourth, the image of Iacchus was taken forth from his shrine and carried in solemn procession along the Sacred Way, over

Margin notes:
The Eleusinian religion.

(1) Triptolemus.

(2) Iacchus.

The rites at Eleusis.

(By the pass of Daphne.)

[5] The feast of the greater Mysteries is referred to. The lesser Mysteries were celebrated early in the year at Agrae, a suburb of Athens.

Mount Aegaleos to Eleusis. The Mystae, as they went, sang the song of Iacchus, and reached the temple of the goddesses, under the Eleusinian acropolis, late at night, by the light of torches. The great day was when they assembled in the Hall of Initiation, and sat around on the tiers of stone-seats. The Hierophant, who always belonged to the Eleusinian royal family of the Eumolpids, displayed the secret things of the worship. Beside him the Torch-holder, the Herald, and the Priest of the Altar, conducted the mystic ceremonies. The Mysteries are mysterious still, so far as most of the details are concerned. Yet we may perhaps say that no definite dogma was taught, no systematic interpretation was laid on the legends; but the "acts" were calculated to arouse men's hopes, mysterious enough to impress their imaginations, and vague enough to suggest to different minds different significances. The rites gave to many an assurance of future weal and even to harder reasoners a certain sense of possibilities in the unknown. And it was believed that the Mystae had an advantage over the uninitiated not only here but hereafter,—an interest as it were with the powers of the other world. So it is said in the old Eleusinian Hymn:

> Bliss hath he won whoso these things hath seen,
> Among all men upon the earth that go;
> But they to whom those sights have never been
> Unveiled have other dole of weal and woe,
> Even dead, shut fast within the mouldy gloom below.

The Eleusinian Mysteries became Panhellenic. All Greeks, not impure through any pollution, were welcome to the rites of initiation, women were not excluded by their sex, nor slaves by their condition. It is probable that the development of the Mysteries owed a good deal to the Pisistratids; and the ground plan of the Hall of Ceremonies, which was erected in their time, can be traced at Eleusis.

Sect. 13. Spread of the Orphic Religion

The Orphic teachers promulgated a new theory of the creation of the world—a theory which may have derived some suggestions from Babylonia. They taught that Time was the original principle; that then Ether and Chaos came into being; that out of these two elements Time formed a silver egg, from which sprang the first-born of the gods, Phanes god of light; the development of the world is the self-revelation of Phanes. It was necessary to bring this cosmogony into connexion with Greek theology. Accordingly, Zeus swallows Phanes and thereby becomes the original force from which the world has to be developed anew. The Thracian god, Dionysus

Marginal notes:

(Telesterion.)

(τὰ δρώμενα.)

Orphic cosmogony.

Myth of

Zagreus, is the son of Zeus and Persephone—and thus closely connected with the underworld. Zeus gives him the kingdom of the universe, while he is still a boy; but he is pursued by the Titans, and when, after many escapes, he takes the shape of a bull, he is rent in pieces by them, but Athena saves his heart. Zeus swallows it, and afterwards brings forth the new Dionysus. The Titans, still wet with the blood of their victim, he strikes with lightning, and the race of men springs from their ashes. So that the nature of men is compact of Titanic and Dionysiac elements, good and bad. The motive of the myth was to awaken in the human soul a consciousness of its divine origin, and help it on its way back to the divine state. To escape from the prison or tomb of the body, to become free from the Titanic elements, penalties and purifications are necessary, and the soul has to pass through a cycle of incarnations. In the intervals between these incarcerations which recur at fixed times the soul exists in the kingdom of Hades. To attain a final deliverance, a man must live ascetically according to rules which the Orphics prescribed, and be initiated in the orgies of Dionysus. Thus they prescribed abstinence from animal food, and imposed necessary ceremonies of purification. They taught the doctrine of judgment after death, and rewards and punishments in Hades, according to men's deeds in the body.

Thus the Orphics reintroduced, as it were, into Greece the Thracian Dionysus, who seemed almost another god when brought face to face with the Dionysus who had been hellenized and sobered since his admission into the society of the Greek gods of Olympus. They adopted and developed the ideas of the Eleusinian Mysteries; and in a poem on the Descent of Orpheus into Hades they described the geography of the underworld. They also aspired to take the place of the old prophets and purifiers; and they sought out and collected the oracles which those prophets had disseminated. Their doctrines were published in poems which were intended to supersede the Theogony of Hesiod; and the surviving fragments of these works show more poetical power than the compositions of the later successors of Homer.

The Orphic religion found a welcome at Athens, and was encouraged by Pisistratus and his sons. Onomacritus, one of the most eminent Orphic teachers, reputed the author of a poem on the "Rites of Initiation," won great credit and influence at the court of the tyrants. We saw how he was supposed to have taken part in preparing an edition of Homer, in which it was suspected that he and his collaborators made interpolations; and how another interpolation led to his banishment, when he was detected in making an addition of

Dionysus Zagreus.

Origin of the human race.

The Orphics in Attica. Onomacritus.

his own to a collection of ancient oracles, which were ascribed to the mythical poet Musaeus.

The Orphic doctrines were taken up by a man of genius, Pythagoras of Samos, who went to Italy and settled at Croton, where he was well received. His philosophy had two sides, the philosophic and the religious. He made important discoveries in mathematics and the theory of music; he recognised the spherical form of the earth, and his astronomical researches led to a considerable step, taken by his followers, in the direction of the Copernican system—the distinction of real and apparent motions. The Pythagoreans knew that the motion of the sun round the earth was only apparent, but they did not discover the revolution of the earth on its axis. They conceived a fire in the centre of the universe, round which the earth turns in twenty-four hours; the five known planets also revolving round it; and the moon and the sun, in a month and a year respectively. We never see the fire, because we live on the side of the earth which is always turned away from it. The whole world is warmed and lit from that fire—the "hearth of the universe." Pythagoras sought to explain the world, spiritual and material, by numbers; and, though he could plausibly defend the idea in general, its absurdity was evident when carried out in detail. His great achievement was the creation of mathematical science.

At Croton he founded a religious sect or brotherhood, organised according to strict rules. The most important doctrine was the transmigration of souls, and the ascetic mode of life corresponded to that of the Orphic sects. In fact, the Pythagoreans were practically an Orphic community. Their brotherhood, which did not exclude women, obtained adherents not only in Croton but in the neighbouring cities, and won a decisive political influence in Italiot Greece. But this influence was exerted solely in the interests of

oligarchy; it would seem indeed that the nobles became members of the religious organisation, in order to use it as an instrument of political power. It was during the ascendency of the Pythagoreans that

a war broke out between Croton and its neighbour Sybaris, which was then subject to a tyranny. The men of Croton harboured the exiles whom Telys, the despot of Sybaris, drove out, and refused his demand for their surrender. Telys led forth a large host; a battle

was fought; and the Sybarites were routed. Then the victors captured Sybaris and utterly blotted it out. New cities were to arise near the place; one was for a few months to resume its name; but the old Sybaris, which had become proverbial throughout Greece for its wealth and luxury, disappeared so completely that its exact site is unknown. The destruction of the rival city was the chief exploit of the Pythagorean oligarchy of Croton; but a strong opposition arose in Croton against the government and against the Pythagorean order. Pythagoras himself found it prudent to escape from the struggle by leaving Croton, and he ended his life at Metapontion. The democratic party was led by Cylon, but the Cylonians did not get the upper hand till more than half a century had passed; and the Pythagorean order flourished in Croton and the neighbouring cities. At length a sudden blow dissolved their power. One day forty brethren were assembled at Croton in the house of Milon. Their opponents set the building on fire, and only two escaped. It was a signal for a general persecution throughout Italy; everywhere the members of the society were put to death or banished.

Pythagoras leaves Croton, c. 510-9 (?).

Suppression of the Pythagoreans, c. 450.

At the time of the fall of the Pythagoreans, the Orphic religion was no longer a danger to Greece. It was otherwise in the lifetime of Pythagoras himself. Then it seemed as if the Orphic doctrines had been revealed as the salvation which men's minds craved; and, if those doctrines had taken firm hold of Greece, all the priesthoods of the national temples would have admitted the new religion, become its ministers, and thereby exercised an enormous sacerdotal power. Nor would the Orphic teachers have failed, if there had not been a powerful antidote to counteract their mysticism. Even as it was, they exercised a permanent influence, stimulating the imaginations of poets, like Aeschylus and Pindar, and diffusing a vivid picture of the world of Hades, which has affected all subsequent literature.

Sect. 14. Ionian Reason

The antidote to the Orphic religion was the philosophy of Ionia. In Asiatic Greece, that religion never took root; and most fortunately the philosophical movement—the separation of science from theology, of "cosmogony" from "theogony"—had begun before the Orphic movement was disseminated. Europe is deeply indebted to Ionia for having founded philosophy; but that debt is enhanced by the fact that she thereby rescued Greece from the tyranny of a religion interpreted by priests. We have met Thales and Anaximander already. Pythagoras, although he and his followers made important advances in science, threw his weight into the scale of mysticism; affected by both the religious and the philosophical movements, he sought to combine them; and in such unions the mystic element always wins the preponderance. But there were others who pursued, undistracted, the paths of reason, and among these the most eminent and influential were Xenophanes and Heraclitus.

No man was more active in the cause of reason than Xenophanes of Colophon, who, after the Persian subjugation of Ionia, migrated to Elea, where he died in extreme old age. But he spent his long life in wandering about the world, and none saw and heard more of many lands and many men than he. The feeble resistance of Ionia to the invader had disgusted him with the Greeks, and produced a reaction in his mind against their religion and their ideals. His experience of many lands helped him to cast away national prejudices, and he spent his strength in warring against received opinions. In the first place he attacked the orthodox religion and showed up the irrational side of gods made in the image of men. If oxen or horses or lions, he said, had hands to make images of their gods, they would fashion them in the shape of oxen, horses, and lions. In the next place, he protested against the accepted teachers of the Greeks, the poets Homer and Hesiod, whom Greece regarded as inspired. All they have taught men, he said, is theft, adultery, and mutual deceit. Again, he ridiculed the conventional ideals of Greek life, the ideal, for instance, of the athlete. He deprecated the folly which showed great honours to a victor in a race or a contest. "Our wisdom is better than the strength of human animals and horses." He carried about and spread his revolutionary ideas from city to city in the guise of a musician, attended by a slave with a cithern. But he was not merely destructive; he had something to put in the place of the beliefs which he overthrew. He constructed a philosophy of which the first principle was god—not like mortals in either form or mind —which he identified with the whole cosmos, and which was thus material, existing in space, and not excluding the existence of particular subordinate gods animating nature. He was also distinguished as a geologist; he drew conclusions from fossils as to the past history of the earth. As a fearless thinker, seeking to break through national prejudices, he is one of the most attractive of the pioneers of Greek thought.

But what especially concerns us here is that Xenophanes rejected Orpheus as utterly as he rejected Hesiod. He would have nothing to do with mysticism and divine revelation; he regarded the Orphic priests as impostors, and he inveighed strongly against Pythagoras. We can hardly over-value his services in thus actively fighting the battle of reason, and diffusing ideas which counteracted not only the comparatively harmless superstitions of the vulgar but also the more serious and subtle danger of the Orphic religion. Long before he died, Greek philosophy had become a living power which no religion would stifle, a waxing force which would hinder sacerdotalism from ever turning back the stream of progress.

The rationalism of Xenophanes affected Heraclitus of Ephesus, a man of very different temper. Heraclitus heartily despised the vulgar—he was an aristocrat in politics—and he wrote in a hard style, for the few. In old age he retreated to the woods to end his life, having deposited the book of his philosophy in the temple of Artemis. A man of greater genius than any of the Ionian philosophers who preceded him, he thought out the "doctrine of the flux," which exercised an immense influence on his successors. This principle was the constant change in all things; existence is change; "we are and we are not." But the process of change observes a certain law; nature has her measures; and thus, while he had developed the doctrine of relativity—"good and bad," he said, "are the same"—he had a basis for ethics. His influence was both subversive and conservative, according as one took hold of the doctrine of the flux or the fixed law of the world.

Heraclitus.

The pantheistic principle of Xenophanes was taken up at Elea by Parmenides, who gave it a new metaphysical meaning. He assumed an eternal unchanging Being, and treated it with the scientific method which he learned from the Pythagoreans. One of the most important services of Parmenides and his followers was their argument that sense is deceptive and leads us into self-contradiction. Here, they said, was the capital error of Heraclitus, who founded his system on the senses.

Parmenides.

With Parmenides and Heraclitus, philosophy in the strict sense, metaphysics as we call it, was fully founded. We have not to pursue the development here; but we have to realise that the establishment of the study of philosophy was one of the most momentous facts in the history of the Greeks. It meant the triumph of reason over mystery; it led to the discrediting of the Orphic movement; it ensured the free political and social progress of Hellas. A danger averted without noise or bloodshed, not at a single crisis but in the course of many years, is a danger which soon ceases to be realised; and it is perhaps hard to imagine that in the days of Pisistratus the religion which was then moving Greece, and especially Attica, bid fair to gain a dominant influence and secure a fatal power for the priests. The Delphic priesthood had, doubtless, an instinct that the propagation of the Orphic doctrines might ultimately redound to its own advantage. Although the new religion had arisen when the aristocracies were passing away and had addressed itself to the masses, it is certain that, if it had gained the upper hand, it would have lent itself to the support of aristocracy and tyranny. The tyrants of Athens might have made an Orphic priesthood an useful instrument of terror; and the brotherhood of Pythagoras was an unmistakable

The religious danger averted.

lesson to Greece what the predominance of a religious order was likely to mean.

We may say, with propriety, that a great peril was averted from Greece by the healthful influence of the immortal thinkers of Ionia. But this, after all, is only a superficial way of putting the fact. If we look deeper, we see that the victory by philosophy over the doctrines of priests was simply the expression of the Greek spirit, which inevitably sought its highest satisfaction in the full expansion of its own powers in the free light of reason.

Legend of the Seven Sages. The sixth century, the most critical period in the mental development of the Greeks, came to be known afterwards as the age of the Seven Sages.[6] The national instinct for shaping legends chose out a number of men who had made some impression by their justice and prudence, and, regardless of dates, invented an ideal community among them, as if they had formed a sort of college; and brought them into connexion with great people, like Lydian kings. Periander, the tyrant of Corinth, was curiously added to the list, which included Solon and Thales. To them were attributed wise maxims like "Know thyself," "Avoid excess," "It is hard to be virtuous." The spirit, which the legend ascribes to these sages and which the lives of Solon and Pittacus displayed, reflects the wisdom, which sought to solve, or rather to evade, the everlasting problem of the discrepancy between man's ideal of justice and the actual ordering of the world, by enjoining a life of moderation. But it is not without significance that, when the Orphic agitation had abated, Greece should have enshrined the worldly wisdom of men who stood wholly aloof from mystic excitements and sought for no revelation, in the fiction of the Seven Sages.

[6] Solon, Periander, Chilon of Sparta, Pittacus, Bias, Thaies, Cleobulus of Lindus.

CHAPTER VIII

THE FOUNDATION OF THE ATHENIAN EMPIRE

Sect. 1. The Position of Sparta and Career of Pausanias

The Persian war, in its effects on Greece, illustrates the operation of a general law which governs human societies. Pressure from without, whether on a nation or a race, tends to promote unity and cohesion within. In the case of a nation the danger of foreign attack increases the sense of unity among individual citizens and strengthens the central power. In the case of a race, it tends to weld the individual communities into a nation or a federation. In the latter case, the chance of realising a complete or permanent unity depends partly on the strength and the duration of the external pressure, partly upon the degree of strength in the instinct for independence which has hitherto hindered the political atoms from cohesion. The Persian danger produced a marked tendency towards unity, but the pressure was acute only for a few years, and lasted in any form only for a few decades; and therefore that tendency was arrested, and the instinct for independence resumed its uncontested sway, before any scheme of Panhellenic federal government had become necessary. On the coast of Asia, where the danger was permanent, an union came into existence.

Now on these principles a philosopher might have predicted that an Hellenic union, whether whole or partial, whether of short or of long duration, would follow the repulse of the Persians; he might have predicted that such a great joint effort would react upon the domestic development of the victorious peoples. But no one could have foreseen what shape the union would take or how the reaction would be directed. The course of Grecian affairs entered upon a new and unexpected way. For the last forty years, Sparta had been the predominant power in continental Greece. She had become the head of a Peloponnesian League, and had intervened with effect in Greek affairs beyond the limits of the Peloponnesus. Her headship in the common resistance to Persia was recognised without murmur or dispute by the allies of northern Greece; in fact, her peninsular league may be said to have widened into the Panhellenic confederacy of the Isthmus. Her admirals had been commanders-in-chief at Salamis and at Mycale; and, if it were said that those naval victories could not be ascribed to Lacedaemonian skill or enterprise, Sparta could point to Thermopylae where her king had been gloriously defeated, to Cithaeron where her general and her spearsmen had won what was after all the decisive contest of the war. A political prophet would therefore have been tempted to predict that Sparta, universally acknowledged before the war to be the leading state of Greece, would after the war be able to convert leadership into dominion. A great national enterprise, conducted under her auspices to a splendid conclusion, must immensely increase the moral strength of her position, and might justly stimulate her ambition; moral power, by dexterous management, can soon be converted into material strength; in short, after the battle of Plataea, the Greek world seemed to lie at Sparta's feet. If such calculations were made, they were doomed to disappointment. Lacedaemon had not the means, and the Lacedaemonian government had not the brains or the spirit to create the means, of carrying out an effective imperial policy.

Sparta; not a sea-power;

For a state which aspired to a truly imperial position in Greece must inevitably be a sea-power. This was determined by the geographical and commercial conditions of the Greek world. So long as the Asiatic Greeks belonged to the Persian dominion, so long as the eastern waters of the Aegean were regarded as a Persian sea, Sparta might indeed hold a dominant position in a Hellas thus restricted. But when the world of free Hellenic states once more extended over the Aegean to the skirts of Asia and to Thrace, Sparta unless she became a sea-power could not extend her influence over this larger sea-bound Greece. She might retain her continental position, but her prestige must ultimately be eclipsed and her power menaced by any city which won imperial authority over the islands and coasts of the Aegean. This was what happened.

her limitations.

The Spartans were a people unable to adapt themselves to new conditions. Their city, their constitution, their spirit were survivals from mediaeval Greece. The government was conservative by tradition; reforms were unwelcome; a man of exceptional ability was regarded with suspicion. They continued to drill their hoplites in the fifth century as they had done in the sixth; the formation of a navy would have seemed to them as unpractical an idea as an expedition against the capital of Persia. And if we follow their conduct of the recent war, we see that their policy was petty and provincial. They had generally acted at the last moment; they had never shown the power of initiation; their view was so limited by the smaller interests of the Peloponnesus that again and again they almost betrayed the national cause. Failing to share in the progress of Greece, utterly wanting in the imperial instinct and the quality of imagination which accompanies it, the city of Lacedaemon was not marked out to achieve a political union of the Hellenic states. She was, however, able to prevent a rival from achieving it; but not before that rival had completely thrown her into the shade.

Unfortunately the events of the years succeeding the battle of Plataea are but very slightly known. Herodotus, who, about half a century later, completed the story, compact of fiction and history, of the Persian war, ends his work at the capture of Sestos. In the meantime the events of that full and momentous half-century had not been recorded, except by bits and scraps; the dates became confused, the details were forgotten; and, when Thucydides, some years after Herodotus, came to investigate the history of this period, the result of his research was a meagre narrative, in a very uncertain chronological setting. The growth of the Athenian empire is the central fact of the period; but before tracing it, we must pause—it will not be for long—over the misfortunes of Sparta.

History of these critical years ill-known

Pausanias, the son of Cleombrotus, had shown, it must be allowed, remarkable military ability in conducting the campaign of Plataea. But his talents as a politician were not equal to his talents as a general. Leaping into fame by his victory, he was led into attempting to play a part for which he was too slight a man. Sparta sent him out, in command of a squadron of ships supplied by her allies, to continue the work of emancipating the eastern Greeks. He sailed first to Cyprus and was successful in delivering the greater part of the island from Persian rule. He then proceeded to Byzantium and expelled the Persian garrison. But here his conduct became ambiguous; he began to play a game of his own. He connived at the escape of some kinsmen of Xerxes who were in the city; and he committed various acts of insolence and oppression to the Greeks. He behaved more as a tyrant than as a general; and he completely ruined all chances that his country had of remaining at the head of the confederacy which the Persian invasion had called into being. The eastern Greeks placed themselves under the protection and headship of Athens. This step was inevitable; the maritime power of Athens marked her out to be leader in the prosecution of the war beyond the sea. But the conduct of Pausanias at Byzantium may well have been the occasion of the formal transference of the

Career of Pausanias

478 B.C. (?).

477 B.C. (?).

leadership of the confederacy from Sparta to Athens. At Sparta itself the reports of the doings of the general aroused alarm and
anxiety. He was recalled to answer the charges. It was said that

His
medism;

he wore Persian dress, and was attended by an Asiatic bodyguard
in his journey through Thrace. For he had indeed been intriguing
with the Persian court. The victor of Plataea offered to enslave his
own city and the rest of Hellas to Xerxes, and to seal the compact
by marrying his daughter. His overtures were welcomed by the
Great King; and Pausanias, being a small man and elated by

recalled
and
acquitted.

vanity, was unable to refrain from betraying, in little things, his
treacherous designs. The Persian intrigue, however, could not at
this time be proved against him; he was punished only for some acts

Proceeds
to Byzan
tium on
his own
account,
477 B.C.
Takes
Sestos;

of injury which he had done to particular persons. He was not sent
out again; but he subsequently hired a trireme for himself and returned to the scene of his former intrigues. He resumed possession
of Byzantium and thus controlled the inner gate of the Euxine; and
he succeeded almost immediately in capturing Sestos, which gave
him control of the outer gate also. This was too much for the Athenians who were extending their political and commercial interests

driven out
by Cimon,
476 B.C.

in those regions, and they sent out a squadron under Cimon, the son
of Miltiades, who recovered Sestos and drove Pausanias out of
Byzantium. The Spartan government, hearing that he was intrigu-

Recalled
to Sparta.

ing in the Troad, sent a herald commanding him to return home. He
obeyed the summons, believing that he could compass an acquittal
by bribes; but it seems that he was already devising a daring and
dangerous plan against the constitution of his own city. The Ephors
threw him into prison; but it was difficult to procure evidence of his
guilt. He was released and challenged inquiry. Everybody knew
that he had not only negotiated with Persia but that he had prepared the way for a revolt of the Helots by promising them emanci-
pation. He dreamed of converting the Spartan state into a true
monarchy. But there were not clear enough proofs to act upon, until
a confidential servant turned informer. Pausanias had entrusted
him with a letter to Artabazus, but the man, who had noticed that
none of the messengers who had been previously dispatched on the
same errand, ever returned, broke the seal and read in the letter
the order for his death. He showed the letter to the Ephors, and
they, wishing to have proof against Pausanias from his own mouth,
contrived a stratagem. A hut with a partition was erected at the
sanctuary of Taenarus. They concealed themselves in one room and
the man remained in the other as a suppliant. Pausanias came to
discover why he was there; the man told him of the letter and re-
proached him. In the conversation, Pausanias admitted the whole

truth.[1] But he received a hint of his danger and fled to the temple of Athena of the Brazen House. He took refuge in a small covered building adjoining the shrine. The Ephors had the doors built up and starved him to death. As he was dying they brought him out, and by the command of the Delphic god he was buried at the entrance to the sacred enclosure. But the starvation within the precincts was an offence against the goddess and brought a curse upon the Spartans. To expiate this they dedicated two brazen statues to Athena of the Brazen House.

The curse of Athena of the Brazen House. (c. 471 B.C. ?).

FIG. 57.—Coin of Pharsalus, fifth century (obverse). Head of Pallas. FIG. 58.—Coin of Elis, fifth century (obverse). Flying eagle [legend: *FAΛEIO*]. FIG. 59.—Coin of Arcadia, fifth century (reverse). Head of Despoena [legend: APKAΔIKON].

Though the adventures of Pausanias are of no great consequence, his career is typical of the Spartan abroad; and it throws some light on years of which we know very little. The Spartan government had sent out another general to replace Pausanias in the Hellespont, but the allies would have no more dealings with Spartan generals; and Sparta made no further attempt to win back the allegiance which the Aegean and Asiatic Greeks had transferred to Athens. On the other hand, she made some attempts at extending her power on the mainland and forming a continental federation. She cast her eyes upon Thessaly, and perhaps hoped that if she brought the far north under her sway, she could extend her influence southward to the Crisaean gulf and form a Lacedaemonian empire on the basis of the Amphictionic league of northern Greece. She sent forth an army under king Leotychidas, who landed in the Pagasaean bay, and showed that he could have easily subjugated the Thessalian states. But like many a Spartan general, he could not resist silver and gold; and the Aleuad princes saved their power by bribing the invader. His guilt was evident, and when he returned home he was condemned to death. He saved himself by fleeing to Tegea, where Athena's sanctuary was ever the refuge of a Spartan king in the day

Sending of Dorcis.

Lacedaemonian expedition against Thessaly, 476 B.C.

---

[1] This anecdote has its improbabilities. The device would have been difficult of execution owing to the long distance of Taenarus from Sparta. Nor is it easy to see why the Ephors should hesitate to act on the letter.

of danger. It is possible that Sparta gained some influence in Thessaly by this enterprise, in which she employed the Peloponnesian fleet; but she made no conquest. Nor did her attempt to reorganise the Amphictionic federation prosper better. She proposed to expel from this league all those states which had joined the Mede—this was aimed at Thebes and Thessaly; and even the states which had not joined the federation against the Mede—this was aimed at Argos. But through the influence of Themistocles, who represented Athens, the proposal was thrown out. The activity of Themistocles in defeating the designs of Sparta at this period is reflected in the story that he tried to induce the Athenians to set fire to the Peloponnesian fleet in Thessalian waters.

Lacedae-
monian
attempt
to annex
the
Amphic-
tionic
league
(476
B.C. ?);
thwarted
by The-
mistocles.

Sparta was unable to prosecute any further plans of empire beyond her own peninsula; she was soon compelled to fight for her position within the Peloponnesus itself. Argos had now recovered somewhat from the annihilating blow which had been dealt her by king Cleomenes, and was entering upon a new constitutional development which was ultimately to shape itself into a democracy. Most of the small towns, which had taken advantage of the prostration of their mistress to throw off her yoke, such as Hysiae and Orneae, were brought back to their allegiance. It might have been harder to cast out the slave lords of Tiryns from the Cyclopean fortress; but a prophet from Phigalia came and stirred them up against Argos; they took the offensive, endured a defeat, and Tiryns was recovered. Thus re-arising, Argos was able to support the Arcadian cities in a combination against the power of Sparta. She entered into alliance with Tegea, but outside the walls of that city the joint forces of the two allies were smitten by the hoplites of Lacedaemon. Yet the city was not taken, and the epitaph of the fallen warriors told how "their bravery hindered the smoke of blazing Tegea from mounting to the sky." Soon after this we find all the Arcadian cities leagued against Sparta,—all except the Mantineans who were never ready to join hands with their Tegeate neighbours. This time Argos sent no help. The Arcadian league sustained a crushing defeat at Dipaea, and Tegea was forced to submit. Thus, through the energy of the young king Archidamus, Sparta maintained her position, but there were grave causes of anxiety for the future. She had to behold the synoecism of the villages of Elis into a city with a democratic constitution; that was a danger in the west. Regenerate Argos was a danger in the east. And even in Arcadia, Sparta was constrained reluctantly to recognise the new synoecism of the Mantinean villages, as a mark of gratitude to the community for holding aloof from the Arcadian league.

Argos
recovers
Tiryns
(468-7
B.C. ?).

Battle of
Tegea,
c. 473 B.C.

Battle of
Dipaea,
471 B.C. ?

Founda-
tion of
Elis, c.
472-1 B.C.
Synoecism
of Man-
tinea.

Thus it was not given to Sparta to strike out a new path; the Persian war left her much where she was before. She had, if anything, diminished rather than increased her prestige, and she had shown the world that she was destined to remain in the old Peloponnesian groove. In the meantime another city had been advancing with rapid strides along a new path, compassing large enterprises, and establishing a large empire.

SECT. 2. THE CONFEDERACY OF DELOS

The lukewarmness of Sparta, exhibited in her failure to follow up the battle of Mycale, had induced the Ionian and other Asiatic Greeks to place themselves under the leadership of Athens. Thus was formed the voluntary confederacy on which an Athenian empire was to rise. The object was not only to protect the rescued cities from reconquest by the barbarian, but also to devastate the country of the Great King, in order to obtain by rapine a set-off against the expenses and losses of the war. The treasury of the league was established in the sacred island of Delos, the ancient centre of Ionian worship, and it was hence called the Confederacy of Delos. The recapture of Sestos was its first achievement.

The league included the Ionian and Aeolian cities of Asia; the islands adjacent to the coast from Lesbos to Rhodes; a large number of towns on the Propontis, and some in Thrace; most of the Cyclades; and Euboea except its southern city Carystus. It was a league of sea-states, and therefore the basis of the contract was that each state should furnish ships to the common fleet. But most of the members were small and poor; many could not equip more than one or two ships; many could do no more than contribute a part of the expenses to the furnishing of a single galley. To gather together a number of small and scattered contingents at a fixed time and place was always a matter of difficulty; nor was such a miscellaneous armament easily managed. It was therefore arranged that the smaller states, instead of furnishing ships, should pay a yearly sum of money to a common treasury. It is uncertain how the amount of these payments was fixed. It seems probable that a calculation was made that all the states, which undertook to pay in money, ought to have been able to contribute between them 100 ships; and that the annual sum of 460 talents was taken as the equivalent of this contribution. Then a careful estimate was made of the resources and capacities of each city; and that sum was proportionally distributed among them. The valuation of the wealth of the confederate cities and the determination of the "contribution" of each was a work of

Confederacy of Delos; its purpose (winter 478-7 B.C.)

(above, p. 310).

(φόρος.)

The
Phoros
fixed and
assigned
by
Aristides.

great difficulty and responsibility; and it was devolved upon Aristides, whose discretion, and the respect in which he was held, fitted
him eminently for the task. His valuation remained in force for
more than fifty years. Thus from the very beginning the Confederacy consisted of two kinds of members, those who furnished ships
and those who paid an equivalent in money—a *phoros,* as it was
called; and the second class was far the larger. For besides those
who could only furnish a ship or two, or even part of a ship, many
of the larger cities preferred the system of money payments, which
did not oblige their burghers to leave home. The tribute was collected by ten Athenian officers, who bore the title of *Hellenotamiae,*
"treasurers of the Greeks." The Council of the Confederates met at
Delos, where the treasury was, and each member had an equal
voice. The large number of votes enabled Athens easily to control
the proceedings of the Council; she could influence the smaller
states, and the number of these votes overcame the weight of any
opposition which the larger states could offer. As leader of the
Confederacy, Athens had the executive entirely in her hands, and
it was of the highest significance that the treasurers were not selected from the whole body of Confederates but were Athenian citizens.
Thus from the first Athens held in her hands the means of gradually, and without any violent revolution, transforming the naval
union into a naval empire.

The
Council.

While the name of Aristides is connected most closely with the
foundation of the Confederacy, there is no doubt that it was due to
his rival Themistocles that Athens took the tide of fortune at the
flood. Themistocles had made his city a sea-power; and this feat
approved him the greatest of all her statesmen. He was a man of
genius. The most reserved of all historians, Thucydides, turns aside
to praise his unusual natural gifts: his power of divining what was
likely to happen, and his capacity for dealing with difficult situa-
tions. We should have expected that the guidance of the policy of
Athens, the organisation of the new Confederacy, would have been
entirely entrusted to Themistocles. Half a century later, when the
democratic development of Athens had advanced farther, this
would probably have been the case. But at this time a man without
powerful connexions could not long maintain his influence over the
people. Themistocles had no party behind him, and the exceptional
ability of the man is shown by nothing so much as by the fact that
in spite of this disadvantage he played such a great part. His rivals,
Aristides and Xanthippus, were representative of the old and considerable party of the Coast, which was associated with the family
of Megacles and Cleisthenes, to which the wife of Xanthippus

Position
of The-
mistocles;
he has no
party to
support
him.

belonged. They are the leaders at Plataea and Mycale; the name of Themistocles does not appear in the second year of the Persian war. The circumstance that Themistocles was not a party leader, that there was no protracted period during which Athens submitted to his influence, might easily lead us to underrate his importance. Though he was not formally or officially the founder of the Confederacy, yet, when Athens undertook the leadership and entered upon the new paths which then opened out before her, she was under the spell of a spirit of which he had been the clearest and earliest interpreter. But his influence had not yet passed away; and, while the fleet was building an empire in the east, there was work for him to do amid the ruins of Athens.

SECT. 3. THE FORTIFICATION OF ATHENS AND THE PIRAEUS

Themistocles, as we saw, made Athens a sea-power. Under his guidance she threw her chief energy into the development of a navy; but, if she had followed that guidance more fully, she would have now cut herself more boldly adrift from the ties which attached her to the continent. It often occurred to the Athenians to regret that Athens was not an island; "if we were islanders," they thought, "we could defy the world." There would always be the Boeotian and the Megarian frontiers. But, if a series of strong fortresses had been regularly maintained on these frontiers, and if Athenian politicians had resolutely eschewed a continental policy, it might have been possible to spend practically all their strength on their ships. In any case, when Athens decided to enter upon a new career, her true policy would have been to come down to the Piraeus. She should have left her old city round the Acropolis and migrated to the shore of the sea which was henceforward to shape her history. The position of the Acropolis was a fatality for Athens; it was too far from the sea and at the same time too near. If it had been as far from the coast as Acharnae, the citizens would almost certainly at this period have transferred their hearths and temples to the hill of Munychia and the shores of the Piraeus. But it was near enough to admit of tolerably quick communication with the harbour; and this geographical circumstance at once saved the old town and weakened the new city. Expediency will induce a monarch, but nothing except necessity will persuade a free people, to take the momentous resolution of leaving the spot where the homes and temples of the community have stood for centuries—the place associated with their dearest memories, their hopes and their fears.

Had Themistocles been a tyrant, we may venture to suppose that

[margin note:] The Acropolis too far from the coast.

he would have left Athens unfortified, built his palace on Munychia, and made Piraeus the centre of government—the city; so that in a few years the old town would have sunk into decay. But since Athens was to remain as before, notwithstanding the new development, and since this new development made the Piraeus of greater strategic importance, it became necessary to fortify and defend two towns within five miles' distance of each other.

The walls of Athens.

After Plataea, the Athenians brought back their families and goods to their desolate habitation. Little of the old town wall was still standing, and they proceeded to build a new wall. The work was done in haste; the material of older buildings and even gravestones were used. The traces of haste can be detected in some of the remains of this wall of Themistocles, near the Dipylon Gate in the north-west of the city. For it was by the advice and under the inspiration of Themistocles that the work was wrought. It embraced a larger circuit than the old enclosure which Pisistratus had destroyed; on the south side it followed the heights of the Pnyx group of hills, and approached the Ilisus. The Peloponnesians looked with jealousy at the rise of the Athenian walls. The activity of Athens in the Persian war and her strong navy made them suspect her ambitions. But they could not prevent her from strengthening her town. The Lacedaemonians sent an embassy, to deprecate fortifications, and to invite the Athenians instead of fortifying their own town to join Sparta in demolishing all fortifications in Greece. But they were not in a position to do more than remonstrate. As the name of Themistocles was associated with the wall, it was inevitable that an anecdote should be circulated, to illustrate the resources and wiles of the Attic Odysseus. At his suggestion, the Spartan envoys were sent back with the answer that the Athenians would send an embassy. When they were gone, he started himself, as one of the ambassadors, but his colleagues were to remain behind till the wall had reached the lowest defensible height. In the meantime, the whole population, men, women, and children, were to press on the work. Having arrived at Sparta, he delayed presenting himself before the assembly, and when he was asked why, he said that his colleagues had been detained and that he expected them every day. Meanwhile persons arriving from Athens assured the Spartans that the wall was being built. Themistocles asked them not to be deceived by such rumours, but to send men of their own to discover whether it was true. At the same time he sent a message to Athens, with instructions that the envoys from Sparta should be detained till he and his colleagues had returned. The wall had now reached a sufficient height; and, the other ambassadors having arrived, Themistocles

The trick of Themistocles.

appeared before the assembly, and declared that Athens had walls and could defend her people. In future, he said, if the Lacedaemonians or their allies have any communication to make, they must deal with us as with men who are capable of deciding their own and Greece's interests. The Lacedaemonians had to put as good a face on the matter as they could. The story has significance in representing Athens as now formally declaring herself the peer of Sparta.

The fortification of Piraeus was likewise taken in hand. A thick wall was built all round the Munychian peninsula, keeping close to the sea, and was continued along the north side of the harbour of Cantharus,—or the Harbour, as it was simply called,—and out to the promontory of Eetionea. The entrances to this chief Harbour and to the two small havens of Munychia and Zea on the east side of the peninsula were fortified by moles.

In the course of the next twenty years the Athenians came to see the disadvantage of the two towns, which ought to have been one. It was borne in upon their statesmen that in the case of an enemy invading Attica with a powerful army, the communications between Athens and the Piraeus might be completely severed, and the folk of the city be cut off from their ships. In order to meet this danger—which would have been most simply met by deserting Athens—a new device was imagined. It was resolved to transform the two towns into a double town, girt by a continuous line of fortification. Two diverging walls were built, to connect Athens with the sea. The northern joined the Piraeus wall, near the Harbour, the southern ran down to the roadstead of Phaleron. By these Long Walls, costly to build and costly to defend, Athens sought to rectify a mistake and adapt her topography to her rôle of mistress of the sea. *The Long Walls, 458 B.C.*

But though this device of Athens to conciliate her past history with her future seems clumsy enough, it answered its purpose fairly well. Her naval power was based upon the only sure foundation, a growing naval commerce. This, in its turn, depended upon the increase of Attic industries, which may be estimated by the enormous number of resident aliens or metics, who settled in Athens or Piraeus for the purpose of manufacture and trade. These metics, who seem to have ultimately approached the number of 10,000, were liable to the same ordinary burdens as the citizens, and, when a property-tax was imposed in time of war, they were taxed at a higher rate. We may well believe that Themistocles was concerned to encourage the growth of a class of inhabitants who were directly or indirectly so profitable to the community. But in our scanty and vague records of this momentous period, it is impossible to define the activity of Themistocles. *The μέτοικοι*

We know that he wished to introduce a system by which a certain number of triremes should be added to the fleet every year; but this idea was not adopted; new ships were built from time to time according as they were needed. But a new system of furnishing them was introduced. The state supplied only the hull and some of the rigging; the duty and expense of fitting the galley, launching it complete, and training the oarsmen, were laid upon the most wealthy burghers, each in his turn. This public burden was called the trierarchy, and the trierarch, who sailed with his ship, was responsible for the good repair of the trireme at the end of the period of his office. One hundred and seventy oarsmen composed of hired foreigners and slaves, and partly of the poorest class of the citizens, propelled each galley; there was a crew of twenty men, to manage the vessel, including the *keleustes* who set the time to the oarsmen; and there were, besides, ten soldiers.

As their navy was from henceforth to be the chief arm of their military power, the Athenians were obliged to make a necessary change in the constitution of their highest military command. Two courses were open to them. They might leave the board of generals as it was, each general being the captain of the hoplites of his own tribe, and institute a new board of admirals. If this arrangement had been made, it would have been necessary to assign to the admirals a higher authority, for the purpose of conducting joint operations by land and sea, so that the position of generals would have been reduced to that of subordinate officers. The other course was to make the generals supreme commanders by land and sea alike—and such had been their virtual position during the Persian invasion. This second plan was adopted, and as a logical consequence the generals were no longer elected one from each tribe, but from the whole people, though in actual practice an attempt was made to secure that each tribe should be represented. The old duties of the generals as commanders of the tribal regiments were undertaken for the infantry by new officers called taxiarchs and for the cavalry by the phylarchs.

The fortification of the city and her harbour was the chief, but it was not the only, work that the masons of Athens were set to do. The Persians had wrecked the houses of Athena on her high hill, and no duty was more pressing for the Athenians, when the danger passed, than to find a dwelling-place for the goddess. There can be little doubt that their first thought was to restore the elder temple, the house which she shared with Erechtheus, the place of the precious emblems of the olive-tree and the salt-spring,—if it were only to make it ready in some temporary fashion to receive the ancient

Introduction of the trierarchy.

Crew: 170 oarsmen, twenty hypêretai, ten epibatai.

Change in the stratêgia.

(See above, p. 248.)

Restoration of the temple of Athena Polias ("House of Erechtheus").

wooden image, which had probably been lodged in a secret hiding-place. It is not clear that they attempted any complete or partial restoration of the younger temple, the House of a Hundred Feet; perhaps they simply swept away the ruins. Probably the walls and columns still partly stood, but the roof and all the woodwork had been destroyed, and the sculptures which adorned the pediments had been cast down and shattered. The limbs and trunks of the giants, strewn among the ruins, were cast away into the rubbish heaps, from which they have been drawn forth recently into new honour, as precious relics of the early art of Greece. In any case, even if they rebuilt in some sort the dismantled temple, the burghers of Athens were not content; they resolved that the lady of their city should have an ampler and more glorious dwelling-house. It was probably when Themistocles was still their guiding statesman that the plan was laid of a second temple near the southern brink of the hill. The foundations of this new temple are still to be seen; but it was never carried out as it was designed; when the time came to rear the walls, the plan was entirely altered; and, as we shall see hereafter, the Parthenon arose on the foundations which were intended for a building of wholly different proportions.

The Heca tompedon

The designed new temple (of Themistocles or Cimon?); remains of its foundations under the Parthenon.

SECT. 4. OSTRACISM AND DEATH OF THEMISTOCLES

For some years Themistocles divided the guidance of public affairs with Aristides and Xanthippus. He superintended the building of the walls, and we have already seen how he effectually opposed the designs of Sparta. But the man of genius had his weaknesses. Like most Greek statesmen, he was accessible to bribes, and perhaps he would hardly have cared to tell how he had become a rich man. It was more serious that his vanity betrayed him into committing public indiscretions. He built near his own house a shrine to "Artemis wisest in Council," on the ground that the counsels which he had offered his country had been wiser than all others. In themselves such things were of little importance; but they conduced to unpopularity and gave opponents a handle for attack. The time and the immediate causes of the banishment of Themistocles are uncertain. Perhaps he tried to carry through measures which were too revolutionary for Aristides, though Aristides was a decided democrat. At all events he succumbed to a coalition of Aristides and Xanthippus, which was doubtless also supported by Cimon, who was rising into prominence through his military successes. Appeal was made to the trial of Ostracism; and the greater number of six thousand sherds bore the name of Themistocles. One of these

(Artemis Aristobule.)

Ostracism of Themistocles, c. 472 B.C.

fatal sherds, perhaps,[2] still exists. The exiled statesman took up his abode in Argos. The presence there of such a crafty and active enemy was not agreeable to Sparta, and he was not left long in peace. When the Persian intrigues of Pausanias were disclosed, the Lacedaemonians discovered that Themistocles was implicated in the scandal. But though Themistocles held communications with Pausanias, communications of a compromising kind, it is not in the least likely that he was really guilty of any design to betray Greece to Persia; it is rather to be presumed that those communications were concerned with the schemes of Pausanias against the Spartan constitution. He was accused of high treason against his country; men were sent to arrest him and bring him to trial; and he fled to Corcyra. The Corcyraeans refused to keep him and he crossed over to Epirus, pursued by Lacedaemonian and Athenian officers. He was forced to stop at the house of Admetus king of the Molossians, though his previous relations with this king had not been friendly. In these western lands, we seem to be translated into a far older time and to visit the homestead of a Homeric king. Admetus was not at home, but Themistocles supplicated the queen and she directed him to take her child and seat himself by the hearth. When the king returned, Themistocles implored his protection; and Admetus hospitably refused to give him up to the pursuers. The Athenians, disappointed of their prey, condemned him as a traitor to outlawry, confiscating his property and dooming his descendants to loss of citizenship. Admetus sent the fugitive overland to Pydna in Macedonia. A vessel carried him to the shores of Ionia. For some years he lay hidden in towns on the Asiatic coast, but when Xerxes died and Artaxerxes came to the throne, he went up to Susa and intrigued at the Persian court. Thus circumstances drove him to follow the example of Pausanias; and, by a curious irony, the two men who might be regarded as the saviours of Greece, the hero of Salamis and the hero of Plataea, were perverted into framing plans for undoing their own work and enslaving the country which they had delivered. It may well have been, however, that Themistocles, who was an able and far-sighted man, merely intended to compass his own advantage at the expense of the Great King, and had no serious thought of carrying out any designs against Greece. He was, as we might expect, more successful than the Spartan schemer. He won high honour in Persia and was given the government of the district of Magnesia, where Magnesia itself fur-

---

[2] Perhaps; for it might have been a sherd on which a vote against Themistocles was recorded, on the occasion of the ostracism of Aristides or of Xanthippus.

ninshed his table with bread, Lampsacus with wine, and Myus with meat.

Themistocles died in Magnesia, and the Magnesians gave him outside their walls the resting-place which was denied to him in his own country.[3] Nor were they content with this; they sought to associate his fame more intimately with their own city. They paid him the honour of a hero, and erected in their market-place a statue of the saviour of Greece, standing naked in the act of pouring a libation over an altar, below which lay a slain bull. It was not long before this scene was wilfully or ignorantly misunderstood and gave rise to a false story. Half a century after the death of Themistocles it was popularly supposed that he had poisoned himself with bull's blood; and the absurd motive of despair at his inability to fulfil his promises to the Persian king was assigned for his self-slaughter. There can be little doubt that this tale, first circulated perhaps by malicious tongues at Athens, was suggested by the bull and the libation-dish in the monument of the Magnesian market-place.

Death of Themistocles.

His statue.

Rumoured suicide

Sect. 5. The Confederacy of Delos becomes an Athenian Empire

The conduct of the war which the Confederacy of Delos was waging against Persia had been entrusted to Cimon, the son of Miltiades. We have seen already how he drove Pausanias out of Sestos and Byzantium. His next exploit was to capture Eion, a town near the mouth of the Strymon, and the most important stronghold of the Persians east of the Hellespont. The place was defended to the uttermost by Boges, its gallant commander, who refused all overtures; and when the food ran out he lit a great funeral pyre. He slew his wife and his children, his concubines and his slaves, and hurled them into the fire. He took all his gold and silver to the top of the wall and flung it into the waters of the Strymon. Then he leaped himself into the flames. Thus the Athenians captured a strong coast-fortress, and they were tempted by the rich cornfields and the forests of timber in the neighbourhood to make a permanent settlement at Eion; but the colonists whom they sent forth were destroyed by the Thracian natives. The day for the establishment of the Athenian power on the lower Strymon had not yet come.

Cimon general of confederate fleet. Capture of Eion, 476-5 B.C.

Doriscus which commanded the mouth of the Hebrus was still in Persian hands, the attempts of the Athenian fleet to take it were

---

[3] It is said that relatives took his bones to Attica and buried them secretly; and it is supposed that his Attic sepulchre can be identified on the shore of the Munychian promontory.

successfully resisted, and we know not what befell it in the end.

Perhaps it fell into the hands of the Thracians. The next enterprise of Cimon was the reduction of the rocky island of Scyrus, a stronghold of Dolopian pirates. While Athens was winning posts on the fringe of the Aegean, it was no less necessary for her to secure intermediate stations; and the importance of Scyrus was its position on the sea-road from Athens to western Thrace. The rude inhabitants were enslaved, and their place was taken by Attic settlers; the

island was in fact annexed to Attica. But Cimon won less glory by the conquest than by the discovery of the bones of Theseus. There was a Delphic oracle which bade the Athenians take up the bones of Theseus and keep them in an honourable resting-place, and perhaps there was a legend that the hero was buried in Scyrus. In any case, whether by chance or after a search, there was found in the island a grave containing a warrior's corpse of heroic size. It was the corpse of Theseus; Cimon brought it back to Athens; and perhaps none of his exploits earned him greater popularity.

A few years later Cimon achieved what was the most brilliant success of his life. Hitherto he had been busy in the northern waters of the Aegean; it was high time that the fleet should sail southward and strike a blow against the Persian power in the seas of Rhodes and Cyprus. It was not only high time, it was imperative; for Xerxes had equipped a great armament—his last resistance to the triumph of Greek arms. Cimon delivered both the Greek and the native coast towns of Caria from Persian rule, and constrained the Lycian communities to enrol themselves in the Confederacy of

Delos. Then at the river Eurymedon in Pamphylia he found the Persian army and the Persian fleet; and overcame them in a double battle by land and sea, destroying 200 Phoenician ships. This victory sealed the acquisition of southern Asia Minor, from Caria to Pamphylia, for the Athenian federation.

The booty which was won in this battle was put to the use of fortifying the Athenian citadel which the Persians had dismantled. Themistocles, who laid his hopes on the Piraeus, would have been content that the Acropolis should have remained unwalled; but the conservative policy of Cimon decided that it should become again the fortress of Athens. The south wall was now built out of the spoils of the Eurymedon.

It could not be said that the Confederacy of Delos had failed to do its work. The victory on the Pamphylian river freed Greece

from all danger on the side of the Persian empire; and Cimon soon followed up his success by reducing some places on the Thracian Chersonese which were still held by the barbarians. But in the interval between the conquest of Scyrus and the battle of the Eurymedon, the confederate fleet had been set to do other work. It had been set to make war upon Greek states, which were unwilling to belong to the league. The first case was one of pure and simple coercion of a foreign city. Carystus, unlike the other cities of her island, had held aloof from the Confederacy; and this anomaly seemed intolerable to Athens, especially as the place was so near the shores of Attica. Carystus was subjugated, and made, in spite of herself, a member of the league. The second case was that of a confederate state which wished to be confederate no longer. Naxos seceded from the league, and the fleet of the allies reduced her by blockade. In the case of Carystus, the Confederacy could defend its act only by the plea of political necessity; in the case of Naxos, it could reasonably maintain its right of forcing the individual mem-

Helles-
pont, 466
B.C. (late
summer).

Reduction
of Cary-
stus,
472-1 B.C.

Revolt
and re-
duction of
Naxos,
469 B.C. ?

FIG. 60.—Coin of Thasos, fifth century (obverse). Satyr and nymph [legend: (Θ)A]. FIG. 61.—Coin of Erythrae, sixth century (obverse). Horseman with horse. FIG. 62.—Coin of Cos, fifth century (obverse). Youth about to hurl quoit; tripod.

bers to fulfil their obligations until the association should be dissolved by the common consent of all. But both acts alike seemed to be acts of tyrannical outrage on the independence of free states, and were an offence to public opinion in Greece. The oppression was all the worse, inasmuch as both Naxos and Carystus were deprived of their autonomy. They became in fact subjects of Athens. They are typical examples of the fashion in which the Athenian empire was built up. Athens was already forging the fetters with which she would bind her allies.

The victory of the Eurymedon left Athens free to pursue this inevitable policy of transforming the Confederacy into an empire. The most powerful confederate state on the Thracian coast was the island city of Thasos. Possessing a considerable fleet, it was doubtless one of those cities which contributed ships. Athens was making new endeavours to plant a settlement on the Strymon and to lay hands on the traffic in those regions. Her interests collided with those of the Thasians, whose prosperity largely depended upon their

Revolt of
Thasos,
465 B.C.

trade in Thrace. A dispute arose about a gold mine and the island-ers revolted. They hoped for support both from Macedonia and from Thrace, since both those countries were interested in excluding Athens from the coast trade of the northern sea-board. They hoped too for help from Sparta; but the Lacedaemonians were hindered from sending succour by a revolt of the Helots. The fleet of the Thasians was defeated by Cimon, and after a long blockade they capitulated. Their walls were pulled down, their ships were handed over to Athens, they gave up all claim to the mine and the mainland, and agreed to pay whatever tribute was demanded.

Surrender, 463 B.C.

The typical instances of these three island cities, Carystus, Naxos, and Thasos, exhibit the methods which Athenian policy fol-lowed in numerous cases which are not recorded. There were now three classes of members in the Confederacy of Delos; there were (1) the non-tributary allies which contributed ships; (2) the tribu-tary allies which were independent; and (3) the tributary allies which were subject. As the Asiatic cities were declining in vigour, and disliked military service and absence from home, they most-ly preferred to discharge their obligations by paying tribute. It was obviously for the interest of Athens that as many members as possible should contribute money, and as few as possible contribute ships. For the ships which the tribute money furnished out were simply an addition to her own fleet, because they were under her direct control. She consequently aimed at diminishing the members of the first class; and soon it consisted of only the three large and wealthy islands, Lesbos, Chios, and Samos. Again, it was to the in-terest of Athens to transfer the members of the second class into the third, and win control over the internal affairs of the cities. New members which were coerced to join were never allowed to preserve absolute autonomy; and all revolting cities were reduced to the con-dition of subjection. But the degrees of subjection were not the same. The position of each city was determined by a special agree-ment with Athens, and the terms of these treaties varied. As a rule, Athens prescribed to her subjects the general form of their constitu-tions, and it need hardly be said that these constitutions were al-ways democratic. The new constitution which she imposed on Ery-thrae, when that city was forced to join the league, has been par-tially preserved on a stone. But there was no general hard and fast system. Each city had its own individual arrangements, its own measure of restricted autonomy. The closer dependence of these tributary states on Athens was in many cases marked by the presence of an Athenian garrison and Athenian civil officers. But there was one burden which was common to all, the obligation of

Three classes of confed-erates.

Erythrae, between 463 and 454 B.C.

furnishing soldiers to the league in time of war. It was a duty which could be demanded only under certain defined conditions, but it was an innovation which altered the original character of the league as a merely maritime confederacy. It seems probable that Athens tried to extend the duty of military service to her autonomous allies, and that this policy caused revolts; a result which was not unwelcome to Athens, as it gave her opportunities to deprive them of autonomy. Ultimately, all the allies seem to have been liable to military service except the three states which furnishd ships, Chios, Lesbos, and Samos.

As the process of turning the Alliance into an Empire advanced, Athens found herself able to discontinue the meetings of the Confederate assembly in the island of Delos. She could now act entirely as she deemed good without going through the form of consulting a body, whose decisions must necessarily be hers, as the great majority of the members were her own subjects. The formal establishment of her empire may be dated ten years after the war with Thasos, when the treasury of the league was transferred from Delos to Athens. This set the seal on the creation of the Athenian empire. The Confederacy of Delos no longer existed; and, though the term *Alliance* was always officially used, men no longer hesitated to use the word *empire* in ordinary speech. The tribute money thus passed from the protection of the Ionian Apollo to the custody of the goddess of the Acropolis; and, in return for her safe keeping, one mina for every talent of the yearly tribute was paid into her own treasury.

The Athenian empire embraced the Aegean Sea with its northern and eastern fringes, from Methone in the north-west to Lycian Phaselis in the south-east.[4] The number of cities which belonged to it at its height was considerably more than 200. We can enumerate more than 260 names from official tribute lists.[5] Large fragments of some of these lists have come down to us in the most trustworthy form—on the original stones themselves. They not only teach us the names of the subject cities, but they tell us the amount of tribute

Treasury transferred to Athens, 454-3 B.C.

($\dot{\alpha}\rho\chi\dot{\eta}$).

Onesixtieth as first-fruits to Athena.

(Quota lists.)

[4] The tributary cities were subsequently (443-2 B.C.) divided into five geographical districts: (1) *Thracian*, from Methone in the west to Aenus in the east; (2) *Hellespontine*, including the Chersonese and the cities on the Propontis and Bosphorus; (3) *Ionian*, from Assos to Miletus; (4) *Carian*, including Caria (with Rhodes, Cos, and adjacent islands) and Lycia, extending to the extreme Phaselis; (5) *Insular*, Aegina, Euboea, the Cyclades (except Melos); with Lemnos and Imbros in the north. But the Carian existed only for a few years. See below, p. 348.

[5] Not the lists of the Hellenic Treasurers, giving the whole amount of tribute paid by each city; but the lists which gave the share of the goddess. Thus in 443 B.C. the tribute of Perinthus brought the goddess 1000 drachmae; therefore it amounted to 60,000 drachmae or 10 talents.

Assession of tribute.

which many of these cities were called upon to pay. At the end of every fourth year the assessment of the tribute was readjusted, the burden was redistributed; and the evidence of the lists permits us to infer that the total amount of the revenue was maintained at 460 talents, as it had been originally fixed by Aristides. For a few years indeed it was temporarily raised to meet the pressure of exceptional needs; but in general it was maintained, and the accession of new members, instead of augmenting the total revenue, diminished proportionally the contributions of all the cities. Moreover every member had a voice in the assessment of its tribute, and could appeal, after the assessment had been made, to the popular courts of Athens.

Jurisdiction of Athens.

One of the most important restrictions on the independence of the cities was the jurisdiction which the Athenians asserted in criminal cases. It was natural that all disputes between Athens and any of her subjects should be decided at Athens; and it was not unreasonable that if the burgher of any allied community committed an act of treason against the empire he should be tried in the imperial city. But Athens sometimes claimed further rights of jurisdiction. In the case of Chalcis, she enacted that all cases in which the penalty was death, banishment, or the loss of civic rights should be sent for judgment to Athens. In this as in other matters, there were various arrangements with the various cities; and some doubtless had more freedom than others. In regard to lawsuits arising out of breach of contract between citizens of Athens and citizens of the allied states, such affairs were regulated by separate international agreements, and decided in the law-courts of the defendant's city. In this matter, and it was important, Athens could take the credit of not using her power for the furtherance of her own interests; and it may sometimes have happened that an Athenian was treated with somewhat less than fairness, when a subject folk had the chance of indulging their bitterness against one of their masters.

Athenian empire opposed to Greek political sentiment.

The Athenian Empire was dissolved half a century after the translation of the treasury from Delos to Athens. We shall see that it began to decline not many years after it had reached the height of its power. We must remember that the first principles of the political thought and political life of Greece were opposed to such an union. The sovereign city-state was the basis of the civilised Hellenic world, and no city-state was ready, if it could help it, to surrender any part of its sovereignty. In the face of a common danger, cities might be ready to combine together in a league, each parting with some of her sovereign powers to a common federal council but preserving the right of secession; and this was the idea of the Contederacy of Delos in its initial form. But even such a voluntary and partial surrender of sovereignty was regarded as a misfortune, so that when the motives which induced a city to join a federation became less strong and pressing, every member was anxious to gain its complete independence and resume the sovereign rights which it had laid down. Such being the free tendencies which swayed the peoples of Greece, it required a mighty arm and constant vigilance in a ruling state to keep her federation or empire together. An empire, however disguised, was always considered an injustice—a defiance to the political morality of Hellas. A Greek felt it a degradation of his dignity, or an infraction of his freedom, not to be the citizen of a free and sovereign city. And he felt this at many points if he belonged to one of the subject allies of Athens; since their self-government was limited in regard to domestic, as well as foreign, affairs. However liberal the general supervision of the mistress might be, the alliance with that mistress was a loss of the best of all good things, liberty, which means the right of governing one's self. If Athens had adopted the policy which was so successfully adopted by Rome, the policy of enlarging herself by admitting the citizens of smaller states to her own citizenship, she might have built up a more enduring fabric of empire. But such a plan was incompatible with the political notions of the Greeks.

Sect. 6. Policy and Ostracism of Cimon

As the Persian War had brought out more vividly the contrast between Greek and barbarian and impressed the Greeks with the ideal unity of their race, so the Confederacy of Delos emphasised a division existing within the Greek race itself, the contrast of Dorian and Ionian. That division was largely artificial. It was the result of mistaken notions about the early history of Greece, and only within very restricted limits did it represent any natural line of cleavage in the Hellenic race. But it had come to be accepted as an axiom and was an important element in the situation. We must probably seek for the origin of the opposition between Dorian and Ionian, as a political doctrine, in the unity of the Peloponnesus. The actual geographical unity produced a political unity, when in the sixth century the Spartan power became dominant; and this was reinforced by the conception of its ethnical unity, as mainly a Dorian country. The identity and exclusiveness of Peloponnesian interests had been apparent at the time of the Persian invasion; and the Peloponnesus not only stood aloof from, but had the air of protesting against, the growth of the Athenian Confederacy.

Antagonism of Dorian and Ionian.

And this confederacy had taken upon itself from the very first an Ionian colour. Athens, believing that she was an Ionian city and the mother of the Ionians of Asia, was gathering her children about her. The shrine of the Delian Apollo, the great centre of Ionian worship, was chosen as the centre of the new Ionian union. The treasures of the league were in the Ionian Apollo's keeping; and in his island the allies met to take counsel together. Thus the Dorian federation of the Peloponnesus under the headship of Sparta stood over against the Ionian federation of the Aegean under the headship of Athens.

For some years the antagonism lay dormant. Sparta was still an ally of Athens against the Mede, and the danger from Persia had not passed away. But the preservation of peace was also due, in some measure, to the policy of the men who guided the fortunes of Athens, Aristides and Cimon. The son of Miltiades had been at first regarded as a youth of little promise. His grandfather was nicknamed "Simpleton"; and he was supposed to have inherited a wit poorer than that of the ordinary Athenian. Fond of the wine-cup and leading a disorderly life, he was not a man of liberal education; and a writer of memoirs, who knew him, described him as Peloponnesian rather than Athenian—uncultivated but honest and downright. He lived with his step-sister Elpinice, and they both affected Lacedaemonian manners. Aristides seems to have discerned his military ability and to have introduced him to public life. His simplicity, geniality, and lavish hospitality rendered him popular; his military successes confirmed his influence. The two guiding principles of Cimon's policy were the prosecution of the war against Persia, and the maintenance of good relations with the Lacedaemonians. He upheld the doctrine of dual leadership: Athens should be mistress of the seas, but she should recognise Sparta as the mistress on the continent. Cimon's sympathy with Sparta and his connexions there became an important political fact, and undoubtedly helped to postpone a rupture between Sparta and Athens.

In this policy Aristides, the leader of the democracy, and Cimon, who was by no means in sympathy with the development of the democratic constitution, had pulled together. After the death of Themistocles they had the whole power in their hands, Cimon being continually re-elected as Strategos, and Aristides having the moral control of the sovereign Assembly. On the death of Aristides, Cimon remained the most powerful statesman in Athens, but his want of sympathy with democracy rendered it impossible that he should retain this power in a state which was advancing on the lines along which Athens was moving now. Younger statesmen arose and

Cimon.

formed a party of opposition against Cimon and the oligarchs who rallied around him. The two chief politicians of this democratic party were Ephialtes, a man of unquestioned probity, whom the oligarchs disliked and feared, and Pericles, the son of Xanthippus, who now began to play a prominent part in the Assembly. After the conquest of Thasos, they charged Cimon with having received bribes from Alexander, the king of Macedon, who was supporting the Thasians, and with having failed to act against Macedonia as it was his duty to act. The accusation appears not to have been pressed hard, and Cimon was acquitted. But it was the first movement of an opposition which was speedily to bring about his fall.

Meanwhile Sparta herself had dealt a blow to his policy. When the victory of the Eurymedon dispelled the fears of Persia which had hovered over Greece till then, Sparta felt herself free to unseal her dormant jealousy of Athens at the first suitable opportunity, and she saw her opportunity in the war with Thasos. But unforeseen events at home hindered her, as we saw, from actual intervention against Athens. The Spartan citizens lived over a perpetual volcano—the servitude of their Perioeci and Helots. The fire which Pausanias thought of kindling burst forth eight years after his death. An earthquake had laid in ruins the villages which composed the town of Sparta, and a large number of the inhabitants were buried in the convulsion. The moment was chosen by the Messenian serfs to shake off the yoke of their detested masters. They annihilated in battle a company of 300 Spartans, but then they were smitten at Isthmus, an unknown place in Messenia, and sought refuge in the stronghold of Ithome. On that steep hill, full of the memories of earlier struggles, they held out for a few years. The Spartans were driven to ask the aid of allies; Plataea, Aegina, and Mantinea sent troops to besiege Ithome. They even asked Athens herself to succour them in their distress. *Earthquake at Sparta, 464 B.C. Revolt of the Helots.*

The democratic politicians lifted up their voices against the sending of any aid; and the event proved them to be perfectly right. But the Athenian folk listened to the counsels of Cimon, who drove home his doctrine of the dual leadership by two persuasive metaphors: "We must not leave Hellas lame; we must not allow Athens to lose her yoke-fellow." Cimon took 4000 hoplites to Messenia, but though the Athenians had a reputation for skill in besieging fortresses their endeavours to take Ithome failed. Then Sparta rounded and smote Athens in the face. She told the Athenians, alone of all the allies who were encamped around the hill, that she required their help no more. We are told that the Lacedaemonians were afraid "of the adventurous and revolutionary spirit" of the *Expedition of Cimon to Messenia, 462 B.C.*

Athenians. But it is strange indeed that they should have dealt thus with a force which was both procured and commanded by a friend so staunch as Cimon.

This incident exploded the Laconian policy of Cimon; it exposed the futility of making sacrifices to court Sparta's friendship, and it revealed the depth of Spartan jealousy. The opposition of Ephialtes and his party to the Messenian expedition received its justification. And meanwhile Ephialtes and Pericles had taken advantage of the absence of the conservative statesman to effect a number of radical reforms which were necessary to complete the democratic constitution. These reforms were extremely popular, and immensely increased the influence of the statesmen who carried them. When then Cimon returned with his policy discredited, they denounced him as a "Philo-Laconian," and felt that they could safely attempt to ostracize him. An ostracism was held, and Cimon was banished. Soon afterwards a mysterious crime was committed. Cimon's chief antagonist Ephialtes was murdered, and no one ever ascertained with surety who the murderers were. He had many bitter foes among the Areopagites whom he had attacked singly and collectively; and there were perhaps some among them who would not have hesitated to wreak such vengeance on their assailant.

Ostracism of Cimon, 461 B.C. Murder of Ephialtes.

The Athenians had presently an opportunity of retaliating on Sparta for her contumely. The blockade of Ithome was continued and the rebels at last capitulated. They were allowed to leave the Peloponnesus unharmed, on the condition that they should never return. The Athenians who had helped to besiege them now found them a shelter. They settled the Messenians in a new home at Naupactus, on the Corinthian Gulf, a place where they had recently established a naval station. In the Altis of Olympia we may still see a memorial of this "Third Messenian War"—the round base of a statue of Zeus which the Lacedaemonians dedicated as a thank-offering for their victory; and we may read the inscribed verses in which they besought the lord Zeus of Olympus to accept the fair image graciously.

Capture of Ithome, 459 B.C.

Messenians settled at Naupactus.

While the Lacedaemonians were wholly intent upon the long siege of the Messenian fort, the Argives, free from the fear of attack on that side, had seized the occasion to lay siege to Mycenae. In the days of Argive greatness this stronghold can hardly have been other than an Argive fortress, and it was probably after the great victory of Cleomenes that with Spartan help the Mycenaeans won for a brief space their ancient independence. During that brief space they had the glory of bearing a hand in the deliverance of Greece. On the summit of their primeval citadel, they built a temple where

Argos reduces and destroys Mycenae (c. 462-0 B.C.). (494 B.C.)

the old palace had stood; and they girdled the city below with a wall. They now defended the fortress for some time, but their supplies were cut off and they were forced to submit. The Argives let them depart whither they would and some found a refuge in Macedonia; but the old town was destroyed, all except the walls which were stronger than the forces of destruction. Argos was once more mistress of her plain.

CHAPTER IX

THE ATHENIAN EMPIRE UNDER THE GUIDANCE OF PERICLES

SECT. 1. THE COMPLETION OF THE ATHENIAN DEMOCRACY

To the Greeks of Cimon's day it might have seemed that the Athenian constitution as it had been fixed by Cleisthenes and further reformed after the battle of Marathon was as democratic as it well could be. But the supreme people was to become in still fuller measure lord in its own house, under the guidance of Ephialtes, whose career was suddenly cut short, and of Pericles, son of Xanthippus, who was to be the most prominent figure in Greece for thirty years. The mother of Pericles belonged to the family, and bore the name, of the daughter of the Sicyonian tyrant, the Agarista whose wooing had been so famous. She was the niece of Cleisthenes the lawgiver, and sister of Megacles who had been ostracized as a friend of the Pisistratids. The young statesman had a military training, but he came under the influence of two distinguished teachers, to whom he owed much. One was a countryman of his own, Damon of Oa, one of the most intellectual Athenians of his day, and renowned as a master of the theory of music. The other was an outlander and a philosopher, Anaxagoras of Clazomenae, whose mechanical theory of the material universe, once for all set in motion by an act of unchangeable mind, freed Pericles from the superstitions of the multitude whom it was his task to guide. To these masters the statesman partly owed his intellectual aloofness; but he did not owe them either his political ideas or the gift of lucid and persuasive speech which was essential to his success. He was indeed a striking contrast to Cimon, the loose and genial boon companion. He seldom walked abroad; he was strict in the economy of his household; he avoided convivial parties; and jealously maintained the dignity of his reserve. His portrait was chiselled by Cresilas. It is something to have the round pedestal on which the original image was set, but we also possess a copy of the portrait. It shows us, not the lofty "Olympian" statesman, but the passionless contemplative face of the friend of Anaxagoras.

The most conservative institution in Athens was the Council of

Pericles.

See above, p. 199.

His teachers.

His reserve.

Portrait.

The Areopagus

Areopagus, for it was filled up from the archons who were taken from the two richest classes in the state. This institution was incompatible with the development of democracy, and it was inevitable that it should be ended or mended. Ephialtes had prepared the way for an attack by accusing individual Areopagites of corruption and fraudulent practices; and then, taking advantage of Cimon's absence in Messenia, he introduced a series of laws which deprived the ancient council of all its powers that had any political significance. Its right to punish the public ministers and officers if they violated the laws, its duties of supervising the administration and seeing that the laws were obeyed, were taken away and transferred to the people. The censorial powers which enabled it to inquire into the lives of private citizens were abolished. Nothing was left to the venerable body but its jurisdiction in homicidal cases, the care of the sacred olive-trees of Athena, and a voice in the supervision of the property of the Eleusinian deities. The functions which it lost passed to the Council of Five Hundred, the Assembly, and the popular law-courts. All impeachments for crimes which threatened the public weal were henceforward brought before the Council or the Assembly; and henceforward the people tried in their own courts officials who had failed to give a satisfactory account of their administration. loses political power.

We have a notable monument of the excitement which this radical change caused at Athens, in a drama of Aeschylus which was performed a few years later. The *Eumenides* describes the trial of Orestes on the hill of Ares for the murder of his mother, and the institution of the court of the Areopagus. The significance of the drama has been often misunderstood. It is no protest after the event; it is no cry to undo what had been done. On the contrary, Aeschylus, so far as his poetical motive permits him to suggest a criticism of recent events, approves of the reform. The Areopagus, he suggests, was instituted as a court, not as a council; its true purpose is to pass a judgment on homicides, like Orestes. The *Eumenides* was calculated to tranquillise those who, awed by the dark and solemn associations which hovered over the hill of Ares, regarded the attack upon it as an impiety. The Eumenides of Aeschylus, 458 B. C.

The dismantling of the Areopagus was an indirect blow to the dignity of the archons, who, by virtue of their office, became Areopagites. About the same time another step was taken on the path of democracy by making the archonship a paid office. Once this was done, there was no longer any reason for confining the post to the two richer classes. The third class, the Zeugitae, were presently made eligible; and it cannot have been long before the Archonship becomes a paid office.

Admission

of Zeugi-
tae to
archon-
ship,
c. 458-7
B.C.

Lot.

Payment
of offices.

Pay of the
judges,
c. 462-1
B.C.

Law of
citizen-
ship,
451-0 B.C.

Thetes, whose distinction from the third class seems to have been yearly becoming fainter, were admitted also.

The two engines of the democratic development were lot and pay. Lot had been long ago introduced; but it had not been introduced in its purest form. The archons and other lesser officers, and the members of the council, were taken by lot from a select number of candidates; but these candidates were chosen by deliberate election. This mixed system was now abolished; the preliminary election was done away with; and the Council of Five Hundred, as well as the archons, were appointed by lot from all the eligible citizens. By this means every citizen had an equal chance of holding political office, and taking a part in the conduct of public affairs.

It is clear that this system could not work unless the offices were paid; for the poor citizens would have been unable to give up their time to the service of the state. Accordingly pay was introduced not only for the archonship, but for the members of the Council. The payment of state offices was the leading feature of the democratic reforms of Pericles.

It was a feature which naturally won him popularity with the masses especially when it was adopted in the case of the popular courts of justice. At the time of the attack on the Areopagus, Pericles carried a measure that the judges should receive a remuneration of an obol a day.[1] Though the measure had the immediate political object of gaining popular support for the attack on the Areopagus, it was a measure which was ultimately inevitable. The amount of judicial business was growing so enormously that it would have been impossible to find a sufficient number of judges ready to attend day after day in the courts without any compensation. But the easily earned pay attracted the poor and idle, who found it pleasant to sit in court listening to curious cases, their sense of self-importance tickled by the flattering respect of the pleaders. Every citizen who wished could place his name on a list from which the list of judges was selected by lot, so many from each tribe; and the courts were empanelled from this list.

It was now to the interest of every Athenian that there should be as few citizens as possible to participate in the new privileges and profits of citizenship. Accordingly, about ten years later the rolls of the burghers were stringently revised; and a law was passed that the name of no child should be admitted whose father and mother were not Athenian citizens legitimately wedded. It was a law which

---

[1] There is some uncertainty whether the amount was one obol or two obols; perhaps the more probable view is that it was one.

would have excluded Themistocles and Cleisthenes the lawgiver, whose mothers were foreigners.

It was a matter of course that in cases of a political character the judges of the heliaea should be swayed by their own political opinions and by the eloquence of the pleaders working upon their emotions. It was inevitable that the legal aspect of such cases should be often lost to sight, and the facts often misjudged. It was an essential part of the democratic intention that the sovereign people should make its anger felt; and if its anger were sometimes, like a king's anger, unfair, that could not be helped. But it was far more serious that in private cases the ends of justice were liable to be defeated, not through intention but through ignorance. We can have no better evidence as to the working of the popular courts than the speeches by which the pleaders hoped to influence the decisions of the judges. Litigants at Athens had to plead their own cases; there was no such institution as court-advocates. But a man might learn off a speech which had been composed for him by another, and recite it in court. Hence there arose a class of professional speech-writers, and many of their speeches have been preserved. From these models of judicial eloquence we learn how pleaders expected to gain sentences in their favour. They make a large use of arguments which are perfectly irrelevant to the case; a plaintiff, for example, will try to demonstrate at great length that he has rendered services to the state and that his opponent has performed none. There was thus no question of simply administering the law. The judges heard each party interpreting the law in its own sense; but they had themselves no knowledge of the law, and therefore, however impartial they sought to be, their decision was unduly influenced by the dexterity of an eloquent pleader, and affected by considerations which had nothing to do with the matter at issue. And there was no appeal from their judgment.

The working of the law-courts.

A feature of the Athenian democracy, not to be lost sight of, is that public burdens were laid upon the rich burghers, which did not fall upon the poor. These were no regular taxes on income or capital, but burdens which were highly characteristic of ancient society, and which might fall to a man's lot only once or twice in his life. We have already seen how trierarchs were taken from the richer classes to equip and man triremes, in which they were themselves obliged to sail, and for which they were entirely responsible. It was a duty which entailed not only an outlay of money, but a considerable sacrifice of time and trouble. There were other burdens also. For example, when the city sent solemn deputations on some

Liturgies, or public burdens.

The trierarchy.

The architheoria.

religious errand, whether to the yearly feast of Apollo at Delos, or to one of the great Panhellenic festivals, or to the oracle of Delphi, a wealthy citizen was chosen to eke out at his cost the money supplied for the purpose by the public treasury, and to conduct the deputation and equip it with magnificence worthy of the occasion. But none of the liturgies, as these public burdens were called, was more important or more characteristic of Athenian life than that of providing the choruses for the festivals of Dionysus. Every year each tribe named one of its wealthy tribesmen to be a *chorêgos*, and his duties were to furnish and array a chorus and provide a skilled trainer to teach it the dances and songs of the drama which it was to perform. Rivalry spurred the *chorêgoi* to ungrudging outlay. He whose chorus was victorious in the tragic or the comic competition was crowned and received a bronze tripod, which he used to set up, inscribed with his own name and that of his tribe, upon a pillar, or sometimes upon a miniature round temple. On the east side of the Acropolis, leading to the theatre, a long street of these choregic monuments recorded the public spirit of the citizens, and this Street of Tripods showed, perhaps more impressively than any other evidence, how much significance the state attached to the theatre and the worship of Dionysus. Never was piety more fully approved as wisdom. The state's endowment of religion turned out to be an endowment of brilliant genius; and the rich men who were called upon to spend their time and money in furnishing the dancers did service to the great masters of tragedy and comedy, and thereby served the whole world.

The chorêgia.

Sect. 2. War of Athens with the Peloponnesians

Alliance of Athens and Argos.

(458 B.C.)

The banishment of Cimon was the signal for a complete change in the foreign policy of Athens. She abandoned the alliance with the Lacedaemonians and formed a new alliance with their enemies, Argos and Thessaly. The new friendship of the Athenian and Argive peoples is reflected in the trilogy which Aeschylus composed about this time on the murder of Agamemnon and the vengeance of Orestes. The dramatist plays pointedly upon the alliance, and perhaps it is a not undesigned compliment to the new ally that he makes Agamemnon lord of Argos and not of newly-destroyed Mycenae. So far, indeed, as the main interests of Athens were concerned, she was not brought into direct collision with Sparta. But these interests forced her into deadly rivalry with two of Sparta's allies. The naval empire of Athens and the growth of her sea-power were rapidly extending her trade and opening new visions of commercial ambition in all quarters of the Greek world. She was competing with, and it seemed likely that she would outstrip, the two great cities of traffic, Corinth and Aegina. With Aegina there had already been a struggle, and now that Athens had grown in power and wealth another struggle was inevitable. The competition of Athenian merchants with Corinth in the west was active, and it was about this time that an Athenian general took Naupactus from the Ozolian Locrians, and secured a naval station which gave Athens a considerable control over the mouth of the Corinthian Gulf. This was a blow which struck home; Athens had now the means of intercepting and harassing the Corinthian argosies which sailed forth with merchandise for the far west. War was a question of months, and the occasion soon came.

Capture of Naupactus.

The Megarians, on account of a frontier dispute with Corinth, deserted the Peloponnesian league and placed themselves under Athenian protection. Nothing could be more welcome to Athens than the adhesion of Megara. Holding Megara, she had a strong frontier against the Peloponnesus, commanding the isthmus from Pagae on the Corinthian, to Nisaea on the Saronic bay. Without any delays she set about the building of a double line of wall from the hill of Megara down to the haven of Nisaea, which faces Salamis, and she garrisoned these "Long Walls" with her own troops. Thus the eastern coast-road was under her control, and Attica had a strong bulwark against invasion by land.

Athens wins Megara, 459 B.C.

Long Walls of Megara.

The occupation of Megara was a new offence to Corinth; and it was an offence to the mistress of the Peloponnesian league. War soon broke out, but at first Sparta took no active part. On the events of the war we are ill-instructed. We find an Athenian squadron making a descent on Halieis, and gaining an advantage over some Corinthian and Epidaurian troops. Then the little island of Cecryphalea, which lies between Aegina and the Argive shore, becomes the scene of a naval combat with a Peloponnesian fleet, and the Athenians prevail. At this point the Aeginetans enter the struggle. They saw that if Corinth sustained a severe defeat, their own fate was sealed; Athens would become absolute mistress in the Saronic sea. A great naval battle was fought near Aegina; the allies of both Aegina and Athens were engaged; and the Athenians, having taken seventy ships, landed on the island and blockaded the town. Thereupon the Peloponnesians sent a force of hoplites to help the Aeginetans; while the Corinthians, advancing over the heights of Geranea, descended into the Megarid, expecting that the Athenians would find it impossible to protect Megara and blockade Aegina at the same time. But they reckoned without a true knowl-

Battle of Halieis, 459-8 B.C

Battle of Cecryphalea.

Battle of Aegina, 458 B.C.

edge of the Athenian spirit. The citizens who were below and above the regular military age were formed into an extraordinary army and marched to the Megarid under the strategos Myronides. A battle was fought; both sides claimed the victory; but, when the Corinthians withdrew, the Athenians raised a trophy. Urged by the taunts of their fellow-citizens, the Corinthian soldiers returned in twelve days and began to set up a counter-trophy, but as they were at work the Athenians rushed forth from Megara and inflicted a severe defeat.

Battle in the Megarid, 458 B.C.

This warfare, round the shores and in the waters of the Saronic bay, is the prelude to more warfare in other parts of Greece; but it is a prelude which has a unity of its own. Athens is opposed indeed to the Peloponnesian alliance; but the war is, so far, mainly conducted by a concert of three states, whose interests lie in the neighbourhood of the Saronic Bay—Corinth, Epidaurus, and Aegina. These states have indeed the Peloponnesian league behind them, and are helped by "Peloponnesian ships" and "Peloponnesian hoplites"; but at the same time, the war has not yet assumed a fully Peloponnesian character.

The year of these successes was a year of intense excitement and strain for Athens; it might fairly be described as an *annus mirabilis* in her history. The victories of Cecryphalea and Aegina were won with only a portion of her fleet. For, in the very hour when she was about to be brought face to face with the armed opposition of rival Greek powers against the growth of her empire and the expansion of her trade, she had embarked in an enterprise beyond the limits of the Greek world. It was an expedition to Egypt, one of the most daring ventures she ever undertook.

Egyptian expedition.

A fleet of 200 Athenian and Confederate galleys was operating against Persia in Cyprian seas, when it was invited to cross over to Egypt. The call came from Inaros, a Libyan potentate, who had stirred up the lands of the lower Nile to revolt against their Persian masters. The murder of Xerxes had been followed by troubles at the Persian court, and it was some time before Artaxerxes was safely seated on his throne; the rebellion of Egypt was one of the consequences of this situation. The invitation of Inaros was most alluring. It meant that, if Athens delivered Egypt from Persian rule, she would secure the chief control of the foreign trade with the Nile valley and be able to establish a naval station on the coast; by one stroke she would far outstrip all the rival merchant cities of Hellas. The nameless generals of the Aegean fleet accepted the call of the Libyan prince. As in the days of remote antiquity, the "peoples of the north" were now to help the Libyans in an attempt to overthrow the lords of Egypt. Of those remote episodes the Greeks knew nothing, but they might remember how Carian and Ionian adventurers had once placed an Egyptian king upon the throne. In another way, an attack on Egypt was a step in a new path. Hitherto the Confederate ships had sailed in waters which were wholly or partly Greek, and had confined their purpose to the deliverance of Greek cities or cities which, like the Carian and Lycian, were in close touch with Greek civilisation. The shores of Cyprus, where Greek and Phoenician were side by side, invited above other shores a squadron of Greek deliverers. But when the squadron crossed over to Egypt, it entered a new sphere and undertook a new kind of work. The Egyptian expedition was an attempt to carry the struggle with Persia into another stage—a stage in which Greece is the aggressor and the invader. This attempt was not destined to prosper; more than a century was still to elapse before the invasion of Xerxes would be avenged. But it is well to remember that the Athenians, in moving on Egypt, anticipated Alexander the Great, and that success was not impossible if Cimon had been their general.

The Athenians sailed up the Nile to find Inaros triumphant, having gained a great victory in the Delta over a Persian army which had been sent to quell him. Sailing up they won possession of the city of Memphis, except the citadel, the "White Castle," in which the Persian garrision held out. After this achievement, we lose sight of the war in Egypt for more than two years, and beyond the protracted blockade of the White Castle we have no record how the Athenian forces were employed. But it was a fatal coincidence that the power of Athens should have been divided at this moment. With her full forces she might have inflicted a crushing blow on the Peloponnesians; with her full forces she might have prospered in Egypt. It was a triumph for the political party which had driven Cimon into banishment that, when half the Athenian fleet was on the banks of the Nile, the hostilities of Corinth and Aegina and their friends should have been so bravely repelled. Nothing impresses one more with the energy of Athens at this crisis than the stone which records the names of the citizens belonging to one of the tribes, who fell in this memorable year:

> Of the Erechtheid tribe,
> These are they who died in the war, in Cyprus, in Egypt, in
> Phoenice, at Halieis, in Aegina, at Megara, in the same year;

and the names follow.

The siege of Aegina was continued, and, within two years after the battle, the Aeginetans capitulated, and agreed to surrender their

Capture of Memphis, 459 B.C. (autumn).

Erechtheid inscription, 459-8 B.C.

Fall of Aegina, 457-6 B.C

Enrolled
in the
Confed-
eracy of
Delos.

fleet and pay tribute to Athens. Few successes can have been more welcome or profitable to the Athenians than this. The island which offended their eyes and attracted their desires when they looked forth from their hill across the waters of their bay was at length powerless in their hands. They had lamed one of their most formidable commercial rivals; they had overthrown one of the most influential cities of Dorian Greece. In the Confederacy, Aegina took her rank with Thasos as the richest of the subject states. For these two island cities the burden of yearly tribute was thirty talents, incomparably larger than the sum paid by any of the other cities whose tribute we know.

Lacedae-
monian
expedition
to north-
ern
Greece,
457 B.C.

In the meantime events in another part of Greece had led the Lacedaemonians themselves to take part in the war, and had transported the main interest of the struggle from the Saronic Gulf to Boeotia. The errand of the Lacedaemonians was an errand of piety, to succour their mother people, the Dorians of the north, one of whose three little towns had been taken by the Phocians. To force the aggressors to restore the place was an easy task for a force which consisted of 1500 Lacedaemonian hoplites and 10,000 troops of the allies. The real work of the expedition lay in Boeotia. It was clearly the policy of Sparta to raise up here a powerful state to hold Athens in check; and this could only be effected by strengthening Thebes and making her mistress of the Boeotian federation.

Restora-
tion of the
hegemony
of Thebes
in
Boeotia.

Accordingly Sparta now set up the power of Thebes again, revising the league, and forcing the Boeotian cities to join it. When the army had done its work in Boeotia, its return to the Peloponnesus was beset by difficulties. To march through the Megarid was dangerous, for the Athenians held the passes, and had redoubled their precautions. And it was not safe to cross the Corinthian Gulf—the way by which they probably had come—for Athenian vessels were now on the watch to intercept them. In this embarrassment they seem to have resolved to march straight upon Athens, where the people were now engaged on the building of Long Walls from the city to the harbour. This course was probably suggested by an Athenian party of oligarchs, who were always abiding an opportunity to overthrow the democracy. The Peloponnesian army advanced to Tanagra, near the Attic frontier; but before they crossed the borders the Athenians went forth to meet them, 14,000 strong, including 1000 Argives and some Thessalian cavalry. The banished statesman, Cimon, now came to the Athenian camp, pitched on Boeotian soil, and sought leave to fight for his country—against Sparta. The request was hastily referred to the Council of Five Hundred at Athens; it was not granted; and all that Cimon could

Battle of
Tanagra,
457 B.C.
(summer).

do was to exhort his partisans to fight valiantly. This act of Cimon prepared the way for his recall; in the battle which followed, his friends fought so stubbornly that none of them survived. There was great slaughter on both sides; but the Thessalian horsemen deserted during the combat, and the Lacedaemonians gained the victory. But the battle saved Athens, and the victory only enabled the victors to return by the Isthmus and cut down the fruit trees of the Megarid.

Athens now desired to make a truce with Sparta in order to gain time. No man was more fitted to compass this than the exile Cimon, whose recent conduct had shown that he was the foe of the foes of Athens, even if those foes were Spartans. The people, at the instance of Pericles, passed a decree recalling him; but when Cimon had negotiated the truce, he withdrew to a distance from Athens, with a tact which we might hardly have expected.

Truce with Sparta; Cimon recalled.

The Lacedaemonians celebrated their victory by a golden shield which they set above the gable of the new temple of Zeus in the altis of Olympia, as a gift from the spoils of Tanagra. But the victory did not even secure Boeotia. Two months after the battle, the Athenians made an expedition into Boeotia under the command of Myronides. A decisive battle was fought at Oenophyta, and the Athenians became masters of the whole land except Thebes. The Boeotian cities were not enrolled in the maritime Confederacy of Delos, but their dependence on Athens was expressed in the obligation of furnishing contingents to her armies. At the same time the Phocians entered into the alliance of Athens, and the Opuntian Locrians were constrained to acknowledge her supremacy. Such were the consequences of Oenophyta and Tanagra. Athens could now quietly complete the building of her Long Walls.

Conquest of Boeotia.

Battle of Oeno-phyta, 457 B.C. (autumn)

These brilliant successes were crowned, as we have seen, by the capture of Aegina; and probably about the same time the acquisition of Troezen gave the Athenians an important post on the Argolic shore. But in the far south their arms were not so prosperous. Since the capture of Memphis, no success seems to have been gained, and the White Castle still held out. After an ineffectual attempt to induce Sparta to cause a diversion by invading Attica, king Artaxerxes sent a large army to Egypt under Megabyzus, who was supported by a Phoenician fleet. Having won a battle, he drove the Greeks out of Memphis and shut them up in Prosopitis, an island formed by a canal which intersected the Canopic and Sebennytic channels of the Nile. Here he blockaded them for eighteen months. At last he drained the canal and turned aside the water, so that the Greek ships were left high and dry, and almost the whole island was

Failure of the Egyptian expedition.

456 B.C.

454 B.C.

reconnected with the banks. Thus the Persians were able to march across to the island. The Greeks having burned their ships retreated to Byblos, where they capitulated to Megabyzus and were allowed to depart. A tedious march brought them to friendly Cyrene, where they found means of returning to their homes. Inaros who kindled the revolt was crucified, though his life had been spared by the terms of the capitulation. Soon afterwards a relief squadron of fifty triremes arrived from Athens. It was attacked by the powerful Phoenician fleet in the Mendesian mouth of the Nile, and only a few ships escaped. The Persian authority was restored throughout the land; the day for Greek control of Egypt had not yet come.

But though the Athenians lost ships and treasure in this daring, ill-fated enterprise, their empire was now at the height of its power. They were even able to make the disaster in Egypt a pretext for converting the Delian confederacy into an undisguised Athenian empire. The triumphant Persian fleet might sail into the Aegean sea; Delos was not a safe treasury; the funds of the league must be removed to the Athenian Acropolis.

Extent of Athenian empire, 456-449 B.C.

The empire of Athens now included a continental as well as a maritime dominion. The two countries which marched on her frontiers, Boeotia and Megara, had become her subjects. Beyond Boeotia, her dominion extended over Phocis and Locris to the pass of Thermopylae. In Argos her influence was predominant, Aegina had been added to her Aegean empire, the ships of Aegina to her navy. Through the subjection of Megara, the conquest of Aegina, and the capture of Troezen, the Saronic bay had almost been converted into an Attic lake.

Expeditions to the Corinthian Gulf, 455 and 453 B.C.

The great commercial city of the isthmus was the chief and most dangerous enemy of Athens, and the next object of the policy of Pericles was to convert the Corinthian Gulf into an Attic lake also, and so hem in Corinth on both her seas. The possession of the Megarid and Boeotia, and especially the station of Naupactus, gave Athens control of the northern shores of the gulf, from within the gate up to the isthmus. But the southern seaboard was still entirely Peloponnesian; and outside the gate, on the Acarnanian coast, there were posts which ought to be secured. The general Tolmides made a beginning by capturing the Corinthian colony Chalcis, opposite Patrae. Then Pericles himself conducted an expedition to continue the work of Tolmides. Having failed to reduce Sicyon he laid siege to Oeniadae, an important and strong-walled mart on the Acarnanian coast, but was unable to take it. Though no military success was gained, the expedition created a sensation, and it seems to have led to the adhesion of the Achaean cities to the Athenian alliance. It is certain at least that shortly afterwards Achaea was an Athenian dependency; and for a few years Athenian vessels could sail with a sense of dominion in the Corinthian as well as in the Saronic bay.

Acquisition of Achaea between 453 and 446.

Sect. 3. Conclusion of Peace with Persia

The warfare of recent years had been an enormous strain on the resources of Athens, and it was found necessary to increase the burden of tribute imposed on her allies. She wanted a relief from the strain, but after the expedition of Pericles three or four years elapsed before peace was concluded. During that interval there seems to have been by mutual consent of the combatants a cessation from military operations. Lacedaemon and Argos first concluded a treaty of peace for thirty years; and then Cimon, who had returned to Athens, negotiated a truce, which was fixed for five years, between the Athenians and Peloponnesians.

Five Years' Truce.

Thirty Years' Peace of Argos and Sparta, 452-1 B.C.

As soon as the peace was arranged, Athens and her allies were able to resume their warfare against Persia, and to no man could that warfare be more safely or fitly entrusted than to the hero of the Eurymedon river. Pericles may have been well pleased to use Cimon's military experience; and an amicable arrangement seems to have been made, Cimon undertaking not to interfere with the policy of Pericles. Gossip said that Cimon's sister had much to do with bringing to pass the reconciliation. "The charms as well as the intrigues of Elpinice appear to have figured conspicuously in the memoirs of Athenian biographers: they were employed by one party as a means of calumniating Cimon, by the other for discrediting Pericles." [2] But we need not heed the gossip. Women played no part in the history of Athena's city.

Pericles and Cimon.

The Phoenician fleet, which had put down the Egyptian rebellion, was afterward sent to re-establish the authority of Artaxerxes in the island of Cyprus; and accordingly Cimon sailed thither with a squadron of 200 vessels. He detached sixty to help a princelet who had succeeded in defying the Persians in the fens of the Delta of the Nile; for the Athenians, even after their calamity, had not entirely abandoned the thought of Egyptian conquest. Then he laid siege to Cition. It was the last enterprise of the man who had conducted the war against Persia ever since the battle of Mycale. He died during the blockade; and his death marks the beginning of a new period in which hostilities between Greek and Persian slumber. But one final success was gained. Raising the siege of

Campaign in Cyprus.

Death of Cimon, 450-49 B.C.

[2] Grote.

Cition, because there was no food, the fleet arrived off Salamis, and the Greeks gained a double victory by sea and land over the Phoenician and Cilician ships.

But this victory did not encourage the Athenians to continue the war. We have no glimpse of the counsels of their statesmen at this moment; but the facts of the situation enable us to understand their resolution to make peace with the Great King. The events of recent years had proved to them that it was beyond the strength of Athens to carry on war at the same time, in any effectual way, with the common enemy of all the Greeks and with her rivals among the Greeks themselves. It was therefore necessary to choose between peace with Persia and peace in Greece. But an enduring peace in Greece could only be purchased by the surrender of those successes which Athens had lately gained. Corinth would never acquiesce, until she had won back her old predominant position in her western gulf; so long as she was hemmed in, as Athens had hemmed her in, she would inevitably seize any favourable hour to strike for her release. Some Athenian politicians would have been ready to retreat from the positions which had been recently seized

and of which the occupation was most galling to Corinth. But Pericles, who had won those positions, was a strong imperialist. The aim of his statesmanship was to increase the Athenian empire and to spread the political influence of Athens within the borders of Greece. He was unwilling to let any part of her empire go, for the sake of earning new successes against the barbarian. The death of Cimon, who had been the soul of the Persian war, may have helped Pericles to carry through his determination to bring that war to an end. And the Great King on his side was disposed to negotiate; for the Greek victory of Cyprian Salamis had been followed by a revolt of Megabyzus, the general who had quelled the insurrection of Egypt.

Accordingly peace was made with Persia. There is a dark mist about the negotiations, so dark that it has been questioned whether a formal treaty was ever concluded. But there can be no reasonable doubt that Athens came to an understanding with Artaxerxes, and that peace ensued; and it is equally certain that there was a definite contract, by which Persia undertook not to send ships of war into the Aegean, and Athens gave a similar pledge securing the coasts of the Persian empire against attack. An embassy from Athens and her allies must have waited on the Great King at Susa; and the terms of the arrangement must have been put in writing. But, on the other hand, there was no treaty as between two Greek states. The Great King would never have consented to treat either with a

Greek city or a federation of Greek cities as an equal. And he certainly did not stoop to the humiliation of formally acknowledging the independence of the Greek cities of Asia. It was enough that he should graciously promise to make certain concessions. But, whatever were the diplomatic forms of the agreement, both parties meant peace, and peace was maintained. It has been called the Peace of Callias; and we have a record which makes it probable that the chief ambassador was Callias, the richest man at Athens, and the husband of Cimon's sister.

The first act in the strife of Greece and Persia thus closes. All the cities of Hellas which had come under barbarian sway had been reunited to the world of free Hellenic states; except in one outlying corner. The Greek cities of Cyprus were left to struggle with the Phoenicians as best they might; and the Phoenicians soon got the upper hand and held it for many years. They tried to extirpate Greek civilisation from the island; but Greek civilisation was a hardy growth, and we shall hereafter see Greek dynasties again in power.

Struggle
of Greek
and Phoe
nician in
Cyprus.

Preva-
lence of
Phoeni-
cians after
the Peace.

SECT. 4. ATHENIAN REVERSES. THE THIRTY YEARS' PEACE

The peace with Persia, however, was not followed by further Athenian expansion within the defined limits; on the contrary, some of the most recent acquisitions of the Athenian empire began to fall away. Orchomenus and Chaeronea and some other towns in western Boeotia were seized by exiled oligarchs; and it was necessary for Athens to intervene promptly. The general Tolmides went forth with a wholly inadequate number of troops. He took and garrisoned Chaeronea, but did not attempt Orchomenus. On his way home he was set upon by the exiles from Orchomenus and some others, in the neighbourhood of Coronea, and defeated. He was himself slain; many of the hoplites were taken prisoners; and the Athenians in order to obtain their release resigned Boeotia. Thus the battle of Coronea undid the work of Oenophyta.

Athens
loses
Boeotia.

Battle of
Coronea,
447 B.C.

Athens had little reason to regret this loss; for dominion in Boeotia was not really conducive to the consolidation of her empire. To maintain control over the numerous city-states of the Boeotian country would have been a constant strain on her military resources, which would hardly have been remunerative. The loss of Boeotia was followed by the loss of Phocis and Locris. It was strange enough that Phocis should fall away. A few years before the Phocians had taken possession of Delphi. The Spartans had sent an army to rescue the shrine from their hands, and give it back to

Sacred
War,
448 B.C.

the Delphians; but as soon as the Spartans had gone, an Athenian army came, led by Pericles, and restored the sanctuary to the Phocians. It was a Sacred War, but so conducted that it did not make a breach of the Five Years' Truce. Yet, although their position at Delphi seemed to depend on the support of Athens, the Phocians now deserted her alliance. The change was due to an oligarchical reaction in the Phocian cities, consequent on the oligarchical rising in Boeotia.

The defeat of Coronea dimmed the prestige of Athenian arms; and still more serious results ensued. Euboea and Megara revolted at the same moment; here too oligarchical parties were at work. Pericles, who was a General, immediately went to Euboea with the regiments of seven of the tribes, while those of the remaining three marched into the Megarid. But he had no sooner reached the island than he was overtaken by the news that the garrison in the city of Megara had been massacred and that a Peloponnesian army was threatening Attica. He promptly returned, and his first object was to unite his forces with the troops in the Megarid, which were under the command of Andocides. But king Pleistoanax and the Lacedaemonians were, between them, commanding the east coast-road. Andocides was compelled to return to Attica by creeping round the corner of the Corinthian Gulf at Aegosthenae and passing through Boeotia. The troops were guided by a man of Megara named Python, and the gratitude of the three tribes "whom he saved by leading them from Pagae, through Boeotia, to Athens" was recorded on his funeral monument. The stone has survived, and the verses written upon it are a touching reminiscence of a moment of great peril. But when the whole army united in Attica, the peril was passed. The return of Pericles had disconcerted king Pleistoanax, who commanded the Lacedaemonians, and having advanced only as far as the Thriasian plain he withdrew, deeming it useless to strike at Athens. Pericles was thus set free to carry out the reduction of Euboea. Histiaea, the city in the north of the island, was most hardly dealt with, probably because her resistance was most obstinate; the people were driven out, their territory annexed to Athens; and the new settlement of Oreos took the place of Histiaea. In other cases the position of each state was settled by an agreement; and the arrangements which were made with Chalcis are still preserved on stone. The alarm of the Athenians is reflected in reductions of tribute which they allowed to their subject states; they feared that the example of Euboea might spread. The truce of five years was now approaching its end, and peace was felt to be so indispensable that they resigned themselves

Loss of Megara.

March of Andocides.

Reduction of Euboea.

to purchasing a more durable treaty by considerable concessions. They had lost Megara, but they still held the two ports, Nisaea and Pagae. These, as well as Achaea, they agreed to surrender, and on this basis a peace was concluded for thirty years between the Athenians and the Peloponnesians. All the allies of both sides were enumerated in the treaty, and it was stipulated that neither Athens nor Lacedaemon was to admit into her alliance an ally of the other, while neutral states might join which ever alliance they chose.

The Thirty Years' Peace. 446-5 B.C

It was a humiliating peace for Athens, and perhaps would not have been concluded but for the alarm which had been caused by the inroad of the Peloponnesians into Attic territory. While the loss of Boeotia was probably a gain, and the evacuation of Achaea might be lightly endured, the loss of the Megarid was a serious blow. For, while Athens held the long walls and the passes of Geranea, she had complete immunity from Peloponnesian invasions of her soil. Henceforth Attica was always exposed to such aggressions. Besides this, her position in the Crisaean Gulf was greatly weakened. The attempt which she had made to win a land-empire had succeeded only for a brief space; the lesson was that she must devote her whole energy to maintaining her maritime dominion. It was a gloomy moment for the Athenians; and it must have required all the tact and eloquence of Pericles to restore the shaken confidence and revive the drooping spirits. Euboea at all events was safe, and men might look back over sixty years to that victory which had been won by their ancestors, in a critical hour, over a joint attack of the Boeotians and Chalcidians. On that occasion a tithe of the spoil had been dedicated to Athena. Pericles now set up a bronze chariot with this tithe, and so associated the earlier victory with his own. The parallel was close; for the rebellion of Euboea had been mainly instigated by the Boeotian oligarchs who freed their own land from Athenian control. The marble base on which the chariot stood, on the Acropolis, has been found, and a few letters of the inscribed verses, which Herodotus read and copied, can be made out. The recollection that the sons of the Athenians "quenched the insolence" of the Boeotians, as those verses have it, was indeed the only consolation that could be offered for the defeat of Coronea. While he made the most of the reduction of Euboea, Pericles may have also dwelt on the prospects of the Attic sea-empire. He may have elated them by words such as he is reported to have used at a later moment of despondency. "Of the two divisions of the world accessible to man, the land and the sea, there is one of which you are absolute masters, and have, or may have, the dominion to any extent you please. Neither the Great King nor any nation on earth

c. 507 B.C. ?

can hinder a navy like yours from penetrating whithersoever you choose to sail." [3]

SECT. 5. THE IMPERIALISM OF PERICLES, AND THE OPPOSITION TO HIS POLICY

The cities of the Athenian alliance might have claimed, when the Persian war was ended, that the "Confederacy" should be broken up and that they should resume their original and rightful freedom. The fair answer to this claim would have been, that peace had indeed come, but that it would endure only so long as a power was maintained strong enough to stand up against the might of Persia. Dissolve the Confederacy, and the cities will severally and speedily become the prey of the barbarian. But in any case, the Confederacy had become an Empire, and Athens was in the full career of an ambitious "imperialist" state. The tributes which she imposed on her subjects were probably not oppressive, and were constantly revised; when the Five Years' Truce was about to be concluded, she reduced the tribute, which had been increased under the stress of the war, to its former amount. She did not force her own coinage upon her subjects; every city might have its own mint, and most of them had. But there was much that was galling in her empire, to communities in which the love of freedom was strongly developed. The revolt and reduction of Euboea showed in its undisguised shape the rule of might. It must however be remembered, in judging of the feelings of the cities towards their mistress, that in nearly every city there were an oligarchical and a democratical party. The democracy was supported by Athens and was generally friendly to her; the oligarchs were always on the watch for an opportunity to rebel. And for this reason, a revolt is not in itself evidence that Athens was unpopular among her allies. The Carian and Lycian cities began to fall away after the peace with Persia; [4] but most of them were only superficially Hellenized, and Athens let them go, not thinking it worth while to take measures for retaining her control of them.

Pericles had been the guide of the Athenian people in the recent war; his counsels had directed their imperial policy. But that policy had not been unchallenged; his leadership had not been unopposed. There was a strong oligarchical party at Athens which not only disliked the democracy of their city, but arraigned her empire. Most of

Reduction of tribute, 450 B.C.

---

[3] Thucydides, ii. 62 (transl. Jowett).
[4] The Carian tribute-district existed only for four years, 443-2—439-8 B.C.; the remnant of the Carian cities were then added to the Ionian district.

this party attacked the imperialist policy of Pericles purely from party motives, and for the purpose of attacking him; but there was one man at least who may claim the credit of having honestly espoused the cause of the allied cities against the unscrupulous selfishness of his own city. This was Thucydides, the son of Melesias, a man who had connexions with many of the allies. He maintained that the tribute should be reserved exclusively for the purpose for which it was levied, the defence of Greece against Persia, and that Athens had no right to spend it on other things, especially on things which concerned herself alone, and did not benefit the cities. It was an injustice that these cities should have to defray any part of the costs of an Athenian campaign in Boeotia or of a new temple in Athens. This was a just view, but justice is never entirely compatible with the growth of a country to political greatness, and Pericles was resolved to make his country great at all hazards. For this purpose his policy towards the allied cities was— in a phrase which seems to have been his own—"to keep them well in hand." It is pleasant to find that voices were raised against his unscrupulous imperialism.

Anti-imperialists: champions of the cities.

The more extreme section of the party which supported Thucydides would not have hesitated to betray Athens into the hands of her foes for the sake of overthrowing the democracy. They had tried to do this at the time of the battle of Tanagra. Much less would they have scrupled to give secret help to the oligarchical parties which worked against Athenian rule in the subject cities. Oligarchy had raised its head in many places during the Five Years' Truce. Oligarchical movements had led to the loss of Boeotia; oligarchical movements had caused the revolts of Megara and Euboea; oligarchy had even prevailed in Phocis. There can be little doubt that this widespread oligarchical activity had its echo in Athens; and that in these years the party opposed to Pericles was loud and aggressive. He met that opposition with remarkable dexterity. He introduced a new policy, which, while it was thoroughly imperialist, was so popular at Athens that his adversaries were silenced.

Oligarchical parties.

Among the measures which Pericles initiated to strengthen the empire of his city, none was more important in its results than the system of settling Athenian citizens abroad. Like measures of many great statesmen, this policy effected the solution of two diverse problems. The colonies which were thus sent to different parts of the empire, served as garrisons in the lands of subject allies, and they also helped to provide for part of the superfluous population of Athens. The first of these Periclean *cleruchies* was established in

THE OUT-SETTLE-MENTS.

Colonisa-

the Thracian Chersonese, under the personal supervision of Pericles himself. Lands were bought from the allied cities of the peninsula, and a thousand Athenian citizens, chiefly of the poor and unemployed, were allotted farms and assigned to the several cities. The payment for the land was made in the shape of a reduction of the tribute. At the same time Pericles restored the wall which Miltiades had built across the isthmus, to protect the country against the Thracians; in view of the rising power of the Thracian prince Teres, this precaution was wise.

The out-settlements in the Chersonese—which were probably followed by out-settlements in Lemnos and Imbros, the island warders of the gate of the Propontis—were the most important of all. The same policy was at the same time adopted in Euboea and some of the islands of the Aegean, and in a mysterious place, the Thracian Brea, which probably lay west of the Strymon. The original act of the colonisation of Brea has been preserved, and the provision that all the settlers shall belong to the two poorest classes of the people, on the Solonian classification, illustrates the character of the Periclean cleruchies. The policy was naturally popular at Athens, since it provided for thousands of unemployed who cumbered the streets; and perhaps it may be regarded as one of the happiest strokes devised by Pericles for increasing his ascendency and confounding his opponents. But it was a policy which was highly unpopular among the allies, in whose territories the settlements were made; and it gave perhaps more dissatisfaction than any other feature of Athenian rule.

Cleruchies
in
Euboea,
Naxos,
Andros,
447 B.C.;

Brea (446
B.C. ?).

Most Athenian citizens were naturally allured by a policy of expansion which made their city great and powerful without exacting heavy sacrifices from themselves. The day had not yet come when they were unwilling to undertake military service, and they were content as long as the cost of maintaining the empire did not tax their purses. The empire furthered the extension of their trade, and increased their prosperity. The average Athenian burgher was not hindered by his own full measure of freedom from being willing to press, with as little scruple as any tyrant, the yoke of his city upon the necks of other communities. So long as the profits of empire were many and its burdens light, the Athenian democracy would feel few searchings of heart in adopting the imperialism of Pericles.

That imperialism was indeed of a lofty kind. The aim of the statesman who guided the destinies of Athens in these days of her greatness was to make her the queen of Hellas; to spread her sway on the mainland as well as beyond the seas; and to make her

political influence felt in those states which it would have been unwise and perhaps impossible to draw within the borders of her
empire. The full achievement of this ideal would have meant the
union of all the Greeks, an union held together by the power of
Athens, but having a natural support in a common religion, common traditions, common customs, and a common language.

Shortly before the loss of Boeotia through the defeat of Coronea, Athens addressed to Greece an open declaration of her Panhellenic ambition. She invited the Greek states to send representatives to an Hellenic congress at Athens, for the purpose of discussing certain matters of common interest. To restore the temples which had been burned by the Persians, to pay the votive offerings which were due to the gods for the great deliverance, and to take common measures for clearing the seas of piracy;—this was the programme which Athens proposed to the consideration of Greece. The invita-tion did not go to the west, for the Italiots and Siceliots were not directly concerned in the Persian war, but it went to all the cities of old Greece, and to the cities and islands which belonged to the Athenian empire. If the congress had taken place it would have inaugurated an amphictiony of all Hellas, and Athens would have been the centre of this vast religious union. It was a sublime pro-ject, but it could not be. It was not to be expected that Sparta would fall in with a project which, however noble and pious it sounded, might tempt or help Athens to strike out new and perilous paths of ambition and aggrandisement. The Athenian envoys were rebuffed in the Peloponnesus, and the plan fell through. Immedi-ately after this, the revolution in Boeotia deprived Athens of her empire on the mainland.

Sect. 6. The Restoration of the Temples

It remained then for Athens to carry out that part of the pro-gramme which concerned herself, and restore in greater splendour the temples of her city and her land. We shall miss the meaning of the architectural monuments which now began to rise under the direction and influence of Pericles, if we do not clearly grasp their historical motive, and recognise their immediate connexion with the Persian war. It devolved upon the city, as a religious duty, to make good the injuries which the barbarian had inflicted upon the habita-tions of her gods, and fully to pay her debt of gratitude to heaven for the defeat of the Mede. And seeing that Athens had won her great empire through that defeat, the gods might well expect that she would perform this duty on no small scale and in no niggardly spirit. In this, above all, was the greatness of Pericles displayed, that he discerned the importance of performing it on a grand scale. He recognised that the city by ennobling the houses of her gods would ennoble herself; and that she could express her own might and her ideals in no worthier way than by the erection of beautiful temples. His architectural plans went farther than this, and we can see that he was influenced by the example of the Pisistratids; but the chief buildings of the Periclean age, it should always be remembered, were, like the Athenian empire itself, the direct consequence of the Persian invasion.

£ 50-30
U.C.

"Athena
Pro-
machos,"
c. 448.

Of the monuments which in the course of twenty years changed the appearance of the Acropolis, one of the first was a gigantic statue of Athena, wrought in bronze. The goddess stood near the west brow of her own hill, looking south-westward, and her helmet and the tip of her lance flashing in the sun could be seen far off at sea. But nothing was so pressing as to carry to completion the new house of the goddess, which had been begun in the days of Themistocles and never finished. The work was now resumed on the same

Temple of
Athena
Polias
(the "Par-
thenon"),
finished
438 B.C.

site, and the same foundations; but it was resumed on an entirely different plan, which was drawn up by the gifted architect Ictinus. The new temple was slightly broader but considerably shorter than it would have been if the old design had been carried out, and instead of foreign Parian marble, native Attic from the quarries of Pentelicus was employed. Callicrates, another expert architect, superintended the execution of the plan which Ictinus had conceived. It is not within our province to enter here into the architectural beauties of this perfect Dorian temple, which came afterwards to be generally known as the Parthenon. The building contained two rooms, between which there was no communication. The eastern room into which one entered from the pronaos was the temple proper, and contained the statue of the goddess. It was about a hundred feet long, and was hence officially called the *Hecatompedos*. The door of the small western room was on the west side of the temple. This chamber was perhaps designed for the habitation of invisible maidens who attend the maiden goddess; it is at least certain that it was called the *Parthenôn*. It is easy to imagine how a word which designated as the room of the Maidens part of the house of the Maiden, could soon come to be associated popularly with the whole building, and the name Parthenon came to mean for the ordinary ear, in defiance of official usage, the temple of Athena Parthenos, and not the chamber of her virgins.

The
statue of
Athena by
Phidias.

The goddess stood in her dwelling, majestic and smiling, her colossal figure arrayed in a golden robe, a helmet on her head, her

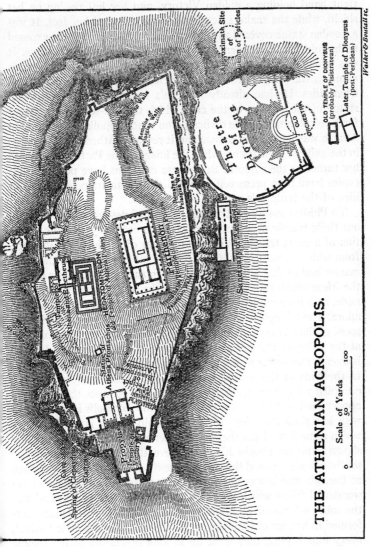

Walker & Boutall sc.

OLD TEMPLE OF DIONYSUS
(probably Pisistratean)

Later Temple of Dionysus
(post-Periclean)

THE ATHENIAN ACROPOLIS.

Scale of Yards

0   50   100

FIG. 63.

right hand holding a golden Victory, and her left resting on her shield, while the snake Erichthonius was coiled at her feet. It was a wooden statue covered with ivory and gold—ivory for the exposed flesh, gold for the raiment—and hence called *chryselephantine*. It was wrought by the Athenian sculptor of genius who has given his name to the plastic art of the Periclean age, Phidias, the son of Charmides. He had already made his fame by another beautiful statue of the goddess of the city, which the out-settlers who went forth to colonise Lemnos dedicated on the Acropolis. The Lemnian Athena was wrought in bronze and it revealed Athena to her people in the guise of their friend, while the image of the Parthenon showed her rather as their queen. Both these creations have perished, but copies have been preserved from which we can frame some far-off idea of the sculptor's work.

To Phidias too was entrusted the task of designing and carrying out those plastic decorations which were necessary to the completion of a great temple. With the metopes of the lofty entablature, from which Centaurs and Giants stood out in high relief, the great master had probably little to do. But in the two pediments and on the frieze which ran round the wall of the temple, within the colonnade, he left monuments of his genius and his skill, for mankind to adore. The triangle above the eastern portal was adorned with the scene of the birth of Athena, who has sprung from the head of Zeus, at the rising of the sun and the setting of the moon; and Iris the heavenly messenger was shown, going forth to carry the good news to the ends of the world. The pediment of the western end was occupied with the passage in the life of the goddess, that specially appertained to Attica—her triumph on the Acropolis in her contest with her rival Poseidon, for the lordship of the land. The olive which came forth from the earth by her enchantment was probably shown; and we should like to believe that at the northern and southern ends reclined the two river gods, Eridanus and Ilisus, each at the side which was nearest his own waters. The subject of the wonderful frieze which encircled the temple from end to end was the most solemn of all the ceremonies which the Athenians performed in honour of their queen. At the great Panathenaic festival, every fourth year, they went up in long procession to her temple to present her with a new robe. The advance of this procession, starting from the western side, and moving simultaneously along the northern and southern sides, to meet at the eastern entrance, was vividly shown on the frieze of the Parthenon. Walking along the peristyle and looking upwards, the spectator saw the Athenian knights—beautiful young men—on horseback, charioteers, citizens

The pedi-ments.

The frieze of cella.

The Pan-athenaic proces-sion.

on foot, musicians, kine and sheep led for sacrifice, stately maidens with sacred vessels, the nine archons of the city, all advancing to the house of Athena where she entertains the celestials on her feast-day. The high gods are seated on thrones, Zeus on one side of Athena, Hephaestus on the other; and near the goddess is a peplos —perhaps the old peplos—in the hands of a priest. The western side of the frieze is still in its place, but the rest has been removed —the greater part to our own island.

Athena Polias had now two houses side by side on her hill. For the old restored temple was not destroyed, nor was her old image removed from it. But in her character of Victory, yet another small habitation was built for her by the architect Callicrates, about the same time,[5] on the bastion which the hill throws out on its south-western side. It was an appropriate spot for the house of Victory. The Athenian standing on that platform saw Salamis and Aegina near him; his eye ranged along the Argolic coast, to the distant citadel of Corinth and the mountains of the Megarid; under the shadow of Victory he could lose himself in reveries of memory and dreams of hope. The motive of the temple, as a memorial of the Persian war, was written clear in the frieze. Whereas the sculptures of other temples of this period only alluded indirectly to that great struggle, by the representation of mythical wars—such as the war of Greek and Amazons, or of Lapiths and Centaurs, or of gods and giants; on the frieze of Athena Nike a battle between the Greeks and Persians is portrayed. It is the battle of Plataea; for Greeks are shown fighting in the Persian host.

But there were other shrines of other gods in Athens and Attica, which had been wrecked by the Persians, and which were now to be restored. From the west side of the Acropolis, as one looks down on the western quarter of the city, no building is so prominent, or can ever have been so prominent, as the Dorian temple of Pentelic marble which crowns the hill of Colonus, and replaced an older temple of the limestone of Piraeus. It is the temple which "the sons of Hephaestus" built for their sire, the god of handicraftsmen, who was always worshipped with special devotion at Athens—it is significant that on the frieze of the Parthenon he sits next the lady of the land. This house of Hephaestus is the only Greek temple that is not a ruin. About the same time, a marble temple of Poseidon rose on the extreme point of southern Attica, the promontory of Sunium. The Persian invasion had probably been fatal to the old temple of poros-stone. Here the sea-god, "to whom men

The old temple.

Temple of Athena Nike.

The temple of Hephaestus (popularly called the Theseum).

The temple of Sunium.

(Σουνι-άρατος.)

---

[5] An inscription, of *c.* 450 B.C., providing for the building of the temple and altar, has been recently discovered.

pray at Sunium," seems to have had his own house, looking down upon his own domain; he was not forced here, as on the Acropolis, to share a sanctuary with Athena; but the goddess had a separate temple of her own hard by.

At the other extremity of the Attic land, the shrine of the goddesses of Eleusis had likewise been destroyed by the barbarians. The rebuilding had been soon begun, but, like the new temple of Athena on the Acropolis, the work had been discontinued owing to the claims of war on the revenue of the state. Under Pericles it was taken up again and completed; Ictinus made the design and Coroebus carried it out. The new Hall of Mysteries was built of the dark stone of Eleusis; one side of it was formed by the rock of the hill under which it was built; and the stone steps around the walls would have seated about 3000. As the place was close to the Megarian frontier, a strong wall with towers was erected round the precincts of the shrine; so that the place had the aspect of a fortress.

These splendid buildings required a large outlay of money, and thus gave the political opponents of Pericles a welcome handle against him. Thucydides was the leader of the outcry. He accused Pericles not merely of squandering the resources of the state which ought to be kept as a reserve for war, but of misappropriating the money of the Confederacy for purely Athenian purposes. Athens, it was said, was "like a vain woman, adorning herself with pendants of precious stones, and statues, and temples that cost a thousand talents." It is certainly true that some money was taken from the treasury of the Hellenotamiae for the new buildings, but this was only a very small part of the cost, which was mainly defrayed by the treasury of Athena and by the public treasury of Athens. There was however a good case against Pericles both on grounds of policy and on grounds of justice. The plea for taking a part of the tribute (perhaps a sixtieth—besides the sixtieth which was consecrated to Athena) doubtless was that the restoration of Greek temples destroyed by the Persians was a duty which devolved upon all the Greeks. But Pericles, with bold sophistry, argued that the allies had no reason to complain, so long as Athens defended them efficiently; this was the contract, and they had no right to interfere in her disposition of the funds. Three years after the Thirty Years' Peace, Thucydides thought that he could bring the question to an issue, and he asked the people to adjudicate by the sherd. But the people voted for the ostracism of Thucydides, and henceforward Pericles had no opponent of influence to thwart his policy or cross his way. The buildings already begun could now be continued without criticism and new works could be undertaken. A great Hall of Music or *Odeon,* intended for the musical contests which had recently been added to the Panathenaic celebrations, was now erected on the east side of the Theatre of Dionysus. Its roof, made of the masts and yard-arms of captured Persian ships, was pointed like a tent, and wits compared it to the helmet of Pericles the strategos. "The trial by sherd is over," says some one in a play which the comic poet Cratinus put on the stage at this time; "so here comes Pericles, our peak-headed Zeus, with the Odeon set on his crown."

Cratinus on Pericles (in the Thrattai).

Though Cimon, when he constructed the southern wall of the Acropolis, also built a new entrance-gate facing south-westward. it was too small and unimposing to relieve the frowning aspect of the walled hill. A more worthy approach, worthy of the Parthenon, was devised by the architect Mnesicles and met the approbation of Pericles. The buildings designed by Mnesicles occupied the whole west side of the hill. In the centre, on the brow of the height and facing westward, was to be the entrance with five gates, and on either side of this two vast columned halls—reaching to the north and south brinks of the hill—in which the Athenians could walk sheltered from sun and rain. Thrown out on the projecting cliffs in front of these halls were to be two spacious wings, flanking the ascent to the central gate. But the plan of Mnesicles took no account of the sanctuaries on the south-western part of the Acropolis, on which his new buildings would encroach. The southern colonnade would have cut short the precinct of Artemis Brauronia and the adjacent southern wing would have infringed on the enclosure of Athena Nike. On the north side there were no such impediments. The priests of these goddesses raised objections to the execution of the architect's plan at the expense of their sacred precincts, and in consequence the grand idea of Mnesicles was only partly carried out. But even after the building had been begun, Pericles and his architect never abandoned the hope that the scruples of the priests might ultimately be overcome; and, while they omitted altogether the southern colonnade and reduced the proportions of the southern wing, they built in such a way that at some future time the structure might be easily enlarged to the measures of the original design. On the northern side, too, the idea of Mnesicles was not completed, but for a different reason. The covered colonnade was never built; it was left to the last, and, when the time came, Athens was threatened by a great war, and deemed it unwise to undertake any further outlay on building. But the north-western wing was built and was adorned with paintings. The greatest paintings that Athens pos-

The new Propylaea.

Pinacotheca.

Polygno-
tus at
Athens,
c. 470-465.

Poecile
Stoa.

sessed were however not on the hill but in buildings below; and they belonged to a somewhat earlier age. It was Cimon who brought Polygnotus of Thasos to Athens, and it was when Cimon was in power that he, in collaboration with Micon, another eminent painter, decorated with life-size frescoes the new Theseum and the Anaceum, on the north side of the Acropolis, and the walls of the Painted Portico in the market-place. We have already cast a glance at the picture of the Battle of Marathon. The most famous of the pictures of the Thasian master was executed, after he had left Athens, for the speech-hall of the Cnidians at Delphi. Its subject was the underworld visited by Odysseus.

If it was vain for Athens to hope that Greece would yield her any formal acknowledgment of headship, she might at all events have the triumph of exerting intellectual influence even in the lands which were least ready to admit her claims. And in the field of art she partly fulfilled the ambition of Pericles, who, when he could not make her the queen, desired that she should be the instructress, of Helas. When Phidias had completed the great statue of Athena in gold and ivory, and had seen it set up in the new temple, he went forth, invited by the men of Elis, to make the image for the temple of Zeus at Olympia. For five years in his workshop in the Altis the Athenian sculptor wrought at the "great chryselephantine god," and the colossal image which came from his hands was probably the highest creation ever achieved by the plastic art of Greece. The Panhellenic god, seated on a lofty throne, and clad in a golden robe, held a Victory in his right hand, a sceptre in his left. He was bearded, and his hair was wreathed with a branch of olive. Many have borne witness to the impression which the serene aspect of this manifest divinity always produced upon the heart of the beholder. "Let a man sick and weary in his soul, who has passed through many distresses and sorrows, whose pillow is unvisited by kindly sleep, stand in front of this image; he will, I deem, forget all the terrors and troubles of human life." An Athenian had wrought, for one of the two great centres of Hellenic religion, the most sublime expression of the Greek ideal of godhead. Nor was Phidias the only Athenian artist who worked abroad; we also find the architect Ictinus engaged in designing temples in the Peloponnesus.

Phidias
goes to
Olympia,
c. 438 B.C.

(E.g. temple of
Apollo at
Phigalia.)

SECT. 7. THE PIRAEUS. GROWTH OF ATHENIAN TRADE

The
Piraeus.

The Piraeus had grown enormously since it had been fortified by Themistocles; it was now one of the great ports and cheaping-towns "in the midst of Hellas," and Pericles took in hand to make it a

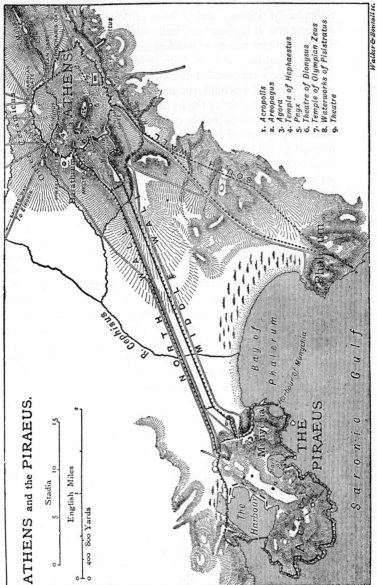

ATHENS and the PIRAEUS.

1. Acropolis
2. Areopagus
3. Agora
4. Temple of Hephaestus
5. Pnyx
6. Theatre of Dionysus
7. Temple of Olympian Zeus
8. Waterworks of Pisistratus
9. Theatre

Walker & Boutall sc.

Fig. 64.

greater and fairer place. There was one weak point in the common defences of Piraeus and Athens. Between Munychia and the extreme end of the southern wall which ran down to the strand of Phaleron, there was an unfortified piece of marshy shore, where an enemy might land at night. This defect might have been remedied by building a cross-wall, but a wholly different plan was adopted.

The middle Long Wall.

A new long wall was built, running parallel and close to the northern wall, and, like it, joining the fortification of Piraeus with the "upper city," as Athens was locally called. The southern or Phaleron wall consequently ceased to be part of the system of defence and was allowed to fall into disrepair. Round the three harbours shipsteads were constructed, in which the vessels could lie high and dry; and on the wharfs and quays new storehouses and buildings of sundry kinds arose for the convenience of shipping and trade. On the east side of the great Harbour the chief traffic was carried on in the

Emporion.

Place of Commerce. This mart was marked off by boundary stones, some of which are still preserved, and was subject to the control of a special board of officers. The most famous of the buildings in the Place of Commerce was the colonnade known as the Deigma or Show-place, where merchants showed their wares. But Pericles was not content with the erection of new buildings; the whole town, which crept up the slopes of Munychia from the quays of the great Harbour, was laid out on a completely new system, which created considerable interest in Greece. It was the rectangular system, on which the main streets run parallel and are cut by cross streets at right angles. The Piraeus was the first town in Europe where this plan was adopted, which we now see carried out on a large scale in many modern cities. The idea was due to Hippodamus, an architect of Miletus, a man of a speculative as well as practical turn, who tried with less success to apply his principles of symmetry to politics, and sketched the scheme of a model state whose institutions were as precisely correlated as the streets of his model town.

The increase of Athenian trade was largely due to the decline of the merchant cities of Ionia, as well as to the blow which was struck to Phoenician commerce by the victory of Greece over Persia. The decay of Ionian commerce is strikingly reflected in the tribute-records of the Athenian Confederacy, where the small sums paid by the Ionians are contrasted with the larger tributes of the cities on the shores of the Propontis. Lampsacus contributes twice as much as

(Tribute of Lampsacus, 12 tals.; of Ephesus, 6.)

Ephesus. Both trade and industry migrated from the eastern to the western and northern shores of the Aegean; and as this change coincided with the rise of her empire, it was Athens that it chiefly profited. The population of Athens and her harbour multiplied; and about this time the whole number of the inhabitants of Attica seems to have been about 250,000—perhaps more than twice as large as the population of the Corinthian state. But nearly half of these inhabitants were slaves; for one consequence of the growth of manufactures was the inflowing of slave "hands" into the manufacturing towns. In towns where the people subsisted on the fruits of agriculture the demand for slaves remained small. It should be observed that, although Greece, and especially Athens, consumed large quantities of corn brought from beyond the seas, this did not ruin the agriculture of Greece; the costs of transport were so great that home-grown corn could still be profitable.

Except in remote or unusually conservative regions, money had now entirely displaced more primitive standards of exchange and valuation. Most Greek states of any size issued their own coins, and their money at this time was in almost all cases silver. Silver had become plentiful, and prices had necessarily gone up. Thus the price of barley and wheat had become two or three times dearer than a hundred years before. Far more remarkable was the increase in the price of stock. In the days of Solon a sheep could be bought for a drachma; in the days of Pericles, its cost might approach fifty drachmae. As money was cheap, interest should have been low; but mercantile enterprise was so active, the demand for capital so great, and security so inadequate, that the usual price of a loan was twelve per cent.

Money plentiful

Rise of prices.

Rate of interest.

SECT. 8. ATHENIAN ENTERPRISE IN ITALY

In the far west Athens was spreading her influence and pushing her trade. She supplied Etruria with her black red-figured pottery, and there was a market for these products of her industry even in the remote valley of the Po. Her ships brought back metal-works from Tuscany, carpets and cushions from Carthage, corn, cheese and pork form Sicily. The Greek cities of Sicily had gradually adopted the Attic standard for their currency; and in the little Italian republic on the Tiber, which was afterwards destined to make laws for the whole world, the fame of the legislation of Solon was so high that envoys were sent to Athens to obtain a copy of the code. Thus Athens had stepped into the place of Chalcis; she was now the chief Ionian trader with Italian and Sicilian lands. Her rival in this western commerce was Corinth, but she was beginning to out-distance the great Dorian merchant-city. In this competition Athens had one advantage. By the possession of Naupactus she could control the entrance to the Corinthian gulf—a perpetual

Athenian trade in the west

menace to Corinth; while the hatred which existed between Corinth and her colony Corcyra prevented this island from being as useful as it should have been to the Corinthian traffic with the west. On the other hand, Corinth had the advantage of having important colonies in the west, with which she maintained intimate relations, especially Syracuse; and these maritime cities were centres of her trade and influence. Next to Athens herself, Syracuse was probably the largest and most populous city in the Greek world. Athens had no colonies and no such centres. The disadvantage was felt by Themistocles, and his active brain devised the occupation of the site of Siris, which had been destroyed by its neighbours, but the scheme was not realised. At length the opportunity came, when Pericles was at the head of affairs; here, as in other cases, it fell upon him to execute ideas of Themistocles.

Sybaris re-occupied, 452-448 B.C.

The men of old Sybaris, who since the destruction of their own town had dwelled in neighbouring cities, thought that they might at length return to build a new Sybaris on the old site; but within five years their old foes, the men of Croton, went up and drove them out. Yet they did not despair, but hoped to compass with the help of others what they had failed to accomplish by themselves. They invited Athens and Sparta to take part in founding a new city. For Sparta the offer had no attraction; but for Athens it was a welcome opportunity. The land of Sybaris was famous for its fertility, and the position was suitable for Athenian commerce. But Pericles determined to give the enterprise an international significance; it was to be more than a mere Athenian speculation. It was proclaimed throughout the Peloponnesus that whosoever wished might take part in the foundation of the new colony. The Peloponnesus—and especially Achaea, with whose cities Athens had been closely connected in recent years—was the mother country of the Greek colonies which fringed the Tarentine gulf; and the idea of Pericles was that the mother country, *under the auspices of Athens,* should establish the new city. Achaea, Arcadia, and Elis responded to the call; New Sybaris was founded; and the Athenian predominance was expressed in the image of Athena with Attic helmet on the coins of the young city.

Sybarites invite Athens to co-operate, 446 B.C.

Foundation of New Sybaris.

But the men of old Sybaris were not content to stand on an equal footing with the colonists who had come to help them from the mother-country. They thought that their old connexion with the place entitled them to a privileged position; they claimed an exclusive right to the most important offices in the state. Such claims could not be tolerated; a battle was fought; and the Sybarites were driven out. But, when the city was thus deplenished, there was a pressing need for men; and for the second time an appeal was made to Athens, but this time from her own children.

To the second appeal Athens, under the guidance of Pericles, responded by an enterprise on a still greater scale. All Greece was now invited to take part in founding a Panhellenic colony. In carrying out this project the right-hand man of Pericles was the Seer and Interpreter (*Exegete*) Lampon, who was closely connected with the Eleusinian worship, and was the highest authority in Athens on all matters pertaining to religion. He obtained from the Delphic god an oracle touching the new colony; it was to be planted where men could drink water by measure and eat bread without measure. At Athens the enemies of Pericles opposed the project, and especially the Panhellenic character which he sought to impress upon it. Cratinus brought out a play deriding Lampon, and asking whether Pericles was a second Theseus who wanted to synoecize the whole of Greece. But Greece responded to the Athenian proposal, and the colony went forth under the guidance of Lampon. Not far from the site of Sybaris they found a stream gushing from a bronze pipe, which was locally known as the Bushel. Here clearly was the measured water to which the oracle pointed; while the land was so fruitful that it might well be said to furnish bread without measure. The place was named Thurii, and the new city was designed by Hippodamus, the architect who had laid out the Piraeus in rectangular streets. The constitution of Thurii was naturally a democracy; but though the influence of the Athenian model might be recognised, the colony adopted not the laws of Solon, but those of Zaleucus, the lawgiver of Locri. Some years after the foundation, the question was asked, Who was the founder? and the Delphic god himself claimed the honour. The coins of Thurii were stamped with Athena's head and an olive branch; and the place became, as it was intended, a centre of Athenian influence in Italy, although the Attic element in the population failed to maintain its predominance.

Drapetides of Cratinus.

Colony of Thurii, 443 B.C.

Sect. 9. Athenian Policy in Thrace and the Euxine

But Athens had greater and more immediate interests in the eastern sea where she succeeded Miletus than in the western where she succeeded Chalcis. The importance of the imports from the Pontus, especially corn, fish, and wood, was more vital than that of the wares which came to her from the west; and hence there was nothing of higher consequence in the eyes of a clear-sighted statesman than the assurance of the line of communication between Athens and the Euxine sea, and the occupation of strong and favourable points on the coasts of the Euxine itself. The outer gate of the Euxine was secured by the possession of the Chersonese which Pericles strengthened, and the inner gate by the control of Byzantium and Chalcedon, members of the Athenian Confederacy. In the Euxine, Athens relied on the Greek towns which, fringing the shores at distant intervals, looked to her for support against the neighbouring barbarians. The corn-market in the Athenian agora was sensitive to every political movement in Thrace and Scythia; and it was necessary to be ever ready to support the ships or trade

Rise of Thracian kingdom, c. 450 B.C.

by the presence of ships of war. The growth of a large Thracian kingdom under Teres and his son Sitalces demanded the attention of Athenian statesmen to these regions more pressingly than ever. The power of Teres reached to the Danube, and his influence to the Dnieper; for he married his daughter to the king of the neighbouring Scythians.

It was in order to impress the barbarians of the Euxine regions with a just sense of the greatness of the Athenian sea-power that

Pericles visits the Euxine.

Pericles sailed himself to the Pontus, in command of an imposing squadron. Of that voyage we know little. It is ascertained that he visited Sinope, and that in consequence of his visit the Athenians gained a permanent footing at that important point. It is probable that he also sailed to the Cimmerian Bosphorus and visited the Archaeanactid lords of Panticapaeum, who were distinguished for many a long year by their abiding friendship to Athens in her good and evil days alike. As Panticapaeum was the centre of the Euxine corn trade, this intimacy was of the highest importance.

The union of the Thracian tribes under a powerful king constrained Athens also to keep a watchful eye upon the north coast of the Aegean and the eastern frontier of Macedonia. The most important point on that coast both from a commercial and a strategic point of view was the mouth of the Strymon, where the Athenians possessed the fortress of Eion. Not far from the mouth was the bridge over which all the trade between Thrace and Macedonia passed to and fro; and up the Strymon valley ran the chief roads into the "Hinterland." The mountains of the neighbourhood were famous for the veins of gold and silver stored in their recesses; the Macedonian king Alexander had tapped a mine near Lake Prasias which yielded daily a silver talent. In the days of Cimon, Athens had attempted to strengthen Eion by established a colony at the

Attempt to colonise the Nine Ways, 465 B.C.

Nine Ways, by the Strymon bridge. We saw how that attempt roused the opposition of Thasos, whose interests it menaced; and, though Thasos was subdued, the colony of the Nine Ways was destroyed by the neighbouring barbarians. Thirty years later, Pericles resumed the project with greater success. Hagnon, son of Nicias, led forth a colony, of Athenians and others, and founded a new city, surrounded on three sides by the Strymon-stream, and called its name Amphipolis. It flourished and became, as was inevitable, the most important place on the coast. But a local feeling grew up unfavourable to the mother-country, and the city was lost to Athens within fifteen years of its foundation, as we shall see hereafter.

Foundation of Ampnipolis, 436 B.C.

SECT. 10. THE REVOLT OF SAMOS

After the ostracism of Thucydides, Pericles reigned, the undisputed leader of Athenian policy, for nearly fifteen years. He ruled as absolutely as a tyrant, and folk might have said that his rule was a continuation of the tyranny of the Pisistratids. But his position was entirely constitutional, and it had the stablest foundation, his moral influence over the sovereign people. He had the power of persuading them to do whatever he thought good, and every year for fifteen years after his rival's banishment he was elected one of the generals. Although all the ten generals nominally possessed equal powers, yet the man who possessed the supreme political influence and enjoyed the confidence of the people was practically chief of the ten and had the conduct of foreign affairs in his hands. Pericles was not irresponsible; for at the end of any official year the people could decline to re-elect him and could call him to account for his acts. When he had once gained the undisputed mastery, the only forces which he used to maintain it were wisdom and eloquence. Whatever devices he may have employed in his earlier career for party purposes, he rejected now all vulgar means of courting popularity or catching votes. He believed in himself; and he sought to raise the people to his own wisdom, he would not stoop to their folly. The desire of autocratic authority was doubtless part of his nature; but his spirit was fine enough to feel that it was a greater thing to be leader of freemen whom he must convince by speech than despot of subjects who must obey his nod. Yet this leader of democracy was disdainful of the vulgar herd; and perhaps no one knew more exactly than he the weak points in a democratic constitution. There is no better equipment for the highest statesmanship than the temper which holds aloof from the public and shows a front of good-natured indifference towards unfriendly criticism; and we may be sure that this quality in the temperament of Pericles helped to establish his success and maintain his supremacy.

Pericles was a man of finer fibre than Themistocles, but he was not like Themistocles a statesman of originative genius. He origi-

Political position of Pericles.

nated little; he elaborated the ideas of others. He brought to perfection the sovereignty of the people which had been fully established in principle long ago; he raised to its height the empire which had been already founded. As an orator he may have had true genius; of that we cannot judge. It was his privilege to guide the policy of his country at a time when she had poets and artists who stand alone and eminent not only in her own annals and those of Greece, but in the history of mankind. The Periclean age, the age of Sophocles and Euripides, Ictinus and Phidias, was not made by Pericles. But Pericles, though not creative, was one of its most interesting figures. Perhaps his best service to Greece was one which is often overlooked: the preservation of peace for twelve years between Athens and her jealous continental neighbours—an achievement which demanded statesmanship of no ordinary tact.

In his military operations he seems to have been competent, though we have not material to criticise them minutely; he was at
Revolt of Samos, 440 B.C.
least generally successful. Five years after the Thirty Years' Peace, he was called upon to display his generalship. Athens was involved in a war with one of the strongest members of her Confederacy, the island of Samos. The occasion of this war was a dispute which Samos had with another member, Miletus, about the possession of Priene. It appears that Athens, some years before, had settled the constitution of Miletus and placed a garrison in the city; and yet we now find Miletus engaged in a struggle with a non-tributary ally, and, when she is worsted, appealing to Athens. The case shows how little we know of the various orderings of the relations between Athens and her allies and subjects. One would have thought the decision of such a case would have rested with Athens from the first. On the appeal, she decided in favour of Miletus, and Pericles sailed with forty-four triremes to Samos where he overthrew the aristocracy, carried away a number of hostages, and established a democratic constitution, leaving a garrison to protect it. The nobles who fled to the mainland returned one night, captured the garrison and handed them over to the Persian satrap of Sardis, with whom they were intriguing. They also recovered the hostages who had
Revolt of Byzantium.
been lodged in the island of Lemnos. Athens received another blow at the same time by the revolt of Byzantium.

Pericles sailed speedily back to Samos and invested it with a large fleet. Hearing that a Phoenician squadron was coming to assist the Samians, he raised the siege and with a part of his armament went to meet it. During his absence the Samians gained some successes against the Athenian ships which were anchored close to the harbour. At the end of two weeks Pericles returned; either the Phoenicians had not appeared after all, or they had been induced to sail home. Well-nigh 200 warships now blockaded Samos, and at the end of nine months the city surrendered. The Samians undertook to pull down their walls, to surrender their ships, and pay a war indemnity which amounted to 1500 talents or thereabouts. They became subject to Athens and were obliged to furnish soldiers to her armies, but they were not made tributary.

Siege and reduction of Samos, 439 B.C.

The Athenian citizens who fell in the war received a public burial at Athens. Pericles pronounced the funeral oration, and it may have been on this occasion that he used a famous phrase of the young men who had fallen. The spring, he said, was taken out of the year.

Byzantium also came back to the confederacy. It had been a trying moment for Athens; for she had some reason to fear Peloponnesian intervention. Sparta and her allies had met to consider the situation; and the Corinthians afterwards claimed, whether truly or not, that they deprecated any interference, on the general principle that every state should be left to deal with her own rebellious allies. However the Corinthians may have acted on this occasion, it was chiefly the commercial jealousy existing between Athens and Corinth that brought on the ultimate outbreak of hostilities between the Athenians and Peloponnesians, which led to the destruction of the Athenian empire.

It seems that during the excitement of the Samian war, Pericles deemed it expedient to place some restraints upon the licence of the comic drama. What he feared was the effect which the free criticisms of the comic poets on his policy might have, not upon the Athenians themselves, but upon the strangers who were present in the theatre, and especially upon citizens of the subject states. The precaution shows that the situation was critical; though the restraints were withdrawn as soon as possible, for they were contrary to the spirit of the time. Henceforward the only check on the comic poet was that he *might* be prosecuted before the Council of Five Hundred for "doing wrong to the people," if his jests against the officers of the people went too far.

Temporary restrictions on Comedy.

Comedy had grown up in Athens out of the mummeries of masked revellers who kept the feasts of Dionysus by singing phallic songs and flinging coarse jests at the folk. It was not till after the Persian war that the state recognised it. Then a place was given at the great festival of Dionysus to comic competitions. To the three days which were devoted to the competitions of tragedies a fourth was added for the new contest. The comic drama then assumed form

472-1 B.C.

and shape. Magnes and Chionides were its first masters; but they were eclipsed by Cratinus, the most brilliant comic poet of the age of Pericles.

There is no more significant symptom of the political and social health of the Athenian state in the period of its empire, than the perfect freedom which was accorded to the comic stage, to laugh at everything in earth and heaven, and splash with ridicule every institution of the city and every movement of the day, to libel the statesmen and even jest at the gods. Such license is never permitted in an age of decadence even under the shelter of religious usage. It can only prevail in a free country where men's belief in their own strength and virtue, in the excellence of their institutions and their ideals, is still true, deep, and fervent; then they can afford to laugh at themselves. The Old Comedy is a most telling witness to the greatness of Athens.

SECT. 11. HIGHER EDUCATION. THE SOPHISTS

Since the days of Nestor and Odysseus, the art of persuasive speech was held in honour by the Greeks. With the rise of the democratic commonwealths it became more important, and the greater attention which was paid to the cultivation of oratory may perhaps be reflected in the introduction of a new class of proper names, which refer to excellence in addressing public assemblies. The institutions of a Greek democratic city presupposed in the average citizen the faculty of speaking in public, and for any one who was ambitious for a political career it was indispensable. If a man was hauled into a law-court by his enemies, and knew not how to speak, he was like an unarmed civilian attacked by soldiers in panoply. The power of clearly expressing ideas in such a way as to persuade an audience was an art to be learned and taught. But it was not enough to gain command of a vocabulary; it was necessary to learn how to argue, and to exercise one's self in the discussion of political and ethical questions. There was a demand for higher education.

This tendency of democracy corresponded to the growth of that spirit of inquiry which had first revealed itself in Ionia in the field of natural philosophy. The study of nature had passed into a higher stage in the hands of two men of genius, whose speculations have had an abiding effect on science. Empedocles distinguished the "four elements," and explained the development of the universe by the forces of attraction and repulsion which have held their place till to-day in scientific theory. He also foreshadowed the doctrine

Marginal notes:
New class of names (e.g. Pythagoras, Anaxagoras).

Science.

of the survival of the fittest. Democritus, of Abdera, a man of vast learning, originated the atomic theory, which was in later days popularized by Epicurus, and in still later by the Roman Lucretius. The scientific imagination of Democritus generated the world from atoms, like in quality but different in size and weight, existing in void space. Such advances in the explanation of nature implied and promoted a new conception of what may be called "methodized" knowledge, and this conception was applied to every subject. The second half of the fifth century was an age of technical treatises; oratory and cookery were alike reduced to systems; political institutions and received morality became the subject of scientific inquiry. Desire of knowledge had led the Greeks to seek more information about foreign lands and peoples; they had begun both to know more of the world and to regard it with a more critical mind; enlightenment was spreading, prejudices were being dispelled. Herodotus, who was far from being a sceptic, fully appreciates the instructiveness of the story which he tells, how Darius asked some Greeks for what price they would be willing to eat the dead bodies of their fathers. When they cry that nothing would induce them to do so, the king calls a tribe of Indians who eat their parents, and asks them what price *they* would accept to burn the bodies of their fathers. The Indians exclaim against the bare thought of such a horror. Custom, Pindar had said and Herodotus echoes, is king of the world; and men began to distinguish between custom and nature. They felt that their own conventions and institutions required justification; the authority of usage and antiquity was not enough; and they compared human society with nature. The appeal to nature led indeed to very opposite theories. In the sight of nature, it was said, all are equal; birth and wealth are indifferent; therefore the state should be built on the basis of perfect equality. On the other hand, it was argued that in the state of nature the strong man subdues the weaker and rules over them; therefore monarchy is the natural constitution. But it matters little what particular inferences were drawn; for no attempt was made to put them into practice. The main point is that the questioning spirit was active; there were clever men everywhere, who refused to take anything on authority; who always asked, how do you know? and claimed to discuss all things in heaven and earth.

It was in this atmosphere of critical inquiry and scepticism that Greece had to provide for the higher education of her youth, which the practical conditions of the democracy demanded. The demand was met by teachers who travelled about and gave general instruction in the art of speaking and in the art of reasoning, and, out of

The sophists.

their encyclopaedic knowledge, lectured on all possible subjects. They received fees for their courses, and were called Sophists, of which name perhaps our best equivalent is "professors." Properly a sophist meant one who was eminently proficient in some particular art—in poetry, for instance, or cookery. As applied to the teachers who educated the youths who were able to pay, the name acquired a slightly unfavourable colour—partly owing to the distrust felt by the masses towards men who know too much, partly to the prejudice which in Greece always existed more or less against those who gave their services for pay, partly too to the jealousy of those who were too poor to pay the fees and were consequently at a great disadvantage in public life compared with men whom a sophist had trained. But this haze of contempt which hung about the sophistic profession did not imply the idea that the professors were impostors, who deliberately sought to hoodwink the public by arguments in which they did not believe themselves. That suggestion—which has determined the modern meaning of "sophist" and "sophistry"—was first made by the philosopher Plato, and it is entirely unhistorical.

Their writings.

The sophists did not confine themselves to teaching. They wrote much; they discussed occasional topics, criticised political affairs, diffused ideas; and it has been said that this part of their activity supplied in some measure the place of modern journalism. But the greatest of the professors were much more than either teachers or journalists. They not only diffused but set afloat ideas; they enriched the world with contributions to knowledge. They were all alike rationalists, spreaders of enlightenment; but they were very various in their views and doctrines. Gorgias of Leontini, Protagoras of Abdera, Prodicus of Ceos, Hippias of Elis, Socrates of Athens, each had his own strongly marked individuality. To Socrates, who has a place apart from the others, we shall revert in a later chapter.

Prodicus.

Supplices 196.

Prota-goras.

Prodicus of Ceos was a pessimist; and it was doubtless he whom the poet Euripides meant by the man who considered the ills of men to be more in number than their good things. It was Prodicus who invented the famous fable of Heracles at the crossway choosing between virtue and pleasure. Of all the sophists Protagoras was perhaps the greatest. He first distinguished the parts of speech and founded the science of grammar for Europe. His activity as a teacher was chiefly at Athens, where he seems to have been intimate with Pericles. The story that Pericles and Protagoras spent a whole day arguing on the theory of punishment—a question which is still unsettled—illustrates the services which the sophists rendered to speculation. The retributive theory of justice, which logically enough led to the trial and punishment of animals and inanimate things, was called in question; and a counter theory started that the object of punishment was to deter. Protagoras was a victim of the religious prejudices of the Athenians. He wrote a theological book, which he published by reading it aloud before a chosen audience in the house of his friend Euripides. The thesis of the work is probably contained in the first sentence: "In regard to the gods I cannot know that they exist, nor yet that they do not exist; for many things hinder such knowledge,—the obscurity of the matter, and the shortness of human life." Protagoras may have himself *believed* in the gods; what he asserted was that their existence could not be a matter of *knowledge*. Unluckily the book itself has perished. For a certain Pythodorus came forward as the standard-bearer of the state religion, and accused Protagoras of impiety. The philosopher deemed it wise to flee from Athens; he sailed for Sicily and was lost at sea. When Euripides makes the choir of Thracian women in his play of *Palamedes* cry bitterly, "Ye have slain, O Greeks, ye have slain the nightingale of the Muses, the wizard bird that did no wrong," the poet was thinking of the dead friend who had come from the Thracian city. The sale of the book of Protagoras was forbidden in Athens, and all copies that could be found were publicly burned.

His flight from Athens. (415 B.C.)

The case of Protagoras was not the only case of the kind. Years before, the philosopher Anaxagoras had been condemned for impiety; years after, Socrates would be condemned. These cases show that the Athenians were not more enlightened than other peoples, or less prejudiced. The attitude of Protagoras to theology was perfectly compatible with a fervent devotion to the religion of the state; but an Athenian jury was not sufficiently well-educated to discern this. When we admire the spread of knowledge and reasoning in the fifth century, we must remember that the mass of citizens was not reached by the new light; they were still sunk in ignorance, suspicious and jealous of the training which could be got only by sons of the comparatively well-to-do, or those who were exceptionally intellectual.

Gorgias was a philosophical thinker and a politician, but he won his renown as an orator and a stylist. He taught Greece how to write a new kind of prose—not the cold style which appeals only to the understanding, but a brilliant style, rhythmic, flowery in diction, full of figures, speaking to the sense and imagination. In the inscription of a statue which his grand-nephew erected to him at Olympia, it is said: "No mortal ever invented a fairer art, to temper

Gorgias of Leontini.

the soul for manlihood and virtue." Wherever he went he was received with enthusiasm; we shall presently meet him as an ambassador at Athens.

Euripides.

His critical spirit.

The sophists were the chief, the professional expounders of the intellectual movement. But the exaltation of reason had a no less powerful supporter in the poet Euripides. He used the tragic stage to disseminate rationalism; he undermined the popular religion from the very steps of the altar. By the necessity of the case he accomplished his work indirectly, but with consummate dexterity. Aeschylus and Sophocles had reverently modified religious legend, adapting it to their own ideals, interpreting it so as to satisfy their own moral standard. Euripides takes the myths just as he finds them, and contrives his dramas so as to bring the absurdities into relief. He does not acquiesce, like the older tragic poets, in the ways of the gods with men; he is not content to be a resigned pessimist. He will receive nothing on authority; he declines to bow to the orthodox opinions of his respectable fellow-countrymen, on such matters as the institution of slavery, or the position of women in society. He refuses to endorse the inveterate prejudice which prevailed even at Athens in favour of noble birth. But perhaps nothing is so significant as his attitude to the contempt which the Greeks universally felt for other races than their own. Nowhere is Euripides more sarcastic than when, in his *Medea,* he makes Jason pose as a benefactor of the woman whom he has basely betrayed, on the ground that he has brought her out of an obscure barbarian home, and enabled her to enjoy the privilege of—living in Greece.

The Antigone, 442 or 441 B.C., March-April.

Yet we need not go to the most daring thinkers, to Euripides and the sophists, to discern the spirit of criticism at work. The Periclean age has left us few more significant, and certainly no more beautiful, monuments than a tragic drama which won the first prize at the great Dionysia a few years after the Thirty Years' Peace. The soul of Sophocles was in untroubled harmony with the received religion; but, living in an atmosphere of criticism and speculation, even he could not keep his mind aloof from the questions which were debated by the thoughtful men of his time. He took as the motive of his *Antigone* a deep and difficult question of political and of ethical science—the relation of the individual citizen to the state. What shall a man do if his duty of obedience to the government of his country conflicts with other duties? Are there any obligations higher than that of loyalty to the laws of his city? The poet answers that there are such,—for instance, certain obligations of religion. He justifies Antigone in her disobedience to the king's decree. The motive lends itself to dramatic treatment, and never has it been handled with such consummate art as by him who first saw its possibilities. But it is worth observing that the *Antigone*, besides its importance in the history of dramatic poetry, has a high significance in the development of European thought, as the first presentation of a problem which both touches the very roots of ethical theory and is, in daily practice, constantly clamouring for solution.

CHAPTER X[1]

THE WAR OF ATHENS WITH THE PELOPONNESIANS (431-421 B.C.)

THE empire and commercial supremacy of Athens had, as we have seen, swiftly drawn a war upon herself and Greece. That war had been indecisive; it had taught her some lessons, but it had not cooled her ambition or crippled her trade; and it was therefore inevitable that she should have to fight again. We have now to follow the second phase of the struggle, up to the culmination of that antagonism between Dorian and Ionian, of which the Greeks of this period never lost sight.

SECT. 1. THE PRELUDE OF THE WAR

The incidents which led up to the "Peloponnesian War" are connected with two Corinthian colonies, Corcyra and Potidaea; Corcyra which had always been an unfilial daughter; Potidaea which, though maintaining friendly relations with Corinth, had become a member of the Athenian Confederacy.

Incident of Epidamnus, 435 B.C.,

(1) One of those party struggles in an insignificant city, which in Greece were often the occasion of wars between great states, had taken place in Epidamnus, a colony of Corcyra. The people, harassed by the banished nobles and their barbarian allies, asked help from their mother-city. Corcyra refused, and Epidamnus turned to

leads to war between Corcyra and Corinth.

Corinth. The Corinthians sent troops and a number of new colonists. The Corcyraeans, highly resenting this interference, demanded their dismissal, and when the demand was refused, blockaded the isthmus of Epidamnus. Corinth then made preparations for an expedition against Corcyra; and Corcyra in alarm sent envoys to Corinth, proposing to refer the matter for arbitration to such Peloponnesian states as both should agree upon. But the Corinthians refused the arbitration, and sent a squadron of seventy-five ships

Corcyraean naval victory

with 2000 hoplites against the Corcyraeans. The powerful navy of Corcyra consisted of 120 ships, of which forty were besieging Epidamnus. With the remaining eighty they won a complete victory

---

[1] The citations from Thucydides in this chapter are taken from Jowett's translation.

over the Corinthians outside the Ambracian gulf; and on the same day Epidamnus surrendered. During the rest of the year Corcyra had command of the Ionian sea and her triremes sailed about damaging the allies of Corinth.

(435 B.C., spring). Surrender of Epidamnus.

But Corinth began to prepare for a greater effort against her powerful and detested colony. The work of preparation went on for two years. The report of the ships she was building and the navies she was hiring frightened Corcyra. For, while Corinth had the Peloponnesian league at her back, Corcyra had no allies, and belonged neither to the Athenian nor to the Spartan league. It was her obvious policy to seek a connexion with Athens, and she determined to do so. The Corinthians hearing of this intention, tried to thwart it; for they had good reason to fear a combination of the Athenian with the Corcyraean navy. And so it came to pass that the envoys of Corcyra and Corinth appeared together before the Assembly of Athens. The arguments which Thucydides has put into their mouths express clearly the bearings of the situation and the importance of the decision for Athens. The main argument for accepting the proffered alliance of Corcyra depends on the assumption that war is imminent. "The Lacedaemonians, fearing the growth of your empire, are eager to take up arms, and the Corinthians, who are your enemies, are all powerful with them. They begin with us, but they will go on to you, that we may not stand united against them in the bond of a common enmity. And it is our business to strike first, and to forestall their designs instead of waiting to counteract them." On this assumption, the alliance of Corcyra offers great advantages. It lies conveniently on the route to Sicily, and it possesses one of the only three considerable navies in Greece. "If the Corinthians get hold of our fleet, and you allow the two to become one, you will have to fight against the united navies of Corcyra and the Peloponnesus. But if you make us your allies, you will have our navy in addition to your own ranged at your side in the impending conflict." The reply of the Corinthian ambassadors was weak. Their appeal to certain past services that Corinth had rendered to Athens could hardly have much effect; for there was nothing but jealousy between the two cities. They might deprecate, but they could not disprove, the notion that Athens would soon have a war with the Peloponnesus on her hands. And as for justice, Corcyra could make as plausible a case as Corinth. The most cogent argument for Corinth was that if Athens allied herself with Corcyra she would take a step which if not in itself violating the Thirty Years' Peace would necessarily involve a violation of it.

434-3 B.C.

Corcyraean and Corinthian embassies at Athens

After two debates the Assembly agreed to an alliance with

Defensive

alliance of
Athens
with
Corcyra.

Corcyra, but of a defensive kind. Athens was only to give armed help, in case Corcyra itself were threatened. By this decision she avoided a direct violation of the treaty. Ten ships were sent to Corcyra with orders not to fight unless Corcyra or some of the places belonging to it were attacked. A great and tumultuous naval

Battle of
Sybota,
433 B.C.
(autumn).

engagement ensued near the islet of Sybota, between Leucimme, the south-eastern promontory of Corcyra, and the Thesprotian mainland. A Corcyraean fleet of 110 ships vas ranged against a Corinthian of 150—the outcome of two years of preparation. The right wing of the Corcyraeans was worsted, and the ten Athenian ships, which had held aloof at first, interfered to prevent its total discomfiture. In the evening the sudden sight of twenty new Athenian ships on the horizon caused the Corinthians to retreat, and the next day they declined battle. This seemed an admission of defeat, and justified the Corcyraeans in raising a trophy; but the Corinthians also raised a trophy, for they had come off best in the battle. They returned home then, and on their way captured Anactorion, which Corcyra and Corinth held in common. Corinth treated the Corcyraeans who had been taken captive in the battle with great consideration. Most of them were men of importance and it was hoped that through them Corcyra might ultimately be won over to friendship with Corinth. It will be seen afterwards that the hope was not ill-founded.[2]

Revolt of
Potidaea
from
Athens.

(2) The breach with Corinth forced Athens to look to the security of her interests in the Chalcidic peninsula, where Corinth had a great deal of influence. The city of Potidaea, which occupies and guards the isthmus of Pallene, was a tributary ally of Athens, but received its annual magistrates from its mother-city, Corinth. Im-

(433 B.C.)

mediately after the battle of Sybota, Athens required the Potidaeans to raze the city-walls on the south side where they were not needed for protection against Macedonia, and to abandon the system of Corinthian magistrates. The Potidaeans refused; they were

(Winter,
433-2 B.C.)

supported by the promise of Sparta to invade Attica, in case Potidaea were attacked by Athens. But the situation was complicated by the policy of the Macedonian king, Perdiccas, who had been formerly the friend of Athens but was now her adversary, because she had befriended his brothers who were leagued against him. He conceived and organised a general revolt of Chalcidice against Athens; and even persuaded the Chalcidians to pull down their cities on the coast and concentrate themselves in the strong inland town of

---

[2] A report of the expenses of Athens on this Corcyraean expedition has been partially preserved on a stone. The ships that sailed first and those that followed are distinguished.

Olynthus. Thus the revolt of Potidaea, while it has its special causes in connexion with the enmity of Athens and Corinth, under another aspect forms part of a general movement in that quarter against the Athenian dominion.

The Athenians began operations in Macedonia, but soon advanced against Potidaea and gained an advantage over the Corinthian general, Aristeus, who had arrived with some Peloponnesian forces. This battle has a particular interest; for a graven stone still speaks to us of the sorrow of Athens for the men who fell fighting foremost before Potidaea's walls and "giving their lives in barter for glory ennobled their country." [3] The Athenians then invested the city. So far the Corinthians had acted alone. Now, seeing the danger of Potidaea, they took active steps to incite the Lacedaemonians to declare war against Athens.

Pericles knew that war was coming, and he promptly struck—not with sword or spear, but with a more cruel and deadly weapon. Megara had assisted Corinth at the battle of Sybota; the Athenians passed a measure excluding the Megarians from the markets and ports of their empire. The decree spelt economical ruin to Megara, and Megara was an important member of the Peloponnesian league; the Athenian statesmen knew how to strike. The comic poets sang how

> The Olympian Pericles in wrath
> Fulmined o'er Greece and set her in a broil
> With statutes worded like a drinking catch:
> No Megarian on land
> Nor in market shall stand
> Nor sail on the sea nor set foot on the strand.[4]

The allies appeared at Sparta and brought formal charges against Athens of having broken the Thirty Years' Peace and committed various acts of injustice. Some Athenian envoys who were at Sparta —ostensibly for other business—were given an opportunity of replying. But arguments and recriminations were superfluous; it did not matter in the least whether Athens could defend this transaction or Corinth could make good that charge. For in the case of an inevitable war the causes openly alleged seldom correspond with the motives which really govern. It was not the Corcyraean incidents, or the siege of Potidaea, or the Megarian decree that caused the Peloponnesian War, though jointly they hastened its outbreak; it was the fear and jealousy of the Athenian power. The only question was whether it was the right hour to engage in that unavoidable

Battle of Potidaea, c. Sept. 432 B.C

Megarian Decree, 432 B.C., autumn.

First Assembly at Sparta

---

[3] This inscription is preserved in the British Museum.
[4] From Aristoph. *Acharnians,* transl. Tyrrell.

struggle. The Spartan king, Archidamus, advised delay. "Do not take up arms yet. War is not an affair of arms, but of money which gives to arms their use, and which is needed above all things when a continental is fighting against a maritime power. Let us find money first, and then we may safely allow our minds to be excited by the speeches of our allies." But the ephors were in favour of war. Sthenelaidas, in a short and pointed speech, put the question, not, Shall we declare war? but Has the treaty been broken and are the Athenians in the wrong? It was decided that the Athenians were in the wrong, and this decision necessarily led to a declaration of war. But before that declaration was made, the approval of the Delphic oracle was gained, and a general assembly of the allies gathered at Sparta and agreed to the war.

'Second Assembly.

Thucydides chose the setting well for his brilliant contrast between the characters and spirits and aims of the two great protagonists who now prepare to stand face to face on the stage of Hellenic history. He makes the Corinthian envoys, at the first assembly in Sparta, the spokesmen of his comparison. "You have never considered, O Lacedaemonians, what manner of men are these Athenians with whom you will have to fight, and how utterly unlike yourselves. They are revolutionary, equally quick in the conception and in the execution of every new plan; while you are conservative— careful only to keep what you have, originating nothing, and not acting even when action is most necessary. They are bold beyond their strength; they run risks which prudence would condemn; and in the midst of misfortune they are full of hope. Whereas it is your nature, though strong to act feebly; when your plans are most prudent, to distrust them; and when calamities come upon you, to think that you will never be delivered from them. They are impetuous and you are dilatory; they are always abroad, and you are always at home. For they hope to gain something by leaving their homes; but you are afraid that any new enterprise may imperil what you have already. When conquerors, they pursue their victory to the utmost; when defeated, they fall back the least. Their bodies they devote to the country, as though they belonged to other men; their true self is their mind, which is most truly their own when employed in her service. When they do not carry out an intention which they have formed, they seem to have sustained a personal bereavement; when an enterprise succeeds they have gained a mere instalment of what is to come; but if they fail, they at once conceive new hopes and so fill up the void. With them alone to hope is to have, for they lose not a moment in the execution of an idea. This is the lifelong task, full of danger and toil, which they are always imposing upon

The contrast, drawn by Thucydides, between the Athenians and Lacedaemonians.

themselves. None enjoy their good things less, because they are always seeking for more. To do their duty is their only holiday, and they deem the quiet of inaction to be as disagreeable as the most tiresome business. If a man should say of them, in a word, that they were born neither to have peace themselves nor to allow peace to other men, he would simply speak the truth."

On the present occasion, however, the Athenians did not give an example of that promptness in action which is contrasted in this passage with the dilatory habits of the Spartans; we shall presently see why. It was the object of Sparta to gain time; accordingly she sent embassies to Athens with trivial demands. She required the Athenians to drive out the "curse of the goddess," which rested on the family of the Alcmaeonidae. This was a raking up of history, two centuries old—the episode of Cylon's conspiracy; the point of it lay in the fact that Pericles, on his mother's side, belonged to the accursed family. Athens replied by equally trivial demands—the purification of the curse of Athena of the Brazen House, and of the curse of Taenarus, where some Helots had been murdered in the temple of Poseidon. These amenities, which served the purpose of Sparta by gaining time, were followed by an ultimatum, in the sense that Athens might still have peace if she restored the independence of the Hellenes. There was a peace party at Athens, but Pericles carried the day. "Let us send the ambassadors away"—he said— "giving them this answer: That we will not exclude the Megarians from our markets and harbours, if the Lacedaemonians will not exclude foreigners, whether ourselves or our allies, from Sparta; for the treaty no more forbids the one than the other. That we will concede independence to the cities, if they were independent when we made the treaty, and as soon as the Lacedaemonians allow their subject states to be governed as they choose, not for the interest of Lacedaemon but for their own. Also that we are willing to offer arbitration according to the treaty. And that we do not want to begin the war, but intend to defend ourselves if attacked. This answer will be just and befits the dignity of the city. We must be aware, however, that the war will come; and the more willing we are to accept the situation, the less ready will our enemies be to lay hands upon us." Pericles was in no haste to draw the sword; he had delivered a blow already by the Megarian decree.

The peoples of Greece were parted as follows on the sides of the two chief antagonists. *Sparta* commanded the whole Peloponnesus, except her old enemy Argos, and Achaea; [5] she commanded the Isthmus, for she had both Corinth and Megara; in northern Greece

Diplomatic futilities.

(Above, p. 311.)

[5] Pellene alone was on the Peloponnesian side.

she had Boeotia, Phocis, and Locris; in western Greece, Ambracia, Anactorion, and the island of Leucas. In western Greece, *Athens* commanded the Acarnanians, Corcyra, and Zacynthus, as well as the Messenians of Naupactus; in northern Greece she had Plataea; and these were her only allies beyond her confederacy. Of that confederacy Lesbos and Chios were now the only two independent states. In addition to the navies of Lesbos, Chios, and Corcyra, Athens had 300 ships of her own.[6]

SECT. 2. GENERAL VIEW OF THE WAR. THUCYDIDES

Perspective of the war of Athens with the Peloponnesians.

The war on which we are now entering is a resumption, on a somewhat greater scale, of the war which was concluded by the Thirty Years' Peace. Here too the Corinthians are the most active instigators of the opposition to Athens. The Spartans are but half-hearted leaders, and have to be spurred by their allies. The war lasts ten years, and is concluded by the Peace of Nicias. But hostilities begin again, and pass for a time to a new scene of warfare, the island of Sicily. This war ends with the battle of Aegospotami, which decided the fate of the Athenian empire. Thus during fifty-five years Athens was contending for her empire with the Peloponnesians, and this conflict falls into three distinct wars: the first ending with the Thirty Years' Peace, the second with the Peace of Nicias, the third with the battle of Aegospotami. But while there is a break of thirteen years between the first war and the second, there is hardly any break between the second war and the third. Hence the second and the third, which have been united in the History of Thucydides, are generally grouped closely together and called by the common name of the "Peloponnesian War." This name is never used by Thucydides; but it shows how Athenian the sympathies of historians have always been. From the Peloponnesian point of view the conflict would be called the "Attic War."

Three periods: (1) 460-445 B.C.; (2) 431-421; (3) 420-404.

It will not be amiss to repeat here what the true cause of the struggle was. Athens was resolved to maintain, in spite of Greece, her naval empire; and thus far she was responsible. But there is no reason to suppose that she had any design of seriously increasing her empire; and the idea of some modern historians that Pericles undertook the war in the hope of winning supremacy over all Hellas is contrary to the plain facts of the case.

This war has attained a celebrity in the world's history which

---

[6] Athens had 1200 cavalry, including mounted archers; 1800 foot archers; 13,000 hoplites for field service; 16,000 hoplites (of elder and younger men, and metics) for garrison service.

considering its scale and its consequences, may seem unmerited. A domestic war between small Greek states may be thought a slight matter indeed, compared with the struggle in which Greece was arrayed against the might of Persia. But the Peloponnesian war has had an advantage which has been granted to no other episode in the history of Hellas. It has been recorded by the first and the greatest of Greek critical historians. To read the book which Thucydides, the son of Olorus, has bequeathed to posterity is in itself a liberal education; a lesson in politics and history which is, as he aimed to make it, "a possession for ever." Only a few years can have separated the day on which Herodotus completed his work and the day on which Thucydides began his. But from the one to the other there is a sheer leap. When political events have passed through the brain of Herodotus, they come out as delightful stories. With the insatiable curiosity of an inquirer, he has little political insight; he has the instinct of a literary artist, his historical methods are rudimentary. The splendid work of Herodotus has more in common with the epic poets who went before him than with the historians who came after him. When he began to collect material for his history, the events of the Persian invasion were already encircled with a halo of legend, so that he had a subject thoroughly to his taste. It is a strange sensation to turn from the naïve, uncritical, entrancing story-teller of Halicarnassus to the grave historian of Athens. The first History, in the true sense of the word, sprang full-grown into life, like Athena from the brain of Zeus; and it is still without a rival. Severe in its reserves, written from a purely intellectual point of view, unencumbered with platitudes and moral judgments, cold and critical, but exhibiting the rarest powers of dramatic and narrative art, the work of Thucydides is at every point a contrast to the work of Herodotus. Mankind might well despair if the science of criticism had not advanced further since the days of Thucydides; and we are not surprised to find that when he deals, on the threshold of his work, with the earlier history of Greece, he fails to carry his sceptical treatment far enough and accepts some traditions which on his own principles he should have questioned. But the interval which divides Thucydides from his elder contemporary Herodotus is a whole heaven; the interval which divides Thucydides from a critic of our own day is small indeed. Reserved as he is, Thucydides cannot disguise that he was a democrat of the Periclean school; he makes no secret of his admiration for the political wisdom of Pericles.

It must be granted that the incidents of the war would lose something of their interest, that the whole episode would be shorn of

The
History of
Thucy-
dides.

Contrast
of Thucy-
dides with
Hero-
dotus.

much of its dignity and eminence, if Thucydides had not deigned to be its historian. But it was not a slight or unworthy theme. It is the story of the decline and fall of the Athenian empire, and at this period Athens is the centre of ecumenical history. The importance of the war is not impaired by the smallness of the states, which were involved in it. For in these small states lived those political ideas and institutions which concerned the future development of mankind far more than any movements in barbarous kingdoms, however great their territory.

The war of ten years, which now began, may seem at first sight to have consisted of a number of disconnected and haphazard incidents. But both the Athenians and the Peloponnesians had definite objects in view. Their plans were determined by the nature of their own resources, and by the geography of the enemy's territories.

Key to the operations of the war.

The key to the war is the fundamental fact that it was waged between a power which was mainly continental and a power which was mainly maritime. From the nature of the case, the land-power is obliged to direct its attacks chiefly on the continental possessions of the sea-power, while the sea-power has to confine itself to attacking the maritime possessions of the land-power. It follows that the small land army of the sea-power, and the small fleet of the land-power, are each mainly occupied with the work of defence, and are seldom free to act on the offensive. Hence the maritime possessions of the maritime power and the inland possessions of the continental power are not generally the scene of warfare. These considerations simplify the war. The points at which the Peloponnesians can attack Athens with their land forces are Attica itself and Thrace. Accordingly Attica is invaded almost every year, and there is constant warfare in Thrace; but the war is hardly ever carried into the Aegean or to the Asiatic coast, except in consequence of some special circumstance, such as the revolt of an Athenian ally. On the other hand the offensive operations of Athens are mainly in the west of Greece, about the islands of the Ionian sea and near the mouth of the Corinthian gulf. That was the region where they had the best prospect, by their naval superiority, of detaching members from the Peloponnesian alliance. Thrace, Attica, and the seas of western Greece are therefore the chief and constant scenes of the war. There are episodes elsewhere, but they are to some extent accidental.

Pericles had completely abandoned the policy of continental enterprise which had led up to the Thirty Years' Peace. That enterprise had been a departure from the policy, initiated by Themistocles, of concentrating all the energy of Athens on the development of her naval power. Pericles returned to this policy without reserve, and he appears, at the outbreak of the war, under the inspiration of the Salaminian spirit. Athens is now to show the same extreme independence of her land, the same utter confidence in her ships, which she had shown when the Mede approached her borders. "Let us give up lands and houses," said Pericles, "but keep a watch over the city and the sea. We should not under any irritation at the loss of our property give battle to the Peloponnesians, who far outnumber us. Mourn not for houses or lands, but for men; men may give these, but these will not give men. If I thought that you would listen to me, I would say to you: Go yourselves and destroy them, and thereby prove to the Peloponnesians that none of these things will move you." For "such is the power which the empire of the sea gives." [7] This was the spirit in which Pericles undertook the war.

The policy of sacrificing Attica was no rash or perverse audacity; it was only part of a well-considered system of strategy, for which Pericles has been severely blamed. His object was to wear out the enemy, not to attempt to subjugate or decisively defeat. He was determined not to court a great battle, for which the land forces of Athens were manifestly insufficient: on land Boeotia alone was a match for her. He adopted the strategy of "exhaustion," as it has been called,—the strategy which consists largely in manœuvring, and considers the economy of one's own forces as solicitously as the damaging of the foe; which will accept battle only under certain conditions; which is always on the watch for favourable opportunities, but avoids great risks. The more we reflect on the conditions of the struggle and the nature of the Athenian resources, the more fully will the plan of Pericles approve itself as the strategy uniquely suitable to the circumstances. Nor will the criticism that he neglected the land defences of Attica, and the suggestion that he should have fortified the frontier against invasions, bear close examination. The whole Athenian land army would have been required to garrison both the Begarian and Boeotian frontiers, and there would have been no troops left for operations elsewhere. Nor would it have been easy for a citizen army to abide on duty, as would in this case have been necessary, for a large part of the year. It was quite in accord with the spirit of the patient strategy of Pericles that he refrained from the temptation of striking a blow at the enemy, when they had resolved on war but were not yet prepared. One effective blow he had indeed struck, the decree against Megara; to damage the foe commercially was an essential part of his method. Within a few years this method would doubtless have been crowned with success

[7] Jowett's translation.

and brought about a peace favourable to Athens, but for untoward events which he could not foresee.

SECT. 3. THE THEBAN ATTACK ON PLATAEA

Theban night attack on Plataea (March 431 B.C.).

The declaration of war between the two great states of Greece was a signal to smaller states to profit by the situation for the gratification of their private enmities. On a dark moonless night, in the early spring, a band of 300 Thebans entered Plataea, invited and admitted by a small party in the city. Instead of at once attacking the chiefs of the party which supported the Athenian alliance, they took up their post in the agora and made a proclamation, calling upon the Plataeans to join the Boeotian league. The Plataeans, as a people, with the exception of a few malcontents, were cordially attached to Athens; but they were surprised, and in the darkness of the night exaggerated the numbers of the Thebans. They acceded to the Theban demand, but in the course of the negotiation discovered how few their enemies were. Breaking down the party-walls between their houses, so as not to attract notice by moving in the streets, they concerted a plan of action. When all was arranged, they barricaded the streets leading to the agora with waggons, and then attacked the enemy before dawn. The Thebans were soon dispersed. They lost their way in the strange town and wandered about, pelted by women from the house-tops, through narrow streets deep in mud, for heavy rain had fallen during the night. A few clambered up the city wall and cast themselves down on the other side. But the greater number rushed through the door of a large building, mistaking it for one of the town-gates, and were thus captured alive by the Plataeans. A few escaped who reached an unguarded gate, and cut the wooden bolt with an axe which a woman gave them.

The 300 were only the vanguard of a large Theban force which was advancing slowly in the rain along the eight miles of road which lay between Thebes and Plataea. They were delayed by the crossing of the swollen Asopus river, and they arrived too late. The Plataeans sent out a herald to them requiring them to do no injury to Plataean property outside the walls, if they valued the lives of the Theban prisoners. According to the Theban account, the Plataeans definitely promised to restore the prisoners, when the troops evacuated their territory. But the Plataeans afterwards denied this, and said that they merely promised (without the sanction of an oath) to restore the prisoners in case they came to an agreement after negotiation. It matters little. The Plataeans as soon as they had conveyed all their property into the city, put their prisoners to

Theban prisoners executed.

death, 180 in number. Even on their own showing they were clearly guilty of an act of ill faith, which is explained by the deep hatred existing between the two states. A message had been immediately sent to Athens. The Athenians seized all the Boeotians in Attica, and sent a herald to Plataea bidding them not to injure their prisoners; but the herald found the Thebans dead. The Athenians immediately set Plataea ready for a siege. They provisioned it with corn, removed the women, children, and old men; and sent a garrison of eighty Athenians.

Athens supports Plataea.

The Theban attack on Plataea was a glaring violation of the Thirty Years' Peace, and it hastened the outbreak of the war. Greece was now in a state of intense excitement at the approaching struggle of the two leading cities; oracles flew about; and a recent earthquake in Delos was supposed to be significant. Public opinion was generally favourable to the Lacedaemonians, who seemed to be the champions of liberty against a tyrannical city.

Both sides meditated enlisting the aid of Persia. The Lacedaemonians negotiated with the states of Italy and Sicily, for the purpose of obtaining a large navy to crush the Athenians. But this scheme also fell through; the cities of the west were too busy with their own political interests to send ships and money to old Greece. Athens indeed had also cast her eyes westward; and when she embraced the alliance of Corcyra, she seems to have been forming connexions with Sicily. At all events, in the same year ambassadors of Rhegium and Leontini appeared together at Athens; and at the same meeting of the Assembly alliances were formed with both cities on the proposal of Callias. The object of Chalcidian Leontini was doubtless to gain support against Corinthian Syracuse; while the motive of Rhegium may have been connected with the affairs of Thurii, the rebellious daughter of Athens herself. But these alliances led to no action of Athens in the west for six years to come.

Treaties of Athens with Leontini and with Rhegium, 433 B.C.

SECT. 4. THE PLAGUE

When the corn was ripe, in the last days of May, king Archidamus with two-thirds of the Peloponnesian army invaded Attica. From the isthmus he had sent on Melesippus to Athens, if even at the last hour the Athenians might yield. But Pericles had persuaded them to receive no embassies, once the enemy were in the field; the envoy had to leave the borders of Attica before the sun set. And Thucydides, after the manner of Herodotus, marks the formal commencement of the war by repeating the impressive words which Melesippus uttered as he stood on the frontier: "This day will be

First invasion of Attica, 431 B.C.

the beginning of many woes to the Greeks." Archidamus then laid siege to Oenoe, a fortress on Mount Cithaeron, but failed to take it, and his delay gave the Athenians time to complete their preparations. They brought into the city their family and their goods, while their flocks and herds were removed to the island of Euboea. The influx of the population into the city caused terrible crowding. A few had the homes of their friends, but the majority pitched their tents in the vacant spaces, and housed themselves, as the peace-party bitterly said, in barrels and vultures' nests. They seized temples and shrines, and even the ancient enclosure of the Pelargicon on the north-west of the Acropolis was occupied, though its occupation was deprecated by a dark oracle. Subsequently the crowding was relieved when the Piraeus and the space between the Long Walls were utilised.

Archidamus first ravaged the plain of Eleusis and Thria. He then crossed into the Cephisian plain by the pass between Mounts Aegaleos and Parnes, and halted under Parnes in the deme of Acharnae, whence he could see, in the distance, the Acropolis of Athens. The proximity of the invaders caused great excitement in Athens, and roused furious opposition to Pericles who would not allow the troops to go forth against them—except a few flying columns of horse in the immediate neighbourhood of the city. Pericles had been afraid that Archidamus, who was his personal friend, might spare his property, either from friendship or policy; so he took the precaution of declaring to his fellow-citizens that he would give his lands to the people, if they were left unravaged. The invader presently advanced northward, between Parnes and Pentelicus, to Decelea, and proceeded through the territory of Oropus to Boeotia.

The Athenians meanwhile had been operating by sea. They had sent 100 ships round the Peloponnesus. An attack on Methone, on the Messenian coast, failed; the place was saved by a daring Spartan officer, Brasidas, who by this exploit began a distinguished career. But the fleet was more successful further north. The important island of Cephallenia was won over, and some towns on the Acarnanian coast were taken. Measures were also adopted for the protection of Euboea against the Locrians of the opposite mainland. The Epicnemidian town of Thronion was captured, and the desert island of Atalanta, over against Opus, was made a guard station. More important was the drastic measure which Athens adopted against her subjects and former rivals, the Dorians of Aegina. She felt that they were not to be trusted, and the security of her positions in the Saronic gulf was of the first importance. So she drove

Athens wins Cephallenia and Sollion. Locrian expedition.

End of the Aeginetans. Aegina becomes

out the Aeginetans and settled the island with a cleruchy of her own citizens. Aegina thus became, like Salamis, annexed to Attica. Just as the Messenian exiles had been befriended by Athens and given a new home, so the Aeginetan exiles were now befriended by Sparta and were settled in the region of Thyreatis, in the north of Laconia. Thyreatis was the Lacedaemonian answer to Naupactus.

part of Attica.

When Archidamus left Attica, Pericles consulted for emergencies of the future by setting aside a reserve fund of money, and a reserve armament of ships. There had been as much as 9700 talents in the treasury, but the expenses of the buildings on the Acropolis and of the war at Potidaea had reduced this to 6000. It was now decreed that 1000 talents of this amount should be reserved, not to be touched unless the enemy were to attack Athens by sea, and that every year 100 triremes should be set apart, with the same object.

£2,619,000

£1,620,000

In winter the Athenians, following an old custom, celebrated the public burial of those who had fallen in the war. The bones were laid in ten cedar boxes, and were buried outside the walls in the Ceramicus. An empty bed, covered with a pall, was carried, for those whose bodies were missing. Pericles pronounced the funeral Panegyric. It has not been preserved; but the spirit and general argument of it have been reproduced in the oration which Thucydides, who must have been one of the audience, has put in his mouth.[8] It is a rare good fortune to possess a picture, drawn by a Pericles and a Thucydides, of the ideal Athens, which Pericles dreamed of creating.

Funeral of those slain in the war.

"There is no exclusiveness," he said, "in our public life, and in our private intercourse. We are not suspicious of one another, nor angry with our neighbour if he does what he likes; we do not put on sour looks at him which, though harmless, are not pleasant. And we have not forgotten to provide for our weary spirits many relaxations from toil; we have regular games and sacrifices throughout the year; at home the style of our life is refined; and the delight which we daily feel in all these things helps to banish melancholy. Because of the greatness of our city the fruits of the whole earth flow in upon us; so that we enjoy the goods of other countries as freely as of our own.

The ideal Athens adumbrated by Pericles.

"Then again our military training is in many respects superior to that of our adversaries. Our city is thrown open to the world, and we never expel a foreigner or prevent him from seeing or learning anything, of which the secret if revealed to an enemy might

[8] We may fancy we can detect some phrases which fell from the lips of Pericles himself: such as "The whole earth is the sepulchre of famous men," or "Athens is the school of Hellas."

profit him. We rely not upon management or trickery, but upon our own hearts and hands. And in the matter of education whereas they from early youth are always undergoing laborious exercises which are to make them brave, we live at ease, and yet are equally ready to face the perils which they face.

"If we prefer to meet danger with a light heart but without laborious training, and with a courage which is gained by habit and not enforced by law, are we not greatly the gainers? Since we do not anticipate the pain, although, when the hour comes, we can be as brave as those who never allow themselves to rest; and thus too our city is equally admirable in peace and in war. For we are lovers of the beautiful, yet simple in our tastes, and we cultivate the mind without loss of manliness. Wealth we employ, not for talk and ostentation, but when there is a real use for it. To avow poverty with us is no disgrace; the true disgrace is in doing nothing to avoid it. An Athenian citizen does not neglect the state because he takes care of his own household; and even those of us who are engaged in business have a very fair idea of politics. We alone regard a man who takes no interest in public affairs, not as a harmless, but as a useless character; and if few of us are originators, we are all sound judges of a policy. The great impediment to action is, in our opinion, not discussion, but the want of that knowledge which is gained by discussion preparatory to action. For we have a peculiar power of thinking before we act and of acting too, whereas other men are courageous from ignorance but hesitate upon reflection."

Then the speaker goes on to describe Athens as the centre of Hellenic culture and to claim that "the individual Athenian in his own person seems to have the power of adapting himself to the most varied forms of action with the utmost versatility and grace." And, he continues, "we shall assuredly not be without witnesses; there are mighty monuments of our power which will make us the wonder of this and of succeeding ages; we shall not need the praises of Homer or any other panegyrist whose poetry may please for the moment, although his representation of the facts will not bear the light of day. For we have compelled every land and every sea to open a path for our valour, and have everywhere planted eternal memorials of our friendship and of our enmity. Such is the city for whose sake these men nobly fought and died; they could not bear the thought that she might be taken from them; and every one of us who survive should gladly toil on her behalf. I would have you day by day fix your eyes upon the greatness of Athens, until you become filled with the love of her; and when you are impressed by the spectacle of her glory, reflect that this empire has been acquired by men who knew their duty and had the courage to do it, who in the hour of conflict had the fear of dishonour always present to them, and who, if ever they failed in an enterprise, would not allow their virtues to be lost to their country, but freely gave their lives to her as the fairest offering which they could present at her feast. The sacrifice which they collectively made was individually repaid to them; for they received again and again each one for himself a praise which grows not old and the noblest of all sepulchres—I speak not of that in which their remains are laid, but of that in which their glory survives and is proclaimed always and on every fitting occasion both in word and deed. For the whole earth is the sepulchre of famous men; not only are they commemorated by columns and inscriptions in their own country, but in foreign lands there dwells also an unwritten memorial of them, graven not on stone but in the hearts of men. Make them your example." [9]

Perhaps we have another funeral monument; a monument in carven stone, of Athenians who were slain in one of the first years of the war. A beautiful relief, found on the Acropolis, shows the helmeted lady of the land, leaning on her spear, with downcast head, and gazing gravely at a slab of stone. It is an attractive interpretation that she is sadly engaged in reading the names of citizens who had recently fallen in defence of her city.

The "Mourning Athena."

Next year the Peloponnesians again invaded Attica, and extended their devastations to the south of the peninsula as far as Laurion. But the Athenians concerned themselves less with this invasion; they had to contend with a more awful enemy within the walls of their city. The Plague had broken out. Thucydides, who was stricken down himself, gives a terrible account of its ravages and the demoralisation which it produced in Athens. The art of medicine was in its first infancy, and the inexperienced physicians were unable to treat the unknown virulent disease, which defied every remedy and was aggravated by the over-crowding, in the heat of summer. The dead lay unburied, the temples were full of corpses; and the funeral customs were forgotten or violated. Dying wretches were gathered about every fountain, seeking to relieve their unquenchable thirst. Men remembered an old oracle which said that "a Dorian war will come and a plague therewith." But the Greek for plague (*loimós*) was hardly distinguishable from the Greek for famine (*limós*)—at the present day they are identical in sound; and people were not quite sure which was the true word. Naturally

430 B.C.: Invasion of Attica.

The Great Plague.

Oracle: λοιμός or λιμός?

---

[9] Jowett's translation.

the verse was now quoted with *loimos;* but, says Thucydides, in case there comes another Dorian war and it is accompanied by a famine, the oracle will be quoted with *limos.*

Origin of the plague.

The same historian—who has given of this pestilence a vivid description, unequalled by later narrators of similar scourges, Procopius, Boccaccio, Defoe—declares that the plague originated in Ethiopia, spread through Egypt over the Persian empire, and then reached the Aegean. But it is remarkable that a plague raged at the same time in the still obscure city of central Italy which was afterwards to become the mistress of Greece. It has been guessed with some plausibility that the infection which reached both Athens and Rome had travelled along the trade-routes from Carthage. The

Effect of the plague on the Athenian population.

Peloponnesus almost entirely escaped. In Athens the havoc of the pestilence permanently reduced the population. The total number of Athenian burghers (of both sexes and all ages) was about 80,000 in the first quarter of the fifth century. Prosperity had raised it to 100,000 by the beginning of the war; but the plague brought it down below the old level which it never reached again.[10]

Sea operations of Athenians.

As in the year before, an Athenian fleet attacked the Peloponnesus, but this time it was the coasts of Argolis,—Epidaurus, Troezen, Hermione, Halieis. The armament was large, 4000 spearmen and 300 horse; it was under the command of Pericles; and it aimed at the capture of Epidaurus, while the Epidaurian troops were absent with their allies in Attica. The attempt miscarried, we know not why; and it is hard to forgive our historian for omitting all the details of this ambitious enterprise, which would have been, if it had succeeded, one of the most important exploits of the war.

Not till the autumn were operations renewed in the west of Greece. The fleet was summoned to the help of the people of Amphilochian Argos, on the eastern shore of the Ambracian gulf. They had been expelled from their own city by their northern neighbours the Ambraciots, and had sought the protection of their southern neighbours the Acarnanians. Athens sent the general Phormio with thirty ships. He stormed Argos, sold the Ambraciots into slavery, and restored the Amphilochians to their city—the most important place in those regions. This was the beginning of a long feud between Argos and Ambracia. In the winter Phormio returned to the west and, making Naupactus his station, guarded the entrance of the Crisaean gulf.

---

[10] The metic class possibly reached the number of 30,000. We cannot estimate the number of slaves in the fifth century; but we know at least that it did not fall far short of that of the free population. At this time they may have numbered about 100,000.

In Thrace meanwhile the siege of Potidaea had been prosecuted throughout the year. The inhabitants had been reduced to such straits that they even tasted human flesh, and in the winter they capitulated. The terms were that the Potidaeans and the foreign soldiers were to leave the city, the men with one garment, the women with two, and a sum of money was to be allowed them. Athens soon afterwards colonised the place. The siege had cost 2000 talents.

Surrender of Potidaea.

Meanwhile the Athenians had been cast into such despair by the plague that they made overtures for peace to Sparta. Their overtures were rejected, and they turned the fury of their disappointment upon Pericles, who had returned unsuccessful from Epidaurus. He was suspended from the post of strategos to which he had been elected in the spring; his accounts were called for and examined by the Council; and an exceptionally large court of 1501 judges was impanelled to try him for the misappropriation of public money. He was found guilty of "theft" to the trifling amount of five talents; the verdict was a virtual acquittal, though he had to pay a fine of ten times the amount; and he was presently re-elected to the post from which he had been suspended. He was in truth indispensable. All the courage, all the patience, all the eloquence of the great statesman were demanded at this crisis. He had to convince Athens that the privileges of her imperial position involved hardships and toils, and that it was dangerous for her to draw back. She must face the fact boldly that if the public opinion of Greece regarded her empire as unjustly gained, it could not safely be laid down. The position of the Imperialist is always vulnerable to assaults on grounds of morality, and the peace party at Athens could make a plausible case against the policy of Pericles. But the imperial instinct of the people responded, in spite of temporary reactions, to his call. Athens was not destined to be guided by him much longer. He had lost his two sons in the plague, and he died about a year later. In his last years he had been afflicted by the indirect attacks of his enemies. Phidias was accused of embezzling part of the public money devoted to the works on the Acropolis, in which he was engaged, and it was implied that Pericles was cognisant of the dishonesty. Phidias was condemned. Then the philosopher Anaxagoras was publicly prosecuted for holding and propagating impious doctrines. Pericles defended his friend, but Anaxagoras was sentenced to pay a fine of five talents, and retired to continue his philosophical studies at Lampsacus. The next attack was upon his mistress, whose name was Aspasia. The comic poet Hermippus charged her likewise with impiety, and

£540,000. Pericles deposed from office of general; tried and fined (c. July, 430 B.C.).

Death of Pericles (autumn 429 B.C.). Attacks upon him. (1) Trial of Phidias (2) Trial of Anaxagoras. £1350. (3) Trial Aspasia, the mistress of Pericles.

The younger Pericles legitimised.

represented her abode as a house of recreation in the worst sense. The pleading of Pericles procured her acquittal, and in the last year of his life the People passed a decree to legitimise her son. The latest words of Pericles express what to the student of the history of civilisation is an important feature of his character—his humanity. "No Athenian ever put on black for an act of mine."

SECT. 5. THE SIEGE AND CAPTURE OF PLATAEA

Third year of the war, 429 B.C.

In the next summer Archidamus was induced by the Thebans, instead of invading Attica, to march across Cithaeron and lay siege to Plataea. Like Elis itself, the Plataean land was sacred,—in memory of the great deliverance of Hellas which had been wrought there; and the Spartan king, when he set foot upon it, called the gods to witness that the Plataeans had first done wrong. He proposed to the Plataeans that they should evacuate their territory, until the end of the war; they might count their trees and their possessions, and all should then be restored to them intact. Having consulted Athens, which promised to protect them, the Plataeans refused, and Archidamus began the siege. The Athenians, however, were true to the policy of avoiding continental warfare, and notwithstanding their promises sent no help. Plataea was a very important position for the Peloponnesians to secure. It commanded the road from Megara to Thebes, by which communications between the Peloponnesus and Boeotia could be maintained most easily without entering Attica.

Site of Plataea.

The visitor to Plataea must not suppose that the city which Archidamus besieged extended over the entire ground plan which now meets his eye. For he sees the circuit of the city as it existed a century later, occupying the whole surface of the low triangular plateau on which the town stood. The Plataea of Archidamus corresponds probably to the southern and higher part of the space occupied by the later town. The wall of the older Plataea cannot have been much more than a mile long; for the small garrison— 400 Plataeans and eighty Athenians—could never have maintained a longer line of defence in a place where nature had done almost nothing to assist them.

The mound.

Having surrounded the city with a palisade to prevent any one from getting out, Archidamus employed his army in building a mound against the southern wall. They worked for seventy days and seventy nights. The Plataeans endeavoured to counteract this by raising the height of their own wall, opposite the mound, by a structure of bricks set in a wooden frame. They protected th[...]

Stratagems of the besieged.

workmen by screens of hide against burning arrows. But as the mound rose higher and higher, a new device was tried. They made a hole in the wall underneath and drew out the earth from the mound. The Peloponnesians met this device by putting into the gap clay packed in baskets of reed; this could not be drawn away quickly like the loose earth. Another plan was then devised by the besieged. They dug a subterranean mine under the wall to some distance beneath the mound, and drew the earth away as they had done before. This effectually retarded the progress of the mound, for, though the besiegers were numerous, they had to carry the earth from a considerable distance. The Plataeans resorted to yet another device. From the two extremities of that portion of the wall which they had raised in height, they built an inner wall, in crescent shape, projecting inwards; so that if the outer wall were taken, the Peloponnesians would have all their labour over again. They also showed ingenuity in frustrating the battering-rams which the besiegers brought against the walls. They placed two poles on the top of the wall, projecting over it; to the ends of these poles they attached a huge beam by means of iron chains. When the engine approached, they let go the beam, which snapped off the head of the battering-ram. The besiegers then made an attempt to set the town on fire. They heaped up faggots along the wall close to the mound, and kindled them with brimstone and pitch. If the prevalent south wind had been blowing down the slopes of the mountain, nothing would have saved the Plataeans from the tremendous conflagration which ensued and rendered the wall unapproachable by the besiegers.

When this device failed the Peloponnesians saw they would have to blockade Plataea. They built a wall of circumvallation, about 100 yards from the city, and dug two fosses one inside and one outside this wall. Then Archidamus left part of his army to maintain the blockade during the winter. The blockaders, of whom about half were Boeotians, established a communication by means of fire signals with Thebes. At the end of another year, the Plataeans saw that they had no longer any hope of help from Athens, and their food was running short. They determined to make an attempt to escape.

The wall of the Peloponnesians looked like a single wall of immense thickness, but it actually consisted of two walls, 16 feet apart. The middle space, which served as quarters for the garrison, was roofed over, and guard was kept on the roof. Along the top there were battlements on each side, and at every tenth battlement there was a tower which covered the whole width from wall to wall.

(1) Raising of the wall. (2) Removing the earth through wall; (3) by a mine.

(4) The inner wall.

The battering rams

The fire.

Blockade autumn 429 to summer 427.

Plan of escape Winter (? Dec.) 428 B.C.

There were passages through the middle of the towers but not at the sides. On wet and stormy nights the guard used to leave the battlements and retire under the shelter of the towers. The escape was attended with much risk and less than half the garrison attempted it. The plan was carefully calculated. They determined the height of the wall by counting and recounting the number of layers of bricks in a spot which had not been plastered; and then constructed ladders of exactly the right length. On a dark night, amid rain and storm, they stole out, crossed the inner ditch, and reached the wall unnoticed. They were lightly equipped, and while their right feet were bare the left were shod, to prevent slipping in the mud. Twelve men, led by Ammeas, ascended first, near two adjacent towers. They killed the guard in each tower, and secured the passages, which they held until all their companions had mounted and descended on the other side. One of the Plataeans, in climbing up on the roof, knocked a brick from one of the battlements; its fall was heard, and the alarm was given. All the besiegers came out on the wall, but in the blackness they could not discover what it was, and no one dared to move from his own place. Moreover the Plataeans in the city distracted their attention, by sallying out on the side opposite to that on which their friends were escaping. The Peloponnesians lit their danger signals to Thebes, but this had also been foreseen by the Plataeans, who by lighting other beacons on their own wall confused the signals of their enemies. But what the Plataeans had most to fear was an attack from a band of 300 men, whose duty it was to patrol outside the wall. While the last of the Plataeans were descending, they arrived with lights. They were thus illuminated themselves and a good mark for the arrows and darts of the Plataeans who were standing along the edge of the outer ditch. This ditch was crossed with difficulty; it was swollen with rain and had a coat of ice too thin to bear. But all got over safely except one archer who was captured on the brink.

Surrender
of Plataea,
427 B.C.

The escape was perhaps effected on the north side of the city. The fugitives at first took the road to Thebes, to put their pursuers off the scent, but when they had left Plataea about a mile behind them, they struck to the right and reached the road from Thebes to Athens near Erythrae. Two hundred and twelve men reached Athens; a few more had started but had turned back before they crossed the wall. This episode is an eminently interesting example of the survival of the fittest; for a melancholy fate awaited those who had not the courage to take their lives in their hands. In the following summer want of food forced them to capitulate at discretion to the Lacedaemonians. Five men were sent from Sparta to decide their fate. But their fate had been already decided through the influence of Thebes. Each prisoner was merely asked, "Have you in the present war done any service to the Lacedaemonians or their allies?" The form of the question implied the sentence, and it was in vain that the Plataeans appealed to the loyalty of their ancestors to the cause of Hellas in the Persian war, or implored the Lacedaemonians to look upon the sepulchres of their own fathers buried in Plataean land and honoured every year by Plataea with the customary offerings. They were put to death, 200 in number, and twenty-five Athenians; and the city was rased to the ground. The Peloponnesians now commanded the road from Megara to Thebes.

It is hard to avoid reproaching the Athenians for impolicy in not coming to the relief of their old and faithful ally, and maintaining a position so important for the communication between the Peloponnese and Boeotia. Their failure to bring succour at the beginning of the siege may be explained by their sufferings from the plague which still prevailed. And in the following year a more pressing danger diverted their attention, the revolt of a member of their maritime confederacy.

Sect. 6. Revolt of Mytilene

Archidamus had invaded Attica for the third time, and had just quitted it, when the news arrived that Mytilene and the rest of Lesbos, with the exception of Methymna, had revolted. This was a great and, as it might seem to Athens, an unprovoked blow. It was not due to any special grievance. The oligarchical government of Mytilene confessed that the city was always well-treated and honoured by Athens. The revolt is all the more interesting and significant on this account. It was a protest of the Hellenic instinct for absolute autonomy against an empire such as the Athenian. The sovereignty of the Lesbian cities was limited in regard to foreign affairs; their relations with other members of the confederacy were subject to control on the part of Athens; and their ships were required for Athenian purposes. Such restraints were irksome, and as they had seen the free allies of Athens, most recently Samos, gradually transformed into subjects, they might fear that this would presently be their own case too. The revolt had been meditated for some years; it was hastened in the end, before all the preparations were made—such as the closing of the harbour of Mytilene by a mole and chain—because the design had been be-

Fourth year of the war, 428 B.C.

trayed to Athens by enemies in Methymna and Tenedos. The Athenians, on the first news, sent ships under Cleïppides to surprise Mytilene at a festival of Apollo, which all the inhabitants used to celebrate outside the walls; but the Mytilenaeans received secret intelligence and postponed the feast. The Lesbians had a large fleet; and the Athenians were feeling so severely the effects of the plague and of the war that the rebellion had a good prospect of success if it had been energetically supported by the Peloponnesians. Envoys who were sent to gain their help, pleaded the cause of Lesbos at the Olympian games which were celebrated this year. At the most august of the Panhellenic festivals, by the banks of the Alpheus, it was a fitting occasion to come forward among the assembled Greeks as champions of the principle of self-government which it is the glory of Greece to have taught mankind. And as Mytilene had no grievance beyond the general injustice of Athens in imposing external limitations on the autonomy of others, her assertion of that principle carried the greater weight. Lesbos was admitted into the Peloponnesian league, but no assistance was sent.

Lesbian
envoys at
Olympia.

The revolt from Athens was accompanied by a constitutional change within the borders of Lesbos itself. Except Methymna in the north, the other cities in the island—Antissa, Eresus, and Pyrrha on her land-locked bay—agreed to merge their own political individualities in the city of Mytilene. By the constitutional process, known as synoecism, Mytilene was now to be to Lesbos what Athens was to Attica. The citizens of Pyrrha, Eresos, and Antissa would henceforward be citizens of Mytilene. Lesbos, with Methymna independent and hostile, would now be what Attica was before the annexation of Eleusis.

Synoe-
cism of
Mytilene.

Meanwhile the Athenians had blockaded the two harbours of Mytilene, and Paches soon arrived with 1000 hoplites, to complete the investment. He built a wall on the land side of the city. At this time the Athenians were in sore want of money, for their funds (with the exception of the reserve) had been exhausted, especially by the expenses of the siege of Potidaea. They were obliged to resort to the expedient of raising money by a property tax.

Autumn,
428 B.C.

This tax, now introduced for the first time, differed both in object and in nature from the property tax of the sixth century. In the first place, it was not imposed permanently but only to meet a temporary crisis; secondly, it was to be used for purely military purposes; thirdly, it was imposed on all property and not merely on land. Economical conditions had changed since the days of Pisistratus, and landed proprietors no longer formed the bulk of the richest men. The four classes of Solon were used for the purpose of

The
Eisphora
(property
tax),
428 B.C.

the assessment; but the minimum incomes for each class were translated into money equivalents, and the capital which such an income implied seems to have been calculated on a sliding scale.[11] Men who had a capital of at least a talent belonged to the highest class; those whose property exceeded half a talent, to the second; one-sixth of a talent qualified for the third; men of less means were exempt. The tax yielded 200 talents.

Probably
a tax on
capital.

£48,000.

Towards the end of the winter, the Spartans sent a man, his name was Salaethus, to assure the people of Mytilene that an armament would be dispatched to their relief. He managed to elude the Athenians and get into the city. The spirits of the besieged rose, and when summer came forty-two ships were sent under the command of Alcidas, and at the same time the Peloponnesians invaded Attica for the fourth time, hoping to distract the attention of the Athenians from Mytilene. The besieged waited and waited, but the ships never came, and the food ran short. Salaethus, in despair, determined to make a sally, and for this purpose armed the mass of the people with shields and spears. But the people, when they got the arms refused to obey and demanded that the oligarchs should bring forth the corn and that all should share it fairly; otherwise, they would surrender the city. This drove the government to anticipate the chance of a separate negotiation on the part of the people; and they capitulated at discretion. Their fate was to be decided at Athens, and meanwhile Paches was to put no man to death.

427 B.C.,
first
months.

May.

Surrender
of
Mytilene.

The fleet of Alcidas had wasted time about the Peloponnesus, and on reaching the island of Myconus received the news that Mytilene was taken. He sailed to Erythrae and there it was proposed to Alcidas that he should attack Mytilene, on the principle that men who have just gained possession of a city are usually off their guard. Another suggestion was that a town on the Asiatic coast should be seized and a revolt excited against Athens in the Ionian district. But these plans were far too good and daring for a Lacedaemonian admiral to adopt. He sailed southward, was pursued by Paches as far as Patmos, and retired into the Peloponnesian waters where he was more at home.

The
expedition
of Alcidas.

The ringleaders of the revolt of Mytilene were sent to Athens, and along with them the Spartan Salaethus, who was immediately put to death. The Assembly met to determine the fate of the prisoners, and decided to put to death not only the most guilty who had

People of
Mytilene
sentenced
to death.

[11] On the ground, doubtless, that rich men got a proportionally larger revenue out of their capital than men of small means (the Zeugitae), whose property consisted often in land solely.

been sent to Athens, but the whole adult male population, and to enslave the women and children. A trireme was immediately dispatched to Paches with this terrible command.

The fact that the Athenian Assembly was persuaded to press the cruel rights of war so far as to decree the extinction of a whole population shows how deep was the feeling of wrath that prevailed against Mytilene. Many things contributed to render that feeling particularly bitter. The revolt had come at a moment when Athens was sore bestead, between the plague and the war. Every Athenian had a grudge against Mytilene; for his own pocket had suffered, through the tax which it had been necessary to impose. And the Imperial pride of the people had been wounded by the unheard-of event of a Peloponnesian fleet sailing in the eastern waters, of which Athens regarded herself as the sole mistress. But above all it was the revolt not of a subject, but of a free ally. Athens could more easily forgive the rebellion of a subject state which tried to throw off her yoke, than repudiation of her leadership by a nominally independent confederate. For the action of Mytilene was in truth an indictment of the whole fabric of the Athenian empire as unjust and undesirable. And the Athenians felt its significance. The mere unreasoning instinct of self-preservation suggested the policy of making a terrible example. It was another question whether this policy was wise.

New class of statesmen.

The calm sense of Pericles was no longer there to guide and enlighten the Assembly. We now find democratic statesmen of a completely different stamp coming forward to take his place. The Assembly is swayed by men of the people—tradesmen, like Cleon, the leather-merchant; Eucrates, the rope-seller; Hyperbolus, the lamp-maker. These men had not, like Aristides, Cimon, and Pericles, family connexions to start and support them; they had no aristocratic traditions as the background of their democratic policy. They were self-made; they won their influence in the state by the sheer force of cleverness, eloquence, industry, and audacity. A man like Cleon, the son of Cleaenetus, whom we now meet holding the unofficial position of leader of the Assembly, must, to attain that eminence, have regularly attended week after week in the Pnyx; he must have mastered the details of political affairs; he must have had the courage to confront the Olympian authority of Pericles, and the dexterity to make some palpable hits; he must have studied the art of speaking and been able to hold his audience. Cleon and the other statesmen of this new type are especially interesting as *the politicians whom the advanced democracy produced and educated*. It would be a grievous error and injustice to suppose that their policy was determined by mere selfish ambition or party malice. Nearly all we know of them is derived from the writings of men who not only condemned their policy but personally disliked them as low-born upstarts. Yet though they may have been vulgar and offensive in their manners, there is abundant evidence that they were able, and there is no proof that they were not generally honest, politicians. To those who regretted the dignity of Pericles, the speech of Cleon or Hyperbolus may have seemed violent and coarse; but Cleon himself could hardly have outdone the coarseness and the violence of the personalities which Demosthenes heaped on Aeschines in a subsequent generation.

These new politicians were for the most part strong imperialists, and Cleon seems to have taken fully to heart the maxim of Pericles, to keep the subject allies "well in hand." It was under his influence that the Assembly vented its indignation against Mytilene by dooming the whole people to slaughter. But when the meeting had dispersed, a partial reaction set in. Men began, in a cooler moment, to realise the inhumanity of their action and to question its policy. The envoys of Mytilene, who had been permitted to come to Athens to plead her cause, seeing this change of feeling, induced the Generals to summon an extraordinary meeting of the Assembly for the following morning, to reconsider the decree. Cleon again came forward to support it on the grounds of both legal justice and good policy. Thucydides represents him as openly asserting the principle that a tyrannical city must use tyrannical methods, and rule by fear, chastising her allies without mercy. The chief speaker on the other side was a certain Diodotus, whose name has won immortality by his action at this famous crisis. Diodotus handled the question entirely as a matter of policy. Cleon had deprecated any appeal to the irrelevant considerations of humanity or pity; Diodotus, carefully avoiding such an appeal, deprecates on his own side with great force Cleon's appeal to considerations of justice. The Mytilenaeans have deserved the sentence of death: certainly; but the argument is entirely irrelevant. The question for Athens to consider is not what Mytilene deserves, but what it is expedient for Athens to inflict. "We are not at law with the Mytilenaeans and do not want to be told what is just; we are considering a matter of policy, and desire to know how we can turn them to account." He then goes on to argue that as a matter of fact the penalty of death is not a deterrent, and that the result of such a severe punishment will be injurious to Athens. A city which has revolted, knowing that whether she comes to terms soon or late the penalty will be the same, will never surrender; money will be wasted in a long block-

Second
meeting
of the
Assembly
Arguments of
Cleon.

Speech of
Diodotus

ade; and "when the place is taken, it will be a mere wreck." Moreover, if the people of Mytilene, who were compelled to join with their oligarchical government in rebelling, are destroyed, the popular party will everywhere be alienated from Athens.

Sentence revoked.

The reasoning of Diodotus, which was based on sound views of Policy, must have confirmed many of the audience who had already been influenced by the emotion of pity. But even still the Assembly was nearly equally divided, and the supporters of Diodotus won their motion by a very small majority. The ship which bore the sentence of doom had a start of about a day and a night; could it be overtaken by the trireme which was now dispatched with the reprieve? The Mytilenaean envoys supplied the crew with wine and barley, and offered large rewards if they were in time. The oarsmen continued rowing while they ate the barley, kneaded with wine and oil, and slept and rowed by turns. The first trireme, bound on an unpleasant errand, had sailed slowly. It arrived a little before the other. Paches had the decree in his hand and was about to execute it, when the second ship sailed into the harbour, and the city was saved.

Execution of Mytilenaean ringleaders. Cleruchy at Mytilene.

The wrath of Athens against her rebellious ally was sufficiently gratified by the trial and execution of those Mytilenaeans who had been sent to Athens as especially guilty. They were perhaps about thirty in number.

Having taken away the Lesbian fleet and rased the walls of Mytilene, the Athenians divided the island, excluding Methymna, into 3000 lots of which 300 were consecrated to the gods. The rest they let to Athenian citizens as cleruchs, and the land was cultivated by the Lesbians, who paid an annual rent.

SECT. 7. WARFARE IN WESTERN GREECE. TRAGIC EVENTS IN CORCYRA

Course of events in western Greece. 429 B.C.

While the attention of Greece was directed upon the fortunes of Plataea and Mytilene, warfare had been carried on in the regions of the west, and the reputation of the Athenian navy had risen higher. The Ambraciots had persuaded Sparta to send an expedition against Acarnania; if the Peloponnesians firmly established themselves there, they might win the whole Athenian alliance in the west. Cnemus was sent with 1000 hoplites in advance; he made an attempt on the important town of Stratus but was forced to retreat. Meanwhile a Peloponnesian fleet was to sail from Corinth to support him. It consisted of forty-seven ships, and had to pass Phormio, who was guarding the entrance of the Corinthian gulf with only twenty. Phormio let them sail into the open sea, preferring to attack them there. By skilful manœuvres he crowded the enemy's ships into a narrow space; a morning breeze helped him by knocking the ships against one another; and when they were in confusion the Athenians dashed in and gained a complete victory. The government at Sparta could not understand how skill could gain such an advantage over far superior numbers; they sent commissioners to make an inquiry; and Cnemus was told that he must try again and be successful. A reorganised Peloponnesian fleet took up a position at Panormus in Achaea, and Phormio was stationed at Rhion on the opposite coast. The object of Cnemus was to lure or drive the enemy into the gulf where their skill in handling their ships would be less decisive than in the open sea. With this purpose he sailed towards Naupactus, and Phormio in alarm sailed along the coast to protect the place. As the Athenian ships moved near the land in single file, the enemy suddenly swung round and rowed down upon them at their utmost speed. The eleven ships which were nearest Naupactus had time to run round the right Peloponnesian wing and escape; the rest were driven aground. Twenty Peloponnesian vessels on the right were in the meantime pursuing the eleven Athenian, which were making for Naupactus. A Leucadian ship was far in advance of the others, closely pursuing an Athenian which was lagging behind. Near Naupactus a merchant vessel lay in their way, anchored in the deep water. The Athenian trireme rowed round it, struck her pursuer amidships, and sank her. This brilliant exploit startled the Peloponnesians who were coming up singing a paean of victory; the front ships dropped oars and waited for the rest. The Athenians, who had already reached Naupactus, saw the situation, and immediately bore down and gained another complete victory.

If this able admiral, Phormio, had lived, he might have extended Athenian influence considerably in western Greece. But, after a winter expedition which he made in Acarnania, he silently drops out of history, and, as we find his son Asopius sent out in the following summer at the request of the Acarnanians, we must conclude that his career had been cut short by death. Asopius made an unsuccessful attempt on Oeniadae, and was slain in a descent on Leucas. The peninsula of Leucas, and the Acarnanian Oeniadae, girt by morasses at the mouth of the river Achelous, were two main objects of Athenian enterprise in the west. Leucas was never won, but four years later Oeniadae was forced to join the Athenian alliance.

Corcyra herself was to be the next scene of the war in the Ionian

Sea. The prisoners whom Corinth had taken in the Epidamnian war had been released on the understanding that they were to win over Corcyra from the Athenian alliance, and their intrigues were effectual in dividing the state and producing a sanguinary revolution. The question between the Peloponnesian and the Athenian alliance was closely bound up with cleavage between the oligarchical and the democratic party. The intriguers in the Corinthian interest and their faction formed a conspiracy to overthrow the democratic constitution. Their first step was to prosecute Peithias, the leader of the people on the charge of scheming to make Corcyra a subject of Athens. He was acquitted, and retorted by summoning their five richest men to take their trial for cutting vine-poles in the sanctuaries of Zeus and Alcinous. They were fined a stater for each pole: such a heavy fine that the culprits sat as suppliants in the sanctuary, imploring that they might pay by instalments. The prayer was refused, and in desperation they rushed into the senate-house and slew Peithias and sixty others who were with him.

(? Gold
stater,
16s.)
Murder of
the popu-
lar gov-
ernment,
427 B.C.
Civil war
in
Corcyra.

The oligarchy now had the upper hand, and they attacked the people, who fled to the acropolis and the Hyllaic harbour. The other harbour, which looks towards the mainland, along with the agora and the lower parts of the city were held by the oligarchs. Next day reinforcements came to both sides: to the people, from other parts of the island; and to the oligarchs, from the mainland. Fighting was soon resumed and the people had the advantage. In order to bar their way to the arsenal, the oligarchs set fire to the houses and buildings in the neighbourhood of the agora.

Next day twelve Athenian ships under Nicostratus arrived from Naupactus. He induced the two parties to come to an agreement, but the democrats persuaded him to leave five Athenian ships to ensure the preservation of order, for they did not trust their opponents. Nicostratus was to take five Corcyraean ships instead, and the crews of them were chosen from the oligarchs; they were in fact to be hostages for the behaviour of their fellows. But they feared they might be sent to Athens, and fled to the refuge of a temple. Nicostratus could not induce them to stir. The people regarded this distrust as a proof of criminal designs, and armed anew. The rest of the oligarchs then fled to the temple of Hera, but the democrats induced them to cross over to an islet off the coast.

Four or five days later a Peloponnesian fleet of fifty-three ships arrived under Alcidas, who had just returned from his expedition to Ionia. In a naval engagement outside the harbour the Corcyraeans fought badly, and the Athenians were forced to retreat; but the Peloponnesians did not follow up their success, and soon afterwards, hearing that an Athenian armament of sixty ships was on its way, returned home.

The democratic party was now in a position to wreak vengeance on its foes, who had gratuitously disturbed the peace of the city and sought to submit it to the yoke of its ancient enemy. The most vindictive and inhuman passions had been roused in the people by the attempt of the oligarchs on their liberty, and they now gave vent to these passions without regard to honour or policy. The 400 suppliants had returned from the island, and were again under the protection of Hera. Fifty of them were persuaded to come forth to take their trial, and were executed. The rest, seeing their fate, aided each other in committing suicide; some hung themselves on the trees in the sacred enclosure. Eurymedon arrived with the Athenian fleet and remained seven days. During this time, the Corcyraeans slew all whom they suspected of being opposed to the democracy, and many victims were sacrificed to private enmity. "Every form of death was to be seen, and everything, and more than everything that commonly happens in revolutions, happened then. The father slew the son, and the suppliants were torn from the temples and slain near them; some of them were even walled up in the temple of Dionysus and there perished. To such extremes of cruelty did revolution go; and this seemed to be the worst of revolutions because it was the first." Eurymedon looked on and did not intervene.

Cruel massacres by the democrats.

While the democracy cannot be excused for these horrible excesses, the fact remains that the guilt of causing the revolution rests entirely with the oligarchs. The chief victims of the democratic fury deserve small compassion; they had set the example of violence. The occurrences at Corcyra made a profound impression in Greece, reflected in the pages of Thucydides. That historian has used the episode as the text for deep comments on the revolutionary spirit which soon began to disturb the states of the Greek world. Party divisions were encouraged and aggravated by the hope or fear of foreign intervention, the oligarchs looking to the Lacedaemonians, and the democrats to the Athenians. In time of peace these party struggles would have been far less bitter. This acute observation is illustrated by a famous modern instance, the French Revolution, where the worst outrages of the revolutionists were provoked by foreign intervention. In that great Revolution too [12] we can verify the Greek historian's analysis of the effect of the revolutionary spirit, when it runs wild, on the moral nature of men. The revolutionists "determined to outdo the report of all who

The revolutionary spirit.

[12] Grote observed this.

had preceded them by the ingenuity of their enterprises and the activity of their revenges. The meaning of words had no longer the same relation to things, but was changed by them as they thought proper. Reckless daring was held to be loyal courage; prudent delay was the excuse of a coward; moderation was the disguise of unmanly weakness; to know everything was to do nothing. Frantic energy was the true quality of a man. The lover of violence was always trusted and his opponent suspected." It was dangerous to be quiet and neutral. "The citizens who were of neither party fell a prey to both; either they were disliked because they held aloof, or men were jealous of their surviving." The laws of heaven as well as of civilised societies were set aside without scruple amid the impatience of party spirit, the zeal of contention, the eagerness of ambition, and the cravings of revenge. These are some of the features in the delineation which Thucydides has drawn of the diseased condition of political life in the city-states of Greece.

Cor-
cyraean
oligarchs
on Istone.

427-5 B.C.
Fall of
Istone,
425 B.C.

But the sequel of the Corcyraean revolution has still to be recorded. About 600 of the oligarchs who escaped the vengeance of their opponents established themselves on Mount Istone in the north-east of the island, and easily becoming masters of the open country they harassed the inhabitants of the city for two years. Then an Athenian fleet, of which the ultimate destination was Sicily, under the command of Eurymedon and Sophocles, arrived at Corcyra; and the Athenians helped the democrats to storm the fort on Mount Istone. The oligarchs capitulated on condition that the Athenian people should determine how they were to be dealt with. The generals placed them in the island of Ptychia, on the understanding that, if any of their number attempted to escape, all should be deprived of the benefit of the previous agreement. But the democrats apprehended that the prisoners would not be put to death at Athens, and they were determined that their enemies should die. A foul trick was planned and carried out. Friends of the prisoners were sent over to the island, who said that the generals had resolved to leave them to the mercy of the democrats, and advised them to escape, offering to provide a ship. A few of the captives fell into the trap and were caught starting. All the prisoners were immediately handed over to the Corcyraeans, who shut them

Massacre
of the
oligarchs.

up in a large building. They were taken out in batches of twenty, and made to march, tied together, down an avenue of hoplites, who smote and wounded any whom they recognised as a personal enemy. Three batches had thus marched to execution, when their comrades in the building, who thought they were merely being removed to another prison, discovered the truth. They called on the Athenians, but they called in vain. Then they refused to stir out of the building or let any one enter. The Corcyraeans did not attempt to force their way in. They tore off the roof, and hurled bricks and shot arrows from above. The captives, absolutely helpless, began to anticipate the purpose of their tormentors by taking their own lives, piercing their throats with the arrows which were shot down, or strangling themselves with the ropes of some beds which were in the place or with strips of their own dress. The work of destruction went on during the greater part of the night; all was over when the day dawned; and the corpses were carried outside the city. Thus ended the Corcyraean revolution, and the last scene was more ghastly even than the first. Eurymedon had less excuse, on this occasion, for refusing to intervene than he had two years before; since the prisoners had surrendered to the Athenians. It was said that he and Sophocles were ready to take advantage of the base trick of the democrats, because, unable to take the captives to Athens themselves, being bound for Sicily, they could not bear that the credit should fall to another. The oligarchical faction at Corcyra was now utterly annihilated, and the democrats lived in peace.

Sect. 8. Campaigns of Demosthenes in the West

During the Corcyraean troubles, the war had not rested in western Greece. An Athenian fleet under the general Demosthenes had sailed round the Peloponnesus and attacked the "island" of Leucas. Demosthenes was an enterprising commander, distinguished from most of his fellows by a certain originality of conception. On this occasion, the idea of making a great stroke induced him to abandon the operations at Leucas,—though the Acarnanians thought he might have taken the town by blockade,— and engage in a new enterprise on the north of the Corinthian gulf. Most of the lands between Boeotia and the western sea—Phocis, Locris, Acarnania—were friendly to Athens. But the hostility of the uncivilised Aetolians rendered land operations in those regions dangerous. Demosthenes conceived the plan of reducing the Aetolians, so that he could then operate from the west on Doris and Boeotia, without the danger of his communications being threatened in the rear. His idea, in fact, was to bring the Corinthian gulf into touch with the Euboean sea. The Spartans, it is to be observed, were at this very time concerning themselves with the regions of Mount Oeta. The appeals of Doris on the south, and Trachis on the north, of the Oetaean range, for protection against

Aetolian expedition, 426 B.C.

Colony or Heraclea.

the hostilities of the mountain tribes, induced the Lacedaemonians to send out a colony, which was established in Trachis not very far from the Pass of Thermopylae, under the name of Heraclea. A colony was an unusual enterprise for Sparta; but Heraclea had a more important significance and intention than the mere defence of members of the amphictiony. It was a place from which Euboea could be attacked; and it might prove of the greatest service, as an intermediate station, for carrying on operations in the Chalcidic peninsula. The fears which the foundation of Heraclea excited at Athens were indeed disappointed; Heraclea never flourished; it was incessantly assailed by the powerful hostility of the Thessalians, and its ruin was completed by the flagrantly unjust administration of the Lacedaemonian governors. But its first foundation was a serious event; and it seems highly probable that Demosthenes, when he formed his plan, had before his mind the idea of threatening Heraclea from the south by the occupation of Doris. But his plan, attractive as it might sound, was eminently impracticable. The preliminary condition was the subjugation of a mountainous country, involving a warfare in which Demosthenes was inexperienced and hoplites were at a great disadvantage. The Messenians of Naupactus represented to him that Aetolia, a land of unwalled villages, could easily be reduced. But the Messenians had their own game to play. They suffered from the hostilities of their Aetolian neighbours and wanted to use the ambition of the Athenian general for their own purpose.

The Acarnanians, who were deeply interested in the defeat of Leucas, were indignant with Demosthenes for not prosecuting the blockade and refused to join him against Aetolia. Starting from Oeneon in Locris, the Athenians and some allies—not a large force—advanced into the country, hoping to reduce several tribes before they had time to combine. But the Aetolians had already learned his plans, and were already collecting a great force. The main chance of Demosthenes lay in the co-operation of the Ozolian Locrians, who knew the Aetolian country and mode of warfare and were armed in the Aetolian fashion. Demosthenes committed the error of not waiting for them. He was consequently unable to deal with the Aetolian javelin-men. At Aegition, rushing down from the hills they wrought havoc among the invaders who had captured the town. A hundred and twenty Athenian hoplites fell—"the very finest men whom the city of Athens lost during the war." Demosthenes did not dare to return to Athens. He remained at Naupactus, and soon had an opportunity of retrieving his fame.

[Aegition = Veluchovos ?].

The Lacedaemonians answered this invasion of Aetolia by sending 3000 hoplites under Eurylochus against Naupactus. Five hundred of these troops came from Heraclea, the newly-founded colony. Naupactus, ill-defended, was barely saved by the energy of Demosthenes, who persuaded the Acarnanians to send reinforcements. Eurylochus abandoned the siege, and withdrew to the neighbourhood of Calydon and Pleuron in southern Aetolia, for the purpose of joining the Ambraciots in an attack upon Argos. Winter had begun when the Ambraciots descended from the north into the Argive territory and seized the fort of Olpae, which stands, a little north of Argos, on a hill by the sea, and was once used as a hall of justice by the Acarnanian league. Demosthenes was asked by the Acarnanians to be their leader in resisting this attack, and a message for help was sent to twenty Athenian vessels which were coasting off the Peloponnesus. The troops of Eurylochus marched from the south across Acarnania and joined their allies at Olpae. The Athenian ships arrived in the Ambracian gulf, and, with the reinforcements which they brought, Demosthenes gave battle to the enemy between Olpae and Argos, and by a skilfully contrived ambuscade annulled the advantage which they had in superior numbers. Eurylochus was slain, and the Peloponnesians delivered themselves from their perilous position—between Argos and the Athenian ships—by making a secret treaty with Demosthenes, in which the Ambraciots were not included. It was arranged that they should retreat stealthily without explaining their intention to the Ambraciots. It was good policy on the part of Demosthenes; for by this treacherous act the Lacedaemonians would lose their character in that part of Greece. The Peloponnesians crept out of Olpae one by one, pretending to gather herbs and sticks. As they got farther away, they stepped out more quickly, and then the Ambraciots saw what was happening and ran out to overtake them. The Acarnanians slew about 200 Ambraciots, and the Peloponnesians escaped into the land of Agraea. But a heavier blow was in store for Ambracia. Reinforcements of that city, ignorant of the battle, were coming to Olpae. Demosthenes sent forward some of his troops to lie in ambush on their line of march. At Idomene, some miles north of Olpae, there are two peaks of unequal height. The higher was seized in advance by the men of Demosthenes; the Ambraciots when they arrived encamped on the lower. Demosthenes then advanced with the rest of his troops and attacked the enemy at dawn, when they were still half asleep. Most were slain, and those who escaped at first found the mountain paths occupied. Thucydides says that during the first ten years of the war "no such calamity happened within so few days to any Hellenic state," and he does not give the numbers of those who perished, because they would appear incredible in proportion to the size of the state. Demosthenes might have captured the city if he had pushed on, but the Acarnanians did not desire a permanent Athenian occupation at their doors; they were content that their neighbour was rendered harmless. A treaty of alliance for 100 years was concluded between the Acarnanians, with the Amphilochians of Argos, and the Ambraciots. Neither side was to be required by the other to join against its own allies in the great war, but they were to help each other to defend their territories. Some time afterwards Anactorion, and then Oeniadae, were won over to the Athenian alliance.

Anactorion,
425 B.C.
Oeniadae
424 B.C.

Sect. 9. Nicias and Cleon. Politics at Athens

The success against Ambracia compensated for the failure in Aetolia, and Demosthenes could now return to Athens. His dashing style of warfare and his bold plans must have caused grave mistrust among the older, more experienced, and more commonplace commanders. Nicias, the son of Niceratus, who seems to have already won, without deserving, the chief place as a military authority at Athens, must have shaken his head over the doings of Demosthenes in the west. Nicias, a wealthy conservative slave-owner, who speculated in the silver-mines of Laurion, was one of the mainstays of that party which was out of sympathy with the intellectual and political progress of Athens, and bitterly opposed to the new politicians like Cleon who wielded the chief influence in the Assembly.

Nicias

The ability of Nicias was irretrievably mediocre; he would have been an excellent subordinate officer, but he had not the qualities of a leader or a statesman. Yet he possessed a solid and abiding influence at Athens, through his impregnable respectability, his superiority to bribes, and his scrupulous superstition, as well as his acquaintance with the details of military affairs. This homage paid to mediocre respectability throws light on the character of the Athenian democracy, and the strength of the conservative party. Nicias belonged to the advocates of peace and was well-disposed to Sparta, so that for several reasons he might be regarded as a successor to Cimon. But his political opponents, though they constantly defeated him on particular measures, never permanently undermined his influence. He understood the political value of gratifying in small ways those prejudices of his fellow-citizens which he shared himself; and he spared no expense in the religious service of the state. As Thucydides says, he thought too much of divination and omens. He had an opportunity of displaying his religious devotion and his liberality on the occasion of the purification of the island of Delos, which was probably undertaken to induce Apollo to stay the plague. The dead were removed from all the tombs, and it was ordained that henceforth no one should die or give birth to a child on the sacred island. Those who were near to either should cross over to Rheneia. The Athenians revived in a new form the old festival, celebrated in the Homeric hymn to Apollo, the festival to which "the long-robed Ionians gathered, and made thee glad, O Phoebus, with boxing, dancing, and song." The games were restored, and horse-races introduced for the first time. Four years later the purification was perfected by the removal of all the inhabitants, and the Persians accorded them a refuge at Adramyttion.

Purification of Delos, 426 B.C.

Quadriennial festival established at Delos.

Conducting such ceremonies, Nicias was in his right place. Unfortunately such excellence had an undue weight; and it should be noted that this is one of the drawbacks of a city-state. In a large modern state, the private life and personal opinions of a statesman have small importance and are not weighed by his fellow-countrymen in the scale against his political ability, save in rare exceptional cases. But in a small city the stateman's private life is always before men's eyes, and his political position is distinctly affected, according as he shocks or gratifies their prejudices and predilections. A mediocre man is able, by judicious conforming, to attain an authority to which his brains give him no claim. Pericles was indeed so strong that his influence could survive attacks on his morality and his orthodoxy. Nicias maintained his position because he never shocked the public sense of decorum and religion by associating with an Aspasia or an Anaxagoras. The Athenian people combined in a remarkable degree the capacity of appreciating both respectability and intellectual power; their progressive instinct was often defeated by conservative prejudices.

Though Nicias was one of those Athenians who were not in full sympathy with the policy of Pericles and approved still less of the policy of his successors, he was thoroughly loyal to the democracy. But an oligarchical party still existed, secretly active, and always hoping for an opportunity to upset the democratic constitution. This party, or a section of it, seems to have been known at this time as the "Young Party." It included, among others who will appear on the stage of history some years later, the orator Antiphon, who was now coming into public notice in connexion with some sensational lawsuits. Against the dark designs of this party, as well

The oligarchical party.

οἱ νεώτεροι

Antiphon.

as against the misconduct of generals, Cleon was constantly on the watch; he could describe himself in the Assembly as the "people's watch-dog." But at present these oligarchs were harmless; so long as no disaster from without befell Athens, they had no chance; all they could do was to make common cause with the other enemies of Cleon, and air their discontent in anonymous political pamphlets. Chance has preserved us a work of this kind, written in one of these years by an Athenian of oligarchical views. Its subject is the Athenian democracy, and the writer professes to answer on behalf of the Athenians the criticisms which the rest of the Greeks pass on Athenian institutions. "I do not like democracy myself," he says; "but I will show that from their point of view the Athenians manage their state wisely and in the manner most conducive to the interests of democracy." The defence is for the most part a veiled indictment; it displays remarkable acuteness, with occasional triviality. The writer has grasped and taken to heart one deep truth, the close connexion of the sea-power of Athens with its advanced democracy. It is just, he remarks, that the poor and the common folk should have more influence than the noble and rich; for it is the common folk that row the ships and make the city powerful, not the hoplites and the well-born and the worthy. Highly interesting is his observation that slaves and metics enjoyed what he considered unreasonable freedom and immunity at Athens: "Why, you may not strike one of them, nor will a slave make way for you in the street." And his malicious explanation is interesting too; the common folk dress so badly that you might easily mistake one of them for a slave or a metic, and then there would be a to-do if you struck a citizen. There is perhaps a touch of malice, too, in the statement that the commercial empire of Athens, which brought to her wharves the delicacies of the world, was affecting her language, as well as her habits of life, and filling it with foreign words.

An important feature in the political history of Athens in these years was the divorce of the military command from the leadership in the Assembly, and the want of harmony between the chief Strategoi and the Leaders of the People. The tradesmen who swayed the Assembly had no military training or capacity, and they were always at a disadvantage when opposed by men who spoke with the authority of a strategos on questions of military policy. Until recent years the post of General had been practically confined to men of property and good family. But a change ensued, perhaps soon after the death of Pericles, and men of the people were elected. The comic poet Eupolis, in a play called the *Demes*—in which the great leaders, Miltiades and Themistocles,

The pseudo-Xenophontic Ἀθηναίων πολιτεία c. 424 B.C.

Cleon's position.

Eupolis on the new generals.

Aristides and Pericles, are summoned back to life that they may
see and deplore degenerate Athens—meditates thus on the contrast between latter-day generals and their predecessors:

> Men of lineage fair
> And of wealthy estate
> Once our generals were,
> The noble and great,
> Whom as gods we adored, and as gods they guided and guarded the state.

> Things are not as then.
> Ah, how different far
> A manner of men
> Our new generals are,
> The rascals and refuse our city now chooses to lead us to war!

Cleon was a man of brains and resolution. He was ambitious to
rule the state as Pericles had ruled it; and for this purpose he saw
clearly that he must gain triumphs in the field as well as in the
Assembly. Hitherto his main activity had been in the law-courts,
where he called officers to account and maintained the safeguards
of popular government. If he was to be more than an opposition
leader, occasionally forcing measures through the Assembly, if he
was to exercise a permanent influence on the administration, he
must be ready, when a good opportunity offered, to undertake the
post of strategos; and, supported by the experience of an able
colleague, he need not disgrace himself. An understanding, therefore, between Cleon and the enterprising Demosthenes was one
which seemed to offer advantages to both; acting together they
might damage both the political and the military position of Nicias.

But before we pass to a famous enterprise, which was probably
the result of such an understanding, we must note the great cost
which the continuation of the war entailed. It was found necessary
to borrow from the temple treasures, at a nominal interest, to
defray the military expenses. But this was not enough. The financiers of Athens—and Cleon must probably bear a large share of
the responsibility—induced the people to raise the tribute of the
subject states. If the tribute was not doubled, it was very nearly
doubled; the total amount, at the lowest estimate, did not fall far
short of 1000 talents. We possess considerable fragments of the
stone on which this assessment was written; it is a monument of
the injustice of a democracy blinded by imperial ambition against
which Thucydides son of Melesias had protested at an earlier stage.
But at this stage, the raising of the tribute was a necessity; Athens
could not retreat. There were indeed still men, especially among
the Young Party, to lift up a voice on behalf of the Cities; and the
glaring injustice of the position of Athens was smartly ridiculed by

Borrow-
ing from
the temple
treasures,
426, 425,
424, 423
B.C.

Raising of
the
tribute,
425 B.C.
Tribute
list.

(Aristo-
phanes,
Wasps,
422 B.C.)

Aristophanes, who ironically suggested in one of his comedies that if the Cities were compelled to do their duty, each would enable twenty Athenians to live in idleness on the fat of the land, "or hare and beestings pudding."

Cleon
introduces
the "trio-
bolon"—
fee of the
dicasts
(probably
425-4
B.C.).

It may seem strange to find that in a time of financial pressure, when it was necessary not only to introduce an extraordinary tax on property but to afflict the allies with heavier burdens, Athens saw fit to increase her domestic expenditure. One of Cleon's most important measures was the raising of the judges' fee from one obol, at which it had been fixed by Pericles, to three obols. It would be a mistake to consider this measure a mere bid for popularity. We shall hardly be wrong in regarding it as an attempt to relieve the distress which the yearly invasions of Attica and losses of the harvests inflicted upon the poorer citizens.

SECT. 10. THE ATHENIAN CAPTURE OF PYLOS

425 B.C.

It was doubtless through the influence of Cleon that Demosthenes, though he received no official command, was sent to accompany the fleet of forty ships which was now ready to start for the west, under Eurymedon and Sophocles. We have already seen this fleet at Corcyra assisting the People against the oligarchical exiles who had established themselves on Mount Istone. Demosthenes accompanied the expedition without any official command. He had a plan in his head for establishing a military post in the western Peloponnesus; and he was allowed to take advantage of the sailing of the fleet and use it according to his discretion. Arriving off the coast of Messenia, Demosthenes asked the commanders to put in at Pylos, but they had heard that the Peloponnesian fleet had already reached Corcyra, and demurred to any delay. But chance favoured the design of Demosthenes. Stress of weather drove them into the harbour of Pylos, and then Demosthenes pressed them to fortify the place. The task was easy; for the place was naturally strong and there was an abundance of material, stone and timber, at hand. The commanders ridiculed the idea. "There are many other desert promontories in the Peloponnesus," they said, "if you want to waste the money of the city." But the stormy weather detained the ships; the soldiers were idle; and at length, for the sake of something to do, they adopted the project of Demosthenes and fell to the work of fortifying Pylos.

Topo-
graphy of
Pylos and
Spha-
cteria.

The features of the scene, which was now to become illustrious by a striking military episode, must be clearly grasped. The high promontory of Pylos or Coryphasion was on three sides encompassed by water. Once it had been an island, but at this time it was connected with the mainland on the north side by a low sand-bar. If we go further back into prehistoric days, Pylos had been part of a continuous line of coast-cliff. In this line three rents were made, which admitted the sea behind the cliff and isolated the islands of Pylos and Sphacteria. Accumulation of sand gradually covered the most northern breach and reunited Pylos with the mainland, but the other openings were never filled up and Sphacteria still remains an island. Originally Pylos and Sphacteria, when they had been severed, formed the sea-wall of one great land-locked bay; but a curving sand-bar has gradually been formed, which now joins the mainland with the southern extremity of Pylos, and secludes a small lagoon of which Pylos forms the western side. It is impossible to say whether the formation of this sand-bar had perceptibly begun in the time of Demosthenes; but in any case it seems probable that it had not advanced so far as to hinder the waters behind Pylos from appearing to be part of a continuous bay. This north corner of the bay—now a marshy lagoon—was sheltered and afforded harbourage for ships; the rest of the bay—the modern bay of Navarino—had no good anchorage; but the whole sheet of water, by virtue of the northern corner, was called a harbour. It follows from what has been said that there were two entrances into the bay: the narrow water which divides Pylos from Sphacteria, and the wide passage which severs the southern point of Sphacteria from the opposite mainland. We must distinguish yet another smaller bay on the north side of the Pylos hill. The sand-bar which there connects Pylos with the mainland is of lunar shape and forms the little circular basin of Buphras, dominated by the height of Pylos on the south and a far lower, nameless hill on the north.

The length of Pylos is less than a mile. On the sea-side it was hard to land, and the harbour side was strongly protected by steep cliffs. Only in three places was it found necessary to build walls: (1) at the south-east corner, where the cliffs slope down to the channel for about 100 yards; (2) along the shore on the south west side close to the entrance to the bay, for four or five hundred yards; (3) the northern defence of the position consisted of a line of land cliffs, which required no artificial fortification except at the western extremity, where they decline before they reach the sea; here another wall was built. One of the soldiers present vividly described to Thucydides the manner in which the fortifications were wrought. Being unprovided with iron tools they brought stones which they picked out, and put them together as they happened to fit; if they required to use mortar, having no hods, they carried it on their

Athenian fortifications of Pylos.

backs, which they bent so as to form a resting-place for it, clasping their hands behind them that it might not fall off.[13] In six days the work was finished, and the fleet went on its way, leaving Demosthenes with five ships to hold Pylos.

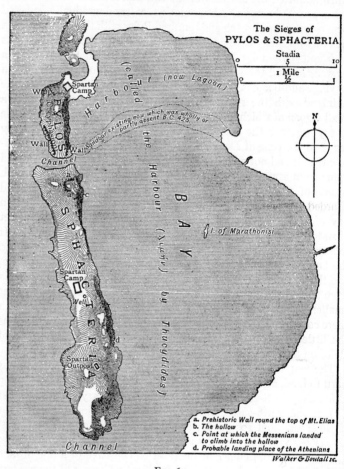

FIG. 65.

Walker & Boutall sc.

a. *Prehistoric Wall round the top of Mt. Elias*
b. *The hollow*
c. *Point at which the Messenians landed to climb into the hollow*
d. *Probable landing place of the Athenians*

The Sieges of PYLOS & SPHACTERIA

Arrival of Lacedaemonians by land and sea.

The Lacedaemonian army under Agis had invaded Attica earlier than usual, before the corn was ripe. Want of food, wet weather, and then perhaps the news from pylos, decided them to return to Sparta after a sojourn of only two weeks within the Attic borders.

[13] Jowett's translation.

They did not proceed immediately to Pylos, but another body of Spartans was sent on; requisitions for help were dispatched to the Peloponnesian allies; and the sixty ships at Corcyra were hastily summoned. These ships succeeded in eluding the notice of the Athenian fleet which had now reached Zacynthus. In the meantime Demosthenes, beset by the Spartan troops, sent two of his ships to overtake the fleet and beg Eurymedon to return to succour him.

The object of the Lacedaemonians was to blockade the hill of Pylos by land and sea, and to prevent Athenian succours from landing. They probably established their camp on the north side of Pylos, so that no ships entering the bay of Buphras could bring help to the fort. They were moreover afraid that the Athenians might use the island of Sphacteria as a basis for military operations, and accordingly Epitadas occupied Sphacteria with 420 Spartans and their attendant Helots. It would have been easy to block the narrow entrance to the bay between Pylos and the island; but there was little use in doing so, as the Athenian ships would be able to enter by the ingress at the south of the island, a passage about three-quarters of a mile wide—far too wide to block with so small a fleet.

Siege of Pylos.

The Lacedaemonians then prepared to attack the place, before help could come to the Athenians. Demosthenes posted the greater part of his force to guard the northern line of defence and the south-eastern corner; while he himself with sixty hoplites and some archers took his stand on the edge of the south-western shore, which though rocky and perilous was the spot where the enemy had the best prospect of effecting a landing. Thrasymelidas was the name of the Spartan admiral. He had forty-three ships, which he brought up in relays, the crews fighting and resting by turns. The great danger was that of running the vessels on reefs. Brasidas who commanded one of the ships was the leading spirit. "Be not sparing of timber," he cried to those who seemed to draw back from the rocks; "the enemy has built a fortress in your country. Perish the ships, and force a landing." But in trying to disembark he was wounded and lost his shield. It was washed ashore and set up in the trophy which the Athenians afterwards erected. The Spartan attack which was renewed on two subsequent days was repelled. It was a singular turn of fortune, says Thucydides,[14] which drove the Athenians to repel the Lacedaemonians, who were attacking them by sea from the Lacedaemonian coast, and the Lacedaemonians to fight for a landing on their own soil, now hostile to them, in the

Attack on Pylos.

repelled.

[14] Jowett's translation.

face of the Athenians. For in those days it was the great glory of the
Lacedaemonians to be an inland people distinguished for their
military prowess, and of the Athenians to be a nation of sailors and
the first naval power in Hellas.

Arrival of
Athenian
fleet.

The fleet from Zacynthus, now augmented to fifty ships by some
reinforcements, at length arrived. But finding the shores of the bay
of Buphras and the island of Sphacteria occupied, they withdrew
for the night to the isle of Prote which was some miles distant. The
next morning they returned, determined to sail into the harbour, if
the enemy did not come out to meet them. The Lacedaemonians
were preparing their ships for action, evidently intending to fight

Battle
in the
harbour.

in the bay. The Athenians therefore rowed in by both entrances;
some of the enemy's vessels which were able to come out to meet
them were captured; and a tremendous struggle ensued close to
the shore. The Athenians were tying the empty beached ships to
their own and endeavouring to drag them away, the Lacedaemonians dashed into the sea and were pulling them back. The Lacedaemonians knew that, if they lost their ships, the party on the
island of Sphacteria would be cut off. Most of the empty ships were
saved; but the fleet was so far damaged and outnumbered that the
Athenians were able to blockade Sphacteria.

Second
stage of
the
episode:
blockade
of Sphac-
teria.

The interest of the story now passes from Pylos to Sphacteria.
The blockade of Demosthenes and his Athenians in Pylos by the
Spartans has changed into a blockade of Epitadas and his Spartans
in Sphacteria by the Athenians. The tidings of this change in the
situation caused grave alarm at Sparta and some of the ephors
came themselves to see what measures could be taken. They decided
that nothing could be done for the relief of the island, and obtained from the Athenian generals a truce for the purpose of sending

Truce.

ambassadors to Athens to ask for peace. The terms of this truce
were as follows: [15]—

The Lacedaemonians shall deliver into the hands of the Athenians at Pylos the ships in which they fought, and shall also bring
thither and deliver over any other ships of war which are in Laconia; and they shall make no assault upon the fort either by sea
or land. The Athenians shall permit the Lacedaemonians on the
mainland to send to those on the island a fixed quantity of
kneaded flour, viz. two Attic quarts of barleymeal for each man,
and a pint of wine, and also a piece of meat; for an attendant half
these quantities; they shall send them into the island under the
inspection of the Athenians, and no vessel shall sail in by stealth.
The Athenians shall guard the island as before, but not land, and

[15] Jowett's translation of Thucydides.

shall not attack the Peloponnesian forces by land or sea. If either party violate this agreement in any particular, however slight, the truce is to be at an end. The agreement is to last until the Lacedaemonian ambassadors return from Athens, and the Athenians are to convey them thither and bring them back in a trireme. When they return, the truce is to be at an end, and the Athenians are to restore the ships in the same condition in which they received them.

In accordance with these terms, sixty ships were handed over and the ambassadors went to Athens. They professed the readiness of Sparta to make peace and pleaded for generous treatment on the part of Athens. At heart most of the Athenians were probably desirous of peace. But the Assembly was under the influence of Cleon, and he, as the opponent of Nicias and the peace-party, urged the Athenians to propose terms which could hardly be accepted. It might seem indeed an exceptionally favourable moment to attempt to undo the humiliation of the Thirty Years' Truce, and win back some of the possessions which had been lost twenty years ago. Not only Nisaea and Pagae, the harbours of the Megarid, but Achaea and Troezen, were demanded as the purchase of the lives of the Spartans in Sphacteria. The embassy returned to Pylos disappointed, and the truce came to an end. But the Athenians refused to give back the sixty ships, on the pretext of some slight infraction of the truce on the part of the Lacedaemonians.

Athens rejects Spartan proposals of peace.

The blockade proved a larger and more difficult matter than the Athenians had hoped. Reinforced by twenty more triremes from Athens, they lay round the island, both in the bay, and, except when the wind was too high, on the seaside; and two ships kept continually cruising round in opposite directions. But their vigilance was eluded, and Sphacteria was secretly supplied with provisions. Large sums were offered to any who succeeded in conveying meal, wine, or cheese to the island; and Helots, who did such service, were rewarded with freedom. When a strong wind from the west or north drove the Athenian ships into the bay, the daring crews of provision-boats beat recklessly into the difficult landing-places on the seaside. Moreover some skilful divers managed to reach the shores of the island,—drawing skins with poppy-seed mixed with honey, and pounded linseed. But this device was soon discovered and prevented.

Protracted blockade.

And besides the difficulty of rendering the blockade complete in a high wind, the maintenance of it was extremely unpleasant. As there was no proper anchorage, the crews were obliged to take their meals on land by turns,—generally in the south part of Sphacteria, which was not occupied by the Spartans. And they depended for

their supply of water on one well, which was in the fort of Pylos.
The supply of food was deficient,—for it had to be conveyed round
the Peloponnesus. At home the Athenians were disappointed at the
protraction of the siege, and grew impatient. They were sorry that
they had declined the overtures of the Lacedaemonians, and there
was a reaction of feeling against Cleon. That statesman took the
bold course of denying the reports from Pylos, and said—with a
pointed allusion to the strategos Nicias—that if the Generals were
men they would sail to the island and capture the garrison. "If I
were commander," he added, "I would do it myself." The scene
which follows is described in one of the rare passages where the
most reserved of all historians condescends to display a little political animosity. Seeing that the people were murmuring at Cleon,
Nicias stood up and offered, on the part of his colleagues, to give
Cleon any force he asked for and let him try. Cleon—says Thucydides[16]—at first imagined that the offer of Nicias was only a pretence and was willing to go; but finding that he was in earnest, he
tried to back out and said that not he but Nicias was general. He
was now alarmed, for he never imagined that Nicias would go so far
as to give up his place to him. Again Nicias bade him take the
command of the expedition against Pylos, which he formally gave
up to him in the presence of the Assembly. And the more Cleon
declined the proffered command and tried to retract what he had
said, so much the more the multitude, as their manner is, urged
Nicias to resign and shouted to Cleon that he should sail. At length,
not knowing how to escape from his own words, he undertook the
expedition and, coming forward, said that he was not afraid of the
Lacedaemonians and that he would sail without withdrawing a
single man from the city, if he were allowed to have the Lemnian
and Imbrian forces now at Athens, the auxiliaries from Aenus who
were targeteers, and four hundred archers from other places. With
these and with the troops already at Pylos he gave his word that he
would either bring the Lacedaemonians alive or kill them on the
spot. His vain words moved the Athenians to laughter; nevertheless
the wiser sort of men were pleased when they reflected that of two
good things they could not fail to obtain one—either there would be
an end of Cleon, which they would have greatly preferred, or, if
they were disappointed, he would put the Lacedaemonians into
their hands.

The story is almost too good to be true. But whether Cleon desired the command or had it thrust upon him against his will, his
words which moved the Athenians to laughter were fully approved

Impati-
tience at
Athens.

Cleon
sent as
com-
mander to
Pylos.

---

[16] Jowett's translation to the end of the paragraph.

by the event. He chose Demosthenes as his colleague; and, invested with the command by a formal vote of the Assembly, he immediately set sail.

In the meantime Demosthenes, wishing like Cleon to bring matters to an issue, was meditating an attack upon Sphacteria. This desert island is about two miles and three-quarters long. At the northern extremity rises a height, higher than the acropolis of Pylos over against it, and on the east side descending, a sheer cliff, into the water of the bay. Some of the Spartans had naturally occupied the summit, but the chief encampment of their small force was in the centre of the island, close to the only well; and an outpost was set on a hill farther to the south. An assault was difficult not only because the landing-places on both sides were bad, but because the island was covered with close bush, which gave the Spartans who knew the ground a great advantage. Demosthenes had experienced in Aetolia the difficulties of fighting in a wood. But one day, when some Athenians were taking their noonday meal on the south shore of the island, the wood was accidentally kindled, and, a wind arising, the greater part of the bush was burnt. It was then possible to see more clearly the position and the numbers of the Lacedaemonians, and, when Cleon arrived, the plan of attack was matured. Embarking at night all their hoplites in a few ships, Cleon and Demosthenes landed before dawn on the south of the island, partly on the seaside and partly on the harbour side, near the spot where the Lacedaemonians had their outpost. The whole number of troops that landed must have been nearly 14,000, against which the Spartans had only 420 hoplites and perhaps as many Helots. And yet a high military authority described the Athenian enterprise as mad. The truth seems to be that it could hardly have succeeded if the Spartan commander had disposed his forces to the best advantage, posting watches at all possible landing-places and organising a proper system of signals.

The outpost was at once overpowered, and light-armed troops advanced towards the main Spartan encampment, along a high ridge on the harbour side of the island. Others moved along the low shore on the seaside; so that when the main body of the Spartans saw their outpost cut to pieces and began to move southward against the Athenian hoplites, they were harassed on either side by the archers and targeteers, whom, encumbered by their arms and in difficult ground, they were unable to pursue. And the attacks of these light-armed troops, as they grew more fully conscious of their own superiority in numbers and saw that their enemy was growing weary, became more formidable. Clouds of dust arose from the

Nature of Sphacteria.

Burning of the wood.

Athenian forces land on Sphacteria.

The attack.

Distress
of the
Spartans.

newly burnt wood—so Thucydides reports the scene from the vivid description of an eye-witness—and there was no possibility of a man's seeing what was before him, owing to the showers of arrows and stones hurled by their assailants which were flying amid the dust. And now the Lacedaemonians began to be sorely distressed, for their felt cuirasses did not protect them against the arrows, and the points of the javelins broke off where they struck them. They were at their wits' end, not being able to see out of their eyes or to hear the word of command, which was drowned by the cries of the enemy. Destruction was staring them in the face, and they had no means or hope of deliverance.[17]

Spartan
retreat to
the hill
(now Mt.
Elias).

At length it was determined that the only chance lay in retreating to the high hill at the north of the island. About a mile had to be traversed to the foot of the hill; but the ground was very difficult. The endurance and discipline of the Spartan soldiers was conspicuously displayed in this slow retreat which was accomplished, with but a small loss, under a burning sun, by men who were suffering from thirst and weary with the distress of an unequal battle. When they had reached and climbed the hill the battle assumed another aspect. On the high ground, no longer exposed on their flanks, and finding a defence in an old Cyclopean wall, which can still be traced round the summit, the Lacedaemonians were able to repel their assailants; and they were determined not to surrender.

The
Messenian
plan.

At length a Messenian captain came to the Athenian generals and said that he knew a path by which he thought he could take some light-armed troops round to the rear of the Spartans. The hill on its eastern side falls precipitously into the bay; but the fall is not direct. The summit slopes down into a hollow, about fifty yards wide, and then the hill rises again into the cliff which falls sheer into the water. But at the south end of the cliff there is a narrow gorge by which it is possible to climb up into the hollow. Embarking in a boat on the eastern side of the island, the Messenians reached the foot of the gorge and climbed up with difficulty, unseen by the Spartans, who neglected what seemed an impracticable part of the hill, and then ascending the summit suddenly appeared above the Lacedaemonians, who were ranged in a semicircle below on the western and northern slopes. The Athenians now invited the defenders to capitulate, and with the consent of their friends on the mainland they laid down their arms. Two hundred and ninety-two, of the four hundred and twenty, survived, and were brought to Athens The high opinion which the Greek world held of the Spartan spirit was expressed in the universal amazement which was caused by this

[17] Jowett's translation.

urrender. Men had thought that nothing could induce the Lacedae-
ionians to give up their arms.

Cleon had performed his promise; he brought back the captives
vithin twenty days. The success was of political rather than mili-
ary importance. The Athenians could indeed ravage Lacedaemo-
ian territory from Pylos, but it was a greater thing that they had
n the prisoners a security against future invasions of Attica and
a means of making an advantageous peace when they chose. It was
he most important success gained in the war, and it was a brilliant
example of the valuable successes that can be gained, as it were
accidentally, in following that system of strategy which Pericles had
aid down at the beginning of the war. This stroke of luck increased
he influence of Cleon. It was necessary for Nicias to do something
o maintain his reputation. Shortly afterwards he led an army into
he Corinthian territory, gained a partial victory at Solygea, and
:hen went on to the peninsula of Methone, between Troezen and
Epidaurus. He built a wall across the isthmus and left a garrison in
Methone. In the following year, he made the more important acquisition of the island of Cythera, from which he was able to make
descents upon Laconia. The loss of Cythera was in itself more serious for Sparta than the loss of Pylos; but owing to the attendant
:ircumstances the earlier event made far greater stir. The Athenians
had now three bases of operation in the Peloponnesus—Pylos,
Cythera, and Methone.

425 B.C.
Activity
of Nicias.

424 B.C.
Capture
of
Cythera.

To none was the discomfit of the Spartans in Messenia sweeter
than to the Messenian exiles who had borne their part in the work
of that memorable day. At Olympia there is a figure of Victory,
hovering aloft in the air, amid wind-blown drapery, while an eagle
flies below her. It is the work of the sculptor Paeonius, and it was
dedicated by the Messenians in the Altis of Zeus, with part of the
spoil they stripped from the hated usurpers of their land.

Victory of
Paeonius.

SECT. II. ATHENIAN CAPTURE OF NISAEA

In each of the first seven years of the war, Attica was invaded,
except twice; on one occasion, the attack on Plataea had taken the
place of the incursion into Attica, and, on another, the Peloponnesian army was hindered by earthquakes from advancing beyond the
isthmus. Every year by way of reply the Athenians invaded the
Megarid twice, in spring and in autumn. The capture of Pylos
affected both these annual events. The invasion of Attica was discontinued, because Athens held the Spartan hostages; and the ela-
tion of the Athenians at their success induced them to undertake a
bolder enterprise against Megara.

429 B.C.
426 B.C.

Capture
of Minoa,
427 B.C.

Minoa, now a hill on the mainland but then an island, lay at th
entrance to the harbour of Nisaea. It was separated from Nisae
by a narrow channel, protected by two projecting towers. Nicia
had destroyed these towers, three years before, and had fortifie
Minoa, so as to blockade completely the port of Nisaea. The Mega
rians then depended entirely on the port of Pagae and their com
munications with the Crisaean Gulf. They were hard pressed; thei
distress was vividly portrayed in the comedy of the *Acharnian*
which was put on the stage two years later. The situation becam
424 B.C.
almost intolerable when a domestic sedition led to the expulsion o
a small party who seized Pagae and cut off Megara from importin
food on that side too. It became a question between allowing th
exiles to return or submitting to Athens. Those who knew that th
return of their rivals from Pagae would mean their own doo
opened secret negotiations with Athens, and offered to betray Me
gara and Nisaea. The Long Walls and Nisaea were held by a Pelo
ponnesian garrison. The generals Hippocrates and Demosthene
organised the enterprise. While a force of 4000 hoplites and 60
horse marched overland by Eleusis, the generals sailed to Minoa
When night fell, they crossed to the mainland. There was a gate i
the eastern wall close to the spot where it joined the fortification o
Nisaea, and near the gate there was a hollow out of which earth t
make bricks had been dug. Here Hippocrates and 600 hoplites concealed themselves, while Demosthenes, with some light-armed Plataeans and a band of the youthful Peripoloi or Patrollers of Attica,
took up a position still nearer the gate, in a sacred enclosure of the
war-god, Enyalios. The conspirators had long matured their plan
for admitting the Athenians. As no boat could openly leave the harbour, owing to the occupation of Minoa, they had easily obtained
permission of the commander of the Peloponnesian garrison to carry
out through this gate a small boat on a cart at night, for the alleged
purpose of privateering. They used to convey the boat to the sea
along the ditch which surrounded Nisasa, and, after a midnight
row, return before dawn, and re-enter the Long Walls by the same
gate. This became a regular practice, so that they carried out the
boat without exciting any suspicion, on the night fixed for executing
the conspiracy. When the boat returned, the gate was opened, and
Demosthenes, who had been watching for the moment, leapt forward and forced his way in, assisted by the Megarians. They kept
the gate open till Hippocrates arrived with his hoplites, and, when
these were inside, the Long Walls were easily secured, the garrison
retreating into Nisaea. In the morning the main body of the Athenians arrived. A scheme for the betrayal of Megara had been con-

certed. The conspirators urged their fellow-citizens to sally forth
and do battle with the Athenians; they had secretly arranged that
the Athenians should rush in, and had anointed themselves with oil,
as a mark by which they should be known and spared in the assault.
But their political opponents, informed of the scheme, immediately
rushed to the gates and declared decisively that they should not be
opened; the battle would have to be first fought inside. The delay
apprised the Athenians that their friends had been baffled, and they
set about blockading Nisaea. Their energy was such that in two
days the circumvallation was practically completed, and the garrison, in want of food (for their supplies were derived from Megara),
capitulated. Thus the Long Walls, which they had built themselves,
and the port of Nisaea had passed again into the hands of the Athenians. They were not, however, destined to take the city on the hill.
The Spartan general Brasidas, who was recruiting in the north-east
regions of the Peloponnesus for an expedition to Thrace, hastened
to the relief of Megara. Nothing more than an indecisive skirmish
took place; the Athenians did not care to risk a battle and they resolved to be content with the acquisition of Nisaea. Soon afterwards
there was a revolution in Megara. The exiles from Pagae were received back; they soon got the power into their hands and murdered
their enemies. A narrow oligarchical constitution was established.
The new order of things, says Thucydides, lasted a very long time,
considering the small number of its authors.

Sect. 12. Athens fails in Boeotia

The recovery of Nisaea which had been lost by the Thirty Years'
Peace was a solid success, and it seemed to the ambitious hopes of
the two generals who had achieved it the first step in the recovery of
all the former conquests of their city. Hippocrates and Demosthenes induced Athens to strive to win back what she had lost at Coronea. But Boeotia was not like Megara; and an attempt on Boeotia
was an unwise reversion to the early continental policy of Pericles,
which Pericles had himself definitely abandoned. The dream of a
second Oenophyta was far less likely to come true than the threat
of a second Coronea. And the enterprise was a departure from the
Periclean strategy, of which Nicias was the chief exponent, and it is
significant that Nicias took no part in it. Moreover at this moment
Athens, as we shall see, ought to have concentrated her forces on the
defence of her Thracian possessions which were in grave jeopardy.
The Boeotian, like the Megarian, plan was formed in concert with
native malcontents who wished to overthrow the oligarchies in the

cities, to establish democratical governments, and probably dissolve
the Boeotian Confederacy. At this time the Confederacy was governed by eleven Boeotarchs, two of whom were chosen by Thebes
and four Councils, of unknown nature and functions.

Plan for
invading
Boeotia.

The new Boeotian plan, in which Demosthenes was now concerned, did not involve such extensive operations and combinations
as that which he had conceived when he invaded Aetolia. But the
two plans resembled each other in so far as each involved operations
from the Crisaean Gulf. Demosthenes, having sailed to Naupactus
and gathered a force of Acarnanians, was to go on to secure Siphae,
the port of Thespiae, on the shore of a promontory beneath Mount
Helicon. On the same day, the Athenian army under Hippocrates
was to enter Boeotia on the north-east and seize the temple of
Apollo at Delium, which stood on the sea-coast over against the
Lelantine plain in Euboea. At the same time Chaeronea, the extreme west town of the land, was to be seized by domestic conspirators. Thus on three sides the Boeotian government was to be
threatened; and the same day was fixed for the three attacks. But
the scheme was betrayed by a Phocian, and frustrated by the
Boeotarchs, who occupied Siphae and Chaeronea with strong forces,
and made a general levy of the Boeotians to oppose the army of
Hippocrates. It mattered little that Demosthenes made a mistake
about the day fixed for the attack; he found himself opposed by a
Boeotian force and could only retire. None of the internal movements in the Boeotian cities, on which the Athenians had counted,
took place.

Battle of
Delium,
474 B.C.

Hippocrates, however, had time to reach and fortify Delium. He
had a force of 7000 hoplites and over 20,000 light-armed troops.
A trench, with a strong rampart and palisade, was drawn round the
temple; and at noon on the fifth day from their departure from
Athens the work was completed. The army then left Delium, to return home. When they crossed the frontier and entered the Athenian territory of Oropus, at about a mile from Delium, the hoplites
halted, to wait for Hippocrates, who had remained behind to give
final directions to the garrison of the temple; the light-armed troops
proceeded on their way to Athens. The hoplites were interrupted in
their rest by a message from Hippocrates, ordering them to form
instantly in array of battle, as the enemy were upon them. The
Boeotian forces had been concentrated at Tanagra, about five miles
from Delium; and they had been persuaded by Pagondas, one of the
Theban Boeotarchs, to follow and attack the Athenians in their
retreat although they had left Boeotia. After a rapid march, Pagondas halted where a hill concealed him from the view of the Athe-

ians and drew up his army. It consisted of 7000 hoplites—the same number as that of the enemy—1000 cavalry, and over 10,000 light-armed men. The Thebans occupied the right wing, in the unique formation of a mass twenty-five shields deep; the other contingents varied in depth. The Athenian line was formed with the uniform and regular depth of eight shields. Hippocrates had arrived and was moving along the lines encouraging his men, when the enemy, who had for some time been visible on the crest of the hill, raised the Paean and charged down. The extreme parts of the wings never met, for watercourses lay between them. But the rest pushed shield against shield and fought fiercely. On the right the Athenians were victorious, but on the left they could not sustain the enormous pressure of the massed Theban force, especially as the Thebans were probably man for man stronger than the Athenians through a laborious athletic training. But even the victory on the right was made of no effect through the sudden appearance of a squadron of cavalry, which Pagondas, seeing the situation, had sent unobserved round the hill. The Athenians thought it was the vanguard of another army and fled. Hippocrates was slain and the army completely dispersed.

The battle of Delium confirmed the verdict of Coronea.

The Boeotians were left masters of the field, but Delium itself was still held by the invader. This led to a curious negotiation. The Athenians demanded their dead, and the Boeotians refused permission to take them unless they evacuated the temple of Apollo. Now if there was an international custom which was universally recognised among the Greeks, even among the barbarous Aetolians, it was the obligation of the victor to allow his defeated opponents to remove and bury their dead, unconditionally. This custom had the sanction of religious feeling and was seldom violated. But in this case the Boeotians had a pretext for departing from the usual practice. They alleged that the Athenians had on their side violated the laws of Hellenic warfare by seizing and fortifying the sanctuary of Delium and living in it, as if it were unconsecrated,—using even the sacred water. There seems little doubt that the conduct of the Boeotians was a greater departure from recognised custom than the conduct of the Athenians. The herald of the Athenians made what seems a foolish reply, to the effect that Delium having been occupied by the Athenians was now part of Attic soil, and that they showed the customary respect for the temple, so far as was possible in the circumstances. "You cannot tell us to quit Boeotia," he said, "for the garrison of Delium is not in Boeotia." The Boeotians made an appropriate answer to the quibble: "If you are in Boeotia, take

Subsequent negotiations.

what is yours; if you are in your own land, do as you like." The dead were not surrendered, and the Boeotians betook themselves

Capture of Delium, 17 days after the battle.

to the blockade of Delium. They took the place by a curious device. They sawed in two and hollowed out a great beam, which they joined together again very exactly, like a flute, and suspended a vessel by chains at the end of the beam; the iron mouth of a bellows directed downwards into the vessel was attached to the beam, of which a great part was itself overlaid with iron. This machine they brought up from a distance on carts to various points of the rampart where vine stems and wood had been most extensively used, and when it was quite near the wall they applied a large bellows to their own end of the beam and blew through it. The blast, prevented from escaping, passed into the vessel, which contained burning coals and sulphur and pitch; these made a huge flame and set fire to the rampart, so that no one could remain upon it. The garrison took flight and the fort was taken.[18] The Boeotians no longer refused to surrender the dead, who included rather less than 1000 hoplites.

SECT. 13. THE WAR IN THRACE. ATHENS LOSES AMPHIPOLIS

The defeat of Delium eclipsed the prestige of Athens, but did not seriously impair her strength. Yet it was a fatal year; and a much greater blow, entailing a permanent loss, was dealt her in her Thracian dominion.

The war in Thrace was always complicated by the neighbourhood of the kingdoms of Thrace and Macedonia. Before the fall of Potidaea the Athenians had formed an alliance with Sitalces, king of

The Thracian kingdom.

Thrace, and made his son Sadocas an Athenian citizen. The realm of Sitalces extended from the Strymon to the Euxine, its coast-line began at Abdera and ended at the mouth of the Ister. His revenue of tribute both from Greek towns and barbarians amounted, in the

£108,000.

reign of his successor, to more than 400 talents—counting only what was paid in the shape of coin. The alliance with Athens seems to have lasted till the king's death. An Athenian ambassador from

425 B.C.

Thrace, in the *Acharnians* of Aristophanes, reports to the Assembly:

> We passed our time
> In drinking with Sitalces. He's your friend,
> Your friend and lover, if ever there was one,
> And writes the name of Athens on his walls.[19]

[18] The description of the engine is a literal version of that of Thucydides Jowett's translation.
[19] Frere.

Perdiccas, the shifty king of Macedonia, played a double game between Athens and Sparta. At one time he helped the Chalcidians against Athens, at another he sided with Athens against her revolted allies. Throughout all changes of fortune, the city of Methone, situated to the south of the mouth of the Haliacmon, held to Athens with unshaken fidelity, though the varying relations between Athens and Perdiccas must have seriously affected the welfare of the Methonaeans. Some decrees relating to Methone have been preserved on a marble, adorned with a relief of the Athenian Demos seated, stretching out his hand to the Demos of Methone, who stands accompanied by a dog.

Double dealings of Macedonia.

Methone.

Perdiccas and the Chalcidians (of Olynthus) feared that the success of Pylos might be followed by increased activity of the Athenians in Thrace, and they sent an embassy to Sparta, requesting help, and expressing a wish that Brasidas might be the commander of whatever auxiliary force should be sent. It was wise policy for Sparta to threaten her rival in Thrace at this juncture, though the prospect of any abiding success was faint. No Spartans went, but 700 Helots were armed as hoplites; the government was glad to take the opportunity of removing another portion of this dangerous element in the population. Having obtained some Peloponnesian recruits and having incidentally, as we have already seen, saved Megara, Brasidas marched northward to the new colony of Heraclea.

Chalcidians and Macedonia appeal to Sparta.

Brasidas was a Spartan by mistake. He had nothing in common with his fellows, except personal bravery, which was the least of his virtues. He had a restless energy and spirit of enterprise, which received small encouragement from the slow and hesitating authorities of his country. He had an oratorical ability which distinguished him above the Lacedaemonians, who were notoriously unready of speech. He was free from political prejudices, and always showed himself tolerant, just, and moderate in dealing with political questions. Besides this, he was simple and straightforward; men knew that they could trust his word implicitly. But the quality which most effectually contributed to his brilliant career and perhaps most strikingly belied his Spartan origin was his power of winning popularity abroad and making himself personally liked by strangers. In Greece, the Spartan abroad was a proverb for insolence and misbehaviour. Brasidas shone out, on a dark background, by his frank and winning manners.

Character of Brasidas

His own tact and rapid movements, as well as the influence of Perdiccas, enabled Brasidas to march through Thessaly, which was by no means well disposed to the Lacedaemonians. When he

Brasidas at Acanthus

reached Macedonia, Perdiccas required his assistance against Arrhabaeus, the king of the Lyncestians, in Upper Macedonia. Brasidas was impatient to reach Chalcidice, and he contrived to make a separate arrangement with Arrhabaeus and abstained from invading Lyncestis, to the disappointment of Perdiccas. He then marched against Acanthus, situated on the base of the peninsula of Acte. The mass of the Acanthians were perfectly content with the position of their city as a member of the Athenian Confederacy; they had no grievance against Athens; and they were unwilling to receive the overtures of Brasidas. They were, however, induced by a small party to admit Brasidas alone into the city, and give him a hearing in the Assembly. From his lips the Acanthians learned the Lacedaemonian programme, and Thucydides has given the substance of what he said. "We declared at the beginning of the war that we were taking up arms to protect the liberties of Hellas against Athens; and for this purpose we are here now. You have a high repute for power and wisdom, and therefore a refusal from you will retard the good cause. Every city which joins me will retain her autonomy; the Lacedaemonians have pledged themselves to me on this point by solemn oaths. And I have not come to be the tool of a faction, or to enslave the many to the few; in that case we should be committing an act worse than the oppression of the Athenians. If you refuse and say that I have no right to thrust an alliance on a people against its will, I will ravage your land and force you to consent. And for two reasons I am justified in doing so. The tribute you pay to Athens is a direct and material injury to Sparta, for it contributes to strengthen her foe; and secondly, your example may prevent others from embracing freedom." When Brasidas retired, there was a long debate; much was said on both sides. The manner of Brasidas had produced a favourable impression; and the fear of losing the vintage was a powerful motive with many for acceding to his demand. The vote was taken secretly and the majority determined to detach themselves from Athens, though they had no practical grievance and were not enthusiastic for the change.[20]

Acanthus was an Andrian colony, and its action led to the adhesion of two other Andrian colonies, Stagira and Argilus; and the

[20] The scene in the Acanthian assembly called forth the admiration of the historian Grote. "There are," he says, "few facts in history wherein Grecian political reason and morality appear to greater advantage than in this proceeding of the Acanthians. The habit of fair, free, and pacific discussion—the established respect to the vote of the majority—the care to protect individual independence of judgment by secret suffrage—the deliberate estimate of reasons on both sides by each individual citizen—all these main laws and conditions of healthy political action appear as a part of the confirmed character of the Acanthians."

relations which Brasidas established with Argilus led to the capture of the most important of all Athenian posts in Thrace, and among the most important in the whole Athenian empire, the city of Amphipolis. This place, of which the foundation has been already recorded, had diminished the importance of Argilus and roused the jealousy of the Argilians; although some of the colonists were of Argilian origin. The coming of Brasidas offered Argilus an opportunity, for which she had been waiting, against the Athenians of Amphipolis. After a cold wintry night march, Brasidas found the Bridge of the Strymon defended only by a small guard, which he easily overpowered. Amphipolis was completely unprepared, but Brasidas did not venture to attack the city at once; he expected the gates to be opened by conspirators within, and meanwhile he made himself master of the territory.

(See above, p. 364.)

That a place of such first-rate importance as Amphipolis should be found unprepared at a time when an energetic enemy like Brasidas was actively engaged against other Athenian cities in the neighbourhood seemed a criminal negligence on the part of the two Strategoi to whom defence of the Thracian interests of Athens was entrusted. These were Thucydides, the son of Olorus, and Eucles. It was inexcusable in Eucles, who was in Amphipolis, to leave the Bridge without an adequate garrison; and it was considered culpable of Thucydides to have removed the Athenian squadron to the island of Thasos, where (it was insinuated) he possessed mines of his own. A message was sent at once to Thucydides; that officer hastened back with seven triremes and reached the mouth of the Strymon in the evening of the same day. But in the meantime Brasidas had offered the inhabitants of Amphipolis such easy terms that they were accepted. He promised every citizen who chose to remain equal political rights, without any loss of property; while all who preferred to go were allowed five days to remove their possessions. Had the Amphipolitans known how near Thucydides was, they would probably have declined to surrender. Thucydides arrived just too late. But he preserved Eion, at the mouth of the river, and repelled an attack of Brasidas.

Revolt of Amphipolis (424 B.C.).

Negligence of Thucydides the historian;

The true blame for the loss of Amphipolis probably rests not on the General, who was in a very difficult position, but on the Athenians, who, instead of making adequate provision for the defence of Thrace, were misled by the new strategy of Demosthenes into the unsuccessful expedition to Boeotia. It must be remembered that Thucydides was responsible for the safety of the whole coast of Chalcidice and Thrace; that at any moment he might be summoned to defend any part of it from Potidaea to the Chersonese; that

therefore either Eion or Thasos was a suitable centre for his headquarters; and that Eion had the disadvantage of having no harbour.
It may be that we are indebted to the fall of Amphipolis for the
great history of the war. The Athenians accused the neglect of their
generals, as having cost them one of their most valuable possessions.

his ban-
ishment.

Thucydides was sentenced to banishment, and it is probable that
Cleon, to whom he bore no good-will, was instrumental in drawing
down upon him a punishment which possibly was not deserved. But
in his exile the discredited general became the greatest of Greek historians. If he had remained at Athens and continued his official
career he might not have concentrated his whole mind on his history. By travelling in foreign lands, among the enemies of Athens
and in neutral states, Thucydides gained a large knowledge of the
Hellenic world and wrote from a wider point of view than he could
have done if he had only had an Athenian experience. "Associating," he says himself, "with both sides, with the Peloponnesians
quite as much as with the Athenians, because of my exile, I was thus
enabled to watch quietly the course of events." Judged in this way,
the fall of Amphipolis, a great loss to Athens, may have been a great
gain to the world.

Reduction
of Acte.

Having secured the Strymon, Brasidas retraced his steps and
subdued the small towns on the high eastern tongue of Chalcidice.
The Andrian Sane and another place held out, and their obscurity
saved them. Brasidas hastened on to gain possession of Torone, the

Capture
of Torone,
424-3 B.C.

strongest city of Sithonia. A small party of the citizens invited and
expected him; but the rest of the inhabitants and the Athenian garrison knew nothing of his coming until the place was in his hands.
Torone was a hill city by the sea. Besides its walls, it had the protection of a fort on a height which rose out of the water and was
connected with the city by a narrow neck of land. This fortress,
known as Lecythus, was occupied by an Athenian garrison. Brasidas halted within about half a mile from the city before daybreak.
Seven bold soldiers, light-armed and carrying daggers, were secretly
introduced by the conspirators. They killed the sentinels on the top
of the hill, and then broke down a postern gate, and undid the bars
of the great gate near the market-place, in order that the men without might rush in from two sides. A hundred targeteers who had
drawn near to the walls dashed in first, and when a signal was given
Brasidas followed with the rest. The surprise was complete. Fifty
Athenian hoplites were sleeping in the agora; a few were cut down;
most escaped to the fort of Lecythus, which was held for some days
and then captured.

Brasidas called an assembly of the Toronaeans, and spoke to

them in words which sounded strange indeed falling from the mouth of an Hellenic victor. He told them that he had not come to injure the city or the citizens; that those who had not aided in the conspiracy to admit him would be treated on a perfect equality with the others; that the Lacedaemonians had never suffered any wrong from Torone; and that he did not think the worse of those who opposed him.

SECT. 14. NEGOTIATIONS FOR PEACE

In the meantime the Athenians had taken no measures to check the victorious winter-campaign of Brasidas. Their inactivity was due to two causes. The disaster of Delium had disheartened them, and rendered the citizens unwilling to undertake fresh toil in Thrace. In Grecian history we must steadfastly keep in view that we are reading about citizen soldiers, not about professional soldiers; and that the temper of the time, whether of confidence or dismay, modifies all the calculations of military and political prudence. Secondly, the peace party, especially represented by the generals Nicias and Laches, took advantage of this depression to work in the direction of peace. The possession of the Spartan captives gave the means of coming to terms with Sparta at any moment, but it was clear that they could not now conclude a peace on such favourable terms as would have been possible a year before. If an able statesman, like Pericles, had at this time possessed the confidence and guided the counsels of the Athenians, he would have persuaded them to postpone all thoughts of peace until the success of Brasidas had been decisively checked and the prestige of Athens in some degree retrieved. This was obviously the true policy, which would have enabled Athens to win the full advantage of the captives of Sphacteria. It was a policy which Cleon, a far abler politician than any of his opponents, must have preached loudly in the Assembly. But the Athenians were not in a mood to weigh considerations of policy; they were swayed by the feelings of the hour, which were flattered by the arguments of the military experts; and they decisively inclined to peace.

Athenian inactivity.

The Lacedaemonians were more deliberately set on peace than the Athenians. Their anxiety to recover the Sphacterian captives increased, and on the other hand they desired to set a term to the career of Brasidas in Chalcidice. They wished to take advantage of the considerable successes he had already won, to extort favourable conditions from Athens before any defeat should undo or reverse his triumphs. Nor was the news of his exploits received at Sparta

Sparta desires peace.

with unmixed feelings of pleasure. They were rather regarded with jealousy and distrust. The victories had not been won by an army of Spartan citizens, but by the brilliant un-Spartan qualities of Brasidas and a force of which the effectiveness entirely depended on its leader. Brasidas had broken through the fetters of Lacedaemonian method, and his fellow-citizens felt that he was a man of different fibre from themselves, and suspected and disliked him accordingly. Moreover the personal influence of king Pleistoanax was thrown weightily into the scale of peace. This king had been banished just before the Thirty Years' Peace, on the ground that he had taken bribes to spare Attica when he invaded it after the deliverance of Megara. He had lived for nearly twenty years in western Arcadia on the mountain of Lycaeon, beside the dread sanctuary of Zeus, of which it was told that whosoever entered it lost his shadow and died before the year was out. Even here Pleistoanax was afraid for his life. His house was half within the precincts, so that in case of danger he could retire into the sacred place without passing his door. But he had influence at Delphi, and whenever the Spartans consulted that oracle they were always bidden to take back into their own land the seed of the demi-god, the son of Zeus, or else they would have to plough with a silver share. The Lacedaemonians at length recalled him, and re-enthroned him as king with ancient and most solemn ceremonies. But his enemies now vexed him with the charge of having bribed the Pythian priestess to procure his recall. Pleistoanax conceived that such charges would fall to the ground if he satisfied the people by negotiating a permanent peace and restoring as speedily as possible the prisoners from their captivity in Athens to their impatient friends at home. And as a matter of fact, Sparta, had everything to gain from making peace at once, unless she was prepared to adopt the Imperial policy of Athens, against which it had been hitherto her rôle to protest. Such a policy might for a time have met with some success if she had put her whole confidence in Brasidas, but must soon have been checked by the naval superiority of her rival.

One year's truce (March 423).

Pleistoanax and Nicias understood each other; and Nicias, a man of commonplace ability and possessed by one idea, played into the hands of Sparta. It was not, however, an easy matter to arrange the exact terms of a durable pacification, while it was important for Athens that the negotiation should be made before she experienced any further losses in Thrace. Accordingly the two states agreed on a truce for a year, which would give them time to arrange quietly and at leisure the conditions of a permanent peace. The truce and some of its conditions were suggested by Athens; the terms were drawn up at Sparta and accepted by the Spartan Assembly; and were then conveyed to Athens, where they were proposed for the acceptance of the Athenian Assembly by Laches. The clauses were the following: (1) Free access to the Delphic oracle was ensured to all. For Athens had been debarred from consulting it during the war. (2) Both parties guaranteed the protection of the treasures of Delphi. (3) During the truce both parties should keep what they had; the Athenians retaining Pylos, Cythera, Argolic Methone, Nisaea, and Minoa. (4) The Lacedaemonians were not to sail, even along their own coasts, in warships or in merchant vessels exceeding a certain size (twelve tons). (5) The free passage of envoys, for the purpose of arranging a peace, was provided for. (6) Neither party was to receive deserters; and (7) disputes, in case they arose, were to be decided by arbitration.

The truce was sworn to. But in the meantime an event happened in Chalcidice which was to disappoint the pacific calculations of the statesmen at Athens and Sparta. The city of Scione on the western prong of the Chalcidian fork revolted from Athens and invited Brasidas, much to that general's surprise. For it was far more hazardous for the towns on the peninsula of Pallene to defy the authority of Athens than for any others; since by the strong city of Potidaea, which stretched entirely across the narrow isthmus, they were isolated and as much exposed to the full force of Athenian power as if they had been islanders. The arrival of Brasidas and the words he spoke to them wound up the men of Scione to the highest pitch of enthusiasm; they set a golden crown on his head, as the liberator of Hellas, and their admiration for him personally was shown by casting garlands on him, as if he were a victorious athlete,—so great was his popularity.

Revolt of Scione.

At this point an Athenian and a Lacedaemonian commissioner arrived to announce the truce, which had in fact been concluded two days before Scione revolted. The Athenians refused to admit Scione to the benefit of the armistice until the authorities at home had been consulted. There was deep indignation at Athens when the news of the defection of Scione arrived; it was practically the rebellion of "islanders" relying on the land-power of Sparta. Cleon was able to take advantage of this exasperation and carry a decree that Scione should be destroyed and all the male inhabitants slain. This incident brings out in an interesting way the geographical difference between the three sea-girt promontories of Chalcidice as to their degrees of participation in the insular character. Acte, with its steep inhospitable shores, is far more continental than insular; Sithonia partakes of both natures more equally, is more strictly a half-island; Pallene is more an island than part of the mainland. And we see the political importance of such geographical differences. The loss of Scione produces an irritation at Athens which the loss of Torone could not inspire.

The revolt of Mende.

The revolt of Scione was followed by that of the neighbouring town of Mende, and although this happened distinctly after the truce had been made, Brasidas did not hesitate to accept the alliance of Mende, his plea being that in certain points the Athenians themselves had broken the truce. The case of Mende differed from that of Scione; for the revolt was the doing not of the people but of an oligarchical faction. Brasidas was then obliged to join Perdiccas in another expedition against Arrhabaeus, king of the Lyncestians. The fact that the Macedonian monarch was contributing to the pay of the Peloponnesian army rendered it necessary for Brasidas to co-operate in an enterprise which was of no interest to the Greeks. Arrhabaeus was defeated in a battle, but a reinforcement of Illyrians came to his help, and the warlike reputation of Illyria was so great that their approach produced a panic among the Macedonians

Perdiccas breaks with Brasidas.

and the whole army of Perdiccas fled, leaving the small force of Brasidas to retreat as best it could. He was in great jeopardy, but effected his retreat successfully. The incident led to a breach between Brasidas and the Macedonians; Perdiccas changed sides once more, and proved his new friendship to Athens by preventing Lacedaemonian troops, which had been sent to join Brasidas, from crossing Thessaly.

The truce observed except in Thrace.

Brasidas returned to Torone and found that an Athenian armament of fifty ships, under Nicias and Niceratus, had recovered Mende, and was besieging Scione. Everywhere else the truce was observed, and by tacit consent the hostilities in Thrace were not allowed to affect the rest of Greece. But it was inevitable that they should frustrate the purpose for which the truce had been concluded. It was impossible that negotiations with a view to the definitive peace should proceed in exactly the same way as had been originally contemplated; by the end of the year there was a marked change in public feeling at Athens and the influence of Cleon was again in the ascendant. If Nicias had played into the hands of Sparta, Brasidas had played into the hands of Cleon and effectually embarrassed the home government. His conduct first in regard to Scione and then in regard to Mende was indefensible and entirely governed by personal considerations. The gold crown of Scione seems to have acted like a potent spell in arousing his ambition, and he began to play a war-game of his own. His policy was the more unhappy, as he was perfectly aware that it was impossible to protect the cities of Pallene against the fleets of their indignant mistress. He effectually hindered the conclusion of peace, which his city sincerely desired. Brasidas and Cleon, Thucydides says, were the chief opponents of the peace; but while the motives of Brasidas were purely personal, the policy of Cleon, whatever his motives may have been, was statesmanlike. He adopted the principle of Pericles that Athens must maintain her empire unimpaired, and he saw that this could not be done without energetic opposition to the progress of Brasidas in Thrace. The charge of Thucydides that Cleon desired war because he could not so easily conceal his own dishonesty in peace, does not carry the least conviction. When the truce expired, Cleon was able to carry a resolution that an expedition should be made to reconquer Amphipolis. It does not appear whether he was himself anxious for the command, in consequence of his previous success at Pylos, or whether the opposition and lukewarmness of the strategoi practically forced him into it. But it is certain that all possible difficulties were thrown in his way by Nicias and the peace party, who in their hearts doubtless hoped for the complete failure of his enterprise.

March
422 B.C.

Sect. 15. Battle of Amphipolis and Peace of Nicias

Cleon set sail with thirty ships, bearing 1200 Athenian hoplites, 300 Athenian cavalry, as well as allies. Taking some troops from the force which was still blockading Scione, he gained a considerable success at the outset by taking Torone and capturing the Lacedaemonian governor; Brasidas arrived too late to relieve it. Cleon went on to the mouth of the Strymon and made Eion his headquarters, intending to wait there until he had augmented his army by reinforcements from Thrace and Macedonia.

Not far from its mouth the stream of the Strymon expands into the lake Kerkinitis; on narrowing again into its proper channel it is forced to bend to the westward in order to skirt a hill, and forms a great loop, before it disgorges its waters into the sea close to the walls of Eion. In this loop the high city of Amphipolis stood, watergirt as its name implies,—the river serving as its natural defence, so that it required artificial bulwarks only on the eastern side. On the right bank of the river, to the west of the town, rose the hill of Cerdylion; on the east were the heights of Pangaeus. A ridge joined Pangaeus with the hill of Amphipolis, and the wall of the city crossed the ridge. The Strymon Bridge was outside the southwestern extremity of the wall; but, since the place had passed into the hands of Brasidas, a palisade had been built connecting the wall

Site of
Amphipolis.

with the bridge. Brasidas with some of his forces took up a commanding position on the hill of Cerdylion, from which he had a wide view of the surrounding country; while other troops remained in Amphipolis under the command of Clearidas, whom he had appointed governor. Their hoplites numbered about 2000.

The discontent and murmurs of his troops forced Cleon to move prematurely. The soldiers had grumbled at leaving Athens under an utterly inexperienced commander to face a general like Brasidas, and they were now displeased at his inaction. In order to do something, Cleon led his army to the top of the ridge, near the city wall, where he could obtain a view of the country beyond, and, as he saw Brasidas on Cerdylion, he had no fear of being attacked. But Brasidas was resolved to attack, before reinforcements should arrive; and, seeing the Athenians move, he descended from Cerdylion and entered Amphipolis. The Athenians, who had reached the ridge, could observe the whole army gathered within the city, and Brasidas himself offering sacrifice at the temple of Athena; and Cleon was presently informed that the feet of men and horses, ready to sally forth, could be seen under one of the gates. Having verified this fact for himself, Cleon gave the signal to wheel to the left and retreat to Eion; it was the only possible line of retreat, and necessarily exposed the unshielded side to an enemy issuing from the city. But he made the fatal mistake of not preparing his men for action, in case they should be forced to fight; he rashly calculated that he would have time to get away. Hence when Brasidas, with 150 hoplites, came forth from one of the gates, ran up the road, and charged the Athenian centre, the left wing, which was in advance, was struck with terror and took to flight. At the same time the rest of the garrison of Amphipolis, led by Clearidas, had issued from a more northerly gate and attacked the Athenian right. Here a stand was made, though Cleon, unused to the dangers of warfare, proved himself no better than many of his hoplites, who were said to be the flower of the army. He fled, and was shot down by a targeteer. But the bravery of Brasidas was doomed as well as the cowardice of Cleon by the equal decree of Death. As he was turning to assist Clearidas, he received a mortal wound and was carried into the city. He lived long enough to be assured of the utter rout of the foe; but his death had practically converted the victory into a defeat. The people of Amphipolis gave him the honours of a hero; they made him their founder, and removed all the memorials of the true founder of their colony, the Athenian Hagnon. Sacrifices were offered to Brasidas, and yearly games celebrated in his honour.

Battle.

Death of
Cleon.

Death of
Brasidas.

The death of Brasidas removed the chief obstacle to peace; for no man was competent or disposed to resume his large designs in Thrace. The defeat and death of Cleon gave a free hand to Nicias and the peace party. The peace party were in truth far more responsible for the disaster than Cleon, whom they had placed in a false position. Thus the battle of Amphipolis led immediately to the conclusion of peace; and the comic poet could rejoice in the destruction of the pestle and mortar—Cleon and Brasidas—with which the spirits of War and Tumult had pounded the cities of Greece. But the desire of peace seems to have been even stronger at Sparta than at Athens, where there was a certain feeling, in spite of the longing for a rest from warfare, that the lustre of the city was tarnished and something strenuous should be done. Menaces of invading Attica were required to apply the necessary pressure; though they could hardly have been seriously contemplated, as long as the captives were in an Athenian prison. Negotiations were protracted during autumn and winter, and the peace was definitely concluded about the end of March.

The Peace, of which Nicias and Pleistoanax were the chief authors, was fixed for a term of fifty years. Athens undertook to restore all the posts which she had occupied during the war against the Peloponnesians; Pylos, Cythera, Methone, Atalanta, and Pteleon in Thessaly. But she insisted upon retaining Sollion and Anactorion, and the port of Nisaea. The Lacedaemonians engaged to restore Amphipolis, and to relinquish Argilus, Stagira, Acanthus, Scolus, Olynthus, Spartolus, which cities, remaining independent, were to pay a tribute to Athens according to the assessment of Aristides. Moreover, the fortress of Panacton, in Mount Cithaeron, which the Boeotians had recently occupied, was to be restored to Athens. Certain towns in the possession of Athens, such as Torone, were to be dealt with at the discretion of Athens. All captives on both sides were to be liberated.[21]

Result of the battle —peace.

(Aristophanes.)

422-1 B.C.

Peace of Nicias, 421 B.C. (March).

[21] The details of this Treaty and of the Truce of 423 B.C. have been given fully by Thucydides, and are of great importance for the study of the diplomatic methods of the Greek states. Other clauses of the Peace of Nicias are as follows: The common temples of Greece are to be free to all. The autonomy of the Delphians and their temple is ensured. Controversies between the contracting parties are to be settled by legal means. The inhabitants of any city handed over to the Athenians are allowed to leave it and take their property with them. Argilus, Olynthus, etc., may become allies of Athens, if they voluntarily consent; and Mecyberna, Sane, and Singe are to be independent. If any matter is forgotten in this contract, the Athenians and Lacedaemonians may make alterations by mutual agreement. The oaths to the Peace are to be renewed every year, and the terms are to be inscribed on pillars at Olympia, Delphi, Isthmus, and on the Acropolis of Athens, and in the Temple of Apollo at Amyclae.

Corinth,
Megara,
Boeotia
refuse to
accept the
Peace.

It appeared immediately that the situation was not favourable to a durable peace; for, when the terms were considered at Sparta by a meeting of deputies of the Peloponnesian allies, they were emphatically denounced as unjust by three important states, Corinth, Boeotia, and Megara. Corinth was indignant at the surrender of Sollion and Anactorion; Megara was furious that Nisaea should be abandoned to the enemy; and Boeotia was unwilling to hand over Panacton. Yet Athens could hardly have demanded less. The consequence was that the Peace was only partial; those allies which were politically of most consequence refused to accept it, and they were joined by Elis; the diplomacy of Nicias was a complete failure, so far as it aimed at compassing an abiding peace. But since the deepest cause of the war lay in the commercial competition between Athens and Corinth, and since the interests of Sparta were not at stake, the treaty might seem at least to have the merit of simplifying the situation.

Cleon's
policy
justified,
if the
Periclean
imperial-
ism was
justified.

But, if we admit the justification of the imperial policy of Pericles, then the policy of vigorous action advocated by Cleon was abundantly justified. It may safely be said that if the conduct of the state had rested entirely with Cleon, and if the military talents of the city had been loyally placed at his disposal, the interests of Athens (as Pericles understood them) would have been far better served than if Nicias and his party had been allowed to manage all things as they willed without the restraint of Cleon's opposition. Few statesmen of the merit of Cleon have come before posterity for judgment at such a great disadvantage, condemned by Thucydides, held up to eternal ridicule by Aristophanes. If we allow for the personal prejudice of Thucydides, these testimonies only show that Cleon was a coarse, noisy, ill-bred, audacious man, offensive to noblemen and formidable to officials—the watchful dog of the people. Nothing is proved against his political insight or his political honesty. The portrait of Aristophanes in the *Knights* carries no more historical value than nowadays a caricature in a comic paper. He too had suffered from the assaults of Cleon, who

> had dragged him to the Senate House,
> And trodden him down and bellowed over him,
> And mauled him till he scarce escaped alive.[22]

The
Peace,
421 B.C.

The Peace of Nicias was celebrated by a play of Aristophanes, which admirably expresses the exuberant joy then felt at Athens, but carefully avoids the suggestion of any noble sentiment that may have quickened the poet's delight in the accomplishment of the

[22] Frere.

policy he had advocated. So Cleon's friends might have said; but we judge Aristophanes unfairly, if we misapprehend the comic poet's function. Comedy did not guide public opinion, but rather echoed it; comedy set up no exalted ideal or high standard of action. The best hits were those which tickled the man in the market-place and more or less responded to his thoughts. Aristophanes had his own political prejudices and predilections; but as a son of Athens he was assuredly proud of the great place which her democracy had won for her in the world. It was the nature and the business of his muse to distort in the mirror of comedy the form and feature of the age; but the poet who was inspired to write the verse

O rich and renowned, and with violets crowned, O Athens, the envied of nations!

cannot have been altogether out of sympathy with those who strove to maintain the imperial position of his country.

Fig. 66.—Coin of Segesta, after 431 B.C. (reverse). River god with hunting-spears; two dogs; term [legend (invisible in reproduction): (ΕΓΕΣ)ΤΑΙΩΝ].

Fig. 67.—Coin of Catane, between 431 and 404 B.C. (obverse). Bay-wreathed Apollo; bell; crayfish [legend: ΚΑΤΑΝΑΙΩΝ].

CHAPTER XI

THE DECLINE AND DOWNFALL OF THE ATHENIAN EMPIRE

SECT. I. NEW POLITICAL COMBINATIONS WITH ARGOS

Sparta and Athens form a defensive alliance.

SPARTA had good reasons for desiring peace; the prospect in the Peloponnesus gave her no little concern. Mantinea had been gradually enlarging her boundaries southwards; and that could not be permitted. Elis was sulky and hostile, because, in a quarrel with Lepreon, Sparta had supported her rival. Far more serious than these minor vexations was the circumstance that the treaty of peace with Argos was about to expire. It had been a consideration of supreme importance for Sparta, when she entered upon the war with Athens, that for the next ten years she was secure on the side of her old Peloponnesian rival. But there was now the chance that Athens and Argos might combine, and, as Argos had not agreed to renew the treaty, there was urgent need to come to terms with Athens. These reasons which recommended the peace to Sparta ought to have prevented Athens from consenting to it. The settlement was a complete failure. Not only did the Corinthians and the other chief allies refuse to accede to it, but the signatories found themselves unable to carry out the terms they had agreed upon. The Chalcidians refused to surrender Amphipolis, and the Spartans could not compel them. Athens therefore justly declined to carry out her part of the bargain. As a way out of this deadlock, the Spartans, impatient at all costs to recover the Sphacterian prisoners, conceived the device of entering into a defensive alliance with their old enemy. This proposal, warmly supported by Nicias, was accepted, and the captives were at length restored,—Athens still retaining Pylos and Cythera.

This approximation between Sparta and Athens led directly to the dissolution of the Peloponnesian league. Corinth, Mantinea, and Elis, considering themselves deserted by their leader, broke with her, and formed an alliance with Argos, who now enters upon the scene. The Chalcidians of Thrace joined. There was, however, little reason to fear or hope that the intimacy between Sparta and Athens could be long or strong, seeing that Athens insisted on keeping Cythera and Pylos until Amphipolis should be restored to her and the other states should accede to the Peace. In the following year these unstable political combinations were upset by a change in the balance of parties at Athens, and by the triumph of the anti-Athenian war-party at Sparta. The opposition to Nicias was led by Hyperbolus, a man of the same class and same kind of ability as Cleon; a comic poet—and no statesman was such a favourite butt of comedy as Hyperbolus—described him as a Cleon in hyperbole. But the party was now strengthened by the accession of a young man of high birth, brilliant intellect, and no morality, Alcibiades, son of Cleinias. Educated by his kinsman Pericles in democratic traditions, he was endowed by nature with extraordinary beauty and talents, by fortune with the inheritance of wealth which enabled him to indulge an inordinate taste for ostentation. He had shocked his kinsfolk and outraged the city, not by his dissoluteness, but by the incredible insolence which accompanied it. The numerous anecdotes of his petulance, which no one dared to punish, need not all be true; but they illustrate the fact that undue respect for persons of birth and wealth had not disappeared in the Athenian democracy. Alcibiades was feared and courted, and pursued by lovers of both sexes. He fought with bravery at Delium, where his life was saved by his friend Socrates the philosopher. It was a celebrated friendship. Intellectual power and physical courage were the only points of likeness between them; socially and morally, as well as in favour and fortune, they were as contrasted as two men well could be. Though Socrates took no interest in politics, he was an unequalled dialectician, and an aspiring statesman found his society a good training for the business of political debate. Alcibiades indeed had not in him the stuff of which true statesmen are made; he had not the purpose, the perseverance, or the self-control. An extremely able and dexterous politician he certainly was; but he wanted that balance which a politician, whether scrupulous or unscrupulous, must have in order to be a great statesman. Nor had Alcibiades any sincere belief in the democratic institutions of his country, still less any genuine sympathy with the advanced democratic party whose cause he espoused. When he said—as Thucydides makes him say—at Sparta, at a

Disruption of Peloponnesian league.

420 B.C.

Hyperbolus.

Alcibiades.

later stage of his career, that democracy is "acknowledged folly," he assuredly expressed what he felt in his heart. Yet at this time his ultimate aim may have been to win such a place as that which Pericles had held, and rule his country without being formally her ruler. At all events he saw his way to power through war and conquest.

The accession of Alcibiades was particularly welcome to the radical party, not so much on account of his family connexions, his diplomatic and rhetorical talents, but because he had a military training and could perform the functions of strategos. Unfitness for the post of strategos was, as we have seen, the weak point in the position of men like Hyperbolus and Cleon. When Alcibiades was elected a strategos and Nicias was not re-elected, the prospects of the radical party looked brighter. The change was immediately felt. Athens entered into an alliance with Argos, and her allies Elis and Mantinea, for a hundred years; [1] and the treaty was sealed by a joint expedition against Epidaurus. Sparta assisted Epidaurus, and then the Athenians declared that the Lacedaemonians had broken the Peace.

The new policy of Athens received a check by the return of Nicias to power and the refusal of the people to re-elect the adventurous Alcibiades; but the alliance with Argos was not broken off.

Sparta, alarmed by the activity of Argos against Epidaurus, resolved to strike a blow, and sent forth in summer an army under king Agis to invade the Argive land. The allies gathered at Phlius, and Corinth, which had no longer any reason to hold aloof, sent a contingent. The Argive troops under Thrasyllus, with their Mantinean and Elean allies, were in every way inferior to the enemy; yet concentrating close to Nemea, they could easily defend the chief pass from the north into the plain of Argos. But Agis outmanœuvred them. Sending the Boeotians along the main road by Nemea, he led his own troops by a difficult mountain path, from the west, and descended into the plain by the valley of the Inachus; the Corinthians and Phliasians he sent over by another pass. Thus the Argives were hemmed in between two armies and cut off from their city. They left their position near Nemea and came down into the plain; the Boeotians appear not to have followed. The soldiers of both Thrasyllus and Agis were confident of victory, but the generals were of another mind. Agis, as well as his antagonist, considered his position precarious, and consequently they came to terms, concluding a truce for four months. On both sides there was

---

[1] A fragment of the stone on which this treaty (given in full by Thucydides) was written was found near the Dionysiac Theatre.

a loud outcry against the generals, and Thrasyllus was nearly stoned to death by his disappointed soldiers.

Athenian forces now arrived at Argos, under Laches and Nicostratus, accompanied by Alcibiades as an ambassador. Stepping beyond his instructions, Alcibiades induced the allies to disregard the truce, on the technical ground that, not having been accepted by the Athenians, it was not valid. The allied troops accordingly crossed the mountains into Arcadia and won Orchomenus. The men of Elis then proposed to move against their own particular foes, the people of Lepreon; and being out-voted they deserted their allies and marched home. The army, thus weakened by the loss of 3000 hoplites, was obliged to hasten southward to protect Mantinea, against which the Lacedaemonians under Agis, along with the men of Tegea, had meanwhile come forth.

And now, at length, a great battle was fought. The exact numbers are not known, but must have approached 10,000 on each side. Coming round the hill of Scope, the spur of Mount Maenalus, which projects into the plain between Tegea and Mantinea, at the point where the territories of the two cities met, the Lacedaemonians found the enemy drawn up for fight and proved their excellent discipline by a rapid formation in the face of the hostile line. They won the battle; but their success was endangered, and its completeness diminished, by a hitch which occurred at the outset. There was a tendency in all Greek armies, when engaging, to push towards the right, each man fearing for his own exposed right side and trying to edge under the screen of his neighbour's shield. Consequently, an army was always inclined to outflank the left wing of the enemy by its own right. On this occasion, Agis observed that the Mantineans, who were on the right wing of the foe, stretched far beyond his own left wing, and fearing it would be disastrously outflanked and surrounded, gave a signal to the troops of his extreme left to make a lateral movement further towards the left; and at the same time he commanded two captains on his right to move their divisions round to fill up the gap thus created. The first order was executed, but the two captains refused to move. The result was that the extreme left was isolated, and utterly routed, while a band of 1000 chosen Argives dashed through the gap. On the right, however, the Lacedaemonians were completely victorious over the Athenians and other allies. The Athenians would have been surrounded and utterly at the mercy of their foes, if Agis had not recalled his troops to assist his discomfited left wing. Both Laches and Nicostratus fell.

The Lacedaemonians returned home and celebrated the feast of the Carnean Apollo in joy. The victory did much to restore the

Battle of Mantinea, 418 B.C. (Scope = hill of Mytika.)

Results of the battle.

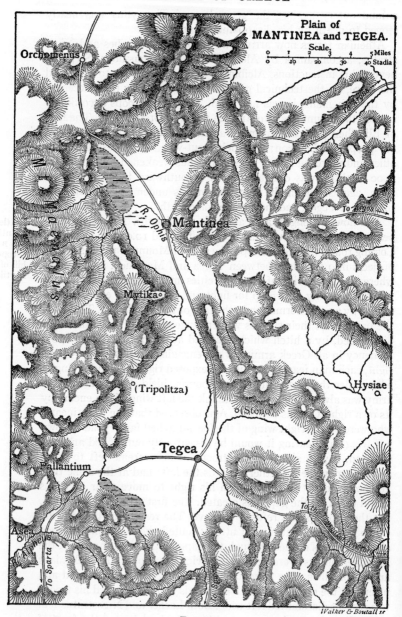

Plain of
MANTINEA and TEGEA.

Scale.

Orchomenus

R. Ophis

Mantinea

Mytika

(Tripolitza)

(Steno)

Hysiae

Tegea

Pallantium

Asea

To Argos

To Sparta

Walker & Boutall sc

FIG. 68.

prestige of Sparta, which had dwindled since the disaster of Sphacteria. The public opinion of Greece had pronounced Sparta to be stupid and inert; it now began to reconsider its judgment. But the victory had direct political results; it transformed the situation in the Peloponnesus. One of those double changes which usually went together, a change in the constitution and a change in foreign policy, was brought about at Argos. The democracy was replaced by an oligarchy, and the alliance with Athens was abandoned for an alliance with Sparta. Mantinea, Elis, and the Achaean towns also went over to the victor. Athens was again isolated.

Argos joins Sparta.

It was probably at this juncture that the advanced democrats in Athens made an attempt to remove from their way the influential man who was their chief opponent, Nicias. It had been due to his counsels that Argos had not been more effectively supported; there was probably a good deal of dissatisfaction at Athens; and, when Hyperbolus proposed that a vote of ostracism should be held, he had good grounds to hope that there would be a decision against Nicias, and no apparent reason to fear for himself. He might calculate that most of the supporters of Nicias would vote against the more dangerous Alcibiades. The calculation was so well grounded that it missed its mark; for Alcibiades, seeing the risk which threatened him, deserted Hyperbolus and the democratic party, and allied himself with Nicias. So it came about that Hyperbolus was ruined by his own machination; all the followers of Nicias and Alcibiades wrote *his* name on their sherds, and he was banished for ten years. His political career had ended. This was the last case of ostracism at Athens; the institution was not abolished, but it became a dead letter. Henceforward it was deemed a sufficient safeguard for the constitution that any man who proposed a measure involving a change in any established law was liable to be prosecuted by the process known as the *Graphê Paranomôn* and incur the penalty of death.

Ostracism of Hyperbolus, 418-7 B.C.

The new alliance of the pious and punctilious Nicias, champion of peace, with the profane and unstable Alcibiades, bent on enterprises of war, was more unnatural than that between the high-born noble and the lamp-maker. But Nicias seems to have been to some small extent aroused from his policy of inactivity. We find him undertaking an expedition against Chalcidice, where nothing had been done since the Peace, except the capture of Scione and the execution of all the male inhabitants.

417 B.C.

421 B.C.

Nicias failed in an attempt on Amphipolis; but in the following year an enterprise in the southern Aegean was attended with success. The island of Melos had hitherto remained outside the sea-

Conquest of Melos, 416 B.C.

Athenian
cleruchs.

lordship of the Athenians, and Athens, under the influence of Alcibiades, now attacked her. The town of Melos was invested in the summer by land and sea, and surrendered at discretion in the following winter. All the men of military age were put to death, the other inhabitants were enslaved, and the island was colonised by Athenians.

Emphasis
laid by
Thucy-
dides
on the
conquest
of Melos.

The conquest of Melos is remarkable, not for the rigorous treatment of the Melians, which is merely another example of the inhumanity which we have already met in the cases of Plataea, Mytilene, Scione, but for the unprovoked aggressions of Athens, without any tolerable pretext. By the curious device of constructing a colloquy between Athenian envoys and the Melian government, Thucydides has brought the episode into dramatic relief. In this scene the Athenians assert in frank and shameless words the "law of nature" that the stronger should rule over the weaker. This was a doctrine which it was Hellenic to follow, but unusual to enunciate in all its nakedness; and in the negotiations which preceded the blockade no Athenian spokesmen would have uttered the undiplomatic audacities which Thucydides ascribes to them. The historian has artfully used the dialogue to indicate the overbearing spirit of the Athenians, flown with insolence, on the eve of an enterprise which was destined to bring signal retribution and humble their city in the dust. Different as Thucydides and Herodotus were in their minds and methods, they had both the same, characteristically Hellenic, feeling for a situation like this. The check of Athens rounded the theme of the younger, as the check of Persia had rounded the theme of the elder, historian; and, although Nemesis, who moves openly in the pages of Herodotus, is not acknowledged by Thucydides, she seems to have cast a shadow here.

Temple of
Athena
Polias
(see
below,
p. 482).
The As-
clepieum.
The Eleu-
sinian
decree
(medim-
nus = 1½
bushels),
418 B.C.

During the years immediately succeeding the Peace there are some signs that the Athenians turned their attention to matters of religion, which had perhaps been too much neglected during the war. It may have been in these years that they set about the building of a new temple for Athena and Erechtheus, concerning which we shall hear again at a later stage. It may have been at this time that Asclepius, the god of healing, came over with his snake from Epidaurus, and established himself in a sanctuary under the south slope of the Acropolis. And it was probably soon after the Peace that a resolution was carried imposing a new tax upon the fruits of the earth for the maintenance of the worship of Eleusis. The farmers of Attica were required to pay $\frac{1}{600}$th of every medimnus of barley and $\frac{1}{1200}$th of every medimnus of wheat. The same burden was imposed upon the allies; and the Council was directed to invite "all

Hellenic cities whom it seemed possible to approach on the matter"
to send first-fruits likewise.

SECT. 2. THE WESTERN POLICY OF ATHENS

During the fifth century the eyes of Athenian statesmen often
wandered to western Greece beyond the seas. We can surprise some
oblique glances, as early as the days of Themistocles, and we have
seen how under Pericles a western policy definitely began. An
alliance was formed with the Elymian town of Segesta, and subsequently treaties of alliance (the stone records are still partly preserved) were concluded (as has been already mentioned) with
Leontini and Rhegium. One general object of Athens was to support
the Ionian cities against the Dorian, which were predominant in
number and power, and especially against Syracuse, the daughter
and friend of Corinth. The same purpose of counteracting the
Dorian predominance may be detected in the foundation of Thurii.
But Thurii did not effect this purpose. The colonists were a mixed
body; other than Athenian elements gained the upper hand; and,
in the end, Thurii became rather a Dorian centre and was no support to Athens. It is to be observed that at the time of the foundation of Thurii, and for nigh thirty years more, Athens is seeking
merely influence in the west, she has no thought of dominion. The
growth of her connexion with Italian and Sicilian affairs was forced
upon her by the conditions of commerce and the rivalry of Corinth.

The treaties with Leontini and Rhegium had led to no immediate
interference in Sicily on the part of the Athenians. The first action
came six years later, on an appeal for help from both cities. Leontini was struggling to preserve her independence against Syracuse,
her southern neighbour. All the Dorian cities, with the exception of
Acragas and Camarina, were on the side of Syracuse, while Leontini had the support of Rhegium, Catane, Naxos, and Camarina.
The continued independence of the Ionian element in western
Greece might seem to be seriously at stake. The embassy of the
Leontines was accompanied by the greatest of their citizens, Gorgias, the professor of eloquence, whose fame and influence were
Panhellenic. We may well believe that when the embassy arrived
the Athenians were far more interested in the great man than in his
mission; that they thronged in excitement to the Assembly, caring
little what he said, but much how he said it. His eloquence indeed
was hardly needed to win a favourable answer. Athens was convinced of the expediency of bringing Sicily within the range of her
politics. It was important to hinder corn and other help being con-

Margin notes:

Alliances
with
Segesta,
c. 454 B.C.

Leontini,
and
Rhegium,
433 B.C.

Thurii
colonised,
443.

Condition
of Sicily,
427 B.C.

448 A HISTORY OF GREECE

veyed from thence to her Peloponnesian enemies; it was important to prevent Syracuse, the friend of Corinth, from raising her head too high; and already adventurous imaginations may have pressed beyond the thought of Athenian influence, and dreamed of Athenian dominion, in the west. Hyperbolus seems to have especially interested himself in the development of a policy in the western Mediterranean. Aristophanes ridicules him for contemplating an enterprise against Carthage herself.

Sicilian expedition under Laches, 427 B.C. An expedition was sent out, under the command of Laches. It achieved little, but, if it had been followed up, might have led to much. Messana was induced to join Athens, who thus obtained free navigation of the Straits. The old alliance with Segesta was renewed, but a severe check was experienced in an attempt to take Inessa. The poor success of this expedition must partly at least be

Fig. 69.—Coin of Naxos, fifth century (reverse). Seated satyr with wine-cup [legend: ΝΑΞΙΟΝ]. Fig. 70.—Coin of Messana, fifth century (obverse). Hare; head of Pan; syrinx [legend: ΜΕΣΣΑΝΙΟΝ]. Fig. 71.—Coin of Selinus, fifth century (obverse). River Hypsas sacrificing at altar; snake round the altar; lake-bird; leaf of selinon [legend: ΗΤΨΑΣ].

set down to the dishonesty of the general Laches and his treasurer. Cleon seems to have called Laches to account for his defalcations, on his return; and a comic poet jested how Laches ate up the Sicilian cheese—Sicily was famous for her cheeses—with the help of his treasurer, the cheese-grater.

Expedition of Eurymedon and Sophocles, 425 B.C. The episode of Pylos and the operations at Corcyra may fairly be regarded as causes which ruined Athenian prospects in Sicily. For these affairs detained the fleet which was bound for the west under the command of Eurymedon and Sophocles, and the delay led to the loss of the one thing which the expedition of Laches had gained, the adhesion of Messana. This city, cleft by adverse political parties, revolted; and the fleet, when at last it came, accomplished nothing worthy of record. Its coming seems rather to have been the occasion for the definite shaping of a movement among almost all the Sicilian states towards peace,—a movement unfavourable to the Athenian designs. When the Athenian generals invited the cities to join in the war against Syracuse, they were answered by the gathering of a congress at Gela, where delegates from all the Siceliot cities met to discuss the situation and consider the possibility of peace. The man who took the most prominent part at this remarkable congress was Hermocrates of Syracuse. He developed what has been justly described as a Siceliot policy. Sicily is a world by itself, with its own interests and politics, and the Greeks outside Sicily should be considered as strangers and not permitted to make or meddle in the affairs of the island. Let the Sicilian cities settle their own differences among themselves, but combine to withstand intervention from Athens or any other external power. Thus the policy of Hermocrates was neither local nor Panhellenic, but Siceliot. It has been compared to the "Monroe doctrine" of the United States. The policy, indeed, was never realised, and we shall see that Hermocrates himself was driven by circumstances to become eminently untrue to the doctrine which he preached. But the Congress of Gela was not a failure; the policy of peace prevented at the time any serious Athenian intervention. Soon afterwards a sedition was disastrous to Leontini. Its oligarchs became Syracusan citizens; Leontini ceased to exist as a city and became a Syracusan fortress. Such an incident, following so hard upon the pacification which Syracusan diplomacy had helped to bring about, must have produced a strange impression on the Siceliots. It seemed clear that Syracuse wanted to get rid of the Athenians only for the purpose of tyrannising over her neighbours. Athens was again invited to intervene, and she did intervene, but not seriously or effectually; and it was not till the year of the conquest of Melos that she resumed her active interest in the politics of western Hellas.

Congress of Gela.

423 B.C.

Sect. 3. The Sailing of the Sicilian Expedition. First Operations in Sicily

In that year there arrived at Athens an appeal for help from Segesta, who was at war with her stronger southern neighbour, Selinus. The appeal was supported by the Leontine democrats, who had no longer a city of their own. Athens sent envoys to Sicily, for the purpose of reporting on the situation and spying out the resources of Segesta, which had undertaken, if the Athenians would send an armament, to provide the expenses of the war. The ambassadors returned with sixty talents of uncoined silver and glowing stories of the untold wealth of the people of Segesta. They described the sacred vessels of gold and the rich plate of the private citizens. Alcibiades and all the younger generation were in favour of

Embassy of Segesta 416 B.C.

responding to the appeal; of vigorously espousing the causes of Segesta against Selinus, of the Leontines against Syracuse. Nicias wisely opposed the notion, and set forth the enormous cost of an expedition which should be really effective. The people, however, elated by their recent triumph over Melos, were fascinated by the idea of making new conquests in a distant, unfamiliar world; the ordinary Athenian had very vague ideas of what Sicily meant; and carried away by dreams of a western empire, he paid no more attention to the discreet counsels of Nicias than to vote a hundred triremes instead of the sixty which were originally asked for.

Athenians
vote
expedition
to Sicily.

But having committed the imprudence of not listening to Nicias when his caution was, from the highest point of view, wisdom, the people went on to commit the graver blunder of electing him as a commander of the expedition which he disapproved. He was appointed as General along with Alcibiades and Lamachus. This shows how great was the consideration of his military capacity, and he was doubtless regarded as a safe makeweight against the adventurous spirit of his colleagues. But though Nicias had shown himself capable of carrying out that Periclean strategy which Athens had hitherto adopted, his ability and temperament were wholly unsuited for the conduct of an enterprise of conquest demanding bolder and greater operations.

(See
above,
p. 383.)

The muti-
lation
of the
Hermae,
415 B.C.

When the expedition was ready to sail in the early summer, a mysterious event delayed it. One morning in May it was found that the square stone figures which stood at the entrance of temples and private houses in Athens, and were known as Hermae, had been mutilated. The pious Athenians were painfully excited. Such an unheard-of sacrilege seemed an evil omen for the Sicilian enterprise, and it was illogically argued that the act betokened a conspiracy against the state. The enemies of Alcibiades seized the occasion and tried to implicate him in the outrage. It was said that a profane mockery of the Eleusinian Mysteries had been enacted in his house,—a charge which may well have been true; and it was argued that he was the author of the present sacrilege and prime mover in a conspiracy against the democracy. It did not appear why a conspirator should thus advertise his plot. But though the theory hardly hung together, it might be good enough for an excited populace. Alcibiades demanded the right of clearing himself from the charge, before the fleet started. In this case, his acquittal was certain, as he was deemed necessary to the enterprise; and his enemies, aware of this, procured the postponement of his trial till his return. The fleet then set sail, and in the excitement of its starting, the sacrilege was almost forgotten. Thucydides says that no armament

Sailing of
the fleet.

so magnificent had ever before been sent out by a single Greek state. There were 134 triremes, and an immense number of smaller attendant vessels; there were 5100 hoplites; and the total number of combatants was well over 30,000. For cavalry they relied on their Sicilian allies; only thirty horse went with the fleet.

A halt was made at Rhegium, where disappointments awaited them. Rhegium adopted a reserved attitude which the Athenians did not expect. The government said that their conduct must be regulated by that of the other Italiot states. This looks as if the Italiots were aiming at a policy of joint interests, such as that which the Siceliots had discussed at the Congress of Gela. In the next place, the Athenians had relied on the wealth of Segesta for supporting their expedition, and they now learned that their spies had been deceived by simple tricks. Gilt vessels of silver had been displayed to them as solid gold; and the Segestaeans, collecting all the plate they could get from their own and other cities, had passed the same service from house to house and led the envoys to believe that each of the hosts who sumptuously entertained them possessed a magnificent service of his own.

This discovery came as an unwelcome surprise to soldiers and commanders alike. It was a serious blow to the enterprise, but no one, not even Nicias, seems to have thought of giving the enterprise up. What then was to be done? A council of war was held at Rhegium. Nicias advocated a course which involved risking and doing as little as possible,—to sail about, make some demonstrations, secure anything that could be secured without trouble, give any help to the Leontines that could be given without danger. Alcibiades proposed that active attempts should be made to win over the Sicilian cities by diplomacy, and that then, having so strengthened their position, they should take steps to force Selinus and Syracuse to do right by Segesta and Leontini. Both Nicias and Alcibiades kept in the forefront the ostensible object of the expedition, to right the wrongs of Leontini and Segesta. But Lamachus, who was no statesman or diplomatist but a plain soldier, regarded the situation from a soldier's point of view. Grasping the fact that Syracuse was the real enemy, the ultimate mark at which the whole enterprise was aimed, he advised that Syracuse should be attacked at once, while her citizens were still unprepared. Fortunately for Syracuse, the bold strategy of Lamachus did not prevail; he had no influence or authority except on the field; and, failing to convince his colleagues, who perhaps contemned him as a mere soldier, he gave his vote to the plan of Alcibiades.

Naxos and Catane were won over; the Athenian fleet made a

The council of war at Rhegium.

demonstration in the Great Harbour of Syracuse and captured a ship. But nothing more had been done, when a mandate arrived from Athens recalling Alcibiades, to stand his trial for impiety. The people of Athens had reverted to their state of religious agony over the mutilation of the Hermae, and the mystery which encompassed it increased their terrors. A commission of inquiry was appointed; false informations were lodged; numbers of arrests were made. Andocides, a young man of good family, was one of the prisoners, and he at length resolved to confess the crime and give the names of his accomplices. His information was readily believed; the public agitation was tranquillised; and all the prisoners whom he accused were tried and put to death. He was himself pardoned, and soon afterwards left Athens. But it is not certain, after all, whether the information of Andocides was true; Thucydides declares that the truth of the mystery was never explained.

It was, indeed, never known for certain who the actual perpetrators were; so far the affair remained a mystery. But the purpose of the deed and the source of its inspiration can hardly be doubtful. It was wrought on the eve of the Sicilian expedition, and can have had no other intention than to hinder the expedition from sailing, by working on the superstitions of the people. If we ask then, who above all others were vitally concerned in preventing the sailing of the fleet, the answer is obvious, Corinth and Syracuse. We are justified in inferring that the authors of the outrage—to us their names would be of only subordinate interest—were men suborned by Corinth, in receipt of Corinthian silver. In the main point, the mutilation of the Hermae is assuredly no mystery.

The investigations in connexion with the Hermae led to the exposure of other profanations, especially of travesties of the Eleusinian mysteries, in which Alcibiades was involved. His enemies of both parties deemed that it was the time to strike. Thessalus, the son of Cimon, preferred the impeachment, which began thus: "Thessalus, son of Cimon, of the deme Laciadae, impeached Alcibiades, son of Cleinias, of the deme Scambonidae, of wrongdoing in respect to the two goddesses, Demeter and Core, by mimicking the mysteries and displaying them to his comrades in his own house, wearing a dress like that which a hierophant with the mysteries wears, and calling himself hierophant." The trireme "Salaminia" was sent to summon Alcibiades to return, but with instructions to use no violence. Alcibiades might have refused, but he did not do so. He went with the Salaminia as far as Thurii, where he made his escape and went into voluntary exile. The Athenians

Recall of Alcibiades.

Meaning of the Hermae mystery.

condemned him to death, along with some of his kinsfolk, and confiscated his property.

In Sicily, when Alcibiades had gone, the rest of the year was
frittered away in a number of small enterprises, which led to nothing. At length, when winter came, Nicias aroused himself to a far
more serious undertaking. By a cunning stratagem he lured the
Syracusan army to Catane for the purpose of making an attack on
the Athenian camp, which they were led to believe they would take
unawares, while in the meantime the Athenian host had gone on
board the fleet and sailed off to the Great Harbour of Syracuse.
Nicias landed and fortified his camp on the south-west side of the
harbour, near the point of Dascon, just south of the temple of the
Olympian Zeus, which he was scrupulous to treat with profound
respect. When the Syracusans returned, a battle was fought, the
first battle of the war. The Athenians had the disadvantage of having no cavalry whatever; but the woeful want of discipline which
prevailed in the ranks of the enemy outbalanced the advantage
they had from 1200 horse. A storm of rain and lightning aided
the Athenians to discomfit their untrained antagonists; but the
cavalry stood the Syracusans in good stead by protecting their
retreat.

Athenian
victory.

A success had now been gained, but the temper of Nicias forbade
it to be improved. On the day ensuing, he ordered the whole army to
embark and sail back to Catane. He had numbers of excellent
reasons,—the winter season, the want of cavalry, of money, of
allies; and in the meantime Syracuse was left to make her preparations. "The Athenian fleet and army was to go on falling away
from its freshness and vigour. All Sicily was to get more and more
accustomed to the sight of the great armada sailing to and fro, its
energies frittered away on small and mostly unsuccessful enterprises, and, when it did strike something like a vigorous blow, not
daring to follow it up." [2]

The winter was employed by both parties in seeking allies. The
Sicels of the island for the most part joined Athens. Camarina,
wooed by both Athens and Syracuse, remained neutral. It is in the
Assembly of Camarina that Thucydides makes Hermocrates reassert the doctrine of a purely Siceliot policy, which he had formulated ten years before at Gela, while an Athenian envoy develops
in its most naked form the theory of pure self-interest, reminding
us of the tone which the Thucydidean Athenians adopted in the
Melian dialogue. A train had been laid for the capture of Messana

[2] Freeman.

before Alcibiades had been recalled, but when the time came for making the attempt, it failed. Alcibiades began the terrible vengeance which he proposed to wreak upon his country by informing the Syracusan party in Messana of the plot.

It seemed, indeed, as if a fatality dogged Athens in her conduct of the expedition which she had so lightly undertaken. If she had committed the command to Alcibiades and Lamachus, without Nicias, it would probably have been a success, resulting in the capture of Syracuse. But, not content with the unhappy appointment of Nicias, she must go on to pluck the whole soul out of the enterprise by depriving it of Alcibiades. That active diplomatist now threw as much energy into the work of ruining the expedition as he had given to the work of organising it. He went to Sparta, and was present at the Assembly which received a Syracusan embassy, begging for Spartan help. He made a vigorous and effective speech. He exposed the boundless plans of Athenian ambition, aiming at conquests in the west (including Carthage), which should enable them to return and conquer the Peloponnesus. These had perhaps been the dreams of Alcibiades himself; but they had certainly never taken a definite shape in the mind of any sober Athenian statesman. Alcibiades urged the Spartans especially to take two measures: to send at once a Spartan general to Sicily to organise the defence,—a general was far more important than an army; and to fortify Decelea in Attica, a calamity which the Athenians were always dreading. "I know," said the renegade, "the secrets of the Athenians." Thucydides shows what defence Alcibiades might have made for his own vindictive—it can hardly be called treacherous— conduct. The description of the Athenian democracy as "acknowledged folly" may well have been a phrase actually used by Alcibiades. Intense hostility animated the exile, but, one asks, Did he act merely to gratify this feeling, or had he not further projects for his own career? If we might trust the speech which Thucydides ascribes to him, his ultimate aim was to win back his country. With Spartan help, presumably, he was to rise on the calamity of Athens, and, we may read between the lines, the "acknowledged folly" was to be abolished. One can hardly see a place for Alcibiades except as a second Pisistratus.

The speech of this powerful advocate turned the balance at a most critical point in the history of Hellas. The Lacedaemonians, who were wavering between the policies of neutrality and intervention, were decided by his advice, and appointed an officer named Gylippus to take command of the Syracusan forces. Corinth too sent ships to the aid of her daughter city.

Alcibiades at Sparta; his speech.

Since the sailing of the expedition, Athens was in a mood of adventurous speculation and sanguine expectancy, dreaming of some great and wonderful change for the better in her fortunes. Aristophanes made this mood of his countrymen the motive of a fanciful comedy, entitled the *Birds,* which he brought out at the Great Dionysia. Some have sought to detect definite political allusions in the story of the foundation of Cloudcuckootown by the birds of the air, under the direction of two Athenian adventurers, Persuasive and his follower Hopeful; but this is to misapprehend the intention of the drama and to do wrong to the poet's art. The significance of the *Birds* for the historian is that it exhibits with good-humoured banter the temporary mood of the Athenian folk.

The Birds of Aristophanes, 414 B.C., March to April.

Sect. 4. Siege of Syracuse, 414 b.c.

The Island of Syracuse, the original settlement of Archias, always remained the heart and centre of the city. However the city might extend over the hill above it, the island was always what the Acropolis was to Athens, what Larisa was to Argos; it was even called the acropolis, a name which was never given to the hill. But the military importance of the *Epipolae,* the long hill which shuts in the north side of the Great Harbour, could not be ignored, although it was only gradually that the Syracusans came fully to recognise its significance. The water between the Island and the mainland had been filled up; this was an inducement to the settlement to creep up the height; and finally the eastern part of the hill, known as *Achradina,* was fortified by a wall running from north to south. At a later period, during the domestic troubles which followed the expulsion of Thrasybulus, the suburb of *Tycha,* northwest of Achradina, was added to the enclosed city. Henceforward the name *Epipolae* was restricted to the rest of the heights, westward from the wall of Tycha and Achradina. It formed a sort of triangle, with this wall as the base and the high point of Euryālus as the vertex.

414 b.c.

Fortification of Achradina;

of Tycha. c. 463.

The Syracusans did something, though not perhaps as much as they might, to prepare for a siege. They reformed their system of military command and elected Hermocrates a general. They fortified the precinct of Apollo Temenites, which was just outside the wall of Achradina, and also strengthened Polichna, the fort south of the hill, near the shrine of Olympian Zeus.

The first brief operation of the Athenians against Syracuse had been made on the table-land west of the Great Harbour. With the second act, which began in the ensuing spring, the scene changes to

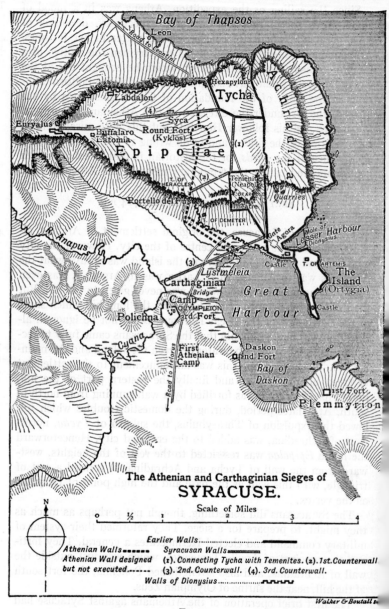

The Athenian and Carthaginian Sieges of
SYRACUSE.

Scale of Miles

| 0 | ½ | 1 | 2 | 3 | 4 |

Earlier Walls............................
Athenian Walls ------   Syracusan Walls ▓▓▓▓▓▓
Athenian Wall designed   (1). Connecting Tycha with Temenites. (2).1st.Counterwall.
but not executed-------   (3). 2nd. Counterwall. (4). 3rd. Counterwall.
Walls of Dionysius.....................

Walker & Boutall sc

Fig. 72.

the north, and the hostilities are enacted on the heights of Epipolae. Hermocrates had realised the necessity of guarding these heights. It was accordingly fixed that a great review should be held of all the fighting population, and a force of 600 was to be chosen for the guard of Epipolae. But the hour had almost passed. At the very moment when the muster was being held below in the meadows on the banks of the Anapus, the Athenians were close at hand. The fleet had left Catane the night before, steered for the bay on the north side of the Epipolae, and set down the army at a landing-place within less than a mile from the height of Euryalus. The soldiers hastened up the ascent, and were masters of Epipolae before the Syracusan host knew what was happening. The six hundred made an attempt to dislodge them, and were repulsed with great loss. The Athenians then fortified a place called Labdalon, near the north cliffs; they have been criticised for not rather fortifying Euryalus.

The Athenians seize Epipolae.

The plan of the siege was to run a wall right across the hill, from the cliffs on the north to the harbour on the south. This would cut off communications by land, while the fleet which was stationed at Thapsus, ready to enter the Great Harbour, would cut off communications by sea. For this purpose, a point was chosen in the centre of the intended line of wall, and a round fort, "the Circle" (*kyklos*), was built there, from which the wall was to be constructed northward and southward. The Syracusans having made a vain attempt to stop the building of the wall, set themselves to build a counter-wall, beginning at the Temenites and running westward, with a view to intercept the southern wall of the Athenians and prevent its reaching the harbour. The Athenians did not try to hinder them, and devoted themselves entirely to the building of their own wall north of the Round Fort; this seemed at first of greater consequence than the southern section, since they had to consider the maintenance of communications with their fleet at Thapsus. But though they were apparently not concerning themselves with the Syracusan builders, they were really watching for a good opportunity. The carelessness of the Syracusans soon gave the looked-for chance. An attack was made on the counter-wall and it was utterly destroyed. The generals then began to look to the southern section of their own wall, and, without waiting to build it on the side of the Round Fort, they began to fortify the southern cliff, near the temple of Heracles, above the marshy ground on the north-west side of the great harbour.

The Athenian wall.

First Syracusan counter wall.

The Syracusans then began a second counter-work, not on the hill, but over this low swampy ground, to hinder the Athenians from bringing their wall down from the cliff to the harbour. This work was not a wall, which would not have been suited to the swampy ground, but a trench with a palisade. At the break of day, the Athenians led by Lamachus descended into the swamp and destroyed the Syracusan works. But what was gained was more than undone by what followed. Troops sallied out of Syracuse; a battle was fought; and Lamachus—the hero Lamachus, as comic poets called him in derision while he lived, in admiration when he died—exposed himself rashly and was slain. This was the third great blow to the prospect of Athenian success. Nicias had been appointed; Alcibiades had been recalled; now Lamachus was gone. To make things worse, Nicias himself was ill.

Death of La-machus.

The southern Athenian wall advanced southward in a double line, and the fleet had now taken up its station in the Great Harbour. The Syracusans, not realising how much they had gained in the death of Lamachus, were prematurely in despair; they changed their generals, and were prepared to make terms. Nicias, strangely swerving from his wonted sobriety, was prematurely elated; he thought that Syracuse was in his hands, and made the fatal mistake of neglecting the completion of the wall on the north side. His neglect was the more culpable as he had received information of the help that was coming for Syracuse from the mother-country. But alike in his normal mood of caution and in his abnormal moment of confidence, Nicias was doomed to do the wrong thing.

All thought of capitulation was abandoned when a Corinthian captain named Gongylus reached Syracuse with the news that Corinthian ships and a Spartan general were on their way. That general had indeed given up the hope of being able to relieve Syracuse, which, from the reports of Athenian success that had reached him, was thought to be past helping; but he had sailed on to the coast of Italy with the aim of saving the Italiot cities. At Locri, Gylippus learned that Syracuse might still be saved, since the northern wall was not yet completed. He immediately sailed to Himera and collected a land force, supplied by Gela, Selinus, and Himera itself, and marched overland to Syracuse. He ascended the hill of Epipolae by the same path on the north side which had been climbed by the Athenian army when they seized the heights; and without meeting any opposition advanced along the north bend of the hill to Tycha and entered the city. Such was the result of the gross neglect of Nicias. If the wall had been finished, the attempt of Gylippus would never have been made; if Euryalus had been fortified, the attempt would probably have failed.

Arrival of Gylippus.

Gylippus immediately undertook the command of the Syracusan army, and inspired the inhabitants with new confidence. He
was as unlike the typical Spartan as Nicias was unlike the typical
Athenian. He had all the energy and resourcefulness of Brasidas,
without that unique soldier's attractive personality. He set him
self instantly to the work of the defence, and his first exploit was
the capture of the fort Labdalon. But the great object was to prevent the Athenians from hemming in the city by completing the
northern section of their wall, and this could be done only by building a new counter-wall. The Athenians themselves began to build
vigorously, and there was a race in wall-building between the two
armies. As the work went on, attacks were made on both sides with
varying success. In the end, the Syracusan builders prevailed; the
Athenian wall was turned, and never reached the northern coast.
This was not enough for Gylippus. His wall was continued to reach
Euryalus, and four forts were erected on the western part of the
hill, so that Syracuse could now hinder help from reaching the
Athenians by the path by which Gylippus had himself ascended. In
the meantime Nicias had occupied Plemmyrion, the headland
which, facing the Island, forms the lower lip of the mouth of the
Great Harbour. Here he built three forts and established a station
for his ships; some of which were now dispatched to lie in wait for
the expected fleet from Corinth. The Syracusans made a sort of
answer to the occupation of Plemmyrion by sending a force of
cavalry to the fort of Polichna to guard the southern coast of the
Harbour. But, though the Athenians commanded the south part
of Epipolae and the entrance to the Harbour, the Syracusan wall
from Tycha to Euryalus had completely changed the aspect of the
situation for Syracuse from despair to reasonable hope.

*Third
Syracusan
counter-
wall.*

The winter had now come and was occupied with embassies and
preparations. Gylippus spent it in raising fresh forces in Sicily.
Camarina, so long neutral, at length joined Syracuse, who had in
fact all Greek Sicily on her side, except her rival Acragas, who
persistently held aloof, and the towns of Naxos and Catane. Appeals of help were again sent to the Peloponnesus. Corinth was
still unremitting in her zeal; and Sparta had sent a force of 600
hoplites—Neodamodes and Helots. Thebes and Thespiae also sent
contingents.

We must go back for a moment to Old Greece. The general war
is being rekindled there, and the war in Sicily begins to lose the
character of a collateral episode and becomes merged in the larger
conflict, in which greater interests than those of Syracuse and Sicily
are at stake. The Spartans had come to the conclusion that they

had been themselves the wrong-doers in the earlier war, and the Athenian successes, especially the capture of Pylos, had been a retribution which they deserved. But now the Athenians had clearly committed a wrong in their aggression on Sicily, and Sparta might with a good conscience go to war against her. The advice of Alcibiades to fortify Decelea was adopted: a fort was built and provided with a garrison under the command of king Agis. From Mt. Lycabettus at Athens one can see the height of Decelea through the gap between Pentelicus on the right and Parnes, of which Decelea is an outlying hill, on the left. It was a good position for reaching all parts of Attica, which could no longer be cultivated, and at the same time maintaining easy communications with Boeotia.

But while the Peloponnesians were carrying the war once more to the very gates of Athens, that city was called upon to send forth a new expedition to the west on a scale similar to the first. Nicias wrote home a plain and unvarnished account of the situation. We are expressly told that he adopted the unusual method of sending a *written* despatch instead of a verbal message; it was all-important that the Athenian Assembly should learn the exact state of the case. He explained that, since the coming of Gylippus and the increase of the numbers of the garrison, and the building of the counter-wall, the besiegers had become themselves besieged. They even feared an attack on their own element the sea, and their ships had become leaky and the crews fallen out of practice. Further successes of the enemy might cut off their supplies, now derived from the cities of Italy. One of two things must be done: the enterprise must be abandoned or a new armament, as strong as the first, must be sent out at once. Nicias also begged for his own recall, on the ground of the disease from which he suffered. The Athenian people repeated its previous recklessness by voting a second expedition, and by refusing to supersede Nicias, in whom they had a blind and touching trust. They appointed Eurymedon and Demosthenes as commanders of the new armament.

Sect. 5. The Second Expedition

"The original interference of Athens in the local affairs of Sicily, her appearance to defend Segesta against Selinus and the Leontines against Syracuse, has grown into a gigantic struggle in which the greater part of the Hellenic nation is engaged. The elder stage of the Peloponnesian War has begun again with the addition of a Sicilian war on such a scale as had never been seen before. In that

Margin notes:

413 B.C.
Occupation of Decelea by the Spartans.

Appeal of Nicias for help.

413 B.C.

elder stage Sicilian warfare had been a mere appendage to warfare in Old Greece. Now Sicily has become the centre of the struggle, the headquarters of both sides." [3]

For Sicily itself, the struggle was now becoming a question of life and death, such as the Persian invasion had been for Greece. Syracuse, under the guidance of Hermocrates and Gylippus, put forth all her energy in the organisation of a fleet, and in the spring she had a navy numbering eighty triremes. The crews were inexperienced, but they could remember that it was under the pressure of the Persian danger that Athens herself had learned her sea skill. Gylippus determined to attack the Athenian station at Plemmyrion by land and sea. By sea the Syracusans were defeated, but while the naval battle was being fought in the harbour, a land force under Gylippus had marched around to Plemmyrion and captured the forts on the headland. The Athenian ships were thus forced back to their station close to their double wall on the north of the Harbour, of which the entrance was now commanded by the Syracusans. The Athenians were thus besieged both by land and sea, and could not venture to send ships out of the Harbour except in a number sufficient to resist an attack. Presently the new Syracusan sea-power achieved the important success of capturing off the Italian coast a treasure-fleet which was on its way from Athens.

Sea battle

At length the news came that the great fleet under Eurymedon and Demosthenes was on its way. It consisted of seventy-three triremes; there were 5000 hoplites and immense numbers of light-armed troops. The chance of Syracuse lay in attacking the dispirited forces of Nicias before the help arrived, and it was obviously the policy of Nicias—a congenial policy—to remain inactive. The Syracusans made a simultaneous assault on the walls by land and on the naval station below the walls by sea. The land attack was beaten off, but two days' fighting by sea resulted in a distinct victory for Syracuse. The Great Harbour was too small for the Athenians to win the advantage of their superiority in seamanship, and their ships were not adapted for the kind of sea-warfare which was possible in a narrow space. The effective use of the long light beaks depended on the possibility of manœuvring. The Syracusans had shaped the beaks of their vessels with a view to the narrow space, by making them short and heavy. On the day after the victory, the fleet of Eurymedon and Demosthenes sailed into the Great Harbour.

Syracusan sea-victory.

Demosthenes saw at once that all was over, unless the Syracusan cross-wall were captured. An attempt to carry it from the

Fruitless attacks on the Syracusan cross-wall

[3] Freeman.

south was defeated, and the only alternative was to march round the west end of the hill and ascend by the old path near Euryalus. It was a difficult enterprise, guarded as the west part of Epipolae was by the forts, as well as the wall, and by a picked body of 600 men who were constantly keeping watch. A moonlight night was chosen for the attempt. The Athenians were at first successful. One fort was taken and the six hundred under Hermocrates himself were repelled. But when one part of their force received a decisive check from the Thespians, the disorder spread to the rest, and they fell back everywhere, driven down the hill on the top of their comrades who had not yet reached the summit. Some, throwing away their shields, leapt from the cliffs. About 2000 were slain.

(August.)

These failures damped the spirits of the army, and Demosthenes saw that no profit could be won by remaining any longer where they were. The only wise course was to leave the unhealthy marsh, while they had still command of the sea, and before the winter came. At Syracuse they were merely wasting strength and money. But though Demosthenes had the sense of the army and the sense of the other commanders with him, he could not persuade Nicias to adopt this course. The same quality of nature which had made Nicias oppose the counsel of Lamachus to attack Syracuse now made him oppose the counsel of Demosthenes to leave Syracuse. Fear of responsibility was the dominant note in the character of Nicias. He was afraid of "Pulydamas and the Trojan women," he was afraid of the censure, perhaps the condemnation, of the Athenian Assembly. Nor would he even accept the compromise of retiring to Catane and carrying on the war on a new plan. Demosthenes and Eurymedon, being two to one, should have insisted on instant departure, but they foolishly yielded to the obstinacy of their senior colleague. In a few days, however, events overbore the resolution of Nicias himself. Gylippus arrived at Syracuse with new contingents he had collected in the islands; and Peloponnesian and Boeotian succours, after a long round-about journey by way of Cyrene, at length reached the Great Harbour. Nicias gave way and everything was ready for departure. But on the night on which they were to start, the enemy suspecting nothing, the full moon suffered an eclipse. The superstitious army regarded the phenomenon as a heavenly warning, and cried out for delay. Nicias was not less superstitious than the sailors. Unluckily his best prophet, Stilbides, was dead, and the other diviners ruled that he must wait either three days or for the next full moon. There was perhaps a difference of opinion among the seers, and Nicias decided to be on the safe side by waiting the longer period. Never was a celestial

Eclipse of the moon, Aug. 27.

Departure postponed.

phenomenon more truly disastrous than that lunar eclipse. With the aid of Nicias, it sealed the doom of the Athenian army.

Religious rites occupied the next few days. But meanwhile the Syracusans had learned of the Athenian intention to abandon the siege; their confidence was raised by the implied confession of defeat; and they resolved not to be content with having saved their city, but to destroy the host of the enemy before it could escape. So they drew up their fleet, seventy-six ships, in the Great Harbour for battle; and eighty-six Athenian ships moved out to meet them. The Athenians were at a disadvantage as before, having no room for manœuvring; and, centre, right, and left, they were defeated. The general Eurymedon was slain. The left wing was driven back on the marshy north-west shore of the harbour, between their own wall and Dascon. A force under Gylippus endeavoured to advance along the swamp of Lysimelea and prevent the crews of their ships from landing, but he was driven off by the Etruscan allies of Athens who had been sent to guard the shore here. Then there was a battle for the ships, and the Syracusans succeeded in dragging away eighteen.

The defeat completed the dejection of the Athenian army; the victory crowned the confidence of their enemies. The one thought of the Athenians was to escape,—the eclipse was totally forgotten; but Syracuse was determined that escape should be made impossible. The mouth of the Great Harbour was barricaded by a line of ships and boats of all kinds and sizes bound together by chains and connected by bridges. The fate of the Athenians depended on their success in breaking through that barrier. They abandoned their posts on the hill and went on board their ships. At this critical moment Nicias revealed the best side of his character. He left nothing undone that could hearten his troops. We are told that, after the usual speech, still thinking, "as men do in the hour of great struggles, that he had not done, that he had not said half enough," [4] he went round the fleet in a boat, making a personal appeal to the trierarch of each ship. "He spoke to them, as men will at such times, of their wives and children and the gods of their country; for men do not care whether their word sound commonplace, but only think that they may have some effect in the terrible moment." [5] The paean sounded, and the Athenian lines sailed forth together across the bay to attack the barrier. When they reached it, Syracusan vessels came out against them on all sides. The Athenians were driven back into the middle of the harbour, and the battle resolved itself into an endless number of separate conflicts. The battle was long and wavered. The

Marginal notes:

Sea-fight in the Harbour, Sept. 3.

Blocking of the Harbour, Sept. 6-8.

Last battle in Harbour Sept. 9.

[4] Thucydides.   [5] Ibid.

walls of the Island, the slopes of Achradina above, were crowded with women and old men, the shores below with warriors, watching the course of the struggle. Thucydides gives a famous description of the scene; one would think that he had been an eye-witness. "The fortune of the battle varied, and it was not possible that the spectators on the shore should all receive the same impression of it. Being quite close and having different points of view, they would some of them see their own ships victorious; their courage would then revive, and they would earnestly call upon the gods not to take from them their hope of deliverance. But others, who saw their ships worsted, cried and shrieked aloud, and were by the sight alone more utterly unnerved than the defeated combatants themselves. Others again who had fixed their gaze on some part of the struggle which was undecided were in a state of excitement still more terrible; they kept swaying their bodies to and fro in an agony of hope and fear, as the stubborn conflict went on and on; for at every instant they were all but saved or all but lost. And while the strife hung in the balance, you might hear in the Athenian army at once lamentation, shouting, cries of victory or defeat, and all the various sounds which are wrung from a great host in extremity of danger." [6] Those motions of human passion, suspense, agony, triumph, despair, which swayed to and fro, in the breasts of thousands, round and over the waters of the Great Harbour on that September day, have been lifted out of the tide of time and preserved for ever by the genius of Thucydides.

In the end the Athenians gave way. They were driven back to the shelter of their own wall, chased by the foe. The crews of the remnant of the navy—which amounted to sixty ships—rushed on shore as best they could. The land forces were in a panic; no such panic had ever been experienced in an Athenian army. Thucydides compares the situation to that of the Spartans in Sphacteria. The generals did not even think of asking for the customary truce to bury the corpses which were strewn over the waters of the bay. Demosthenes proposed that they should make another attempt to pass the barrier at daybreak; their ships were even now rather more numerous than those of the enemy; but the men positively refused to embark. Nothing remained but to escape by land. If they had started at once, they would probably have succeeded in reaching shelter at Catane or inland among the friendly Sicels. But Hermocrates contrived a stratagem to delay their departure, so as to give him time to block the roads. Taking advantage of the known fact that there were persons in Syracuse who intrigued with the besieg-

[6] Jowett's translation.

ers, he sent some horsemen who rode up within earshot of the Athenian camp, and feigning to be friends stated that the roads were guarded and that it would be well to wait and set out better prepared. The message was believed. The Athenians remained the next day, and the Syracusans blocked the roads.

In his picture of the sad start of the Athenians on their forlorn retreat, Thucydides outdoes his wonderful powers of description. They had to tear themselves away from the prayers of their sick and wounded comrades, who were left to the mercy of the enemy. They could hardly make up their minds to go. The bit of hostile soil under the shelter of their walls had come to seem to them like their home. Nicias, notwithstanding his illness, rose to this supreme occasion as he had never risen to another. He tried to cheer and animate the miserable host—whose wretched plight was indeed of his own making—by words of hope They set forth, Nicias leading the van, Demosthenes the rear, along the western road which crosses the Anapus and passes the modern village of Floridia. The aim was to reach Sicel territory first, and then get to Catane as they could; for it would have been madness to attempt the straight road to Catane round the west of Epipolae under the Syracusan forts. The chief difficulty in their way was a high point called the Acraean cliff, approached by a rugged pass, which begins near Floridia. It was not till the fourth day that, having toiled along the pass under constant annoyance from darters and horsemen, they came in sight of the cliff, and found that the way was barred by a wall, with a garrison of Syracusan hoplites behind it. To attempt to pass was impossible; they retreated on Floridia in a heavy thunderstorm. They now moved southwards, and abandoning the idea of reaching the Sicel hill-land from this point, marched to the Helorine road, which would take them in the direction of Gela. During the sixth day's march a sort of panic seems to have fallen on the rear of the army under Demosthenes; the men lagged far behind and the army was parted in two. Nicias advanced with his division as speedily as he could. There were several streams to cross, and it was all-important to press on before the Syracusans had time to block the passages by walls and palisades. The Helorine road approaches the shore near the point where the river Kakyparis flows into the sea. When they reached the ford, the Athenians found a Syracusan band on the other side raising a fortification They drove the enemy away without much difficulty and marched as far as the river Erineos, where they encamped for the night. On the next morning a Syracusan herald drew near. He had news to tell. The rear of the army had been surrounded the day before, in the olive garden of Polyzalus,

Retreat of Athenians, Sept. 11.

Sept. 16.

(R. Cassibile.)

(R. Elanici, or Cavallata?)

through which the Helorine road passed, and had been forced to surrender. The lives of the 6000 men were to be spared. Demosthenes did not condescend to make terms for himself, and when the capitulation had been arranged he sought death by his own hand, but the enemy, who desired to secure a captive general, intercepted the stroke. Having sent a messenger, under a truce, to assure himself of the truth of the tale, Nicias offered terms to the Syracusans —that the rest of the army should be allowed to go free on condition that Athens should repay the costs of the war, the security being a hostage for every talent. The terms were at once rejected. The Syracusans were bent on achieving the glory of leading the whole army captive. For that day the miserable army remained where it was, worn out with want of food. Next morning they resumed the march and, harassed by the darts of the enemy, made their way to the stream of the Assinaros. Here they found a hostile force on the opposite steep bank. But they cared little for the foe, for they were consumed with intolerable thirst. They rushed down into the bed of the river, struggling with one another to reach the water. Th Syracusans who were pursuing came down the banks and slaughtered them unresisting as they drank. The water was soon foul, but muddy and dyed with blood as it was, they drank notwithstanding and fought for it.

Sept. 17.
Sept. 18.

(R. Falconara).

Athenians surrender.

At last Nicias surrendered. He surrendered to Gylippus, for he had more trust in him than in the Syracusans. The slaughter, which was as great as any that had been wrought in the war, was then stayed and the survivors were made prisoners. It seems that a great many of the captives were appropriated for their own use by the individual victors; and their lot may have been comparatively light.

Treatment of the prisoners.

But the fate of the state-prisoners was cruel. Seven thousand were thrown into the stone-quarries of Achradina—deep, unroofed dungeons, open to the chills of night and the burning heat of the day— on a miserable allowance of food and water. The allies of the Athenians were kept in this misery for seventy days; the Athenians themselves were doomed to endure the torture for six months longer, throughout the whole winter. Such was the vengeance which Syracuse wreaked upon her invaders. The prisoners who survived the ordeal were put to work in the public prison or sold. Some were rescued by young men who were attracted by their manners. Others owed mitigation of their lot, even freedom, to the power which an Athenian poet exercised over the hearts of men, in Sicily as well as in his own city. Slaves who knew speeches and choruses of the plays of Euripides by heart, and could recite them well, found favour in the sight of their masters; and we hear of those who, after many days, returned to their Athenian homes and thanked the poet for their deliverance.

Some mystery has hung round the fate of the two generals, Demosthenes and Nicias, but there is no doubt that they were put to death without mercy, and some reason to suppose that they were not spared the pain of torture. Hermocrates and Gylippus would have wished to save them, but were powerless in face of the intense feeling of fury against Athens which animated Syracuse in the hour of her triumph. If a man's punishment should be proportionate not to his intentions but to the positive sum of mischief which his conduct has caused, no measure of punishment would have been too great for the deserts of Nicias. His incompetence, his incredible bungling, ruined the expedition and led to the downfall of Athens. But the blunders of Nicias were merely the revelation of his own nature, and for his own nature he could hardly be held accountable. The whole blame rests with the Athenian people, who insisted on his playing a part for which he was utterly unsuited. It has already been observed that one dominant note of the character of Nicias was fear of responsibility. Throughout the whole war there was no post which so absolutely demanded the power of undertaking full responsibility as that of chief commander in this great and distant expedition. And yet Nicias was chosen. The selection shows that he was popular as well as respected. He was popular with his army, and he seems to have been hardly a sufficiently strict disciplinarian. It has been well said that in the camp he never forgot that the soldiers whom he commanded had votes in the Ecclesia which they might use against himself when they returned to Athens. Timid as a general, timid as a statesman, hampered by superstition, the decorous Nicias was a brave soldier and an amiable man, whose honourable qualities were the means of leading him into a false position. If he had been less scrupulous and devout, and had been endowed with better brains, he would not have ruined his country. "Given the men a people chooses," it has been said, "the people itself, in its exact worth and worthlessness, is given." In estimating the character of the Athenian people, we must not forget their choice of this hero of conscientious indecision.

So deep is the pity which the tragic fate of the Athenians excites in us that we almost forget to sympathise with the sons of Syracuse in the joy of their deliverance. Yet they deserve our sympathy; they had passed through a sore trial, and they had destroyed the powerful invader who had come to rob them of their freedom. To celebrate the anniversaries of their terrible victory they instituted games which they called Assinarian, after the river which had wit-

Fate of
Nicias and
Demo-
sthenes.

Institu-
tion of the
Assinarian
games.

The coin-
engravers
of
Syracuse.

nessed the last scene. In connexion with these games, some beautiful coins were struck. Perhaps there is nothing which enlists our affections for Syracuse so much as her coins. And it was at this very period that she brought the art of engraving coin-dies to perfection. Never in any country, in any age of the world, was the art of engraving on metal practised with such high inspiration and such consummate skill as in Sicily. No holy place in Hellas possessed diviner faces in bronze or marble than the faces which the Sicilian cities circulated on their silver money. The greatest of the Sicilian artists were Syracusan, and among the greatest of the Syracusan were Evaenetus and Cimon. The die-engraver's achievements may seem small, compared with the life-size or colossal works of a sculptor, yet, as creators of the beautiful, Evaenetus and his fellows may claim to stand in the same rank as Phidias. Their heads of Persephone and of the water-nymph Arethusa encircled by dolphins, their wonderful four-horsed chariots, seem to invest Syracuse with a glory to which she hardly attained. In the years after the defeat of Athens there were several issues of large ten-drachm medallions, modelled on those "Damaratean" coins which had commemorated Gelon's victory at Himera.[7] The engraving of these was committed to Cimon and Evaenetus and a nameless artist—perhaps a greater than either—of whom a single medallion, an exquisite Persephone crowned with barley, has been found on the slopes of Aetna.

New
issues of
"Dama-
ratea,"
412-406
B.C.

Sect. 6. Consequences of the Sicilian Catastrophe

Was the
Sicilian
expedition
a foolish
under-
taking?

The Sicilian expedition was part of the general aggressive policy of Athens which made her unpopular in Greece. Unjust that policy was; but this enterprise was not more flagrantly unrighteous than some of her other undertakings, and it had the plausible enough pretext of protecting the weaker cities in the west against the stronger. More fruitful is the question whether the expedition was expedient from a purely political point of view. It is often said that it was a wild venture, an instance of a whole people going mad, like the English people in the matter of the Crimean War. It is hard to see how this view can be maintained. If there were ever an enterprise of which the wisdom cannot be judged by the result, it is the enterprise against Syracuse. All the chances were in its favour. If the advice of Lamachus had been taken and Syracuse attacked at once, there cannot be much doubt that Syracuse would have fallen at the outset. If Nicias had not let precious time pass and delayed the completion of the wall to the northern cliff of Epipolae, the doom of the

[7] See above, p. 291.

city was sealed, Gylippus could never have entered. The failure was due to nothing in the character of the enterprise itself, but entirely to the initial mistake in the appointment of the general. And it was quite in the nature of things that the Athenian sea-power, predominant in the east, should seek further expansion in the west. An energetic establishment of Athenian influence in that region was recommended by the political situation. It must be remembered that the most serious and abiding hostility with which Athens had to reckon was the commercial rivalry of Corinth; and the close alliance of Corinth with her Dorian daughters and friends in the west was a strong and adequate motive for Athenian intervention. The necessity of a counterweight to Corinthian influence in Sicily and Italy had long ago been recognised; some attempts had been made to meet it; and when peace with Sparta set Athenian forces free for service outside Greece and the Aegean, it was natural that the opportunity should be taken to act effectively in the west.

The infatuation of the Athenian people was shown not in willing the expedition, but in committing it to Nicias—instead of Demosthenes, who was clearly marked out for the task—and then in recalling Alcibiades. These blunders seemed to point to something wrong in the constitution or its working. They did in fact show that an expedition of that kind was liable to be mismanaged when any of the arrangements connected with its execution depended on a popular assembly, or might be interfered with for party purposes.

Cause of the failure.

And after the disaster of the Assinaros there was a feeling that some change must be made in the administration. Athens was hard pressed by the Lacedaemonian post at Decelea, which stopped cultivation and became a refuge for deserting slaves. Of these slaves, who numbered about 2000, we can hardly doubt that many belonged to the gangs which worked in the mines of Laurion. In any case, one most disastrous effect of the seizure of Decelea was the closing of the mines; since even southern Attica was at the mercy of the Lacedaemonians. Thus one of the chief sources of Athenian revenue was cut off; she was robbed of her supply of "Laureot owls"; and in a few years we find her melting gold dedicatory offerings to make gold coins, and even coining in copper. The mines of Laurion were not to be opened again till three-quarters of a century had passed.

Closing of the mines of Laurion, 413 B.C. Gold coinage at Athens (407); copper coinage (406).

Thus the treasury was at a low ebb, and there were no men to replace those who were lost in Sicily It was felt that the committees of the Council of Five Hundred were hardly competent to conduct the city through such a crisis; a smaller and more permanent body was required; and the chief direction of affairs was entrusted to a

Extraordinary administration of the Probuloi at Athens.

board of Ten, named *Probuli,* which practically superseded the Council for the time being.

Tribute of the Confederacy abolished.

A very important change in the system of taxation was made at the same time. The tribute, already as high as it could be put with impunity, was abolished; and was replaced by a tax of 5 per cent on all imports and exports carried by sea to or from the harbours of the Confederacy. It was calculated that this duty would produce a larger income than the tribute, and it would save the friction which generally occurred in the business of collecting the tribute and caused more than anything else the unpopularity of Athens. But further, the change had a great political significance. The duty was collected in the Piraeus as well as elsewhere, and thus fell on Athens herself. This might prove a step towards equalising Athens with her allies, and converting the Confederacy or dominion into a national state.

The financial pressure was shown by the dismissal of a body of Thracian mercenaries who had arrived too late to sail to Sicily. They returned home under the conduct of Diitrephes, who was instructed to employ them, on the road, in any way he could against the enemy. Sailing northward between Euboea and the mainland, they disembarked on the coast of Boeotia, and reaching the small town of Mycalessus at daybreak, captured it. "Nothing was ever so unexpected and terrible." The Thracians showed their barbarity in massacring all the inhabitants,—nay, every living thing they saw. They broke into a boys' school and killed all the children.

Reforms did not avert the dangers which threatened Athens. The tidings of the great calamity which had befallen the flower of her youth in Sicily moved Hellas from end to end. The one thought of enemies, neutrals and subjects alike, was to seize the opportunity of shattering the power of Athens irretrievably. Messages came from some of the chief allies, from Euboea, from Lesbos, from Chios, to Agis at Decelea, to the ephors at Sparta, declaring that they were ready to revolt, if a Peloponnesian fleet appeared off their coasts. A fleet was clearly necessary to do the work that was to be done; a naval policy was forced upon Sparta by the case. It was decided that a hundred ships should be equipped, of which half, in equal shares, were to be supplied by Sparta and Boeotia. Athens also spent the winter in building triremes, and fortified Cape Sunium to protect the arrival of her corn-ships.

King Agis while he was at Decelea possessed the right of sending troops wherever he chose. He received the overtures from Euboea and Lesbos and promised assistance. But Spartan interference in these islands was deferred owing to the more pressing demands of

Chios, which were addressed directly to Sparta and were backed by the support of a great power, whose voice for many years had not been heard in the sphere of the politics of Hellas. Persia now enters once more upon the stage of Greek history, aiming at the recovery of the coast cities of Asia Minor, and for this purpose playing off one Greek power against another. The Sicilian disaster suggested to Tissaphernes, the satrap of Sardis, and to Pharnabazus, the satrap of Hellespontine Phrygia, that it was the moment to wrest from Athens her Asiatic dominions. This must be done by stirring up revolt and by a close alliance with Sparta. Each satrap was anxious to secure for himself the credit of having brought about such a profitable alliance, and each independently sent envoys to Lacedaemon, Pharnabazus urging action in the Hellespont, Tissaphernes supporting the appeal of Chios. The Chian demand, which had the powerful advocacy of Alcibiades, carried the day.

Persia comes on the stage again.

In the following summer the rebellion against Athens actively began. The appearance of a few Spartan ships was the signal for the formal revolt of Chios, and then in conjunction with the Chian fleet they excited Miletus, Teos, Lebedus to follow in the same path. Methymna and Mytilene lost little time in joining the movement and were followed by Cyme and Phocaea. The Athenian historian has words of commendation for the city which played the chief part in this rebellion. "No people," says Thucydides, "as far as I know, except the Chians and Lacedaemonians (but the Chians not equally with the Lacedaemonians), have preserved moderation in prosperity, and in proportion as their city has gained in power have gained also in the stability of their government. In this revolt they may seem to have shown a want of prudence, yet they did not venture upon it until many brave allies were ready to share the peril with them, and until the Athenians themselves seemed to confess that after their calamity in Sicily the state of their affairs was hopelessly bad. And, if they were deceived through the uncertainty of human things, the error of judgment was common to many who, like them, believed that the Athenian power would speedily be overthrown." [8]

412 B.C.

Revolt of Athenian allies.

This successful beginning led to the Treaty of Miletus between Sparta and Persia. In the hope of humbling to the dust her detested rival, the city of Leonidas now sold to the barbarian the freedom of her fellow-Greeks in Asia. The Persian claim was that Athens had usurped the rights of the Great King for well-nigh seventy years over the Asiatic cities, and that arrears of tribute were owing to him for all that time. Sparta recognised the right of the Great King to all the dominion which belonged to him and his forefathers,

Treaty of Miletus.

[8] Jowett.

and he undertook to supply the pay for the seamen of the Peloponnesian fleet operating on the Asiatic coast, while the war with
Athens lasted. It may be said for Sparta that she merely wanted to
get the money at the time, and had no intention of honourably
carrying out her dishonourable undertaking, but hoped to rescue the
Greek cities in the end. But the treaty of Miletus opened up a new
path in Greek politics, which was to lead the Persian king to the
position of arbiter of Hellas.

Fig. 73.—Coin of Rhodes (obverse). Head of Apollo. Fig. 74.—Coin of
Ialysus (Rhodes), fifth century (obverse). Part of winged boar; helmet
[legend: ΙΑΛΥΣΙΟΝ].

Warfare in 412-11 B.C.

Meanwhile Athens had not been idle. Straitened by want of
money, she had been forced to pass a measure to touch the reserve
fund of 1000 talents. She blockaded a Corinthian fleet, destined for
Chios, on the Argolic coast; she laid Chios itself waste, and blockaded the town; she won back Lesbos, and gained some successes at
Miletus. But Cnidus rebelled; the Peloponnesians gained an advantage in a naval engagement at the small island of Syme, and this was
followed by the revolt of Rhodes. Thus by the spring of the next
year the situation was that Athens had her northern and Hellespontine confederacy intact, but that on the western coast of Asia little
of importance remained to her but Lesbos, Samos, Cos, and Halicarnassus. She was confronted by a formidable Peloponnesian fleet,
supported by Persia and by a considerable reinforcement from
Sicily—twenty-two vessels under Hermocrates, the return of Syracuse for her deliverance.

Battle of Syme (Jan. ? 411).

It could not be said indeed that all things had gone smoothly between Persia and Lacedaemon. Differences had arisen as to the
amount of the subsidies, and a new treaty was concluded in which
the rights of the king were less distinctly formulated. In the meantime Alcibiades had been cultivating the friendship of Tissaphernes
at Miletus, and had on that account become an object of suspicion
at Sparta. He had a bitter enemy in king Agis, whose wife he had
seduced. Seeing that his life was in danger, he had left Miletus and
gone to the court of the satrap, where he began a new series of

Alcibiades leaves Sparta, 412 B.C. (autumn).

machinations with a view to his own return to Athens. Indeed his work at Sparta had now been done, and political changes which were in the air at Athens invited the formation of new schemes. The man who had done much to bring about the alliance of Tissaphernes with Sparta now set himself to dissolve that union and bring about an understanding between the satrap and Athens. It was a matter of supreme moment to Athens to break the formidable union of Persia with her enemies, and the accomplishment of this service would go far to restore Alcibiades to his country.

Sect. 7. The Oligarchic Revolution

At Athens in these months there was distress, fear, and discontent. How deeply the people felt the pressure of the long war is uttered in the comedy of *Lysistrate* or "Dame Disbander" which the poet Aristophanes brought out at this crisis. The heroine unites all the women of the belligerent cities of Greece into a league to force the men to make peace. Under the ribald humour there pierces here and there a note of pathos not to be found in the poet's earlier peace plays, the *Acharnians* and the *Peace*. War is not a time for marrying and giving in marriage. "Never mind us married women," says Lysistrate; "it is the thought of the maidens growing old at home that goes to my heart." "Do not men grow old too?" asks a Probulos who argues with her. "Ah, but it is not the same thing. A man, though his hair be gray, can soon pick up a young girl; but a woman's season is short, and, if she miss her chance then, no one will marry her."

The Lysistrate of Aristophanes, 411 B.C., Jan.-Feb.

But the fear of Persia was the shadow which brooded darkest over Athens at this time, and there was also a lurking suspicion of treachery, a dread that the oligarchical party were planning a revolution or even intriguing with the enemy at Decelea. Two months after the *Lysistrate,* at the great feast of Dionysus, Aristophanes brought out a play whose plot had nothing to do with politics—the "Celebrants of the Thesmophoria." But the fears that were in the hearts of many were echoed by the poet, when his chorus called upon Athena, "the sole keeper of our city," to come as *the hater of tyrants.*

Thesmo-phoria-zusae (March to April, 411 B.C.).

Lovers of the democracy might well pray to the guardian lady of the city. The opportunity for which the oligarchs had waited so long had come at last. For outside their own ranks there was a large section of influential men who were dissatisfied with the existing forms of government and, though opposed to oligarchy, desired a modification of the constitution. There was a fair show of reason for argu-

The moderate revolutionists.

ing that the foreign policy had been mismanaged by the democracy, and that men of education and knowledge had not a sufficient influence on the conduct of affairs. The chief of those who desired to see the establishment of a moderate polity—neither an extreme democracy nor an oligarchy, but partaking of both—was Theramenes, whose father Hagnon was one of the Probuli. The watchword of Theramenes and his party was "the old constitution of our fathers." By this they meant not the constitution of Solon, but the constitution before Solon. They interpreted the whole history of Athens in accordance with their political views. They condemned Solon as the author of democracy, the first of a long line of mischievous demagogues; they made out that the Areopagus, and not Themistocles, was the hero of Salamis; they branded Aristides, founder of the Delian confederacy, for organising a system which fed 20,000 idlers on the allied cities; they represented Pericles as a man of no ideas of his own, but depending upon others to prompt him. After two centuries of evil government, the Athenians must go back to the times before Solon and revive in some new form the constitution of Dracon. This "constitution of Dracon," of which the chief feature was a Council of Four Hundred, had never existed; it was fathered upon Dracon by Theramenes and his friends.

The extreme oligarchs, though the ideal of Theramenes was not theirs, were ready in the first instance to act in concert with the moderate party for the purpose of upsetting the democracy. The soul of the plot was Antiphon of Rhamnus, an eloquent orator and advocate, who had made his mark in the days of Cleon. He was unpopular, on account of his undisguised oligarchical views; the historian Thucydides describes him as "a man who in virtue fell short of none of his contemporaries"; and by *virtue* is meant disinterested and able devotion to his party. Other active conspirators were Pisander, who had been in old days a partisan of Cleon, and Phrynichus, who was one of the commanders of the fleet stationed at Samos. The prospects of the movement were good; it was favoured by the Probuli and by most of the officers of the fleet. Moreover, the Athenians—as they had shown already by the appointment of the Porbuli—were in a temper, with the fear of Persia before their eyes, to sacrifice their constitution if such a sacrifice would save the city. Alcibiades had entered into negotiations with the officers at Samos, promising to secure an alliance with Tissaphernes, but representing the abolition of democracy as a necessary condition. Most of the oligarchical conspirators were pleased with the scheme, and even the army was seduced by the idea of receiving pay from the Great King. Some indeed of the more sagacious thought they saw through the designs of Alcibiades; and Phrynichus, who aspired himself to be the leader of the revolution, detected a rival and tried by various intrigues to thwart him. Alcibiades was certainly no friend of oligarchy; but it was his policy in any case to upset the existing democracy, which would never recall him. If an oligarchy were established, he might intervene to restore the democracy, and in return for such a service all would be forgiven. But he would have to be guided by events.

Pisander was sent to Athens to prepare the way for the return of Alcibiades and a modification of the democracy. The people were at first indignant at the proposals to change the constitution and recall the renegade; the Eumolpidae denounced the notion of having any dealings with the profaner of the Mysteries. But the cogent argument that the safety of Athens depended on separating Persia from the Peloponnesians, and that this could be managed only by Alcibiades, and that the Great King would not trust Athens so long as she was governed by a popular constitution, had its effect; and there was moreover powerful but secret influence at work through the Hetaeriae or political clubs. It was voted that Pisander and other envoys should be sent to negotiate a treaty with Tissaphernes and arrange matters with Alcibiades.

Pisandros at Athens

(? Feb.)

It appeared at once that Alcibiades had promised more than he could perform. There had indeed been a serious rupture between Tissaphernes and Sparta. Lichas, a Spartan commissioner who conferred with the satrap, denounced the terms of the treaties. He pointed out the monstrous consequences of the clause which assigned to the king power over all the countries which his ancestors had held; for this would involve Persian dominion over Thessaly and other lands of northern Greece. On such terms, he said, we will not have our fleet paid, and he asked for a new treaty. Tissaphernes departed in anger. But when it came to a question of union with Athens, Tissaphernes showed that he did not wish to break with the Peloponnesians. He proposed impossible conditions to the Athenian envoys, and then made a new treaty with the Spartans, modifying the clause to which Lichas objected. The territory which the Spartans recognised as Persian was now expressly confined to Asia.

Sparta and Tissaphernes.

But though the reasons for a revolution, so far as they concerned Tissaphernes and Alcibiades, seemed thus to be removed, the preparations had advanced so far that the result of the mission of Pisander produced no effect on the course of events. The conspirators did not scruple to use menaces and even violence; Androcles, a strong democrat, who had been prominent in procuring the condemnation of Alcibiades, was murdered. Some others of less note

The revolution at Athens.

were made away with in like manner; and there was a general feel-ing of fear and mistrust in the city. But there was a widespread conviction that the existence of Athens was at stake and that some change in the constitution was inevitable. The news that Abydus and Lampsacus had revolted may have hastened the final act. The revolution was peaceably effected through the co-operation of the Ten Probuli. A decree was passed that the Probuli and twenty others chosen by the people should form a commission of thirty who should jointly devise proposals for the safety of the state and lay them before the Assembly on a fixed day. When the day came, the Assembly met at the temple of Poseidon at Colonus, about a mile from the town. After preliminary measures to secure impunity for a proposal involving a subversion of existing laws, a radical change was brought forward and carried. The sovereign Assembly was to consist in future not of the whole people, but of a body of about Five Thousand, those who were strongest physically and financially. A hundred men were to be chosen, ten by each tribe, for the purpose of electing and enrolling the Five Thousand. Pay for almost all pub-lic offices was to be abolished. To these revolutionary measures a saving clause was attached; they were to remain in force "as long as the war lasts"; and thus the people were more easily induced to pass them.

But this was only preliminary; a constitution had still to be framed. When the Five Thousand were elected, they chose a com-mission of one hundred men to draw up a constitution. The scheme which they framed is highly remarkable as a criticism on certain defects in the constitution which was now to be overthrown. The body of Five Thousand were not to act as an Assembly; there was in fact to be no Assembly. The Five Thousand were to be divided into four parts, and each part was to act as Council for a year in turn. The Council would elect the higher magistrates from its own number. Thus the difficulties of administration which arose in the double system, where the Council's action was hampered by the Assembly, would be done away with; and the inclusion of the gen-erals and magistrates in the Council was a necessary consequence. Under the democracy, the holders of office could influence the Assembly against the Council; under the new scheme there would be no room for such collisions.

One fatal defect in this scheme was the size of the administrative body, and if it had been tried we may be sure that it would not have worked. But it was never tried. It passed the Assembly as a scheme to come into force in the future; but in the meantime a further pro-

(End of April.)
(April to May,
411 B.C.)

(May.)

Scheme of a polity.

Council of Four Hundred.

posal of the Hundred commissioners enacted that the state should be administered by a Council of Four Hundred, in which each of the ten tribes was to be represented by forty members. It would seem, but it is not quite certain, that the election of the Council was managed in the following way. The Assembly which created it chose five men under the title of *presidents,* who were empowered to nominate one hundred councillors, and each of these councillors co-opted three others; but both the presidents in their nomination and the one hundred councillors in their co-option were limited to a number of candidates who were previously chosen by the tribes. The Four Hundred were instituted as merely a provisional government, but the entire administration was placed in their hands, the management of the finances, and the appointment of the magistrates. The Five Thousand were to meet only when summoned by the Four Hundred, so that the Assembly ceased to have any significance, and the provisional constitution was an unadulterated oligarchy. The Council of Four Hundred was proclaimed to be a revival of the imaginary constitution of Dracon, under which Athens flourished before demagogues led her into evil paths; but the whole fabric of Cleisthenes, the ten tribes and the dems, was retained. The existing Council of Five Hundred went out of office before the end of the civil year, and seven days later the administration of the Four Hundred began. Throughout these transactions intimidation was freely used by the conspirators, and we are told that they went with hidden daggers into the council-chamber and forced the Five Hundred to retire. Thucydides admires the ability of the men who carried out this revolution. "An easy thing it certainly was not, one hundred years after the fall of the tyrants, to destroy the liberties of the Athenian people, who were not only a free, but during more than one-half of this time had been an imperial people." [9]

It may be asked why a provisional government was introduced, instead of proceeding at once to the establishment of the permanent constitution which the Hundred commissioners had framed. Here we touch upon the inwardness of the political situation: the two constitutions betray the double influence at work in the revolution. The establishment of the Four Hundred was a concession made to Antiphon and the oligarchs by Theramenes and the moderates, who regarded it as only preliminary; while the oligarchs hoped to render it permanent.

Marginal notes:

5 proedroi

Council of Five Hundred goes out of office, 14 Thargelion (end of May); Four Hundred enter on office, 22 Thargelion, 411 B.C.

[9] Jowett.

SECT. 8. FALL OF THE FOUR HUNDRED. THE POLITY. THE DEMO-
CRACY RESTORED

For more than three months the Four Hundred governed the city with a high hand, and then they were overthrown. Their success had been largely due to the absence of so many of the most democratic citizens in the fleet at Samos; and it was through the attitude of the fleet that their fall was brought about. The sailors rose against the oligarchic officers and the oligarchs of Samos, who were conspiring against the popular party and had murdered the exile Hyperbolus. The chief leaders of this reaction were Thrasybulus and Thrasyllus, who persuaded the soldiers and sailors to proclaim formally their adhesion to the democracy and their hostility to the Four Hundred. The Assembly, which had been abolished at Athens, was called into being at Samos, and the army, representing the Athenian people, deposed the Generals and elected others. The Athenians at Samos felt that they were in as good a position as the Athenians at Athens, and they hoped still to obtain the alliance of Persia, through the good offices of Alcibiades, whose recall and pardon were formally voted. Thrasybulus fetched Alcibiades to Samos, and he was elected a General. The hoped-for alliance with Persia was not effected, but it was at least something that Tissaphernes did not use the large Phoenician fleet which he had at Aspendus against the Athenians, and that his relations with the Peloponnesians were becoming daily worse. He went to Aspendus, but he never brought the ships, and it was a matter of speculation what the object of his journey was. Thucydides records his own belief that Tissaphernes "wanted to wear out and to neutralise the Hellenic forces; his object was to damage them both, while he was losing time in going to Aspendus, and to paralyse their action and not strengthen either of them by his alliance. For if he had chosen to finish the war, finished it might have been once for all, as any one may see." [10] The Athenians at Samos now proposed to sail straight to Athens and destroy the Four Hundred. The proposal shows how much the fleet despised the Peloponnesian navy, which, under its incompetent admiral Astyochus, had been spending the summer in doing nothing. But to leave Samos would have been madness, and Alcibiades saved them from the blunder of sacrificing Ionia and the Hellespont. Negotiations were begun with the oligarchs at Athens, and Alcibiades expressed himself satisfied with the Assembly of Five Thousand, but insisted that the Four Hundred should be abolished.

[10] Jowett.

As a matter of fact the overtures from Samos were welcome to the majority of the Four Hundred, who were dissatisfied with their colleagues and their own position. The nature of an oligarchy which supplants a democracy was beginning to show itself. "The instant an oligarchy is established," says Thucydides, "the promoters of it disdain mere equality, and everybody thinks that he ought to be far above everybody else. Whereas in a democracy, when an election is made, a man is less disappointed at a failure because he has not been competing with his equals." [11] Moreover, the Four Hundred were at first professedly established as merely a temporary government, preliminary to the establishment of a polity which would be less an oligarchy than a qualified democracy. Such a polity was the ideal of Theramenes, and he was impatient to constitute it. Thus there was a cleavage in the Four Hundred, the extreme oligarchs on one side, led by Antiphon and Phrynichus, the moderate reformers on the other, led by Theramenes. While the moderates had the support of the army at Samos behind them, the extreme party looked to the enemy for support and sent envoys to Sparta for the purpose of concluding a peace. In the meantime they fortified Eetionea, the mole which formed the northern side of the entrance to the Great Harbour of Piraeus. The object was to command the entrance so as to be able either to admit the Lacedaemonians or to exclude the fleet of Samos.

When the envoys returned from Sparta without having made terms, and when a Peloponnesian squadron was seen in the Saronic gulf, the movement against the oligarchs took shape. Phrynichus was slain by foreign assassins in the market-place. The soldiers who were employed in building the fort at Eetionea were instigated by Theramenes to declare against the oligarchy, and, after a great tumult at the Piraeus, the walls of the fort were pulled down, to the cry of "Whoever wishes the Five Thousand, and not the Four Hundred, to rule, let him come and help." Nobody in the crowd really knew whether the Five Thousand existed as an actually constituted body or not. When the fort was demolished, an Assembly was held in the theatre on the slope of Munychia; the agitation subsided, and peaceable negotiations with the Four Hundred ensued. A day was fixed for an Assembly in the theatre of Dionysus, to discuss a settlement on the basis of the constitution of the Five Thousand. But on the very day, just as the Assembly was about to meet, the appearance of a Lacedaemonian squadron, which had been hovering about, off the coast of Salamis, produced a temporary panic and a general rush to the Piraeus. It was only a fright, so far as the Piraeus was concerned, but there were other serious dangers

Movement against the Four Hundred.

[11] Jowett. Ibid.

ahead, as every one saw. The safety of Euboea was threatened, and the Athenians depended entirely on Euboeo, now that they had lost Attica. The Lacedaemonian fleet—forty-two ships under Agesandridas—doubled Sunium and sailed to Oropus. The Athenians sent thirty-six ships under Thymochares to Eretria, where they were forced to fight at once and were utterly defeated. All Euboea then revolted, except Oreus in the north, which was a settlement of Athenian cleruchs.

Revolt of Euboea (early in September).

At no moment perhaps—since the Persian War—was the situation at Athens so alarming. She had no reserve of ships, the army at Samos was hostile, Euboea, from which she derived her supplies, was lost, and there was feud and sedition in the city. It was a moment which might have inspired the Lacedaemonians to operate with a little vigour both by land and sea. Athens could not have resisted a combined attack of Agis from Decelea and Agesandridas at the Piraeus. But the Lacedaemonians were, as Thucydides observes, very convenient enemies, and they let the opportunity slip. The battle of Eretria struck, however, the hour of doom for the oligarchs. An Assembly in the Pnyx deposed the Four Hundred, and voted that the government should be placed in the hands of a body consisting of all those who could furnish themselves with arms, which body should be called the Five Thousand. Legislators (*nomothetae*) were appointed to draw up the details of the constitution, and all pay for offices was abolished. Most of the oligarchs escaped to Decelea, and one of them betrayed the fort of Oenoe on the frontier of Boeotia to the enemy. Two—Antiphon and Archeptolemus—were executed.

(Sept.) "Polity" or moderate democracy established at Athens.

The chief promoter of the new constitution was Theramenes. It was a constitution such as he had conceived from the beginning, though apparently not actually the same as that which had been proposed by the Hundred commissioners. Thucydides praises it as a constitution in which the rule of the many and the rule of the few were fairly tempered. It was the realisation of the ultimate intentions of most of those who had promoted the original resolution. It is certain that Theramenes, from the very beginning, desired to organise a polity, with democracy and oligarchy duly mixed; his acquiescence in a temporary oligarchy was a mere matter of necessity; and the nickname of *Cothurnus*—the loose buskin that fits either foot—given to him by the oligarchs was not deserved.

Battle of Cynossema, 411 B.C.

In the meantime the supine Spartan admiral Astyochus had been superseded by Mindarus, and the Peloponnesian fleet, invited by Pharnabazus, sailed for the Hellespont. The Athenian fleet under Thrasybulus and Thrasyllus followed, and forced them to fight in the straits. The Athenians, with seventy-six ships, were extended along the shore of the Chersonese, and the object of the Peloponnesians, who had ten more ships, was to outflank and so prevent the enemy from sailing out of the straits, and at the same time to press their centre in upon the land. The Athenians, to thwart this intention, extended their own right wing, and in doing so weakened the whole line. The Peloponnesians were victorious on the centre, but Thrasybulus, who was on the right wing, took advantage of their disorder in the moment of victory and threw them into panic. The engagement on the Athenian left was round the Cape of Cynossema, out of sight of the rest of the battle, and resulted after hard fighting in the repulse of the Peloponnesians. This victory heartened the Athenians; it was followed immediately by the recovery of Cyzicus, which had revolted. Mindarus had to send for the squadron which lay in the waters of Euboeo; but only a remnant reached him: the rest of the ships were lost in a storm off Mt. Athos. Another Athenian success at Abydus closed the military operations of the year. Tissaphernes was ill satisfied with the success of Athens, and when Alcibiades paid him a visit at Sardis during the winter, he arrested him. But Alcibiades made his escape.

The Peloponnesians were now vigorously supported by Pharnabazus, who was a far more valuable and trustworthy ally than Tissaphernes. In the spring Mindarus laid siege to Cyzicus, and the satrap supported him with an army. The Athenian fleet of eighty-six ships succeeded in passing the Hellespont unseen, and in three divisions, under Alcibiades, Theramenes, and Thrasybulus, took Mindarus by surprise. After a hard-fought battle both by land and sea, the Athenians were entirely victorious, Mindarus was slain, and about sixty triremes were taken or sunk. This annihilated the Peloponnesian navy. A laconic despatch, announcing the defeat to the Spartan ephors, was intercepted by the Athenians; "Our success is over; Mindarus is slain; the men are starving; we know not what to do." Sparta immediately made proposals of peace to Athens on the basis of the *status quo*. It would have been wise of Athens to accept the offer, and obtain relief from the pressure of the garrison at Decelea. But there is no doubt that the feeling in the navy was entirely against a peace which did not include the restoration of the power of Athens in the Aegean and Asia Minor; and the victory of Cyzicus seemed to assure the promise of its speedy recovery, notwithstanding the purse of Pharnabazus. The Spartan overtures were rejected.

The victory of Cyzicus led to a restoration of the unity of the Athenian state, which for a year had been divided into two parts,

Battle of Cyzicus, 410 B.C.

Restoration of Athenian democracy.

centred in Athens and Samos. The democratic party at Athens, encouraged by the success of the thoroughly democratic navy, were able to upset the polity of Theramenes and restore the democracy with the unlimited franchise and the Cleisthenic Council of Five Hundred. The most prominent of the leaders of this movement was Cleophon the lyremaker, a man of the same class as Hyperbolus and Cleon, and endowed with the same order of talent. Like Cleon he was a strong imperialist, and he was now the mouthpiece of the prevailing sentiment for war. His financial ability seems to have been no less remarkable than that of Cleon. The remuneration of offices, which was an essential part of the Athenian democracy, was revived as a matter of course; but Cleophon instituted a new payment, for which his name was best remembered by posterity. This was the "Two-obol payment." Though we know that it was introduced by Cleophon, it is not recorded for what purpose it was paid or who received it. Some have supposed that it was simply the wage of the judges,—that the old fee of three obols was revived in the reduced form of two obols. But this can hardly be the case. The two-obol payment is mentioned in a manner which implies that it was something completely novel. The probability is that it was a disbursement intended to relieve the terrible pressure of the protracted war upon the poor citizens whose means of livelihood was reduced or cut off by the presence of the enemy in Attica; and we may guess that the pension of two obols a day was paid to all who were not in the receipt of other public money for their services in the field, on shipboard, or in the law courts. To give employment to the indigent by public works was another part of the policy of Cleophon, who herein followed the example of Pericles. In the first years of this statesman's influence the building of a new temple of Athena on the Acropolis was brought to a completion. It rose close to the north cliff, on the place of the oldest of all the temples on her hill, the house which from the beginning she shared with Erechtheus. He shared the new temple too,—or the old temple, as it might well be called, since, though younger than the Parthenon, it stood on the elder site and held the ancient wooden statue of the goddess and sheltered those two significant emblems, her own olive and her rival's salt-spring. Athena now possessed two noble mansions. But the newer building on the older site was burned down by chance about two years after its completion, and was not rebuilt for some time, so that the ruins of the temple which still stand are not, stone for stone, a memorial of the days of Cleophon. But it is well to remember that it was in years of sore need that the graceful Ionic temple with the Porch of the Maidens was built in its first shape.

Diobelia.

The new temple of Athena Polias (so-called Erechtheum).

The years following the rejection of the Spartan overtures were marked by operations in the Propontis and its neighbourhood. The Athenians, under the able and strenuous leadership of Alcibiades, slowly gained ground. Thasos and Selymbria were won back. At Chrysopolis a toll station was established at which ships coming from the Euxine had to pay one-tenth of the value of their freight. Then Chalcedon was besieged and made tributary; and finally Byzantium was starved into capitulation, so that Athens once more completely commanded the Bosphorus. Meanwhile Pharnabazus had made an arrangement to conduct Athenian envoys to Susa for the purpose of coming to terms with the Great King. Nearer home, Athens lost Nisaea to the Megarians; and Pylus was at length recovered by Sparta.

As the distinctive feature of the last eight years of the Peloponnesian War was the combination between Persia and Sparta, we may divide this period into three parts, according to the nature of the Persian co-operation. During the first two years it is the satrap Tissaphernes who supports the Peloponnesian operations, and Athens loses nearly all Ionia. Then the satrap Pharnabazus takes the place of Tissaphernes as the active ally of the Peloponnesians; the military operations are chiefly in the Hellespont; and Athens gradually recovers many of her losses. But the affairs of the west had begun to engage the attention of the Great King, Darius, who, aware that the jealousy of the two satraps hinders an effective policy, sends down his younger son Cyrus to take the place of Tissaphernes at Sardis, with jurisdiction over Cappadocia, Phrygia, and Lydia. The government of Tissaphernes is confined to Caria. The arrival of Cyrus on the scene marks a new turning-point in the progress of the war.

It was a strange sight to see the common enemy of Hellas ranged along with the victors of Plataea against the victors of Salamis. It was a shock to men of Panhellenic feeling, and it was fitting that at the great Panhellenic gathering at Olympia a voice of protest should be raised. Men of western Hellas beyond the sea could look with a calmer view on the politics of the east, and it was a man of western Hellas, the Leontine Gorgias himself, who lifted up an eloquent voice against the wooing of Persian favour by Greek states. "Rather," he said, "go to war against Persia."

Sect. 9. Downfall of the Athenian Empire

Prince Cyrus was zealous; but his zeal to intervene actively and furnish pay to the Peloponnesian seamen might have been of little

Recovery of Thasos; occupation of Chrysopolis, 410 B.C.; recovery of Colophon by Thrasyllus, 409 B.C.; Athenians lose Pylus and Nisaea, 409 B.C.; capture of Chalcedon and Byzantium, 408.

Three periods of union between Persia and Peloponnesians: (1) 412-11, (2) 410-7, (3) 407-5.

Gorgias at Olympia, 408 B.C. (July to August).

Lysander

use, were it not for the simultaneous appointment of a new Spartan admiral, who possessed distinguished ability and inordinate ambition. This was Lysander, who was destined to bring the long war to its close. He gained the confidence of his seamen by his care for their interests, and he won much influence over Cyrus by being absolutely proof against the temptation of bribes,—a quality at which an oriental greatly marvelled. In prosecuting the aims of his ambition Lysander was perfectly unscrupulous, and he was a skilful diplomatist as well as an able general.

While Cyrus and Lysander were negotiating, Alcibiades, after an exile of eight years, had returned to his native city. He had been elected strategos, and had received an enthusiastic welcome. Time had, in some measure, dulled the sense of the terrible injuries which he had inflicted on his country, and his share in the recent recovery of the Hellespontine cities had partly at least atoned. But it was rather hope for future benefits than forgiveness for past wrongs that moved the Athenians to let bygones be bygones. They trusted in his capacity as a general, and they thought that by his diplomatic skill they might still be able to come to terms with Persia. So a decree was passed, giving him full powers for the conduct of the war, and he was solemnly freed from the curse which rested upon him as profaner of the Eleusinian rites. He had an opportunity of making his peace with the divinities of Eleusis. Ever since the occupation of Decelea, which he had done so much to bring about, the annual procession from Athens along the Sacred Way to the Eleusinian shrine had been suspended, and the mystic Iacchus had been conveyed by sea. Under the auspices of Alcibiades, who protected the procession by an escort of troops, the solemnity was once more celebrated in the usual way. It is possible that, if he had been bold enough to seize the opportunity of this tide of popularity, he might have established a tyranny at Athens; but he probably thought that such a venture would hardly be safe until he achieved further military or diplomatic successes. The opportunity was lost and did not recur. A slight incident completely changed the current of feeling in Athens. An Athenian fleet was at Notion, keeping guard on Ephesus, and Lysander succeeded in defeating it and capturing fifteen ships. Though Alcibiades was not present at the battle, he was responsible, and lost his prestige at Athens, where the tidings of a decisive victory was confidently expected. New generals were appointed immediately, and Alcibiades withdrew to a castle on the Hellespont which he had provided for himself as a refuge in case of need. Conon succeeded him in the chief command of the navy.

The Peloponnesians during the following winter organised a fleet

of greater strength than they had had for many years—140 ships;
but Lysander had to make place for a new admiral, Callicratidas.
The Peloponnesians at first carried all before them. The fort of
Delphinion in Chios, and the town of Methymna in Lesbos were
taken; Conon, who had only seventy ships, was forced into a battle
outside Mytilene and lost thirty triremes in the action. The re-
mainder were blockaded in the harbour of Mytilene. The situation
was critical, and Athens did not underrate the danger. The gold and
silver dedications in the temples of the Acropolis were melted to
defray the costs of a new armament; freedom was promised to
slaves, citizenship to resident aliens, for their services in the emergency; and at the end of a month Athens and her allies sent a fleet
of 150 triremes to relieve Mytilene. Callicratidas, who had now 170
ships, left 50 to maintain the blockade and sailed with the rest to
meet the foe. A great battle was fought near the islets of the Arginusae, south of Lesbos, and the Athenians were victorious. Seventy
Spartan ships were sunk or taken, and Callicratidas was slain. An
untimely north wind hindered the victors from rescuing the crews of
their wrecked ships, as well as from sailing to Mytilene to destroy
the rest of the hostile fleet.

Battle of
Arginu-
sae, 406
B.C.

The success had not been won without a certain sacrifice; twenty-
five ships had been lost with their crews. It was believed that many
of the men, floating about on the wreckage, might have been saved
if the officers had taken proper measures. The commanders were
blamed; the matter was taken up by politicians at Athens; the generals were suspended from their office and summoned to render
an account of their conduct. They shifted the blame on the trierarchs; and the trierarchs, one of whom was Theramenes, in order to
shield themselves, accused the generals of not having issued the
orders for rescue until the high wind made the execution impossible.
We are not in a position to judge the question; for the decision must
entirely depend on the details of the situation, and as to the details
we have no certainty. It is not clear, for instance, whether the storm
was sufficiently violent to prevent any attempt at a rescue. The pre-
sumption is, however, that the Athenian people were right in the
conviction that there had been criminal negligence somewhere, and
the natural emotion of indignation which they felt betrayed them
into committing a crime themselves. The question was judged by
the Assembly, and not by the ordinary courts. Two sittings were
held, and the eight generals who had been present at Arginusae
were condemned to death and confiscation of property. Six, including Thrasyllus and Pericles, son of the great statesman, were executed; the other two had prudently kept out of the way. Whatever

Trial of
the
generals.

were the rights of the case, the penalty was unduly severe; but the worst feature of the proceedings was that the Assembly violated a recognised usage[12] of the city by pronouncing sentence on all the accused together, instead of judging the case of each separately. Formally illegal indeed it was not; for the supporters of the generals had not the courage to apply the *Graphe Paranomon*. Protests had no effect on the excited multitude, thirsty for vengeance. It was an interesting incident that the philosopher Socrates, who happened on the fatal day to be one of the prytaneis, objected to putting the motion. All constitutions, democracy like oligarchy and monarchy, have their own dangers and injustices; this episode illustrates the gravest kind of injustice which a primary Assembly, swayed by a sudden current of violent feeling and unchecked by any responsibility, sometimes commits,—and repents.

The victory of Arginusae restored to the Athenians the command of the eastern Aegean, and induced the Lacedaemonians to repeat the same propositions of peace which they had made four years ago after the battle of Cyzicus: namely, that Decelea should be evacuated and that otherwise each party should remain just as it was. Through the influence of the demagogue Cleophon, who is said to have come into the Assembly drunk, the offer was rejected. Nothing was left for the Spartans but to reorganise their fleet. Eteonicus had gathered together the remnants of the ships and gone to Chios, but he was unable to pay the seamen, who were forced to work as labourers on the fields of Chian farmers. In the winter this means of support failed, and threatened by starvation, they formed a conspiracy to pillage the town of Chios. The conspirators agreed to wear a straw in order to recognise one another. Eteonicus discovered the plot, but there were so many straw-bearers that he shrank from an open conflict, and devised a stratagem. Walking through the streets of Chios, attended by fifteen armed men, he met a man who suffered from ophthalmia, coming out of a surgeon's house, and seeing that he wore a straw, ordered him to be put to death. A crowd gathered and demanded why the man was put to death; the reply was "Because he wore a straw." When the news spread, every straw-bearer was so frightened that he threw his straw away. The Chians then consented to supply a month's pay for the men, who were immediately embarked.

This incident shows that money had ceased to flow in from Persia. It was generally felt that if further Persian co-operation was to be secured and the Peloponnesian cause to be restored, the command of the fleet must again be entrusted to Lysander. But there

Conspiracy of the straw-bearers at Chios.

Lysander in command again, 405 B.C.

[12] The principle was formulated in the Psephism of Cannōnus.

was a law at Sparta that no man could be navarch a second time. On this occasion the law was evaded by sending Lysander out as secretary, but on the understanding that the actual command lay with him and not with the nominal admiral. Lysander visited Cyrus at Sardis, asserted his old influence over him, and obtained the money he required. With the help of organised parties in the various cities, he soon fitted out a fleet. An unlooked-for event gave him still greater power and prestige. King Darius was very ill, his death was expected, and Cyrus was called to his bedside. During his absence, Cyrus entrusted to his friend Lysander the administration of his satrapy, and the tribute. He knew that money was no temptation to this exceptional Spartan, and he feared to trust such power to a Persian noble.

His influence with Cyrus.

With these resources behind him, Lysander speedily proved his ability. Attacked at Ephesus by the Athenian fleet under Conon, he declined battle; then, when the enemy had dispersed, he sailed forth, first to Rhodes, and then across the Aegean to the coast of Attica, where he had a consultation with Agis. Recrossing the Aegean, he made for the Hellespont and laid siege to Lampsacus. The Athenian fleet of 180 ships reunited and followed him thither. Lampsacus had been taken before they reached Sestos, but they determined now to force him to accept the battle which he had refused at Ephesus, and with this view proceeded along the coast till they reached Aegospotami, "Goat's rivers," an open beach without harbourage, over against Lampsacus. It was a bad position, as all the provisions had to be fetched from Sestos at a distance of about two miles, while the Peloponnesian fleet was in an excellent harbour with a well-supplied town behind. Sailing across the strait, the Athenians found the enemy drawn up for battle but under orders not to move until they were attacked, and in such a strong position that an attack would have been unwise. They were obliged to return to Aegospotami. For four days the same thing befell. Each day the Athenian fleet sailed across the strait and endeavoured to lure Lysander into an engagement; each day its efforts were fruitless. From his castle in the neighbourhood Alcibiades descried the dangerous position of the Athenians, and riding over to Aegospotami earnestly counselled the generals to move to Sestos. His sound advice was received with coldness, perhaps with insult. When the fleet returned from its daily cruise to Lampsacus, the seamen used to disembark and scatter on the shore. On the fifth day Lysander sent scout ships which, as soon as the Athenian crews had gone ashore for their meal, were to flash a bright shield as a signal. When the signal was given, the whole Peloponnesian squadron, consisting

Victory of Lysander at Aegospotami (end of summer, 405 B.C.).

of about 200 galleys, rowed rapidly across the strait and found the Athenian fleet defenceless. There was no battle, no resistance. Twenty ships, which were in a condition to fight, escaped; the remaining 160 were captured at once. It was generally believed that there was treachery among the generals, and it is possible that Adeimantus, who was taken prisoner and spared, had been bribed by Lysander. All the Athenians who were taken, to the number of three or four thousand, were put to death. The chief commander Conon, who was not among the unready, succeeded in getting away. Greek ships usually unshipped their sails when they prepared for a naval battle, and the sails of the Peloponnesian triremes had been deposited at Cape Abarnis, near Lampsacus. Informed of this, Conon boldly shot across to Abarnis, seized the sails, and so deprived Lysander of the power of an effective pursuit. It would have been madness for the responsible commander to return to Athens with the tidings of such a terrible disaster; and Conon, sending home twelve of the twenty triremes which had escaped, sailed himself with the rest to the protection of Evagoras, the king of Salamis in Cyprus. Never was a decisive victory gained with such small sacrifice as that which Lysander gained at Aegospotami.

Situation at Athens.

The tidings of ruin reached the Piraeus at night, and "on that night not a man slept." The city remembered the cruel measure which it had once and again meted out to others, as to Melos and Scione, and shuddered at the thought that even such measure might now be meted out to itself. It was hard for the Athenians to realise that at one blow their sea-power was annihilated, and they had now to make preparations for sustaining a siege. But the blockade was deferred by the policy of Lysander. He did not intend to attack Athens but to starve it into surrender, and with this view he drove all the Athenian cleruchs whom he found in the islands to Athens, in order to swell the starving population. Having completed the subjugation of the Athenian empire in the Hellespont and Thrace, and ordered affairs in those regions, Lysander sailed at length into the Saronic gulf with 150 ships, occupied Aegina, and blockaded the Piraeus. At the same time the Spartan king Pausanias entered Attica, and, joining forces with Agis, encamped in the Academe, west of the city. But the walls were too strong to attack, and at the beginning of winter the army withdrew, while the fleet remained near the Piraeus. As provisions began to fail, the Athenians made a proposal of peace, offering to resign their empire and become allies of Lacedaemon. The envoys were turned back at Sellasia; they would not be received by the ephors unless they brought more acceptable terms; and it was intimated that the demolition of the Long Walls for a length of ten stades was an indispensable condition of peace. It was folly to resist, yet the Athenians resisted. The demagogue Cleophon, who had twice hindered the conclusion of peace when it might have been made with honour, first after Cyzicus, then after Arginusae, now hindered it again when it could be made only with humiliation. An absurd decree was passed that no one should ever propose to accept such terms. But the danger was that such obstinacy would drive the enemy into insisting on an unconditional surrender; for the situation was hopeless. Theramenes undertook to visit Lysander and endeavour to obtain more favourable conditions, or at all events to discover how matters lay. His real object was to gain time and let the people come to their senses. He remained three months with Lysander, and when he returned to Athens, he found the citizens prepared to submit on any terms whatever. People were dying of famine, and the reaction of feeling had been marked by the execution of Cleophon, who was condemned on the charge of evading military service. Theramenes was sent to Sparta with full powers. It is interesting to find that during these anxious months a decree was passed recalling to Athens an illustrious citizen, who had been found wanting as a general, but whose genius was to make immortal the war now drawing to its close—the historian Thucydides.

Athens submits.

An assembly of the Peloponnesian allies was called together at Sparta to determine how they should deal with the fallen foe. The general sentiment was that no mercy should be shown; that Athens should be utterly destroyed and the whole people sold into slavery. But Sparta never felt the same bitterness towards Athens as that which animated Corinth and Thebes; she was neither a neighbour nor a commercial rival. The destruction of Athens might have been politically profitable, but Sparta, with all her faults, could on occasion rise to nobler views. She resolutely rejected the barbarous proposal of the Confederacy; she would not blot out a Greek city which had done such noble services to Greece against the Persian invader. That was more than two generations ago, but it was not to be forgotten; Athens was saved by her past. The terms of the Peace were: the Long Walls and fortifications of the Piraeus were to be destroyed; the Athenians lost all their foreign possessions, but remained independent, confined to Attica and Salamis; their whole fleet was forfeited; all exiles were allowed to return; Athens became the ally of Sparta, pledged to follow her leadership. When the terms were ratified, Lysander sailed into the Piraeus. The demolition of the Long Walls immediately began. The Athenians and their conquerors together pulled them down to the music of

Conditions of Peace imposed on Athens.

404 B.C. April.

flute-players; and the jubilant allies thought that freedom had at length dawned for the Greeks. Lysander permitted Athens to retain twelve triremes, and, having inaugurated the destruction of the fortifications, sailed off to reduce Samos.

It is not to be supposed that all Athenians were dejected and wretched at the terrible humiliation which had befallen their native city. There were numerous exiles who owed their return to her calamity; and the extreme oligarchic party rejoiced in the foreign occupation, regarding it as an opportunity for the subversion of the democracy and the re-establishment of a constitution like that which had been tried after the Sicilian expedition. Theramenes looked forward to making a new attempt to introduce his favourite polity. Of the exiles, the most prominent and determined was Critias, son of Callaeschrus, and a member of the same family as the lawgiver Solon. He was a man of many parts, a pupil of Gorgias and a companion of Socrates, an orator, a poet, and a philosopher.

Institution of the Thirty by the psephism of Dracontides (summer, 404).

A combination was formed between the exiles and the home oligarchs; a common plan of action was organised; and the chief democratic leaders were presently seized and imprisoned. The intervention of Lysander was then invoked for the establishing of a new constitution, and awed by his presence, the Assembly passed a measure proposed by Dracontides, that a body of Thirty should be nominated, for the purpose of drawing up laws and managing public affairs until the code should be completed. The oligarchs did not take the trouble to repeal the law which would expose the proposer of the measure to prosecution by the Graphe Paranomon; they felt sure of their power. Critias, Theramenes, and Dracontides were among the Thirty who were appointed.

Suspected oligarchical intrigues.

The ruin of the power of Athens had fallen out to the advantage of the oligarchical party, and it has even been suspected that the oligarchs had for many years past deliberately planned to place the city at the mercy of the enemy, for the ulterior purpose of destroying the democracy. The part played by Theramenes in the condemnation of the generals who had the indiscretion to win Arginusae, the parts he subsequently played in negotiating the Peace and in establishing the oligarchy, the serious suspicions of treachery in connexion with the disaster of Aegospotami, have especially suggested this conjecture. The attempt of the Four Hundred on a previous occasion to come to terms with Sparta may be taken into account, and the comparatively lenient terms imposed on Athens might seem to point in the same direction. One thing seems certain. The oligarchic party had been distinctly aiming at peace, and the repeated opposition of Cleophon (impolitic, as we have seen) indicates that he suspected oligarchical designs. It must also be admitted that the conduct of the Athenians in fixing their station at Aegospotami, and delivering themselves to the foe like sheep led to the altar, argues a measure of folly which seems almost incredible, if there were not treachery behind; and the suspicion is confirmed by the clemency shown to Adeimantus. It must, however, be acknowledged that it is hard to understand how the treason could have been effectually carried out without the connivance of Conon, the commander-in-chief; yet no suspicion seems to have been attached to him. The whole problem of the oligarchic intrigues of the last eight years of the war remains wrapped in far greater mystery than the mutilation of the Hermae.

Sect. 10. Rule of the Thirty and Restoration of the Democracy

The purpose for which the Thirty had been appointed was to frame a new constitution; their powers, as a governing body, were only to last until they had completed their legislative work. The more part of them, however, with Critias, who was the master spirit, had no serious thoughts of constructing a constitution; they regarded this as merely a pretext for getting into power; and their only object was to retain the power in their own hands, establishing a simple oligarchy. In this, however, they were not absolutely unanimous. One of them at least, Theramenes, had no taste for pure oligarchy, but was still genuinely intent on framing a polity, tempered of both oligarchic and democratic elements. This dissension in the views of the two ablest men, Critias and Theramenes, soon led to fatal disunion.

Rule of the Thirty, c. Sept. 404 to May 403.

The first measures of the Thirty were, however, carried out with cordial unanimity. A Council of Five Hundred, consisting of strong supporters of oligarchy, was appointed, and invested with the judicial functions which had before belonged to the people. A body of Eleven, under the command of Satyrus, a violent, unscrupulous man, was appointed for police duties; and the guard of the Piraeus was committed to a body of Ten. The chief democrats, who on the fall of Athens had opposed the establishment of an oligarchy, were then seized, tried by the Council, and condemned to death for conspiracy. So far there was unanimity; but at this point Theramenes would have stopped. At such times, moderate counsels have small chance of winning, ranged beside the extreme policies of resolute men like Critias, who had come back in a bitter and revengeful spirit against democracy, relentlessly resolved to exercise an ab-

First measures.

Disunion.

solute despotism and expunge all elements of popular opposition. A polity on the broad basis which Theramenes desired was as obnoxious to Critias as the old democracy; into which, he was convinced, it would soon deviate. He and his colleagues were therefore afraid of all prominent citizens of moderate views, whether democratic or oligarchic, who were awaiting with impatience the constitution which the Thirty had been appointed to prepare,—the men on whom the polity of Theramenes, if it came into existence, would mainly rest.

The Thirty had announced as part of their programme that they would purge the city of wrong-doers. They put to death a number of men of bad character, including some notorious informers; but they presently proceeded to execute, with or without trial, not only prominent democrats, but also men of oligarchical views who, though unfriendly to democracy, were also unfriendly to injustice and illegality. Among the latter victims was Niceratus, the son of Nicias. To the motives of fear and revenge was soon added the appetite for plunder; and some men were executed because they were rich, while many fled, happy to escape with their lives. Even metics, who had little to do with politics, were despoiled; thus the speech-writer Lysias and his brother Polemarchus, who kept a lucrative manufactory of shields, were arrested, and while Lysias succeeded in making his escape, Polemarchus was put to death. And while many Athenians were removed by hemlock or driven into banishment, others were required to assist in the revolting service of arresting fellow-citizens, in order that they might thereby become accomplices in the guilt of the government. Thus the philosopher Socrates and four others were commanded with severe threats to arrest an honest citizen, Leon of Salamis. Socrates refused without hesitation to do the bidding of the tyrants; the others were not so brave. Yet Socrates was not punished for his defiance; and this immunity was perhaps due to some feeling of piety in the heart of Critias, who had been one of his pupil-companions; a feeling which might be safely indulged, as the philosopher was neither wealthy nor popular.

To these judicial murders and this organised system of plundering, Theramenes was unreservedly opposed. The majority of the Council shared his disapprobation; and he would have been able to establish a moderate constitution, but for the ability and strength of Critias. His representations, indeed, induced the Thirty to broaden the basis on which their power rested by creating a body of 3000 citizens, who had the privilege of bearing arms and the right of being tried by the Council. All outside that body were liable

Tyranny.

Attitude of Theramenes.

to be condemned to death by sentence of the Thirty, without a trial. The body of 3000 had practically no political rights, and were chosen so far as possible from known partisans of the government, the staunchest of whom were the thousand knights. This measure naturally did not satisfy Theramenes; his suggestions had, in fact, been used with a purpose very different from his,—to secure, not to alter, the government.

In the meantime the exiles whom the oligarchy had driven from Athens were not idle. They had found refuge in those neighbouring states—Corinth, Megara, and Thebes—which had been bitter foes of Athens, but were now undergoing a considerable change of feeling. Dissatisfaction with the high-handed proceedings of Sparta, who would not give them a share in the spoils of the war, had disposed them to look with more favour on their fallen enemy, and to feel disgust at the proceedings of the Thirty, who were under the aegis of Lysander. They were therefore not only ready to grant hospitality to Athenian exiles, but to lend some help towards delivering their city from the oppression of the tyrants. The first step was made from Thebes. Thrasybulus and Anytus, with a band of seventy exiles, seized the Attic fortress of Phyle, in the Parnes range, close to the Boeotian frontier, and put into a state of defence the strong stone walls, whose ruins are still there. The Thirty led out their forces—their faithful knights and Three Thousand hoplites—and sat down to blockade the stronghold. But a timely snowstorm broke up the blockade; the army retired to Athens; and for the next three months or more nothing further was done against Thrasybulus and the men of Phyle.

The oligarchs were now in a dangerous position, menaced without by an enemy against whom their attack had failed, menaced within by a strong opposition. They saw that the influence of Theramenes, who was thoroughly dissatisfied with their policy, would be thrown into the scale against them, and they resolved to get rid of him. Having posted a number of devoted creatures, armed with hidden daggers, near the railing of the council-house, Critias arose in the assembled Council and denounced Theramenes as a traitor and conspirator against the state,—a man who could not be trusted an inch, in view of those repeated tergiversations which had won him the nickname of the "Buskin." The reply of Theramenes, denouncing the impolicy of Critias and his colleagues, is said to have been received with applause by most of the Council, who really sympathised with him. Critias, seeing that he would be acquitted by the Council, resorted to an extreme measure. He struck the name of Theramenes out of the list of the Three Thou-

The exiles.

Thrasybulus seizes Phyle, c. Dec. 404. First expedition of the Thirty against Thrasybulus, Dec. 404 or Jan. 403.

Death of Theramenes, c. Jan. 403.

sand;[13] and then along with his colleagues condemned him to death, since those who were not included in the list could not claim the right of trial. Theramenes leapt on the sacred Hearth and appealed for protection to the Council; but the Council was stupefied with terror, and at the command of Critias the Eleven entered and dragged the suppliant from the altar. He was borne away to prison; the hemlock was immediately administered; and when he had drunk, he tossed out a drop that remained at the bottom of the cup, as banqueters used to do in the game of kottabos, exclaiming, "This drop for the gentle Critias!" There had perhaps been a dose of truth in the reproaches which the gentle Critias had hurled at him across the floor of the council-chamber. Theramenes may have been shifty and unscrupulous where means and methods were concerned. But in his main object he was perfectly sincere. He was sincere in desiring to establish a moderate polity which should unite the merits of both oligarchy and democracy, and avoid their defects. There can be no question that he was honestly interested in trying this political experiment. And the very nature of this policy involved an appearance of insincerity and gave rise to suspicion. It led him to oscillate between the democratic and oligarchical parties, seeking to gain influence and support in both, with a view to the ultimate realisation of his middle plan. And thus the democrats suspected him as an oligarch, the oligarchs distrusted him as a democrat. In judging Theramenes, it seems fair to remember that a politician who in unsettled times desires to direct the state into a middle course between two opposite extremes can hardly avoid oscillation more or less, can rarely escape the imputation of the Buskin.

After the death of Theramenes, the Thirty succeeded in disarming, by means of a stratagem, all the citizens who were not enrolled in the list of the Three Thousand, and expelled them from the city. But with a foe on Attic ground, growing in numbers every day, Critias and his fellows felt themselves so insecure, that they took the step of sending an embassy to Sparta, to ask for a Lacedaemonian garrison. The request was granted, and 700 men, under Callibius, were introduced into the acropolis. The Thirty would never have resorted to this measure except under the dire pressure of necessity; for not only was it unpopular, but they had to pay the strangers out of their own chest.

Spartan garrison occupies the Acropolis.

---

[13] An appearance of legality seems to have been given to this act. A law was passed—presumably on the spot—that persons who had opposed the Four Hundred in 411 B.C., or taken part in destroying the fort at Eetionea, should be excluded from the constitution.

It was perhaps in the first days of the month of May that it was resolved to make a second attempt to dislodge the democrats from Phyle. A band of the knights and the Spartan garrison sallied forth; but near Acharnae they were surprised at night and routed with great loss by Thrasybulus. This incident produced considerable alarm at Athens, and the Thirty had reason to fear that many of their partisans were wavering. Deciding to secure an eventual place of refuge in case Athens should become untenable, they seized Eleusis and put about 300 Eleusinians to death. This measure had hardly been carried out when Thrasybulus descended from Phyle and seized the Piraeus. He had now about 1000 men, but the Piraeus, without fortifications, was not an easy place to defend. He drew up his forces on the hill of Munychia, occupying the temples of Artemis and the Thracian goddess Bendis, which stood at the summit of a steep street; highest of all stood the darters and slingers, ready to shoot over the heads of the hoplites. Thus posted, with his prophet by his side, Thrasybulus awaited the attack of the Thirty, who had led down all their forces to the Piraeus. A shower of darts descended on their heads as they mounted the hill, and, while they wavered for a moment under the missiles, the hoplites rushed down on them, led by the prophet, who had foretold his own death in the battle and was the first to perish. Seventy of the enemy were slain; among them Critias himself. During the truce which was then granted for taking up the dead, the citizens on either side held some converse with one another, and Cleocritus, the herald of the Eleusinian Mystae, impressive both by his loud voice and by his sacred calling, addressed the adherents of the Thirty: "Fellow-citizens, why seek ye to slay us? why do ye force us into exile? us who never did you wrong. We have shared in the same religious rites and festivals; we have been your schoolfellows and choir-fellows; we have fought with you by land and sea for freedom. We adjure you, by our common gods, abandon the cause of the Thirty, monsters of impiety, who for their own gains have slain in eight months more Athenians than the Peloponnesians slew in a war of ten years. Believe that we have shed as many tears as you for those who have now fallen." This general appeal, and individual appeals in the same tone, at such an affecting moment, must have produced an effect upon the half-hearted soldiers of the Thirty, who had now lost their able and violent leader. There was dissension and discord not only among the Three Thousand and the Council, but among the Thirty themselves. It was felt that the government of the Thirty could no longer be maintained, and that if the oligarchy was to be rescued a

Second expedition against Phyle, beginning of May, 403 B.C.

Battle of Munychia

Death of Critias.

new government must be installed. A general meeting of the Three
Thousand deposed the Thirty and instituted in their stead a body
of Ten, one from each tribe. One member of the Thirty was re-
elected as a member of the new government, but the rest withdrew
to the refuge which they had provided for themselves at Eleusis.
The new body of Ten represented the views of those who were
genuinely devoted to oligarchy, but disapproved of the extreme
policy of Critias and his fellows. They failed to come to terms with
Thrasybulus, who was every day receiving reinforcements both in
men and arms; the civil war continued; and it soon appeared that
it would be impossible for Athens to hold out against the democrats in the Piraeus without foreign aid.

An embassy was accordingly dispatched by the Ten to Sparta;
and about the same time the remnant of the Thirty at Eleusis sent
a message on their own account for the same purpose. Both embassies represented the democrats at Piraeus as rebels against the
power of Sparta. The Lacedaemonian government, through the
influence of Lysander, was induced to intervene in support of the
Ten. Lysander assembled an army at Eleusis, and forty ships were
sent under Libys to cut off the supplies which the democrats received by sea. The outlook was now gloomy for Thrasybulus and
his company; but they were rescued by a disunion within the
Lacedaemonian state. The influence of Lysander, which had been
for the last years supreme, was perceptibly declining; the king
Pausanias was his declared opponent; and many others of the governing class were jealous of his power, vexed at his arrogance, perhaps suspicious of his designs. The oligarchies which he had created
at Athens and in the other cities of the Athenian empire had dis-
graced themselves by misgovernment and bloodshed; and the disgrace was reflected upon the fame of their creator. Lysander had
hardly begun his work when Pausanias persuaded the ephors to entrust to himself the commission of restoring tranquillity at Athens;
and Lysander had the humiliation of handing over to his rival the
army which he had mustered. A defeat convinced Thrasybulus that
it would be wise to negotiate; and on the other hand Pausanias deposed the irreconcilable Ten, and caused it to be replaced by another Ten of more moderate views. Both parties then, the city and
the Piraeus alike, submitted themselves to Spartan intervention,
and Sparta, under the auspices of king Pausanias, acquitted herself
uncommonly well. A commission of fifteen was sent from Lacedaemon to assist the king, and a reconciliation was brought about. The
terms were a general and mutual pardon for all past acts; from
which were excepted only the Thirty, the Ten who had held the

Marginal notes:

The first
board of
Ten.

Oligarchs
appeal to
Sparta
(late
spring,
403).
Sparta in-
tervenes.

Pausanias
in com-
mand.

Second
board of
Ten.

End of the
civil war
in Attica.

Piraeus under the Thirty, the Eleven who had carried out the judicial murders perpetrated by the Thirty, and the Ten who had succeeded the Thirty. All these excepted persons were required to give an account of their acts if they wished to remain at Athens. Eleusis was to form an independent state, and any Athenian who chose might migrate to Eleusis within a specified time.

The evil dream of Athens was at last over: a year and half of oligarchical tyranny, and foreign soldiery on the Acropolis. She owed her deliverance to the energy of Thrasybulus and the discretion of Pausanias. Pausanias displayed his discretion further by not meddling with the reconciled parties in their settlement of the constitution. It was decreed, on the motion of Tisamenus, that "lawgivers" should be appointed to revise the constitution, and that in the meantime the state should be administered according to "the laws of Solon and the institutions of Dracon." The union of the two names is significant of the conciliation. Provisionally, then, the franchise was limited to those who belonged to the first three Solonian classes—those who could at least serve as hoplites. It is noteworthy that there was an idea afloat of making the possession of landed property a qualification for political rights. But it was a totally unpractical idea. Such a test would have excluded rich men; it would have included many of the fourth class. In the end, no new experiment was tried. The lawgivers restored the old democracy with its unlimited franchise, and Athens entered upon a new stage of her career. The amnesty was faithfully kept; the democrats did not revenge themselves on the supporters of the oligarchical tyranny. But it was easier to forgive than forget; and for many years after the reconciliation a distinction was drawn, though not officially, yet in the ordinary intercourse of life, between the "men of the city" and the "men of the Piraeus"—the men who had fought for freedom and those who had fought against it. That was almost inevitable; and so long as the oligarchs held Eleusis, there might even be some ground for suspecting the loyalty of their old supporters. After about two years of independent existence, Eleusis was attacked by Athens; the Eleusinian generals were captured and put to death, and the town resumed its old place as part of Attica. Henceforward, for well-nigh three generations, the Athenian democracy was perfectly secure from the danger or fear of an oligarchical revolution. That hideous nightmare of the Thirty had established it on a firmer base than ever.

September, B.C. 403.

Nomothetes appointed. Provisional arrangement.

(See below, p. 573.)

CHAPTER XII

THE SPARTAN SUPREMACY AND THE PERSIAN WAR

Sect. I. The Spartan Supremacy

Sparta drawn into founding an empire.

SPARTA had achieved the task which she had been pressed to undertake, and had undertaken somewhat reluctantly, the destruction of the Athenian empire. It was a task which, though not imposed by the unanimous voice of Greece, appealed to a most deeply-seated sentiment of the Greeks, their love of political independence. The Athenian empire had been an outrage on that sentiment, and, apart from all calculations of particular interest, the humiliation of the great offender must have been regarded, even by those who were not her enemies, with an involuntary satisfaction. The avowed aim of Sparta throughout had been to restore their liberty to those states which had been "enslaved" by Athens, and protect the liberty of those whom her ambition threatened. Now that this object was accomplished as fully as could be desired, it would have been correct for Sparta to retire into her old position, leaving the cities which had belonged to the Athenian empire to arrange their own affairs,—if her deeds were to be in accordance with her professions. The alternative course for a state in the position of Sparta was to enter frankly upon the Athenian inheritance, and pursue the aims and policy of Athens as an imperial power. Other states might have adopted this course with advantage both to themselves and Greece; for Sparta it was impossible. And so when Sparta, unable from the nature of her institutions and the character of her genius to tread in the footsteps of her fallen rival, nevertheless resolved to take under her own dominion the cities which she had gone forth to deliver from all dominion, she not only cynically set aside her high moral professions, but entered on a path of ambition which led to calamity for herself and distress for Greece. The main feature of Greek history for the thirty years after Aegospotami is Sparta's pursuit of a policy of aggrandisement beyond the Peloponnesus; the opposition which this policy calls forth leads both to the revival of Athens as a great power and to the rise of Thebes. In the end Sparta is forced to retire into the purely Peloponnesian position for which her institutions fitted her. In the making of those institutions an activity beyond the Peloponnesus had not been contemplated; and they were too rigid to be adapted to the enlarged sphere of an Aegean dominion. Nothing short of a complete revolution in the Spartan state could have rendered her essay in empire a success; but the narrow Spartan system was too firmly based in the narrow Spartan character to suffer such a revolution.

We may wonder how far the general who had placed his country in the position of arbitress of Greece appreciated the difficulty of reconciling the political character of Lacedaemon with the rôle of an imperial city. Un-Spartan as he was in many respects, Lysander had possibly more enlightened views as to the administration of an empire than his countrymen. A story is told that when Callibius, the Spartan harmost of Athens, was knocked down by a young athlete whom he had insulted, and appealed to Lysander, he was told that he did not know how to govern freemen. To deal with freemen abroad was what the average Spartan could not do; and it was such men as Callibius that Lysander had to use for the establishment of the empire which he had resolved to found. In each of the cities which had passed from Athenian into Spartan control, a government of ten members was set up, and its authority was maintained by a Lacedaemonian *harmost* with a Lacedaemonian garrison. The cities were thus given over to a twofold oppression. The foreign governors were rapacious and were practically free from home control; the native oligarchies were generally tyrannical, and got rid of their political opponents by judicial murders; and both decarchs and harmost played into each other's hands. Lysander exercised with a high hand and without farsightedness the dictatorship which was his for the time and might at any hour be taken from him. He was solely concerned to impose a firm military despotism on the states which had been rescued from the Athenian Confederacy.

It is obvious that the Athenian and Spartan empires had little in common. They were, first of all, sharply contrasted through the fact that the Spartan policy was justified by no public object like that to which the Confederacy owed its origin. And this contrast was all the more flagrant, considering that after the battle of Aegospotami there was the same demand for a Panhellenic confederacy, with the object of protecting the Asiatic Greeks from Persia, as there had been after the battle of Mycale. But so far from connecting her supremacy with such an object, Sparta had abandoned the Asiatic Greeks to the Great King as the price of Persian help. Athens had won her power as the champion of the eastern Greeks;

Unfitness of Sparta for empire.

Decarchies.

Harmosts (= "regulators").

Contrast between Athenian and Spartan empires.

Sparta had secured her supremacy by betraying them. In the second place, the methods of the two states in exercising their power were totally different. The grievances against Athens, though real, were mainly of a sentimental nature. The worst Athens had done was to deprive some Confederate cities of autonomy; there were no complaints of tyranny, rapine, or oppression. But under the Lacedaemonian supremacy men suffered from positive acts of injustice and violence, and might seek in vain at Sparta for redress. The spirit of the system which Lysander instituted may be judged from the statement that the will of any Spartan citizen was regarded as law in the subject states. The statement comes from a friend of Lacedaemon.

Lysander's recall.

The position of power which Lysander had attained in the eyes of the world, and enjoyed without moderation, could not fail to excite jealousy and apprehension at Sparta itself. He held a sort of royal court at Samos, and the Samians accorded him divine honours by calling after his name a feast which had hitherto been a feast of Hera. He was recalled to Sparta, and he obeyed the summons, bearing a letter from the satrap Pharnabazus to justify him. But when it was opened, instead of being an encomium, it was found to be a deed of accusation; and Lysander was covered with ridicule

403 B.C.

as the victim of a Persian trick. He was permitted to escape from the situation on the plea of visiting the temple of Zeus Ammon in the Libyan oasis, in accordance with a vow. But his work remained. Lacedaemon upheld her uncongenial military despotism, modifying Lysander's system only so far as not to insist on the maintenance of the decarchies, but to permit the cities to substitute other forms of government, under the aegis of the harmost. Financially, the empire was so constituted as to secure an income of a thousand talents to meet the expenses of Sparta in maintaining her system. The receipt of such an income was a political innovation, and its administration involved money transactions of a nature and on a scale which would have been severely condemned by "Lycurgus." The admission into the treasury of a large sum of gold and silver which had been brought to Sparta by Lysander was a distinct breach of the Lycurgean discipline. Thus, inflexible as the Spartan system was, the necessities of empire compelled it to yield at one point, and a point where attack is wont to be especially insidious.

404-371 B.C.

The supremacy of Sparta lasted for a generation, though with intervals in which it was not effective; and its history for more than half of the period is mainly determined by her relations with Persia. As it had been through Persia that she won her supremacy, so it was through Persia that she lost it, and through Persia that she once more regained it.

SECT. 2. THE REBELLION OF CYRUS AND THE MARCH OF THE TEN THOUSAND

We now come to an episode which takes us into the domestic history of Persia, out of the limits of Greek geography into the heart of the Persian empire. On the death of Darius, his eldest son Artaxerxes had succeeded to the throne, notwithstanding the plots of his mother Parysatis, who attempted to secure it for her younger and favourite son Cyrus. In these transactions Tissaphernes had supported Artaxerxes, and when Cyrus returned to his satrapy in Asia Minor, Tissaphernes was set to watch him. False suspicions and calumnies frequently lead to the actual perpetration of the crimes which they attribute; and perhaps if he had not been suspected, Cyrus would not have formed the plan of subverting his brother and seizing the kingship. But it is far more likely that from the first Cyrus had hoped and resolved to succeed to his father's throne. For his success he relied largely on an army of Greek mercenaries which he began to enlist. The revolutions which had passed over Greek cities in recent years, both in Asia and Europe, threw into the military market large numbers of strong men eager for employment and pay. They were recruited for the prince's service by Clearchus, a Spartan, who had held the post of harmost, but had been repudiated and expelled by the ephors when he attempted to make himself tyrant of Byzantium, like a new Pausanias. Moreover, the Lacedaemonian government, which owed much to Cyrus, was induced to support him secretly, and sent him —avowedly for another purpose—seven hundred hoplites. The army which Cyrus mustered when he set forth on his march to Susa amounted to 100,000 oriental troops, and about 13,000 Greeks, of which 10,600 were hoplites.

The purpose of the march was at first carefully concealed from the troops, nor was the secret communicated to any of the officers except Clearchus. The hill tribes of Pisidia were often troublesome to Persian satraps, and their reduction furnished a convenient pretext. Among those who were induced, by the prospect of high pay under the generous Persian prince, to join this Pisidian campaign was Xenophon, an Athenian knight, who was one of the pupils and companions of the philosopher Socrates. His famous history of the *Anabasis* or Up-going of the Greeks with Cyrus, and their subsequent retreat, has rendered the expedition a household word.

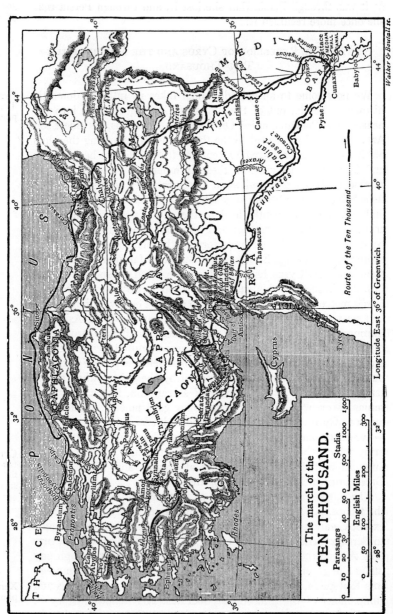

The march of the
TEN THOUSAND.

Route of the Ten Thousand..........

Longitude East 36° of Greenwich

Walker & Boutall sc.

FIG. 75.

The charm of the *Anabasis* depends on the simple directness and fulness with which the story is told, and the great interest of the story consists in its breaking new ground. For the first time we are privileged to follow step by step a journey through the inner parts of Asia Minor, into the heart of the Persian empire beyond the Euphrates and the Tigris. There is a charm of actuality in the early chapters, with their recurring phrases, like brief entries in a diary, —the days' marches from one city to another, the number of parasangs, and the lengths of the halts, all duly set out. "Hence Cyrus marches two stages, ten parasangs, to Peltae, an inhabited city; and here he remained three days."

Setting forth from Sardis, Cyrus took the south-easterly road, which led across the upper Maeander to the Phrygian Colossae, where he was joined by the troops of one of his Greek captains, the Thessalian Menon; and thence onward to Celaenae, where he awaited the arrival of Clearchus. So far, the march had been straight to the ostensible destination, the country of Pisidia; but now Cyrus turned in the opposite direction, and, descending the Maeander, marched northward to Peltae and Ceramon Agora or Potters' Mart. Then eastward, to the city called Cayster-Plain, close to the fort of Ipsus. Here the Greeks demanded their arrears of pay, and Cyrus had no money to satisfy them. But he was relieved from the difficulty, which might well have proved fatal to his enterprise, by the Cilician queen Epyaxa, wife of Syennesis, who arrived well laden with money. Her coming must have been connected with private negotiations between Cyrus and the Cilician governor. As the route of Cyrus lay through Cilicia, a country barred on all sides by difficult passes, it was of the greatest moment for Cyrus to come to an understanding with the ruler; and on the other hand it was the policy of Syennesis so to order his ways that whether Cyrus succeeded or failed he might in either event be safe. As the plan of Cyrus was still a secret, it was a prudent policy to entrust the delicate negotiations to no one less safe than the queen. Having pacified the demands of his Greek mercenaries, Cyrus proceeded (by Thymbrion and Tyriaeon) to Iconium; and thence by the road, which describes a great southern curve through Lycaonia, to Tyana. The Greeks were allowed to plunder Lycaonia, a rough country with rough people, as they passed through it. The arrangement with Syennesis seems to have been that he should make a display of resisting Cyrus, and Cyrus make a display of circumventing him. To carry out this arrangement, Menon's division, accompanied by the queen Epyaxa, diverged from the route followed by the rest of the army, and

Marginal notes:

March through Asia Minor.

Ceramon Agora (now Iskam Keui).

crossed the Taurus into Cilicia by a shorter route. Perhaps they struck off at Barata and passed by Laranda, on a road that led to Soli. Thus Syennesis, who, as a loyal servant of the Great King, hastened to occupy the Cilician gates, the pass for which the main army of Cyrus was making, found himself taken in the rear by Menon. It was therefore useless to remain in the pass, and he retreated to a mountain stronghold: what more could a loyal servant of the Great King be expected to do? The army of Cyrus then coming up from Tyana, by Podandus, found the impregnable pass open, and descended safely to Tarsus, where it met Menon. The city and palace of the prince of Cilicia were pillaged; this perhaps was part of the pretence. It was at all events safe now for Syennesis to enter into a contract with Cyrus (a compulsory contract, the Great King would understand) to supply some money and men.

It must have been dawning on the Greek troops for some time past, and at Tarsus they no longer felt any doubt, that they had been deceived as to their ultimate destination. They had long ago passed Pisidia, the ostensible object of their march, and the true object was now clear to them. They flatly refused to advance further. It was a small thing to be asked to take the field against the forces of the Great King; but it was no such light matter to be asked to undertake a march of three months into the centre of Asia. To be at a distance of three months from the sea-coast was a terrible idea for a Greek. Clearchus, a strict disciplinarian—a man of grim feature and harsh voice, unpopular with his men—thought to repress the mutiny by severity; but the mutiny was too general to be quelled by coercion. Then he resorted to a stratagem, which he carried out with admirable adroitness. Calling his soldiers together, he stood for some time weeping before he spoke. He then set forth the cruel dilemma in which their conduct had placed him: he must either break his plighted faith with Cyrus or desert them; but he did not hesitate to choose; whatever happened, he would stand by them, who were "his country, his friends, and his allies." This speech created a favourable impression, which was confirmed when Cyrus sent to demand an interview with Clearchus and Clearchus publicly refused to go. But the delight of the troops was changed into perplexity when Clearchus asked them what they proposed to do: they were no longer the soldiers of Cyrus, and could not look to him for pay, provisions, or help. He (Clearchus) would stand by them, but declined to command them or advise them. The soldiers—some of them in the secret confidence of their captain—discussed the difficulty, and it was decided to send a deputation to Cyrus, to ask him to declare definitely his real intentions. Cyrus told the deputation that his purpose was to march against his enemy Abrocomas—Persian general in Syria—who was now on the Euphrates, and offered higher pay to the Greeks, a daric and a half instead of a daric a month. The soldiers, finding themselves in an awkward pass, agreed to continue the march,—reluctant, but hardly seeing any other way out of the difficulty; though many of them must have shrewdly suspected that they would deal with Abrocomas on the Euphrates even as they had dealt with the hillmen of Pisidia.

(Daric a month = c. 9d. a day.)

The march was now eastward by Adana and Mopsuestia, across the rivers Sarus and Pyramus, and then along the coast to Issus, where Cyrus found his fleet. It brought him 700 hoplites sent by the Lacedaemonians. Here too he was reinforced by 400 Greek mercenaries who had deserted from the service of the Persian general Abrocomas, the enemy of Cyrus, who had fled to the Euphrates, instead of holding the difficult and fortified passes from Cilicia into Syria, as a loyal general of the King should have done. So Cyrus now, with his Greek troops increased to the total number of 14,000, passed with as much ease through the Syrian gates, owing to the cowardly flight of Abrocomas, as he had before passed through the Cilician gates, owing to the prudent collusion of Syennesis. The Syrian gates are a narrow pass between the end of Mount Amanus and the sea, part of the coast road from Issus to Myriandrus. At Myriandrus the Greeks bade good-bye to the sea, little knowing how many days would pass, how many terrible things befall them, before they hailed it again. They crossed Mount Amanus by the pass of Beilan, which Abrocomas ought to have guarded, and in a twelve days' march, passing by the park and palace of Belesys, satrap of Syria, they reached Thapsacus and beheld the famous Euphrates. Here a new explanation was necessary as to the object of the march, and Cyrus had at last to own that Babylon was the goal,—that the foe against whom he led the army was the Great King himself. The Greek troops murmured loudly and refused to cross the river; but their murmurings here were not like their murmurs at Tarsus, for they had guessed the truth long since; and their complaints were only designed to extort promises from Cyrus. The prince agreed to give each man a present of five minae at the end of the expedition—more than a year's pay at the high rate of a daric and a half. But while the rest of the Greeks were making their bargain, Menon stole a march on them, inducing his own troops to cross the river first—a good example, for which Cyrus would owe him and his troops particular thanks.

Issus: new reinforcements.

Arrival at Thapsacus.

About £20.

About August 1.

Abrocomas had burned the ships, but the Euphrates was—a very unusual circumstance at that season—shallow enough to be forded; a fact of which Abrocomas was conceivably aware. The army accordingly crossed on foot and continued the march along the left bank; an agreeable march until they reached the river Chaboras, beyond which the desert of "Arabia" began: a plain, Xenophon describes it, smooth as a sea, treeless; only wormwood and scented shrubs for vegetation, but alive with all kinds of beasts strange to Greek eyes, wild asses and ostriches, antelopes and bustards. The tramp through the desert lasted thirteen days, and then they reached Pylae, at the edge of the land of Babylonia, fertile then with its artificial irrigation, now mostly a barren wilderness. Soon after they passed Pylae, they became aware that a large host had been moving in front, ravaging the country before them.

Preparations of Artaxerxes.

Artaxerxes on his part had made somewhat tardy preparations to receive the invaders. It seems indeed to have been hardly conceived at the Persian court that the army of Cyrus would ever succeed in reaching Babylonia. The city of Babylon was protected by a double defence against an enemy approaching from the north,—by a line of wall and a line of water, both connecting the Euphrates with the Tigris. The enemy would first have to pass the Wall of Media, 100 feet high and 20 feet broad, built of bricks with bitumen cement; and they would then have to cross the Royal Canal, before they could reach the gates of Babylon. To these two lines of defence a third was now added, in the form of a trench about forty miles long, joining at one end the Wall of Media and at the other the Euphrates, where a space of not more than seven yards was left between the trench and the river. To defend a country so abundantly guarded by artificial fortifications, the king was able to muster immediately an army of about 400,000; but this did not seem enough when the danger became imminent, and orders were sent to Media that the troops of that province should come to the aid of Babylonia. There was some delay in the arrival of these forces, and Artaxerxes probably did not wish to risk an action until their arrival had made his immense superiority in numbers overwhelming. This may explain the extraordinary circumstance that when the army of Cyrus came to the foss which had been dug expressly to keep them out, they found it undefended, and walked at their ease over the narrow passage between the trench and the river.

Battle of Cunaxa (summer, 401).

But now it was hardly possible for Artaxerxes to let his foes advance further, though there was still no sign of the troops from the east. Two days after passing the trench, the army of Cyrus reached the village of Cunaxa, and suddenly learned that the king's host was approaching. The oriental troops under Ariaeus formed the left wing of Cyrus, who himself occupied the centre with a squadron of cavalry; the Greeks were on the right, resting on the river Euphrates. The Persian left wing, commanded by Tissaphernes, consisted of cavalry, bowmen, and Egyptian footmen, with a row of scythe-armed chariots in front. The king was in the centre with a strong bodyguard of horse. Cyrus knew the oriental character, and he knew that if the king fell or fled, the battle would be decided and his own cause won. He accordingly formed a plan of battle which would almost certainly have been successful, if it had been adopted. He proposed that the Greeks should shift their position further to the left,—to a considerable distance from the river,—so that they might immediately attack the enemy's centre where the king was stationed. But Clearchus, to whom Cyrus signified his wishes, made decided objections to this bold and wise plan. Unable to rise, like Cyrus, to the full bearings of the situation, he ruined the cause of his master by pedantically or timorously adhering to the precepts of Greek drill-sergeants, that it is fatal for the right wing to allow itself to be outflanked. And besides the consideration which Cyrus had in view, the advantage of bringing about with all speed the flight of Artaxerxes, there was another consideration which would not have occurred to Cyrus, but which ought to have occurred to Clearchus. The safety of Cyrus himself was a matter of the first importance to the Greeks,—how important we shall see in the sequel. It was useless for the Greeks to cut down every single man in the Persian left, if while they were sweeping all before them the prince for whom they fought were slain. Syrus did not press the matter, and left it to Clearchus to make his own dispositions. The onset of the Greeks struck their enemies with panic before a blow was struck. On the other side, the Persian right, which far outflanked the left wing of Cyrus, was wheeled round, so as to take the troops of Ariaeus in the rear. Then Cyrus, who was already receiving congratulations as if he were king on account of the success of the Greeks, dashed forward with his 600 horse against the 6000 who surrounded Artaxerxes. The impetuous charge broke up the guard, and, if the prince had kept command over his passions, he would have been the Great King within an hour. But unluckily he caught sight of his brother, whom he hated with his whole soul, amid the flying bodyguard. The bitter passion of hatred overmastered him, and he galloped forward, with a few followers, to slay Artaxerxes with his own hand. He had the satisfaction of wounding him slightly with a javelin; but, in the mellay

Greeks victorious;

Cyrus slain.

which ensued, he was himself wounded in the eye by a Carian soldier, and falling from his horse, was presently slain. The news of his death was the signal for the flight of his Asiatic troops.

The vivid narrative of Xenophon, who took part in the battle, preserves the memory of these remarkable events. At the time he saw little of the battle, and he could have known little of the arrangements and movements of the Persians. But before he wrote his own book, he had the advantage of reading a book written by another Greek, who had also witnessed those remarkable events, but from the other side. This was Ctesias, the court physician, who was present at the battle and cured Artaxerxes of the breast-wound which Cyrus had dealt him. The book of Ctesias is lost, but some bits of his story have drifted down to us in the works of later writers who had read it, and afford us a glimpse or two into the Great King's camp and court about this eventful time.

The work of Ctesias.

Ability of Cyrus; possible consequences of his success.

For the Greek band, which now found itself in the heart of Persia, girt about by enemies on every side, the death of Cyrus was an immediate and crushing calamity. But for Greece it was probably a stroke of good fortune,—though Sparta herself had blessed the enterprise. Cyrus was a prince whose ability was well-nigh equal to his ambition. He had proved his capacity by his early successes as satrap; by the organisation of his expedition, which demanded an exceptional union of policy and vigour, in meeting difficulties and surmounting dangers; by his recognition of the value of the Greek soldier. Under such a sovereign, the Persian realm would have thriven and waxed great, and become once more a menace to the freedom of the European Greeks. Who can tell what dreams that ambitious brain might have cherished, dreams of universal conquest to be achieved at the head of an invincible army of Grecian foot-lancers? And in days when mercenary service was coming into fashion, the service of Cyrus would have been popular. Whatever oriental craft and cruelty lurked beneath, he had not only a frank and attractive manner, but a generous nature, which completely won such an honest Greek as Xenophon, the soldier and historian. He knew how to appreciate the Greeks, as none of his country ever knew before; he recognised their superiority to the Asiatics in the military qualities of steadfastness and discipline; and this undisguised appreciation was a flattery which they were unable to resist. If Cyrus had come to the throne, his energy and policy would certainly have been felt in the Aegean world; the Greeks would not have been left for the next two generations to shape their own destinies, as they did, little affected by the languid interventions of Artaxerxes. Perhaps the stubborn stupidity of Clearchus on the field of Cunaxa, with his hard-and-fast precepts of Greek drill-sergeants, saved Hellas from becoming a Persian satrapy.

But such speculations would have brought little comfort, could they have occurred, to the 10,000 Greeks who, flushed with the excitement of pursuit, returned to hear that the rest of their army had been defeated, to find their camp pillaged, and then to learn on the following morning that Cyrus was dead. The habit of self-imposed discipline which Cyrus knew so well how to value stood the Greeks in good stead at this grave crisis; and their easy victory had given them confidence. They refused to surrender, at the summons of Artaxerxes. For him their presence was extremely awkward, like a hostile city in the midst of his land; and his first object was at all hazards to get them out of Babylonia. He therefore parleyed with them, and supplied them with provisions. The only desire of the Greeks was to make all the haste they could homeward. By the road they had come it was nearly 1500 miles to Sardis; but that road was impracticable; for they could not traverse the desert again unprovisioned. Without guides, without any geographical knowledge—not knowing so much as the course of the Tigris— they had no alternative but to embrace the proposal of Tissaphernes, who undertook to guide them home by another road, on which they would be able to obtain provisions. Following him—but well in the rear of his troops—the Greeks passed the Wall of Media, and crossed two navigable canals, before they reached the Tigris, which they passed by its only bridge, close to Sittace. Their course then lay northward, up the left bank of the Tigris. They passed from Babylonia into Media, and, crossing the lesser Zab, reached the banks of the greater Zab without any incident of consequence. But here the distrust and suspicion which smouldered between the Greek and the Persian camps almost broke into a flame of hostility, and Clearchus was driven into seeking an explanation with Tissaphernes. The frankness of the satrap disarmed the suspicions of Clearchus; Tissaphernes admitted that some persons had attempted to poison his mind against the Greeks, but promised to reveal the names of the calumniators, if the Greek generals and captains came to his tent the next day. Clearchus readily consented, and induced his four fellow-generals—Agias, Menon, Proxenus, and Socrates— to go to Tissaphernes, though such blind confidence was ill justified by the character of the crafty satrap. It was a fatal blunder—the second great blunder Clearchus had made—to place all the Greek commanders helplessly in the power of the Persian. Clearchus had been throughout an enemy of the Thessalian Menon; and it may be

Greeks refuse to surrender.

Treacherous seizure of Clearchus and the generals.

that he suspected Menon of treason, and that his desire to convict his rival in the tent of Tissaphernes blinded his better judgment. The five generals went, with twenty captains and some soldiers; the captains and soldiers were cut down, and the generals were fettered and sent to the Persian court, where they were all put to death.

Tissaphernes had no intention of attacking the Greek army. He had led them to a place from which it would be extremely difficult, if not impossible, to return to Greece, and he imagined that when they found themselves without any responsible commanders they would immediately surrender. But if in the first moments of dismay the prospect seemed hopeless, the Greeks speedily rallied their courage, chose new generals, and resumed their northward march. It was the Athenian Xenophon, a man of ready speech and great presence of mind, who did most to infuse new spirit into the army and guide it amidst the perils and difficulties which now beset it. Though he had no rank, being merely a volunteer, he was elected a general, and his power of persuasion, united with practical sense, won for him a remarkable ascendency over the men. He tells us how, on the first dreary night after the betrayal of the generals, he dreamed that he saw a thunderbolt striking his father's house and flames wrapping the walls about. This dream gave him his inspiration. He interpreted it of the plight in which he and his fellows were; the house was in extreme danger, but the light was a sign of hope. And then the thought was borne in on him that it was foolish to wait for others to take the lead, that it would be well to make a start himself.

It was bold indeed to undertake a march of uncertain length—terribly long—without guides and with inexperienced officers, over unknown rivers and uncouth mountains, through the lands of barbarous folks. The alternative would have been to found a Greek city in the centre of Media; but this had no attraction: the hearts of all were set upon returning to the Greek world. It would be long to tell the full diary of the adventures of their retreat; it is a chronicle of courage, discipline, and reasonableness in the face of perils which nothing but the exercise of those qualities in an unusual measure would have been able to surmount. Their march to the Carduchian mountains, which form the northern boundary of Media, was harassed by the army of Tissaphernes, who however never ventured on a pitched battle. When they entered Carduchia, the Greeks passed out of the Persian empire; for the men of these mountains were independent, wedged in between the satrapies of Media and Armenia. The passage through this wild country was the most dangerous and destructive part of the whole retreat. The

Kurdi-
stan.

savage hillsmen were implacably hostile, and it was easy for them to defend the narrow precipitous passes against an army laden with baggage, and fearing, at every turn of the winding roads, to be crushed by rocky masses which the enemy rolled down from the heights above. After much suffering and loss of life, they reached the stream of the Centrites, a tributary of the Tigris, which divides Carduchia from Armenia. The news of their coming had gone before; and they found the opposite bank lined with the forces of Tiribazus, the Armenian satrap. The Carduchian hillsmen were hanging on their rear, and it needed a clever stratagem to cross the river safely. It was now the month of December, and the march lay through the snows of wintry Armenia. They had sore struggles with cold and hunger; but they went unmolested, for they had made a compact with Tiribazus, undertaking to abstain from pillage. The direction of the march lay north-westward; they crossed the two branches of the Euphrates, and their route perhaps partly corresponded to that which a traveller follows at the present day from Tavriz to Erzerum. When they had made their way through the territories of the martial Chalybes and other hostile peoples, they reached a city—a sign that at last they were once more on the fringe of civilisation. It was the city of Gymnias, a thriving place which perhaps owed its existence to neighbouring silver mines. Here they had a friendly welcome, and learned with delight that they were not many days' journey south of Trapezus. A guide undertook that they should have sight of the sea after a five days' march. "And on the fifth day they came to Mount Theches, and when the van reached the summit a great cry arose. When Xenophon and the rear heard it, they thought that an enemy was attacking in front; but when the cry increased as fresh men continually came up to the summit, Xenophon thought it must be something more serious, and galloped forward to the front with his cavalry. When he drew near, he heard what the cry was—*The Sea, the Sea!*" The sight of the sea, to which they had said farewell at Myriandrus, and which they had so often despaired of ever again beholding, was an assurance of safety at last attained. The night watches in the plains of Babylonia or by the rivers of Media, the wild faces in the Carduchian mountains, the bleak highlands of Armenia, might now fade into the semblances of an evil dream.

A few more days brought the army to Trapezus—to Greek soil and to the very shore of the sea. Here they rested for a month, supporting themselves by plundering the Colchian natives, who dwelled in the hills round about, while the Greeks of Trapezus supplied a market. Here they celebrated games and offered their

Buhtan-Tchai.

They cross the Kara Su and Murad Su.

Gumish.

Reach the Euxine Sea.

At Trapezus (first months of 400 B.C.).

sacrifices of thanksgiving to Zeus Soter,—in fulfillment of a vow they had made on that terrible night on the Zab after the loss of their generals.

Ten thousand Greek soldiers dropt down from the mountains, like a sudden thunderbolt from heaven, were a surprise which must have caused strange perplexity to the Greeks of the coast,— to Trapezus and her sister Cerasus, and to their common mother Sinope. It was a somewhat alarming problem: more than a myriad soldiers, mostly hoplites, steeled by an ordeal of experience such as few men had ever passed, but not quite certain as to what their next step should be, suddenly knocking at one's gates. And they were not an ordinary army, but rather a democracy of ten thousand citizens equipped as soldiers, serving no king, responsible to no state, a law unto themselves, electing their officers and deciding all matters of importance in a sovereign popular assembly,—as it were, a great moving city, moving along the shores of the Euxine; what might it, what might it not, do? For one thing, it might easily plant itself on some likely site within the range of Sinope's influence, and conceivably out-top Sinope herself.

The Ten Thousand themselves thought only of home—the Aegean and the Greek world. Could they have procured ships at once, they would not have tarried to perplex Sinope and her daughter cities. To Xenophon, who foresaw more or less dimly the difficulties which would beset the army on its return to Greece, the idea of seizing some native town like Phasis and founding a colony, in which he might amass riches and enjoy power, was not unwelcome; but when it was known that he contemplated such a plan, though he never proposed it, he well-nigh forfeited his influence with the army. In truth, a colony at Phasis, in the land of the Golden Fleece, founded by the practical Xenophon, might have been the best solution of the fate of the Ten Thousand. The difficulties which they had now to face were of a different kind from those which they had so successfully surmounted, demanding not so much endurance and bravery as tact and discretion. Now that they were no longer in daily danger of sheer destruction, the motive for cohesion had lost much of its strength. If we remember that the army was composed of men of different Greek nationalities, brought together by chance, and that it was now united by no bond of common allegiance but was purely a voluntary association, the wonder is that it was not completely disorganised and scattered long before it reached Byzantium. It is true that the discipline sensibly and inevitably declined; and it is true that the host dissolved itself at Heraclea into three separate bands, though only to be presently reunited. But it is a remarkable spectacle, this large society of soldiers managing their own affairs, deciding what they would do, determining where they would go, seldom failing to listen to the voice of reason in their Assemblies, whether it was the voice of Xenophon or of another.

The last stages of the retreat, from Trapezus to Chalcedon, were accomplished partly by sea, partly by land, and were marked by delays, disappointments, and disorders. It might be expected that on reaching Chalcedon the army would have dispersed, each man hastening to return to his own city. But they were satisfied to be well within the Greek world once more, and they wanted to replenish their empty purses before they went home. So they still held together, ready to place their arms at the disposal of any power who would pay them. To Pharnabazus, the satrap of the Hellespontine province of Persia, the arrival of men who had defied the power of the Great King was a source of alarm. He bribed the Lacedaemonian admiral Anaxibius, who was stationed at the Bosphorus, to induce the Ten Thousand to cross over into Europe. Anaxibius compassed this by promises of high pay; but the troops, who were admitted into Byzantium, would have pillaged the city when they discovered that they had been deluded, if Xenophon's presence of mind and persuasive speech had not once more saved them from their first impulse. After this they took service under a Thracian prince, Seuthes was his name, who employed them to reduce some rebellious tribes. Seuthes was more perfidious than Anaxibius, for he cheated them of the pay which they had actually earned. But better times were coming. War broke out—as we shall presently see—between Lacedaemon and Persia, and the Lacedaemonians wanted fighting men. The impoverished army of Cyrus, now reduced to the number of 6000, crossed back into Asia, and received an advance of pay. Here our interest in them ends, if it did not already end when they reached Trapezus,—our interest in all of them, at least, except Xenophon. Once and again Xenophon had intended to leave the army since its return to civilisation, and he had steadfastly refused all proposals to elect him commander; but his strong ascendency among the soldiers and his consequent power to help them had rendered it impossible for him on each occasion to abandon them in their difficulties. Now he was at last released, and returned to Athens with a considerable sum of money. It is probable that his native city, where his master Socrates had recently suffered death, proved uncongenial to him; for he soon went back to Asia to fight with his old comrades against the Persians. When Athens presently became an ally of Persia against

It reaches Chalcedon.

At Byzantium

Employed by Sparta, 399 B.C.

Career of Xenophon.

Xenophon
lives at
Scillus in
Triphylia
till 370
B.C.

Sparta, Xenophon was banished, and more than twenty years of his life were spent at Scillus, a Triphylian village, where the Spartans gave him a home. Afterwards the sentence of exile was revoked, and his last years were passed at Athens.

On a country estate near that Triphylian village, not far from Olympia, Xenophon settled down into a quiet life, with abundant leisure for literature; and composed, among other things of less account, the narrative of that memorable adventure in which Xenophon the Athenian had played such a leading part. Of the environment of his country life in quiet Triphylia he has given a glimpse, showing us how he imprinted his own personality on the place. He had deposited in the great temple of Artemis at Ephesus a portion of a ransom of some captives taken during the retreat, to be reserved for the service of the goddess. This deposit was restored to him at Scillus, and with the money Xenophon bought a suitable place for a sanctuary of Ephesian Artemis. "A river Selinus flows through the place, just as at Ephesus a river Selinus flows past the temple; and in both streams there are fishes and shellfishes, but in the place at Scillus there is also all manner of game. And Xenophon made an altar and a temple, with the sacred money, and henceforward he used every year to offer to the goddess a tithe of the fruits of his estate, and all the citizens and neighbours, men and women, took part in the feast. They camped in tents, and the goddess furnished them with meal, bread, wine, and sweetmeats, and with a share of the hallowed dole of the sacrifice, and with a share of the game. For Xenophon's lads and the lads of the neighbours used to hunt quarry for the feast, and men who liked would join in the chase. There was game both in the consecrated estate and in Mount Pholoe, wild swine, and gazelles, and stags. That estate has meadowland and wooded hills—good pasture for swine and goats, for cattle and horses; and the beasts of those who fare from Sparta to the Olympian festival—for the road wends through the place—have their fill of feasting. The temple, which is girt by a plantation of fruit trees, is a small model of the great temple of Ephesus; and the cypress-wood image is made in the fashion of the Ephesian image of gold." Here Xenophon could lead a happy, uneventful life, devoted to sport and literature and the service of the gods.

Signifi-
cance
of the
expedition
of Cyrus.

At a casual glance the expedition of Cyrus may appear to belong not to Greek but to Persian history; and the retreat of the Ten Thousand may be deemed matter for a book of adventures, and a digression which needs some excuse in a history of Greece. But the story of the upgoing and the home-coming of Xenophon and his fellows is in truth no digression. It has been already pointed out how vitally the interests of Hellas, according to human calculation, were involved in the issue of Cunaxa; and how, if the arbitrament of fortune on that battlefield had been other, the future of Greece might have been other too. But the whole episode—the upgoing, the battle, and the home-coming—has an importance, by no means problematical, which secures it a certain and conspicuous place in the procession of Grecian history. It is an epilogue to the invasion of Xerxes and a prologue to the conquest of Alexander. The Great King had carried his arms into Greece, and Greece had driven him back; that was a leading epoch in the combat between Asia and Europe. The next epoch will be the retribution. The Greeks will carry their arms into Persia, and Persia will fail to repel them. The success of Alexander will be the answer to the defeat of Xerxes. For this answer the world has to wait for five generations; but in the meanwhile the expedition of the soldiers of Cyrus is a prediction, vouchsafed as it were by history, what the answer is to be. Xenophon's *Anabasis* is the continuation of Herodotus; Xenophon and his band are the reconnoitrers who forerun Alexander. And this significance of the adventure, as a victory of Greece over Persia, was immediately understood. A small company of soldiers had marched unopposed to the centre of the Persian empire, where no Greek army had ever won its way before; they had defeated almost without a blow the overwhelming forces of the king within a few miles of his capital; and they had returned safely, having escaped from the hostile multitudes, which did not once dare to withstand their spears in open warfare. Such a display of Persian impotence surprised the world; and Greece might well despise the power whose resources a band of strangers had so successfully defied. No Hellenic city indeed had won a triumph over the barbarian; but all Hellenic cities alike had reason to be stirred by pride at a brilliant demonstration of the superior excellence of the Greek to the Asiatic in courage, discipline, and capacity. The lesson had, as we shall see, its immediate consequences. Only a year or two passed, and it inspired a Spartan king—a man, indeed, of poor ability and slight performance—to attempt to achieve the task which fate reserved for Alexander. But the moral effect of the Anabasis was lasting, and of greater import than the futile warfare of Agesilaus. Considering these bearings, we shall have not said too much if we say that the episode of the Ten Thousand, though a private enterprise so far as Hellas was concerned, and though enacted beyond the limits of the Hellenic world, yet occupies a more eminent place on the highway of Grecian history than the contemporary transactions of Athens and Sparta and the other states of Greece.

Sect. 3. War of Sparta with Persia

The enterprise of Cyrus had immediately affected the position and prospects of the Greek cities of Ionia. In accordance with their contract the Spartans had handed over the Asiatic cities to Persia, retaining only Abydus, on account of its strategic importance. Cyrus, however, bidding for Greek support, had instigated the Ionian cities to revolt from their satrap, Tissaphernes, and to place themselves under his protection. Tissaphernes was in time to save Miletus; but all the other cities received Greek garrisons, and thus, when Cyrus disappeared into the interior of Asia, they had practically passed out of Persian control. After the defeat of Cyrus at Cunaxa, Tissaphernes returned to the Aegean coast as governor of all the districts which had been under Cyrus, and with the general title of commander of Further Asia, implying supremacy over the adjacent satrapies. His first concern was to recover the Greek cities of the coast, and he attacked Cyme. The Asiatic Greeks were greatly alarmed, and they sent to Sparta an appeal for her protection.

The relations of Sparta to Persia were no longer the same; since the help given to Cyrus was an act of war against the king. The successful march of the Ten Thousand inspired Greece with a feeling of contempt for the strength of the Persian empire. The opportunity of plundering the wealthy satrapies of Pharnabazus and Tissaphernes was a bait for Spartan cupidity; the prospect of gaining signal successes against Persia appealed to Spartan ambition. These considerations induced Sparta to send an army to Asia, and this army was increased by the remains of the famous Ten Thousand, who (as already stated) crossed over from Thrace and entered the service of Sparta. Much might have been accomplished with a competent commander, but the general Thibron was unable to maintain discipline among his men, and the few successes achieved fell far short of Sparta's reasonable hopes. Thibron was superseded by Dercyllidas, a man who had the repute of being unusually wily. Taking advantage of a misunderstanding between the two satraps, Dercyllidas made a truce with Tissaphernes and marched with all his forces into the province of Pharnabazus, against whom he had a personal grudge. A recent occurrence rendered it possible for him to get into his hands the Troad—or Aeolis, as it was called—with speed and ease. The government of this region had been granted by Pharnabazus to Zenis, a native of Dardanus. When he died, leaving a widow, a son, and daughter, Pharnabazus was about to choose another subsatrap; but the widow, whose name was Mania, present-

Tissaphernes, as commander of Asia, plans to recover the Greek cities,

which appeal to Sparta.

Sparta sends an army, 400 B.C.,

under Thibron (400-399 B.C.), who is succeeded by Dercyllidas (399 B.C.)

The Troad.

Mania,

ed a petition that she should be permitted to fill the post which her husband had held. "My husband," she argued, "paid his tribute punctually, and you thanked him for it. If I do as well, why should you appoint another? If I am found unsatisfactory, you can remove me at any moment." She fortified her arguments by large presents of money to the satrap, his officers, and concubines; and won her request. She gave Pharnabazus full satisfaction by her regular payments of tribute, and under her vigorous administration the Aeolid became a rich and well-defended land. A body of Greek mercenaries was maintained in her service, and immense treasures were stored in the strong mountain fortresses of Scepsis, Gergis, and Cebren. She even reduced some coast towns in the south of the Troad, and took part herself, like the Carian Artemisia, in military expeditions. But she had for son-in-law an ungrateful traitor, Meidias of Scepsis, whom she treated with trust and affection. In order to possess himself of her power, he strangled her, then killed her son, and laid hold of the three fortresses which controlled the district, along with all the treasure. But Pharnabazus refused to recognise the murderer of Mania, and sent back the gifts of Meidias with the message: "Keep them till I come to seize both them and you. Life would not be worth living if I avenged not the death of Mania." murdered by her son-in-law.

As Meidias was expecting with alarm the vengeance of Pharnabazus, the Spartan army appeared on the scene. Dercyllidas became master of the Aeolid without any opposition, since the garrisons of the cities did not acknowledge Meidias,—excepting only the forts of Scepsis, Gergis, and Cebren. The garrison of Cebren soon surrendered; at Scepsis, Meidias came forth to a conference, and Dercyllidas, without waiting to confer, marched up to the gates of the town, so that Meidias, in the power of the enemy, could do nothing but order them to be opened; and his unwilling orders likewise threw open the gates of Gergis. His own private property was restored to Meidias, but all the treasures of Mania were appropriated by the Spartan general; for the property of Mania belonged to her master Pharnabazus, and was therefore the legitimate booty of the satrap's enemy. This booty supplied Dercyllidas with pay for his eight thousand soldiers for nearly a year; and it was noticed that the conduct of the heroes of the Anabasis showed a signal improvement from this time forward. The Aeolid now served the Spartans against the satrapy of Pharnabazus somewhat as Decelea had served them in Attica; it was a fortified district in the enemy's country. Sparta, hoping that these successes would induce Persia to make terms and acquiesce in the freedom of the Greek cities, concluded truces with Tissaphernes and Pharnabazus, and sent up am- Dercyllidas gains the Troad; (398 B.C.)

besieges
and
captures
Atarneus
(398-7
B.C.);
goes to
Caria
(397 B.C.).

bassadors to Susa to treat with the Great King. Dercyllidas mean
while crossed into Europe and occupied himself with restoring the
cross-wall which defended Sestos and the other cities of the Chersonese against the incursions of the Thracians, the inhabitants
gladly furnishing pay and food to the army. On returning to Asia,
the Spartan commander captured, after a long siege, the strong
town of Atarneus. Then by special orders from home he proceeded
to Caria.

The Spartan overtures were heard unfavourably at Susa, for the
king had been persuaded by his able satrap Pharnabazus to prosecute the war by sea. The Spartans could not cope in mere numbers
with the fleet which Phoenicia and Cyprus could furnish him; but
everything would depend on the commander. Here fortune played
into his hands. There was an enemy of Sparta, an experienced naval
officer, who was ready to compass heaven and earth to work the

downfall of her supremacy. The Athenian admiral Conon, whom
we last saw escaping from the surprise of Aegospotami, was burning
to avenge the disgrace of that fatal day. He had found hospitality
and protection at the court of Evagoras, king of the Cyprian
Salamis; and through him had entered into communication with
Ctesias, the Greek physician, whom we already met at Cunaxa.
Ctesias had the ear of the queen-mother Parysatis, and through her

influence and the advice of Pharnabazus Conon was appointed to
command a fleet of 300 ships which was prepared in Phoenicia and
Cilicia. Under his command, such a numerous navy was extremely
formidable, but the Lacedaemonian government does not seem to
have realised the danger, owing perhaps to their experience of the
ineffectiveness of previous Persian armaments; and they committed
the mistake of throwing all their vigour into the land warfare, and
neglecting their sea-power, which was absolutely vital for the maintenance of their supremacy. But when Conon, not waiting for the
complete equipment of the fleet, sailed to Caunus in Caria with
forty ships, the Spartans were obliged to move. They sent a fleet of
120 ships under Pharax to blockade Caunus and Conon's galleys in
the harbour, and ordered Dercyllidas to Caria. The joint forces of
Tissaphernes and Pharnabazus first raised the siege of Caunus and
then confronted Dercyllidas in the valley of the Maeander. A panic
which seized some of the troops of the Spartan general might have
been fatal, but the reputation of the Ten Thousand, whose valour
Tissaphernes had experienced, rendered that satrap unwilling to

risk a battle, and a conference issued in an armistice. But Sparta
had now decided to conduct the war against Persia with greater

vigour and on a larger scale; and Dercyllidas had to make way for no less a successor than one of the Spartan kings.

Agesilaus, who now comes upon the scene, had been recently raised to the regal dignity in unusual circumstances. When Lysander retired from public affairs to visit the temple of Zeus Ammon, he had neither discarded ambition nor lost his influence. He conceived the plan of making a change in the Spartan constitution which can hardly be described as less than revolutionary. The idea was that the kingship should be no longer confined to the Eurysthenid and Proclid families in which it was hereditary by law, but that the kings should be elected from all Heraclids. The Spartan king was not a king in our sense of the word; he was not a sovereign, he was rather a grand officer of state; but the scheme to make the office elective, instead of hereditary, was nevertheless momentous. It meant immediately that Lysander should hold the military functions which belonged to the kings, the command of the army abroad, *for life;* he could no longer be deposed or recalled at the end of a term of office. And in the hands of a man like Lysander this permanent office might become something very different from what it was in the hands of the ordinary Proclid or Eurysthenid; the proportion between the power of king and ephor might be considerably shifted. Lysander's project might well have proved the first step to a sort of *principate;* which might have partially adapted Spartan institutions to the requirements of an imperial state. Lysander did not conceive the possibility of carrying this bold innovation by a *coup d'état;* his plan was to bring religious influence to bear on the authorities; and he secretly employed his absence from Sparta in attempting to enlist the most important oracles in favour of his design. But the oracles received his proposal coldly; it sounded far too audacious. He succeeded, however, in winning over some of the Delphic priests, who aided him to invent oracles for his purpose: a rumour was spread that certain sacred and ancient records were preserved at Delphi, never to be revealed until a son of Apollo appeared to claim them; and at the same time people began to hear of the existence of a youth named Silenus, whose mother vouched that Apollo was his sire. But the ingenious plot broke down at the last moment; one of the confederates did not play his part; and the oracles bearing on the Spartan kingship were never revealed. Lysander then abandoned his revolutionary idea, and took advantage of the death of king Agis to secure the sceptre for a man whom he calculated he could direct and control. The kingship descended, in the natural course, on Leotychidas, the son of Agis; but it was common-

Agesilaus

Revolutionary scheme of Lysander.

The plot abandoned.

Accession
of
Agesilaus,
398 B.C.

ly believed that this youth was illegitimate, being really the son of
Alcibiades. There were doubts on the matter; but the suspicion was
strong enough to enable the half-brother of Agis, Agesilaus, supported by the influence of Lysander, to oust his nephew and assume
the sceptre.

His char-
acter.

Lysander was deceived in his man; the new king was not of the
metal to be the kingmaker's tool. Agesilaus had hitherto shown only
one side of his character. He had observed all the ordinances of
Lycurgus from his youth up; had performed all duties with cheerful
obedience; had shown himself singularly docile and gentle; had
never asserted or put himself forward among his fellow-citizens. But
the mask of Spartan discipline covered a latent spirit of pride and
ambition which no one suspected. Agesilaus, though strong and
courageous, was of insignificant stature and lame. When he claimed
the throne, an objection was raised on the ground of his deformity;
for an oracle had once solemnly warned Lacedaemon to beware of a
halt reign. But like all sacred weapons this oracle could be blunted
or actually turned against the adversaries. The god did not mean,
said Lysander, physical lameness; but the reign of one who was not
truly descended from Heracles. Yet those Spartans who believed in
literal interpretation of divine words were ill content with the
preference of Agesilaus.

The new king displayed remarkable discretion and policy by his
general demeanour of deferential respect to the other authorities.
This had the greater effect, as the kings were generally wont to
make up by their haughty manners for their want of real power.
Agesilaus made himself popular with everybody, and he maintained
as king the simplicity which had marked his life as a private citizen.
He was unswervingly true to his friends; but this virtue declined to
vice, when he upheld his partisans in acts of injustice.

Domestic
condition
of Sparta.

Not long after his accession, a serious incident occurred which
gives us a glimpse of the social condition of the Lacedaemonian
state at this period and shows that while the government was struggling to maintain its empire abroad, it was menaced at home by
dangers which the existence of that empire rendered graver every
year. Commerce with the outside world and acquisition of money
had promoted considerable inequalities in wealth; and in consequence the number of Peers or fully enfranchised Spartan citizens
was constantly diminishing, while the class of those who had become too poor to pay their scot to the *syssitia* was proportionally
growing. These disqualified citizens were not degraded to the rank
of Perioeci; they formed a separate class and were named Inferiors: a stroke of luck might at any moment enable one of them to

The
Inferiors
(Hypo-
meius).

pay his subscription, and restore him to full citizenship. But the Inferiors naturally formed a class of malcontents; and the narrow, ever narrowing, oligarchy of Peers had to fear that they might make common cause with the Perioeci and Helots and conspire against the state. Such a conspiracy was hatched, but was detected in its first stage through the efficient system of secret police which was established at Sparta. The prime mover seems to have been a young man of the Inferior class named Cinadon, of great strength and bravery. The ephors learned from an informer that Cinadon had called his attention in the market-place to the small number of *Spartans* compared with the multitude of their *enemies*—one perhaps in a hundred. All alike, Inferiors, Neodamodes, Perioeci, Helots, were, according to Cinadon, his accomplices; "for hear any of them talk about the Spartans, he talks as if he could eat them raw." And when Cinadon was asked where the conspirators would find arms, he pointed to the shops of the ironsmiths in the market-place, and added that every workman and husbandman possessed tools. On the ground of information which was perhaps more precise than this, the ephors sent for Cinadon, whom they had often employed on police service, and sent him on a mission of this kind, but with an escort which arrested him on the road, put him to the torture, and wrung from him the names of his accomplices. It would have been dangerous to arrest him in Sparta and so spread the alarm before the names of the others were known. Asked why he conspired, Cinadon said: "I wished to be inferior to none in Sparta." He was scourged round the city, and put to death with his fellows.

Recollecting the histories of other states we cannot forbear wondering that an ambitious general like Lysander did not attempt to use for his own purposes this mass of discontent, into which Cinadon's abortive conspiracy opens a glimpse. There was something in the Spartan air which made a peer rarely capable of disloyalty to the privileges of his own class.

Marginal note: Conspiracy of Cinadon, 397 B.C.

SECT. 4. ASIATIC CAMPAIGNS OF AGESILAUS. BATTLE OF CNIDUS

It was arranged that Agesilaus should take the place of Dercyllidas; that he should take with him a force of 2000 Neodamodes, and a military council of thirty Spartans, including Lysander.

In the Spartan projects at this juncture we can observe very clearly the effect of the episode of the expedition of Cyrus and the Ten Thousand in revolutionising the attitude of Greece towards Persia and spreading the idea that Persia was really weak. The

Marginal note: 396 B.C.

High
flying
plans of
Agesilaus;

Spartan leaders seemed to have regarded the lands of the Great King as a field of easy conquest for a bold Greek. King Agesilaus, especially, who now began to disclose the consuming quality of ambition, dreamed of dethroning the Great King himself, and felt no doubt that he would at least speedily deliver the Asiatic coast from Persian control. But he lived sixty years too soon; and in any case this respectable Spartan was not the man to settle the "eternal question." He regarded himself as a new Agamemnon going forth to capture a new Troy; and, to make the illusion of resemblance complete, he sailed with part of his army to Aulis, to offer sacrifice there in the temple of Artemis as the "king of men" had done before the sailing of the Greeks to Ilium. If Agesilaus had subverted the Persian empire, the sacrifice at Aulis would have seemed an interesting instance of a great man's confidence in his own star.

his dis-
play at
Aulis.

But the performance of Agesilaus can only provoke the mirth of history, especially as the solemnity was not successfully carried out. The Spartan king had not asked the permission of the Thebans to sacrifice in the temple; and a body of armed men interrupted the proceedings and compelled him to desist. It was an insult which Agesilaus never forgave to Thebes.

Lysander expected that the real command in the war would devolve upon himself, and on arriving in Asia he acted on that assumption. He was soon undeceived. Agesilaus had no intention of being merely a nominal chief; and he checked his councillor's self-sufficiency by invariably refusing the petitions which were presented to him through Lysander. This policy was effectual; Lysander, smarting under the humiliation, was sent at his own request on a separate mission to the Hellespont, where he did useful work for Sparta. The satraps in the meantime had renewed with Agesilaus

396 B.C.

the truce they had made with Dercyllidas, but it was soon broken by Tissaphernes. Agesilaus made a feint of marching into Caria,

Campaign
of Agesi-
laus in
Phrygia
(autumn).

and then suddenly, when Tissaphernes had completed his dispositions for defence, turned northwards to Phrygia and invaded the satrapy of Pharnabazus. Here he accomplished nothing of abiding importance but secured a vast quantity of booty, with which he enriched his friends and favourites—it was no temptation to himself. The historian Xenophon, who has left us a special work on the life and character of Agesilaus, tells many anecdotes of this campaign, to illustrate the merits of his hero. Those incidents which

Anecdotes
of
Agesilaus.

bring out his humanity have more than a personal interest for us; they must be taken in connexion with the general fact that the Greeks of the fourth century were more humane than the Greeks of the fifth. We are told that Agesilaus protected his captives against ill-usage; they were to be treated as men, not as criminals. sometimes slave-merchants, fleeing out of the way of his army, abandoned on the roadside little children whom they had bought. Instead of leaving these to perish by wolves or hunger, Agesilaus had them removed and given in charge to natives who were too old to be carried into captivity. But Agesilaus did not scruple to use the captives, without regard to their feelings, as "object-lessons" for his own soldiers. At Ephesus, where the winter was passed in drill, he conceived the idea of showing his troops the difference between good and bad training. He caused the prisoners to be put up for auction naked, so that the Greek soldiers might see the inferior muscles, the white skin, and the soft limbs of the Asiatics whose bodies were never exposed to the weather nor hardened by regular gymnastic discipline. The spectacle impressed the Greeks with their own superiority; but it was an outrage, though not intended as such, on the captives; for, while all Greeks habitually stripped for exercise, Asiatics think it a shame to be seen naked.

Having organised a force of cavalry during the winter, Agesilaus took the field in spring, and gained a victory over Tissaphernes on the Pactolus, near Sardis. The general ill-success of Tissaphernes was made a matter of complaint at Susa. The queen-mother Parysatis, who had never forgiven him for the part he played in the disaster of her beloved Cyrus, made all efforts to procure his downfall; and Tithraustes was sent to the coast to succeed him and put him to death. An offer was now made by Tithraustes to Agesilaus, which it would have been wise to accept. He was required to leave Asia, on condition that the Greek cities should enjoy complete autonomy, paying only their original tribute to Persia. Agesilaus could not agree without consulting his government at home, and an armistice of six months was concluded,—an armistice with Tithraustes, not with Persia; for Agesilaus was left free to turn his arms against Pharnabazus.

In his second campaign in Phrygia, the Spartan king was supported by a Paphlagonian prince named Otys, as well as by Spithridates, a Persian noble whom Lysander had induced to revolt. The province was ravaged up to the walls of Dascylion, where Pharnabazus resided, and the Spartan troops wintered in the rich parks of the neighbourhood, well supplied with birds and fish. The train of Pharnabazus, who moved about the country with all his furniture, was captured; but a dispute over the spoil alienated the oriental allies of Agesilaus, who was the more deeply chagrined at their departure, as he was warmly attached to a beautiful youth, the son of Spithridates. The Greek occupation of Phrygia was brought to an

Campaign in Lydia, 395 B.C. (spring).

Death of Tissaphernes.

Second invasion of the satrapy of Pharnabazus by Agesilaus (autumn).

end by an interesting scene—an interview between the Persian satrap and the Lacedaemonian general. Agesilaus arrived first at the appointed place and sat down on the grass to wait. Then the servants of Pharnabazus appeared and began to spread luxurious carpets for their master. But Pharnabazus seeing the simple seat of Agesilaus went and sat down beside him. They shook hands, and Pharnabazus made a speech of dignified remonstrance. "I was the faithful ally of Sparta when she was at war with Athens; I helped her to victory; I never played her false, like Tissaphernes; and now, for all this, you have brought me to such a plight that I cannot get a dinner in my own province save by picking up what you leave. All my parks and hunting grounds and houses you have ravaged or burnt. Is this justice or gratitude?" After a long silence, Agesilaus explained that being at war with the Great King he had to treat all Persian territory as hostile; but invited the satrap to throw off his allegiance and become an ally of Sparta. "If the king sends another governor and puts me under him," said Pharnabazus, "then I shall be glad to become your friend and ally, but now, while I hold this post of command for him, I shall make war upon you with all my strength." Agesilaus was delighted with this becoming reply. "I will quit your territory at once," he said, "and will respect it in future, so long as I have others to make war upon." Farewells were said and Pharnabazus rode away; but his handsome son, dropping behind, said to Agesilaus, "I make you my guest," and gave him a javelin. Agesilaus accepted the proffered friendship and gave in exchange the ornaments of his secretary's horse. The incident had a sequel. In later years this young Persian, ill-treated by his brothers, fled for refuge to Greece, and did not seek in vain the protection of his guest-friend Agesilaus.

His success in Phrygia rendered Agesilaus more than ever disposed to attempt conquests in the interior of Asia Minor. But in the meantime he had mismanaged matters of greater moment. Before he marched against Pharnabazus, he had received a message from Sparta, committing to him the supreme command by sea. The preparation of an adequate fleet was urgent. Conon, with eighty sail—the rest of the armament was not yet completed—had induced Rhodes to revolt and had captured a corn fleet which an Egyptian prince had despatched to the Lacedaemonians. Agesilaus took measures for the equipment of a fleet of 120 triremes at the expense of the cities of the islands and coast-land; but he committed the blunder of entrusting the command to Pisander, his brother-in-law, a man of no experience. After his Phrygian expedition, Agesilaus had been himself recalled to Europe for reasons which will presently

(395 B.C.)

be related; while Pharnabazus went to discharge the functions of joint-admiral with Conon, who had visited Susa in person, to stimulate Persian zeal and obtain the necessary funds. In the middle of the summer the fleet of Conon and Pharnabazus, having left Cilician waters, appeared off the coast of the Cnidian peninsula. The numbers are uncertain, but the Persian fleet was overwhelmingly larger than that of Pisander, who sailed out from Cnidus to oppose it with desperate courage. The result could not be doubtful. Pisan-

Battle of Cnidus (Aug. 394 B.C.)

Fig. 76.—Coin of Cnidus (obverse). Head of Aphrodite. Fig. 77.—Coin of Elis (obverse). Head of Hera [legend: *FA*].

der's Asiatic contingents deserted him without fighting, and of the rest the greater part were taken or sunk. Pisander fell in the action. The Greek cities of Asia expelled the Spartan garrisons and acknowledged the overlordship of Persia. Thus Conon, in the guise of a Persian admiral, avenged Athens and undid the victory of the Aegospotami in a battle which was almost as easily won. The maritime power of Sparta was destroyed, and the unstable foundations of her empire undermined.

SECT. 5. SPARTA AT THE GATES OF THE PELOPONNESUS (THE "CORINTHIAN WAR")

At the same time, she was suffering serious checks nearer home. While Agesilaus was meditating his wonderful schemes against Persia, war had broken out in Greece between Sparta and her allies; and the turn it took rendered it imperative to recall him from Asia. It is necessary to go back a little to explain.

After the battle of the Goat's River, Sparta had kept for herself all the fruits of victory. She had taken over the maritime empire of her prostrate foe, and enjoyed its tribute. Her allies had got nothing; and yet they had made far greater sacrifices than Sparta herself throughout the Peloponnesian war. Any demands made by Corinth and other allies who had borne the burden and heat of those years were haughtily rejected. Lacedaemon felt herself strong enough to treat her former friends with contempt. She further exhibited her despotic temper by her proceedings within the Peloponnesus against those who had displeased her. Elis had given her repeated and recent grounds of offence, and Elis was now chastised. King Agis invaded and ravaged the country, and imposed severe conditions on the Eleans. They were deprived of their Triphylian territory, of Cyllene their port, and of other places; and were compelled to pull down the incomplete fortifications of their city. The only grace accorded to them was that they should still have the privilege of conducting the Olympian festival. The Spartans indulged another grudge by expelling from Naupactus and Cephallenia the residue of the Messenians, who had settled in those places.

Fate of Elis, 399 B.C.

The Messenians.

The exercise of authority within the Peloponnesus was regarded by Sparta as an ordering of her own domain; but she also began vigorously to assert her power in the north of Greece. She resuscitated into new life her colony of Heraclea, near Thermopylae, and pushing into Thessaly she placed a Lacedaemonian garrison and harmost in Pharsalus.

Spartan activity north of Thermopylae.

When war broke out between Persia and Sparta, it was the policy of Persia to excite a war in Greece against her enemy, and fan the smouldering discontent of the secondary Greek powers into a flame. The satrap Tithraustes sent a Rhodian agent, named Timocrates, with fifty talents to bribe the leading statesmen of the chief cities to join Persia in a league of hostility against Sparta. Timocrates visited Argos, Corinth, and Thebes, and gained over some of the most influential people. But it really required only an assurance of Persian co-operation, and then a favourable occasion, to raise a general resistance to the ascendency of Lacedaemon. The first aggression, however, came from Lacedaemon herself. A trifle, a border dispute between Phocis and Opuntian Locris, furnished the occasion, the Locrians appealing to Thebes, the Phocians to Lacedaemon, for support. The Lacedaemonians, according to their friend Xenophon, rejoiced to have a pretext for attacking Thebes and chastising her insolence. A double invasion of Boeotia was arranged, king Pausanias advancing from the south, and Lysander coming down from Heraclea, on the north.

Mission of Tithraustes, 395 B.C.

Outbreak of war in Boeotia.

Thus threatened, Thebes turned for aid to her old enemy for whose utter destruction she had pleaded a few years agone. Athens had been steadily recovering a measure of her prosperity; the oligarchical party seems to have already merged its own ambitions in loyalty to the democratic majority which had shown such generosity in the day of its triumph; and in the debate on the Theban request for aid, men of all parties alike voted to seize the opportunity for attempting to break free from Spartan rule. The decision

Athens combines with Thebes.

was felt to be bold, since the Piraeus was unfortified; but there was also a feeling that the tide was at the flood—Conon was sailing the southeastern seas, Rhodes had revolted,—the moment must not be lost. So there was concluded an "eternal alliance between the Boeotians and Athenians"; the phrase, pregnant with the irony of history, has been preserved on a fragment of the original treaty-stone, and it shows at least the enthusiastic hopes of the hour.

When Lysander approached Boeotia, he was joined by Orchomenus, which was always bitterly hostile to Theban supremacy in Boeotia. He and Pausanias had arranged to meet near Haliartus, which is about half-way between Thebes and Orchomenus. It is uncertain whether Lysander was too soon or Pausanias too late; but Lysander arrived in the district of Haliartus first and attacked the town. From their battlements the men of Haliartus could descry a band of Thebans coming along the road from Thebes, some time before the danger was visible to their assailants; and they suddenly sallied forth from the gates. Taken by surprise and attacked on both sides, Lysander's men were driven back, and Lysander was slain. His death was a loss to Sparta, which she could not make good. He had made her empire such as it was; and she had no other man of first-rate ability. But the death of the Spartan Lysander was no loss to Greece.

Siege of
Haliartus.

Death of
Lysander.

Pausanias soon came up, and his first object was to recover the corse of his dead colleague. He was strong enough to extort this from the Thebans and Haliartians, but an Athenian army came up at the same moment to their assistance, under the leadership of Thrasybulus. Pausanias was in a difficult predicament. To fight meant to incur defeat; but to acknowledge weakness by asking for a burial truce was galling to Spartan pride. A council of war, however, decided to beg for a truce; and, when the Thebans, contrary to usage, would grant it only on condition that the Peloponnesian army should leave Boeotia, the terms were accepted. The Spartans vented their sorrow for the loss of Lysander in anger against their king. He was condemned to death for having failed to keep tryst with Lysander and for having declined battle. It is not clear whether the first charge was well founded; as for the second, no prudent general could have acted otherwise. Pausanias, who had discreetly refrained from returning to Sparta, spent the rest of his life as an exile at Tegea.

The result of this double blow to the Spartans—their prestige tarnished and their ablest general fallen—was the conclusion of a league against her by the four most important states. Thebes and Athens were now joined by Corinth and Argos. This alliance was

Confederation
against
Sparta.

soon increased by the adhesion of the Euboeans, the Acarnanians, the Chalcidians of Thrace, and other minor states. Perhaps the most active spirit in this insurgent movement was the Theban Ismenias. This leader succeeded in expelling the Spartans from their northern post Heraclea, and spreading the Theban alliance among the peoples of those regions. Sparta lost her foothold in Thessaly, and the Phocians, who were under the protection of a Spartan harmost, were defeated.

The Confederates at the Isthmus, spring, 394 B.C.

Thus the situation of Greece and the prospects of Sparta were completely changed. The allies, when spring came, gathered together their forces [1] at the Isthmus, and it was proposed by one bold Corinthian to march straight on Sparta and "burn out the wasps in their nest." But the Lacedaemonians were already advancing through Arcadia to Sicyon, from which place they crossed over, by Nemea, to the southern shores of the Saronic gulf—a movement somewhat hampered by the allies, who had reached Nemea. The allies then took up a post near Corinth, and a battle was fought. The

Battle of Corinth (July).

number of combatants on each side was unusually large for a Greek battle. The Spartans on their wing decisively routed the Athenians, and though on the other wing their subjects were routed, it was distinctly a Spartan victory. The losses of the Confederates were more than twice as great as those of their foes. Some unrecorded feat of arms was achieved in this battle by five Athenian horsemen who lost their lives; and in the burying-ground outside the Dipylon Gate of Athens, we may still see the funeral monument of one of these "five knights," Dexileos, a youth of twenty who is portrayed, according to Greek habit, not in the moment of his death but in the moment of victory, spearing a hoplite who has fallen under his horse's hoofs. Strategically, the Confederates lost nothing, the victors gained nothing by the battle of Corinth. The Isthmus was left under the control of the Confederates, who were now free to oppose Agesilaus in Boeotia.

Return of Agesilaus to Europe.

For Agesilaus was bearing down on Boeotia. The battle of Haliartus and the events which followed had decided the ephors to recall him from Asia, his presence being more pressingly needed in Europe; and with a heavy heart he was constrained to abandon his dazzling visions of Persian conquest. Agamemnon had to return to Mycenae without having taken Troy. He marched overland by a route which no army had traversed since the expedition of Xerxes, through Thrace and Macedonia. At Amphipolis he received the

---

[1] Amounting altogether to 24,000 hoplites, 1550 cavalry, besides light troops. The Lacedaemonian forces at the battle of Corinth were 13,500 hoplites, 600 cavalry.

news of the victory of Corinth, not excessively inspiriting. But even
as he marched the fate of his country's empire was being decided.
The victory of Conon at Cnidus was the knell of the ambitions of
Agesilaus. When his army reached Chaeronea the sun suffered an
eclipse; and the meaning of the phenomenon was explained by the
news, which presently arrived, of the battle of Cnidus. To conceal
from his army the full import of this news was the first duty of the
general; and the second was to hasten on a battle, while it could
still be concealed. Agesilaus had been reinforced by some contingents from Lacedaemon, as well as by troops from Phocis and Orchomenus; but his main force consisted of the soldiers whom he had
brought from Asia, among whom were some of the famous Ten
Thousand, including Xenophon himself. The Confederate army
which had fought at Corinth was now in Boeotia, though hardly in
the same strength, as a garrison must have been left to defend their
important position near the Isthmus. The Confederates established
their camp in the district of Coronea, a favourable spot for blocking
against a foe the road which leads to Thebes from Phocis and the
valley of the Cephisus. On the field where the Boeotians had thrown
off Athenian rule half a century before, Athenians and Boeotians
now joined to throw off the domination of Lacedaemon. Agesilaus
advanced from the Cephisus. He commanded his own right wing,
and the Argives who were on the Confederate left fled before him
without striking a blow. On the other side, the Thebans on the Confederate right routed the Orchomenians on the Lacedaemonian left.
Then the two victorious right wings wheeling round met each other,
and the real business of the day began. The object of Agesilaus was
to prevent the Thebans from joining and rallying their friends. The
encounter of the hoplites is described as incomparably terrible by
Xenophon, who was himself engaged in it. Agesilaus, whose bodily
size was hardly equal to such a fray, was trodden underfoot, and
rescued by the bravery of his bodyguard. The pressure of the deep
column of the Thebans pushed a way through the Lacedaemonian
array. Agesilaus was left master of the field; he erected a trophy;
and the Confederates asked for the burial truce. But though the
battle of Coronea, like the battle of Corinth, was a technical victory
for the Spartans, history must here again offer her congratulations
to the side which was, superficially, defeated. In the chief action of
the day, the Thebans had displayed superiority and thwarted the
attempt of their enemy to cut them off. It was a great moral encouragement to Thebes for future warfare with Lacedaemon. And immediately, it was a distinct success for the Confederates. When an
aggressor cannot follow up his victory, the victory is strategically

Eclipse of
sun, Aug.
14, 394
B.C.

Battle of
Coronea,
394 B.C.

A HISTORY OF GREECE

equivalent to a repulse. Agesilaus immediately evacuated Boeotia—
that was the result of Coronea. He crossed over to the Peloponnesus
from Delphi, as the Confederates commanded the road by Corinth.

Spartans
blockaded
in the
Peloponnesus.
It was round Corinth that the struggle of the next years mainly
centred, in fitting accordance with the object of the war. Sparta was
fighting for domination beyond the Peloponnesus; her enemies were
fighting to keep her within the Peloponnesus. The most effective
way of accomplishing this design was to hold the gates of the peninsula, between the Corinthian and Saronic gulfs, and not let her
pass out. With this view long walls were built binding Corinth, on
the one hand with its western port Lechaeon, and on the other with
its eastern port at Cenchreae. Thus none could pass from the Peloponnesus into Northern Greece without dealing with the defenders
of these fortifications. Never had Lacedaemon been more helpless;
almost a prisoner in her peninsula, and her maritime empire dissolved. This momentary paralysis of Lacedaemon proved the salvation of Athens.

393 B.C.
Pharna-
bazus on
the Greek
coast.
The restoration of Athens to her place among the independent
powers of Greece at this juncture came about by curious means.
The satrap Pharnabazus who had done so much to aid Lysander in
destroying her, now helped to bring about her resurrection. He had
not forgiven Sparta for the injury which Agesilaus had inflicted on
his province, and this rankling resentment was kept alive by the
circumstance that, while the other Asiatic cities had unanimously
declared against Sparta after the battle of Cnidus, Abydus alone
held out against himself under the Spartan Dercyllidas. He exhibited his wrath by accompanying Conon and the fleet, in the following spring, to the shores of Greece, to ravage the Spartan territory
and to encourage and support the Confederates. A Persian satrap
within sight of Corinth and Salamis was a strange sight for Greece.
His revengefulness stood Athens in good stead. When he returned
home, he allowed Conon to retain the fleet and make use of it to
Rebuild-
ing of the
Long
Walls of
Athens.
rebuild the Long Walls of Athens and fortify the Piraeus. He even
supplied money to inflict this crushing blow on Sparta, a blow which
completely undid the chief result of the Peloponnesian war. The
two long parallel walls connecting Athens with the Piraeus were
rebuilt; [2] the port was again made defensible; and the Athenians
could feel once more that they were a free and independent people
in the Grecian world. Conon who had wrought out their deliverance
erected a temple to the Cnidian Aphrodite in the Piraeus, as a
monument of his great victory. Never since the day of Salamis was

[2] The building of the walls was begun before the battle of Cnidus; the completion was due to Conon.

there such cause for rejoicing at Athens as when the fortifications were completed at the end of the autumn. As rebuilder of the walls Conon might claim to be a second Themistocles. But the comparison only reminds us of the change which had come over Greece in a hundred years. It was through Persian support that Athens now under the auspices of Conon regained in part the position which she had won by her championship of Hellas against Persia under the auspices of Themistocles. She did not regain her former ascendency or her former empire, but she was restored to an equality with the other powerful states of Greece; she could feel herself the peer of Thebes, Corinth, and Argos, and of Sparta, now that Sparta had fallen from her high estate. The Athenians could now calmly maintain that defiance which they had boldly offered to Sparta by their alliance with Thebes. About the same time the northern islands of Lemnos, Imbros, and Scyrus seem to have been reunited to Athens, and she recovered her control of Delos which the Spartans had taken from her. Chios too became her ally.

It was of vital importance to the Lacedaemonians to gain command of the gates of the Peloponnesus by capturing some part of the line of defence; and thus Corinth becomes the centre of interest. The Lacedaemonians established their headquarters at Sicyon, and from this base made a series of efforts to break through the lines of Corinth—efforts which were ultimately successful. Unluckily the chronology is obscure; and it cannot be decided whether these operations were partly concurrent with, or altogether subsequent to, the rebuilding of the Long Walls of Athens. In Corinth itself there was a considerable party favourable to Sparta. This party seems to have arranged a plot for violently overthrowing the oligarchy which was in power; but the design was suspected and prevented by the government, who caused the friends of Sparta to be massacred in cold blood, in the market-place and theatre, on the last day of the feast of Euclea. The Corinthian government at the same time drew closer the bonds which attached it to the enemies of Sparta. By a remarkable measure Corinth and Argos united themselves into a federal state; the boundary pillars were pulled up; the citizens enjoyed common rights. It would be interesting to know how this federal constitution was framed; but such an union had no elements of endurance; it was merely a political expedient.

Union of Corinth and Argos (392 B.C.)

A considerable number of the philo-Laconian party had escaped; some still remained in the city; and these now managed to open a gate in the western wall and admit Praxitas, the commander at Sicyon, with a Lacedaemonian *mora* of 600 hoplites. Praxitas secured his position between the two walls by constructing a ditch

Praxitas at Corinth.

and palisade, across the intermural space, on the side of Corinth.

Battle of
the Long
Walls.

The Corinthians and their allies came down from the city; the palisade was torn up; a battle was fought; and the Lacedaemonians, completely victorious, captured the town of Lechaeon, though not the port. Praxitas then pulled down part of the walls, and made incursions into the Corinthian territory on the side of the Saronic bay. But when winter set in, he disbanded his army, without making any provision for keeping the command of the Isthmus; and the Athenians came, with carpenters and masons, and repaired the breach in the walls.

Mercenary
troops:
their
growing
importance.

A warfare of raids was at the same time constantly carried on by the hostile parties, from their posts at Corinth and Sicyon. In this warfare a force of mercenaries, trained and commanded by the Athenian Iphicrates, was especially conspicuous. They were armed as peltasts, with light shield and javelin, and this armour was far better suited for the conditions of camp life and the duties of the professional soldier, than the armour of a hoplite. The employment of mercenaries had been growing,—destined ultimately to supplant the institution of citizen armies. It was the wilder parts of Greece, like Crete, Aetolia, Acarnania, that chiefly supplied the mercenary troops. Iphicrates of Rhamnus, an officer of great energy and talent, recognised the importance of the professional peltast as a new element in Hellenic warfare, and immortalised his name in military history by reforming the peltast's equipment. His improvements consisted in lengthening the sword and the javelin, and introducing a kind of light leggings, known as "Iphicratid" boots. It is difficult to appreciate the full import of these changes; but they were clearly meant to unite effectiveness of attack with rapidity of motion.

Reforms
of Iphicrates.

Agesilaus
captures
Lechaeon,
391 B.C.

This enterprising officer and his peltasts won the chief honours of the "Corinthian War." Agesilaus had been sent out to gain some more permanent successes than those which had been achieved by Praxitas. His brother Teleutias co-operated with him by sea; the Long Walls were stormed, and the port of Lechaeon was captured. In the following year he went forth again. It was the time of the Isthmian festival, and the games were about to be held in the precincts of Poseidon at Isthmus. Agesilaus marched thither, interrupted the Corinthians and Argives who were beginning the celebration, and presided at the contest himself. When he retired, the Corinthians came and celebrated the festival over again; some athletes won the same race twice.

(390 B.C.,
spring.)

Spartans
capture
Piraeon.

Agesilaus then captured the port of Piraeon, on the promontory which forms the northern side of the inmost recess of the Corinthian gulf. The importance of this capture lay in the fact that Piraeon connected Corinth with her allies in Boeotia; its occupation was a threat to Boeotia; and the Boeotians immediately sent envoys to Agesilaus. The position was now reversed; the Spartans commanded the Isthmus passage, and by possessing Sicyon, Piraeon, Lechaeon, as well as Sidon and Crommyon on the Saronic gulf, they entirely closed in Corinth, except on the side of Argolis. If Agesilaus felt himself the arbiter of Greece, his triumph was short. The situation was rescued by Iphicrates.

In the garrison at Lechaeon there were some men of Amyclae, whose custom and privilege it was to return to their native place to keep the local feast of Hyacinthus. The time of this feast was now at hand, and they set out to return home by Sicyon and Arcadia, the only way open to them. But as it was not safe for a handful of men to march under the walls of Corinth, they were escorted most of the way to Sicyon by a *mora* of 600 Lacedaemonian hoplites. As this escort was returning to Lechaeon, Iphicrates and his peltasts issued from the gates of Corinth and attacked them. The heavy spearmen were worn out by the repeated assaults of the light troops with which they were unable to cope, and a large number were destroyed. This event, though less striking and important, bore a resemblance to the famous calamity of Sphacteria. In both cases, Spartan warriors had been discomfited in the same way by the continuous attacks of inaccessible light troops; and in both cases a blow was dealt to the military prestige of Lacedaemon. The success of Iphicrates was a suggestive sign of the future which might be in store for the professional peltast. To Agesilaus the news came at a moment when he was regarding with triumphant arrogance his captives and the Theban envoys. His pride was changed into chagrin; the army was plunged into sorrow; and only the relatives of those soldiers who had fallen in the battle moved about with the jubilant air of victors. Leaving another division as a garrison in Lechaeon, Agesilaus returned home, skulking through Sicyon and the Arcadian cities at night, in order to avoid unkind remarks. Piraeon, Sidon, and Crommyon were soon recovered by Iphicrates; and the garrison of Lechaeon seems to have done no more than keep the gates of the Peloponnesus open. This was the result of the "Corinthian" war. Sparta had succeeded in breaking down the barrier which was to shut her out from North Greece; but she had sustained a serious loss and damage to her reputation.

The light troops of Iphicrates vanquish Spartan hoplites.

Sect. 6. The King's Peace

We must now turn from the Isthmus of Corinth to the eastern coasts of the Aegean. The Lacedaemonians ascribed the success of

Efforts towards a peace, 392 B.C.

their opponents to the support of Persia, and drew the conclusion that their chance lay in detaching Persia to their own side. With this view they had dispatched Antalcidas to open negotiations with Tiribazus. The proposals of Sparta were (1) that the Hellenic cities of Asia should be subjects of the king; this was the price of Persian help; (2) that all other Hellenic cities should be independent; this was aimed at the Confederates—at the supremacy of Thebes in Boeotia, and at the union of Corinth with Argos. The Athenians and their allies sent Conon and other envoys to counteract the mission of Antalcidas, and perhaps it was at this time also that they sent the orator Andocides to Sparta to consider terms of peace. Both the mission of Andocides and the mission of Antalcidas were alike unsuccessful. Tiribazus, who was favourable to Sparta and threw Conon into prison, was recalled; and his successor Struthas had no Spartan leanings. The object of Antalcidas was indeed ultimately reached, but its attainment was postponed for four or five years, and the war went on as before.

Warfare in Asia;

The military events of these years are not of great interest; our knowledge of them is meagre. In Asia, the Spartan cause revives. Thibron is sent out once more, and though he sustains a severe defeat at the hands of Struthas, it is not until he has won over Ephesus, Magnesia, and Priene. Soon Cnidus and Samos follow

in Europe.

the example of these cities. Agesilaus invades Acarnania, and forces the Acarnanians to join the Lacedaemonian league; his colleague Agesipolis carries out one of those invasions of Argolis which lead to nothing. Then the Spartans use Aegina as a base for harassing Attica, and a warfare of surprises is carried on between the harmosts of Aegina and Athenian admirals. The harmost Gorgopas captured four ships of an Athenian squadron; the Athenian Chabrias than landed in Aegina, laid an ambush, and killed Gorgopas. Teleutias, the brother of Agesilaus, was sent to Aegina soon afterwards. He made an attack on the Piraeus at daybreak, and towed away some of the galleys lying in the harbour. In old Greece the war was on the whole advantageous to Sparta, though no decisive success was gained.

Taxation at Athens: (1) Euripides' tax of $\frac{1}{40}$th; (2) war tax, 390, 389 B.C.

But the most important event was the recovery of Athenian dominion on the Propontis. At this moment Athens was in great financial straits, for she had ceased to receive Persian subsidies. When an indirect impost of $\frac{1}{40}$th had been tried and found insufficient, a direct war-tax was levied. For the Athenians had determined to operate both in the south and in the north; in the south to assist their friend Evagoras who was revolting from the Great King, in the north to recover control of the road to the Euxine Sea.

Thrasybulus, the restorer of the democracy, sailed with a fleet of forty ships to the Hellespont, and gained over to the Athenian alliance the islands of Thasos and Samothrace, the Chersonesus, and the two cities which commanded the Bosphorus, Byzantium and Chalcedon. Proceeding to Lesbos, he defeated and slew the Spartan harmost, and established Athenian supremacy over most of the island. He also won Clazomenae. The original object for which he had been sent out was to assist Rhodes in maintaining her independence against the efforts of Sparta to regain the mastery of the island. But to act with effect it was necessary to raise money, and the Athenian fleet coasted round Asia Minor, levying contributions. These exactions appear to have been a renewal of the tax of 5 per cent which Athens imposed on the commerce of her allies after the Sicilian expedition. It seemed like the beginning of a new empire. Aspendus in Pamphylia was one of the places visited, and the visit was fatal to Thrasybulus. The violent methods of his soldiers enraged the inhabitants; they surprised him at night in his tent and slew him. Athens had now lost the two men of action to whom, since the death of Pericles, she owed most, Conon and Thrasybulus.

Conon, who soon after his imprisonment by Tiribazus died in Cyprus, had broken down the maritime dominion of the Lacedaemonian oppressor and had given Athens the means of recovering her independence and her sea-power. Thrasybulus had given to the Athenian democracy a new life and breathed into it a new spirit of conciliation and moderation. He strikes us—we know too little of him—as an eminently reasonable citizen, one of those men who command general confidence, and are not biassed by prejudice or ambition. The virtues of Thrasybulus were moral rather than intellectual. After his death insinuations were made against his integrity; and one of his friends named Ergocles was found guilty of embezzlement of money collected on the expedition of Thrasybulus and was put to death. But the statements of an advocate—and we have no other evidence—carry no weight.

The success of Thrasybulus in re-establishing a toll for the advantage of Athens on merchandise passing through the Bosphorus was almost immediately endangered by Anaxibius, whom Sparta promptly sent out to act against Athens and Pharnabazus. He deprived Athens of her tolls by seizing the merchant vessels. Iphicrates was dispatched to oppose him with 1200 peltasts, and the Hellespont became the scene of the same kind of warfare of raids and surprises which we saw carried on at Aegina. At last Iphicrates saw a favourable opportunity for a decisive blow. Anaxibius had gone to place a garrison in Antandrus, which he had just gained over. Iphicrates crossed by night from the Chersonese and laid an ambush on the return route, near the gold mines of Cremaste. The troops of Anaxibius marched in careless order, traversing the narrow mountain passes in extended single file, without the slightest suspicion that an enemy lay in the way. Suddenly, as they were coming down from the mountains into the plain of Cremaste, the peltasts of Iphicrates leaped out. Anaxibius saw at a glance that the case was desperate. The scattered hoplites had no chance against the peltasts. "I must die here," he said to his men, "my honour demands it; but do you save yourselves." A devoted youth who constantly accompanied him fell fighting by his side. This exploit of Iphicrates ensured the command of the Hellespont and Bosphorus to Athens.

Unfortunately for Athens, the political situation changed and other great powers intervened. At the beginning of the fourth century there were three great powers which aimed at supremacy over portions of the Greek world—Persia, Sparta, and the tyrant of Syracuse, Dionysius. At first, however, it was not a case of these three great powers uniting in a sacred alliance for the suppression of liberty. Dionysius did not intervene in the east; and Persia and Sparta contested the supremacy over the Asiatic Greeks. Thus Persia, in the cause of her own supremacy in Asia, made common cause with liberty elsewhere. The general military failure of Sparta forced her to seek a reconciliation with Persia on the basis of abandoning Asia. One of the obstacles to the accomplishment of this object was the influence of the satrap Pharnabazus who cherished bitter hostility to the country of Dercyllidas and Agesilaus. On the other hand, Athens had taken an ambiguous step which could not fail to create distrust and resentment at the Persian court. If Athens was indebted to Persia for the restoration of her walls, she had also been befriended and supported by Evagoras, prince of Salamis, the friend of Conon, and she had bestowed upon him her citizenship in recognition of his services. Thus, when he revolted from Persia, Athens was in an embarrassing position. The support of Persia against Sparta was all-important to her. Artaxerxes was her ally; but Evagoras was her citizen too, and a Greek. Against her own apparent interests, Athens sent ten ships to assist her Cypriote friend; and, though they were captured by a Lacedaemonian admiral and never actually served against the Persians, the incident was calculated to dispose the Great King to entertain the overtures of Sparta. The diplomatist Antalcidas went up to Susa and renewed his proposals. Backed by the influence of Tiribazus he overcame the reluctance of Artaxerxes, who was personally prepossessed

Athens votes to assist Evagoras, 390 B.C.

Spartan diplomacy at Susa.

against Sparta, and induced him to agree to enforce a general pacification, on the same conditions which had been proposed before. Opposition on the part of Pharnabazus was removed by summoning him to court to marry a daughter of Artaxerxes.

The diplomacy of Sparta was successful not only at Susa; it was successful also at Syracuse, and obtained an auxiliary force of twenty triremes from the tyrant Dionysius.

Sparta supported by Syracuse.

With the support of the west and the east, Sparta was able to force the peace upon Hellas. When Antalcidas and Tiribazus returned to the coast, they found Iphicrates blockading the Spartan fleet at Abydus. Antalcidas dexterously rescued the fleet from this predicament, and was able, when the Syracusan vessels joined him, as well as Persian reinforcements, to blockade the Athenians in the Hellespont and prevent corn vessels from reaching Athens. The coasting trade of Attica was at the same time suffering grievously through the raids from Aegina, which have already been mentioned. Hence peace was expedient for Athens; and the allies could not think of continuing the war without her. The representatives of the belligerents were summoned to Sardis, and Tiribazus read aloud the edict of his master, showing them the royal seal. It was to this effect:—

387 B.C.

"King Artaxerxes thinks it just that the cities in Asia, and the islands of Clazomenae and Cyprus, shall belong to him. Further, that all the other Greek cities, small and great, shall be autonomous; except Lemnos, Imbros, and Scyrus, which shall belong to Athens, as aforetime. If any refuse to accept this peace I shall make war on them, along with those who are of the same purpose, both by land and sea, with both ships and money."

The peace which the King sent down, 387-6 B.C.

The representatives were to report to the cities the terms of the peace, and then meet at Sparta to declare their acceptance. All accepted; but the Thebans raised a difficulty by claiming to take the oath on behalf of all the Boeotian cities as well as of themselves. Such a proposal would clearly place the Boeotian cities in a different class from the other cities of Greece, which took the oath each for itself. It was an attempt to assert the dependence of the Boeotian communities on Thebes, whereas one of the chief objects of the peace was to assert their autonomy. Agesilaus was secretly pleased with the opposition of Thebes: he hoped that the Thebans would persist in it and give him the opportunity of attacking and subduing their detested city. But they submitted in time and disappointed his vengeance.

(386 B.C.)

The King's Peace was inscribed on stone tablets, which were set up in the chief sanctuaries of the Greek states. There was a feeling among many that Greece had suffered a humiliation in having to submit to the arbitration of Persia. Both Spartans and Athenians had alike used Persian help, when they could get it, but never before had the domestic conflicts of Hellas been settled by barbarian dictation and under a barbarian sanction. It was Sparta's doing. She constituted herself the minister of the Great King's will in order to save her own position; and the Greeks of Asia were left to

FIG. 78.—Alliance coin of Ephesus, *c.* 394-3 B.C. Obverse: Young Heracles strangling snakes [legend: ΣΥΝ(μαχικόν)]. Reverse: bee [legend: ΕΦ, and below ΠΕ]. FIG. 79.—Coin of Lampsacus, *c.* 394-3 B.C. Obverse: Young Heracles strangling snakes. Reverse: winged horse.

endure oriental methods of government. Athens, though she had lost what Thrasybulus had won for her, was allowed to retain her old insular dependencies in the North Aegean; a concession which shows that it was thought necessary to bribe her into accepting the peace, and that Sparta was more eagerly bent on weakening the other confederates. In truth, the main objects were to break up the Boeotian league and to separate the Argives from Corinth.

Federal movements.

But it was an age of federal experiments, and the King's Peace, while it dissolved the leagues of Argos and Thebes, led to a federal movement in another quarter. Ephesus, Samos, Cnidus, and Iasus, flung back into the power of Persia, formed an alliance with

Coinage.

Rhodes, and in token thereof these cities issued alliance coins of the Rhodian standard, engraven with a picture of the infant Heracles strangling the snakes. It was an alliance for mutual protection of their liberties. These were days in which, from one end of the Greek world to the other, smaller states, seeing their freedom threatened by Persia, Sparta, or Syracuse, were inclined to draw together into small federations. And from one end of the Greek world to the other there seems to have spread a fellow-feeling among these smaller states, a consciousness that their cause was the same. In the west, Croton and Zacynthus, viewing with alarm the extension of the Syracusan empire, seem to have had a secret understanding, and it is most curious that they too engraved on their money the same symbolic scene. Again on the Propontis, at Cyzicus and Lampsacus, this properly Theban token reappears,

It is hazardous to draw conclusions from coins as to definite political relations without some further evidence; but Heracles strangling the snakes seems to have been adopted at this period by tacit unanimity, if nothing more, as an emblem of liberty.

FIG. 80.—Alliance coin of Samos, *c.* 394-3 B.C. Obverse: Young Heracles strangling snakes [legend: ΣΥΝ(μαχικόν)]. Reverse: scalp of lion [legend: ΣΑ].

CHAPTER XIII

THE REVIVAL OF ATHENS AND HER SECOND LEAGUE

SECT. I. HIGH-HANDED POLICY OF SPARTA

THE gates of the Peloponnesus were again open to Sparta without dispute; she was supported by Persia, and she had no complications in Asia to divide her energy. Accordingly she was able to renew the despotic policy which had been inaugurated for her by Lysander. Arcadian Mantinea was the first to suffer. The Mantineans were accused of various acts of disobedience and disloyalty to Sparta, and commanded to pull down their walls. When they refused, king Agesipolis—son of the exiled Pausanias—marched out against them. The city of Mantinea stood in a high plain, without any natural defences, depending entirely on its walls of unburnt brick. The river Ophis flowed through the town; and, a blockade proving tedious, Agesipolis dammed the stream at the point of issue. The water rose and undermined the walls; and when one of the towers threatened to fall, the people surrendered. Their punishment was severe. Mantinea ceased to be a city, and was broken up into its five constituent villages. Those who originally belonged to the *village* of Mantinea remained on the site of the city; the rest had to pull down their houses and move each to the village where his property was. The loss of civic life meant to a Greek the loss of all his higher interests.

Agesilaus, who had once gone forth to destroy the Persian power, zealously supported the King's Peace. When some one suggested that it was at least curious to find the Spartans medizing, he rejoined, "Rather say that the Persians are laconizing." Each way of putting it expressed a measure of the truth. But some of the Lacedaemonians, including king Agesipolis, were opposed to the recent policy of their government, and thought it ill-done to abandon the Greeks of Asia. Some years after the Peace, there seems to have been floating in the air a vague idea, which might or might not take shape, of organising another Asiatic expedition. It was to animate this idea that the Athenian orator Isocrates published a festal speech when the Greek nation was assembled at the Olym-

The dissolution of the city of Mantinea (386-5 B.C.).

'The Panegyric of Isocrates (composed 381), 38c.

pian festival. He advocated a grand Panhellenic union against Persia, under the common headship of Sparta and Athens—Sparta taking the command by land, Athens by sea. It was the third occasion on which a renowned master of style had broached the same idea at the same gathering-place. Nearly thirty years ago, it had been recommended by the florid eloquence of Gorgias; more recently it had been advocated with gracious simplicity of Lysias; and now the rich periods of Isocrates urged it once more upon Greece. The project—in the ideal form in which Isocrates imagined it—was at this moment chimerical. A hundred years before, it had been hard enough to compass a practical co-operation between Greek powers of equal strength and pretensions, in a war of defence; it was hopeless to think of such co-operation now for a war of aggression. Sparta and Athens were quarrelling, as the orator complains, over the tribute of the Cyclad islands; and neither was likely to yield to the other without a clear award of war. And other troubles were brewing in another quarter.

(See above, p. 483; and below, p. 545.)

The contest of east and west had been going on meanwhile in Cyprus, an island whose geographical situation has marked it out, like Sicily, to be a meeting-place of races. We have already met a man who played an eminent part in that struggle, Evagoras the prince of Salamis. He belonged to the Teucrid family which had reigned there in the days of Darius and Xerxes, but had been supplanted by a Phoenician dynasty about the middle of the fifth century. Evagoras, crossing over from the Cilician Soli, won back the sceptre of his race by a daring surprise. He governed with conspicuous moderation, discretion, and success; setting himself to the work of reviving the cause of Hellenism, which had lost much ground during the past half-century; and pursuing this task by entirely peaceful means. After Aegospotami, the city of Evagoras became the refuge for large numbers of Athenians who had settled down in various parts of the Athenian empire and could no longer remain securely in their homes. For the first sixteen years of his reign Evagoras was a faithful tributary of the Great King, and we have seen how his influence at Susa assisted Conon. But soon after the battle of Cnidus he became involved in war, both with Persia and with some of the Phoenician cities in the island. The Peace expressly recognised the sovereignty of Artaxerxes over Cyprus, and as soon as it was concluded, Persia began to concentrate her forces against Evagoras and a recalcitrant king of Egypt, with whom Evagoras was leagued. A severe defeat at sea shut Evagoras up in Salamis; but he held out so dauntlessly, and the war had already cost Persia so much, that Tiribazus agreed to leave him his prin-

Evagoras of Cyprus.

411-10 B.C.

386 B.C.

(Acoris.) 386-4 B.C.

cipality, on condition that he should pay tribute "as a slave to his lord." Evagoras refused; he would only pay it as one king to an-

381 B.C.

other. The negotiations were ruptured for a moment on this point of honour, but a dispute between the satrap and his subordinate general resulted in the removal of Tiribazus, and his successor permitted Evagoras to have his way.

His death. The Salaminian despot had thus gained a moral triumph. He did not survive it many years, and the story of his death is curious. A certain man named Nicocreon formed a plot against his life, and being detected was forced to fly. He left a daughter behind him in Salamis under the care of a faithful eunuch. This servant privily acquainted both Evagoras and his son Pnytagoras with the existence of this young lady and her uncommon beauty, and undertook to conduct them to her bedchamber, each without the knowledge

374 B.C.

of the other. Both kept the assignation and were slain by the eunuch, who thus avenged his master's exile. Another son of Evagoras, named Nicocles, succeeded him, and pursued the same Hellenizing policy. One of the great objects of these enlightened princes was to keep their country in touch with the intellectual and artistic movements of Greece. Nicocles was a student of Greek philosophy, and a generous friend of the essayist, Isocrates, to whose pen we are indebted for much of what we know of the career of Evagoras.

Mace-
donia,
383 B.C.

Towards the close of the almost single-handed struggle of Salamis against Persia, the eyes of Greece were directed to a different quarter of the world. Events were passing in the north of the Aegean, which riveted the attention of Sparta and Athens; their Greek brethren of Cyprus and the Asiatic coast seem to be quite forgotten; for a while the oriental question almost passes out of the pages of Greek history. Yet it was destined that from that very region on the north-west corner of the Aegean should issue the force which should not only reclaim for European influence Cyprus and all the Greek cities of Asia, but bear Greek light into lands of which Agesilaus had never dreamed. That force was being forged in the Macedonian uplands; and some who were children when Isocrates published his Panegyric against the Barbarian lived to see the Barbarian succumb to a Greek power.

It was indeed only indirectly that the southern Greeks had now to concern themselves with their backward brethren of Macedonia. One of the chief obstacles to the development of this country was its constant exposure to the attacks of its Illyrian neighbours; and an Illyrian invasion, supported by domestic disloyalty, compelled king Amyntas—he was the nephew of Perdiccas—to flee

385 B.C.

from his kingdom. Amyntas, soon after his accession, had con-

cluded a close defensive and commercial alliance for fifty years
with the Chalcidian league, which had been formed by Olynthus
and comprised the towns of the Sithonian promontory. It was, as
we observed already, an age of small federations. At the moment of
his retreat Amyntas handed over to the Chalcidians the lower
districts of Macedonia and the cities lying round the Thermaic
gulf. The Macedonian cities readily embraced an union which could
protect them against the Illyrians, and the league spread from the
maritime towns up the country and included even Pella. Perfect
equality and brotherhood between the members was the basis of this
Chalcidian confederacy. All the cities had common laws, common
rights of citizenship, intermarriage and commerce; Olynthus did
not assume a privileged position for herself. The neighbouring
Greek cities were also asked to join, and some of them, Potidaea for
instance, accepted the offer. But it was always a sacrifice for a
Greek city to give up its hereditary laws and surrender any part
of its sovereignty, whatever compensating advantages might be
purchased; and there was consequently more reluctance among the
Chalcidians than among the less developed Macedonians to join
the league. The Olynthians, as their work grew, conceived the idea
of a confederate power which should embrace the whole Chalcidic
peninsula and its neighbourhood. Once this ambition took form,
it became necessary to impose by force their proposition upon those
who declined to accept it freely. The strong cities of Acanthus and
Apollonia resisted, and sent envoys to Sparta to obtain her help.
Moreover Amyntas had recovered his throne, and when the Olynthians refused to abandon the cities which he had handed over to
them, he too looked for aid to Sparta. These appeals directed the
eyes of Greece upon the Chalcidian confederacy. It was the Lacedaemonian policy to oppose all combinations and keep Greece disunited—a policy which was popular, in so far as it appealed to that
innate love of autonomy which made it so difficult to bring about
abiding federal unions in Greece. The ambassadors had little difficulty in persuading the Lacedaemonians and their allies that the
movement in Chalcidice was dangerous to the interests of Sparta,
and should be crushed at the outset; and they argued that the very
liberality of the principles on which it was founded made the league
more attractive and therefore more dangerous. A vote of assistance
to Acanthus and Apollonia was passed, and a small advance force
was immediately sent under Eudamidas. Though unable to meet the
confederate army in the field, this force was sufficient to protect
the cities which had refused to join the league, and it even induced
Potidaea to revolt.

The Chal-
cidian
Con-
federacy.

The citadel of Thebes seized by the Spartans, (383 or) 382 B.C.

The expedition against the Chalcidian Confederacy led unexpectedly to an important incident elsewhere. Phoebidas, the brother of Eudamidas, was to follow with larger forces, and, as the line of march lay through Boeotia, a party in Thebes favourable to Sparta thought to profit by the proximity of Spartan troops for the purpose of a revolution. Leontiadas, the most prominent member of this party, was then one of the polemarchs. He concerted with Phoebidas a plot to seize the Cadmea—the citadel of Thebes—on the day of the Thesmophoria; for on that day the citadel was given up to the use of the women who celebrated the feast. The plot succeeded perfectly; the acropolis was occupied without striking a blow; the oligarchical Council was intimidated by Leontiadas; and his colleague, the other polemarch, Ismenias was arrested. The leading anti-Spartans fled from Thebes, and a government friendly to Sparta was established. This was a great triumph for Sparta, a great satisfaction to Agesilaus, although, as a violation of peace, it caused a moment's embarrassment. Was the government to recognise the action of Phoebidas and profit by it? Spartan hypocrisy compromised the matter; Phoebidas was fined 100,000 drachmae for his indiscretion, and the Cadmea was retained. Then Ismenias was tried by a body of judges representing Sparta and her allies, and was condemned on charges of Medism and executed. That Sparta, after the King's Peace, should condemn a Theban for Medism, was a travesty of justice.

With the fortress of Thebes in her hands, Sparta had a basis for extending her power in central Greece and might regard her supremacy as secured. She restored the city of Plataea, which she had herself destroyed well-nigh fifty years agone, and gathered all the Plataeans who could be found to their old home. But her immediate attention was fixed on the necessity of repressing the dangerous league in the north of Greece, and continuing the measures which had been interrupted by the enterprise of Phoebidas in Boeotia. The popular brother of Agesilaus, Teleutias, was sent to conduct the war; but, although he was aided by Amyntas, and by Derdas, a prince of Upper Macedonia, who supplied good cavalry, it proved no easy matter to make head against the league. In front of the walls of Olynthus, Teleutias sustained a signal defeat and was himself slain. The war was fatal to a king as well as to a king's brother. Agesipolis, who was next sent out at the head of a very large force, caught a fever in the intolerable summer heat. He was carried to the shady grove of the temple of Dionysus at Aphytis, but he died there; and his body, stowed in honey, was brought home for burial. His successor, Polybiadas, was more successful. He

Restoration of Plataea, 382-1 B.C.

(381 B.C.)

(380 B.C.)

forced the Olynthians to sue for peace and dissolve their league. They and all the Greek cities of the peninsula were constrained to join the Lacedaemonian alliance, and the maritime cities of Macedonia were restored to the sway of Amyntas. Thus Sparta put down an attempt to overcome that system of isolation, which placed Greek cities at a great disadvantage, when they had barbarian neighbours. If Sparta had not happened to be so strong at this moment, the Chalcidian league might have grown into a power, which would have considerably modified the development of Macedonia. All that Sparta did, although for a moment it made her power paramount in northern Greece, fell out ultimately to the advancement and profit of Macedon.

Suppression of the Chalcidian League, 379 B.C.

About the same time, the Lacedaemonians were making their heavy hand felt in the Peloponnesus. Soon after the King's Peace they had forced the Phliasians to recall a number of banished aristocrats. Disputes arose about the restoration of confiscated property, and the exiles appealed to Sparta, where they had a zealous supporter in Agesilaus. War was declared; Agesilaus reduced the city of Phlius by blockade, and compelled it to receive a Lacedaemonian garrison for six months, until a commission of one hundred, which he nominated, should have drawn up a new constitution.

Sparta tyrannises over Phlius; blockade, 381-79 B.C.

Thus the Lacedaemonians, in alliance with the tyrant Dionysius and the barbarian Artaxerxes, tyrannised over the Greeks for a space. Some demonstrations were made, some voices of protest were raised, in the name of the Panhellenic cause. At the Olympian festival which was held about two years after the King's Peace, the Athenian orator Lysias warned the assembled Greeks of the dangers which loomed in the east and in the west, from Persia and from Sicily, and uttered his amazement at the policy of Lacedaemon. A magnificent deputation had been sent by Dionysius to this festival, and the inflammatory words, perhaps the direct instigation, of the speaker incited some enthusiastic spectators to attack the gorgeous pavilion of the Syracusan envoys. The outrage was prevented; but the occurrence shows the beginning of that tide of feeling to which Isocrates appealed, four years later, when in his festal oration he denounced the Lacedaemonians, as sacrificing the freedom of Greece to their own interests and treacherously aiding foreigners and tyrants.

(384 B.C.) Olympiac oration of Lysias.

Even Xenophon, the friend of Sparta's king, the admirer of Sparta's institutions, is roused to regretful indignation at Sparta's conduct, and recognises her fall as a just retribution. "The Lacedaemonians, who swore to leave the cities independent, seized the acropolis of Thebes, and they were punished by the very men, single-handed, whom they had wronged, though never before had they been vanquished by any single people. It is a proof that the gods observe men who do irreligious and unhallowed deeds." In this way the pious historian introduces the event which prepared the fall of Sparta and the rise of Thebes.

SECT. 2. ALLIANCE OF ATHENS AND THEBES

The deliverance of Thebes.

The government of Leontiadas and his party at Thebes, maintained by 1500 Lacedaemonians in the citadel, was despotic and cruel, like that of the Thirty at Athens. Fear made the rulers suspicious and oppressive; for they were afraid of the large number of exiles, who had found a refuge at Athens and were awaiting an opportunity to recover their city. Athens was now showing the same goodwill to the fugitives from Thebes which Thebes, when Athens was in a like plight, had shown to Thrasybulus and his fellows. One of the exiles, named Pelopidas, of more than common daring and devotion, resolved to take his life in his hands and found six others to associate in his plans. No open attack was to be thought of; Thebes must be recovered by guile, even as by guile it had been won. There were many in Thebes who were bitter foes of the ruling party, such as Epaminondas, the beloved friend of Pelopidas, but most of them deemed the time unripe for any sudden stroke for freedom. Yet a few were found ready to run the risk; above all, Phyllidas, who was the secretary of the polemarchs and therefore the most useful of confederates, and Charon, a citizen of good estate, who offered his house as a place of hiding for the con-

379-8 B.C. (winter).

spirators. The day on which the two polemarchs, Archias and Philippus, were to go out of office was fixed for the enterprise. On the day before, Pelopidas and his six comrades crossed Cithaeron in the guise of huntsmen, and nearing Thebes at nightfall, mixed with the peasants who were returning from the fields, got them safely within the gates, and found safe hiding in the abode of Charon. The secretary Phyllidas had made ready a great banquet for the following night, to which he had bidden the outgoing polemarchs, tempting them by the promise of introducing them to some high-born and beautiful women, whose love they desired. During the carouse a messenger came with a letter for Archias, and said that it concerned serious affairs. "Business to-morrow," said Archias, placing it under his pillow. On the morrow it was found that this letter disclosed the conspiracy. The polemarchs then called for the women, who were waiting in an adjoining room. Phyllidas said that they declined to appear till all the attendants were dismissed. When no one remained in the dining hall but the polemarchs and a few friends, all flushed with wine, the women entered and sat down beside the lords. They were covered with long veils; and even as they were bidden lift them and reveal their charms, they buried daggers in the bodies of the polemarchs. For they were none other than Pelopidas and his fellows in the guise of women. Then they went and slew in their houses Leontiadas and Hypatas, the two other chief leaders of the party, and set free the political prisoners. When all this was done, Epaminondas and the other patriots, who were unwilling to initiate such deeds themselves, accepted the revolution with joy. When day dawned, an assembly of the people was held in the Agora, and the conspirators were crowned with wreaths. Three of them, including Pelopidas, were appointed polemarchs, and a democratic constitution was established.

The rest of the exiles and a body of Athenian volunteers presently arrived, on the news of the success. The Spartan commander of the Cadmea had sent hastily, on the first alarm, for reinforcements to Thespiae and Plataea, but those that came were charged and repelled, outside the gate. Then in the first flush of success the patriots resolved to storm the Cadmea, strong as the place was. But the labour and the danger were spared them. Amazing as it may seem, the Lacedaemonian harmosts decided to capitulate at once. Two of these commanders were put to death on their return to Sparta, and the third was banished. The chagrin of the ephors and Agesilaus was intense; king Cleombrotus was immediately sent with an army to Boeotia, but accomplished nothing.

Cadmea surrendered.

Athens was formally at peace with Sparta, and was not disposed to break with her, however great may have been the secret joy felt at the events in Boeotia. But the march of the Athenian volunteers to Thebes was an awkward incident, the more so as there were two strategi among them. Lacedaemonian envoys arrived to demand explanation and satisfaction; and their statements were reinforced by the neighbourhood of the army of king Cleombrotus. There was indeed nothing to be said for the conduct of the two strategi. They had abused their position and brought their city into danger and embarrassment. We can only approve the sentence of the Athenians, which executed one and banished the other.

Athens disowns the action of the Athenian volunteers, and punishes the generals.

But if these Athenian generals were indiscreet, it was as nothing beside the indiscretion of a Lacedaemonian commander, which now precipitated the breach between the two states. A not ignoble sympathy might have been pleaded by the two Athenians; but no excuse could be urged for the rash enterprise of the Spartan harmost

The raid of Sphodrias.

of Thespiae, who aspired to be a second Phoebidas. His name was Sphodrias, and he conceived the plan of making a night march to Athens and surprising Piraeus on the landside. To seize Piraeus, the seat of Athenian merchandise, would be a compensation for the loss of Thebes. But the plan was, if not ill-considered, at least ill carried out. Day dawned when he had hardly passed Eleusis; and there was nothing to do but to turn back. He retreated, laying waste the districts through which he passed.

Great wrath was kindled in Athens by this unprovoked deed of hostility. The envoys had not yet gone; they were immediately thrown into prison, but escaped by declaring that the Spartan government was not responsible for the raid, and would speedily prove its innocence by the condemnation of Sphodrias. The assurance was belied; Sphodrias was not condemned. His son and the son of Agesilaus were lovers, and the king's influence saved him. Agesilaus is reported to have said: "Sphodrias is guilty, of course; but it is a hard thing to put to death a man who, as child, stripling, and man, lived a life of perfect honour; for Sparta needeth such soldiers." This miscarriage of justice was a grave mistake of policy; and the high-handed insolence of the Spartan oligarchs was set in a more glaring light by contrast with the fair-mindedness which the Athenian people had displayed in promptly punishing its own generals for a similar though certainly less heinous act. The Athenian generals had at least not invaded Lacedaemonian territory. It was debated at the time, and has been debated since, whether Sphodrias acted wholly of his own accord; some thought that the suggestion came from king Cleombrotus, and the theory was started that the Thebans were the prime instigators—an unlikely theory, which was evidently based on the fact that Thebes was the only gainer by the raid. It seems most probable that the private ambition of Sphodrias, who thought he had a chance of emulating Phoebidas, was alone responsible.

Alliance of Athens with Thebes, 378 B.C.

The raid and acquittal of Sphodrias drove Athens, against her will, into war with Sparta and alliance with Thebes; it stirred her for a while to leave her rôle of neutral spectator and assume that of an active belligerent. For the next six years, Athens and Sparta are at war, though such a war was contrary to the interests of both states, but especially to the interests of Sparta.

SECT. 3. THE SECOND ATHENIAN LEAGUE AND THE THEBAN REFORMS

The raid of Sphodrias was the direct occasion of the Second Athenian Confederacy. For many years back, ever since the battle of Cnidus, Athens had been gradually forming bonds of alliance with various states in Thrace, the Aegean, and the coast of Asia Minor. The breach with Sparta induced her now to gather together these separate connexions into a common league, with the express object of protecting the independence of the Greek states against the oppression of Sparta. When men thought of the old Confederacy of Delos, they might fear that the second Athenian league would be soon converted into a second Athenian empire. But Athens anticipated such alarms by establishing the confederacy on a different system, which provided safeguards against the dangers of Athenian preponderance and Athenian encroachment. In the archonship of Nausinicus, Aristoteles of the deme of Marathon proposed in the Assembly a decree which embodied the principles of the league. The sway of Persia over the Greeks of Asia was explicitly recognised, so that the field of operations was to be European Greece and the Islands. The league, which was purely defensive, was constituted in two parts, Athens on one side, her allies on the other. The allies had their own synedrion or congress which met in Athens, but in which Athens had no part. Both the synedrion of the Confederates and the Athenian Assembly had the right of initiating measures, but no measure passed by either body was valid until it had been approved by the other body also. While this system gave Athens a weight and dignity equal to that of all her allies together, it secured for the allies an independence which they had not possessed under the old league, and they had the right of absolute veto on any Athenian proposal which they disliked. It was necessary for the members of the league to form a federal fund; their payments were called *syntaxeis* ("contributions"), and the word *phoros* ("tribute"), which had odious memories connected with the confederacy of Delos, was avoided. It was especially enacted that the practice of Athenian outsettling in the lands of the allies, which had formerly helped and supported the Athenian empire, was not to be permitted. No Athenian was to acquire home or farm, "by purchase or mortgage, or any other means whatever," in the territory of any of the confederates. But the administration of the federal fund and the leadership of the federal army were in the hands of Athens.

Good fortune has preserved to us the original stone, shattered in about twenty pieces, with the decree which founded the confederacy, and we find the purpose of the league definitely declared: "To force the Lacedaemonians to allow the Greeks to enjoy peace in freedom and independence, with their lands unviolated." It was no doubt Callistratus, the ablest statesman and orator of the day, who did most to make the new scheme a success; but, though he

Second
Athenian
Con-
federacy.

378-7 B.C.

Calli-
stratus.

may be called the Aristides of the Second Confederacy, Callistratus certainly did not mean the combination against Sparta as seriously as Aristides meant the combination against Persia. The policy which Callistratus generally pursued was based on harmony with Sparta and antagonism to Thebes. It is sometimes said that at this period there were two parties contending for the guidance of the foreign policy of Athens, one friendly and the other obstinately hostile to Boeotia. But, though Thebes had some friends at Athens, we have no good grounds for speaking of a Theban or Boeotian party. It might be truer to say that there was an anti-Spartan faction, which might often seek a Theban alliance as a means to an end. At this juncture Callistratus was astute enough to see not only that it would be useless to oppose the feeling against Sparta, but also that an opportunity which might never recur was offered for increasing the power of Athens. He therefore abandoned for the time his permanent policy, and threw himself heartily into a scheme of which the most remarkable feature was union with Thebes.

The chief cities which first joined the new league were Chios, Byzantium, Mytilene, Methymna, and Rhodes; then most of the towns of Euboea joined, and, what was most important and wonderful, Thebes enrolled her name in the list of the confederates. The Thracian cities, and several other states, including Corcyra, Jason the despot of Pherae in Thessaly, and Alcetas a prince of Epirus, presently brought up the whole tale of members to about seventy. But though the league, drawn on such liberal lines, evoked some enthusiasm at first, and the adhesion of Thebes gave its inauguration a certain *éclat*, it had no vital elements of growth or permanence, and never attained high political importance. The fact is, that the true interest of Athens, as Callistratus knew, was peace with Sparta, and was consequently repugnant to the avowed object of the confederacy. Hence the confederacy was doomed either to fall asunder, or to become the tool of other designs of Athens as soon as Sparta had been taught a lesson and the more abiding interest of Athens could safely assert itself again over the temporary expedient of an unnatural alliance with Thebes.

It was a moment at which the chief Greek states were setting their houses in order. Thebes was making herself ready and dight for a new career; Sparta was remodelling her league,[1] and Athens her finances. A property tax, such as had first been introduced in the third year of the Peloponnesian war, was revived, and a new

Eisphora or property-tax at Athens. $\frac{1}{500}$ of capital.

---

[1] In nine divisions:—1, 2, Arcadia; 3, Elis; 4, Achaea; 5, Corinth and Megara; 6, Sicyon, Phlius, the Acte of Argolis; 7, Acarnania; 8, Phocis, Locris; 9, Olynthus and other Thracian cities.

assessment of property was made. One-fifth of the actual capital of each citizen was inscribed in the register, and the tax (probably about one per cent) was imposed on this fraction, not on the whole capital. The revenue from this impost seems to have amounted annually to about sixty talents. For the purpose of levying the tax the whole body of burghers was divided into 20 symmories, and the richest citizens in each symmory were responsible to the treasury for the total sum due on the properties of all the citizens who belonged to it. By this means the State relieved itself from the friction which is generally caused by the collection of direct imposts, and the revenue accruing from the tax was realised more promptly and easily than if the government had to deal immediately with the individual burghers. Thus Athens tried the novel experiment of a system of joint responsibility, such as in later days was to be introduced and established in an empire of which Athens was only an insignificant town.

£14,400.

(Roman Empire.)

At Thebes the attention of the government was chiefly bestowed on military affairs. A ditch was dug and a rampart raised round part of the Theban territory as a defence against the inevitable Lacedaemonian invasions. But this precaution was of small moment in comparison with the creation of a new troop of 300 hoplites, all chosen young men of the noblest families, who had proved their eminent strength and endurance in a long training in the wrestling school. Each man had his best friend beside him; so that the Sacred Band, as it was called, consisted of 150 pairs of comrades, prepared to fight and fall together. In battle, it was to stand in front of the other hoplites. At the same time, we may be sure, much was done to improve the army in other points. Opportunely for Thebes there had arisen, to guide her to success when her chance came, a man of rare ability, in whom nature seemed to have united the best features of Greek character and discarded the defects. This was Epaminondas, the friend of Pelopidas. He was a modest, unambitious man, who in other circumstances would probably have remained in obscurity, unobtrusively fulfilling the duties of a citizen and soldier. But the revolution stimulated his patriotism and lured him into the field of public affairs, where his eminent capacity, gradually revealing itself, made him, before eight years had passed, the most influential man in his city. He had devoted as much time to musical as to gymnastic training; unlike most of his countrymen, he could play the lyre as well as the Theban flute; and he had a genuine interest in philosophical speculation. A Tarentine friend, who had been much in his company, asseverated that he never met a man who knew more and talked less than Epaminondas. But the

Sacred Lochos.

Epaminondas.

Theban statesman could speak when he chose, or when the need demanded; and his eloquence was extremely impressive. Exceptional in his indifference to the prizes of ambition, he was also exceptional in his indifference to money, and he died poor. Not less remarkable was his lack of that party spirit, which led to so many crimes in Greece. He could not share in strong political hatred or lust for revenge; and we have already seen that his repugnance to domestic bloodshed kept him from taking a part in the fortunate conspiracy of Pelopidas.

Sect. 4. The Battle of Naxos and the Peace of Callias

578-1 B.C.

The following eight years are marked by a successful defensive war of Thebes against Spartan invasions; by a decrease of Spartan prestige; by the extension of the Theban supremacy over the rest of Boeotia. At the same time, Athens prosecutes a naval war against the Lacedaemonian Confederacy, and gains considerable successes; but the strain on her resources which this war entails, and a growing jealousy of Thebes, combine to induce her to come to terms with Sparta.

Boeotia invaded by Agesilaus, 378, 377 B.C. Defeat and death of Phoebidas, 377 B.C. Cleombrotus marches to Cithaeron, 373 B.C.

Two invasions of Boeotia conducted by Agesilaus himself in successive summers achieved nothing; and the Thebans had the satisfaction of slaying Phoebidas, who had won his fame by the capture of their acropolis. The other king, Cleombrotus, did even less than Agesilaus, for he found the passes of Cithaeron held by the foes, and could not enter Boeotia. After this, the Thebans had time to attack the Boeotian cities and drive out the Spartan garrisons; so that by the end of four years the Boeotian confederacy once more extended over all Boeotia, the local governments being overthrown and the foreign harmosts expelled. Only in the extreme west, in Orchomenus and Chaeronea, were the Lacedaemonians able to hold their ground. In the course of this resuscitation of the Boeotian league one notable exploit was wrought by Pelopidas and the Sacred Band. At Tegyra, on the road from Orchomenus to Locris, in a narrow pass, the Thebans routed twice as many Lacedaemonian troops, and slew both the Spartan generals. As in the case of all Spartan defeats, the moral effect was of far greater import than the actual loss in the field. Perhaps it was about this time that Athens won back Oropus, which had been lost to her in the year of the Four Hundred.

Battle of Naxos, 376 (September).

In the meantime there had been war too on the seas. When the invasions of Boeotia fell out so badly, Sparta had bethought herself of equipping a naval armament to cut off the corn ships which bore grain to Attica from the Euxine. The ships reached Geraestus, the south point of Euboea; but a fleet of sixty galleys under the Spartan Pollis hindered them from rounding the Cape of Sunium, and Athens was menaced with famine. Eighty triremes were speedily fitted out and sent forth from the Piraeus, under the command of Chabrias, to recover the mastery of the sea. Chabrias sailed to Naxos, which had seized this moment to desert the Athenian Confederacy, and beleaguered the city. Pollis hurried to the rescue, and a battle was fought in the sound between Paros and Naxos. The Athenians gained a complete victory, and only eleven of the Lacedaemonian vessels escaped. Even these would have been disabled, had not Chabrias desisted from the action, for the purpose of saving some of his own men who were overboard or in disabled ships. The lesson which the Athenian people taught its generals after the battle of Arginusae had not been forgotten. Though the battle of Naxos had not the important consequences of the battle of Cnidus, it was more gratifying to Athens. The Cnidian victory had been won indeed under the command of an Athenian, but by Persian men and ships; the victory gained by Chabrias was entirely Athenian. It led immediately to an enlargement of the Confederacy. The triumphant fleet sailed round the Aegean, enrolled seventeen new cities, and collected a large sum of money. Athens had also to reassert her authority at Delos. For the inhabitants of the island who chafed at the administration of their temple by the Athenian *amphictiones,* as the sacred overseers were entitled, had attempted, doubtless with Lacedaemonian help, to recover control of the sanctuary. An interesting entry in the Delian accounts of these years, preserved on a stone, tells how seven ringleaders of the movement were punished by fines and perpetual banishment "for having led the amphictiones forth from the temple and beaten them."

Insurrectionary movement at Delos, 376 B.C.

Next year, the fleet was sent to sail round the Peloponnesus under the command of Timotheus, son of Conon. This circumnavigation of the Peloponnesus was an assertion by Athens that her naval power was once more dominant; it was intended to frighten Sparta, to extend Athenian influence in western Greece, and to act in the Corinthian Gulf, in case the Spartans tried to throw an army into Boeotia by the port of Creusis. The islands of Corcyra and Cephallenia, the king of the Molossi, some of the Acarnanians, were won over to the Athenian alliance by the discreet policy of Timotheus, who also gained a trifling victory over some hostile ships. But there was a darker side to this triumphant expedition. The cost of the war was proving to be greater than Athens could well bear, and Timotheus failed to obtain from home the money requisite to pay

376 B.C. Expedition of Timotheus

his seamen. In this strait, he was obliged to ask each trierarch to advance seven minae for the payment of his crew; and Athens herself sent a request to Thebes for some contribution towards the expense of the naval operations, on the ground that the enterprise of Timotheus had been undertaken partly at Theban instigation. The refusal of this demand, along with a growing jealousy of Theban success, and the somewhat grave financial difficulties of the moment, combined to dispose Athens towards peace with Sparta; and this was in fact her wisest policy. Negotiations were opened and carried to a successful issue; but the peace was no sooner made than it was broken. For Timotheus, who was ordered to return home from Corcyra and reluctantly obeyed, halted at Zacynthus on his way, landed some Zacynthian exiles who were with him, and fortified a post for them on the island.[2] The Zacynthians straightway complained to Sparta; Sparta demanded satisfaction from Athens; and when this was refused, the incident was treated as a breach of contract and the war was resumed.

The first object of Sparta was to regain her power in the west, and undo the work of Timotheus. The best of the winnings of that general had been Corcyra, and Corcyra once more became the scene of a "Peloponnesian" war. With the help of their confederates, including Corinth, the Lacedaemonians launched an armament of sixty ships, conveying 1500 mercenary hoplites, to gain possession of the island; and at the same time a message was dispatched to Dionysius of Syracuse requesting his aid, on the ground that Sicily had her interests in Corcyraean politics. The armament was commanded by the Spartan Mnasippus. He drove the Corcyraean fleet into the harbour, which he blocked with his own ships, and he invested the city by land, so that the supplies of the inhabitants were cut off. The island was a rich prize for the soldiers to whose depredations it was now given over. The tillage was goodly, the crofts and farmhouses exceeding fair; and so plentiful was the wine that the troopers would drink none that was not of the finest sort. Urgent messages were sent to Athens by the Corcyraeans, who soon began to feel the pinch of famine. So great was the misery that slaves were cast out of the gates; even some citizens deserted, but were whipped back to the walls by the Lacedaemonian commander. But he deeming that he had the city in his hands grew careless in his confidence; and from the watch-towers on their walls the besieged could observe that the watch was sometimes relaxed. An

---

[2] The settlement of democratic exiles was enrolled in the Athenian Confederacy; and "the people of the Zacynthians at Nêllon" appears as the last of the additions to the list of members on the Confederacy stone.

(£28.)

Peace, 374

Lacedaemonian attack on Corcyra, 374-3 B.C.

opportune moment was seized for a sally, which resulted in a completer success than they looked for. The professional soldiers, who had not been paid and detested their general, showed no zeal in withstanding the hot onslaught of the desperate men who poured forth from the gates. Mnasippus was slain, and the besiegers fell back to their camp. The beleaguerment was thus broken up, and the Corcyraeans were safe until the coming of the expected help from Athens. But they were delivered from all constraint even before that tardy help came; for the Lacedaemonians evacuated the island almost immediately after the defeat. Then at last the Athenian fleet sailed into the roads of Corcyra.

It was from no want of goodwill on the part of the Athenian people that the help had not come in time to save Corcyra much of the misery which she had suffered. A tale hangs by the delay of the fleet. On the first appeal, it was resolved to send sixty ships at once, and 600 peltasts were sent in advance and successfully introduced into the city. It was befitting that Timotheus should return to the scene of his former achievements, and the command of the fleet was entrusted to him. He found himself in an awkward position, owing to one of the gravest defects in the machinery of Athenian administration. The people had voted a certain measure, appointing him to carry it out; but had omitted to vote or consider the necessary ways and means. It consequently devolved upon Timotheus to find the men and the money. For this purpose he cruised with some of his ships in the Northern Aegean, visiting Thessaly, Macedonia, and Thrace, while the main part of the fleet awaited his return at the island of Calauria. But meanwhile the need of Corcyra was sore, and more pressing messengers were arriving in Athens. The long tarrying of the general excited public indignation; his appointment was annulled; and Iphicrates, in conjunction with Chabrias and Callistratus, was charged to sail at once to Corcyra.

Callistratus was the most eloquent orator of the day. Chabrias, a tried soldier who had served under Cypriote and Egyptian kings, we have already met as the victor of Naxos. Iphicrates, who had come to the front by his boldness and success in the Corinthian war, had for the last fifteen years served as a captain of peltasts under the princes of Thrace, and had married a daughter of king Cotys. A comic poet gives a picturesque description of his barbaric wedding. In the market-place a plentiful feast is set out for a throng of wild-haired Thracians. There are immense brazen cauldrons of broth, and the king girding himself up, serves it with his own hands in a golden basin. Then the wine and water are tempered in

Difficulties and delays of Timotheus.

Iphicrates in Thrace

(c. 378 B.C.)

the mixing-bowls, and the king goes around tasting each bowl, until he is the first drunk. But an adventurous life among the "butter-eating" barbarians does not seem to have wholly satisfied Iphicrates. He served the King of Persia in Egypt and then returned to Athens, and this expedition to Corcyra seems to have been his first service after his return. It was well and capably performed. The people in their excitement gave him a freer hand than they had given to Timotheus. He was able to put hard pressure on the trierarchs; he was allowed to impress seamen, and to make use of the galleys which guarded the Attic coast, and even the two sacred vessels, the *Salaminia* and *Paralus*. By these unusual efforts a fleet of seventy triremes was put together, but before it was quite ready to sail Timotheus returned. His cruise had been successful in raising money and men, and adding new members to the Confederacy; but it was thought that neither necessity nor success could excuse the singular inopportuneness of the delay. Ill-luck seemed to wait upon Timotheus. The funds which he brought back proved insufficient to meet the obligations which they ought to have defrayed, and a fraud was suspected. Iphicrates and Callistratus, his political rivals, lodged an indictment against him, but as they had to sail immediately to the west, the trial was postponed till the autumn.

On his way out Iphicrates learned the news of the deliverance of Corcyra, so that he was able to send back those ships whose true duty was the defence of Attica. But there was still work to be done. The appeal which the Lacedaemonians sent to the tyrant Dionysius had not been in vain, and ten Syracusan triremes were even then approaching Corcyra. They stopped at a point in the north of the island, that the crews might rest after the long voyage; and there Iphicrates whose scouts had watched for their approach captured them, all but one vessel. This prize raised the welcome sum of sixty talents, but it was not long before Iphicrates, even as Timotheus, found himself embarrassed for want of money. Callistratus went back to Athens, promising to persuade the people either to keep the fleet regularly paid or to make peace. Meanwhile the crews of Iphicrates obtained subsistence by labour on the Corcyraean farms.

If Corcyra had fallen, there can be little question that Timotheus would have been sacrificed to the displeasure of the Athenian people. But the good tidings from the west restored the public good-humour, and this was fortunate for the discredited general. His trial came on towards the end of the year. His military treasurer was tried at the same time, found guilty of malversation, and condemned to death. But Timotheus himself was acquitted. He had

Margin notes:

(375-4 B.C.)

Return of Timotheus.

372 B.C. Capture of the reinforcements from Syracuse.

Trial of Timotheus, 373 (Nov.).

indeed unusually powerful support. Two foreign monarchs had condescended to come to Athens to bear testimony in his favour, the Epirot king Alcetas, and Jason the despot of Thessalian Pherae. It was through Timotheus that these potentates had joined the Athenian league; and it was through them that he had been able to transport across Thessaly and Epirus the 600 peltasts who had been sent in advance to Corcyra. The interest of Jason—of whom more will have to be said presently—was particularly effective. Timotheus entertained these distinguished guests in his house in Piraeus, but he was obliged to borrow bedding, two silver bowls, and other things from his rich neighbour, the banker Pasion, in order to lodge them suitably. Though acquitted, Timotheus was discredited in public opinion, and he soon left Athens to take service in Egypt under the Great King.

Sparta had lost heart at the decisive check which she had received in Corcyra, and the discouragement was increased by a series of terrible earthquakes, in which Poseidon seemed to declare his wrath. She was therefore disposed to peace, and she thought to bring peace about, as before, through the mediation of Persia. Antalcidas was once more sent up to the Persian court. But this intervention from without was not really needed. Athens, uneasy under the burdens of the war and feeling rather jealousy of Thebes than bitterness against Sparta, was also well inclined to peace, and the influential orator Callistratus made it the object of his policy. The recent aggressions of Thebes against the Phocians, who were old allies of Athens, tended to estrange the two cities; and to this was added the treatment of that unfortunate little mountain burg, Plataea, by her Theban enemies. Restored Plataea had perforce been enrolled in the Boeotian confederacy, but she was secretly scheming for annexation to Attica. Suspecting these plots, Thebes determined to forestall them, and a small Theban force, surprising the town one day when the men were in the fields, took possession of it and drove all the Plataeans forth from Plataean soil. Many of the people, thus bereft of land and city, found a refuge at Athens; where the publicist Isocrates took up their cause and wrote his *Plataeic Discourse,* a denunciation of Thebes. This incident definitely, though not formally, loosened the bonds between the two northern powers.

The overtures came from Athens and her Confederacy. When the Lacedaemonian allies met at Sparta in spring, three Athenian envoys appeared at the congress. Of these the chief spokesman was Callistratus, and one of his associates was Callias, Torchbearer of the Eleusinian Mysteries, who had also worked to bring about the

Marginal notes:

Plataea seized by Thebes.

371 B.C. Peace of Callias

abortive peace three years before. Thebes likewise sent ambassadors, one of whom was Epaminondas. The basis of the peace which was now concluded was the principle which had been affirmed by the King's Peace, the principle of the autonomy of every Hellenic city. The Athenian and Lacedaemonian Confederacies were thus both rendered invalid. No compulsion could be exercised on any city to fulfil engagements as member of a league. Cities might co-operate with each other freely so far as they chose, but no obligation could be contracted or enforced. Yet while Athens and Sparta resigned empire, they mutually agreed to recognise each other's predominance, that of Athens by sea, that of Sparta on land—a predominance which must never be asserted by aggression and must always be consistent with the universal autonomy.

The Boeotian question.

The question immediately arose whether the Boeotian League was condemned by this doctrine of universal autonomy. Sparta and Athens, of course, intended to condemn it. But it might be pleaded that the Confederacy of Boeotian cities under the presidency of Thebes was not on the same footing as the Confederacies which had been formed, for temporary political purposes, without any historical or geographical basis of union, under the presidencies of Athens and Sparta. It might be contended that Boeotia was a geographical unity, like Attica and Laconia, and had a title to political unity, too, especially as the League was an ancient institution. The question came to the issue when it was the turn of Thebes to take the oath. Her representative Epaminondas claimed to take it on behalf of the Boeotian cities; and Thebes, represented by him, was not so easily cowed as when she made the same claim at the conclusion of the King's Peace. He seems to have developed the view that Boeotia was to be compared to Laconia, not to the Lacedaemonian Confederacy; and when Agesilaus asked him,

Thebes excluded.

curtly and angrily: "Will you leave each of the Boeotian towns independent?" he retorted: "Will *you* leave each of the Laconian towns independent?" The name of Thebes was thereupon struck out of the treaty.

There was an argument as well as a sting in this retort of Epaminondas. The argument was: Sparta has no more right to interfere in the internal affairs of Boeotia than we have to interfere in the domestic administration of Laconia; Laconia, Boeotia, Attica, each represents a distinct kind of constitution, and each constitution is justified; the union of Boeotia in a federation is as natural as the union of Attica in a single city, as legitimate as the union of Laconia in its subjection to the Spartan oligarchy. The union of Boeotia, like the union of Laconia, could not have been realised and could not be maintained without the perpetration of outrages upon the freewill of some communities. Yet it is hardly legitimate for one state to say to another: "We have committed certain acts of violence, but you must not interfere; for at a remote period of history which none of us remember, your ancestors used even more high-handed methods for similar purposes, and you now maintain what they established." But the tyrannical method by which Laconia was governed was certainly a weak point in the Spartan armour; and the reply of Epaminondas may have well set Greece thinking over a question of political science. Setting aside the arguments of diplomacy, the point of the situation was this: Thebes could never become a strong power, the rival of Sparta or of Athens, except at the head of an united Boeotia, and it was the interest of Athens and Sparta to hinder her from becoming such a power.

So far as the two chief contracting parties were concerned, this bargain—which is often called the "Peace of Callias"—put an end to a war which was contrary to the best interests of both. They were both partly to blame, but Sparta was far more to blame than her old rival. Her witless policy in overlooking the raid of Sphodrias had caused the war; for it left to Athens no alternative but hostility. At the end of four years, they seemed to have come to their senses; they made peace, but they were stupid enough to allow the incident of Zacynthus to annul the bargain. Three more years of fighting were required to restore their wits. But, although Athens was financially exhausted by her military efforts, the war had brought its compensations to her. The victory of Naxos, the circumnavigation of the Peloponnesus and revival of her influence in Western Greece, were achievements which indisputably proved that Athens was once more a first-rate Hellenic power, the peer of Sparta; and this fact was fully acknowledged in the Peace of Callias. But the true policy of Athens—from which the raid of Sphodrias had forced her—was that of a watchful spectator; and this policy she now resumes, though only for a brief space, leaving Sparta and Thebes in the arena. As for Sparta, she had lost as much as Athens had gained; the defeat of Naxos, the defeat of Tegyra, the failure at Corcyra, had dimmed her prestige. After the King's Peace, she had begun her second attempt to dominate Greece; her failure is confessed by the Peace of Callias. If a third attempt was to be successful, it was obvious that it must begin by the subjugation of Thebes.

Positions of Athens and Sparta.

SECT. 5. ATHENS UNDER THE RESTORED DEMOCRACY

When Pericles declared that Athens was the school of Greece, this was rather his ideal of what she should be than a statement of a reality. It would have surprised him to learn that, when imperial Athens fell from her throne, his ideal would be fulfilled. This was what actually happened. It was not until Athens lost her empire that she began to exert a great decisive influence on Greek thought and civilisation. This influence was partly exerted by the establishment of schools in the strict sense—the literary school of Isocrates and the philosophical school of Plato—which attracted to Athens men from all quarters of the Hellenic world. But the increase in the intellectual influence of Athens was largely owing to the fact that she was becoming herself more receptive of influence from without. She was becoming Hellenic as well as Athenian; she was beginning to become even something more than Hellenic. This tendency towards cosmopolitanism had been promoted by philosophical speculation, which rises above national distinctions; and it is manifested variously in the pan-Hellenism of Isocrates, in the attitude of such different men as Plato and Xenophon towards Athens, in the increasing number of foreign religious worships established at Athens or Piraeus, in a general decline of local patriotism, and in many other ways. There was perhaps no institution which had a wider influence in educating Greek thought in the fourth century than the theatre; its importance in city life was recognised by practical statesmen. It was therefore a matter of the utmost moment that the old Athenian comedy, turning mainly on local politics, ceased to be written, and a new school of comic poets arose who dealt with subjects of general human interest. Here Athens had a most effectual instrument for spreading ideas. And the tragedies of the fourth century, though as literature they were of less note and consequence than the comedies, were not less significant of the spirit of the time. They were all dominated by the influence of Euripides, the great teacher of rationalism, the daring critic of all established institutions and beliefs. And the comic poets were also under his spell.

Influence of Athens on Greece.

It can easily be seen that the cultivation of these wider sympathies was connected with the growth of what is commonly called "individualism." By this it is meant that the individual citizen no longer looks at the outside world through the medium of his city, but regards it directly, as it were, with his own eyes and in its bearings on him individually. He is no longer content to express his

Growth of individualism.

religious feelings, simply as one member of the state, in the common usages of the state religion, but seeks to enter into an immediate personal relation with the supernatural world. And since his own life has thus become for him something independent of the city, his attitude to the city itself is transformed. The citizen of Athens has become a citizen of the world. His duty to his country may conflict with his duty to himself as a man; and thus patriotism ceases to be unconditionally the highest virtue. Again, men begin to put to themselves, more or less explicitly, the question, whether the state is not made for the individual and not the individual for the state, —a complete reversal of the old unquestioning submission to the authority of the social organism. It followed that greater demands were made upon the state by the citizen for his own private welfare; and that the citizen, feeling himself tied by no indissoluble bond to his country, was readier than formerly to seek his fortune elsewhere. Thus we find, in the single field of military service, Athenian officers acting independently of their country, in the pay of foreign powers, whenever it suited them—Conon, Xenophon, Iphicrates, Chabrias, and others.

A vivid exaggerated description of this spirit has been drawn by Plato in one of his famous contributions to political science, the *Republic*. "The horses and asses," he says "have a way of marching along with all the rights and dignities of freemen; and they will run at anybody whom they meet in the street if he does not leave the road clear for them: and all things are just ready to burst with liberty." [3] When he describes the excessive freedom of democracy, he is dealing with the growth of individualism, as a result of freedom in its constitutional sense; but his argument that individualism is the fatal fruit of a democratic constitution rests largely on the double sense of the word "freedom." The notable thing is that no man did more to promote the tendencies which are here deplored by Plato than Plato himself and his fellow philosophers. If any single man could be held responsible for the inevitable growth of individualism, it would be perhaps Euripides; [4] but assuredly, next to Euripides, it would be Plato's revered master, Socrates, the son of Sophroniscus.

When the history of Greece was being directed by Pericles and Cleon, Nicias and Lysander, men little dreamed either at Athens or elsewhere that the interests of the world were far more deeply con-

Socrates, the sculptor, son of Sophroniscus (born c. 469 B.C.).

[3] Transl. Jowett.
[4] Euripides first; for, though he did not exert nearly as great influence on the world as Socrates, he reached a larger public in his own and the two next generations.

cerned in the doings of one eccentric Athenian who held aloof from public affairs. The work of Pericles and Lysander affected a few generations in a small portion of the globe; but the spirit of that eccentric Athenian was to lay an impress, indelible for ever, upon the thought of mankind. The ideas which we owe to Socrates are now so organically a part of the mind of civilised men, so familiar and commonplace, that it is hard to appreciate the intellectual

His spirit. power which was required to originate them. Socrates was the first champion of the supremacy of the intellect as a court from which there is no appeal; he was the first to insist, without modification or compromise, that a man must order his life by the guidance of his own intellect, without any regard for mandates of external authority or for the impulses of emotion, unless his intellectual approves. Socrates was thus a rebel against authority as such; and he shrank from no consequences. He did not hesitate to show his companions that an old man has no title to respect because he is old, unless he is also wise; or that an ignorant parent has no claim to obedience on the mere account of the parental relation. Knowledge and veracity, the absolute sovereignty of the understanding, regardless of consequences, regardless of all prejudices connected with family or city—this was the ideal of Socrates, consistently and uncompromisingly followed.

His method. But men using their intellects often come to different conclusions. The command issued by an authority which Socrates may reject has been, directly or ultimately, the result of some mental process. It is manifest that we require a standard of truth and an explanation of the causes of error. The solution of Socrates is, briefly, this. When we make a judgment, we compare two ideas; and in order to do so correctly it is obvious that these ideas must be clear and distinct; error arises from comparing ideas that are un-

Definitions. defined and vague. Definition was thus the essential point—and it was an essential novelty—in the Socratic method for arriving at truth. Its necessity is a commonplace now; and we have rather to guard against its dangers.

Founder of utilitarianism. The application of this method to ethics was the chief occupation of Socrates, for the interests of human life and its perplexities entirely absorbed him. In the history of ethics his position is supreme; he was the founder of utilitarianism. He arrived at the doctrine by analysing the notion of "good"; the result of his analysis was that "the good is the useful." Closely connected was the principle that virtue is happiness, and this was the basis of the famous Socratic paradox that no man willingly does wrong, but only through ignorance, for there is no man who would not will his own happiness. It is easy to point out the errors of this startling statement; it is perhaps easier to forget how much wrong-doing is due to the confused thinking of clouded brains and the ignorance of untrained minds.

The man who had no respect for authority was not likely to except the gods from the range of his criticism; and the popular religion could not sustain examination. Socrates was as little orthodox as Anaxagoras and other "impious" philosophers; but he made no new departure in the field of theology. He doubtless believed in the existence of a God; but as to the nature of the divine principle he was probably what we call an "agnostic," as he certainly was in regard to the immortality of the soul.

Attitude to theology

Socrates then was the originator of a new logical method, the founder of utilitarianism, and, above all, the unsparing critic of all things in heaven and earth—or rather on earth only, for he disdained things in heaven as uninteresting and irrelevant,—a fearless critic, undeterred by any feeling of piety or prejudice. He never wrote anything, he only conversed. But he conversed with the ablest young men of the day who were destined afterwards to become immortal themselves as thinkers; he communicated to them —to Plato, to Aristippus, to Euclides—his own spirit of scepticism and criticism; he imbued them with intellectual courage and intellectual freedom. He never preached, he only discussed; that was the Socratic method—dialectic or the conversational method. He did not teach, for he professed to have no knowledge; he would only confess that he was exceptional in knowing that he knew nothing: this was the Socratic irony. He went about showing that most popular notions, as soon as they are tested, prove to be inconsistent and untenable; he wished to convince every man he met that his convictions would not stand examination. We can easily conceive how stimulating this was to the young men, and how extremely irritating to the old. Haunting the market-places and the gymnasia Socrates was always ready to entrap men of all ages and ranks into argument, and many a grudge was owed him by reverend and conceited seniors, whose foggy minds he exposed to ridicule by means of his prudent interrogations. Though no man ever taught more effectually than Socrates, he was not a teacher, he had no course of lectures to give, and therefore he took no fee. Herein lay his distinction from the sophists, to whom by his speculation, his scepticism, his mastery of argument, his influence over young men, he naturally belongs, and with whom he was generally classed. He soon became a notorious figure in the streets of Athens; nature had marked him out among other men by his grotesque satyr-like face.

His scepticism and irony.

Criticism
of demo-
cracy.

Though he was the child of democracy, born to a heritage of freedom in a city where the right of free discussion was unrestrained, the sacred name of democracy was not more sheltered than anything else from the criticism of Socrates. He railed, for instance, at the system of choosing magistrates by lot, one of the protections of democracy at Athens. He was unpopular with the mass, for he was an enemy of shams and ignorance and superstition. Honest democrats of the type of Thrasybulus and Anytus, who did their duty but had no desire to probe its foundations, regarded him as a dangerous freethinker who spent his life in diffusing ideas subversive of the social order. They might point to the ablest of the young men who had kept company with him, and say: "Behold the fruits of his conversation! Look at Alcibiades, his favourite companion, who has done more than any other man to ruin his country. Look at Critias, who, next to Alcibiades, has wrought the deepest harm to Athens; who, brought up in the Socratic circle, first wrote a book against democracy, then visited Thessaly and stirred up the serfs against their masters, and finally, returning here, inaugurated the reign of terror. Look, on the other hand, at Plato, an able young man, whom the taste for idle speculation, infused by Socrates, has seduced from the service of his country. Or look at Xenophon, who, instead of serving Athens, has gone to serve her enemies. Truly Socrates and his propaganda have done little good to the Athenian state." However unjust any particular instance might seem, it is easy to understand how considerations of this kind would lead many practical unspeculative men to look upon Socrates and his ways with little favour. And from their point of view, they were perfectly right. His spirit, and the ideas that he made current, were an insidious menace to the cohesion of the social fabric, in which there was not a stone or a joint that he did not question. In other words, he was the active apostle of individualism, which led in its further development to the subversion of that local patriotism which had inspired the cities of Greece in her days of greatness.

His
teaching
suspected
and un-
popular.

And this thinker, whose talk was shaking the Greek world in its foundations, though none guessed it, was singled out by the Delphic priesthood for a distinguished mark of approbation. In the truest oracle that was ever uttered from the Pythian tripod, it was declared that no one in the world was wiser than Socrates. We know not at what period of the philosopher's career this answer was given, but, if it was seriously meant, it showed a strange insight which we should hardly have looked for at the shrine of Delphi. The Delphic priesthood were skilful enough in adjusting their

He re-
ceives the
approval
of Delphi.

policy to the changing course of events; but they cannot be suspected of brooding over the mysteries of things to come, or feeling the deeper pulsations of the thoughts of men. The motive of the oracle concerning the wisdom of Socrates is an unsolved problem. If it were an attempt to enlist his support, in days when religion was threatened by such men as Anaxagoras, it shows an unexpected perception of his importance, united with a by no means surprising blindness to the significance of his work.

Socrates died five years after the fall of the Athenian empire, and the manner of his death set a seal upon his life. Anytus, the honest democratic politician who had been prominent in the restoration of the democracy, came forward, with some others, as a champion of the state religion, and accused Socrates of impiety. The accusation ran: "Socrates is guilty of crime, because he does not believe in the gods recognised by the city, but introduces strange supernatural beings; he is also guilty, because he corrupts the youth." The penalty proposed was death; but the accusers had no desire to inflict it; they expected that, when the charge was lodged in the archon's office, Socrates would leave Attica, and no one would have hindered him from doing so. But Socrates was full of days—he had reached the age of seventy—and life spent otherwise than in conversing in the streets of Athens would have been worthless to him. He surprised the city by remaining to answer the charge. The trial was heard in a court of 501 judges, the king-archon presiding, and the old philosopher was found guilty by a majority of sixty. It was a small majority, considering that the general truth of the accusation was undeniable. According to the practice of Athenian law, it was open to a defendant when he was condemned to propose a lighter punishment than that fixed by the accuser, and the judges were required to choose one of the two sentences. Socrates might have saved his life if he had proposed an adequate penalty, but he offered only a small fine, and was consequently condemned, by a much larger majority, to death. He drank the cup of doom a month later, discoursing with his disciples as eagerly as ever till his last hour.

The actual reply of Socrates at his trial has not been preserved, but we know its tone and spirit and much of its tenor. For it supplied his companion Plato, who was present, with the material of a work which stands absolutely alone in literature. In the *Apology of Socrates*, Plato has succeeded in catching the personality of the master and conveying its stimulus to his readers. There can be no question that this work reproduces the general outline of the actual defence, which is here wrought into an artistic form. And we see

Trial of Socrates 399 B.C.

His death.

Plato's Apology

Socrates
justly con-
demned.

how utterly impossible it was for Socrates to answer the accusation. He enters into an explanation of his life and motives, and has no difficulty in showing that many things popularly alleged against him are false. But with the actual charge of holding and diffusing heterodox views he deals briefly and unsatisfactorily. He was not condemned unjustly—according to the law. And that is the intensity of the tragedy. There have been no better men than Socrates; and yet his accusers were perfectly right. It is not clear why their manifesto for orthodoxy was made at that particular time; but it is probable that twenty years later such an action would have been a failure. Perhaps the facts of the trial justify us in the rough conclusion that two out of every five Athenian citizens then were religiously indifferent. In any case the event had a wider than a merely religious significance. The execution of Socrates was the protest of the spirit of the old order against the growth of individualism.

Seldom in the course of history have violent blows of this kind failed to recoil upon the striker and serve the cause they were meant to harm. Socrates was remembered at Athens with pride and regret. His spirit began to exercise an influence which the tragedy of his death enhanced. His companions never forgave the democracy for putting their master to death; he lived and grew in the study of their imaginations; and they spent their lives in carrying on his work.

They carried forward his work, but they knew not what they were doing. They had no suspicion that in pursuing those speculations to which they were stimulated by the Socratic method they were sapping the roots of Greek city life as it was known to the men who fought at Marathon. Plato was a true child of Socrates, and yet he was vehement in condemning that individualism which it had been the lifework of Socrates to foster. Few sights are stranger than Plato and Xenophon turning their eyes away from their own free country to regard with admiration the constitution of Sparta, where their beloved master would not have been suffered so much as to open his mouth. It was a distinct triumph for the Lacedaemonians when their constitution, which the Athenians of the age of Pericles regarded as old-fashioned machinery, was selected by the greatest thinker of Athens as the nearest existing approach to the ideal. Indeed the Spartan organisation, at the very time when Sparta was making herself detested throughout Greece, seems to have attracted general admiration from political thinkers. It attracted them because the old order survived there,—the citizen absolutely submissive to the authority of the state, and not looking beyond it. Elsewhere they were troubled by the problem of reconciling the authority of the state with the liberty of the individual citizen; at Sparta there was no such trouble, for the state was absolute. Accordingly they saw in Sparta the image of what a state should be; just because it was relatively free from that individualism which they were themselves actively promoting by their speculations in political philosophy. How freely such speculations ranged at this time is illustrated by the fact that the fundamental institution of ancient society, slavery, was called in question. It had indeed been called in question by Euripides, and the heterodox "modern" views of Euripides were coming into fashion. One thinker expounded the doctrine that slavery was unnatural. Speculation even went so far as to stir the question of the political subjection of women. The *Parliament of Women,* a comedy of Aristophanes, ridicules women's rights; and in Plato's ideal *Republic* women are on a political equality with men. Socialistic theories were also rife, and were a mark for the mockery of Aristophanes in the same play. Plato seized upon the notion of communism and made it one of the principles of his ideal state. But his object was not that of the ordinary "collectivist," to promote the material well-being of all; but rather to make his citizens better, by defending them against poverty and ambition. Before he died, Plato had come to the conviction that communism was impracticable, and in the state which he adumbrated in his old age he recognised private property— though he vested the ownership not in the individual but in the family.

Lycophron's view of slavery. Aristophanes' Ecclesiazusae, (392 or) 389 B.C. Communism in Plato's Republic. Private property in the Laws.

In this period—during the fifty years after the battle of Aegospotami—the art of writing prose was brought to perfection at Athens; and this is closely connected with the characteristic tendency which has engaged our attention. While Socrates and others had been bringing about a revolution in thought, the Sicilian Gorgias and other professors of rhetoric or style had been preparing an efficient vehicle for diffusing ideas. Prose is the natural instrument of criticism and argument; it is a necessary weapon for intellectual persuasion; and therefore the fourth century is an age of prose. The circumstance that the great Athenian poets of the fifth century had no successors in the fourth does not prove any decline in brains or in imagination. If Plato had been born half a century earlier he would have been a rival of Aeschylus and Sophocles. If Aeschylus and Sophocles had been born two or three generations later they would have expressed their genius in prose. Euripides, who has come under the influence of the critical spirit, seems sometimes like a man belated; he uses the old vehicle to convey thoughts for which it was hardly suited. It must always be remembered that

Development of prose.

the great dramatic poems of the fifth century bore an inalienable religious character; and, as soon as the day came when the men of the highest literary faculty were no longer in touch with the received religion, drama of the old kind ceased to be written. That is why the fourth century is an age of prose; tragic poetry owes its death to Euripides and the Socratic spirit. The eager individualism of the age found its natural expression in prose, whose rhythmical periods demanded almost as much care and art as poetry; and the plastic nature of the Greek language rendered it a most facile instrument for the purposes of free thought and criticism.

Thus Athens became really a school for Greece, as soon as that individualism prevailed which Pericles had unwittingly foreshadowed in the very same breath: "I say that Athens is the school of Hellas, and that the individual Athenian in his own person seems to have the power of adapting himself to the most varied forms of action with the utmost versatility and grace."[5]

It must never be forgotten that it is to the democratic Athenian law-courts that the perfecting of Attic prose was mainly due. This institution had, as we saw, called into being a class of professional speech-writers. But there were many who were not content with learning off, and reciting in court, speeches which a speech-writer like Lysias wrote for them, but wished to learn themselves the art of speaking. For those who aspired to make their mark in debates in the Assembly, this was a necessity. The most illustrious instructor in oratory at this period was Isocrates. But the school of Isocrates had a far wider scope and higher aim than to teach the construction of sentences or the arrangement of topics in a speech. It was a general school of culture, a discipline intended to fit men for public life. Questions of political science were studied, and Isocrates likes to describe his course of studies as "philosophy." But it was to Plato's school in the Academy that the youths of the day went to study "philosophy" in the stricter sense. The discipline of these two rival schools—for there was rivalry between them, though their aims were different—was what corresponded at Athens to our university education. And the pupils of Isocrates, as well as those of Plato, had to work hard. For thoroughness of method was one of the distinctive characteristics of Isocrates. His school attained a pan-Hellenic reputation; pupils came to him from all quarters of the world. "Our city," he says, "is regarded as the established teacher of all who speak or teach others to speak. And naturally so, since men see that our city offers the greatest prizes to those who possess this faculty—provides the most numerous

Higher education at Athens: Plato and Isocrates.

[5] Jowett's translation

and various schools for those who having resolved to enter the real contests desire a preparatory discipline—and further affords to all men that experience which is the main secret of success in speaking." [6] The tone of the teaching of Isocrates harmonised with the national position which he held. He took a large view of all things; there was nothing narrow or local in his opinions. And not less important than the width of his horizon was the high moral tone in which his thoughts were consistently pitched. Isocrates discharged not only the duties which are in modern times discharged by university teachers, but also the functions of a journalist of the best kind. Naturally nervous and endowed with a poor voice, he did not speak in the Assembly, but when any great question moved him he would issue a pamphlet, in the form of a speech, for the purpose of influencing public opinion. We may suspect that the Athenians appreciated these publications more for their inimitable excellence of style than for their political wisdom.

Isocrates a pamphleteer.

A highly remarkable passage of Isocrates expresses and applauds the wide-minded cosmopolitanism which was beginning to prevail in Greece. He says that "Athens has so distanced the rest of the world in power of thought and speech that her disciples have become the teachers of all other men. She has brought it to pass that the name of Greek should be thought no longer a matter of race but a matter of intelligence; and should be given to the participators in our culture rather than to the sharers of our common origin." [7] Thirty or forty years earlier, no one perhaps, except Euripides, would have been bold enough to speak like that. But Isocrates did not see that this enlightenment which he admires was closely connected with the decay of public spirit which he elsewhere deplores. It is curious to find the man who approves of citizenship of the world looking back with regret to the days of Solon and proposing to revive the old powers of censorship which the court of the Areopagus possessed over the lives of Athenian citizens.

Cosmopolitanism in the Panegyric Speech of Isocrates, 381 B.C.

Idealisation of 6th century, Athens.

(Areopagitikos, 355-4 B.C.)

The form and features of an age are wont to be mirrored in its art; and one effective means of winning a concrete notion of the spirit of the fourth century is to study the works of Praxiteles and compare them with the sculptures which issued from the workshop of Phidias. Just as the citizen was beginning to assert his own individuality as more than a mere item in the state, so the plastic artist was emancipating his art from its intimate connexion with the temples of the gods, and its subordination to architecture. For in the fifth century, apart from a few colossal statues like those which Phidias wrought for Athens and Olympia, the finest works

Individualistic character of the art of 4th century.

---

[6] Translated by Jebb.   [7] *Ibid.*

of the sculptor's chisel were to decorate frieze or pediment. In the fourth century the architect indeed still required the sculptor's service; Scopas, for instance, was called upon in his youth to decorate the temple of Athena Alea at Tegea, in his later years to make a frieze for the tomb of a Carian prince; but, in general, the sculptor developed his art more independently of architecture, and all the great works of Paxiteles were complete in themselves and independent. And, as sculpture was emancipating itself from the old subordination to architecture, so it also emancipated itself from the religious ideal. In the age of Phidias, the artist who fashioned a god sought to express in human shape the majesty and immutability of a divine being; and this ideal had been perfectly achieved. In the fourth century the deities lose their majesty and changelessness; they are conceived as physically perfect men and women, with human feelings though without human sorrows; they are invested with human personalities. The contrast may be seen by looking at the group of gods in the frieze of the Parthenon, and then at some of the works of Praxiteles: the Hermes, which was set up in the temple of Hera at Olympia, and is preserved there; the Aphrodite of Cnidus—a woman shrinking from revealing her beauty as she enters the bath; or the Satyr, with the shape of a man and the mind of a beast. Thus sculpture is marked by "individualism" in a double sense. Each artist is freer to work out an individual path of his own; and the tendency of all artists is to portray the individual man or woman rather than the type, and even the individual phase of emotion rather than the character.

The general spirit of the Athenians in their political life corresponds to this change. Men came more and more to regard the state as a means for administering to the needs of the individual. We might almost say that they conceived it as a co-operative society for making profits to be divided among the members; this at least was the tendency of public opinion. They were consequently more disinclined to enter upon foreign undertakings which were not either necessary for the protection and promotion of their commerce or likely to fill their purses. The fourth century was therefore for Athens an age of less ambition and glory, but of greater happiness and freedom, than the fifth.

Athenian com- merce.

The decisive circumstance for Athens was that, while she lost her empire, she did not lose her commerce. This was a cruel blow to Corinth, since it was to destroy Athenian trade that Corinth had brought about the war. The fact shows on how firm foundations Athenian commerce rested. The only rival Athens had to fear was Rhodes, which was becoming a centre of traffic in the south-eastern Mediterranean, but was not destined to interfere seriously with Athenian trade for a long time yet. The population of Attica had declined; plague and war reduced the number of adult male citizens from at least 35,000 to 21,000. But that was not unfortunate, for there were no longer outsettlements to receive the surplus of the population; and even with the diminished numbers there was a surplus which sought employment in foreign mercenary service. The mercantile development of Athens is shown by the increase of the Piraeus at the expense of the city, in which many plots of ground now became deserted, and by the growth of private banks. It had long been a practice to deposit money in temples, and the priesthoods used to lend money on interest. This suggested to money-changers the idea of doing likewise; and Pasion founded a famous house at Athens, which operated with a capital of fifty talents, and had credit at all Greek centres of commerce. Thus business could be transacted by exchanging letters of credit instead of paying in coin; and the introduction of this system, even on such a small scale, shows the growth of mercantile activity. Money was now much more plentiful, and prices far higher, than before. This was due to the large amount of the precious metals, chiefly gold, which had been brought into circulation in the Greek world in the last quarter of the fifth century. The continuous war led to the coining of the treasures which had been accumulating for many years in temples; and the banking system circulated the money which would otherwise have been hoarded in private houses. But, although the precious metals became plentiful, the rate of interest did not fall; men could still get 12 per cent for a loan of their money. This fact is highly significant; it shows clearly that industries were more thriving and trade more active, and consequently capital in greater demand. The high rate of interest must always be remembered when we read of a Greek described as wealthy with a capital which would nowadays seem small. Thus a fortune of 50 talents, little more than 10,000 English pounds, would yield an income of nearly £1500; and that sum had an enormously greater purchasing power than the equivalent weight of gold to-day. Such incomes were extremely rare.

Communistic ideas were a consequence, perhaps inevitable, of the growth of individualism and the growth of capital. The poorer burghers became more and more acutely alive to the inconsistency between the political equality of all citizens and the social and economical advantages enjoyed by the rich. Political equality seemed to point to social equality as its logical sequel; in fact, full and equal political equality could not be secured without social equality

Banks.

Rate of interest.

Socialism

also, since the advantages of wealth necessarily involve superiorities in political influence. Thus, just as in modern Europe, so in ancient Greece, capital and democracy produced socialists, who pleaded for a levelling of classes by means of a distribution of property by the state. Aristophanes mocked these speculations in his *Parliament of Women* and his *Wealth*. The idea of communism which Plato develops on lines of his own in the *Republic* was not an original notion of the philosopher's brain, but was suggested by the current communistic theories of the day. It is well worthy of consideration that the Athenians did not take the step from political to social democracy; and this discretion may have been partly due to the policy of those statesmen who, doubtless conscious of the danger, regarded the theoric fund as an indispensable institution.

The changed attitude of the individual to the state is shown by the introduction of a fixed remuneration of half a drachma to Athenian citizens for attending the meetings of the Assembly; and the rise in prices is illustrated by the subsequent increase of this remuneration. For the regular sessions, in which the proceedings were unattractive, the pay was raised to a drachma and a half; for the other meetings, which were more exciting, it was fixed at a drachma. The remuneration for serving in the law-courts was not increased; it was found that half a drachma was sufficient to draw applicants for the judge's ticket. Payment for the discharge of political duties was part of the necessary machinery of the democracy, but the distribution of "spectacle-money" to the poor citizens was a luxury which involved an entirely different principle. It is uncertain when the practice of giving the price of his theatre ticket to the poor Athenian was first introduced; it has been attributed to Pericles, but it is possible that it was not introduced till Athens began to recover after the fall of her empire. In any case, the principle became established in the fourth century of distributing "theoric" moneys, which were supposed to be spent on religious festivals; the citizens came to look forward to frequent and large distributions; the surplus revenue of the state, instead of being saved for emergencies, was placed in the theoric fund; and this theoric fund became so important that it ultimately required a special minister of finance to manage it. Those statesmen under whose guidance the theoric doles were most liberal had naturally the greatest influence with the mass of the citizens; and consequently finance acquired a new importance, and financial ability was developed in a very high degree. The state thus assumed the character of a commercial society; dividends were a political necessity, and in order to meet it heavier taxation was demanded. We have seen how, when war broke out

Ecclesi-
azusae,
389 B.C.
Plutus,
388, B.C.

Ecclesi-
astic pay
(intro-
duced be-
fore 389
B.C.).

ὁ ἐπὶ τὸ
θεωρικόν.

with Sparta, in a year in which the Second Athenian Confederacy was formed, a property-tax was imposed, and the properties of the citizens were assessed anew for this purpose.

Thus the state provided for the comfort of its poorer burghers at the expense of their wealthier fellows. It is, as it were, publicly recognised as a principle of political science that the end of the state is the comfort and pleasure of its individual members; and everything has to be made subordinate to this principle which is outwardly embodied in the theoric fund. This principle affected the foreign policy of Athens, as we have already observed. When she took the step of sending out settlers to Samos and elsewhere, in defiance of the public opinion of Greece, her chief motive was doubtless pecuniary profit.

Constitutionally, the restored Athenian democracy was a remarkable success. The difficulties which the democratic statesmen encountered after the overthrow of the Thirty had been treated with a wisdom and moderation which are in striking contrast with the violence and vengefulness shown in other Greeks states at similar crises. Most democratic men of means had been robbed of property under the tyranny of the oligarchs, and the property had been sold. Were the purchasers to be compelled to restore it without compensation? Were all the acts of the Thirty to be declared illegal? Such a measure would have created a bitter and discontented party in the state. Some of the chief democratic leaders voluntarily resigned all claim to compensation for the property they had lost, and this example promoted a general inclination on both sides to concession and compromise. The wisdom and tact displayed in this matter were not the least of the services which Thrasybulus and his fellows rendered to their country. No oligarchical conspiracy endangered the domestic peace of Athens again; no citizen, if it were not a philosophical speculator, called the democracy in question.

The constitution in the 4th century.

At this epoch the laws were revised, and the register of burghers was revised, but the constitution was left practically unaltered. A change, indeed, was made in the presidency of the Assembly, which had hitherto belonged to the *prytaneis* or board of Ten, selected every seven days from the presiding tribe in the Council. The close organic relation between the Council and Assembly rendered it needful that members of the Council should preside in the Assembly but the presidency of the Assembly was now divorced from the presidency of the Council and invested in a body of nine, selected one from each of the nine tribes which were not presiding. This change was obviously designed to form a check on the administration. The presiding tribe in the Council could no longer deal direct-

Change in the presidency of the Assembly: probably in 403-2 B.C.

The nine proedroi.

ly with the Assembly, but was obliged to present its measures to the people through an intermediate body, which belonged indeed to the Council but not to its own part of the Council. The year in which these reforms were probably made witnessed also the introduction of a new alphabet as the official script of the state. The old Attic alphabet, with its hard-worked vowels doing duty for more than one sound, was discontinued; and henceforward the stones which record the public acts of the Athenian people are inscribed in the Ionic alphabet, with separate signs for the long and short *e* and *o*, and distinct symbols for the double consonants.

It is plain that Athens needed, at this period, not men of genius or enthusiasm, but simply men of ability, for the conduct of her affairs. She had no great aims to achieve, no grave dangers to escape, which demanded a Pericles or a Themistocles; a man of genius would have found no scope in the politics of Athens for two generations after the fall of her empire. Men of great ability she had, men who were thoroughly adequate to the comparatively un-ambitious rôle which she had wisely imposed upon herself— Agyrrhius, Callistratus, and afterwards Eubulus. To us they are all shadowy figures. Agyrrhius inaugurated the profit-system which afterwards resulted in the institution of the theoric fund; and it was he who opposed and discredited the extreme anti-Spartan policy of the heroes of Phyle. His nephew Callistratus enjoyed a longer career and played a greater part in the affairs of Greece, conspicuous as the founder of the Second Confederacy, as the negotiator of the Peace of Callias, and then as the opponent of Epaminondas. His policy throughout was consistent and reasonable. He aimed at rendering Athens powerful enough to be independent of Sparta; he desired that Sparta and Athens should stand side by side as the two leading states in Greece; and he recognised that the neighbourhood of Attica to Boeotia necessarily laid upon Athens the policy of oppos-ing the aggrandisement of Thebes.

Agyrrhius and Callistratus might once and again fill the office of strategos; but, like Cleon and Hyperbolus, they exercised their in-fluence as recognised—practically, official—advisers of the Assem-bly. The art of war became every year more and more an art, and little could be accomplished except by generals who devoted their life to the military profession. Such were Timotheus, the hero of Leucas; Chabrias, the victor of Naxos; and above all Iphicrates, whom we have met in so many places and in so many guises. Timo-theus was a rich man; his father Conon had left him a fortune, and he could afford to serve his country and his country only. But Cha-brias and Iphicrates enriched themselves by taking temporary ser-

Introduc-
tion of the
Ionic
alphabet
in the
archon-
ship of
Euclides,
403-2 B.C.

Agyrrhius.

Calli-
stratus.

Military
men.

vice under foreign masters; Iphicrates even went so far as to support the Thracian king, whose daughter he had wedded, against Athens. All these military men preferred to dwell elsewhere than at Athens. Abroad they could live in luxury and ostentation; while at Athens men lived simply and moderately, and public opinion was unfavourable to sumptuous establishments. The attitude of the generals to the city became much more independent when the citizens themselves ceased to serve abroad regularly, and hired mercenaries instead. The hiring of the troops and their organisation devolved upon the general, and he was often expected to provide the means for paying them too. Here we touch on a vice in the constitutional machine, which was the cause of frequent failures in the foreign enterprises of Athens during this period. No systematic provision was made that, when the people voted that a certain thing should be done, the adequate moneys at the same time should be voted. Any one might propose a decree, without responsibility for its execution; and at the next meeting of the Assembly the people might refuse to allow the necessary supplies, or no one might be ready to move the grant. In the same way, supplies might be cut off in the middle of a campaign. This defect had not made itself seriously felt in the fifth century, when the leading generals were always statesmen too, with influence in the Assembly; but it became serious when the generals were professional soldiers whom the statesmen employed. During the ten years after the Peace of Callias, Athens was actively engaged in a multitude of enterprises of foreign aggrandisement; but she achieved little, and the reason is that her armaments were hardly ever adequate. The difficulties of her financiers, who had always to keep a theoric reserve, must be taken into consideration.

CHAPTER XIV

THE HEGEMONY OF THEBES

SECT. 1. JASON OF PHERAE; AND THE BATTLE OF LEUCTRA

THE balance of power in Greece had been swayed for a hundred years by the two rivals Sparta and Athens; and now the Peace of Callias had formally adjusted an equilibrium between them. But this dual system was threatened from the very outset by formidable dangers. It was clear that new forces had arisen within the last few years, which would dispute the leadership of Hellas with the two older states. There had been a development of military power in the north, and two cities had come into dangerous prominence, Thebes and Pherae.

Of the rise of Pherae we know less than of the rise of Thebes. At the time of the Peace of Callias we make the sudden discovery that the Thessalian cities which were usually in a state of feud have been united, and that Thessaly has consequently become one of the great powers of Greece. This was the doing of one man. There had arisen at Pherae a despot, who was not merely vigorous and warlike, but whose ambition ranged beyond the domestic politics of Thessaly and sought to play a great part on the wider stage of Hellas. Jason had established his dominion by means of a well-trained body of 6000 mercenaries, and also doubtless by able diplomacy. The most influential citizen of Pharsalus exposed at Sparta the ambitious and menacing views of Jason, and urged the importance of checking his career before he became too powerful; but Sparta, pressed by other more importunate claims, declined to interfere. Then Pharsalus yielded to the solicitations of Jason, and helped to install him as *Tagus* of an united Thessaly. The power of the despot extended on one side into Epirus, where Alcetas, prince of the Molossi, became his vassal; and on the other side to Macedonia.

A monarch, endowed with uncommon political and military ability, at the head of all Thessaly, with the best cavalry in Greece at his command, seemed likely to change the whole course of Hellenic affairs. That he aimed at becoming the first power in Hellas—at attaining the *hegemony* or leadership, as it was called—there can be

Jason of Pherae.

371 B.C.

no question; nor, considering the weakness and jealousies of the southern Grecian states, would this object, with his resources, be difficult of achievement. But, if his ambition was not bounded by Thessaly, neither was it confined to Hellas. His dream was to lead Hellas against Persia, and overthrow the power of the Great King. How serious he was in his great projects is shown by the fact that he set about building a navy. Thessaly was again to become a sea-power, as in the days of legendary story, when the Argo ventured forth from the land-locked bay of Iolcus.

The power of Sparta had evidently declined, but she was still regarded as holding the highest position in Greece; and it was the first object of Jason to weaken her still further and dethrone her from that place. His second immediate object was to gain control of the key of southern Greece—the pass of Thermopylae; and as this was commanded by the Spartan fortress of Heraclea, these two objects were intimately connected. His obvious policy was to ally himself with Sparta's enemy, Thebes; and Thebes, in her isolated position, leapt at his alliance. The treaty between the Boeotian and Thessalian federations was probably concluded not long before the Peace of Callias. According to the terms of that Peace, all parties were to recall their armaments from foreign countries and their garrisons from foreign towns. Athens promptly recalled Iphicrates from Corcyra, but Sparta on her side failed to fulfil the contract. King Cleombrotus had, shortly before, led an army to Phocis, and now, instead of disbanding it, he was ordered to march against Thebes and compel that state to set free the Boeotian cities. One voice, perhaps, in the Spartan assembly was raised against this violation of the recent oaths, a violation which was also unfair to the allies who served in the Lacedaemonian army. But in this hour Sparta was led on, as one of her admirers said, by a fatal impulse inspired by the gods; the feeling of hatred against Thebes, diligently fostered by Agesilaus, swept away all thoughts of policy or justice; and the voice which was raised for justice and policy was scornfully cried down. The duel between Thebes and Sparta was inevitable; and all Greece, confident in Spartan superiority, looked to see Thebes broken up into villages or wiped out from among the cities of Hellas. Even Thebes herself hardly hoped for success. But Sparta would have done well to disband the army of Cleombrotus, and organise a new force with the help of those allies who were willing to support her.

Sparta (contrary to treaty) orders Cleombrotus to march against Thebes.

471 B.C. Protest of Prothous.

The object of Cleombrotus, who was posted near Chaeronea, in the gate between Phocis and Boeotia, was to reach Thebes; and, as we have seen in the case of former military operations in this country, his direct road lay along the western and southern banks of Lake Copais, by Coronea and Haliartus. The aim of the Thebans was to prevent him from reaching his objective; and they posted their forces nigh to Coronea, where, nearly a quarter of a century before, a confederate army had waylaid Agesilaus. But Cleombrotus disappointed his enemy; he marched southward by a difficult road round Mount Helicon to Thisbe, and thence pounced on the port of Creusis, which he captured along with twelve Theban ships in the harbour; and, by this swift stroke having secured his rear, he advanced northward along the road to Thebes.

When he reached the height of Leuctra, he found that the way was barred by the Theban army. Leuctra lies on the hills which form the south limit of a small plain, somewhat more than half a mile broad, traversed by the brook of the upper Asopus. The road from the coast to Thebes crosses it and ascends the hills on the northern side, where the Boeotarchs and their army were now drawn up. The round top of one of these low hills, just east of the road, was levelled and enlarged to form a smooth platform. Here the Theban hoplites of the left wing were posted, and the artificial mound marks their place to this day. The numbers of the two hosts are uncertain; the Lacedaemonians, in any case considerably superior, may have been about eleven, the Theban about six, thousand

strong. But the military genius of one of the Boeotarchs, now for the first time fully revealed, made up for the deficiency in strength. Instead of drawing out the usual long and shallow line, Epaminondas made his left wing deep. This wedge, fifty shields deep, of irresistible weight, with the Sacred Band, under the captaincy of Pelopidas, in front, was opposed to the Spartans who, with Cleombrotus himself, were drawn up on the right of the hostile army. It was on his left wing that Epaminondas relied for victory; the shock between the Spartans and Thebans would decide the battle; it mattered little about the Boeotians on the centre and left, whom he could not entirely trust. The Thespians, who were present by constraint, were at the last moment permitted to depart; but their retreat was cut off and they were driven back to the camp by the Phocians and other of the Lacedaemonian allies, who, by detaching themselves for this purpose, weakened their own army without effecting an useful result.

The battle began with an engagement of the cavalry. In this arm the Lacedaemonians were notoriously weak; and now their horsemen, easily driven back, carried disorder into the line of foot. Cleombrotus, who was confident of victory, then led his right wing down the slopes—the centre and left being probably impeded in

their advance by the cavalry; and on his side Epaminondas with
the Theban left moved down from their hill, deliberately keeping
back the rest of the line. The novel tactics of Epaminondas decided
the battle. The Spartans, twelve deep, though they fought ever so
bravely, could not resist the impact of the Theban wedge led by
Pelopidas. King Cleombrotus fell, and after a great carnage on both

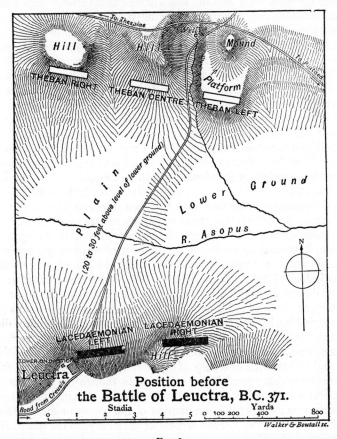

FIG. 81.

sides the Thebans drove their enemies up the slopes back to their
camp. In other parts of the field there seems to have been little
fighting or slaughter; the Lacedaemonian allies, when they saw the
right wing worsted, retired without more ado.

A thousand Lacedaemonians had fallen, including four hundred Spartans; and the survivors acknowledged their defeat by demanding the customary truce to take up the dead. It might be thought that they would have immediately retreated to Creusis, the place of safety which the dead king had prudently provided in their rear. It is not likely that the enemy, whom they still considerably outnumbered, would have attempted to stop their way, or even to harass them seriously from behind. The Thebans could hardly realise the victory which they had never expected; it was more than enough to have defeated the Lacedaemonians in the open field, to have slain their king, and to have compelled them to evacuate Boeotia. But the Lacedaemonian army remained in its entrenchments on the hill of Leuctra, in the expectation of being reinforced by a new army from Sparta and retrieving the misfortune. A messenger was sent home with the inglorious tidings, and the shock was borne there with that studied self-repression which only the discipline of Sparta could inculcate in her citizens. The remaining forces of the city were hastily got together, and placed under the command of Archidamus, son of Agesilaus. Some of the allied states sent aid, and the troops were transported by ship from Corinth to Creusis.

But all this took time, and meanwhile Thebes had not been idle. Two messengers were sent with the good news, to Athens and to Thessaly. At Athens the wreathed messenger was received with an ominous silence. The Theban victory was distinctly unwelcome there; it opened up an indefinite prospect of warfare and seemed likely to undo the recent pacification; while the Athenians were far less jealous of Sparta than of Thebes. At Pherae the tidings had a very different reception. Jason marched forthwith to the scene of action, at the head of his cavalry and mercenaries, flying so rapidly through Phocis that the Phocians, his irreconcilable enemies, did not realise his presence until he had passed. He cannot have reached Leuctra until the sixth or seventh day after the battle. The Thebans thought that with the help of his forces they might storm the Lacedaemonian entrenchments, dangerous though the task would be. But for the policy of Jason the humiliation already inflicted on Sparta was enough; the annihilation of the enemy or any further enhancement of the Theban success would have been too much. He dissuaded the Thebans from the enterprise, and induced them to grant a truce to the Lacedaemonians, with leave to retire unharmed. This the Lacedaemonians were now forced to accept, notwithstanding the approach of reinforcements. For their position was totally altered through the presence of the seasoned troops of Jason, and it was clear that the foe would not wait to attack them till the ex-

Margin notes:

Position at Leuctra after the battle.

Army of relief under Archidamus. Reception of the news at Athens.

Jason of Pherae marches to Leuctra.

Truce. The Lacedaemonians evacuate Boeotia.

pected reinforcements arrived. The retreat was carried out at night, for the leaders suspected the good faith of their opponents. On the coast the defeated troops met the army of Archidamus, which had come in vain, and all the forces were disbanded.

Such were the circumstances of the Lacedaemonian evacuation of Boeotia after the battle of Leuctra, according to the historian whose authority we are naturally inclined to prefer. But the memory of Xenophon might have misled him in regard to some of the details, and there was another account from which it might be inferred that events moved more rapidly. There is something to be said for the view that the army of Archidamus was not dispatched as a relief force after the battle of Leuctra, but was already on its way before the battle was fought; that Cleombrotus had the alternative of waiting for Archidamus before he ventured on an action, and that his visit to Creusis was, in fact, connected with the expected arrival of reinforcements; that Jason too was hastening to support the Thebans, and that the messenger who bore the news of victory met him on his southward march. On this view the truce might have been concluded on the morrow of the battle, and we avoid the difficulty of supposing that the defeated army decided to remain for a week on the hill of Leuctra, when the road to Creusis was open behind them.

Another view of the evacuation of Boeotia.

The question is of little moment save in so far as it concerns the movements of the Tagus of Thessaly. The significance of the sequel of the battle lies in the prominent part which he played as a mediator; and we should like well to know whether his original purpose was to fight side by side with his Theban allies. We also hear darkly of his avowed intention to bring help by sea; and we are tempted to speculate at what point the new Thessalian navy would have acted at this crisis.

Jason's fleet.

Jason returned to his northern home, but on his way he dealt another blow at Sparta on his own account, by dismantling Heraclea, the fort which controlled the pass of Thermopylae. He thus compassed an object of great importance for his further designs. These designs he soon began to unfold. He fixed on the next celebration of the Pythian festival as a time to display his greatness and his power to the eyes of assembled Hellas. He sent mandates around to the Thessalian cities to prepare oxen, sheep, and goats for the sacrifice at Delphi, offering a gold crown as a prize for the fairest ox. And he issued commands that the armed host of the Thessalians should be ready to march with him to keep the feast. He proposed to usurp the rights of the Amphictyonic board, and preside himself over the games. A rumour was set afloat that he intended to seize

Jason at Thermopylae.

His schemes.

the treasures of the temple; but it is hard to believe that an aspirant to the hegemony of Greece would have perpetrated an act so manifestly impolitic. Apollo told the Delphians, who were fluttered by the report, that he would himself guard his treasure.

But the priests were soon to breathe freely; the Phocians were to be spared the mortification of seeing the hated Thessalian in their land. One day Jason held a review of his cavalry, and afterwards sat to hear petitions. Seven young men, to all appearance wrangling hotly, drew near to lay their dispute before him, and slew him where he sat. The death of Jason was the knell of all his plans. The unity of Thessaly, the high position which it had attained among the Grecian powers, depended entirely on him. The brothers who succeeded to his place were slight insignificant men, without the ability, even if they had possessed the will, to carry out his far-reaching

designs. It is the bare truth to say that the blades of the seven young men changed the course of history. Jason was well on his way to attain in eastern Greece the supreme position which his great fellow-despot Dionysius held in the west. Nor is it extravagant to suppose that under him Thessaly might have accomplished part of the work which was reserved for Macedonia. Politically, indeed, his work is to be condemned. He had not laid the foundations of a national unity in Thessaly; the unity which he had compassed was held by military force only and his own genius. We cannot congratulate a statesman on a result of which the stability hangs on the chances of his own life. In this respect Jason stands in the same rank with Epaminondas.

The death of the Thessalian potentate decided that, of the two northern states which had recently risen into prominence, Boeotia, not Thessaly, should take the torch from Sparta.

The significance of the battle of Leuctra is perhaps most clearly revealed in the fact that, during the wars between Sparta and Thebes which followed it, the parts hitherto played by the two states are reversed. Thebes now becomes the invader of the Peloponnese, as Sparta before had been the invader of Boeotia. Thebes is now the aggressor; it is as much as Sparta can do to defend her own land. The significance of Leuctra is also displayed in the effect which it produced upon the policy of Athens, and in its stimulating influence on the lesser Peloponnesian states, especially Arcadia, which was wakened up into new life.

The supremacy of Thebes was the result of no overmastering imperial instinct and was inspired by no large idea, but it brought about some beneficial results. Sparta had greviously abused the dominion which had fallen into her hands; and the period of Theban greatness represents the reaction against the period of Lacedaemonian oppression. The two objects of Theban policy are to hinder Sparta from regaining her old position in the Peloponnesus, and to prevent the revival of Jason's power in Thessaly.

Although no express record has been handed down as to constitutional changes, there is some evidence which has suggested the belief that the Thebans drew tighter the bond which united the Boeotian communities by transforming the federation into a national state. Thebes, seemingly, became in Boeotia what Athens was in Attica; the other cities, Coronea, Thespiae, Haliartus, and the rest, were uncitied and became as Marathon and Eleusis; their citizens exercised their political rights in an Assembly at Thebes. If this be so, we may suspect that Epaminondas played the part of legendary Theseus; but the new constitution had no elements of stability, and it endured but for a few years.

Sect. 2. Policy of Thebes in Southern Greece, Arcadia and Messenia

The defeat of a Lacedaemonian army in the open field by an enemy inferior in numbers was a thrilling shock to the Greeks, who deemed it part of the order of nature that the Spartan hoplites should be invincible except in front of an overwhelmingly larger force. The event was made more impressive by the death of king Cleombrotus; a Spartan king had never fallen in battle since Leonidas laid down his life at the gates of Greece. The news agitated every state in the Peloponnesus. The harmosts, whom Sparta had undertaken to withdraw three weeks before, when she signed the Peace, were now expelled from the cities; there was an universal reaction against the local oligarchies which had been supported by Sparta and had excited universal discontent; and these democratic revolutions flooded the land with troops of dangerous exiles. The contagion spread even to Argos, though Sparta had no influence there, and broke out with such violence that many citizens were cudgelled to death by the infuriated people.

Democratic movements throughout the Peloponnesus

Scytalism, or cudgelling, at Argos.

But it was in Arcadia that the most weighty political results followed. A general feeling, which had perhaps been growing for some years back, now took definite shape, that the cities of Arcadia must combine together to oppose an united front to Lacedaemonian pretensions. The only way in which each city could hope to preserve her independence against the power of Sparta was by voluntarily surrendering a portion of that independence to a federal union of her sister cities. The most zealous advocate of the Pan-Arcadian

Pan-Arcadian League.

idea was the Mantinean Lycomedes, a native of the district which had been more cruelly used than all others by the high-handed policy of Lacedaemon. The fall of Sparta was the signal for the Mantineans to rebuild their walls, desert their villages, and resume the dignity and pleasures of city life. The old king Agesilaus had the insolence to remonstrate; he requested them at least to ask the gracious permission of Sparta, but he had no power to enforce his request.

The Mantineans resolved that their city should not again be captured, as king Agesipolis had captured it, by means of its own river. They dug a new bed, so that the Ophis when it approached the south-eastern wall parted into two channels and, having described a great loop, reunited its waters on the north-western side. In this loop the city of Mantinea rose again, and by this means the river, which had proved itself a danger, was forced to become a fortification, entirely encompassing the walls. The stone foundations of the wall enable us to trace the circuit of the city; but they were only the base for a superstructure which, like the buildings of the town, was of brick. The ten gates were curiously constructed, no two alike, yet all elaborations of a principle which was adopted by the builders of the fortress of Tiryns—the principle of exposing the undefended right side of an approaching enemy to the defenders who manned the walls and flanking towers. The general design may be best grasped by conceiving the wall not as a continuous circle but as composed of ten separate pieces, which did not join but overlapped, while the gates connected the overlapping ends.

Mantinea, arisen from her ruins, and the other towns of Arcadia —with the important exceptions of Tegea, Orchomenus, and Heraea—now agreed to form a Pan-Arcadian union and constitute a federal state. Several reasons made it expedient to establish a new

seat as the federal capital of the country. The Arcadian cities were too small for the purpose. The selection of one of them would have excited the jealousies of the other, and it was intended that there should be no Thebes in the Arcadian state. The site chosen for the new city was in the western of the two large plains which define the geographical character of central Arcadia. It lay, in a long narrow irregular shape, on both sides of the river Helisson. Not far off rose Lycaeon, the mountain to which the Arcadian folk attached their most sacred associations; and in the centre of the market-place was built a shrine of Zeus of that holy hill. The town was entitled to its name of Megalopolis, or Great City, by the large circuit of its double wall, a circuit of five miles and a half—a somewhat rough piece of work, built of stone in the lower courses and brick above, and furnished with towers at intervals.

It must be kept in view that Megalopolis had a double character. It was to be the federal capital, but it was also to be one of the federal cities. Apart from its relation to all Arcadia, it had a special relation to its own plain. The change which had come to pass in the eastern plain, so long ago that no man could tell when, by the founding of Tegea and Mantinea, was now brought to pass in the western plain. The village communities of the surrounding districts were induced to exchange their separate existence for joint life in a city. Lying close to the north-western frontier of Laconia, Megalopolis would be a bulwark against Sparta on this side, corresponding to Tegea on the north. It is natural to compare it with Mantinea, which arose in its new shape at the same time. Both cities seem to have had a similar system of fortification, double walls of stone and brick, strengthened by towers; but Megalopolis, which was the larger, was also the stronger by nature. For Mantinea lay on a dead level, all its strength was due to art; Megalopolis lay on sloping irregular ground, offering hills of which the architect could take advantage. The difference is illustrated by the fact that the little theatre in Mantinea rested on a stone substructure, while the huge theatre in Megalopolis is cut out of a hill.

The Federal Constitution was modelled on the ordinary type of democratic constitutions. There was an Assembly, which met at stated periods to consider all important questions. Every citizen of the federal communities was a member of this Assembly, of which the official title was the *Ten Thousand*. The name indicates an approximate, not an exact, number, like the Five Thousand in the constitution of Theramenes at Athens. We have no information as to the working of this body, but from the analogy of other ancient federations it is probable that the votes were taken by cities, the vote of each city being determined by the majority of the votes of those of its citizens who were present. The Ten Thousand made war and peace, concluded alliances, and sat in judgment on offenders against the League. There was also a *Council*, composed of fifty members from the various cities, and this body had doubtless the usual executive and deliberative functions which belonged to the Greek conception of a Council.

On the south side of the river stood the Thersilion, the federal building in which meetings of the Arcadian league were held. The foundations of this spacious covered hall have been recently laid bare, and display an ingenious arrangement of the internal pillars,

Assembly of the Myrioi.

Council of Damiorgoi.

converging in lines whereby as few as possible of a crowded audience might be hindered from seeing and hearing. It is an attempt to apply the principle of the theatre to a covered building. The Thersilion stood close in front of the hill from which the theatre was hewn, and the place of political deliberation seemed part of the same structure as the place of dramatic spectacles. For the Doric portico, which adorned the southern side of the federal house, faced the audience; the orchestra in which the chorus danced and the actors sometimes played stretched from the circle of seats up to the steps of the portico. Such was the original arrangement, changed in later years; and it illustrates the fact that the stone theatres which began to spring up throughout Greece in the fourth century were intended as much for political assemblies as for theatrical representations.

Fig. 82.—Coin of Arcadia. Obverse: head of Zeus laureate. Reverse: Pan on mountain; syrinx below [legend: APK (monogram); and ΟΛΥ($\mu\pi$os) on the mountain]. Fig. 83.—Coin of Messene. Obverse: head of Demeter, corn-crowned. Reverse: Zeus with thunderbolt and eagle [legend: ΜΕΣΣΑΝΙΩΝ].

The river Helisson divides Megalopolis into two nearly equal parts; and it would seem that this division corresponded to the double character of the place. The city of Megalopolis, in the strict sense, was on the northern side; there was the market-place on the bank of the river, there was the hall in which the Council of the Megalopolitan state met together. But the southern half of Megalopolis was federal ground; here was the federal Hall of Assembly, here was the theatre, which was in fact an open-air hall for federal meetings. Here, we may suppose, were the dwellings of the permanent armed force, 5000 strong, which was maintained by the Federation; here were lodgings for the "Ten Thousand" when they assembled to vote on the affairs of the Arcadian state.

Buleute-
rion.

Eparitoi
(federal
army).

Tegea had hitherto been a sort of Laconian outpost, and a revolution was necessary to bring about its adhesion to the new federation. With the help of a Mantinean band, the philo-Laconian party

Tegea
joins the
League,
370 B.C.

was overthrown, and 800 exiles sought refuge at Sparta. This blow stung Sparta to action. She might brook the resuscitation of Mantinea, she might look on patiently at the measures taken by the presumptuous Arcadians for managing their own affairs; but it was too much to see Tegea, her steadfast ally, the strong warder of her northern frontier, pass over to the camp of the rebels. Agesilaus led an army into Arcadia, and displayed the resentment of Sparta by ravaging the fields of Mantinea; neither he nor the federal forces risked a conflict.

In view of this Spartan invasion, which came to so little, the Arcadians had sought the help of foreign powers. To Athens their first appeal was made. The tidings of Leuctra had excited in that city mixed feelings of pleasure and jealousy. The humiliation of Sparta opened up a prospect of regaining empire, notwithstanding the undertakings of the recent peace; but the triumph of Thebes was unwelcome and dangerous. These hopes and fears spurred Athens to new activity. Shortly after the battle of Leuctra she showed her appreciation of the changed condition of Hellas by inviting delegates from the Peloponnesian cities to pledge themselves anew to the King's Peace (which, it must always be remembered, was the basis of the Peace of Callias) and to pledge themselves to one another for mutual help in case of hostile attack. Elis, refusing to recognise the autonomy of some of her subjects, was forced to hold aloof; but most of the other states swore to the alliance. It was a contract between Athens and her allies on one side, and the former allies of Sparta on the other. By virtue of this act of alliance, Athens was bound to help Mantinea and the Arcadian cities whenever they were threatened by an invasion. But it appeared that, though ready to usurp the place of Sparta, she was not ready to renew the war with her old rival. Perhaps a change of feeling had been wrought in the course of the nine or ten months which had run since the congress at Athens; the violence of the democratic movements in the Peloponnese may have caused disgust; certain it is that Athens refused the Arcadian appeal; she seems to have contemplated a policy of neutrality.

Close of
371 B.C.

The rebuff at Athens drove Arcadia into the arms of Thebes. The battle which had been fought to secure the unity of Boeotia had been the means of promoting the unity of Arcadia; and there was a certain fitness in the northern state coming to the aid of its younger fellow. But it was not mere sympathy with federal institutions that induced Thebes to send a Boeotian army into the Peloponnesus. To keep Sparta down and prevent her from recovering her influence was the concern of Thebes, and an united Arcadia was the best instrument that could be devised for the purpose. At this juncture, the situation in northern Greece permitted Thebes to comply with the Arcadian request. The Phocians and Ozolian Locrians, the Locrians of Opus, the Malians, had sought her alliance after Leuctra, and even the Euboeans had deserted to her; so that all central Greece, as far as Cithaeron, was under the Boeotian influence. But if the request had come some months sooner, it would have been impossible to grant it; for Jason of Pherae was then alive, preparing to march to Delphi, and the Boeotian forces could not have left Boeotia.

Boeotians invade Laconia. It was already winter when the Theban army, led by Epaminondas, accompanied by his fellow Boeotarchs, arrived in Arcadia to find that Agesilaus had withdrawn from the field. But, though the purpose of the expedition was thus accomplished, the Arcadians persuaded Epaminondas not to return home without striking a blow at the enemy. To invade Laconia and attack Sparta herself was the daring proposal—daring in idea at least; for within the memory of history no foeman had ever violated Laconian soil, the unwalled city had never repelled an assault. There was little danger, with an army of such size as that which was now assembled; and a march to the gates of Sparta would drive home the lesson of Leuctra. The invaders advanced in four divisions by four roads, converging on Sellasia, and met no serious attempt to block their way; some neodamodes and Tegeate exiles were annihilated by the Arcadians. Sellasia was burnt, and the united army descended into the plain on the left bank of the Eurotas. The river which separated them from Sparta was swollen with winter rains, and this probably saved the city; for the bridge was too strongly guarded to be safely attacked. Epaminondas marched southward a few miles further, as far as Amyclae, where he crossed the stream by a ford. But Sparta was now saved. On the first alarm of the coming invasion, messages had flown to the Peloponnesian cities which were still friendly; and these—Corinth, Sicyon, Phlius, Pellene, and the towns of the Argolic coast—had promptly sent auxiliary forces. The northern roads being barred by the enemy, these forces were obliged to land on the eastern shore of Laconia and make their way across Mount Parnon. They reached the Eurotas bridge, after the invaders had moved to Amyclae; and their coming added such strength to the defence of Sparta that Epaminondas did not attack it, but contented himself with marching up defiantly to its outskirts. It was indeed a sufficient revenge even for Theban hatred to have wounded Sparta as none had wounded her before, to have violated the precinct of the Laconian land. The consternation of the Spartans at a calamity

which, owing to the immunity of ages, they had never even conceived as possible, can hardly be imagined. The women, disciplined
though they were in repressing their feelings when sons or husbands
perished in battle, now fell into fits of distress and despair: for, unlike the women of so many other Greek cities, they had never looked
upon the face of an enemy before. Old Agesilaus, who loathed the
Theban above all other names, was charged with the defence; and
his task was the harder, since he had to watch not only the foe, but
the disaffected. Freedom had been promised to 6000 helots who
came forward to serve: but this aid was a new danger.

It is needless to say that the loss of a few hundred soldiers on the
field of Leuctra had nothing to do with the impotence displayed by
Sparta at this crisis. And if Leuctra had been won by superior generalship, it was not inferior generalship that exposed Laconia. The
disease lay far deeper. The vigour of Sparta was decaying from the
mere want of men; it has been calculated that at this time there
were not more than 1500 with full citizenship. Not merely constant
warfare, but, far more, economical conditions, brought about this
dispeopling. Since money had begun to flow into Laconia, and since
a new law permitted citizens to alienate their holdings, the inevitable result ensued; the small lots which meagrely supported each
Spartan were gathered into large estates; and with the lots the
citizens disappeared. This disease which was sapping the energies of
his enemy cannot have escaped the view of Epaminondas, and his
next step is significant.

Having ravaged southern Laconia, from the banks of the Eurotas
to the foot of Taygetus, as far as Gytheion—where they failed, we
know not why, to take the arsenal—the allies returned to Arcadia.
But, though it was midwinter, their work was not over yet; a far
greater blow was still to be inflicted on Sparta. Epaminondas led
them now into another part of the Spartan territory, the ancient
Messenia. The serfs, who belonged to the old Messenian race, arose
at their coming; and on the slopes of Mount Ithome the foundations of a new Messene were laid by Epaminondas. The ancient
heroes and heroines of the race were invited to return to the restored
nation; the ample circuit of the town was marked out, and the first
stones placed, to the sound of flutes. Ithome was the citadel, and
formed one side of the town, whose walls of well-wrought masonry
descended the slopes and met in the plain below. The Messenian
exiles who had been wandering over the Greek world had now a
home once more.

Messene, like Megalopolis, was founded by "synoecizing" the
districts round about. But its political position was entirely differ-

Depopu-
lation of
Sparta.

Founda-
tion of
Messene,
winter,
370-69
B.C.

ent from that of Megalopolis. Messene was not a federal capital; it was the Messenian state—a city with the whole country for its territory. Corone and Methone were not cities like Mantinea and Clitor; they were places like Brauron and Marathon; their inhabitants possessed the citizenship of Messene, but it was only under Mount Ithome that they could exercise their burgher-rights. The relation of Messene to Messenia was that of Athens to Attica, not that of Megalopolis to Arcadia.

Thus not only a new stronghold but a new enemy was erected against Sparta in Sparta's own domain. All western Laconia, all the land between Ithome and the sea (except Asine and Cyparissia), were subtracted from the Spartan dominion; all the perioeci and helots became the freemen of a hostile state. Under the auspices of Thebes an old act of injustice was undone, and the principle of autonomy was strikingly affirmed. But, besides the glory which Thebes won by so popular an act, besides the direct injury inflicted on Sparta and the establishment of a hostile fort, the policy of Epaminondas was calculated to produce a result of greater importance. The loss of Messenia would accelerate that process of decline in the Spartan state, which had already advanced so far. The fewer the lots, the fewer the citizens, according to the indissoluble connexion between land and burgher-rights on the Lycurgean system. It was high time for Sparta to reform her constitution.

The stone which bears witness to the invasion of Laconia.

The Arcadians celebrated this memorable invasion of Laconia by dedicating with part of the spoil a group of statues to the Delphian god. The verses of dedication signify that the indigenous people from sacred Arcadia, having laid Lacedaemon waste, set up the monument as a witness to future generations. The statues are gone, but the verses on their stone have come to light in our own day.

In the meantime Sparta had begged aid from Athens, and Athens had decided to depart from her position of neutrality. A vote was passed, strongly supported by the orator Callistratus, to send the entire force of the city under Iphicrates to assist Sparta. This was evidently the most politic course for Athens to adopt. Sparta was a necessary makeweight against Thebes. Nor is it doubtful that, notwithstanding all their rivalries, no such antipathy parted Athens from Sparta as that which existed between the two states and Thebes. Iphicrates marched to the Isthmus and occupied Corinth and Cenchreae, thus commanding the line of Mount Oneion. His object, it must be clearly understood, was not to prevent the enemy from leaving the Peloponnesus, but to protect the rear of his own army marching into a hostile country. He advanced into Arcadia, but found that the Thebans and their allies had left Laconia, and

Athens sends an army to rescue Sparta.

Sparta was no longer in danger. He therefore drew back to Corinth, and harassed the Boeotian army on its return march, without attempting to bar its passage. For the object of the Athenian expedition was simply to rescue Sparta, not, except so far as Sparta's peril might demand, to fight with the Thebans.

But the hasty vote to march to the rescue was soon followed by a deliberate treaty of alliance; and Athens definitely ranged herself with Sparta against Boeotia and Arcadia. She was already meditating schemes of extending her empire; she was nourishing the hope of recovering the most precious of all her former imperial possessions, the Thracian Amphipolis. With such designs it was impossible to remain neutral; and, as we shall see, there was some danger of a collision with Thebes in Macedonia.

Fighting went on in the Peloponnese between the Arcadians and the allies of Sparta; and a few months later Epaminondas (who had been re-elected Boeotarch in his absence at the beginning of the year) appeared again at the head of the Boeotian army. The Spartans and Athenians had occupied the line of Mount Oneion; this time the object was to keep out the Thebans. But Epaminondas broke through their lines, joined his allies, won over Sicyon and Pellene, and failed to win Phlius. A new succour for Sparta arrived at this moment from over-seas. Twenty ships bearing 2000 Celtic and Iberian mercenaries came from her old ally, the tyrant of Syracuse, to whom she had once sent aid in an hour of peril, and who had more than once sent succour to her. Their coming seems to have decided Epaminondas to return home, though he had accomplished but little, and his political opponent Meneclidas took advantage of the general disappointment to indict him for treason. The result was that Epaminondas was not re-elected Boeotarch for the following year.

To establish her supremacy, Thebes was adopting the same policy as Sparta. She placed a harmost in Sicyon; as the Boeotian cities had formerly been garrisoned by Sparta, the Peloponnesian cities were now to be garrisoned by Thebes. Messenia and Arcadia were to be autonomous, but the Thebans desired to be regarded as both the authors and preservers of that autonomy. As a mistress, distant Thebes might be more tolerable than neighbouring Lacedaemon; but the free federation of Arcadia determined to be free in very deed. Sparta was now sunk so low that the Arcadians—with friendly Messene on one side, and friendly Argos on the other—could hope to maintain their liberty with their own swords, without foreign aid. Their leading spirit Lycomedes animated them to this resolve of independence and self-reliance. "You are the only indigenous natives of the Peloponnesus, and you are the most numerous and hardiest nation in Greece. Your valour is proved by the fact that you have been always in the greatest request as allies. Give up following the lead of others. You made Sparta by following her lead; and now if you follow the lead of Thebes, without yourselves leading in turn, she will prove perhaps a second Sparta." In this mood the Arcadians displayed a surprising activity and achieved a series of successes. The two important cities, Heraea in the west, and Orchomenus in the north, which had hitherto stood aloof, were forced to join the league, which now became in the fullest sense Pan-Arcadian. Some of the northern villages of Laconia were annexed, and the Triphylian towns sought in the league a support against the hated domination of Elis. The federal forces were active in the opposite quarters of Argolis and Messenia. Against all this activity Sparta felt herself helpless. But a second armament of auxiliaries arrived from her friend, the tyrant of Syracuse, and thus reinforced she ventured to take the field, and marched into the plain of Megalopolis. But the expedition was suddenly interrupted; time had been wasted, and the Syracusan force, in accordance with its orders, was obliged to return to Sicily. Its way lay through Laconia, in order to take ship at Gytheion; and the enemy tried to cut it off in the mountain defiles. The Spartan commander Archidamus, who was in the rear, hastened to the rescue, and dispersed the Arcadians with great loss. Not a single Lacedaemonian was killed, and the victory was called the "tearless battle." The joy displayed in Sparta over this slight success showed how low Sparta had fallen.

It may be thought that Dionysius might have kept his troops at home, if they were charged to return before they had well time to begin to fight. But the truth is, that these troops were for some months inactive in Greece, while an attempt was being made to bring about a general peace. The initiative came from Ariobarzanes, the Persian satrap of Phrygia, who sent to Greece an agent well furnished with money; and this move on the part of Persia was probably suggested by Athens. The Syracusan sovereign also intervened in the interests of peace, and the stone remains on which the Athenians thanked Dionysius and his sons for being "good men in regard to the people of the Athenians and their allies, and helping the King's Peace." Thus the King's Peace was the basis of the negotiations of the congress which met at Delphi. Both Athens, which was doubtless the prime mover, and Sparta were most anxious for peace; but each had an ultimate condition from which she would not retreat. Sparta's very life seemed to demand the recovery of Messenia, and Athens had set her heart on Amphipolis. But neither

Spring,
368 B.C.

Sparta receives help from Dionysius. The tearless battle, 368 (late summer ?).

Congress of Delphi, 368 B.C. (summer).

condition would be admitted by Thebes, and consequently the negotiations fell through. They led, however, to independent negotiations of various states with Persia, each seeking to win from the king a recognition of its own claims. Pelopidas went up to Susa on behalf of Thebes to obtain a royal confirmation of the independence of Messenia. The Athenians sent envoys to convince the king of their rights to Amphipolis. Arcadia, Elis, and Argos were also represented. Pelopidas was entirely successful. The king issued an order to Greece, embodying the wishes of Thebes: Messenia and Amphipolis to be independent, the Athenians to recall their warships. The question of Triphylia—whether it was to be dependent on Elis or a part of Arcadia—was decided in favour of Elis; this decision in a matter of absolute indifference to Persia was clearly due to Pelopidas, and indicates strained relations between Thebes and Arcadia. Pelopidas returned with the royal letter, but it found no acceptance in Greece, either at the congress of allies which was convoked at Thebes, or when the document was afterwards sent round to the cities. Arcadia would not abandon Triphylia, and Lycomedes formally protested against the headship of Thebes.

Greek envoys at Susa, 367 B.C.

Persian rescript.

The answer of Thebes to this defiance of her will was an invasion of the Peloponnesus. The line of Mount Oneion was still defended, but negligently; and Epaminondas passed it with Argive help. His object was not to depress Sparta further, for Sparta was now too feeble to be formidable, but to check the pretensions of Arcadia. And this could only be done through strengthening Theban influence in the Peloponnesus by winning new allies. Accordingly, Epaminondas advanced to Achaea, and easily gained the adhesion of the Achaean cities.

Third expedition of Epaminondas into the Peloponnesus, 366 B.C.

But the gain of Achaea was soon followed by its loss. Counter to the moderate policy of Epaminondas, the Thebans had insisted on overthrowing the oligarchical constitutions and banishing the oligarchical leaders; these exiles from the various cities banded together, and recovered each city successively, overthrowing the democracies and expelling the harmosts. Henceforward Achaea was an ardent partisan of Sparta.

Achaea won and lost, 366 B.C.

The unsettled state of the Peloponnesus was conspicuously shown by the events which happened at Sicyon. When the Theban harmost was installed in the acropolis, the oligarchy had been spared; but soon afterwards one of the chief citizens, named Euphron, brought about the establishment of a democracy, and then, procuring his own election as general, organising a mercenary force, and surrounding himself with a bodyguard,—the usual and notorious steps of a despot's progress,—made himself master of the city and har-

Sicyon: Euphron becomes tyrant, 368 B.C.

bour. The Arcadians had helped Euphron in his first designs, but the intrigues of his opponents were so skilful, that Arcadia again intervened and restored to Sicyon the exiles whom the tyrant had

driven out. Euphron fled from the city to the harbour, which he surrendered to the Lacedaemonians; but the Lacedaemonians failed to hold it. Sicyon, however, was not yet delivered from her tyrant.

He was restored by the help of Athenian mercenaries. Afterwards, seeing that he could not maintain himself without the support of Boeotia, he visited Thebes, and was slain on the Cadmea in front of the Hall of Council, by two Sicyonian exiles who had dogged him. His assassins were tried and acquitted at Thebes, but at Sicyon his memory was cherished and he was worshipped as a second founder of the city. The fact shows that under the rule of Euphron the masses of the people were happier than under the political opponents whom he had so mercilessly treated. His son succeeded to his power.

The expedition of Epaminondas was attended with results which were in the end injurious to Thebes. The relations with Arcadia became more and more strained. But in the same year Oropus was wrested from Athens and occupied by a Theban force. The Athenians were unable to cope alone with Thebes; they called on their

allies, but none moved to their aid. The moment was seized by Arcadia. Lycomedes visited Athens and induced the Athenians, smarting with resentment against their allies, to conclude an alliance with the league. Thus Athens was now in the position of being an ally of both Arcadia and Sparta, which were at war with each other; and Arcadia was the ally of Athens and Thebes, which were also at war with each other. The visit of Lycomedes incidentally led to a disaster for Arcadia which outweighed the benefit of the alli-

ance. The ambassador, on his way back, was slain by some exiles into whose hands he fell; and the league lost its ablest statesman.

This change in the mutual relations among the Greek states, brought about by the seizure of Oropus, was followed by another change, brought about by an Athenian plot to seize Corinth. The object was to secure permanent control over the passage into the Peloponnesus. But the plot was discovered and foiled by the Corinthians, who then politely dismissed the Athenian soldiers stationed at various posts in the Corinthian territory. But by herself

Corinth would have been unable to resist the combined pressure of Thebes on one side and Argos on the other; and, as Sparta could not help her, she was driven to make peace with Thebes. She was joined by her neighbour Phlius and by the cities of the Argolic coast; all these states formally recognised the independence of Messene, but did not enter into any alliance with Thebes, or give any pledge to obey her headship. They became, in fact, neutral.

It was a blow to Sparta, who still refused to accept a peace on any terms save the restoration of Messenia. The Messenian question gave political speculators at Athens a subject for meditation. Was the demand of Sparta just? The publicist Isocrates argued the case for Sparta in a speech which he put in the mouth of king Archidamus. Another orator, Alcidamas, vindicated in reply the liberty of the Messenians and declared a principle which was far in advance of his time, "God has left all men free; nature has made no man a slave."

If we survey the political relations of southern Hellas at this epoch, we see Thebes, supported by Argos, still at war with Sparta, who is supported by Athens; Achaea actively siding with Sparta; Elis hostile to Arcadia; the Arcadian league at war with Sparta, in alliance with Athens, in alliance with, but cool towards, Thebes, and already—having lost its leader Lycomedes—beginning to fall into disunion with itself.

Summary of the situation.

Fig. 84.—Coin of Cleitor (obverse). Radiate head of Apollo. Fig. 85.—Coin of Amyntas (obverse). Horseman with spear. Fig. 86.—Coin of Larissa, fourth century. Obverse: head of nymph. Reverse: horse feeding [legend: ΛΑΡΙΣΑΙΩΝ].

The peace with Corinth and others of the belligerent states marks the time at which Peloponnesian affairs cease to occupy the chief place in the counsels of Thebes, and her most anxious attention turns to a different quarter. For Sparta is disabled, and the mistress of Boeotia recognises that it is with Athens that the strife for headship will now be. While events were progressing in the Peloponnesus, as we have seen, Athens was busily engaged in other parts of the world with a view to restoring her maritime empire; and we have now to see how she succeeded, and how Thebes likewise was pushing her own supremacy in the north.

SECT. 3. POLICY AND ACTION OF THEBES IN NORTHERN GREECE

Death of
Amyntas.

The same year which saw the death of Jason of Pherae saw the death of another potentate in the north, his neighbour and ally Amyntas of Macedonia. We have seen how Amyntas had to fight for his kingdom with the Chalcidian league; how he was driven out of his land and restored; and how the league was crushed by the power of Sparta. Both Jason and Amyntas were succeeded by an Alexander. At Pherae, the power first passed to Jason's brothers, of whom one murdered the other and was in turn murdered by his victim's son,—Alexander, whose reign was worthy of its sanguinary inauguration. The Thessalian cities refused to bow down to the supremacy of Pherae, now that Pherae had no man who was worthy to be obeyed; and to resist Alexander of Pherae they invoked the aid of Alexander of Macedonia. The aid was given, and Larissa, Crannon, and other cities passed under Macedonian sway. But this was not the purpose of the Thessalians, to exchange a native for a foreign ruler; and accordingly they invoked the help of Thebes against both Alexanders alike. It was sound policy on the part of Thebes to accede to the request. It was impossible to discern yet what manner of man the successor of Jason might prove to be; and it was important, from the Boeotian point of view, to hinder the reunion of Thessaly under a monarch. The conduct of an expedition was entrusted to Pelopidas, who brought Larissa and other towns in the northern part of Thessaly under a Theban protectorate.

369 B.C.

First expe-
dition of
Pelopidas
to Thes-
saly, 369
B.C.

Thessalian
league.

At the same time, the Thessalians sought to strengthen their position by a federal union,—a political experiment which had been tried in Thessaly before. The little we know of the league which was established about this time suggests rather the revival of an old system than a new creation. The country was divided into four political divisions corresponding to the old geographical districts; at the head of each was a polemarch, who had officers of horse and foot under him; and at the head of the league was an archon, elected if not for life at least for longer than a year. Thus the organisation was military; but there are indications that it grew out of an old amphictionic association. There is no reason to think that Pelopidas had more to do with the establishment of the Thessalian federation than Epaminondas with that of the Pan-Arcadian league; the part of Thebes in either case was simply to support and confirm.

Tetrads.

Archon.

Macedonia offered no obstacles to the operations of Pelopidas in Thessaly, for it was involved in a domestic struggle. One of the nobles. Ptolemy of Alorus, rebelled against the king, and was supported by the king's unnatural mother Eurydice. The two parties called upon Pelopidas to adjudicate between them, and he patched up a temporary arrangement and concluded a Theban alliance with Macedonia. Hardly had he turned his back when Ptolemy murdered Alexander and married Eurydice. But it seemed as if the paramours would not be permitted to reap the profits of their crime. Another pretender to the throne had gathered an army of mercenaries and occupied all the land along the Chalcidian frontier. Help, however, was at hand. An Athenian fleet was cruising in the Thermaic gulf, under the command of Iphicrates. The queen visited the admiral on the coast, accompanied by her two sons, Perdiccas and Philip,—the brothers of Iphicrates, since he had been adopted as a son by Amyntas,—and persuaded him to help her in her need. By his exertions the pretender was expelled, and the succession of Perdiccas was secured under the regency of Ptolemy.

The interests of Athens on the Chalcidian and the adjacent coasts had forced that state to keep an ever-watchful eye on political events in Macedonia and to seek influence at the court of Aegae. The intervention of Iphicrates was not the first case in which Athenian power had settled a dynastic question. His settlement was more abiding than that of Pelopidas; we may conjecture that the opportune appearance of the Athenian fleet was due to the circumstance that Thebes had interfered. But Thebes was resolved to continue her interference, and oust the Athenian influence. Pelopidas, again dispatched to the north, compelled the regent Ptolemy to enter into alliance with Thebes and assure his fidelity by furnishing a number of hostages. Among the young Macedonian nobles who were sent as pledges to Thebes was the boy Philip, who was destined to be the maker of Macedonia, and was now to be trained for the work in the military school of Boeotia, under the eye of Epaminondas himself.

Having thus brought Macedonia within the circle of the Theban supremacy, Pelopidas on his way home visited the camp of the despot of Pherae. But he did not know that Alexander had become the ally of Athens—an inevitable combination, since it was the interest of both to oppose Theban expansion in the north. Supported by Athens, the despot could defy Thebes, and he detained his visitor Pelopidas as a hostage. A Boeotian army marched to rescue the captive; but an armament of 1000 men arrived by sea from Athens, and the invaders, who were commanded by incompetent generals, were out-manœuvred and forced to retreat. Epaminondas was serving as a common hoplite in the ranks, and but for his presence the army would have been lost. The soldiers unani-

Murder of Alexander of Macedon, 369-8 B.C. Revolt of Pausanias.

Intervention of Iphicrates.

Second expedition of Pelopidas to Macedonia and Thessaly, 368 B.C.

Pelopidas detained by the despot of Pherae.

Theban invasion of Thessaly to rescue Pelopidas, 368 B.C.

(autumn),
unsuccess-
ful.
Second
invasion
of Thes-
saly to
rescue
Pelopidas,
367 B.C.
(first
months),
successful.

mously invited him to take the command, and he skilfully extri-
cated them from a dangerous position and managed their safe retreat. This exploit secured the re-election of Epaminondas as
Boeotarch, and he immediately returned to Thessaly at the head
of another army to deliver his friend. It was necessary to apply a
compulsion severe enough to frighten the tyrant, but not so violent
as to transport him with fury, which might be fatal to his prisoner.
This was achieved by dexterous military operations, and Pelopidas
was released in return for a month's truce. It seems probable that
at the same time Epaminondas freed Pharsalus from the rule of
Pherae. But it was not the interest of Thebes to overthrow the
tyrant or even limit his authority to his own city. It was well that
he should be there, as a threat to the rest of Thessaly; it was well
that Thessaly should be unable to dispense with Theban protection.
The power of Alexander extended over Phthiotis and Magnesia,
and along the shores of the Pagasaean Bay, and to neighbouring
towns like Scotussa. His tyranny and brutality seem to have been
extreme, though the anecdotes of his cruelty cannot be implicitly
trusted. We read that he buried men alive, or sewed them up in the
hides of wild beasts for his hounds to tear. We read that he massacred the inhabitants of two friendly cities. We read that he worshipped as a divine being the dagger with which he had slain his
uncle, and gave it the name of "Sir Luck"—an anecdote indicating
a strain of madness which often attends the taste for cruelty. Ex-
cellently invented, if not true, is the story that, having seen with
dry eyes a performance of the *Troades* of Euripides, a drama un-
utterably sad, the tyrant sent an apology to the actor, explaining
that his apparent want of emotion was due to no defect in the
acting, but to a feeling of shame that tears for the sorrows of
Hecuba should fall from the eyes of one who had shown no pity for
so many victims.

It has been said that the chief desire of Athens at this time was
to regain the finest jewel of her first empire, Amphipolis. The fleet,
under Iphicrates, was cruising and watching, with this purpose in
view; but the hopes of success—which depended much on the goodwill of Macedonia—were lessened by the ties which Ptolemy had
contracted with Thebes. And, besides losing Macedonian support,
Athens was impeded by the cities of the Chalcidian league, who now
broke away from the Athenian alliance and made a treaty with
Amphipolis.

Meanwhile Athens began to act in the Eastern Aegean. The opportunity was furnished by the revolt of her friend Ariobarzanes,
the satrap of Phrygia. It was the policy of Athens to help the satrap

without breaking with the Great King, from whom she still hoped
to obtain a recognition of her claim to Amphipolis. A fleet of thirty
galleys and 8000 troops was sent under her other experienced general Timotheus, and he accomplished more in the east than Iphicrates had accomplished in the north. He laid siege to Samos, on
which Persia had laid hands, contrary to the King's Peace; and
took it at the end of ten months. At the same time he lent assistance
to Ariobarzanes, who had to maintain himself against the satraps
of Lydia and Caria; and as a reward for these services Athens obtained the cession of two cities in the Thracian Chersonese—Sestos
and Crithote.

Timo-
theus
sent to
Asia
Minor,
366 B.C.
He
captures
Samos,
365 B.C.

Of these acquisitions Sestos was of special value, from its position
on the Hellespont, securing to Athens control at this point over the
ships which supplied her with corn from the Euxine coasts. But
more than this, she now regained a foothold in the peninsula which
Miltiades had won for her, and she hoped to make it entirely her
own up to a line drawn across the isthmus north of Cardia, marked
at one point by an altar of "Zeus of Boundaries." Timotheus himself began the work of expansion by annexing Elaeus near the southern extremity. Thus Athens began to revive her old empire, but in
Samos she revealed her designs even more clearly. This island was
not treated as a subject ally, but was appropriated as Athenian
territory. Outsettlers were sent from Athens to occupy Samos, and
thus the system of cleruchies, which had been the most unpopular
feature of the first Confederacy, and had been expressly guarded
against at the formation of the second Confederacy, was renewed.
It did not indeed violate the letter of the constitution of the league,
which only bound Athens not to force outsettlers upon members of
the league; but it was distinctly a violation in spirit. The treatment
of Samos showed Greece that Athens was bent on rising again to her
old Imperial position; while the second Confederacy was based on
the principle that she had renounced such pretensions for ever.

Athens
gets
Sestos.

Delighted with the achievements of Timotheus, the Athenians
appointed him to command the fleet which had been operating for
years on the Macedonian coast under Iphicrates, whose failure was
strikingly contrasted with the success of Timotheus. It must be remembered that while Iphicrates was hindered by the hostility of the
regent of Macedon, Timotheus was helped by the friendship of the
satrap of Phrygia; but Timotheus possessed a diplomatic dexterity
which Iphicrates never displayed. And now fortune favoured the
diplomatist. Shortly before his new appointment, the regent
Ptolemy was assassinated by the young king Perdiccas, who thus
avenged his brother Alexander. The change in the holders of power

Murder of
the regent
Ptolemy;
Perdicas
in power,
365 B.C.

led to a change in policy. Macedonia freed itself from the influence of Thebes, and the young king sought the support of Athens. And so Timotheus, not only untrammelled by Macedonian opposition, but even aided by Macedonian auxiliaries, set about the reduction of towns around the Thermaic gulf. He compelled Methone and Pydna to join the Athenian confederacy; and in the Chalcidic peninsula he made himself master of Potidaea and Torone. The acquisition of these Chalcidic towns was valuable in itself and Potidaea was occupied by Athenian outsettlers; but the main purpose of the general was to weaken the resources of Olynthus, which, at the head of the Chalcidian states, gave powerful support to its ally Amphipolis, the supreme object coveted by Athens, whose rights to it had been recently recognised by the Persian king. A famous mercenary captain named Charidemus, who had previously served under Iphicrates, was now secured again by Timotheus; but two efforts to capture Amphipolis were repelled. The work of Brasidas was not destined to be undone.

Successes
of Timo-
theus in
the
Chalcidic
region
(364-2
B.C.).

It was high time for Thebes to interfere. If the successes of Timotheus were allowed to continue, Athens would soon recover Euboea, and the adhesion of that island was, from its geographical position, of the highest importance to Boeotia. But in order to check the advance of her neighbour it would be necessary for Thebes to grapple with her on her own element. By the advice of Epaminondas, in spite of the advice of Meneclidas, it was resolved to create a navy and enter upon the career of a sea-power. This was a momentous decision, which demanded a careful consideration of ways and means. Given the problem, to break the power of Athens, there can be no question that Epaminondas advised the only possible method of solving it. But it might be well to consider whether its solution was a necessity for Thebes. The history of Boeotia had marked it out as a continental power; and it would have been wiser to consolidate its sway on the mainland. The maintenance of a navy involved financial efforts which could not be sustained by any but a great commercial state; and the cities of Boeotia had no trade. It was the natural antipathy of the two neighbours far more than any mature consideration of her own interests that drove Boeotia to take this indiscreet step. Yet the step had immediate success. A hundred triremes were built and manned and sent to the Propontis under the Boeotarch, Epaminondas.

Boeotian
navy.

364 B.C.

The sailing of this fleet was a blow to Athens, not from any victory that it gained—there was no battle—but from the support and encouragement which it gave to those members of the Confederacy which were eager to break their bonds. The establishment of the cleruchies of Samos had created great discontent and apprehension among the Athenian allies, and they wanted only the support of a power like Thebes to throw off the federal yoke. Byzantium openly rebelled; Rhodes and Chios negotiated with Epaminondas; and even Ceos, close to Attica itself, defied Athens. When the Theban fleet returned home, Chabrias recalled Ceos to its allegiance, and a new act of treaty was drawn up; but a second rebellion had to be put down at Julis before the island acquiesced in Athenian sway. The expedition of Epaminondas also served to support the enemies of Athens, who opposed her advance in the Chersonese; namely, the free city of Cardia, and the Thracian king Cotys, who was aided by his son-in-law Iphicrates. This general, superseded by Timotheus, had not ventured to return to Athens, and now sided with her enemies.

Revolts of Athenian allies, 364 B.C. Revolts of Ceos, 364 and 363 B.C.

While the young Theban navy went forth to oppose Athens in the Propontis, a Theban army had marched against the ally of Athens, Alexander of Pherae, whose hand, strengthened by a mercenary force, had been heavy against the Thessalians. Once more, but for the last time, Pelopidas entered Thessaly at the head of an army to assist the Federation. Before he left Thebes, the sun suffered an eclipse, and this celestial event, interpreted by the prophets as a sign of coming evil, cast a gloom over his departure.

Third expedition of Pelopidas to Thessaly, 364 B.C.

Eclipse of the sun, July 13.

At Pharsalus he was joined by forces of the Thessalian league, and immediately advanced against Pherae itself. Alexander came forth to meet him with a large force, and it was a matter of great importance, for the purpose of barring the Theban advance, to occupy the heights known as the Dog's Heads, on the road from Pharsalus to Pherae. The armies reached the critical spot nearly at the same time, and there was a rush for the crests. The Theban cavalry beat off the cavalry of the foe, but lost time in pursuing it, and in the meantime the infantry of Alexander seized the hills. In the battle which followed the object of the Thebans was to drive the enemy from this position. Having been repeatedly repelled, Pelopidas, by a combined assault of horse and foot, at length won the summit and forced the enemy to give way. But in the moment of victory the impetuous general espied the hated despot in whose dungeon he had languished, and yielding to an irresistible fit of passion, aggravated by the excitement of battle, he forgot the duties of a general and rushed against his enemy. Alexander withdrew into the midst of his guards, and Pelopidas, plunging desperately after him, was overwhelmed by numbers. It was even so that Cyrus threw away his victory at Cunaxa. The death of Pelopidas was not fatal to his followers, who routed the enemy with heavy loss; but it

Battle of Cynoscephalae.

Death of Pelopidas.

Thessaly
becomes a
Boeotian
depend-
ency,
363 B.C.

was a sore blow both to his own Thebes, of which he had been the deliverer and strong pillar, and to Thessaly, of which he had been the protector. In the following year an army was sent against Pherae, and avenged his death. Alexander was obliged to relinquish all his possessions except his own city and submit to the headship of Thebes.

It was about this time that Thebes shocked the Hellenic world by the destruction of her venerable rival, the Minyan Orchomenus. Some Theban exiles induced the horsemen of Orchomenus to join them in a plot to subvert the constitution. But, the hearts of the principal conspirators failing them before the day of action came, they informed the Boeotarchs; the horsemen were promptly seized and condemned to death; and the Assembly passed a resolution to rase Orchomenus and enslave its people. The Thebans rejoiced at a fair pretext to wreak the hatred of ages upon their unhappy neighbour. They marched forth and executed the doom; the men were slain because they resisted, the rest of the folk were enslaved. It was a deed on which Greece cried shame; and, if the moderate and humane Boeotarch, who was then in the Hellespontine regions, had been present to control the counsels of his country, it would possibly never have been committed.

SECT. 4. THE BATTLE OF MANTINEA

While Thebes was intent on opposing Athens, now her only serious rival, she had kept aloof from the Peloponnesus. But the course of affairs there was soon to demand a new intervention. The interest now centres on the relations of Elis with Arcadia; and the decisive element in the situation is the rift in the Arcadian league, perceptibly widening every month.

Her rights over Triphylia were the chief question of political importance for Elis. They had been recognised in the Persian rescript, but Arcadia refused to admit them and Thebes did not interfere. Thus Elis found herself in the same plight as Sparta in regard to the Arcadian league. It had always been a principle of Lacedaemonian policy to preserve against Elis the independence of her two southern neighbours, the Pisatans and the Triphylians. But now Sparta was only too ready to renounce this policy and recognise the Elean claim, for the sake of winning an ally. It was in the nature of things that the two states should combine to recover Messenia and Triphylia. Thus there came to pass a change for the better in the prospect of Sparta: enemies had risen up against Arcadia on the north and on the west, and Thebes held aloof. The Spartans had recently gained a welcome success in the recovery of Sellasia, with the help of a force which had been sent to their aid by the second Dionysius of Syracuse.

Besides Triphylia there were certain places on the mountainous frontier between Elis and Arcadia to which Elis professed to have claims. One of these was Lasion, in the high plateau of Pholoe, north-east of Olympia. The Eleans occupied the district, but were speedily driven out by the Pan-Arcadian *eparitoi*, who were always ready for such emergencies. The plains of Elis were far more assailable than the highlands of Arcadia, and the Arcadians were able to carry the war to the very heart of their foe. The Olympian festival would fall next year, and they were resolved that it should not be celebrated under the time-honoured presidency of Elis. They marched to Olympia, and occupied and fortified the Hill of Cronus, which looks down upon the Altis. Then they made an attack on the unwalled city of Elis, in concert with the democratic faction. But the attempt at a revolution failed and the Arcadians were repulsed.

Outbreak of war between Elis and Arcadia, 365 B.C. First Arcadian invasion of Elis, 365 B.C.

In the following year a second invasion reduced the Eleans to such distress that they implored Sparta to make a diversion and draw off the Arcadian forces. In answer to this prayer Archidamus occupied Cromnon, a fort which commands the road from Megalopolis to Messenia, with a garrison of 200 men. The importance of this step is shown by the fact that not only did the Arcadians promptly leave Elis, but they were also joined by allies, Argives as well as Messenians, to besiege Cromnon. A Spartan post there cut off the communication between the Arcadian and the Messenian capitals and was a threat to both. Archidamus at first tried to create a second diversion by ravaging northern Laconia, which was now politically part of Arcadia. When this failed, he made an attempt to relieve Cromnon, but was driven back with some loss. A second attempt at rescue would have been successful, if it had been better concerted, but it led to the capture of almost the whole garrison; an event which ten years before would have sent a shock through the Hellenic world, but now seemed an ordinary occurrence.

Second Arcadian invasion, 364 B.C.

The Arcadians were again free to continue their designs in Elis. The time of the Olympian games was approaching, and the people of Pisa, the ancient possessors of the sanctuary, who had by no means forgotten the rights which Elis had usurped in days long gone by, were installed as presidents of the festival. It was fully expected that the feast would not pass without battle and bloodshed. The hill of Cronus had been occupied for a year by the Arcadian garrison, but now the whole army of the federation, as well as 2000 spearmen from Argos and 400 cavalry from Athens, arrived

The Olympian games, 364 B.C., July, celebrated by the Pisatans (Ol. 104).

to protect the solemn celebration. The day came round and the games began. The horse race was run and won. The next contest was the pentathlon, which demanded excellence in five different kinds of athletic prowess—in running, wrestling, hurling the javelin, throwing the disc, and leaping. The first event, the race, was over when the company became aware that the men of Elis were marching up to the bank of the Cladeus, which bounded the western side of the Altis. The soldiers took up their position on the opposite bank, but the games went on. Those competitors who had not failed in the race proceeded to the wrestling; but as the spectators, when the alarm was given, moved from the race-course into the Altis, to be nearer the scene of action, the wrestling match was held in the open space between the race-course and the Great Altar, under the terrace of the Treasure-houses. The Eleans, who were supported by an Achaean force, performed a sacrifice, and then, charging across the stream with unexpected boldness, drove back the Arcadian and Argive line into the Altis. A battle ensued in the southern part of the holy precinct, between the Hall of Council and the great Temple of Zeus. But the colonnades of these and other adjacent buildings gave shelter and points of vantage to the defenders; and the Eleans, when their captain fell, retired across the stream to their camp. The Arcadians improvised a fortification on the western side of the Altis, using for this purpose the tents of the spectators: and the men of Elis, seeing that it would be useless to repeat their attack, returned home, obliged to content themselves with declaring the festival to be null and void, and marking the year in their register as an "An-Olympiad." The religious sentiment of Greece was outraged by these violent scenes at a sanctuary which belonged to all Greece rather than to any single state; and there can be no question that the general sympathy—independently of all political considerations —was on the side of Elis, whose presidency was regarded in Hellas as part of the order of nature, and was strongly adverse to the Arcadian intruders supporting with arms the antiquated rights of Pisa. But it was far worse when the Arcadians began to make free use of the sacred treasures of Olympia, for the purpose of paying the federal army. This was an act of sacrilegious spoliation which could not be defended, and it was disastrous to the Arcadian Federation.

It was inevitable that, when the first impulse of enthusiasm which drove the Arcadian cities to unite together had spent itself, the old jealousies would emerge again and imperil the Pan-Arcadian idea. So it was that the two neighbours, Mantinea and Tegea, whose common action had been the chief cause of the federal union, began

Battle in the Altis.

Spoliation of the Olympian treasures.

Divisions in the Arcadian League.

to resume something of their traditional enmity. The scandal of Olympia gave Mantinea, who was jealous of Megalopolis also, a fair opportunity to secede from the League, which had put itself so signally in the wrong. This step necessarily involved the consequence that Mantinea would definitely range herself with the other camp in the Peloponnesus—with Sparta, Elis, and Achaea. And thus the traditional policies of Mantinea and Tegea were reversed. Tegea, the support of Sparta, had become the life and soul of the anti-Spartan movement; Mantinea, the state which Sparta had uncitied, was now Sparta's support. Though the Arcadian Assembly resented and tried to punish the protest of Mantinea, the pressure of public opinion induced it to forbid any further plundering of the Olympian sanctuaries.

When this resolution was taken, the weakness of the Arcadian League was exhibited. There was no money in the federal treasury to pay the standing army, and without this army it would be impossible for Arcadia to maintain herself against enemies on three sides—not to speak of disaffected Mantinea—without the protection of Thebes. But there was a strong feeling throughout the country against a Theban protectorate, and a large number of wealthy Arcadians, who shared this feeling, proposed to solve the difficulty by enrolling themselves in the corps of *Eparitoi* and serving without pay. Occupying this position they would be able to dictate the policy of the League. There was little doubt that the predominance of this party would soon bring Arcadia into alliance with Sparta, which was no longer dangerous to Arcadian liberty. But such a political revolution would be fatal to Theban influence, which rested on the antagonism between Arcadia and Sparta; it might even imperil the independence of Messenia.

To meet this danger of an alliance between Sparta and Arcadia, Thebes was constrained to send a fourth expedition into the Peloponnese. It was imperative to support the Theban party in Arcadia. Both parties alike were probably satisfied with the resolution of the Assembly to make peace with Elis and acknowledge her rights at Olympia. Each city swore to the peace. At Tegea the solemnity of the oath led to an incident. Arcadians from other places had gathered together for the occasion, which they celebrated by feast and merriment. The commander of the Boeotian garrison ordered the gates to be shut and arrested the leaders of the anti-Theban party. Most of the Mantineans present had left the town at an early hour, but there were a few among the prisoners; and the energetic protests of Mantinea frightened the faint-hearted harmost into releasing all his prisoners and excusing his act by a false explanation.

Fourth Theban invasion of the Peloponnesus, 362 B.C.

The *coup* had doubtless been planned long beforehand, and consent obtained from the highest quarter. Epaminondas, when complaint was made at Thebes, approved the act of arrest, and condemned the act of release. At the same time he declared to the Arcadian League that it had no right to make peace with Elis without consulting Thebes. "We will march into Arcadia," he said, "and assist our friends."

The threat was seriously meant, and the friends and enemies of Thebes prepared for war. Athens, the ally of both Sparta and Arcadia, could now fulfil without difficulty the double obligation, by supporting those Arcadians who were on Sparta's side. The common dread of Thebes was reflected in the quintuple alliance which Athens (with her allies), Mantinea, Elis, Achaia, and Phlius formed for the sake of mutual protection.[1] Part of the text of this treaty is preserved to us on fragments of one of the original marble copies. It is worthy of remark that the Mantineans, who seem to have been the only Arcadian community that entirely dissociated itself from the government at Megalopolis, appear in the treaty as "the Arcadians"—thus claiming to be the true representatives of their country.

The Boeotian force in its full strength, accompanied by all the allies of central Greece who were pledged to follow Thebes into the field, went forth under Epaminondas to bring back the unruly Peloponnesians under Boeotian control. The Phocians alone refused to go; the terms of the alliance which bound them to Boeotia obliged them to bear aid only if Boeotia were itself attacked. When he reached Nemea, Epaminondas halted his army, with the hope of intercepting the forces which Athens prepared to send to her allies. But the Athenian forces came not and he advanced to Tegea, the chief centre of Theban influence in the peninsula, which he had appointed as the meeting-place for all his allies—Arcadian, Argive, and Messenian. His enemies were also gathering to the rival city of Mantinea, and a Spartan army under old Agesilaus was expected there. Epaminondas marched to attack them before the Spartans and Athenians arrived, but found their position too strong and retired to his camp in Tegea. Learning that Agesilaus had already set out, he determined to strike a second blow at Sparta. He would have found the place as unprotected as "a nest of young birds," if his plan had not been thwarted by a Cretan runner who carried the news to Agesilaus. The king immediately returned on his steps; and when Epaminondas after a night's march reached Sparta, he found

The quintuple alliance, summer, 362 B.C.

March of Epaminondas to Sparta.

---

[1] The preliminaries must have been arranged in the early summer, but the date of the final treaty was later than the battle of Mantinea.

it prepared and defended. Baffled in this project by an incalculable chance, Epaminondas promptly resolved to attempt another surprise. He foresaw that the army at Mantinea would immediately march to the rescue of Sparta, and that Mantinea would consequently be inadequately guarded. His camp at Tegea commanded the direct road from Mantinea to Sparta, so that the enemy would be obliged to march by the longer western road. Moving rapidly he reached Tegea, where he rested his hoplites, but he sent on his cavalry to surprise Mantinea. The army had departed, as he calculated, and the people were out in the fields, busy with the harvest. But in the same hour in which the Theban horse approached from the south, a body of Athenian cavalry had reached the city. They had not yet eaten or drunk, but they rode forth and drove the assailants back. The conflict between the two weary troops of horsemen was sharp, and was marked by the death of Gryllus, the son of Xenophon the historian.

He returns to Tegea.

Cavalry battle at Mantinea.

The allied army, learning that Sparta was no longer in danger, soon returned from its fruitless excursion to its former post, now reinforced by both the Spartan and Athenian contingents. Foiled in his two projects of surprise, Epaminondas was obliged to attack the united enemy at Mantinea; the difficulty of supplying his army with provisions, and the anxiety of his allies to return home as soon as possible, rendered it imperative to bring the campaign to a swift decision. The enemy occupied the narrow part of the plain, south of Mantinea, where ridges of the opposite mountains approach each other; the object of Epaminondas was to sweep them out of his way and take the city. But instead of marching straight for the gap, he adopted a strategical movement which puzzled his antagonists. He led his army north-westwards to a point in the hills near the modern Tripolitza, and then moved a short distance along the skirts of the mountain so as to approach the right wing of the foe. He then halted and formed in battle array. The enemy were deceived by the indirect advance. Seeing him march obliquely towards the hills, they concluded that he would not attack that day, and even when he changed his direction and advanced towards them, persisted in their false opinion.

Epaminondas adopted the same tactics by which he had won at Leuctra. On the left he placed the Boeotian hoplites, under his own immediate command, in a deep column, destined to break through the right wing of the enemy before the rest of the armies could come to blows. The oblique advance, besides its chief purpose of deceiving the foe, had the further advantage of assisting the peculiar tactics of the general; for, when he formed his line, there was obvi-

Dispositions of Epaminondas.

ously a far greater distance between his right and the hostile left than that which divided his left from the hostile right. The Mantineans (since it was their territory) had the place of honour on the extremity of the enemy's right wing, and the Lacedaemonians were next them; the Athenians were on the farthest left; and both wings were protected by squadrons of horse. Epaminondas placed his own cavalry in deep column in front of the deep column of infantry. But there was one danger against which he had to guard. When the Boeotian column charged, the Athenian left might wheel round and attack it on the unshielded side—a movement which could be executed owing to the distance dividing them from his own right. To meet this danger, he sent a body of horse and foot to occupy a rising ground, out in the plain, considerably in advance of his line; this body could attack the Athenians in the rear if they tried such a movement.

With an extraordinary lack of perception, the Lacedaemonians and their allies witnessed these manœuvres without understanding their drift; and it was not until Epaminondas began to advance in full march against them, that they realised his meaning and rushed tumultuously to arms. All fell out as he designed. His cavalry routed their cavalry, and the force of his wedge of hoplites, led by himself, broke through the opposing array and put the Lacedaemonians to flight. It is remarkable indeed how the tactical lesson of Leuctra seems to have been lost on the Spartans. The men of Achaea and Elis and the rest, when they saw the flight of the right wing, wavered before they came into collision with their own opponents. It is not quite clear what happened, but here again Mantinea seems to repeat Leuctra: the charge of the Theban left decided the battle; with the exception of cavalry engagements, there was but little and desultory fighting along the rest of the line.

It was a great Theban victory, and yet a chance determined that this victory should be the deathblow to the supremacy of Thebes. As he pursued the retreating foe, at the head of his Thebans, Epaminondas received a mortal thrust from a spear. When the news spread through the field, the pursuit was stayed and the effect of the victory was undone; the troops fell back like beaten men. "So striking a proof has hardly ever been rendered, on the part of soldiers towards their general, of devoted and absorbing sentiment. All the hopes of this army, composed of such diverse elements, were centred in Epaminondas; all their confidence of success, all their security against defeat, were derived from the idea of acting under his orders; all their power, even of striking down a defeated enemy,

Death of
Epami-
nondas.

appeared to vanish when those orders were withdrawn."[2] And there was no one to take his place. In his dying moments, before the point of the fatal spear was extracted, Epaminondas asked for Iolaidas and Daiphantus, whom he destined as his successors. He was told that they were slain. "Then," he said, "make peace with the enemy." Peace was made on condition that things should remain as they were; Megalopolis and Messenia were recognised—the abiding results of Theban policy. In this peace Sparta would not acquiesce; she still persisted in refusing to recognise the independence of Messenia, but her allies would not listen to her protests.

The military genius of Epaminondas, the qualities of mind and character which distinguished him among his countrymen, and the actual work which he accomplished in the deliverance of Messenia and the support of Arcadia, must not be suffered to obscure the fact that his political faculty was mediocre. What could be done by the energy and ability of a general, or by the discretion of a magistrate, that he did; but he failed to solve the fundamental problems which demanded solution at the hands of a statesman who aimed at making his country great. It was necessary to create an efficient machinery, acting on definite principles, for conducting the foreign affairs of Boeotia—like the machinery which existed at Sparta. This was the only possible substitute for brains, which were not plentiful in Boeotia; Epaminondas could not hope to communicate any part of his own virtue to his successors. It was necessary to decide whether it was possible or desirable for Boeotia to enter into competition with Athens as a maritime power. If the decision were affirmative, it was of capital importance to organise the navy on a sound financial foundation. There is no sign that Epaminondas grappled with the problems of government and finance; his voyage to the Propontis was an experiment which had no results. Nor does he seem to have taken steps to secure Boeotia on the side of her dangerous Phocian neighbours, though he had the insight to organise anew the Amphictionic League and make it an instrument of Theban policy. Above all, he did not succeed in accomplishing the first thing needful, the welding together of Boeotia into a real national unity. He aspired to expand Boeotia into an empire; the worst of it was that no one had come before him to make it into a nation. That which mythical Lycurgus and Theseus had done for Sparta and Athens had never been done for Thebes by any of her numerous heroes. Epaminondas seems to have attempted to unify Boeotia; if he had known how to build such an unity on solid foun-

The work of Epaminondas.

dations, he might have bestowed on Thebes a future of glory which he would not have lived to see. But his ambition—for his country, not for himself—was too impatient and imaginative. The ardour of his patriotism impelled him to enter upon paths of policy which his countrymen felt no resistless impulse to pursue; the successes of Thebes were achieved by his brains, not by her force. He bore his country aloft on the wings of his genius, but did not impart to her frame the principle of that soaring motion; so that when the shaft pierced the heart of her sustainer, she sank to the earth, never to rise again. Epaminondas was a great general; he was not a great statesman.

Sect. 6. The Last Expedition of Agesilaus

To no one in Greece can the supremacy of Thebes have come as a sorer trial than to the Spartan king Agesilaus. He who had once dreamed of conquering Persia had lived to see his own inviolable land twice trodden by an invader, his own city quake twice before an enemy at her doors. But he had at least the consolation of out-living the triumph of the Theban, and seeing the brief supremacy pass away. The death of Epaminondas, of which he could not mis take the significance, did not restore Messenia or give Sparta any immediate power; but, Epaminondas dead and Arcadia spent, Sparta had now a prospect of regaining something of her old in-fluence. With her own diminished population she could do little; it would be necessary to follow the general example and take mer-cenary forces into her pay; but to do this a well-filled treasury was needful. Accordingly we find Sparta, as well as Athens, busy beyond the sea, taking part in the troubles which in these years agitated the western portion of the Persian kingdom, and lending help to the satraps and dynasts who were rebelling against the Great King. The object of Athens was territory, the object of Sparta was money. While Timotheus had been engaged in winning Samos, Agesilaus had visited Asia Minor and done his utmost in support of Ario-barzanes—for the sake of gold. And after the battle of Mantinea, he again went forth in a guise which differed little from that of a mercenary in foreign service.

Sparta in want of money.

365 b.c.

The revolt in the Persian empire.

The borders of Western Asia, from the Hellespont to the Nile, were in revolt against the Great King. The expedition of Cyrus was only the first of a series of rebellions which troubled the reign of Artaxerxes. We have seen how Cyprus rebelled and was subju-gated, but Egypt still defied the Persian power, and its success set a bad example to the satraps of the adjoining countries. The Athe-

nian general Chabrias had helped the Egyptians to strengthen their
country by a scientific system of defences, but he was recalled to
Athens after the King's Peace; and the Athenian whom we next
find in Egypt is fighting on the other side—the free-lance Iphicrates,
giving sound military advice to the Persian commander, which the
Persian commander does not follow. Soon after this the satraps of
Asia began to rebel—first in Cappadocia, then in Phrygia, then
successively in Ionia, Caria, and Lydia—and the insurrection extended to Phoenicia and Syria. A scheme of co-operation was
formed between the satraps and the Egyptian king Tachos, who
had recently come to the throne, and Sparta decided to support this
coalition. Athens held aloof, but Chabrias went once more to Egypt
as a volunteer.

At the head of a thousand men, and accompanied by thirty
Spartans as advisers, Agesilaus set sail for the Nile. It is said that
the small figure, the lame leg, and the plain dress of the experienced
old soldier made a bad impression in Egypt; in any case he was not
given the supreme command of the army as he expected. When a
sufficient force was gathered, Tachos, accompanied by Agesilaus
and Chabrias, made an expedition to Phoenicia, to act there against
the Persian troops; but they were obliged to return almost immediately in consequence of a revolt against Tachos, headed by his
cousin Nektanebos. The Spartan king, who considered that he had
been slighted by Tachos, supported the rival; and Tachos fled to
Susa and made his peace with the Persian monarch. Another com-
petitor then arose, but was defeated by the effective support which
Agesilaus gave to Nektanebos. In consequence of these struggles for
the Egyptian throne nothing was done against Persia, and the great
coalition signally failed. Ariobarzanes of Phrygia, the friend of
Timotheus, was betrayed and crucified; another satrap was murdered; the rest made their submission to their king. Within a year
Western Asia was entirely subject to Artaxerxes.

But Sparta had won from the futile project what she really
wanted. She might shelter her dignity under the pretext that she
had gone forth to punish the Persian king for recognising the independence of Messenia, but every one knew that her motive was to
replenish her treasury. Nektanebos presented her with 230 talents,
in return for the support of Agesilaus. It was the last service the
old king was destined to perform for his country. Death carried
him off—he was eighty-four years old—at the Harbour of Menelaus
on the way to Cyrene, and his embalmed body was sent home to
Sparta.

Though not in any sense a great man, though not in the same

373 B.C.

Agesilaus
in Egypt,
361 B.C.

Death of
Agesilaus,
winter,
361-0
B.C. (?).

rank as Lysander, Agesilaus had been for forty years a prominent figure in Greece. There is something melancholy about his career. He could remember the outbreak of the Peloponnesian War; he had seen the triumph of Sparta, and had conducted her policy during a great part of thirty years of supremacy; and then, as an old man, he shared in her humiliation. He had begun by dreaming of the conquest of Persia; he had been forced to abandon such dreams; and he had translated his ardour into a bitter hatred against an Hellenic city. It is tragic to see him, at the age of eighty-three, going forth against Persia once more, not now for conquest or glory, but to earn by any and every means the money needed by his indigent country.

CHAPTER XV

THE SYRACUSAN EMPIRE AND THE STRUGGLE WITH CARTHAGE

WE have seen how the war in Greece, in its last stage, after the collapse of the Sicilian expedition, ceased to be a mere domestic struggle among Greek states and became part of the greater struggle between Greek and barbarian. We have now to see how the strife of Greek and barbarian was renewed at the same moment in the west. It is indeed remarkable how these two episodes in the great conflict between Asia and Europe run parallel though separate courses in the fifth century. The victory of Himera, which beat back the Carthaginian invader from the shores of Sicily, was won in the same year which saw the repulsion of the Persian invader from the shores of Attica. After these triumphs of Hellas, both Persia and Carthage had long lain quiescent, and left the Greek cities of east and west to live undisturbed at war or in peace among themselves. It was not till the mightiest city of eastern and the mightiest city of western Hellas came to blows and wore one another out in the conflict, that the barbarian foes, discerning the propitious hour, once more made their voices heard in the Grecian world. Sicily with an exhausted Syracuse, the Aegean with an exhausted Athens, invited Carthage and Persia alike to make an attempt to enlarge their borders at the expense of the Greek.

Parallel between struggle of western Greeks with Carthage and eastern Greeks with Persia.

SECT. I. CARTHAGINIAN DESTRUCTION OF SELINUS AND HIMERA

After she had achieved the repulse and utter confusion of Athens, it might have seemed likely that Syracuse would succeed in founding a Sicilian empire. Her first task would be to reduce Catane and Naxos; and, when this was done, the other cities, including luxurious Acragas, would hardly be able to resist. This prospect was disappointed by the intervention of a foreign enemy. But, though the victory of Syracuse over Athens did not lead to a Syracusan empire, as the victory of Athens over Persia had led to an Athenian empire, it was followed, as in the case of Athens, by a further advance in the development of democracy. Had Hermocrates remained at Syracuse, in possession of his old influence, a change in this direc-

Results of the Syracusan victory.

Advance in democracy.

613

tion would hardly have come to pass. But he was appointed to command the auxiliary fleet which Syracuse sent to Sparta's help in the Aegean; and, when he had gone, the democratic mood of the citizens, excited by their recent efforts, vented itself in a decree pronouncing the deposition and banishment of Hermocrates. This was the work of his political opponent Diocles, who was a thoroughgoing democrat. Diocles bore the same name as a far earlier lawgiver—belonging to the same class and age as Charondas and Zaleucus—who had drawn up the laws on which the Syracusan constitution rested. The accidental identity of name led in subsequent ages to a confusion, and we find later writers ascribing to the democratic reformer, who rose into prominence now, the legislation of his ancient namesake. In his popular innovations Diocles borrowed ideas from the enemy whom his country had just overthrown. The Athenian use of lot in the appointment of magistrates was adopted. Hitherto the generals were also the presidents of the sovereign assembly, and had the unrestricted power of dismissing it at discretion. Diocles seems to have taken away this political function from the generals, and assigned the presidency of the assembly to the new magistrates, but with much smaller powers. The presidents, as we shall presently see, were able only to fine a speaker who was out of order; they could not silence him or break up the assembly.

Diocles:

his reforms.

Such was the position of the greatest Sicilian city—a full-blown democracy, but without her chief citizen to whom above all others she owed the deliverance from her danger—when the island was exposed for the second time to a Carthaginian invasion. The occasion of the war was the same which had brought about the Athenian invasion—the feud between Selinus and Segesta concerning some fields on their common frontier. In both cases, the dispute of these towns was a pretext, not the deeper cause. As Athens thought that the time had come for extending her commerce in the west, so Carthage deemed that the day had dawned for asserting anew her power in Sicily; and there were those who had not let fade the memory of the humiliation endured at Himera seventy years before and longed to take a late revenge.

Pretext and cause of the war with Carthage.

Segesta, with no Athens to protect her now, ceded the disputed lands; but Selinus went on to exact further cessions, and the Elymian city appealed to Carthage. One of the two shophets or judges in that republic was Hannibal, the grandson of Hamilcar, who had been slain at Himera. The desire of vengeance, long deferred, dominated Hannibal, now almost an old man; and his influence persuaded the Senate to accept Segesta's offer to become a Carthaginian dependency in return for Carthaginian help. A grand expe-

410 B.C.

dition was fitted out, and Hannibal was named commander. Sixty warships were got ready, 1500 transports, 100,000 foot, 4000 horse. The fleet was not intended to take a part in the offensive warfare; it was stationed at Motya to be a protection for Phoenician Sicily and a security in case of discomfiture. The army landed at Lilybaeum and marched straight to Selinus. This city had never been besieged before within the memory of its folk; immunity had made it secure; the fortifications had been neglected. The Selinuntines were engaged in building a temple of vast proportions to Apollo, or perhaps Olympian Zeus, when they were brought face to face with the sudden danger from Carthage. The house of the god was never completed; of the "pillars of the giants" which were to support the massive roof some stand in their places on the eastern hill, but the great drums and the capitals of others must be looked for, some miles away, in the quarries from which they were hewn, left there when the Carthaginian destroyer came. There was no time to repair adequately the walls of the acropolis, on the central hill. Hannibal surrounded it and a breach was soon made; but the place was not in the foe's hands for nine days, owing to the stubborn resistance which the inhabitants were able to offer in the narrow streets. The Siceliot sister cities were not prompt in aid; Syracuse promised to come to the rescue, and sent a force under Diocles, which arrived too late. Selinus was the first Siceliot city which was stormed and sacked by the barbarian; she was not to be the last. The people were slaughtered without mercy, only some women and children who took refuge in the temples were spared (not from any respect of the holy places) and carried into bondage. Those who escaped from the sack fled to Acragas. Thus Selinus fell, after a brief life of two centuries and a half.

Hannibal had now done the work which Carthage had given him to do; but he had still to do the work which he had imposed upon himself. His real motive, in undertaking the public duty of the Selinuntine war, was to carry out the private duty of ancestral vengeance. Against Selinus he had no personal grudge, and there he did not carry the work of destruction further than military considerations required. The buildings on the western hill, where he had pitched his camp, suffered much; but the injuries sustained by the temples on the acropolis and on the eastern hill are due, not to Hannibal's army, but to the earthquakes of later ages. It was to be different in the case of the city which he now turned to attack. At Selinus, Hannibal was merely the general of Carthage; at Himera, he was the grandson of Hamilcar.

Hannibal designed to capture Himera by his land forces alone;

Second Carthaginian invasion, 409 B.C. Siege of Selinus.

Destruction of Selinus.

Hannibal as avenger.

and in this absence of a Carthaginian fleet Hannibal's siege of
Himera differs from Hamilcar's. The Greeks of Sicily were now
bestirring themselves; the terrible fate of one of their chief cities
had aroused them to a sense of their peril. The naval power which
was supporting Sparta in the Aegean had been long ago recalled;
and a force of 5000, including 3000 Syracusans, under Diocles, came
to the relief of Himera. This city had time to prepare for the danger
which she must have foreseen. But the besiegers, by means of mines,
opened a breach in the wall; and, although they were repelled and
the defenders made a successful sally, the prospects of Himera
looked black, when the fleet of 25 ships, which had returned from
the Aegean, appeared in front of the city. Hannibal saved the situation by a stratagem. He spread abroad a report that he intended
to march on Syracuse and take it unprepared. Diocles, thoroughly
deceived, decided to return home and carry off the citizens of
Himera, leaving the empty town to its fate. He induced half the
population to embark in the ships, which, as soon as they had set
the passengers in safety at Messana, were to return for the rest.
Diocles and his army departed in haste, not even waiting to ask
Hannibal for the dead bodies of those who had fallen in fight outside the walls; and for this neglect he was greatly blamed. When
Hannibal saw that half his prey had escaped him, he pressed the
siege more vehemently, determined to force an entry before the
ships returned. The fate of thousands, the vengeance of Hannibal,
might turn on the event of a few minutes. On the third day, the
vessels of safety hove in sight of the straining eyes of the Himeraeans. It seemed that Hannibal was to be baulked of his revenge.
But the gods of Canaan prevailed in that hour of suspense. Before
the ships of rescue could reach the harbour, the Spanish troops of
Hannibal burst through the breach, and the town was in the hands
of the avenger. On the spot where Hamilcar, according to the story,
had offered up his life to the gods of his country, a solemn rite was
held; 3000 men, who had survived the first indiscriminate slaughter,
were sacrificed with torture to appease his shade. Himera, the offending city, was swept utterly out of the world and its place knew
it no more.

Having thus accomplished his duty to his country and his gods,
Hannibal returned triumphant to Africa. The position which Carthage won in Sicily by this year's work, and her new policy of
activity there, are reflected in the coinage of Segesta and Panormus.
The transformation of Segesta into a Carthaginian dependency was
displayed by the fact that she ceased to coin her own money. But
Carthage also showed that she intended to keep a firmer hand on

her Phoenician dependencies. These cities had hitherto paid homage to Hellenic influences by adopting a coinage of Hellenic character, with Hellenic inscriptions. This coinage now comes to an end at Panormus, and is replaced by a coinage, of Greek type indeed, but with a Phoenician legend—the word *Ziz*. The change seems to have been made just before the invasion, and it was significant of an anti-Greek movement. But the curious thing is that Himera—the city which was to be one of the first victims of the new policy heralded in this numismatic reform—abandoned her old coinage with the cock, and struck a new coinage with a sea-horse, on the Punic model of Panormus. Are we to suppose that Himera, aware of the peril which menaced her, thought to avert it by a timely approach

New coinage at Panormus with mysterious legend—Ziz.

Change in Himera's coinage

Fig. 87.—Coin of Syracuse, *c.* 410 B.C., engraved by Cimon (obverse). Head of Arethusa, amid dolphins [legend: ΣΥΡΑΚΟΣΙΩΝ; signature of ΚΙΜΩΝ on dolphin below]. Fig. 88.—Silver coin of Panormus. Obverse: female head with sphendone. Reverse: dog; mussel above [Punic legend: ZIZ].

of friendship to her Phoenician neighbour, and that this coinage was part of a policy of Punicism, intended to be only temporary?

Syracuse, although she had sought to do something for Selinus and had done something for Himera, felt no call to come forward as a champion against the new aggressive policy of Carthage. It was reserved for one of her citizens to attempt on his private responsibility the warfare which she declined to undertake against the Phoenician foe. The exile Hermocrates returned to Sicily, enriched by the gifts of the satrap Pharnabazus. His own city refused to withdraw the sentence of banishment, for a man of his views and abilities seemed dangerous to the democratic constitution. Hermocrates then resolved to earn his recall by performing conspicuous services to the Hellenic cause in Sicily,—by winning back the Greek territory which the Phoenician had taken, by carrying Greek arms into Phoenician territory itself. He had built five triremes, he had hired 1000 mercenaries, and he was joined by 1000 Himeraean fugi-

Return of Hermocrates, 408 B.C.

His warfare against

the Phoe-
nician
cities.
Selinus re-
occupied

tives. With these he marched to the spot where Selinus had once been, and made the place a centre for a "crusade" against the Phoenician. He repaired the fortifications of the acropolis on the central hill; and the remains of the well-built wall betray, by the capitals of columns used in the building, the circumstances of its erection. The adventure prospered; the band of Hermocrates soon increased to 6000, and he was able to devastate the lands of Motya and Panormus, and to drive back the forces which came out to meet him. In the same way he ravaged the territory of Solus and the now Carthaginian Segesta. These successes of Hermocrates were of greater significance than the actual injury dealt to the enemy. He had done what had not been done before (since the days of Dorieus[1]); he had broken into the precincts of Phoenician Sicily, and set an example to many subsequent leaders.

FIG. 89.—Coin of Syracuse, engraved by Cimon (obverse). Head of Arethusa [legend: ΑΡΕΘΟΣΑ; signature of ΚΙΜΩΝ on headband]. FIG. 90.—Coin of Acragas (obverse). Eagle tearing hare; shell as symbol of the seashore [legend: ΑΚΡΑΓΑΝΤΙΝΩΝ]. FIG. 91.—Coin of Acragas (obverse). Hare on rocks, under two eagles; head of Pan [legend: ΣΤΡΑΤΩΝ].

Hermo-
crates at
Himera,
407 B.C.:

he sends
the bones
of the
dead to
Syracuse;

he breaks
into Syra-
cuse and
is slain.

Hermocrates was bent, above all things, on regaining his own country. Diocles and his political opponents were still powerful in the city, and able to hinder the revulsion of feeling which his successes caused from having any practical effect. Accordingly he made another attempt to soften the hearts of his fellow-citizens. It was a well-calculated move. He marched to the ruins of Himera, collected the unburied bones of the soldiers of Diocles which Diocles had neglected, and sent them on waggons to Syracuse, himself remaining as an exile outside the Syracusan borders. He hoped to awaken the religious sentiment of the citizens in his own favour and at the same time to turn it against his rival. The bones were received and Diocles was banished; but Hermocrates was not recalled. Having failed to compass his restoration by persuasion, the exile resolved to compass it by force; and he was encouraged by his numerous partisans in Syracuse. He was admitted with a small band at the

[1] See above, p. 199.

gate of Achradina, and posted himself in the adjacent agora waiting for the rest of his forces to arrive. But they tarried too long; the people, learning that Hermocrates was in the city, rushed to the market-place; the small band was soon overcome and Hermocrates was slain. The Syracusans in these days were inspired with an instinctive rather than well-founded dread of tyranny; and this dread was stronger than admiration for Hermocrates. Their instinct was right; tyranny was approaching, but *he* was not the man. They little guessed that their future master was an obscure follower of Hermocrates, who was wounded that day in the agora and left for dead.

(Diony-
sius.)

Sect. 2. Carthaginian Conquest of Acragas

The private warfare of Hermocrates in western Sicily had naturally provoked the wrath of the Carthaginians. Embassies passed between Carthage and Syracuse, Carthage regarding Syracuse as answerable for the acts of a Syracusan. But diplomacy was merely a matter of form; the African republic had resolved to make all Greek Sicily subject to her sway. She made ready another great expedition—as great as if not greater than that which had been sent against Selinus; and at the same time she took the novel step of founding a colony on Sicilian soil. If Hermocrates had lived, Himera might have been partially restored like Selinus; but the destroyers of Himera now founded a city in the neighbourhood which was to take Himera's place. On the hill above the "hot baths of the Nymphs," where of Pindar sings, the Carthaginian colonists built their town. But it was not destined to retain its Phoenician character. The Greek strangers who were admitted to dwell in it transformed it before long into a Greek city; the *Thermae* of Himera preserved the memories of Himera, and the people were known as Thermites or Himeraeans indifferently.

Founda-
tion of
Cartha-
ginian
colony at
Thermae,
407 B.C.

(Ter-
mini.)

Acragas, the city which faces Carthage, was the first object of attack to the invaders who now came to conquer and enslave all Greek Sicily. Since the days of Theron, Acragas had held aloof from all struggles in the island and was now at the height of her prosperity. But she was enervated by peace and luxury, and, when the day of trial came, she was found wanting. How far her citizens were prepared to endure the hardships of military life may be inferred from the law—passed with a view to the present peril—that none of the men in the watch-towers should have more than a mattress, two pillows, and a quilt. Such were the austerities of the men of Acragas. But at least they paid homage to the different discipline of Sparta. They invited Dexippus, a Spartan who was then at Gela,

Prepara-
tions of
Acragas

to undertake the conduct of the defence. A body of Campanian mercenaries was hired; and they could rely on the assistance of their old rivals the Syracusans, as well as of the other Greek cities, who were fully conscious that the peril of Acragas was their own. And Acragas herself behaved well. Notwithstanding her habits of ease, and her old practice of holding aloof, she refused the tempting offer of the invader that she should now purchase immunity by remain-

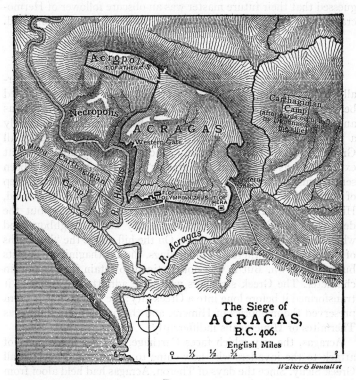

The Siege of
ACRAGAS,
B.C. 406.

English Miles

Walker & Boutall sc

FIG. 92.

ing neutral. She was true to her own race; she might remain indifferent when it was a struggle between Dorian and Ionian, but it was another case when the whole of Sicilian Hellas was threatened by the Phoenician.

406 B.C.

Siege of
Acragas.

The army of Carthage was again under the command of Hannibal, who felt that he was too old for the work, and was assisted by his cousin Himilco. They pitched their main camp on the right bank of the river Hypsas, south-west of the city, and stationed some forces in another small camp on the eastern hill, beyond the river Acragas, to act against Greek aids coming from the east. The point of attack was the part of the western wall close to the chief western gate. But the ground, though lower here, was still difficult for a besieger, and Hannibal determined to raise an immense causeway from which the wall could be more effectively attacked. The tombs of the neighbouring necropolis supplied stones for the work; but, as the tomb of Theron was being broken down, it was shaken by a thunderbolt, and the seers advised that it must be spared. Then a pestilence broke out in the Carthaginian camp, and carried off Hannibal himself. It seemed that the gods were wroth and demanded a victim; Himilco lit the fires of Moloch and sacrificed a boy. The causeway was then completed, but no further injury was done to the sepulchres.

The causeway

Plague. Death of Hannibal.

An army was already on its way to the relief of Acragas—30,000 foot and 5000 horse from Syracuse, Gela, and Camarina. When they approached the city they were met by the forces which had been placed for this purpose on the eastern hill; a battle was fought, a victory gained, and the Greek army took possession of the lesser Carthaginian camp. Meanwhile the routed barbarians fled for refuge to the main camp, and their flight lay along the road beneath the southern wall of the city. There was a general cry to sally forth and cut them off; but the generals refused. The moment was lost; but presently the people, yielding to an impulse which the generals could not resist, went forth from the eastern gates to meet their victorious allies. A strange scene followed. A tumultuous assembly was held outside the walls; the Acragantine commanders were accused of failing in their duty; and, when they essayed to defend themselves, the fury of the people burst out and four generals were stoned to death. The direction of the defence seems now to have been shared by Dexippus within the city and Daphnaeus, the commander of the Syracusan troops, without. Though the hostile camp was too strong to be attacked, the prospect looked favourable for Acragas. The Punic army, diminished though it had been by the plague, was sore bestead for lack of supplies, and it seemed certain that hunger and mutinous soldiers would soon force Himilco to raise the siege. But he learned that provision-ships were coming from Syracuse to Acragas; he sent in haste for the Carthaginian vessels at Panormus and Motya, put out to sea with forty triremes, and intercepted the supplies. This not only saved his leaguer, but even reversed the situation. The besieged city now began to suffer from scarcity of food. And as soon as supplies began to run short, the

Relief army arrives.

Acragantines murder their generals.

weak point in the position of the Acragantines was displayed. They had found it needful to rely on mercenaries, and hirelings were not likely to serve long when rations ran short. The Campanians were easily induced to transfer their services from Acragas to Carthage. But this was not all. It was commonly believed that Dexippus—like most Spartans abroad, incapable of resisting a bribe—received fifteen talents from Himilco and induced the Italiot and Siceliot allies to desert Acragas as a sinking ship. But, whatever the conduct of Dexippus may have been, the discredit of this desertion cannot rest entirely with him.

The defence, which had been maintained for eight months with foreign aid, was now left to the men of Acragas alone. They showed at once that they were shaped of different stuff from the men of Selinus. Overcome with despair, they resolved to save their lives and abandon their city and their gods. Such a resolution, taken by the people of a great city, is unique in Greek history. It did not befit the men who had rejected the overtures of Hannibal, but it was what we might expect from the men who murdered their generals. They marched forth at night, men, women, and children, without let or hindrance from the foe; "they were compelled to leave, for the barbarians to pillage, those things which made their lives happy."[2] The old and sick could not set out on the long journey to Gela, the place of refuge, and were left behind; some too remained who chose to perish at Acragas rather than live in another place. The army of Himilco entered the city in the morning and sacked it, slaying all whom they found, and despoiling and burning the temples. The great house of Olympian Zeus—the largest Greek temple in Europe—was still unfinished, and the sack of Himilco decided that it should never be completed. But Acragas was not to be destroyed like Selinus; it was intended to be a Carthaginian city in a Carthaginian Sicily. Himilco made the place his winter quarters; Gela would be the next object of his attack, when the spring came round.

SECT. 3. RISE OF DIONYSUS

For the catastrophe of Acragas the chief blame was laid upon the Syracusan generals, who deserted her in the critical hour. The Acragantines were not slow to make them responsible for their own unheroic flight. At Syracuse itself there was a feeling that these generals were hardly the men to meet the great jeopardy in which

[2] Diodorus, from Philistus.

Sicily now stood; and there was one man who saw in the jeopardy the opportunity of his own ambition. It was Dionysius, a man of obscure birth, who had been a clerk in a public office. He had been a partisan of Hermocrates, by whose side he had stood in the last fatal fray, and had been wounded and left for dead. Recently he had marked himself out by his energy and bravery before the walls of Acragas. He saw the incompetence of the democratic government of his city; he saw that in the present peril it might be overthrown, and he determined to overthrow it. An assembly was held to consider the situation. Dionysius arose and in a violent harangue accused the generals of treachery. His language was intended to stir up the hearers to fury; he called upon the people to rise up themselves and destroy the traitors without trial. His violence transgressed the constitutional rules of the assembly, but the presidents had no power to bridle him; they imposed a fine—the only resource they had; but a wealthy friend, Philistus the historian, came forward and paid the fine, bidding the speaker go on, for as often as a fine was imposed he would pay it. Dionysius carried his point. The generals were deposed, and a new board was appointed, of which Dionysius was one. This was only the first step on the road which was to lead to the *tyrannis*. His next success was to procure the recall of the partisans of Hermocrates who had been condemned to exile; these old comrades might be useful to him in his designs. At the same time he sought to discredit his colleagues; he kept entirely apart from them and spread reports that they were disloyal to Syracuse. Presently he openly accused them, and the people elected him sole general with sovereign powers to meet the instant danger. This office, held before, as we have reason to think, by Gelon and Hiero, did not set him above the laws; nor was the office illegal, though extraordinary; it may be compared to the Roman dictatorship. But it was the second step to the tyranny. The next step, as history taught him—the story of Pisistratus, for instance—was to procure a bodyguard. The Assembly at Syracuse, which had perhaps begun to repent already of having placed so much power in the hands of one man, would certainly not have granted such an instrument of tyranny. But Dionysius was ingenious; he saw that the thing might be done elsewhere. He ordered the Syracusan army to march to Leontini, which, it will be remembered, was now a Syracusan dependency. He encamped near the town, and during the night a rumour was spread abroad that the general's life had been attempted and he had been compelled to seek refuge in the acropolis. An assembly was held next day, nominally an assembly of Syracusan citizens, which, when Dionysius laid bare the designs

Diony-
sius:

comes for
ward for
the first
time; his
violent
speech.

Philistus
the his-
torian.
The
despot's
progress:
(1) Dio-
nysius
general;

(2) Dio-
nysius
στρατηγὸς
αὐτοκρά-
τωρ;

(3) gets a
body-
guard.

of his enemies, voted him a bodyguard of 600; this he soon increased to 1000; and he had won over the mercenaries to his cause.

These were the three steps in the "despot's progress" which rendered Dionysius lord and master of Syracuse. His intrigues had won him first a generalship, then sole generalship with unlimited military powers, and finally a bodyguard. Syracuse, unwilling and embarrassed, submitted with evident chagrin, but was dominated by the double dread of the mercenaries and the Carthaginians. The democracy of course was not formally overthrown; Dionysius held no office that upset the constitution. Things went on as at Athens under Pisistratus; the Assembly met and passed decrees and elected magistrates.

Democratic constitution formally continues.

The justification of the power of Dionysius lay in the need of an able champion to oppose Carthage, and his partisans represented him as a second Gelon. But, though Dionysius was in later years to prove himself among the chief champions of Hellenic Sicily against the Punic power, his conduct at this crisis did not fulfil the hopes of those who thought to compare him with the hero of Himera. The Carthaginians were already encamped at Gela. Their first act was to remove a colossal brazen statue of Apollo which stood, looking over the sea, on the hill to the west of the city. The Geloans defended their walls with courage and zeal, and when Dionysius arrived with an army of Italiots and Siceliots, and a fleet of fifty ironclad ships to co-operate, it seemed as if Gela would escape the doom of Acragas. An excellent plan was arranged for a combined attack on the Carthaginian camp, which lay on the west side of the town. The plan failed, because the concert was not accurately carried out. The Siceliots who were to assault the eastern side of the camp arrived late on the spot, and found the enemy, who had already repelled the attack of the Italiots and the fleet on the southern and western sides, free to meet them in full force. This hitch in the execution of the plan was hardly a mere blunder. Dionysius with his mercenaries had undertaken to issue from the western gate of Gela and drive away the besiegers, while the rest of his army were attacking the camp. It seems, however, that Dionysius took no part in the fighting, and alleged that he was retarded by difficulties in crossing the town from the eastern to the western gate. We shall probably do no injustice to Dionysius if we conclude that it was through his dispositions that the Siceliots failed to act in concert with the Italiots. The action which he took after the defeat shows that he was half-hearted in the work. He decided in a private council, as Diocles had decided at Himera, that the defence must be abandoned and the whole people of Gela removed. At the first

Siege of Gela, 405 B.C.

Plan of concerted attack; its failure.

Strange conduct of Dionysius.

watch of the night he sent the multitude forth from the city, and followed himself at midnight. His way to Syracuse led by Camarina, and here too Dionysius ruled that the whole people must forsake their home. The road to Syracuse was full of the crowds of helpless fugitives from the two cities.

It was generally thought that these strange proceedings of Dionysius were carried out in collusion with the barbarians; that he had deliberately betrayed to them Gela, which might have been defended, Camarina, which had not yet been attacked. The Italiot allies showed not their disgust only, but their apprehension that the war was practically over, by marching immediately home. The horsemen of Syracuse seized the occasion for a desperate attempt to subvert the new tyrant. They rode rapidly to the city, plundered the house of Dionysius, and maltreated his wife although she was the daughter of Hermocrates. When Dionysius heard the news, he hastened to Syracuse with a small force. He reached the gate of Achradina by night and, being refused admittance, burned it down with a fire of reeds supplied by the neighbouring marsh. In the market-place he easily overmastered a handful of opponents; the remnant fled to Aetna, which now became, "in a better cause, what Eleusis was to Athens after the overthrow of the Thirty."[3]

In what concerns the charge that the Syracusan tyrant had a secret understanding with Carthage, there is a strong case against him; the events are scarcely intelligible on any other view. But it was no more than a temporary disloyalty to the cause of Hellas and Europe, for which he was hereafter to do great feats. His first motive was the selfish motive of a tyrant. He wanted time to lay stable foundations for his still precarious power at Syracuse; and he judged that it would be a strong support to obtain a recognition of his power from the Carthaginian republic. The Punicism of the lord of Syracuse was not more unscrupulous than the Medism of the ephors of Sparta, to which it is the western parallel.

The treaty, which was now agreed upon between Himilco and Dionysius, was drawn up on the basis of *uti possidetis*. Each party retained what it actually held at the time. Syracuse acknowledged Carthage as mistress of all the Greek states on the northern and southern coasts, and also of the Sican communities. Acragas, what was left of Selinus, Gela, and Camarina, were all to be henceforward under Punic sway; and, on the north coast, Carthage had advanced her frontier to include the territory of Himera in which she had planted her first colony.[4] But all these cities were not to hold the

Gela and Camarina dispeopled.

Suspicions of good faith of Dionysius.

Revolt of the horsemen,

put down by Dionysius.

Aetna.

Policy of Dionysius

The treaty between Carthage and Dionysius, 405 B. C.

Carthaginian Sicily:

---

[3] Freeman.
[4] In the treaty, the old Phoenician colonies, sisters of Carthage, seem to have been spoken of as if they were her own daughter colonies.

subjects and tributaries.

same relation to their mistress. Acragas and Selinus, like Thermae, were subjects in the full sense of the word; but Gela and Camarina were to be only tributary and unwalled cities. The Elymian towns are not mentioned; but we have seen how Segesta became a subject of Carthage by her own act, and we can hardly doubt that Eryx was forced into the same condition.

Independent states: position of Leontini.

The terms of the treaty provided for the independence of the Sicel communities and of the city of Messana. But it provided also for the independence of Leontini, and this was a point in which it departed from the basis *uti possidetis*, Leontini being a dependency of Syracuse. It was clearly a provision extorted from Dionysius, and intended by Himilco to be a source of embarrassment to Syracuse. On the other hand, as a counter-concession, nothing was said about the dependence of Naxos or Catane, so that Syracuse might have a free hand to deal with her old enemies, without fear of violating the treaty. Such was the new arrangement of the map of Sicily at the end of the second Carthaginian invasion. An accidental consequence of that invasion had been to establish Dionysius as tyrant of Syracuse. This consequence enabled Himilco to bring his work to a conclusion more easily and quickly than he had hoped; he could not foresee that the undoing of his work would be the ultimate result.

Clause of guaranty.

The Carthaginians guaranteed to maintain the rule of Dionysius, who was soon to prove one of their most powerful foes. For Dionysius this guaranty, "the Syracusans shall be subject to Dionysius," was the most important clause in the treaty,—some suppose that it was a secret clause. It was for the sake of this recognition and the implied promise of support that he stooped to betray Sicilian Hellas. We shall see how he redeemed this unscrupulous act of expediency by creating the most powerful Hellenic state in the Europe of his day.

SECT. 4. FIRST YEARS OF DIONYSIUS

For half a century after the fall of Athens it seemed likely that the destinies of Europe would be decided by a Greek city in the western Mediterranean. Under her new lord Dionysius, Syracuse had become a great power, a greater power than any that had yet arisen in Europe. In strength and dominion, in influence and promise, she outstripped all the cities of the mother-country; and, in a general survey of the Mediterranean coasts, she stands out clearly as the leading European power. The Greek states to which the Persian King sent down his Peace were now flanked on either side by two great powers, and a political prophet might have been tempted

Great position of Syracuse.

to foretell that the communities of old Greece were doomed to perish between the monarchies of Susa and Syarcuse, which threatened their freedom on the east and on the west. Those who were tempted to spy into the future might have conjectured that the ultimate conflict with Persia was reserved for a Sicilian conqueror, who should one day extend his dominion over eastern Greece and the Aegean and, as autocrat of Europe, oppose the autocrat of Asia. Though this was not to be, though the expansion of Sicily was arrested, and the power which was to subdue Asia arose on the borders of Old Greece, yet we shall see that in many ways the monarchy of Dionysius foreshadowed the monarchy of Philip and Alexander. It is in Sicily, not in Old Greece, that we see the first signs of a new epoch, in which large states are to take the place of small, and monarchy is to supersede free institutions.

The tyranny of Dionysius lasted for thirty-eight years, till the end of his life. All that time it was maintained by force; all that time it was recognised as a violation of the constitution and an outrage on the freedom of the people. The forms of the constitution were still maintained; the folk still met and voted in the Assembly; and Dionysius was either annually re-elected, or permanently appointed, general with absolute powers. But all this was pure form; his position was a fact, which had no constitutional name, and which made the constitution of none effect. And it was by compulsion and not of their freewill that the mass of the citizens continued to obey him; his bodyguard of foreign mercenaries was the support of his power. More than one attempt was made to throw off the yoke, but his craft and energy defeated the most determined efforts of his adversaries. Yet the unusual ability of Dionysius would not have availed, more than the spearmen who were ever within call, to extend his unlawful reign to a length which a tyrant's reign seldom reached, if he had not discovered and laid to heart what may be called a secret of tyranny. While he did cruel and oppressive deeds for political purposes, he never committed outrages to gratify personal desires of his own. He scrupulously avoided all those acts of private insolence which have brought the reigns of Greek tyrants into such ill repute. Many a despot had fallen by the hand of fathers or lovers, whom the dishonour of their nearest and dearest had spurred to the pursuit of vengeance at the risk of their own lives. Dionysius eschewed this mistake; his crimes and his enemies were political. When his son seduced a married woman, the discreet tyrant rebuked him. "It is well for you to chide me," said the young man, "but you had not a tyrant for your father." "And if you go on doing this sort of thing," retorted Dionysius, "you will not have

The statecraft of Dionysius, and the secret of his long reign.

a tyrant for your son." This notable moderation of Dionysius in private life was perhaps the chief cause of the duration of his tyranny; beyond the common motive of patriotism, men had no burning personal wrongs to spur them to encounter the danger of driving a dagger to the despot's heart. But, besides this discretion which made his government tolerable, his successes abroad counted for something, and it was more than once borne in on Syracuse that his rule was necessary to protect her against her enemies. And we shall see that Dionysius was fully conscious that it conduced to his own safety that there should be enemies against whom she needed a protector.

Fortification of the Island.

The first concern of the new tyrant was to establish himself in a stronghold. As we have seen, the acropolis of Syracuse was not, as in other cities, the hill, but the Island; and it was the Island which Dionysius made his fortress. He built a turreted wall on the north side of the isthmus so as to bar the Island off from the mainland, and he built two castles, one close to, if not on, the isthmus, the other at the southern point of the island. Whoever entered the Island from Achradina had to pass under five successive gates; and no one was allowed to dwell within the island fortress except those whom Dionysius regarded as his own friends and supporters. The scheme of fortifications took in the Lesser Harbour, which, with its new docks, became under Dionysius the chief arsenal of the Syracusan naval power. The mouth of this port was entirely closed by a mole, the galleys passing in and out through a gate, which was only wide enough to allow one to pass at a time.

Besides these defences of stone, Dionysius strengthened his position by dealing rich rewards to confirm in their allegiance his friends and hirelings, and by forming a class of New Citizens out of enfranchised slaves. The forfeited estates of his enemies supplied him with the means of carrying out both these acts of policy.

Revolt against Dionysius

It was not long before he had an unwelcome occasion of putting to the test both the walls of his fortress and the hearts of his followers. The most favourable opportunity for any attempt to overthrow the tyrant was when the Syracusan army was in the field. When the citizens had arms in their hands and were formed in military ranks, the word of a patriot could more easily kindle them to action than when they were engaged in their peaceable occupations at home. Dionysius led out the army against Herbessus, one of the cities of the Sicels. Mutinous talk passed from mouth to mouth, and the disaffected citizens slew one of the tyrant's officers who rebuked them. Then the mutiny broke out loud and free. Dionysius hastened to Syracuse and shut himself up in his fastness;

the revolted citizens followed and laid siege to their own city. They sent messages to Messana and Rhegium, asking these cities to help them to win back their freedom; and a succour of eighty triremes came in answer to their help. By sea and land they pressed Dionysius so hard in his island fortress that his case seemed desperate, and some of his mercenary troops went over to the enemy. Dionysius called a council of his most trusted friends. Some bade him flee on a swift horse; others counselled him to stay till he was driven out. Heloris used a phrase which became famous: "Sovereign power is a fair winding-sheet." Dionysius followed the counsel of those who bade him stay, but he resorted to a piece of craft which was more successful than he could well have hoped. He entered into negotiation with his besiegers and asked for permission to quit Syracuse with his own goods. They willingly agreed to the proposal and allowed him five triremes, and they were so convinced of his good faith that they dismissed a company of cavalry which had come to their aid from Aetna. But, meanwhile, Dionysius had sent a secret message to the Campanian mercenaries of Carthage, who had been left by Himilco in some part of Sicily. Twelve hundred in number, they were permitted to come to the help of the tyrant, whose lordship had been recognised and guaranteed by Carthage in the recent treaty. The besiegers, thinking that the struggle was over, had half broken up their leaguer, and were in complete disorder; the Campanians occupied the hills of Epipolae without resistance; Dionysius sallied forth, and decisively, though without much shedding of blood, defeated the rebels in the neighbourhood of the theatre—a quarter of the city which we now find for the first time called *Neapolis*. Dionysius used his victory mildly. Many of the rebels fled to Aetna and refused to return to Syracuse, but those who returned were received kindly and not punished. As for the Campanians, to whom Dionysius owed his rescue, they did not return to the service of Carthage, but made a new home in the west of Sicily, in the Sican town of Entella. They induced the inhabitants to admit them as new citizens, and one night they arose and slew all the men and married the women. Thus was formed the first Italian settlement on Sicilian soil.

When the revolt broke out, we saw Dionysius aiming an attack at a Sicel city. The first step in the expansion of Syracusan power, which was the object of the tyrant's ambition, was the reduction of the Greek cities of the eastern coast and the neighbouring Sicel towns. The Sicel towns were putting on more and more of an Hellenic character, and the reign of Dionysius marks a stage of progress in their Hellenization. We get a glimpse of political parties striving

Siege of
Syracuse,
403 A.D.

Revolt
sup-
pressed by
Campanian
help.

Entella;
first
Italian
settlement
in Sicily.
Designs of
Dionysius
on the
Sicels.

in Sicel just as in Greek cities; and we find Henna ruled by a tyrant of Greek name. To attack the Sicels was indeed a breach of the treaty with Carthage; but for the present Dionysius gained no success which obliged Carthage to intervene. He entered Henna indeed, but only to overthrow the local tyrant and leave the inhabitants to enjoy their freedom; he attacked Herbita, but his attack was fruitless. With the Greek cities which stood in his way he was more

Aetna taken.

successful. First of all he captured Aetna, the refuge of Syracusan exiles and malcontents, and these dangerous enemies dispersed we know not whither. Then he turned against the two Ionian cities, Catane and Naxos. In fear of such an attack Catane had taken the

FIG. 93.—Alliance coin (hemidrachm, enlarged) of Leontini and Catane. Obverse: head of Apollo wreathed with bay; bay leaf and berry [legend: ΛΕΟΝ (τινων)]. Reverse: bull (river Simaethos): fish below [legend: KATA-NAION].

Alliance of Catane and Leontini, 404 B.C.

precaution of allying herself with Syracuse's former vassal, Leontini. The sole record we have of this alliance is a beautiful little silver coin, with a laurelled head of Apollo and the names of the two cities—one of an issue which was struck in token of the treaty. But

Catane and Naxos taken by treachery.

the support of Leontini did not avail. Both Catane and Naxos were won by gold, not by the sword; traitors opened the gates to the Dorian tyrant.

Fate of Catane and Naxos.

In his treatment of these cities Dionysius showed himself in his worst light. All the inhabitants of Naxos and Catane alike were sold as slaves in the Syracusan slave-market. Catane was given over to Campanian mercenaries as a dwelling-place, and thus became the second Italian town in Sicily. But the city of Naxos, the most ancient of all the Siceliot cities, was not even given to a stranger to dwell in; the walls and the houses were destroyed; the territory was bestowed upon the Sicels, the descendants of the original possessors; and a small settlement near the old site barely maintained the memory of the name. Dionysius was one of the ablest champions of

Greek Sicily against the Phoenician; yet here he appears in the character of a destroyer, dealing to Greek civilisation blows such as we should expect only from the Phoenician foe. It is certain indeed that the severity of the doom which he meted out to these cities was meant to serve a purpose, for wanton severity was never practised by Dionysius. We may suspect what that purpose was. The conquest of Naxos and Catane was of far less consequence to the lord of Syracuse than the recovery of Leontini. To win back this lost Syracusan possession was the first object of all in the eyes of a Syracusan ruler. Dionysius had already called upon the Leontines to surrender, but in vain; and perhaps he thought that the siege of the place would be long and tedious. When he pronounced the doom of Naxos and Catane, he was in truth besieging Leontini with most effectual engines; and when he approached with his army and summoned the Leontines to migrate to Syracuse and become his subjects under the name of Syracusan citizens, they did not hesitate to prefer that unwelcome change to the risk of faring still worse than the folks of Catane and Naxos.

(The Naxian Neapolis.)

Recovery of Leontini.

If we glance over Sicily at this moment, it comes upon us as a shock to discover that of all the cities of Greek Sicily which enjoyed sovereign powers at the time of the Athenian invasion, there remained now not a single independent community, outside Syracuse herself, with exception of Messana, who still kept watch upon her strait. The Carthaginians and Dionysius between them had swept all away.

The recovery of the Leontine territory was a success which probably gratified the Syracusans as well as their master. It was indeed a direct defiance of Carthage, for the treaty had guaranteed the independence of Leontini. But Dionysius knew that a struggle with Carthage must come, and was not unwilling that it should come soon. He determined to equip Syracuse against all enemies who should come against her, and we next find him engaged in fortifying the city on an enormous scale. The fortification of the Island had been intended mainly for his own safety against domestic enemies; but the works which he now undertook were for the city and not for the tyrant. The Athenian siege of Syracuse taught him lessons which he had taken to heart. It taught him that the commanding heights of Epipolae must not be left for an enemy to seize, and therefore that it must become part of the Syracusan city, enclosed within the circuit of the Syracusan wall. It taught too the decisive importance of the western corner at Euryalos, and the necessity of constructing a strong fortress at that point, which has been called "the key of Epipolae and of all Syracuse." The walls were built in an incredibly

Fortification of Epipolae.

short space of time by 60,000 freemen, under the supervision of Dionysius himself. He seems to have inspired the citizens with the ambition of making their city the most strongly fortified place in the whole Greek world. The northern wall, from Tycha to Euryalos, a distance of more than three miles, was completed in twenty days. The striking ruins of the massive castle of Euryalos, with its curious underground chambers, are a memorial indeed of a tyrant's rule; but they are more than that; they are a monument of Greek Syracuse at the period of her greatest might—when she became for a moment the greatest power in Europe.

It was no small thing to have carried out this enormous system of fortifications which made Syracuse the vastest of all Greek cities; but Dionysius showed his surpassing energy and resource in preparing for offensive as well as for defensive warfare. In military innovations he is the forerunner of the great Macedonians and the originator of the methods which they employed. He first thought out and taught how the heterogeneous parts of a military armament— the army and the navy, the cavalry and the infantry, the heavy and the light troops—might be closely and systematically co-ordinated so as to act as if they were a single organic body. He first introduced, his engineers first invented, the catapult, which, if it did not revolutionise warfare in general like the discovery of gunpowder, certainly revolutionised siege warfare, and introduced a new element into military operations. An engine which hurled a stone of two or three hundredweight for a distance of two or three hundred yards was extremely formidable in close quarters. In naval warfare he was also an innovator; he constructed ships of huger size than had ever been built before, with five banks of oars. He largely increased the fleet, which, counting vessels of both the larger and the smaller kind, seems to have numbered about 300 galleys.

Improvements of Dionysius in warfare.

SECT. 5. FIRST PUNIC WAR OF DIONYSIUS

First Punic War, 398-7 B.C.

When his preparations were complete, Dionysius went forth to do what no Greek leader in Sicily had ever done before. He went forth not merely to deliver Greek cities from Phoenician rule, but to conquer Phoenician Sicily itself. Marching along the south coast he was hailed as a deliverer by the Greek dependencies of Carthage, both by the tributary towns Gela and Camarina, and the subject town of Acragas. Thermae on the northern coast likewise joined him, and of the two Elymian towns, Eryx received his overtures, while Segesta remained faithful to her Punic mistress. At the head of a host, which for a Greek army seems immense—80,000 foot, it is said, and more than 3000 horse—Dionysius advanced to test his new siege engines on the walls of Motya. This city, which now for the first and for the last time becomes the centre of a memorable episode in history, was like the original Syracuse, an island town; but, though it was joined to the mainland by a causeway, the town did not like Syracuse spread to the mainland. It was surrounded entirely by a wall, of which traces still remain; and the bay in which it lay was protected on the sea side by a long spit of land. The men of Motya were determined to withstand the invader to the uttermost, and the first measure they took was to insulate themselves completely by breaking down the causeway which bound them to the mainland. Thus they hoped that Dionysius would have to trust entirely to his ships to conduct the siege, and that he would be unable to make use of his artillery. But they knew not the enterprise of Dionysius nor the excellence of his engineer department. The tyrant was determined to assault the city from solid ground, and to bring his terrible engines close to the walls. He set the crews of his ships to the work of building a mole far greater than the causeway which the Motyans had destroyed; the ships themselves, which he did not destine to play any part in the business of the siege, he drew up on the northern coast of the bay. The mole of Dionysius at Motya forestalls a more famous mole which we shall hereafter see erected by a greater than Dionysius at another Phoenician island town, older and more illustrious than Motya.

While the mole was being built, Dionysius made expeditions in the neighbourhood. He won over the Sicans from their Carthaginian allegiance, and he laid siege to Elymian Segesta and Campanian Entella. Both these cities repelled his attacks, and leaving them under blockade he returned to Motya when the solid bridge was completed. In the meantime, Carthage was preparing an effort to rescue the menaced city. She tried to cause a diversion by sending a few galleys to Syracuse, and some damage was caused to ships that were lying in the Great Harbour. But Dionysius was not to be diverted from his enterprise; he had doubtless foreseen such an attempt to lure him away, and knew that there was no real danger. Himilco, the Carthaginian admiral, seeing that Dionysius was immovable, sailed with a large force to Motya and entered the bay, with the purpose of destroying the Syracusan fleet, which was drawn up on the shore. Dionysius seems to have been taken by surprise. For whatever reason, he made no attempt to launch his galleys; he merely placed archers and slingers on those ships which would be first attacked. But he brought his army round to the peninsula which forms the western side of the bay, and on the shores

Siege of Motya.

The mole.

(Compare the mole of Alexander the Great at Tyre.)

of this strip of land he placed his new engines. The catapults hurled deadly volleys of stones upon Himilco's ships, and the novelty of these crushing missiles, which they were quite unprepared to meet, utterly disconcerted the Punic sailors, and the Carthaginians retreated. Then Dionysius, who was no less ready to treat earth as water than to turn sea into land, laid wooden rollers across the neck of land which formed the northern side of the bay, and hauled his whole fleet into the open sea. But Himilco did not tarry to give him battle there; he went back to Carthage, and the men of Motya were left unaided to abide their fate.

(The hele-poleis.)

As the site of the island city required a special road of approach, so its architecture demanded a special device of assault. Since the space in the city was limited, its wealthy inhabitants had to seek dwelling-room by raising high towers into the air; and to attack these towers Dionysius constructed siege towers of corresponding height, with six storeys, which he moved up near the walls on wheels. These wooden *belfries*, as they were called in the Middle Ages, were not a new invention, but they had never perhaps been built to such a height before, and it is not till the Macedonian age, which Dionysius in so many ways foreshadows, that they came into common use. It was a strange sight to see the battle waged in mid-air. The defenders of the stone towers had one advantage; they were able to damage some of the wooden towers of the enemy by lighted brands and pitch. But the arrangements of Dionysius were so well ordered that this device wrought little effect; and the Phoenicians could not stand on the wall which was swept by his catapults, while the rams battered it below. Presently a breach was made, and the struggle began in earnest. The Motyans had no thought of surrender; dauntless to the end they defended their streets and houses inch by inch. Missiles rained on the heads of the Greeks who thronged through, and each of the lofty houses had to be besieged like a miniature town. The wooden towers were wheeled within the walls; from their topmost storeys bridges were flung across to the upper storeys of the houses, and in the face of the desperate inhabitants the Greek soldiers rushed across these dizzy ways, often to be flung down into the street below. At night the combat ceased; both besiegers and besieged rested. The issue was indeed certain; for however bravely the Motyans might fight, they were far outnumbered. But day after day the fighting went on in the same way, and Motya was not taken. The losses on the Greek side were great, and Dionysius became impatient. Accordingly he planned a night assault, which the Motyans did not look for, and this was successful. By means of ladders a small band entered the part of the town

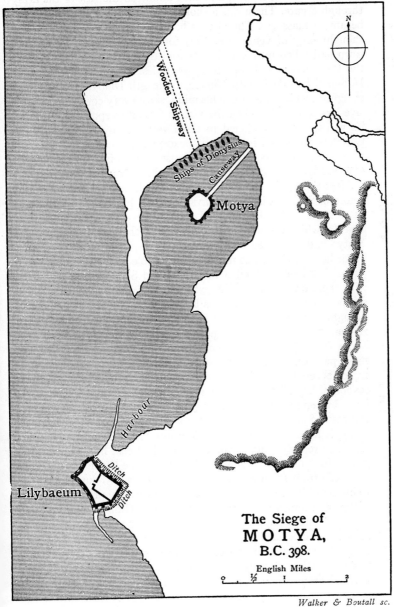

FIG. 94.

The Siege of
MOTYA,
B.C. 398.

English Miles

Walker & Boutall sc.

which was still defended, and then admitted the rest of the army through a gate. There was a short and sharp struggle, which soon became a massacre. The Greeks had no thought of plunder, they thought only of vengeance. Now for the first time a Phoenician town had fallen into their hands, and they resolved to do to it as the Phoenicians had done to Greek cities. They remembered how Hannibal had dealt with Himera. At length Dionysius stayed the slaughter, which was not to his mind, since every corpse was a captive less to be sold. Then the victors turned to spoil the city, and its wealth was abandoned to them without any reserve. All the prisoners were sold into slavery, except some Greek mercenaries, whose treachery to the Hellenic cause was expiated by the death of crucifixion. A Sicel garrison was left in the captured city.

After this achievement, the like of which had not been wrought before in Sicilian history, Dionysius retired for the winter to Syracuse. Next spring he marched forth again to press the siege of Segesta, which was still under blockade. In the meantime the fall of Motya had awakened Carthage into action; she saw that she must bestir herself, if she was not to let her whole Sicilian dominion slip out of her hands. Himilco was appointed Shophet and entrusted with the work of saving Punic Sicily. He collected a force, which seems to have been at least as large as that which Dionysius had brought into the field, and set sail with sealed orders for Panormus. A small portion of the armament was sunk by Leptines, brother of Dionysius, who was in command of the Syracusan fleet; but the main part disembarked in safety. And then events happened in rapid succession, which are hard to explain. Himilco first gains possession of Eryx by treason; then he marches to Motya and captures it; and when Motya is lost, Dionysius raises the siege of Segesta and returns to Syracuse. The loss of Eryx could not be provided against; but it is hard to discern why Dionysius should have made no attempt to relieve Motya, whose capture had cost him so much the year before, or why he should have allowed the Carthaginian army to march from Panormus to Eryx and Motya without attempting to intercept it. He could not have more effectually pressed the siege of Segesta than by dealing a decided check to Himilco. Not knowing the exact circumstances, not knowing even the number of the two armies, we can hardly judge his action; but it may be suspected that Dionysius was by nature a man who did not care to risk a pitched battle, unless the advantage were distinctly on his own side. It is to be remembered that he won nearly all his successes by sieges and surprises, by diplomacy and craft, and that the name of this great military innovator is not associated with a single famous battle in the open field. When he had once allowed Motya to be taken, his retreat is not surprising; for he had no base in the western part of the island, and we are told that his supplies were failing. He had now lost all that he had won in the first campaign. Motya, however, was wiped out as a Phoenician city, though it was not to be a Greek or Sicel stronghold. Himilco, instead of restoring the old colony, founded a new city hard by to take its place. On the promontory of the mainland which forms the south side of the Motyan bay arose the city of Lilybaeum, which was henceforward to be the great stronghold of Carthaginian power in the west of the island. The sea washed two sides of the town, and the walls of the other two sides were protected by enormous ditches cut in the rock. The history of Lilybaeum is the continuation of the history of Motya; but it was not destined to be taken either by a Greek or a Roman besieger.

End of Motya. Foundation of Lilybaeum (Marsala).

Having driven the invader from Phoenician Sicily, and having laid the foundations of a new city, Himilco resolved to carry his arms into the lands of the enemy and to attack Syracuse itself. But he did not go directly against Syracuse. Before he attempted that mighty fortress, he would try the easier task of capturing Messana. The fall of this city would be a grievous blow to Hellas, and it would be no mean vengeance for the fall of Motya. The walls of Messana had been allowed to fall into decay, and the place was an easy prey for the Carthaginians; but the greater part of the inhabitants escaped into fortresses in the neighbouring hills. The Carthaginian general had to wreak his vengeance on the stones. He rased the walls and the edifices, and the work was done so well that no man, we are told, would have recognised the site.

Himilco takes and destroys Messana.

If the triumphant demolition of the Sicilian city which watched the strait was a sore blow to the Hellenic cause, Himilco sought at the same moment to deal another blow to that cause by the foundation of a new Sicilian city in another place. It was his policy to cultivate the friendship of the Sicels and to foment the dislike which they felt towards the lord of Syracuse. Dionysius too had sought to win influence over the native race, and we saw how he gave them the territory of Naxos. The Carthaginian general grasped at the idea of erecting a new town for these very Sicels of Naxos, on the heights of Taurus which rise above the old site. Such was the strange origin of the strong city of Tauromenion, with its two rock citadels, one of the fairest sites in Sicily. It was the second foundation of Himilco in the same year; and both his foundations were destined signally to prosper. Lilybaeum became more famous than Motya, and Tauromenion has had a greater place in history than

Foundation of Tauromenium.

Naxos. As a founder of cities Himilco has a high title to fame; he was, like Dionysius, a creator as well as a destroyer. The creation of new cities and the destruction of old, by Greeks and Phoenicians alike, was a characteristic feature of this epoch.

Dionysius was preparing in the meantime to protect Syracuse. He committed the command of the fleet, which appears to have been now about 200 strong, to his brother Leptines; and fleet and army together moved northward to Catane. In the waters near the shore of Catane a naval battle was fought, and the Greek armament was defeated with great loss. It was indeed far outnumbered by the fleet of the Phoenicians, who also used their transport vessels as warships; but the cause of the disaster was the bad generalship of Leptines, who did not keep his ships together. The rout was witnessed by Dionysius from the shore, and it might have been retrieved by a victory on the land. Himilco and his army had not yet arrived on the scene, for an eruption of Aetna had made the direct road impassable and forced them to make a long détour. Dionysius again shrank from risking a battle, though the men of Sicily were eager to fight; he retreated to the walls of Syracuse. This city was the last bulwark of Greek Sicily, and with it the cause of Greek civilisation was in jeopardy. It was a moment at which the Siceliots might well sue for help from their fellow-Greeks beyond the sea. Dionysius dispatched messages to Italy, to Corinth, and to Sparta, imploring urgently for succour.

It was not long before the victorious Carthaginian fleet sailed into the Great Harbour, and the Carthaginian army encamped hard by, along the banks of the Anapus. The mass of the host encamped as well as it could in the swamp, but the general pitched his tent on the high ground of Polichna, within the precinct of the Olympian Zeus. This insult to the religion of Hellas was followed up by a more awful sacrilege, when Himilco pillaged the temple of Demeter and Kore on the southern slope of Epipolae. When the barbarians began to perish in the plague-stricken marsh, the pestilence was imputed to the divine vengeance for these acts of outrage. The besiegers must have sat for no brief space before the walls of Syracuse. The messengers of Dionysius had time to reach the Peloponnesus and return with succour—thirty ships under a Lacedaemonian admiral. Himilco had time to build three forts to protect his army and his fleet—one near his own quarters at Polichna, one at Dascon, on the western shore of the harbour, and one at Plemmyrion. After the arrival of the auxiliaries, the capture of a Punic cornship was the occasion of a small naval combat in the harbour; only a few of the

Sea-fight at Catane.

Retreat of Dionysius.

Panic siege of Syracuse.

Carthaginian ships were engaged, and the Syracusans were victorious.

Within the town there was deep dissatisfaction with Dionysius and his conduct of the war, and the citizens thought that they might reckon on the sympathy of their Peloponnesian allies with an attempt to cast off the tyrant's yoke. At an assembly which the tyrant convened the feeling of dissatisfaction broke openly forth, and the lord of Syracuse could not only read in the faces but hear in the words of the citizens the depth of their hatred. But the movement of revolution was checked by the Peloponnesians, who said that their business was to help Dionysius against the Carthaginians, not to help the Syracusans against Dionysius. So the danger passed over, but the tyrant had a warning, and he put on winning manners and courted popularity. Feeling in Syracuse against the tyrant.

The deadly airs of the swamp, in the burning heat of summer, were doing their work. The army of Himilco was ravaged by pestilence; soon the soldiers fell so fast that they could not be buried. The hour had now come for the men of the city to complete the destruction which their fens had begun. It was just such a case as called forth the energy and craft of the ruler of Syracuse and showed him at his best. He devised his attack with great skill. Eighty galleys, under Leptines and the Spartan captain, were to attack the Carthaginian fleet, which was anchored off the shore of Dascon. He himself led the land forces, marching by a roundabout road on a moonless night, and suddenly appeared at dawn on the west side of the Punic camp. He ordered his horsemen and a thousand mercenaries to attack the camp here; but the horsemen had secret commands to abandon the hired soldiers once they were in the thick of the fight, and ride rapidly round to the east of the camp, where the true attack was to be made. The attack on the west was only a feint, to distract the attention of the enemy from the other side; and for this purpose Dionysius sacrificed the lives of the hirelings whom he did not trust. The real attack on the east was made on the forts of Dascon and Polichna. Dascon was assailed by the horsemen along with a special force of triremes which had been sent across the bay; Dionysius himself went round to lead the attack on Polichna. The plan was carried out with perfect success. The thousand hirelings were cut to pieces, the forts were captured, and the victory on the land was crowned by the destruction of the Carthaginian fleet. The Syracusan galleys bore down upon the enemy, before they had time fully to man their vessels, much less to row well out to sea, and the beaks of the triremes crashed into defenceless timber. There was Plague in Carthaginian camp. Dionysiu. attacks the Carthaginians. Defeat of Carthaginians.

slaughter, but hardly a fight; and then the land troops, fresh from *their* victory, rushed down to the beach and set fire to the transports and all vessels which had not left the shore. A wild scene followed. A high wind propagated the flames; the cables were burnt asunder; and the bay of Dascon was filled with drifting fireships, while amid the waters despairing swimmers were making for the shore.

Double-
dealing of
Dionysius

Fate had indeed delivered the barbarians into the hands of the Greeks; and the Greeks were determined to wreak their vengeance to the uttermost and extirpate the destroyers of Messana. Dionysius had approved himself the successor of Gelon; the double victory of Dascon was worthy to be set beside the victory of Himera. But Dionysius was not capable of absolute sincerity in the part he played as the champion of Hellas; he could not act to the end as a Syracusan patriot with singleness of heart. This was the fatality of his position as a tyrant, conscious that his autocracy rested on unstable foundations. He fought against Carthage, but it was always with the resolve that the power of the Carthaginians should not be annihilated in Sicily. The Punic peril was a security for his tyranny,

His policy
in regard
to Car-
thage.

by making him necessary to Syracuse. The Syracusans must look to him as their protector against the ever-present barbarian foe. This was another secret of tyranny discovered by Dionysius. The Punic subtlety of Himilco, enlightened by passages in the tyrant's past career, formed no doubt a shrewd idea of this side of his policy; the Carthaginian saw that his hope of safety lay in bargaining with Dionysius. Secret messages passed; and Dionysius agreed to allow Himilco along with all those who were Carthaginian citizens to sail

Escape of
Himilco
by collu-
sion of
Dionysius.

away at night. In payment for this collusion he received three hundred talents. Dionysius recalled his reluctant army from their assaults on the camp, and left it in peace for three days. On the fourth night Himilco set sail with forty triremes, leaving his allies and his mercenaries to their fate. It was an act of desertion which was likely to repel mercenary soldiers from the Carthaginian service in the future; and this was doubtless foreseen by the crafty tyrant. But the squadron of fugitive triremes did not escape untouched. The noise of the oars as they sailed out of the Harbour was detected by the Corinthian allies, and they gave the alarm to Dionysius. But Dionysius was purposely slow in his preparations to pursue, and the impatient Corinthians sailed out without his orders and sank some of the hindmost of the Punic vessels. Having connived at the escape of Himilco, the tyrant was energetic in dealing with the remnant of Himilco's host. The Sicel allies had escaped to their own homes, and only the mercenaries were left. These were slain or made slaves, with the exception of a band of strong and valiant Iberians who were taken into the service of the tyrant.

Thus ended the first struggle of Dionysius with Carthage, and it ended in a complete triumph for the Greek cause. The dominion of the African city was now circumscribed within its old western corner; and the greater part of the rest of Sicily was subject, directly or indirectly, to the rule of the lord of Syracuse. Both from Greek and from barbarian Sicily, a famous city had been blotted out; but Motya had been revived in Lilybaeum, and Messana was soon to rise again upon her ruins.

SECT. 6. SECOND PUNIC WAR, AND SICEL CONQUESTS OF DIONYSIUS

The equivocal policy of Dionysius in his hostilities to Carthage was manifested clearly enough in the course which he pursued after his great victory. It was the most favourable moment that had yet come in the struggle of centuries, for driving the barbarians out and making Sicily a Greek island from the eastern to the western shore. Carthage could not readily gather together such another armament as that which had been destroyed. No patriot leader who was devoted to the Greek cause heart and soul, with singleness of aim, would have failed to follow up the great success by an invasion of western Sicily. But the preservation of his own precarious despotism was the guiding principle of Dionysius; and he saw in the barbarian corner of the island a palladium of his power.

The next Punic War broke out five years later, and part of the meantime had been occupied by Dionysius in extending his power over the Sicels. He annexed to his dominion Morgantina, Cephaloedion, and Henna itself; he made treaties with the tyrants of Agyrion and Centuripa, and with other places. But among all the Sicel towns, that which it was most important for him to win was the new foundation of the Carthaginian on the heights of Taurus. He laid siege to Tauromenium in the depth of winter. Operations of war in the winter season are one of the features of the reign of Dionysius, which separate it from the habits of older Greece and link it to the age of the Macedonian monarchy. The tyrant himself led his men on a wild and moonless night up the steep ascent to the town. One of the citadels was taken, and the assailants entered the place. But the Syracusan band was outnumbered and surrounded, six hundred were killed, and the rest were driven down the cliffs. Of these Dionysius was one; he reached the bottom barely alive, after that precipitous descent.

Sicel conquests of Dionysius (between 396 and 393 B.C.)

Unsuccessful assault on Tauromenium.

Conquest of Solus.

In the course of the extension of his power on the northern coast, Dionysius had advanced to the limits of the Phoenician corner, and had won possession, through domestic treachery, of Solus, the most easterly of the three Phoenician cities. Of the circumstances we know nothing, but the conquest would seem to have been rather a piece of luck than part of any deliberate plan of aggression on the part of the Greek tyrant. No treaty appears to have been concluded between Carthage and Syracuse after the defeat of Himilco, so that the capture of Solus was not a violation of peace, but only an occasion for the reawakening of hostilities which had been permitted to sleep by tacit consent. At all events, it must have had something to do with the renewal of the war,—a renewal for which our records assign no causes.

Second Punic War, 392 B.C.

At the opening of the second war we find a Carthaginian general commanding the Phoenician forces of the island, but without any troops, so far as we know, from Africa. The general was Mago, who in the previous war had been commander of the fleet. His army was doubtless considerably inferior to the forces which Dionysius could muster; certain it is that on this occasion Dionysius did not hesitate to give him battle and did not fail to defeat him. Carthage saw that she must make a more vigorous effort, and she gave Mago a large army—80,000 men, it is said,—to retrieve his ill success. To meet the invader, Dionysius entered into a close league with the strongest Sicel power in the land, his fellow-tyrant Agyris of Agyrium. This is the special feature of the second Punic War: the cause of Europe is upheld by a federation of the two European powers of the island, Sicel and Greek. The Carthaginian army advanced into Sicel territory, seeking to win the Sicel towns. But Agyris and his men waged a most effectual manner of warfare, cutting off all the foraging parties of the enemy and thus starving them by degrees. This they were able to do from their knowledge of their native hills. But it seems that the Syracusans were dissatisfied with this slow method, which was thoroughly to the taste of Dionysius. What happened is not clear; but we learn that the Syracusans marched away from the camp, and that Dionysius replaced them by arming the slaves. Then the Greeks and the Sicels must have won some unrecorded success, or the Carthaginian host must have been already terribly deplenished by the want of food; for we next find Mago suing for peace.

Victory of Dionysius.

League of Dionysius with Agyris.

Terms of the Peace.

This peace, although it is said to have been based on the treaty which Dionysius had made twelve years before, was in truth altogether different; for the parts of the two powers were reversed. All the Greek communities of Sicily were now placed under the direct or indirect power of Syracuse. The Carthaginian power was confined to the western corner. Nothing is said of Solus; it must have been now handed over to Carthage, if Mago had not already recovered it by arms. But the most striking provision of the treaty is that which placed "the Sicels" under the rule of Dionysius. Nothing is said of Agyrium, and we are almost driven to wonder whether there was here any treachery to Agyris, of whom we hear nothing further. But there was a special clause touching Tauromenium; and acting on this clause Dionysius immediately took possession of the town, expelled the Sicels, and established in the fortress one of those mercenary settlements which were characteristic of his age. Such was the end of the two Punic wars, which were in truth rather but a single war broken by an interval of quiescence.

Dionysius wins Tauromenium

Sect. 7. The Empire of Dionysius

Having made himself master of all Greek Sicily, the lord of Syracuse began to extend the compass of his ambition beyond the bounds of the island. He began to plan the conquest of Greek Italy. Hitherto the Sicilian cities, though they had constant dealings with the colonies of the Italian mainland, had never sought there, or anywhere out of their own island, a field for conquest or aggression. The restriction of Siceliot ambition to Sicilian territory was the other side of the doctrine preached by Hermocrates that the Siceliots should not allow Greeks from beyond the sea to interfere in the affairs of Sicily. We are reminded of the policy which has been followed on a greater scale by the United States on the American continent. Here, as in other things, Dionysius was an innovator; he set the example of enterprises of conquest beyond the sea. Into the enterprise of Italian conquest he was naturally led on by his dealings with the fellow-cities of the strait, Messana and Rhegium.

For Messana was a city once more; it had been rebuilt by Dionysius himself. He settled in it colonists from Locri and Medma in Italy, and 600 Messenians from old Greece, who had been wandering about homeless since Sparta had driven them from Naupactus. But this favour to the Messenians displeased the Spartans, and as Dionysius clave to the friendship of Sparta he yielded to their protests. He removed the exiles from Messana, but he made for them a secure though less illustrious home. He founded the city of Tyndaris on a high hill to the west of Mylae, and fortified it strongly; the walls and towers, which still remain, are a good specimen of the fortifications of Dionysius.

The restoration of Messana and the foundation of Tyndaris were

Messana restored 396 B.C. (Messenians driven from Naupactus, 401-400 B.C.) Foundation of — Tyndaris by Dionysius, 395 B.C.

no pleasant sight to the Ionian city across the strait; these new cities seemed to Rhegium a Syracusan menace. The men of Rhegium sought to make a counter-move by founding a city themselves between Tyndaris and Messana. They gathered together the exiles from Catane and Naxos and settled them on the peninsula of Mylae; but the settlement lasted only for a moment; almost immediately the town of Mylae was captured by its neighbours of Messana, and the exiles were driven out to resume their wanderings.

Apart from his political hostility to Rhegium, Dionysius is said to have borne it a private grudge. He had asked the men of Rhegium to give him one of their maidens to wife, and they had answered that they would give him none but the hangman's daughter.

Locri, Rhegium's neighbour, then granted him the request which Rhegium refused; Locri was his faithful ally; and now. when the conclusion of peace with Carthage left him free to pursue his Italian designs, it was Locri that he made his base of operations. The first object was to capture Rhegium; its position on the strait dictated this, apart from all motives of revenge or hatred. Accordingly starting from Locri with army and fleet, he laid siege to Rhegium by

land and sea. But the confederate cities of the Italian coast came to the assistance of a member of their league; the Italiot armament worsted the fleet of Dionysius in or near the strait, and Dionysius escaped with difficulty to the opposite coast.

Rhegium was thus relieved, and Dionysius now directed his hostilities against the Italiot federation. He made an alliance with the Lucanians, to the intent that they and he should carry on war in common against the Italiot cities, they by land and he by sea. In accordance with this treaty, the Lucanians invaded the land of Thurii. The men of Thurii retorted by invading Lucania in considerable force; but they sustained a crushing defeat at the hands of

the barbarians. Most of the Thurians were slain, but some escaped to the shore and swam out to ships which they descried coasting along. By a curious chance, the ships were the fleet of Syracuse, and Leptines, the tyrant's brother, was once more the commander. He received the fugitives, and did more; he landed and ransomed them

from the Lucanians. He did even more than this; he arranged an armistice between the Lucanians and the Italiots. In acting thus, he clearly went beyond his powers; he had been sent to co-operate with the Lucanians against the Italiots, and he had no right to conclude an armistice in such circumstances, without consulting his brother. It is not surprising that Dionysius deposed him from the command

In the following year Dionysius took the field himself. He opened the campaign by laying siege to Caulonia, the northern neighbour of Locri. The Italiots, under the active lead of Croton, collected an army of 15,000 foot and 2000 horse, and entrusted the command to Helōris, a brave exile of Syracuse, who burned with hatred against the tyrant who had banished him. The federal army marched forth from Croton to relieve Caulonia, and when Dionysius learned of its approach, he decided to go forth to meet it; for his own forces, 20,000 foot and 3000 horse, were considerably superior. Luck favoured him. Near the river Elleporus which flows into the sea between Caulonia and Croton, the tyrant heard that the enemy were encamped within a distance of five miles, and he drew up his men in battle array. Heloris, less well-informed, rode forward in front of his main army, with a company of 500 men, and suddenly found himself in the presence of the Syracusan host. He did not quail or flee. Sending back a message to hasten the rest of his army, he and his little band stood firm against the onset of the invaders. Heloris fell himself, and the main army, coming up company by company, in haste and disorder, was easily routed by Dionysius. Ten thousand fugitives escaped to a high hill, but it was a poor hill of refuge, for there was no spring of water and they could not hold out. The next morning they besought Dionysius, who kept watch around the hill throughout the night, to set them free for a ransom. Dionysius refused; he would accept only unreserved surrender. But he was cruel only to grant them a greater mercy than they could themselves have dared to ask. When they came down the hill, Dionysius himself told their number with a wand as they filed past him, and each man deemed that his doom would be bondage if not death. But Dionysius let them all depart, without even exacting a ransom. This act of mercy, which was notable as compared not only with other acts of the tyrant, but with the ordinary practice of the age, produced a great sensation. There is no reason for imputing it to a magnanimous impulse; it was a deliberate act of policy. Dionysius did not wish to be generous, but he wished to be regarded as generous and win over the Italiot cities. For this purpose he made up his mind to sacrifice 10,000 ransoms. His wisdom was soon approved. The communities to which the captives belonged gratefully voted him golden crowns, and made separate treaties with him. In this way he accomplished his purpose; with Rhegium, Caulonia, and Hipponion he still remained at war, but these states were now isolated and the league was broken up. Rhegium bought off his hostilities for the time by surrendering its fleet. Caulonia was captured

Dionysius besieges Caulonia, 389 B.C.

Battle of the Elleporus, 389 B.C.

Dionysius' politic act of mercy.

His treaties with the Italiot cities.

Submission of Rhegium: capture of Caulonia, 389 B.C.

and abolished, and its territory given to Locri; Hipponion was likewise taken and destroyed; but the peoples of both these cities were
transplanted to Syracuse and became Syracusan citizens.

But Dionysius had not yet finished with Rhegium. He created a
pretext for renewing hostilities and he laid siege to the city. The
men of Rhegium had now no friends to help them, but, under their
general Phyton, whom the tyrant vainly endeavoured to bribe, they
held out for ten months, and were reduced to surrender in the end
by starvation. Dionysius accepted ransoms for those who could find
the money; the rest of the inhabitants were sold. Phyton was selected for special vengeance. He was scourged through the army,
and then drowned with all his kin. Thus Dionysius gained what
hitherto had been one of his most pressing desires—possession of
the city which had so long hated and defied him. He was now master of both sides of the strait, and held the fortress which was the
bulwark of Greek Italy. Eight years later he captured Croton, and
his power in Italy reached its greatest height.

But in the meanwhile the unresting lord of Syracuse had turned
his eyes to a region of enterprise further afield. The needs of his
treasury, if nothing else, bent his attention to commerce. We touch
here upon that side of ancient enterprise which has been persistently
and provokingly withdrawn from our vision, because the writers of
antiquity never thought of lingering on the ordinary business transactions which were happening every day before their eyes. Many
things that are now dark would be cleared up if we had more knowledge of the operations of Greek trade. Dionysius saw an opening
for Sicilian commerce along the eastern and western coasts of the
Hadriatic sea, in whose waters the ships of Corcyra, Athens, and
Taras hitherto had chiefly plied. He set about making the Hadriatic
a Syracusan lake, by means of settlements and alliances. He founded settlements in Apulia, which he probably hoped ultimately to
incorporate in his dominion. He settled a colony and fixed a naval
station in the island of Issa, whose importance as a strategic post
has been more than once illustrated in subsequent history. He took
part with the Parians in colonising Pharos, on an island not far from
Issa. A Syracusan colony was planted at Ancon, and, even if the
colonists were, as they are said to have been, exiles and foes of
Dionysius, we may be sure that the merchant ships of Syracuse
were welcome at the wharfs of Ancon. The northern goal of these
merchant ships was near the mouth of the Po, at a spot where there
was already a mart for diffusing Greek merchandise in Cis-Alpine
Gaul, and beyond the Alps into northern Europe. This was the
Venetian Hadria, city of marshes and canals, which was now col-

onised by Dionysius, to be in some sort—as has been aptly observed —a forerunner of Venice itself. It was in one of these outlying posts of the Hellenic world that the historian, to whom we owe our best knowledge of the Sicilian history of this time, probably wrote his works. Philistus had held posts of high trust under Dionysius, and had even been the commandant of the Syracusan citadel; but in later years he incurred his master's displeasure or suspicion, and chose as his place of banishment some city on the Hadriatic, possibly Hadria. In connexion with these Hadriatic designs, touching which we have only the most fragmentary records, Dionysius formed an alliance with Alcetas of Molossia, whose unstable position in his own kingdom made him willing to be a dependent on the strong ruler of Syracuse. Thus Dionysius made his influence predominant at the gates of the Hadriatic.

Molossia

The Syracusan empire—we may survey it, when it reached its widest extent—consisted, like most other empires, partly of immediate dominion and partly of dependent communities. The immediate dominion was both insular and continental; it included the greater portion of Sicily and the southern peninsula of Italy, perhaps as far north as the river Crathis. But this dominion was not homogeneous, in the relations of its various parts to the government at Syracuse. There was first of all the old territory of the Syracusan republic. There were secondly, a number of military settlements; an institution of Dionysius which has been compared to the military colonies of Rome. Such, for example, was Croton on the mainland; such in Sicily were Henna and Messana; such was Issa in the Hadriatic. Outside these direct subjects was the third class of the allied cities, which, though absolutely subject to the power of Dionysius, had still the management of their less important affairs in their own hands. To this class belonged the old Greek cities of Sicily—like Gela and Camarina; new colonies, like Tyndaris; some Sicel states like Agyrium and Herbita.

Greatest extent of Syracusan Empire. Its character. I. Immediate dominion. (a) Territory of Syracuse. (b) Military Colonies (c) Allied cities.

Beyond the sphere of direct dominion stretched the sphere of dependencies—the allies, whose bond of dependence was rather implied than formally expressed. Here belonged the cities of the Italiot league, Thurii and the rest, north of the Crathis river; here belonged some of the Iapygian communities in the heel of Italy; and here the kingdom of Molossia beyond the Ionian sea, and some Illyrian places on the Hadriatic coast. The Crathis may be regarded as the line between the two, the outer and the inner, divisions of the empire of Dionysius. But it is remarkable that at one time he planned a wall and ditch, which should run across the isthmus from Scylletion to the nearest point on the other sea—a distance of about

II. Dependencies.

Scheme of fencing off the extremity of Italy.

twenty miles—and thus sever, as it were, the toe of Italy from the mainland and make it a sort of second Sicily.

The finances of Dionysius.

The acquisition and maintenance of this empire, the building of ships and ship-sheds, the payment of mercenary soldiers, the vast fortifications of Syracuse, both of the island and of the hill—all this, along with the ordinary expenses of government and the state of a despot's ccurt, demanded an enormous outlay. To meet this outlay Dionysius was forced to resort to extraordinary expedients. In the first place, he oppressed the Syracusans by a burdensome taxation. He imposed special taxes for war, special taxes for building ships; and he introduced an onerous tax on cattle. It is said that the citizens paid yearly into the treasury at the rate of twenty per cent of their capital. In the second place, he had recourse to various expedients affecting the coinage. Thus he issued debased four-drachm pieces of tin instead of silver; and in one case of financial need he paid a debt by placing on each coin an official mark which rendered it worth the double of its true value. But such expedients were not enough. Dionysius was an unscrupulous rifler of temples. Thus, when he took Croton, he carried off the treasures of a temple of Hera. In an earlier year he sailed like a pirate to Etruria, swooped down on a rich temple at the port of Agylla, and bore off booty which amounted to the value of 1500 talents. The plunder of a sanctuary on distant barbarian shores might seem a small thing, but no awe of divine displeasure restrained Dionysius from planning a raid upon the holiest place of Hellenic worship. He formed the design of robbing the treasury of Delphi itself, with Illyrian and Molossian help; but the plan miscarried. It is little wonder that the tyrant had an evil repute in the mother-country.

SECT. 8. DEATH OF DIONYSIUS. ESTIMATE OF HIS WORK

Outbreak of Third Punic War, 383 B.C.

It was only for a moment that the dominion of the Syracusan despot reached its extreme limits. He had hardly won the city and lands of Croton, when his borders fell back in the west of his own island. A new war with Carthage had broken out, and this time if Dionysius was not the first to draw the sword, he at least provoked hostilities. He entered into alliances with some of the cities dependent on Carthage—possibly Segesta or Eryx. Of the campaigns we know almost nothing, except their result. First we find Carthage helping the Italiots with whom the tyrant was at war. Next we find a Carthaginian force in Sicily commanded by Mago. In a battle fought at Cabala—a place unknown—the Syracusans won a great victory and Mago was killed. While negotiations for peace were

Battle of Cabala. Battle of Cronion, 379 B.C. Peace, 378 B.C.

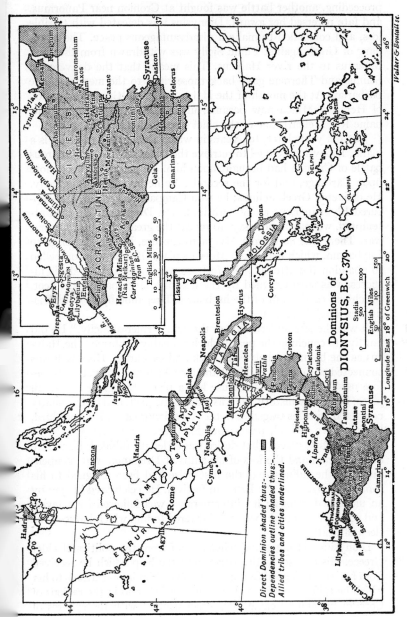

Walker & Boutall sc.

Direct Dominion shaded thus:—
Dependencies outline shaded thus:—
Allied tribes and cities underlined.

Dominions of DIONYSIUS, B.C. 379.

Fig. 95.

proceeding, another battle was fought at Cronion near Panormus, and fate reversed her award. Dionysius was defeated with terrible loss, and compelled to make a disadvantageous peace. The boundary of Greek against Punic Sicily was withdrawn from the river Mazarus to the river Halycus. This meant that the deliverer of Selinus and Thermae gave back those cities to the mercies of the barbarian. At the mouth of the Halycus, the old Greek foundation of Heraclea Minoa now became, under the corresponding Punic name Ras Melkart, one of the chief strongholds of Punic power.

Ras Melkart.

Just ten years later, ten years in which the history of Sicily is a blank, Dionysius essayed to retrieve the losses which the disastrous battle of Cronion had brought upon him. He made war once more upon Carthage, and for the second time he invaded Punic Sicily. He delivered Greek Selinus; he won Campanian Entella; and captured Elymian Eryx along with its haven Drepanon. He then attempted, we may almost say, to repeat the great exploit of his first war. There was no more a Motya to capture, but he laid siege to Lilybaeum, which had taken Motya's place. But he was compelled to abandon the attempt; the fortress was too strong; and his ill-success was soon crowned by the loss of a large part of his fleet, which was carried out of the harbour of Drepanon by an enterprising Carthaginian admiral.

Fourth Punic War, 68 B.C.

It was the last undertaking of the great "ruler of Sicily." He did not live to conclude the peace which probably confirmed the Halycus as the boundary between Greek and barbarian. His death was connected with a side of his character which has not yet come before us. The tyrant of Syracuse has a place, though it is a small place, in literary history. He was a dramatic poet, and he frequently competed with his tragedies in the Athenian theatre. He won third, he won even second, prizes; but his dearest ambition was to be awarded a first place. That desire was at length fulfilled; his failure at Lilybaeum and the loss of his ships at Drepanon were compensated by the tidings that the first prize had been assigned to his *Ransom of Hector* at the Lenaean festival. He celebrated his joy by an unwonted carouse; his intemperance was followed by a fever; and a soporific draught was administered to him which induced the sleep of death.

Death of Dionysius, 367 B C.

Dionysius as a tragic poet.

Dionysius did not stand wholly aloof from the politics of elder Greece. His alliance with Sparta, and the help which he received from her at the siege of Syracuse, involved him in obligations to her which he fulfilled on more than one occasion; and in the regions of Corcyra his empire came into direct contact with the spheres of

Relations of Sicily to Eastern Greece in time of Dionysius.

some of the states of the mother-country. But these political relations are an unimportant part of his reign. His reign, as a whole, lies apart from the contemporary politics of elder Greece. Yet, from some points of view, it possesses more significance in Grecian, and in European, history than the contemporary history of Sparta and Athens.

In the first place, Dionysius stands out as one of the most prominent champions of Europe in the long struggle between the Asiatic and the European for the possession of Sicily. He did what no champion had done before; he carried the war into the enemy's precinct. He well-nigh achieved what it was reserved for an Italian commonwealth to achieve actually, the reclaiming of the whole island for Europe, the complete expulsion of the Semitic intruder. In the second place, he stands out as the man who raised his own city not only to dominion over all Greek Sicily but to a transmarine dominion, which made her the most powerful city in the Greek world, the most potent state in Europe. The purely Sicilian policy is flung aside, and Syracuse becomes a continental power, laying one hand on that peninsula to which her own island geographically belongs, and stretching out the other to the lands beyond the Hadriatic. And, thirdly, this empire, though it is thinly disguised like the later empire of Rome under constitutional forms, is really a monarchical realm, which is a foreshadowing of the Macedonian monarchies and an anticipation of a new period in European history. Again in the art of war Dionysius inaugurated methods which did not come into general use till more than half a century later; some of his military operations seem to transport us to the age of Alexander the Great and his successors. In another way too Dionysius anticipated the age of those monarchs; statues were set up representing him in the guise of Dionysus, the god by whose name he was called. Here indeed he did not stand alone among his contemporaries; the Spartan Lysander also had been invested with attributes of divinity.

But in one respect Dionysius was far from being a forerunner of the Macedonian monarchs: he was not an active or deliberate diffuser of Hellenic civilisation. On the contrary he appears rather as an undoer of Hellenic civilisation. He destroys Hellenic towns, and he replaces Hellenic by Italian communities; he cultivates the friendship of Gauls and Lucanians, to use them against Greeks, not to make them Greeks. This side of the policy of Dionysius, the establishment of Italian settlements in Sicily, points in a different direction; it points—unintentionally, indeed, so far as he was con-

Significance of Dionysius in history. Champion of Europe against the Semite

Extra-Sicilian Empire

Anticipation of the Macedonian monarchies. Military improvements. Deification.

Dionysius not a Hellenizer: First signs of the expansion of the Italian race.

cerned—to the expansion of Italy, it points to the Italian conquest of Sicily which was to be accomplished more than a century after his death.

Why Dionysius did not do more.

Dionysius then has the significance of a pioneer. But there is something else to be said. Original and successful as he was, great things as he did, we cannot help feeling that he ought to have done greater things still. A master of political wisdom, an originator of daring ideas, a man of endless energy, remarkably temperate in the habits of his life, he was hampered throughout by his unconstitutional position. The nature of tyranny imposed limitations on his work. He had always to consider first the security of his own unchartered rule; he could never forget the fact that he was a hated master. He could therefore never devote himself to the accomplishment of any object or the solution of any problem with the undivided zeal which may animate a constitutional prince who need never turn aside to examine the sure foundations of his power. We saw how the tyrant's warfare against Carthage was affected by these personal calculations. The Syracusan tyranny accomplished indeed far more than could have been accomplished by the Syracusan democracy; Dionysius as a tyrant wrought what he could never have wrought as a mere statesman governing by legitimate influence the counsels of a free assembly. But he illustrates—and all the more strikingly, as the pioneer of the great monarchies of the future—the truth to which attention has been called before, that the tyrannies and democracies of Greek cities were in their nature not adapted to create and maintain large empires.

Sect. 9. Dionysius the Younger

Dionysius II., 367 B.C.

The empire of Dionysius, which he had made fast, to use his own expression, "by chains of adamant"—a strong army, a strong navy, and strong walls—descended to his son, Dionysius, a youth of feeble character, not without amiable qualities, but of the nature that is easily swayed to good or evil and is always dependent on advisers.

Dion, brother-in-law and son-in-law of Dionysius the elder.

At first he was under the influence of Dion, who had been the most trusted minister of the elder Dionysius in the latter part of his reign, holding the office of admiral, and allied by a double marriage with the tyrant's family. The tyrant had espoused Dion's sister Aristomache; and Dion married one of the daughters of this marriage, Arete, his own niece. The other daughter was given to Dionysius, her half-brother. Another man, possessing the pride, wealth, and ability of Dion, might have sought to fling aside Dionysius, and if he did not seize the tyranny himself, at all events to secure it for the sons of his sister, the brothers of his wife, Hipparinus and Nysaeus. But Dion was not like other men; his aspirations were loftier and less selfish. His object was not to secure tyranny for any man, but to get rid of tyranny altogether. But this was not to be done by a revolution; the democracy which would have risen on the ruins of the despotism would have been in Dion's eyes as evil a thing for Syracuse as the despotism itself. For Dion had imbibed, and thoroughly believed in, the political teaching of his friend, Plato the philosopher. His darling project was to establish at Syracuse a constitution which would so far as possible conform to the theoretical views of Plato, and which would probably have taken the shape of a limited kingship, with some resemblance to the constitution of Sparta. And this could never have been brought about by a pure vote of the Syracusan people; the ideal constitution must be imposed upon them for their own good. The sole chance lay in persuading a tyrant to impose limitations on his own absolute power and introduce the required constitution. "Give me," says Plato himself, "a city governed by a tyranny, and let the tyrant be young, with good brains, brave, and generous, and let fortune bring in his way a good lawgiver"—then a state has a chance of being well governed. Dion saw in young Dionysius a nature which might be moulded as he wished,—a nature, perhaps, which he missed in his own nephews, Hipparinus and Nysaeus. He devoted himself loyally to Dionysius, who looked up to his virtue and experience, and he set himself to interest the young ruler in philosophy and make him take a serious view of his duties. But his chief hope lay in bringing the tyrant under the attraction of the same powerful personality which had exercised a decisive and abiding influence over himself. Plato must come to Syracuse and make the tyrant a philosopher. The treatment which Plato had experienced on the occasion of a previous visit to Sicily, at the hands of the elder Dionysius, was not indeed such as to encourage him to return. But he yielded, reluctantly, to the pressing invitation of the young ruler and the urgent solicitations of Dion, who represented that now at last the moment had come to call an ideal state into actual existence.

It was the vision of a "dreamer dreaming greatly"; and that a statesman of Dion's practical experience and knowledge of human nature should have allowed himself to be guided by such a dream may seem strange to us; to us to whom the history of hundreds of societies throughout a period of more than two thousand years has brought disillusion. It has indeed seemed so curious that some have concluded that Dion was throughout plotting to dethrone Dionysius, that the philosophical scheme was part of the plot, and Plato

His political aspirations.

Plato's influence on Dion.

c. 388 B.C

Plato's second visit to Sicily.

Serious intention to form an ideal state.

an unconscious tool of the conspiracy. But the good faith of Dion seems assured. We must remember that a state founded on philosophical principles was a new idea, which was not at all likely to seem foredoomed to failure to any one who was enamoured of philosophy; for such a state had never been tried, and consequently there was no example of a previous failure. On the contrary, there was the example of Sparta as a success. The political speculators of those days always turned with special predilection to Sparta, as a well-balanced state, and it was believed that her constitution and discipline had been called into being and established for all time by the will and fiat of a single extraordinarily wise lawgiver. Why then should not Dionysius and Dion, under the direction of Plato, do for Syracuse what Lycurgus had done for Lacedaemon? And Dion doubtless thought that his own experience would enable him to adjust the demands of speculation to the rude realities of existence.

No welcome could have been more honourable and flattering than that which Plato received. He engaged the respect and admiration of Dionysius, and the young tyrant was easily brought to regard tyranny as a vile thing and to cherish the plan of building up a new constitution. The experiment would probably have been tried, if Plato, in dealing with his pupil, had acted otherwise than he did. The nature of Dionysius was one of those natures which are susceptible of impressions and capable of enthusiasm, but incapable of persevering application. If Plato had contented himself with inculcating the general principles which he has expounded with such charm in his *Republic*, Dionysius would in all likelihood have attempted to create at Syracuse a dim adumbration of the ideal state. It is hardly likely that it would have been long maintained: still, it would at least have been essayed. But Plato insisted on imparting to his pupil a systematic course of philosophical training, and began with the science of geometry. The tyrant took up the study with eagerness; his court was absorbed in geometry; but he presently wearied of it. And then influences which were opposed to the scheme of Dion and Plato began to tell.

One of the first acts of the new reign had been to recall from exile the historian Philistus. He was entirely adverse to the proposed reforms, and wished that the tyranny should continue on its old lines. He and his friends insinuated that the true object of Dion was to secure the tyranny for one of his own nephews, as soon as Dionysius had laid it down. They did everything to turn Dionysius against Dion, and at last an indiscreet letter of Dion gave them the means of success. Syracuse and Carthage were negotiating peace, and Dion wrote to the Carthaginian Judges not to act without first consulting

Plato's course of instruction.

Philistus recalled: opposed to Dion's scheme.

him. The letter was intercepted, and though its motive was doubt-less perfectly honest, it was interpreted as treason. Dion was ban-ished from Sicily, but was allowed to retain his property; and the party of Philistus won the upper hand. Plato remained for a while in the island; Dionysius was jealous of the esteem which he felt for Dion, and desired above all things to win the same esteem for him-self. But the philosopher's visit had been a failure; he yearned to get back to Athens, and at length Dionysius let him go.

Banish-ment of Dion.

Plato returns to Athens.

So ended the notable scheme of founding an ideal state, the real-isation of which would have involved the disbandment of the mer-cenary troops and thereby the collapse of the Syracusan empire. It is easy to ridicule Plato for want of tact in his treatment of the young tyrant; it is easy to flout him as a pedant for not distinguish-ing between an Academy and a Court. But Plato was perfectly right. The only motive which had brought him to Sicily was to pre-pare the way for founding a state fashioned more or less according to his own ideal. Now the first condition of the life of such a state was that a king should be a philosopher. Therefore, as Dionysius—not Plato—was to be king in the new state, it was indispensable that Dionysius should become a philosopher. Plato had not the smallest interest in imparting to the tyrant a superficial smattering of philosophy, enough to beguile him into framing a Platonic state. For that state would have been still-born, since it lacked the first condition of life, a true philosopher at its head. If Dionysius had not the stuff of a true, but only of a sham, philosopher, it was useless to make the experiment. Plato adopted the only reasonable course; he was true to his own ideal.

Sect. 10. Dion

Strange as it may appear, after such experiences, Plato seems to have returned once more to Sicily, at the urgent invitation of Dio-nysius. He can have had no more expectations of making a phi-losopher out of the tyrant, and his chief motive must have been to bring about the recall of Dion and reconcile him to Dionysius, who appears to have lured the philosopher by the hope that this might be accomplished. Plato was received and entertained with as great honour as before, but his visit was fruitless. Probably the tyrant ascertained that Dion was in the meantime using his wealth to make silent preparations for winning his way back to Syracuse and overthrowing the tyranny. Dionysius therefore took the precaution of confiscating Dion's property; and then Plato returned to Athens as soon as he could. Dion also betook himself to Old Greece and

Third visit of Plato to Syracuse.

Dion at Athens.

made Athens his headquarters. Presently the tyrant committed a needless act of tyranny; he compelled Dion's wife Arete to marry another man. At length Dion deemed that the time for action had come. With a very small force, packed into not more than five merchant ships, he set sail from Zacynthus, to encounter the mighty armaments of Dionysius. His coming was expected, and the admiral Philistus had a fleet in Italian waters to waylay him. But Dion sailed straight across the open sea to Pachynus. His plan was to land in Western Sicily, collect what reinforcements he could, and march on Syracuse. It was a bold enterprise, but Dion knew that the character of the tyrant was feeble, and that the Syracusans pined to be delivered from his tyranny. Driven by a storm to the Libyan coast, the ships of the deliverer finally reached Heraclea Minoa, now a Carthaginian port, in southwestern Sicily. Here they learned that Dionysius had departed for Italy with eighty ships, and they lost no time in marching to Syracuse, picking up reinforcements, both Greek and Sicel, on their way. The Campanian mercenaries who were guarding Epipolae were lured away by a trick; and, making a night march from Acrae, Dion and his party entered Syracuse amid general rejoicings. The Assembly placed the government in the hands of twenty generals, Dion among them. The fortress of Epipolae was secured; no part of Syracuse remained in possession of Dionysius except the Island, and against this Dion built a wall of defence from the Greater to the Lesser Harbour. Seven days later Dionysius returned.

While Syracuse was rocking with the first enthusiasm at her deliverance, the deliverer was the popular hero. But Dion was not a man who could hold the affections of the people, for he repelled men by his exceeding haughtiness. And it was seen too that he was determined masterfully to direct the Syracusans how they were to use their freedom. Dionysius, shut up in the Island, resorted to artifices to raise suspicion against him in the minds of the citizens. And a rival appeared on the scene who possessed more popular manners than Dion. This was a certain Heraclides, whom the tyrant had banished, and who now returned with an armament of ships and soldiers. The Assembly elected him admiral. Dion undid this act on the ground that his own consent was necessary; and then came forward himself to propose Heraclides. This behaviour alienated the sympathies of the citizens; they did not want another autocrat. Soon afterwards Heraclides won an important sea-fight, defeating Philistus, who had returned from Italy with his squadron. The old historian himself was taken and put to death with cruelty. Dionysius thus lost his best support, and presently he escaped from the

357 B.C.

Dion sails
for Sicily,
August.

Enters
Syracuse.

Dionysius
holds the
Island.

Hera-
clides.

Death of
Philistus.

Island, taking his triremes with him, but leaving a garrison of mercenaries and his young son Apollocrates in command.

Soon after this the influence of Dion waned so much that the Syracusans deposed him from the post of general, and appointed twenty-five new generals, among them Heraclides. They also refused to grant any pay to the Peloponnesian deliverers who had come with Dion. The Peloponnesians would have gladly turned against the Syracusans if Dion had given the signal; but Dion, though self-willed, was too genuine a patriot to attack his own city, and he retired to Leontini with 3000 devoted men.

Dion withdraws to Leontini, 356 B.C.

The Syracusans then went on with the siege of the island fortress, 'and so hard pressed was the garrison that it determined to surrender. Heralds had been already sent to announce the decision to the Syracusans, when in the early morning reinforcements arrived— soldiers and provisions, brought by a Campanian of Naples, by name Nypsius, who, eluding the notice of the enemy's ships, sailed into the Great Harbour. The situation was changed, and negotiations were immediately broken off. At first fortune favoured the Syracusans. Heraclides put out to sea, and won a second sea-fight, sinking or capturing whatever warships had been left behind by Dionysius or were brought by Nypsius. At this success the city went wild with joy and spent the night in carousing. Before the dawn of day, when soldiers and generals were alike sunk in a drunken sleep, Nypsius and his troops issued from the gates of the island, and surmounting the cross wall of Dion by scaling-ladders, slew the guards and took possession of Lower Achradina and the Agora. All this part of the city was sacked; full leave was given to the mercenaries to do as they listed; they carried off women and children and all the property they could lay hands on. Next day all the citizens who had taken refuge in Epipolae and the Upper Achradina, looking helplessly at what had been done, and seeing that the barbarians were beginning their horrible work again, voted to call Dion to the rescue. Messengers riding as swiftly as they could reached Leontini towards evening. Dion led them to the theatre, and there before the gathered folk the envoys told their tale and implored Dion and the Peloponnesians to forget the ingratitude of Syracuse and come to her help. Dion made a moving speech; he would in any case go, and, if he could not save his city, he would bury himself in her ruins; but the Peloponnesians might well refuse to stir for a people which had entreated them so ill. A shout went up that Syracuse must be rescued; and for the second time Dion led the Peloponnesians to her deliverance. They set out at once, and a night march brought them to Megara, five or six miles from Syracuse, at

Arrival of Nypsius (Numsius).

Dion recalled

the dawn of day. There dreadful tidings reached them. Nypsius, knowing that the rescue was on its way and deeming that no time was to be lost, had let loose his barbarians again into the city at midnight. They no longer thought of plunder, but only of slaying and burning. At this news the army of rescue hurried on to save what might still be saved. Entering by the Hexapylon on the north, Dion cleared his way before him through Achradina, and reached the cross-wall which he had himself built as a defence against the Island. It was now broken down, but behind its ruins Nypsius had posted a body of his mercenaries, and this was the scene of the decisive struggle. Dion's men carried the wall, and the foe was driven back into the fortress of Ortygia.

The opponents of Dion, who had not fled, were humbled. Heraclides besought his pardon, and Dion was blamed for not putting him to death. It was at all events foolish magnanimity which consented to the arrangement that Dion should be general with full power on land, and Heraclides by sea. The old dissensions soon broke out, and presently we find a Spartan named Gaesylus reconciling the rivals and constraining Heraclides to swear solemnly to do nothing against Dion.

Nypsius seems to have disappeared from the scene, and it was not long before the son of Dionysius, weary of the long siege, made up his mind to surrender the Island to Dion. During all these dreadful events Dion's sister Aristomache and his wife Arete had been kept in the Island. Dion now took back his wife.

The time at last came for Dion to show what his political aims really were. He professed to have come to give Syracuse freedom; but the freedom which he would have given her was not such as she herself desired. The Syracusan citizens wanted the restoration of their democracy; but to Dion democracy seemed as bad a form of government as tyranny. If, taught by experience, he no longer dreamed of a Platonic state, he desired to establish an aristocracy, with some democratic limitations, and with a king, or kings, as in Sparta. With this purpose in view he sent to Corinth for helpers and advisers; and he expressed his leanings to the Corinthian oligarchy by an issue of coins, with a flying horse, modelled on the Pegasi of Corinth. But though Dion hoped to establish a state in which the few should govern the many, he made a grave mistake in not immediately placing himself above the suspicion of being a selfish power-seeker—a possible tyrant. The Syracusans longed to see the fortress of the tyrant demolished, and if Dion had complied with their wish he might have secured for himself abiding influence. But though he did not live in the fortress he allowed it to remain,

rescues Syracuse.

Surrender of the Island.

Dion's political aim:

a modified aristocracy.

and its existence seemed a standing invitation to tyranny. Dion had no intention of allowing the Syracusans to manage their own affairs, and the enjoyment of power corrupted him. His authority was only limited by the joint command of Heraclides, and at last he was brought to consent that his rival should be secretly assassinated. After this he was to all purposes tyrant, though he might repudiate tyranny with his lips.

Dion becomes a tyrant.

Among those who had come with him from elder Greece to liberate Syracuse was a pupil of Plato named Callippus; and this man plotted to overthrow Dion, who trusted him implicitly. Aristomache and Arete suspected him and taxed him with treachery; nor were they assured until he had taken the most solemn oath that a mortal could take. He went to the precinct of the great goddesses Demeter and Persephone; the priest wrapped him in the purple robe of the queen of the underworld and gave him a lighted torch; in this guise he swore that he plotted no evil design against Dion. But so little regard had Callippus for religion that he chose the festival of the Maiden by whom he had sworn for the execution of his plot. He employed some men of Zacynthus to murder Dion, and then seized the power himself.

Plot of Callippus;

his oath.

Murder of Dion, 354 B.C., June.

The tyranny of Callippus lasted for about a year. Then, while he was engaged in an attack on Catane, the two sons of the elder Dionysius by his second wife, Hipparinus and Nysaeus, came to Syracuse and won possession of Ortygia. These brothers were a worthless pair, drunken and dissolute. Hipparinus held the island for about two years; then he was murdered in a fit of drunkenness, and was succeeded by Nysaeus, who ruled Ortygia five years longer. It is not certain how far these tyrants were able to assert their authority over Syracuse outside the precincts of the Island.

Tyranny of Callippus, 354-3 B.C. of Hipparinus, 353-1 B.C. of Nysaeus, 351-46 B.C.

During all these changes Dionysius was living at Locri, the native city of his mother, and ruling it with a tyrant's rod. His cruelty and the outrages which he committed on the freeborn maidens of the city provoked universal hatred. At length he saw the chance of recovering Syracuse. Leaving his wife and daughters at Locri with a small garrison, he sailed to Ortygia and drove out Nysaeus. As soon as he had gone the Locrians arose and easily overcame his mercenaries. The enormities of which the tyrant had been guilty may best be measured by the brutal thirst of vengeance which now consumed the citizens of Locri. No supplications, no intervention, no offers of ransom could turn them away from wreaking their pent-up hatred on the wife and daughters of Dionysius. The women were submitted to the most horrible tortures and insults before they were strangled; the sea was sown with their ashes.

Second tyranny of Dionysius, 346 B.C.

Fate of his wife and daughters.

SECT. 11. TIMOLEON

At this moment tyrannies flourished in Sicily. Besides Syracuse, the cities of Messana, Leontini, and Catane, and many Sicel towns were under the yoke of tyrants. Syracuse was at least half free; Dionysius held only the Island. But the Syracusans, for lack of another leader, looked for help and guidance, in their struggle against their own tyrant, to the man who had made himself lord of Leontini.

Hiketas. This was a certain Hiketas, a man ill to deal with, who was a follower of Dion, but after Dion's death caused his wife and sister to be drowned while they were sailing to the Peloponnesus. This Hiketas was aiming at becoming himself lord of Syracuse, and he hoped to accomplish his purpose with the help of Carthage. But he

Sicilian appeal to Corinth. veiled his designs, and he supported an appeal which the Sicilian Greeks now addressed to Corinth. It was an appeal for help both against the plague of tyranny which was rampant in Sicily and against the Carthaginians, who were preparing a great armament to descend upon the troubled island. The Syracusans selected Hiketas as their general.

Corinth's response. Corinth, ever a solicitous mother to her colonies, was ready to respond to the appeal; and the only difficulty was to find a suitable commander. Some one in the assembly, by a sudden inspiration,

Timoleon. arose and named Timoleon, the son of Timodemus. Belonging to a noble family, and notable by his personal qualities, Timoleon was living under a strange cloud, through a deed which some highly praised and others severely blamed. He had saved his brother's life in battle at the risk of his own; but, when that brother afterwards plotted to make himself tyrant, Timoleon and some friends put him to death. His mother and many others abhorred him as guilty of a brother's blood; while others admired him as the slayer of a tyrant. In the light of his later deeds, we know that Timoleon was actuated by the highest motives of duty when he consented to his brother's death. Ever since that terrible day he had lived in retirement, but when his name was mentioned in the Assembly all approved, and Teleclides, a man of influence, expressed the general thought by saying, "We shall decide that he slew a tyrant, if he is successful; that he slew his brother, if he fails." The enterprise was to be Timoleon's ordeal.

The sailing of Timoleon, 344 B.C. With ten ships of war, a few fellow-citizens, and about 1000 mercenaries, Timoleon crossed the Ionian sea, guided, it was said, by the track of a flaming torch, the emblem of the Sicilian goddesses Demeter and Persephone. At Rhegium, now free from the rule of tyrants, he met with a warm welcome. But he found a Carthaginian fleet awaiting him there, and likewise ambassadors from Hiketas, who demanded that the ships and soldiers should be sent back to Corinth, since the Carthaginians would not permit them to cruise in Sicilian waters. As for Timoleon himself, Hiketas would be pleased to have his help and counsel. Timoleon had no thought of heeding such a message. It was not to set up the rule of Hiketas at Syracuse that he had come, or to submit to the dictation of the foes of Hellas. But the difficulty was to leave the roadstead of Rhegium in face of the Punic fleet. Here Timoleon showed caution and craft. He pretended to agree to the proposals, but he asked that the whole matter and the intentions of Hiketas should be clearly stated in the presence of the Rhegine people. With the connivance of the Rhegines, time was wasted, and the Carthaginians and the ambassadors of Hiketas were detained in the Assembly, until the Corinthian ships had put out to sea, Timoleon himself slipping away just in time to embark in the last of them. He made straight for Tauromenium.

It will be remembered that Tauromenium, planted by Himilco to be a Sicel city, had been taken by Dionysius to be an abode for his mercenaries. Amid the troubles after the tyrant's death it had gained its independence, and a citizen named Andromachus had become the foremost man in its public affairs. Andromachus induced his fellow-citizens to offer a home to the homeless Naxians whose parents Dionysius had so cruelly dispossessed. The Naxians came back to the hill which looked down on the place of their old city; Naxos revived in Tauromenium. And the Naxians were the first Sicilians to welcome the deliverer of Sicily to her shores. Timoleon's first success was at Hadranum, the Sicel town where the great Sicilian fire-god Hadranus had his chief abode. The men of Hadranum were at discord among themselves; some would summon Hiketas, others invited Timoleon; and both Hiketas and Timoleon came. It was a race between them to get to Hadranum first. Timoleon, the later to arrive, surprised the enemy as they were resting outside the town, and defeated them, although in numbers they were five to one. The gates of the city were then thrown open and Hadranum became the headquarters of Timoleon's army. Soon afterwards Hiketas suborned two men to assassinate the Corinthian leader, but the plot was frustrated at the last moment; and henceforth the belief gained ground that Timoleon was hedged about by some divine protection. The fire-god of Hadranum too had shown by miraculous signs that he approved of the stranger's enterprise. Other cities now allied themselves with Timoleon; and presently Dionysius sent a message to him, proposing to surrender the Island, and asking only

Timoleon comes to Tauromenium.

Settlement of Naxians there by Andromachus.

Battle of Hadranum.

to be allowed to retire in safety to Corinth, with his private property. The offer was at once accepted; the fortress, and the mercenaries who guarded it, and all the war gear were transferred to Timoleon. Dionysius lived the rest of his life at Corinth in harmless obscurity. Many anecdotes were told of the trivial doings of the fallen lord of Sicily and his smart sayings. When some one contrasted his fortune with that of his father, he remarked, "My father came into power when democracy was hated, but I when tyranny was envied."

The end of Dionysius.

Having won Ortygia sooner and more easily than could have been hoped, it remained for Timoleon to liberate the rest of Syracuse, which was in the hands of Hiketas. But Hiketas had powerful allies. A hundred and fifty Carthaginian ships, under the command of Mago, sailed into the Great Harbour, and a Carthaginian force was admitted into Syracuse. The Corinthian commander in the Island—Timoleon himself still abode at Hadranum—was hard pressed; but presently Mago and Hiketas went off to besiege Catane, and Neon making a successful sally occupied Achradina. At the same time reinforcements from Corinth, which had been for some time delayed in Italy by the Carthaginian fleet, arrived in Sicily. It was now time for Timoleon himself to appear at Syracuse. He pitched his camp on the south side, on the banks of the Anapus. Then another piece of luck befell him. The Greek mercenaries, both his own and those of Hiketas, used to amuse their idle hours by fishing for eels at the mouth of the river; and as they had no cause of quarrel, though they were ready to kill each other for pay, they used to converse amicably on such occasions. One of Timoleon's soldiers observed that the Greeks ought to combine against the barbarians, and the words coming to the ears of Mago caused him to conceive suspicions of Hiketas; he suddenly sailed off with all his fleet; but when he reached Carthage he slew himself and his countrymen crucified his corpse. This story, however, can hardly be the whole explanation of Mago's strange behaviour.

Carthaginians at Syracuse supporting Hiketas.

Thus freed from his most formidable foe, Timoleon soon drove Hiketas from Epipolae, and Syracuse was at length completely free. The Syracusans had found a deliverer who did not, like Dion, seek to be their master; and the fortress of Dionysius was pulled down. This act of demolition seemed the seal and assurance of their deliverance. But the city was dispeopled and desolate, grass grew in the market-place; and the first task of the deliverer was to repopulate it with new citizens. The Corinthians made proclamations at the festivals of elder Greece, inviting emigrants to resettle Syracuse; men whom the tyrants had banished flocked back; and 60,000 men in all gathered both from west and east, with women and children,

Syracuse repeopled.

and restored the strength of the city. The laws of Diocles were issued anew, and the democratic constitution was revived and in some respects remodelled. The most important innovation was the investing of the *amphipolos* or priest of Olympian Zeus with the chief magistracy. The priest was annually elected and gave his name to the year; but, as he was chosen by lot out of three clans, his promotion to be the first magistrate of the republic was a limitation of the democracy. Such was the renovation of Syracuse; and her new freedom was expressed, on some coins which were now issued, by the symbol of an unbridled steed.

Demo-cracy.

Coinage.

Timoleon then went on to do for other towns in Sicily what he had done for Syracuse. Many tyrants submitted; even Hiketas, who had withdrawn to Leontini. There was also work to be done against the Carthaginians, who were intent upon recovering lost ground and were preparing for another great effort to drive the Greeks out of Sicily. Five years after Timoleon had landed in the island, a large armament sailed from Carthage and put in at Lilybaeum. It consisted of 200 galleys and 1000 transports; there were 10,000 horses—some for war chariots; and the total number of the infantry was said to be 70,000. The flower of the host was the "Sacred Band" of 2500 Carthaginian citizens, men of birth and wealth. Hamilcar and Hasdrubal, the commanders, decided to march right across Sicily against Syracuse. But Timoleon did not await them there; he would try to encounter them west of the Halycus, in Punic not in Grecian territory. Collecting such an army as he could—it amounted to no more than 10,000—he set out. On the march he was deserted by 1000 mercenaries who clamoured for arrears of pay and murmured at being led against such overwhelming odds; and with difficulty could he persuade the rest to go on. The Carthaginians were encamped on the west bank of the Crimisus, a branch of the river Hypsas, not that which washes Acragas, but that which flows through the territory of Selinus. The city of Entella, now held by Campanians, was situated on the Crimisus, and it may be that the Punic army had halted with the hope of taking it.

Tyrants suppressed in Sicily.

Carthaginian expedition against Sicily, 339 B.C.

The field of the battle which was now fought between the Greeks and Phoenicians on the banks of the Crimisus is unknown. In the morning the Greeks ascended a hill which divided them from the river, and on their way they met mules laden with wild celery, a herb which was used to wreathe sepulchral slabs. The soldiers were depressed by an incident which seemed ominous of evil; but of the same herb were wrought the crowns of victors in the Isthmian games, and Timoleon hastened to interpret the chance as an augury

Battle of the Crimisus (June). (σέλινον.)

of victory. He wreathed his head with the celery, and the whole host followed his example. Then two eagles appeared in the sky, one bearing a serpent—another fortunate omen. The Greeks halted on the hilltop, striving to pierce the mist which enveloped the ground below them; and when it melted away they saw the enemy crossing the stream. The war-chariots crossed first, and behind came the Sacred Band. Timoleon saw that his chance lay in attacking before the whole army had crossed. He sent down his cavalry to lead the attack and himself followed with the foot. The war-chariots prevented the horses from approaching the Sacred Band; so Timoleon ordered the cavalry to move aside and assail the flank of the foe, leaving the way clear for the infantry. It is not recorded how the infantry swept away the war-chariots, but they succeeded in reaching the Sacred Band. The Carthaginians, firm and immovable, withstood the onset of the spears; and the Greeks, finding that all their thrusting could not drive back or pierce the shield wall, flung down their spears and drew their swords. In the sword fight it was no longer a matter of weight and courage; skill and lithesome movements told; and the Greeks, superior in these qualities, utterly smote the Sacred Band. Meanwhile the rest of the Punic army had crossed the river, and although the flower of it was destroyed, there were still enormous numbers to deal with. But fortune followed Timoleon. Clouds had gathered and were hanging over the hills, and suddenly there burst forth a tempest of lightning and wind-driven rain and hail. The Greeks had their backs to the wind; the rain and hail drove into the faces of the enemy, who in the noise could not hear the commands of their officers. When the ground became muddy, the lighter armour of the Greeks gave them a great advantage over their foes, who floundered about, weighed down by their heavy mail. At length the Carthaginians could no longer stand their ground, and when they turned to fly they found death in the Crimisus. Rapidly swollen by the rain, the river was now rushing along in a furious torrent, which swept men and horses to destruction. It is said that 15,000 prisoners were secured; that 10,000 men had been killed in the fight, not counting those who perished in the river; rich spoils of gold and silver were taken in the camp. The choicest of the arms were sent to the Isthmus to be dedicated in the temple of Poseidon.

The battle had fallen out clean contrary to what was like to have been. Timoleon had gained a victory which may be set beside Gelon's victory at Himera. But he did not follow it up; he made no attempt to cut short the Phoenician dominion in Sicily. Perhaps his inaction was due less to unwillingness than to embarrassments which threatened Syracuse. The tyrant of Catane, who had gone over to Timoleon, declared against him. Hiketas seems to have seized again the tyranny at Leontini; and Timoleon found himself engaged in a war with these two tyrants, Mamercus and Hiketas, who were aided by Carthaginian mercenaries. At last both the tyrants were captured. The Syracusans put them both to death, and slew the wife and daughter of Hiketas, in retaliation for the murder of the wife and sister of Dion. The Messanians also put to death their oppressor, Hippon, with torture, and the schoolboys were taken to the theatre to witness a tyrant's death. Other cities under the yoke of tyranny were likewise liberated, and some dispeopled towns, like Acragas and Gela, were colonised. After twenty years of troubles Sicily was to have a respite now. Carthage made peace, the Halycus being again fixed as the frontier, and she undertook to do nothing to uphold tyrants in Greek cities.

Tyranny reviving is suppressed.

Peace with Carthage.

Timoleon had now delivered Sicily both from domestic despots and from foreign foes, and having achieved his task he laid down the powers which had been granted to him for its performance. Among the great men in Greek history he holds a unique place; for the work which he accomplished was inspired neither by selfish ambition nor by patriotism. He sought no power for himself; he laboured in a strange land for cities which might adopt him but were not his own. Patriotism, indeed, in the widest sense, might stimulate his ardour, when he fought for Hellas against the Phoenician. But of Greek leaders who achieved as much as he, there is none whose conduct was, like Timoleon's, wholly guided by simple devotion to duty. The Syracusans gave him a property near Syracuse, and there he dwelt till his death, two years after his crowning victory. Occasionally he visited the city when the folk wished to ask for his counsel, but he had become blind and these visits were rare. He was lamented by all Greek Sicily, and at Syracuse his memory was preserved by a group of public buildings called after him.

The Timo leonteion.

The land had rest for twenty years after Timoleon's death; the direct results of his work did not amount to more than that. A tyrant arose then of a worse type than the elder Dionysius, and his hand was heavy upon Sicily. But the career of Agathocles lies outside the limits of this history.

Sect. 12. Events in Great Greece

In these days, troubles and dangers beset the Greeks of Italy no less than their brethren of Sicily. On the mainland, as in the island, the Hellenic name seemed like to have been blotted out,—there by the Phoenicians and the Italian mercenaries, here by the native races. The power of the elder Dionysius had kept at bay the Lucanians, the Messapians, the Iapygians, and other neighbours who pressed on Great Greece; but when his son was attacked by Dion, the Syracusan empire dissolved of itself, and the barbarians of Italy, having no great power to fear, began anew to descend from the mountains on the Greek settlements of the coast. A number of tribes in the toe of the peninsula banded themselves together in a league with their federal capital at Consentia; and this Brettian league, as it was called, aimed at subduing all the Greek cities of the promontory. Terina, Hipponion, New Sybaris on the Traeis, and other places were captured. Men were not blind to the danger which menaced Western Hellas, of being sunk under a tide of barbarism; one of the objects of Plato and Dion had been to drive all the barbarian mercenaries out of Greek Sicily. But in Italy the peril was greatest, and there was sore need of help from without. The appeal of Syracuse to her mother Corinth and the coming of Timoleon put it into the mind of Taras, hard bestead by the neighbouring peoples, to ask succour of her mother Sparta. The appeal came at a favourable moment. Sparta was not in a position to undertake any political scheme at home, and king Archidamus eagerly embraced the chance of going forth to fight for Hellas against the barbarians of the West, even as his father Agesilaus, sixty years ago, had fought against the barbarians of the East. He got together a band of mercenaries, chiefly from the Phocian survivors of the Sacred War,[4] and sailed to Italy. For four or five years seemingly he strove against the barbarians, but without winning any decisive success, and was finally killed at Mandonia in a battle with the Lucanians. The ineffectual expedition of Archidamus was a striking contrast to the brilliant achievements of Timoleon. But Taras was not ungrateful for his efforts. She had commemorated her appeal to Sparta by minting beautiful gold pieces, on which the infant Taras was shown supplicating Poseidon of Cape Taenarus. The tragic issue of that appeal suggested a motive for another series of coins, and called forth one of those pathetic allusions which Greek art could achieve with matchless grace. Taras is represented riding on his dolphin and sadly contemplating a helmet; it is the helmet of the Spartan king who had fallen in his service.

Taras was soon forced to seek a new champion. She invited Alexander of Molossia, the uncle of Alexander the Great, and this king saw and seized the chance of founding an empire in the West—of doing there on a small scale what his nephew was accomplishing on

The Brettian league.

c. 356 B.C.

King Archidamus sails to Italy, 343 B.C.

Battle of Mandonia, 338 B.C.

Expedition of Alexander of Epirus, 334 B.C.

[5] See below, p. 686.

a mighty scale in Asia. He was an able man and success attended
his arms. On the east coast of Italy he subdued the Messapians, and
pushed as far north as Sipontum, which he captured. In the west he
smote the Brettian league, seizing Consentia and liberating Terina.
His power was so great in the south that Rome made a treaty with
him; and it is possible that his designs reached to Sicily. The welcome given to this ally and deliverer was also reflected in the money
of Taras; coins were struck with the seated eagle of Dodona and the
thunderbolt of Zeus beside it. But Taras presently felt her own freedom menaced by the conqueror, and she renounced her alliance.
War ensued, Thurii upholding Alexander. The barbarians profited
by these struggles to rise against their conqueror, and a battle was
fought at Pandosia. During the engagement, a Lucanian exile in the
Tarentine army stabbed the king in the back, and the design of an
Epirote empire bestriding the Hadriatic perished with him. This
befell not long after the overthrow of the Persian monarchy on the
field of Gaugamela. But Alexander's work had not been futile;
henceforward Taras was able to keep the upper hand over her Italian neighbours.

Battle of
Pandosia,
331-30
B.C.
Alex-
ander's
death.

Fig. 96.—Gold coin of Taras (reverse). Taras on dolphin; contemplating helmet [legend: ΤΑΡΑΣ; below ΚΑΛ].   Fig. 97.—Gold coin of Taras (reverse).
Infant Taras supplicating Poseidon on throne [legend: ΤΑΡΑΝΤΙΝΩΝ].

CHAPTER XVI

THE RISE OF MACEDONIA

AFTER the battle of Mantinea, when Thebes retired from her aggressive policy, Athens stood forth the most important state in Old Greece. She would have been free to devote all her energies to re-establishing her power on the coasts of the northern Aegean and by the gates of the Pontic waters, and would doubtless have successfully achieved this main object of her policy, if two outlying powers had not suddenly stepped upon the scene to thwart her and cut short her empire. These powers, Caria and Macedon, lay in opposite quarters of the Greek world. Both were monarchies, both were semi-Hellenic. Macedon was a land-power; Caria was both a land-power and a sea-power, but it was as a sea-power that she was formidable to Athens. Of the two, it was Caria which seemed to Greece the country with a future and to Athens the dangerous rival. Of Macedonia little account was taken by the civilised world, and Athens expected that she could always manage it. No prophet in his happiest hour of clairvoyance could have predicted that within thirty years Caria would have sunk back into insignificance, leaving nothing to posterity save the sepulchre of her prince, while Macedon would bear the arts and wisdom of Hellas to the ends of the earth.

SECT. I. ATHENS REGAINS THE CHERSONESE AND EUBOEA

The death of Epaminondas delivered Athens from her most dangerous and active enemy; but the intrigues which he had spun against her in the north bore results after his death. Alexander of Pherae, who had become the ally of the Thebans, seized the island of Peparethus with his pirate ships and defeated an Athenian armament under Leosthenes. He then repeated the daring enterprise of the Spartan Teleutias, sailing rapidly into the Piraeus, plundering the shops, and disappearing as rapidly with ample spoil. The Athenians replied by making a close defensive and offensive alliance with the federal state of the Thessalians. The stone of the treaty is preserved. The allies of both parties are included. The Thessalians

Thessalian alliance of Athens.

668

bind themselves not to conclude the war against Alexander without the Athenians, and the Athenians in like wise "without the president (archon) and league of the Thessalians"; and the treasurers of Athens are directed to pull down the stêlê on which the former alliance with Alexander had been inscribed.

But the Athenians vented their indignation within their own walls. Since the capture of Oropus there had been signs of smouldering discontent at the conduct of affairs. Callistratus had been indicted and acquitted in the matter of Oropus; but his credit had been roughly shaken, and Alexander's insult to the city at her very doors excited the popular wrath to such a pitch that the statesman as well as the defeated admiral was condemned to death, and escaped only by a timely flight. Thus the ablest Athenian statesman of the fourth century passed from the stage, and no sympathy followed him. Some years later he ventured to return from his Macedonian exiie, hoping that the wrath of his countrymen would have passed away. Their wrath had passed, but it had not been replaced by regret. On reaching Athens he sought the refuge of suppliants at the altar of the Twelve Gods; but no voice was raised to save him, and the executioner carried out the doom of the people. The Athenians were always austere masters of their statesmen, and it sometimes appears to us—though in truth we seldom have sufficient knowledge of the circumstances to justify a confident judgment— that they unreasonably expected an ingathering where no seed had been sown.

Condemnation and exile of Callistratus.

The public indignation which had been aroused by the daring stroke of the tyrant of Pherae was enhanced by the bad tidings which came from Thrace. King Cotys, the reviver of the Odrysian power, had succeeded in laying hold of Sestos and almost the whole peninsula which guards the entrance to the Propontis, in spite of the Athenian fleet. Soon afterwards the old king was murdered and his realm was divided among his three sons. This change was advantageous to Athens, as she could play off one Thracian prince against another. The territory on the Propontis fell to Cersobleptes, who was supported by the Euboean Charidemus, a mercenary captain who had frequently been employed in the service of Athens, and had married, like Iphicrates, a daughter of the Thracian king. Cersobleptes engaged to hand over to Athens the entire Chersonese, except Cardia, "the enemy of Athens," which was to remain independent. But there was no fleet on the spot to enforce the immediate fulfilment of the promise; and, when an admiral was presently sent out, he was defeated by Charidemus. At length a capable man was sent, Chares, a daring, dissolute, and experienced son of Ares, who

The Thracian Chersonese.

Death of king Cotys, 360-59.

Cersobleptes and his brothers succeed Cotys.

357 B.C.
Recovery
of the
Cherso-
nesus and
settle-
ment of
cleruchies.

Recovery
of
Euboea,
357 B.C.

speedily captured Sestos and punished the inhabitants for their unfaithfulness by an unmerciful slaughter. Cersobleptes was forced to change his attitude, and the peninsula was recovered. The Athenians, adopting the same policy which they had followed in Samos, sent outsettlers to the Chersonese. In the same year Euboea was won back to the Athenian league, and there even seemed a fair prospect of accomplishing what of all things would have rejoiced them most, the recovery of long-lost Amphipolis. But their new scheme against Amphipolis may be said to open, in a certain way, a new chapter in the history of Greece.

SECT. 2. PHILIP II. OF MACEDONIA

The man for whom Macedonia had waited long came at last. We have met once and again in the course of our history kings of that ambiguous country—Hellenic, and yet not Hellenic: Alexander playing a double part at Plataea; Perdiccas playing, with consummate skill, a double part in the war of Sparta and Athens. But now the hour of Macedonia has come, and we must look more closely at the cradle of the power which was destined to change the face not only of the Greek but of the oriental world.

In their fortress of Aegae the Macedonian kings had ruled for ages with absolute sway over the lands on the northern and northwestern coasts of the Thermaic Gulf, which formed Macedonia in the strictest sense. The Macedonian people and their kings were of Greek stock, as their traditions and the scanty remains of their language combine to testify. They were a military people, and they extended their power westward and northward over the peoples of the hills, so that Macedonia in a wider sense reached to the borders of the Illyrians in the west and of the Paeonians in the north. These hill tribes, the Orestians, Lyncestians, and others, belonged to the Illyrian race, and they were ever seeking to cast off the bond of subjection which attached them to the kings of Aegae. In Illyria and Paeonia they had allies who were generally ready to support them in rebellion; and the dangers which Macedonia had constantly to encounter and always to dread from half-subjugated vassals and warlike enemies had effectually hindered her hitherto from playing any conspicuous part in the Greek world.

Thus the Macedonian kingdom consisted of two heterogeneous parts, and the Macedonian kings had two different characters. Over the Greek Macedonians of the coast the king ruled immediately; they were his own people, his own "Companions." Over the Illyric folks of the hills he was only overlord; they were each subject to its cwn chieftain, and the chieftains were his unruly vassals. It is clear that Macedonia could never become a great power until these vassal peoples had been completely tamed and brought under the direct rule of the kings, and until the Illyrian and Paeonian neighbours had been taught a severe lesson. These were the tasks which awaited the man who should make Macedonia. The kings had made some efforts to introduce Greek civilisation into their land. Archelaus, who succeeded Perdiccas, had been a builder and a roadmaker, and following the example of Greek tyrants, he had succeeded in making his court at Pella centre for famous artists and poets. Euripides, the tragic poet, Timotheus, the most eminent leader of a new school of music, Zeuxis the painter, and many another, may have found pleasure and relief in a change from the highly civilised cities of the south to a new and fresher atmosphere, where there were no politicians. It is sometimes said that Macedonia was still in the Homeric stage of development. There is truth in this; but the position of the monarch was different from that of the Homeric king. No law bound the Macedonian monarch; his will was binding on his subjects; and against him they had only one solitary right. In the case of a capital charge, the king could not put a Macedonian to death without the authority of a general Assembly. This was the charter of Macedonian liberty. Fighting and hunting were the chief occupations of this vigorous people. A Macedonian who had not killed his man wore a cord round his waist; and until he had slain a wild boar he could not sit at table with the men. Like the Thracians, they drank deep; Bacchic mysteries had been introduced; it was in Macedonian air, on the banks of Lake Ludias, that Euripides drew inspiration for his *Bacchae*.

King Archelaus

We have seen how Perdiccas slew his guardian and stepfather Ptolemy and reigned alone. Six years later the Illyrians swooped down upon Macedonia, and the king was slain in battle. It was a critical moment for the kingdom; the land was surrounded by enemies, for the Paeonians at the same time menaced it in the north, and from the east a Thracian army was advancing to set a pretender on the throne. The rightful heir, Amyntas, the son of the slain king was a child. But there was one man in the land who was equal to the situation—this child's uncle, Philip; and he took the government and the guardianship of the boy into his own hands. We have already met Philip as one of the hostages who were carried off to Thebes. He had lived there for a few years, and drunk in the military and political wisdom of Epaminondas and Pelopidas. We know not why he was allowed to return to his home soon after the death of Ptolemy; perhaps it was thought that his affections had been

Perdiccas sole king, 365 B.C.;

slain 359 B.C.

Philip, guardian of Amyntas, 359 B.C.

Philip returns to Macedonia, 364 B.C.

firmly won by Thebes and that he would be more useful to her in Macedonia.

Philip was twenty-four years old when he was called upon to rescue his country and the dynasty of his own house. The danger consisted in the number of his enemies,—foreign invaders, and domestic pretenders, and pretenders supported by foreign powers. Philip's first step was to buy off the Paeonians by a large sum of money, his next to get rid of the pretenders. One of these, Argaeus, was assisted by Athens with a strong fleet. Philip defeated him, and did all in his power to come to terms with Athens. He released without ransom the Athenians whom he had made prisoners in the battle; and he renounced all claim to the possession of Amphipolis, which his brother king Perdiccas had occupied with a garrison. Gold easily induced the Thracians to desert the pretender whom they had come forth to support.

Philip disposes of the pretenders, 359 B.C.;

FIG. 98.—Coin of Archelaus I. (obverse). Horseman with two spears. FIG. 99.—Coin of Perdiccas III. (obverse). Head of Heracles. FIG. 100.—Coin of Philip II. Obverse: head of laureate Zeus. Reverse: horse and jockey; thunderbolt below [legend: ΦΙΛΙΠΠΟΥ].

But the Paeonians were quieted only for the moment, and the Illyrians were still in the land, besetting Macedonian towns. It was necessary to deal with these enemies once for all, and to assert decisively the military power of Macedon. Philip had new ideas on the art of war, and he spent the winter in remodelling and training his army. When the springtide came round he had 10,000 footsoldiers and 600 horsemen, thoroughly disciplined and of great physical strength. With this force he marched against the Paeonians and quelled them in a single battle. He then turned against the Illyrians, who refused to evacuate the towns they held in the Lyncestian territory. A great battle was fought, in which Philip tested his new military ideas; the Illyrians left 7000 on the field; and the vassals of the highlands, who had supported the invaders, were reduced to abject submission.

defeats the Paeonians, 358 B.C. (spring); the Illyrians, 358 B.C.

When he had thus established his power over his dependencies and cleared the land of foes, Philip lost little time in pushing eastward, on the side of Thrace. The motive for this rapid advance was the imperative necessity of obtaining gold. Without gold Philip could not develop his country or carry out his military schemes; the Macedonians were not a commercial folk; and therefore his prospects depended on possessing land which produced the precious ore. In Mount Pangaeus on his eastern frontier there were rich sources of gold; and, incited by him, a number of people from the opposite island of Thasos, where the art of mining was well understood, had crossed over to Crenides on that mountain and formed a settlement. But in order to control the new mines it was indispensable to become master of the great fortress on the Strymon, the much-coveted Amphipolis. The interests of Philip thus came into direct collision with the interests of Athens. Here Philip revealed his skill in diplomacy. When he released the Athenian prisoners, he professed to resign all claim to Amphipolis; and on this basis negotiated a peace with Athens. When the treaty was concluded, a secret article was agreed upon, by which Philip undertook to conquer Amphipolis for Athens, and Athens undertook to surrender to him the free town of Pydna. It is probable that this secret engagement was not made until Philip had actually attacked Amphipolis, and the Amphipolitans—preferring Athens to Macedon—had sent a request for Athenian succour. The moment was inconvenient, as the forces of Athens could not be spared from the Chersonese; and the Athenians, failing to grasp the situation, trusted the promises of Philip. Of course Philip deceived them, and they deserve no sympathy; for their own part of the agreement was a shameful act of treachery to Pydna, their ally. Their orators might cry out against the perfidy of the Macedonian; but the truth is that they thought to make Philip a tool of their own designs and he showed them that in diplomacy he was not their dupe but their master.

When Philip had taken Amphipolis, he converted the Thasian settlement of Crenides into a great fortress, which he called after his own name, Philippi. He had thus two strong stations to secure Mount Pangaeus; and the yield of the gold mines, which were soon actively worked, amounted to at least 1000 talents a year. No Greek state was so rich. The old capital, Aegae or Edessa, was now definitely abandoned, and the seat of government was established at Pella, the favourite residence of Archelaus. This coming down from Aegae to Pella is significant of the opening of a new epoch in Macedonian history.

Not long afterwards Philip captured Pydna. If the seizure of Amphipolis was an injury to Athens, the capture of Pydna was an insult. He then took Potidaea, but instead of keeping it for himself,

Thasian settlement at Crenides, 359 B.C.

Philip's treaty with Athens, and secret agreement.

Philip attacks Amphipolis, 357 B.C.

Philip takes Pydna and Potidaea, c. B.C. 356; his alliance with Olynthus.

handed it over to the Olynthians, to whom he also ceded Anthemus. The Olynthians, alarmed by his operations on the Strymon, had made proposals to Athens for common action against Macedon. The Athenians, trusting Philip, had rejected the overtures. But when they found that they had been duped, they would have been ready and glad to co-operate with Olynthus; and it was to prevent such a combination that Philip dexterously propitiated the Olynthians—intending to devour them on some future day. With the exception of Methone, the Athenians had no foothold now on the coasts of the Thermaic Gulf.

They formed alliances[1] with the Thracians of the west, who were indignant at the Macedonian occupation of Crenides, and with the Paeonian and Illyrian kings, who were smarting under their recent discomfitures. But Philip prevented the common action of the allies. He forced the Paeonians to become his vassals; his ablest general—his only general, he used to say himself—Parmenion inflicted another overwhelming defeat on the Illyrians; and the Thracians, again bought off, renounced their rights to Mount Pangaeus.

Defeat of Illyrians, 356 B.C., autumn.

But the successes cost Philip little. Having established his mining town, he assumed the royal title, setting his nephew aside, and devoted himself during the next few years to the consolidation of his kingdom, and the creation of a national army. It was in these years that he made Macedonia. His task, as has been already indicated, was to unite the hill tribes, along with his own Macedonians of the coast, into one nation. The means by which he accomplished this was military organisation. He made the highlanders into professional soldiers and kept them always under arms. Caught by the infection of the military spirit, seduced by the motives of emulation and ambition, they were to forget that they were Orestians or Lyncestians, and blend into a single homogeneous Macedonian people. To complete this consummation would be a work of years, but Philip conceived the project clearly and set about it at once. "A professional army with a national spirit—that was the new idea." Both infantry and cavalry were indeed organised in territorial regiments; perhaps Philip could not have ventured at first on any other system. But common pride and common desire of promotion, common hope of victory, tended to obliterate these distinctions, and they were done away with under Philip's son. The heavy cavalry were called "Companions" of the king and "Royal" soldiers, and they were more honourable than the infantry. Among the infantry

The making of Macedonia.

Hetairoi.

Argyraspides.

[1] A treaty of alliance in summer 356, between Athens, the Thracian king Cetriporis and his brothers (these were the nephews of Cersobleptes and ruled in western Thrace), Lyppeios the Paeonian, and Grabos the Illyrian, is extant

there was one body of "Royal" guards, the silver-shielded *Hypaspistae*.

The famous Macedonian phalanx, which Philip drilled, was merely a modified form of the usual battle-line of Greek spearmen. The men in the phalanx stood freer, in a more open array, and used a longer spear; so that the whole line, though still cumbrous enough, was more easily wielded, and the effect was produced not merely by the sheer pressure of a heavy mass of men but by the skilful manipulation of weapons. Nor was the phalanx intended to decide a battle, like the deep columns of Epaminondas; its function was to keep the front of the foe in play, while the cavalry, in wedge-like squadrons, rode into the flanks. It was by these tactics that Philip had won his victory over the Illyrians.

But Greece paid little heed to the things which Philip was doing. The Athenians might indeed encourage his Illyrian and Paeonian enemies, and urge the Thracians to drive him from Mount Pangaeus, but though he had outwitted them, they could not yet see that he was an enemy of a different stamp from a Cotys or a Cersobleptes; having managed Macedonia for a hundred years, they had little fear that as soon as they had the time to spare they would easily manage it again. When Philip married Olympias, the daughter of an Epirot prince, the event could cause no sensation; the birth of a son a year later stirred no man's heart in Greece; for who, in his wildest dreams, could have foreseen in the Macedonian infant the greatest conqueror who had yet been born into the world? If it had been revealed to men in that autumn that a power had started up which was to guide history into new paths, they would have turned their eyes not to Pella but to Halicarnassus.

Birth of Alexander, c. Oct. 356 B.C.

SECT. 3. MAUSOLUS OF CARIA

Caria, like Macedonia, was peopled by a double race, the native Carians and the Greek settlers on the coast. But the native Carians were further removed than the Illyrians from the Greeks: the Illyrians spoke a tongue of the same Indo-Germanic stock as the Greeks; the Carians belonged to an older race which held the region of the Aegean before Greeks and Illyrians came. Yet the Carians were in closer touch with Greece than the Greeks of Macedonia. The Greeks of Caria were always abreast of Greek civilisation, and they had assimilated and tutored the natives of the land. Tralles and Mylasa were to all appearance Greek towns; Greek was the dominant language of the country. A province of the Persian empire, Caria had yet a certain independent bond of union among her cities in an Amphictionic League which met in the temple of Zeus at Lagina. It was a religious union, though it might be used for purposes of common political action. But political unity was given to Caria not by federation but by monarchy. A citizen of Mylasa named Hecatomnus succeeded in establishing his rule over the whole land, soon after the death of Tissaphernes, and the Great King esteemed it his most prudent policy to acknowledge the "dynast of Caria" as his official satrap. Both Hecatomnus and his son Mausolus,[2] who succeeded to his power, never failed to pay their tribute to the treasury of Susa or to display the becoming submission to the Persian king; only once—as we have seen—when all the western satraps rebelled, did Mausolus fall short in his loyalty. The Carian Dynasts—they never assumed the royal title— thus secured for themselves a free hand. With the constitutions of the Carian cities their sovereignty did not interfere. Thus even in their own city, Mylasa, the popular Assembly still passes decrees, and these decrees are ratified not by Mausolus but by the "Three Tribes"—perhaps a sort of aristocratic council. In fact Hecatomnus and Mausolus held in relation to the Carian states an analogous position to that which Pisistratus and his sons held in the Athenian state; they were the actual rulers but officially they did not exist. The differences were that the Carian dynast held the official position of Persian satrap, and was "tyrant" of a number of states which were independent of each other.

These native satraps brought the Greek towns of the coast, Halicarnassus, Iasus, Cnidus, perhaps Miletus itself, gradually under their power; and Mausolus annexed the neighbouring land of Lycia. Thus at the time of Philip's accession to the throne of Macedonia a rich and ambitious monarchy had arisen on the south-eastern shores of the Aegean. To develop his power, it was desirable for Mausolus to win the lordship of the islands adjacent to his coasts, and it was clearly necessary to form a strong navy. The change of the satrap's residence from inland Mylasa to Halicarnassus on the sea is thus politically significant; Caria was to become a sea-power. Mausolus built himself a strong castle on the little island of Zephyrion in front of the city, and constructed two harbours, one for ships of war, the other for ships of trade.

The great islands of Rhodes, Cos, and Chios, which Mausolus especially coveted, belonged to the Athenian alliance. But recently there was much discontent at the Athenian supremacy, and there were good grounds for this feeling. The reversion to the policy of

Heca-
tomnus,
c. 395-90
to 377
B.C.

Extra-
constitu-
tional
position
of the
Carian
tyrants.

---

[2] The true form is Maussôllos, but for literary purposes Mausolus is consecrated by *Mausoleum*.

cleruchies in neighbouring Samos, as well as in distant Potidaea, excited apprehensions for the future; and the exactions of the rapacious and irresponsible mercenaries whom Athens regularly employed, but did not regularly pay, caused many complaints. There were moreover strong oligarchical parties in these states which would be glad to sever connexion with Athens. The scheme of the Carian prince was first to induce these islands to detach themselves from Athens and then to bring them under his own sway. He fanned the flame of discontent, and the three islands jointly revolted from the Athenian alliance and were supported by Byzantium.

Revolt of Chios, Cos, and Rhodes, 357 B.C.

Athens immediately sent naval forces to Chios under Chabrias and Chares, two of the generals of the year, and the town was attacked by land and sea. But in trying to enter the harbour, Chabrias, who led the way, was assailed on all sides and fell fighting. Thus the Athenians lost the most gallant of their soldiers—a commander of whom it was said that he never spared himself and always spared his men. The attack on Chios was abandoned, and the Chians, much elated, and commanding a fleet of 100 ships, proceeded to aggressive warfare against the outsettlers of Athens, and blockaded Samos. With only sixty ships Chares could do nothing; and as many more were hastily sent under the command of Timotheus and Iphicrates. Under three such generals much might be expected from such a fleet; but more would probably have been accomplished under any one of them alone. They relieved Samos and made an unsuccessful diversion to the Propontis, hoping to take Byzantium. Then they sailed to Chios, and concerted a plan of attack in the straight between the island and the mainland. But the day proved stormy, and the two veteran admirals, Iphicrates and Timotheus, deemed that it would be rash to fight. Chares, however, against their judgment, attacked the enemy, and being unsupported was repulsed with loss.

Athenian attack on Chios; death of Chabrias 357 B.C.

356 B.C.

Battle of Embata.

The ineffectual operations of two such tried and famous generals were a cruel disappointment to the Athenians, who had given them an adequate fleet. Chares, furious at the behaviour of his colleagues, formally accused them of deliberate treachery, and was supported by the orator Aristophon. The charge was that they had received bribes from the Chians and the Rhodians. Counter-charges were brought against Chares by Timotheus and Iphicrates, but the sympathies of Athens were altogether given to the commander who erred on the side of boldness. Iphicrates, however, had less political influence and therefore fewer enemies than Timotheus, and he knew how to conciliate the people; he was accordingly acquitted. Timotheus, always haughty and unpopular, probably assumed a posture

Trial of Timotheus and Iphicrates, 355 B.C. (?).

Condemnation of Timotheus (£27,000); his death.

as haughty and unbending as ever, Aristophon probably pressed him hard, and he was fined 100 talents. Rich as he was, he was unable to pay this enormous sum, and he withdrew to Chalcis where he died soon afterwards. Thus within twelve months the Athenians lost the two men, Chabrias and Timotheus, who had built up their second empire. They afterwards recognised that the measure which they had dealt out to Timotheus was hard, and they permitted his son—who had himself been tried and acquitted on the same charge —to settle the fine by a payment of ten talents.

Chares in Asia Minor, 355 B.C.

Chares now went forth as sole commander to sustain the war against the recreant allies; but he went unfurnished with money to pay his troops. He found the means of supplying this deficiency in the disturbed state of Asia Minor. The satrap of Hellespontine Phrygia, Artabazus, had rebelled, but was not strong enough to hold his own against the king's troops. Chares came to his rescue, gained a brilliant victory over the satraps who were arrayed against him, and received from the grateful Artabazus money which enabled him to pay and maintain the army. The victory and the money pleased the Athenians, but Artaxerxes was deeply incensed. The news presently reached Athens that the Great King was equipping a vast armament in Syria and Cilicia to avenge the audacity of Chares. How much truth there was in this report it is impossible to say; but it evoked an outburst of patriotism and supplied the Athenian orators with material for invectives and declamations. Men began to talk in earnest of realising the dream of Isocrates, of convoking a pan-Hellenic congress and arming Hellas against the barbarian. Demosthenes, who was now beginning to rise into public notice, delivered in these days a speech which was more to the point than many of his later more famous orations. He showed that the alarm was premature; and that the notion of sending round appeals to the cities of Greece was foolish; "your envoys will do nothing more than rhapsodise in their round of visits." The truth was that Athens could in no case think of embarking at this juncture in a big war; she had not the means. Isocrates himself raised his voice for peace in a remarkable pamphlet, distinguished by the nobility of tone and the width of view which always mark his writings. It was a scathing condemnation of Imperialism. Passing from the momentary state of affairs, he looked out into the future and boldly declared that the only salvation for Athens lay in giving up her naval empire. "It is that," he said, "which brought us to this pass; it is that which caused the fall of our democracy." He showed the calamities which the empires of Athens and Sparta had drawn upon themselves and Greece. But it is to be observed that, when a mo-

Demosthenes' speech On the Symmorics

Isocrates on the Peace, 355 B.C.

(404 B.C.)

ment had come at which his favourite plan of a common attack on Persia seemed at length feasible, he was wise enough not to advise it. He looks to Thrace, not to Persia, to find lands for endowing those needy Greeks who were roving about for subsistence.

In the end prudent counsels prevailed; Chares was recalled; negotiations were opened with the revolted allies, and a peace was made.[3] Athens recognised the independence of the three islands, Chios, Cos, and Rhodes, and of the city of Byzantium. It was not long before Lesbos also severed itself from the Athenian alliance, which thus lost all its important members in the eastern Aegean: and in the west Corcyra fell away about the same time. *Peace, 354 B.C.*

All happened as Mausolus foresaw. He helped the oligarchies to overthrow the popular governments, and then gave them the protection of Carian garrisons. But the prince did not live to develop his empire. Soon after the success of his policy against Athens, he died, leaving his power to his widow Artemisia. The opportunity was seized by the democrats of Rhodes to regain their freedom, and they appealed to Athens. After what had passed they had little right to expect a hearing; and under the influence of the wise and pacific statesmen who now controlled the Assembly, their appeal was refused—in spite of the hot and somewhat sentimental pleadings of Demosthenes, who upheld the extraordinary doctrine that Athens was bound, whenever she was called upon, to intervene to support democracy against oligarchy. Artemisia soon recovered her grip on Rhodes. *Death of Mausolus 353 B.C.*

353 B.C.

Caria remained for another twenty years under dynasts of the house of Hecatomnus, until it submitted to Alexander the Great. The expansion of the Carian power, which seemed probable under the active administration of Mausolus, was never fulfilled. Though we know nothing of his personal character, the outward appearance of Mausolus is familiar to us, the islanders of the north, who possess in our capital his genuine portrait, and the headless figure of his queen. The colossal statue, made, at latest, soon after his death, represents a man of a noble cast of face, of a type presumably Carian, certainly not Greek, and with the hair curiously brushed back from the brow. This statue stood, along with that of Artemisia, within the sepulchral tomb which he probably began and which she certainly completed. Such a royal tomb seems to take us back to the days of prehistoric Greece; it strikes one almost like a glorified resurrection of one of the old chamber sepulchres of the Leleges *The statues of Mausolus and Artemisia (in the British Museum).*

The tomb of Mausolus.

[3] The war which this peace brought to an end is generally called, by a misleading translation of ὁ συμμαχικὸς πόλεμος, the Social War. This Latinism might well disappear from histories.

which are strewed about the Halicarnassian peninsula. It rose above the harbour at Halicarnassus, conspicuous from the sea, crowned with a chariot on its apex. The building was adorned with friezes,

wrought by four of the most illustrious sculptors of the day, of whom Scopas himself was one. The precious fragments of these works of art are the legacy which the Carian realm has bequeathed to mankind—these and a new word which the tomb of Mausolus added to the vocabularies of Europe.

SECT. 4. PHOCIS AND THE SACRED WAR

In the meantime, another of the states of northern Greece seemed likely to win the position of supremacy which Thessaly had seemed on the eve of winning, and which Boeotia had actually held for a few years. Phocis now came forward in her turn and enjoyed a brief moment of expansion and conquest—a flashlight which vanished almost as soon as it appeared. In succession to the national leaders, Jason of Pherae and Epaminondas of Thebes, we now meet Onomarchus of Elatea.

Position of Phocis.

Into this career of aggrandisement Phocis was thrust by the aggression of her neighbours rather than lured by the lust of conquest. The Phocians had never been zealous adherents of the Boeotian alliance, which they were forced to join after the battle of Leuctra, and they cut themselves loose from it after the death of Epaminondas. But though Thebes could no longer maintain her wider supremacy in Greece, an independent Phocis was a source of constant danger to her in her narrower supremacy in Boeotia, as the western cities of the land could always find in Phocis a stay and support for their own independence. It was therefore deemed necessary by the politicians of Thebes to strike a blow at their western neighbours. One of the instruments of which Epaminondas had made use to promote his city's influence in the north was the old Amphictionic League, which for a hundred years had never appeared on the scene of history. At an assembly of this body, soon after Leuctra, the Thebans accused the Spartans of having seized the Cadmea in time

Sparta fined.

of peace. The Spartans were sentenced to pay a fine of 500 talents; the fine could not indeed be exacted, but they were doubtless excluded from the temple of Delphi. The Thebans resolved to wield against Phocis the same engine which they had wielded against Sparta. The nature of the pretext is uncertain, but it was not difficult to find a misdemeanour which would seem grave enough to the

Phocians fined.

Thessalians and Locrians, inveterate enemies of Phocis, to justify a sentence of condemnation. A number of rich and prominent Phocians were condemned to pay large fines for sacrilege, and when these sums were not paid within the prescribed time, the Amphictions decreed that the lands of the defaulters should be taken from them and consecrated to the Delphian god, and a tablet with the inscribed decree was set up at Delphi.

The men who were implicated in the alleged sacrilege determined to resist, and they appealed to their fellow-countrymen, in whatever form of federal assembly the Phocian cities used to discuss their common interests, to protect themselves and their property against the threatened danger. The man who took the lead in organising the resistance was Philomelus, a wealthy citizen of Ledon. He discerned clearly that mercenaries would be required to defend Phocis against her enemies—Boeotians, Locrians, and Thessalians —and made the bold and practical proposal that Delphi should be seized, since the treasures of Delphi would supply at need the sinews of war. It is hardly likely that he openly avowed the true reason of the importance of seizing Delphi; it was enough to assert the old rights of the Phocians over rocky Pytho—rights for which he could appeal to the highest authority, the sacred text of Homer[4]— and to point out that the Delphians were implicated in the injust decrees of the Amphictions. The proposals of Philomelus were adopted, and he was appointed general of the Phocian forces, with full powers. His first step was to visit Sparta, not only as the enemy of Thebes, but as being in the same case as Phocis, lying under an Amphictionic sentence which had recently been renewed and confirmed. King Archidamus welcomed the proposals of the Phocian plenipotentiary, but Sparta stood in a rather awkward position. Hitherto she had always supported the Delphians in maintaining their independence against Phocian claims, as, for instance, when in the days of Pericles she restored them to their shrine after the Phocians with Athenian aid had dispossessed them. It would consequently have been a flagrant inconsistency in Spartan policy to turn against the Delphians now; so that Archidamus did not openly avow his sympathy with the Phocian cause, but privately he supported it by placing fifteen talents in the hands of Philomelus. With this sum and fifteen talents from his own purse, Philomelus was able to hire some mercenaries, and with their help to seize Delphi. The Locrians of neighbouring Amphissa, whom the Delphians had summoned to their aid, arrived too late and were repulsed. Philomelus did no hurt to the people of Delphi, excepting only the clan of the Thracidae, bitter anti-Phocians, whom he put to death.

Philomelus.

450 B.C. sqq.

Phocians seize Delphi. c. 356 B.C.

[4] In the Homeric Catalogue, Pytho is said to be possessed by two Phocian chiefs.

The first object of Philomelus was to enlist Hellenic opinion in his favour. He had the secret sympathy of Sparta, and he might count on the friendship of Athens, who had always been an ally of Phocis and was now an enemy of Thebes. He sent envoys to Sparta, to Athens, to Thebes itself, to explain the Phocian position. These envoys were instructed to say that in seizing Delphi the Phocians were simply resuming their rights over the temple, which belonged to them and had been usurped by others, and to declare that they would act merely as administrators of the Panhellenic Sanctuary, and were ready to allow all the treasures to be weighed and numbered, and to be responsible to Greece for their safety. In consequence of these embassies Sparta came forward from her reserve and openly allied herself with Phocis, while Athens and some smaller states promised their support. The Thebans and their Amphictionic friends resolved to make war.

In the meantime, Philomelus had fortified the Delphic sanctuary by a wall, and had collected an army of 5000 men, with which he could easily hold the position. It was his wish that the oracular responses from the mystic tripod should continue to be given as usual to those who came to consult Apollo, and he was anxious above all to receive some voice of approval or encouragement from the god. But the Delphian priestess was stubborn to the Phocian intruder, and refused to prophesy. He tried to seat her by force upon the tripod, and in her alarm she bade him do as he would. He eagerly seized these words as an oracular sanction of his acts. It soon became necessary to raise more money for paying the mercenaries, and for this purpose Philomelus, refraining as long as he could from touching the treasures of the shrine, levied a contribution from the rich Delphians. At first he had to deal only with the Locrians, whom he finally defeated in a hot battle near the Phaedriad cliffs which rise sheer above Delphi. The loss of the Locrians was heavy; some of them, driven to the edge, hurled themselves down the cliffs.

This victory forced the Thebans to prepare actively to intervene. The Amphictionic assembly met at Thermopylae, and it was decided that an Amphictionic army should enforce the decree of the league against the Phocians, and rescue Delphi from their power. Philomelus, with the forces which he had, might hold his own against the Locrians, but not against the host which would now be arrayed against him. There were only two means of saving Phocis. One was the active support of Athens or Sparta, or both; the other was the organisation of a large army of mercenaries. As neither Athens nor Sparta showed willingness to give any immediate assistance, nothing remained but the other alternative. And that alternative, as Philomelus must have foreseen from the beginning, would not be possible without the control of far larger sums of money than could either be contributed by the Phocian cities or extorted from the Delphian proprietors. No resource remained but to make use of the treasures of the temple. At first Philomelus was scrupulous. He only *borrowed* from the god enough to meet the demand of the moment; but, as habitude blunted the first feelings of scrupulousness, and as needs grew more pressing, the Phocians dealt as freely with the sacred vessels and the precious dedications as if they were their own. By offering large pay Philomelus assembled an army of 10,000 men, who cared little whence the money came. An indecisive war with the Thebans and Locrians was waged for some time, till at length the Phocians underwent a severe defeat near Neon on the north side of Mount Parnassus. The general fought desperately, and, covered with wounds, he was driven to the verge of a precipice where he had to choose between capture and self-destruction. He hurled himself from the cliff and perished.

Battle of Neon, 354 B.C.; death of Philomelus.

The Thebans imagined that the death of Philomelus meant the doom of the Phocian cause, and they retired after the battle. But it was not so. In Onomarchus of Elatea, who had been associated with him in the command of the army, he had a successor as able as himself. The retreat of the enemy gave Onomarchus time to reorganise the troops and collect reinforcements; and he not only coined the gold and silver ornaments of the temple, but beat the bronze and iron donatives into arms for the soldiers. He then entered upon a short career of signal successes. Westward, he forced Locrian Amphissa to submit; to northward he reduced Doris, and crossing the passes of Mount Oeta he made himself master of Thermopylae, and captured the Locrian Thronion near the eastern gate of the pass. Eastward, he took possession of Orchomenus and restored those of the inhabitants who had escaped the sword of the Thebans ten years before.

Onomarchus succeeds Philomelus.

The Thebans meanwhile were hampered by want of money, and, having neither mines like Philip nor a rich temple like Phocis, they decided to replenish their treasury by sending out a body of troops on foreign service. We have already seen Sparta and Athens raising money by the same means, and the Theban soldiers who now went forth under Pammenes hired themselves out to the same Persian satrap Artabazus, for whom the Athenian Chares had won a victory over the army of the king. Pammenes was equally successful, but it does not seem that his expedition profited the Boeotian treasury; for he presently became suspected by Artabazus, who threw him into prison.

Among the most important uses to which Onomarchus applied the gold of Delphi was the purchase of the alliance of the tyrants of Pherae. By this policy Thessaly was divided; and the Thessalian league, beset by the hostility of Pherae, was unable to co-operate with the Thebans against Phocis. But the Thessalians, being hard pressed, turned for help to their northern neighbour, Philip of Macedon, and his intervention south of Mount Olympus marks a new stage in the course of the Sacred War.

Philip's capture of Methone, 353 B.C. He enters Thessaly;

Philip had lately deprived Athens of her last ally on the Thermaic Gulf by the capture of Methone, the Athenian expedition of relief coming too late to save it. He readily acceded to the request of the Thessalians to act as their general; it was a convenient occasion to begin the push southward, and lay the foundation of Macedonian supremacy in Greece, plans which were now coming within the range of practical effort. Against the forces which Philip led to the support of the Thessalian league, it was hopeless for Lycophron of Pherae to stand alone; the tyrant was lost unless he were succoured by the arm of those who had already furnished him with gold. Nor

defeats a Phocian army;

did the Phocians leave him unsupported. The strength of Onomarchus was now so great that he could spare a force of 7000 men for a campaign in the north. But his brother Phayllus, to whom he entrusted the command, was beaten out of Thessaly by Philip. Then

suffers two defeats and is expelled from Thessaly by Onomarchus.

Onomarchus went forth himself, at the head of the whole Phocian host (about 20,000), to rescue his ally. Far superior in numbers, he defeated the Macedonian army in two battles with serious loss; Philip was compelled to withdraw into Macedonia; and Onomarchus delivered Thessaly into the hands of Lycophron.

Height of the Phocian supremacy, 353-2 B.C.

At this moment, the power of the Phocians was at its height. Their supremacy reached from the shores of the Corinthian Gulf to the slopes of Olympus. They were masters of the pass of Thermopylae, and they had two important posts in western Boeotia, for,

Coronea.

in addition to Orchomenus, they won Coronea immediately after the Thessalian expedition. If all these things had befallen at some other epoch, the Phocian power might have endured for a time, and the name of their able leader might have been more familiar to posterity. But Onomarchus had fallen on evil days. He and his petty people were swept away in the onward course of a greater nation and a greater chief.

Philip drives the Phocians from Thessaly.

Philip of Macedon speedily retrieved the humiliation which he had suffered at the hands of his Phocian foes. In the following year he descended again into Thessaly, and Onomarchus went forth again to succour his ally or dependent. In the preceding campaign Philip had captured the port of Pagasae, and placed in it a Macedonian garrison. It was important not only for Pherae, but for Athens, that this post should not remain in his hands, and Chares was sent with an Athenian fleet to assist the Phocians in recovering it. The decisive battle was fought at a place unknown, near the Pagasaean Gulf. The numbers of the infantry were nearly equal, but Philip's cavalry and his tactics were far superior. More than a third of the Phocian army was slain or made prisoners, and Onomarchus was killed. Pherae was then captured and Lycophron driven from the land; and Philip, having thus become master of Thessaly, prepared to march southward for the purpose of delivering the shrine of Apollo from the possession of the Phocians, whom he professed to regard as sacrilegious usurpers.

Phocis was now in great need, and her allies—Sparta, Achaea, and Athens—at length determined to give her active help. The Macedonian must not be permitted to pass Thermopylae. The statesman Eubulus, whose influence was now predominant at Athens, and was chiefly directed to the maintenance of peace, acted promptly on this occasion, and sent a large force under Nausicles to defend the pass. Philip at once recognised that it would be extremely hazardous to attempt to force the position, and he retired. He was a prince who knew when to wait and when to strike. Thus Phocis was rescued for the time; she was indebted both to Sparta and Achaea who had sent her aid, but most of all to Athens.

Eubulus rescues Phocis.

In supporting Phocis, the Spartans had objects of their own in view. They had not abandoned their hopes of winning back Messenia and destroying Megalopolis. It was therefore their policy to sustain Phocis, in order that Phocis might keep Thebes so fully occupied that they would have a free hand in the Peloponnesus without fear of Theban interference. The successes of Onomarchus in his first Thessalian campaign encouraged Sparta to prepare for action, and Megalopolis, made aware of the danger, applied to Athens for help. It was a request which no practical statesman could have entertained, and it had no chance of being granted under the régime of as wise a head as Eubulus. Orators like Demosthenes, who constituted themselves the opponents of Eubulus, might invoke the old principle that it was the policy of Athens to keep Sparta weak. But this was an obsolete maxim, for there was now no serious prospect of Sparta becoming formidably strong. It was no concern of Athens to meddle in the Peloponnesus now. Her true policy was to keep on friendly terms with Sparta, and, in conjunction with her, to support the Phocian state against Thebes, Thessaly, and Macedon. This was the policy which Eubulus followed.

Megalopolis applies to Athens, end of 353 B.C.

Demosthenes' speech for the Megalopolitans.

The war broke out in the Peloponnesus soon after the check of

War in the Peloponnesus, 352 B.C.

Philip at Thermopylae. While Athens held aloof, Achaea and Elis'
Phlius and Mantinea, supported Sparta, and the Phocians sent 3000
men to her help. But all these forces were outnumbered by the
Messenians, Arcadians, and Argives, to whom the Thebans had
sent a considerable aid. A series of engagements were fought; they
were almost all indecisive; but they rescued Messenia and the Arcadian capital, and frustrated the plans of Lacedaemon.

Phayllus.

The death of Onomarchus devolved the leadership of the Phocian
league upon his brother Phayllus. At first the Phocians barely
maintained their posts in western Boeotia; but presently—after the
return of the auxiliaries whom they had sent to the Peloponnesus—
they conquered Epicnemidian Locris and laid siege to Naryx, which

350 B.C.

they ultimately captured. Thus Phayllus maintained the power of
Phocis for about two years; then he was carried off by disease, and
was succeeded by his nephew, Phalaecus, son of Onomarchus. Un-

Pha-
laecus.

der Phalaecus the war dragged on for a few more years, without any
notable achievement, the Thebans winning battles of no importance
and ravaging Phocis, the Phocians retaining their grip on western
Boeotia.

The posi-
tion and
policy of
Phocis.

The rise of Phocis to its momentary position as one of the leading
powers in Greece depended on two conditions—the possession of
Delphi and the possibility of hiring mercenaries. It is therefore clear
that Phocis could not easily have come to the front before the fourth
century, when mercenary service had come widely into vogue. But
these two essential features of the Phocian power, the occupation of
Delphi and the employment of mercenary troops, gave it a bad
name. Historians echo the invectives of the enemies of Phocis, and
give the impression that during the Sacred War the sanctuary of
Apollo was in the hands of sacrilegious and unscrupulous barbarians. Tales were told how the dedicatory offerings were bestowed
upon the loose favourites of the generals—how Philomelus gave a
golden wreath to a dancing girl, or Phayllus a silver beaker to a
flute-player. It matters little whether such scandals are true or false;
if true, they would only show that the generals were not above petty
peculations. But the Phocians were not alien desecrators of the
shrine of Apollo. They could establish as good a claim to Delphi as
many claims founded on remote events in the past; and they certainly desired to maintain the Panhellenic dignity and sanctity of
the shrine and the oracle as high as ever under their own administration. But they regarded Delphi not only as a Panhellenic sanctuary, but as a national sanctuary of Phocis; somewhat in the same
way as Athens employed the treasures of her temples for national
purposes of defence in the Peloponnesian war, so Phocis felt justi-

fied in employing the treasures of Apollo for the national interest of Phocis. Throughout all, the Phocian statesmen could have maintained that they were only borrowing from the god loans which would be gradually paid back after the restoration of peace.

Recently there has come to light, among the original documents inscribed on the stones of Delphi, a striking disproof of the old view which conceived the Phocians of Onomarchus and Phayllus as a band of robbers holding their orgies in a holy place. The temple of the god which had been built by the Alcmaeonids was destroyed by an earthquake nearly twenty years before the Phocian usurpation. The work of rebuilding had been begun, perhaps soon after, but had advanced slowly, and when Philomelus seized Delphi the completion of the temple was still far off. The work was carried out under a commission of "Temple-builders," in which all the Amphictionic states were represented; and this body administered a fund set apart for the building. During the Phocian usurpation the council of Temple-builders still held their meetings; the work still went on; the skilful artisans in Corinth and elsewhere wrought the stone material and transferred it to Delphi, as if nothing had befallen; the payments were made, as usual, from the fund; and the accounts were kept—we have some of them still. Those Amphictionic states which were at war with Phocis, like Thebes and Thessaly, were naturally not represented at the meetings of the board of the Temple-builders, but Delphian members were always present; and after Locris had been conquered by Phayllus we find Locrians also attending the meetings.[5] Thus the completion of the temple of Apollo was not suspended while the Phocians held the sanctuary; and the Dorian and Ionian states continued to take their part in the Panhellenic work of supervising the structure, as if nothing had happened to alter the centre of the Greek world.

The building of the temple of Apollo not interrupted during the Phocian occupation. Destruction of the Second Temple of Delphi, 373 B.C. Council of Naopoioi

SECT. 5. THE ADVANCE OF MACEDONIA

The Macedonian monarch was now master not only of the Thermaic Gulf and the mouth of the Strymon, but of the basin of Pagasae, and he was beginning to create a fleet. His marauding vessels, let loose in the northern Aegean, captured the cornships of Athens, descended on her possessions and dependencies—Lemnos, Imbros, and Euboea—and once even insulted the coast of Attica

[5] Thus in B.C. 351-50 the members present are a Delphian, a Sicyonian, a Corinthian, and two Argives; in B.C. 349-48, a Delphian, an Athenian, two Locrians, a Megarian, an Epidaurian, a Lacedaemonian, a Corinthian, two Phocians.

itself. The most important interests of Athens centred round the Hellespont and Propontis; and it was obviously her policy to form a close combination with the Thracian king Cersobleptes, with a view to offering common resistance to the advance of the new northern power on the Thracian side. It was an effort in this direction when Aristocrates proposed a resolution in honour of Charidemus, the adventurer who had become the brother-in-law and the chief minister of the Thracian king. The resolution was impeached as illegal, and the accuser was supplied with a speech by the young politician Demosthenes. The legal objections were probably cogent, but the opponents of the proposal might wisely have confined themselves to this aspect of the question. They went on to impugn the expediency of the measure; and the speech of Demosthenes against Aristocrates was calculated, so far as a single speech could have a political effect, to alienate a power which it was distinctly the interest of Athens to conciliate.

Demosthenes' speech against Aristocrates, 352 B.C.

But it mattered little. No sooner had Philip returned from Thessaly than he moved against Thrace. Supported by a rival Thracian prince and by the cities of Byzantium and Perinthus, he advanced to the Propontis, besieged Heraeon-Teichos the capital of Cersobleptes, and forced that potentate to submit to the overlordship of Macedon. The movements of Philip had been so rapid that Athens had no time to come to the rescue of Thrace. When the news arrived there was a panic, and an armament was voted to save the Chersonese. But a new message came that Philip had fallen ill; then he was reported dead; and the sending of the armament was postponed. Philip's illness was a fact; it compelled him to desist from further operations, and the Chersonesus was saved.

Philip in Thrace, 352 B.C., autumn.

Submission of Cersobleptes to Philip.

Eight years had not elapsed since Philip had mounted the throne of Macedon; and he had shifted the balance of power in Greece, and altered the whole prospect of the Greek world, for those who had eyes to see. He had created an army, and a thoroughly adequate revenue; he had made himself lord of almost the whole sea-board of the northern Aegean from the defile of Thermopylae to the shores of the Propontis. The only lands which were still excepted from his direct or indirect sway were the Chersonesus and the territory of the Chalcidian league. He was ambitious to secure a recognised hegemony in Greece; to hold such a position as had been held by Athens, by Sparta, and by Thebes in the days of their greatness; to form, in fact, a confederation of allies, which should hold some such dependent relation towards him as the confederates of Delos had held towards Athens. Rumours were already floating about that his ultimate design was to lead a Panhellenic expedition against the Per-

Position of Philip at the end of 352 B.C.

sian king—the same design which was ascribed to Jason of Pherae. Though the Greek states regarded Philip as in a certain sense an outsider, both because Macedonia had hitherto lain aloof from their politics and because absolute monarchy was repugnant to their political ideas, it must never be forgotten that Philip desired to identify Macedonia with Greece, and to bring his own country up to the level of the kindred peoples which had so far outstripped it in civilisation. Throughout his whole career he regarded Athens with respect; he would have given much for her friendship, and he showed that he deemed it one of his misfortunes that she compelled him to be her foe. He was himself imbued with Greek culture; and if the robust Macedonian enjoyed the society of the somewhat rude boon companions of his own land with whom he could drink deep, he knew how to make himself agreeable to Attic philosophers or men of letters whom he always delighted to honour. He chose an accomplished man of letters, Aristotle of Stagira, who had been educated at Athens, to be the instructor of his son Alexander. This fact alone sets Philip in the true light, as a conscious and deliberate promoter of Greek civilisation.

His Hellenism.

Greece saw with alarm the increase of the Macedonian power, though men were yet far from apprehending what it really meant. No state had been directly hit except Athens—though the day of Chalcidice was at hand; and it was now too late for Athens to retrieve her lost position, either alone or with any combination she could form, against a state which possessed an ample revenue and a well-drilled national army, under the sovereign command of the greatest general and diplomatist of the day. The only event which could now have availed to stay the course of Macedon would have been the death of Philip. But the Athenians did not apprehend this; they still dreamed of recovering Amphipolis. Their best policy would have been peace and alliance with Macedonia. There can be little question that Philip would have gladly secured them the Chersonese and their cornships; for the possession of the Chersonese had not the same vital importance for him as Amphipolis, or as the towns around the Thermaic Gulf.

Position of Athens.

In these years, Athens was under the guidance of a cautious statesman, Eubulus, who was a marvellously able minister of finance. He was appointed chancellor of the Theoric Fund for four years, and this office, while it was specially concerned with the administration of the surplus of revenue which was devoted to theoric purposes, involved a general control over the finances of the state. He pursued a peace policy; yet it was he who struck the one effective blow that Athens ever struck at Philip, when she hindered him

Eubulus, in charge of the Theoric Fund, 354-50 B.C., and probably, 350-346 B.C.

from passing Thermopylae. But Eubulus wisely refused to allow Athens to be misled into embarking in unnecessary wars in the Peloponnesus or Asia Minor; and frankly accepted the peace which had concluded the war of Athens with her allies. The mass of the Athenians were well contented to follow the counsel of a dexterous financier, who, while he met fully all the expenses of administration, distributed large dividends of festival-money. The news of Philip's campaign in Thrace may have temporarily weakened his influence; it was felt that there had been slackness in watching Athenian interests in the Hellespontine regions; and his opponents had a fair opportunity to inveigh against an inactive policy.

Demosthenes, born c. 384 B.C.

The most prominent among these opponents was Demosthenes, who had recently made a reputation as a speaker in the Assembly. The father of Demosthenes was an Athenian manufacturer, who died when his son was still a child; his mother had Scythian blood in her veins. His guardians dealt fraudulently with the considerable fortune which his father had left him; and when he came of age he resolved to recover it. For this purpose he sat at the feet of the orator Isaeus, and was trained in law and rhetoric. Though he received but a small portion of his patrimony, the oratory of Demosthenes owed to this training with a practical purpose many qualities which it would never have acquired under the academic instruction of Isocrates. He used himself to tell how he struggled to overcome his natural defects of speech and manner, how he practised gesticulation before a mirror and declaimed verses with pebbles in his mouth. In the end he became as brilliant an orator as the Pnyx had ever cheered; perhaps his only fault was a too theatrical manner. His earlier political speeches are not monuments of wisdom. He came forward as an opponent of the policy of Eubulus, and so we have already met him supporting the appeals of Rhodes and Megalopolis. The advance of Philip to the Propontis gave him a more promising occasion to urge the Athenians to act, since their own interests were directly involved. And the effort of Demosthenes was more than adequate. The harangue, which is known as the First Philippic, one of his most brilliant and effective speeches, calls upon the Athenians to brace themselves vigorously to oppose Philip "our enemy." He draws a lively picture of the indifference of his countrymen and contrasts it with the energy of Philip "who is not the man to rest content with that he has subdued, but is always adding to his conquests, and casts his snare around us while we sit at home postponing." Again: "Is Philip dead? Nay, but he is ill. What does it matter to you? For, if this Philip die, you will soon raise up a second Philip by your apathy." Demosthenes proposed a scheme

His first Philippic.

for increasing the military forces of the city; and the most essential part of the scheme was that a force should be sent to Thrace of which a quarter should consist of citizens, and the officers should be citizens. At present the numerous officers whom they elected were kept for services at home: "You choose your captains, not to fight but to be displayed like dolls in the market-place."

Demosthenes was applauded, but nothing was done. His ideal was the Athens of Pericles; but he lived in the Athens of Eubulus. In the fourth century the Athenians were quite capable of holding their own among their old friends and enemies, the Spartans and Thebans and the islanders of the Aegean; with paid soldiers and generals like Iphicrates and Chares they could maintain their position as a first-rate power. But against a large, vigorous land-power with a formidable army their chances were hopeless; for, since the fall of their empire, the whole spirit of the people had tended to peace and not to war; they were no longer animated by the idea of empire; and the memories of the past, which Demosthenes might invoke, were powerless to stir them to action. The orations of Demosthenes, however carefully studied, however imbued with passion, could not change the character of his countrymen; their spirit did not respond to his, and, not being under the imperious dominion of an idea, they saw no reason for great undertakings. Nor was the condition of Athens as ill as the opponent of Eubulus painted it. Under the administration of Eubulus the fleet was increased, the building of a new arsenal was begun, new ship-sheds were made, and the military establishment of Athens was in various ways improved. She was still the great sea-power of the Aegean, and strong enough to protect her commercial interests.

The next stage in the development of Macedonia was the incorporation of Chalcidice, and as soon as Philip recovered from his illness he turned his attention to this quarter. If the Olynthians had treated Philip honourably, they would probably have been left a self-governing community, with their territory intact, dependent on Macedonia. But they treated both Athens and Philip badly. They first made a close alliance with Philip to rob Athens; and then, when they had received from Philip Anthemus and Potidaea, they turned round and made peace with Athens, a power with which Philip was at war, and recognised the right of Athens to Amphipolis. At the time Philip was otherwise engaged; but three years later he sent a requisition to Olynthus, demanding the surrender of his half-brother, a pretender to the Macedonian throne, to whom they had given shelter. The demand was refused and Philip marched against Chalcidice. One after another the cities of the Olynthian

Peace of the Chalcidian league with Athens, 352 B.C.

Philip reduces Chalcidice, 349 B.C.

confederacy opened their gates to him; or if they refused, like Stagira, they were captured.

In her jeopardy Olynthus sought an alliance with Athens, and on this occasion both the leaders of the Athenian Assembly and the advocates of a war policy found themselves in harmony. It was during the debates on the question of alliance that Demosthenes pronounced his Olynthiac orations, which were animated by the same spirit as his Philippic, and were in fact Philippics. At this juncture the Athenians seem to have been awakened to the necessity of action sufficiently to embolden Demosthenes to throw out the unpopular suggestion that the Theoric Fund should be devoted to military purposes; and he repeats his old plea for citizen-soldiers. An alliance was concluded and mercenaries were dispatched to the Chalcidian peninsula under Chares and Charidemus (who had left the service of Cersobleptes). More troops would certainly have followed, and Philip might have been placed in some embarrassment, especially as Cersobleptes had rebelled. But he diverted the concern

of Athens in another direction, and so divided her forces. He had long been engaged in intrigues in Euboea, and now Eretria revolted and drove out Plutarch, the tyrant who held the city for Athens. Neighbouring Chalcis, and Oreos in the north, followed the example; Euboea was in a state of revolt. It is just possible that, if Athens had left Euboea alone, and concentrated all her military power in Chalcidice, she might have saved Olynthus for the time. The division of her forces was certainly fatal; and Demosthenes deserves great credit for opposing any interference in Euboea. But the Athenians would have been strong-minded indeed if they had done nothing to regain the neighbouring island, while they dispatched all

their troops to succour an ally. The expedition to Euboea, which was now entrusted to the general Phocion, might better never have been sent; but beforehand there seemed no reason why it should not succeed. Phocion's only exploit was to extricate himself from a dangerous position at Tamynae, by winning a battle, but he returned to Athens without having recovered any of the rebellious cities. The enemy had taken a number of prisoners, for whose ransom Athens

had to pay fifty talents; and it was decided that there was nothing for it but to acknowledge the independence of Euboea, with the exception of Carystus, which remained loyal.

Meanwhile Philip was pressing Olynthus hard, and urgent appeals were sent to Athens. This time Demosthenes had his way, and

2000 citizen-soldiers sailed for the north. But it was too late. Olynthus was captured before they reached it; and Philip showed no mercy to the city which had played him false. The place was des+royed and the inhabitants scattered in various parts of Macedonia, some set to work as slaves in the royal domains. The other cities of the confederacy were practically incorporated in Macedonia; but they still continued to exist as cities and manage their local affairs. There was no question of their extermination.

Demosthenes had opposed the expedition to Euboea, and thereby hangs a story. He had a bitter foe in a rich man, named Meidias, who was a supporter of Eubulus. Their personal hostility was re-awakened in the debates over the Euboean question, and Meidias seized the occasion of the great Dionysiac feast to put a public affront on his enemy. Demosthenes had undertaken the duty of supplying a chorus for his tribe, and on the day of the performance, when he appeared in the sacred robe of a choregus, Meidias struck him in the face. The outrage involved contempt of a religious festival, and Demosthenes instituted proceedings against his insulter. The speech which he composed for the occasion contains fine scathing invective. The description of Meidias vulgarly displaying his wealth may be quoted to illustrate contemporary manners. "Where," Demosthenes asks, "are his splendid outlays? For myself, I cannot see unless it be in this—that he has built a mansion at Eleusis large enough to darken all the neighbourhood—that he keeps a pair of white horses from Sicyon, with which he conducts his wife to the mysteries or anywhere else he fancies—that he sweeps through the market-place with three or four lackeys all to himself, and talks about his bowls and drinking-horns and saucers, loud enough to be heard by the passers-by."[6] But Demosthenes consented to compromise the matter for a small sum before it was brought to an issue, and there can be little question that his consent was given from political motives. On the capture of Olynthus the different parties drew together and agreed to co-operate; and this new political combination rendered it necessary for Demosthenes, however reluctant, to patch up the feud with Meidias.

Demosthenes insulted by Meidias 348 B.C.

Sect. 6. The Peace of Philocrates

Her recent military efforts had exhausted the revenue of Athens; there was not enough money in the treasury to pay the judges their daily wage. Peace was clearly a necessity, and this must have been fully recognised by Eubulus. But there was great indignation at the fall of Olynthus, and the feeling that a disaster had been sustained was augmented by the fact that there were a considerable number

---

[6] Translation by Professor Butcher.

of Athenians among the captives. Accordingly the pressure of popular opinion, which was for the moment strongly aroused against Philip, induced Eubulus to countenance the dispatch of envoys to the cities of the Peloponnesus, for the purpose of organising a national resistance in Hellas against the man who had destroyed Olynthus. It is probable that this measure was advocated by Demosthenes; in later years, a national resistance to Philip was his favourite idea. It was an effort foredoomed to failure, as Eubulus knew perfectly well; yet it served his purpose, for it protected him against suspicions of being secretly friendly to Philip. On this occasion the orator Aeschines, famous as the antagonist of Demosthenes, first came prominently forward. He had begun life as an usher in a school kept by his father, he had then been a tragic actor, and finally a public clerk. He was now sent to rouse the Greeks of the Peloponnesus against Macedonia, and he used such strong language in disparagement of Philip, especially at Megalopolis, that no one could accuse him of "philippizing." The mere fact that envoys were sent to Megalopolis—whose application for help had so recently been rejected by Athens—is enough to cast suspicion on the whole round of embassies as a farce, got up to satisfy public opinion at home. Demosthenes, like other politicians, saw the necessity of peace and worked towards it.

Aeschines at Megalopolis, 347 B.C.

Philip desired two things, to conclude peace with Athens and to become a member of the Amphictionic Council. Towards this second end a path was prepared by the Thebans, who along with the Thessalians addressed an appeal to Philip that he would undertake the championship of the Amphictionic League and crush the Phocians. In Phocis itself there had recently been domestic strife; Phalaecus had been deposed from the generalship, but he had a party of his own and he held Thermopylae with the strong places in its neighbourhood. When it was noised abroad that Philip was about to march southward in answer to the Theban prayer, the Phocians invited Athens and Sparta to help them once again to hold the gates of Greece. Both Athens and Sparta again responded to the call; but the call had come from the political opponents of Phalaecus, and he refused to admit either Spartan or Athenian into the pass. Phalaecus seems to have previously assisted the enemies of Athens in Euboea; and statesmen at Athens might now feel some uneasiness, whether he would not turn traitor and surrender the pass to Philip. It was another reason for acquiescing in the necessity of making peace.

Philip's intervention sought by Thebes.

The ambiguous position of Phalaecus.

The first overtures came from Athens. Ten Athenian envoys, and one representative of the Synedrion of Athenian allies, were sent to

First embassy to Philip, end of 347 B.C.

Pella to negotiate terms of peace with the Macedonian king. Among the envoys were Philocrates, who had proposed the embassy, Aeschines, and Demosthenes. The terms to which Philip agreed were that Athens and Macedon should each retain the territories of which they were actually in possession at the time the peace was concluded; the peace would be concluded when both sides had sworn to it. Both the allies of Macedonia and those of Athens were to be included, with two exceptions: Philip refused to treat with Halus in Thessaly—a place which he had recently attacked—or with the Phocians, whom he was determined to crush.

(Halon-nesus.)

By these terms, which were perfectly explicit, Athens would surrender her old claim to Amphipolis, and on the other hand Philip would recognise Athens as mistress of the Chersonese. The two exceptions which Philip made were inevitable. Halus indeed was a trifle which no one heeded; but it was an essential part of the Macedonian policy to proceed against Phocis. To the envoys, whom the king charmed by his courteous hospitality at Pella, he privately intimated that he was far from being ill-disposed to the Phocians; and perhaps a few of them hoped that there was something in the assurance. But in truth the Athenian statesmen troubled themselves little about Phocis; some of them, like the Theban proxenos Demosthenes, were more disposed to lean towards Thebes. It would be necessary to keep up the appearance of protecting an ally,— though relations with that ally had recently grown somewhat strained; but neither Eubulus nor Demosthenes would for a moment have dreamed of forgoing the peace for the sake of supporting Phocis against her enemies.

There were a few Thracian forts, belonging to Cersobleptes, which Philip was anxious to capture before the peace was made; and, when the envoys left Pella, he set out for Thrace, having given them an undertaking to respect the Chersonese. The envoys returned home bearing with them a friendly letter from Philip to the Athenian people, and they were followed in a few days by three Macedonian delegates, appointed to receive the oaths from the Athenians and their allies. How important this negotiation was for Philip is proved by the fact that two of these deputies were the two greatest of his subjects, Parmenio and Antipater. On the motion of Philocrates, the Peace was accepted by Athens on the terms which Philip offered, though there were dissentient voices against the exclusion of Phocis and Halus; but the murmurs of the opposition were silenced by the plain speaking of Eubulus, who showed that if the terms were rejected the war must be continued. And some of the ambassadors disseminated the unofficial utterances of Philip, that

Peace accepted and sworn to at Athens, 346 B.C., March.

he would not ruin the Phocians and that he would help Athens to win back Euboea and Oropus. The upshot was that Phocis was not mentioned in the treaty; she was tacitly, not expressly, excluded.[7]

The Peace was now concluded on one side, and it remained for the envoys of Athens to administer the oath to Philip and his allies. It was to the interest of Athens that this act should be accomplished as speedily as possible, for Philip was entitled to make new conquests until he swore to the Peace, and he was actually engaged in making new conquests in Thrace. The same ambassadors who had visited Macedonia to arrange the terms of a treaty now set forth a second time to administer the oaths.

Meanwhile Philip had taken the Thracian fortresses which he had gone to take, and had reduced Cersobleptes to be a vassal of Macedonia. When he returned to Pella, he found not only the embassy from Athens, but envoys from many other Greeks states also, awaiting his arrival with various hopes and fears. He was beginning to be recognised as the arbiter of northern Hellas.

So far as the formal conclusion of the Peace went, there was no difficulty. But the Athenian ambassadors had received general powers to negotiate further with Philip, with a view to some common decision on the settlement of the Phocian question and northern Greece. The treaty was a treaty of "peace and alliance," and, if Philip could have had his way, the alliance would have become a bond of close friendship and co-operation. And it was in this direction that Eubulus and his party were inclined cautiously to move. Athens might have now taken her position as joint arbitrator with Philip in the settlement of the Amphictionic states. Both Philip and Athens had a common interest in reducing the power of Thebes; and, if it was the interest of Athens that Phocis should not be utterly destroyed, Philip had no special enmity against Phocis, whose strength was now exhausted; the Phocian "sacrilege" was a convenient pretext to interfere and step into the place of Phocis in the Delphian Amphictiony. A common programme was discussed, and might easily have been concerted between Philip and the ambassadors. To treat the Phocians with clemency and to force Thebes to acknowledge the independence of the Boeotian cities would have been the basis of common action; the restoration of Plataea was mentioned; and while Philip promised to secure the restitution to Athens of Euboea and Oropus, Athens would have supported the admission of Macedonia into the Amphictionic Council. Aeschines

---

[7] The express exclusion was not necessary, since Procis did not belong to the Athenian symmachy or confederacy in the strict sense, and had no voice in the Synedrion of the Athenian allies.

was the chief mouthpiece of the counsels of Eubulus. But the project of an active alliance was opposed strenuously by Demosthenes, and as Demosthenes had great and daily increasing influence with the Athenian Assembly, it would have been unsafe for Philip to conclude any definite agreement with the majority of the embassy. The policy of Demosthenes was to abandon the Phocians to their fate and to draw closer to Thebes; so that, when his city had recovered from her financial exhaustion, Thebes and Athens together might form a joint resistance to the aggrandisement of Macedonia. In consequence of this irreconcilable division, which broke out in most unseemly quarrels among the ambassadors, nothing more was done than the administration of the oath. The envoys accompanied the king into Thessaly, and at Pherae the oath was administered to the Thessalians, his allies. A peace was then arranged with Halonnesus, and the envoys returned to Athens, leaving Philip to proceed on his own way.

Embassy returns tc Athens, June, 346 B.C.

It now remained to be seen whether Eubulus would carry the Assembly with him in favour of a rational policy of co-operation with Macedon, or would be defeated by the brilliant oratory of his younger rival. Philip's course of action would depend on the decision of the Assembly.

It was a calamity for Athens that at this critical moment there was no strong man at the helm of the state. The Assembly was swayed between the opposite counsels of Demosthenes, whose oratory was irresistible, and of Eubulus, whose influence had been paramount for the past eight years. When the ambassadors returned, Demosthenes lost no time in denouncing his colleagues, as having treacherously intrigued with Philip against the interest of the city. His denunciation was successful for a moment, and the usual vote of thanks to the embassy was withheld. But the success was only for a moment; Aeschines and his colleagues defended their policy triumphantly before the Assembly; and it was clear that the programme which they had discussed with Philip would have been satisfactory to the people. The Assembly decreed that the treaty of peace and alliance should be extended to the posterity of Philip. It further decreed that Athens should formally call upon the Phocians to surrender Delphi to the Amphictions, and should threaten them with armed intervention if they declined. Demosthenes appears to have made no opposition to this measure against the Phocians; and it seemed that the policy of co-operation with Philip was about to be realised.

Philip in the meantime advanced southward. The pass of Thermopylae was held by Phalaecus, who had been reinforced by some

Lacedaemonian troops; but Phalaecus had opened secret negotiations with Pella some months before; and the hostile vote of the
Athenians decided him to capitulate on condition of departing unhindered where he would.

Before he reached Thermopylae, Philip had addressed two friendly letters to Athens, inviting her to send an army to arrange the
affairs of Phocis and Boeotia. Indisposed as the Athenian citizens
were to leave Athens on military service, they lent ready ears to the
absurd terrors which Demosthenes conjured up, suggesting that
Philip would detain their army as hostages. Accordingly they contented themselves with sending an embassy (on which Demosthenes
declined to serve) to convey to Philip an announcement of the decree which they had passed against the Phocians. Thus swayed between Eubulus and Demosthenes, the Athenians had done too
much or too little. They had abandoned the Phocians, and at the
same time they resigned the voice which they should, and could,
have had in the political settlement of northern Greece.

As it was clear that Philip could not trust Athens, owing to the
attitude of Demosthenes, he was constrained to act in conjunction
with her enemy, Thebes. The cities of western Boeotia, which had
been held by the Phocians, were restored to the Boeotian confederacy. The doom of the Phocians was decided by the Amphictionic

Council which was now convoked. If some of the members had had
their way, all the men of military age would have been cast down a
precipice; but Philip would not have permitted this, and the sentence was as mild as could have been expected. The Phocians were
deprived of their place in the Amphictionic body; and all their cities
(with the exception of Abae) were broken up into villages, so that
they might not again be a danger to Delphi. They were obliged to
undertake to pay back, by instalments of sixty talents a year, the
value of the treasures which they had taken from the sanctuary.
The Lacedaemonians were also punished for the support which they
had given to Phocis, by being disqualified to return either of the
members who represented the Dorian vote. The place which Phocis
vacated in the Council was transferred to Macedonia, in recognition
of Philip's services in expelling the desecrators of the temple.

The Athenian declaration against Phocis exempted Athens from
the penalty which was inflicted on Sparta at this Amphictionic
meeting. But this was small comfort, and when the Athenians realised that they had gained nothing and that Thebes had gained all
she wanted, they felt with indignation that the statesmanship of
their city had been unskilful. The futility of their policy had been
mainly due to Demosthenes, who had done all in his power to

thwart Eubulus; and he now seized the occasion to discredit that statesman and his party. He encouraged his fellow-countrymen in the unreasonable fear that Philip would invade Attica, and the panic was so great that they brought their families and movable property from the country into the city. The fear was soon dispelled by a letter from Philip himself; but Demosthenes had succeeded in creating a profound distrust of Philip, and there was soon an opportunity of expressing this feeling.

An occasion offered itself to Philip almost immediately to display publicly to the assembled Greek world the position of leadership which he had thus won. It so happened that the celebration of the Pythian games fell in the year of the Peace. It will be remembered how the despot of Pherae, when he had made himself ruler of Thessaly, was about to come down to Delphi and assume the presidency of the Pythian feast, when he was cut down by assassins. The ambitions and plans of Pherae had passed to Pella, and Greece, which had dreaded the claims of the Thessalian tyrant, had now to bend the knee before the Macedonian king. Athens sulked; she sent no deputy to the Amphictionic meeting which elected Philip president for the festival, no delegates to the festival itself. This marked omission was a protest against the admission of Macedonia to the Amphictionic League, and Philip understood it as such. But he did not wish to quarrel with Athens; he hoped ultimately to gain her goodwill; and instead of marching into Attica, whither his Thessalian and Theban friends would have only too gladly followed him, he contented himself with sending an embassy to notify to the Athenian people the vote which made him a member of the Amphictiony and to invite them to concur. The invitation was in fact an ultimatum. Eubulus and his party had lost their influence in the outburst of anti-Macedonian feeling which Demosthenes had succeeded in stirring up. But the current had gone too far, and Demosthenes had some difficulty in allaying the spirits which he had conjured up. The Assembly was ready, on the slightest encouragement, to refuse its concurrence to the Amphictionic decree, and Demosthenes was forced to save the city from the results of his own agitation by showing that it would be foolish and absurd "to go to war now for the shadow at Delphi." Rarely had Athens been placed in such an undignified posture—a plight for which she had to thank the brilliant orator whom a malignant fate had sent to guide her on a futile path. From this time forward Demosthenes was the most influential of her counsellors.

Neither Demosthenes, the eloquent speaker, nor Eubulus, the able financier, saw far into the future. The only man of the day per-

Pythian games, 346 B.C.: Philip president.

Inconsistency of Athens.

Demosthenes' speech on the Peace.

700 A HISTORY OF GREECE

The
political
insight
and fore-
sight of
Isocrates.

haps who grasped the situation in its ecumenical aspect, who descried, as it were from without, the place of Macedonia in Greece
and the place of Greece in the world, was the nonagenarian Isocrates. He had never ventured to raise his voice in the din of party
politics; he had kept his garments unspotted from the defilement of
public life; and when he condescended to give political advice to
Greece, it was easy for the second-rate statesman as well as the
party hack to laugh at a mere man of study stepping into a field
where he had no practical experience. But Isocrates discerned the
drift of events, where the orators who madly declaimed in the Pnyx
were at fault; and the view which he took of the situation after the
conclusion of the Peace of Philocrates simply anticipated the decrees of history. He explained his view in an open letter to king
Philip. He had, long since, seen the endless futility of perpetuating
that international system of Greece which existed within the memory of men: a number of small sovereign states, which ought by
virtue of all they had in common to form a single nation, divided
and constantly at feud. The time had come, he thought, to unite
Greece, now that there had arisen a man who had the brains, the
power, and the gold to become the central pivot of the union.
Sovereign and independent the city states would of course remain;
but they might be drawn together into one fold by a common hope
and allegiance to a common leader. And under such a leader as
Philip there was a great programme for Greece; and not a mere
programme of ambition, undertaken for the sake of something to
do, but an enterprise which was urgently needed to meet a pressing
social danger. We have already seen how Greece was flooded for
many years past with a superfluous population who went about as
armed rovers, attached to no city, hiring themselves out to any
state that needed fighting men, a constant menace to society. A
new country to colonise was the only remedy for this overflow of
Greece, as Isocrates recognised. And the new country must be won
from the barbarian. The time had come for Hellas to take the offensive against Persia, and the task appointed for Philip was to lead
forth the hosts of Hellas on this splendid enterprise. If he did not
destroy the whole empire of the Great King, he might at least annex
Asia Minor "from Cilicia to Sinope" to the Hellenic world and appropriate it to the needs of the Hellenic folk.

Ten years later the fulfilment of this task which Isocrates laid
upon Philip was begun, not indeed by Philip himself, but by his
successor. We shall see in due time how the fulfilment surpassed the
utmost hopes of the Athenian speculator. But it is fair to note how
justly Isocrates had discerned the signs of the times and the tend-

ency of history. He saw that the inveterate quarrel between Europe and Asia, which had existed since the "Trojan war," was the great abiding fact; he foresaw that it must soon come to an issue; and throughout the later part of his long life he was always watching for the inevitable day. The expedition of Cyrus and the campaign of Agesilaus were foreshadowings of that day; and it had seemed for a moment that Jason of Pherae was chosen to be the successor of Agamemnon and Cimon. Now the day had come at last; the choice of destiny had fallen upon the man of Macedonia. And Isocrates knew that this expansion of Greece would meet Greece's chief practical need. It is instructive to contrast his sane and practical view of the situation of Greece with the chimerical conservatism of some of his contemporaries. This conservatism, to which the orator Demosthenes gave a most noble expression, was founded on the delusion that the Athens of his day could be converted by his own eloquence and influence into the form and feature of the Periclean city. That was a delusion which took no account of the change which events had wrought in the Athenian character; it was a noble delusion which could have misled no great statesman or hardheaded thinker. It did not mislead Isocrates; he appreciated the trend of history, and saw the expansion of Greece, to which the world was moving.

SECT. 7. INTERVAL OF PEACE AND PREPARATIONS FOR WAR (346-1 B.C.)

Having gained for Macedonia the coveted place in the religious league of Greece, Philip spent the next year or two in improving his small navy, in settling the administration of Thessaly, and in acquiring influence in the Peloponnesus. It may fairly be said that Thessaly was now joined to Macedonia by a personal union. The Thessalian cities elected the Macedonian king as their *archon*—the old name of tagus with its Pheraean associations was avoided,—and he set four governors over the four great divisions of the country. South of the Corinthian Isthmus, Philip adopted the old policy of Thebes, offering friendship to those states which needed a friend to stand by them against Sparta. His negotiations gained him the adhesion of Messenia and Megalopolis, Elis and Argos. In Megalopolis they set up a bronze statue of Philip, while Argos had a special tie with Macedon, since she claimed to be the original home of the Macedonian kings.

Nor did Philip yet despair of achieving his chief aim, the conciliation of Athens. No one knew how to bribe better than he, and we

Philip elected archon of Thessaly;

four tetrarchies of Thessaly.

may be sure that he gave gold without stint to his Athenian supporters. The Athenians naturally preferred peace to war; and the
political party which was favourable to friendly relations with
Philip was still strong and might at any moment regain its power.
The influence of the veteran Eubulus, who seems to have withdrawn somewhat from public affairs, was on that side; there were
Aeschines and Philocrates who had been active in the negotiation of
the Peace; and there was the incorruptible soldier Phocion, who was
a remarkable figure at Athens, although he had no pretensions to
eminence either as a soldier or as a statesman. He was marked
among his contemporaries as an honest man, superior to all temptations of money; and, as the Athenians always prized this superhuman integrity which few of them attempted to practise, they
elected him forty-five times as strategos, though in military capacity he was no more than a respectable sergeant. But his strong common sense, which was impervious to oratory, and his exceptional
probity made him an useful member of his party.

There was one man in Athens who was firmly resolved that the
peace should be no abiding peace, but a mere interval preparatory
to war. Demosthenes, supported by Hypereides, Lycurgus, and
others, spent the time in inflaming the wrath of his countrymen
against Philip and in seeking to ruin his political antagonists. These
years are therefore marked by a great struggle between the parties
of war and peace; the influence of Demosthenes being most often
in the ascendency and ultimately emerging victorious.

After Philip's installation in the Amphictionic Council, Demosthenes lost no time in striking a blow at his opponents. He brought
an impeachment against Aeschines for receiving bribes from the
Macedonian king and betraying the interests of Athens in the negotiations which preceded the Peace. Men's minds were irritated by
the triumph of Thebes, and Demosthenes might have succeeded in
inducing them to make Aeschines a scapegoat, if he had not committed a fatal mistake. He associated with himself in the prosecution a certain Timarchus, whose early life had been devoted to vices
which disqualified him from the rights of a citizen; and thus
Aeschines easily parried the stroke by bringing an action against
Timarchus and submitting his private life to an annihilating exposure. The case of Demosthenes was thereby discredited, and he
was obliged to let it drop for the time.

A year or so later we find Demosthenes going forth on a mission
to the cities of the Peloponnesus, to counteract by his oratory the
influence of Philip. But his oratory roused no echoes, and Philip had
good reason to complain of invectives which could hardly be justi-

The
Peace-
party at
Athens.

The War
party.

Demo-
sthenes
impeaches
Aeschines,
346-5 B.C.

Aeschines
against
Timar-
chus.

Demo-
sthenes in
the Pelo-
ponnese,
344 B.C.

fied from the lips of the representative of a power which was at peace and in alliance with Macedonia. An embassy came from Pella to remonstrate with the Athenians on their obstinate misconstruction of Macedonian motives, and Demosthenes seized the occasion to deliver one of his uncompromising anti-Macedonian harangues. The basis of his reasoning in this Philippic, and in the political speeches which followed it during the next few years, is the proposition that Philip desired and purposed to destroy Athens. It was a proposition of which he had no valid proof; and it was actually untrue, as the sequel showed. The Second Philippic.

We are not told what answer Athens sent to Pella, but it would seem that she complained of the terms of the recent Peace as unfair, and specially mentioned her right to Halus. This island off the coast of Thessaly, a place of no value whatever, had belonged to the Athenian Confederacy, but it had been seized by pirates, and the pirates had been expelled by Philip's soldiers. Philip sent an embassy with a courteous message, requesting Athens to propose emendations in the terms of the Peace, and offering to give her Halonnesus. But the place was of so little consequence to Athens or any one, that it served as an excellent pretext for diplomatic wrangling, and Demosthenes could persuade the people to refuse Halonnesus as it was offered, and demand that it should not be "given" but "given back." Besides the "restoration" of this worthless island, Athens made the proposal that the basis of the Peace should be altered, and that each party should retain, not the territories which were actually in its possession when the treaty was concluded, but the territories which lawfully belonged to it. This proposal was preposterous; no peace can be made on a basis that leaves open all the debated questions which it is the object of the treaty to settle. Athens also complained of the Thracian fortresses which Philip captured and retained after the negotiation had begun. On this question Philip was legally in the right, but he offered to submit the matter to arbitration. Athens refused the offer on the plea that suitable arbiters could not be found. She thus showed that she was not in earnest; her objection was as frivolous as her proposal. Demosthenes was responsible for the attitude of the city, and his intention was to keep up the friction with Macedonia and prevent any conciliation. Halus.

The ascendency which Demosthenes and his fellows had now won emboldened them to make a grand attack upon their political opponents, and thereby deal Philip a sensible blow. Hypereides brought an accusation of treachery against Philocrates, whose name was especially associated with the Peace, and so formidable did the prospect of the trial seem, in the present state of popular opinion, Impeachment and flight of Philocrates, 343 B.C.

Impeach-
ment of
Aeschines,
343 B.C.

that Philocrates fled, and he was condemned to death for contempt of court. Encouraged by this success, Demosthenes again took up his indictment against Aeschines, but Aeschines stood his ground; and one of the most famous political trials of antiquity was witnessed by the Athenian public. We can still hear the two rivals scurrilously reviling each other and vying to deceive the judges; for they published their speeches after the trial, to instruct and perplex posterity. It is in these documents, burning with the passions of political hatred, that the modern historian, picking his doubtful way through lies and distortions of fact, has to discover the course of the negotiations which led to the Peace of Philocrates.

Demo-
sthenes
on the
malversa-
tion of the
embassy.

The speech of Demosthenes, in particular, is a triumph in the art of sophistry. No politician ever knew better than he how short is the memory of ordinary men for the political events which they have themselves watched and even helped to shape by their votes and opinions; and none ever traded more audaciously on this weakness of human nature. Hardly four brief years had passed since the Peace was made, and Demosthenes, confident that his audience will remember nothing accurately, ventures lightly to falsify facts which had so lately been notorious in the streets of Athens. Disclaiming all responsibility for a peace which he had himself worked hard to bring about but now seeks to discredit, he discovers that the Phocians were basely abandoned and imputes their fate to Aeschines. Against Aeschines there was in fact no case; the charge of receiving bribes from Philip was not supported by any actual evidence. The reply of Aeschines, which as an oratorical achievement is not inferior to that of his accuser, rings less falsely. Eubulus and Phocion,

Aeschines
acquitted.

men of the highest character, supported Aeschines, but the public feeling was so hostile to Philip at this juncture, that the defendant barely escaped.

That Aeschines and many others of his party received money from Philip we may well believe—though the reiterations of Demosthenes are no evidence. But to receive money from Philip was one thing and to betray the interests of Athens was another. It must be proved that a politician had sacrificed the manifest good of his country, or deserted his own political convictions, for a sackful of silver or gold, before he could be considered unconditionally a traitor. Public opinion in Greece thought no worse of a man for accepting a few talents from foreigners who were pleased with his policy; although those few public men—Demosthenes was not among them—who made it a rule never to accept an obol in connexion with any political transaction were respected as beings of superhuman virtue. Philip, who unlocked many a city by golden keys, was doubtless generous to the party whose programme was identical with his own interests; and it may be that Aeschines and others, who were not in affluent circumstances, would have been unable to devote themselves to public affairs if the king had not lined their wallets with gold.

Meanwhile Philip was seeking influence and intriguing in the countries which lay on either side of Attica,—in Megara on the west, and Euboea on the north-east. An attempt at a revolution in Megara was defeated, and the city allied itself with its neighbour and old enemy Athens. But in Euboea the movements supported by Macedonia were more successful. Both in Eretria and in Oreus oligarchies were established, really dependent on Philip. But in Chalcis, which from its strategic position was of greater importance, the democracy held its ground, and sought an equal alliance with Athens, to which Athens gladly consented.

Alliances of Athens with Megara and Chalcis, 343-2 B.C. Philo-Mace-donian oligarchies in Euboea.

Events in another quarter of Greece now caused a number of lesser Greek states to rally round Athens, and so bring within the field of near possibilities a league such as it was the dream of Demosthenes to form against Macedonia. By his marriage with an Epirot princess, it naturally devolved upon Philip to intervene in the struggles for the Epirot throne which followed her father's death. He espoused the cause of her brother Alexander against her uncle Arybbas, marched into the country, and established Alexander in the sovereignty. Epirus would now become dependent on Macedonia, and Philip saw in it a road to the Corinthian Gulf and a means of reaching Greece on the western side. His first step was to annex the region of Cassopia (between the rivers Acheron and Oropus) to the Epirote league of which his brother-in-law was head; and his eyes were then cast upon Ambracia, which stood as a barrier to the southward expansion of Epirus. But the place which he desired above all was doubtless Naupactus, the key to the Corinthian Gulf, now in the hands of the Achaeans. For compassing his schemes in this quarter his natural allies were the Aetolians. They too coveted Naupactus and would have held it for him; and they were the enemies of the Ambraciots and Acarnanians, whom he hoped to render dependent on Epirus. The evident designs of Philip alarmed all these peoples, and not only Ambracia, Acarnania, and Achaea, but Corcyra also, sought the alliance of Athens.

Philip in Epirus.

Philip, however, judged that the time had not come for further advances on this side, and some recent movements of Cersobleptes decided him to turn now to one of the greatest tasks which were imposed upon the expander of Macedonia—the subjugation of Thrace. Since the Persians had been beaten out of Europe, Thrace had been subject to native princes, some of whom—Teres, Sitalces, Cotys—we have seen ruling the whole land from the Strymon's to the Danube's mouth. It was now to pass again under the rule of a foreigner, but its new lords were Europeans who would lead Thracian soldiers to avenge upon Asia the oriental yoke which had been laid upon their ancestors. Of the Thracian expedition of Philip we know as little as of the Thracian expedition of Darius. Unlike Darius, he did not cross the rivers of the north or penetrate into any part of Scythia, but his campaign lasted ten months, and he spent a winter in the field in that wintry land, suffering from sickness as well as from the cold. In war Philip never spared himself either hardship or danger. Demosthenes in later years described his reckless energy, ruthless to himself, in a famous passage: "To gain empire and power he had an eye knocked out, his collar-bone broken, his arm and his leg maimed; he abandoned to fortune any part of his body she cared to take, so that honour and glory might be the portion of the rest."

The Thracian king was dethroned, and his kingdom became a tributary province of Macedon. There is still in the land a city which bears Philip's name, and is the most conspicuous memorial of that great and obscure campaign. Philippopolis on the Hebrus was the chief of the cities which the conqueror built to maintain Macedonian influence in Thrace.

This conquest was not an infringement of the Peace, for Cersobleptes had not been admitted to the treaty as an ally of Athens. But it affected nearly and seriously the position of Athens at the gates of the Black Sea. The Macedonian frontier was now advanced to the immediate neighbourhood of the Chersonese, and Athens had no longer Thracian princes to wield against Philip. The prospect did not escape Demosthenes, and he resolved to force on a war,— though both his own country and Philip were averse to hostilities. Accordingly he induced Athens to send a few ships and mercenaries under a swashbuckler named Diopeithes, to protect her interests in the Chersonese. There had been some disputes with Cardia touching the lands of the Athenian outsettlers, and Diopeithes lost no time in attacking Cardia. Now Cardia had been expressly recognised as an ally of Philip in the Peace, and thus the action of Diopeithes was a violation of the Peace. The admiral followed up this aggression by invading some of Philip's Thracian possessions, and Philip then remonstrated at Athens. Their admiral was so manifestly in the wrong that the Athenians were prepared to disown his conduct, but Demosthenes saved his tool and persuaded the people to sustain Diopeithes. He followed up his speech on the

Chersonese question, which scored this success, by a loud call to war—the harangue known as the Third Philippic. The orator's thesis is that Philip, inveterately hostile to Athens and aiming at her destruction, is talking peace but acting war; and, when all the king's acts have been construed in this light, the perfectly sound conclusion is drawn that Athens should act at once. The proposals of Demosthenes are to make military preparations, to send forces to the Chersonese, and to organise an Hellenic league against "the Macedonian wretch."

Envoys were sent here and there to raise the alarm. Demosthenes himself proceeded to the Propontis and succeeded in detaching Byzantium and Perinthus from the Macedonian alliance. At the same time Athenian troops were sent into Euboea; the governments in Oreus and Eretria were overthrown, and these cities joined an independent Euboeic league, of which the Synod met at Chalcis. The island was thus liberated from Macedon without becoming dependent on Athens.

Demosthenes at Byzantium, 341 B.C. The Euboeic Federation, 341 B.C.

All these acts of hostility were committed without an overt breach of the Peace between Athens and Philip. But the secession of Perinthus and Byzantium was a blow which Philip was not prepared to take with equanimity. When he had settled his Thracian province, he began the siege of Perinthus by land and sea. There was an Athenian squadron in the Hellespont which barred the passage of the Macedonian fleet, but Philip caused a diversion by sending land troops into the Chersonese, and by this stratagem got his ships successfully through. The siege of Perinthus marks, for eastern Greece, the beginning of those new developments of the art of besieging, which in Sicily had long since been practised with success. But all the engines and rams, the towers and the mines of Philip failed to take Perinthus on its steep peninsular cliff. His blockade on the seaside was inefficient, and the besieged were furnished with stores and men from Byzantium. The Athenians were still holding aloof. They had addressed a remonstrance to Philip for violating the Chersonese and capturing some of their cruisers. Philip replied by a letter in which he rehearsed numerous acts of Athenian hostility to himself. But the decisive moment came when the king suddenly raised the siege of Perinthus and marched against Byzantium, hoping to capture it by the unexpectedness of his attack. Athens could no longer hold aloof when the key of the Bosphorus was in peril. The marble tablet on which the Peace was inscribed was pulled down; it was openly war at last. A squadron under Chares was sent to help Byzantium, and Phocion presently followed with a second fleet. Other help had come from Rhodes and Chios, and Philip was

Philip lays siege to Perinthus, 340 B.C.

then to Byzantium.

compelled to withdraw into Thrace, baffled in both his undertakings. It was the first triumph of Demosthenes over the arch-foe, and he received a public vote of thanks from the Athenian people.

But one wonders that the naval power of Athens had not made itself more immediately and effectively felt. The Macedonian fleet was insignificant; it could inflict damage on merchant-vessels or raid a coast, but it had no hold on the sea. The Athenian navy was 300 strong and controlled the northern Aegean; and yet it seems that in these critical years there was no permanent squadron of any strength stationed in the Hellespont. Naval affairs had been by no means neglected. Eubulus had seen to the building of new shipsheds and had begun the construction of a magnificent arsenal, close to the harbour of Zea, for the storage of the sails and rigging and tackle of the ships of war. But these luxuries were vain, if the ships themselves were not efficient, and the group-system on which the

The naval reform of Demosthenes.

ships were furnished worked badly. Demosthenes had long ago desired to reform this system, which had been in force for seventeen years. The 1200 richest citizens were liable to the trierarchy—each trireme being charged on a small group, of which each member contributed the same proportion of the expense. If a large number of ships were required, the group might consist of five persons; if a small, of fifteen. This system bore hardly on the poorer members of the partnership, who had to pay the same amount as the richer, and some were ruined by the burden. But the great mischief was that these poorer members were often unable to pay their quota in time and consequently the completion of the triremes was delayed. The influence of Demosthenes was now so enormous that he was able, in the face of bitter opposition from the wealthy class, to introduce a new law, by which the cost of furnishing the ships should fall on each citizen in proportion to his property. Thus a citizen whose property was rated as exceeding thirty talents, would henceforward, instead of having to pay one-fifth or perhaps one-fifteenth of the cost of a single trireme, be obliged to furnish three triremes and a boat.

So popular was Demosthenes, by the successes of Euboea and Byzantium, that he was able to accomplish a still greater feat. Years before he had cautiously hinted at the expediency of devoting the Festival Fund to military purposes; he now persuaded the Athenians to adopt this highly disagreeable measure. The building of the arsenal and ship-sheds was interrupted also, in order to save the expenses.

Philip in Thrace, 340-339 B.C.

Philip in the meantime had again withdrawn into the wilds of Thrace. The Scythians near the mouth of the Danube had rebelled, and he crossed the Balkan range to crush them. In returning to Macedon through the land of the Triballi, in the centre of the peninsula, he had some sore mountain warfare and was severely wounded in the leg. But Thrace was now safe, and he was free to deal with Greece.

Sect. 8. Battle of Chaeronea

Philip had no longer the slightest prospect of realising the hope, which he had cherished both before and after the Peace of Philocrates, of establishing friendly relations with Athens. The influence of the irreconcilable orator was now triumphant; through the persistent agitation of Demosthenes, coldness and quarrelling had issued in war; and Macedonia had received a distinct check. There was nothing for it now but to accept the war and bring the Macedonian cavalry into play. There were two points where Athens could be attacked effectively, at the gates of her own city, and at the gates of her granary in the Euxine. But a land-power like Macedonia could not operate effectively in the Propontis, unless aided by allies which possessed an effective navy; and Philip had experienced the truth of this when he laid siege to Perinthus and Byzantium. And in that quarter he had now to reckon not only with the Athenian sea-power but with the small navies of the Asiatic islands, Rhodes, Cos, and Chios, which had recently come to the rescue of the menaced cities. For these island states calculated that, if Philip won control of the passage between the two continents, he would not only tax their trade, but would soon cross over to the conquest of Asia Minor, and their fleets would then be appropriated to form the nucleus of a Macedonian navy. Now that Athens had been awakened from her slumbers, it was abundantly evident that the only place where Macedonia could inflict upon her a decisive blow was Attica.

Philip makes up his mind to the war with Athens.

On her side Athens had lightly engaged in a war, for which she had not either fully counted the cost or meditated an adequate programme. In truth the Athenians had no craving for the war; and they were not driven to it by an imperious necessity, or urged by an irresistible instinct, or persuaded by a rational conviction of its expediency. The persistent and crafty agitation of Demosthenes and his party had drawn them on step by step; their natural feeling of irritation at the rise of a new great power in the north had been sedulously fed and fostered by that eloquent orator and his friends, till it had grown into an unreasoning hatred of the Macedonian king, whose character, aims, and resources were totally misrepre-

Dangerous position of Athens.

sented. But now that war was declared, what was to be the plan of action? Athens had not even an able general who could make an effective combination. She controlled the sea, and it was something that Euboea had shaken off the Macedonian influence. In Chalcis, Athens had a point of vantage against Boeotia, and from Oreus she could raid the Thessalian coast and operate in the bay of Pagasae. But when Philip advanced southward, and passed Thermopylae, which was in his hands, the Athenian superiority at sea was of no use, for his communications were independent of the sea. There was no means of offering serious opposition if he marched on Attica; and the citizens were hardly likely at the bidding of Demosthenes to ascend their ships as they had done at the bidding of Themistocles. If events fell out according to the only probable forecast which could be made—on the assumption of Demosthenes that the invasion of Attica and ruin of Athens were the supreme objects of Philip —the Athenians had to look forward to the devastation of their country and the siege of their city. How was this peril to be met? They were practically isolated; for they had no strong continental power to support them; what could Megarians or Corinthians, Ambraciots or Achaeans, do for them against the host of Philip and his allies? "Ah, if we were only islanders!" many an Athenian must have murmured in these critical years. It was the calamity of Athens, as it has been the calamity of Holland, that she was solidly attached to the continent. Now that the crisis approaches nearer, it is borne in upon us more and more how improvident the policy of Athens had been. If she had accepted Macedonian friendship and kept a strong naval force permanently in the Propontis, assuring herself of undisputed control of her own element, she would have been perfectly safe. The constant presence of a powerful fleet belonging to a predominant naval state may be in itself a strategic success equivalent to a series of victories. But, though we have almost no notices of the movements of the Athenian galleys at this time, we cannot help suspecting that the naval power of Athens was inefficiently handled.

Demosthenes had never had a free hand until the siege of Byzantium; till then, he could do little more than agitate. When at length he became in the full sense of the word the director of Athenian policy, his energy and skill were amazing. But we cannot help asking with what hopes he was prepared to undertake the responsibility of bringing an invader into his country and a besieger to the walls of his city. The answer is that he rested his hope on a single chance. From the beginning of his public career Demosthenes had a strong leaning to Thebes; it has been already mentioned that he was

Theban leanings of Demosthenes.

Theban proxenos at Athens. This was a predilection which it behoved him to be very careful of airing; for the general feeling in his city was unfriendly to Thebes. The rhetorical tears which Demosthenes shed over the fate of the Phocians were not inconsistent with his attachment to the enemies of Phocis; for he never raised his voice for the victims of Theban hatred until their doom was accomplished. The aim of his policy was to unite Athens in alliance with Thebes. It was a difficult and doubtful game. Could Thebes be induced to turn against her Macedonian ally, who had recently secured for her the full supremacy of Boeotia, and who, she might reasonably reckon, would continue to support her as an useful neighbour to Attica? On this chance, and a poor chance it seemed, rested the desperate policy of Demosthenes. If Thebes joined Philip, or even gave him a free passage through Boeotia, the fate of Attica was sealed. But if she could be brought to desert him, her well-trained troops, joined with those of Athens, might successfully oppose his invasion.

The invasion was not long delayed; and it came about in a curious way. During the recent Sacred War, the Athenians had burnished anew and set up again in the sanctuary of Delphi the donative which they had dedicated after the victory of Plataea, being gold shields with the inscription, "From the spoils of Persians and Thebans, who fought together against the Greeks." Such a re-dedication, while Delphi was in the hands of the Phocians, who had been condemned as sacrilegious robbers, might be regarded as an offence against religion; at all events, the Thebans and their friends had an excellent pretext to revenge themselves on Athens for that most offensive inscription, which had perpetuated the shame of Thebes for a century and a half. The Thebans themselves did not come forward, but their friends of the Locrian Amphissa arranged to accuse the Athenians at the autumn session of the Amphictionic Council and propose a fine of fifty talents. At this session Aeschines was one of the Athenian deputies and he discovered the movement which was afoot against his city. He was an able man and he forestalled the blow by dealing another. The men who had been incited to charge Athens with sacrilege had been themselves guilty of a sacrilege far more enormous. They had cultivated part of the accursed field which had once been the land of Crisa. Aeschines arose in the assembly and, in an impressive and convincing speech which carried his audience with him, called upon the Amphictions to punish the men who had wrought this impious act. On the morrow at break of day the Amphictions and the Delphians, armed with pickaxes, marched down the hill to lay waste the places which had been un-

Meeting of the Amphictionic Council, autumn, 340 B.C.

Speech of Aeschines, who retorts sacrilege on the Locrians

lawfully cultivated, and, as they did so, were assaulted by the Amphissians, whose city is visible from the plain. The Council then resolved to hold a special meeting at Thermopylae, in order to consult on measures for the punishment of the Locrians, who, to their former crime, had added the offence of violating the persons of the Amphictionic deputies.

By this promptness and eloquence the Athenian orator had secured a great triumph. He had completely turned the tables on the enemies, Amphissa and Thebes, who must have been prepared to declare an Amphictionic war against Athens, in case she declined, as she certainly would have done, to pay the fine. They calculated of course on the support of Philip of Macedon. But it was now for Athens to take the lead in a sacred war against Amphissa; and it was a favourable opportunity for her to make peace with Philip—so that the combination should be Philip and Athens against Thebes, instead of Philip and Thebes against Athens. It was not to be expected that this advantage which Aeschines had gained would be welcome to Demosthenes; for it was the object of Demosthenes to avoid an embroilment with Thebes. Accordingly he persuaded the people to send no deputies to the special Amphictionic meeting and take no part in the proceedings against Amphissa. He upbraided Aeschines with trying to "bring an Amphictionic war into Attica": a strange taunt to the man who had prevented the declaration of an Amphictionic war against Athens.

Thus, although the attack upon Athens must have been prepared at Theban instigation, the incident was converted, through the policy of Demosthenes, into a means of bringing Athens and Thebes closer together. Athens and Thebes alike abstained from attending the special meeting. The Amphictions, in accordance with the decisions of that meeting, marched against the Amphissians, but were not strong enough to impose the penalties which had been decreed. Accordingly, at the next autumn session, they determined to invite Philip to come down once more to be leader in a sacred war.

Philip did not delay a moment. An Amphictionic war, from which both Athens and Thebes held aloof, was a matter which needed prompt attention. When he reached Thermopylae, he probably sent on, by the mountain road which passes through Doris to Amphissa. a small force to occupy Cytinion, the chief town on that road. Advancing himself through the defile of Thermopylae into northern Phocis, he seized and refortified the dismantled city of Elatea. The purpose of this action was to protect himself in the rear against Boeotia, and preserve his communications with Thermopylae, while he was operating against Amphissa. But while he halted at Elatea,

Athens does not follow up the stroke of Aeschines.

The Amphictions proceed against Amphissa, 339 B.C. The Amphictions call in Philip, 338 B.C., spring.

he sent ambassadors to explore the intentions of Thebes. He declared that he intended to invade Attica, and called upon the Thebans to join him in the invasion, or, if they would not do this, to give his army a free passage through Boeotia. This was a diplomatic method of forcing Thebes to declare herself; it does not prove that Philip had any serious intention of marching against Attica, and his later conduct seems to show that he did not contemplate such a step.

Alarm at Athens.

But in Athens, when the news came that the Macedonian army was at Elatea, the folk fell into extreme panic and alarm. It would seem that Philip's rapid movements had brought him into central Greece far sooner than was expected; and the news of his arrival, which must have been transmitted by way of Thebes, was accompanied by the rumour that he was about to march on Athens. And thus the Athenians in their fright connected the seizure of Elatea with the supposed design against themselves, although Elatea had no closer connexion than the pass of Thermopylae with an attack on Athens. For a night and a day the city was filled with consternation, and these anxious hours have become famous in history through the genius of the orator Demosthenes, who in later years recalled to the people the scene and their own emotions by a picturesque description which no orator has surpassed.

Athens sends ten envoys to Thebes.

On the advice of Demosthenes, the Athenians dispatched ten envoys to Thebes; everything depended on detaching Thebes from the Macedonian alliance. And it seemed at least possible that this might be effected. For, though there were probably few in Thebes who were inclined to be friendly to Athens, there was a party of some weight which was distinctly hostile to Macedonia. Moreover, there was a feeling of soreness against Philip for having seized Nicaea, close to Thermopylae, and replaced its Theban garrison by Thessalians. The envoys, of whom Demosthenes was one, were instructed to make concessions and exact none.

The ambassadors of Athens and Macedon met in the Boeotian capital, and their messages were heard in turn by the Theban assembly. It would be too much to say that the fate of Greece depended on the deliberations of this assembly, but it is the mere truth that the Theban vote not only decided the doom of Thebes itself, but determined the shape of the great event to which Greece had been irresistibly moving.

Situation of Thebes

In considering the situation which the rise of Macedon had created we have hitherto stood in Pella or in Athens; we must now for a moment take our point of view at Thebes. The inveterate rivalry and ever-smouldering hate which existed between Thebes and

Athens was a strong motive inducing Thebes to embrace an opportunity for rendering Athens harmless. But it would require no great foresight to see that, by weakening her old rival, Thebes would gravely endanger her own position. So long as Philip had a strong Athens to reckon with, it behoved him to treat Thebes with respect, but, if Athens were reduced to nothingness, Thebes would be absolutely in his power, and probably his first step would be to free the cities of Boeotia from her domination. To put it shortly, the independent attitude which Thebes had hitherto been able to maintain towards her friend Macedonia depended on the integrity of Athens. Thus the positions of Thebes and Athens were remarkably different. While Athens could with impunity stand alone as Philip's enemy, when Thebes was Philip's friend, Thebes could not safely be Philip's friend unless Athens were his enemy. The reason of this difference was that Athens was a sea-power.

To a Theban statesman then, possessing any foresight, the subjugation of Athens would have been feared as the prelude to the depression of Thebes; and it would have seemed wiser to join in a common resistance to Philip. This sound reasoning was quickened by the eloquence of Demosthenes and the offers of Athens. The Athenians were ready to pay two-thirds of the expenses of the war: they abandoned their claim to Oropus, and they recognised the Boeotian dominion of Thebes—a dominion which they had always condemned before as an outrage on the rights of free communities. But professing now, through the mouth of Demosthenes, to be the champion of Hellenic liberty, Athens scrupled little to sacrifice the liberties of a few Boeotian cities. By these concessions she secured the alliance of Thebes, and Demosthenes won the greatest diplomatic success that he had yet achieved—the consummation to which his policy had been directed for many years.

The first concern of Philip was to do the work which the Amphictions had summoned him to perform; but he is completely lost to our sight in this campaign. We only know that the allies followed him into Phocis and gained some advantages in two engagements, but that he ultimately captured not only Amphissa, cutting up a force of mercenaries that Athens had sent thither, but also Naupactus, thus gaining a point of vantage against the Peloponnesus. He then turned back to carry the war into Boeotia, and when he entered the great western gate of that country close to Chaeronea, he found the army of the allies guarding the way to Thebes, and prepared to give him battle. He had 30,000 foot soldiers and 2000 horse, perhaps slightly outnumbering his foes.

Their line extended over about three and a half miles, the left

Thebes forms an alliance with Athens against Philip, 338 B.C., spring.

Philip captures Amphissa, summer, 338 B.C.

wing resting on Chaeronea and the right on the river Cephisus. The Theban hoplites, with the Sacred Band in front, under the command of Theagenes, did not occupy the left wing, as when Epaminondas led them to victory at Leuctra and at Mantinea, but were assigned the right, which was esteemed the post of honour. In the centre were ranged the troops of the lesser allies, Achaeans, Corinthians, Phocians, and others, whom Demosthenes boasted of having rallied to the cause of Hellenic liberty. On the left stood the Athenians under three generals, Chares, Lysicles, and Stratocles, of whom Chares was a respectable soldier with considerable experience and no talent, while the other two were incompetent. Demosthenes himself was serving as a hoplite in the ranks.

Battle of Chaeronea, August (Metageitnior 7), 338 B.C.

Of the battle we know less perhaps than of any other equally important engagement in the history of Greece. But we can form a general notion of the tactics of Philip. The most formidable part of the adverse array was the Theban infantry; and accordingly he posted on his own left wing the phalanx, with its more open order and long pikes, to try its strength against the most efficient of the old-fashioned hoplites of Greece. On the flank of this wing he placed his heavy cavalry, to ride down upon the Thebans when the phalanx had worn them out. The cavalry was commanded by Alexander, now a lad of eighteen, and, many hundred years after, "the oak of Alexander" was shown on the bank of the river. The right wing was comparatively weak, and Philip planned that it should gradually give way before the attack of the Athenians, and draw them on, so as to divide them from their allies. This plan of holding back the right wing reminds us of the tactics of Epaminondas; but the use of cavalry to decide the combat is the characteristic feature of Philip's battles.

The Athenians pressed forward, fondly fancying that they were pressing to victory, and Stratocles in the flush of success cried, "On to Macedonia!" But in the meantime the Thebans had been broken by Alexander's horsemen: their leader had fallen, and the comrades of the Sacred Lochos were making a last hopeless stand. Philip could now spare some of his Macedonian footmen, and he moved them so as to take the Athenians in flank and rear. Against the assault of these trained troops the Athenians were helpless. One thousand were slain, two thousand captured, and the rest ran, Demosthenes running with the fleetest. But the Sacred Band did not flee. They fought till they fell, and it is their heroism which has won for the battle of Chaeronea its glory as a struggle for liberty. When the traveller, journeying on the highway from Phocis to Thebes, has passed the town of Chaeronea, he sees at the roadside the tomb where those heroes were laid, and the fragments of the lion which was set up to keep a long ward over their bones.

Signifi-
cance of
battle of
Chae-
ronea.
(1) mili-
tary;

An epitaph which was composed in honour of the Athenian dead suggested the consolation that God alone is sure of success, men must be prepared to fail. It is true, but in this case the failure cannot be imputed to the chances of war. When the allies opened the campaign the outlook was not hopeless; if they had been led by a competent general they might have reduced the Macedonian army to serious straits amid the valleys of Phocis and the hills of Locris. But to oppose to a Philip, the best they had was a Chares. The war was really decided in Locris by the strategical inferiority of the Athenian and Theban generals; and the inevitable sequel of the blunders there was the catastrophe in Boeotia. The advantage in numerical strength with which the allies started had been lost, and when they stood face to face with the advancing foe at Chaeronea, all the chances were adverse to any issue save defeat, in a battle in the open against a general of such pre-eminent ability. Men must be prepared to fail when they have no competent leader.

(2) politi-
cal.

If the chances of another issue to the battle of Chaeronea have been exaggerated, the significance of that event has been often misrepresented. The battle of Chaeronea belongs to the same historical series as the battles of Aegospotami and Leuctra. As the hegemony or first place among Greek states had passed successively from Athens to Sparta, and to Thebes, so now it passed to Macedon. The statement that Greek liberty perished on the plain of Chaeronea is as true or as false as that it perished on the field of Leuctra or the strand of the Goat's River. Whenever a Greek state became supreme, that supremacy entailed the depression of some states and the dependency or subjection of others. Athens was reduced to a secondary place by Macedon, and Thebes fared still worse; but we must not forget what Sparta, in the day of her triumph, did to Athens, or the more evil things which Thebes proposed. There were, however, in the case of Macedonia, special circumstances which seemed to give her victory a more fatal character than those previous victories which had initiated new supremacies.

Greek
feelings
towards
Macedon.

For Macedon was regarded in Hellas as an outsider. This was a feeling which the southern Greeks entertained even in regard to Thessaly when Jason threatened them with a Thessalian hegemony; and Macedonia, politically and historically as well as geographically, was some steps further away than Thessaly. If Thessaly was hardly inside the inner circle of Hellenic politics, Macedonia was distinctly outside it. To Athens and Sparta, to Corinth and Argos and Thebes, the old powers, who, as we might say, had known each other all their lives as foes or friends, and had a common international history, the supremacy of Macedonia seemed the intrusion of an upstart. And, in the second place, this supremacy was the triumph of an absolute monarchy over free commonwealths, so that the submission of the Greek states to Macedon's king might be rhetorically branded as an enslavement to a tyrant in a sense in which subjection to a sovereign Athens or a sovereign Sparta could not be so described. For these reasons the tidings of Chaeronea sent a new kind of thrill through Greece. And the impression that there was something unique in Philip's victory might be said to have been confirmed by subsequent history, which showed that the old Greek commonwealths had had their day and might never again rise to be first-rate powers.

SECT. 9. THE SYNEDRION OF THE GREEKS. PHILIP'S DEATH

Isocrates just lived to hear the tidings of Chaeronea, and died consoled for the fate of his fallen fellow-citizens by the thought that the unity of Hellas was now assured. But a Greek unity, such as he dreamed of, was by no means assured. The hegemony of Macedonia did as little to unite the Greek states or abolish the separatist tendency as the hegemony of Athens or of Sparta. But we must see how Philip used his victory.

He treated Thebes just as Sparta had treated it when Phoebidas surprised the citadel. He punished by death or confiscation his leading opponents; he established a Macedonian garrison in the Cadmea, and broke up the Boeotian league, giving all the cities their independence, and restoring the dismantled towns of Orchomenus and Plataea. But if his dealing with Thebes did not go beyond the usual dealing of one Greek state with its vanquished rival, his dealing with Athens was unusually lenient. The truth was that Athens did not lie defenceless at his feet. He might invade and ravage Attica, but when he came to invest Athens and Piraeus, he might find himself confronted by a task more arduous than that which had thwarted him at Perinthus and Byzantium. The sea-power of Athens saved her, and not less, perhaps, the respect which Philip always felt for her intellectual eminence. Now, at last, by unexpected leniency, he might win what he had always striven for, the moral and material support of Athens. And in Athens men were now ready to listen to the voices which were raised for peace. The policy of Demosthenes had failed, and all desired to recover the 2000 captives and avert an invasion of Attica soil. There was little disposition to hearken to the advice of Hyperides, who proposed to

Philip harsh to Thebes;

lenient to Athens.

enfranchise and arm 150,000 slaves. Among the captives was an orator of consummate talent, named Demades, who belonged to the peace party and saw that the supremacy of Macedon was inevitable. An anecdote was noised abroad that Philip, who spent the night after the battle in wild revelry, came reeling drunk to the place where his prisoners were and jeered at their misfortune, making merry, too, over the flight of the great Demosthenes. But Demades stood forth and ventured to rebuke him: "O king, fortune has given you the rôle of Agamemnon, and you play the part of Thersites!" The words stung and sobered the drunken victor; he flung away his garlands and all the gear of his revel, and set the bold speaker free. But whether this story be true or not, Demades was politically sympathetic with Philip and was sent by him to negotiate peace at Athens.

Philip offered to restore all the prisoners without ransom and not to march into Attica. The Athenians on their side were to dissolve what remained of their confederacy, and join the new Hellenic union which Philip proposed to organise. In regard to territory, Oropus was to be given to Athens, but the Chersonesus was to be surrendered to Macedonia. On these terms peace was concluded, and the Athenian people thought that they had come off well. Philip sent his son and two of his chief officers to Athens, with the bodies of the Athenians who had been slain. They were received with great honour, and a statue of the Macedonian king was set up in the market-place, a token of gratitude which was probably genuine. Demosthenes himself afterwards confessed with a snarl that Philip had been kind.

It was now necessary for Macedonia to win the recognition of her supremacy from the Peloponnesian states. Philip marched himself into Peloponnesus, and met with no resistance. Sparta alone refused to submit, and the conqueror bore down upon her, with the purpose of forcing on her a reform of the constitution and the abolition of her peculiar kingship, which seemed to him like a relic of the dark ages. But something mysterious happened which induced him to desist from his purpose, and a poet of Epidaurus, who was at that time a boy, told in later years how the god Asklêpios had intervened to save the Spartan state—

> What time king Philip unto Sparta came,
> Bent on abolishing the royal name.

But Sparta, though her kings were saved, had to suffer at the hands of Philip what she had before suffered at the hands of Epaminondas, the devastation of Laconia and the diminution of her territory. The frontier districts on three sides were given to her neighbours, Argos, Tegea, Megalopolis, and Messenia. Having thus displayed his arms and power in the south, the Macedonian king invited all the Greek states within Thermopylae to send delegates to a congress at Corinth; and, with the sole exception of Sparta, all the states obeyed.

Synedrion at Corinth, 338 B.C.

It was a Federal congress: the first assembly of an Hellenic Confederacy, of which the place of meeting was to be Corinth, and Macedonia the head. The aim of the Confederacy was understood from the first; but it would seem that it was not till the second meeting, a year later, that Philip announced his resolve to make war upon Persia, in behalf of Greece and her gods, to liberate the Greek cities of Asia, and to punish the barbarians for the acts of sacrilege which their forefathers had wrought in the days of Xerxes. It was the formal announcement that a new act in the eternal struggle between Europe and Asia was about to begin, and Europe, having found a leader, might now have her revenge for many a deed of insolence. The federal gathering voted for the war and elected Philip general with supreme powers. It was arranged what contingents in men or ships each city should contribute to the Panhellenic army; the Athenians undertook to send a considerable fleet.

Second Synedrion at Corinth, 337 B.C.

The league which was thus organised under the hegemony of Macedon had the advantage of placing before its members a definite object to be accomplished, and, it might be thought, a common interest. But if Themistocles found it hard to unite the Greek states by a common fear, it was harder still for Philip to unite them by a common hope; and the idea which Macedon promulgated produced no Panhellenic effort, and awakened but small enthusiasm. Yet the Congress of Corinth has its significance; it is the counterpart of that earlier congress which met at the Isthmus, when Greece was trembling at the thought of the barbarian host which was rolling towards her from the east. She had so long since ceased to tremble that she had almost forgotten to remember before the day of vengeance came; but with the revolution of fortune's wheel, that day came duly round, and Greece met once more on the Isthmus to concert how her ancient tremors might be amply avenged. The new league did not unite the Greeks in the sense in which Isocrates hoped for their union. There was a common dependency on Macedon, but there was no zeal for the aims of the northern power, no faith in her as the guide and leader of Greece. Each state went its own private way; and the interests of the Greek communities remained as isolated and particular as ever. A league of such members could not be held together, the peace which the league stipulated could not be maintained, without some military stations in the midst of the

Comparison of the Synedrion of the Isthmus of 480 B.C. with that of 338 B.C.

Unity of Greece not achieved.

country; and Philip established three Macedonian garrisons at important points: at Ambracia to watch the west, at Corinth to hold the Peloponnesus in check, and at Chalcis to control north-eastern Greece.

The designs of Philip probably did not extend beyond the conquest of western Asia Minor, but it was not fated that he should achieve this himself. In the spring after the congress, his preparations for war were nearly complete, and he sent forward an advance force under Parmenio and other generals to secure the passage of the Hellespont and win a footing in the Troad and Bithynia. The rest of the army was soon to follow under his own command.

Parmenio,
Amyntas,
and
Attalus
invade
Asia
Minor,
336 B.C.

But Philip, as a frank Corinthian friend told him, had filled his own house with division and bitterness. A Macedonian king was not expected to be faithful to his wife; but the proud and stormy princess whom he had wedded was impatient of his open infidelities. Nor was her own virtue deemed above suspicion, and it was even whispered that Alexander was not Philip's son. The crisis came when Philip fell in love with a Macedonian maiden of too high a station to become his concubine—Cleopatra, the niece of his general Attalus. Yielding to his passion, he put Olympias away and celebrated his second marriage. At the wedding feast, Attalus, bold with wine, invited the nobles to pray the gods for a *legitimate* heir to the throne. Alexander flung his drinking-cup in the face of the man who had insulted his mother, and Philip started up, drawing his sword to transpierce his son. But he reeled and fell, and Alexander jeered, "Behold the man who would pass from Europe to Asia, and trips in passing from couch to couch!" Pella was no longer the place for Alexander. He took the divorced queen to Epirus, and withdrew himself to the hills of Lyncestis, until Philip invited him to return. But the restless intrigues of the injured mother soon created new debates, and when a son was born to Cleopatra, it was easy to arouse the fears of Alexander that his own succession to the throne was imperilled. Philip's most urgent desire was to avoid a breach with the powerful king of Epirus, the brother of the injured woman. To this end he offered him his daughter in wedlock, and the marriage was to be celebrated with great pomp in Pella, on the eve of Philip's departure for Asia. But it was decreed that he should not depart. Olympias was made of the stuff which does not hesitate at crime, and a tool was easily found to avenge the wrongs of the wife and assure the succession of the son. A certain Pausanias, an obscure man of no merit, had been grossly wronged by Attalus, and was madly incensed against the king, who refused to do him justice.

Philip
divorces
Olympias
and
marries
Cleopatra.

On the wedding day, as Philip, in solemn procession, entered the theatre a little in advance of his guards, Pausanias rushed forward with a Celtic dagger and laid him a corpse at the gate. The assassin was caught and killed, but the true assassin was Olympias; and it was Alexander who reaped the fruits of the crime. Willingly would we believe that he knew nothing of the plot, and that a man of such a generous nature never stooped to thoughts of parricide. Beyond dark whispers, there is no evidence against him; yet it would be rash to say that his innocence is certain.

Murder of Philip, 336 B.C. (summer).

To none of the world's great rulers has history done less justice than to Philip. This failure in appreciation has been due to two or perhaps to three causes. The overwhelming greatness of a son greater than himself has overshadowed him and drawn men's eyes to achievements which could never have been wrought but for Philip's lifetime of toil. In the second place, we depend for our knowledge of Philip's work almost entirely on the Athenian orators, and especially on Demosthenes, whose main object was to misrepresent the king. And we may add, thirdly, that we possess no account of one of the greatest and most difficult of his exploits, the conquest of Thrace. Thus through chance, through the malignant eloquence of his opponent, who has held the ears of posterity, and through the very results of his own deeds, the maker and expander of Macedonia, the conqueror of Thrace and Greece, has hardly held his due place in the history of the world. The importance of his work cannot be fully understood until the consequences which it devolved upon his son to carry out have been studied. The work of Alexander is the most authentic testimony to the work of Philip.

Injustice done to Philip by posterity.

But there was one notable man of the day whose imagination grasped the ecumenical importance of the king of Macedon. A pupil of Isocrates, Theopompus of Chios—who played some part in the politics of his own island—was inspired by the deeds of Philip to write a history of his own time, with Philip as its central figure. In that elaborate work, the loss of which is irreparable, Theopompus exposed candidly and impartially the king's weaknesses and misdeeds; but he declared his judgment that Europe had never produced so great a man as the son of Amyntas.

The Philippic Histories of Theopompus.

It is part of the injustice to Philip that the history of Greece during his reign has so often been treated as little more than a biography of Demosthenes. Only his political opponents would deny that Demosthenes was the most eloquent of orators and the most patriotic of citizens. But that oratory in which he excelled was one of the curses of Greek politics. The art of persuasive speech is in-

Demosthenes as an orator.

dispensable in a free commonwealth, and, when it is wielded by a statesman or a general,—a Pericles, a Cleon, or a Xenophon,—is a noble as well as useful instrument. But once it ceases to be a merely auxiliary art, it becomes dangerous and hurtful. This is what had happened at Athens. Rhetoric had been carried to such perfection that the best years of a man's youth were absorbed in learning it, and when he entered upon public life he was a finished speaker, but a poor politician. Briefly, orators took the place of statesmen, and Demosthenes was the most eminent of the class. They could all formulate striking phrases of profound political wisdom; but their school-taught lore did not carry them far against the craft of the Macedonian statesman. The men of mighty words were as children in the hands of the man of mighty deeds. The Athenians took pleasure in hearing and criticising the elaborate speeches of their orators; and the eloquence of Demosthenes, though it was thoroughly appreciated, imposed far less on such connoisseurs than it has imposed upon posterity. The common sense of a plain man could easily expose his sophistries; he said himself that the blunt Phocion was the "chopper" of his periods.

The policy of Demosthenes.

Demosthenes used his brilliant gift of speech in the service of his country; he used it unscrupulously according to his light—the light of a purblind patriotism. He could take a lofty tone; he professed to regard Philip as a barbarian threatening Hellas and her gods. There is no need to show that, judged from the point of view of the history of the world, his policy was retrograde and retarding. We cannot fairly criticise him either for not having seen, even as fully as Isocrates, that the day for the expansion of Greece had come, and that no existing Greek commonwealth was competent to conduct that expansion; or if he did vaguely see it, for having looked the other way. All he saw, or at least all he cared, was that the increase of Macedonia meant the curtailment of Athens; and his political life was one long agitation against Macedonia's resistless advance. But it was nothing more than a busy and often brilliant agitation, carried on from day to day and from month to month, without any comprehensive plan. A fervent patriot does not make a great statesman. Demosthenes could devise reforms in special departments of the administration; he could admonish his fellow-citizens to be up and doing; but he did not grapple seriously with any of the new problems of the day; he did not originate one fertile political idea. A statesman of genius might conceivably have infused fresh life into Athens by effecting some radical change in her constitution and finding for her a new part to play. The fact that no such statesman arose is perhaps merely another side of the fact that her part as a chief actor was over. It has often been said that the Demosthenic Athenians were irreclaimable. They certainly could not have been reclaimed by Demosthenes; for Demosthenes, when all is said, was a typical Demosthenic Athenian.

CHAPTER XVII

THE CONQUEST OF PERSIA

SECT. I. ALEXANDER'S FIRST DESCENT ON GREECE

Alexander surrounded by foes. ON his accession to the throne of Macedon, Alexander found himself menaced by enemies on all sides. The members of the Confederacy of Corinth, the tributary peoples of the province of Thrace, the inveterately hostile Illyrians, all saw in the death of Philip an opportunity, not to be missed, for undoing his work; and in Asia, Attalus, the father of Cleopatra, espoused the claim of Cleopatra's infant son. Thus Alexander stood within a belt of dangers like that by which his father, at the same crisis in *his* life, had been encompassed; and the difference of the means which sire and son adopted to deal with the jeopardy showed the difference in temperament be-**His methods unlike Philip's.** tween the two men. If Alexander had followed the slow and sure methods of his father, he would have bought off the barbarians of the north, effected a reconciliation with Attalus, and deferred the Greek question till he had thoroughly established his power in Macedonia; then, by degrees, he could have recovered in a few years the dominion which Philip had won, and undertaken the expedition against Persia which Philip had planned. But such cautious calculations did not suit the bolder genius of Philip's son. He refused to yield to any of his foes; he encountered the perils one after another, and overcame them all.

First of all, he turned to Greece, where the situation looked serious enough. Athens had hailed the news of Philip's death with undisguised joy, and at the instance of Demosthenes had passed a decree in honour of his murderer's memory. Trumpets were sounding for war; messengers were flying to Attalus and to Persia; and Greece was incited to throw off the Macedonian yoke. Ambracia expelled her garrison, and Thebes attempted to expel hers.

Importance of Thessaly. But the insurrection of Thessaly was of far greater importance than the hostile agitations in the southern states. The Thessalian cavalry was an invaluable adjunct to the Macedonian army, and it was of more material consequence to a Macedonian king to be the archon of the Thessalian Federation than to be acknowledged as general of the Confederacy of Corinth. Yet it was hardly altogether the need of quickly securing Thessaly that urged Alexander to deal with Greece before he dealt with any other portion of his empire. He wished above all things to save Greece from herself. His timely appearance, before the agitation could develop into a fully declared rebellion, might prevent the cities from committing any irreparable action, which would necessitate a condign punishment, or even harsh measures. He would march south, not to chastise or judge the Greeks, but to conciliate them and obtain recognition as successor to his father's place in the amphictiony of Delphi and in the league of Corinth.

He advanced to the defile of Tempe, but found it strongly held by the Thessalians. Instead of attempting to carry a position which was perhaps impregnable, he led his army farther south along the coast, and cutting steps up the steep side of Ossa he made a new path for himself over the mountain and descended into the plain of the Peneus behind his enemy. Not a drop of blood was shed. A Thessalian assembly elected Alexander to the archonship, and he guaranteed to the communities of the land the same rights and privileges which they had enjoyed under his father. The conciliation of Thessaly led, without a blow, to the adhesion of its southern neighbours, Malis and Dolopia. At Thermopylae the young king was recognised by the amphictiony, and as he marched southward not a hand was raised against him; he had swooped down so quickly that nothing was ready to resist. The Athenians sent a repentant embassy, which the king received kindly without any reference to the public jubilations over his father's murder; and the Congress of the Confederacy met at Corinth to elect Alexander general in his father's place.

Alexander was chosen supreme general of the Greeks for the invasion of Asia; and it was as head of Hellas, descendant and successor of Achilles, rather than as Macedonian king, that he desired to go forth against Persia. But his election by the Greek Confederacy at Corinth had more of historical fitness than political significance. The contingents which the Greek states furnished as members of the league were small, and the idea of the expedition failed to arouse any national feeling. Yet the welcome, though halfhearted and hypocritical, which was given to Alexander at Corinth, and the vote, however perfunctory, which elected him leader of the Greeks, were the fitting prelude to the expansion of Hellas and the diffusion of Hellenic civilisation, which destiny had chosen him to accomplish. He was thus formally recognised as what he in fullest verity was, the representative of Greece. Of all those who thronged

336 B.C., late summer.

Alexander elected General of the Greeks

at Corinth round the royal youth, to observe him with curious gaze or flatter him with pleasant words, some may have foreseen that he would be a conqueror of many lands, but none can have suspected how his conquests would transform the world; for few realised that the world was waiting to be transformed. Outside the gates of Corinth, according to a famous story, the king found the eccentric philosopher Diogenes, sitting in the barrel, which served him as a home, and asked him to name a boon. "Stand out of the sun," was the brief reply of the philosopher. "Were I not Alexander," said the king to his retinue, "I should like to be Diogenes." The incident may never have happened, but the anecdote happily brings face to face the enthusiast who carried individual liberty to the utmost verge of independence and the enthusiast who dreamed of making his empire conterminous with the globe. For the individualism which Diogenes caricatured was sister to the spirit of cosmopolitanism which Alexander's empire was to promote.[1]

Meanwhile some domestic dangers had been cleared violently out of his path. His stepmother, her father, and her child had all been done away with. Attalus had been murdered in Asia, in accordance with the king's commands. But Alexander was not responsible for the death of Cleopatra and her infant. This was the work of Olympias, who, thirsty for revenge, caused the child to be slaughtered in its mother's lap, and forced Cleopatra to hang herself by her own belt.

Sect. 2. Alexander's Campaigns in Thrace and Illyria

There were symptoms of disquietude in Thrace; there were signs of a storm brewing in the Illyrian quarter; and it would have been impossible for the young king to invade Asia, with Thrace ready to revolt in his rear, and Macedonia exposed to attack from the west. It was indispensable to teach the Thracians a lesson, and especially the Triballi, who had never been chastised for the check which they had inflicted on Philip. The Triballi lived beyond the Haemus, and when Alexander, having crossed Mount Rhodope, reached the foot of one of the western passes of Mount Haemus, he found the steep defile defended by mountaineers. They had hauled up a multitude of their war-chariots to the top of the pass, in order to roll them upon the Macedonians and then, rushing down themselves, to fall upon the disordered array. There was no other way of crossing the mountain, and the mountain must be crossed. Alexander showed here again the same temper and the same resource which he had

Alexander marches against the Triballi, 335 B.C.

Shipka Pass.

---

[1] Cp. above, p. 560.

shown at Tempe; when he had made up his mind that an object must be attained, he never hesitated to employ the boldest or most novel means. He ordered the infantry to advance up the path, opening the ranks when possible to let the chariots roll through, but when that was impossible, he directed them to fall on their knees and, holding their shields locked together, to form a roof on which the chariots could fall and roll harmlessly away. The device was successful. The volleys of the cars rattled over the locked shields, and notwithstanding the shock not a man was killed. When the barbarians had exhausted these ponderous missiles, the pass was easily taken, and the Macedonians descended into the country of the Triballi. At the news of Alexander's approach the Triballi had sent their wives and children to an island named Peuce, in the Danube; and then, waiting until he advanced into their land, stole behind him to seize the mountain passes in his rear. Learning of this movement, Alexander marched rapidly back, forced the enemy to fight and dispersed them with great loss. He then proceeded on his way to the bank of the Danube. He had foreseen that it might be necessary to operate on that river, perhaps to make a demonstration in the country of the Getae on the northern bank; and he had prepared for this emergency by adopting the same plan as Darius in his famous Thracian expedition. He instructed his ally Byzantium to dispatch ships to sail up the river. The garrison in the island of Peuce were supported by a host of Scythian friends on the left bank of the stream, and Alexander saw that with his few Byzantine galleys it would be hopeless to attack the island until he had secured the Scythian shore. The problem was to throw his troops across the river without the enemy's knowledge, and this must be done in the darkness of one night. The ships were too few in number; but all the fishing-boats in the neighbourhood were collected, and tent-skins filled with hay were tied firmly together and strung across the stream. Landing on the other bank, led by the king himself, a large band of horse and foot advanced under the cover of the long corn at dawn of day, and the barbarian host arose to see the Macedonian phalanx unfolded before them. Startled as much by the terrible promptitude of their foe as by the formidable array which faced them, they withdrew into their poorly fortified town, and when Alexander followed them at the head of his cavalry, they fled with all their horses could carry into the wilds of the north. Empire beyond the Danube was not sought by Alexander, and he did not pursue. He marked the term of his northern conquest by sacrificing solemnly on the banks to Zeus Soter, Heracles, and the river-god himself.

On the Danube, May.

This exploit led to the surrender of the Triballi in the island, and all the neighbouring tribes south of the river hastened to assure the king of their submission. There came also from unknown homes far up the river, or perhaps in the Dalmatian mountains, an embassy of Celts, huge-limbed, self-confident men, who had heard of Alexander's deeds and were fain to be his friends. Curious to know what impression the Macedonian name had made upon that distant folk, Alexander asked them what they feared most. "We fear nothing," they said, "if it be not lest the sky fall." "Braggarts!" said Alexander afterwards. But before two generations had passed away these men of mighty limbs and mighty words were destined to roll down in a torrent upon Greece and Asia, and to wrest for their own habitation a part of Alexander's conquests.

Alexander's work was done in Thrace, but as he marched homewards he learned that the Illyrians were already in the gate of Macedonia, and that not a moment must be lost if the country was to be saved from an invasion. Philip had secured the Macedonian frontier on the Illyrian side by a number of fortresses, near the sources of the Haliacmon and Apsus; and Pelion, which was the strongest of these strongholds, the key-fortress of the mountain gate, had now fallen into the hands of Clitus, the Illyrian chief. To reach Pelion as quickly as possible, before the arrival of the Taulantines, a folk in alliance with Clitus, was the object of Alexander. His march was threatened by the Autariats, another hostile folk, whom Clitus had engaged to waylay him; but this danger was prevented by the friendly king of the Agrianes, who invaded the Autariat territory and fully occupied the fighting-men. Marching rapidly up the valley of the Erigonus, Alexander encamped near Pelion. The heights around were covered with Illyrians, and Clitus, as was the custom of his people before a battle, sacrificed three boys, three maidens, and three black rams. But before they came to the actual attack, the hearts of the Illyrians failed them, and deserting all their points of vantage and leaving their sacrifice incomplete, they retired into the fastness. Alexander intended to blockade the place next day by a circumvallation, but the Taulantines arrived in a large force, and he saw that his men were too few to deal at once with the foes within and the foes without the walls, nor were his provisions sufficient for a protracted siege. It was absolutely necessary to withdraw from his present position; but it was a task of extreme peril to retreat in these defiles, with hostile Pelion in the rear and Taulantine troops occupying the slopes and heights. This task, however, was carried out successfully, through the amazingly swift and skilful manœuvring of the highly drilled Macedonian soldiers; the enemy were driven from their flanking positions, and the river was crossed with much trouble yet without the loss of a man. At the other side of the river, Alexander's communications were safe; he could obtain provisions and reinforcements as he chose, and might wait, at his ease, for an opportunity to strike. The moment soon came. The enemy, seeing in Alexander's retreat a confession of fear, neglected all precautions and formed a camp without rampart or outpost before the gates of the fortress. Taking a portion of his army and bidding the rest follow, Alexander set out at night and surprised the slumbering camp of the barbarians. A carnage followed and a wild flight, and the Macedonians pursued to the Taulantine mountains. At the first alarm, Clitus rushed into the gates of Pelion and set the town on fire, before he joined the flight.

Macedonian victory

This discomfit of the Illyrians was a no less striking proof of Alexander's capacity than his exploits in Thrace. These months of incessant toil had earned him a rest, but there was to be no rest yet for the young monarch. Even as the tidings of the Illyrian danger had reached him before the left Thrace, so now, while he was still at Pelion, the news came that Thebes had rebelled. He must now speed to Greece as swiftly as seven days agone he had sped to the Illyrian hills. No need was more pressing than to crush this revolt before it spread.

Sect. 3. Alexander's Second Descent on Greece

The agitation against Macedon had not ceased during the past year in the cities of Greece, and it was now fomented by the gold and the encouragement of Persia. Five years before, at the outbreak of the war, Athens had sent ambassadors to Susa begging for subsidies from Artaxerxes, but the Great King would not break with Philip then, and sent them away with "a very haughty and barbarous letter" of refusal. The Phrygian satrap, however, perhaps on his own responsibility, sent useful help to Perinthus in its peril, and Persia gradually awoke to the fact that Macedonia was a dangerous neighbour. The new king, Darius, saw the necessity of embarrassing Alexander in Europe, so as to keep him as long as possible from crossing into Asia, where the Macedonian forces under Parmenio were holding their own. For this purpose he stirred up thoughts of war in Greece and sent subsidies to the Greek states. To many cities these overtures were welcome, but especially to Thebes, under the shadow of the Macedonian garrison. Three hundred talents were offered to Athens and publicly declined; but Demosthenes privately accepted them, to be expended in the interests of the Great King.

Greek cities negotiating with Persia against Macedonia.

It is not probable that any city entered into a formal contract with Persia, but the basis of the negotiations was the King's Peace, of fifty years ago, the Greeks admitting the rights of the Persian empire over their brethren in Asia, who on their part were awaiting with various feelings the approach of the Macedonian deliverer.

As the patriots had often prayed for the death of Philip, so now they longed for the death of his youthful son, an event which might have hurled back Macedon into nothingness for ever. Rumours soon spread that the wish was fulfilled. Alexander was reported to have been slain in Thrace; Demosthenes produced a man who had seen him fall; and the Theban fugitives in Athens hastened to return to their native city and incite it to shake off the Macedonian yoke. Two captains of the garrison were caught outside the Cadmea and murdered, and the Thebans then proceeded to blockade the citadel by a double rampart on the south side, where there was no city wall outside the wall of the citadel. Greece responded to the Theban leading, which Demosthenes, Lycurgus, and the other Athenian patriots had prompted and encouraged. There were movements against Macedon in Elis and Aetolia; the Arcadians marched forth to the Isthmus; and the Athenians sent arms to Thebes, though they sent no men. The hopes of the patriots ran high; the fall of the Cadmea seemed inevitable.

Suddenly a report was whispered in Thebes that a Macedonian army was encamped a few miles away at Onchestus. As Alexander was dead, it could only be Antipater—so the Theban leaders assured the alarmed people. But messengers soon came, affirming that it was certainly Alexander. Nay, then, said the leaders, since King Alexander is dead, it can only be Alexander of Lyncestis.

But it was indeed the king Alexander. In less than two weeks he had marched from Pelion to Onchestus, and on the next day he stood before the walls of Thebes. He halted first on the northeastern side of the city, near the sanctuary of the Theban hero, Iolaus; he would give the citizens time to make their submission. But they were in no mind to submit, and some of their light-armed troops, rushing out of the gates, attacked the outskirts of the Macedonian camp. On the morrow Alexander moved his whole army to the south side of the city, and encamped close to the Cadmea, without making any attack on the walls, still hoping that the city would surrender. But the fate of Thebes was precipitated by one of his captains, by name Perdiccas, who was in charge of the troops which guarded the camp on the side of the Cadmea. Stationed within a few yards of the Theban earthworks, Perdiccas, without waiting for orders, dashed through the outer rampart and fell upon the Theban guards.

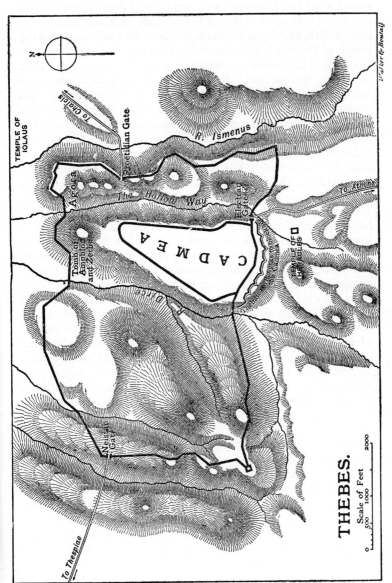

FIG. 101.

He was supported by a fellow-officer; and Alexander, when he observed what had happened, sent archers and light troops to their

(The Hollow Way.)

aid. The Thebans who manned the rampart were driven along the gully, which, running along the east side of the Cadmea, passes the temple of Heracles outside the walls. When they reached this temple they rallied and turned on their assailants and routed them back along the "hollow road." But, as they pursued, their own ranks were broken, and Alexander, watching for the moment, brought his phalanx into action and drove them within the Electran gate. They had no time to shut the gate before some Macedonians pushed in along with the fugitives; and there were no men on the walls to shoot the enemy down, for the men who should have defended the walls had been sent to the blockade of the citadel. Some of the Macedonians, who thus entered, made their way to the Cadmea, and joining with the garrison they sallied out close to the Ampheion,

(Tomb of Amphion and Zethus.)

where the main part of the Theban forces was drawn up. Others, having mounted the bastions, helped their friends without to climb the walls, and the troops thus admitted rushed to the market-place. But the gate was now in the possession of the Macedonians; the city was full of them; and the king himself was everywhere. The Theban cavalry was broken up, and fled through the streets and the open gates into the plain; the foot soldiers saved themselves as they could; and then a merciless butchery began. It was not the Macedonians who were zealous in the work of slaughter, but the old enemies of Thebes, the Phocians, the Plataeans and other Boeotian peoples, who now wreaked upon the proud city of the seven gates vengeance for the wrongs and insults of many generations. Six

The destruction of Thebes.

thousand lives were taken before Alexander stayed the slaughter. On the next day he summoned the Confederates of Corinth to decide the fate of the rebellious city. The judges meted out to Thebes the same measure which Thebes would have once meted out to Athens. The sentence was that the city should be levelled with the dust and her land divided among the Confederates; that the remnant of the inhabitants, with the women and children, should be sold into bondage, except the priests and priestesses of the gods, and those burghers who had bonds of guest-right with the Macedonians; and that the Cadmean citadel should be occupied by a garrison. The severe doom, showing how deeply the masterful city was abhorred, was carried out; and among the ruined habitations, on which the Macedonian warders looked down from the fortress walls, only one solitary house stood, making the desolation seem more desolate, the house of Pindar, which Alexander expressly spared.

The Boeotian cities were at length delivered from the yoke of their imperious mistress; Plataea and Orchomenus re-arose from their ruins. The fall of Thebes promptly checked all other movements in Greece; the Arcadian forces withdrew from the Isthmus; Elis and Aetolia hastened to retrieve their hostile attitude. The news reached Athens during the festival of the Mysteries. The solemnity was interrupted, and in a hurried meeting of the Assembly it was resolved, on the proposal of Demades, to send an embassy to welcome Alexander on his safe return from his northern campaign, and to congratulate him on the just chastisement which he had inflicted upon Thebes. The same people passed this decree who, a few days before, on the proposal of Demosthenes, had resolved to send troops to the aid of that luckless city. Alexander demanded—and it was a fair demand—that Demosthenes and Lycurgus and the other agitators who kept the hostility to Macedonia alive, and were largely responsible for the disaster of Thebes, should be delivered to him; for so long as they were at large there was no security that Athens would not entangle herself in further follies. When the demand was laid before the Assembly, Demosthenes epigrammatically expressed his own view of the situation by advising the people not to hand over their sheep-dogs to the wolf. Phocion said in downright words that Alexander must be conciliated at any cost; let the men whose surrender he demanded show their patriotism by sacrificing themselves. But it was finally decided that Demades, who had ingratiated himself with the Macedonian king, should accompany another embassy and beg that the offenders might be left to the justice of the Athenian people. Alexander, still anxious to show every consideration to Athens, withdrew his demand, insisting only on the banishment of the adventurer Charidemus, of Thracian notoriety.

Athens congratulates Alexander on the fall of Thebes.

With the fall of Thebes Alexander's campaigns in Europe came to an end. The rest of his life was spent in Asia. The European campaigns, though they filled little more than a year, and though they seem of small account by the side of his triumphs in the east, were brilliant and important enough to have won historical fame for any general. In his two descents into Greece, first to conciliate and afterwards to punish, in his expedition to the Danube, and in his Illyrian campaign, he had given tokens of the rare strategic capacity, the originality of conception, the boldness of resolution, the rapidity of action, and those other qualities which served Alexander's genius and soon found a more spacious sphere for their manifestation when they bore him toward the unknown limits of the eastern world.

SECT. 4. PREPARATIONS FOR ALEXANDER'S PERSIAN EXPEDITION. CONDITION OF PERSIA

Having spent the winter in making his military preparations and setting in order the affairs of his kingdom for a long absence, Alexander set forth in spring for the conquest of Asia. Of his plans and arrangements we know almost nothing, but we may say with confidence that his scheme of conquest was well considered, and that he did not go forth as an adventurer to take whatever came in his way. His original scheme of conquest was afterwards merged in a second and larger scheme, of which he had no conception when he went forth from Macedonia, for he had not the requisite geographical knowledge of central Asia. But in the first instance his purpose was to conquer the Persian kingdom, to dethrone the Great King and take his place, to do unto Persia what Persia under Xerxes had essayed to do unto Macedonia and the rest of Hellas. To carry out this design the first thing needful was to secure Thrace in the rear, and that had been already done. In the conquest itself there were three stages. The first step was the conquest of Asia Minor; the second was the conquest of Syria and Egypt; and these two conquests, preliminary to the advance on Babylon and Susa, would mean not merely acquisitions of territory, but strategic bases for further conquest. The weak point in Alexander's enterprise was the lack of a fleet capable of coping with the Persian navy, which was 400 strong. Here the Confederacy of Corinth should have come to his help; Athens alone could have furnished over 200 galleys. And Alexander doubtless counted on obtaining the support of Athens and the other Greek cities ultimately. But he desired aid rendered with goodwill, and he made no effort to extort ships or men. The loosely organised league of Corinth had undertaken to supply fixed contingents, but the fulfilment of these promises was not strictly exacted.

To secure Macedonia against her neighbours and subjects during his absence, Alexander was obliged to leave a large portion, perhaps as much as one half, of the national army behind him. The government was entrusted to his father's minister, Antipater. It is said that the king made dispositions before his departure as one who expected never to return. He divided all his royal domains and forests and revenues among his friends; and, when Perdiccas asked what was left for himself, he replied, Hope. Then Perdiccas, rejecting his own portion, exclaimed "We who go forth to fight with you

Marginal notes:

The scheme of Alexander's conquests.

Want of a fleet.

Provisions for the government of Macedonia.

need share only in your hope." The anecdote at least illustrates the enthusiasm with which Alexander infected his friends and officers on the threshold of a venture, of which the conception was almost as wonderful as its success.

The Persian empire was weak and loosely knit, and it was governed now by a feeble monarch. Two generations had passed since Greece beheld its weakness memorably demonstrated by the adventures of Xenophon's Ten Thousand; and since then we have seen it, on the western side, rent and riven by revolts. Artaxerxes Ochus displayed more strength than his predecessors. He re-established his power in Asia Minor, he quelled rebellions in Phoenicia and Cyprus, and even conquered Egypt, which had long set at nought the Persian efforts to regain it. The king, Nektanebos, was driven back from Pelusium to Memphis, and from Memphis he fled to Ethiopia. The Persian king had no thought of holding the land of the Nile by kindness; as soon as he had Memphis in his power he displayed the intolerance of the fire-worshipper. He drowned the holy bull, Apis, and inaugurated the ass as the sacred animal of Egypt. This stupid outrage made the Persian rule more detested than ever. Ochus was assassinated, the victim of a palace conspiracy; and after two or three years of confusion the throne passed to a distant member of the Achaemenid house, Darius Codomannus, destined to be the last successor of his great namesake. He was a mild and virtuous prince, beloved by his followers, but too weak, both in brains and will, for the task to which fate had doomed him.

It cannot be gainsaid that, if Darius had been able and experienced in war and capable of leading men, he had some enormous advantages. In the first place, he had the advantage in the sheer weight of human bodies. Had the myriads which he could muster been divided into troops of thirty men, and a soldier of Alexander's army allotted as a cupbearer to each troop, many a company would have gone unserved. In the second place, while the coffers of Pella are said to have been emptied before Alexander set foot in Asia, the Great King commanded untold wealth. The treasury of Susa was full, and in the palace of Persepolis were hoarded inexhaustible stores of gold. In the third place, he had a navy which controlled the seaboard of Asia Minor, Syria, and Egypt, and ought, if it had been handled ably, to have placed insuperable obstacles in the way of an invader who had no adequate sea-power. And fourthly, although there was no cohesion in the vast empire or unity of centralisation, there was, for that very reason, little or no national discontent in the provinces. Egypt was an exceptional case. The revolts which occurred from time to time were not national movements, but the

State of Persia.

Ochus (acceded, 358 B.C.) conquers Egypt.

Murder of Ochus, 338 B.C. Accession of Darius, 335 B.C.

Advantages on the side of Persia in the approaching struggle.

disaffections of ambitious satraps. If the Persian monarch was not loved, at least he was not hated; and the warlike barbarians of the east, from far Hyrcania or the banks of the Oxus, were always ready to follow him and glad to fight in his cause. It was quite feasible, so far as the state of feeling in the provinces was concerned, to

organise an effective defence of the empire. But all these advantages were as naught, for lack of a master mind and a controlling will. Multitudes were useless without a leader, and money could not create brains. Moreover Persia was behind the age in the art of warfare. She had not kept pace with the military developments in Greece during the last fifty years, and, though she could pay Greek mercenaries, and though these formed in fact a valuable part of her army, they could have no effect on the general character of the tactics of an oriental host. The Persian commanders had no notion of studying the tactics of their enemy and seeking new methods of encountering them. They had no idea of shaping strategic plans of their own; they simply waited on the movements of the enemy. They trusted, as they had always trusted, with perfect simplicity, in numbers, individual bravery, and scythe-armed chariots. The only lesson which the day of Cunaxa had taught them was to hire mercenary Greeks.

The strength of the army which Alexander led forth against Persia is said to have been 30,000 foot and 5000 horse, thus preserving the large proportion of cavalry to infantry, which was one of the chief novelties of Philip's military establishment. We have seen how Philip organised the national army of Macedonia, in the chief divisions of the phalanx, the light infantry or hypaspists, and the

heavy cavalry. Alexander led to Asia six regiments of the phalanx, and in the great engagements which decided the fate of Persia these formed the centre of his array. They were supported by Greek hoplites, both mercenary and confederate; the mercenary were com-

manded by Menander, the confederate by Antigonus. The hypaspists, led by Nicanor, son of Parmenio, had their station on the right wing, and the first regiment of these was the royal guard, called the *agēma*. Philotas, another son of Parmenio, was commander of the

heavy cavalry, in eight squadrons; one of which, the "royal squadron," under Clitus, corresponded to the *agēma* of the light armed foot. This Macedonian cavalry was always placed on the right, while on the left rode the splendid Thessalian cavalry under Callas, with

a corps of other Greek horse attached. Both the right and the left wings were strengthened by light troops, horse and foot, accoutred according to their national habit, from Thrace, Paeonia, and other countries of the Illyrian peninsula.

Sect. 5. Conquest of Asia Minor

The forces which had been operating in Asia under Parmenio while Alexander was detained in Europe had been endeavouring to establish a footing in Aeolis and Mysia, and secure a base on the Propontis for further advance. The Great King had empowered Memnon of Rhodes, an able mercenary captain, who in recent years had come to the front, to oppose the van of the Macedonian invasion. The most pressing need of the Persians was to recapture Cyzicus, which was in the hands of Parmenio. In this Memnon failed; but he occupied Lampsacus, he forced the Macedonians to raise the siege of Pitane and beat them back to the coast of the Hellespont. But he could not or did not press his advantage, and the shores where Alexander's host would land were safe in Macedonian possession.

Successes of Parmenio, 335 B.C.

The fleet transported the army from Sestus to Abydus, while Alexander himself proceeded to Elaeus, where he offered a sacrifice on the tomb of Protesilaus, the first of the mythical Greeks who landed on the shore of Asia in the Trojan war, and the first who fell. Praying that he might be luckier than Protesilaus, Alexander sailed across to the "Harbour of the Achaeans," and in the mid-strait made libations to Poseidon and the Nereids from a golden dish. The first to leap upon the Mysian strand, he crossed the plain of Troy and went up to the hill of Ilion, where he performed a sacrifice in the temple of Athena, in the poor town which stood cn the ruins of six prehistoric cities. It is said that he dedicated his own panoply in the shrine, and took down from the wall some ancient armour, preserved there as relics of the war of Priam and Agamemnon. He sacrificed to Priam to avert his anger from one of the race of Neoptolemus; he crowned the tomb of Achilles his ancestor; and his bosom-friend Hephaestion cast a garland upon the grave of Patroclus, the beloved of Achilles. He commanded that Ilion should rise again from its ruins, as a favoured city enjoying the rights of self-government and immunity from taxation. These solemnities on the hill of Troy are significant as revealing the spirit which the young king carried into his enterprise. They show how he was imbued with Greek scriptures and Greek traditions; how his descent from Achilles was part of his life, part of his inspiration; how he regarded himself as chosen to be the hero of another episode in the drama, whereof the first act had been illustrated by the deeds of that glorious ancestor.

The crossing of the Hellespont, 334 B.C.

Alexander at Troy.

Advance of a Persian army to the Granicus Meanwhile the satraps of the Great King had formed an army of about 40,000 men to defend Asia Minor. If he had entrusted the command to the Rhodian Memnon, it is possible that some effective defence might have been made; but he committed the characteristic blunder of a Persian monarch, and consigned the army to the joint command of a number of generals, including Memnon and several of the western satraps. The Persian commanders were jealous of the Greek, and against his advice they decided to risk a battle at once. Accordingly they advanced from Zelea, where they had mustered, to the plain of Adrastea, through which the river Granicus flows into the Propontis, and posted themselves on the steep left bank of the stream, so as to hinder the enemy from crossing. Alexander and

Advance of Alexander. his army advanced eastward from Abydus, and received the submission of Lampsacus, and then of Priapus, a town near the mouth of the Granicus. It was impossible for him to avoid the combat, which the Persians desired; he could not march southward, leaving them in his rear. But he courted the combat even more than they; for the worst thing that could have befallen him (as Memnon knew well) was that the hostile army should persistently retire before him, eating up the provisions of the country as it retreated.

Position of the armies. With his heavy infantry in two columns and his horse on the wings, Alexander marched across the Adrastean plain. The Persians had made the curious disposition of placing their cavalry along the river bank and the Greek hoplites on the slopes behind. As cavalry in attack has a great advantage over cavalry in defence, Alexander saw that the victory could best be won by throwing his own squadrons against the hostile line. Parmenio advised him to wait till the following morning and cross the river at daybreak before the foe were drawn up in array. "I should be ashamed," said the king, "having crossed the Hellespont, to be detained by a miserable stream like the Granicus"; an answer such as Alexander loved to give, veiling under the appearance of negligent daring a self-confidence which was perfectly justified by his strategic insight.

Battle of the Granicus (334 B.C., May-June) Drawing up his army in the usual way (which has been described above), with the six regiments of the phalanx in the centre, entrusting the left wing to Parmenio and commanding the right himself, Alexander first sent across the river his light cavalry to keep the extreme left of the enemy engaged, and then led his heavy Macedonian cavalry against the Persian centre. Alexander himself was in the thickest of the fight, dealing wounds and receiving blows. After a sharp mellay on the steep banks, the Persian cavalry was broken and put to flight. The phalanx then advanced across the

river against the Greek hoplites in the background, while the victorious cavalry cut them up on the flanks.

This victory, in winning which Alexander drank to the full the
mad excitement of battle, cost few lives to the Macedonians and
cleared out of their way the only army which was to oppose their
progress in Asia Minor. But it was very far from laying Asia Minor
at the conqueror's feet. There were strong places, which must be
taken one by one—strong places on the coast, which could be supported by the powerful Persian fleet. Of all things, the help of the
Athenian navy would have best bestead Alexander now, and he did
not yet despair. After the skirmish of the Granicus, when he divided
the spoil, he sent 300 Persian panoplies to Athens, as an offering to
Athena on the Acropolis, with this dedication: "Alexander, son of
Philip, and the Greeks (except the Lacedaemonians), from the barbarians of Asia." But Athens had no zeal for the cause of the Greeks
and Alexander against the barbarians.

The victor entrusted the satrapy of Hellespontine Phrygia to
Callas, making no change in the method of the Persian administration; and marched southward to occupy the satrapy of Lydia and
the rock of Sardis, girt with its threefold wall. It was a little more
than 200 years since Cyrus had overthrown the Lydian kingdom
and Sardis had become the chief burg of Persian power in the west.
The citadel was strong and capable of a stout defence, but it now
passed with its treasures unresistingly into the hands of the Greek
conqueror. For this prompt submission the Lydians received their
freedom and the ancestral constitution, which had been suspended
during the long period of Persian domination. Alexander resolved to
build a temple to the Olympian Zeus on the citadel. It was said that
a thunder shower falling on the site of the royal palace showed him
the fitting place for the sanctuary; the spot where a more famous
thunder shower had quenched the pyre of the last Lydian king.

Parmenio's brother, Asander, was appointed satrap of Lydia, and
Alexander turned to deal with the Ionian cities. Here, as was to be
expected, everything depended on the strength of the political
parties. The democrats welcomed the Greek deliverer; but the
oligarchs supported the Persian cause, and wherever they were in
power, admitted Persian garrisons. In Ephesus the oligarchy had
got the upper hand, but on the approach of Alexander's army the
garrison left the city and the people began to massacre the oligarchs.
Alexander pacified these troubles and established a democratic constitution. He abode some time in the city, and during this sojourn
the painter Apelles executed a famous picture of the king, wielding

Submis-
sion of
Lydia.

lightning in his hand, which was set up in the temple of Artemis.

The next stage in the advance of Alexander was Miletus, and here for the first time he encountered resistance. The Persian garrison was commanded by a Greek, who had at first meditated surrender, but learning that the Persian fleet was at hand in full force, decided to brave a siege. In an earlier episode of the struggle between Europe and Asia, we witnessed memorable operations in the Latmian gulf and the Milesian harbours, which the retreat of the sea has blotted from the map. The isle of Lade, then associated with the triumph of Asia, was now to play a part in the triumph of Europe. The Macedonian fleet, of 160 galleys, sailed into the bay and occupied the harbour of Lade, before the great fleet of the enemy arrived. When the Persian vessels came and saw that they had been forestalled, they anchored off the promontory of Mycale. The city of Miletus consisted of two parts, an outer city which Alexander easily occupied as soon as he came up, and an inner city strongly fortified with wall and fosse. Alexander threw up a rampart round the inner city, and placed troops in the island of Lade. Miletus was easily stormed by the Macedonian siege engines, and the fleet blocking the harbour hindered the Persian squadron from bringing help.

Parmenio had urged the king to risk a battle on the water, though the enemy's ships were nearly three to one, but Alexander rejected the advice. He had judged the whole situation, and he had made up his mind that the Persian sea-power would have to be conquered on land. If Athens had sent him naval reinforcements it might have been otherwise, but he now despaired of active help from Greece, and he decided that it was an useless drain on his treasury to main-

tain 160 galleys, too few to cope with the 400 of the enemy. Accordingly he disbanded the fleet, after the fall of Miletus, and proceeded to blockade the sea by seizing all the strong places on the shores of the Eastern Mediterranean. The execution of this design occupied him for the next two years, but it brought with it the conquest of Asia Minor, Syria, and Egypt.

The manifest objection to the dissolution of the naval force was that, in case a decisive defeat at the hands of the Great King should compel him to retreat, he would have no fleet to transport his army from Asia to Europe, and the fleet of the enemy, by occupying the straits at either end of the Propontis, could entirely cut him off. But Alexander trusted his own strategy; he knew that he would not be compelled to retreat.

As for Asia Minor, the next and the hardest task was the reduction of Caria and the capture of Halicarnassus. The remnant of the host which fled from the Granicus, and the Rhodian Memnon himself, had rallied here and rested their last hopes in the strong city of Mausolus, with its three mighty citadels. The Great King had now entrusted to Memnon the general command of the fleet and the coasts, and Memnon had dug a deep fosse round Halicarnassus, furnished the place with food for a long siege, and placed garrisons in the smaller neighbouring towns. Halicarnassus was to be the centre of a supreme resistance.

There had once been a chance that Alexander himself might have been, by a personal right, lord of Halicarnassus. The prince Pixodarus, one of the brothers of Mausolus, had wished to form an alliance of marriage with the house of Macedon, and Alexander had thought of offering himself as a bridegroom for his daughter. But Philip would not hear of such a match, and Pixodarus had given the maiden to a Persian noble, who had succeeded to the dynasty after his father-in-law's death. There was indeed another claimant to the dynasty, Ada, wife and sister of Idrieus. She had succeeded her husband as ruler, and had been driven out by her brother Pixodarus. She now sought the protection of Alexander, and when he captured Halicarnassus, he assigned to her the satrapy of Caria. It was destined that women should represent Caria in the two great collisions of Greece with Persia, in the days of Alexander as in the days of Xerxes; the submission of Ada atoned for the bravery of Artemisia.

The last rulers of the dynasty of Mausolus

Ada.

Having made a futile attack on Myndus, Alexander filled up the moat with which Memnon had encompassed Halicarnassus, and brought his towers and engines against the walls. A breach was made on the north-east side near to the gate of the road to Mylasa, but Alexander, who hoped to induce the town to surrender, forbore to order an attack. His hands were almost forced by two soldiers of the phalanx, who, one day drinking together in their tent and bragging of their prowess, flushed with wine and the zeal of rivalry, put on their armour, and marching up to the wall, challenged the enemy to come out. The men on the wall seeing them alone rushed out in numbers, and the twain were hard pressed till their comrades came to the rescue, and there was a sharp fight under the walls. But even now, Alexander would not order an attack on the breach, and the besieged built a new crescent wall connecting the two points between which the wall had been broken down, and maintained themselves behind it for a time. At length they made a great excursion against the camp of the besiegers at two different places. On both sides they were driven back in confusion, and in their haste to shut the gates they left many of their fellows to perish. At this moment an assault would doubtless have carried the Macedonians within the walls, but Alexander gave the signal to retire, still intent on sav-

Siege of Halicarnassus, autumn, 334 B.C.

ing the city. Memnon saw that the prospect of holding out longer was hopeless, and he determined to withdraw the garrison to the citadel of Salmacis and the royal fortress on the island in the harbour. He fired the city at night before he withdrew, and the place was in flames when the Macedonians entered. Alexander destroyed what the fire spared, and left a body of mercenary soldiers under Ptolemy to blockade Salmacis and support the princess of Caria.

Division of the army.

The cold season was approaching and Alexander divided his army into two bodies, one of which he sent under Parmenio to winter in Lydia, while he advanced himself with the other into Lycia. He gave leave to a few young officers who had been recently wedded to return to their Macedonian homes, charging them with the duty of bringing reinforcements to the army in spring, and appointing Gordion in Phrygia as the mustering-place of the whole host.

Lycia submits. Advance through Pamphylia and Pisidia.

Alexander met with no resistance from the cities of the Lycian League, and he left the constitution of the confederacy intact. From the rich frontier town of Phasēlis he advanced along the coast of Pamphylia, receiving the submission of Perge and Aspendus and other maritime cities; and then he turned inland from Perge, and fought his way through the Pisidian hills, taking with some trouble Sagalassus, the chief fastness of the Pisidian mountaineers. He descended to Celaenae, the strong and lofty citadel of the Phrygian satrapy, and leaving a garrison there, he marched on to Gordion on the Sangarius, the capital of the ancient kingdom of Phrygia.

Trans- actions in the Aegean.

While he was winning the Lycian and Phrygian satrapies, he lost, for the moment, some points in the Aegean. Memnon, appointed commander of the Persian fleet, had taken Chios, reduced the greater part of Lesbos, and laid siege to Mytilene. He died during the siege, but Mytilene soon surrendered, and then Tenedos was compelled to recognise the "Peace which the king sent down." The great danger for Alexander was that these successes might encourage the Greeks to revolt, and ten Persian ships sailed as far west as Siphnos for the purpose of exciting a movement in Hellas. But eight of these vessels were captured by some Macedonian triremes which ran over from Chalcis, and the project of a Greek rising was not carried out.

At Gordion, 333 B.C.

At Gordion, the appointed mustering-place, Alexander's army reunited, and new troops arrived from Macedonia to replace those who had been left to garrison the subjugated countries and cities. On the citadel of Gordion stood the remains of the royal palaces of Gordius and Midas, and Alexander went up the hill to see the chariot of Gordius and the famous knot which fastened the yoke. Cord of the bark of a cornel-tree was tied in a knot which artfully concealed the ends, and there was an oracle that he who should loose it would rule over Asia. Alexander vainly attempted to untie it, and then drawing his sword cut the knot and so fulfilled the oracle. From Gordion Alexander marched by Ancyra into Cappadocia. Having received the submission of Paphlagonia and asserted rather than confirmed his authority over the Cappadocian satrapy, he marched southward to Tyana and the Cilician gates. It was well that Alexander should show himself for a moment in the centre of Asia Minor, but the reduction of these wild regions and of the southern coast of Pontus was a task which might safely be postponed. The Cilician gates might have easily been defended by the garrison which the satrap Arsames had posted in the pass. Alexander, with the hypaspists and other light troops, leaving the rest of his army in camp, marched up at night to surprise the station. As soon as the guards heard the footfalls of the approachers they fled; and then Alexander at the head of his cavalry moved so rapidly on Tarsus that Arsames, amazed at his sudden appearance, fled without striking a blow.

Advance to Cilicia

Here a misadventure happened which well-nigh changed the course of history. After a long ride under a burning sun, the king bathed in the cool waters of the Cydnus, which flows through Tarsus. He caught a chill which resulted in violent fever and sleepless nights, and his physicians despaired of his life. But Philip of Acarnania, who was eminent for his medical skill, recommended a certain purgative. As he was preparing the draught in the king's tent, a letter was placed in Alexander's hands. It was from Parmenio, and was a warning against Philip, alleging that Darius had bribed him to poison his master. Alexander taking the cup, gave Philip the letter to read, and, while Philip read, Alexander swallowed the medicine. His generous confidence was justified, and under the care of Philip he soon recovered from his sickness.

At Tarsus.

SECT. 6. BATTLE OF ISSUS

The Great King had already crossed the Euphrates at the head of a vast host. He had let the invader subjugate Asia Minor, but he now came in person to bar his further progress. Alexander did not hurry to the encounter, and his delay, as we shall see, turned to his profit in an unexpected manner. Sending forward Parmenio with part of the army to secure the passes from Cilicia into Syria, Alexander himself turned to subdue western Cilicia. He first visited Anchialus, noted for the statue of the Assyrian king Sardanapalus, and the famous inscription: "Sardanapalus founded Anchialus and

Reduction of Cilicia. At Anchialus.

Tarsus on the same day. But thou, O stranger, eat, drink, and sport; all else is worthless." Having seen this comment on his own ambi-

At Soli.

tious dreams, Alexander went on to Soli, the city of "solecisms," an ultimate Greek outpost, where men had almost forgotten Greek institutions and Greek speech. From here he made an excursion against the Cilician hill-folks, and reduced the whole district in seven days. He then returned eastward, and advanced to Issus

At Issus, 333 B.C., Oct.

under Mount Amanus.

Darius was on the other side of the mountains, in the plain of Sochoi, on ground which was highly favourable for deploying his host. There were two roads from Issus into Syria. One led directly over difficult mountain-passes, while the other wound along the coast to Myriandros and then crossed Mount Amanus. The second road, along which we formerly accompanied Cyrus and Xenophon,

At Myriander.

was now chosen by Alexander. Leaving his sick at Issus, he marched forward to Myriandros, but was detained there by a violent storm of rain, for it was already the beginning of winter. The Great King, informed by Arsames of the rapid approach of Alexander, expected every day to see him descending from the mountains. And when he came not, owing to the delays in Cilicia, it was thought that he held back through fear, and did not venture to desert the coast. Accord-

Advance of the Persians to Issus,

ingly Darius and his nobles decided to seek Alexander. The Persian army crossed the northern passes of Amanus and reached Issus, where they tortured and put to death the sick who had been left behind. Alexander cannot be blamed for this disaster, for he could not foresee that his enemies would commit such an incredible military error as to abandon the open position in which their numerical superiority would tell for a confined place where the movements of a multitude would be cramped. To Alexander the tidings that Darius was at Issus was too good to be true, and he sent a boat to

and return of Alexander.

reconnoitre. When he was assured that the enemy had thus played into his hands, he marched back from Myriandros through the sea-gates into the little plain of Issus.

Position of the armies at Issus.

The plain of Issus is cut in two by the stream of the Pinarus, which was to play the same part in the coming battle as the Granicus had played in the plain of Adrastea. Here, as in that first skirmish, it fell to Alexander to attack the Persians, who had themselves no plan of attack; and here as there the Persians were defended by the natural entrenchment of a steep-banked river. The Macedonian columns defiled into the plain at dawn, and when Darius learned that they were approaching he threw across the river 50,000 cavalry and light troops to cover the rest of the army while it arrayed itself for battle. As his host was numbered by tens of thousands and the plain was only three miles broad, it is clear that most of his troops were forced to remain behind as reserves. The whole front was composed of hoplites—30,000 Greek mercenaries, and regiments of orientals called *Kardakes;* the left wing touched the lower slopes of the mountains and curved round, following the line of the hill, so as to face the flank of the enemy's right wing. When the array was formed, the cavalry was recalled to the north of the river, and posted on the right wing, near the sea, where the ground was best adapted for cavalry movements.

Alexander advanced, his army drawn up on the usual plan, the phalanx in the centre, the hypaspists on the right. At first he placed the Thessalian as well as the Macedonian cavalry on the right wing, in order to strengthen his own cavalry attack, but when he saw that all the Persian cavalry was concentrated on the sea side, he was obliged to transfer the Thessalians to their usual position on his own left. In order to meet the danger which threatened the flank and rear of his right wing from the Persian forces on the slope of the mountain, he placed a column of light troops on the extreme right, to form a second front. As in the engagement on the Granicus, the attack was to be made by the heavy cavalry on the left centre of the enemy's line. But it was a far more serious and formidable venture. Those who had read the story of the battle of Cunaxa might despise an Asiatic multitude, but Darius had 30,000 Greek mercenaries who knew how to stand and to fight. And if Alexander was defeated, his retreat was cut off.

Arrangement of Alexander's troops.

The Persian left did not sustain Alexander's onset at the head of his cavalry. The phalanx followed more slowly, and in crossing the stream and climbing the steep bank the line became dislocated, especially at one spot, and the Greek hoplites pressed them hard on the river-brink. If the phalanx had been driven back, Alexander's victorious right wing would have been exposed on the flank and the battle lost; but the phalangites stood their ground obstinately, until the hypaspists were free to come to their help by taking their adversaries in the flank. Meanwhile Alexander's attack had been directed upon the spot where the Great King himself stood in his warchariot, surrounded by a guard of Persian nobles. There was a furious, mellay, in which Alexander was wounded in his leg. Then Darius turned his chariot and fled, and this was the signal for an universal flight on the left. On the sea side the Persian cavalry crossed the river and carried all before them; but in the midst of their success the cry that the king was fleeing made them waver, and they were soon riding wildly back, pursued by the Thessalians. The whole Persian host was now rushing northward towards the

Battle.

passes of Amanus, and thousands fell beneath the swords of their pursuers. Darius did not tarry; he forgot even his mother and his wife who were in the camp at Issus; and when he reached the mountain he left his chariot, his shield, and his royal cloak behind him, and mounting a swift mare rode for dear life.

Having pursued the Great King till nightfall and found his relics by the wayside, Alexander returned to the Persian camp. He supped

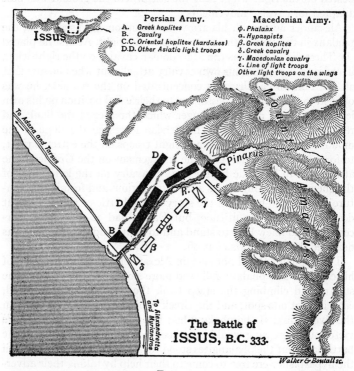

Persian Army.
A. Greek hoplites
B. Cavalry
C.C. Oriental hoplites (kardakes)
D.D. Other Asiatic light troops

Macedonian Army.
φ. Phalanx
α. Hypaspists
β. Greek hoplites
δ. Greek cavalry
γ. Macedonian cavalry
ε. Line of light troops
Other light troops on the wings

The Battle of
ISSUS, B.C. 333.

Walker & Boutall sc.

FIG. 102.

in the tent of Darius, and there fell upon his ears a noise and the wailing of women from a tent hard by. He asked who the women were, and why they were lodged so near, and learned that it was the mother and wife and children of the fugitive king. They had been told that Alexander had returned with the shield and cloak of Darius, and, supposing that their lord was dead, had broken out into lamentation. Alexander sent one of his companions to comfort them with the assurance that Darius lived, and that they would receive, while they were in Alexander's power, all the respect and consideration due to royal ladies; for Alexander had no personal enmity against Darius. No act of Alexander, perhaps, astonished his contemporaries more than this generous treatment of the family of his royal rival. His ideal hero Achilles would not have resisted the charm of the captive queen Statira, the most beautiful of women. But the charms of love had no temptation for Alexander; and his behaviour to the captives was prompted not only by his natively humane and generous feelings, but by the instinct and policy of a royal invader to display respect for royalty as such.

Thus was the Persian host, which had come to "trample down" Alexander and his little army, annihilated on the plain of Issus. A city, which still retains the name of Alexander, was built in commemoration of the battle, at the northern end of the sea-gates. The road was now open into Syria; this was the immediate military result of the battle of Issus. Just as the small fight on the Granicus had cleared the way for the acquisition of Asia Minor, so the fight on the Pinaros cleared the way for the conquest of Syria and Egypt. The rest of the work would consist in tedious sieges. But the victory of Issus had, beyond its immediate results, immense importance through the prestige which it conferred on the victor. He had defeated an army ten times as great as his own, led by the Great King in person, whom he had driven back over the mountains in ignominious flight; he had captured the mother of the Great King, and his wife and his children. Darius himself unbent his haughty Persian pride, when he had reached safety beyond the Euphrates, so far as to make the first overtures to the conqueror. He wrote a letter, in which he complained that Alexander was an unprovoked aggressor, begged that he would send back the royal captives, and professed willingness to conclude a treaty of friendship and alliance. It was much for a Persian king to bring himself to write this, but such a condescending appeal required a stern reply. We are fortunate enough to possess the text of Alexander's answer, which seems to have been published as a sort of manifesto to Europe as well as Asia. It was to this effect:—

Foundation of Alexandria at Issus (Alexandretta)

"Your ancestors invaded Macedonia and the rest of Greece, and without provocation inflicted wrongs upon us. I was appointed leader of the Greeks, and crossed over into Asia for the purpose of avenging those wrongs; for ye were the first aggressors. In the next place, ye assisted the people of Perinthus, who were offenders against my father, and Ochus sent a force into Thrace, which was part of our empire. Further, the conspirators who slew my father were suborned by you, as ye yourselves boasted in your letters.

A state document of Alexander: letter to Darius, 333 B.C.

Thou with the help of Bagoas didst murder Arses [son of Ochus] and seize the throne unjustly and contrary to the law of the Persians, and then thou didst write improper letters regarding me to the Greeks, to incite them to war against me, and didst send to the Lacedaemonians and others of the Greeks, for the same purpose, sums of money (whereof none of the other cities partook, but only the Lacedaemonians); and thine emissaries corrupted my friends and tried to dissolve the peace which I had brought about in Greece. Wherefore I marched forth against thee, who wert thus the aggressor in the quarrel. I have overcome in battle, first thy generals and satraps, and now thyself and thine host, and possess thy land, through the grace of the gods. Those who fought on thy side and were not slain, but took refuge with me, are under my protection, and are glad to be with me, and will fight with me henceforward. I am lord of all Asia, and therefore do thou come to me. If thou art afraid of being evilly entreated, send some of thy friends to receive sufficient guarantees. Thou hast only to come to me to ask and receive thy mother and wife and children, and whatever else thou mayest desire. And for the future, whenever thou sendest, send to me as to the Great King of Asia, and do not write as to an equal, but tell me whatever thy need be, as to one who is lord of all that is thine. Otherwise I will deal with thee as an offender. But if thou disputest the kingdom, then wait and fight for it again, and do not flee; for I will march against thee wherever thou mayest be."

The treasures which Darius had brought with him into Syria had been sent for safety to Damascus when he crossed the passes of Mount Amanus. Accordingly Alexander sent Parmenio to take possession of them. Parmenio found at Damascus some Greek envoys who had arrived at the camp of Darius a short time before the battle—one Spartan, one Athenian, and two Thebans. Alexander detained the Spartan as a prisoner, kept the Athenian as a friend, and let the Thebans go free. His clemency to the Thebans was due to a certain compunction which he always felt for the hard measure dealt out to their city; while a personal motive dictated his favour to the Athenian, Iphicrates, son of the great general of the same name, whose memory was highly esteemed in Macedonia. The incident showed that Greece, which had openly chosen Alexander for her leader, was secretly intriguing with Persia. When it was known that Darius was crossing the Euphrates, men were hoping and praying at Athens that the Macedonians would be trodden down by the Persian host. A hundred fast-sailing Persian ships appeared at Siphnos, and Agis the Spartan king visited the commanders, asking for money and galleys to carry out a project of rebellion against

Greek intrigues with the Persian king.

Persian squadron at Siphnos. Activity of Agis.

Macedonia. At Athens, Hypereides agitated for open war, but Demosthenes prudently counselled his fellow-citizens to wait until the expected catastrophe of Alexander had become an accomplished fact. Then the news came that the leader of the Greeks had won a brilliant victory, and Greece had to cloak her disappointment. The Persian squadron hurried back to save what could be saved on the Asiatic coast, and only thirty talents and ten vessels could be spared to Agis, who used them to secure the island of Crete.

Disappointment in Greece at the news of Issus.

SECT. 7. CONQUEST OF SYRIA

It might seem that the course plainly marked out for the victor of Issus was to pursue and overwhelm Darius before he should have time to collect another army; and this is what Darius himself would

Strategic plan of — Alexander's conquest.

FIG. 103.—Coin of Phaestus in Crete (obverse). Resting Heracles; bow and quiver on tree; vase behind [legend: ΦΑΙΣΤΙ(ων)]. FIG. 104.—Coin of Cydonia (obverse). Ivy-crowned head of Dionysus. FIG. 105.—Coin of Cnossus (obverse). Head of Argive Hera.

have done if he had been Alexander. But it would have been a strategical error to plunge into the heart of the Persian empire, leaving Syria and Egypt unsubdued behind him and a Persian fleet controlling the coast. The victory of Issus did not seduce Alexander into swerving from his inevitable course; the strategic value of that victory was simply that it opened the gates to Syria and Egypt. As the subjugation of Asia Minor was the strategic condition of subjugating Syria and Egypt, so the conquest of Syria and Egypt was the strategic condition of conquering Mesopotamia and Iran. It was the more imperative to follow this logical order of conquest, since Phoenicia supplied the main part of the hostile navy, and nothing but the reduction of the Phoenician towns would effectually break down the sea-power of Persia. No one could swoop more swiftly than Alexander when it was the hour to swoop; but never did he display his superior command of the art of war more signally

than when he let the royal prey escape him and quietly carried out
the plan of conquest which he had predestined.

Conditio'
of Phoe-
nicia

The Persian kings had allowed the Phoenician traders to go on
their own way, and meddled little with their prosperous cities, so
long as the Phoenician navy was at the disposal of Persia. If these
strong and wealthy semi-insular cities of the coast, cut off as they
were from the inner country by the high range of Lebanon, had
formed a solid federal union, they might have easily succeeded in
winning complete independence in the days of Persian decadence.
But though Tyre, Sidon, and Aradus were bound together by a federal bond, their commercial interests clashed and their jealousies
hindered a hearty national effort. This had been illustrated by a
recent experience. When Sidon revolted from Persia, in the reign of
Artaxerxes Ochus, her two sister cities promised at a federal meeting to stand by her. But both Tyre and Aradus selfishly calculated

FIG. 106.—Silver coin of Sidon (? 374-62 B.C.). Obverse: galley in front of
city wall; below two lions. Reverse: king and charioteer in chariot; below
goat (incuse). FIG. 107.—Silver coin of Sidon (330 B.C.). Obverse: king in
chariot; servant with sceptre and flask behind [Phoenician legend: 'AB
(? Abdalonymus)]. Reverse: galley; waves.

that if Sidon were crushed and punished, her trade would come to
themselves, and they left her to maintain the struggle alone. She
succumbed to the power of Ochus, her town was burnt down, and
she lost her rights as a city.

The divisions, which prevented the Phoenicians from becoming
a nation, were profitable to Alexander. If their united fleet, which
was now acting ineffectually in Aegean waters, had acted energetically in defence of their own coast against the Macedonian, their
cities would have been impregnable even to Alexander. But those
cities could not trust each other. Byblus, which had in some measure taken the place of Sidon, and Aradus sent their submission to
the conqueror of Issus; while dismantled Sidon, which still contributed some ships to the fleet, hoped to be reinstated in her old
position by the favour of Persia's foe. Her hope was not disap-

pointed. Alexander restored to Sidon her constitution and her territory.

It cannot have been long after this that a kingling of Sidon was laid in a resting-place worthy of the great conqueror himself. His sculptured sarcophagus, recently dug up in a burying-ground of the Sidonian kings, is one of the most beautiful achievements of Greek art. But we may well associate this monument with Alexander, rather than with the obscure Phoenician for whose ashes it was made. For in two of the vivid scenes which are represented in coloured relief upon its sides, Alexander appears on horseback. One of these is a passage from the battle of Issus. There is a mellay in the centre; the king charges on this side; a general, perhaps Parmenio, on that. The other scene is a lion-hunt, and here, if Alexander were not marked out by the royal fillet, we might almost recognise him by his eager straining face.

The sarco-phagus (vulgarly called of Alex-ander).

Alexander advanced southward towards Tyre. Ambassadors from this city met him on the road, professing the readiness of the Tyrians to do his will. Alexander expressed his intention of visiting the city, in order to sacrifice in the famous temple of Heracles. But a Macedonian visit was far from the wish of the men of Tyre. Persia was not yet subdued, and their policy was to await the event, and avoid compromising themselves by a premature adhesion to Macedonia. They felt secure on their island rock, which was protected by eighty ships, apart from the squadron which was absent in the Aegean. Accordingly they invited Alexander to sacrifice in Old Tyre on the mainland, but refused to "receive either Persian or Macedonian into the city."

Tyre de-fies Alex-ander, 333 B.C., Dec.

To subdue Tyre was an absolute necessity, as Alexander explained to a council of his generals and captains which he called together. It was not safe to advance to Egypt, or to pursue Darius, while the Persians were lords of the sea; and the only way of wresting their sea-power from them was to capture Tyre, the most important naval station on the coast; once Tyre fell, the Phoenician fleet, which was the most numerous and strongest part of the Persian navy, would come over to Macedon, for the rowers would not row or the men fight when they had no habitations to row or fight for. The reduction of Cyprus and Egypt would then follow without trouble. Alexander grasped and never let go the fact that Tyre was the key to the whole situation.

It was easy to say that Tyre must be captured; but it was not easy to say how, without a powerful navy, its capture could be achieved. This was perhaps the hardest military task that Alexander's genius ever encountered. The city, girt by walls of great

Siege of Tyre, Jan to July, 332 B.C.

height and magnificently strong masonry, stood on an island severed from the continent by a sound of more than half a mile in
width. On the side which faced the mainland were the two harbours:
the northern or Sidonian harbour with a narrow mouth, and the
southern or Egyptian. It might seem utterly hopeless for an enemy,
vastly inferior at sea, to attempt a siege of the island Rock. And in

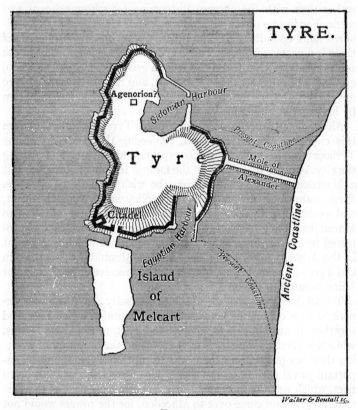

FIG. 108.

truth there was only one way for a land-power to set about the task.
Those thousand yards of water must be bridged over and the isle
annexed to the mainland. Without hesitation Alexander began the
building of the causeway. The first part of the work was easy, for
the water was shallow; but when the mole approached the island,
the strait deepened, the workmen came within range of the walls,

and the difficulties of the task began. Triremes issued from the havens on either side to shoot missiles at the men who were at work. To protect them Alexander erected two towers on the causeway, and mounted engines on the towers to reply to the missiles from the galleys. He attached to these wooden towers curtains of leather to screen both towers and workmen from the projectiles which were hurled from the city walls. But the men of Tyre were ingenious. They constructed a fire-ship filled with dry wood and inflammables, and choosing a day on which a favourable wind blew, they towed it close to the dam and set it on fire. The device succeeded; the burning vessel soon wrapt the towers and all the engines in flames, and the triremes which had towed it up discharged showers of darts at the Macedonians who attempted to extinguish the fire. The Tyrians too rowed across from their island in boats and tore up the stakes at the unfinished part of the mole.

Undismayed by this disaster, which seemed to show the hopelessness of the enterprise, Alexander only went to work more vigorously. It was necessary to take Tyre, and he was determined that Tyre should be taken. He widened the causeway throughout its whole length, so that it could accommodate more towers and engines, before he attempted to complete it. He saw that it would be needful to support his operations from the causeway by operations from shipboard; and he went to Sidon to bring up a few galleys which were stationed there. But at this moment the aspect of affairs was suddenly changed by the accession to Alexander of naval forces which enabled him to cope with Tyre at an advantage on her own element. The squadrons of Aradus and Byblus which were acting in the Aegean, learning that their cities had submitted to Alexander, left the fleet and sailed to Sidon, which the Macedonians had chosen as their naval station. These Phoenician ships were about eighty; and at the same time there came nine galleys from Rhodes and ten from Lycia and Cilicia. The adhesion of the kings of Cyprus presently followed, and reinforced the fleet at Sidon by 120 ships. With a fleet of about 250 triremes at his command, Alexander was now far stronger at sea than the merchants of Tyre, and though the siege of the mighty stronghold was still a formidable task, it was no longer superhuman.

While the fleet was being made ready in the roads of Sidon, and the engineers were fabricating new siege-engines to batter down the walls of Tyre, Alexander made an expedition, at the head of his light troops, to punish the native brigands who infested the hills of Antilibanon, and made the traffic between the coast and the hinterland unsafe. Perhaps it was now that he received an embassy from

Embassy
from
Darius.

the Great King, offering an immense ransom for the captives of the royal house, and the surrender of all the lands west of the Euphrates; proposing also that Alexander should marry the daughter of Darius and become his ally. The message was discussed in a council, and Parmenio said that if he were Alexander he would accept the terms. "And I," said the king, "would accept them if I were Parmenio." Alexander was resolved to carry out his plan of conquest to the end; he would agree to no compromise. He bade the ambassadors say that he would receive neither money nor provinces in lieu of the whole empire of Darius, for that all the land and possessions of Darius were his; he would marry the daughter of Darius if he chose, whether Darius willed it or not; and if Darius wished for any boon he must come himself and ask it.

From Sidon Alexander bore down upon Tyre with his whole fleet, hoping to entice the Tyrians into an engagement. He commanded the right wing, while the left was committed to the charge of Craterus, and Pnytagoras the king of Cypriote Salamis. When the fleet hove in sight, the men of Tyre were astonished and dismayed. Before, they would gladly have given battle, but they saw that they had no chance against so many, and they drew up their triremes in close array to block the mouths of their harbours. Alexander set the Cyprian vessels on the north side of the mole to blockade the Sidonian harbour, and the Phoenician on the south side to blockade the Egyptian harbour. It was opposite this harbour, on the mainland, that his own pavilion was placed.

The mole had now been carried up to the island, and engineers, the best that Phoenicia and Cyprus could furnish, had prepared the engines of war. All was ready for a grand attack on the eastern wall. Some of the engines were placed on the mole, others on transport ships or superannuated galleys. But little impression was made on the wall, which on this side was 150 feet high and enormously thick; and the besieged replied to the attack with volleys of fiery missiles from powerful engines, which were mounted on their lofty battlements. Moreover, the machine-bearing vessels could not come close enough to the walls for effective action; huge stones lying under the water hindered their approach. Alexander decided that these must at all cost be removed; and galleys with windlasses were anchored at the spot in order to drag the boulders away. It was a slow task, and was thwarted by the Tyrians. Covered vessels shot out of the havens and cut the anchor-ropes of the galleys, so that they drifted away. Alexander tried to meet this by placing boats similarly decked close to the anchors; but even this failed, since Tyrian divers swam under water and cut the cables. The only resource was to attach the anchors with chains instead of ropes, and by this means the stones were hauled away and the ships could approach the wall.

The Tyrians now resorted to a last device. They spread the sails of all the ships which were riding at the entrance of the northern harbour, and behind this curtain of canvas, which screened them from the observation of the enemy, they manned seven triremes, three five-oared and three four-oared boats, with the coolest and bravest of their seamen, and waiting for the hour of noon, when the sailors of the besieging vessels used generally to disembark and Alexander himself used to retire to his tent, they rowed noiselessly towards the Cyprian squadron, which was taken completely by surprise, sank some of the vessels at once, and drove the rest on the strand. It happened that on this day Alexander remained for a shorter time than usual in his pavilion; and when he returned to his station with the Phoenician ships on the south side of the mole, discovering what had happened, he stationed the main part of these ships close to the Egyptian harbour to prevent the enemy from making any movement on this side, and taking with him some five-oared boats and five swift-sailing galleys he sailed round the island. The men in the city saw Alexander and all that he did, and signalled to their own crews who were engaged in battering the stranded Cyprian vessels; but the signals were not seen or heard until Alexander was close upon them. When they saw him coming, they desisted from their work and made all speed for the haven, but the greater number of their boats were disabled by Alexander's vessels before they reached the harbour mouth. Henceforward the ships of Tyre lay useless in the harbours, unable to do anything for the defence of the island.

It was now a struggle between the engineers of Tyre and the engineers of Alexander. The wall opposite to the mole defied all machines of battery and methods of assault, and the northern part of the same eastern wall, though the big stones had been cleared away from the water below it, proved equally impracticable. Accordingly the efforts of the besiegers were united upon the south side near the Egyptian harbour. Here at length a bit of the wall was torn down, and there was fighting in the breach, but the Tyrians easily repelled the attack. It was an encouragement for Alexander, it showed him the weak spot, and two days later he prepared a grand and supreme assault.

The vessels with the siege engines were set to work at the southern wall, while two triremes waited hard by, one filled with hypaspists under Admetus, the other with a phalanx regiment, ready as soon as the wall yielded to hurl their crews into the breach. Ships were stationed in front of the two havens, to force their way in at a favourable moment, and the rest of the fleet, manned with light troops and furnished with engines, were disposed at various points round the island, to embarrass and bewilder the besieged and hinder them from concentrating at the main point of attack. A wide breach was made, the two triremes were rowed up to the spot, the bridges were lowered, and the hypaspists, Admetus at their head, first mounted the wall. Admetus was pierced with a lance, but Alexander took his place, and drove back the Tyrians from the breach. Tower after tower was captured; soon all the southern wall was in the hands of the Macedonians, and Alexander was able to make his way along the battlements to the royal palace, which was the best base for attacking the city. But the city had been already entered from other points. The chains of both the Sidonian and the Egyptian harbours had been burst by the Cyprian and Phoenician squadrons; the Tyrian ships had been disabled; and the troops had pressed into the town. The inhabitants made their last stand in a place called the Agenorion. Eight thousand are said to have been slain, and the rest of the people, about 30,000, were sold into slavery, with the exception of the king, Azemilco, and a few men of high position, who were set at liberty.

The siege had been long and wearisome, but the time and the labour were not too dear a price. The fall of Tyre gave Alexander Syria and Egypt, and the naval supremacy in the eastern Mediterranean. He performed the sacrifice to Heracles in the temple to which the Tyrians had refused him access, and celebrated the solemnity with a torch procession and games. The communities of Syria and Palestine, that had not submitted, like Damascus, after the victory of Issus, submitted now after the capture of Tyre, and he encountered no resistance in his southern march to Egypt, until he came to the great frontier stronghold, Gaza, the city of the Philistines.

Southward advance of Alexander.

Siege of Gaza, Oct.-Nov. 332 B.C.

Girt with a stout wall Gaza stood on a high rising-ground, and more than two miles of sand lay between the city and the seashore, so that a fleet was no help to a besieger. The place had been committed by Darius to the care of Batis, a trusty eunuch, and had been well furnished with provisions for a long siege. Batis refused to surrender, trusting in the strength of the fortifications, and at the first sight the engineers of Alexander declared that the wall could never be stormed on account of the height of the hill on which it stood. But Alexander was now accustomed to overcome the insuperable, and the conqueror who sacked Tyre was not ready to turn away from the walls of Gaza. He could not leave such an important post on the line from Damascus to Egypt in the hands of the enemy. He ordered ramparts to be thrown up round the city, in order that the siege engines mounted on this elevation might be on a level with the wall. The best chance seemed to be on the south side, and here the work was pushed on rapidly. When the engines were placed in position, Alexander offered a sacrifice, and a bird of prey flying over the altar dropped a stone on the king's garlanded head. The sooth-sayer interpreted the meaning of the sign: "O king, you will take the city, but you must take good heed for your own safety on this day." Alexander was cautious for a while, but when the besieged

FIG. 109.—Silver coin of Tyre (331 B.C.). Obverse: Melkart with bow on sea-horse; waves; dolphin. Reverse: owl with crook and flail (Egyptian emblems of royalty). FIG. 110.—Coin of Barce (reverse). Three silphion plants; owl, jerboa, and chameleon between them [legend: BAPKAIΩN]. FIG. 111.— Coin of Cyrene (obverse). Head of Zeus Ammon; olive spray.

sallied forth from the gates and attacked the Macedonians who were working the engines on the rampart, and pressed them hard, he rushed to their aid, and was wounded in the shoulder by a dart from a catapult. Thus part of the sign had come true; the other part was in time fulfilled. The engines which had been used in the siege of Tyre arrived by sea; the rampart was widened and raised to a greater height; and underground mines were dug beneath the walls. The walls yielded in many places to the mines and the engines, but it was not till the fourth attack that the Macedonians succeeded in scaling the breaches and entering the city. The slaughter was great-er than in Tyre; the women and children were sold into bondage; and the place became a Macedonian fortress.

SECT. 8. CONQUEST OF EGYPT

Egypt was now absolutely cut off from Persia; the gate to that sequestered land was open, and Alexander had only to march in. The Egyptians had not the vigour to offer any national resistance to

Alexander enters Egypt, c. Nov. 332 B.C.

the Greek invader; and Mazaces the Persian satrap, seeing Phoenicia and Syria in Alexander's power, the Macedonian navy in the
roadstead of Pelusium, and no help at hand, thought only of making
his submission and winning the conqueror's grace. Sending his fleet
up the Pelusiac branch of the Nile to meet him at Memphis, Alexander journeyed thither by way of Heliopolis. In the capital of the

At
Memphis.
Pharaohs, where he was probably proclaimed king, he sacrificed to
Apis and the other native gods, and thereby won the goodwill of the
people, who contrasted his piety with the bigotry of the Persian
monarch Ochus, who had killed the sacred bull. But while the new
king showed that he would treat the native religion and customs
with respect, he also made it clear that Greek civilisation was now
to pour into the exclusive regions of the Nile. He held athletic games
and a poetical contest at Memphis; and the most famous artists
from Greece came to take part in it.

Founda-
tion of
Alex-
andria,
331 B.C.
Jan. (?).
From Memphis he sailed down the river to Canopus, and took a
step which, if he had never performed another exploit in his life,
would have made his name memorable for ever. He chose the
ground, east of Rhacotis, between Lake Mareotis and the sea, as the
site of a new city, over against the island of Pharos, famous in
Homeric song, and soon to become more famous still as the place of
the first lighthouse, one of the seven wonders of the world. The king
is said to have himself traced out the ground plan of *Alexandria*—
the market-place and the circuit of the walls, the sanctuary of Isis
and the temples of the Hellenic gods. He joined the mainland with
the island by a causeway seven stades (nearly a mile) in length, and
thus formed two harbours. The subsequent history of Alexandria,
which has held its position as a port for more than 2000 years,
proves that its founder had a true eye in choosing the site of the
most famous of his new cities. The greatness of the place as a mart
of the world far surpassed any purposes or hopes that Alexander
could have formed; but his object in founding it can hardly be
doubted. Alexandria was not intended to supersede Memphis as the
capital of Egypt; it was intended to take the place of Tyre as the
commercial centre of Western Asia and the Eastern Mediterranean.
And there was a good reason for diverting the lines of traffic from
the Phoenician to the Egyptian coast. For it was naturally the
policy of Alexander to transfer the trade of the world, so far as
might be, into the hands of Greeks; but any new emporium rising
on the ruins of Tyre or Sidon would have soon become predomi-
nantly Phoenician, owing to the Phoenician genius for trade; whereas on the Egyptian coast Greek traders would encounter no such

rivalry. It was thus with a view to the commercial interests of his own race that Alexander founded the port of Egypt.

In the official style of the Egyptian monarchy the Pharaohs were sons of Ammon, and as the successor of the Pharaohs Alexander assumed the same title. It was therefore necessary in order to regulate his position that an official assurance should be given by Ammon himself that Alexander was his son. To obtain such a declaration and satisfy fully the formalities required by the priests, Alexander undertook a journey to the oracular sanctuary of Ammon in the oasis of Siwah. And this motive is alone sufficient to explain the expedition. But it may well be that in Alexander's mind there was a vague notion that there was something divine about his own origin, something mystical in his mother's conception, and that, like Achilles, he was somewhat more than an ordinary man. Proceeding along the coast to Paraetonion, he was there met by envoys who conveyed the submission of Cyrene. By this acquisition the western frontier of the Macedonian empire extended to the border of the Carthaginian sphere of rule. Alexander then struck across the desert to visit that Egyptian temple which was most famous in the Greek world, the temple as it was always called of Zeus Ammon. There were no tracks to guide the travellers, for the south wind had ploughed up the sand and obliterated the road-marks; and stories were told in the camp of miraculous guidance vouchsafed to the favourite of the god. Ptolemy, son of Lagus, who was destined hereafter to rule over Egypt and Libya, recorded in his Memoirs that two snakes moved in front of the troops and showed the way; while Aristobulus, another companion of the king, spoke of the guidance of two crows. A certain mystery enveloped this expedition. It is said that Alexander told no man what he asked the god or what the god replied, save only that the answer pleased him. But it is certain that the priests had made such dispositions that Ammon spoke and recognised him as his son. The very route by which Alexander returned to Memphis is uncertain, for the same two companions differ; Ptolemy stating that he fared direct across the desert, and Aristobulus that he returned by Paraetonion.

At Memphis he organised the government of Egypt, entrusting it to two native monarchs, and appointing separate Greek governors for the adjoining districts of Arabia and for Libya. But the control of the finances was placed in the hands of a special minister, Cleomenes of Naucratis. Several military commanders were also appointed, and it would seem that Alexander instituted this divided command as a safeguard against the danger of a rebellion. For,

Amen Ra

Alexander's visit to temple of Zeus Ammon (first months of 331 B C.).

Organisation of Egypt.

geographically situated as Egypt was, an ambitious commander might have a fair prospect of holding the country against his lord; and its recent history as a Persian province had illustrated the difficulty of dealing with it. If this be so, Alexander inaugurated a policy which was followed, in later days and in another form, by his Roman successors.

SECT. 9. BATTLE OF GAUGAMELA, AND CONQUEST OF BABYLONIA

The new lord of Egypt and Syria returned with the spring to Tyre. The whole coastland was now in his possession, and he controlled the sea; the time had come to advance into the heart of the Persian empire. Having spent some months in the Phoenician city, busied with various matters of policy and administration, as well as with plans for his next campaign, he set forth at the head of 40,000 infantry and 7000 horse, and reached Thapsacus on Euphrates at the beginning of August. The building of two bridges had been already begun, but the Persian Mazaeus, who was stationed with troops on the further shore, had hindered their completion. When Alexander arrived, he withdrew; the bridges were finished, and the army passed over. The objective of Alexander was Babylon. At that time of year it would have been mad to follow the direct route down the Euphrates which was traversed by Cyrus and the Ten Thousand. Alexander chose the other road, across the north of Mesopotamia and down the Tigris on its eastern bank. Throughout the Asiatic campaigns of Alexander we are struck by the perfect organisation of his transports and supplies; but we are struck even more by the certainty of his movements through strange lands, as if he had a map of the country before him. His intelligence department must have been excellent, and though our records give us no intimations on the subject, it has been supposed with much plausibility that here the invader received help from the Jews, who ever since the Captivity were scattered about Media and Babylonia. It is certain that Alexander had shown special favour to the race of Israel at the foundation of Egyptian Alexandria; he had invited a Jewish colony to settle there, enjoying the rights of citizens, and yet living in a separate quarter and keeping their own national customs.

From some Persian scouts who were captured it was ascertained that Darius, with a yet larger multitude than that which had succumbed at Issus, was on the other side of the river, determined to contest the passage. Alexander crossed the Tigris, not at Nineveh, the usual place of crossing, but higher up at Bezabde. On the same night the moon went into eclipse, and men anxiously sought in the

Alexander crosses the Euphrates and marches to the Tigris.

Eclipse of the moon, Sept. 20, 331 B.C.

phenomenon a portent of the issue of the coming struggle for the lordship of Asia.

Marching southward for some days, Alexander learned that Darius was encamped in a plain near Gaugamela on the river Bumōdus. The numbers of the army were reported at 1,000,000 foot and 40,000 horse. Having given his men four days' rest, Alexander moved on by night and halted on a hill looking down on the plain where the enemy lay prepared for battle. A council of war was held, and the question was discussed whether the attack should be made immediately; but Parmenio counselled a day's delay, for the purpose of reconnoitring fully the enemy's position and discovering whether perchance covered pits had been dug or stakes laid in the ground. Parmenio's counsel was followed, and the troops pitched their camp in the order in which they were to fight. Alexander rode over the plain and found that the Persians had cleared it of all bushes and obstacles which might impede the movements of their cavalry or the effect of their scythed chariots.

Alexandei reaches the plain of Gaugamela.

Sept. 30.

The following night was spent by the Persians under arms, for their camp was unfortified and they feared a night attack. And a night attack was recommended by Parmenio, but Alexander preferred to trust the issue to his own generalship and the superior discipline of his troops, and not to brave the hazards of a struggle in the dark. He said to Parmenio, "I do not steal victory," and under the gallantry of this reply he concealed, in his usual manner, the prudence and policy of his resolve. A victory over the Persian host, won in the open field in the light of day, would have a far greater effect in establishing his prestige in Asia than an advantage stolen by night.

Night be fore the battle.

The Great King, according to wont, was in the *centre* of the Persian array, surrounded by his kinsfolk and his Persian bodyguard. On either side of them were Greek mercenaries, Indian auxiliaries with a few elephants, and Carians whose ancestors had been settled in Upper Asia. The centre was strengthened and deepened by a second line, composed of the Babylonian troops, and the men from the shores of the Persian Gulf, and the Uxians who dwelt east of Susa, and the Sitacenes. On the *left* wing, the Cadusians from the shores of the Caspian and the men of Susa were nearest the centre; next came a mixed host of Persian horse and foot; and at the extreme left were the troops from the far east, from Arachosia and Bactria. This wing was covered by 1000 Bactrian cavalry, 100 scythe-armed chariots, and the Scythian cavalry from the desert districts of Lake Aral. On the *right* were the contingents of the Caucasian folks; the Hyrcanians and Tapurians from the south-

Battle of Gaugamela, Oct. 1, 331 B.C.

The Persian order of battle.

eastern shores of the Caspian; the Parthians, who were destined in the future to found a new oriental monarchy; the Sacae from the slopes of the Hindu-Kush; the Medes, and the dwellers in Mesopotamia and northern Syria.

The Macedonian order of battle.

Against this host, of which the cavalry alone is said to have been as numerous as all the infantry of the enemy, Alexander descended the hill in the morning. On his *left* wing—commanded as usual by Parmenio—were the cavalry of the Thessalian and confederate Greeks; in the *centre* the six regiments of the phalanx; and on the *right*, the hypaspists, and the eight squadrons of the Companions, the royal squadron of Clitus being at the extreme right. Covering the right wing were some light troops, spear-throwers and archers. The line was far outflanked on both sides by the enemy, and the danger which Alexander had most to fear, as at the battle of Issus, was that of being attacked in rear or flanked; only that, whereas in the plain of Issus his right alone was threatened, here both wings were in peril. He sought to meet these contingencies by forming behind each wing a second line, which by facing round a quarter or half circle could meet an attack on flank or rear. Behind the *left* wing were placed Thracian foot and horse, some Greek confederate cavalry, and Greek mercenary cavalry; behind the *right*, the old Greek mercenaries under Cleander, the Macedonian archers, some of the Agrianian spear-throwers, the mounted pikemen, the light Paeonian cavalry; and, at the extreme right, to bear the brunt of a flank assault, the new Greek mercenaries under Menidas.

As he advanced, Alexander and his right wing were opposite to the centre of the enemy's line, and he was outflanked by the whole length of the enemy's left. He therefore bore obliquely to the right, and, even when the Scythian horsemen riding forward came into contact with his own light troops, he continued to move his squadrons of heavy cavalry in the same direction. Darius saw with anxiety that this movement would soon bring the Macedonian right outside the ground which he had carefully levelled and prepared for the action of his scythed chariots, and, as he had set no small part of his hopes in the deadly effect of these chariots, he commanded the Scythian and Bactrian cavalry to ride round and deliver a flank-charge, in order to hinder any further advance towards the right.

Cavalry battle on the extreme right.

The charge was met by the new mercenaries of Menidas; but they were too few, they were driven back, until the Paeonians and the old mercenaries were bidden to come to their support. Then the barbarians gave way, but in a short while, reinforced by more troops, they returned to the charge. The battle raged, and it was well if the Macedonians, far outnumbered, could hold their ground.

Meanwhile Darius had loosed his scythed cars, to whirl destruction into the ranks of the Companions and the hypaspists. But the archers and the Agrian spear-throwers received them with showers of spears and arrows; some of these active hillsmen seized the reins of the horses and pulled the drivers from their seats, while the hypaspists, swiftly and undismayed, opened their ranks, and the terrible chariots rattled harmless down the intervals.

The attack of the scythe-chariots frustrated.

The whole Persian line was now advancing to attack, and Alexander was waiting for the moment to deliver his cavalry charge. He had to send his mounted pikemen to the help of the light cavalry, who were being hard pressed on the right by the Scythians and Bactrians; and as a counter-check to this reinforcement, squadrons of Persian cavalry were dispatched to the assistance of their fellows. By the withdrawal of these squadrons a gap was caused in the left wing, and into this gap Alexander plunged at the head of his cavalry column and split the line in two. Thus the left side of the enemy's centre was exposed, and turning obliquely Alexander charged into its ranks. Meanwhile the bristling phalanx was moving forward and was soon engaged in close combat with another part of the Persian centre. The storm of battle burst with wildest fury round the spot where the Persian king was trembling, and what befell at Issus befell again at Gaugamela. The Great King turned his chariot and fled. His Persians fled with him, and swept along in their flight the troops who had been posted in the rear.

Charge of Alexander.

Flight of Darius.

Thus the Persian centre and the neighbouring part of the left wing were cut down or routed by the phalanx, the hypaspists, and the Companions. And in the meantime, the severe struggle of the light cavalry on the uttermost left had also ended in victory for the Macedonians.

The regiments of the phalanx in their rapid advance had failed to keep abreast, and it would seem that when the regiment of Craterus, on the extreme left, was already far forward in the thick of the fight, the regiment commanded by Simmias, second from the left, was considerably in the rear. From his position Simmias saw that the Thessalian cavalry on the left wing were pressed hard by their adversaries, and he halted his regiment, in order apparently to make a movement to assist them. But the Indian and Persian cavalry of the hostile centre rushed through the gap in the phalanx and rode straight onward to the Macedonian camp, unhindered by the rear line of the left wing who did not expect an enemy on that side. The captives in the camp burst out and helped their friends to murder the Thracians who had been set to guard it. The Greek mercenaries and Thracians of the rear line soon perceived what had

Gap in the phalanx.

Attack on the Macedonian camp.

happened; they turned round, attacked the plunderers in the rear, and overcame them.

Meanwhile Parmenio was hard bestead. The Mesopotamians and Syrians of the extreme Persian right had attacked his cavalry in the flank or rear. Parmenio sped a messenger to Alexander entreating aid, and Alexander desisted from the pursuit of his fleeing rival, to restore the battle on his left wing. Riding back with his Companions he encountered a large body of cavalry, Persians, Parthians, and Indians, in full retreat, but in orderly array. A desperate conflict ensued, perhaps the most fearful in the whole battle, the Persians fighting not for victory but for life. Sixty of the Companions fell, but Alexander was again victorious and rode on to the help of

Victory on the Macedonian right.

Parmenio. But Parmenio no longer needed his help. Not the least achievement of this day of great deeds was the brilliant fighting of the Thessalian cavalry, who not only sustained the battle against the odds which had wrung from Parmenio the cry for aid, but in the end routed their foemen before Alexander could reach the spot. The battle was won, and the fate of the Persian empire was decided.

Pursuit of Darius as far as Arbela.

Alexander did not tarry on the field. He lost not a moment in resuming the chase which he had abandoned, and, riding eastward throughout the night on the tracks of the Persian king, he reached Arbela on the morrow. It befell now as it had befallen after Issus. He did not take the king, but found at Arbela his chariot, his shield, and his bow. Darius fled into the highlands of Media, and Ariobarzanes with a host of the routed army hastened southward to Persia. Alexander did not follow either king or satrap, but pursued his way to Babylon.

Babylon submits to Alexander.

It might have been expected, and Alexander seems to have expected, that the men of Babylon, trusting in their mighty walls, would have offered to the victor of Gaugamela the same defiance which the men of Tyre offered to the victor of Issus. He was disappointed. When he approached the city, with his army arrayed for action, the gates opened and the Babylonians streamed out, led by their priests and their chief men. The satrap Mazaeus, who had fought bravely in the recent battle, surrendered the city and citadel. In Babylonia, Alexander followed the same policy which he had already followed in Egypt. He appeared as the protector of the national religions which had been depressed and slighted by the fire-worshippers. He rebuilt the Babylonian temples which had been destroyed, and above all he commanded the restoration of the marvellous temple of Bel, standing on its eight towers, on which the rage of Xerxes had vented itself when he returned from the rout of

Salamis. The Persian Mazaeus was retained in his post as satrap of Babylonia.

SECT. 10. CONQUEST OF SUSIANA AND PERSIS

Having rested his army in the luxurious and wonderful city of the Euphrates, the conqueror advanced south-eastward to Susa, the summer residence of the Persian court. Susa had been already secured for him by Philoxenus, whom he had dispatched thither from Arbela with some light troops. In the citadel he found enormous treasures of gold and silver and purple. Among other precious things at Susa was the sculptured group of the tyrant-slayers, Harmodius and Aristogiton, which Xerxes had carried off from Athens; and Alexander had the pleasure of sending back to its home this historical monument, now more precious than ever through its own strange history.

Alexander at Susa, Dec. 331 B.C.

Statue-group of Harmodius and Aristogiton.

Though it was mid-winter, Alexander soon left Susa to accomplish one of the most arduous adventures that he ever undertook. He had won the treasures of Susa, but there were immense treasures still in the palaces of Cyrus and Darius in the heart of the Persian highlands, and these were guarded not only by the difficulties of the mountainous approaches, but by the army which Ariobarzanes had rescued from the overthrow of Gaugamela. Perhaps the reason for Alexander's haste in pressing on to Persis was the fear that Darius might descend with a new force from Media, if time were given him before Ariobarzanes was crushed. But whatever were his reasons, it seemed to him of the greatest moment to secure Persis immediately. His road lay south-eastward, and when he had crossed the river Pasitigris, the first obstacle that he encountered was the independent tribe of the Uxian hillsmen, on whom the Persian kings themselves were accustomed to bestow gifts for their goodwill. The barbarians held the passes through which the road lay, but a night march by a difficult mountain path enabled Alexander to surprise them, and the Uxians henceforward were forced to pay yearly gifts to the lord of Asia—a hundred horses, five hundred draught oxen, and thirty thousand sheep.

(Kārūn.)

The Uxian pass.

The Macedonian army was now in the midst of a region which was unknown to Greek charts. Alexander's advance is a march not only of conquest but of discovery, and opens a new epoch in the history of geographical science by revealing Central Asia to the knowledge of Europe.

Leaving half of his army with Parmenio to proceed more slowly

Storming
of the
Persian
Gates,
Jan.
330 B.C.
along the main road, Alexander led the other half (including the
Macedonians, both horse and foot) by a shorter path through the
hills to the narrow defile which formed the entrance to Persis and
was called the Persian Gates. Ariobarzanes was posted there with
40,000 foot and 700 horse, guarding the rocky pass which he had
fortified by a wall. An attack, easily repelled, showed Alexander
that the pass was impregnable; yet it must be carried, for this was
the only road to the royal cities of Persia. For a moment Alexander
was baffled; never perhaps—not even before Tyre—was he encountered by a problem more desperate to all seeming. But he learned
from a prisoner of some extremely perilous paths leading round,
through the forests which covered the mountains, to the back of the
pass. At this season the snow made these paths more dangerous
than ever, and they might well seem hopeless to men weighed down
with heavy armour; but they were the only hope and Alexander did
not hesitate. He left Craterus with part of the troops in front of the
pass, with orders to attack as soon as he heard the Macedonian
trumpets sounding from above on the other side. With the rest of
his force, including most of the cavalry, three regiments of the
phalanx, the hypaspists, and other light troops, he set forth at
night, and marched quickly eleven miles along the precipitous
snowy track, intersected frequently by deep gullies. When the point
was reached at which he was to turn in order to descend on the
Persian camp, he again divided his forces, and sent one division forward to bridge the river Araxes and cut off the Persian retreat.
Taking the hypaspists, the royal squadron of the Companions, one
regiment of the phalanx, and some light troops, he raced down upon
the camp and destroyed or routed three successive sets of outposts
before the day dawned. Instead of raising the alarm, the sentinels
scattered on the mountain, and when the Macedonian trumpets
pealed on the brink of his entrenchments, Ariobarzanes was taken
completely by surprise. Attacked on both sides, in front by Craterus
who stormed up the wall of rock, and in the rear by Alexander, the
Persians were cut to pieces or fell over precipices in their flight.
Ariobarzanes with a small band escaped into the mountains.

The royal palaces of Persia, to which Alexander now hurried with
the utmost speed, stood in the valley of Mervdasht, fertile then but
desolate at the present day, and close to the city of Istachr, which
the Persians deemed the oldest city in the world. In Istachr itself
there was a royal house too, but the great palaces stood some miles
away, close beneath the mountain, upon a lofty platform against a
background of black rock. The platform was mounted by magnificent staircases, and it bore, besides massive propylaea, four chief

buildings, the small palace of Darius, the larger palace of Xerxes, and two great pillared halls. The impressive ruins tell a trained eye how to reconstruct the general plan of the royal abode, and there can be no question that Achaemenian architecture had wrought here its greatest achievements, greater than the palace of Susa which Alexander had seen, greater than that of Ecbatana which he was soon to see. This cradle of the Persian kingdom, to which, city and palace together, the Greeks gave the name of *Persepolis*, was "the richest of all the cities under the sun." It is said that 120,000 talents were found in the treasury; an army of mules and camels were required to remove the spoils. This store of gold, so long withdrawn from use, was now suddenly to be restored to circulation and perturb the markets of the world.

Not far off, two days' journey northward up the winding valley of the Murghab, was Pasargadae, the city of Cyrus. The maker of Persia built it close to the field where he had shattered the host of the Median king; and the place is still marked by his tomb, and the stones of other buildings, on some of which the traveller may read the words "I am Cyrus the king, the Achaemenian." In Pasargadae too Alexander found a store of treasure. Pasargadae.

For four months he made the Persian palaces his headquarters, during which time he received the submission of Caramania or Kirman, and made some excursions to punish the robbers who infested the neighbouring mountains. But the most famous incident connected with the sojourn at Persepolis is the conflagration of the palace of Xerxes. The story is that one night when Alexander and his companions had drunk deep at a royal festival, Thais, an Attic courtesan, who was of the company, mindful of her country and all the wrongs which Xerxes had wrought, flung out among the tipsy carousers the idea of burning down the house of the malignant foe who had burned the temples of Greece. The mad words of the woman inspired a wild frenzy, and whirled the revellers forth, armed with torches, to accomplish the barbarous deed. Alexander hurled the first brand, and the cedar wood-work of the palace was soon in flames. But before the fire had done its work the king's head was cool, and he commanded the fire to be quenched. It is folly to attempt to read into this act a deliberate policy; it was the wild freak of a moment, repented the next. Jan.-
April,
330 B.C. Burning
of the
palace of
Xerxes.

SECT. 11. DEATH OF DARIUS

In the meantime king Darius remained in Ecbatana, surrounded by the adherents who were faithful to him, chiefly the satraps of those lands which were still unconquered—Media itself and Hyrcania, Areia and Bactria, Arachosia and Drangiana. It is probable that after the Gaugamela battle Alexander hoped to receive some proposal from his defeated foe, more submissive and acceptable than that which had been sent after Issus. He would have been ready perhaps to leave to Darius the eastern part of his dominions, with the royal title, though as a dependent vassal, and to content himself for a while with the empire which he had won, including Susa and Persepolis. It may have been with the hope of receiving overtures that he tarried so long in Persis. But Darius gave no sign. Media was defensible; he had a large army from the northern satrapies; and he had Bactria as a retreat, if retreat he must.

The spring was advanced when Alexander left Persis for Ecbatana. The direct road did not lie by Susa, but much farther east through the land of Paraetacene. He made all speed, when the news reached him by the way, that Darius was at Ecbatana with a large army, prepared to fight. But when after a succession of forced marches he drew nigh to the city, he found that Darius had flown eastward, following the women and heavy baggage which had been sent on to the Caspian Gates, and taking the treasures with him. It is said that the reason of this retreat was the default of some Cadusian and Scythian troops which had failed to arrive in time. When he reached the Median capital, Alexander was detained by the need of arranging certain matters before he pursued his rival into the northern wilds. He paid off the Thessalian troops and the other Greek confederates, giving them a handsome donative and a conduct to the Aegean; but any who chose to enrol themselves anew in his service and share in his further course of conquest might stay, and not a few stayed. Parmenio was entrusted with the care of seeing that the treasures of Persis were transported and safely deposited in the strong keep of Ecbatana, where they were to remain in charge of the treasurer Harpalus and a large body of Macedonian troops. Parmenio was then to proceed northward to Cadusia, and along the shores of the Caspian Sea, where he was to meet the king.

With the main part of the army Alexander hurried on, merciless to men and steeds, bent on the capture of Darius. His way lay by Ragae, and when he reached that place, a little to the south of the modern capital of Persia, he found that the fugitive was already well beyond the Caspian Gates, which lie a long day's journey to the east. Despairing of overtaking him, Alexander rested some days at Ragae before he advanced towards Parthia through the Caspian pass. But meanwhile doom was stealing upon Darius by another way. His followers were beginning to suspect that ill-luck dogged

Alexander at Ecbatana.

(Rayy.)

Darius seized by Bessus.

him, and when he proposed to stay and risk another battle instead of continuing his retreat to Bactria, none were willing except the remnant of Greek mercenaries, who were still faithful to the man who had hired them, and perhaps dreaded punishment as recusants to the Greek cause. Bessus, the satrap of Bactria, was a kinsman of the king, and it was felt by many that he might be able to raise up again the Achaemenian house, which Darius had been unable to sustain. A plot was formed; Darius was seized and bound in the middle of the night, set in a litter, and hurried on as a prisoner along the road to Bactria. This event disbanded his army. The Greek mercenaries went off northwards into the Caspian mountains, and many of the Persians turned back to find pardon and grace with Alexander. They found him encamped on the Parthian side of the Caspian Gates, and told him the new turn of events. When he learned that his old rival was a prisoner and that Bessus was now his antagonist, Alexander resolved on a swift and hot pursuit. Leaving the main body of the army to come slowly after, he set forth at once with his cavalry and some light foot, and sped the whole night through, not resting till next day at noon, and then another evening and night at the same breathless speed. Sunrise saw him at Thara. It was the place where the Great King had been put in chains, and it was ascertained from his interpreter, who had remained behind ill, that Bessus and his fellows intended to surrender Darius if the pursuit were pressed. There was the greater need for haste. The pursuers rode on throughout another night; men and horses were dropping with fatigue. At noon they came to a village where the pursued had halted the day before, and Alexander learned that they intended to force a march in the night. He asked the people if there was no short way, and was told that there was a short way, but it was waterless. Alexander instantly dismounted five hundred of his horsemen and gave their steeds to the officers and the strongest men of the infantry who were with him. With these he started in the evening, and having ridden about forty-five miles came up with the enemy at break of day. The barbarians were straggling, many of them unarmed; a few who made a stand were swept away, but most of them fled when they saw that it was Alexander. Bessus and his fellow-conspirators bade their prisoner—no longer, seemingly, in chains—mount a horse; and when Darius refused, they stabbed him and rode their ways, wounding the litter-mules too and killing the drivers. The beasts, sore and thirsty, strayed about half a mile from the road down a side valley, where they were found at a spring by a Macedonian who had come to slake his thirst. The Great King was near his last gasp. If he could have spoken Greek, or if the stranger

The pursuit of Darius.

had understood Persian, he might have found words to send a message of thanks to his conqueror for the generous treatment of his wife and mother who were then assuredly in his thoughts; afterwards men had no scruple in placing appropriate words in the mouth of the dying monarch. It is enough to believe that he had the solace of a cup of water in his supreme moments and thanked the Macedonian soldier by a sign. Alexander viewed the body, and is related to have thrown his own cloak over it in pity. It was part of his fair luck that he found Darius dead; for if he had taken him alive, he would not have put him to death, and such a captive would have been a perpetual embarrassment. He sent the corpse with all honour to the queen-mother, and the last of the Achaemenian kings was buried with his forefathers at Persepolis.

SECT. 12. SPIRIT OF ALEXANDER'S POLICY AS LORD OF ASIA

Change in Alexander's aims.

Before we follow Alexander on his marches of conquest and discovery into the regions which were then in European eyes the Far East, we may pause to observe his attitude as ruler and king; for the months which passed between the battle of Gaugamela and the pursuit of Darius were a critical period, which witnessed a remarkable change in his conception of his duty and in his political aims.

His tolerant policy.

From the very beginning he had shown to the conquered provinces a tolerance, which was not only prompted by generosity but based on political wisdom. He had not attempted to apply an artificial scheme to all countries, but had permitted each country to retain its national institutions. One general principle, indeed, he did adopt—the division of power; and this was a notable improvement on the Persian method. Under the Persian kingdom the satrap was usually sole governor, controlling not only the civil administration, but the treasury and the troops. Alexander in most cases committed only the internal administration to the governor, and appointed beside him, and independent of his authority, a financial officer and a military commander. This division of authority was a security against rebellion. We have already seen, in Egypt and Babylonia, how in matters of religion Alexander was, like all the Greeks, broad-minded and tolerant.

His policy as successor of the Great King.

But the Macedonian king, the commander-in-chief of the Greek confederates, had set forth as a champion of Greeks against mere barbarians, as a leader of Europeans against effeminate Asiatics, as the representative of a higher folk against beings lower in the human scale. All the Greeks and Macedonians who followed him regarded the east as a world to be plundered and rifled by their higher

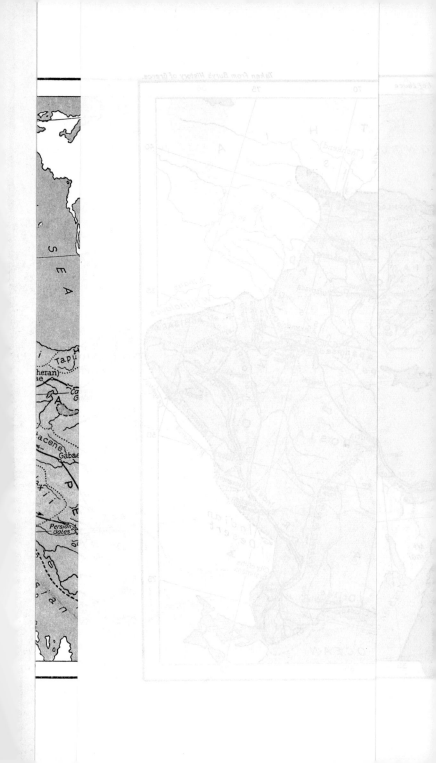

intelligence and courage, and considered the orientals as inferiors meant by nature to be their own slaves. "Slaves by nature" they seemed to the political wisdom of Aristotle himself, Alexander's teacher; and the victories of Issus and Gaugamela were calculated to confirm the Europeans in their sense of unmeasured superiority. But, as Alexander advanced, his view expanded, and he rose to a loftier conception of his own position and his relation to Asia. He began to transcend the familiar distinction of Greek and barbarian, and to see that, for all the truth it contained, it was not the last word that could be said. He formed the notion of an empire, both European and Asiatic, in which the Asiatics should not be dominated by the European invaders, but Europeans and Asiatics alike should be ruled on an equality by a monarch, indifferent to the distinction of Greek and barbarian, and looked upon as their own king by Persians as well as by Macedonians. The idea begins to show itself after the battle of Gaugamela. The Persian lords and satraps who submit are received with favour and confidence; Alexander learns to know and appreciate the fine qualities of the Iranian noblemen. Some of the eastern provinces are entrusted to Persian satraps, for example Babylonia to Mazaeus, and the court of Alexander ceases to be purely European. With oriental courtiers, the forms of an oriental court are also gradually introduced; the Asiatics prostrate themselves before the lord of Asia; and presently Alexander adopts the dress of a Persian king at court ceremonies, in order to appear less a foreigner in the eyes of his eastern subjects. The idea which prompted this policy was new and bold, and it harmonised with the great work of Alexander,—the breaking down of the barriers between west and east; but it was accompanied by a certain imperious self-exaltation, which we do not find in the earlier part of Alexander's career, and it involved him in troubles with his own folk. The Macedonians strongly disapproved of their king's new paths; they disliked the rival influence of the Asiatic nobles, and their prejudices were shocked at seeing Alexander occasionally assume oriental robes. The Macedonian royalty was indeed inade-- quate for Alexander's imperial position; but it is unfortunate that he had no other model than the royalty of Persia, hedged round by forms which were so distasteful to the free spirit of Greece. The life of Alexander was spent in solving difficult problems, political and military; and none was harder than this, to create a kingship which should conciliate the prejudices of the east without offending the prejudices of the west.

CHAPTER XVIII

THE CONQUEST OF THE FAR EAST

Sect. I. Hyrcania, Areia, Bactria, Sogdiana

Conquest
of
Hyrcania
(Taba-
ristan and
Mazen-
deran),
330 B.C.

THE murderers of Darius fled, Bessus to Bactria, Nabarzanes to Hyrcania; and the direction of their flight determined the course of Alexander's advance. He could not pursue Bessus while there was an enemy behind him in the Caspian region, and therefore his first movement was to cross the Elburz chain of mountains which separate the south Caspian shores from Parthia, and subdue the lands of the Tapuri and Mardi. The Persian officers who had retreated into these regions submitted, and were received with favour; the life of Nabarzanes was spared. The Greek mercenaries who had found refuge in the Tapurian mountains capitulated. All who had entered the Persian service, before the Synedrion of Corinth had pledged Greece to the cause of Macedon, were released; the rest were compelled to serve in the Macedonian army for the same pay which they had received from Darius. The importance of the well-wooded southern coast of the Caspian was understood by Alexander, and he sent orders to Parmenio to go forth from Ecbatana and take possession of the Cadusian territory on the south-western side of the sea.

(Astra-
bad.)
(Near
Meshed.)

He himself could not tarry. Having rested a fortnight at Zadracarta and held athletic games, he marched eastward to Susia, a town in the north of Areia, and was met there by Satibarzanes, governor of Areia, who made his submission and was confirmed in his satrapy. Here the news arrived that Bessus had assumed the style of Great King with the name of Artaxerxes, and was wearing his turban "erect." Alexander started at once on the road to Bactria. His way would have lain by Merv; in the wilds of Central Asia the beaten ways of traffic remain the same for thousands of years. But he had not gone far when he was overtaken by the news that Satibarzanes had revolted behind him. There was nothing to be done but to return and secure the province of Areia; for this province did not stand alone; it would certainly be upheld in its hostility by the neighbouring countries of Arachosia and Drangiana, which formed the satrapy of Barsaentes, one of the murderers of Darius. Hurrying back in forced marches with a part of his army, Alexander appeared before Artocoana, the capital of Areia, in two days; Satibarzanes galloped away to seek Bessus in Bactria, and his troops who fled to the mountains were pursued and overcome. There was no further resistance, and the conqueror marched southwards to Drangiana. His road can hardly be doubtful—the road which leads by Herat into Seistan. And it is probable that Herat is the site of the city which Alexander founded to be the capital and stronghold of the new province, Alexandria of the Areians. The submission of Drangiana was made without a blow; the satrap, who had fled to the Indians, was given up by them and put to death.

At Prophthasia, the capital of the Drangian land, there befell a tragedy, whereof we know too little to judge the rights and wrongs of the case. It came to Alexander's ears that Philotas, the son of Parmenio, was conspiring against his life. The king called an assembly of the Macedonians and stated the charges against the general. Philotas admitted that he had known of a plot to murder Alexander and said nothing about it; but this was only one of the charges against him. The Macedonians, although many of them were ill-content with the developments of their king's policy in the east, found Philotas guilty, and he was pierced by their javelins. The son dead, it seemed dangerous to let the father live, whether he was involved or not in the treasonable designs of Philotas. A messenger was despatched with all speed to Media, bearing commands to some of the captains of Parmenio's army to put the old general to death. If the guilt of Philotas was assured—and we have no reason to doubt it—we can hardly, so far as Philotas is concerned, blame Alexander for his rigorous measures, which it must have been painful for him to adopt. A crime which might have been pardoned in Macedonia could not be dealt gently with in a camp in distant lands, where not only success but safety depended on loyalty and discipline. But the death of Parmenio was an arbitrary act of precaution against merely suspected disloyalty; there seem to have been no proofs against him, and there was certainly no trial.

In the meantime Alexander had changed his plans. Instead of retracing his steps and following the route to Bactria, which he had originally intended to take, he resolved to fetch a circle, and marching through Afghanistan, subduing it as he went, he would cross the Hindu-Kush mountains and descend on the plain of the Oxus from the east. First he advanced southwards to secure Seistan and the north-western regions of Baluchistan, then known as Gedrosia. The Ariaspae, a peaceful and friendly people whom the Greeks called "Benefactors," dwelt in the south of Seistan. Alexander passed part

Alexandria Areiôn (Herat). Occupation of Drangiana.

Execution of Barsaentes.

(? Farah in Seistan.)

The conspiracy of Philotas.

Fate of Parmenio.

Alexander winters in Seistan, 330-29 B.C.

of the winter among them, and gratified them by a small increase of territory, and made them free, subject to no satrap. The neighbouring Gedrosians volunteered their submission, and a Gedrosian satrapy was constituted with its capital at Pura. When spring came, Alexander pushed north-eastward up the valley of the Halmand to Candahar. And in pronouncing the name of Candahar, we are perhaps pronouncing the name of the great conqueror; for the chief

city which he founded in Arachosia was probably on the site of Candahar, which seems to be a corruption of its name, Alexandria. The way led on over the mountains, past Ghazni, into the valley of the upper waters of the Cabul river, and Alexander came to the foot of the high range of the Hindu-Kush. The whole massive complex of mountains which diverge from the roof of the world, dividing southern from central, eastern from western Asia—the Pamirs, the Hindu-Kush, and the Himalayas—were grouped by the Greeks under the general name of Caucasus. But the Hindu-Kush was distinguished by the special name of Paropanisus, while the Himalayas

were called the Imaus. At the foot of the Hindu-Kush he spent the winter, and founded another Alexandria to secure this region, somewhere to the north of Cabul; it was distinguished as Alexandria of the Caucasus. While he was in these parts he learned that Satibarzanes was still abroad in Areia, inflaming a rebellion; some forces were sent to crush him; a battle was fought and Satibarzanes was killed.

The crossing of the Caucasus, undertaken in the early spring, was an achievement which, for the difficulties overcome and the hardships of cold and want endured, seems to have fallen little short of Hannibal's passage of the Alps. The soldiers had to content themselves with raw meat and the herb of silphion as a substitute for

bread. At length they reached Drapsaca, high up on the northern slope—the frontier fortress of Bactria. Having rested his way-worn army, Alexander went down by the stronghold of Aornus into the plain, and marched through a poor country to Bactra, the chief city of the land, which has preserved its old site but has changed its name to Balkh.

The pretender, Bessus Artaxerxes, had stripped and wasted eastern Bactria up to the foot of the mountains, for the purpose of checking the progress of the invading army; but he fled across the Oxus when Alexander drew near, and his native cavalry deserted him. No man withstood the conqueror, and another province was added without a blow to the Macedonian empire. Alexander lost no time in pursuing the fugitive into Sogdiana. This is the country which lies between the streams of the Oxus and the Jaxartes. It was

other regions from the river Sogd, which flows through it,
[...]

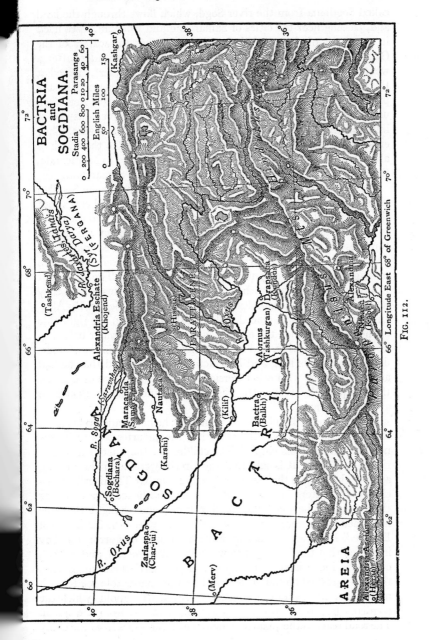

FIG. 112.

called Sogdiana from the river Sogd, which flows through the land
and, passing near the cities of Samarcand and Buchara, loses itself
in the sands of the desert before it approaches the waters of the
(R. Sarav-   Oxus. Bessus had burned his boats, and when Alexander, after a
shan.)   weary march of two or three days through the hot desert, arrived at
the banks of the Oxus, he was forced to transport his army by the
primitive vehicle of skins, which the natives of Central Asia then
used and still use to-day. Alexander's soldiers, however, instead of
inflating the sheep-skins with air, stuffed them with rushes. They
crossed the river at Kilif, where its banks contract to the width of
about two-thirds of a mile, and advanced on the road to Maracanda,
the chief city of the country, easily recognised as Samarcand.

Bessus had no support north of the Oxus. He had some Sogdian
allies, at the head of whom were Spitamenes and Dataphernes; but
these men had no intention of sacrificing their country to the cause
of the pretender. Thinking that Alexander's only object was to capture Bessus, and that he would then withdraw from Sogdiana and
fix the Oxus as the northern boundary of his dominion, they sent a
message to him offering to surrender the usurper. The king sent
Ptolemy, son of Lagus, with 6000 men to secure Bessus, whom they
found in a walled village, deserted by his Sogdian friends. By Alexander's orders he was placed, naked and fettered, on the right side
of the road by which the army was marching. Alexander halted as
he passed the captive, and asked him why he had seized and murdered Darius, his king and benefactor. Bessus replied that he had
acted in concert with other Persian nobles, in the hope of winning
the conqueror's favour. He was scourged and sent to Bactra to
await his doom.

River   But Alexander did not arrest his march; he had made up his mind
Jaxartes   to annex Sogdiana. Not the Oxus but the Jaxartes was to be the
(Syr
Darya).   northern limit of his empire. The children of the waste called this
river the Tanais. It is said that the Greeks were deceived into im-
(Don.)   agining that it was the same river as the familiar Tanais which dis-
charges its waters into the Maeotic lake, and hence regarded it as
the boundary between Asia and Europe, and thought that the
herdsmen of the north, who dwelt beyond it, were "the Scythians of
Europe." But they can hardly have fallen into this error, for they
imagined that the Caspian Sea was a gulf of the ocean, and the two
errors are inconsistent. Having seized and garrisoned Samarcand,
the army pushed on north-eastward by the unalterable road which
nature has marked out, and occupied seven strongholds which the
Sogdians had built as defences against invaders from the north.
The road reaches the Jaxartes where that river issues from the chilly

vale of Fergana and deflects its course to flow through the steppes. It was a point of the highest importance; for Fergana forms the vestibule of the great gate of communication between south-western Asia and China—the pass over the Tian-shan mountains, which descends on the other side into the land of Kashgar. Here Alexander, with strategic insight, resolved to fix the limit of his empire, and on the banks of the river he founded a new city which was known as Alexandria the Ultimate. There is no doubt about the situation; it is the later Khodjend.

The conqueror, judging from the ease with which he had come and conquered Arachosia and Bactria, seems not to have conceived that it might be otherwise beyond the Oxus. But the chiefs of Sogdiana were not as the Persian grandees; they were ready to dare greatly for their freedom against the European invader. As he was designing his new city, Alexander received the news that the land was up in arms behind him. Spitamenes was the leader of the movement, and was supported by Oxyartes and other leading Sogdians. The few Macedonian soldiers left in the seven strongholds had been overpowered, and the garrison of Samarcand was besieged in the citadel. A message had gone forth into the western wastes, and the Massagetae and other Scythian tribes were flocking to drive out the intruder. It was a dangerous moment for Alexander. He first turned to recover the fortresses, and in two days he had taken and burned five of them. Cyrupolis, the largest and strongest, caused more trouble; but Alexander, with a few companions, contrived to creep under the wall by the bed of a dry stream, and threw open a gate to the troops. The resistance of the inhabitants was furious, and the king was wounded in the mellay. The fall of Cyrupolis was followed by the capitulation of the seventh town, and the remnant of the indwellers of all these places were led in chains to take part in peopling the new Alexandria.

The next task should have been the relief of Samarcand, but Alexander found himself confronted by a new danger, and could send only a few thousand troops to succour the besieged garrison. The herdsmen of the north were pouring down to the banks of the Jaxartes, ready to cross the stream and harass the Macedonians in the rear. It was impossible to move until they had been repelled and the passage of the river secured. The walls of Alexandria were hastily constructed of unburnt clay and the place made fit for habitation in the short space of twenty days. Meanwhile the northern bank was lined by the noisy and jeering hordes of the barbarians, and Alexander determined to cross the river. The offerings were not favourable; they betokened, said the seer, personal danger to the

king; but Alexander would be mocked no longer. Bringing up his missile-engines to the shore, he dismayed the shepherds, who, when stones and darts began to fall among them from such a distance and unhorsed one of their champions, retreated some distance from the bank. The army seized the moment to cross; the Scythians were routed, and Alexander, at the head of his cavalry, pursued them far into the steppes. Parched by the intense summer heat, the king was tempted to drink of the foul water of the desert, and he fell dangerously ill. Thus was the presage of the offerings fulfilled.

Luckily Alexander soon recovered, for ill tidings came from the south. When the relieving force approached Maracanda, Spitamenes had fled westward to the town of Sogdiana, which probably answers to Buchara. The Macedonians marched after him, hoping to drive him utterly out of the land, but they were indiscreet, and the whole detachment was cut off. Learning of this disaster, Alexander hurried to Samarcand with cavalry and light troops, covering the distance, it is said, in three days,—a forced march of between fifty and sixty miles a day, which seems almost impossible for foot soldiers, however lightly equipped, in the heat of a Sogdian summer. At his coming, Spitamenes, who had returned to the siege of Samarcand, again darted westward, and Alexander followed in pursuit. Visiting the spot where the unlucky corps had been cut down on the banks of the Sogd, the king buried the dead; then crossing the river, he pursued the fugitive chieftain and his Scythian allies to the limits of the waste. He swept on to Sogdiana, ravaging the land; then marching south-westward to the Oxus, he crossed into western Bactria and spent the winter at Zariaspa. The Bactrian cities of Zariaspa and Bactra bore somewhat the same relation to one another as the Sogdian cities of Maracanda and Sogdiana.

At Zariaspa, Bessus was formally tried for the murder of Darius, and was condemned to have his nose and ears cut off and be taken to Ecbatana to die on the cross. The Greeks, like ourselves, regarded mutilation as a barbarous punishment, and it is not pleasant to find Alexander violating this sentiment. But the adoption of oriental punishments in dealing with orientals must be judged along with the adoption of other oriental customs. Every conqueror of an alien race finds himself in a grave embarrassment. Is he to offend his ideals and fall away from his convictions by acquiescing in outlandish usages antagonistic to his own? Or is he, stiffnecked and inflexibly true to the principles of his own civilisation, to remain out of touch with his new subjects? Is he to adopt the policy which will be most effective in administering the conquered land, or is he to impose a policy which works and is approved in his home-

Alexander in western Sogdiana; winters, 328-7 B.C., at Zariaspa (Charjui).

Fate of Bessus.

country, but may be useless or fatal elsewhere? Alexander did not adopt the second method. It was the task of his life to spread Greek civilisation in the East. But he saw that this could not be done by an outsider—a general of Hellas or basileus of Macedonia,—he must meet the orientals on their own ground; he must become their king in their own way. The surest means of planting Hellenism in their midst was to begin by taking account sympathetically of their prejudices. Alexander therefore assumed the state of Great King, surrounded himself with Eastern forms and pomp, exacted self-abasement in his presence from oriental subjects, and adopted the maxim that the king's person was divine. He was the successor of Darius, and he regarded the murder of that monarch as a crime touching himself, inasmuch as it was a crime against royalty. It was therefore an act of deliberate policy that he punished the king-slayer in Eastern fashion, as an impressive example to his Eastern subjects. Oriental policy of Alexander;

The misfortune was that Alexander's assumption of oriental state, and the favour which he showed to the Persians, were highly unpopular with the Macedonians. It was hard always to preserve a double face, one for his Companions, another for his Persian ministers. Nor was it Alexander's policy to maintain this difference for ever. He hoped ultimately to secure uniformity in the relations of Macedonians and Persians to their common king. Meanwhile, in the intervals of rest between military operations, discontent smouldered among the Macedonians. Though they were attached to their king, and proud of the conquests which they had helped him to achieve, they felt that he was no longer the same to them as when he had led them to victory at the Granicus. His exaltation over obeisant orientals had changed him, and the execution of his trusted general Parmenio was felt to be significant of the change. unpopular with the Macedonians.

These feelings of discontent accidentally found a mouthpiece about this time. Rebellious movements in Sogdiana brought Alexander over the Oxus again before the winter was over, and he spent some time at Samarcand. One of the most unfortunate consequences of the long-protracted sojourn in the regions of the Oxus was the increase of drunkenness in the army. The excessively dry atmosphere in summer produces an intolerable and frequent thirst; and it was inevitable that the Macedonians should slake it by wine—the strong wine of the country—if they would not sicken themselves by the brackish springs of the desert or the noisome water of the towns. Alexander's potations became deep and habitual from this time forth. One night in the fortress of Samarcand the carouse lasted far into the night. Greek men of letters, who accompanied the army, sang the praises of Alexander, exalting him above the Dioscuri, 327 B.C. (first months.) Alexander at Samarcand.

whose feast he was celebrating on this day. Clitus, his foster-brother, flushed with wine, suddenly sprang up to denounce the blasphemy, and once he had begun, the current of his feelings swept him on into a denunciation and disparagement of Alexander. It was to the Macedonians, he said—to men like Parmenio and Philotas—that Alexander owed his victories; he himself had saved Alexander's life at the Granicus. These were the two sharpest stings; and they stirred Alexander's blood to fury. He started to his feet and called in Macedonian for his hypaspists; none obeyed his drunken orders; Ptolemy and other banqueters forced Clitus out of the hall, while others tried to restrain the king. But presently Clitus made his way back and shouted from the doorway some insulting verses of Euripides, signifying that the army does the work and the general reaps the glory. The king leapt up, snatched a spear from the hand of a guardsman, and rushed upon his foster-brother. Drunk though he was, the aim was sure—Clitus sank dead to the ground. An agony of remorse followed. For three days the murderer lay in his tent, without sleep or food, cursing himself as the assassin of his friends. The army sympathised with his grief; they tried the dead man and resolved that he had been justly slain. The tragedy was attributed to the anger of Dionysus, because the day was his festival and the Dioscuri had been celebrated instead.

Murder of Clitus.

The tragic issue of this miserable drunken brawl is a lurid spot in Alexander's life, but it was a slight matter compared with an act which is said to have marked his invasion of Sogdiana. When we saw him first cross the Oxus in pursuit of Bessus, we did not pause to witness his treatment of a remarkable town which lay on his way. The Branchidae, who had charge of the temple and oracle of Apollo twenty miles from Miletus, are charged with having betrayed the treasures of the sanctuary. Their lives were not safe from the anger of the Milesians, and Xerxes transported them into Central Asia, where no Greek vengeance could pursue them. They were established in Sogdiana, not far from the place where Alexander crossed, —a solitary little settlement, which, though severed so long from Hellas, preserved its Greek religion and Greek customs, and had not forgotten the Greek speech. It is easy to imagine what excitement was stirred there by the coming of a Greek army. The folk come forth joyously to bid Alexander welcome and offer him their fealty. But Alexander remembered only one thing—the ancestors of this people had committed a heinous crime against Apollo, and had sided with Persia against Greece. That crime had never been forgotten by the men of Miletus, and the king called upon the Milesians in his army to pronounce sentence upon the Branchidae. The

The town of the Branchidae (near Kilif).

Milesians could not agree, and Alexander himself decided the fate of the town. Having surrounded it with a cordon of soldiers, he caused all the inhabitants to be massacred and the place to be utterly demolished. Few of the children of the children's children of the original transgressors could have been still alive; most of the victims would have belonged to the fifth degree of descent. We cannot imagine a fouler enforcement of the savage principle that the crimes of the fathers should be visited to distant generations. Such is the shocking story which has blackened Alexander's fame; fortunately we can safely reject it as untrue; it was not related in the memoirs of the two oldest and best authorities, Ptolemy and Aristobulus. Alexander committed some cruel deeds, but none so appalling as this massacre would have been.

There were more hostilities in western Bactria and western Sogdiana, until at last, overawed by Alexander's success, the Scythians, in order to win his favour, slew Spitamenes. With this chieftain the resistance expired, and it only remained to reduce the rugged southeastern regions of Sogdiana, which were called Paraetacene. The Sogdian Rock, which commands the pass into these regions, was occupied by Oxyartes, and a band of Macedonian soldiers captured it by an arduous night-climb. Among the captives was Roxane, the daughter of Oxyartes; and the love of Alexander, who had been always indifferent to women, was attracted by the beauty and manners of the Sogdian maiden. It was characteristic of him that, notwithstanding the adverse comment which such a condescension would excite among the proud Macedonians, he resolved to make her his wife, and, on his return to Bactra after subjugating other fortresses in Paraetacene, he divided a loaf of bread with his bride according to the fashion of the country, and celebrated the nuptials. There was policy in this marriage as well as inclination. It was symbolic of the union of Asia and Europe, of the breaking down of the barrier between barbarian and Hellene, and of Alexander's position as an oriental king.

About this time an attempt seems to have been made to render uniform the court ceremonial. The Persian nobles were not well pleased that, whereas they were compelled to abase themselves to the ground before the divinity of the king, the Macedonians and Greeks were excused from the obeisance. Most of the Greeks would have been pliant enough, but there was one prominent man of letters who stood out against the usage and drew upon himself displeasure by the utterance of bold truths. This was Callisthenes, a nephew of Aristotle. He was composing a history of the campaigns of Alexander, whose exploits he ungrudgingly lauded; he had joined

Reduction of Paraetacene (Hissar)

Marriage of Alexander with Roxane, 327 B.C.

Callisthenes of Olynthus,

the army, he used to say, to make *him* famous, not to win fame himself. It is related that Hephaestion and a number of others arranged a plan for surprising the king's guests at a banquet into making the obeisance. Alexander, raising his golden cup, drank to each guest in order,—first to some of those who were privy to the plan; each arose and prostrated himself and was then kissed by the king. Callis-

thenes, when his turn came, drained the cup and went to receive the kiss, without doing obeisance; Alexander would not kiss him; and he turned away, saying, "I go the poorer by a kiss!" Incidents of this kind created a coolness between the king and his historian. One of the duties of Callisthenes and the other philosophers and literary men who accompanied Alexander's progress was to educate the pages, the noble Macedonian youths who attended on the king's person; and over some of these Callisthenes had great influence.

One day at a boar-hunt a page named Hermolaus committed the indiscretion of forestalling the king in slaying the beast; and for this breach of etiquette he was flogged and deprived of his horse. Smarting under the dishonour, Hermolaus plotted with some of his comrades to slay Alexander in his sleep. But on the appointed night Alexander sat up carousing till dawn, and on the next day the plot was betrayed. The conspirators were arrested, and put to death by

the sentence of the whole army. Callisthenes was also handfasted on the charge of being an accomplice, and was afterwards hanged. Hermolaus was indeed one of his warmest admirers, but it is not clear what the evidence against the historian was. On the one hand, Ptolemy and Aristobulus asserted independently that the pages declared under torture that Callisthenes had incited them; on the other hand, Alexander is said to have stated in a letter that the torture had failed to elicit the name of any accomplice. The deeper cause may be that Alexander suspected Callisthenes as an agent of the anti-Macedonian party in Greece.

Before the end of summer, Alexander bade farewell to Bactria and set forth to the conquest of India. Three years had passed since the death of Darius, three unique years in the annals of the world. In that time the western conqueror, disarranging the cycles of Asiatic history, had subdued Afghanistan, and cast his yoke over the herdsmen of the north as far as the river Jaxartes. He was the first and last western conqueror of Afghanistan; he was the first but not the last invader. He was the first European invader and conqueror of the regions beyond the Oxus, anticipating by more than two thousand years the conquests which have been achieved by an European power within the memory of the present generation. His next enterprise forestalled our own conquest of north-western India.

But England made her conquests from the south, Russia hers from the north; Alexander was the only European conqueror who marched straight from the west to the Indus and the Oxus.

The Macedonian monarch's work in Bactria and Sogdiana was an unavoidable sequel of his succession to the Persian empire. He had to set up a barrier against the unsettled races of the waste, who were a perpetual menace to the civilisations of the south. He founded a number of settlements in these regions, not only for the purpose of military garrisons, but also probably with the hope of gradually training the herdsmen to more settled ways of life. If so, it was a vain hope. History has shown that there is only one means of forcing the shepherd races to become reluctant tillers of the soil. Not until they have been encompassed on all sides by civilisation, and driven within a narrow geographical area, will they adopt, under the stress of necessity, the regular and laborious life of agriculture. The iron pressure of Russia's embrace is gradually narrowing the grounds of the nomads in Central Asia; in the days of Alexander they had end-less space behind them and an indefinite future before them.

SECT. 2. THE CONQUEST OF INDIA

In returning to Afghanistan, Alexander seems to have followed the main road from Balkh to Cabul, crossing the Hindu-Kush by a pass more westerly than that by which he had come. Reaching Alexandria in ten days, he went on to another town, which, if he had not refounded, he had at all events renamed, Nicaea, and which is possibly to be sought in Cabul itself. Here he stayed till the middle of November, finding much to do both in organising the province and in preparing for further advance. He had left a large detachment of his army in Bactria, but he had enrolled a still larger force—30,000—of the Asiatics of those regions,—Bactrians, Sogdians, Dahae, and Sacae. The host with which he was now to descend upon India must have been at least twice as numerous as the army with which he had crossed the Hellespont seven years before. It had increased as it rolled on, and the augmentations far more than counterbalanced the reductions caused by leaving detachments in each new province, and the losses due to warfare or disease.

During these years Alexander's camp was his court and capital, the political centre of his empire,—a vast city rolling along over mountain and river through Central Asia. Men of all trades and callings were there, some indispensable for the needs of the king and his army, others drawn by the prospect of making profits out of the spoil-laden soldiers: craftsmen of every kind, engineers, physi-

Halt at Nicaea (Cabul or Bagram?) 327 B.C.

Alexander's camp.

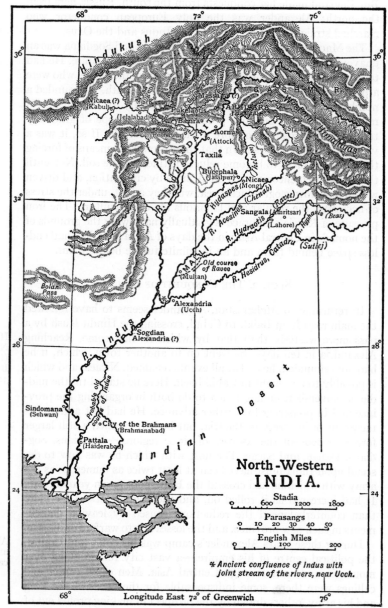

North-Western
INDIA.

Stadia
0   600   1200   1800

Parasangs
0   10   20   30   40   50

English Miles
0   100   200

* Ancient confluence of Indus with
joint stream of the rivers, near Ucch.

Longitude East 72° of Greenwich

Walker & Boutall sc.

FIG. 113.

cians, and seers; cheapmen and money-changers; literary men, poets, musicians, athletes, jesters; secretaries, clerks, court attendants; a host of women and slaves. In many of the halting-places athletic and musical contests were held, serving both to cheer the Greeks by reminding them of their home country and to impress the imagination of the barbarians. A Court Diary was regularly kept—in imitation of the court journal of Persia—by Eumenes of Cardia, who conducted all the political correspondence of Alexander.

Alexander had no idea of the shape or extent of the Indian peninsula, and his notion of the Indian conquest was probably confined to the basins of the Cophen and the Indus. He was not the first invader speaking an Aryan language who went down through the north-western hills into the plains of India. Centuries and centuries before, Aryan herdsmen had flowed down in successive waves and found an abiding home there. From Central Asia, from the regions of the Hindu-Kush, bringing with them their old hymns, some of which we still possess, they came down into the lands of the Indus, "the glorious giver of wealth," and turned to a settled agricultural life. Strangely different was the civilisation which grew up in northern India among the men who called upon *Dyaus pitar* from that of their speech-brethren who worshipped *Zeus patêr* on the shores of the Aegean. The castes of the Brahmans and the warriors, the inhuman asceticism of the Brahman's life, the political influence of these religious men, must have seemed repulsive and outlandish to the free and cheerful temper of the Greeks. The great Darius had partially annexed the lands of the Indus, and they constantly supplied troops to his successors. Scylax of Caryanda had sailed down the Indus by his orders and probably published an account of the voyage. The stories that were told about the wonders of India excited the curiosity of the Greek invaders. It was a land of righteous folks, of strange beasts and plants, of surpassing wealth in gold and gems. It was supposed to be the ultimate country on the eastern side of the world, bounded by Ocean's stream.

State of India.

(R. Cabui.)

At this time north-western India was occupied by a number of small heterogeneous principalities and village communities. The northern districts of the land between the Indus and the Hydaspes—the stream which we now call the Jhelum—were ruled by Omphis, a prince whose capital was at Taxila near the Indus. His brother Abisares was the ruler of Hazara and the adjacent parts of Cashmir. Beyond the Hydaspes was the powerful kingdom of Porus, who held sway as far as the Acesines or "dark-hued," which we know as the Chenab, the next of the "Five Rivers." East of the Chenab. in the lands of the Ravee and the Bëas, were other small

Omphis

(Takka cila.)
(The Pau rava.)
(Asikni.)

principalities, and also free "kingless" peoples, who owned no master. These principalities and free communities differed much in manners and religion; they had no tendency to unity or combination; the free tribes feared and hated the princes; the princes strove with one another. And these states were not all of the same race.

Most perhaps were Aryan; but some, like the Malli, belonged to the old "Dravidian" stock, whom even in the Punjab the Aryans had not entirely dispossessed or subdued. An invader, therefore, had no common resistance to fear; he had to deal with the states one by one; and he could be assured that many would welcome him out of hatred for their neighbours. The prince of Taxila hoped great things from the Macedonian conqueror, especially the downfall of his rival Porus. He visited Alexander at Nicaea, laid himself and his kingdom at the great emperor's feet, and promised his aid in subduing India. Other chiefs on the hither side of the Indus also made submission.

Alexander's direct road from the high plain of Cabul into the Punjab lay along the right bank of the Cophen or Cabul river, through the great gate of the Khyber Pass. But it was impossible to advance to the Indus without securing his communications, and for this purpose it was needful to subjugate the river-valleys to the left of the Cabul, among the huge western spurs of the Himalaya mountains.

It was perhaps not far from Jelalabad that the army came to a city which was called Nysa. The name immediately awakened in the minds of all the Greeks the memory of their god Dionysus. For Mount Nysa was the mythical place where he had been nursed by nymphs when he was born from the thigh of Zeus. The mountain was commonly supposed to be in Thrace; but an old hymn placed it "near the streams of Nile"; it had no place on the traveller's chart. But here was an actual Nysa; and close to the town was a hill whose name resembled *mêros*, the Greek word for "thigh," and whose slopes were covered with the god's own ivy. Therefore Nysa, they said, was founded by Dionysus; the god had fared eastward to subdue India; and now Alexander was marching on his tracks. Everywhere on their further march the Greeks and Macedonians were alert to discover traces of the progress of the bacchic god.

For the purposes of this campaign Alexander divided his army. Hephaestion, taking three regiments of the phalanx, half the Macedonian cavalry, all the mercenary cavalry, advanced by the Khyber Pass, with orders to construct a bridge across the Indus. The king, with the rest of the army, including the light troops, plunged into the difficult country north of the river; and the winter was spent in

warfare with the hardy hill-folks, especially the Aspasians and
Assacenes, and in capturing their impregnable fortresses, in the dis-   (Açrakas.)
trict of the Kunar, in remote Chitral, and in the Panjkar and Swat
valleys. It would be interesting to follow the exploits of the Macedonian army in these wilds, but we cannot identify the places with
certainty. Massaga, of the Assacenian people, in the Swat valley,
was one of the most important strongholds that Alexander captured; we cannot point it out on the map, but Dyrta, another fortress of the same people, may be fairly sought in Dir. The most
wonderful exploit of all was the scaling and taking of the rock of   Aornus
Aornus, which was probably somewhere near Amb, on the right
bank of the Indus, about sixty miles above the confluence of that
river with the Cabul. When by a miracle of boldness and patience
he captured this fortress, Alexander had to return on his steps as far
as Dir to suppress a revolt of the Assacenes.

After this severe winter campaign the army rested on the hither   Crossing
bank of the Indus until spring had begun, and then, with the solem-   of the
nity of games and sacrifices, crossed the river and marched a three   Indus
days' journey eastward to Taxila. The rich country of these Aryan   Attock,
husbandmen was a striking and pleasant contrast to the barren   326 B.C
abodes of the shepherds of Bactria and Sogdiana. The prince of
Taxila met Alexander with obsequious pomp, and other lesser
princes assembled at the city to do him homage. The administration
of the recent conquests was now arranged. A new satrapy, embracing the lands west of the Indus, was established and entrusted to
Philip, son of Machatas; Macedonian garrisons were placed in
Taxila and some other places east of the Indus, and Philip was
charged with the general command of these troops. This shows the
drift of Alexander's policy. The Indus was to be the eastern boundary of his direct sway; beyond the Indus, he purposed to create no
new provinces, but only to form a system of protected states, over
which the governor of the frontier province would have a general
supervision.

Alexander then marched by a southward road to the Hydaspes,
where he was to meet the only power in the land which could hope
to resist his progress. Prince Porus had sent a defiance, and having
gathered an army from thirty to forty thousand strong, was encamped on the left bank of the river, to contest the crossing. Moreover, Abisares of Cashmir promised him aid, although he had sent
marks of homage to Alexander. The boats which had been constructed on the Indus for transporting the troops were, by Alexander's orders, sawn in two or three pieces according to their size
and conveyed on carts to the Hydaspes. After a march, which was

made slow and toilsome by the heavy tropical rain, the invaders encamped on the right bank of the river, near Jalalpur, and saw the lines of Porus on the opposite shore, protected by a multitude of elephants, his most formidable weapon of war. It was useless to think of crossing in the face of this host; for the horses, who could not endure the smell and noise of the elephants, would certainly have been drowned; and the men would have found it almost impossible to land, amid showers of darts, on the slimy, treacherous edge of the stream. All the fords in the neighbourhood were watched. Alexander adopted various measures to deceive and puzzle the enemy. He collected large stores of corn, as if he had made up his mind to remain for many days where he was; he spread the rumour that he intended to wait till the season of rains was over; and he kept his troops in constant motion, sending detachments hither and thither. Then one night his trumpets blew, his cavalry rode down to the edge of the water, and to the eyes of the enemy it seemed that the whole army was about to cross. Porus moved his elephants up to the bank and set his host in array. But it proved to be a false alarm. The same feint was repeated again and again. Each night the Macedonian camp was in motion as if for crossing; each night the Indians stood long hours in the wind and rain. But when he saw that the noise was never followed by action, Porus became weary of these useless nightly watches and disregarded the alarms of a faint-hearted foe. Alexander meanwhile was maturing a plan which he was able to carry out when he had put Porus off his guard.

About sixteen miles upwards from the camp, the Hydaspes makes a bend, changing its course from south to westward, and opposite the jutting angle a thickly wooded island rose amid the stream, while a dense wood covered the right shore. Here Alexander determined to cross. He caused the boats to be conveyed thither and re-made in the shelter of the wood close to a deep ravine; he had prepared skins stuffed with straw, such as he had used in passing the Oxus. When the time came, he led a portion of his troops to the wooded promontory, marching at a considerable distance from the river in order to avoid the observation of the enemy. A sufficient force was left in the camp under the command of Craterus, with orders not to cross, unless Porus either moved his entire army from its present position or was defeated and routed. Other forces were posted at points between the camp and the island, to cross and help at the right moment. The king arrived at the appointed spot later in the evening, and throughout the wet stormy night he directed the preparations for passing the swollen stream. Here, on the right bank, he posted the regiments of heavy infantry which he had brought with him,—a precaution, probably, against the possible arrival of Abisares.

The wind and rain, which had effectually concealed all the noise from the ears of hostile outposts on the bank, abated before dawn, and the passage began. Alexander led the way in a barque of thirty oars; and the island was safely passed; but land was hardly reached before they were descried by Indian scouts, who galloped off at full speed to warn their chieftain. The king, who was the first to leap ashore, waited till the cavalry had been disembarked and marshalled, but on advancing he discovered that he had landed not on the bank but on an island which was parted from the bank by a small channel now swollen with rain. It was some time before a passage for wading could be found, and the water was breast-high. At last the whole force was safely landed on the bank, and Alexander ordered his men for the coming battle—the third of the three great battles of his life. It was to be won without any heavy infantry; he had with him only 6000 hypaspists, about 4000 light foot, 5000 cavalry, including 1000 Scythian archers. Taking all the cavalry with him, he rode rapidly forward towards the camp of Porus, leaving the infantry to follow. If the whole host of Porus should come out to meet him, he would wait for the infantry, but if the enemy showed symptoms of retreating, he would dash in among them with his superior cavalry. Presently he saw a troop coming; it was the son of Porus at the head of 1000 horsemen and sixty warchariots, too late to impede the landing of the Macedonians. As soon as he perceived the small number of the foe, Alexander charged and easily drove them back, slaying the prince and four hundred of his men.

But Porus himself was advancing with his main army, having left a small force to guard the river-bank against Craterus. When he reached sandy ground, suitable for the movements of his cavalry and war-chariots, he drew up his line of battle. In front of all he arranged two hundred elephants at intervals of 100 feet, and at some distance behind them his infantry, who numbered 20,000 if not more. On the wings he placed his cavalry—perhaps 4000. Alexander waited for the hypaspists, and drew them up opposite to the elephants. It was impossible to attack in front, for neither horse nor foot could venture in between these beasts which stood like towers of defence, the true strength of the Indian army. The only method was to begin by a cavalry attack on the flank; and Seleucus and the other captains of the infantry were bidden not to advance until they saw that both the horse and the foot of the foe were tumbled into confusion by the flank assault. Alexander determined to concentrate

Battle of the Hydaspes

his attack on the left wing; perhaps because it was on the river-side and he would be within easier reach of his troops on the other bank. Accordingly he kept all his cavalry on his right wing. One body was entrusted to Coenus, who bore well to the right, and was ready to strike in the rear, and to deal with the body of horse stationed upon the enemy's right wing, in case they should come round to assist their comrades on the left. The mounted Scythian archers rode straight against the front of the enemy's cavalry—which was still in column formation, not having had time to open out—and harassed it with showers of arrows; while Alexander himself, with the

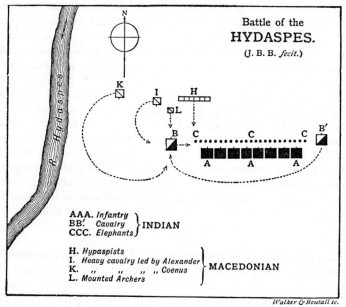

Battle of the
HYDASPES.
(J. B. B. *fecit.*)

AAA. *Infantry* ⎫
BB.' *Cavalry* ⎬ INDIAN
CCC. *Elephants* ⎭

H. Hypaspists ⎫
I. *Heavy cavalry led by Alexander* ⎪
K.   ,,   ,,   ,,   ,,   Coenus ⎬ MACEDONIAN
L. Mounted Archers ⎭

Walker & Boutall sc.

Fig. 114.

rest of the heavy cavalry, led the charge upon the flank. Porus—who had committed the fatal mistake of allowing the enemy to take the offensive—brought up his remaining squadrons from the right wing as fast as he could. Then Coenus, who had ridden round close to the river-bank, fell upon them in the rear. The Indians had now to form a double front against the double foe. Alexander seized the moment to press hard upon the adverse squadrons; they swayed backwards and sought shelter behind the elephants. Then those elephant riders who were on this side of the army drove the beasts against the Macedonian horses; and at the same time the Macedonian footmen rushed forward and attacked the animals which were now turned sidewards towards them. But the other elephants of the line were driven into the ranks of the hypaspists, and dealt destruction, trampling down and striking furiously. Heartened by the success of the elephants, the Indian cavalry rallied and charged, but beaten back by the Macedonian horse, who were now formed in a serried mass, they again sought shelter behind the elephantine wall. But many of the beasts were now furious with wounds and beyond control; some had lost their riders; and in the mellay they trampled on friends and foes alike. The Indians suffered most, for they were surrounded and confined to the space in which the animals raged; while the Macedonians could attack the animals on side or rear, and then retreat into the open when they turned to charge. At length, when the elephants grew weary and their charges were feebler, Alexander closed in. He gave the order for the hypaspists to advance in close array shield to shield, while he, re-forming his squadrons, dashed in from the side. The enemy's cavalry, already weakened and dislocated, could not withstand the double shock and was cut to pieces. The hypaspists rolled on upon the enemy's infantry, who, though they had hitherto taken no serious part in the fight, soon broke and fled. Meanwhile the generals on the other side of the river, Craterus and the rest, discovering that fortune was declaring for Alexander, crossed the river without resistance and arrived in time to consummate the victory by pursuing the fugitives. Porus, who had shown himself a mediocre general but a most valiant soldier, when he saw most of his forces scattered, his elephants lying dead or straying riderless, did not flee—as Darius had twice fled—but remained fighting, seated on an elephant of commanding height, until he was wounded in the right shoulder, the only part of his body unprotected by mail. Then he turned round and rode away. Alexander, struck with admiration at his prowess, sent messengers who overtook him and induced him to return. The victor, riding out to meet the old prince, was impressed by his stature and beauty, and asked him how he would fain be treated. "Treat me like a king," said Porus. "For my own sake," said Alexander, "I will do that; ask a boon for thy sake." "That," replied Porus, "containeth all."

And Alexander treated his captive royally. He not only gave him back his kingdom, henceforward to be a protected state under Macedonian suzerainty, but largely increased its borders. This royal treatment, however, though it pleased the generous impulses of Alexander, was inspired by deep policy. He could rest the security of

The Indian rally.

his rule beyond the Indus on no better base than the mutual jealousy of two moderately powerful princes. He had made the lord of Taxila as powerful as was safe; the reinstatement of his rival Porus would be the best guarantee for his loyalty. But on either side of the Hydaspes, close to the scene of the battle, two cities were founded, which would serve as garrisons in the subject land. On the right hand, the city of Bucephala, named after Alexander's steed, which died here—probably shortly before the battle—of old age and weariness; on the left, Nicaea, the city of victory.

Leaving Craterus to build the cities, Alexander marched northwards to subdue the Glausae, a hill-folk on the border of Cashmir, and at the same time to intimidate Abisares. Then keeping near the skirts of the hills, he crossed the Acesines, more than a mile and a half broad, with great peril and some loss, into the territory of a namesake and nephew of Porus. This Porus was at enmity with his uncle, who probably claimed overlordship over him; he had sent messages of submission to Alexander before the battle; but, disappointed and frightened at the favour which the conqueror had shown his uncle, he fled eastward. Alexander himself hastened in pursuit, crossing the Hydraotis, which, unlike the Acesines, was easily passed, but he left Hephaestion to march southward and subdue the land of the younger Porus, as well as the free communities between the two rivers,—all this northern portion of the "doab" or interfluvial tract to be added to the realm of the elder Porus. The news that the Cathaeans, a free and warlike people, whom Porus and Abisares had, some time before, failed to conquer, were determined to give him battle, diverted Alexander from the pursuit. He advanced against their chief town Sangala, strongly walled and protected on one side by a hill and on the other by a lake. It was probably near Amritsar, to the north-west of Lahore. The Cathaeans, supported by some neighbouring tribes, had made a stockade with a triple line of waggons round the hill. After a severe struggle the entrenchment was carried and the defenders retreated into the city. They tried to escape through the lake under the cover of night, but Alexander discovered the plan and lined the shores with soldiers. Then the place was stormed, and slighted; the neighbouring peoples submitted; and all this land was likewise placed under the lordship of Porus. Thus of the four river-bounded tracts which compose the Punjab, the largest, between Indus and Jehlum, belonged to Omphis of Taxila, while the three others, between Jehlum and Bëas, were assigned to Porus.

Alexander now advanced to the Hyphasis, or Bëas, and reached it higher up than the point where it joins the Sutlej to form the

Çatadru or "Hundred Streams." It was destined to be the land-mark of his utmost march. He wished to go farther and explore the lands of the Ganges, but an unlooked-for obstacle occurred. The Macedonians were worn out with years of hard campaigning, and weary of this endless rolling on into the unknown. Their numbers had dwindled; the remnant of them were battered and grown old before their time. The terrible rains which had beaten incessantly upon them since the crossing of the Indus and had made their lab-ours doubly laborious were the last weight in the scale. Their gear was worn out; the hoofs of their horses, as one of the campaigners described, were rubbed away by the long rough journeys; their arms were blunted and broken in hard combats; the bodies of the veter-ans were enveloped in Indian rags, for their Greek clothes were worn out. All yearned back to their homeland in the west. They had won glory enough; why heap up toil on toil and peril upon peril? On the banks of the Hyphasis the crisis came; the men resolved to go no farther, and their resolution was strengthened by the information that they would have to cross the Indian desert, a journey of eleven days, before they reached the fertile regions of the Ganges. At a meeting of the officers which Alexander summoned, Coenus was the spokesman of the general feeling. The king, not a little vexed, dis-missed them, and summoning them on the morrow, declared that he purposed to advance himself, but would constrain no man to fol-low him; let the Macedonians go back to Macedonia and tell how they abandoned their king in a hostile land. He retired to his tent, and for two days refused to see any of his Companions, hoping that their hearts would be softened. But though his resentment made them unhappy, the Macedonians did not relent or go back from their purpose. On the third day, Alexander offered sacrifices pre-liminary to crossing the river. But the victims—and this was as-suredly no freak of chance—gave unfavourable signs. Then the king yielded, and signified to the obdurate army that he had decided to return. When his will was made known, the way-worn veterans burst into wild joy; the more part of them shed tears. They crowded round the royal tent, blessing the unconquered king, that he had permitted himself to be conquered for once, by his Macedonians. On the banks of the Hyphasis Alexander erected twelve towering altars to the twelve great gods of Olympus, as a thank-offering for having strewn his wonderful path with victories and led him safely within reach of the world's end.

Within reach of the world's end, and not to reach it—this was the disappointment which befell Alexander at the Hyphasis. To under-stand fully the measure of this disappointment we must realise his

The term of Alex-ander's march.

The army refuses to advance.

Alexander's conception of the geography of Asia.

geographical conceptions. Of the southern extension of Asia in the great Indian promontory, and Further India with its huge islands, he knew nothing; of the vastness of China, of the existence of Siberia he had not the least suspicion. He supposed that the Ganges discharged its waters into the ocean which bounded the earth on the east, as the Atlantic bounded it on the west; and he imagined that this eastern sea, washing the base of the further slopes of the Hindu-Kush and Pamir mountains, and rounding the northern shores of Scythia, was continuous with the Caspian. And just as he planned to navigate the southern ocean, from the mouth of the Indus to the Arabian Gulf, or perhaps even round Libya to the Pillars of Heracles,—plans of which we shall presently speak,—so he probably dreamed of navigating the eastern ocean from the mouth of the Ganges and winning round to the shores of Scythia and Hyrcania. On annexation or effective conquest beyond the Hyphasis the mind of Alexander does not seem to have been bent. He had only a small army with him, for he had dropped large detachments on his way from the Jehlum to the Bëas; and he expected no hostilities from the tranquil dwellers of the Ganges. His expedition would have been in the first instance a journey of exploration; circumstances might have made it a march of conquest.

Alexander is often represented as a madman, dazzled by wild and whirling visions of dominion and glory, impelled by an insatiable lust of conquest for conquest's sake. But in judging his schemes, which in themselves seem wild to us who know the configuration of the earth, we must contract our imagination to the compass of his false notions and imperfect knowledge. If the form and feature of the earth were what he pictured it to be, twenty years would have sufficed to make his empire conterminous with its limits. He might have ruled from the eastern to the western ocean, from the ultimate bounds of Scythia to the shores of Libya; he might have brought to pass in the three continents an universal peace, and dotted the habitable globe with his Greek cities. Alexander was ambitious, but ambition did not blind him; he was perfectly capable of discerning shine from substance. The advance to the Indus was no mere wanton aggression, but was necessary to establish secure routes for Indian trade, which was at the mercy of the wild hill-tribes; and the subjugation of the Punjab was a necessity for securing the Indus frontier. The solid interests of commerce underlay the ambitions of the Macedonian conqueror. It is not without significance that Phonician merchants accompanied his army.

Alexander retraced his steps to the Hydaspes, on his way picking up Hephaestion, who had founded a new city on the banks of the

Acesines. On the Hydaspes, Craterus had not only built the two cities at the scene of the great battle, but had also prepared a large fleet of transports, which was to carry part of the army down the river to reach the Indus and the ocean. The fleet was placed under the command of Nearchus, and the king's own ship was piloted by Onesicritus, who afterwards wrote a book on Alexander's expedition. The rest of the army, divided into two parts, marched along either bank, under Hephaestion and Craterus.

As they advanced they swept the southern portions of the doabs, reducing the tribes which did not submit. The only formidable resistance that they encountered was from the free and warlike tribe of the Malli, whose territory stretched on both sides of the Ravee. Having routed a large host of these Indians on the southern bank of the river, Alexander pursued them to their chief city, which is probably to be sought at the site of the modern Multan. Since then the Ravee has changed its bed; in the days of Alexander it used to flow into the Chenab below Multan. Here he met with a grave adventure. The city had been easily taken, and the Indians had retreated into the citadel. Two ladders were brought to scale the earthen wall, but it was found hard to place them beneath the shower of missiles from above. Impatient at the delay, Alexander seized a ladder and climbed up under the cover of his shield. Peucestas, who bore the sacred buckler from the temple of Ilion, and Leonnatus followed, and Abreas ascended the other ladder. When the king reached the battlement, he hurled down or slew the Indians who were posted at that spot. The hypaspists, when they saw their king standing upon the wall, a mark for the whole garrison of the fortress, made a rush for the ladders, and both ladders broke under the weight of the crowd. Only those three—Peucestas, Leonnatus, and Abreas— reached the wall before the ladders broke. His friends implored Alexander to leap down; he answered their cries by leaping down among the enemy. He alighted on his feet. With his back to the wall he stood alone against the throng of foes, who recognised the Great King. With his sword he cut down their leader and some others who ventured to rush at him; he felled two more with stones; and the rest, not daring to approach, pelted him with missiles. Meanwhile his three companions had cleared the wall of its defenders and leapt down to help their king. Abreas fell slain by a dart. Then Alexander himself received a wound in the breast. For a space he stood and fought, but at last sank on his shield fainting through loss of blood. Peucestas stood over him with the holy shield of Troy, Leonnatus guarded him on the other side, until rescue came. Having no ladders, the Macedonians had driven pegs into the wall, and a few had

Siege of
Multan.

Alexander
wounded.

clambered up as best they could and flung themselves down into the fray. Some of these succeeded in opening one of the gates, and then the fort was taken. No man, woman, or child in the place was spared by the infuriated soldiers, who thought that their king was dead. But though the wound was grave, Alexander recovered. The rumour of his death reached the camp where the main army was waiting at the junction of the Ravee with the Chenab, and it produced deep consternation and despair. Reassuring letters were not believed; so Alexander caused himself to be carried to the banks of the Ravee and conveyed by water down to the camp. When he drew near, the canopy which sheltered his bed in the stern of the vessel was removed. The soldiers, still doubting, thought it was his corpse they saw, until the barque drew close to the bank and he waved his hand. Then the host shouted for joy. When he was carried ashore, he was lifted for a moment on horseback, that he might be the better seen of all; and then he walked a few steps for their greater reassurance.

Alex-
ander's
rashness
in endan-
gering his
person.

This adventure is an extreme case of Alexander's besetting weakness, which has been illustrated in many other of his actions. In the excitement of battle, amid the ring of arms, he was apt to forget his duties as a leader. Though one of the most consummate generals that the world has seen, he took a far keener delight in fighting in the thickest of the fray, or heading a charge of cavalry, than in manœuvring an army or contriving strategical operations. His eyes and ears were ever filled

With the brilliance of battle, the bloom and the beauty, the splendour of spears.

He could not resist the temptations of danger, and he had hardly conducted a single campaign in which he had not been wounded. On the last and most flagrant occasion, when some of his intimate friends upbraided him for acting as a soldier instead of acting as a general, he was deeply hurt; for his conscience pricked him. To have endangered his own safety was a crime against the whole army.

325 B.C.

The Malli made a complete submission, and their example was followed by the Oxydraces, their southern neighbours, who were also renowned for their warlike character. These lower parts of the Punjab were not added to the dominion of Porus, but were placed in direct dependence on the satrapy which had been committed to Philip. When Alexander had recovered from his wound, the fleet sailed downward past the junction of the Hyphasis, and the Indian tribes submitted, presenting to the conqueror the characteristic products of India, gems, fine draperies, tame lions and tigers. At the place where the united stream of the four lesser rivers joins the mighty flow of the Indus, the foundations were laid of a new Alexandria, to be the great trade centre between the Punjab and the territory of the lower Indus, and to be the bulwark of the southern frontier of the province of Philip. The next stage of the southward advance was the capital town of the Sogdi, which lay upon the river. Alexander refounded it as a Greek colony, and built wharfs; it was known as the Sogdian Alexandria and was destined to be the residence of a southern satrapy which was to extend to the seacoast. This province was committed to Peithon, the son of Agenor.

(The Panjnab.) Alexandria (Uchh). Foundation of Sogdian Alexandria (? Alor, or, higher up, Sirwahi).

The principalities of the rich and populous land of Sind were distinguished from the states of the north by the great political power enjoyed by the Brahmans. Under the influence of this caste, which was vehemently opposed to the intrusion of the outlanders, the princes either defied Alexander or, if they submitted at first, speedily rebelled. The spring was spent in reducing these regions, and it was nearly midsummer when the king reached Patala at the vertex of the Indus delta. On the tidings of an insurrection in Arachosia, he had dispatched Craterus with a considerable portion of the army to march through the Bolan Pass into southern Afghanistan and put down the revolt. Alexander himself designed to march through Baluchistan, and Craterus was ordered to meet him in Kirman, near the entrance of the Persian Gulf. Another division of the host was to go by sea to the mouth of the Tigris. The king fixed upon Patala to be for the Indian empire what the most famous of his Alexandrias was for Egypt. He charged Hephaestion with the task of fortifying the citadel and building an ample harbour. Then he sailed southward himself to visit the southern ocean. It was the season at which the monsoons blow from the south-west, and the Macedonians, accustomed to the tideless midland sea, were at first sorely perplexed by the ebb and flow of the oceanic tide, at this time especially high and violent in the main arm of the river. Several ships were lost, but the sailors soon mastered the secret of the times and tides, and Alexander fared out into the open sea. He sacrificed to Poseidon; he poured drink-offerings from a golden cup to the Nereids and Dioscuri, and to Thetis the mother of his ancestor Achilles, and then hurled the cup into the waves. This ceremony inaugurated his plan of opening a seaway for commerce between the West and the Far East. The enterprise of discovering this seaway was entrusted to Nearchus, an officer who was an intimate companion of his own and possessed the confidence of the troops. Alexander started on his land-march in the early autumn, but Nearchus and the fleet were

Patala (Hyderabad).

Alexander sails in the Indian Ocean.

to wait till October, in order to be helped forward by the eastern monsoons.

SECT. 3. ALEXANDER'S RETURN TO BABYLON

No enterprise of Alexander was so useless, and none so fatal, as the journey through the desert of Gedrosia, the land which is now known as the Mekran. Of the inhospitable character of the country he must have had general information, but he had no idea of the hardships and terrors of the march which awaited him. His guiding motive in choosing this route was to make provisions for the safety of the fleet, to dig wells and store food at certain places along the coast. He also had in view the subjugation of the Orītae, a hardy warlike people who dwelled in the mountains on the eastern limit of the wilderness. But if it had been only a matter of subduing the

FIG. 115.—Coin of Alexander. Obverse: head of Heracles, in lion's skin. Reverse: eagle-bearing Zeus, and prow of galley in field [legend: ΑΛΕΞΑΝΔΡΟΥ].

Orites, this could easily have been accomplished by an expedition from Patala. The march through the Mekran and the voyage of Nearchus were interdependent parts of the same adventure; and so timid were the mariners of those days that the voyage into unknown waters seemed far more formidable than the journey through the waste.

March of Alexander through the Mekran [August, Sept., Oct.), 325 B.C.

With perhaps thirty thousand men, Alexander passed the mountain wall which protects the Indus delta, and crossing the river Arbis, he reduced the Oritae to subjection. He chose their chief village Rambacia for the foundation of a colony, the Orite Alexandria; it was important to have stations on his projected ocean-route. Then he descended into the waste of Gedrosia. No resistance met him here, for there was no folk to resent his intrusion; only a few miserable villages in the hills, or more miserable fishing hamlets on the coast. The army moved painfully through the desert of rocks and sand, waterless and barren; and part of the scanty provisions that the foragers obtained had to be stored on the shore for the coming of the fleet. It was often almost impossible to step through the deep sinking sand; the pitiless heat rendered night marches necessary; and those marches were frequently of undue length, owing to the need of reaching a spring of water. Alexander himself is said to have trudged on foot and shared all the hardships of the way. It was doubtless the non-combatants and camp-followers who suffered most. At length the waste was crossed; and, leaving the coast regions, the remnant of the army marched north to Pura, the residence of the satrapy of Gedrosia. It is said that the survivors, exhausted and dishevelled, were the smaller part of the army which had set forth from India two months before; and the losses of that terrible Gedrosian journey exceeded the losses of all Alexander's campaigns. But this is probably a heightened statement of the calamities of the march.

Having rested at Pura, the king proceeded to Kirman, where he was joined by Craterus, who had suppressed the revolt in Arachosia. Presently news arrived that the fleet had reached the Kirman coast, and soon Nearchus arrived at the camp and relieved Alexander's anxiety. He too had a tale to tell of hardships and perils. The hostile attitude of the Indians, when Alexander's back was turned, had forced him to start a month before the season of the east winds; and contrary south winds kept him for twenty-four days in a haven at some distance to the west of the delta. Then a storm wrecked three of his ships near Cocala. During the rest of their voyage the seafarers were sore bestead by want of sweet water and provisions. But the king was overjoyed that they had arrived at all. Nearchus was dismissed to complete the voyage by sailing up the Persian Gulf and the Pasitigris river to Susa; Hephaestion was sent to make his way thither along the coast; while Alexander himself marched through the hills by Persepolis and Pasargadae.

The voyage of Nearchus, Oct.-Dec. 325 B.C.

(? Karachi.)

It was high time for Alexander to return. There was hardly a satrap, Persian or Macedonian, in any land, who had not oppressed his province by violence and rapacity; and some, in the expectation that the king would never come back from the Far East, had formed plots for establishing independent principalities. In Kirman, in Persis, and at Susa, the most pressing business of the king was to re-establish his authority by punishing without favour or mercy the governors and officers who were found guilty of treason and oppression. Many satraps were deposed or put to death; Atropates of Media was one of the few who had been faithful to his charge. But the military garrison of Media had not behaved so well; and none of Alexander's dooms at this juncture was more effective than the execution of two officers and six hundred soldiers for having plun-

Misconduct of Alexander's governors, and his dealings with them.

dered the temples and sepulchres of that province. Of all evil deeds, that perhaps which most vexed the king was the opening and plundering of the sepulchre of Cyrus at Pasargadae; it was more than a common sacrilege, it was an outrage against the majesty of kings. He tortured the Magians who were the guardians of the tomb, but did not discover the author of the outrage.

Flight of Harpalus.

One guilty minister fled at Alexander's approach. This was the treasurer Harpalus, who had once before been untrue to his charge, but had been forgiven and entrusted with the royal treasures of Persia. He squandered his master's money in riotous living at Babylon, and as the news of these scandals reached Alexander in India, he deemed it prudent to move westward. Taking a large sum of money, he went to Cilicia, and hiring a bodyguard of 6000 mercenaries, he lived in royal state at Tarsus with Glycera, an Athenian courtesan. On Alexander's return, Tarsus was not safe, and he fled to Greece, where we shall meet him presently.

Alexander's policy: the the fusion of Greeks and Asiatics;

Having punished with a stern hand the misrule of his satraps, Macedonian and Persian alike, Alexander began to carry out schemes which he had formed for breaking down the barrier which divides the East from the West. He had unbarred and unveiled the Orient to the knowledge and commerce of the Mediterranean peoples, but his aim was to do much more than this; it was no less than to fuse Asia and Europe into a homogeneous unity. He devised various means for compassing this object. He proposed to transplant Greeks and Macedonians into Asia, and Asiatics into Europe, as permanent settlers. This plan had indeed been partly realised by the foundation of his numerous mixed cities in the Far East. The second means was the promotion of intermarriages between Persians and Macedonians, and this policy was inaugurated in magnificent fashion at Susa. The king himself espoused Statira, the daughter of Darius; his friend Hephaestion took her sister; and a large number of Macedonian officers wedded the daughters of Persian grandees. The nuptials were celebrated on the same day and according to the Persian fashion; Alexander is said to have feasted 9000 guests. Of the general mass of the Macedonians 10,000 are said to have followed the example of their officers and taken Asiatic wives; all those were liberally rewarded by Alexander. He looked forward to the offspring of these unions as a potent instrument for the further fusing of the races. It is to be noticed that Alexander, already wedded to the princess of Sogdiana, adopted the polygamous custom of Persia; and he even married another royal lady, Parysatis, daughter of Ochus. These marriages were purely dictated by policy; they were meant as an example; for Alexander never came

**means for accomplishing this:
(1) transplantation and colonisation;
(2) intermarriage;**

under the influence of women. The bridals of Susa were a lesson in political marriages on a vast scale.

But the most effective means for bringing the two races together vas the institution of military service on a perfect equality. With this purpose in view, Alexander, not long after the death of Darius, had arranged that in all the eastern provinces the native youth should be drilled and disciplined in Macedonian fashion and taught to use the Macedonian weapons. In fact, Hellenic military schools were established in every province, and at the end of five years an army of 30,000 Hellenized barbarians was at the Great King's disposition. At his summons this army gathered at Susa, and its arrival created a natural, though unreasonable, feeling of discontent among the Macedonians, who divined that Alexander aimed at making himself independent of their services. His schemes of transforming the character of his army were also indicated by the enlistment of Persians, Bactrians, Areians, and other orientals in the Macedonian cavalry regiments, and the enrolling of nine distinguished Persians in the royal Agema itself. The general dissatisfaction was not allayed by the king's liberality in defraying all the debts of the soldiers—amounting perhaps to two millions.

(3) equal military service.

Alexander left Susa for Ecbatana in spring. He sailed down the river Pasitigris to the Persian Gulf, surveyed part of the coast, and sailed up the Tigris, removing the weirs which the Persians had constructed to hinder navigation. The army joined him on the way, and he halted at Opis. Here he held an assembly of the Macedonians, and formally discharged all those—about 10,000 in number—whom old age or wounds had rendered unfit for warfare, promising to make them comfortable for life. He fondly thought that his words would be welcomed with delight, but he was disappointed. The smouldering discontent found a voice now. The cry was raised, "Discharge us all"; and some tauntingly added, "Go and conquer with your father Ammon." The king may well have been taken aback. The men who on the banks of the Hyphasis had declared themselves worn out with war and toil and sick with yearning for their homes, were now indignant when he honourably discharged their veterans. Alexander leapt down from the platform into the shouting throng; he pointed out thirteen of the most forward rioters, and bade his hypaspists seize them and put them to death. The rest were cowed. Amid a deep silence the king remounted the platform, and in a bitter speech he discharged the whole army. Then he retired into his palace, and on the third day summoned the Persian and Median nobles and appointed them to posts of honour and trust which had hitherto been filled by Macedonians. The names of

Macedonian mutiny at Opis.

the Macedonian regiments were transferred to the new barbarian army. When they heard this, the Macedonians, who still lingered in their quarters, miserable and uncertain whether to go or stay, appeared before the gates of the palace. They laid down their arms submissively and implored admission to the king's presence. Alexander came out, and there was a tearful reconciliation, which was sealed by sacrifices and feasts. This dramatic incident possesses no historical importance like the action of the troops on the Hyphasis, and it is only significant in so far as it marks the last futile explosion of Macedonian sentiment against the liberal policy of the king, the final protest of men who knew that they would have to acquiesce in a new order of things.

The veterans started for home under the leadership of Craterus and Polyperchon; they left behind the children whom Asiatic women had borne to them, the king promising to bring them up in Macedonian fashion. Craterus was to supersede Antipater as regent of Macedonia, and Antipater was to come out to Asia with a fresh supply of troops. This arrangement was desirable, on account of the estranged relations which existed between Antipater and the queen-mother, whose letters to Alexander were always teeming with mutual accusations.

The summer and early winter were spent at the Median capital. Here a sorrow, the greatest that could befall him, befell Alexander. Three thousand professional players or "Dionysiac artists," as they were called, had arrived from Greece; and Ecbatana was festive

with revels and dramatic exhibitions. In the midst of the gaiety, Hephaestion fell ill, languished for seven days, and died. Alexander was plunged into despair at losing the friend of his bosom; he fasted three days, and the whole empire went into mourning; it is said that he crucified the miserable physician whose skill had been found wanting. Inconsolable the lonely monarch might well be. He could have other boon companions, other faithful counsellors and devoted servants; but he knew that he would never find another to whom he would be simply "my friend Alexander" and not "my lord the king." The body was sent to Babylon to be burned; 10,000 talents were set apart for a funeral of unsurpassed magnificence.

Alexander set out for Babylon towards the end of the year, and on his way he enjoyed the excitement of hunting down the Cossaeans, a hill-folk of Luristan, who made brigandage their trade. The slaughter of these robbers, who were chased to their mountain nests, was described as an offering to the spirit of Hephaestion. As Alexander advanced to Babylon, ambassadors from far lands came to his camp. The Bruttians, Lucanians, and Etruscans, the Carthaginians and the Phoenician colonies of Spain, Celts, Scythians of the Black Sea, Libyans, and Ethiopians had all sent envoys to court the friendship of the monarch who seemed already to be lord of half the earth. A feeling of dread was beginning to quiver faintly through the western world that the conqueror of the East would presently turn the path of his progress to the West. Carthage might feel a tremor lest he should come against her as the champion of Hellenic Sicily and do unto her what he had done to elder Tyre. But from the city of Italy, which was destined to destroy the power of Carthage and become the partial inheritor of Alexander's empire, no ambassador came.

(No embassy from Rome.)

When Alexander approached within sight of Babylon, he was met by a deputation of priestly star-gazers who counselled him not to enter the city, for their god Bel had revealed to them that it would not be for his profit. He replied to the Chaldaeans with a verse of Euripides—"The best seer he who guesseth well," and entered at the head of his army. One of his first cares was to take measures for the rebuilding of the temple of Bel, unduly retarded by the wilful neglect of the Chaldaean priests, who were unwilling to appropriate their revenues to the purpose. It has been thought that their attempt to divert the king from entering Babylon may have had a motive connected with their negligence.

Arrival at Babylon. The warning of the Chaldeans; and the temple of Bel.

SECT. 4. PREPARATIONS FOR AN ARABIAN EXPEDITION. ALEXANDER'S DEATH

Ever since the successful voyage of Nearchus, the brain of Alexander was filled with maritime enterprises. He was bent on the exploration of the northern and the southern oceans. He had already sent Heraclides and a company of shipwrights to the Hyrcanian mountains, to cut wood in the forests and build a fleet to navigate the Caspian Sea and discover its supposed communication with the eastern ocean. But his more immediate and serious enterprise was the circumnavigation and conquest of Arabia. His eastern empire was not complete so long as this peninsula lay outside it. He knew of the rich spice-lands of Arabia Felix, but he had no conception of the vast extent of the desert which renders a land invasion so difficult and so unremunerative. The possession of this country of sand, however, was not his main object; it was only an incident in the grand range of his plans. His visit to India and the voyage of Nearchus had given him new ideas; he had risen to the conception of making the southern ocean another great commercial sea like the Mediterranean. He proposed to make the seaboard of the Persian

Alexander's designs on Arabia;

Gulf a second Phoenicia, and he sent to the Syrian coast for seamen to colonise the shores of the mainland and the islands. He hoped to establish a regular trade route from the Indus to the Tigris and Euphrates, and thence to the canals which connected the Nile with the Red Sea. If he had lived to accomplish this he might have renewed the project of king Necho and hewn a water-way through the neck of Suez. Mighty Babylon would then be in close connexion with the new oceanic trade; argosies from Alexandria or Patala could sail into her wharves. Alexander destined Babylon to be the capital of his empire, and doubtless it was a wise choice. But its character was now to be transformed. It was to become a naval station and a centre of maritime commerce. Alexander set about the digging of a great harbour, with room for a thousand keels, and designed the building of shipsteads.

his preparations;   The fleet of Nearchus sailed up the Euphrates and met the king at Babylon. But this fleet was not sufficient for the approaching enterprise. Orders had been sent to Phoenicia for the building of new warships: twelve triremes, three quadriremes, four quinqueremes, and thirty of the smaller thirty-oared barques. These were constructed in pieces, conveyed overland to Thapsacus on Euphrates, and there put together. Other ships, of cypress wood, were also built in Babylonia. The expedition was to set forth in the summer, and the king occupied part of the intervening time in a voyage down

his voyage to the Babylonian marshes.   the Euphrates to visit the Pallacopas canal. The snows of winter melting in the late spring-tide on the north slopes of the Armenian mountains used to swell the waters of the Euphrates and force it to overflow its banks in the Babylonian plain. About ninety miles below Babylon a canal had been dug to drain the superfluous waters into the marshes which stretched for leagues and leagues southwestward. In the autumn the canal was closed by a sluice to prevent the water leaving its bed. But the sluice was out of working order, and Alexander devised a better place, connecting the canal with the river at a different point. He sailed up the canal, lost his way for a while among the swamps, and selected a site for a new city, whose building was immediately begun. We may guess that the city was meant to be the first of a string of fortresses stretching across the desert from Babylonia to the Red Sea.

Reform of the phalanx.   On his return to Babylon, he found some new western troops which had arrived from Caria and Lydia, and also a body of 20,000 Persians who had been recruited by Peucestas. He proceeded to carry out a sweeping military reform, at which his mind must have been working for some time past. It was nothing less than a complete transformation of his father's phalanx,—in fact, of the Hellenic hoplite system. Alexander had done much with the well-drilled phalanx; but his experience had taught him that it was far from being the ideal infantry. The advantages of its sheer weight and solid strength were more than counterbalanced by its want of mobility. Alexander invented a means of increasing the mobility with as little as possible diminution of the weight. He inserted the fresh body of 20,000 Persians into the Macedonian phalanx in the following way. The old depth of the file, namely sixteen men, was retained, but of these only four were Macedonian pikemen—the men of the first three ranks and the hindmost man of all. The twelve intervening places—the fourth to the fifteenth ranks—were filled by Persians lightly armed with their native bows and javelins. This new phalanx required a new kind of tactics, which must have consisted in opening out the ranks, so as to allow the archers and javelin-men to deploy into the intervals and discharge their missiles, and then closing up again, in order to advance in a serried mass, each file bristling with three, no longer with five, spear-points. It was a thoroughly original idea, this combination of heavy and light troops into a tactical unity; but it would need all the skill of the great master to bring it to perfection. The strange thing is to find Alexander introducing this new system, which implied a complete change in the drill, on the very eve of his setting forth on the Arabian expedition. We are tempted to think that he had already made experiments—perhaps with that army of 30,000 orientals, drilled in Macedonian fashion, who had come to him at Susa. The tactical reform had also its political bearings. It was another step in the direction of fusing the Macedonian and Persian together, and marrying Europe with Asia.

There was one thing, very near to the king's heart, still to be accomplished before he set out—the funeral of Hephaestion. The oracle of Ammon had been consulted touching the honours which should be paid to the dead man, and had ordained that he might be honoured as a hero. In accordance therewith, Alexander ordered that chapels should be erected to Hephaestion in Egyptian Alexandria and other cities. Never were obsequies so magnificent as those which were held at Babylon; the funeral pyre, splendidly decked with offerings, towered to the height of 200 feet.

All was in readiness at length for the expedition to the south. On a day in early June a royal banquet was given in honour of Nearchus and his seamen, shortly about to start on their oceanic voyage. As Alexander was retiring to his chamber at a late hour, a friend named Medius carried him off to spend the rest of the night in a bout of hard drinking. On the morrow he slept long; in the evening he dined

Funeral of Hephaestion, May 323 B.C.

Illness of Alexander, 16th day of Daesius (June 1 ?); 17th;

18th;

with Medius, and another carousal followed. After a bath and a meal in the early hours of the morning, he fell into a feverish sleep. On awaking, he insisted upon preparing the daily sacrifices according to his wont; but the fever was still on him, he could not walk, and was carried to the altar on a couch. He spent the day in bed, actively engaged with Nearchus in discussing the expedition, which he fixed for four days hence. In the cool of the evening he was conveyed to the river and rowed across to a garden villa at the other

19th-24th;

side. For six days he lay here in high fever, but regularly performing the sacrifices, and daily perforce deferring the departure of the expedition for another and yet another day. Then his condition grew

25th;

worse, and he was carried back to the palace, where he won a little sleep, but the fever did not abate. When his officers came to him they found him speechless; the disease became more violent, and a rumour spread among the Macedonian soldiers that Alexander was dead. They rushed clamouring to the door of the palace, and the

27th.

bodyguards were forced to admit them. One by one they filed past the bed of their young king, but he could not speak to them; he could only greet each by slightly raising his head and signing with his eyes. Peucestas and some others of the Companions passed the night in the temple of Serapis and asked the god whether they should convey the sick man into the temple, if haply he might be cured there by divine help. A voice warned them not to bring him,

Death of Alexander, 28th of Daesius (= June 13). His work and what he might have done.

but to let him remain where he lay. He died on a June evening, before the thirty-third year of his age was fully told. Such is the punctilious and authentic account of the last illness of Alexander, as it was recorded in the Court Diary; but it is not sufficient to enable us to discover the precise nature of the fatal disease.

The untimely deaths of sovereigns at particular junctures have often exercised an appreciable influence on the course of events; but no such accident has diverted the paths of history so manifestly and utterly as the death of Alexander. Twelve years had sufficed him to conquer western Asia, and to leave an impress upon it which centuries would not obliterate. And yet his work had only been begun. Many plans for the political transformation of his Asiatic empire had been initiated,—plans which reveal his originality of conception, his breadth of grasp, his firm hold of facts, his faculty for organisation, his wonderful brain-power,—but all these schemes and lines of policy needed still many years of development under the master's shaping and guiding hand. The unity of the realm, which was an essential part of Alexander's conception, disappeared upon his death. The empire was broken up among a number of hard-headed Macedonians, capable and practical rulers, but with-

out the higher qualities of the founder's genius. They maintained
the tolerant Hellenism which he had initiated,—his lessons had not
been lost upon them; and thus his work was not futile; the toils of
even those twelve marvellous years smoothed the path for Roman
sway in the East, and prepared the ground for the spread of an
universal religion.

It is impossible to write the history of Alexander so as to produce
a true impression of his work, because, in the records which we have,
the general and soldier fills the whole stage and the statesman is, as
it were, hustled out. The details of administrative organisation are
lost amidst the sounding of trumpets and the clashing of spears. But
it is the details of administration and political organisation which
the historical inquirer craves to know, and especially the constitution of the various new-founded cities in the Far East, those novel
experiments which set Macedonian, Greek, and oriental inhabitants
side by side. By their silence on these matters the Companions of
Alexander, who wrote memoirs about him, unwittingly did him a
wrong, and hence there has largely prevailed an unjust notion that
he only knew and only cared how to conquer.

It is hardly open to question that this brilliant lord of well-trained
myriads would have advanced to the conquest of the West; nor can
we affect to doubt that, succeeding where one of his successors   (Pyrrhus.)
failed, he would have annexed Sicily and Great Hellas, conquered
Carthage, and overrun the Italian peninsula. To apprehend what
his death meant for Europe we need not travel farther in our speculations. To the Indies he would certainly have returned and carried
out with fresh troops that project of visiting the valley of the
Ganges which had been frustrated by his weary army. As it was, he
had left no lasting impression upon Indian civilisation; and his successors soon abandoned their hold upon the Punjab. It is needless
to add that if Alexander had lived another quarter of a century, he
would have widened the limits of geographical knowledge. The true
nature of the Caspian Sea would have been determined; the southern extension of the Indian peninsula would have been discovered;
and an attempt would have been made to repeat the Phoenician
circumnavigation of Africa. Nor could Alexander have failed, in his
advanced position on the Jaxartes, to have learned some facts about
the vast extension of the Asiatic continent to the east and north,
and the curiosities of Chinese civilisation.

His sudden death was no freak of fate or fortune; it was a natural
consequence of his character and his deeds. Into thirteen years he
had compressed the energies of many lifetimes. If he had been content with the duties of a general and a statesman, laborious and

wearing though those duties would have been both to body and to brain, his singularly strong constitution would probably have lasted him for many a long year. But the very qualities of his brilliant temper which most endeared him to his fellows, a warrior's valour and a love of good fellowship, were ruinous to his health. He was covered with scars; and he had probably never recovered from that terrible wound which had been the price of his escapade at Multan. Sparing of himself neither in battle nor at the symposion, he was doomed to die young.

SECT. 5. GREECE UNDER MACEDONIA

The tide of the world's history swept us away from the shores of Greece; and, borne breathlessly along from conquest to conquest in the triumphant train of the Macedonian, we could not pause to see what was happening in the little states which were looking with mixed emotions at the spectacle of their own civilisation making its way over the earth. Alexander's victory at the gates of Issus and his ensuing supremacy by sea had taught many of the Greeks the lesson of caution; the Confederacy of the Isthmus had sent congratulations and a golden crown to the conqueror; and when, a twelvemonth later, the Spartan king Agis, a resolute man without any military ability, renewed the war against Macedonia, he got no help or countenance outside the Peloponnesus. Some hot spirits at Athens proposed to support the movement, but the people were discreetly restrained not only by Phocion and Demades but by Demosthenes himself. Agis induced the Arcadians, except Megalopolis, the Achaeans, except Pellene, and the Eleians, to join him; and having mercenary troops besides, he got together a considerable army. It was easy to gain a few successes, before the regent of Macedonia, then occupied with a rising in Thrace, had time to descend on the

Battle of Megalopolis, 331 B.C.

Peloponnesus. The chief object of the allies was to capture Megalopolis, and the federal capital of Arcadia was in the strange position of being besieged by the Arcadian federates. Antipater, as soon as the situation in Thrace set him free, marched southward to the relief of Megalopolis, and easily crushed the allies in a battle fought hard by. Agis fell fighting, and there was no further resistance; Sparta sent up hostages to Alexander, who accorded the conquered Greeks easy terms.

So long as Darius lived, many of the Greeks cherished secret hopes that fortune might yet turn against Alexander, and maintained clandestine intrigues with Persia. But on the news of his death such hopes expired, and tranquillity prevailed in Hellas. It was not till Alexander's return from India that anything happened to trouble the peace. And in the meantime Greece was experiencing a relief which she had needed for two generations. A field had been opened to her superfluous children, who were pouring by thousands, or rather tens of thousands, into Asia, to find careers, if not permanent homes.

For Athens the twelve years between the fall of Thebes and the death of Alexander were an interval of singular well-being. The conduct of public affairs was in the hands of the two most honourable statesmen of the day, Phocion and Lycurgus. Supported by the orator Demades, Phocion was able to dissuade the people from embarking in any foolhardy enterprises; and Demosthenes was sufficiently clear-sighted not to embarrass, but, when needful, to support, the policy of peace. Phocion probably did not grudge him the signal triumph which he won over his old rival, Aeschines; for this triumph had only a personal, and not a political, significance. Shortly before Philip's death, Ctesiphon had proposed to honour Demosthenes, both for his general services to the state and especially for his liberality in contributing from his private purse towards the repair of the city-walls, by crowning him publicly in the theatre with a crown of gold. The Council had passed a resolution to this effect; but Aeschines lodged an accusation against the proposer, whose motion technically exposed him to the Graphe Paranomon, and consequently the Council's resolution was not brought before the people. The matter remained in abeyance for about six years, neither party venturing to bring it to an issue, Aeschines by following up his indictment or Ctesiphon by forcing him to bring it into court. The collapse of the attempt of Agis to defy Macedonia probably encouraged Aeschines to face his rival at last. In a speech of the highest ability Aeschines reviewed the public career of Demosthenes, to prove that he was a traitor and responsible for all the disasters of Athens. The reply of Demosthenes, a masterpiece of splendid oratory, captivated the judges; and Aeschines, not winning one-fifth part of their votes, left Athens and disappeared from politics. It is not unfair to say that it was Demosthenes the orator, not Demosthenes the statesman, who convinced the Athenian judges. Apart from his Speech on the Crown, which has been described as the funeral oration on Greek freedom, Demosthenes fell almost silent during these years; he saw that public action on his part would be useless; but perhaps he worked underground.

In these two speeches in the matter of the crown, the most interesting passage is where Aeschines reflects on the changes which had recently come to pass over the face of the earth. We want to know

Athens.

Attitude of Demosthenes.

Speeches on the Crown, 330 B.C.

Aeschines on the strange events of his time.

what the Greeks thought of those startling changes, what they felt as they saw the fashion of the world passing and the things which had seemed of great weight and worth in Hellas becoming of small account. Aeschines thus utters their surprise:—

"All manner of strange events, utterly unforeseen, have befallen in our lifetime. Our extraordinary experiences will seem to those who come after us like a curious tale of marvels. The king of the Persians, who dug the canal through Athos, who bridged the Hellespont, who demanded earth and water from the Greeks, who dared in his letters to declare, 'I am the lord of all the world from the rising to the setting of the sun,' is at this moment struggling not for domination over other men, but to save his own life and limb. Thebes, even Thebes our neighbour, has been snatched, in the space of a single day, out of the midst of Hellas—justly, for her policy was false; but assuredly she was rather blinded by a heaven-sent infatuation than misled by human perversity. And the poor Lacedaemonians, who once lifted themselves up to be leaders of the Greeks, must now go up to Alexander as hostages and throw themselves upon the mercy of the potentate whom they wronged. Our own city, once the asylum of the Greek world, whither all men looked for help, has now ceased to strive for the leadership of the Greeks, for the very ground of her home is in danger."

Athenian activity in the west.

The Macedonian empire had not yet lasted long enough to turn the traffic of the Mediterranean into new channels, and Athens still enjoyed great commercial prosperity. She sent a colony to some unknown place on the Hadriatic seaboard, to be a base of protection against the Etruscan rovers, the big menacing eyes of whose pirate crafts were a constant terror to traders in those seas. And although peace was her professed policy, she did not neglect to make provision for war, in case a favourable opportunity should come round, in the revolution of circumstance, for regaining her sovereignty on sea. Money was spent on the navy, which is said to have been increased to well-nigh 400 galleys, and on new ship-sheds. The handsome "marble storehouse for the hanging shipgear," designed by the architect Philo, was completed at the harbour of Zea. It was expressly provided that the cases which lined the walls and pillars of this cool triple-aisled arcade should be open, "in order that those who pass through may be able to see all the gear that is in the gearstore."

Skeuotheke of Philo.

Financial ministry of Lycurgus.

The man who was mainly responsible for this naval expenditure was Lycurgus. It is significant of the spirit of Athens at this time that while Phocion and Demades were the most influential men in the Assembly, the finances were in the charge of a statesman who had been so signally hostile to Macedonia that Alexander had demanded his surrender. In recent years considerable changes had been made in the constitution of the financial offices. Eubulus had administered as the president of the Theoric Fund. But now we find the control of the expenditure in the hands of a Minister of the Public Revenue, who was elected by the people and held office for four years, from one Panathenaic festival to another. Lycurgus was entrusted with this post for twelve years; for the first period in his own name; for the two succeeding periods his activity was cloaked under the names of his son and another nominal minister. He acted, of course, in conjunction with the Council, but the influence of the more permanent and experienced minister upon that annual body was inevitably very great. The new system, it is evident, was a distinct improvement on the old. It was much better that the administration of the revenue should be managed by one competent statesman, unhampered by colleagues, and that his tenure of office should not be limited to a year. The post practically included the functions of a minister of public works, and the ministry of Lycurgus was distinguished by building enterprises. He constructed the Panathenaic stadion on the southern bank of the Ilisus. He rebuilt the Lycean gymnasium, where in these years the philosopher Aristotle used to take his morning and evening "walks," teaching his "peripatetic" disciples. It lay somewhere to the east of the city, under Mount Lycabettus. But the most memorable work of Lycurgus was the reconstruction of the theatre of Dionysus. It was he who built the rows of marble benches, climbing up the steep side of the Acropolis, as we see them to-day; and his original stage-buildings can be distinguished, amidst the ruins, from the mass of later additions and improvements. He canonised, as it were, the three great tragic poets, Aeschylus, Sophocles, and Euripides, by setting up their statues in the theatre, and by carrying a measure that copies of their works should be officially prepared and preserved by the state.

In connexion with the prosperity of Athens and her large public outlay, it is important to observe that the silver mines of Laurion, which had been closed when the Spartans occupied Decelea and had been neglected—for want of capital and enterprise—throughout the whole first half of the fourth century, had been reopened and were working vigorously. They seem to have been managed largely on a new principle, namely by private companies. The historian Xenophon had written a pamphlet on the subject of the mines as a neg-

338-326 B.C.

The stadion; the gymnasium at the temple of Apollo Lyceus;

theatre;

canonical copies of the tragic poets.

Working of the Laurion silver mines.

Xenophon, De Vectigal., 355 B.C.

lected source of revenue, and it would be interesting to know whether the revival of the industry is to be ascribed directly or indirectly to the influence of his exhortations.

The institution of the ephebi, c. 336 B.C.

No sign of the times, which followed the defeat of Chaeronea, is more striking than the framing of a new system for drilling the young burghers of Athens in the duties of military life. The training began when the youth, having completed his eighteenth year, came of age and was enrolled in the register of his deme; and it lasted for two years. During these two years the young citizen was known as an *ephēbos*, and might not appear either as prosecutor or defendant

FIG. 116.—An ephebus taking oath (from a cylix in the British Museum).

in the law-courts except in a few cases expressly specified. The general supervision over all the Attic ephebi was committed to a marshal (*kosmētēs*), who was elected by the Athenian Assembly; and under him were ten masters of discipline (*sōphrŏnistai*), one for each tribe. The institution had a religious consecration. The first act in the service of the ephebi was solemnly to "go round the temples" under the conduct of the masters. Then they served for a year on duty in the guard-houses at Munychia and along the coast, receiving regular military instruction from special drill-masters, who trained them in the exercises of the hoplites, and taught them how to shoot with bow and javelin and to handle artillery. The ephebi of each tribe ate together at barrack messes which were managed by the masters of discipline. At the end of the first year they appeared before an Assembly in the theatre, and when they had made a public display of their proficiency in the art of warfare, each received from the city a shield and a spear. The second year was spent in patrolling the frontiers of the land and guarding the prisons. The garrison and patrol duties had always devolved upon the young men of Attica, but they were now organised into a new and thorough scheme of discipline,—a mild Attic approach to the stern system of Sparta. It almost strikes one as a conscious effort to arrest the decline of the citizen army in the face of the encroachments of the mercenary system. The ephebi in their characteristic dress, the dark mantle and the broad-brimmed hat, are a graceful feature in Athenian life and art from this time forward.

It is significant that the whole revival, stimulated by the disaster of Chaeronea, was marked by a religious character. Lycurgus, who belonged to the priestly family of the Eteobutads, was a sincerely pious man, and impressed upon his administration the stamp of his own devotion. Never for a hundred years had there been seen at Athens such a manifestation of zealous public concern for the worship of the gods. The two chief monuments of the Lycurgean epoch —the Panathenaic stadion and the theatre of Dionysus—were, it must always be remembered, religious, not secular, buildings.

Thus Athens discreetly attended to her material well-being, and courted the favour of the gods, and the only distress which befell her was a dearth of corn. But on the return of Alexander to Susa, two things happened which imperilled the tranquillity of Greece.

Alexander promised the Greek exiles—there were more than 20,000 of them—to procure their return to their native cities. He sent Nicanor to the great congregation of Hellas at the Olympian festival, to order the states to receive back their banished citizens. A general reconciliation of parties was a just and politic measure; but it could be objected that, by the terms of the Confederation of Corinth, the Macedonian king had no power to dictate orders to the confederates in the management of their domestic affairs. Only two states objected, Athens and Aetolia; and they objected because, if the edict were enforced, they would be robbed of ill-gotten gains. The Aetolians had possessed themselves of Oeniadae and driven out its Acarnanian owners; by Alexander's edict the rightful inhabitants would now return to their own city and the intruders be dislodged. The position of Athens in Samos was similar; the Samians would

The exiles

324 B.C.

now be restored to their own lands, and the Athenian settlers would have to go. Both Athens and Aetolia were prepared to resist.

Another desire was expressed by Alexander at the same time, which was readily acquiesced in. He demanded that the Greeks should recognise his divinity. Sparta is reported to have replied indifferently, "We allow Alexander to call himself a god, if he likes." There was not a sensible man at Athens who would have thought of objecting; even the bitterest patriots would have allowed him to be "the son of Zeus or Poseidon, or whomever he chose." If the Greeks of Corinth looked up to Alexander as their chieftain and protector— and this was actually their position in regard to him—there was no incongruity in the idea of officially acknowledging his divinity. Ever since the days in which an Homeric king "was honoured as a god by the people," there was nothing offensive or outlandish to a Greek ear in predicating godhood of a revered sovereign or master. Divine honours had been paid to Lysander; and the Greeks, in complying with Alexander's desire, did not commit themselves more than the pupil of the Academy who erected an altar to his master Plato.

Sect. 6. The Episode of Harpalus and the Greek Revolt

Meanwhile an incident had happened which might induce some of the patriots to hope that Alexander's empire rested on slippery foundations. Harpalus had arrived off the coast of Attica with 5000 talents, a body of mercenaries, and thirty ships. He had come to excite a revolt against his master. A gift of corn had formerly secured him the citizenship of Athens, but the Athenians prudently refused to harbour him, coming in this guise. He sailed away to Cape Taenaron, always a refuge of adventurers, and leaving his men and ships there, returned to Athens with a sum of about 700 talents.

He was now received, since he did not come with an armed array, but after a while messages arrived both from Macedonia and from Philoxenus, Alexander's financial minister in western Asia, demanding his surrender. It would have been an act of war to protect the runaway treasurer and his stolen moneys; but the Athenians, on the proposal of Demosthenes, adopted a clever device. They arrested Harpalus, seizing his treasure, and said that they would surrender him to officers expressly sent by Alexander; but declined to give him up to Philoxenus or Antipater.

It was not long before Harpalus escaped; he returned to Taenaron, and was shortly afterwards murdered by one of his fellow-adventurers.

The stolen money was deposited in the Acropolis, under the

charge of specially-appointed commissioners, of whom Demosthenes was one. It was known by report that the sum was about 700 talents, but Demosthenes and his fellows had strangely omitted to make any official entry or report of the amount. Suddenly it was discovered that only 350 talents were actually in the Acropolis. Charges immediately circulated against the influential politicians, that the other 350 talents had been received in bribes by them before the money was deposited in the citadel. Men of opposite sides were suspected; Demades, for example, as well as Demosthenes. But, apart from the suspicion of bribery, manifest blame rested upon Demosthenes for having grossly neglected his duty. He was responsible for the custody of the treasure, for which Athens was responsible to Alexander. He was bound to demand an investigation, and on his motion the people directed the Council of Areopagus to hold an inquiry. Philoxenus furnished the account-book of Harpalus, which had come into his hands. By this evidence it was proved that 700 talents had been delivered for safe-keeping in the Acropolis; the entries ceased at this point. It was also shown that certain Athenians had previously been bribed; but Demosthenes was not among them. Other evidence was necessary to show how the missing half of the 700 talents had disappeared. We know not what this evidence was, but the court of Areopagus satisfied themselves that a number of leading statesmen had received considerable sums. Demosthenes appeared in their report as the recipient of twenty talents. The proofs against him were irrefutable, for he confessed the misdemeanour himself, and sought to excuse it by the paltry and transparent subterfuge that he had taken it to repay himself for twenty talents which he had advanced to the Theoric Fund. But why should he repay himself, without any authorisation, out of Alexander's money, for a debt owed him by the Athenian state? There can be little doubt that Demosthenes took the money not for personal gratifications, but for the good of his party. It was all the more necessary for his party to clear themselves from implication in such corrupt transactions. We therefore find Hypereides coming forward as a public prosecutor of Demosthenes. We possess considerable portions of his speech; and we have in its complete form another speech, written for one of the other prosecutors by a miserable hack named Dinarchus. The charges against Demosthenes were twofold: he had taken money, and he had culpably omitted to report the amount of the deposit and the neglect of those who were set to guard it. For the second offence alone he deserved a severe sentence. The judges were not excessively severe, if we consider that his behaviour had placed the city in a most embarrassing position

The Harpalus scandal:

bribery and peculation.

Demosthenes a receiver of twenty talents.

towards Alexander. He was condemned to pay a fine of fifty talents. Unable to pay it, he was imprisoned, but presently effected his escape. It was a venial offence in the eyes of Greece for a statesman to take a bribe, provided he did not take it to injure his country; and in the view of public opinion the moral character of Demosthenes was little damaged by this tortuous transaction. He was not on a level with men like Nicias and Phocion, whom millions would not have tempted; but then nobody ever supposed that he was incorruptible. Yet there were two circumstances which aggravated the case. The money of which Demosthenes partook was stolen money, which Athens was about to sequester for Alexander; and he was himself a commissioner responsible for its safety. It was far from being an ordinary case of corruption.

If Alexander had lived, the Athenians might have persuaded him to let them remain in occupation of Samos; for he was always disposed to be lenient to Athens. When the tidings of his death came, men almost refused to credit it; the orator Demades forcibly said, "If he were indeed dead, the whole world would have smelt of his corpse." The patriots had been building on the slender hopes of some disaster; and the greatest disaster of all had befallen. It had been recognised as madness to defy the power of Alexander; but it did not seem rash to strike for freedom in the unsettled condition of things after his death. Athens revolted from Macedonia; she was joined by Aetolia and many states in northern Greece, and she secured the services of a band of 8000 discharged mercenaries who had just returned from Alexander's army. One of their captains, the Athenian, Leosthenes, occupied Thermopylae, and near that pass the united Greeks gained a slight advantage over Antipater, who had marched southward as soon as he could gather his troops together. The Thessalian cavalry had deserted him, and no state in north Greece except Boeotia remained true to Macedonia. The regent shut himself in the strong hill-city of Lamia, which stands over against the pass of Thermopylae under a spur of Othrys; and here he was besieged during the winter by Leosthenes. These successes had gained some adherents to the cause in the Peloponnesus; and, if the Greeks had been stronger at sea, that cause might have triumphed, at least for a while. But the strange thing was that, notwithstanding the improvements of recent years in her naval establishment, Athens seems to have been able to set afloat no more than 170 warships against 240 of Macedon. The brave general Leosthenes was hampered by a Council of War, in which the various allies were represented—reminding us of the days of the Persian invasion; yet, if a fatal stone had not put an end to his life during the beleaguerment, more would probably have been effected for the cause of the allies. In spring the arrival of Leonnatus, governor of Hellespontine Phrygia, at the head of an army, raised the siege of Lamia. The Greeks marched into Thessaly to meet the new army before it united with Antipater; a battle was fought, in which the Greeks had the upper hand, and Leonnatus was wounded to death. Antipater arrived the next day, and, joining forces with the defeated army, withdrew into Macedonia, to await Craterus, who was approaching from the east. When Craterus arrived, they entered Thessaly together, and in an engagement at Crannon, in which the losses on both sides were light, the Macedonians had a slight advantage. This battle apparently decided the war, but the true cause which hindered the Greeks from continuing the struggle was not the insignificant defeat at Crannon, but the want of unity among themselves, the want of a leader whom they entirely trusted. They were forced to make terms singly, each state on its own behoof.

Battle of Crannon, 322 B.C., Aug.

Hypereides pronounced a funeral oration, distinguished by that lucidity of which he was a perfect master, over those who had fallen in this hopeless war; and gave his due—it is not for us to say that he gave more than his due—to Leosthenes, who "succeeded in what he undertook, but not in escaping fate." There is a fine passage which distorts indeed the historical perspective, but well displays the spirit of the patriots. "In the dark underworld—suffer us to ask—who are they that will stretch forth a right hand to the captain of our dead? May we not deem that Leosthenes will be greeted with welcome and with wonder by those half-gods who bore arms against Troy? Ay, and there, I deem, will be Miltiades and Themistocles, and those others who made Hellas free to the glory of their names."[1]

Funeral speech of Hypereides.

Athens submitted when Antipater advanced into Boeotia and prepared to invade Attica. She paid dearly for her attempt to win back her power. Antipater was not like Alexander. He was an able man, warmly devoted to the royal house of Macedon; but he did not share in Alexander's sympathies with Greek culture, he had no soft place in his heart for the memories and traditions of Athens. He saw only that, unless strong and stern measures were taken, Macedonia would not be safe against a repetition of the rising which he had suppressed. He therefore imposed three conditions, which Phocion and Demades were obliged to accept: that the democratic constitution should be modified by a property qualification; that a Macedonian garrison should be lodged in Munychia; and that the agitators, Demosthenes, Hypereides, and their friends, should be surrendered.

Terms imposed on Athens.

[1] Translated by Professor Jebb.

Demosthenes had exerted eloquence in gaining support for the cause of the allies in the Peloponnesus, and his efforts had been rewarded by his recall to Athens. As soon as the city had submitted, he and the other orators fled. Hypereides with two companions sought refuge in the temple of Aeacus at Aegina, whence they were taken to Antipater and put to death. Demosthenes fled to the temple of Poseidon in the island of Calauria. When the messengers of Antipater appeared and summoned him forth, he swallowed poison, which he had concealed, according to one story, in a pen, and was thus delivered from falling into the hands of the executioner.

The constitutional change which was carried out at the dictation of the Macedonian general would have been judged by Aristotle an improvement. The institutions were not changed, but the democracy was converted into a "polity" or limited democracy—such as Theramenes had striven for—by a restriction of the franchise. All citizens whose property amounted to less than 2000 drachmae were deprived of their civic rights. It is said that this measure erased 12,000 names from the burgher lists, and that 9000 citizens remained. A large number of the poorer people thus disfranchised left Attica and settled in Thrace, where Antipater gave them land; perhaps these settlers included some of the outdwellers of Samos, who were now turned adrift, being obliged to quit the island and make way for the rightful possessors.

SECT. 7. ARISTOTLE AND ALEXANDER

It was through an accident that Alexander was brought into contact with the one other man of his time whose genius was destined to move the world. Aristotle's father had been court physician of Amyntas II., and Aristotle was meant to follow his father's profession. At the age of seventeen he went to Athens, where he was under the guardianship of a certain Proxenus, to whose son Nicanor—the same Nicanor who made public Alexander's edict at Olympia—he afterwards betrothed his only daughter. At first Aristotle studied in the school of Isocrates, but when Plato returned from Sicily he came under the influence of that philosopher's idealism, and this decided him for the "life of speculation," which he regards—and it is the deliberate judgment of his mature years—as the only life that is perfectly happy. After Plato's death he spent some years on the north-eastern coasts of the Aegean, at Assos and Mytilene, and then received the call from Philip to undertake the education of the crown prince. As yet he had won no eminent reputation for wisdom

---

Marginal notes:

Death of Demosthenes, 322 B.C., Oct.

Introduction of property qualification at Athens.

(£80.)

Aristotle, born 384-3, c. 367 B.C.

Called to Pella, 343-2 B.C.

or learning, and Philip probably chose him because his father had been connected with the Macedonian court. The instruction which Aristotle imparted to Alexander was perhaps chiefly literary and philological; he came as a tutor, not as a philosopher. We know nothing of the mutual relations between the brilliant master and his brilliant pupil; they were men of different and hardly sympathetic tempers; we may suspect that Aristotle was fainer to curb than spur the ardent straining spirit of Alexander. Certainly the episode led to no such maintenance of intimacy afterwards as it might have led to if Plato had been the teacher. On his return to Athens, Aristotle founded his school of philosophy, and the Lyceum soon took the place formerly occupied by the Academy, which ever since the discomfiting adventures in Sicily had withdrawn itself more and more from the public attention. He taught for twelve or thirteen years—and these years were doubtless the time of his most effective philosophical activity—and died not long after the death of Alexander.

c. 335 B.C.

Death, 322 B.C.

Never were there more wonderful years than these in which the brains of Alexander and Aristotle were ceaselessly working. It is not an overstatement to say that there is no one to whom Europe owes a greater debt for the higher education of her peoples than to Aristotle. The science of the laws of thought is still taught mainly as he first worked it out. There are no better introductions to ethical and political speculation than his fundamental treatises on ethical and political science. Nor was it a small thing that his system controlled the acutest minds of the Middle Ages, whose reasoning faculties, though cabined by the imminence of a narrowly interpreted theology, were amazingly powerful and subtle.

Debt of Europe to Aristotle.

But Aristotle, supreme as he was in abstract reasoning, zealous as he was in collecting and appreciating concrete facts, was not without prejudices. As a boy, in the narrow self-satisfied community of little remote Stagira, he had imbibed the dislike which was openly or secretly felt towards Athens in all the Chalcidian regions. And, though he established his abode at Athens, he never overcame this distrust; he always remained a citizen of Stagira and lived in Athens as a stranger. This initial prejudice prevented him from ever judging with perfect impartiality the Athenian institutions, which he took as the type of democracy. He was also prejudiced against Macedonia. The Chalcidians looked upon their Macedonian neighbours as far below themselves in civilisation; and Aristotle's experience of the court of Pella, where he must have been a spectator of the scandalous quarrels between Philip and Olympias, did not create a favourable impression. He was thus disposed to hold his sympathies entirely aloof from the enterprises of Alexander. But not

Aristotle's prejudices,

against Athens

and Macedonia,

only did he not sympathise, he disapproved. For he was wedded to
the idea of the small Greek republic; he condemned the large state.

Moreover, he held firmly to the Hellenic conviction that Hellenes
were superior by nature to peoples of other race, and he was thus
opposed to the most original and enlightened feature of Alexander's
policy—the ruling of Greeks and barbarians on an equality. Owing
to this attitude of coldness and distrust towards the Macedonians,
he missed a great opportunity. Alexander's expedition threw open
to science a new field of discovery in natural history; and we can
imagine what endless pains the king would have given himself, if
Aristotle had urged him to collect extensive observations on the
animal and vegetable kingdoms in the various countries and cli-
mates through which he passed.

It is a strange sensation to pass from the view of the state which
Alexander was fashioning to the sketch of an ideal state which was
drawn by the most thoughtful of men at the same time. Aristotle
desires a little north-country city, situated in a compact, defensible
territory; close to the sea and yet not on the coast, having a harbour
within easy reach, but quite disconnected, so that the precincts of
the city may not be contaminated and its indwellers troubled by the
presence of a motley crowd of outlanders, cheapmen, and mariners,
such as throng a seaport's quays. He will not have his city a centre
of trade; it is to import and export only for the purposes of its own
strict needs. It is to be a tiny city, the number of the burghers so
limited that each one may be able to know all about each of the
others. The burghers are to have equal rights; their early manhood
is to be spent on military duties; when they come to middle life they
are to be eligible for political offices; in their old age they are to act
as priests. Subject to this citizen aristocracy, but entirely excluded
from the franchise, are to be the artisans and merchants. Part of
the land is to be public—the yield to be devoted to maintaining the
worship of the gods and providing the public meals of the city; part
is to be the private property of the citizens; and the fields are to be
tilled by slaves or labourers of non-Hellenic race. Such was the little
exclusive community which Aristotle designed, while his former
pupil was setting in motion schemes for world-wide commerce,
shattering the barriers which sundered nation from nation, building
an empire which should include millions, founding cities composed
of men of divers races, hewing his way through a maze of new political problems which were beyond Aristotle's horizon. The republic
of Aristotle's wish is not quickened like Plato's by striking original
ideas; it is a commonplace Greek aristocracy with its claws cut,
carefully trimmed and pruned, refined by a punctilious education,

without any expansive vitality, and like Sparta leaving no room for the free development of the individual citizens. If the cities of Hellas had been moulded and fashioned on the model of the city of the philosopher's wish, they would hardly have done what they did for European civilisation.

We may wonder whether Aristotle divined before his death that the Hellenic cities were not to have the last word in the history of men. More probably the untimely end of Alexander reassured him that the old fashion of things would soon go on again as before. The brilliant day of the Greek city states had indeed drawn to a close so suddenly that they could not be expected to grasp the fact; and no people that has ever borne the torch of civilisation has been willing, or even able, to recognise that the hour of relinquishing sovereignty has come. The Greeks may well be excused if they were reluctant to acquiesce in the vicissitude which forced them to sink into a subordinate place. But it is thus that the austere laws of history reward the meritorious. The republics of Greece had performed an imperishable work; they had shown mankind many things, and, above all, the most precious thing in the world, fearless freedom of thought.

CHRONOLOGICAL TABLE

B.C.

c. 3000—2200	Beginning of Bronze Age in Crete. Early "Minoan" Age of Cretan civilisation. Greece occupied by Greek-speaking peoples.
s. 2200—2000	Middle "Minoan" Age, Period I.; building of first palaces of Cnossus and Phaestus. Second (Brick) City of Troy.
c. 2160—2000	11th Dynasty in Egypt.
c. 2200—1400	Crete leading power in Aegean.
c. 2000—1300	Hittite power predominant in Asia Minor.
c. 2000—1850	Middle "Minoan" Age, Period II. 12th Dynasty in Egypt.
c. 1850—1600	Middle "Minoan" Age, Period III.
c. 1600—1500	Late "Minoan" Age, Period I.
c. 1600—1100	"Mycenaean" Age in Greece.
1580—1321	18th Dynasty in Egypt (Thothmes III., 1500—1450; Amenhotep III., 1414—1383; Amenhotep IV., 1383—1350).
c. 1500	Foundation of Sixth City of Troy.
c. 1500—1400	Late "Minoan" Age, Period II.
c. 1400	Fall of Cnossus and Phaestus.
c. 1400—1100	Late "Minoan" Age, Period III. Great power of Mycenae. Achaean principalities in Peloponnesus and Crete.
1287	Battle of Cadesh between Egypt and Hittites. Dardanians fight with Hittites against Egypt.
c. 1250	Fifth City of Troy.
1225—1215	Reign of Mernptah in Egypt.
1223	Achaeans join in raid on Egypt.
c. 1200—1180	Trojan War.
c. 1180—1100	Early poems on Trojan War.
c. 1180—700	Aegean trade partly in hands of Phoenicians.
c. 1130—1100	Thessalian and Boeotian conquests. Beginnings of Achaean migration to Asia Minor. Beginning of Iron Age.
c. 1100—1000	Ionian colonisation in Asia Minor. Dorian conquests in Peloponnesus and Crete. Greek colonisation in Cyprus. Beginning of Dorian colonisation in Asia Minor.
c. 900—800	Homer composes the *Iliad* and *Odyssey*.
c. 800—700	Rise of aristocracies throughout Greece.
c. 750	Hesiod.
[776	[Traditional date of First Olympiad.
735	" " foundation of Naxos (Sicily).
734	" " " Corcyra.
734	" " " Syracuse.
728	" " " Catane and Leontini.
728	" " " Megara (Hyblaean).
721	" " " Sybaris.
715	" " " Zancle.
707	" " " Taras.
703	" " " Croton.
688	" " " Gela.
648]	" " " Himera.]
709	King Sargon of Assyria sets up stêlê in Cyprus.

B.C.

c. 700	Midas king of Phrygia. Deioces founds Median monarchy. Athenian conquest of Eleusis.
687—652	Reign of Gyges king of Lydia.
683—2	List of annual archons at Athens begins.
681—68	Reign of Assarhaddon king of Assyria.
679	Assarhaddon defeats the Cimmerians under their leader Teuspa.
c. 672	Assyrian conquest of Egypt.
668—26	Reign of Assurbanipal king of Assyria.
[668	Traditional date of battle of Hysiae, in which Argos defeats Sparta.
664	Traditional date of ancient sea-battle of Corinth with Corcyra.]
664	Fortress of Defenneh (Daphnae) in Egypt built by Psammetichus I.
660—20	Conjectural limits of date of Pheidon king of Argos.
650—600	Age of law-givers in Greece.
	Rise of tyrannies in Ionia. Foundation of tyrannies in Sicyon, Corinth, and Megara.
	Ardys and Sadyattes reign in Lydia. Ardys drives out the Cimmerians.
	The league of Calauria.
c. 650—25	Reign of Phraortes king of Media.
645	Egypt throws off yoke of Assyria.
c. 632	Cylon attempts to seize tyranny at Athens.
c. 635	Foundation of Naucratis.
c. 630	Foundation of Cyrene.
630—600	Approximate limits of Spartan conquest of Messenia.
625	Nabopolassar founds new Babylonian kingdom.
c. 621	Legislation of Dracon at Athens.
612	Fall of Nineveh. Nabopolassar of Babylonia and Cyaxares of Media conquer and divide Assyria.
c. 610	Thrasybulus tyrant of Miletus.
605	Nebucadnezar succeeds Nabopolassar.
c. 600	War of Athens and Mytilene on the coast of the Hellespont.
	Sappho, Alcaeus, Pittacus, flourish at Mytilene.
	Periander tyrant of Corinth.
594—89	Nubian expedition of Psammetichus II. Inscription of Greek mercenaries at Abu Simbel.
594—3	Archonship of Solon. *Seisachtheia*.
593—1	(?) Continuation of Solon's legislation.
590—89	Sacred War against Crisa.
	Cleisthenes of Sicyon flourishes.
585	May 28: Eclipse of sun. Drawn battle of Cyaxares king of Media with Alyattes king of Lydia.
	Thales flourishes.
583—1	Archonship of Damasias at Athens.
582	First Pythiad.
572	Eleans win control of the Olympian games.
c. 570	Athenian conquest of Salamis.
569	Accession of Amasis to throne of Egypt.
562	Death of Nebucadnezar.
560	Croesus succeeds to throne of Lydia.
c. 560—50	War of Sparta with Tegea.
561—60	Archonship of Comeas. Pisistratus seizes tyranny.
c. 559—6	Miltiades becomes tyrant in Thracian Chersonese.
556—5	First exile of Pisistratus.
550—49	? Restoration of Pisistratus; and his second exile.
c. 550	Spartan conquest of Thyreatis.
548—7	Temple of Apollo at Delphi burnt down.

B.C.	
546	Cyrus king of Persia conquers Lydia, and captures Sardis.
546—5	Persian conquest of Asiatic Greeks.
540—39	Second restoration of Pisistratus.
538	Cyrus takes Babylon.
528—7	Death of Pisistratus.
526	Polycrates, tyrant of Samos, abandons alliance with Amasis and joins Persia.
525	Death of Amasis king of Egypt.
	Persian conquest of Egypt: battle of Pelusion.
c. 525	Spartans attack Samos.
c. 523	Death of Polycrates.
522	Death of Cambyses king of Persia.
521	Accession of Darius.
520	First capture of Babylon by Darius.
519	Second capture of Babylon by Darius.
514	Conspiracy of Harmodius and Aristogiton.
c. 512	First European expedition of Darius: conquest of Thrace.
510	Fall of the Pisistratid tyranny. Spartans in Attica. Athens joins Peloponnesian league.
	War of Sybaris and Croton.
508—7	Archonship of Isagoras. Spartans under Cleomenes invade Attica; besieged in the Acropolis. Beginning of reforms of Cleisthenes.
506	Peloponnesian army invades Attica.
	Athenians defeat (1) Boeotians, (2) Chalcidians: acquire Chalcidian plain.
506	Athens acquires Oropus (land of the Graeans).
503—2	First civil year in the Cleisthenic system.
501	Institution of the *Ten* stratêgoi of the tribes at Athens.
499	Outbreak of Ionic revolt.
c. 498	Athens at war with Aegina.
c. 497	Ionians and allies at Sardis: burning of Sardis.
496	(?) Revolt of Thrace; Scythians drive Miltiades from Chersonese.
494	Battle of Lade; Persians capture Miletus.
c. 494	Battle of Sêpeia (Spartans under Cleomenes defeat Argives).
493—2	Archonship of Themistocles.
c. 492	Athens coerces Aegina. Battle of the Helorus.
492	Mardonius subdues Thrace and Macedonia.
c. 491	Gelon becomes tyrant of Gela.
490	Expedition of the Persians under Datis of Greece. Destruction of Eretria. Battle of Marathon.
489	Expedition of Miltiades to Paros.
c. 489	Death of Cleomenes.
488	Victory of Gelon in chariot-race at Olympia.
487	Ostracism of Hipparchus the Pisistratid.
	War of Athens with Aegina.
487—6	Archons begin to be appointed by lot. Strategoi supersedes the Polemarch.
486	Ostracism of Megacles. Pindar's *7th Pythian*.
486—5	Egypt revolts against Persia.
485	Death of Darius. Accession of Xerxes.
484	Ostracism of Xanthippus son of Arriphron.
484—3	Persia recovers control of Egypt.
483	Persians hew canal through Mount Athos.
483—2	Discovery of a new vein of silver in mine-fields of Laurion.
482	Ostracism of Aristides.
	Increase of Athenian fleet. Pythian victory of Hieron in horse-race.

B.C.

481	Xerxes comes down to Sardis.
480	Spring: Athens recalls ostracized citizens.
	August: Xerxes enters Greece. Battles of Artemisium and Thermopylae.
	September: Battle of Salamis.
	October 2: Eclipse of the sun.
	Olynthus given to the Chalcidians.
	Carthaginians invade Sicily. Battle of Himera.
479	Mardonius in Attica. August: Battle of Plataea; and battle of Mycale. Ionians revolt from Persia.
478	Athenians capture Sestos. Foundation of Confederacy of Delos (478-7 winter).
	Death of Gelon: his brother Hieron succeeds to his power. Pythian victory of Hieron in horse-race. *3rd Pythian Ode* of Pindar.
478—6	Fortification of Athens.
477—6	Pausanias at Byzantium: driven out by Cimon.
476	Lacedaemonian expedition to Thessaly (?). Victory of Hieron in horse-race at Olympia (*1st Olymp. Ode* of Pindar; *5th Ode* of Bacchylides).
476—5	Cimon captures Eion.
474	Battle of Cyme.
474—3	Cimon conquers Scyrus.
472	Olympian victories of Hieron in horse-race and Theron in chariot-race. *2nd and 3rd Olympians* of Pindar. The *Persae* of Aeschylus.
472—1	Athenians reduce Carystus. Ostracism of Themistocles. Death of Theron of Acragas. Synoecisms of Elis and Mantinea.
c. 471	Flight of Themistocles. Battle of Dipaea.
471—70	War of Hieron with Thrasydaeus of Acragas.
470	Pythian victory of Hieron in chariot-race. Pindar's *1st Pythian. 4th Ode* of Bacchylides.
470—69	Revolt and reduction of Naxos.
468	Olympian victory of Hieron in chariot-race. *3rd Ode* of Bacchylides. Olympian victory of a boy of Tiryns in boxing.
	Battle of the Eurymedon.
468—7	Argos reduces Tiryns (?).
467	Death of Hieron.
465	Revolt of Thasos.
465—4	Attempt to colonise the Nine Ways.
464	Earthquake at Sparta. Revolt of helots. Siege of Ithome. Accession of Artaxerxes to throne of Persia.
463	Surrender of Thasos.
463—2	Cimon in Messenia.
463—1	Ephialtes influential at Athens. The Areopagus deprived of its powers.
462—60	Argos reduces Mycenae. Pay introduced at Athens for the judges of the heliaea. Influence of Pericles begins.
461	Ostracism of Cimon.
461—60	Alliance of Athens and Argos.
459	Athens wins Megara. Long Walls of Megara built. Athenian expedition to Egypt.
	Capture of Ithome. Messenians settled at Naupactus. Capture of Memphis.
459—8	Battle of Halieis. Battle of Cecryphalea.
458	*Oresteia* of Aeschylus. Zeugitae admitted to archonship. Battle of Aegina. Battle in the Megarid.
	Building of Long Walls of Athens.

B.C.

457 Lacedaemonian expedition to Phocis and Boeotia. Battle of Tanagra. Athenian conquest of Boeotia (battle of Oenophyta; autumn).

457—6 Athenian conquest of Aegina.

456 Megabyzus arrives in Egypt with army and fleet.

456—5 Expedition of Tolmides to Corinthian Gulf.

454 Catastrophe of Egyptian expedition.

454—3 Treasury of confederacy of Delos transferred from Delos to Athens.

453 Expedition of Pericles to Corinthian Gulf.

453—46 Inclusion of Achaea in Athenian empire.

452—1 Thirty years' Peace between Argos and Lacedaemon. Five years' Truce between Athenians and Peloponnesians.

451—50 Law of citizenship at Athens.

450—49 Cimon in Cyprus. Death of Cimon.

448 Peace with Persia. Sacred War. Athens invites the Greeks to restore the temples.

447 Athens loses Boeotia (battle of Coronea). Cleruchies sent to the Chersonese, Euboea, etc.

447—6 Revolt and reduction of Euboea. Athens loses Megara.

446—5 Thirty years' Peace between Athens and Peloponnesians. Foundation of New Sybaris.

443 Foundation of Thurii.

443—2 Division of Athenian confederacy into five districts.

442 Ostracism of Thucydides, son of Melesias.

440 Revolt of Samos, and Byzantium.

439 Reduction of Samos.

438 Chryselephantine Athena set up in the Parthenon.

436 Foundation of Amphipolis.

436—5 Sedition at Epidamnus.

435 Sea-victory of Corcyra over Corinth (spring).

433 Defensive alliance of Athens with Corcyra. Battle of Sybota (autumn). Treaties of Athens with Rhegion and Leontini.

433—2 Revolt of Potidaea (winter).

432 The "Megarian decree" passed at Athens (autumn). Battle of Potidaea (c. Sept.).

432—1 Assemblies at Sparta decide on war.

431 *First year of the Peloponnesian War.*—Theban attack on Plataea (March). First Peloponnesian invasion of Attica (May). Athens wins Sollion and Cephallenia; takes Thronion and Atalanta; expels Aeginetans from Aegina.

430 *Second year of the War.*—Outbreak of plague at Athens. Second invasion of Attica. Expedition of Pericles to Argolis and his failure at Epidaurus. Pericles deposed from strategia, tried, fined, and reappointed strategos. Phormio operates in the west: captures Amphilochian Argos. Surrender of Potidaea.

429 *Third year of the War.*—Peloponnesians besiege Plataea. Sea-victories of Phormio. Death of Pericles (autumn).

428 *Fourth year of the War.*—Third invasion of Attica. Revolt of Mytilene.

427 *Fifth year of the War.*—Fourth invasion of Attica. Surrender of Mytilene. Surrender of Plataea. Civil war breaks out in Corcyra. Athens captures Minoa. Expedition of Laches to Sicily.

426 *Sixth year of the War.*—Aetolian expedition of Demosthenes. Battle of Olpae. Purification of Delos.

B.C.	
425	*Seventh year of the War.*—Fifth invasion of Attica. Athenians send an expedition to Sicily. Occupation of Pylos; and capture of Spartans in Sphacteria. Triumph of the democracy in Corcyra. Athens wins Anactorion, and occupies Methone. Athens raises the tribute of her allies. Introduction of the triobolon (?). *Acharnians* of Aristophanes. Antiphon's *De Choreuta.* Congress of Gela.
424	*Eighth year of the War.*—Athens wins Oeniadae; captures Nisaea, with the Long Walls of Megara, and Cythera. Athenian invasion of Boeotia; battle of Delion. Brasidas in Thrace. Revolt of Acanthus, Amphipolis, and other cities. Banishment of Thucydides, the historian. *Knights* of Aristophanes.
423	*Ninth year of the War.*—Negotiations for peace. One year's truce (March). Revolt of Scione. *Clouds* of Aristophanes. Leontini annexed by Syracuse.
422	*Tenth year of the War.*—Battle of Amphipolis. Peace negotiations. *Wasps* of Aristophanes.
421	Peace of Nicias (March). *Peace* of Aristophanes. Capture of Scione.
421—20	Defensive alliance between Athens and Sparta.
420	Alliance of Athens with Argos.
418	Battle of Mantinea. Argos forms alliance with Sparta. Eleusinian decree.
417	Ostracism of Hyperbolus. Nicias in Chalcidice.
416	Conquest of Melos. Embassy of Segesta to Athens.
415	Mutilation of the Hermae at Athens. Athenian expedition to Sicily. Recall of Alcibiades.
414	Spring: *Birds* of Aristophanes. Siege of Syracuse. Glyippus arrives in Sicily.
413	Spartans occupy Decelea. Second Athenian expedition to Sicily. Great battle in the Syracusan Harbour (Sept. 9). Disaster of the Athenians.
412	Revolt of Athenian allies. Treaty of Miletus (between Sparta and Persia). Alcibiades leaves Sparta.
411	Battle of Syme (Jan.). Revolt of Rhodes. Pisander at Athens (*c.* Feb.). Revolt of Abydus and Lampsacus (April). Assembly at Colonus and provision made for a new Constitution (May). Council of Four Hundred comes into office (early in June), and governs till September. Revolt of Euboea (Sept.). Four Hundred overthrown and Polity established (Sept.). Battle of Cynossema. *Lysistrate* and *Thesmophoriazusae* of Aristophanes. Evagoras becomes king of Salamis.
410	Battle of Cyzicus. Restoration of Democracy at Athens. Athens recovers Thasos. [Pseudo-Lysias] *For Polystratus.*
409	Athens recovers Colophon; loses Pylos and Nisaea. Carthaginian invasion of Sicily. Destruction of Selinus and Himera.
408	Athens recovers Chalcedon and Byzantium. Gorgias at Olympia. Warfare of Hermocrates in western Sicily.
407	Cyrus comes down to the coast. Battle of Notion. Alcibiades at Athens. Battle of Mytilene. Death of Hermocrates. Foundation of Thermae.
406	Battle of Arginusae. Trial of the Generals. Siege of Acragas.
406—5	Conspiracy of strawbearers at Chios.

B.C.

405 Lysander navarch. Cyrus called to Susa. Battle of Aegospotami (end of summer).
Dionysius becomes tyrant of Syracuse; and makes peace with Carthage.

405—4 Blockade of Athens.

404 Surrender of Athens. Long Walls pulled down (April). Psephism of Dracontides (summer) and rule of the Thirty. Thrasybulus seizes Phyle (Dec.). Alliance of Catane and Leontini.

404—3 First expedition of Thirty against Thrasybulus. Death of Theramenes.

403 Lacedaemonian garrison at Athens. Second expedition against Thrasybulus (May).
Thrasybulus seizes Piraeus. Battle of Munychia. King Pausanias at Athens. Fall of Thirty (Sept.). Recall of Lysander. Lysias' *Against Eratosthenes*.
Revolt at Syracuse against Dionysius.

403—2 Archonship of Euclides.

403—400 Sicel war of Dionysius. His reduction of Naxos and Catane.

401 Expedition of Cyrus. Battle of Cunaxa (summer).

400 Thimbron in Asia Minor (end of summer).

399 Dercyllidas succeeds Thimbron, and gains the Troad. War of Sparta and Elis. Death of Socrates.

398 Sparta makes truce with the satraps; sends embassy to Susa. Accession of Agesilaus. Dionysius captures Motya.

398—7 Dercyllidas in the Chersonese; takes Atarneus (397, first months).

397 Dercyllidas in Caria; makes truce with the satraps. Conon appointed commander of Persian fleet. Conspiracy of Cinadon at Sparta.
Himilco's expedition to Sicily. Siege of Syracuse. Foundation of Lilybaeum.

396 First campaign of Agesilaus in Phrygia (autumn). Restoration of Messana. Acoris becomes king of Egypt.

396—3 Sicel war of Dionysius.

395 Campaign of Agesilaus in Lydia. Death of Tissaphernes. Second campaign of Agesilaus in Phrygia. Revolt of Rhodes. War breaks out in Boeotia. Battle of Haliartus and death of Lysander. Accession of Agesipolis at Sparta. Athens begins to rebuild her Long Walls. Foundation of Tyndaris.

395—4 Confederation of Athens, Thebes, etc., against Sparta.

394 Battle of Corinth (July). Battle of Cnidus (Aug.). Eclipse of sun (Aug. 14). Battle of Coronea (Aug.). Foundation of Mylae.

393 Completion of Long Walls of Athens.

392 Union of Corinth and Argos. Battle of the Long Walls (of Megara). First embassy of Antalcidas to Susa. Second Punic War of Dionysius.

391 Spartans capture Lechaeon. Dionysius besieges Rhegion.

390 Agesilaus celebrates Isthmian games and captures Piraeon. Iphicrates gains a victory over Spartan hoplites. Teleutias captures an Athenian squadron. Evagoras revolts from Persia. Alliance of Athens with Evagoras and Acoris. Hecatomnus has become satrap of Caria (between 395 and 390).

390—89 Tax of $\frac{1}{40}$th; and a war-tax introduced at Athens.

389 Successes of Thrasybulus in the Hellespont. Dionysius besieges Caulonia. Battle of the Elleporus. *Ecclesiazusae* of Aristophanes.

B.C.

388	Death of Thrasybulus (first months). Warfare of Anaxibius and Iphicrates in the Hellespont.
388—7	Second mission of Antalcidas to Susa.
387	Capture of Rhegion by Dionysius. Chabrias sent to help Evagoras.
387—6	The King's Peace.
386	Evagoras defeated at Cition. Chabrias in Egypt.
386—4	Persian siege of Cypriote Salamis.
386—5	Breaking up of Mantinea.
384	Speech of Lysias at Olympic games (July-Aug.). Orontes makes peace with Evagoras.
384—2	Formation of the Chalcidian Confederacy.
383—78	Third Punic War of Dionysius.
383	Death of Acoris.
382	Spartans seize citadel of Thebes (summer).
382—1	Restoration of Plataea.
381	Defeat of Spartans at Olynthus. Siege of Phlius begins. Persia concludes Peace with Evagoras. Accession of Nektanebos I. in Egypt.
380	Accession of king Cleombrotus at Sparta. Olympic games for which Isocrates wrote his *Panegyric*.
379	Suppression of Chalcidian League. Battles of Cabala and Cronion in Sicily.
379—8	Spartans expelled from Theban citadel (winter). Raid of Sphodrias.
378	Alliance of Athens with Thebes. Boeotia invaded by Agesilaus. Iphicrates in Thrace; his marriage (?). Peace of Syracuse with Carthage.
378—7	Foundation of Second Athenian Confederacy. Property tax at Athens.
377	Boeotia invaded by Agesilaus. Defeat of Phoebidas. Mausolus becomes satrap of Caria.
376	Battle of Naxos. Western expedition of Timotheus. Rebellion at Delos. Iphicrates in Persian service.
375—3	Iphicrates and Pharnabazus in Egypt. Jason of Pherae a member of Athenian League.
374	Peace between Athens and Sparta. Death of Evagoras; accession of Nicocles.
374—3	Peace broken. Lacedaemonians at Corcyra.
373	Iphicrates sent to Corcyra. Trial of Timotheus. Earthquakes in Greece; destruction of temple of Delphi (?).
371	Peace of Callias (June). Battle of Leuctra (July). Accession of Agesipolis II. at Sparta.
371—69	Foundation of Arcadian League, and of Megalopolis.
370	[Epaminondas a Boeotarch.] Rebuilding of Mantinea. Death of Jason of Pherae. Accession of Cleombrotus II. at Sparta.
370—69	First Boeotian invasion of Peloponnesus.
369	[Epaminondas a Boeotarch.] Foundation of Messene (first months). Alliance of Athens and Sparta (spring). Second Boeotian invasion of Peloponnesus. First Thessalian expedition of Pelopidas.
369—8	Murder of Alexander of Macedon, and intervention of Iphicrates.
368	Heraea and Orchomenus join Arcadian League. Congress of Delphi (summer). Tearless Battle. Euphron tyrant of Sicyon. Second Thessalian expedition of Pelopidas, and his captivity. First expedition to rescue him. Fourth Punic war of Dionysius.

B.C.	
367	[Epaminondas a Boeotarch.] Greek envoys at Susa. Second expedition to rescue Pelopidas. Death of Dionysius I. Ariobarzanes revolts from Persia.
366	Third Boeotian invasion of Peloponnesus. Thebans seize Oropus. Alliance of Athens with Arcadia. Death of Lycomedes. Timotheus in eastern Aegean. Isocrates' *Archidamus*.
366—5	Partial peace in Peloponnesus.
365	Timotheus wins Samos. Murder of Macedonian regent Ptolemy. Timotheus wins Potidae and other towns of Chalcidian region. War breaks out between Arcadia and Elis.
364	[Epaminondas a Boeotarch.] Naval expedition of Epaminondas. Third Thessalian expedition of Pelopidas. Eclipse of sun, July 13. Battle of Cynoscephalae. Destruction of Orchomenus. Pisatans celebrate Olympian games; battle in the Altis. Athens obtains Sestos. Timotheus besieges Amphipolis.
363	Timotheus recovers Byzantium. Nektanebos I. succeeded by Tachos.
363—2	Timotheus again besieges Amphipolis. Revolts of satraps against Persia.
362	[Epaminondas a Boeotarch.] Battle of Mantinea. Athenian fleet sent to Hellespont. Ariobarzanes crucified.
361	Agesilaus in Egypt. Accession of Nektanebos II. Battle of Peparethus.
361—60	Death of Agesilaus (?).
360—59	Death of king Cotys, and division of Thrace.
359	Death of Perdiccas and accession of Amyntas.
358	Victories of Philip over Paeonians and Illyrians. Death of Artaxerxes II.; accession of Artaxerxes III. Ochus.
357	Athens recovers the Chersonese and Euboea. Philip captures Amphipolis. Revolt of Chios, Cos, and Rhodes from Athens. Death of Chabrias. Dion returns to Sicily.
356	Illyrian victory of Philip. Battle of Embata. Phocians seize Delphi. Revolt of Artabazus and Orontes. Arrival of Nypsius at Syracuse.
356—5	Philip captures Pydna and Potidaea. Birth of Alexander. Composition of Xenophon's *De Vectigalibus*.
355	Chares in Asia Minor; defeats Tithraustes. Isocrates' *De Pace*. Trial of Timotheus and Iphicrates (?).
355—4	Peace of Athens with Rhodes, Cos, etc. Isocrates' *Areopagiticus*.
354	Battle of Neon. Death of Philomelus. Murder of Dion.
354—3	Demosthenes' *On the Symmories*. Tyranny of Callippus at Syracuse.
354—50	Eubulus in charge of the Theoric Fund.
353	Philip captures Methone. Power of Onomarchus in Thessaly. Eubulus hinders Philip from attacking Phocis. Demosthenes' *For the Megalopolitans*. Death of Mausolus. Demosthenes' *For the Freedom of the Rhodians*.
353—1	Hipparinus tyrant of Syracuse.
352	Cersobleptes of Thrace submits to Macedon. Demosthenes' *Against Aristocrates*. Artabazus flees to Macedonia, and Artaxerxes makes peace with Orontes.
351	Revolt of Phoenicia against Persia; revolt in Cyprus. Demosthenes' *First Philippic*. Idrieus succeeds Artemisia in Caria. Nysaeus becomes tyrant at Syracuse.
350	Phocion in Cyprus helping to suppress revolt.
349	Phocion in Euboea. Philip reduces Chalcidice. Alliance of Athens with Olynthus. Demosthenes' *Olynthiacs*.

NOTES AND REFERENCES

[The following notes are partly illustrative partly justificatory. Only in the case of the first sections of Chapter I., where the material is chiefly archaeological, is a select bibliography given. The following abbreviations are used:—
C.I.G.=Boeckh's Corpus Inscriptionum Graecarum.
C.I.A.=Corpus Inscriptionum Atticarum.
Hicks=E. L. Hicks, Manual of Greek Historical Inscriptions.
Ditt.=W. Dittenberger, Sylloge Inscriptionum Graecarum (Ditt.²=2nd ed. vol. i).]

CHAPTER I

P. 5.—Home of the Greek invaders: cp. Kretschmer, Einleitung in die Geschichte der griechischen Sprache.

P. 6.—Pre-Hellenic names on both sides of the Aegean: Kretschmer, *op. cit.* 401 *sqq.*

P. 6. *Sect.* 2.—Sources: Architectural remains *in situ* and objects in Museums.—Modern researches and expositions: For *Crete*, Cnossus: A. J. Evans, Reports of excavations at Cnossus, in Annual of British School at Athens, vols. vi.-x.; and Palace of Minos, vol. i. 1921. Phaestus: Accounts of Italian excavations in Monumenti antichi vols. xii. *sqq.* and in Rendiconti dell'a Accademia dei Lincei, vols xii, *sqq.* For Cretan systems of writing: A. J. Evans, Scripta Minoa, vol. i. 1909 (also, Cretan Pictographs, 1895, and Further Discoveries of Cretan and Aegean Script in Journal of Hellenic Studies, 1898). General: R. M. Burrows, The Discoveries in Crete, 1907; C. H. and H. B. Hawes, Crete the Forerunner of Greece, 1911. *For Melos:* Excavations at Phylakopi in Melos, conducted by the British School at Athens, 1904. *For Troy* (second city): Schliemann, Ilios, 1881, Troja, 1884; Schuchhardt, Schliemann's Excavations (E.T.), 1891.

P. 9.—Survival of Eteocretan language in Eastern Crete: The Praesus inscriptions have been studied by R. S. Conway, Pre-Hellenic Inscriptions of Praesos in Annual of Brit. Sch. at Athens, viii. 125 *sqq.*, x. 115 *sqq.* He regards the language as Indo-Germanic.

P. 9.—Melos: Four settlements have been explored at Phylakopi, the earliest unwalled, the second and third "pre-Mycenaean" fortresses, the fourth of the Mycenaean age.

P. 11.—Cretan Pottery: On chronological classification, see D. Mackenzie's article in Journal of Hellenic Studies, xxvi. A. J. Evans, Essai de classification des époques de la civilisation minoienne, 1906.

P. 14.—Gournia: see H. B. Hawes (with others), Gournia, Vasiliki and other Prehistoric Sites on the Isthmus of Hierapetra, Crete. Palaikastro: see reports of British excavations in Ann. British School at Athens, vols. viii. *sqq.*

P. 14.—Hagia Triada: This residence flourished in the periods known as Midde Minoan 3 and Late Minoan 1. A catastrophe befell it before the end of the latter period, *i.e.* before B.C. 1500. This was also the period of the prosperity of Zakro, a small port on the east coast of the island (a few miles south of Palaikastro), where ships trading with Egypt and Libya called. It was excavated by D. G. Hogarth in 1901; see articles in Ann. British School at

Athens, vii., and Journal of Hell. Studies, xxii. 500 seal impressions in clay were found in a house which seems to have belonged to a gold merchant.

P. 15.—Labyrinth: For other labyrinths, in Egypt (at Hawara, see Herodotus ii. 148), in Lemnos, and at Clusium, see Burrows, *op. cit.* 108 *sqq.*

P. 16.—Cretan trade and industry: Evidence that the early Cretans practised purple-dyeing has been found by R. C. Bosanquet at the island of Leuce, which lies off the south-east coast, and at Palaikastro. See Ann. British School at Athens, ix. 276, and Journal of Hell. Studies, xxiv. 321.

P. 16.—Minos: Ridgeway, in his Minos the Destroyer rather than the Creator of the so-called "Minoan" Culture of Cnossus (Proceedings of Brit. Academy, vol. iv.), insists on the tradition (preserved in the Parian Chronicle, also in Diodorus and Plutarch) that there were two kings of the name Minos, the earlier *c.* 1406 B.C., the later *c.* 1229 B.C., out of whom Herodotus has made one person (i. 171 and 173, iii. 122). He finds Minos I. in *Iliad* xiv. 321, Minos II. in *Odyssey* xi. 322 and xix. 169. He regards Minos I as an Achaean and the destroyer of Cnossus; Minos II. as the king of the traditional thalassocracy and perhaps the leader of the Achaeans who invaded Egypt in 1223, B.C.

P. 16.—Minoa: For places of this name see Fick, Vorgriechische Ortsnamen, 1905, p. 27. It is uncertain whether the name Minoa in Sicily is of early origin, but there is an old legend that Minos went to Sicily to seek Daedalus (Herodotus vii. 169).

P. 17. Sect. 3.—Sources: Architectural remains on sites and objects in Museums, especially in the National Museum at Athens.—Modern expositions and researches: Schliemann, Mycenae 1878, Ithaca 1879, Orchomenos 1881, Tiryns 1886; Rodenwaldt, G., Tiryns, Die Ergebnisse der Ausgrabungen, vol. ii. 1912; Schuchhardt, *op cit.*; H. Bulle, Orchomenos, 1907; Wace and Thompson, Prehistoric Thessaly, 1912; Tsuntas, Μυκῆναι καὶ Μυκηναῖος πολιτισμός, 1893; Tsountas and Manatt, The Mycenaean Age, 1897; Perrot and Chipiez, Histoire de l'Art: vi. La Grèce préhistorique, 1895; Ridgeway, The Early Age of Greece, vol. i. 1901. H. R. Hall, Aegean Archaeology, 1915; Cp. also J. G. Frazer's commentary on Pausanias, vol. iii. for Tiryns and Mycenae.

P. 20.—The hall of the women at Tiryns: This identification—it is not quite certain—is due to Dr. Dörpfeld.

P. 20.—On the resemblances and differences between the Cretan and mainland palaces, see the investigation of D. Mackenzie in Ann. of British School at Athens, vols. xi. *sqq.*; and F. Noack, Homerische Paläste, 1903.

P. 25.—For the spearmen on the gravestone (cp. illustration, fig. 15) discovered in the lower town of Mycenae, see Tsuntas, Ἐφημερὶς ἀρχαιολογική, 1896, 1 *sqq.*

P. 27.—Mycenaean pottery: Furtwängler and Löschke, Myken. Thongefässe, 1879; Myken. Vasen, 1886.

P. 29.—Menelaion: Mycenaean fortress at Sparta, excavated by the British School at Athens, see Annual B.S.A. vol. xv.

P. 31.—Cadmeia: for excavations see American Journal of Archaeology, xi (1907).

P. 31.—Orchomenus: see Bulle, *op. cit.* Orchomenus had pottery of its own, the so-called Minyan ware, thin and of grey biscuit colour. Specimens of it have been found at Troy. The resemblance of Minyae to Minos has been invoked to support a connexion with Crete.

P. 32.—Castle of Gla: De Ridder, Bull. de corr. hell. 1894, 271 *sqq.*; Noack, Ath. Mitth. 1894, 405 *sqq.*

P. 32.—Pylus: Round tombs of the Second Late Minoan period have been excavated.—A prehistoric settlement has recently been discovered at Olympia.

P. 32.—Leucas: Dörpfeld has striven to establish that the Homeric Ithaca is identical with Leucas (in which he has discovered Mycenaean remains) and not with the smaller island known as Ithaca in historical times.

P. 32.—Thessaly: see Wace and Thompson, *op. cit.* The bronze age begas later in Thessaly than in southern Greece. "Minoan" culture reached Thessaly in the Second, but was not diffused till the Third, Late Minoan period. Round "tholos" tombs have been found also at Sesklo, and at Kapakli near Iolcus.

P. 33.—Mycenaean pottery in Egypt: Petrie, Journal Hell. Studies, xii. 199 sqq.

P. 33.—Strictly speaking, objects with the names of Amenhotep III. and Taia furnish only a major limit of time; and if only one such object had been found, or if all the objects had been found in one grave, we could not safely draw any further conclusion than that the aera of the Mycenaean civilisation was subsequent to the accession of Amenhotep. The cogency of the chronological argument rests on the circumstance that these objects have been found in different graves, and so far apart as Mycenae and Ialysus. It would be very hard to account for this on the theory, say, that the Mycenaean aera did not begin till the thirteenth century. The argument is strengthened by similar evidence from Cyprus.

P. 33.—Influence of Egypt on Aegean civilisation: cp. A. J. Evans, The Eastern Question in Anthropology, address at British Association, 1896.

Sect. 4.—Sources: Ruins of Hissarlik (Troy); Homer.—Modern Expositions: W. Dörpfeld, Troja and Ilion, 2 vols. 1902; W. Leaf, Troy, A study in Homeric Geography, 1912.

P. 38.—Peoples of the north who invaded Egypt: cp. W. Max Müller, Asien und Europa, 354-386. (1) Under Mernptah, in B.C. 1223. The invaders were the Libyans, along with a number of allies who are described as "northlanders" and "from the isles of the sea." These allies were the Akhaivasha= Achaeans; Shardana (who appear as a bodyguard under Mernptah's father Ramses II.)=Sardinians (it is presumed that their home is to be sought in Asia Minor, cp. Sardis, and that afterwards they lived in the western Mediterranean and gave its name to Sardinia); Shakarsha or Shakalsha=(?) Sikels (but cp. Sagalassus); Tursha=Tyrseni, Tyrrhenians; Luku or Lykki=Lycians. The invaders were defeated. (2) Under Ramses III. (in his 8th year, c. 1194) "the islands were unquiet" and Egypt was threatened on its Eastern frontier by Pulusatu or Pulishta=Philistines; Tikkarai, who have been identified with the Teucrians (a Thraco-Phrygian people, probably connected with the foundation of Salamis in Cyprus); Shakalsha; Danauna=Danaoi; Vasha-sha.

P. 39.—Hittite Empire: On the connexion of the absence of Mycenaean remains in western Asia Minor with the Hittite Empire, see Hogarth, Ionia and the East, 1908.

P. 41.—This theory of the source of Trojan wealth is propounded in the important work of Leaf, op cit. He has established that the Trojan war is an historical fact, has shown how the background of Homer corresponds to the geographical conditions, and has made it highly probable that the Trojan Catalogue in Iliad ii. is a document of the 12th century.

P. 42.—It has been suggested by Mr. Leaf that the story of the sack of Laomedon's Troy by Heracles may have been based on a memory of the fall of the Fifth City (which must have occurred before B.C. 1500).

P. 42.—Menelaus and Helen: This story is accepted as roughly true by J. L. Myres, The Dawn of History, 1911, p. 210.

P. 42.—The Greek forces against Troy: Enumerated in the Homeric Catalogue in Iliad, Book ii., the genuineness of which has been successfully defended by T. W. Allen, The Homeric Catalogue of Ships, 1921.

Sects. 5 and 6.—Chief Source: Homer.

P. 44.—The art of writing in Greece: Written memorials of the second millennium in the Aegean area have been found almost exclusively in Crete. But we may, with virtual certainty, infer that the art was practised in Greece in the heroic age. (1) The influence of Crete on Greece in other respects makes it a priori probable. (2) The legendary tradition of the invention of letters by Cadmus has considerable importance. (3) There are distinct archaeological traces of early writing outside Crete. For instance: at Mycenae, in a house on the acropolis, a stone vessel with hieroglyphs, and, in a chamber-tomb in the lower town, an amphora, with three linear signs; at Orchomenus, a vase with four linear signs. The evidence is collected in Evans Scripta Minoa, vol. i. The preservation of the clay tablets in Crete is a lucky accident, but endless memorials of Cretan writing *on other material* must have perished. The absence of memorials on the Greek mainland does not prove a negative or even an improbability.

P. 44.—Cremation: see Ridgeway, Early Age of Greece, i. 481 *sqq.*

Pp. 53 *sqq.*—For comparison of early Greek institutions with Roman and Teutonic, cp. Freeman, Comparative Politics (2nd ed. 1896). But though I have adopted, in the text, the view which regards these institutions as characteristically Aryan, I own that I feel grave doubts as to is truth, since we find similar institutions (the Council, and the assembly of the folk) among primitive non-Aryan peoples (*e.g.* in South Africa).

P. 45.—Family property in land: P. Guiraud, La Propriété foncière en Grèce, 1893.

Sects. 7, 8, and 9.—Chief sources: *Primary:* Homer; Hesiod's Theogony; fragments of Cyclic and Hesiodic poems. *Derivative:* (1) fragments of Hecataeus, Acusilaus, Charon, Pherecydes of Athens, Hellanicus; Herodotus; Thucydides i. 1-21; (2) fragments of Ephorus; Diodorus Siculus; Strabo; Pausanias.

P. 49.—Aetolia illyricized: cp. Kretschmer, *op. cit.* 254 *sqq.*

P. 51, *note.*—Pelasgians: Herodotus says that a non-Greek language which he regards as Pelasgian, was still spoken in his day in two little towns east of Cyzicus. This, so far as it goes, is against the view that the Pelasgians were Greeks.

P. 52.—Achaean immigration into the Peloponnesus: Bury, Journal Hell. Studies, xi. 217 *sqq.*

P. 52.—Boeotians from Mt. Boeon: Hoffmann, De mixtis Graecae linguae dialectis, 34.

Pp. 53 *sqq.*—On the course of the Dorian invasion cp. Wilamowitz-Möllendorff, Euripides, Herakles, i.[2] 14 *sqq.*—Argos claimed to be the premier Dorian state of the Peloponnese; hence Temenos was the eldest of the three great-grandchildren of Hyllus, who according to the legend (see Sect. 11 of this chapter) led the Dorian invasion. It may be held that this preserves a genuine reminiscence of the priority of the Dorian settlement of Argos.

P. 55.—Nisa: Wilamowitz-M., Hom. Unt. 252-3.

P. 55.—The comparative lateness of the Dorian conquest of Aegina is rendered probable by the nature of a "Mycenaean" gold treasure discovered there: A. J. Evans, Journal Hell. Studies, xiii. 195 *sqq.* (See Fig. 28.)

P. 57.—Aeolians of Aetolia: Thucydides iii. 102; Strabo x. 34.

P. 56, *note* 1.—The etymological connexion of *Achaean* with *Aeolian* is a view of Fick.

P. 60.—Magnesia: On the origin of the Magnesians, Wilamowitz-Möllendorff, Hermes, 1895, 177 *sqq.*

P. 60, *note* 1.—Ionian dialect: cp. Hoffmann, Der ionische Dialekt, 1898.

P. 61.—Homer: cp. P. Cauer, Grundfragen der Homerkritik; and G. Murray, Rise of the Greek Epic.

P. 61.—The Homer of the Iliad, a dweller in Chios: Fick, Die Erweiterung der Mênis, Bezzenberger's Beiträge zur Kunde der indogermanischen Sprachen, 1899, 20 *sqq.* The great rôle which Hector plays in the Iliad may be connected with the fact that Hector was a name in the royal family of Chios, which connected itself with Hector of Troy.

P. 61.—Sun rising over the sea, Il. xxiii. 227: κροκόπεπλος ὑπεὶρ ἅλα κίδναται Ἠώς; and xxiv. 13.

P. 62.—The general fact of an Ionizing of original Aeolic lays has been shown by Fick; but it is unnecessary to suppose that the Iliad as a whole and the Odyssey as a whole were first written in Aeolic.

P 62.—Expurgation: see G. Murray, *op. cit.*

P. 63.—Leleges and Carians: Paton and Myres, Journal Hell. Studies, 1896, 242 *sqq.* Tombs at Assarlik: Paton, *ib.* 1887, 67 *sqq.*

P. 63.—Alleged Carian inventions: At the best, "invent" must be explained to mean "introduce among the Greeks." The shield-handle was used, for example, by the Hittites.

P. 63.—Apollo Lykios: cp. Kretschmer, *op. cit.* p. 370.—But I cannot believe that the Trm̃mili were first called Lycians by the Greeks. It seems far more probable that the name Lycia is not to be separated from Lycaonia, and that *Lyk-* was a name by which the peoples of south-western Asia Minor were known in the Eastern Mediterranean and in Egypt (Luku). It was the name Lycia which suggested to the Greeks the identification of the Trm̃milian god with Appolo Λύκιος.

Sect. 10.—Chief sources: passages in Homer; Herodotus, i. 1-5, 105, and other passages; (for alphabet) early inscriptions.

P. 70.—For mining in Greek islands, Ardaillon, Les Mines du Laurion, 1899.

P. 70.—Alphabet: Evans (in his Scripta Minoa I.) discusses the possibility that the Phoenicians derived their alphabet from a Cretan script, through the Philistines. A certain number of the Phoenician letters are identical with Minoan signs.

P. 71.—Date of Introduction of Greek alphabet: Wilamowitz-M. would put the reception of writing "in the tenth cent. at latest" (Hom. Unt. 287); and so too A. J. Evans, Scripta Minoa I. p. 73.

P. 71, *note* 1.—The reading of the second verse of the inscription is very uncertain.

Sect. 11.—Chief sources: *Primary:* (1) Hesiod and "Hesiodic" fragments; (2) fragments of Hecataeus, Acusilaus, etc.; Herodotus; Thucydides i. 1-21. *Derivative:* Diodorus, Books iv. v., fragments of vi. vii.; the Bibliotheca of Pseudo-Apollodorus; Pausanias.

P. 71, *note* 2.—Grote, History of Greece, pt. i. cap. xvii.

P. 72.—The Ionians are *mentioned* once in the Iliad, where the Athenians are meant (xiii. 685).

CHAPTER II

P. 80.—Influence of land-system on colonisation: Guiraud (*op. cit.* Bk. i. cap. vi.), who, however, exaggerates it.

P. 82, *Sect.* 2.—Sources: scattered: largely in the works mentioned under Chap. I. Sects. 4-6. Add Pseudo-Scymnus.

P. 82.—The Euxine was also called the Axine or inhospitable ("Αξενος, Pind. Pyth. iv. 203); and it has been conjectured (by E. Meyer) that the sea was called the "Ascanian" from the (Phrygian) Ascanians, and that "Αξενος was a Greek corruption of this name.

P. 82.—Odyssey and the Euxine: Wilamowitz-Möllendorff, Hom. Unt. 163 *sqq.*

P. 83.—Dates of colonies in Pontus and Propontis: The dates assigned seem untrustworthy. Thus 757-6 B.C. is given for both Cyzicus and Trapezus (and in the Parian Marble for Syracuse). Sinope: 1st colony, 676 B.C., and 2nd colony of Cyzicus, 676 B.C. 2nd colony of Sinope, 631 B.C.; same year as colonisation of Cyrene. Cp. E. Meyer, *op. cit.* ii. p. 443. The dates for Chalcedon vary between 687 and 677 B.C.; the date for Byzantium is 660-59. Other dates are: Astacus, 712-11; Acanthus, Stagira, Abdera, and Lampsacus, 654; Istrus, 656; Olbia, 645; Perinthus, *c.* 600; Odessus, in the reign of the Median king Astyages (*c.* 585).

P. 86, *Sect.* 3.—Sources: Primary: coins; [traditions]. *Derivative:* (1) [Antiochus of Syracuse]; (2) Thucydides vi. 1-5; fragments of Philistus and

Ephorus; (3) fragments of Timaeus; Diodorus iv. v., and fragments of viii.; Strabo v. vi.; Pseudo-Scymnus.

P. 87.—Cyme: The statement that Cyme was older than any Greek settlement in either Italy or Sicily seems to rest entirely on a statement of Ephorus (Strabo v. 4. 4), who was a native of the mother-city Aeolian Cyme. Taking into account the motive of local patriotism, we need not lay any stress on his statement, which can hardly be maintained. Certainly Cyme is not older than the eighth century. Helbig, Das homerische Epos, Exkurs 1; Busolt, op. cit. i. 392, note.

P. 88.—Origin of name Graius, Graecus, Greek (Busolt, op. cit. i.[1] 44, who has since changed his view): cp. E. Meyer, op. cit. p. 471.

P. 88.—Position of Sicily in history: Freeman, History of Sicily, i. cap. 1.

P. 91.—Exact datings of Siceliot colonies uncertain: Mahaffy, Problems of Greek History, Appendix. The chronology given by Thucydides (doubtless derived from Antiochus) depended on the fact that Archias, the founder of Syracuse, was reckoned as the tenth descendant from Temenus, and the date of Temenus and the return of the Heraclidae was supposed to be (so Ephorus) 1069 B.C. This (ten generations being counted as 334 years gives 735 B.C. for Archias. As it was universally admitted that Naxos was the oldest Greek foundation in Sicily, the Syracusan chronographers gave it the priority of a year over Syracuse: hence Naxos, 735 B.C.; Syracuse, 734 B.C.

P. 96.—Foundation of Taras: View that the Partheniae were pre-Dorian Greek inhabitants of the Peloponnese (whom he regards as Achaeans): Geffcken, Jahrbb. für klass. Phil., B. 147, pp. 177 sqq. If this view is right, we ought perhaps to connect the Partheniae specially with the Taenarus peninsula.

P. 98.—Name Hellênes: Bury, Journal Hell. Studies, xvi. 217 sqq.

P. 99, Sect. 4.—Sources: Hesiod; Thucydides i. 13-15.

P. 99.—Family system of property: Guiraud, op. cit.

P. 100.—For the probable date of Hesiod and the Hesiodic school, see T. W. Allen, Journal Hell. Studies, xxxv. 85 sqq.

P. 102.—Shipbuilding: C. Torr, Ancient Ships. Significance of Briareos: ib.

P. 103.—Battle between Corinth and Corcyra: The date has the authority of Thucydides, i. 13.

P. 103, Sect. 5.—Sources: Primary: fragments and Callinus and Archilochus; cuneiform inscriptions of Assarhaddon and Assurbanipal; coins. Derivative: (1) Herodotus i. 6-15; [Xanthus]; (2) fragments of Nicolaus of Damascus.

P. 104.—Gyges and Cimmerians: Gelzer, Das Zeitalter des Gyges, Rheinisches Museum, 1875, 230 sqq.; 1880, 514 sqq.; E. Meyer, op. cit. i. p. 543 sqq., and ii. pp. 455 sqq. The entrance of the Bithynians from Thrace into Asia Minor and the occupation of Bithynia seems to have taken place soon before the Cimmerian invasion. It may be regarded as a continuation of the Phrygian immigrations. Bithynia is not mentioned in the Catalogue in Iliad ii.

P. 104.—Sardanapalus has been identified with other Assyrian kings; but he was doubtless suggested by Assurbanipal (E. Meyer, op. cit. i. p. 481).

P. 105.—Sarcophagus with Cimmerians (sixth cent.): A. S. Murray, Terracotta Sarcophagi, Greek and Etruscan, in the British Museum, 1898.

P. 105.—"It was some satisfaction to Assurbanipal to record": The account given by Assurbanipal of the submission, the revolt, and the death of Gyges is as follows (translated from the Assyrian by G. Smith, History of Assurbanipal, p. 64; cp. p. 73):—Gyges, king of Lydia, a district which is across the sea, a remote place of which the kings my fathers had not heard speak of its name. The account of my grand kingdom in a dream was related to him by Assur, the God my creator: "Of Assurbanipal, king of Assyria, the beloved of Assur, king of the Gods, lord of all, his princely yoke take." The day [he saw that] dream his messenger [he sent to pray for my friendship]. That dream [which he saw] by the hand of his envoy he sent and repeated [to me]. From the midst of the day when he took the yoke of [my kingdom], the Cimmerians, wasters of [his] people, who did not fear my fathers and me, and did not take the yoke of my kingdom, he captured, in the service of Assur and Ishtar, the Gods my lords. From the midst of the chiefs of the Cimmerians, whom he had taken, two chiefs in strong fetters of iron and bonds of iron, he bound, and with numerous presents he caused to bring to my presence. His messengers whom, to pray for my friendship, he was constantly sending, he wilfully discontinued; as the will of Assur, the God my creator, he had disregarded; to his own power he trusted and hardened his heart. His forces to the aid of Psammetichus (king) of Egypt, who had thrown off the yoke of my dominion, he sent; and I heard [of it] and prayed to Assur and Ishtar thus: "Before his enemies his corpse may they cast, and may they carry captive his attendants." When thus to Assur I had prayed he requited me. Before his enemies his corpse was thrown down, and they carried captive his attendants. The Cimmerians, whom by the glory of my name he had trodden under him, conquered and swept the whole of his country. . . . (Ardys) his son sat on his throne, that evil work at the lifting up of my hands, the Gods my protectors in the time of the father his begetter had destroyed. By the hand of his envoy he sent [word] and took the yoke of my kingdom thus: "The king whom God has blessed art thou; my father from [thee] departed and evil was done in his time; I am thy devoted servant, and my people all perform thy pleasure."

P. 106.—Coin of Phanes of Halicarnassus: This Phanes may be the grandfather of Phanes, son of Glaucus (mentioned in Herodotus iii. 4), who dedicated a costly bowl found at Naucratis.

Pp. 106-7.—Coinage: P. Gardner, Types of Greek Coins, 41 *sqq.*; and Earliest Coins of Greece Proper, in Proceedings of British Academy, vol. v.

P. 107, Sect. 6.—Sources: *Primary*: inscription of Abu Simbel; inscriptions of Naucratis; archaeological remains at Naucratis and Defenneh. *Derivative*: Herodotus ii.

P. 107.—Defenneh: Flinders Petrie, Tanis, Part ii. 1888.

P. 108.—Naucratis: Naukratis, Part I., by Flinders Petrie, 1886; Part II. by E. A. Gardner and F. Ll. Griffith, 1888. Solon describes Naucratis in the line (Bergk, fr. 28): Νείλου ἐπὶ προχοῆσι Κανωβίδος ἐγγύθεν ἀκτῆς.

P. 108.—Abusimbel inscription (Röhl, Inscr. Gr. Ant. 482): Perhaps belongs to the time of Psammetichus I. (so Kirchhoff), but it seems more reasonable to connect it with the Ethiopian expedition of his grandson Psammetichus II., whom Herodotus calls Psammis (Her. ii. 161). The mercenaries who inscribed their names were from Colophon, Teos, and Ialysus.

P. 108, Sect. 7.—Sources: *Primary*: fragments of Eugammon. *Derivative*: Herodotus iv.; Pindar, Pyth. iv. v. ix

P. 110.—Arcesilas vase: The inscriptions are: in the upper field, Ἀρκεσίλας (the seated king); Σοφορτος (the man with outstretched finger, speaking to the king); [στ]αθμός (the scale); ἱρμοφόρος (the man with the sack); Ὀρυξο[s] (?; second man with sack, looking backward); σλιφομαχος (σιλφομαξος?=silphion-kneader; man pointing upward). Below: φύλακος and μαεν(?). See Jahn, Berichte der sächsischen Ges. der Wiss. 1867, 94 *sqq.*

P. 110.—Libyan flavour in the Telegony: Wilamowitz-M., Hom. Unt. 186.

P. 111, Sect. 8.—Sources: *Primary*: fragments of Archilochus. *Derivative*: passages in Aristotle's Politics, iv. v.

P. 112.—Eclipse of sun (Archil. frag. 74, Bergk): April 6, 648 B.C. is sometimes designated as the first precise date in Greek history; but it is quite uncertain whether the poet himself saw the eclipse he refers to. The lines of Archilochus are:

Ζεὺς πατὴρ Ὀλυμπίων
ἐκ μεσημβρίης ἔθηκε νύκτ' ἀποκρύψας φάος
ἡλίου λάμποντος.

CHAPTER III

P. 113, *Sects.* 1 and 3.—Sources: *Primary:* fragments of laws quoted in Plutarch's Lycurgus; fragments of Tyrtaeus and Alcman. *Derivative:* (1) Herodotus (i. 65; iv. 147, etc.; vi. 51, etc.); Xenophon's Polity of the Lacedaemonians; Aristotle, Pol. ii. and fragments of Polity of Lacedaemonians; (2) Strabo viii.; Diodorus vii. (frags.); Plutarch's Lycurgus; Pausanias iii. (various passages).

P. 117.—The view that the importance of the Ephors was comparatively late is supported (though, of course, not proved) by the fact that they are not mentioned in the fragments of Tyrtaeus or in the old laws preserved by Plutarch (Lyc. 6).

P. 117, *note 3.*—Names of kings of Eurypontid house significant (Anaxidamus, Damaratos, etc.): E. Meyer, *op. cit.* ii. 562.

P. 120, *Sect.* 2.—Sources: *Primary:* fragments of Tyrtaeus. *Derivative:* (1) [Rhianus]; (2) Diodorus xv. 66; Pausanias iv.; Justin iii. 4, 5.

P. 120.—"First Messenian War": only early source, Tyrtaeus (fr. 5, Bergk); but it would be unsafe to regard as certain his statement that the war lasted nineteen years and was concluded in the twentieth. Nor can we press chronologically his description of its heroes as πατέρων ἡμετέρων πατέρες (Niese. Hermes, xxvi. 1 *sqq.*). It is noteworthy that in Od. xxi. 13-15 Messene is regarded as part of Lacedaemon.

P. 123.—Sparta in seventh century: cp. E. Meyer, *op. cit.* ii. 562 *sqq.*

P. 128.—Lycurgus: cp. E. Meyer, Rhein. Museum, 42, pp. 88 *sqq.*; Wilamowitz-M., Hom. Unt. 284 *sqq.* There can be little doubt that the name meant wolf-driver not light-worker; so Apollo Lykios was a wolf-god, not a light-god. The Lycaean mountain in Arcadia was possibly so called because it was infested with wolves.

P. 130, *Sect.* 4.—Sources: *Primary:* (1) Laws of Gortyn; (2) Aristotle, Pol. ii. 7; passages in Plato's Republic and Laws. *Derivative:* Strabo x. 4.

P. 133, *Sect.* 5.—Sources: *Primary:* architectural remains at Olympia. *Derivative:* Herodotus vi. 127; Ephorus (ap. Strabo viii. 3. 33); Aristotle, Pol. ii. 6, v. 10; 'Αθην. Πολ. 10; and frags. 480, 481; Pausanias v. and vi.

P. 133.—Pheidon of Argos: The traditional date of Pheidon's reign, in the first half of the eighth century, rests on late combinations. (1) Ephorus counted him as tenth in descent from Temenus, and so determined his date (on the calculation of three generations to a hundred years) as 803-770. (2) The derivation of the dynasty of the Macedonian kings, from Temenus of Argos, affected Pheidon's date. Karanos, the first in the list of these kings (he is not heard of till the fourth century B.C.), was made a brother of Pheidon, and seventh in descent from Temenus (or eleventh from Heracles). As it was believed (unhistorically) that the Median dynasty succeeded the Assyrian in 884, it seemed desirable to make the Macedonian dynasty at least as old; consequently Karanos and Pheidon were placed about 884, the older date of Lycurgus. Then, when Lycurgus, on account of the Olympian disc of Iphitus, was moved down to the time of the first Olympiad, those who adopted this system moved Pheidon also, and 798 was determined as the first year of Pheidon. Then fifty years later, 748, he celebrated the eighth Olympiad. Busolt, Griechische Geschichte i.[2] 612 *sqq.* (who calls attention to the chronological scheme of Argive history, on the basis of 50 and 30: 798, succession of Pheidon; 748, Pheidon's Olympiad; 718, first war for Thyreatis; 668, battle of Hysiae; 548 (= 668 − 4 × 30), second war for Thyrea). On the other hand, Herodotus implies that Pheidon ruled at Argos in the first quarter of the sixth century; for he makes his son Lacedas one of the suitors of Agarista. But we cannot lay much stress on this: his source is evidently a romantic tale, not serious history. Such a late date is inconsistent with the fact that the measures used at Athens before Solon's reform were Pheidonian; and it may be added that if he had been a contemporary of Solon we should probably have known more about him. While some scholars accept the tradition which placed him in the eighth century, the view that he lived in the seventh has been strengthened by the careful investigation of Busolt (*loc. cit.*). To the arguments which have been urged by others I would add one more. If the traditional date (first half of eighth century) were true, it is almost inconceivable that the romance of the wooing of Agarista would have made Pheidon a contemporary of Cleisthenes of Sicyon; on the other hand, this is by no means unintelligible, if Pheidon flourished in the middle, and third quarter, of the seventh century. Story could violate chronology by bringing Solon into relation with Croesus, but it would never have dreamed of bringing Lycurgus into relation with Croesus. I may further observe that the decline in the Argive power after Pheidon's death synchronises most happily with the Messenian war in the last quarter of the seventh century. The weakness of Argos left Sparta free to deal with Messenia.

P. 135.—The story of the struggle of the Eleans and Pisatans for Olympia rests on Elean tradition. The certain facts seem to be that the Elean control of the games dates from 572 B.C., and that for some years before there was a struggle. The Eleans represented this struggle as begun by the Pisatans (Pausanias vi. 22. 4), they themselves having been in possession of Olympia since the Olympiad of Pheidon. But it may be questioned whether this is true. The mere fact that the Elean control of the festival is dated from 572 B.C. (Eusebius i. 198, ed. Schöne) makes it probable that till then the festival was administered by the Pisatans.—The institution of the Ἑλλανοξίκαι, as umpires, may be referred to 572 B.C. or shortly after.—The struggle between Elis and Pisa may probably be illustrated by a treaty, graven on a bronze tablet discovered at Olympia (now in the British Museum), between the men of Elis and the men of Arcadian Heraea. We may guess (cp. Busolt, Griechische Geschichte, i.[2] 706; von Scala, Staatsverträge, No. 27) that it belongs to a year shortly before 572 B.C.; the aid of Heraea would have been very valuable to Elis in the war with Pisa. As this is the earliest extant treaty between two Greek states, I may add a translation of it here:—

"The treaty (*vratra*) between the Eleans and Heraeans.

"There shall be an alliance for a hundred years; this year shall be the first. If any need arise, either in word or deed, they shall help one another, both in other matters and in war. But if they do not so help, the transgressors shall pay a talent of silver to Zeus of Olympia as a fine. If any injure this writing, whether a private man (*Fέτας*) or magistrate (*τελεστά*) or deme, he (or it) shall be liable to the sacred penalty herein written" (Text: C.I.G. 11; Collitz, Sammlung der Dialektinschriften, 1149; Hicks, Greek Historical Inscriptions, 8).

P. 135.—The first Olympiad: Records of the Olympian victors seem to have been kept by the Eleans since the early part of the sixth century; but the Olympian list, as a whole, with the dates of the eighth and seventh centuries, seems to have been first worked out by Hippias of Elis at the very end of the fifth century. The Olympiads were first used as a system of chronological reckoning in the third century by the Siceliot Timaeus. The untrustworthy character of the Olympian list and of the generally accepted early dates in Greek history was pointed out by Professor Mahaffy. See Problems in Greek History, 217 *sqq.* Appendix. His arguments have been reinforced by Busolt, *op. cit.* 2nd ed. i. 586 *sqq.*

P. 137.—For extent of Argive power to the south, cp. Herodotus i. 82

P. 137, Sect. 6.—Sources: *Primary:* fragments of Archilochus, Alcaeus, Sappho. *Derivative:* Thucyd. i. 13; Aristotle, Pol. iv. and v.

P. 141, Sect. 7.—Sources: *Primary:* fragments of Theognis. *Derivative:* (1) Herodotus iii. 48-53, v. 67-8, 92, vi. 126-130; (2) Aristotle, Pol. iv. and v.; frags. of Nicolaus of Damascus; Pausanias v. 17; Diogenes Laertius i. 7. 2.

P. 141.—"Age of the Despots," a misleading expression. Cp. Mahaffy, Problems in Greek History, 79.

P. 143.—Corcyra's sea-power in the latter part of the seventh century is illustrated by the epitaph on Arniadas, who was slain fighting "hard by the ships" (παρὰ ναυσίν) near the mouth of the river Arachthus (Hicks, 2).

P. 145.—Corinthian invention of roof-tiles: Dörpfeld, Introduction to Tsountas-Manatt, Mycenaean Age.

P. 145.—Old (double) temple of Corinth = the temple of Apollo mentioned by Pausanias. This is indicated by the orientation of Corinth determined by the American excavations.

P. 145.—The "chest of Cypselus": Interesting restoration by Mr. H. Stuart Jones in Journal Hell. Studies, xiv. 30 sqq. and Plate 1.

P. 147.—Orthagoras: Aristotle, Pol. v. 12. Presumably Andreas took the name Orthagoras when he became tyrant. Cp. Busolt (op. cit. i. 661), who calculates that the date of the foundation of the Sicyonian tyranny was about 665. The date of Cleisthenes, c. 600-570, is certain.

P. 149, Sect. 8.—Sources: Primary: Homeric Hymn to Pythian Apollo. Derivative: Aeschines, c. Ctes. 107-112; Marmor Parium, 37; Strabo ix. 3; Plutarch, Solon, 11; Pausanias x. 37; Hypothesis to Pindar's Pythian Odes.

P. 149.—Crisa=Cirrha: E. Meyer, op. cit. ii. p. 669.

P. 149.—Date of Homeric Hymn to Pythian Apollo: prior to the Sacred War, as its tenor shows.

P. 150, note.—The part ascribed to Solon in the Sacred War is very doubtful (E. Meyer, op. cit. ii. p. 670), but the Athenians doubtless, as an Amphictionic state, sent aid, perhaps under Alcmeon as polemarch (Plut. Sol. 11).

P. 150.—"Crisaean Gulf": the name remained in common use long afterwards; it is always used by Thucydides.

P. 150.—First Pythiad=582 B.C. (not 586): the scholiasts on Pindar calculated the Pythiads on this assumption.

P. 150.—Old stadion in the plain below Crisa: cp. Pindar, Pyth. xi. 49.

CHAPTER IV

P. 155.—Sources: Primary: Homeric Hymn to Demeter; fragments of Solon; [laws of Solon]; [register of Archons]. Derivative: (1) Herodotus (various passages); Thucydides ii. 15; [Cleidemus]; fragments of Androtion; Aristotle, Politics and Ἀθηναίων Πολιτεία; fragments of Polemon and others; (2) Plutarch, Theseus and Solon; Pausanias i.

P. 156.—Eridanus: Dörpfeld, Ath. Mitth. 1888, 211 sqq.

P. 156.—Cecrōpes (like Dolopes, Dryopes, etc.): An inference from Cecrops. Cp. E. Meyer, op. cit. ii. 68; Wilamowitz-M., Aristoteles und Athen, i. 128.

P. 156.—Athena and Poseidon Erechtheus: Miss Harrison, Mythology and Monuments of Ancient Athens, Introduction.

P. 157.—Conquest of Attica: E. Meyer, op. cit. ii. 340-1.

P. 158.—It is probable that Theseus was originally connected with Thessaly: cp. J. Töpffer, Theseus und Peirithoos, Aus der Anomia, 30 sqq.

P. 160.—Neleids: J. Töpffer, Attische Genealogie.

P. 161, note.—Codrus: Story of disguise first appears in Pherecydes (middle of fifth century), fr. 10; that Codrus fell in battle is the assumption of the painter of the red figured cylix (shown in text): cp. Busolt, op. cit. ii. 128.

P. 161.—For kings and regents and position of the Medontids, see Wilamowitz-Möllendorff, Hermes, 1898, 126 sqq. Acastus and his successors beside the basilês fainéants correspond to the Pippins and Charles Martel in the days of the last Merovingian kings of Gaul.

P. 162.—Origin of Ionic tribes in Attica: Wilamowitz-M., Aristoteles und Athens, i. 141. Names of tribes, Busolt, *op. cit.* ii. 103.

P. 165, *note.*—Suggestions respectively of Wachsmuth and Rohde.

P. 165.—The Eumolpids, who traced themselves to Poseidon, were the royal house of Eleusis, and they retained the priesthood after the incorporation in Attica. Their Thracian descent was a legend which had obtained credence as early as the fifth century. There may, however, have been Thracian settlers at Eleusis; this is an obscure question. For Thracians in Phocis: Helianicus, frag. 71; Thucydides ii. 29. There was a clan of Thracidae (Θρᾳκίδαι) at Delphi: Diodorus xvi. 24.

P. 165.—Date of Eleusinian Hymn: cp. Wilamowitz-M., Aus Kydathen, 125; Hom. Unt. 208. But it need not have been composed *before* the destruction of Eleusinian independence; it may have been composed soon afterwards.

P. 165.—On the treaty between Athens and the Eleusinian dynasty—a treaty which was doubtless *written*—see Wilamowitz-Möllendorff, Aristoteles und Athen, ii. 38 *sqq.; R.* von Scala, Staatsverträge des Altertums, i. No. 18.

P. 167.—Timocracy before Solon: Three classes, not four; Solon made the citizens who had a smaller income than two hundred medimni into a fourth class, called the Thêtes. *Pentacosiomedimni may* have been a name invented officially for the highest class when the timocracy was organised; but it may also, as I suggest, have been a popular name for the rich (like our millionaire, though applied to income, not to capital).

P. 168.—The Demiurgi: Their political position both under the timocracy and under Solon's constitution is obscure. Yet that they had political rights, whether they acquired land or not, I consider certain. The mere fact that they stand out as a distinct social class, and are not simply merged in the Thêtes, shows their importance; and the probable view that one of the thesmothetes was a demiurgos implies that they had political rights. For the thesmothetes, cp. Busolt, *op. cit.* ii. 178, and 179 *note.*

P. 170.—Athenian navy in second half of seventh century: That the Athenians had then a small fleet of penteconters is not only a necessary inference from the institution of the naucraries, but is implied by the Athenian operations at the Hellespont *c.* 600 B.C.

P. 170.—The league of Calauria: Wilamowitz-Möllendorff, Die Amphiktionie von Kalaurea, in the Nachrichten der Gött. gel. Gesellschaft, 1896, 188 *sqq.*

P. 170.—Temple of Poseidon at Calauria, excavated by Wide and Kjellberg: Ath. Mitth. 1895, 267 *sqq.*

P. 171.—Epimenides: an Attic hero made into a Cretan. Cp. E. Meyer, *op. cit.* ii. 748-9. Diels argues with considerable force that he was a real person, Sitzungsberichte der Berliner Akademie, 1891, 387.

P. 175.—Monetary reform of Solon: the conclusions of P. Gardner (see above, p. 858, note on pp. 113-4) are here adopted.

CHAPTER V

P. 182.—Sources, as for Chapter IV., with a few inscriptions, architectural remains, etc.

P. 183.—Conquest of Salamis, date of: Wilamowitz-Möllendorff, Aristoteles und Athen, ii. 267.—A Megarian tradition ascribed the conquest to the treachery of a banished Megarian family, the Dorykleioi: Pausanias i. 40. 4. Cp. Töpffer, Quaestiones Pisistrateae, 56.

P. 184.—Salaminian decree: Concerns the Salaminians (not, as was hitherto supposed, the cleruchs): A. Wilhelm, Altattische Schriftdenkmäler, in Ath. Mitth. 1899, 466 *sqq.* The date cannot be determined with certainty.

P. 184.—Stêlê of Aristion from his tomb near Brauron (C.I.A. i. 464): Wilamowitz-M., *op. cit.* i. 14.

P. 185.—Chronology of the exiles of Pisistratus: C. Cichorius, Die Chronologie des Pisistratus (in Kleinere Beiträge zur Geschichte, 1894). But the dates cannot be determined with certainty.

P. 185.—Sons of Pisistratus: Wilamowitz-M., *op. cit.* i. 109 *sqq.*; J. Töpfer, in Hermes, 29, 463 *sqq.*

P. 187.—Hektemors: Cauer, Parteien und Politiker in Megara und Athen, 95 *sqq.*

P. 187.—Land-taxes: thus we may reconcile Aristotie, 'Aθ. Πολ. 16. 4 (δεκάτην) with Thucydides vi. 54 (εἰκοστὴν μόνον).

P. 187.—Mines of Laurion: Ardaillon, *op. cit.*

P. 189.—The presence of the Athenians on the Heliespontine shores in the first (?) half of the sixth century is illustrated by an inscription found at Sigeum (now in the British Museum), *in the Attic dialect and in the Attic alphabet*, on a pillar which supported the sculptured portrait of a certain Phanodicus of Proconnesus—probably the tyrant of that city—who presented the city hall (πρυτανεῖον) of the Sigeans with a mixing-bowl, a stand for it, and a strainer. Phanodicus sent the pillar with his bust, and an Ionic inscription recording his gift; the men of Sigeum added an Attic version below (C.I.G. 8; Hicks, 7).

P. 190.—The story of the Pisistratean commission on the Homeric poems has been definitely disproved by Mr. T. W. Allen in the Classical Quarterly, vol. vii. p. 33 *sqq.*, 1913.

P. 191.—Temple of Athena, Hecatompedon, excavated 1885-6: Dörpfeld, Ath. Mitth. 1886, 337 *sqq.* This is the temple of Athena in Herod. viii. 51, 53, and is distinct from the older temple which she shared with Erechtheus (Iliad ii. 547; Herod. viii. 55), and which stood on the site of the later "Erechtheum." Against this view, however, it is urged that there are no traces of an older building on that site. Cp. G. Körte, Rhein. Museum, 1898, 239 *sqq.*, who holds that the Hecatompedon was a double temple, of Athena and Erechtheus —Inscription concerning the Hecatompedon temple, C.I.A. iv. 1, 138; Wilhelm, *op. cit.* 491-2.—The Gigantomachy may be post-Pisistratean (last quarter of sixth cent.): see H. Schrader, Ath. Mitth. 1897, 59 *sqq.*

P. 191.—Pisistratus also built a temple to the Pythian Apollo (the Pythion) S.W. of the temple of Zeus. Hippias dedicated an altar in the temenos (Thucydides vi. 54), and a fragment of the inscription has been found (C.I.A. iv. 373 E; Hicks, 9).

P. 192.—Supposed sanctuary of Dionysus in Limnae: Dörpfeld, Ath. Mitth. 1895, 161 *sqq.*; but there are serious difficulties in the identification.

P. 193.—Theseus: cp. E. Meyer, *op. cit.* ii. p. 775.

P. 193.—Aqueducts (excavated by Dörpfeld): Ath. Mitth. 1894, 248 *sqq.*; 1895, 161 *sqq.*; 1896, 265 *sqq.*

P. 193.—Walls of Athens: Wilamowitz-M., Aus Kydathen, 97 *sqq.*

P. 194.—Tegea to harbour no Messenians: Aristotle (frag. 73 in Müller, Fr. Hist. Graec. ii. 134), who quotes from the stêlê on which the treaty was engraved, and which was set up on the banks of the Alpheus (at Olympia?).

P. 195.—Corinth ranged against Argos: A bronze helmet (in the British Museum) from Olympia records a victory won by the Argives over Corinth, conjecturally about 500 B.C. (C.I.G. 29; Hicks, 10).

P. 195.—Exclusion of Attic pottery from Argos (Herod. v. 88): J. C. Hoppin, Class. Review, 1898, Feb., 86.

P. 197.—Temple of Apollo: Remains of pediment sculptures, Homolle, Bull. de corr. hell. 1896, 650 *sqq.* Cp. Bury, in Hermathena, 1899, 1 *sqq.*

P. 198.—Anchimolius (Herodotus) is called Anchimolus in Aristotle's Constitution of Athens, 19. 5.

P. 197.—Siphnian treasury: This (the original) identification is strongly supported by the order in Pausanias; but M. Homolle now regards it as the Cnidian treasury.

P. 198.—Athens a member of the Peloponnesian League: Wilamowitz-M.,
Aus Kydathen, 116; Aristoteles und Athen, ii. 78. Cp. Thucyd. vi. 82.

P. 201.—Political reorganisation of Attica by Cleisthenes: cp. Wilamowitz-
M., Aristoteles und Athen, ii. 145 *sqq.*

P. 203.—Cleisthenic cycle: B. Keil, Hermes, 1894, 321 *sqq.*

P. 206.—Date of alliance between Athens and Plataea (see Thucydides iii.
55): According to the text of Thucydides iii. 68, the date would be $5\frac{20}{18}$
B.C., which can hardly be right. Busolt proposes a slight emendation (Gr.
Geschichte, ii. 399), which would give $5\frac{10}{9}$ B.C.

P. 207.—Inscription of Athenian stoa at Delphi: Dittenberger, Sylloge[2], 3
(Hicks, 20); Wilamowitz-M., Arist. u. Athen, ii. 287.

P. 207.—History of Oropus: Wilamowitz-M., Hermes, 21, 97 *sqq.*

CHAPTER VI

P. 208, *Sect.* 1.—Sources: *Primary:* inscriptions of Assarhaddon and Assurbanipal. *Derivative:* (1) Herodotus, Bk. i.; [Xanthus]; Bacchylides, Ode 3;
fragments of Ctesias; (2) fragments of Nicolaus of Damascus; Diodorus,
fragments of Bk. ix.; Justin (=Pompeius Trogus), Bk. i.

P. 208.—Sargon stêlê: Schrader, Die Sargonstele des Berliner Museums, in
the Abhandlungen of the Berlin Academy, 1881.

P. 212.—Croesus inscription at Ephesus: Hicks, 4; Dittenberger[2], 1.

P. 213.—*Medism:* significance of the term; cp. Mahaffy, Hermathena, 1879,
459.

P. 214.—546 B.C.: Received date of fall of Sardis, but it is far from certain.
Busolt is in favour of 541 B.C.

P. 215.—The date of the red-figured vase (preserved in the Louvre), on
which the pyre of Croesus is represented (reproduced in text), might be
roughly between 510 and 490 B.C. Miss Harrison, Classical Review, 1898, Feb.
p. 84; A. H. Smith, Journal of Hell. Studies, 1898, 267-8.

P. 216. *Sect.* 2.—Sources: Herodotus i.; Justin and fragments as in Sect. 1.

P. 219, *Sect.* 3.—Sources: Herodotus iii.; Justin and fragments as in Sect. 1.

P. 222, *Sect.* 4.—Sources: *Primary:* inscription of Behistun; fragments of
Hecataeus. *Derivative:* Herodotus iii. 61-96, 133 *sqq.*; v. 52, etc.

P. 223.—Royal Road: cp. Macan's Herodotus, vol. ii. App. xiii.

P. 224.—Maps: cp. J. L. Myres, An Attempt to Reconstruct the Maps used
by Herodotus, in Geographical Journal, Dec. 1896.

P. 224.—"Text of Anaximander's map": phrase of E. Meyer.

P. 225, *Sect.* 5.—Sources: *Derivative:* Herodotus, Bk. iv.; cp. frags. of
Ctesias, and Strabo, Bk. vii. c. 2.

P. 228.—Scythian expedition of Darius: cp. Macan, Herodotus, vol. ii.
App. ii. iii.; Bury, Classical Review, July 1897. The story was first seriously
criticised by Grote.

P. 229, *Sect.* 6.—Sources: *Primary:* [Hecataeus]. *Derivative:* Herodotus,
Bks. v. and vi. 1-42.

P. 232.—Darius and the Athenians: "as has been well observed"—by Grote.

P. 234.—Inscription of Chares: Hicks, 6. There was also a dedication of
one Histiaeus in this temple (Hicks, 5): he *may* be the tyrant of Miletus.

P. 234.—Letter of Darius to Gadates, preserved on a stone: Dittenberger,
Sylloge[2], 2.

P. 235, *Sect.* 7.—Sources: *Primary:* inscriptions. *Derivative:* (1) Herodotus
vi. 43 *sqq.*; (2) Plato, Menexenus; [Lysias] Epitaphios; frags. of Ctesias;
Justin ii.; Nepos, Miltiades; Plutarch, Aristides 5, Parallels 305; De malign.
Herod.; Pausanias i. 15 and 32.

P. 237.—Decree to march to Marathon: τὸ Μιλτιάδου ψήφισμα. The source is Demosthenes, De fals. leg. 303, with Schol., and Aristotle, Rhet. iii. 10.

P. 240.—Battle of Marathon, reconstruction of: Macan, *op. cit.* vol. ii. Appendix x.; Review of Macan's work in Athenaeum, 21st Dec. 1895; cp. Bury, Class. Review, March 1896.—For an acute and interesting treatment of the Marathonian problem, see Mr. J. A. R. Munro's article in the Journal of Hellenic Studies, xix., 1899.

P. 242.—Callimachus inscription: C.I.A. iv. 153, 350: Köhler, Hermes, 1896, 150. Two other epigrams on battle of Marathon, C.I.A. i. 333: cp. Wilhelm, Ath. Mitth. 1899, 489 *sqq.*

P. 242.—Shield incident: A guess as to its significance, Bury, Class. Review, Feb. 1896. The doubt of Herodotus would, of course, be explained, if Alcmaeonids were his informants.

Sect. 8.—Sources: Herodotus, passages in Bks. v. and vi.

P. 245.—Athens and Aegina: Wilamowitz-M., Aristoteles und Athen, ii. 280 *sqq.*; Macan, *op. cit.* vol. ii. App. viii.

P. 247, *Sects.* 9, 10.—Sources: Pindar, Pyth. 7 (486 B.C.) ; Herodotus viii. 104, and other passages; Thucydides i. 93; Aristotle, Ἀθηναίων Πολιτεία; Plutarch's Themistocles and Aristides.

P. 249.—Annual Procheirotonia whether an "ostrakophoria" should be held: Arist. Ἀθ Πολ. 43.

P. 249, *note.*—Solon's law against neutrality—ostracism—Graphe Paranomon; Mahaffy, Hermathena, 1881, 87.

P. 251.—Maronea identified with Camareza: Ardaillon, Les Mines du Laurion.

CHAPTER VII

P. 252, *Sects.* 1-8.—*Primary:* Aeschylus, Persae; contemporary epigrams (ascribed to Simonides) ; passages in Pindar. *Derivative:* (1) Herodotus vii.-ix.; fragments of Ctesias; (2) Diodorus xi.; Justin ii.; Nepos, Themistocles and Aristides; Plutarch, Themistocles and Aristides.

P. 252.—The whole story of the Persian invasion has been fully and critically treated in G. B. Grundy, The Great Persian War, 1901, and R. W. Macan, Herodotus, Books vii.-ix., Appendix volume.

Pp. 260 *sqq.*—Thermopylae and Artemisium: criticism of the account of Herodotus, Bury, in Annual of the British School at Athens, vol. ii.

P. 265.—Oracle of the wooden wall: Acropolis not left without a garrison; Bury in Classical Review, Dec. 1896.

P. 268.—Battle of Salamis; cp. Grundy, and Macan, *opp. citt.*, where references to previous researches will be found.

P. 268.—Aristides at Salamis; Bury, Class. Review, *loc. cit.*

P. 271.—Prize of wisdom: The anecdote that each general wrote his own name first and that of Themistocles second cannot, of course, be taken seriously; but even the statement that a prize for wisdom was offered at all may be rejected. In fact, the story carries with it its own refutation: *no prize was awarded,*—because none was offered.

P. 271.—The epitaphs: Wilamowitz-Möllendorff, Simonides der Epigrammatiker, in Nachrichten der K. Ges. der Wiss. zu Göttingen, 1897, 307 *sqq.* Stone with the Corinthian epitaph: Dragumês, Ath. Mitth. 1897, 52.

P. 277, *Sect.* 7.—Besides sources mentioned above, inscription on base of Delphic tripod (most recent ed.: Dittenberger, Syll.² 7).

P. 277.—Battle of Plataea; G. B. Grundy, The Topography of the Battle of Plataea, 1894; Woodhouse, Journal of Hell. Studies, 1898, 33 *sqq.*; Grundy, and Macan, *opp. citt.*

P. 281.—"Distressed in soul": καίπερ ἀχνύμενος θυμόν, Pindar, Isth. vii. 5.

P. 283.—Stone of Tantalus: Pindar, *ib.* 10.

P. 284, *Sects.* 9-11.—Sources: *Primary:* Sicilian Odes of Pindar and Bacchylides. *Derivative:* (1) Herodotus vii. 153-167; (2) Pindaric scholia; Diodorus xi.; Xenophon's Hiero.

P. 287.—Position and title of the Syracusan tyrants: στρατηγὸς αὐτοκράτωρ? Freeman, History of Sicily, ii. 499 *sqq.;* Bury, Class. Rev., March 1899.

P. 293.—Hieron's victories in the games were: Horse-races at Pytho, 482, 478 B.C.; horse-races at Olympia, 476 and 472 B.C.; chariot-race at Pytho, 470 B.C.; chariot-race at Olympia, 468 B.C. The dates of the victories of 476 and 472 are now absolutely determined by the List of Olympian victors (Oxyrhynchus Papyri, ii. pp. 87-8).

P. 296, *Sects.* 12, 13.—Homeric Hymn to Demeter; Orphica (ed. Abel); material collected in Lobeck's Aglaophamus [cp. Kern, De Orphei, Epimenidis, Pherecydis theogoniis; and Rohde's Psyche].

P. 300.—Orphic Theology: cp. Gomperz, Griechische Denker, i. 65 *sqq.;* E. Meyer, *op. cit.* pp. 727 *sqq.* The dangers of the Orphic movement, and philosophy as an antidote: cp. E. Meyer, *ib.* pp. 749 *sqq.*

P. 301.—Orphic interpolation in Odyssey: Wilamowitz-M., Hom. Unters. 199 *sqq.*

P. 303, *Sect.* 14.—Sources: *Primary:* fragments of early philosophers. *Derivative:* their lives in Diogenes Laertius.

P. 304.—Xenophanes: cp. sympathetic portrait in Gomperz, *op. cit.* 127 *sqq.*

CHAPTER VIII

Pp. 307 and 332.—Sources: *Primary:* inscriptions; scattered notices in Herodotus; Thucydides, i. 89-117, 128-138; fragments of Timocreon, Ion, Stesimbrotus, Cratinus, Eupolis; [Hellanicus]. *Derivative:* (1) [Cleidemus]; [Ephorus]; [Androtion]; (2) Aristotle, Ἀθηναίων Πολιτεία; Diodorus, xi. 37-xii. 28; Plutarch: Themistocles, Aristides, Cimon, Pericles; Nepos: Themistocles, Aristides, Pausanias, Cimon. [The sources are collected in G. F. Hill's Sources for Greek History, 478-431 B.C.]

P. 309.—It is very difficult to fix the chronology of the years 478-445. In most cases I concur with Busolt.

P. 312.—Argos recovers Tiryns: Date seems to be later than Aug. 468, for in the recently discovered List of Olympian Victors (Oxyrhynchus Papyri, ii. p. 89) we find that in that year the Boys' boxing-match was won by a Tirynthian (. . . ης Τιρύνθιο[ς παίδων π]ύξ). The conclusion is not indeed quite certain: the victor might have been an exile.

P. 316.—Traces of haste in Themistoclean walls: Use of inscribed stones: C.I.A. i. 479, etc.; Hicks, 13, 14.

P. 316.—Heights of the Pnyx: The name Pnyx was given to the whole complex of hills S.W. of Athens (Nymph Hill, Pnyx, and Museum): Plato, Critias, 112A.

P. 317.—Relation of Athens to Lacedaemon after the Persian war, and at the time of the building of her walls: The significance of the interference of Sparta in the matter of the walls is clearer, if Athens was still regarded as a member of the Peloponnesian League,—and it seems to me that Wilamowitz-Möllendorff is right in insisting on this. It is a point which Athenian writers would naturally ignore. Thus by building her walls in spite of Lacedaemonian protests, Athens withdrew from the League and declared herself the peer of Sparta.

P. 317.—Harbours of the Munychian peninsula: I have followed the current view as to the identity of the harbours; but I must note that this has recently been called in question by Angelopulos, Περὶ Πειραιῶς καὶ τῶν λιμένων αὐτοῦ, 1898, whose arguments I cannot test.

P. 320, note.—Ostracism: Two sherds are also extant with the name of Xanthippus and one with that of Megacles. The Themistocles sherd reads: Θεμιστοκλῆς Φρεάρριος: R. Zahn, Ath. Mitth. 1897, 345.

P. 321.—Origin of story of suicide of Themistocles: Rhusopulos, Ath. Mitth. 1896, 18 sqq.; P. Gardner, Class. Review, Feb. 1898, 21.

P. 324.—Stone of treaty of Athens with Erythrae: C.I.A. i. 9 (cp. 10 and 11); Hicks, 23; Ditt.² 8. Fragments of similar treaties with Miletus and Colophon: C.I.A. iv. 22a and i. 13.

P. 325.—Quota-lists: We have fragments, varying in length, of quota-lists for every year from 454-3 to 436-5 B.C.: C.I.A. i. 226-244 and iv. pp. 71-2. The pieces preserved from the stones of the following years up to 425-4 B.C. are very slight: ib. 245-258. Cp. Hill, Sources for Greek History, chap, ii.; Hicks, 30, 35.

P. 330.—Revolt of Helots: Memorial at Olympia: Hicks, 17 (Pausanias v. 24. 1).

P. 330.—Mycenae: Temple and city-walls belong to period of her independence. Cp. Bury, Hermathena, 1898.

CHAPTER IX

P. 332.—Sources: see sources for Chapter VIII.

P. 339.—Erechtheid inscription: C.I.A. i. 433; Hicks, 19; Dittenberger², 9. Date: cp. Busolt, Griechische Geschichte, iii. 305.

P. 343.—Women at Athens: I adapt the observation of Wilamowitz-M. (Aristoteles und Athen, ii. 100, note), "Es ist kein kleines Zeichen von der Würde der attischen Geschichte, dass nur ein Weib in ihr vorkommt, das aber beherrscht sie: die Jungfrau von der Burg."

P. 344.—Peace of Callias: cp. Bury, Hermathena, 1898.

P. 346.—March of Andocides: Köhler, Hermes, 1889, 92 sqq. (C.I.A. ii. 1675).

P. 346.—Treaty with Chalcis: C.I.A. iv. 27a; Hicks, 28; Dittenberger², 17.

P. 347.—Marble base with a few letters of the inscribed verses: C.I.A. i. 334; Hicks, 27.

P. 349.—For the feeling in the allied cities against the great statesmen of the democracy, especially Themistocles and Pericles, the lost work of Stesimbrotus of Thasos, entitled Concerning Themistocles, Thucydides, and Pericles, may be cited as evidence. We know the tone of the work (composed c. 430 B.C.) from quotations and references; the author collected all the stories, true and untrue, that he could hear of, to the disadvantage of Pericles and Themistocles. But there is no doubt that his political views were oligarchical; and therefore he cannot be used as evidence for the sentiments of the democrats or the mass of the citizens in Thasos or anywhere else.

P. 350.—Colony to Brea: C.I.A. i. 31; Hicks, 29; Dittenberger², 19. Colony to Eretria: C.I.A. i. 339; Dittenberger², 18.

P. 351, Sects. 6 and 7.—Architectural sources: architectural remains and sculptures.

P. 352.—Parthenôn, the name (which in itself might mean the chamber either of the Parthenos or of the Parthenoi): cp. Furtwängler, Meisterwerke der griechischen Plastik, 172.—The temple seems to have been finished so far as to be ready for use in 438 B.C., when the statue of Athena was set up; but the decorations were not complete for some years later.

P. 355.—Temple of Hephaestus: popularly called the Theseum. This temple, set on the hill of Colonos Agoraios, must have been always a conspicuous building, and no traveller could have failed to mention it in a description of Athens. Any one, standing on the Acropolis and looking westward, will convince himself of this. The only temple which can correspond to it in the description of Pausanias is that of Hephaestus. But the last doubts as to the identification would be set at rest if B. Sauer has rightly explained some of the sculptures as referring to Hephaestus (Das sogenannte Theseion und sein plastischer Schmuck, 1899).

P. 357.—Original design of the Propylaea: Dörpfeld, Ath. Mitth. 1885, 38 sqq., 131 sqq.

P. 361.—Population of Attica, c. 432 B.C.: Beloch, Die Bevölkerung der griechisch-römischen Welt, 54 sqq. He reckons the total population at about 235,000 (including 100,000 slaves). This is probably an understatement. He reckons the population of the Peloponnesus, at the same period, at 350,000, and the total population of Greece (including Macedonia, Chalcidice, Crete, and the Cyclades; excluding Asiatic Greece) at upwards of 3,000,000 (including 1,000,000 slaves).—For Athens itself, with the Piraeus, he reckons about 110,000 to 115,000 (namely, 30,000 citizens, 20,000 to 25,000 metics, and 60,000 slaves: the greater part of the citizen population lived in the country).

P. 362.—Reoccupation of Sybaris, foundation of New Sybaris and of Thurii: Busolt, op. cit. iii. 518 sqq.

P. 364.—The friendship of Athens with the lords of Bosporus in the fourth century is illustrated by an Attic inscription of 347-6 B.C. in honour of the sons of Leucon (who had reigned over the Bosporane kingdom as "archon of Bosporus and Theodosia, king of the Sindi, the Toreteis, the Dandarii, and the Psessi": see C.I.G. ii. 2134a; Ditt.[2] 128): C.I.A. iv. 2, 109b; Hicks, 111; Ditt.[2] 129.

P. 368, Sect. 11.—Cp. Gomperz, Griechische Denker, i. pp. 306-413.

CHAPTER X

P. 374.—Sources: Primary: inscriptions; Thucydides, Books i.-v.; Aristophanes: Acharnians, Knights, Wasps, Peace. Derivative: [Ephorus]; Plutarch's Pericles and Nicias; Diodorus xii. 31-74.

P. 376, note.—Expenses of Athens in the Corcyraean Expedition: C.I.A. i. 179; Hicks, 41; Ditt.[2] 26.

P. 383.—Strategy of Pericles: H. Delbrück, Die Strategie des Perikles erläutert durch die Strategie Friedrichs des Grossen, 1890. He calls the strategy employed by Pericles (as explained above) "Ermattungsstrategie," as opposed to "Niederwerfungsstrategie."

P. 390.—Expedition to Epidaurus: it has been suggested that the very brie and inadequate treatment of this episode by Thucydides, his omission to ex plain how and why the enterprise failed—in contrast with his full accounts oi events of less moment—is an instance of partiality; and that it is one of those rare cases in which he allowed his personal prepossessions to influence his presentation of history. In his treatment of the statesmen, Cleon and Hyperbolus, he failed to control his prejudice against them. But I doubt whether admiration of Pericles was his motive for passing so lightly over the failure at Epidaurus.

P. 391.—Athenian colonists sent to Potidaea: Record of this on a stone: C.I.A. i. 340; Hicks, 45; Ditt.[2] 28.

P. 391.—Aspasia: cp. Wilamowitz-Möllendorff, Aristoteles und Athen, ii. 99.

P. 392.—Plataea: extent of the city: cp. Frazer, Pausanias, vol. v. 88 *sqq.* Mr. Grundy (Topography of Battle of Plataea, 53 *sqq.*) thinks the older Plataea was the N.W. corner of the later town.

P. 396.—Sending of Paches: part of the decree providing for the furnishing of transport-ships for the expedition of Paches is preserved: C.I.A. iv. 2, 35*c*; Ditt.² 27. Cp. Busolt, Philologus, L. 583 *sqq.*

P. 399.—Mytilenaean prisoners who were put to death: "a little more than a thousand," according to our text of Thucydides (iii. 50), which, since only the ringleaders are meant, seems to be nonsense. The difficulties are well set out by J. Steup in his note on the passage in Classen's edition. The suggestion (made independently by Mahaffy and Schütz) "a little more than thirty" (Λ for Α) is highly probable.

P. 400.—The cleruchies of Lesbos: Fragment of the decree preserved: C.I.A. i. 96; Ditt.² 29. It is an error to suppose that the cleruchs enjoyed their lots without leaving Athens: Dittenberger, *ib.*

P. 401.—Naval victories of Phormio: Commemorated perhaps by a dedication at Dodona with the words, "the Athenians from the Peloponnesians, having conquered in a sea-fight": Ditt.² 30.

P. 401.—The "peninsula" of Leucas: The canal of Periander, which had completely insulated it, seems to have been silted up, for Thucydides mentions that ships were hauled across the isthmus.

P. 403.—The revolutionary spirit: This was not a new thing, we meet it in the days of Theognis at Megara.

P. 405.—Aetolian campaign of Demosthenes: Woodhouse, Aetolia, 57 *sqq.*, 340 *sqq.* Identification of Aegition: *ib.* 363.

P. 408.—Defeat of Ambraciots and capture of Anactorion: A statue of Athena Nike was set up with spoils won on these occasions and at the capture of Istone in Corcyra in the same year: the monument was restored in the next century and a fragment of a decree relating to it has been preserved (C.I.A. iv. 2, 189*c*; Ditt.² 136): Behr in Hermes, 1895, 447.

P. 408, *Sect.* 9.—Additional sources: Pseudo-Xenophon, Constitution of the Athenians; Antiphon, de Choreuta and fragment of Contra Philinum.

P. 409.—οι νεώτεροι: Aristophanes, Wasps, 890.

P. 409.—Antiphon: date of his orations Contra Philinum and De Choreuta now fixed as 425 B.C. by Keil: Hermes, 1894, 337-9.

P. 410.—The people's dog: Aristophanes, Knights, 1023.

P. 411.—The money borrowed from the temple treasures was paid back, after the Peace of Nicias; fragments of the accounts are preserved: C.I.A. i. 273; Hicks, 46.

P. 411.—Tribute of 425-4 B.C., not less than 960 talents: cp. Wilhelm, Epigraphischer Bericht aus Griechenland (*supra cit.*), p. 43. Fragments are preserved both of the assessment-list (C.I.A. i. 37) and of the quota-list (C.I.A. i. 259).

P. 412.—Topography of Pylos and Sphacteria: see excellent description and accurate map of G. B. Grundy, J.H.S. 1896, 1 *sqq.*

P. 413.—That the bay and lagoon were continuous in 424 B.C. must be inferred from the account of Thucydides.

P. 413.—Wall on S.E. corner of Pylos: R. Burrows, J.H.S. 1896, 64, and 1898, 149.

P. 420.—Prehistoric wall on Mt. Elias: Burrows, *ib.* 1896, p. 59.

P. 420.—Ascent of Messenians on S.E. side of Mt. Elias: Burrows, *ib.* pp. 61 *sqq.*

P. 421.—425-4 B.C.: An inscription (imperfect) is preserved of Athenians and soldiers in Athenian service who fell during this year. One citizen fell at Pylos: C.I.A. i. 446; iv. 1, p. 46; Ditt.² 32.

P. 421.—Inscription on base of the Victory of Paeonius: Hicks, 49.

P. 421.—Decrees relating to Methone: C.I.A. i. 40; Hicks, 44; Ditt.² 33.

P. 429.—The case for Thucydides: cp. Delbrück, Die Strategie des Perikles 178 *sqq.*

P. 431.—The importance of the fact that armies were not professional has been well brought out by Grote.

P. 434.—Perdiccas changed sides once more: fragments of his treaty with Athens are preserved, C.I.A. i. 42, 43, iv. 1, 141. Athens seems to have acted as mediator between him and Arrhabaeus (so the name is spelt on the stone). About the same time the Athenians concluded a treaty with the Bottiaeans, C.I.A. i. 52, 53, iv. 1, 142.—It is interesting to observe that they were also negotiating in these years with Persia, and a treaty was concluded with Darius II. See Andocides, De pace 29, and the decree conferring proxenia on Heraclides of Clazomenae (Aristotle, 'Aθ. Πολ. 41) for his services in the negotiation (Köhler, Hermes, 27, 68 sqq.).

P. 435.—'Aμφίπολις, meaning of the name: Thucydides, iv. 102.

CHAPTER XI

P. 440.—Sources: Primary: Thucydides v.-viii.; Xenophon, Hellenica, i. ii.; [Philistus]; Andocides, De mysteriis (399 B.C.), De reditu; Speech against Andocides (=Pseudo-Lysias, 6); Speech for Polystratus (=Pseudo-Lysias, 20); Aristophanes: Birds, Lysistrata, Thesmophoriazusae. Derivative: [Ephorus]; Aristotle, 'Aθην. Πολ.; [Timaeus]; Diodorus xii. 75, xiii. 104, xiv. 3-5, 32, 33; Plutarch, Lives of Nicias, Alcibiades, Lysander.

P. 442.—A fragment of the stone: C.I.A. iv. 1, 46b; Hicks, 52.

P. 443.—Battle of Mantinea: Scope=Mytika: W. Loring, J.H.S. 1895, 83.

P. 445.—Athens was again isolated. Some sentences were accidentally omitted here from the text; in which it was stated that Argos was very soon induced (418-7 B.C.) to form a new alliance with Athens. This was brought about by the exertions of Alcibiades. Some fragments of the treaty stone are preserved: C.I.A. i. 50 (new bits have been found by Wilhelm, op. cit. 43).

P. 445.—Nicias in Thrace: There was another Thracian expedition in the following year under Chaeremon, not mentioned by Thucydides, but referred to on a stone which records the payments made from the treasures of Athena for military and other purposes during the years 418-14 B.C. The expedition to Melos is also mentioned: C.I.A. i. 180-3; Hicks, 53; Ditt.² 37.

P. 446.—Attention to religious matters: also to the worship of Hephaestus: cp. C.I.A. iv. 1, 35b, p. 64; and Wilhelm, Epigraphischer Bericht aus Griechenland (in the Anzeiger of the Vienna Academy, 1897, n. xxvi.).

P. 446.—Eleusinian decree, date of: A. Körte, Ath. Mitth. 1896, 320 sqq. (Foucart, Lipsius, Sauppe, and others had placed it before the Peloponnesian war.) Text in C.I.A. iv. 1, 27b; Ditt.² 20.

P. 447.—Treaty with Leontini: C.I.A. iv. 1, p. 13; Hicks, 40; Ditt.² 24; with Rhegium: C.I.A. ib.; Hicks, 39; Ditt.² 25.

P. 448.—Laches and the cheese: Aristophanes, Wasps, 924.

P. 449.—Siceliot policy of Hermocrates, his "colonial statesmanship": Freeman, History of Sicily, iii. 50 sqq.

P. 452.—Inscriptions (414-13 B.C.) pertaining to sale of confiscated property of those who were condemned for mutilating the Hermae: C.I.A. i. 274-281; iv. 1, p. 35; 2, p. 73; 3, pp. 176-178; Hicks, 55; Ditt.² 38-45.

P. 452.—Motive of mutilation of the Hermae: cp. Wilamowitz-Möllendorff, Aristoteles und Athen, ii. 113.

P. 454.—Corinth too sent ships: At this time the Athenians kept a strict guard on the mouth of the Corinthian Gulf. Their control of the gulf, in the year 413 B.C. apparently, is illustrated by the Lycon inscription: C.I.A. iv. 1, 3, n. 53b; Dittenberger², 46.

P. 467.—The revived Damaratea, the Assinarian games: Evans, Syracusan Medallions, 141 sqq.

P. 473, Sects. 7 and 8.—There is one original document bearing on the revo-

lution of 411 B.C.—*the* (Pseudo-Lysiac) Speech for Polystratus. Date 410 B.C.:
see Wilamowitz-Möllendorff, Aristoteles und Athen, ii. 356 *sqq.*

P. 476.—The oligarchic revolution: For the constitutional events of 411
B.C., Wilamowitz-Möllendorff, Aristoteles und Athen, ii. 113 *sqq.*, especially
for the unrealised constitution drawn up by the Commission of a Hundred.

P. 479.—Phrynichus was slain by foreign assassins. The man who struck
the blow escaped; his comrade, an Argive, was caught and tortured, according
to Thucydides. But on the fall of the Four Hundred, Thrasybulus of Calydon
and Apollodorus of Megara claimed the glory of having slain Phrynichus, and
rewards were decreed to these: Lysias, c. Agoratum, 71 (cp. Περὶ τοῦ σηκοῦ,
4). A decree giving further rewards to Thrasybulus, a gold vase, and citizenship, was passed in 409 B.C. and is preserved on a stone: C.I.A. i. 59; Hicks,
56; Dittenberger², 50.

P. 481.—"Our success is over," adopting the reading ἔρρει τὰ καλά (so
Grote): ἔρρει τὰ κᾶλα is the other reading: "our timber (ships) is rotting."

P. 482.—Diobelia, what it was: Wilamowitz-Möllendorff, Aristoteles und
Athen, ii. 212. For payments of the diobelia in 410-9 and 407-6 B. c., C.I.A.
i. 188, 189a; Dittenberger², 51.   á

P. 482.—Erechtheum: building-inscriptions; C.I.A. i. 321; iv. i. pp. 75,
148; Michaelis, Ath. Mitth. 1889, 349 *sqq.*

P. 483.—Capture of Selymbria by Alcibiades: Decree defining conditions
of its new alliance with Athens: C.I.A. iv. i. 61a; Hicks, 58; Dittenberger, 53.

P. 485.—The indignation of the Athenians at the time of the trial of the
Generals was inflamed by the circumstance that it was the season of the
festival of the Apaturia, a time for family reunions, and the relatives of the
doomed men put on black. This trial was an instructive example of the evils
of having no court of revision to correct the dooms of the Assembly.

P. 491, Sect. 10.—Additional sources: Lysias, Against Eratosthenes, and
Περὶ τῆς πολιτείας (403 B.C.), Δήμου καταλύσεως ἀπολογία (c. 402 B.C.),
Against Agoratus (400-398 B.C.), Against Philo (before 395 B.C.), Περὶ
δημεύσεως τῶν τοῦ Νικίου ἀδελφοῦ (c. 396 B.C.), For Mantitheus (c. 392 B.C.);
Isocrates, Against Callimachus (399 B.C.). [For the chronology of 404-3 B.C.,
see Busolt, Aristoteles und Xenophon, in Hermes, 1899.]

P. 494.—Law passed before the execution of Theramenes: Aristotle,
'Αθ. Πολ. 37.

P. 497.—Idea of making landed property a condition of political rights:
This was proposed by Phormisius, and we have a fragment of a speech of
Lysias opposing it (Περὶ πολιτείας, Or. 34).

CHAPTER XII

P. 498, Sects. 1 and 3-6.—Sources: *Primary:* inscriptions; Andocides, **On
the Peace** (391 B.C.); Lysias, Against Alcibiades I. and II. (395 B.C.), Against
Ergocles and Against Philocrates (389 B.C.), Against Epicrates (c. 389 B.C.),
On the Property of Aristophanes (c. 387 B.C.), Against Evandrus (382 B.C.);
Xenophon, Hellenics, iii. iv. and v. 1. *Derivative:* [Ephorus]; Diodorus, xiv.
12-xv. 110; Plutarch, Lives of Lysander, Agesilaus, Artaxerxes; Nepos, Lives
of Conon, Thrasybulus, Agesilaus, Iphicrates.

P. 501, Sect. 2.—Sources: *Primary:* Xenophon's Anabasis; fragments of
Ctesias. *Derivative:* Plutarch's Life of Artaxerxes.

P. 515.—Xenophon composed the Anabasis: he cloaked his authorship
under the pseudonym "Themistogenes of Syracuse": Xen. Hell. iii. 2.

P. 527.—Treaty stone of alliance of Boeotians and Athenians: C.I.A. ii. 6;
Hicks, 65; Ditt.² 61.

P. 528.—Adhesion of the Euboeans: The treaty of Athens with Eretria
has been partly preserved: C.I.A. ii. 7b; Ditt.² 62; cp. Hicks, 66.

P. 528.—Battle of Corinth: Besides the monument of Dexileos with the inscription (C.I.A. ii. 2084; Hicks, 69; Ditt.[2] 67), there is a funeral inscription enumerating the knights who fell at Corinth and at Coronea: C.I.A. ii. 1673; Hicks, 68; Ditt.[2] 68. Ten, besides the phylarch, fell at Corinth, one at Coronea.

P. 530.—Building of walls had begun in the archonship of Diophantus= 395-4 B.C.: cp. C.I.A. iv. 2, 830b.

P. 530.—Temple to Cnidian Aphrodite (near Eetionea): inscription, C.I.A. iv. 2, 830c; Ditt.[2] 64.

P. 531.—Athens recovered her control of Delos; it is uncertain at what time, but before 390-89 B.C. Delos had been freed from Athenian rule after Aegospotami: decree of Lacedaemonians probably relating thereto, Hicks, 61; Ditt.[2] 101.

P. 531.—Chios became her ally: see the treaty of Athens with Phaselis (between 394 and 388 B.C.), in which the alliance with Chios (Diodorus xiv. 84) is referred to: C. I. A. ii. 11; Hicks, 73; Ditt.[2] 72.

P. 535.—Exactions of Thrasybulus= $\frac{1}{20}$th on commerce: This seems to follow from the phrase τὴν ἐπὶ Θρασυβούλου εἰκοστήν in the Athenian decree respecting an alliance with Clazomenae (see below). Cp. Swoboda, Ath. Mitth. 1882, 174.

P. 536.—Unfortunately for Athens: the King's Peace was a blow to Athens, since she was gradually recovering a *commercial* empire. This is illustrated by the negotiations for a treaty with Clazomenae (387 B.C.), which was broken off when the Peace restored Clazomenae to Persia: inscription, C.I.A. ii. 14b (pp. 397, 423), iv. 2, 14b; Ditt.[2] 73; cp. Hicks, 76.

P. 536.—Evagoras, an Athenian citizen: fragment of decree concerning citizenship, Hicks, 72.

P. 538.—Alliance coins: Head, Historia numorum, 495, 516, 540, etc.

CHAPTER XIII

P. 540, Sects. 1-4.—Sources:*Primary:* inscriptions; Isocrates, Panegyricus, Plataeicus, Evagoras, Nicocles; Lysias, c. Evandrum (382 B.C.), Olympiacus (384 B.C.); Xenophon, Hellenica, v. 2—vi. 3; [Ephorus]. *Derivative:* Diodorus, xv. 2-50; Plutarch: Agesilaus, Pelopidas; Nepos: Timotheus, Chabrias, Pelopidas.

P. 543.—Amyntas concluded an alliance with the Chalcidians: A mutilated copy of the treaty is preserved on a stone, Dittenberger[2], 77; Hicks, 74. Date: between 389 B.C. (when Amyntas, son of Arrhidaeus, came to the throne) and 383 B.C.

P. 543.—Amyntas recovered his throne: The Athenians helped him (schol. Aesch., De falsa leg. 26), but it is doubtful whether the inscription relating to an alliance between Amyntas and Athens (Dittenberger[2], 78; cp. Hicks, 77; C.I.A. ii. 15b) is to be referred to this occasion.

P. 545.—Lysias at Olympia: The true date is 384 B.C. (not 388 B.C.); so Grote, Freeman, and others.

P. 549.—The original stone of the decree founding the Confederacy: C.I.A. ii. 17; Hicks, 81; Dittenberger[2], 80. The list of allies is as follows:—Chios, Tenedos, Mytilene, Methymna, Rhodes, Poeessa in Ceos, Byzantium, Perinthus, Peparethus, Sciathus, Maronea, Dion, Paros, O———, Athenae Diades (in Euboea), P———, Thebes, Chalcis, Eretria, Arethusa, Carystus, Icus, Palaesciathus, . . .; the demos of Corcyra, Abdera, Thasos, Chalcis (at Mt. Athos), Aenus, Samothrace, Dicaeopolis, Acarnania, Pronnoi in Cephallenia, Alcetas, Neoptolemus, Jason (erased), Andros, Tenos, Hestiaea, Myconos, Antissa, Eresus, the Astraiusioi (?), Iulis in Ceos, Carthaea, Coresia in Ceos, Elaeus, Amorgos, Selymbria, Siphnos, Sicinos, Dion in Thrace, Neopolis in Thrace, Nellon in Zacynthus.

P. 550.—The chief cities were Chios, Byzantium, etc.: Chios had already made an alliance with Athens, for the extant treaty (C.I.A. ii. 15, and iv. 2, 15c; Dittenberger², 75; Hicks, 80) must be referred, as Köhler has shown, to a year or two after the King's Peace, not to the year 378-7 B.C.—Fragments of the treaty with Byzantium are extant: C.I.A. ii. 19; Hicks, 78; Dittenberger², 79.—Decree admitting Methymna to the Confederacy; C.I.A. iv. 2, 18b; Dittenberger², 82.—Treaty with Chalcis (377 B.C.): C.I.A., ii. 17b; Hicks, 79; Dittenberger², 81.—We have not the treaty with Mytilene, but we have a stone of 368-7 B.C. with an Athenian decree, in which the valuable services of Mytilene to Athens during the years of war 377-1 are acknowledged: C.I.A. ii. 52c; Hicks, 85; Dittenberger², 91.

P. 550.—Several other states: Corcyra, Acarnania, and Cephallenia: decree admitting them to the League (375 B.C.): C.I.A. ii. 49; Hicks, 83; Dittenberger², 83.—the treaty with Corcyra: C.I.A. ii. 49b (and iv. 2, p. 14); Dittenberger², 84.

P. 553.—Delian accounts (for 377-4 B.C.) preserved on a stone: "the Sandwich Marble": C.I.A. ii. 814; Hicks, 82; Dittenberger², 86.

P. 555.—A comic poet: Anaxandrides in the Protesilaus (41 in Kock's Comicorum Att. Frag. vol. 2).

P. 560, Sect. 5.—Sources: Primary: works of Isocrates and Plato; Xenophon's Memorabilia and Apologia Socratis; Aristophanes' Ecclesiazusae and Plutus; fragments of "Middle Comedy"; Aristotle, Politics and Ethics.

P. 561.—Athenian officers in the pay of foreign powers: Such men were often looked on with disfavour when they returned home rich, and were suspected of dishonesty and treachery. See Lysias, On the Property of Aristophanes (Or. 19; c. 387 B.C.): cp. Jebb, Attic Orators², vol. i. 234.

P. 564.—They might point to the ablest of the young men and say: cp. Gomperz, Griechische Denker ii. 75-8. An excellent impartial account of the trial of Socrates, ib.

P. 568.—Education at Athens: The school and aims of Isocrates: Jebb, Attic Orators, vol. ii.

P. 570.—On commerce, prices, banks, etc.: cp. Beloch, Griechische Geschichte, ii. 336 sqq.

P. 571.—This decline in the number of Athenian citizens implies a decline in the free population (including metics) of about 150,000-140,000 to about 80,000. Cp. Beloch, Bevölkerung der griechisch-römischen Welt, 99. He assumes a large decline in the number of slaves (from 100,000 to 55,000); and it may be observed that the closing of the mines of Laurion in the Deceleic war supports the view that there was a considerable decline—The number 21,000 is strictly recorded as the number of citizens in the last quarter of the fourth century (Ctesicles, in Athenaeus, vi. 272B); but there is no reason to suppose that there was much change during the fourth century, and we may reasonably assume 20,000 as roughly true for the end of the Peloponnesian war.

P. 571.—In regard to the high rate of interest, the great risk of trade in ancient times must be borne in mind.

P. 573.—Democratic leaders resigned claim to compensation: especially Thrasybulus and Anytus: Isocrates, Callimachus, 23.

CHAPTER XIV

P. 576.—Sources: Primary: inscriptions; Xenophon, Hellenics, vi. 4-vii.; [Ephorus]. Derivative: Diodorus xv. 51-89; Plutarch: Pelopidas, Agesilaus; Nepos: Pelopidas, Epaminondas; Pausanias, passages in Bks. viii. and ix.

P. 576.—The name of Jason of Pherae, who had joined the Athenian League in 375 B.C., is erased on the stone (Dittenberger, Sylloge², 80): it must have been erased between 373 B.C. (when he was at Athens for the trial of Timotheus) and his death 370 B.C.; perhaps in 372 B.C.

P. 578.—It may be noticed that the tactics of Delium (424 B.C.) were in some measure an anticipation of the tactics of Leuctra.

P. 581.—Another account of the events after Leuctra: I infer this account from Diodorus xv. 54; his authority was doubtless Ephorus.

P. 583.—Tightening of Boeotian unity; Köhler, Hermes, 1889, 638 *sqq.*

P. 583, *Sect.* 2.—Additional sources: architectural remains of Mantinea, Megalopolis, and Messene.

P. 583.—Many citizens cudgelled to death: more than twelve hundred according to Diodorus xv. 58; The number seems incredible.

P. 584.—Date of foundation of Megalopolis: Niese (in Hermes, 1899, Beiträge zur Geschichte Arkadiens, 527 *sqq.*) concludes for spring 369.

P. 584.—Geography of Arcadia: cp. Mahaffy, Rambles and Studies, chap. xii.

P. 585.—Council of Fifty Damiorgoi: inscription: Ditt.[2] 106 (Hicks, 171). Date: middle of fourth century.

P. 586.—The Thersilion: cp. Excavations at Megalopolis (1892), 17 *sqq.*

P. 586.—The two parts of the city of Megalopolis: Bury, Journal of Hell. Studies, 1898, 15 *sqq.*

P. 590.—Decline of Sparta: cp. Pöhlmann, Grundriss der gr. Geschichte, 237, who thinks that the process which resulted in the concentration of the landed property in the hands of a few had begun before the 4th century. Law permitting alienation of the κλῆρος: law of the ephor Epitadeus, Plutarch, Agis 5 (from the context the date of his ephorate seems to have been somewhere about 400 B.C.).

P. 590.—Arcadian statues to Apollo, and inscription: Pausanias x. 9. 5; Pomtow, Ath. Mitth. xiv. 1889, 15 *sqq.*

P. 599.—The Athenian occupation of Samos and the consequent imitation there of Athenian institutions are illustrated by a stone of 346-5 B.C., giving a list of treasures in the temple of Hera: Hicks, 90.

P. 600.—The operations of Timotheus in Chalcidice and against Amphipolis are illustrated by a stone on which honours are decreed to Menelaus, a Pelagonian who assisted him: C.I.A. ii. 55; Hicks, 92; Ditt.[2] 102. The inscription shows that the war in these regions was protracted into 362 B.C.

P. 601.—Ceos: C.I.A. iv. 2, 54*b*; Hicks, 93; Ditt.[2] 101.

P. 603.—Arcadian occupation of Olympia: Illustrated by an inscription conferring privileges on certain Sicyonians: Ditt.[2] 98.

P. 604.—It is interesting to find that the treasures which the Arcadians took from Olympia were paid back: the record is an Argive inscription, Fränkel, Sitzungsberichte of the Berlin Academy, 1898, p. 635.

P. 606.—Text of quintuple alliance treaty: C.I.A. ii. 57*b* and 112; Hicks, 94; Ditt.[2] 105.

P. 606.—The Phocians refused to go: It is to be noted that there was a Phocian, anti-Theban party at Delphi: C.I.A. ii. 54; Hicks, 91; Ditt.[2] 100.

P. 607.—Battle of Mantinea: The left wing of Epaminondas was drawn up not further north than Scope (Mytika): W. Loring, J.H.S. 1895, 87-8.

P. 610, *Sect.* 6.—Sources: Diodorus, xv. 90-94; Xenophon, Agesilaus; Plutarch, Agesilaus; Nepos, Agesilaus. [Compare Judeich, Kleinasiatische Studien, 164 *sqq.*]

P. 611.—Chabrias in Egypt: Ambassadors of Tachos seeking help at Athens: C.I.A. ii. 60; Hicks, 95. Inscription (near Memphis) of Greek mercenaries serving under Chabrias: C.I.G. 4702; Hicks, 96.

CHAPTER XV

P. 613.—Sources: *Primary:* [Philistus]; Platonic and Pseudo-Platonic Epistles. *Derivative:* Diodorus xiii. xiv. and xvi.; Plutarch, Lives of Dion and

Timoleon; Nepos, Lives of Dion and Timoleon; Justin (= Pompeius Trogus)
xx. xxi.

P. 617.—Panormitan coinage with ZIZ. This word has been supposed to
be the Phoenician name of Panormus; it might mean the "bright." It appeared
on an older issue of Panormitan coins, and seems to have been originally connected specially with Panormus; but at this period it was adopted by other
non-Greek towns of Sicily (both Phoenician and Elymian). It has been suggested that it was interpreted as a symbol of Sicily (possibly with a play on
Sik-). See Holm, Geschichte Siciliens, iii. 647-50.

P. 623.—The constitutional position of Dionysius was probably similar to
that of Gelon (cp. above, p. 299).

P. 630.—Alliance of Catane and Leontini: A. J. Evans, Numismatic Chronicle, xvi. 1896.

P. 636.—The aversion of Dionysius to pitched battles has been pointed out
by Freeman.

P. 643.—Ruler of Sicily: ὁ Σικελίας ἄρχων, as he is called in the Athenian
decrees in his honour (preserved on stone) of B.C. 393, 36⅝, and 36⅔ (C.I.A.
ii. 8, 51, 52=Hicks, G. Hist. Inscr. 71, 84, 88=Dittenberger, Sylloge², 66,
89, 90).

P. 647.—Extent of the Syracusan empire; cp. A. J. Evans, Supplement i.
to Freeman's History of Sicily, vol. iv. Hadriatic Colonies: Supplement ii.
ib. Finance: Supplement iii. ib.

P. 666.—"Archidamus eagerly embraced," etc.: It may be noted that in
356 B.C. Isocrates had urged Archidamus inopportunely to lead an expedition
against Persia: Isocrates, Letter 9 (to Archidamus).

P. 667.—Tarentine coins alluding to appeal to Sparta and death of Archidamus: A. J. Evans, Horsemen of Tarentum (cp. Pl. v. 1; Pl. iv. 9 and 10).

P. 666.—Expedition and alliances of Alexander of Epirus: Evans, ib. (83-
85). The influence of Timoleon's example is illustrated by the circumstance
that Alexander adopted Timoleon's Syracusan type of Zeus Eleutherios for his
Italian coins: Evans, in Freeman's Sicily, iv. p. 350.

CHAPTER XVI

P. 668.—Sources: *Primary:* inscriptions; speeches of Demosthenes and
Aeschines, and works of Isocrates (see below under separate sections); fragments of Theopompus; [Ephorus]. *Derivative:* Diodorus xv. 95, xvi.; Plutarch, Lives of Demosthenes and Phocion; Justin, Bks. vii.-ix.; Pseudo-
Plutarch, Lives of Ten Orators (viz. of Demosthenes and Aeschines).

P. 668.—Stone of Thessalo-Athenian treaty: C.I.A. iv. 2, 59b; Hicks, 97;
Ditt.² 108.

P. 670.—Recovery of Euboea: Decree (357-6 B.C.) regarding a rearrange-
ment of the alliances with the Euboean towns: C.I.A. ii. 64 and iv. 2, p. 22;
Hicks, 181; Ditt.² 109. The decree shows that the four chief cities, Chalcis,
Eretria, Carystus, and Oreus, were loyal to Athens throughout the war and
averse to Boeotian rule.—Inscription regarding an attack upon Eretria during the war: C.I.A. ii. 65; Ditt.² 110.

P. 670, *Sect.* 2.—Additional sources: *Primary:* [Thrasybulus]. *Derivative:*
Herodes Atticus, Περὶ πολιτείας; Arrian's Tactics.

P. 673.—Philip's capture of Amphipolis: For the proceedings against the
philathenian party in Amphipolis on its capture, C.I.G. 2008; Hicks, 98;
Ditt.² 113: a decree of perpetual exile against Philon and Stratocles.

P. 674, *note.*—Thracian alliances: C.I.A. ii. 66b; Hicks, 109; Ditt.² 114.

P. 674.—"A professional army with a national spirit": Hogarth, Philip and
Alexander of Macedon, 51. In his account of the phalanx Mr. Hogarth seems
somewhat to exaggerate its mobility.

P. 675, *Sect. 3.*—Special sources: Demosthenes: On the trierarchical Crowᵢ (359 B.C.), Against Androtion, and Against Timocrates, and Against Leptines (355-4 B.C.), On the Symmories (354 B.C.), For the Rhodians (353 B.C.); Isocrates: On the Peace (55 B.C.), Areopagiticus (355-4 B.C.), Περὶ ἀντιδόσεως (353 B.C.).

P. 675.—The fact that Carians saw much of the world in mercenary service, since the days of Psammetichus and Amasis, helped to keep the country abreast of civilisation.

P. 676.—Position of the Carian princes (like that of the Attalids of Pergamon); cp. Mahaffy, Hermathena, 1897, 389 *sqq.* Inscriptions illustrating the position of Mausolus at Mylasa, Iasus, etc.: Ditt.² 95, 96; Hicks, 101, etc.

P. 677.—Revolt of Athenian allies: This led to the introduction of Athenian garrisons into some of the allied cities which had not revolted, *e.g.* Andros: C.I.A. ii. 62; Hicks, 103; Ditt.² 111.

P. 677.—Chares, however, was successful in preventing the Byzantines from joining forces with the other hostile states. A decree bearing on this: C.I.A. ii. 69; Ditt.² 116.

P. 678.—It is noteworthy that in the speech on the Symmories there is no mention of Philip; a supposed allusion does not really refer to him, as Mahaffy has shown (Greek Literature, ii. 105: cp. Butcher, Demosthenes, 39).

P. 679.—Pleadings of Demosthenes for Rhodes: The received date (on the authority of Dionysius of Halicarnassus) is 351-50 B.C.; but the difficulties of this date have been pointed out by Judeich (Kleinasiatische Studien, 186-9). There can be hardly any doubt that the true date is 353 B.C., second half of the year.

P. 680., *Sect. 4.*—Special source: Demosthenes, For the Megalopolitans (353 B.C.).

P. 680.—Thebes and Amphictiones make war: An account of moneys paid to the Thebans by their amphictionic allies for urging this war during some three years (perhaps the first three, 355-2 B.C.): Collitz, Sammlung der gr. Dialektinschriften, i. 705; Ditt.² 120.

P. 687.—Accounts of the Council of Naopoioi: B.C.H. 1896, 197; Sammlung der gr. Dialektinschriften, ii. 2502; Ditt.² 140. At the beginning of the war the building seems to have been interrupted for a few years: cp. Ditt. *loc. cit.* p. 217.

P. 687, *Sect. 5.*—Special sources: Demosthenes: Against Aristocrates (352 B.C.), First Philippic (351 B.C.), Olynthiacs (349 B.C.), Against Meidias (348 B.C.).

P. 691.—Treaty of Chalcidians with Athens (? 351-50 B.C.): C.I.A. ii. 105; Ditt.² 121.

P. 693, *Sect. 6.*—Special sources: Demosthenes: On the Peace (346 B.C.), On the Embassy (343 B.C.), On the Crown (330 B.C.); Aeschines: Against Timarchus (346-5 B.C.), On the Embassy (343 B.C.), Against Ctesiphon (330 B.C.); Isocrates, Philip (346 B.C.); Hypereides, For Euxenippus, 39, 40.

P. 698.—Phocians obliged to undertake to pay back: Accounts of these repayments: Ditt.² 141, 142, 143.

P. 700.—Demosthenes and the Peace of Philocrates: see the sensible remarks of Holm, History of Greece (E.T.), iii. 257 *sqq.*

P. 700.—Isocrates: In 370 B.C. Isocrates seems to have looked to Dionysius of Syracuse to be the saviour of Greece: Isocrates, Letter 1 (to Dionysius).

P. 701, *Sect. 7.*—Special sources: Demosthenes: Second Philippic (344 B.C.), On the Chersonese and Third Philippic and Fourth Philippic (341 B.C.), On the Embassy and On the Crown, as before; Hegesippus (Pseudo-Demosth.), On Halonnesus; Aeschines, as before; Letter of Philip; Isocrates, Panathenaicus (339 B.C.).

P. 707.—Chares sent to Byzantium: He had already been operating in these regions: cp. C.I.A. ii. 116; Hicks, 114; Ditt.² 145: a decree (beginning of 340 B.C.) touching Elaeus, a city of the Chersonese which was throughout loyal to Athens.

P. 708.—Siege of Byzantium. Important help was given to Athens by Tenedos on this occasion: C.I.A. ii. 117; Hicks, 116; Ditt.[2] 146.

P. 717, Sect. 9.—Special sources: *Primary:* Isocrates, Letter 3 (to Philip); Pseudo-Demosthenes, On the Treaty with Alexander (335 B.C.); Circular Letter of Philip Arrhidaeus (319 B.C.), in Diodorus xviii. 56; fragments of Hypereides, In reply to Aristogeiton; Isyllus. *Derivative:* Justin, Bk. ix.

P. 718.—Philip at Sparta: Isyllus of Epidaurus: Wilamowitz-Möllendorff, Isyllos von Epidauros, 30 *sqq.*

The lines are:—

ἐγ κείνοισι χρόνοις ὅκα δὴ στρατὸν ἦγε Φίλιππος
εἰς Σπάρτην, ἐθέλων ἀνελεῖν βασιληίδα τιμήν.

P. 719.—Synedrion of 337 B.C.: Fragment of the oath taken by the members: Wilhelm, Archaeol.-Epigr. Mittheilungen aus Oesterreich, 1894, p. 35; Ditt.[2] 149.

CHAPTERS XVII AND XVIII

SOURCES: *Primary:* [Aristobulus], [Ptolemy], [Callisthenes], [Onesicritus], [The Court Journal of Alexander], [Journal of Nearchus], [Cleitarchus], [Chares of Mytilene], [Anaximenes of Lampsacus]. *Derivative:* Arrian's Anabasis; Plutarch's Life of Alexander; Quintus Curtius; Diodorus xvii.; Justin xi. xii.; passages in Strabo (collected by A. Miller, Die Alexandergeschichte nach Strabo, 1882). (Fabulous, but contaning a fact or two: Pseudo-Callisthenes.)

P. 739.—Democratic constitution at Ephesus: The establishment of democratic constitutions by Alexander is illustrated by his decree in the form of a letter to the people of Chios: Ditt.[2] 150.

P. 743, Sect. 6.—Special source: *Derivative* (from Callisthenes): Polybius xii. 17-22.

P. 745.—Battle of Issus: The resemblance of the tactics of Alexander to the tactics of Cromwell has been instructively pointed out by Mahaffy (Greek Life and Thought[2], 32). "Each of them fought most of his battles by charging with his heavy cavalry on the right wing, overthrowing the enemy's horse, and then, avoiding the temptation to pursue, charging the enemy's infantry in flank, and so deciding the issue."

P. 745.—The numbers of the Oriental troops at Issus (80,000 is stated) are probably exaggerated.

P. 747.—Genuineness of this letter of Alexander (and of most of his letters which are quoted or referred to): Pridik, De Alexandri Magni epistularum commercio, 1893.

P. 756.—The submission of the Jews is a certain inference from the situation, though the account of his visit to Jerusalem by Josephus (Ant. xi. 8) is a fable.

P. 759.—Alexander's visit to temple of Amon: cp. Mahaffy, History of Egypt under the Ptolemaic dynasty, 14 *sqq.*

P. 760.—"It has been supposed": by Professor Mahaffy, Greek Life and Thought[2], 506.

P. 767.—Burning of Persepolis: Gutschmid regarded it as a symbolic act, Geschichte Irans, p. 1.

P. 770.—The satrapies. But it seems to have become ultimately the policy of Alexander to appoint only Macedonian governors. At his death only three satrapies (Media, Parthia, Paropanisadae) were held by orientals. Cp. Gutschmid, *op. cit.* p. 7.

P. 772.—Chronology of the years 330-327: Hogarth, Philip and Alexander of Macedon, Appendix.

P. 774.—Identifications of Drapsaca and Aornus, of Cyropolis and various places in Sogdiana: F. v. Schwarz, Alexander des Grossen Feldzüge in Turkestan (a valuable contribution to the subject by a man who knows the ground), 1893.

P. 776.—The Caspian: The view that Alexander did not suppose the Caspian to be an inlet of the ocean, but identified the Jaxartes with the Don seems to be less likely. Herodotus seems to have known the view that the Caspian was a gulf as well as the view that it was a lake.

P. 777.—The opposition to Alexander in Sogdiana was perhaps aggravated by the intensity of the Zoroastrian faith (Gutschmid, *op. cit.* II).

P. 778.—Scythians beyond the Jaxartes: It has been thought that here we have the first trace of a Turkish people in history. The king's brother is called Carthasis (Curtius vii. 7. I), which, Nöldeke observed, might be Turkish *kardâshy* "his brother" (Gutschmid, *op. cit.* 2).

P. 779.—Intemperance promoted by the dryness of the air, and want of good water: cp. Schwarz, *ib.* 44-5, who points out the similar experience of the Russians in these regions. Drunkenness among the Europeans in Turkestan was shocking until General v. Kauffmann introduced the use of tea in the army.

P. 780.—We must unquestionably reject the episode of the Branchidae, because the act was so unlike Alexander, and the sources for the story are late. The argument for it was the difficulty in understanding why it should have been invented, whereas we could understand its being passed over in silence both in the Court Diary and by the companions of Alexander (Ptolemy, Aristobulus, Callisthenes) who wrote the history of his campaign. The story may be regarded as definitely exploded by Mr. Tarn's paper in the Classical Review, vol. xxxvii., 1922.

P. 781.—Alexander's indifference to women. Little importance need be attached to the passing connexion with Barsine, daughter of Memnon, after the capture of Damascus (Plut. Al. 22).

P. 785.—The extant Periplus, ascribed to Scylax, is a later work under a false name.

P. 786.—Conjectural identifications of Nysa and other places in the Cabul and Swat regions: cp. J. W. M'Crindle, Invasion of India by Alexander the Great (2nd ed. 1896). On the ancient geography of the Punjab, see this work and Cunningham's Geography of Ancient India. Nysa, near Aegae in Euboea, was specially associated with Dionysus, cp. Soph. Antig. 1131, Stephanus *sub voc.*

P. 787.—Massaga: According to the account of Diodorus (xvii. 84), Alexander was guilty of gross treachery on this occasion. This does not appear in the narrative of Arrian.

P. 789.—Battle of the Hydaspes: Alexander left his heavy infantry on the right side of the river at the point where he crossed, probably a precaution against Abisares. This was seen by Rüstow and Köchly.

P. 806.—I have not mentioned the scythed chariots which Arrian places in front of each wing, because they played no part in the battle as he describes it.—My account of the engagement differs in an important point from that of Rüstow and Köchly. They and other interpreters assume that the cavalry on the right wing of Porus remained idle throughout the battle. But surely Porus, when he found that the attack was entirely on his left wing, brought round the other half of his cavalry, and did not leave it inactive throughout the battle. And this is the most reasonable interpretation of Arrian's words (v. 17): οἵ τε Ἰνδοὶ τοὺς ἱππέας πάντοθεν ξυναλίσαντες κ.τ.λ.

P. 806.—It seems a gross exaggeration, for instance, to compare the march through Gedrosia with Napoleon's retreat from Moscow.

P. 806.—Date of Alexander's death: Court Journal (in Plutarch, Al. 77), τῇ τρίτῃ φθίνοντος (Δαισίου)=28th (27th if a short month) of Daesius. The correspondence of the Macedonian with Roman months is uncertain; but we have a statement in a MS. of Pseudo-Callisthenes, which may well be trustworthy, and would enable us to interpret the date. According to one reading (ed. Müller, 151) Alexander "died on the 4th of Pharmuthi"; and in 323 B.C.

the 4th of the Egyptian month Pharmuthi fell on the 13th of June (Unger, Philologus, 1882, 82 *sqq.*).

P. 807.—Seventy towns are said to have been founded by Alexander. We know only of about forty. The uncertainty about their constitutions may be illustrated by the different accounts which Diodorus and Curtius give of Alexandria under Caucasus.

P. 808.—In Alexander's camp the war in Arcadia was likened to a war of mice (Plut. Ages. 15).

P. 808, *Sect.* 5.—Sources: *Primary:* inscriptions; Aeschines, Against Ctesiphon; Demosthenes, On the Crown; Lycurgus, Against Leocrates; Aristotle, Constitution of the Athenians; architectural remains. *Derivative:* Life of Lycurgus; Plutarch, Lives of Demosthenes and Phocion; Diodorus, Bk. xvii. 62, 63.

P. 809.—Aeschines, quotation from: Against Ctesiphon, 132-4.

P. 810.—Etruscan rovers: decree (325-4 B.C.): C.I.A. ii. 809; Ditt.² 153. Hypereides delivered a speech Περὶ τῆς φυλακῆς τῶν Τυρρηνῶν, aind Dinarchus wrote a Τυρρηνικός.

P. 810.—Skeuotheke of Philo: Ditt. 352.

P. 812.—Ephebi: cp. Wilamowitz-Möllendorff, Aristoteles und Athen, i. 191 *sqq.*

P. 813.—Dearth of corn from 330-325 B.C.: marble stele with honorary decrees for Heraclides of Cypriote Salamis, who during these years gave large gifts of corn to Athens: C.I.A. iv. 2, 179 *b*; Ditt.² 152. Cp. C.I.A. ii. 808, l. 40.

P. 814.—Deification of Alexander: Mahaffy, Problems of Greek History, 165 *sqq.;* Wilamowitz-Möllendorff, Aristoteles und Athen, i. 337-8.

P. 814, *Sect.* 6.—Sources: *Primary:* Hypereides, Against Demosthenes, Epitaphios; Dinarchus: Against Demosthenes, Against Aristogiton, Against Philocles. *Derivative:* Diodorus, Bk. xvii. 108, 109, 111; xviii. 2-18; Lives of Hypereides and Demosthenes (in the Lives of Ten Orators).

P. 814.—Harpalus affair: cp. Mahaffy, *op. cit.* 146.

P. 819.—Aristotle: Wilamowitz-Möllendorff, Aristoteles and Athen, i. 311 *sqq.*

INDEX

INDEX

A.

Abae, 698
Abantes, 53
Abarnis, 488
Abdera, 219
Abisares, 785, 787, 789, 792
Abreas, 795
Abrocomas, 505
Abusimbel, inscription of, 108
Abydus, 85, 476, 481, 516, 530, 537, 738
Acanthus, 428, 543
Acarnania, 342, 400-1, 405, 406, 408, 534, 705
Acesines, 785, 792
Achaea (Peloponnesian), 52; its colonies, 95; dependent on Athens, 343; resumes independence, 347; adheres for a moment to Thebes, 595; supports Sparta, 596, 606; member of quintuple alliance, 608; allied with Athens, 705; sends troops to Chaeronea, 715; moves against Macedonia, 808
Achaeans, their invasion of Greece, 5 sq., 37 sq.; in Crete, 37; in Argolis 37; emigration to Asia Minor, 56 sqq.; emigration to Peloponnesus, 51; in Phthia, 38; genealogy of, 73
Achaeus, 72
Acharnae, 31, 495
Achilles, 44, 61; shield of, 43; worship on Pontic coast, 85
Acrae, 94, 656
Acragas, 94, 286; under Theron, 288, 292, 294, 395, 459; Carthaginian conquest of, 619-21, 626, 665
Acte of Argolis, 550
Acusilaus, 72
Ada, 741
Adeimantus, 266
Adeimantus, Athenian general, 488
Admetus, 74
Admetus, general of Alexander, 755
Admetus of Molossia, 320
Adramyttion, 409
Adrastea, plain of, 738
Adrastus, hero, 148, 151
Aegae (Macedonia), 670, 673
Aegean civilisation, early, 6
Aegidae, at Sparta, 114

Aegimius, 73
Aegina, 55; coinage of, 106-7, 143; in Calaurian league, 169; weights and measures, 170; wars with Athens, 195, 245-47; at Salamis, 266, 272; temple of Athena at, 273; battle of, 337; subdued by Athens, 339; inhabitants expelled from, 386; colonised by Athens, ib.; 534
Aegition, 406
Aegospotami, battle of, 487
Aeolians, and Aeolis, 56; cities of, 57; genealogy of, 72 sq.
Aeolus, 72
Aeschines, career of, 694; at Megalopolis, 694; ambassador to Philip, 695-6; partisan of Eubulus, 693; defends his policy, 697; impeached, 702; Against Timarchus, 702; impeached again, 704; De falsa Legatione, ib.; paid by Philip, 704-5; speech at Delphi against the Locrians, 712; Against Ctesiphon, 809; on Alexander's conquests, ib.
Aeschylus, 240, 285, 293; Persae, 294; Eumenides, 333; Orestea, 336; official ed. of his works, 811
Aesymnetes, 141
Aetna, 294, 296, 625
Aetolia, illyricized, 49; Athenians attack, 405 sq., 813
Afghanistan, 773, 782
Africa, Phoenician colonies in, 91
Agamemnon, 42
Agarista, 148
Agariste, mother of Pericles, 332
Agathyrsi, 227
Agema, 736
Agesandridas, 480
Agesilaus, 519; accession, 520; Asiatic campaign of, 521 sqq.; in Boeotia, 528-9; at the Isthmus, 532-3; in Acarnania, 534; hatred of Thebes, 521, 537, 577; supports King's Peace, 540; reduces Phlius, 545; shields Sphodrias, 548; invades Boeotia, 552; action at the Peace of Callias, 558; 584; in the campaign of Mantinea, 606 sqq.; expedition to Egypt and death, 610-12
Agesipolis, king, 534, 540, 544
Agids, 73, 114
Agis I., 442-3, 460, 480, 487, 488, 519, 526
Agis II., 748, 808

865

N.

O.